The Orient in Western Art

The publisher would like to thank Ms Asiyeh Ziai and Mr Jean-Philippe Follet
for their invaluable help and cooperation on this project.

Project Coordination: Agnès de Gorter
Picture Research: Mathilde Decorbez

Original title: *L'univers des Orientalistes*
ISBN 2-84459-001-2

Translation from the French: Harriet de Blanco, Peter Field, Françoise Jones,
Doris Wolstencroft, in association with Cambridge Publishing Management
Editing: Chris Murray, in association with Cambridge Publishing Management
Typesetting: Cambridge Publishing Management

Project Coordination: Kristin Zeier

Printed in France

ISBN 3-8331-1961-6

10 9 8 7 6 5 4 3 2 1
X IX VIII VII VI V IV III II I

Gérard-Georges Lemaire

The Orient in Western Art

With a preface by Geneviève Lacambre

KÖNEMANN

Contents

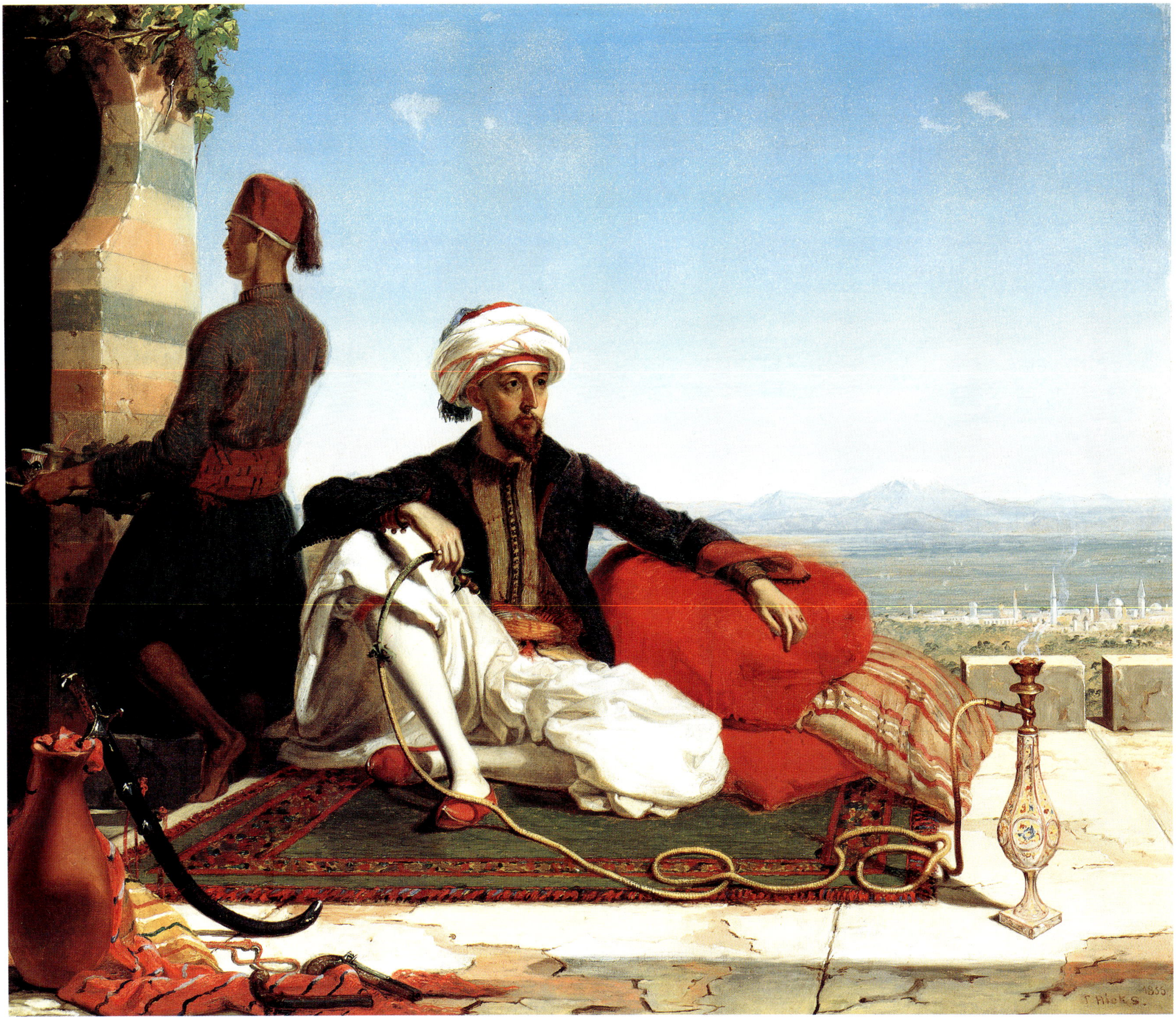

Advocat Taylor with a View of Damascus,
Thomas Hicks, 1855
Oil on canvas, 62.5 x 75.5 cm
(National Portrait Gallery,
Smithsonian Institution, Washington).

Preface

by Geneviève Lacambre

Where exactly was the Orient that was so vividly depicted by the Orientalists? The concept of the Orient is after all a broad and uncertain one; in fact we ought more accurately speak of the Orients. In this book "the Orient" refers to the countries along the eastern and southern seaboard of the Mediterranean; to what is sometimes called the Levant or simply "the East." At times it also refers to Moorish Spain. At once a geographical and a cultural concept, it is inextricably linked with Islam.

This Orient (stretching from Egypt through Palestine to Greece, which shook off the Turkish yoke during the Romantic period) is perceived as the birthplace of our civilization – and of our duality. It is a region that is part of us and yet not quite part of us – unlike the countries where wholly different cultures have developed, such as the Far East of China and Japan, the pre-Columbian Americas, or the islands of the Pacific. The spread of Islam and the rise of the Ottoman Empire meant that for centuries this ancestral Orient was relatively inaccessible, except for merchants welcomed in the ports of the Levant or ambassadors and their retinues.

During the 19th century major changes in Europe – notably the French Revolution and the fierce struggle for a balance of powers that ensued – led to an opening up of the Orient. Bonaparte's expedition to Egypt, Greek independence, the control of the route to the Indies, and the ever-present "Eastern Question" (Europe's growing role in the East) all contributed to the gradual weakening of the once mighty Ottoman Empire. Opportunities for travel improved along with trade; sea transport became cheap and reliable. So, on 20 April 1824, the French artist Eugène Delacroix was able to note in his journal, "I came out of Leblond's. It was certainly a question of Egypt: one can go there for very little. God willing I shall go!" We know that he never made the journey, but some years later, at a time when the French were starting to colonize North Africa, Delacroix visited Morocco and glimpsed the women of Algiers, the subject of one of his finest Orientalist works. As the colonial armies advanced, it was soon possible for artists to journey farther and farther, right into the desert; some became more or less permanent residents in the Orient.

Published tourist guides soon multiplied and a new "grand tour," which replaced the once-obligatory journey to Italy, could be made along the entire eastern seaboard of the Mediterranean. The Moorish buildings of medieval Spain could also be included in the tour, and Venice and Marseilles became the "gates to the Orient."

Usually painters could make this journey only once, and so their accumulated sketches and ideas had to last them a lifetime. One of the most profitable journeys was that of Delacroix, who discovered in Morocco a passion for life and a sense of nature which, he wrote, "is always stifled in our countries"; he marveled in particular at the sheer animal vitality of rearing horses and their spirited riders. There, under a sun that eliminated shadow and brought colors to brilliant life, he found his inspiration for colorful and violent hunting scenes that recall those of Rubens. By comparison, Alexandre Decamps was struck by the stark contrast between the brightness of light-drenched walls and the deep shadows in the labyrinthine alleys of Smyrna.

Artists found what suited their temperament. And though the Orient added to their repertoire of subjects, most of the time it scarcely had any effect on the way they painted. Their country of origin and their masters were the prime influences on the subjects they painted and the way they painted them.

After the picturesque approach to ruined monuments so carefully delineated by the Frenchman Adrien Dauzats and the Scotsman David Roberts, the following generation brought with them a down-to-earth naturalism, as we can see in the works of Gustave Guillaumet and Léon Belly. Now the traditional concern with fine turbans and opulent, richly embroidered costumes gave way to an interest in the rags of snake-charmers or the simple but ample robes that offered protection from the heat of the sun. The Orient in fact became one of the most popular settings for genre painting. In large part this was because Orientalism was strongly affected by the tastes of the buying public. The French artist Eugène Fromentin complained that if you wanted to earn a living you had to abandon the idea of painting what you had really seen and felt, and instead paint the sort of pictures which people expected.

Towards 1880 it was even hoped that an Orientalism that had been vulgarized to the point of absurdity would die out. This, however, was not to be, for the establishment of colonies increased both the opportunities for travel and also a keen interest in foreign parts among those who stayed at home.

Orientalism was not, however, limited to the picturesque depiction of contemporary city streets, vast deserts, intimate interiors, colorful casbahs and festivals, and scenes of rural life. Artists applied to the East all the genres beloved of the academies, including history painting. Archaeological discoveries and the heroes of romantic literature provided new sources of inspiration, from Byron's Sardanapalus to Cleopatra. And then of course there was still the Bible, which was increasingly portrayed in terms of contemporary life in Palestine. Some artists, such as William Holman Hunt and James Tissot, even traveled to Palestine and Egypt in order to observe the light, the landscapes, and the costumes of the region so that they could depict scenes from the Gospels as authentically as possible.

There was, however, another Orientalism – that of the artists who never made the journey. Though they knew the Orient only at second-hand, through pictures and literature, they were often the most original, sometimes the most profound, Orientalists. Personal accounts were often very important; we know of the effect of Lady Mary Wortley Montagu's letters on the imagination of the French artist Jean Auguste Dominique Ingres, the creator of so many odalisques and the celebrated *Turkish Bath*, one of the key works of Orientalism.

The world of the Orientalists was, moreover, limited to a Western (figurative) approach to art that was quite the opposite of the Islamic (largely decorative) tradition that daily confronted every painter who traveled in the East. Islamic art in its many forms, well known in the West through faithful representations by European artists of its architecture and day-to-day objects, such as tiles, carpets, screens, and *narghiles*, was not the starting point for a change in the way Western artists painted – as *japonisme* was for Manet, the Impressionists, and the Nabis in the last third of the 19th century. Genuine aesthetic wonder of the kind experienced by Matisse and Klee was rare.

Even if the 19th-century colonial impulse was essential in opening up access to some of these seemingly mythical lands, it would be quite wrong to see Orientalism as "merely a product of colonialism." A propagandistic colonial art did indeed exist, especially after the French occupation of areas of North Africa during the 1830s, then just after World War I, and subsequently in the 1930s. But its area of concern was far larger than the Mediterranean, reaching sub-Saharan Africa and South East Asia, and its purpose was quite specific.

A sociological analysis of the motives behind Orientalist art has yet to be undertaken; Arabic commentators such as the Egyptian scholar Mohammed Mahmoud Khalil consider Western Orientalist art as essentially a search for the decorative. But it is permissible to believe that many Orientalists were motivated by a sincere desire to return to the roots of civilization, to a more authentic life far from the fumes of industrial civilization. They also had a great desire to capture the picturesque and the beautiful, a desire that is one of the fundamental aims of painting.

Gérard-Georges Lemaire describes all these aspects of the quest for the Orient, from the Renaissance to the many forms that developed during the 19th century, and on into the 20th century, a time when Orientalism became closely linked with the emergence of modern art. His journey is both chronological and geographical, though it is anything but linear. The many fascinating images he shows us are invitations to go on a journey, real or imaginary.

A Thousand and One Nights,
Georges Rouault, 1942
Oil on canvas, 57 x 47.3 cm
(Musée des Beaux-Arts,
La Chaux-de-Fonds).

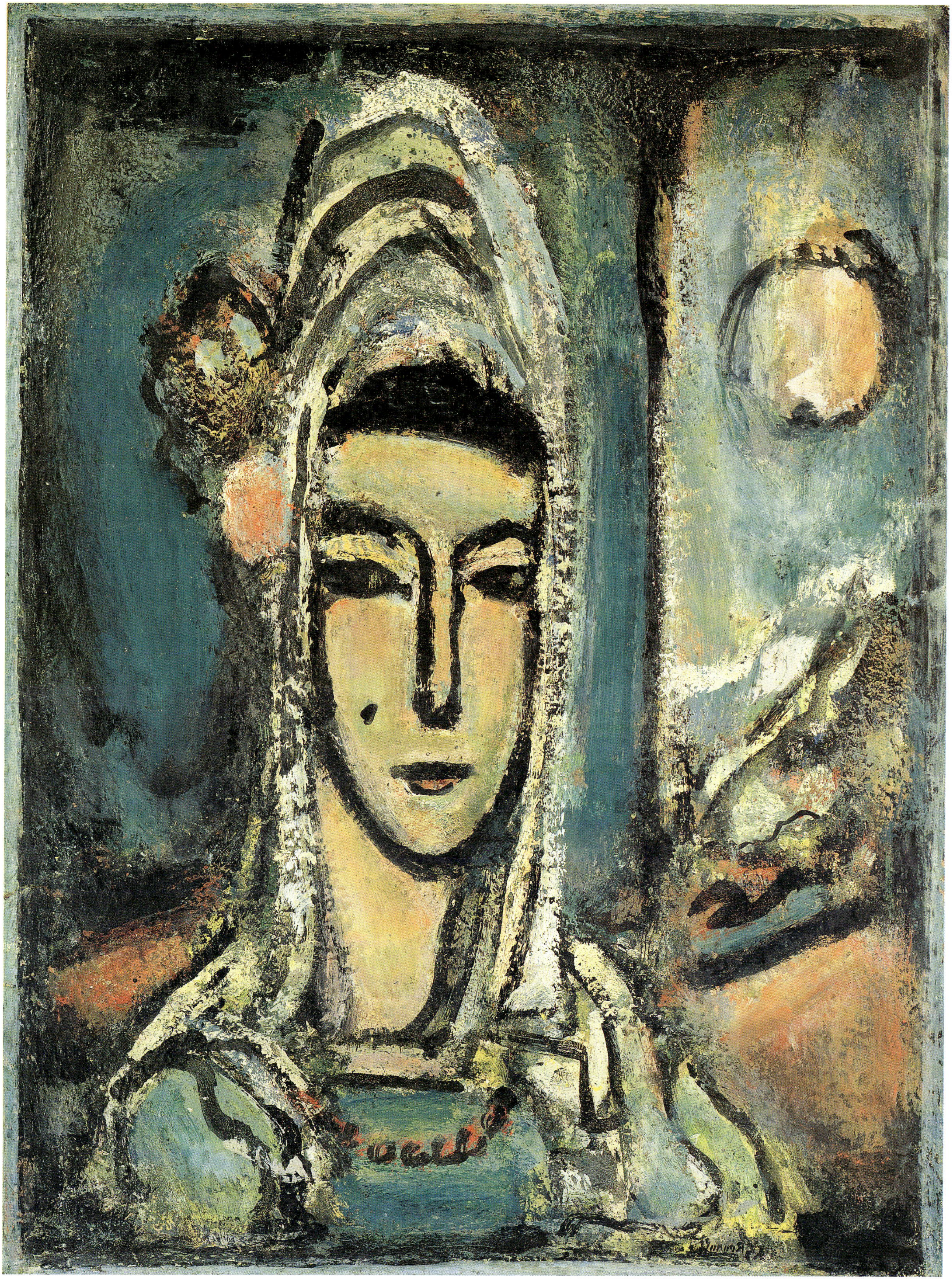

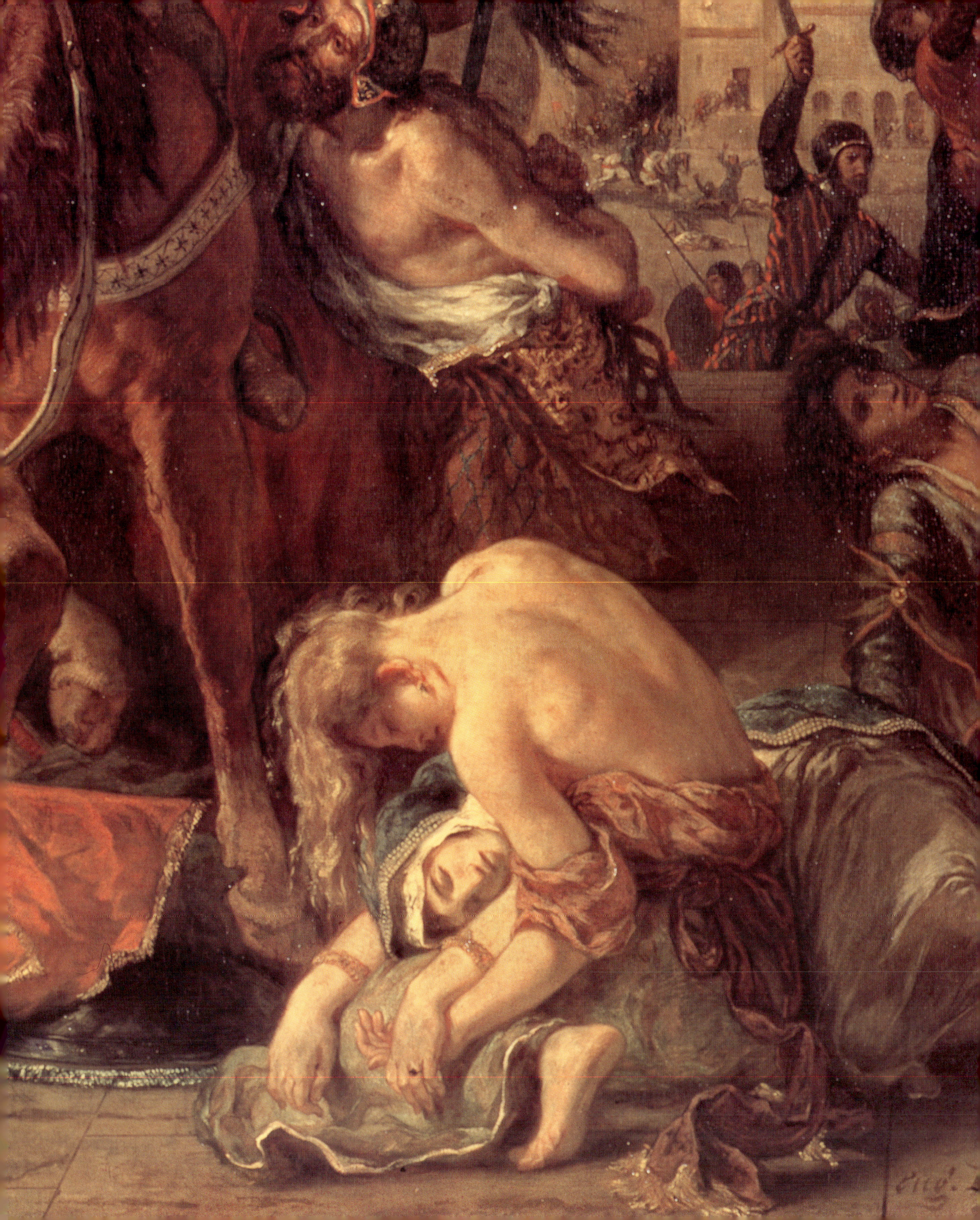

INTRODUCTION

The Paradoxes of Europe's Fascination with the Orient

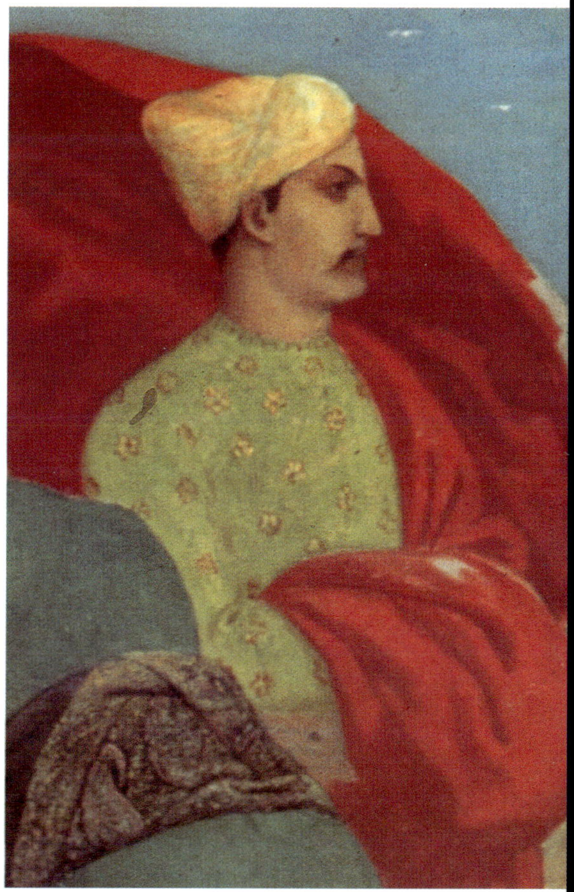

The Capture of Constantinople by the Crusaders, 12 April 1204, Eugène Delacroix, 1840
Oil on canvas, 411 x 497 cm
(Musée du Louvre, Paris).

Page 11,
Marseilles, Gateway to the Orient,
Pierre Puvis de Chavannes, 1869 (detail)
Canvas mounted on a wall,
425 x 565 cm
(Musée des Beaux Arts, Marseilles).

For over two thousand years the Orient has exercised an irresistible fascination over Western minds, and still does so today. What are the roots of this fascination?

The decision by Emperor Constantine in 312 A.D. to adopt Christianity as his state religion sealed the fate of the Roman Empire during its decline. The political, military, economic and even cultural identity that the Romans had been able to impose throughout their empire for centuries was replaced with another form of identity – religious unity – that was to be maintained against all odds during the 'barbarian' (in other words 'pagan') invasions. The story of the conversion of the Frankish king Clovis, who was completely reinvented in the interests of the faith, is one of the most striking examples of this use of religion for political ends. From Charlemagne in the 8th century to Emperor Charles V in the 16th century, powerful rulers would attempt to recreate the Roman Empire in the name of the Christian faith.

The fact that the new religion had its roots in the Bible, in other words in the Jewish tradition, meant that it was from the beginning ambiguously anchored to the world of the East. When the Jews were dispersed in A.D. 70, becoming a landless race, they settled in many parts of the West, and in doing so played a key role in introducing the Orient into Europe.

The advent of Islam completely altered the situation that had arisen in Europe after the migration of Asian peoples into Europe and their unlikely conversion to Christianity. Appearing in the 7th century A.D., Islam was a monotheistic religion that (like Judaism and Christianity) saw itself as the inheritor of the biblical tradition. Its expansion appeared irresistible and the nations of the West now had to face an enemy they saw as unbelievers – an enemy who, in their turn, considered their adversaries infidels.

In Spain, the extraordinary rise of Arab civilization during the Cordoba Caliphate led inevitably to a clash between the Arab world and the empire created by Charlemagne, a clash that gave rise to a myth

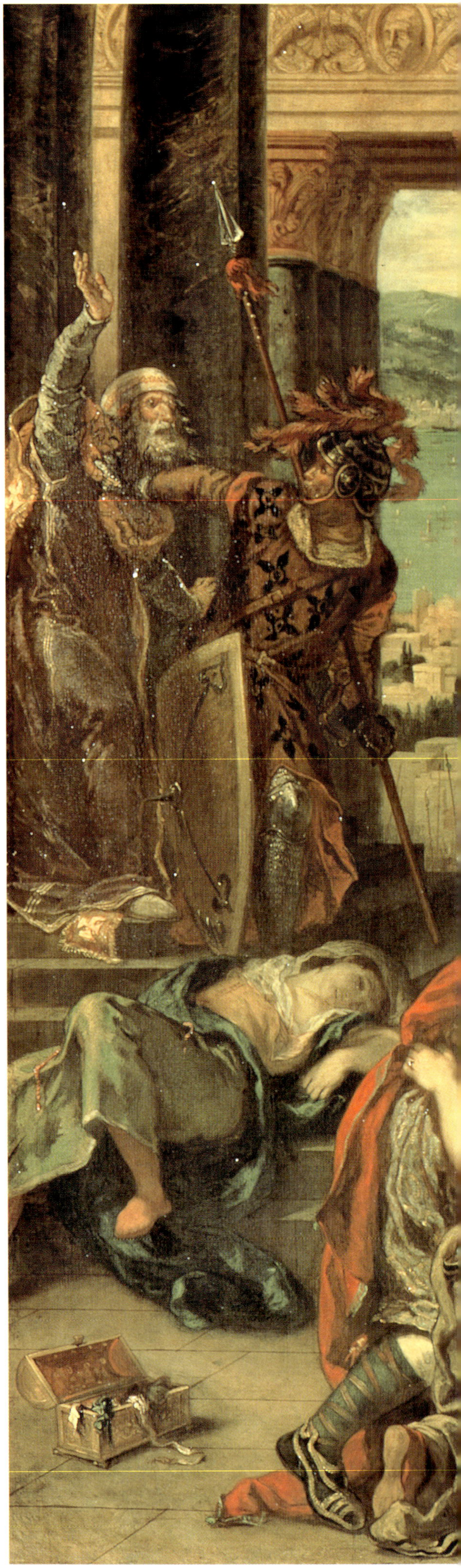

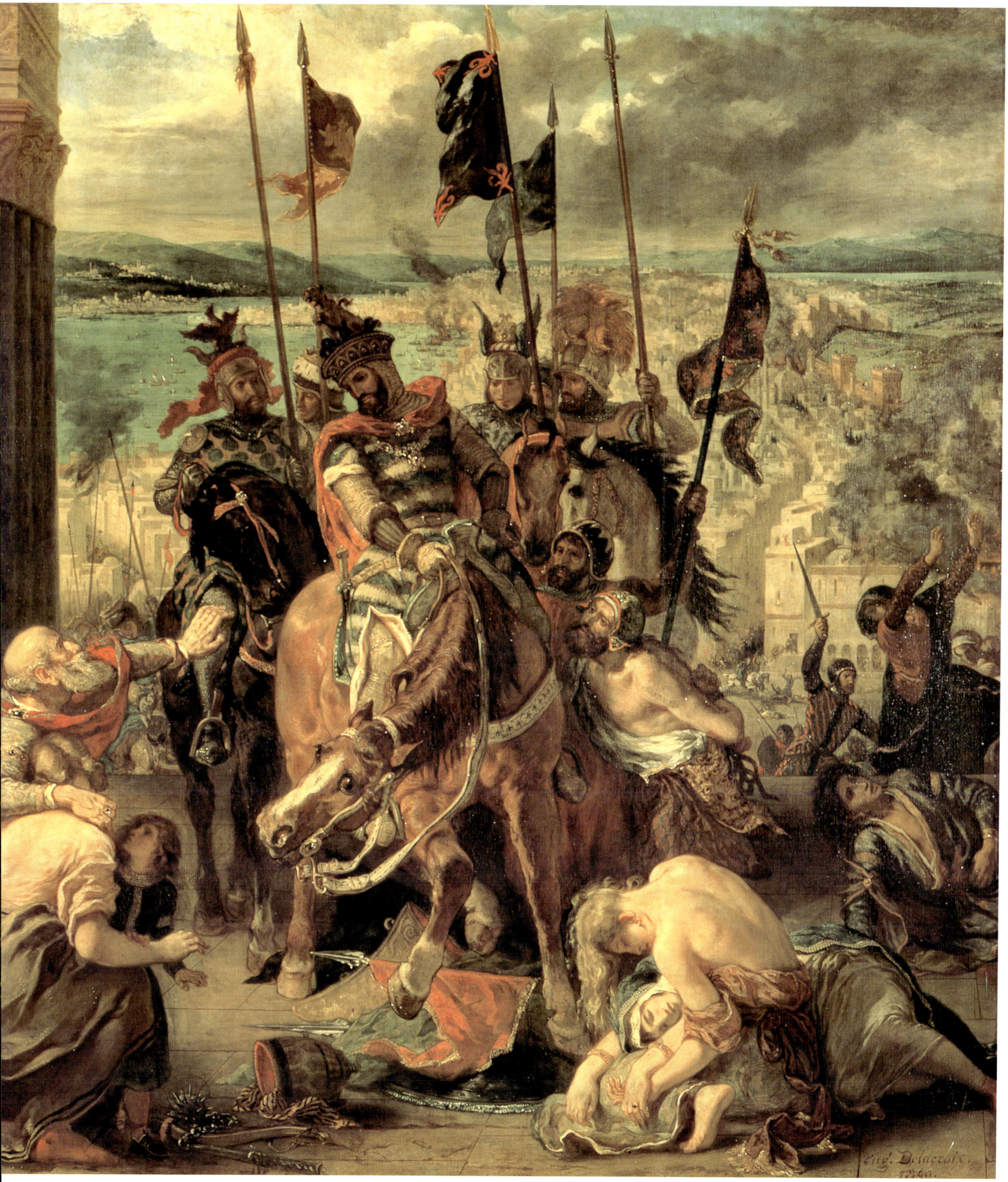
Eug. Delacroix.

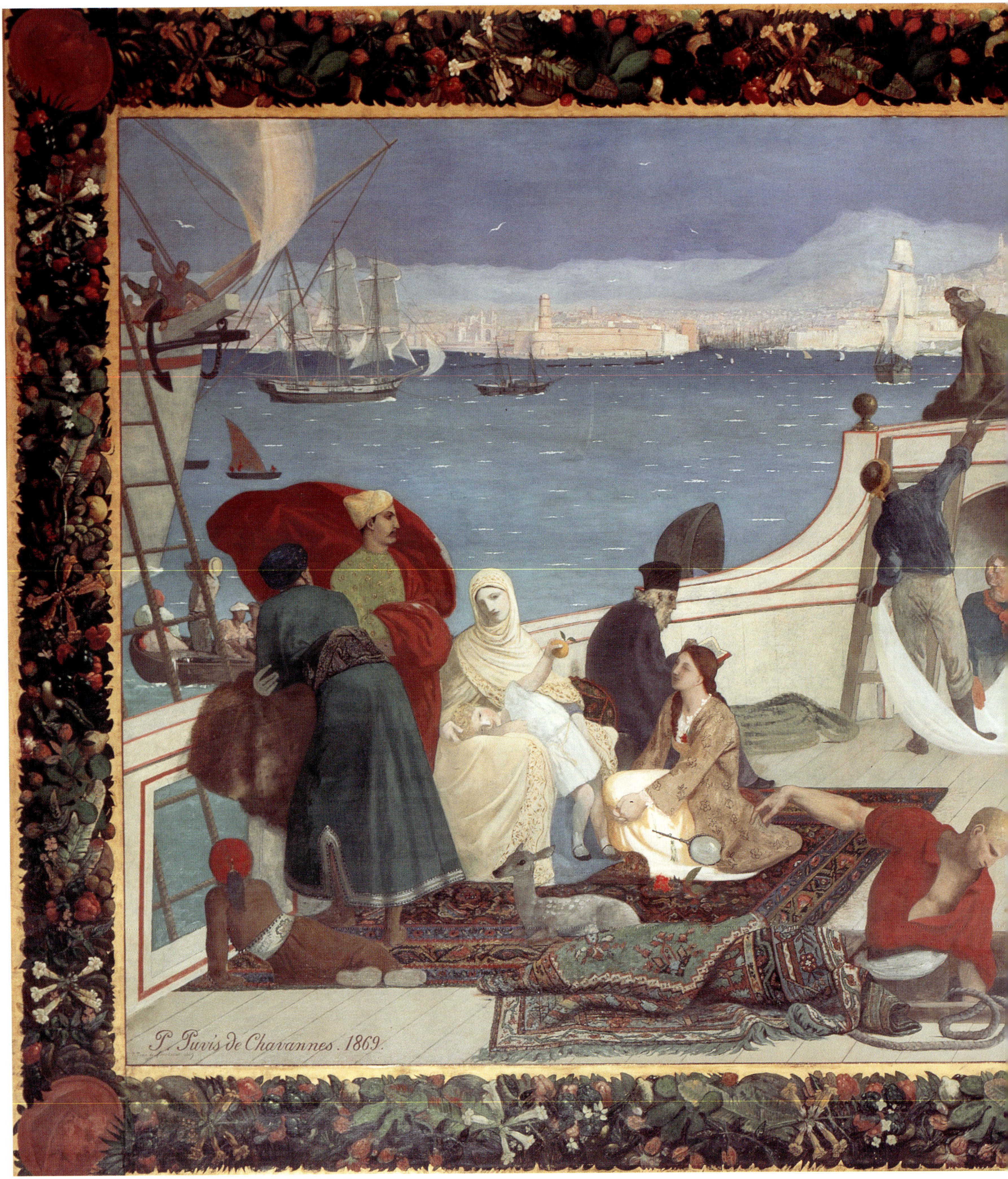
P. Puvis de Chavannes. 1869.

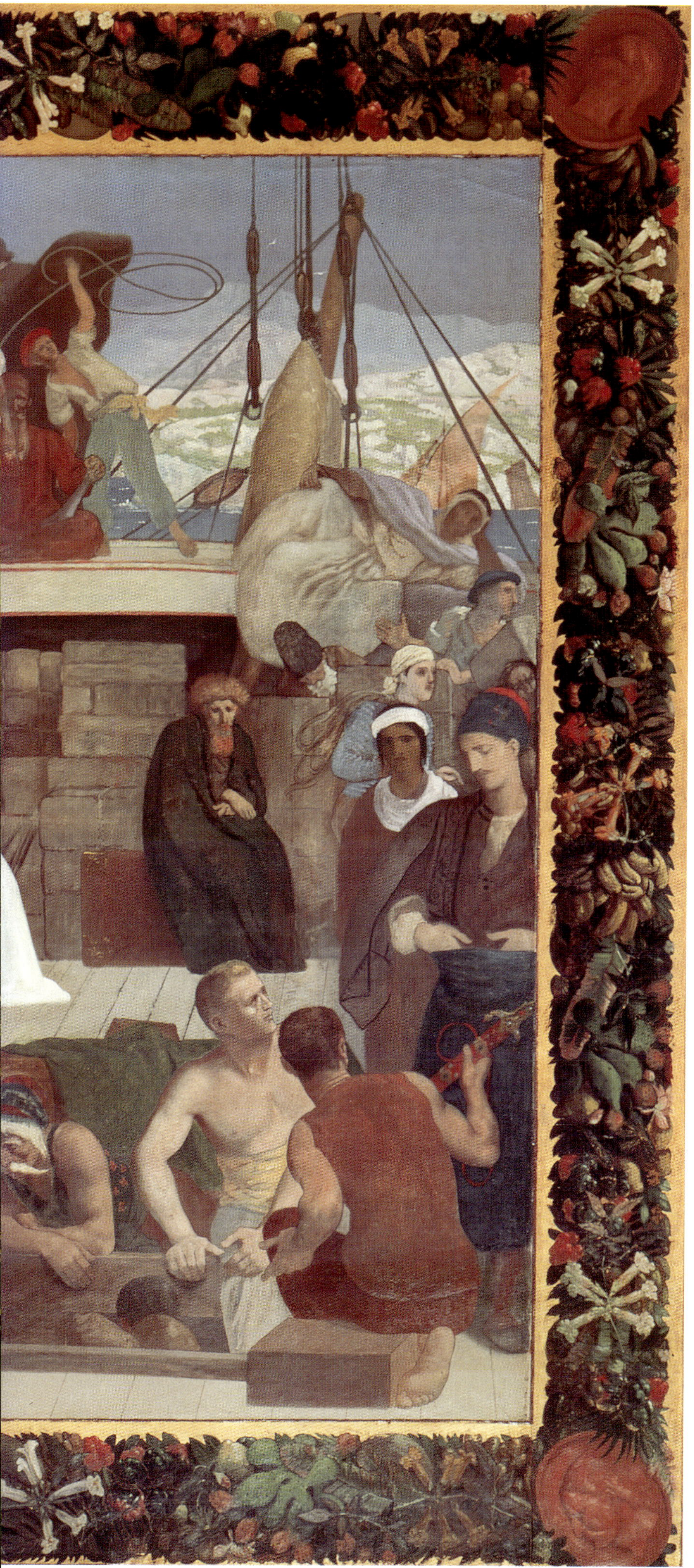

Marseilles, Gateway to the Orient, Pierre Puvis de Chavannes, 1869
Canvas mounted on a wall, 425 x 565 cm
(Musée des Beaux-Arts, Marseilles).

that lies at the root both of French literature and of a European conception of the world that would nowadays be seen as an ideology.

The *Chanson de Roland* (The song of Roland), the first known *chanson de geste* (medieval epic poem) and the one that provided the foundation of all the heroic literature of the French Middle Ages, tells the story of the king of the Franks' seven-year war in Spain. Unable to take Saragossa, Charlemagne negotiated with the Moorish leader Marsile for the right to pull back across the Pyrenees once peace terms had been agreed. However, Marsile's army – at least according to this version of events – attacked Charlemagne's rearguard at Roncesvalles (Roncevaux), where the paladin Roland died bravely fighting against overwhelming odds to defend his king. In righteous reprisal, Charlemagne pursued the Saracens and crushed them, and then fought the final, fateful battle with a Babylonian admiral who had come to the aid of his Muslim ally. Charlemagne was now able to complete the conversion of Spain. The historical reality, however, was very different. In 778 Charlemagne had sacked Pamplona, a Christian city, and when he pulled out of Spain, his Iberian expedition a failure, the Basques took their revenge by massacring his army's rearguard. These inglorious facts, admitted by Charlemagne's own secretary and biographer, Einhard, 40 years later, were in time falsified into legend that had a clear political purpose.

It will come as no surprise that the *Chanson de Roland* has been dated to the period of the First Crusade: it is generally thought that it was composed between 1090 and 1130. In 1095 Urban II made his call to arms at Clermont in France, launching a momentous military and political movement that was to last for two centuries. From the First Crusade preached by Peter the Hermit, to the Eighth Crusade launched by Urban IV in 1263, and including the Fourth Crusade, which did not even reach the Holy Land, knights and villeins from every corner of Europe threw themselves into the adventure in the hope of delivering the Holy Sepulchre from the hands of the infidel.

Despite the inconclusive results of these incredible military adventures, the Crusades, inspired by tremendous outbursts of piety, created a sense of identity with which the West could begin to define and justify itself in its dealings with the rest of the world.

Relations with the Muslim world were not exclusively belligerent, however. At times, cultures that appeared to be in complete opposition managed to fuse, as happened after the Normans conquered Palermo in 1071 – the flourishing Arab-Norman culture that emerged there made this Sicilian city the intellectual capital of the West.

This was because the philosophy, science, medicine, poetry, and arts that the Arabs had cultivated allowed the West to renew its links with part of its lost classical inheritance. As Gustave Cohen astutely remarks in his book *La Grande Clarté du Moyen Âge* (The great mediaeval enlightenment): "They [medieval scholars] translated certain medical and scientific works and often philosophy as well into Latin from the Arabic documents which had themselves been translated from the Greek of Aristotle or Strabo. This is an incontestable fact, based on well-attested cases such as that of Gerard of Cremona, and no-one can deny that the introduction of Aristotle's writings at the end of the 12th century – so fundamental for the development of the scholastic philosophies of the 13th century – is attributable to them." He goes on to argue that "the Arab world played the role of envoy for Greek philosophy and transmitted it along with its own interpretations and commentaries, though its influence was no less decisive for that." And the same can be said for literature and also for painting, which culminated in Spanish Mozarabic art, a distinctive blending of Christian and Islamic styles.

The Great Schism of East and West in 1054 split the Christian world after centuries of violent and often bloody struggles against heresy. The differences between dogmas and rites in the Byzantine Empire and in the West meant that the artistic forms attached to these Christian traditions drew ever further apart. However, by a strange quirk of history, it was the Christian East that provided the foundation for the great artistic revolution of the Renaissance, with Venice being the mainspring. St. Mark's Basilica in Venice is unquestionably the greatest work to result from this appropriation of Byzantine art and its translation into Catholic iconography. This transfer broke the rigidity of Byzantine art and in so doing gave rise to a line of painters who, from Cimabue to Giotto, went on to forge a new visual language – one that would dominate Western art until the early years of the 20th century.

The ever-present East, so near and yet so far, so terrible and so entrancing, the object of a thousand desires and illusions, has never ceased to haunt the West; it is a spectre that obsesses us, by turns seductive and haunted by our deepest fears. Where Western art is concerned, it disguised the Jewish origins of Christianity by presenting all biblical characters in accordance with very abstract conventions. Raphael did not break with this tradition, any more than Giotto did. Attempts were made to push this East back into the ghettos of the mind, just as the Jewish communities in cities throughout Europe were firmly confined within their very real ghettos. But the East continued inexorably to exert its influence on the imagination of the West – a West that found it hard to unite when its interests were threatened in Jerusalem and Constantinople, or even when Ottoman forces stood at the very gates of Vienna.

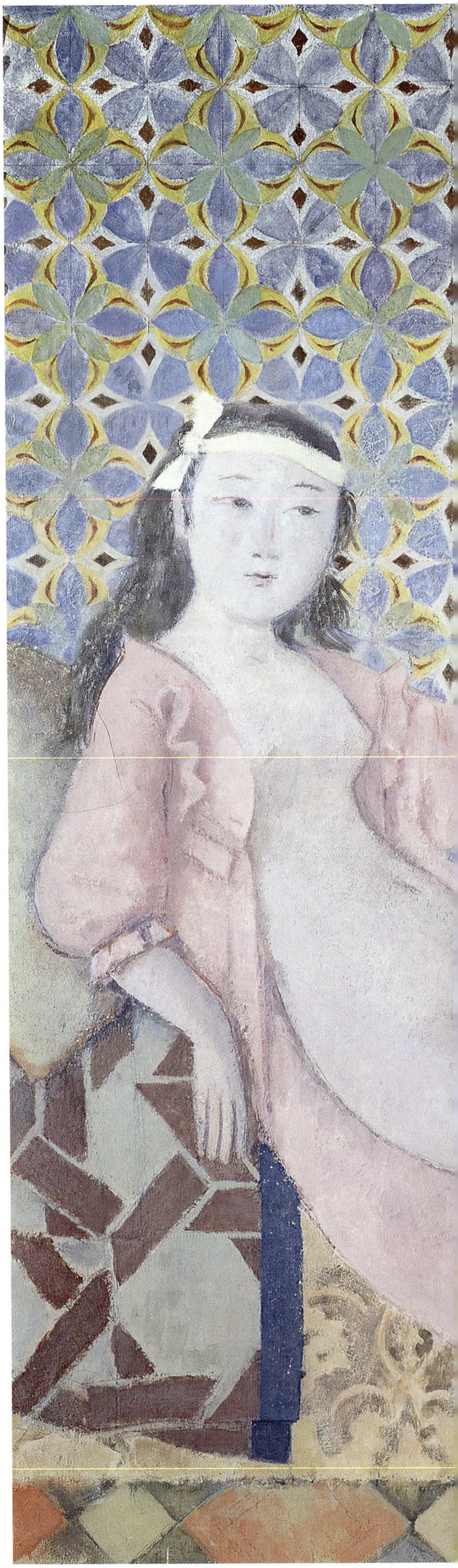

The Turkish Bedroom, Balthus (Balthazar Klossowski de Rola), 1963–1966
Casein and tempera on canvas, 180 x 210 cm
(Musée National d'Art Moderne, Centre Georges Pompidou, Paris).

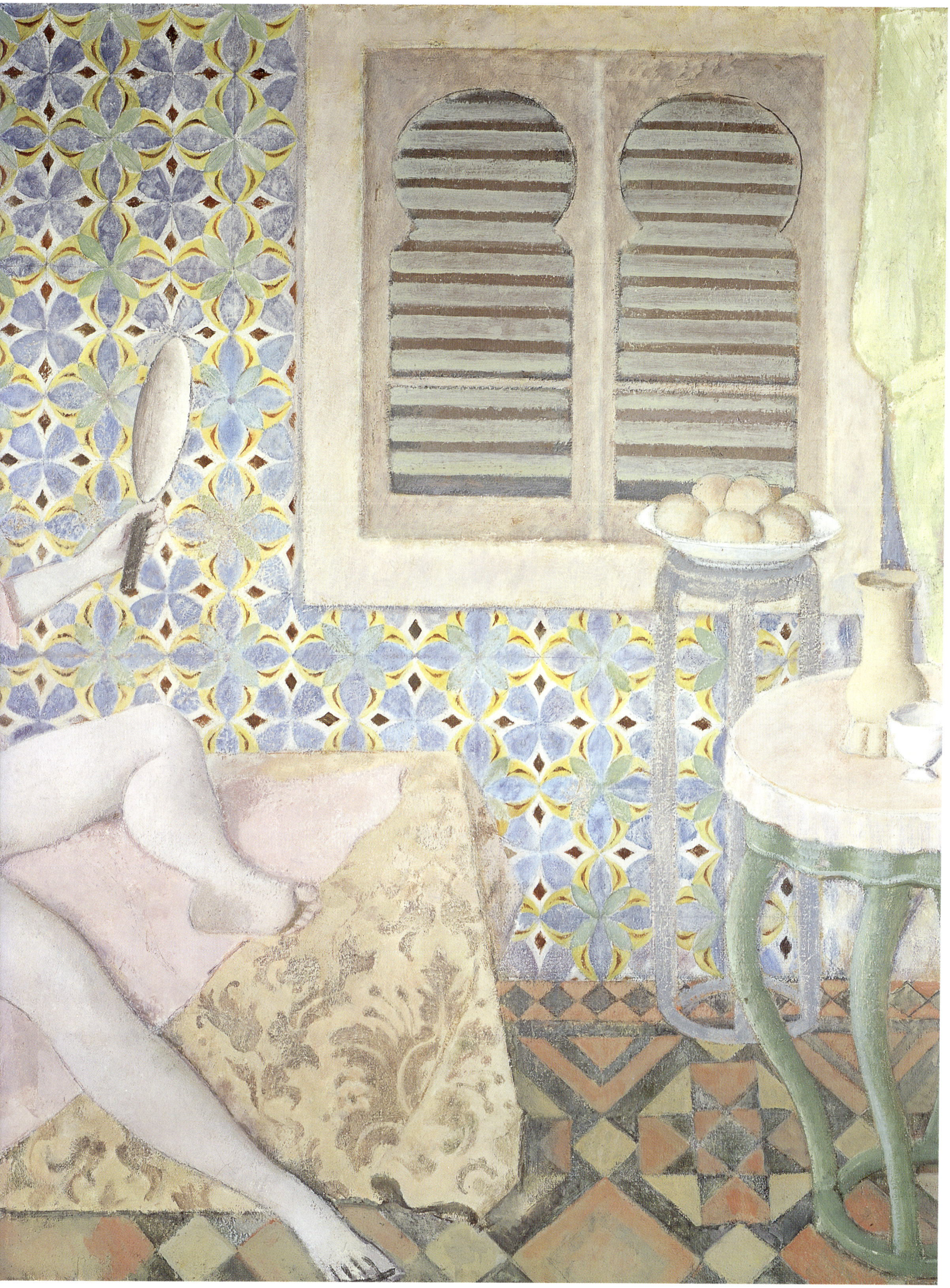

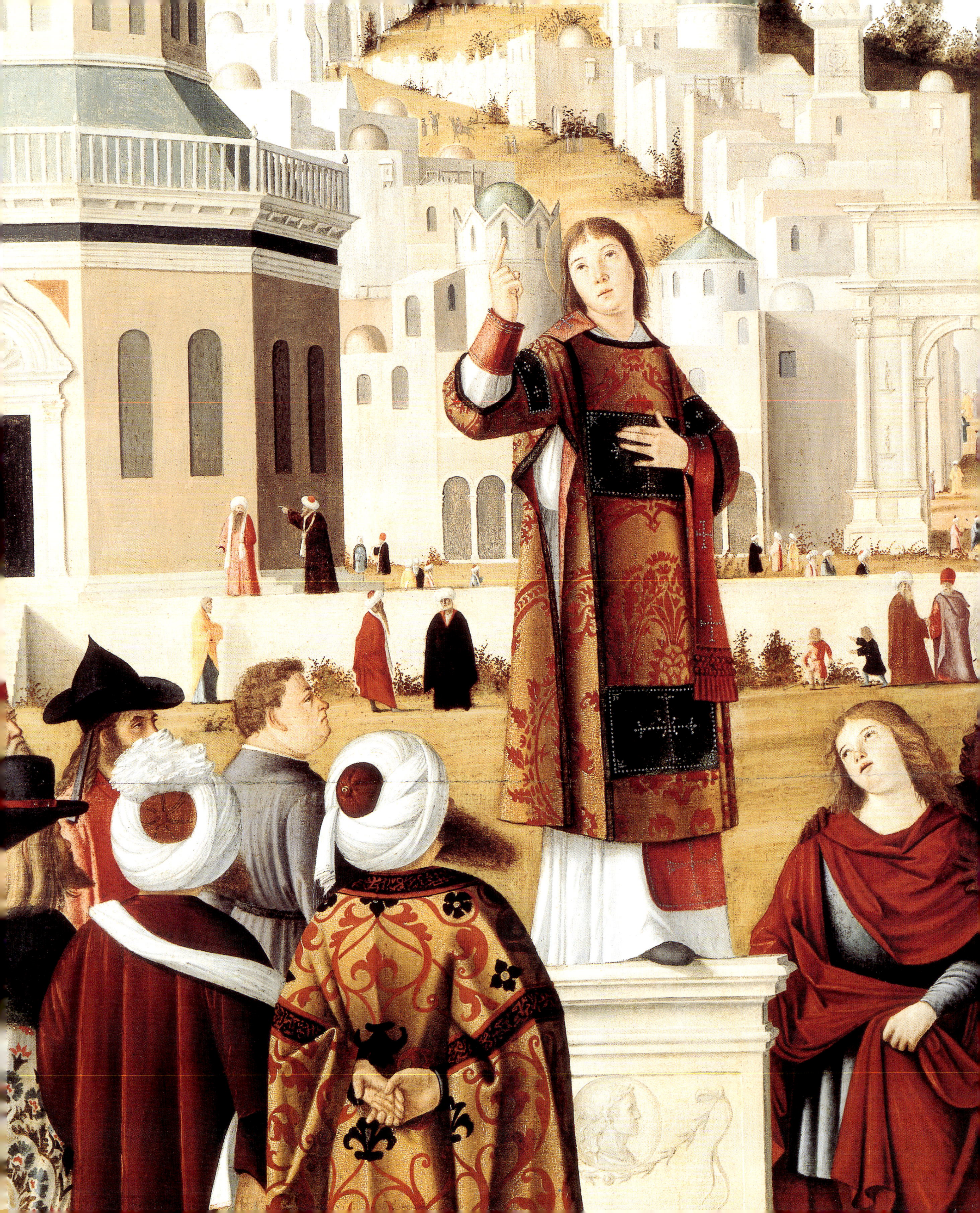

CHAPTER I

Orientalism from the 15th to 17th Century

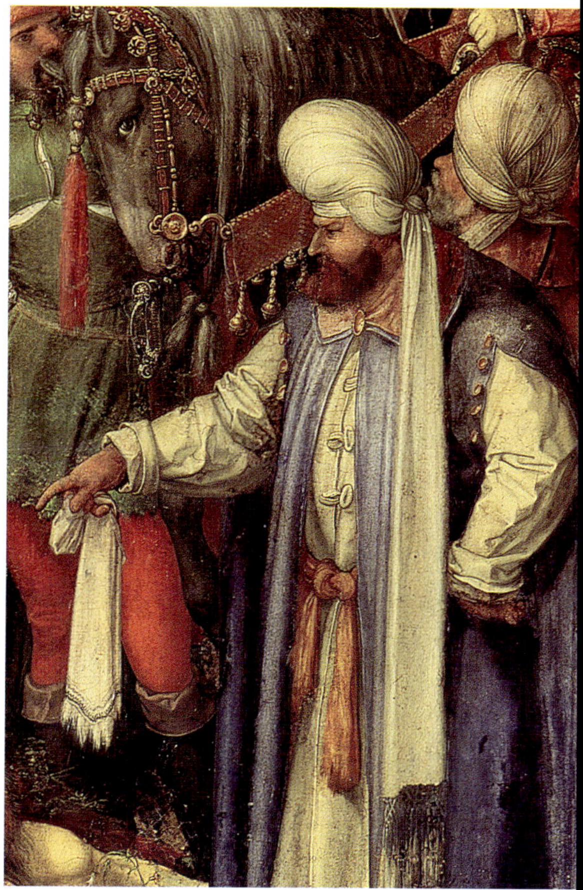

This devastating loss of Constantinople, the capital of the Eastern Empire, took place in the year 1453 from the birth of the Savior, on the twenty-ninth of March (some say it was in April and others say it was in May); it had been a part of Christendom for eleven hundred and ninety years. But it is a most remarkable thing and worthy of note, that Constantinople, rebuilt and raised up by Constantine, son of Saint Helen, to resemble Rome, was captured, pillaged, and put into the power of the Turks by another Constantine, son of another Helen; this was to be an everlasting and irreparable loss to the whole of Christianity. After it had been captured in this way, Mehemet, determined to make it the center of his empire, hastened to repair the walls and some other areas that had been ruined.

Navigations et pérégrinations orientales
(Travels in the Orient by land and sea),
Nicolas de Nicolay, 1567

Renaissance Art and the Orient

Venice – where East meets West

There is no doubt that the fall of Constantinople to Ottoman forces in 1453 was the beginning of a new geopolitical order in the Renaissance world. It was one of the two defining moments in the founding of the modern world, the second being Columbus' discovery of America in 1492. And as the nations of Europe were discovering new continents and taking possession of rich lands, in Europe they saw themselves increasingly threatened by an empire rallied under the green standard of Islam and the white crescent moon of the Ottomans. The opulent and cultured Byzantine (Eastern Roman) Empire, which had been the object of so much covetousness and the source of so many theological disputes, had at last fallen to an empire that had nothing in common with the Christian world. The fall of the Byzantine Empire to the Ottomans was to have a profound impact on Western culture.

The Republic of Venice, La Serenissima ('the most serene'), claimed exclusive rights to sea trade with the Orient until the very end of the Middle Ages. It had slowly but surely carved out an important naval empire in the Mediterranean, though it was an 'empire' with scarcely any territory except for a few ports where ships could take on water and provisions, and where small forts stood to protect them. After Constantinople had fallen to Mehmed II the Conqueror, Venice found itself facing a powerful naval force that could find shelter and support all along the coast of an empire that seemed to be expanding unstoppably. Venice was the only Western port where Turkish merchant ships could dock in times of peace, and where the merchants of the Levant could benefit not only from the commodities traded but also the protection offered by the Fondaco dei Turchi, a Turkish trading post on the Grand Canal in Venice. So it is no surprise to see, in Vittore Carpaccio's painting *The Miracle of the Relics of the Cross*, which he completed in 1494, that at the end of a Venetian alley or *calle* alongside the Fondaco dei Tadeschi (as it once appeared, for it was destroyed by fire in 1505), two Eastern visitors walking and conversing peacefully in the midst of peddlers and passers-by, who are not in the least intrigued by their presence as the Procession of the Holy Cross passes over the old Rialto Bridge.

Relations with the Eastern powers were of great importance to the Republic, which extended its economic liaisons throughout the Mediterranean. The painting *An Audience with a Venetian Embassy* (long attributed wrongly to Bellini) has been the object of endless debates over the site of the event. Some claim that it is in Turkey, which seems unlikely; others have proposed Damascus. The Orientalist Scherer has argued convincingly that the picture depicts Venetian ambassador Trevisano in Cairo in 1512. The vizier who is welcoming the ambassador wears a pointed turban also found in the St. Mark cycle by Gentile Bellini, and the costumes are identical to those worn by the Selenites in Carpaccio's St. George paintings.

The Oriental figures in Carpaccio are not based on travelers' first-hand accounts, which were still rare and fragmentary, but on people living and working in Venice. In fact, he painted several portraits of Oriental sailors and merchants from life between 1501 and 1505, when he was working on the legend of St. George, who was himself an Eastern figure (many believed that he was born in Cappadocia in central Turkey). Similarly, in 1511 the German artist Albrecht Dürer painted *A Turkish Family* from life. He stayed in Venice and was therefore able to observe these travelers from the most distant shores of the Mediterranean at his leisure.

It is clear, then, that by the end of the 15th century relations with the Near East had changed profoundly. This, despite the incessant conflicts that would follow, allowed for richer and more numerous cultural exchanges and, at the very least, a greater familiarity with certain national types, their dress, and their customs.

Renaissance fact and fantasy

It was undoubtedly Gentile Bellini who introduced the Orient into Venetian painting. After a thorough apprenticeship in the studio of his father, Jacopo Bellini, Gentile worked on a range of important commissions in Venice, including the refurbishment of the Hall of the Grand Council in the Doge's Palace, and a number of portraits, notably one of Emperor Frederick III, who visited Venice in 1469 (a portrait that has not survived). In 1479 he accompanied an embassy to Constantinople at the express demand, it is said, of Mehmed II the Conqueror. He painted the portrait of the powerful ruler with the greatest simplicity. His sharp profile is silhouetted against a dark background, and only the rounded Romanesque arch bordering the image is richly decorated, as is a carpet sewn with precious stones that lies over a balustrade. His dreamy gaze somewhat softens the resolute character of his features and the hardness of his mouth. His informal pose is very similar to the pose he takes in a famous Turkish watercolor depicting him in the act of smelling the perfume of a red rose. A longstanding anecdote recounted by the Renaissance writer on art Carlo Ridolfi has it that Bellini left the court of the great sovereign after an episode that was bound to test his nerve. One day, while the painter was discussing a *Beheading of St. John the Baptist*, the Grand Sultan suggested that some of the anatomical details in the painting were incorrect. In order to prove this to Bellini, he had a slave executed in front of the painter's very eyes. The fate of the sultan's portrait itself was also unusual: it was sold in the bazaar by his son, who rejected all Western influence, and bought by Venetian merchants.

Gentile Bellini had appreciated both the beauty and splendor of the Orient, and after his return to Venice he retained a great love for the East. He gave a dazzling demonstration of this in two pictures that the Scuola Grande of St. Mark's commissioned from him in 1504. His brother Giovanni was to finish them in 1507, shortly after Gentile's death. In *St. Mark Preaching in Alexandria*, Gentile depicts the patron saint of Venice perched on an unusual platform that resembles a small bridge. In front of him is an extraordinary audience of veiled women with extravagant head-dresses. They are listening attentively; behind them stand the Venetians (no doubt members of the Scuola Grande) and a group of turbaned Oriental dignitaries. It is clear that Gentile drew his information from Vercelio's album of costumes and the pages of Nicolas de Nicolay's *Navigations et pérégrinations orientales* (Travels in the Orient by land and sea) (1567). As represented by Gentile, the setting – his conception of Alexandria in the 1st century A.D. – is a surprising combination of Venice and Constantinople. The temple (a church transformed into a mosque by the addition of minarets) in front of which the scene takes place is a building that owes as much to the great Hagia Sofia in Constantinople (with its overabundance of buttresses) as to St. Mark's Basilica in Venice. This setting is in effect an *ideal* Oriental city that is even furnished with an obelisk. In Vittore Belliniano's *Martyrdom of St. Mark*, which was painted a little later (after 1515, and completed around 1528), the drama unfolds under the gaze of a huge Oriental crowd in multicolored turbans who are in a setting that is wholly Eastern.

Vittore Carpaccio first revealed his precocious talent in the studios of the Bellini, and it is likely that he discovered the bewitching forms of the Orient there too. In the cycle of paintings he completed between 1501 and 1507 for the Scuola di San Giorgio degli Schiavoni, an institution reserved for Dalmatians staying in Venice, he tells the heroic story of their patron saint, St. George, who fights a dragon and so saves the life of the imprisoned daughter of the king of Selene (present-day Libya). On the first panel in the series, *St. George and the Dragon*, if the church on the right looks much like S. Ciraco in Ancona, then the monumental gates of Selene undeniably resemble the gates of Cairo. The other buildings shown derive from Venetian architecture of the time, vaguely orientalized. In the *Triumph of St. George* we see the hero killing the monster in front of the king and his court. The city of Selene has certainly been wholly invented.

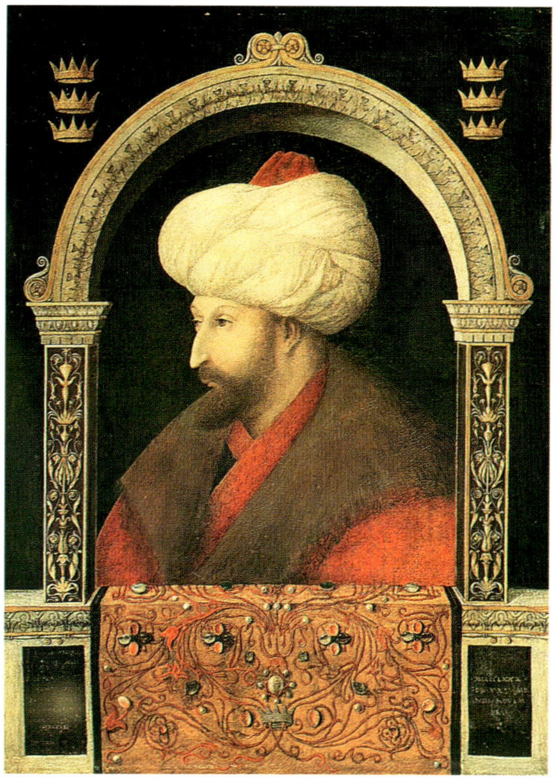

Mehmed II, Gentile Bellini, 1480
Oil on canvas, 69.9 x 52.1 cm
(National Gallery, London).

Page 18
St. Stephen Preaching, Vittore Carpaccio, c. 1514 (detail)
Oil on canvas, 148 x 195 cm
(Musée du Louvre, Paris).

Page 19
Martyrdom of the Ten Thousand, Albrecht Dürer, 1508 (detail)
Wood transferred onto canvas 99 x 87 cm
(Kunsthistorisches Museum, Vienna).

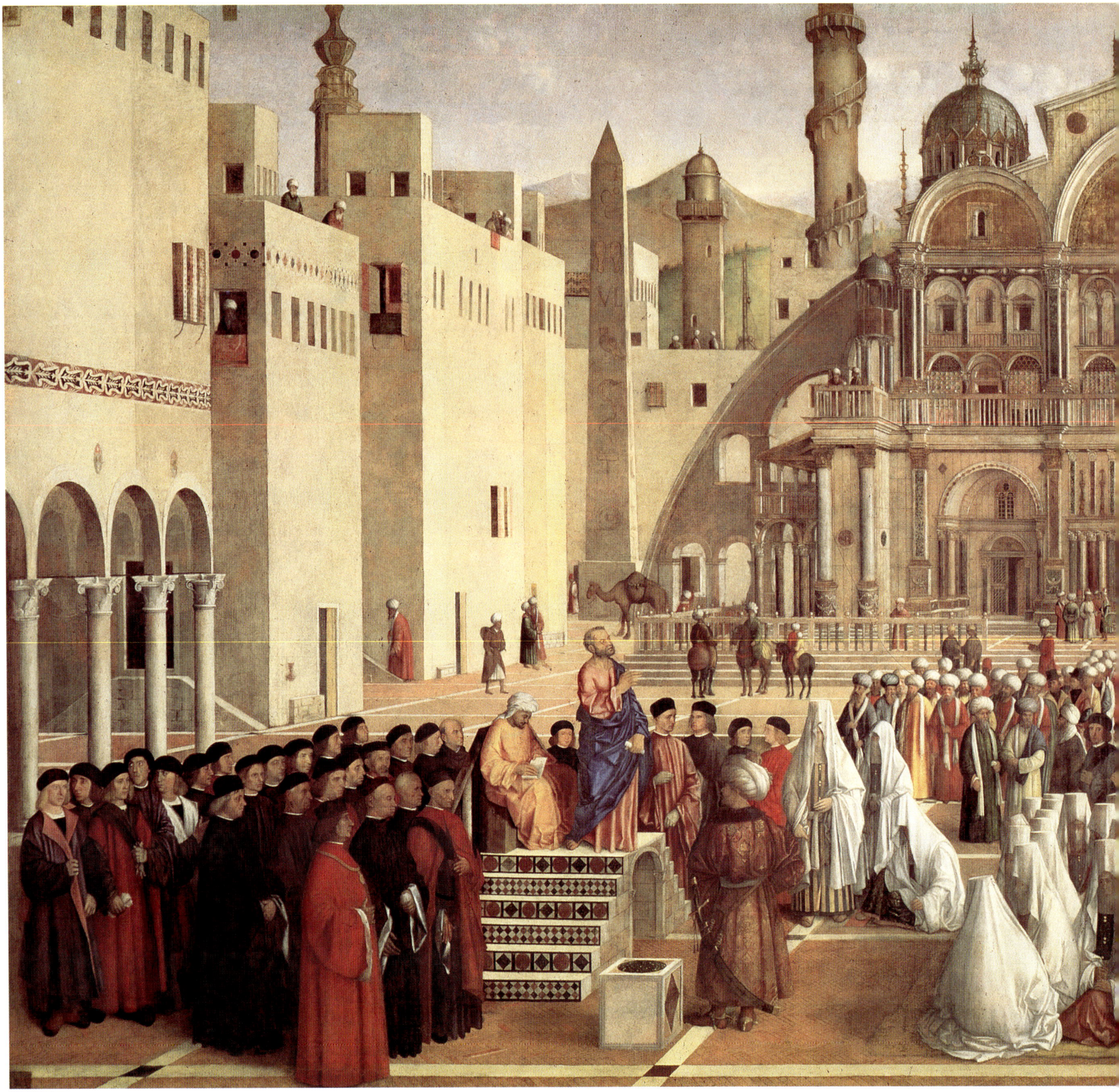

St. Mark Preaching in Alexandria
(or *St. Mark Preaching in Egypt*),
Gentile and Giovanni Bellini, 1504–1507
Oil on canvas, 347 x 770 cm
(Pinacoteca de Brera, Milan).

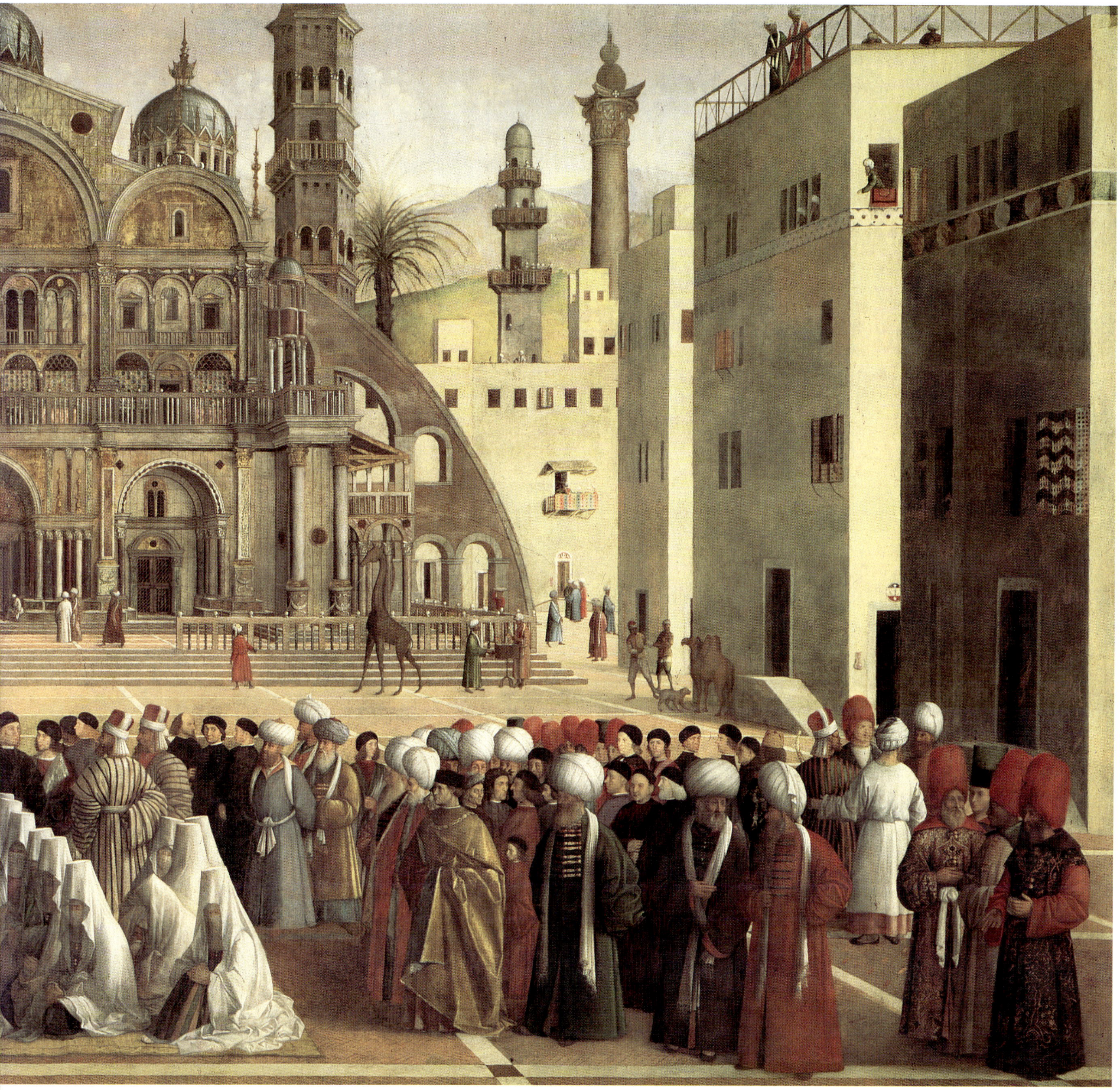

In the center of the square the painter has placed a temple constructed on the model of both the Holy Sepulchre and the Temple of Solomon in Jerusalem, both inspired by Erhard Reuwich's widely influential wood prints, which were published in Mainz in 1486 as illustration to Bernhard von Breydenbach's *Perigrinationes in Terram Sanctum* (Travels in the Holy Land). Some commentators have thought they recognized the mosque of Kubbet-es-Sakbra in Jerusalem, retouched and altered to suit the architectural tastes of the Venetians. The tower on the left is a mixture of various Eastern buildings. In the heart of the city, however, we can clearly make out the tower of the Holy Sepulchre. In *St. George Baptizing the Selenites*, the three musicians on a broad platform to the left of the other musicians are authentic Oriental figures from the artist's own day. The tower on the horizon ends in a minaret, whilst a slightly orientalized Romanesque baptistery occupies the center of the composition. In short, Carpaccio's Orient is composed of both authentic and imaginary elements. It is an Orient seen through the prism of the Venetian aesthetic, a Venetian ideal projected onto the Muslim world.

The most complete expression of an Orientalism based on fact rather than fantasy is to be found in the series *Scenes from the Life of St. Stephen*, which Carpaccio painted between 1511 and 1520. In *St. Stephen and his Six Companions Made Deacons by St. Peter* we see a group of people from the Levant. One of them is wearing a hat very similar to that worn by John Palaeologus in Pisanello's celebrated medallion portrait, and also that worn by a figure in the Piero della Francesca frescos at Arezzo. In Carpaccio's *St. Stephen Preaching*, now in the Louvre in Paris, we can make out, in the crowd around the saint, who is preaching from a platform, several wealthy Orientals in splendid clothes. In the background the city of Jerusalem is visible, here rendered with great precision; the artist was clearly inspired by a view of Jerusalem that came into the possession of the Marquis of Gonzaga in 1511. The mountain landscape, however, is without doubt Venetian. In *St. Stephen Disputing with the Doctors*, the learned doctors also wear superb Oriental costumes. As usual, Carpaccio here presents a subtle and disconcerting contrast with his own culture: behind the porticos we can see spectators in Venetian costume, probably members of the scuola for whom he worked. In the last painting in the cycle, the *Martyrdom of St. Stephen*, he re-uses Reuwich's image of Jerusalem – and here the people who judge, condemn, and fiercely stone the saint are, of course, Orientals.

The most enigmatic picture of the late Venetian Renaissance is still Giorgione's *The Three Philosophers*; commentaries on it are legion. Some scholars see it as the representation of the three ages of human life, others as an allegory of the three major religions, Christianity, Judaism, and Islam. No one has ever been able to solve the mystery as there are as yet no documents to provide a definitive answer; to make things even more difficult, the work is thought to have been completed by another painter, Sebastiano del Piombo. We know that it was given its present title in 1525, but in the inventory to the Archduke Léopold Guillaume it was registered under the name *The Mathematicians*. We also know that it was painted for Taddeo Contarini, whose family had links with the East: one of his relatives had been an official in Constantinople and another, Andrea Gritti, doge of Venice from 1523, had been close to Sultan Bayezid II. In remaining a

The Three Philosophers,
Giorgione, c. 1508
Oil on canvas, 123.3 x 144.5 cm
(Kunsthistorisches Museum, Vienna).

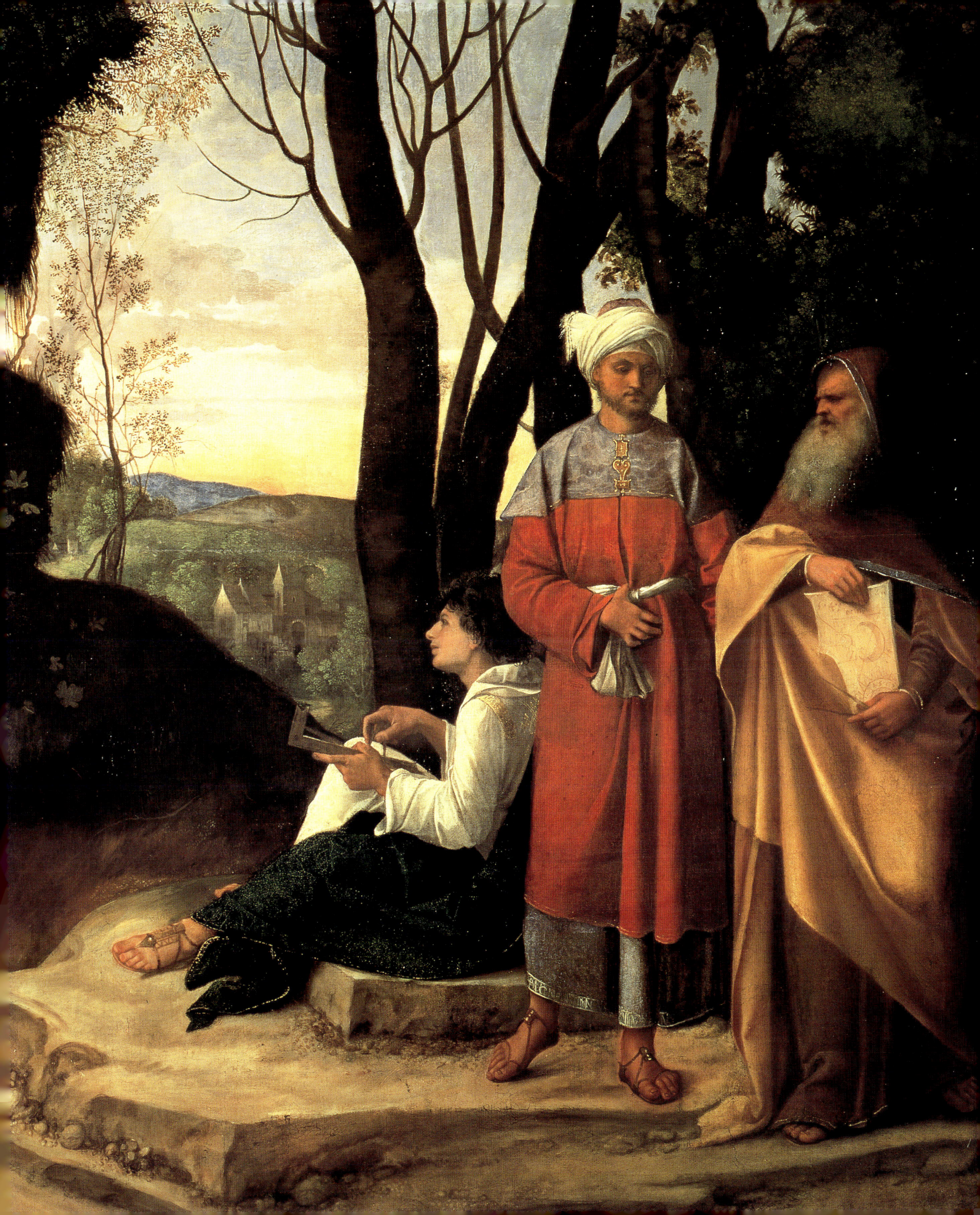

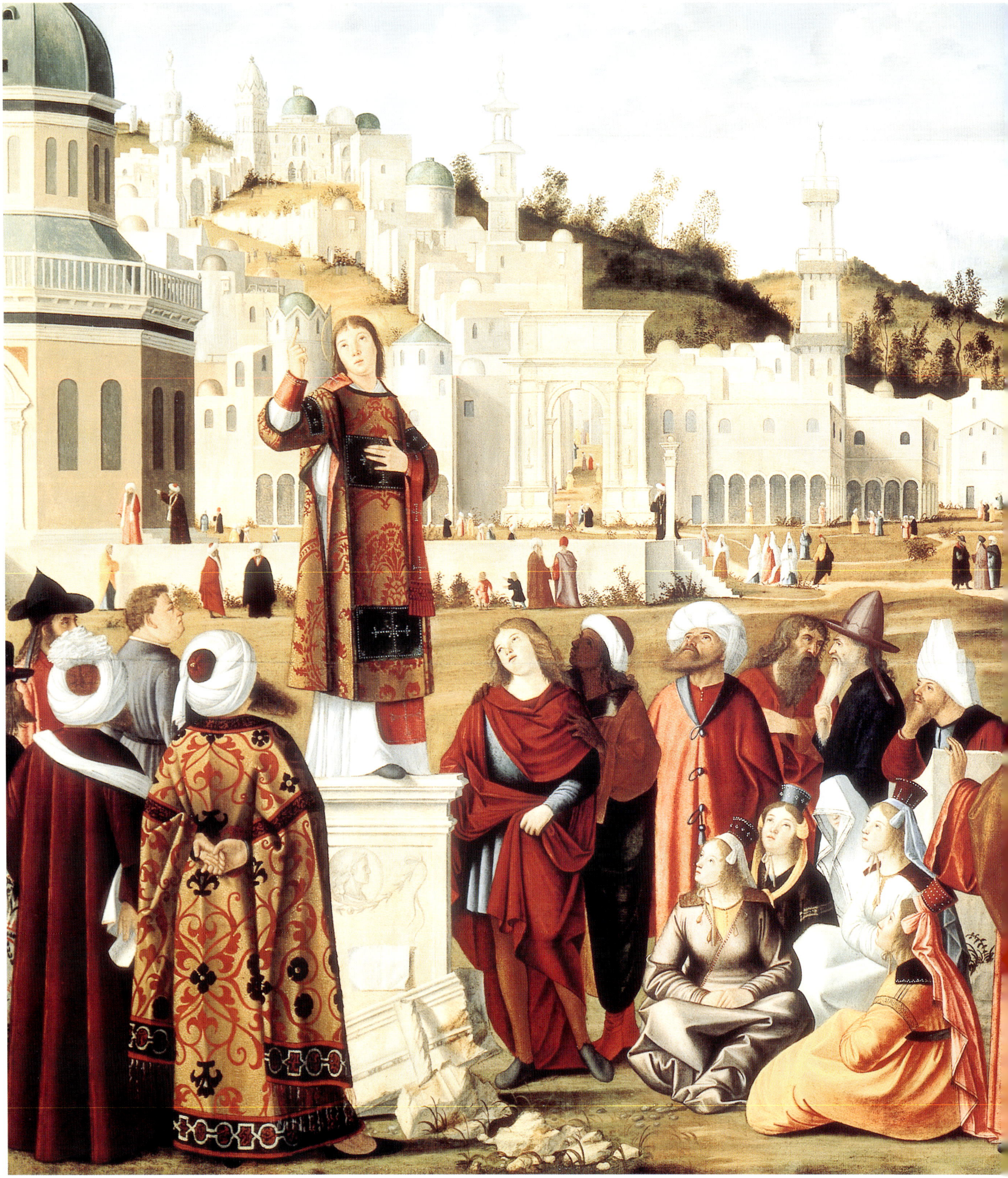

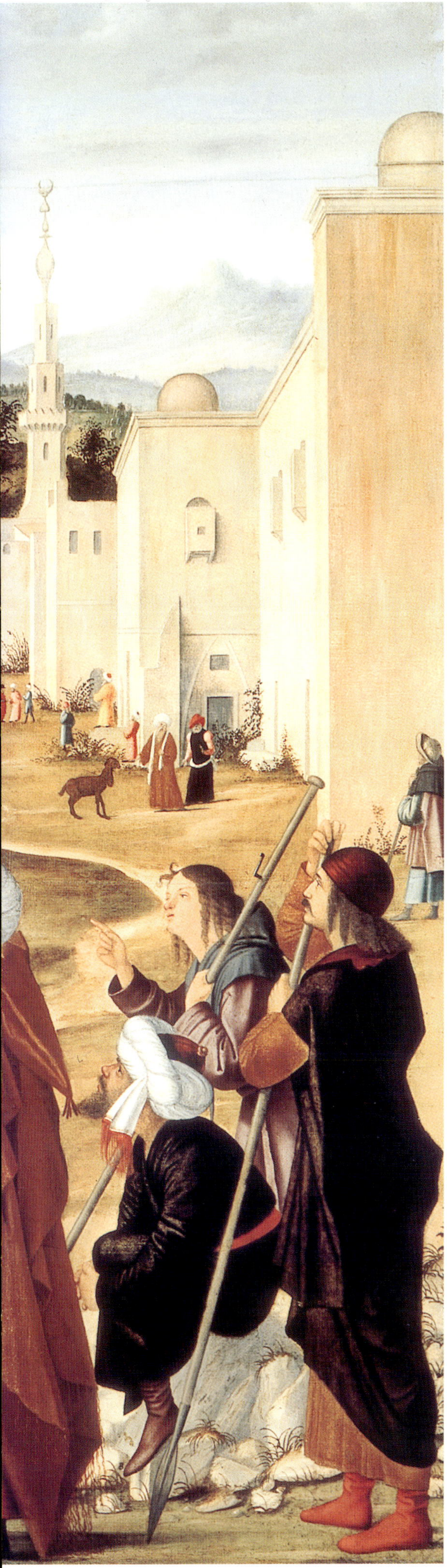

mystery, the picture has come to symbolize the complex and contradictory relations that grew up between two opposing ways of viewing existence and representing the universe: the aged Jewish sage can be seen as the meeting point between the two poles represented by the Arab who is standing and the ancient Greek who is seated next to him.

An interest in the Orient soon spread beyond Venice. In 1506 Albrecht Dürer made a second journey to Italy, living the life of a well-to-do and much-admired gentleman. It was in this year that he painted his *Martyrdom of the Ten Thousand*, a popular subject with his contemporaries, but one that he interpreted in an original way. The massacre, on Mount Ararat, was of ten thousand Roman legionaries (among them St. Maurice) who had refused to sacrifice to the gods of Rome while fighting Shapur, the king of Persia, for control of Armenia. This painting was, it

St. Stephen Preaching,
Vittore Carpaccio, c. 1514
Oil on canvas, 148 x 195 cm
(Musée du Louvre, Paris).

Circe the Sorceress,
Dosso Dossi (Giovanni Luteri), c. 1516
Oil on wood, 176 x 174 cm
(Galleria Borghesi, Rome).

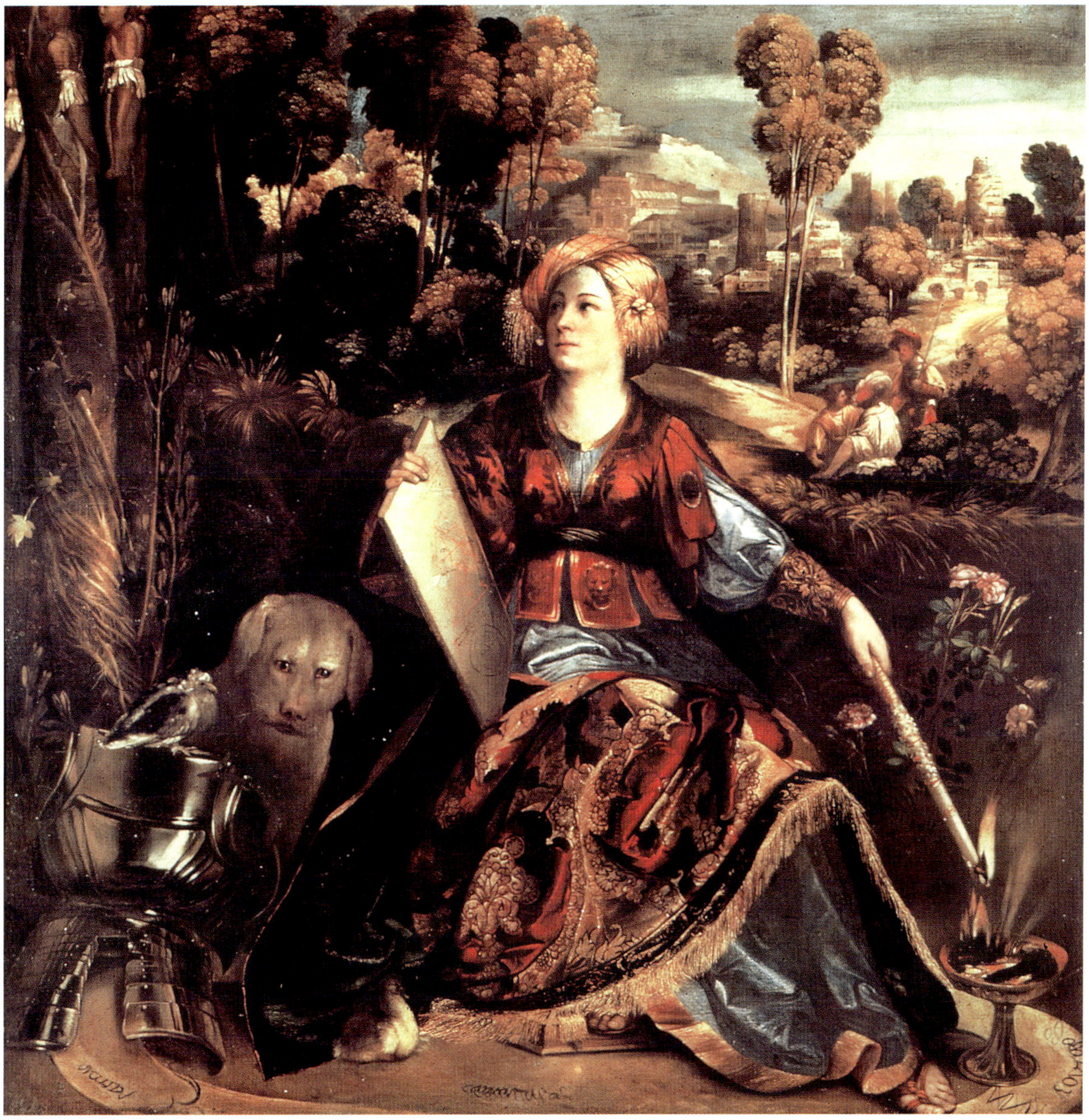

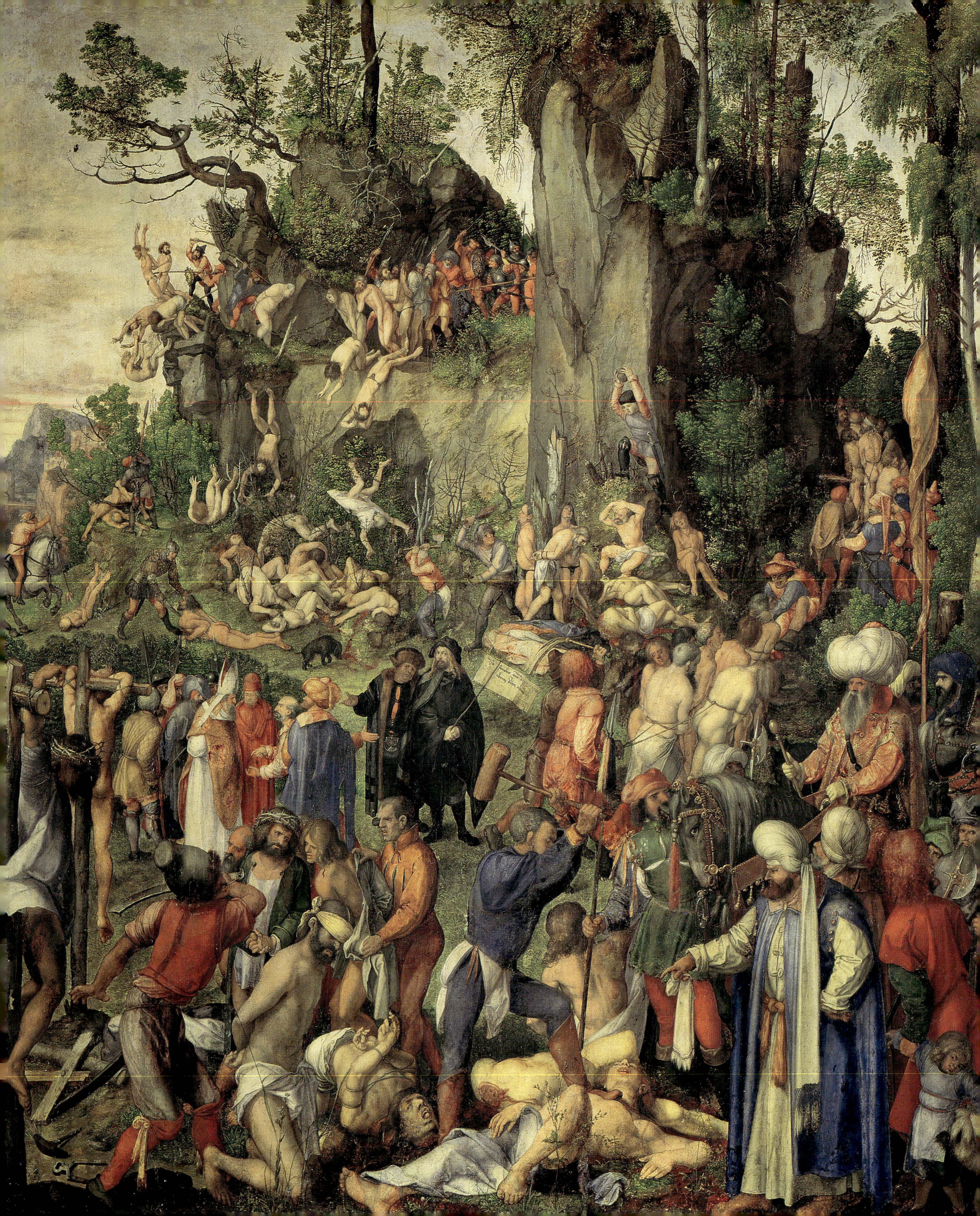

goes without saying, a metaphor for the wars against the Ottomans, who had by now extended their empire into the Balkans.

In Rome between 1512 and 1513 the Italian artist Pinturicchio painted *The Dispute of St. Catherine of Alexandria* for the apartments of Pope Alexander VI Borgia in the Vatican. He shows the patron saint of philosophers debating with the 52 pagan doctors, most of whom are sages or Oriental theologians, brought together by Emperor Maximian to refute her arguments and convince her to abjure her faith. Catherine is represented with the face of Lucrezia Borgia, the Pope's daughter. Next to her is the son of Mehmed II, Djem, who requested the assistance of the Knights of Rhodes against his brother Bayezid and who was to have a miserable end as a prisoner of the Pope, probably assassinated. In 1529 the German artist Albrecht Altdorfer painted the *Battle of Alexander* for the Duke of Bavaria, who was a close ally of Emperor Charles V. This subject, too, had a clear Eastern theme, for the defeat of Issos by Alexander the Great precipitated the fall of the Persian king Darius III.

Dosso Dossi of Ferrara also alluded to the Orient in a painting usually known as *Circe the Sorceress* (c. 1523). In fact, the subject of this canvas has caused a good deal of debate: it is not known definitively whether it portrays Circe, who in Homer's *Odyssey* transforms the companions of Odysseus into swine; or whether it depicts Melissa in the epic *Orlando Furioso* by Ariosto, one of Dossi's close friends. It is highly likely that Dossi did in fact have Ariosto's poem in mind, for Roger (Ruggiero) the Saracen, one of the central characters of this epic, was the supposed founder of the legendary house of d'Este. Ariosto had dedicated his work to Leopoldo d'Este, the brother of Duke Alfonso, who was the reigning prince.

Parmigianino's superb *Turkish Slave*, painted between 1527 and 1530, was perhaps also inspired by the verses of Ariosto. The beautiful young woman is the precursor of innumerable sultanas who would in time take up residence in the palaces, salons, and drawing rooms of Christendom.

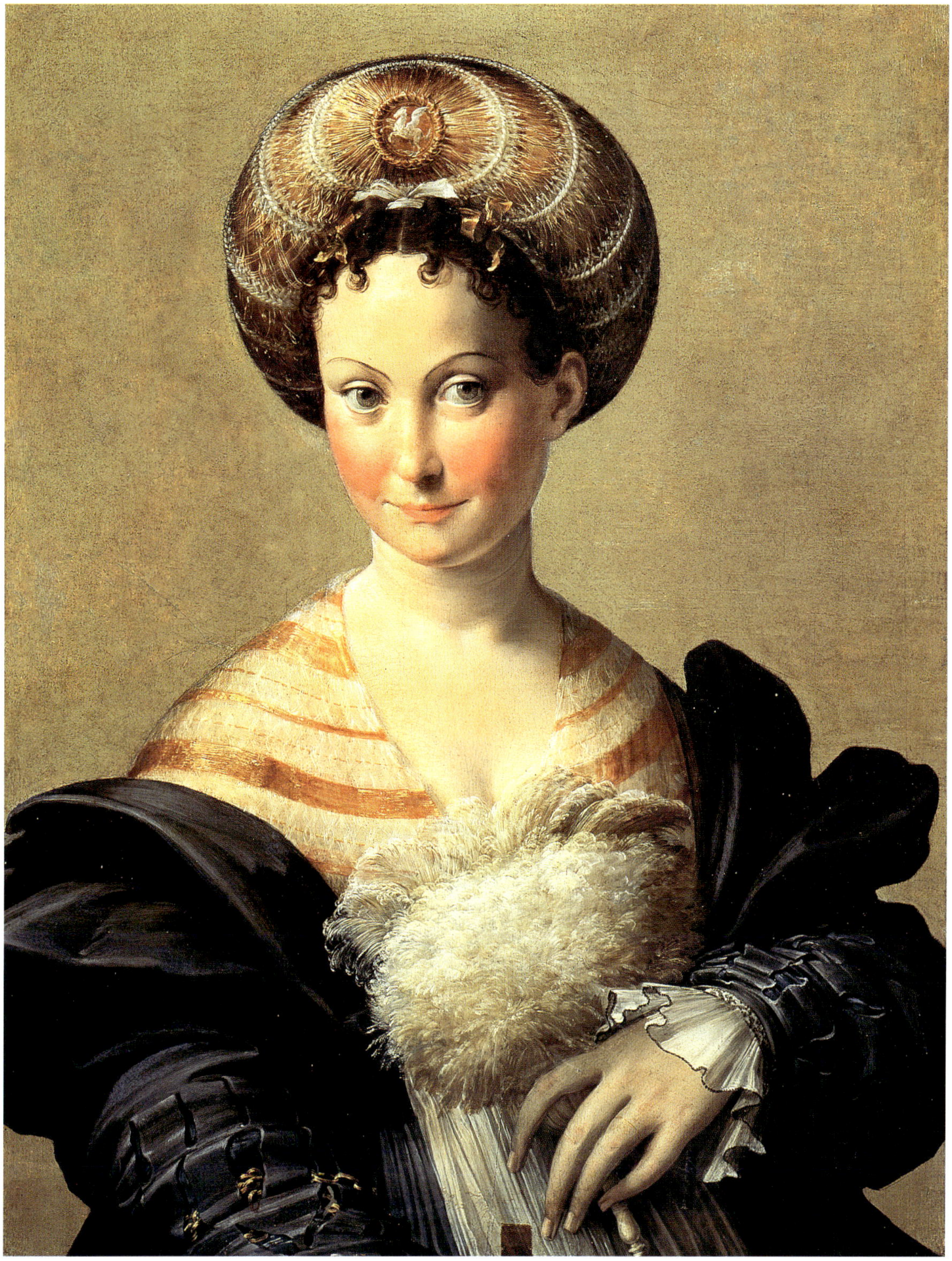

Opposite
Martyrdom of Ten Thousand, Albrecht Dürer, 1508.
Wood transferred to canvas, 99 x 87 cm (Kunsthistorisches Museum, Vienna).

Turkish Slave, Parmigianino (Francesco Mazzola), 1527–1530, Oil on wood, 68 x 53 cm (Galleria Nazionale, Parma).

Near and Far – the Orient During the 17th Century

The Battle of Lepanto, *(sic: italic)*

Veronese (Paolo Caliari), 1581–1582

Oil on canvas, 169 x 137 cm

(Galleria dell'Accademia, Venice).

Allegory of the Battle of Lepanto (also known as *Sebastiano Venier, Victor at Lepanto, Giving Thanks to Christ*,

Veronese (Paolo Caliari), 1581–1582

Oil on canvas, 285 x 565 cm

(The Doges' Palace, Sala del Collegio, Venice).

Fear and Fascination

During the 17th century two great embassies to Versailles brought countries that were distant and still largely unknown into the heart of Europe. The first represented Mawlay Ismail, the Sultan of Morocco, who presented the French king with two lions, a panther, and four ostriches. To thank the Sherifian sultan, Louis XIV in return sent him sumptuous gifts. A French witness to the reception, no doubt with chivalric literature in mind, noted that, "it is true that the gallantry of the Moors has always been held in esteem." Two years later it was the turn of the King of Siam's emissary to astonish and dazzle the court of the French king. Development of commercial relations with both the Near and the Middle East on the one hand, and the fact that the Turkish fleet controlled part of the Mediterranean on the other, meant that treaties had to be made with these two kingdoms, which seemed to have come straight out of the pages of fairy stories.

French relations with the Ottoman Empire, however, were seriously affected when, in 1664, French troops were sent to assist the Austrians at St. Gotthard and the Venetians in Crete. The Venetian defeat was so crushing that Louis XIV decided to recall his ambassador from Constantinople, Monsieur de La Haye Vautelet. On learning this news the Sultan became angry and resolved to send a message to the Sun King requesting him to replace the ambassador as soon as possible. As his messenger he chose Suleyman Aga, whose rank was more or less equivalent to that of a king's courtier. Louis XIV thought that the Grand Sultan was sending him an ambassador, an honor that until then had been reserved for the Habsburg Emperor. Suleyman Aga arrived in Paris amid great pomp in November 1669. His taste and refinement were impressive, and it is thanks to him that the habit of coffee-drinking was introduced into France. This may seem a rather modest achievement, but it was to have a profound effect on European social and intellectual life through the opening of establishments where wits, writers, painters, novelists, philosophers, musicians and actors could meet – an important cultural practice which, developed in the Islamic world, was taken up and adapted to European uses and customs. On 5 December he was received at the chateau of St. Germain-en-Laye. But the ceremony did not go off as well as was expected, for the king was deeply disappointed to learn that Suleyman Aga did not hold the rank of ambassador. In order to avenge this affront to royal dignity, the king asked Molière to write a comedy ridiculing the Turks. The great playwright started immediately, collaborating with the composer Jean-Baptiste Lully to create the *Bourgeois Gentilhomme*. The first showing of this comedy-ballet was at Chambord on 14 October 1670. But the king let Molière know that he was far from pleased with the comedy as it did not ridicule the Turks, as the king had wished, but Frenchmen disguised as Turks.

Relations with the Ottoman Empire had long become difficult as both East and West were attempting to gain control of the Mediterranean. In the 16th century this had led to one of the decisive events in the West's relations with the Ottoman Empire, the Battle of Lapanto in 1571, which was a victory for the West. The Venetian artist Veronese painted his *The Battle of Lepanto* shortly afterwards. He was not the only artist to celebrate this unexpected victory

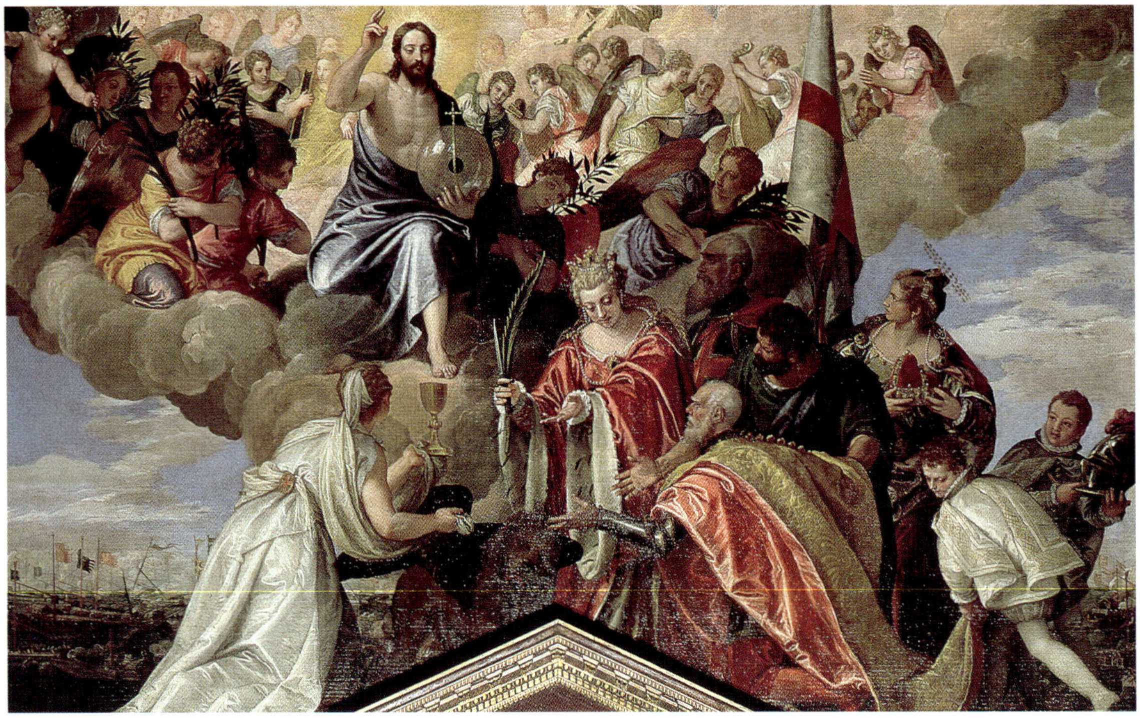

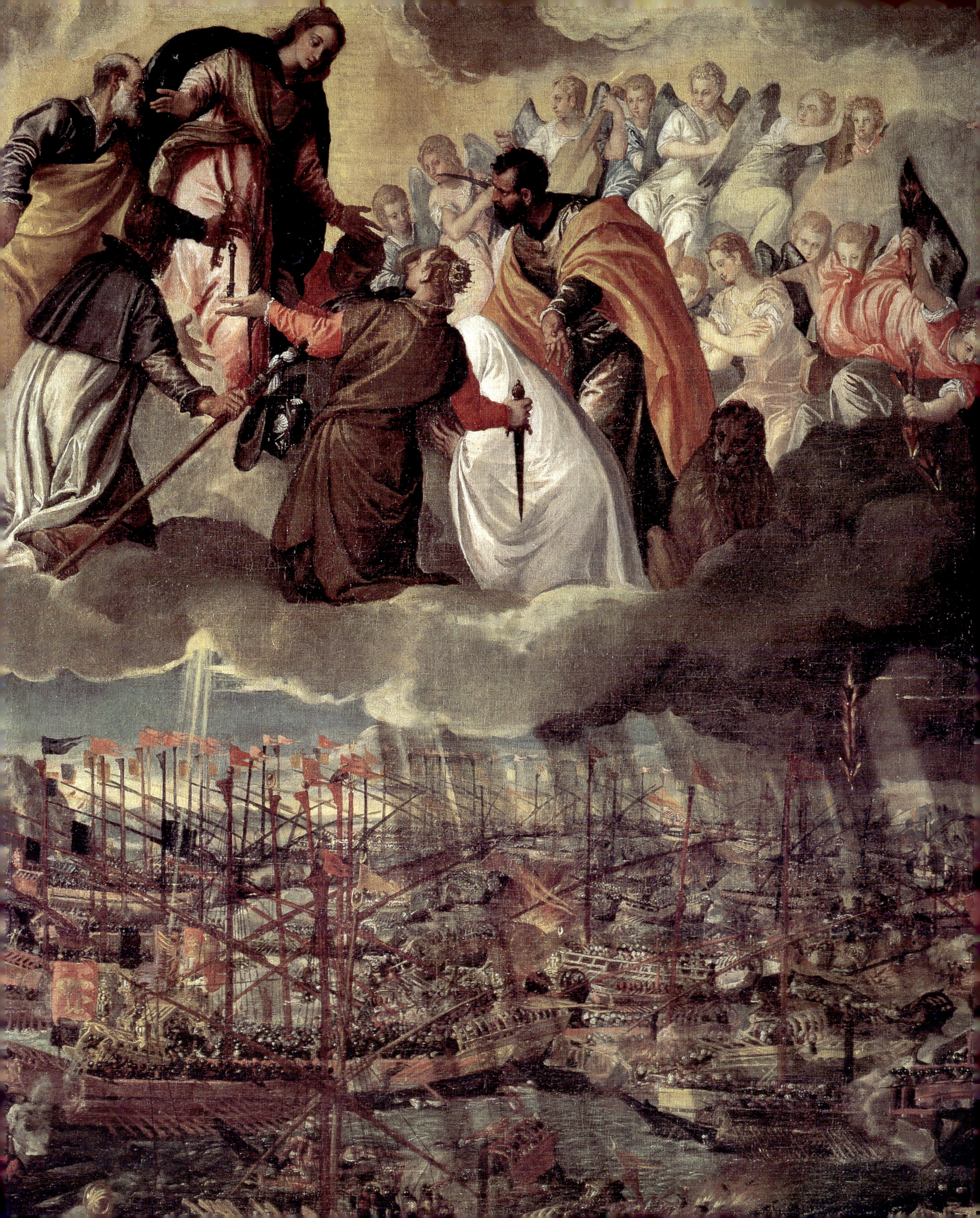

that made the Islamic threat less oppressive. An immense fresco by Tintoretto, painted in the Doge's Palace in Venice, had already commemorated the event (unfortunately, this painting was destroyed in a fire). Titian painted an allegory of King Philip II of Spain that included the triumphal date, and frescos depicting the battle adorned the Roman palace of Marco Antonio Colonna who, as the admiral of the papal fleet, had played a key role in the victory. Veronese shows the 269 ships of the European force battling with the Ottoman galleys under a sky full of dark clouds pierced by bolts of lightning, a feature that lends the scene a miraculous quality. The terrible hand-to-hand fighting, which came to stand as a powerful symbol of the hard-won deliverance of the West – and in which such figures as the Spanish writer Miguel de Cervantes and the French soldier Louis Balbis de Berton de Crillon took part – is described with a wealth of astonishing detail under the banners and oriflammes of the Genoese admiral Andrea Doria and the Venetian admiral Sebestiano Venier.

The decisive naval battle of Lepanto, fought on 7 October 1571, allowed a much-needed period of respite. It was now possible for European nations to convince themselves that the Ottoman expansion, which until then had appeared irresistible, was no longer an imminent threat. The victory brought a deep sense of relief to the Christian world. The nations of Europe had found only a semblance of unity in this new crusade led by Don Juan of Austria, but the victory was highly symbolic: the incontestable supremacy of the Turkish fleet was now in question. This, however, did little to actually check the success of the sultan's forces on land and sea. In the same year as his defeat at Lapanto, Selim occupied Cyprus and within only a few years had rebuilt and even expanded his fleet, retaking Tunisia from the Spanish in 1574. Azerbaijan and Georgia became provinces of the Ottoman Empire in 1608, and a revolt in the principalities of Walachia and Moldavia on the lower Danube was suppressed by the Ottomans after a long and bitter campaign. The peace treaty signed with the Austrians in 1606 marked the height of Ottoman power in Europe.

Incessant wars did not, however, damage the extraordinary prosperity that trade with the countries of the East brought. And with trade came a greater knowledge of the East. Hundreds of travelers returned from their journeys bringing a wealth of information on the customs of Oriental peoples. The young Frenchman Jean Thévenot arrived in Constantinople in 1655 while the Venetian fleet was blockading the Dardanelles. He spent nine months there, gleaning useful information about the city itself, of which he gives a detailed description, and also about the customs of the Turks. He then made his way to Egypt, where he stayed for two years. In his *Voyage du Levant* (Voyage to the Lavant), published in 1665, he attempted to rid himself of prejudice and to show his fellow-countrymen another philosophy of existence and a different form of social life. Jean-Baptiste Tavernier, the son of a Protestant cartographer in Paris, visited Constantinople and then Isfahan, the capital of Persia. Five other journeys followed; and between 1676 and 1679 he published three volumes that give a rich and remarkably accurate account of the Turkish and Persian civilizations. Another Frenchman, Jean Chardin, left Paris for the East in 1644, returning in 1670 but leaving for the East again in 1671 to travel there for a further six years. He, too, was a Protestant and traveled because he was unable, at a time when Protestants were being harshly discriminated against in France, to find employment in his own country. He acquired a profound knowledge of Persia and his works describe with exceptional insight not only the political system, administration, religion, customs, and sights of the country, but also its science and industrial arts. His *Voyages du chevalier de Chardin en Perse et autres lieux de l'Orient* (The Chevalier de Chardin's travels in Persia and other Oriental lands) was read by Montesquieu in his château at La Brède and formed an important source for his famous *Lettres Persianes* (Persian letters), in which he satirizes European institutions and values by seeing them through the innocent eyes of two Persian visitors. This abundance of literature made a major contribution to changing how Europeans viewed the East.

The theater in France during the 17th century, the *grand siècle*, found useful themes in both the ancient and modern Orient. Pierre Corneille wrote no less than three plays inspired by the East – *Nicomède*, *Rodogune*, and *Sophonisbe* – while Jean Racine was inspired by the illustrations in Ricaut's book *Relation de l'empire ottomane* (An account of the Ottoman Empire) "to dress our lovers in the Turkish manner," as it was noted at the time. For *Bajazet*, a tragedy that deals with an almost contemporary question, he drew his information from de Cesy and de La Haye, ambassador at the Sublime Porte, as Constantinople was sometimes called. Despite Racine's efforts at authenticity, Madame de Sévigné wrote that "everyone reproaches him for not having been Turkish enough." His *Esther* is the story of a courtesan who reigned over the affections of the king of Persia – the connection with Madame de Maintenon and Louis XIV was immediately apparent – and the heroine of his *Bérénice* is the "Queen of Palestine."

Artists were still interested in using Moorish or Oriental characters drawn from such works as Ariosto's *Orlando Furioso* (notably Armina the sultana, whose enchanted pavilion resembles a kiosk similar to those in the Grand Seraglio), and Tasso's epic *Gerusalemme Liberata* (Jerusalem delivered). Few painters, however, made their way to the

Solomon and the Queen of Sheba,
Frans II Francken, between 1606 and 1617
Oil on wood, 131 x 116 cm
(Musée des Beaux-Arts, Quimper).

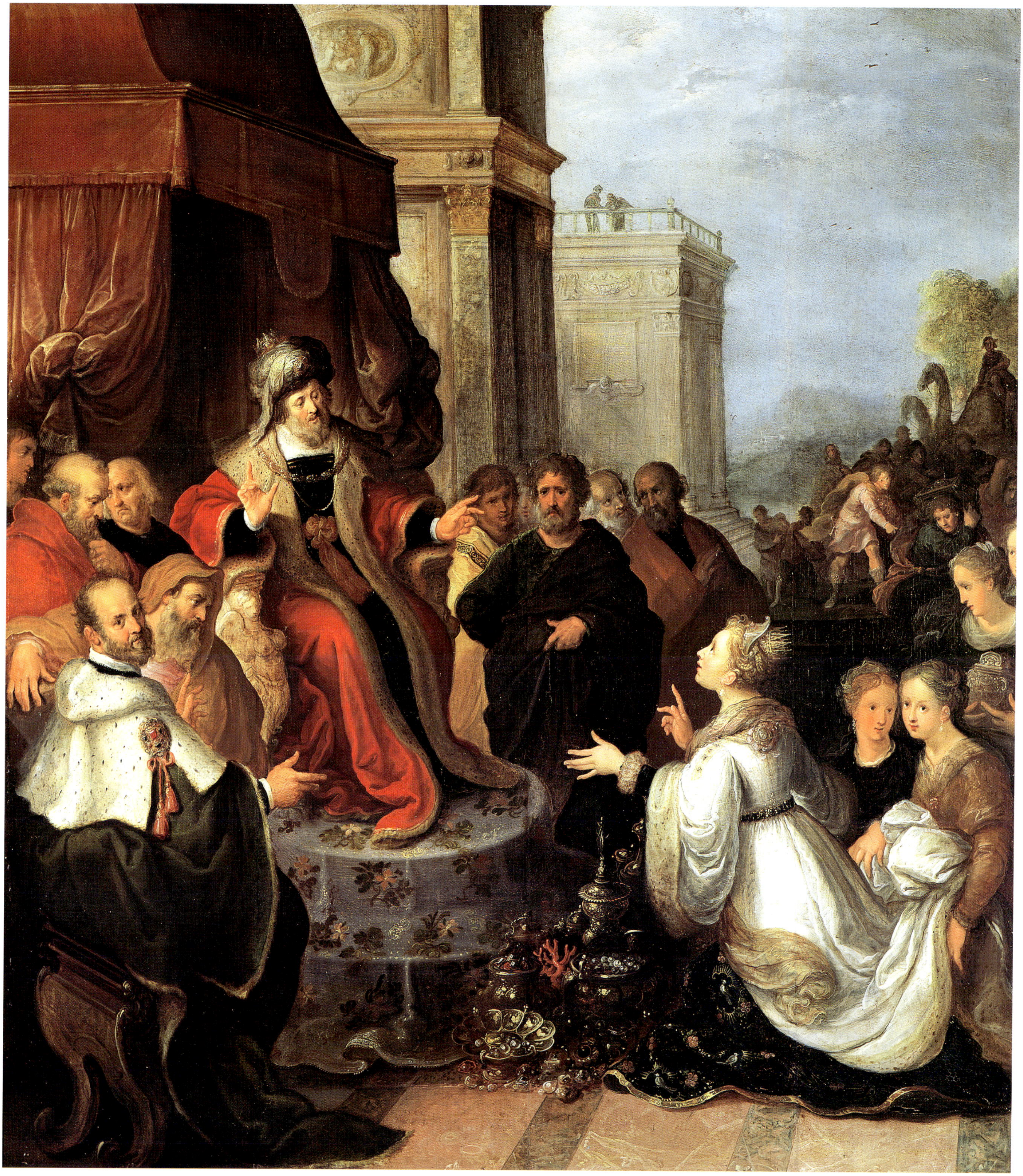

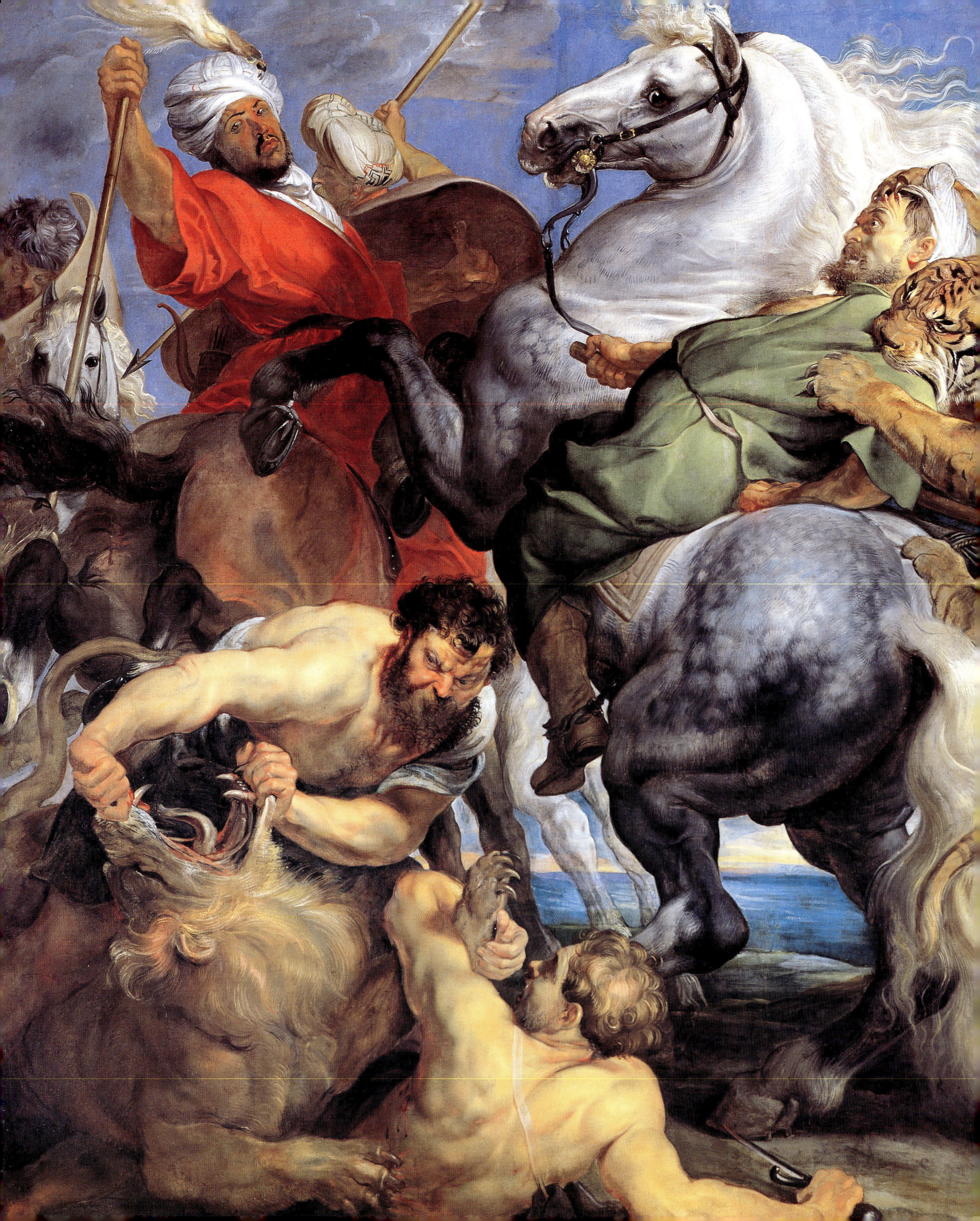

East. Simon Vouet, having visited London in 1605, spent an entire year in Constantinople in 1610, when he was only 20 years old. Unfortunately, his work shows no trace of his experiences in the capital of the Ottoman Empire.

ART AND UNCERTAINTY

Vouet was in fact typical, for despite greater contact with the East, most Western artists were uncertain about how to assimilate the Orient into their work. Little by little it did enter painting, but it did so timidly, ,poradically, and without a clear logic. Across Europe, responses varied widely.

When the envoy of Mawlay Ismail, the Sultan of Morocco, presented himself with great splendor to the court of Louis XIV, the artist Antoine Coypel was present; he had been charged with immortalizing the extraordinary event. He produced several paintings, the most instructive and entertaining of which is without doubt *The Moroccan Ambassador at the Comédie Italienne*. Morocco fascinated Peter Paul Rubens, too: he painted a portrait of Mawlay Ahmed, a picture that is in fact a copy of a canvas (now lost) painted by Jan Vermeyen, the creator of a group of tapestries entitled *The Conquest of Tunisia* that celebrate Emperor Charles V's victorious campaign in North Africa. Vermeyen had accompanied the emperor on this military campaign and depicts him in the company of the young Moroccan prince, Ahmed, before the walls of a besieged city. Rubens made great use of this portrait as a prototype for the Oriental figures he included in many of his pictures, for example his *Tiger Hunt* of 1618. It was executed for Maximilien von

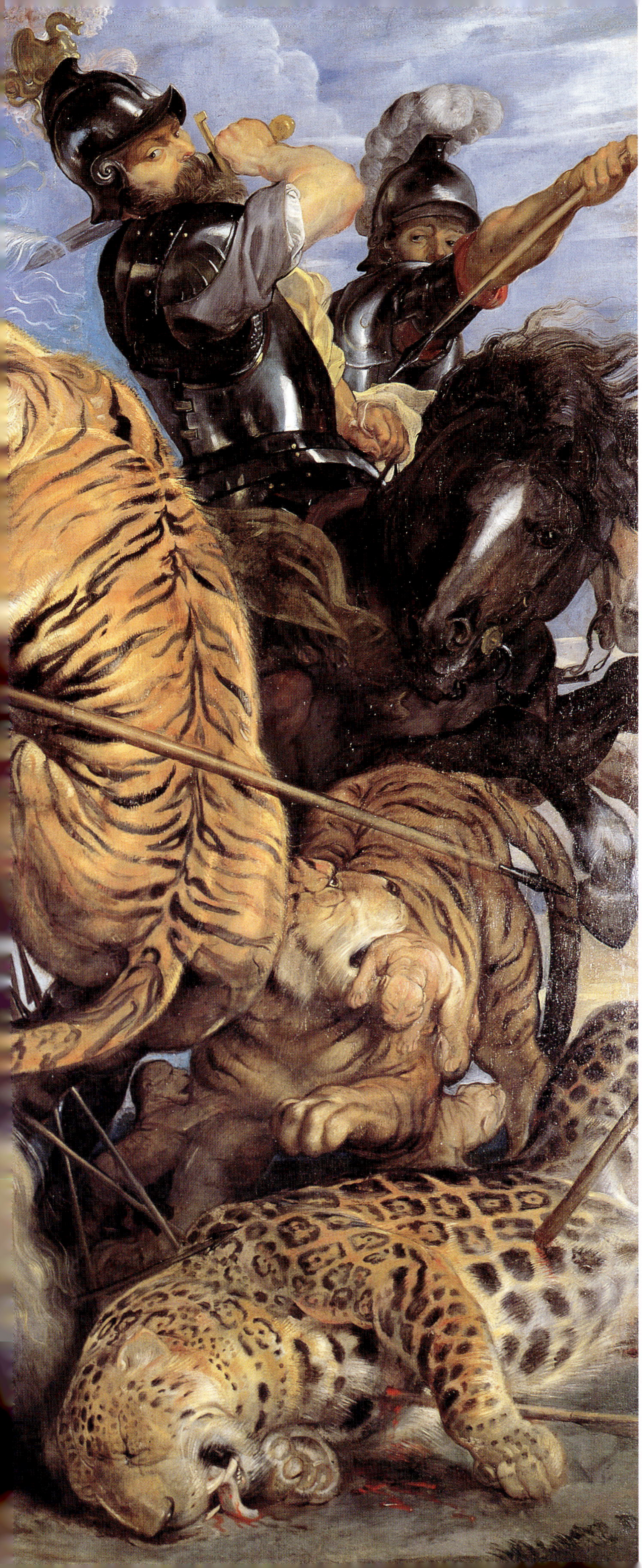

The Tiger Hunt,
Peter Paul Rubens, c. 1616
Oil on canvas, 256 x 324 cm
(Musée des Beaux-Arts, Rennes).

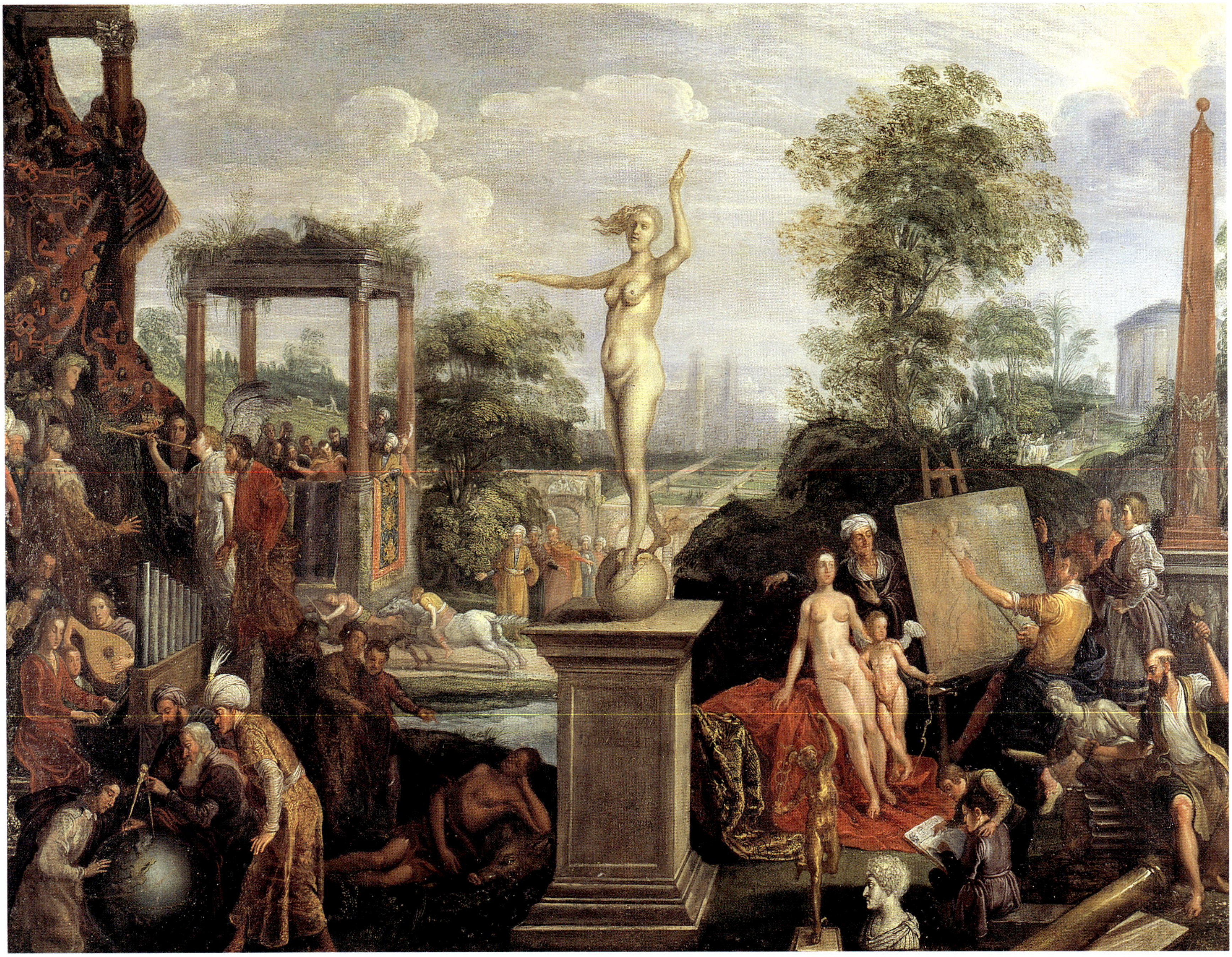

Allegory,
Frans II Francken, 1628
Oil on copper, 48 x 66 cm
(Musée du Périgord, Périgueux).

Wittelsbach, the Elector of Bavaria, who had rebuilt the castle of Schlossheim and asked the painter to depict different types of hunting (for wild boar, tigers, crocodiles, and lions) to decorate its walls. Rubens also shows his penchant for the Orient in his religious paintings, as in his eleven versions of *The Adoration of the Magi* and his *Epiphany* in the Prado.

Some artists were generally content to introduce just a few notes of authenticity to lent credibility to a host of implausibilities or pure speculation. Trophisme Bigot, in his *St. Sebastian Attended by St. Irene*, dressed the attractive servant who holds the lamp that lights the scene in a turban painted in minute detail. Similarly, in his *Annunciation* (1624), Claude Vignon was equally attentive to the costumes of the Magi, each of whom symbolizes a continent, and in his *David with the Head of Goliath* he crowned David with very unusual 'Oriental' headgear. In paintings such as *Lot's Daughters*, *The Queen of Sheba*, *Esther*, and *Ahasuerus Displaying his Treasures to Marduk*, he makes a clear effort to introduce authentic objects, finery, and costumes, while the rest of the composition is invented. The Flemish painter Frans II Francken, in his various versions of *Solomon and the Queen of Sheba*, puts the accent on Solomon's opulent ceremonial robes, but also uses a camel and a few unknown trees to vaguely suggest an Eastern setting. Sometimes sitters liked the incongruity of dressing up as people from the Near

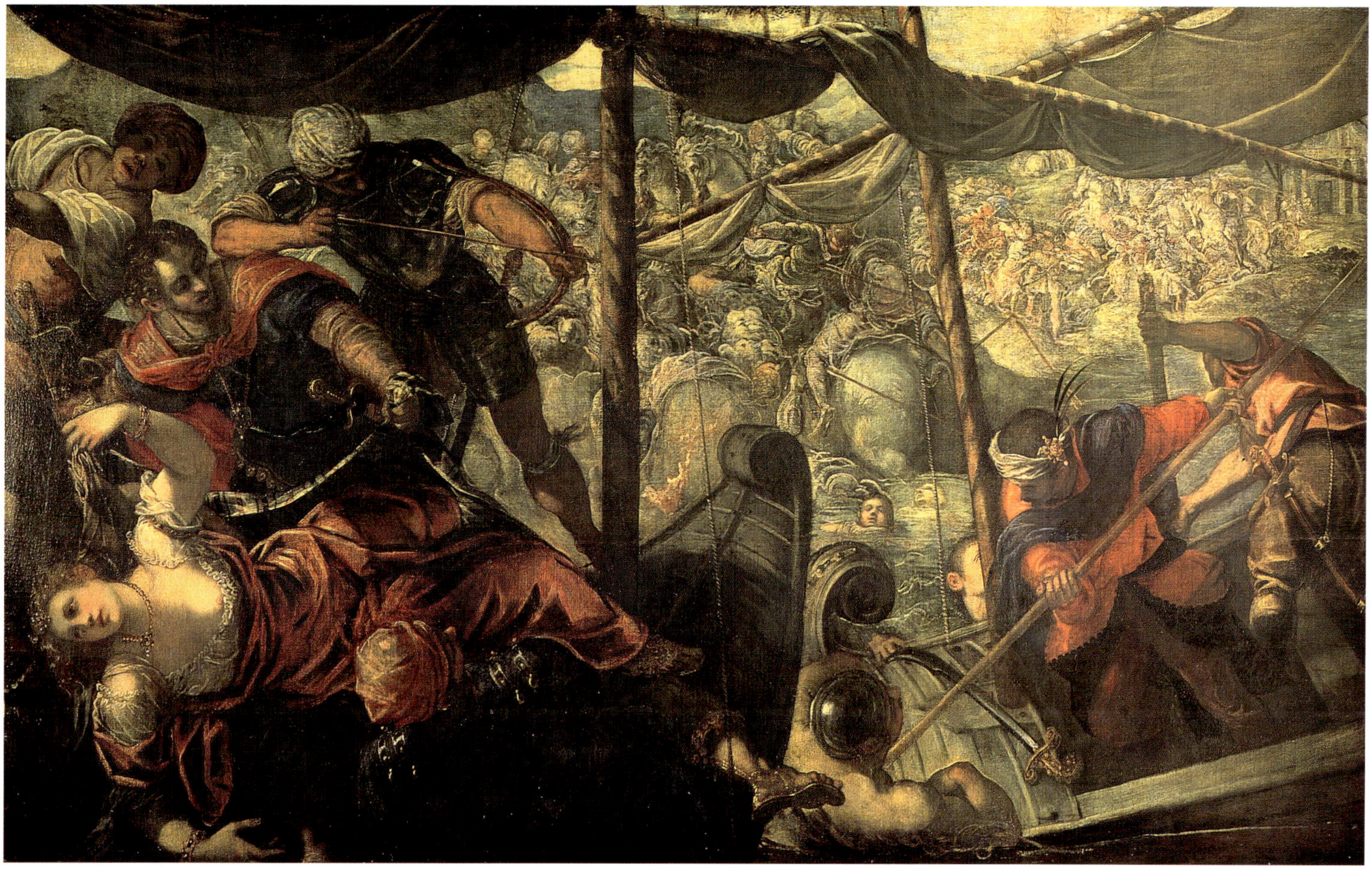

Battle Between Turks and Christians (or *Abduction of Helen*), Tintoretto (Jacopo Robusti), c. 1580
Oil on canvas, 186 x 307 cm
(Museo del Prado, Madrid)

or Middle East; Van Dyck, for example, painted the Englishman Robert Shirley dressed as a Persian and wearing a turban.

Frans II Franken, a painter from Antwerp, was struck by the journey made by the envoys of Shah Abbas I, King of Persia. This great Safavid ruler, a descendant of Caliph Ali, wishing to get to know the West better and to forge relations with certain of its countries, despatched emissaries to Tsar Boris Godunov in Moscow, to the King of Bohemia, to Philip II in Valladolid, and to the King of Portugal in Lisbon. Franken represents him favorably in his *Allegory* (1628), showing Shah Abbas as a new Caesar saluted by the trumpet of Renown. He appears as the wise protector of the liberal arts: painters, sculptors, and musicians work in the foreground, encouraged by Love and Venus. Behind, a horse race between a kiosk and an obelisk unmistakably reminds us of the Hippodrome in Constantinople. This reference may well have had a political significance, since the Persia empire had once reached as far as ancient Byzantium. In the distance, cupolas and minarets strengthen the impression of an Islamicized East.

The fear inspired by the civilizations that followed the Prophet was deeply felt, and the struggle against Ottoman forces became a common theme in the decoration of palaces all over Europe. The palace of Troia near Prague gives a vivid demonstration of this, almost to the point of obsession in fact, the fireplaces being lavishly decorated with chained Turkish soldiers and the trophies of victories that were still unlikely. In 1641, the Neapolitan painter Andrea di Lione painted a *Battle Against the Turks*. This appears to be a depiction of the famous Papal Legate, St. John of the Marches, who went to fight in Hungary, which was still threatened by the Ottoman invaders. It is all the more likely that the work was executed at the time when Urban VIII authorized devotion to this military and spiritual hero, who had died in Naples in 1476. Many painters took up this type of subject: the Italian artist Mola painted an impressive *Oriental Archer*, the Spaniard Carducho a *Massacre of the German Carthusians*, and the French artist Courtois, known as Le Bourguignon (the Burgundian), several canvases depicting cavalry engagements between Turks and Christians. Salvatore Rosa and the school of the Neapolitan Falcone also adopted this theme. Around 1580 Tintoretto had demonstrated a similar interest in topical events. Long thought to be an *Abduction of Helen*, his *Battle Between Turks and Christians* (around 1580) in fact alludes to the pirate raids that grew more numerous after the famous Barbary pirate Baba Aroudj (Khayr ad-Din), known to Europeans as Barbarossa, made an alliance with the Sublime Porte. It was he who abducted the daughter of the Venetian governor of Corfu, Cecilia Venier-Masso. The painting is full of authentic details, especially the costumes of the captains and the Turkish soldiers. It was acquired by the Spanish artist Velazquez on behalf of King Philip IV of Spain. It is thought that this painting made a pair with *The Escape*, which is now in Dresden Museum. Two naked women, still wearing chains, are climbing down a rope from the top of a tower to a boat waiting for them below; one of them is falling into the arms of a knight.

It was always timely to remember the constant danger posed by the Muslim world. An illustration of this is *The Surrender of Seville*, painted by the Spanish artist Francisco de Zurbarán in 1628. It refers to the recapture of the capital of Andalusia by the Spaniards in 1248 after a siege lasting 16 months. Zurbarán painted the picture for the Order of Mercy (the founder of which had taken part in this siege), at the same time as a series of canvases destined for the order. If the clothes worn by the victor of Seville, the most Catholic King Ferdinand III, are authentic, those of King Achacafs, who is kneeling to present him with the keys of the city, resemble those of the Turkish corsairs who criss-crossed the Mediterranean, preying on the ships of the Spanish fleet and even having the audacity to threaten galleons returning from America when they were just off the coast of Galicia.

But the appeal and the mystery of this threatening Orient were also quite amply expressed in painting. Veronese, for example, endows figures from the Scriptures with the appearance of Muslim potentates in such works as *Feast in the House of Simon, The Pharisee*, and *The Last Supper*. In *The Wedding at Cana*, destined for the refectory of the Convent of S. Giorgio Maggiore in Venice, the painter places his artist friends (Titian, Tintoretto, and Bassano) on an equal level with the great rulers who are present – Charles V, Emperor of the Holy Roman Empire, and Suleyman II, the Grand Sultan of the Ottoman Empire, the two most powerful sovereigns of their time. The princes' table is remarkable: Oriental dignitaries mingle with the patricians and beauties of Venice, who are served by black cupbearers.

So, despite a political situation that was always precarious, and a growing interest in

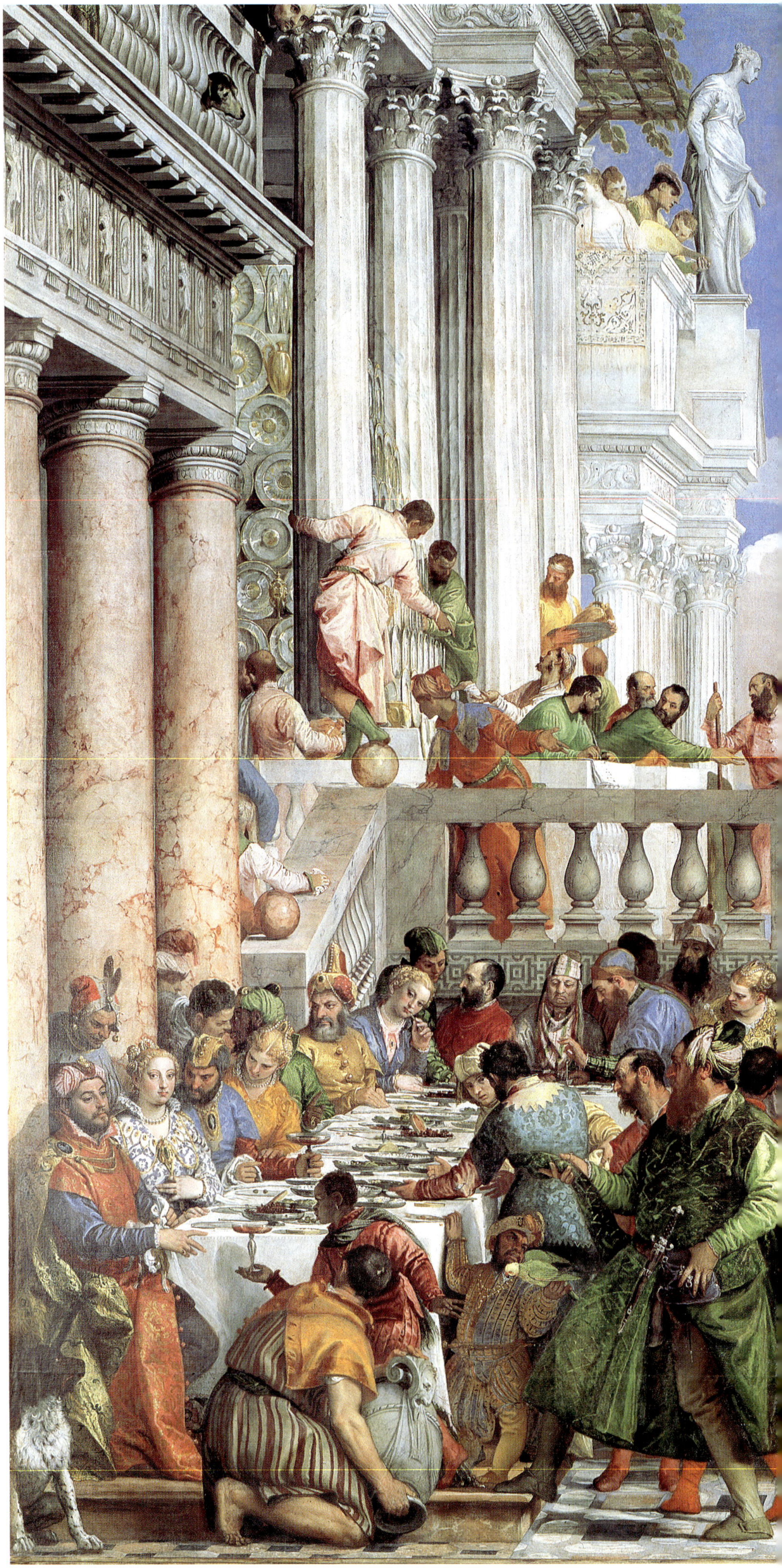

The Wedding at Cana,
Veronese (Paolo Caliari), 1562–1563
Oil on canvas, 677 x 994 cm
(Musée du Louvre, Paris).

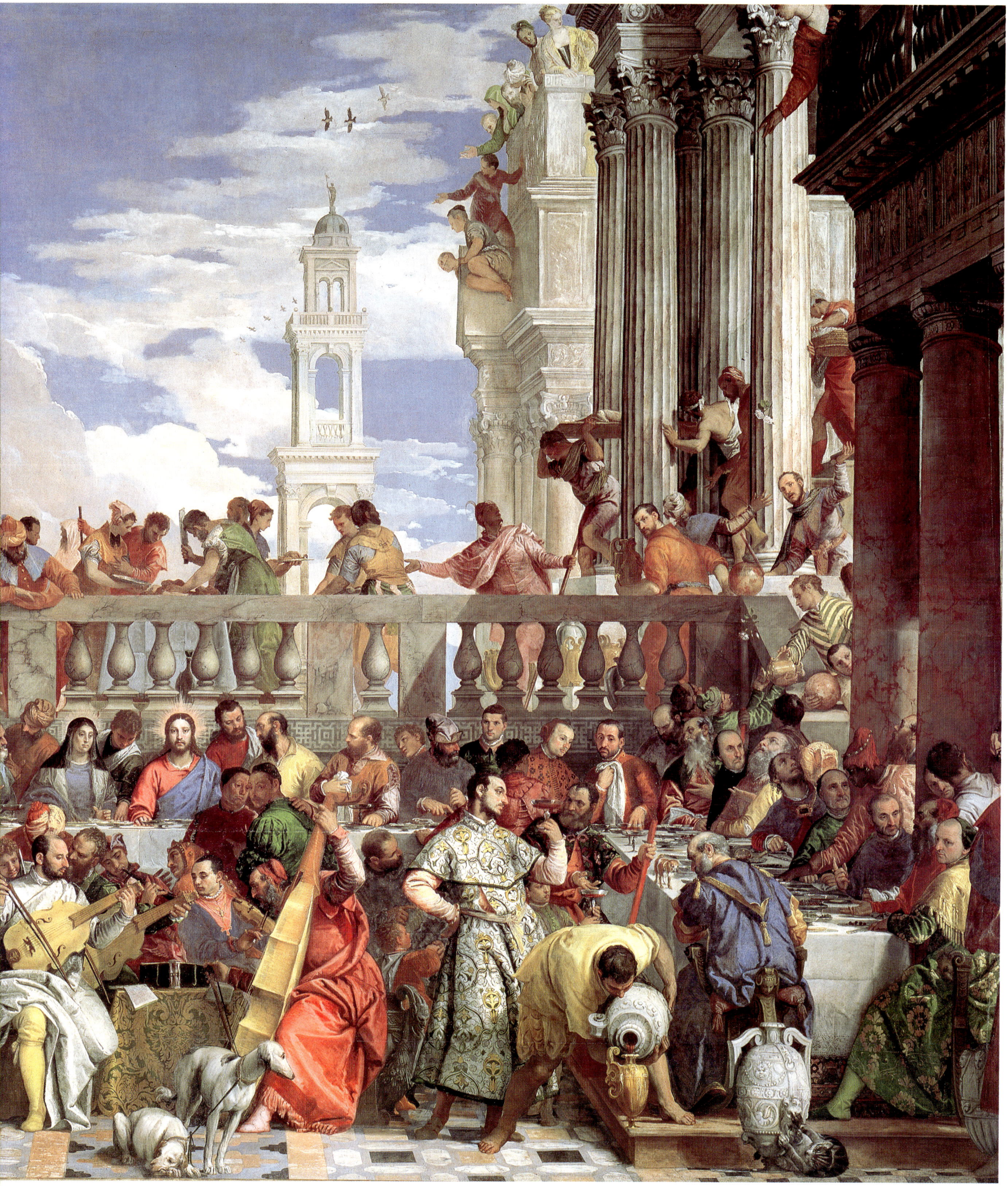

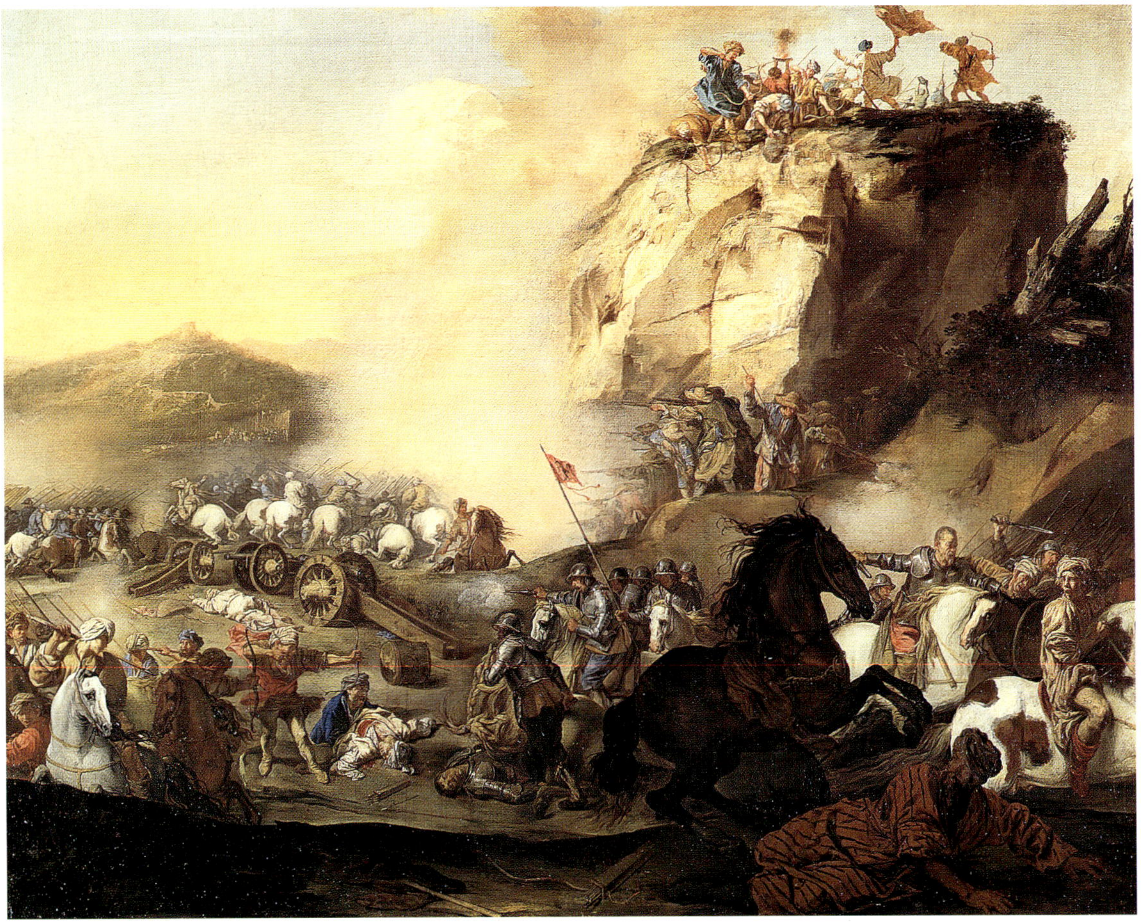

Battle Against the Turks,
Andrea di Lione, 1641
Oil on canvas, 103 x 130 cm
(Musée du Louvre, Paris).

Panthée Led Before Cyrus,
Laurent de La Hyre, c. 1633 (detail)
Oil on canvas, 143 x 120 cm
(Musée Municipal de La Louvière, Montluçon).

another concept of civilization as symbolized by the Ottomans, in general Western art did not appear concerned with reflecting this cultural and political game of mirrors. On the contrary, in religious art in particular painters retained and even strengthened the convention used in depicting scenes from the Old and New Testaments. The ancient East was also dealt with in terms of iconographic traditions that owed little to historical accuracy. Simon Vouet, who as we have seen had spent a year in Constantinople when he was only 20, is one of the clearest examples of this. His numerous religious paintings never show any real Oriental influence. But there were a few attempts to include a little more realism, even if only in the details; an example is a canvas by Laurent de La Hyre, *Panthée Led Before Cyrus*. A subject already painted by Hardy in 1624 and Tristan in 1639, the story told by the Greek historian Xenophon shows Queen Panthée as a prisoner, led with her servants before the founder of the Persian empire, Cyrus the Great. Araspe unveils her before her conqueror, who interrupts the degrading act with a compassionate gesture that shows him sensitive to the beauty of the beautiful Panthée. The treasures strewn at the prince's feet – jewels, incense burners, ewers, cups, caskets, and a thousand precious and curious objects, including turbans decorated with ostrich plumes – give a semblance of verisimilitude to this episode, even though the reconstruction is wholly imaginary. Towards 1630 the painter brought the story of Panthée and Cyrus to its happy conclusion with *Cyrus Announces to Araspe that Panthée has Obtained his Mercy*. Here again we see the same acid colors, with delicate greens and turquoise blues, and the same plumed Persian trappings spread out in front of the unfortunate queen, who is still half naked – eroticism was indeed to be a key feature of Orientalism in Western art.

Though on the whole Western artists of the 16th century were unable to successfully assimilate the Oriental world into their work, there was one artist who found in it a profound aspect of spirituality: Rembrandt.

Rembrandt's Orient

Rembrandt Harmenszoon van Rijn was the son of an affluent Leiden miller and a Catholic who converted to Protestantism. What lay behind his deep, obsessive attraction to the Orient? He doubtless owed it to his parents, and especially his mother, whom he depicts in a magnificent portrait as an old woman attentively reading an enormous, almost disproportionately large Bible that seems almost crushingly heavy (1631). He never traveled and never wanted to, for he found inexhaustible treasure in reading the Old Testament. While remaining a member of the Calvinist church, which sometimes censured his behavior, Rembrandt gradually drew closer to the Mennonites, an Anabaptist sect to which several of his friends belonged, including the art dealer Hendrick van Uylenburch, with whom he lodged in Amsterdam between 1632 and 1635 and whose niece, Saskia, was to become his wife. This religious community claimed a direct and spontaneous relationship with God. It appears that Rembrandt did not join the sect, but he clearly had a deep sympathy for it. Did

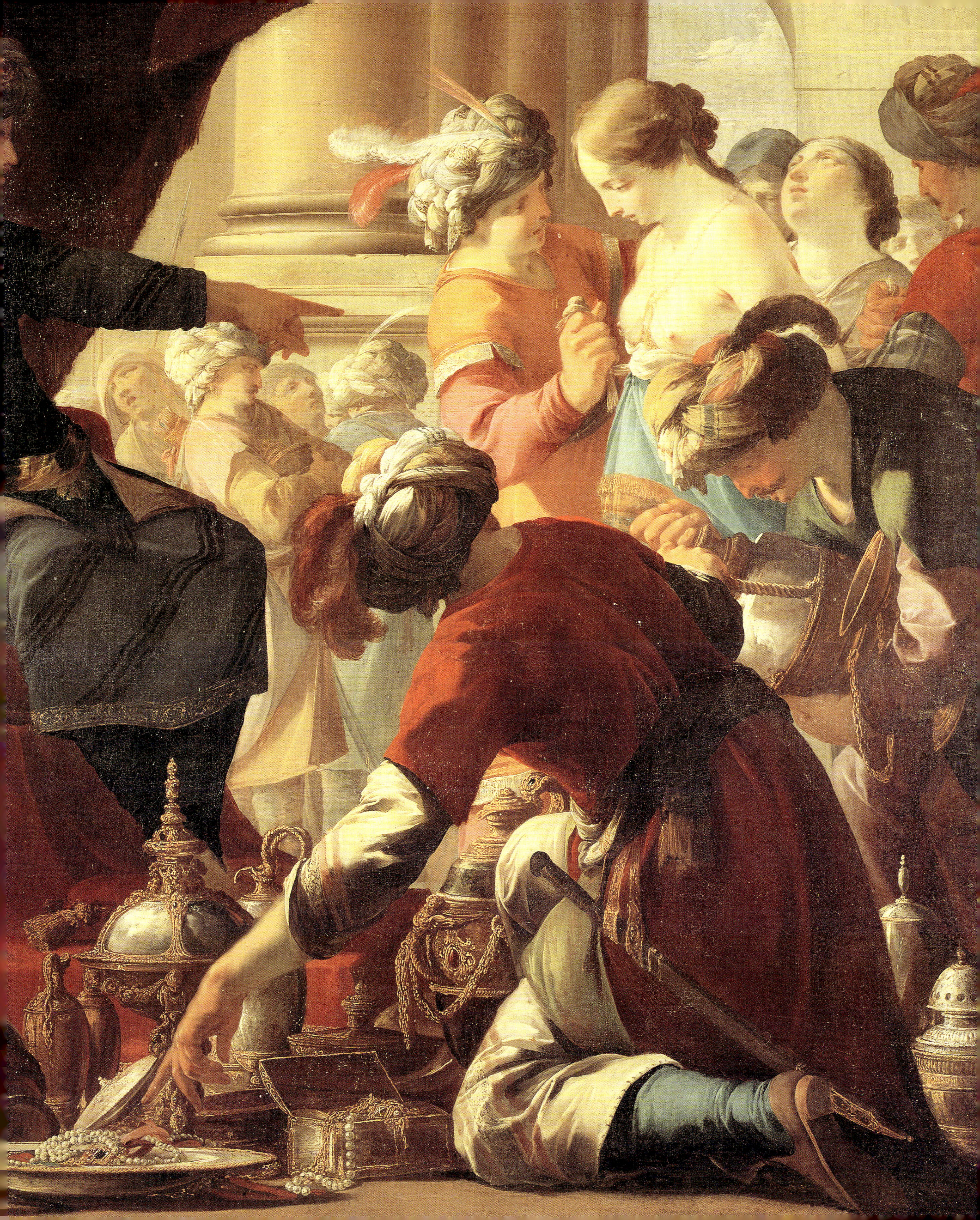

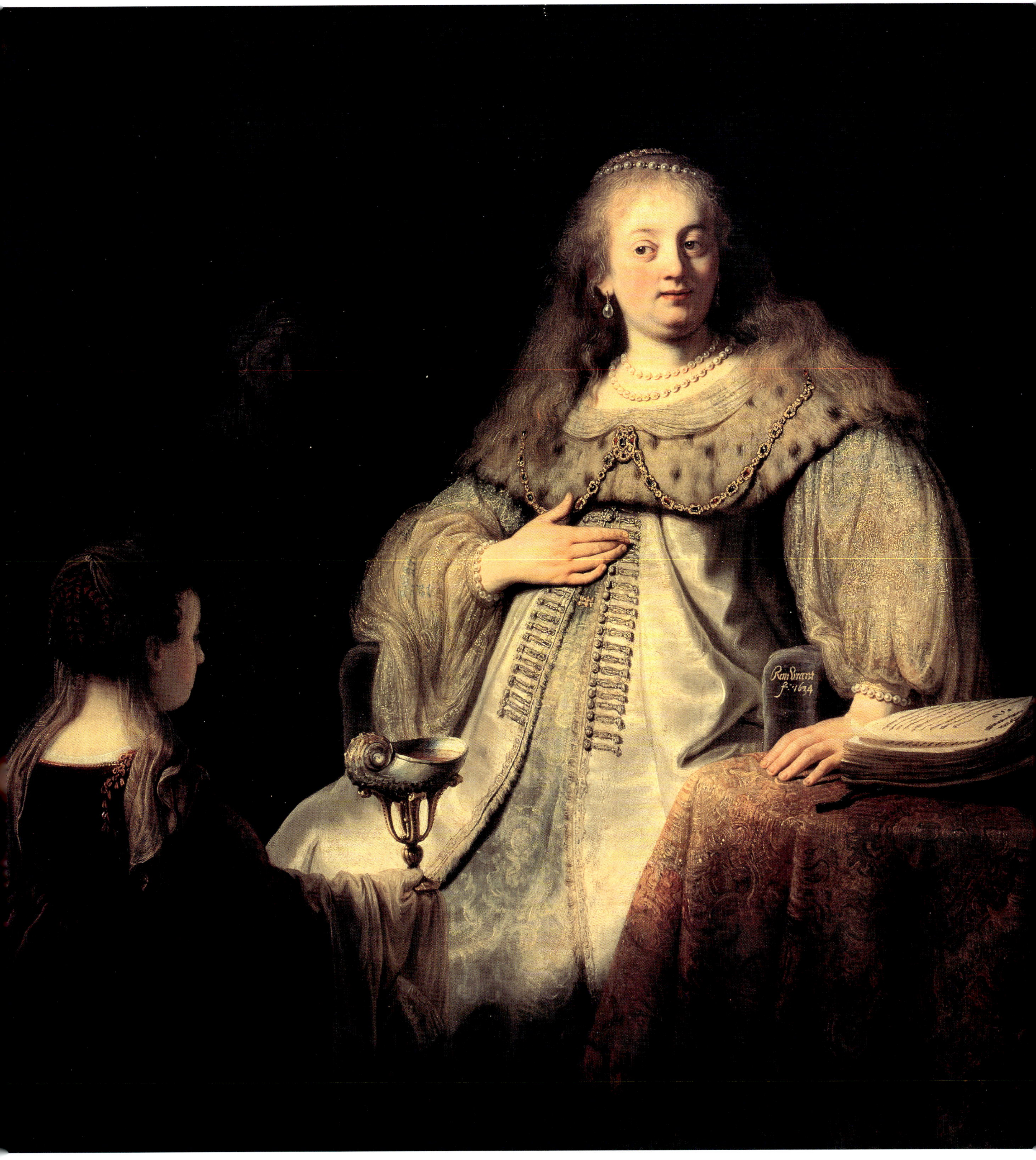

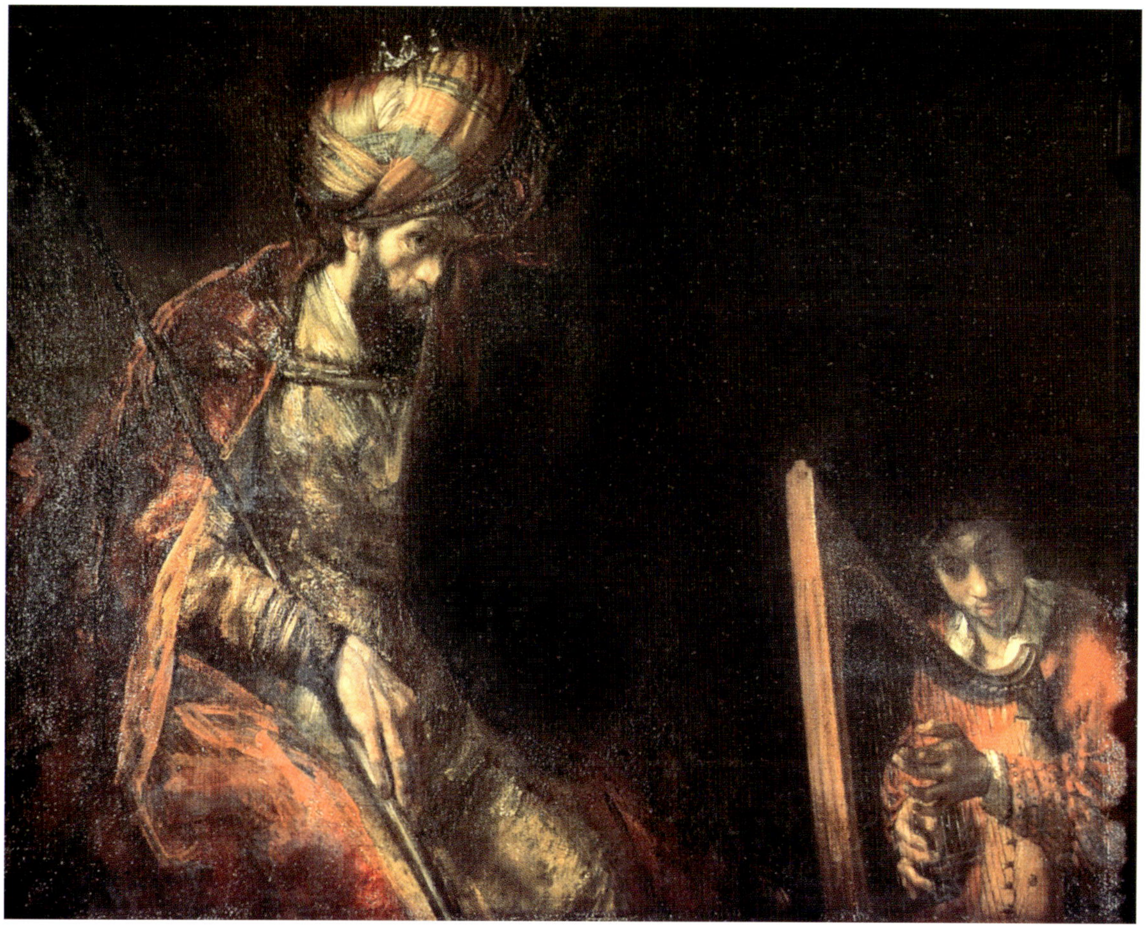

he feel a secret desire to convey his own response to the Bible, not as regards its theological interpretation, but in terms of a direct and intense response to its spiritual truth? He never stopped recounting the life of Christ, depicting Him among His disciples, or suffering the many torments of the Passion. As an artist, Rembrandt attempted to bring the events and key figures of the New Testament, from the Virgin Mary to the Apostles, before the eyes of his contemporaries in a way that confirmed their spiritual reality while in no way detracting from their humanity.

It was the biblical Orient that appeared in his earliest works, for example in *Balaam's Ass* (1626), which was inspired by a painting by his master, Lastman, and in *David Presenting the Head of Goliath to Saul* (1625–1627). In these canvases he already shows a clear taste for the theatrical, both in terms of dramatic intensity, and in terms of richly ornamented clothes, which he delights in depicting in vivid detail. His idea of the East rapidly became opulent and excessive, as we can see in compositions like *Judas Returning the Thirty Pieces of Silver* (1629), *David Playing the Harp before Saul* (c. 1630), and the extraordinary *Presentation at the Temple* (1631), in which he insists on giving the Temple the appearance of a synagogue. The luxuriant character of his imaginary Orient was to grow not only as he advanced in years but also as he increasingly refined his art, as his *Sophonisba Receiving the Poisoned Chalice* (1634) shows. Here, the Carthaginian princess Sophonisba, refusing to become a captive of the Romans, appears triumphant; as she prepares to die by her own hand, there is no trace of the victim about her. As a young servant holds out to her a precious cup – a rare shell mounted on a golden stem – she stands out against the darkness as if she herself were the source of all the light, ready to gain her liberty at the price of her own life. And what can we make of *Belshazzar's Feast* (c. 1635)? The powerful King of Babylon pulls back in astonishment as he sees the Hebrew words *Mene, mene, tekel, upharsin* written in letters of fire, announcing his imminent death and the destruction of his kingdom. In 1640, in the *Visitation*, Rembrandt attempted to make the scene as realistic as possible, producing a feeling both of simplicity (in the attitude and clothing of Anne and the Virgin) and of sumptuousness (the composition itself and the little black servant who is taking off Mary's mantle).

With Rembrandt it is not unusual to find contemporary subjects treated in an orientalized fashion; or, conversely, biblical themes treated as though they were subjects from the artist's own day. Examples include *Jacob Blessing the Son of Joseph* (1656), and *Samson Blinded by the Philistines* (1638), which forms part of a cycle on which he worked for ten years. His *Jewish Bride* (1665) transforms a ceremony that he could well have attended into a vision of antiquity that possesses a dreamlike quality.

By contrast, the setting of *Christ and the Woman Taken in Adultery* (1644) is monumental and the number of characters enormous, as though he had transposed an episode from the New Testament into the Old. Rembrandt's passion for this fabulous Orient, for an East both sumptuous and violent, comes across in an unusual self-portrait. He clearly had a particular taste for this genre, for he executed over a hundred self-portraits during his life, disguising himself as a young soldier, an old commander, a Spanish gentleman, a Dutch magistrate, and so on, only rarely appearing as an artist (as in *The Artist Drawing at the Window*, an etching dating from 1648). In his self-portrait *The Oriental Prince* (1631) he

David Playing the Harp before Saul,
Rembrandt van Rijn, c. 1655
Oil on canvas, 130 x 164.3 cm (Mauritshuis, La Haye).

Sophonisba Receiving the Poisoned Chalice (or *Artemisia*), Rembrandt van Rijn, 1634
Oil on canvas, 142 x 153 cm
(Museo del Prado, Madrid).

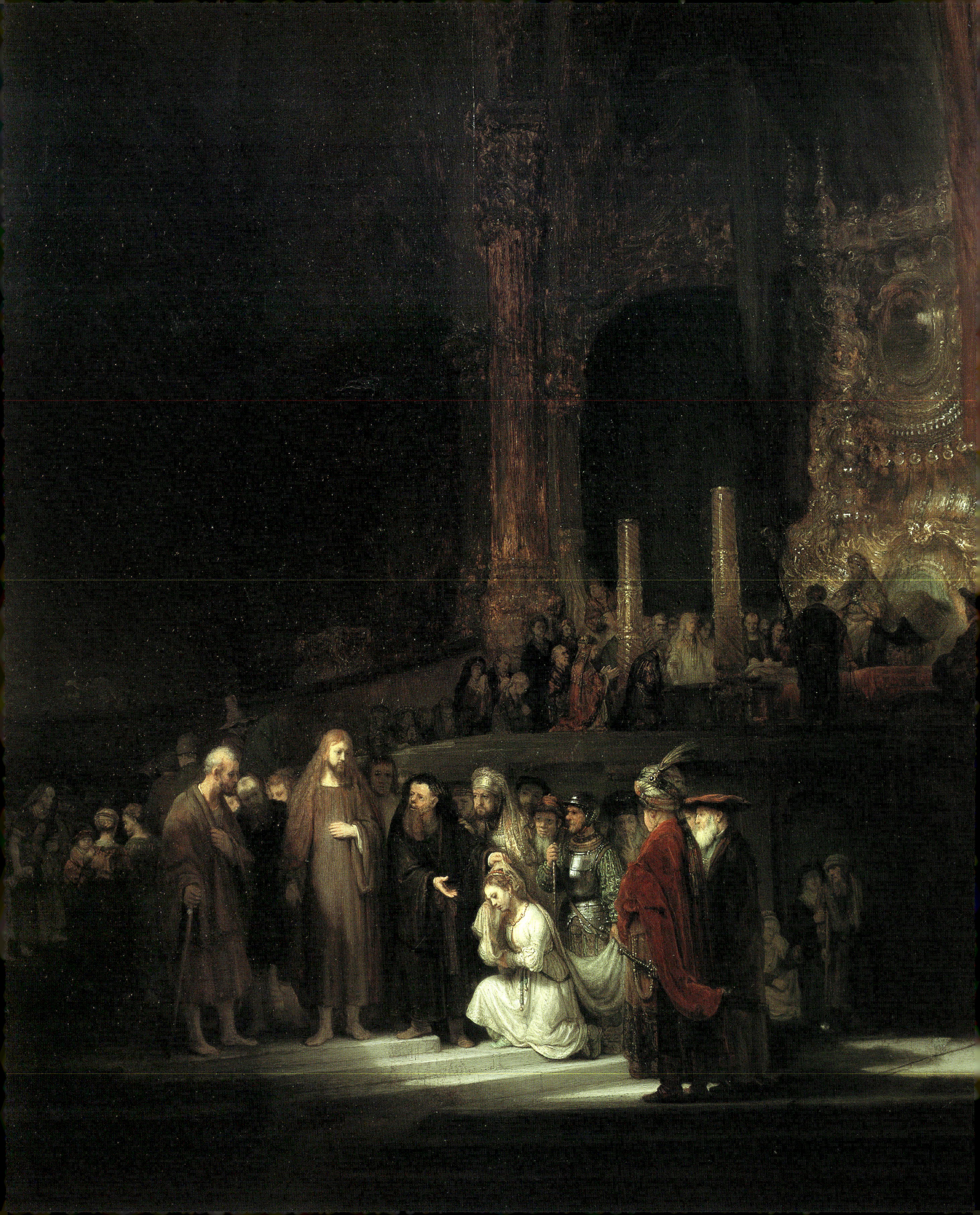

presents himself draped in a dark, sober mantle, but wearing a golden robe. The setting is simple, almost stark, with a pale circle of light on a wall contrasting with the enveloping shadows. In the foreground a dog is sitting on tiles. The painter's attitude appears equivocal: in his fine costume he gives the impression of being proud and haughty, and yet at the same time aware that he is slightly ridiculous.

However, the most striking aspect of Rembrandt's attitude to the Orient was his strong feeling for the Jewish world. In 1639 he decided to purchase a large house in Sin Anthonies Breestraat, next to that of his friend Uylenburch, which was near the artists' quarter but, more particularly, at the entrance to Amsterdam's Jewish quarter. There is no doubt that the painter felt drawn to the Jewish tradition. On this issue Emmanuel Berl writes that Rembrandt was "At once the opposite and the complementary of Spinoza, who inclined towards Christianity as Rembrandt did towards Judaism [...] The more Christian Rembrandt felt, the closer he approached the Jews by and in his spirit, to the point where one asks whether he was not himself Jewish, although there is nothing in his ancestry which gives us leave to suppose this..." He was particularly fascinated by the Portuguese synagogue in Amsterdam, the one the philosopher Spinoza attended. He painted portraits of rabbis (such as *Portrait of an Old Rabbi*) and used models from the ghetto, as in *David Playing the Harp*, where he chose an adolescent who bore a curious resemblance to his own son, Titus.

Finally, in his large and remarkable collection of studio props and equipment there were many rare books, prints, and works of art, including a portfolio of views of Turkey by Melchior Lorch, Hendrik van Aest and other artists, as well as some Persian miniatures. Around 1655 he copied some of these – including *Shah Jehan on Horseback, Holding a Falcon* and *The Emperor Jahangir Receiving a Message* – in watercolor, or pen, brush and sepia. He also engraved *The Persian* and two Oriental heads (c. 1635).

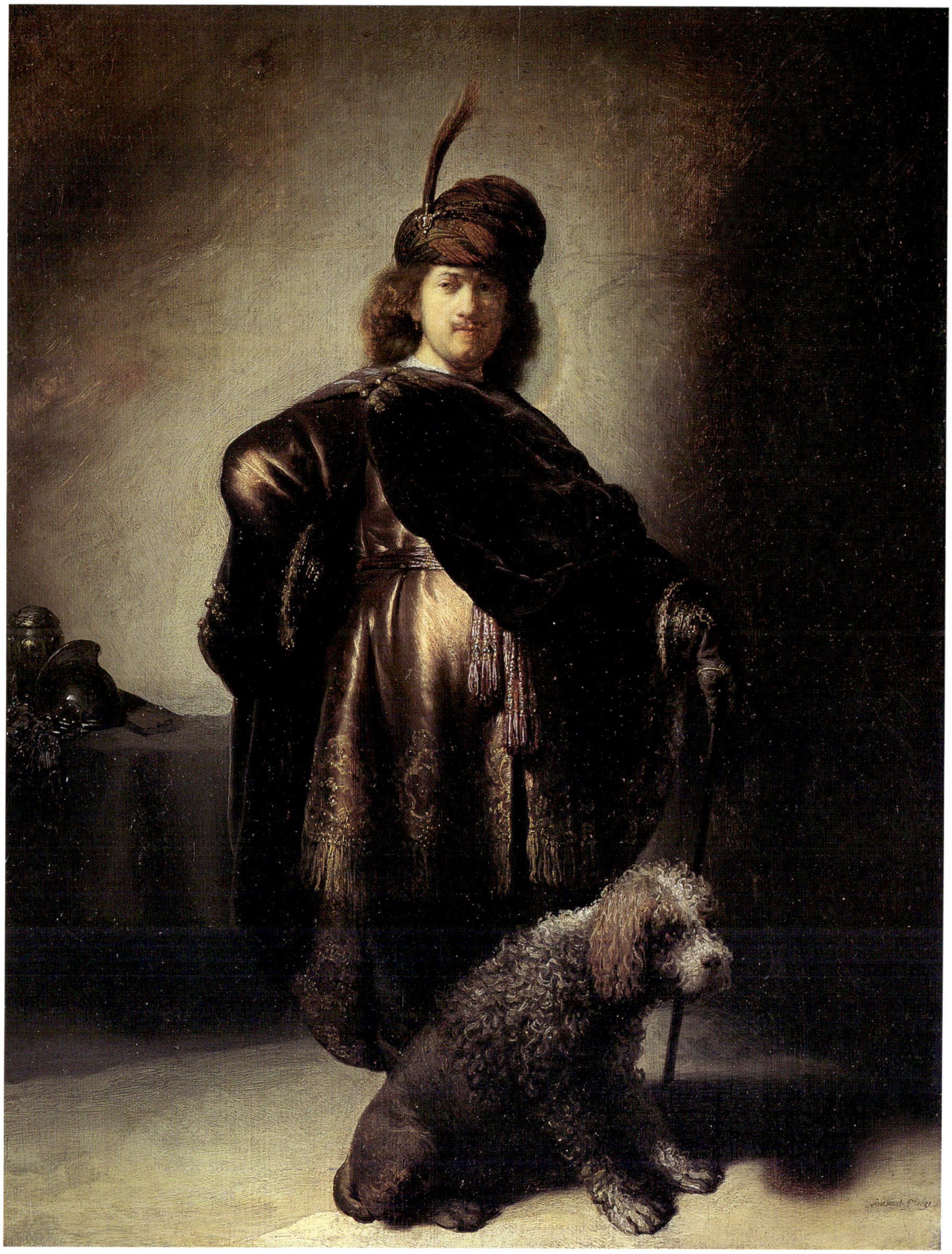

To understand Rembrandt's fascination with the Oriental dimension of Christian spirituality we have merely to observe the strange and disconcerting resemblance between his portrait of an old rabbi of 1661 and the portrait of Homer he painted shortly afterwards, between 1662 and 1663. Deep in Rembrandt's imagination there was a sort of forgotten or abandoned culture, an ideal world that was a perfect synthesis of classical Greco-Latin civilization, the Jewish tradition, and Christian belief.

Self-portrait with Dog,
Rembrandt van Rijn (attributed to), 1631
Oil on wood, 63 x 56 cm
(Musée du Petit Palais, Paris).

Christ and the Woman Taken in Adultery,
Rembrandt van Rijn, 1644
Oil on wood, 83.8 x 65.4 cm
(National Gallery, London).

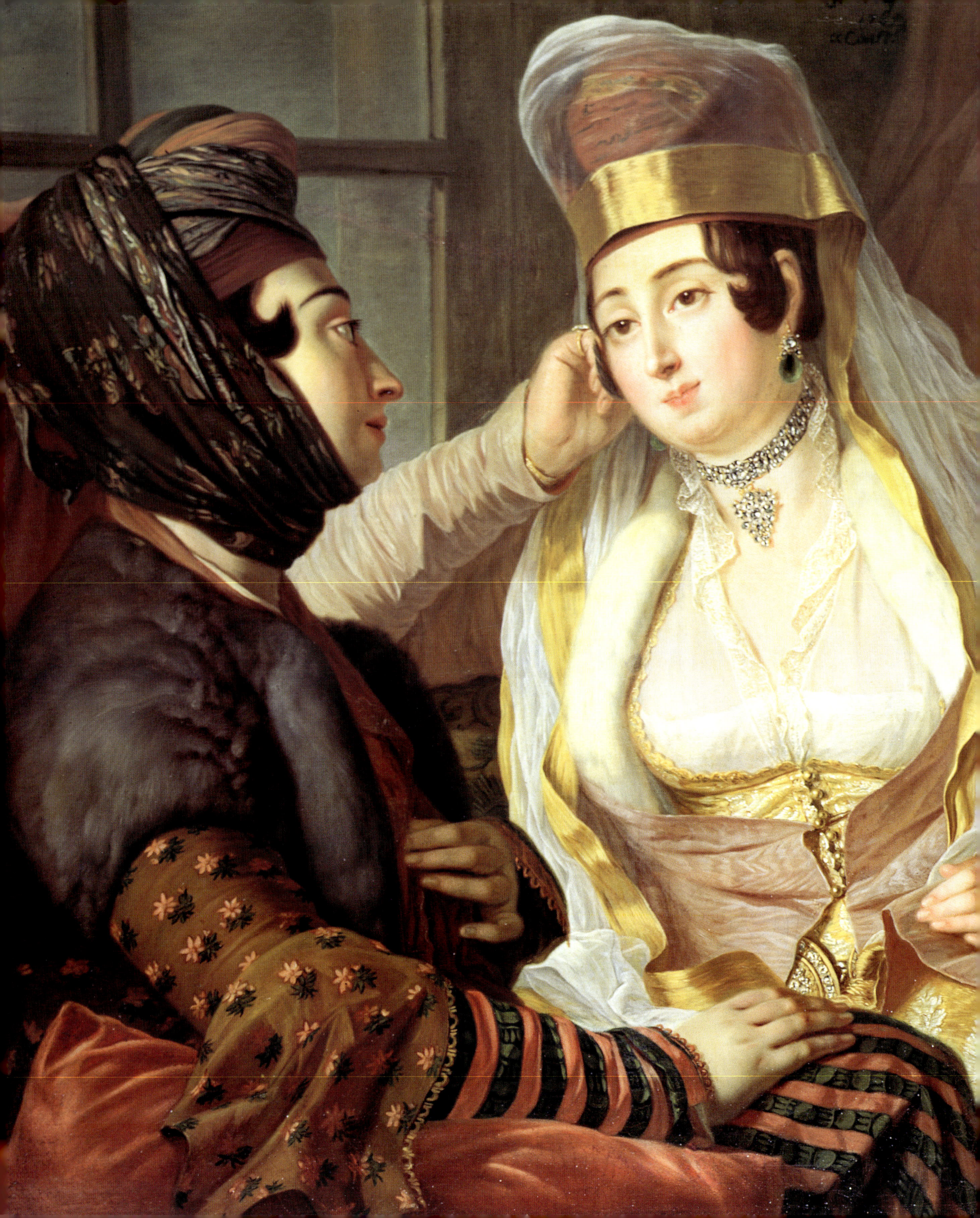

CHAPTER II

Orientalism in the 18th Century

The curiosity of the inhabitants of Paris is really quite beyond bounds. When I arrived, I was looked at as if I had come straight from heaven: old people, men, women, children, all wanted to see me. If I was in the Tuileries gardens, I would immediately see a circle of people forming around me: the women themselves were like a rainbow that surrounded me, in colors of a thousand shades; if I was at the theater, I would straightaway find a hundred opera glasses trained on me; in short, never was a man so much in the public gaze as I was. It sometimes made me smile to hear people who had hardly ever left their own houses saying to each other: "One must admit that he really does have a Persian air about him. How very remarkable!" I found portraits of myself everywhere; I saw myself reproduced in all the shops, on every mantelpiece – so afraid were people that they might not see enough of me.

Lettres Persanes (Persian letters),
Montesquieu, 1721

The Turkish Fashion

Page 46
Maltese Women,
Antoine de Favray, undated (detail)
Oil on canvas, 93 x 124 cm
(Musée des Augustins, Toulouse).

Page 47
The Sultan at her Toilette
Pithou the Younger, Sèvres porcelain.
After the painting by Charles Amédée
Philippe Van Loo, 1783 (detail)
(Musée National du Château Versailles).

Page 49
The Queen Sultana,
Joseph-Marie Vien, 1748
Oil on paper, 26.5 x 20.5 cm
(Musée du Petit-Palais, Paris).

Pages 50–51
Africa, Giambattista Tiepolo,
1752–1753 (detail)
Fresco (Résidence des Princes-évêques, Würtzburg).

The end of the 17th century marked the real beginning of Europe's fascination with the Orient. The Ottoman Empire in particular, a source both of wonder and of fear, now provided a new style, a new aesthetic, that had a marked impact on Western literature, fashion, and above all painting well into the 18th century. Remarkably, this craze for things Turkish (*turqueries*) was matched by a vogue for things Chinese (*chinoiserie*), the two unrelated styles developing side by side. Both became aspects of Rococo, an elegant, playful, and decorative style that would later be seen as an expression of the frivolity of the *ancien régime*.

There were a number of reasons why Europe began taking a greater interest in the East at this time. The first was political. The siege of Vienna by Ottoman armies in 1683 sent shock waves through Europe, and was the pretext for what has been described as the "last Western crusade." The Ottoman Empire had in fact now attained its greatest extent and soon would begin a slow and irreversible decline. Nevertheless, it was still enormously powerful, extending into Asia and Africa and controlling almost a third of Europe – the whole of the Balkans from Bulgaria to Serbia, right to the gates of its old rival, the Venetian Republic. After a highly dramatic moment, when the Ottomans seemed on the point of absorbing Vienna into its empire, the Christian world could breathe again.

An interest in the East was also encouraged by growing trade links. France in particular had continued to enjoy close relations with the Great Sultan: the development of trade routes had led to the creation of the Compagnie du Levant (Levant company), and to the huge expansion of the port of Marseilles, which benefited from the right of passage granted by Moka. From the 17th century onwards, Marseilles became highly prosperous, extending its commercial activities as far as the ports of the Levant, the Barbary Coast, and the states of the Indian Ocean, and little by little it overtook Venice, whose influence continued to wane. When the French artist Joseph Vernet received a commission from the Marquis de Marigny, brother of Madame de Pompadour, for an important set of pictures representing French ports, he painted two views of Marseilles, one of them showing groups of Muslim merchants going about their business on the quaysides. This canvas, which was exhibited at the Salon of 1755, won him further orders: the Duc de Luynes requested a view of "a port with the costumes of different nations," and Lenoir asked for a picture showing the "loading of merchandise and figures dressed in Levantine and Greek garb." Vernet soon developed a taste for these exotic scenes, typical subjects being *The Turkish Fisherman*, *Greek Woman Emerging from the Bath*, and *Turkish Bathers*, works that inspired a book of engravings by Jean-Baptiste Van Mour.

The rapid development of contacts between East and West also encouraged scientists, especially botanists and geographers, to make their own journeys of discovery, the result often being books of exploration and discovery that were eagerly read by their contemporaries. Diplomats attempted to set down in learned works the knowledge they had acquired of countries that still, to European eyes, either possessed a mythical character or appeared appallingly barbaric. In 1714 Charles de Ferriol, the French ambassador in Constantinople, published a book on the customs of the Ottoman Empire illustrated with engravings by Le Hay of paintings by Van Mour – *Receuil de cent estampes représentant différentes nations du Levant* (Collection of one hundred engravings depicting the different nations of the Levant) – an album that was long used as a principal source of information on the Ottoman Empire not only by scholars, but also by artists and writers.

However, it was the appearance of the collected letters of the Englishwoman Lady Mary Wortley Montagu that had the greatest impact on the public imagination. Her literary style, her exquisite eye for detail, and her revealing accounts of the lives of Muslim women made her collected letters an exceptional and fascinating account of life in the Ottoman Empire. Of the several portraits of

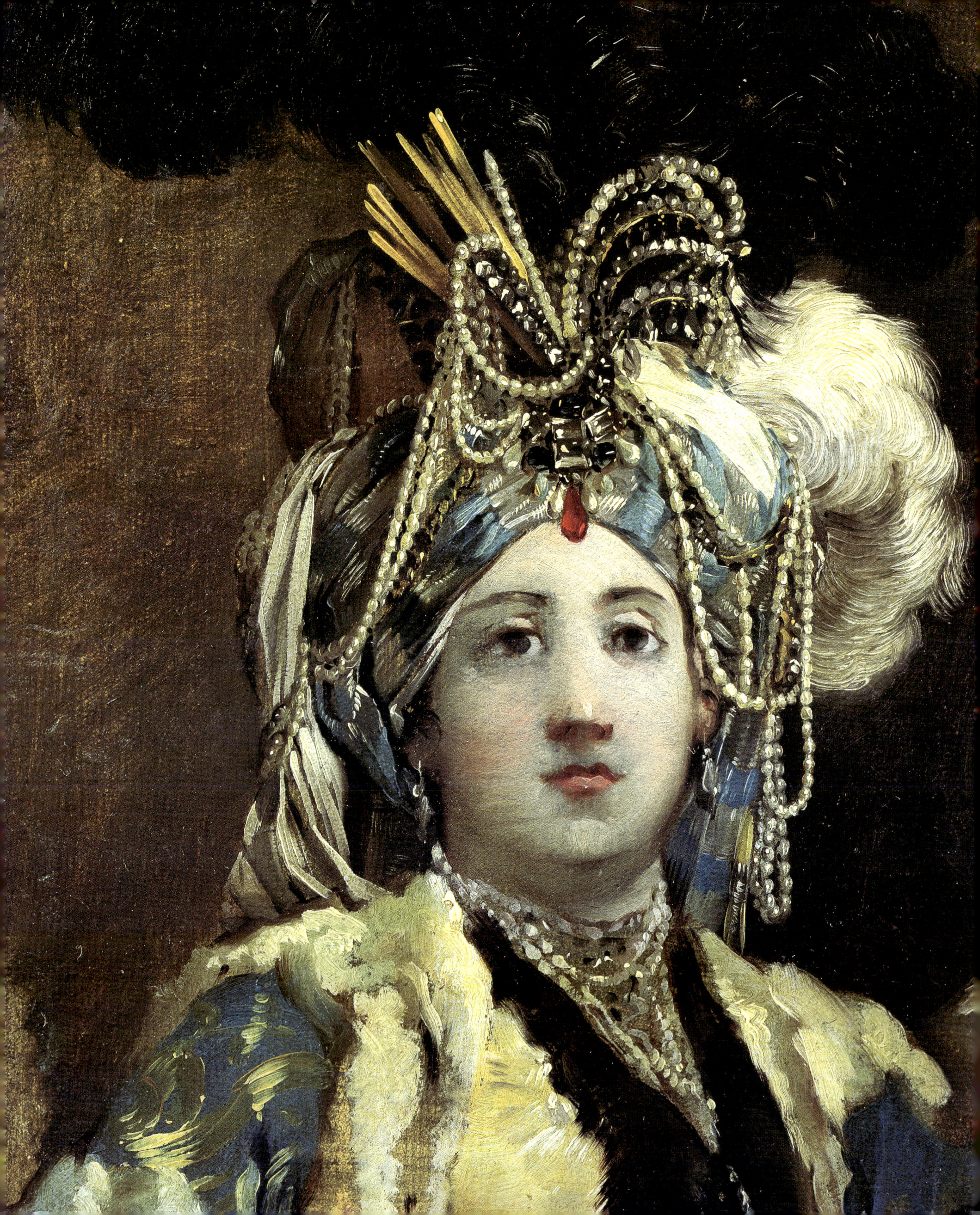

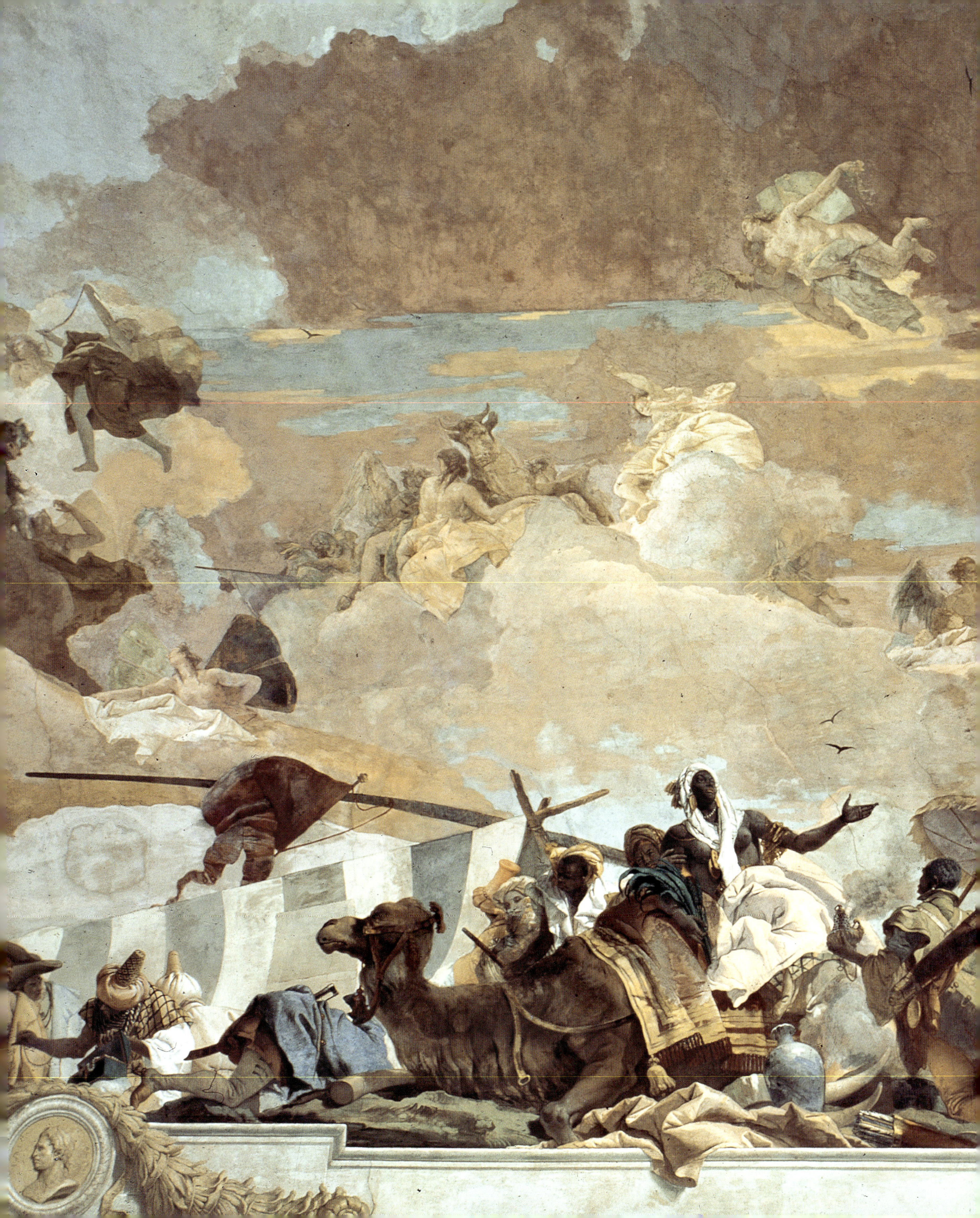

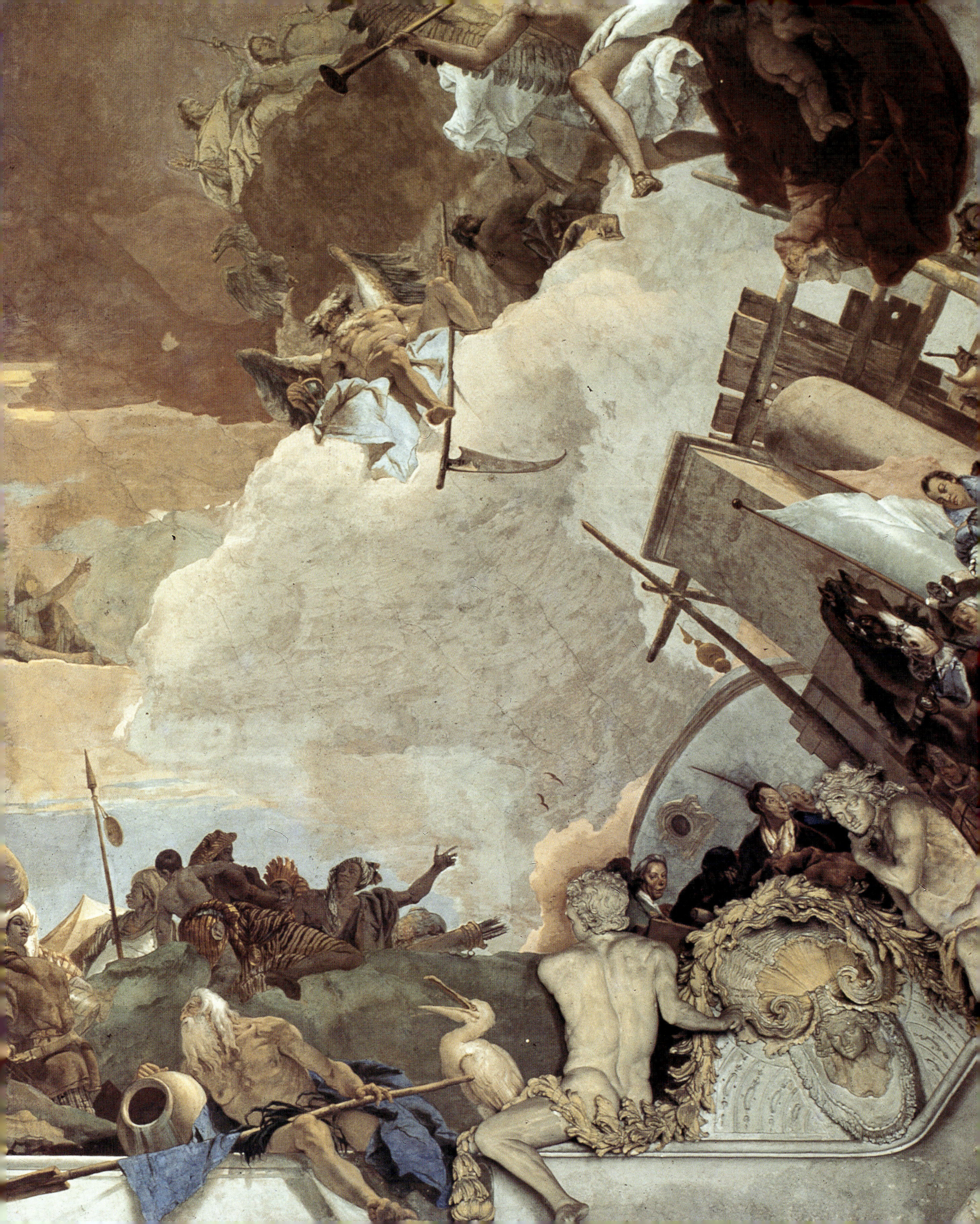

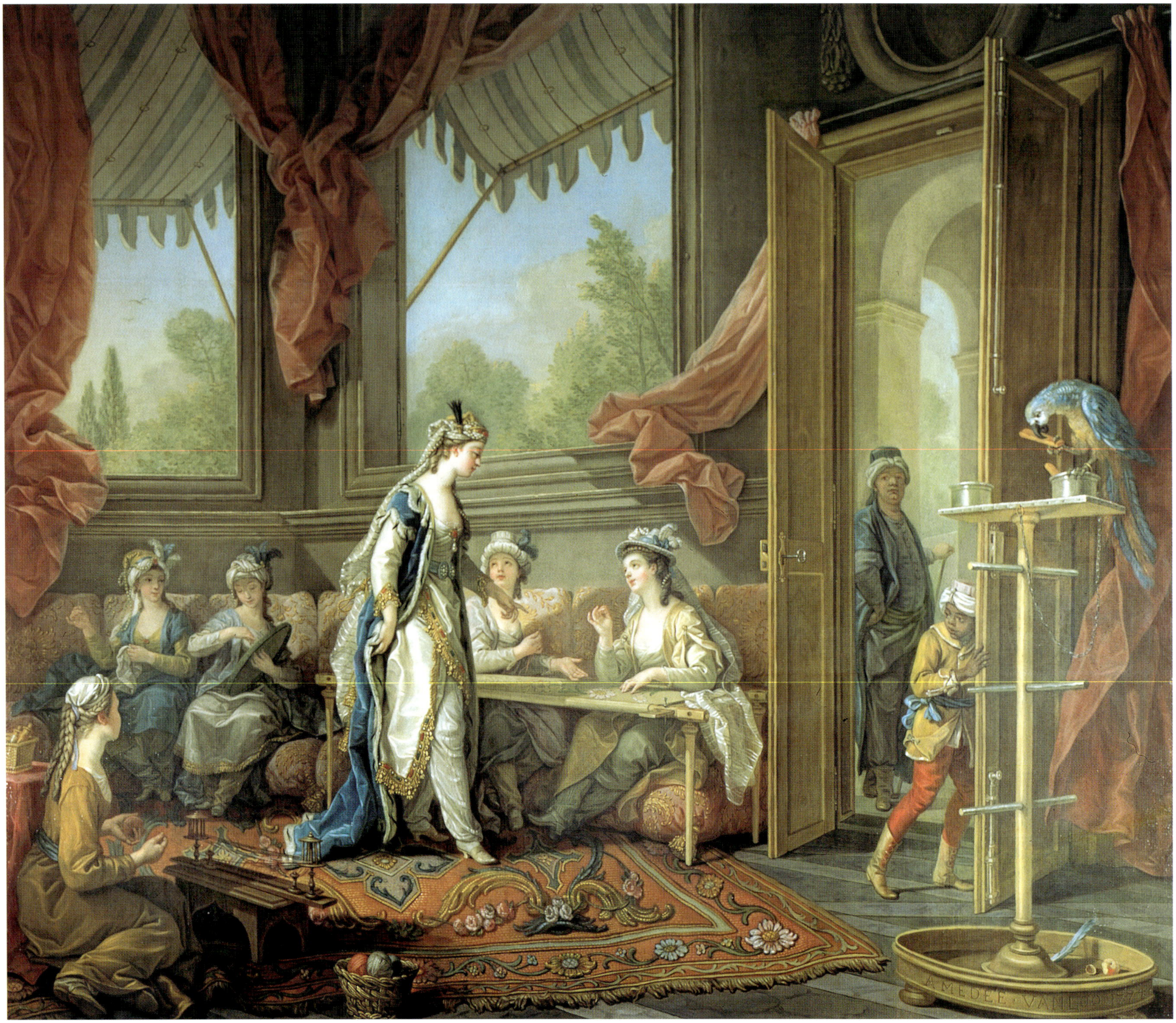

The Sultana Sets Work for the Odalisques,
Charles Amédée Philippe Van Loo, 1773
Oil on canvas, 320 x 480 cm
(Musée Jules Chéret, Nice).

Madame Grassini in the Role of Zaire,
Élisabeth Vigée-Lebrun, c. 1805
Oil on canvas, 127 x 95 cm
(Musée des Beaux-Arts, Rouen).

Lady Montagu, the one by Jonathan Richardson, who shows her in a gold-trimmed silk caftan and embroidered ermine cap, is particularly striking. Born into an aristocratic family, and related to the novelist Henry Fielding, author of the novel *Tom Jones*, she was a woman of spirit, highly literate, and very beautiful. She possessed an uncommon intelligence and real literary talent, and became acquainted with many of the writers and intellectuals of her day, including the poet Alexander Pope (with whom she later famously quarrelled). In 1716 she married Wortley Montagu, a brilliant statesman, and almost immediately followed him to Constantinople, where he had been sent as Britain's ambassador. The letters she wrote to friends over the next two years of her stay in Constantinople were published in 1763, shortly after her death.

There was also a new vogue for Arabic and Persian literature. In 1704 the first volume of a French version of *A Thousand and One Nights* appeared, translated by the extraordinarily learned scholar of Middle Eastern languages, Antoine Galland. This was a key

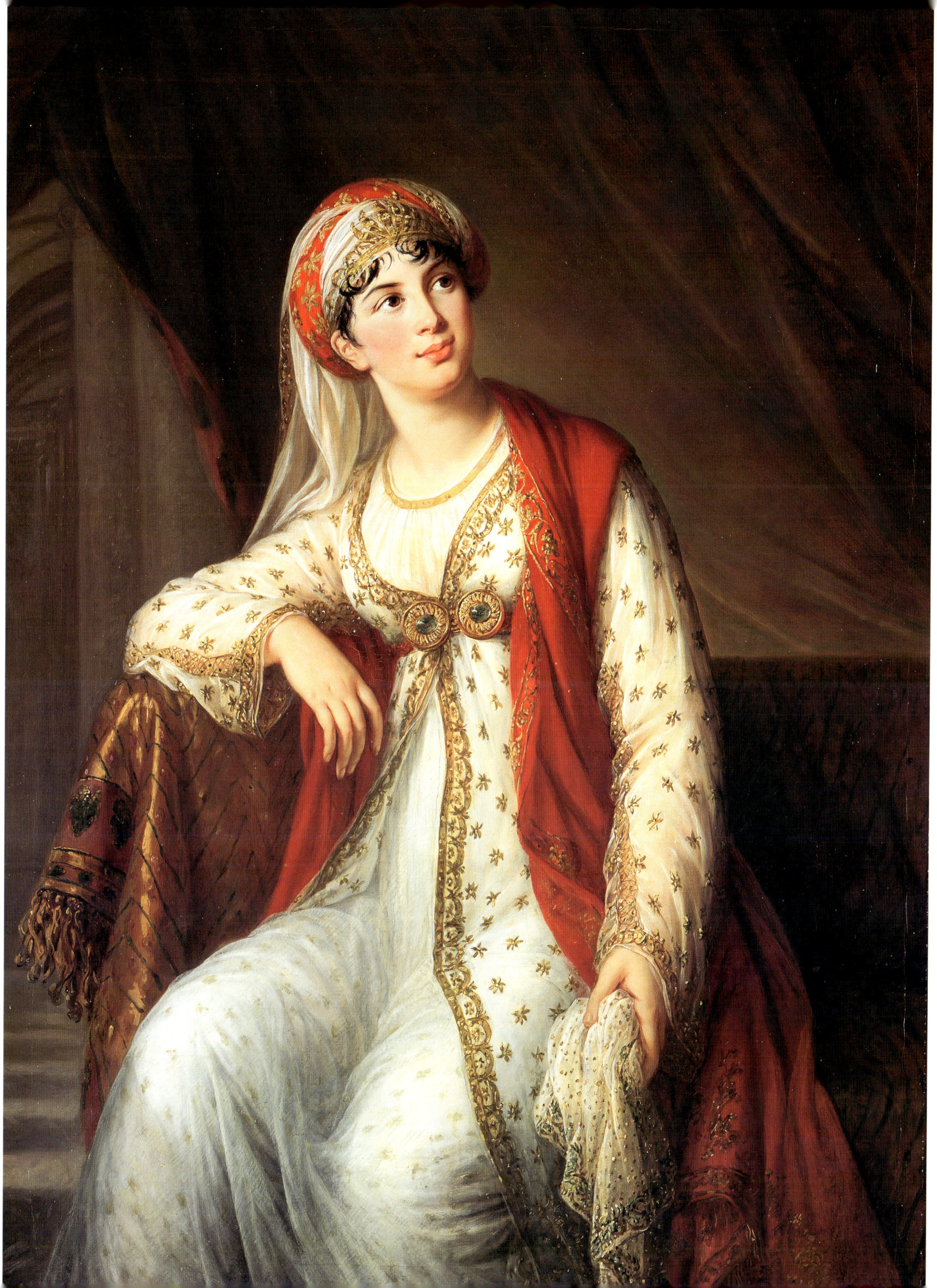

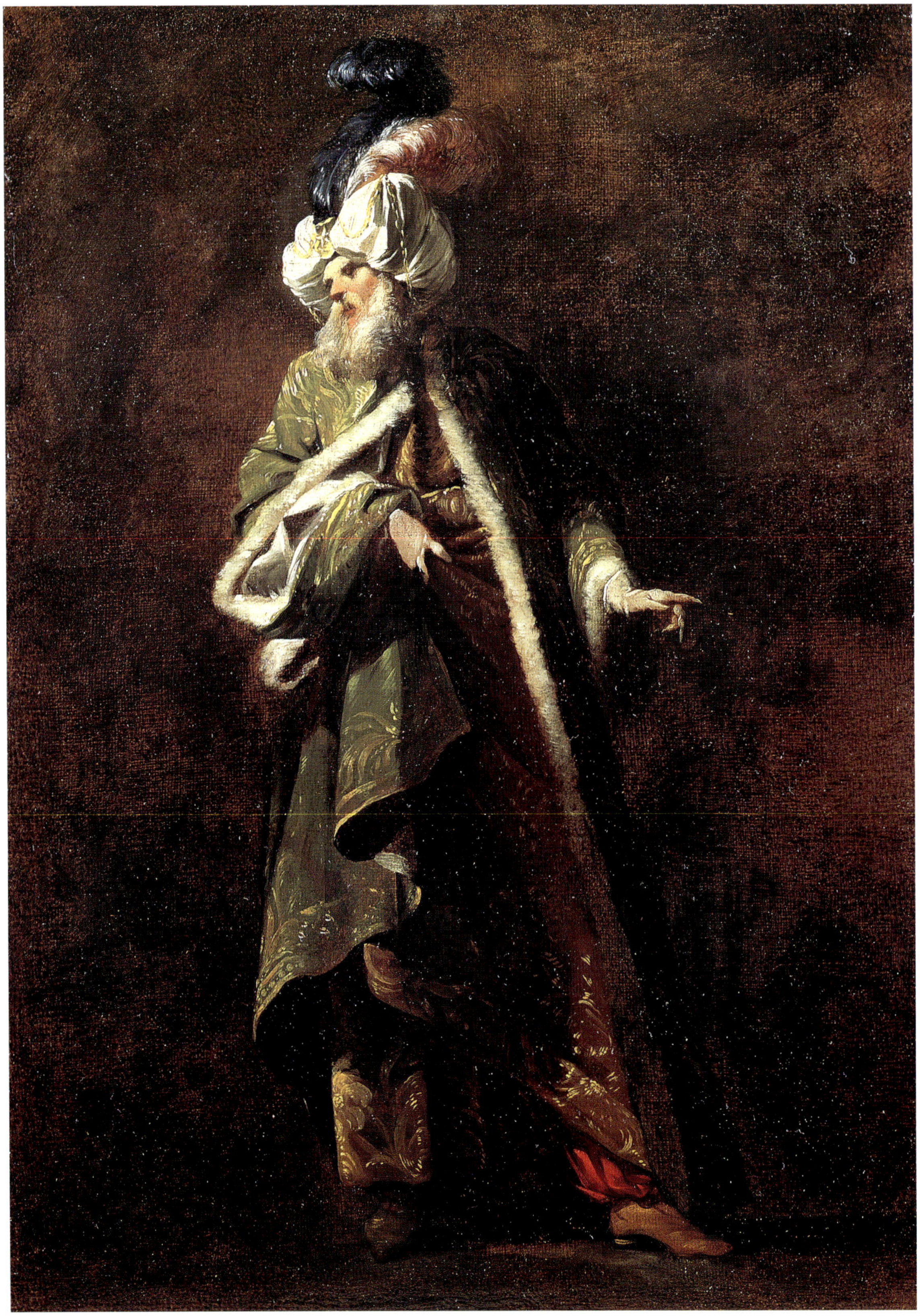

A Teacher of the Law, Jean Barbault, 1748
Oil on canvas, 66 x 49 cm
(Musée du Louvre, Paris).

The Queen Sultana, Jean Barbault, c. 1748
Oil on canvas, 29 x 22 cm
(Musée du Louvre, Paris).

moment in the emergence of a direct knowledge of Arabic culture. François Pétis de la Croix soon followed his example, writing *Mille et un jours* (Thousand and one days), which appeared between 1710 and 1712, for Marie-Adelaïde de Savoie, the wife of the Duke of Burgundy. While the *Thousand and One Nights* tells the story of a man who is mortally afraid of women, François Pétis de la Croix' version tells the story of a princess who is afraid of men. Though he pretended to have heard the stories from "the Chief Sufi of Isfahan, Dervish Moclès," Pétis de la Croix was himself the real author of these tales, which he wrote entirely according to his own fanciful inclinations. Similarly, a now forgotten French author, Fromaget, wrote fantastic tales inspired by the Muslim world, though again without the least concern for truth or accuracy. His *Le Cousin de Mahomet* (Mohammed's cousin) appeared in 1742, followed eight years later by *Kara-Moustapha et Bah-Levi* (Kara Mustafa and Bar-Levi), which contemporaries thought "a very amusing tale."

Philosophy did not escape this groundswell, either. For the French thinker Montesquieu, the sumptuous and exotic embassy of the Persian envoys, who were received in Paris in 1715, was one of the main inspirations for his satirical *Lettres Persanes* (Persian letters), which appeared in 1721. For many of the details he consulted the writings of Jean Chardin. Voltaire, likewise, was happy to employ the appeal of the Orient, notably in the moral tales *Zaïre* (1731) and *Candide* (1759). He even wrote an essay entitled *Mahomet*, a rare French attempt at a portrait of the Prophet. Voltaire's contemporary, Denis Diderot, used Montesquieu's stratagem of seeing one culture through the eyes of another by depicting the young King Louis XV as a sultan in his novel *Les Bijoux indiscrets* (The indiscreet jewels). The French poet André Chénier, born in Constantinople of a Greek mother had, from childhood, maintained both a hatred of the Turks and a boundless love for the culture of classical Greece, both of which he incorporated into his own works.

This version of the Orient soon became fashionable and influential. When Madame de Pompadour moved into the Palace of Versailles to become Louis XV's official mistress, she decorated her apartments with a range of exotic objects. She had herself painted as a sultana by Natoire, and hung on her walls three paintings of sultanas by her protégé Carle Van Loo – one is shown doing needlework, another taking coffee, and the

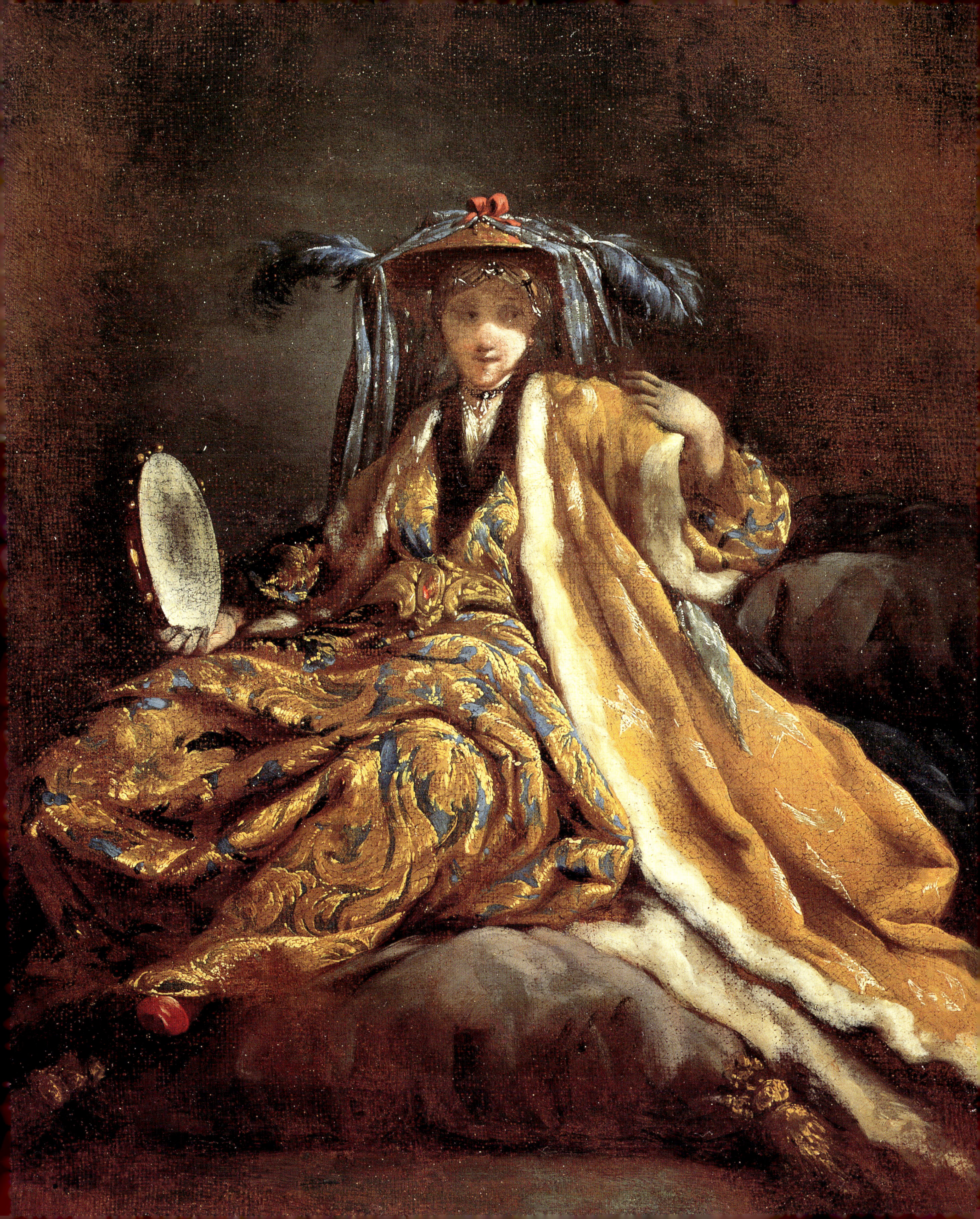

Seated Persian,
Jean-Antoine Watteau, 1715
Red chalk and *pierre noire* on parchment,
30 x 19 cm (Musée du Louvre, Paris).

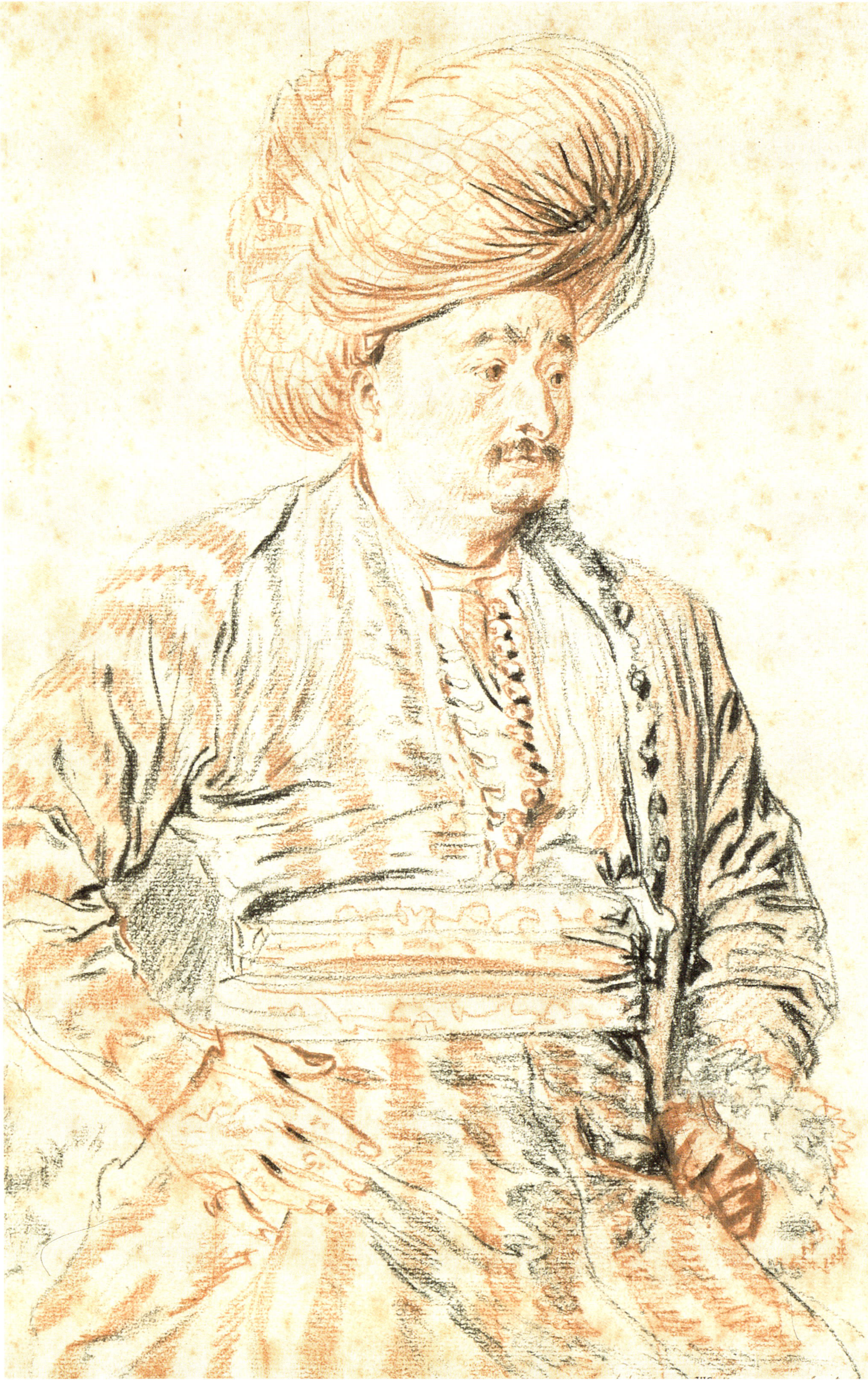

third is playing the guitar. When Marie-Antoinette became Queen of France, she in her turn adopted this style and wore sultana's clothes and Levantine-style robes. This craze had already spread throughout Europe, starting in England. Hence we find Philippa Rooper, Lady Sunderlin, and Lady Cottrel-Darmel in Oriental costume in portraits by Sir Joshua Reynolds, and Mrs Thomas Gage wearing similar clothes in a portrait by the American artist John Singleton Copley.

But perhaps the most extravagant expression of this penchant for things Oriental was the remarkable masquerade organized by the students of the Académie de France in Rome in 1744, the Masquerade of the Sultan at Mecca, which included allegorical floats. The artist Joseph Marie Vien took part by contributing several paintings (*Black Sultana, White Sultana* and *The Moghul Ambassador*), as did Jean Barbault. Four years later Jacques-François Martin left a magnificent depiction of this occasion, his *Sultan's Caravan at Mecca*, showing the horses and floats processing round a Baroque square that has been recreated in Oriental style with a wealth of impressive detail. When we take a look at the magnificent drawings for the costumes by Vien and Barbault, for which well-known actresses posed, it is easy to see how much care the artists took over the minute detail of Oriental dress – though this did not stop their unbridled and fantastic imaginations from running to extravagant excesses.

Oriental splendors in the heart of Paris

On 7 February 1715 the Persian delegation of Reza Bey, the "Intendant of the Province of Erevan," was received in Paris. It was a major event and did not fail to make a deep impression on the public imagination. The artist Antoine Coypel was commissioned to paint the main official picture: *Louis XIV Receiving the Persian Envoys in the Hall of Mirrors at the Palace of Versailles*. The French statesman Saint-Simon wrote in his journal that the Sun King, then in the twilight of his long reign, was "extremely flattered to receive a Persian delegation without his having requested the visit.... He wishes the entire court to be the last word in splendor." In the painting, we see Louis XIV receiving the emissaries' homage while holding in his hand the presents that he is about to offer them, "a hundred and four pearls, two hundred turquoises, and two golden boxes containing a balm." The artist Jean-Antoine Watteau took advantage of the occasion to do at least five studies of members of Reza Bey's entourage.

The arrival in 1721 of Mehemed Effendi, envoy of the Sublime Porte, was even more spectacular. An historic event, it confirmed Louis XV's commitment to the politics of "alliance with the devil," a policy begun by François I and renewed by Louis XIV. Artistically, to quote the 19th-century writers the Goncourt brothers, it made Turkey "one of the provinces of Rococo." The inhabitants of the capital saw the processions of this 80-strong delegation as a magical spectacle, something rich, extravagant, and exotic. The artist Charles Paroncel was commissioned to immortalize this embassy, the result being his *Mehemed Effendi Entering the Tuileries on 21 March 1721*, of which he provided two versions. Pierre-Denis Martin (Martin the Younger) painted: *Mehemed Effendi Leaving the Audience with the King on the 21 of March 1721*. These pictures were not shown to the public until the Salon of 1746. A third artist, Monsieur d'Ulin, was entrusted with portraying *The Reception for the Ambassador of the Sublime Porte with his Son, and his Meeting with Monsieur le Blanc, Minister for War, at the Hôtel des Invalides*, a canvas that was exhibited at the Salon of 1738.

Mehemed Effendi made a great impression on the ladies and gentlemen of the court; the Duchess of Orléans enthusiastically declared in one of her letters that he "must be a distinguished man indeed, for he understood so much." The man whom the King received standing was certainly a refined and cultured person. He showed great interest in all manner of things, including the arts, and without hesitation went to Coypel's studio to pose for the great painting of his audience with the king (a work which has, unfortunately, been lost).

Turkish masquerades and languorous sultanas

Literature and the theater supplied numerous Oriental subjects for painters of this period, though they encouraged fantasies rather than a realistic appreciation of life in the East. And strange as it may seem, it was the literature of the 17th century that often provided artists with subjects. Jean-François de Troy, for example, took from Racine's tragedy *Esther* the subject for his cartoon *Esther Fainting* (1737), which was made into tapestry by the Gobelins factory. This play, which was first performed by the young ladies of Saint-Cyr in 1689, had not been performed again until 1727. Others, however, were struck by more recent plays, an example being Nicolas Lancret, who, taking his inspiration from contemporary works, painted *Turkish Lover* to match his *Grecian Beauty*, two canvases that were to be hung in Monsieur de Boullonge's Paris mansion. Similarly, Jean-Antoine Watteau, who often painted the actors in costume at the Théâtre de la Foire and the Comédie Italienne, included a Turkish man conversing with an odalisque in his *Actors at a Fairground* (c. 1710). And when in 1761 the playwright Charles-Simon Favart produced a play entitled *Les trois sultanes* (The three sultanas), with his wife in the leading role, the Swiss artist Liotard painted a miniature of her in Turkish costume. This same play also inspired one of Fragonard's best-known paintings, *In the Seraglio*.

Generally speaking, the Orient was presented in terms of an imaginary world, the character of which was based on festivals and masquerades rather than fact. Jean-Antoine Watteau provides a particularly good example of this in his *Carnival in Venice* (1717), in which one of the characters, dressed as a Turk, is performing a dance step. Unfortunately, his *Sultana* of 1705 has completely disappeared. In the same spirit, in 1740 Jacques de Lajoue painted two great decorative panels that were presented at the Salon the same year. One was

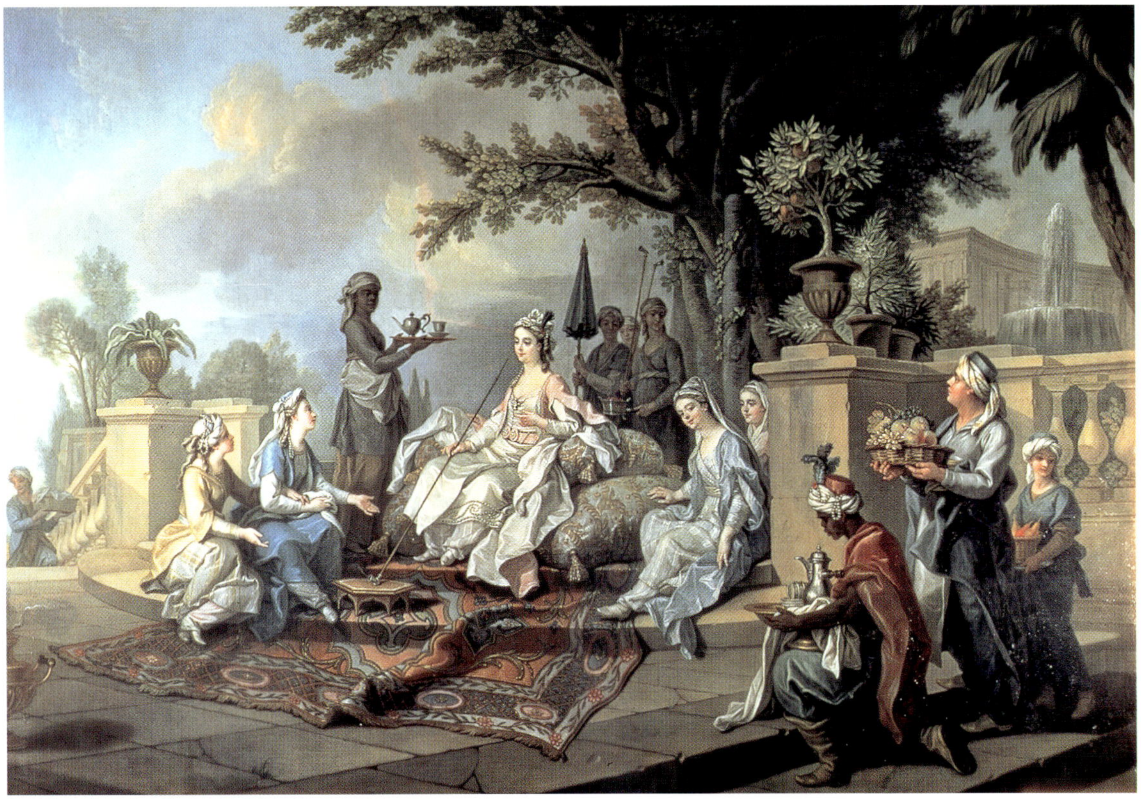

entitled *Marble Chamber with Turkish Figures* and the other *Garden with Oriental Figures*, both pure fictions in the Rococo style. Charles Amédée Philippe Van Loo took a similar line in the cartoon *The Favourite Sultana with her Women, Served by Black and White Eunuchs* (1773), which formed part of a Turkish ensemble created by the Gobelins tapestry factory that included *The Sultana's Repast*, *The Sultana Orders Work from Her Odalisques*, and *Fête Champêtre Given by Odalisques*.

Portraying courtesans as languorous sultanas became a cliché, as did the habit of showing kings and princes in the guise of a pasha or sultan. A fine example is *The Pasha Entertaining his Mistress with a Concert*, which Carle Van Loo painted in 1737 as a compliment to his wife, the singer Christine Somnis. François Boucher, who made this the main motif in his art, painted *Dark Odalisque* in 1745, using his wife as model. This picture, in which real people appear as fictitious characters, is certainly an allusion to Madame de Pompadour, who is pretending to look at the necklace on a low table with great interest. François Boucher also painted *Blonde Odalisque*, this time using the attractive Victoire O'Murphy as his model. In these two works it is only the title and woman's coquettish manner that form any kind of link with the East. Boucher did not, however, limit himself to such playfully erotic scenes. His *Sultana Reading*, a drawing in black crayon and white chalk, brilliantly illustrates how he was able to take a fashionable subject and give it undeniable feeling and meaning. Here he gives a fairly accurate idea of an Oriental figure, even though the model is clearly Western. The picture was so successful that it was imitated by artists such as Leprince,

The Favorite Sultana with her Women, Served by Black and White Eunuchs,
Charles Amédée Philippe Van Loo, 1773
Oil on canvas, 320 x 480 cm
(Musée Jules Chéret, Nice).

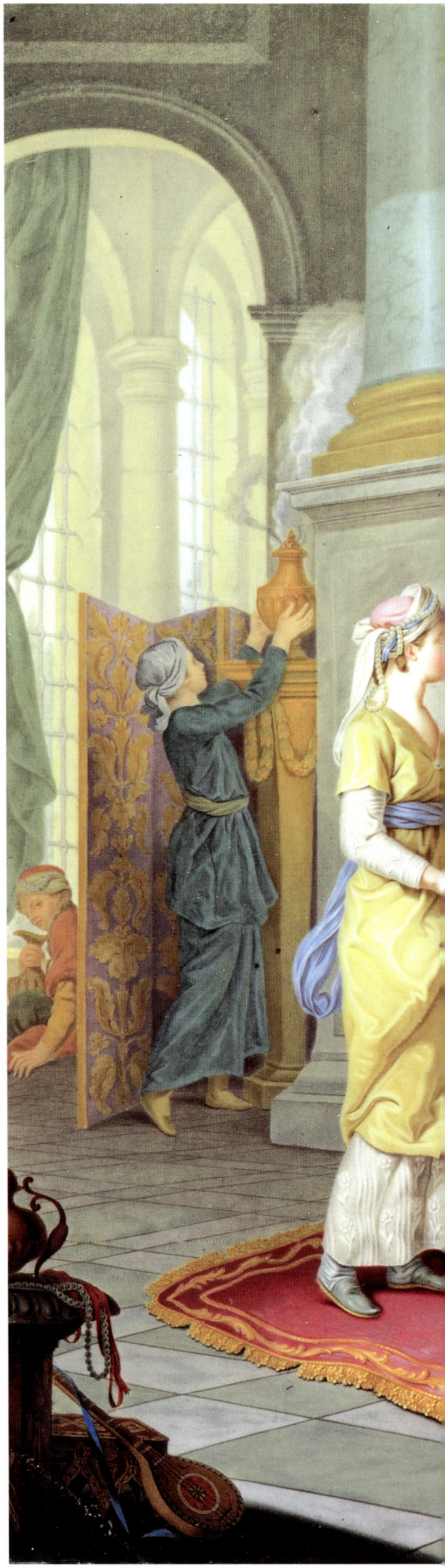

The Sultana at her Toilette,
Pithou the Younger, Sèvres porcelain,
After the painting by Charles Amédée
Philippe Van Loo, 1783
(Musée National du Château, Versailles).

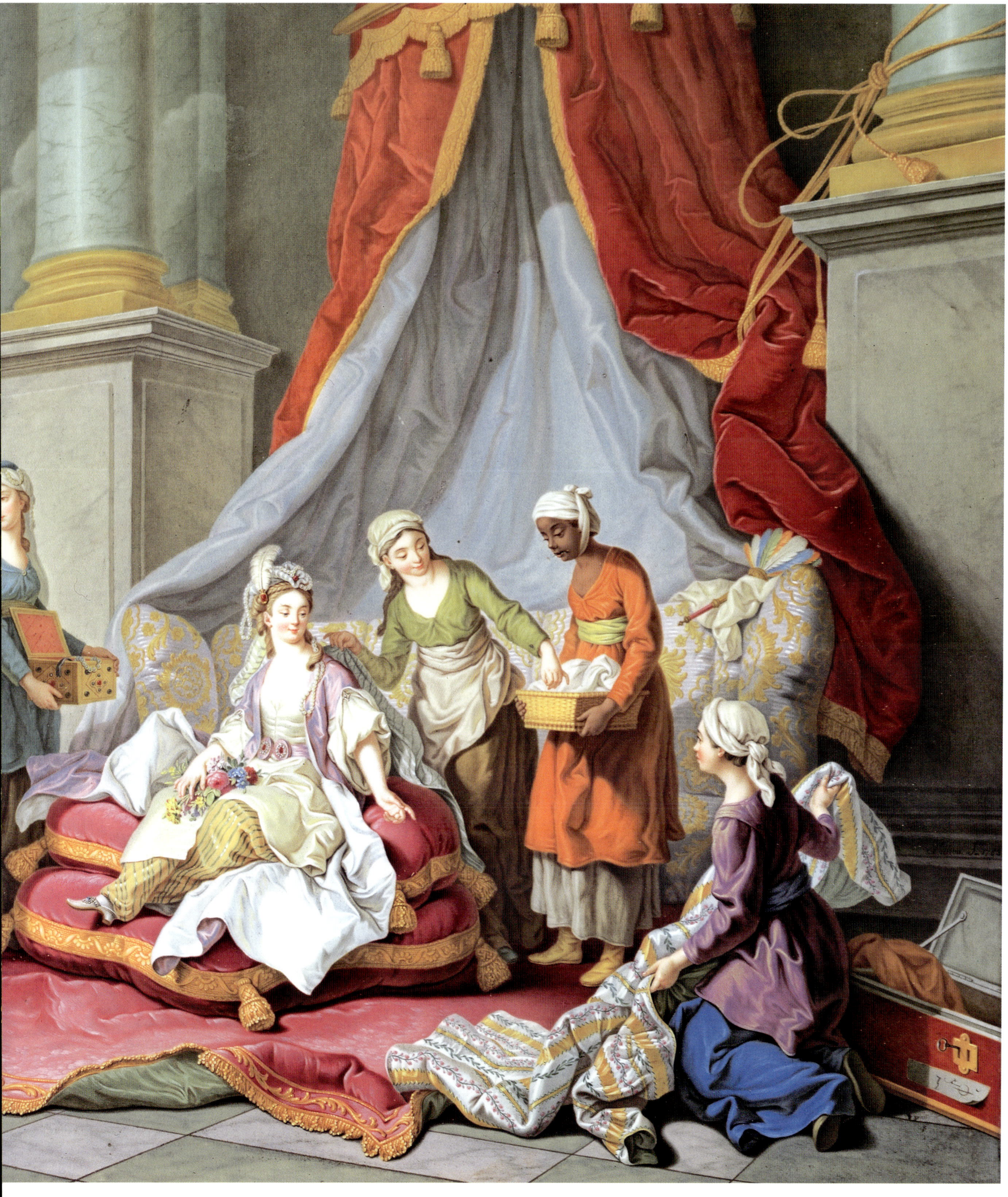

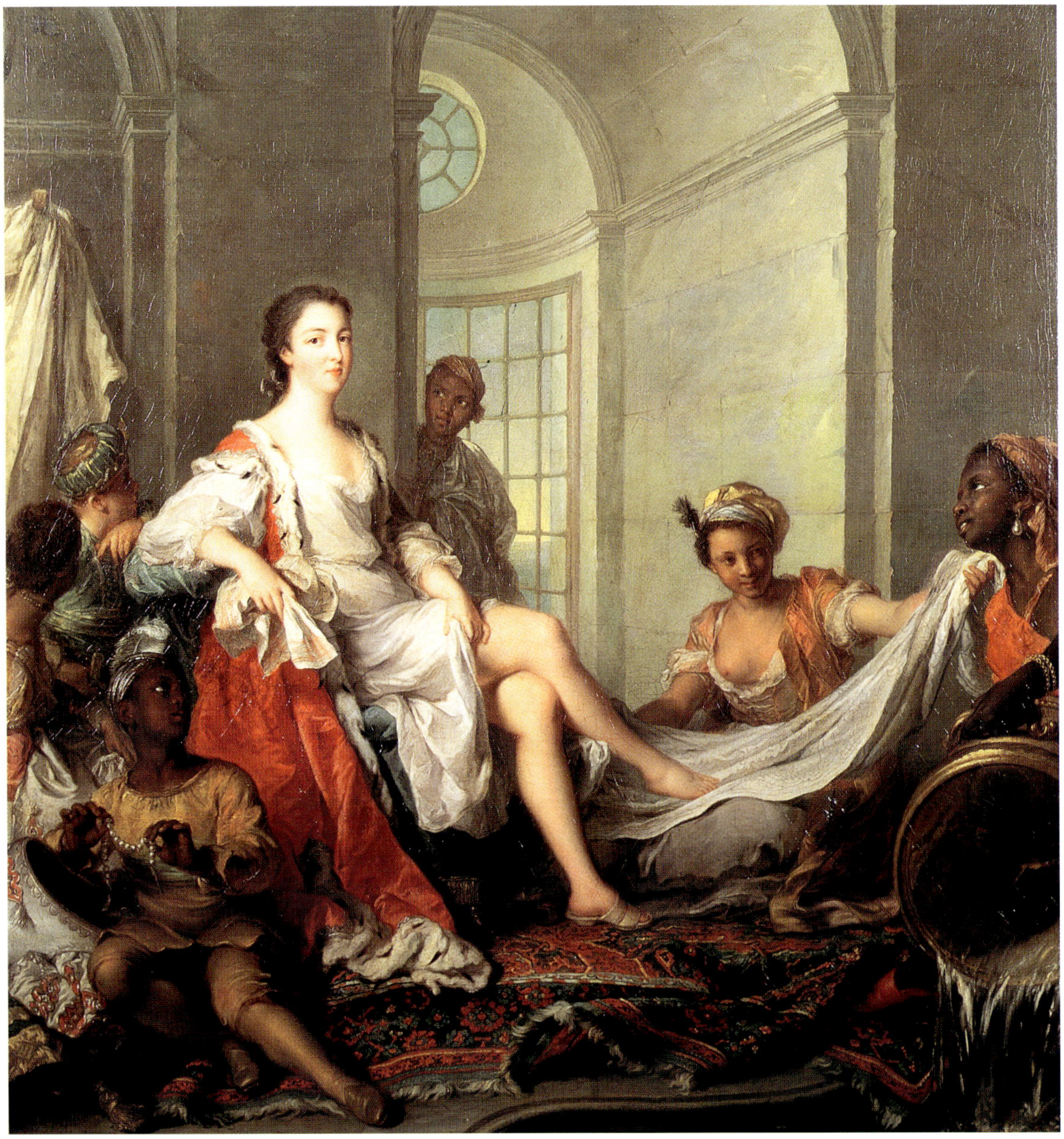

Mademoiselle de Clermont at her Bath, Attended by Slaves,
Jean- Marc Nattier, 1733
Oil on canvas, 110 x 106 cm
(Wallace Collection, London).

Portrait of the Pasha Mehmed Said, Bey of Rovurelia, Ambassador of Sultan Mahmud I at Versailles,
Jacques Aved, 1742
Oil on canvas, 238 x 161 cm
(Musée National du Château, Versailles).

Liotard, and Duflos, who made an engraving of the original.

Oriental themes were exploited by many artists. Charles Amédée Philippe Van Loo painted a *Sultana Playing the Tschegour* for Madame de Pompadour's bed-chamber. Jean-Baptiste Leprince produced canvases on subjects that touch on two popular European themes in relation to the Orient, eroticism and violence. Hunting was another popular Oriental theme. In 1736 Leprince produced *Leopard Hunt* when Louis XV had the gallery on the second floor of Versailles decorated for use as a gaming room. The set theme was that of "hunting scenes in foreign countries," and the results were wildly exotic. Leprince was first asked to portray "a Turk assailed by tigers"; in the end he replaced the Turk with a Persian and tigers with leopards. His fellow artists on the project were Pater (who painted *Chinese Hunt*), Parrocel (*Elephant Hunt*), Carle Van Loo (*Bear Hunt*), De Troy (*Lion Hunt*), and Lancret (*Tiger Hunt*). In 1738 Leprince returned there again with Van Loo and Parrocel to work on other hunting scenes (ostrich, wild bull, and crocodile hunts).

It was Jean-Honoré Fragonard, however, who shone most brilliantly in the Oriental genre, a fine example being his delightful *Sultana with a Pearl* (c. 1775). He had already painted a number of portraits of women in the guise of Levantine princesses, works with titles like *Little Sultana*, *Little Sultana with a Letter*, and *Great Sultana*. A typical version of this theme, painted in pearly tonalities, shows a young woman, dreamy and slightly melancholy, holding a letter in her hand. She is wearing a gray dress, with baggy pantaloons and a wide, cabochon-studded belt. A gentle, delicate twilight surrounds her. The fact that Fragonard painted several variations on this theme shows the importance he placed on this composition, and the care he took over transforming a small exercise in the Oriental genre into masterpieces of sensitivity and refined sensuality. In 1752, the year when he won the Académie's Grand Prix, Fragonard turned to a very different Oriental subject, *Jeroboam Sacrificing to Idols*, which depicts Jeroboam, the first king of Israel, offering a sacrifice to the Golden Calf. From this subject the artist has created a spectacular vision that tries to go beyond the conventional images of Oriental antiquity. Much later, around 1775, he devoted himself to a more sensual and less dramatic subject in *The Pasha*, which probably depicts King Solomon.

A taste for the Orient was not of course confined to French artists; several Venetian painters specialized in the "Turkish look." The Guardi in particular were well-known for this, especially Gianantonio Guardi (Guardi the Elder). He painted 43 small canvases for the collection of Marshal Mathias van der Schulemberg, a great soldier in the service of Venice who acquired a magnificent collection of pictures that he kept at his house in Verona, where the artist Giovanni Piazzetta was put in charge of them. In order to be able

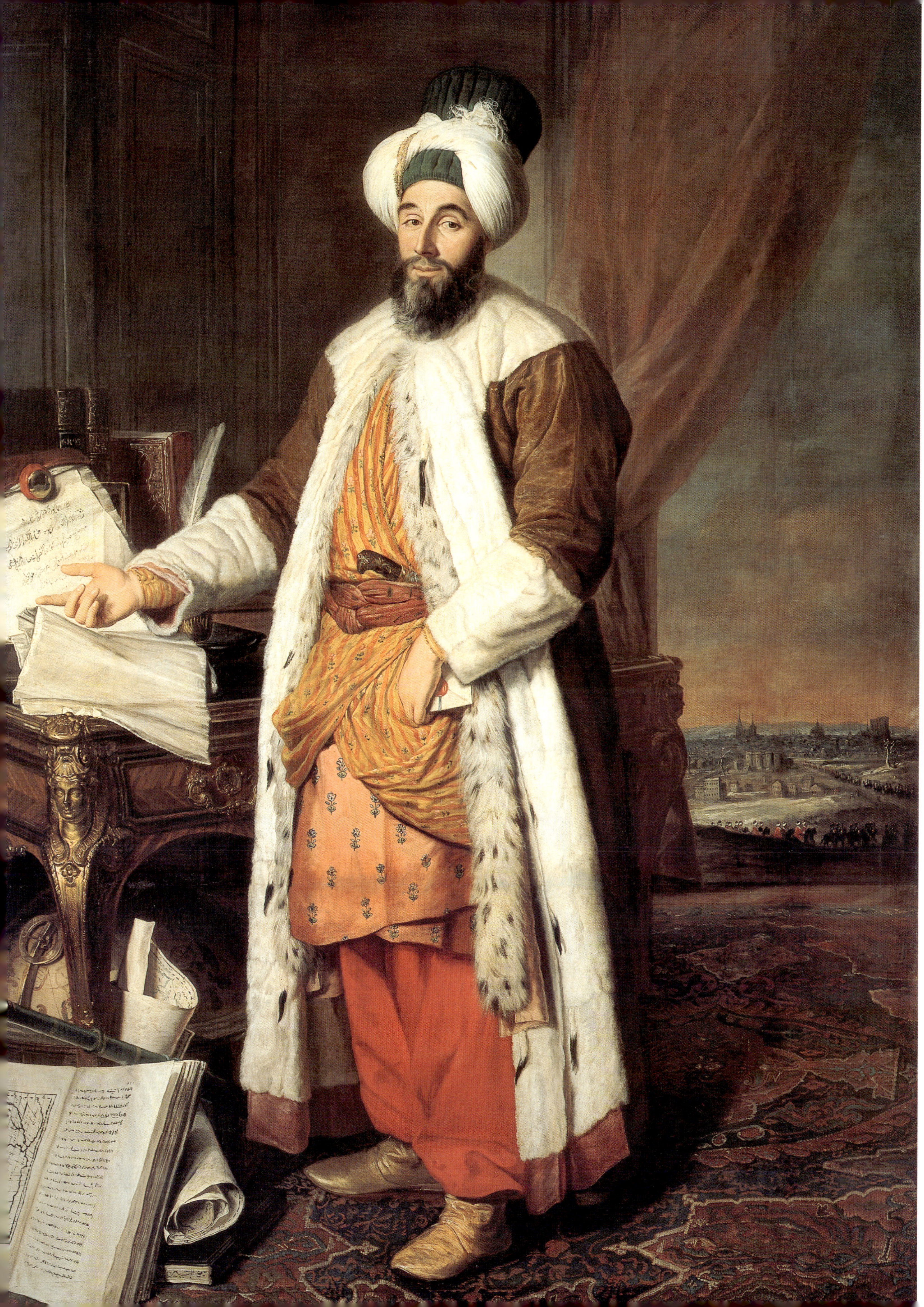

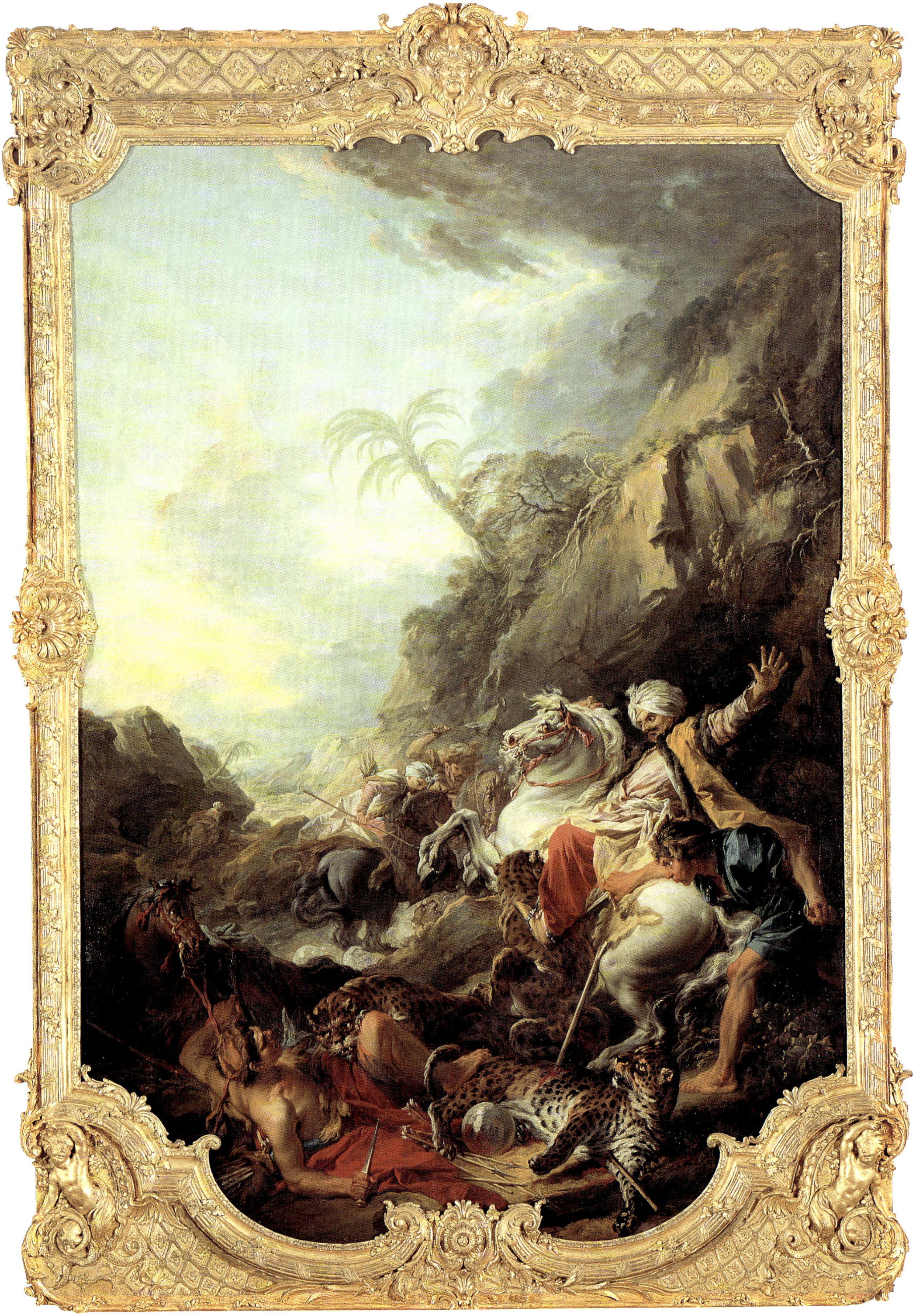

Leopard Hunt,
François Boucher, 1736
Oil on canvas, 174 x 129 cm
(Musée de Picardie, Amiens).

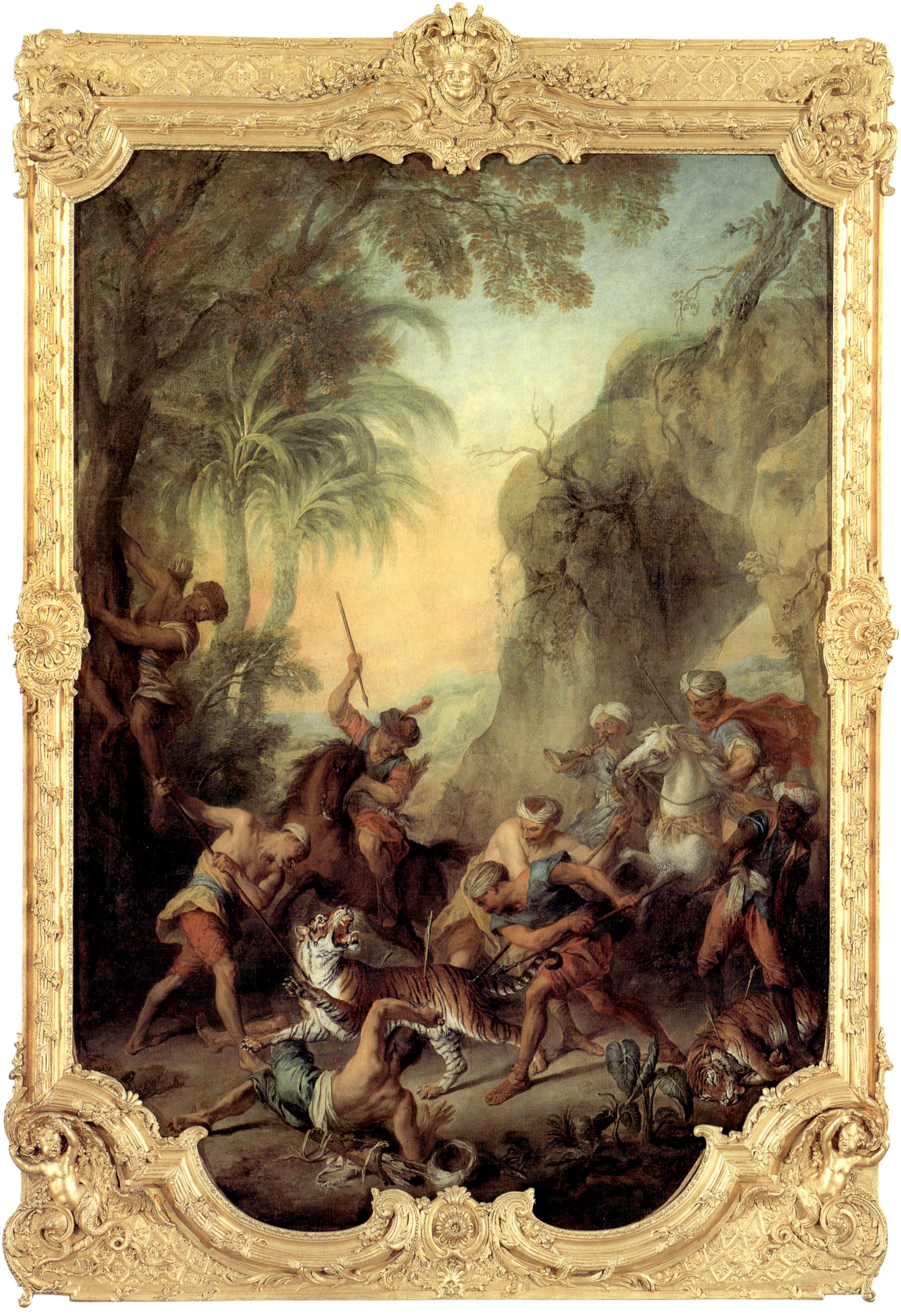

Tiger Hunt,
Nicolas Lancret, 1736
Oil on canvas, 177 x 129 cm
(Musée de Picardie, Amiens).

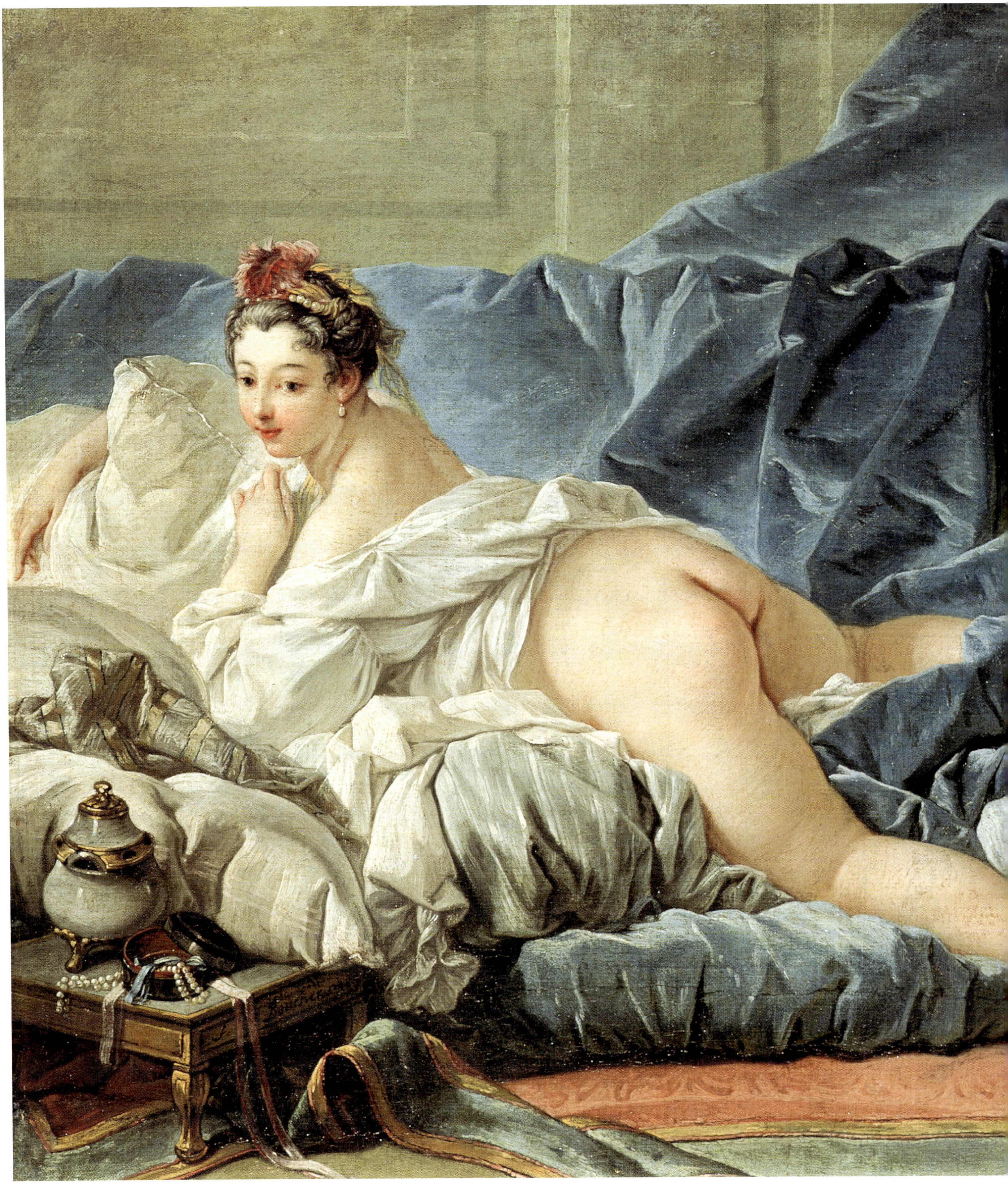

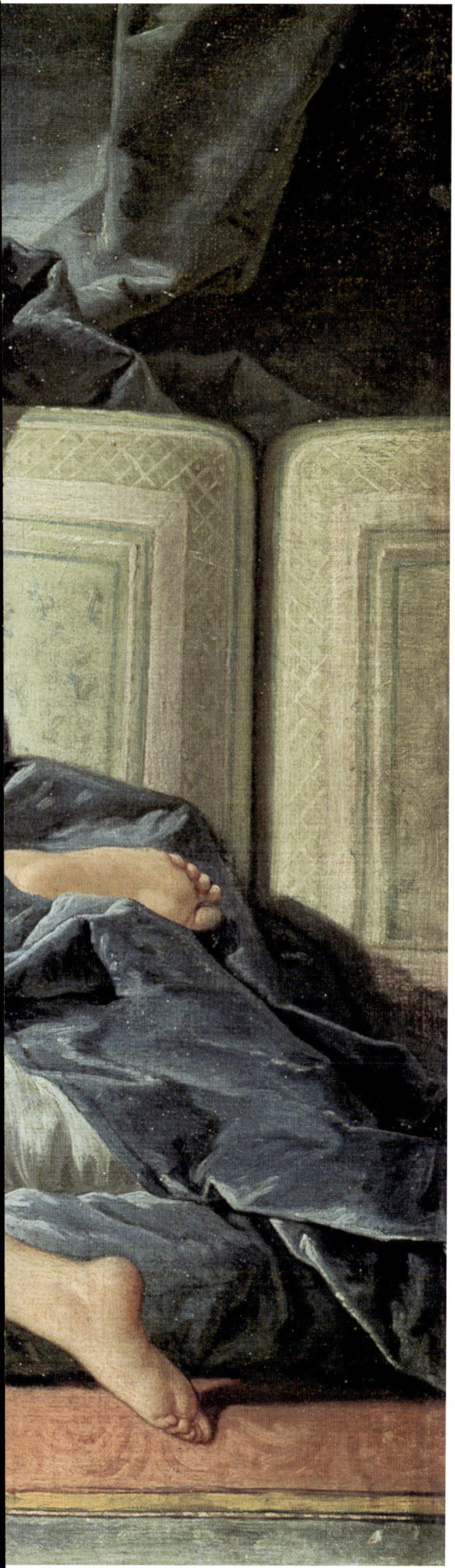

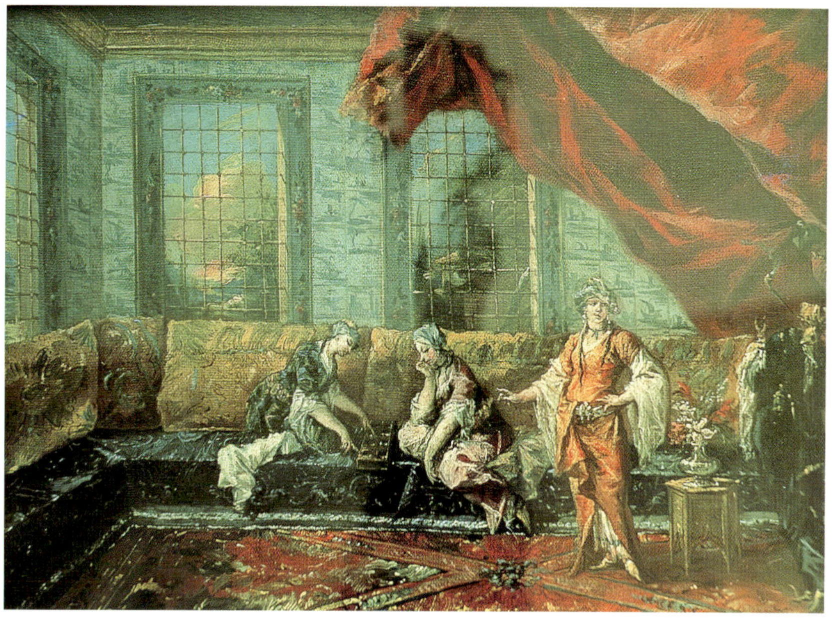

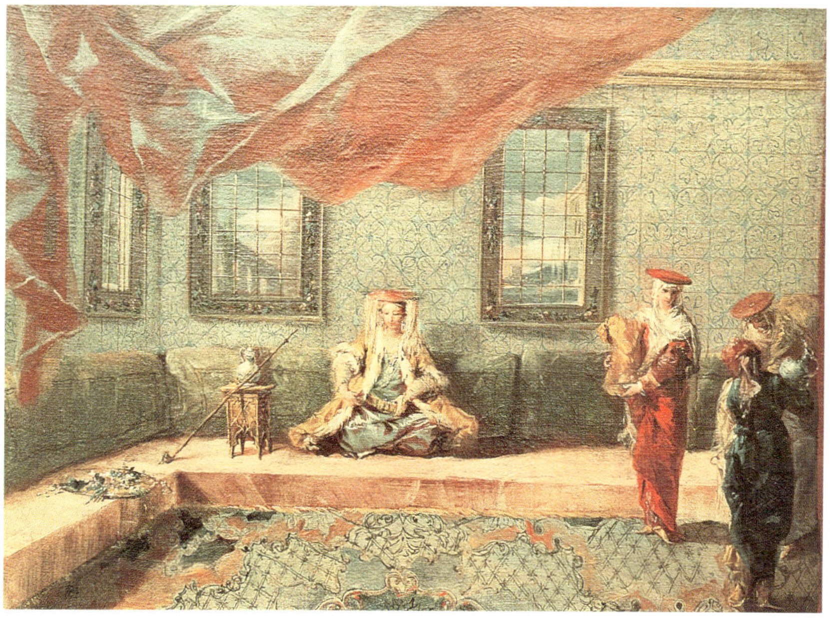

Harem scene, Francesco (or Gianantonio) Guardi, 1742–1743 Oil on canvas, 46 x 64 cm (Kunstmuseum, Düsseldorf).

Scene in a harem, Gianantonio Guardi, 1742–1743 Oil on canvas, 46.5 x 64 cm (Thyssen-Bornemisza Collection, Lugano).

Opposite
Dark Odalisque, François Boucher, 1745 Oil on canvas, 53 x 64 cm (Musée du Louvre, Paris).

to carry out this major commission in the space of a single year (1742 to 1743), Gianantonio relied on the help of his younger brother, Francesco, the famous landscape painter. Both artists were clearly inspired by Van Mour's collection of prints *Différents nations du Levant* (The different nations of the Levant), and both were determined not to succumb to the Baroque fantasies that were so popular at the time.

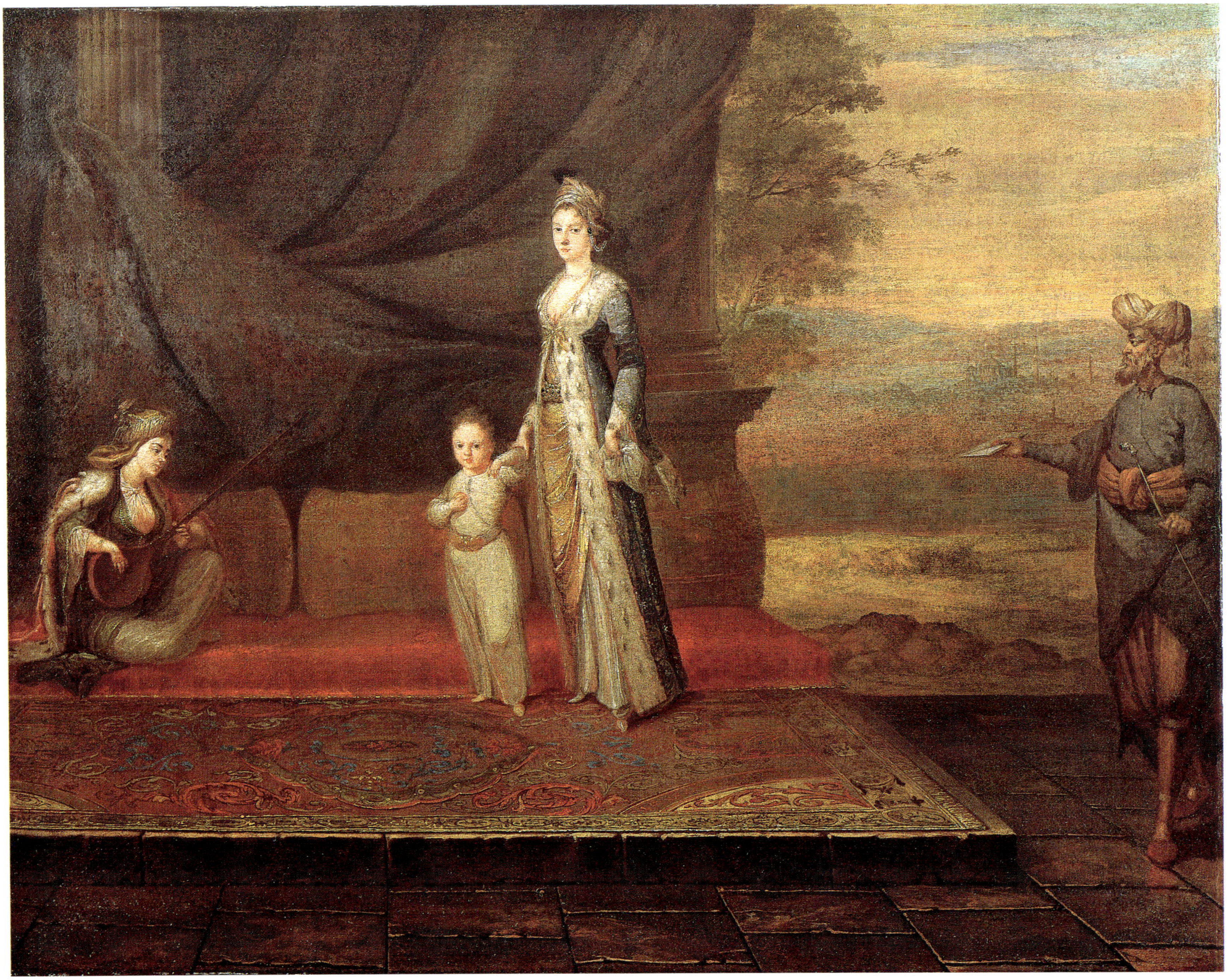

The First Orientalists

Portrait of Lady Montagu, Jean-Baptiste Van Mour, undated. Oil on canvas, 33 x 25 cm (private collection).

Pomp and circumstance in the drawings of Van Mour

Jean-Baptiste Van Mour had been almost completely forgotten before being rehabilitated by Alexandre Bopp, who does justice to him in his *Peintres du Bosphore au XVIIe siècle* (17th-century painters of the Bosporus), an invaluable work that has never been surpassed. Not much is known of Van Mour's career. In 1699 he was already in Constantinople, probably, Bopp tells us, at the request of Monsieur de Ferriol, ambassador of the King of France. Van Mour painted at least a hundred small pictures depicting Ottoman costumes, as well as many portraits of people at the Sultan's court. Showing the same fastidious attention to detail, he also produced an exhaustive catalog of the extraordinary range of nationalities who lived side by side in the capital of the Ottoman Empire, which was then at the very height of its power – Hungarians, Walachians, Tartars, Greeks, Franks (as people of European origin were known), Turks, and many other ethnic groups. This enormous project resulted in the publication in 1712 of the *Recueil de cent estampes représentant différentes nations du Levant* (Collection of a hundred engravings depicting the different nations of the Levant), which was greeted with great excitement in Paris. It was so successful that his engravings became known all over Europe and were shamelessly plagiarized, particularly in Germany, Spain, and Italy. Watteau took a keen interest in the collection, and entrusted François Boucher with the task of creating versions of two of the images. The first version was described as "an Oriental standing, full face, one hand on hip, the left hand extended towards the right. He is wearing a robe and a fur-trimmed turban," a description that related it to Plate 80 of the collection, *Walachian Gentleman*. The second version is entitled *Standing Slave Playing the Guitar*, which is based on Plate 70, *Greek Islander Playing the Tabour*. Throughout the 18th century and beyond, Van Mour's album was to be by far the best source of visual information on life in the Levant.

Van Mour worked very hard and his studio soon became a meeting place for elegant society figures in Pera, the European quarter of Constantinople. He met Lady Mary Wortley Montagu, wife of the British ambassador and author of the letters that made such an important contribution to Western knowledge of the Ottoman way of life. Van Mour painted two portraits of her, the first of which shows her alone in a park and wearing magnificent Oriental dress. The second depicts her in the company of her son Edward; a girl seated to one side of her plays a musical instrument known as the tschegour, and on the other side a messenger opens a letter. In October 1719 the new ambassador received the painter warmly, as his secretary noted: "A French painter came to show his Excellency the sketches for some pictures showing Turkish women bathing, and others dancing. The Ambassador immediately requested him to finish these pictures."

It is clear that the high esteem in which Van Mour was held by his contemporaries was based as much on the finesse of his style as on the variety of subjects he depicted, though he did in fact take an interest in all aspects of Turkish life. He particularly liked to depict the entrance to the port of Constantinople and also great monuments. He was even more interested in sketching ceremonies and festivals, and has left a charming and minutely observed account of the official ceremonies in the Seraglio. With such works as *The Ambassador's Procession through the Second Court of the Seraglio, at the Moment when Dishes of Pilaff are Distributed to the Janissaries*, *Presentation of the Marquis of Bonnay's Children to the Grand Vizier*, *Ambassador Calkoen's Audience with Sultan Ahmet III on 14 September 1727*, and *Ambassador d'Andrezel's Audience with Sultan Ahmet III on 17 October 1724*, he provides a detailed and accurate description not only of the ceremonies and the varied ceremonial costumes worn, but also of the

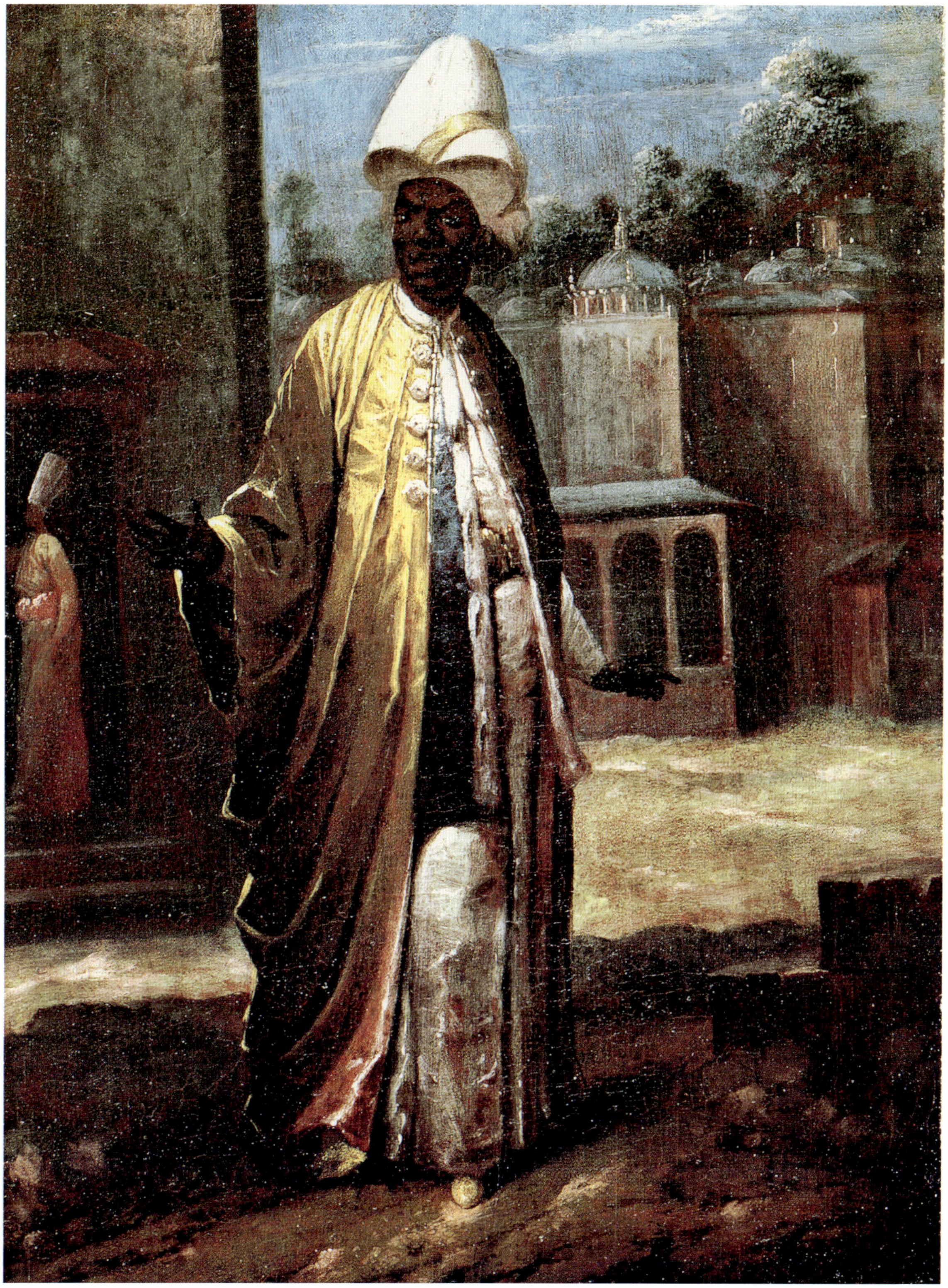

Portrait of a Black Dignitary,
Jean-Baptiste Van Mour, undated.
Oil on wood, 33 x 26 cm
(Musée des Beaux-Arts, Valenciennes).

subtleties of protocol and rank at the court of the Great Sultan. Van Mour also charted historical events, as in the series of pictures he painted when a revolt overthrew Sultan Ahmet III. In his *Rebel Attack on the Vizier's Palace, September 1730*, for example, he depicts the court of the Seraglio during the Revolution of 1730, showing a number of scenes and episodes simultaneously. One of the pictures contains a view of the meat market (Etmeidan), where we see the leader of the insurgents, a simple sailor named Patrona Halil, surrounded by his lieutenants, who include a fruit seller and a coffee merchant. A full-length portrait of Patrona Halil is attributed to Van Mour, but is not fine enough to be by his hand.

Van Mour clearly enjoyed depicting celebrations; an example is his *Turkish Wedding*, which he set before the walls of Rumeli Hissar, an imposing castle on the shores of the Bosporus. Other such works include *Armenian Wedding*, *Greeks Dancing the Khora*, and *Fête Champêtre in Turkey*. He also had a talent for gracefully capturing the quieter moments of daily life, as in *Woman Doing Embroidery*, *Armenian Women Embroidering*, *Turkish Musician and Interior Scene*, *Woman Talking with an Armenian Noble*, *Armenian Interior*, *Dancers in the Harem*, and *Reception in a Harem*.

Van Mour showed great sensitivity and thoroughness in the way he researched the manners and costumes of the different people who made up the gigantic ethnic and religious mosaic of Constantinople. His *Jewish Money-Changer* and *Jewish Woman in Ceremonial Dress* shows just how thoroughly he could steep himself in a given milieu in order to capture its own unique character without resorting to a facile display of exotic "local color." This meant that he was able to paint the ceremonies of the Whirling Dervishes, for example, without crudely exaggerating the scenes of ecstatic dancing. He excelled in depictions of people, places, and events, neatly capturing the magnificence of a ceremonial robe, the dignified solemnity of a procession snaking over a hill, or the quiet magic of a shadowy interior. He clearly loved life in the Orient and wanted to render it as it was, in all its individuality; it was precisely because he treated it with respect and affection that he was able to bring it so vividly before the viewer.

A Swiss at the court of the Grand Sultan

Jean-Étienne Liotard, the son of a Geneva merchant, showed a talent for drawing and painting when he was very young: his first known pictures are portraits of his twin brother, Jean-Michel. He learned the essentials of his craft in Paris, in the studio of the skilled miniaturist Jean-Baptiste Massé. Soon after engraving Watteau's *Sick Cat* in 1726, he started to earn a living from his own work, hoping to make his name as a portraitist. He painted only one religious work in his entire life: *David and Abimelech*, which was refused by the Académie in 1735. He also made some fine copies of the Old Masters, Titian in particular. Despite his technical skill as an artist, Liotard was not attracted to the grand subjects of traditional painting; he preferred to take his subjects from the world around him. In 1736, after entering the service of the Marquis of Puysieux, the French ambassador to the Kingdom of the Two Sicilies, he spent four months in Naples before moving on to Rome, where he painted the portraits of Pope Clement XII, Cardinal Biancheri, and the Englishman James Stuart and his family.

However, a chance meeting was to change the whole course of his life. He was in a café in Rome, probably in the Piazza di Spagna or the area around it, then the center of the Eternal City's literary and cultural life, when he heard an Englishman singing the praises of Liotard's recent copy of the Medici Venus; his admirer was Sir William Ponsonby. Nothing came of this until they were introduced in Florence in 1737 and Ponsonby offered Liotard the opportunity to accompany him to Constantinople. They sailed from Naples on the *Clifton*, stopping to take on water at Capri, Messina, Syracuse, and Malta, then at the ports of the Levant. At each port Liotard drew enthusiastically, often capturing the likenesses of the notables who received his illustrious patron. At Paros he painted Signora Lenetta Shepri, and at Chios Madame Vestali and her sister, Maroudia. When he reached Smyrna he portrayed Madame Marigot, her superb, luxuriant hair cascading from under a little lace bonnet; and also Monsieur Péleran, the French consul, and his wife, who dressed as an Amazon and wore a strange, pointed hat. He was amazed by the beauty of the women of Smyrna, who were dressed "in flowered, low-necked dresses which reveal the bosom below the covering muslin, their figures accentuated by belts clasped with broad gold or silver buckles, pearl bracelets glistening on their bare arms, a secret voluptuousness, the promise of ecstasy." In the margins of his sketchbooks he made numerous notes on the details of the women's costumes, from their lace aprons to their shoes embroidered with gold or silver, their petticoats trimmed with red, and their red stockings bordered with gold. Most of his drawings were done with red chalk and *pierre d'Italie* (a drawing stick made of fine clay) and have a delicate grace that shows he was supremely able to combine simplicity and rigorous technique. The simple naturalness of the pose his sitters adopt often contrasts with the richness of the cushions around them and also with the sumptuousness of their clothes, which he renders with rare sensitivity.

Liotard lived in Constantinople for five years, and those five years were well spent. An English merchant, Mr Levett, took an interest in the young artist and procured commissions for him. Liotard started by painting the portraits of his benefactors, first that of Sir William Ponsonby, whom he shows in Turkish costume, wearing a red and white turban, a broad green sash, and a red robe, his colorful figure standing out sharply from the neutral background. When he painted John Montagu, the Earl of Sandwich, he portrayed him in the same costume – only the color of the sash and the shape of the turban are different. The Earl is shown pointing with his index figure, his figure standing against a theatrical back-

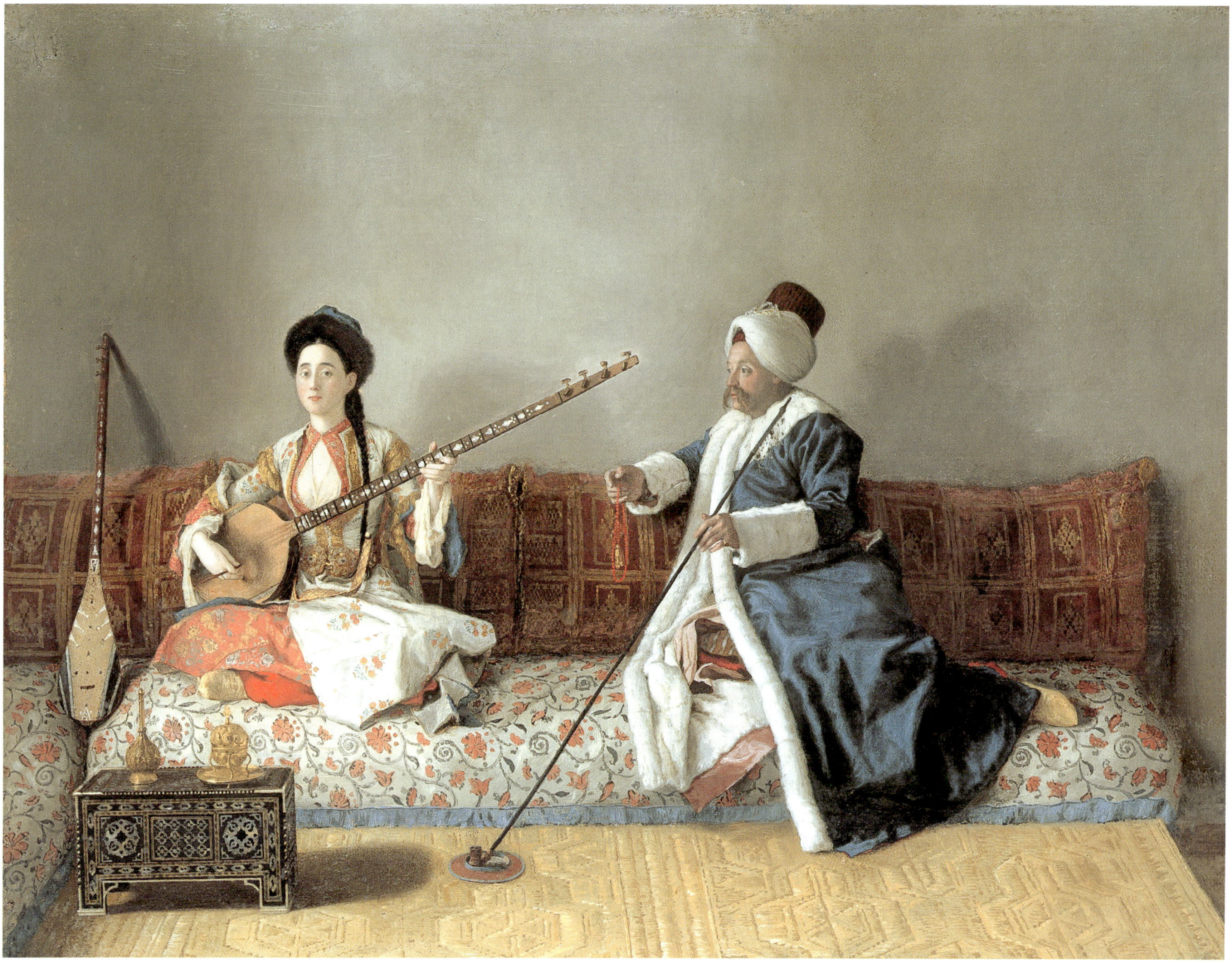

drop. Liotard also posed his friend, Mr Levett, on a divan. He is impressively mustachioed after the Turkish fashion, and wears a tall fur hat that gives him an imposing air. In the painting that Liotard produced from this drawing, the English merchant wears a turban and holds a long Turkish pipe; he is seated on a divan in the company of Mademoiselle Hélène Glavany (daughter of the former French consul in the Crimea), who is wearing traditional Tartar costume and playing a stringed instrument.

Orders flowed in and Liotard was asked to immortalize the Dutch ambassador, Cornelis Calkoen. On a journey between the Greek Islands and the Bosporus, Liotard met Richard Pococke, a man of exceptional culture who was an archaeologist, theologian, and indefatigable traveler rolled into one. For his portrait, Pococke chose to assume an austere appearance, wrapped in a long, dark mantle trimmed with black fur, and with a black fur hat on his head. He holds a book in his hand and leans on a stele on which there is a carved relief; in the background, a view of the Golden Horn can be discerned. Liotard then worked on a portrait of Mrs Tyrell, the wife of the British consul, before going on to draw men on low divans, smoking long hookahs, the glass bowl of which rests on richly patterned carpets, as in *An Effendi* and the pastel *Gentleman in Turkish Costume, Seated on a Sofa and Smoking the Chibouk*. When Liotard was allowed into the Sultan's entourage, he produced a

Portrait of M. Levett and of Mlle Glavany Seated on a Sofa, Jean-Étienne Liotard
Oil on card, 24.7 x 36.4 cm
(Musée du Louvre, Paris).

remarkable portrait of the dwarf Ibrahim, an attaché in the service of the Grand Sultan, managing to endow the poor, ill-favored man with true nobility, and to bring out a fascinating intelligence behind his unprepossessing features. The Grand Vizier asked for a portrait showing him in his ceremonial robes, the resulting pastel being one of exemplary sobriety. Liotard also painted Adig-Aga, the Great Treasurer of the Mosques, and "Akmed, the Pasha of Caramanie," who was really the Frenchman Claude-Alexandre, the Comte de Bonneval, who had been made general-in-chief of the Bombardiers – a man whom Casanova described as "a fat old man, dressed in the French manner, with a cheerful disposition." Works such as *Four Turkish Musicians* and *Two Levantine Violinists* were extremely popular, but it was in his depictions of women that Liotard excelled, whether European women of quality, or Turkish women caressing the strings of an instrument, dancing, or just walking in the street. His greatest work started as a drawing: *Frankish Woman of Pera Receiving a Friend.* From this developed a pastel in which the beautiful European woman is shown alone, and also a pastel on parchment showing a bathroom scene, *Frankish Woman and Her Servant.* In this second pastel, the young woman is perched on extraordinarily high pattens and is wearing a yellow-striped jacket and wide, white trousers embroidered with flowers, and a tall red and white head-dress. Her hand is extended in the direction of a little servant girl, who is carrying a pot of henna. Behind them is a fountain, set against a bare wall.

In the autumn of 1742 Liotard left Turkey for Moldavia (in what is now Romania), his plan to marry a young Greek girl called Mimica having come to a sudden end; the Prince of Moldavia's invitation to join him at Jassy perhaps helped him to forget this disappointment. He stayed six months, painting the portraits of the prince, his wife, a Prince Scarlati, and the Patriarch of Jerusalem, and drawing the nobles of the court. And it was here, in this distant land, that he created one of his most beautiful pictures, his *Young Man in Oriental Costume,* in which he depicts his subject full face and

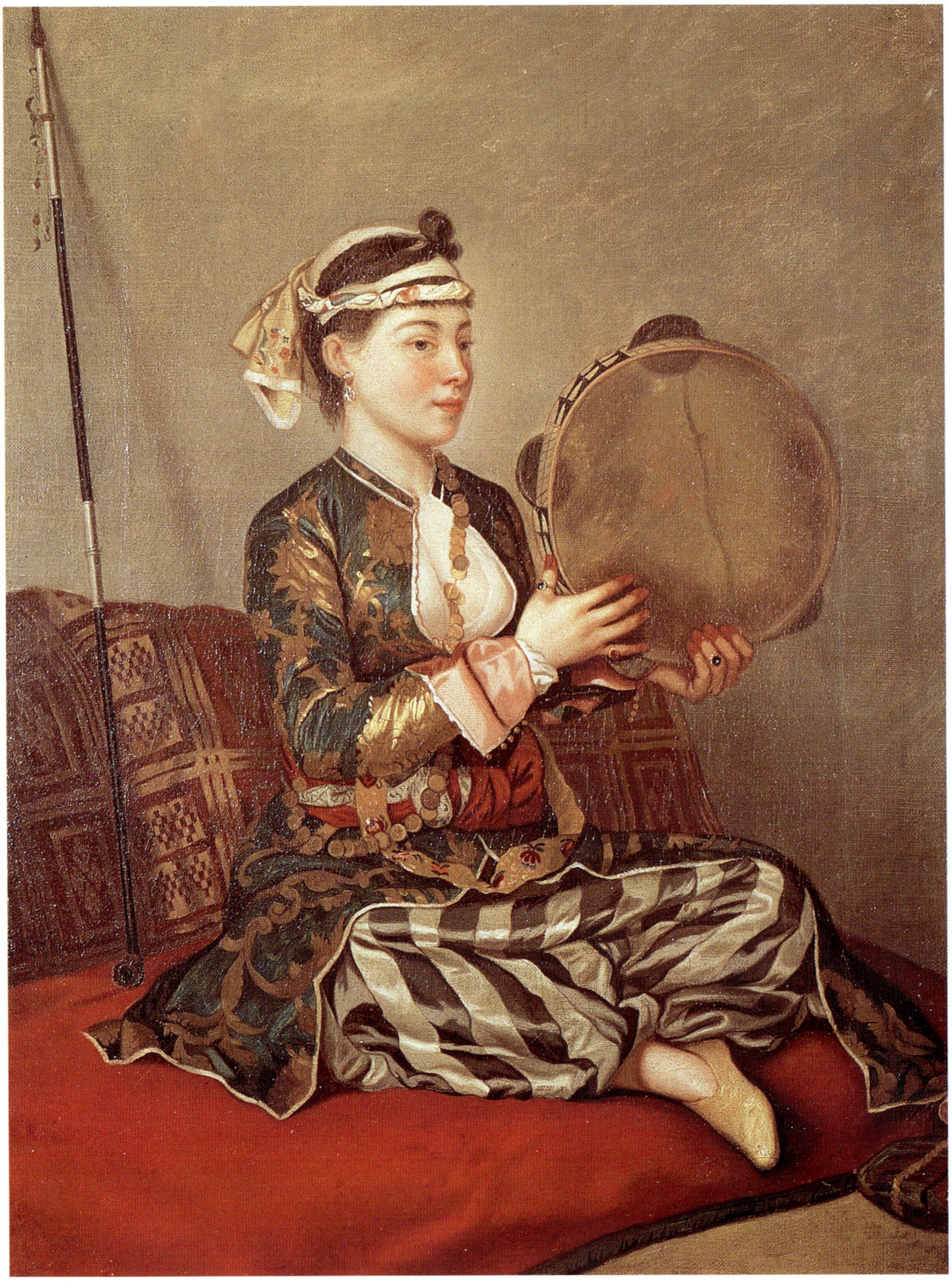

Girl in Turkish Costume with Tambourine,
Jean-Étienne Liotard,
between 1738 and 1743
Oil on canvas, 63.5 x 48.5 cm
(Musée d'Art et d'Histoire, Geneva).

Opposite
Portrait of Mary Gunning, Countess of Coventry,
Jean-Étienne Liotard, 1749
Pastel on parchment, 23.5 x 19 cm
(Musée d'Art et d'Histoire, Geneva).

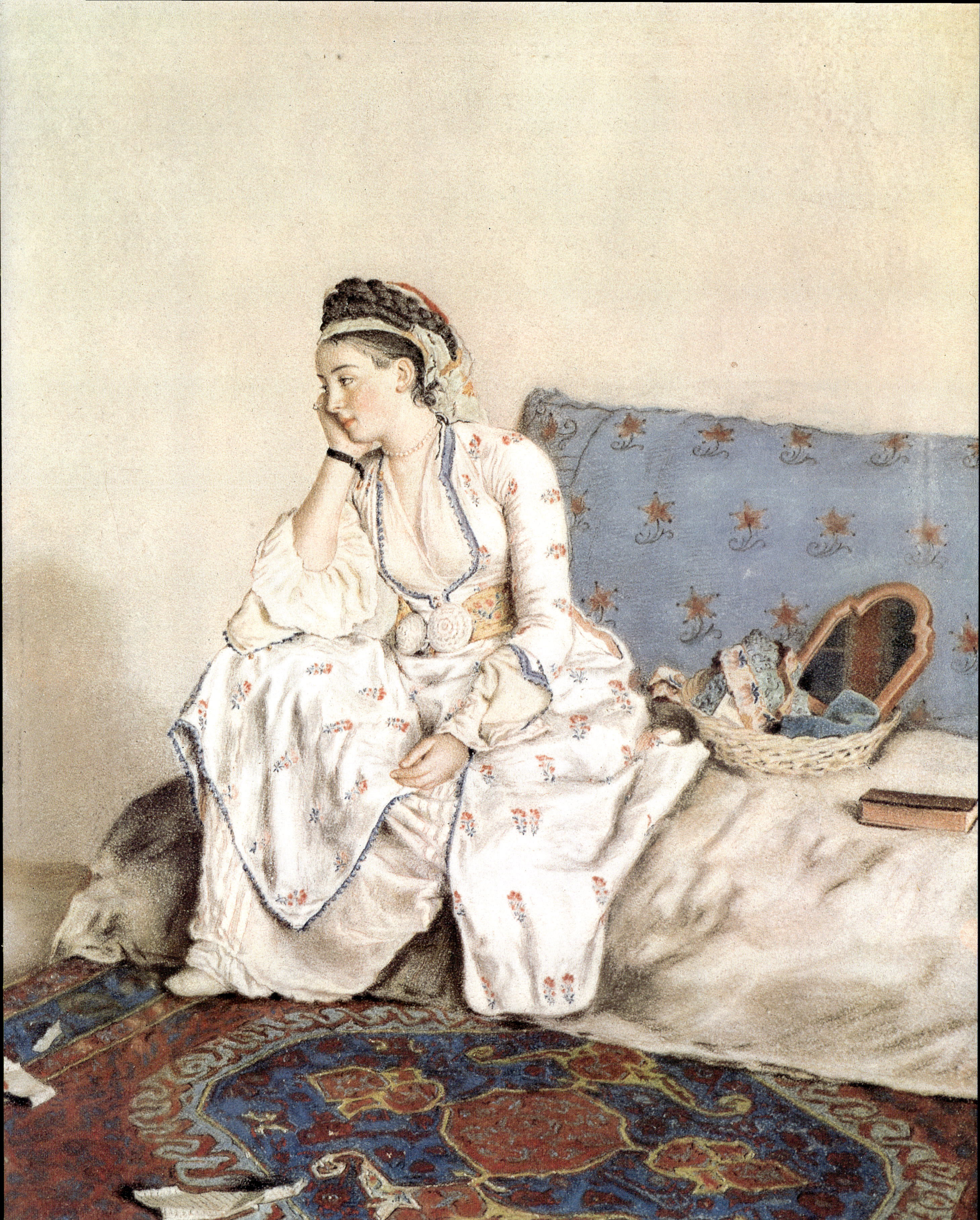

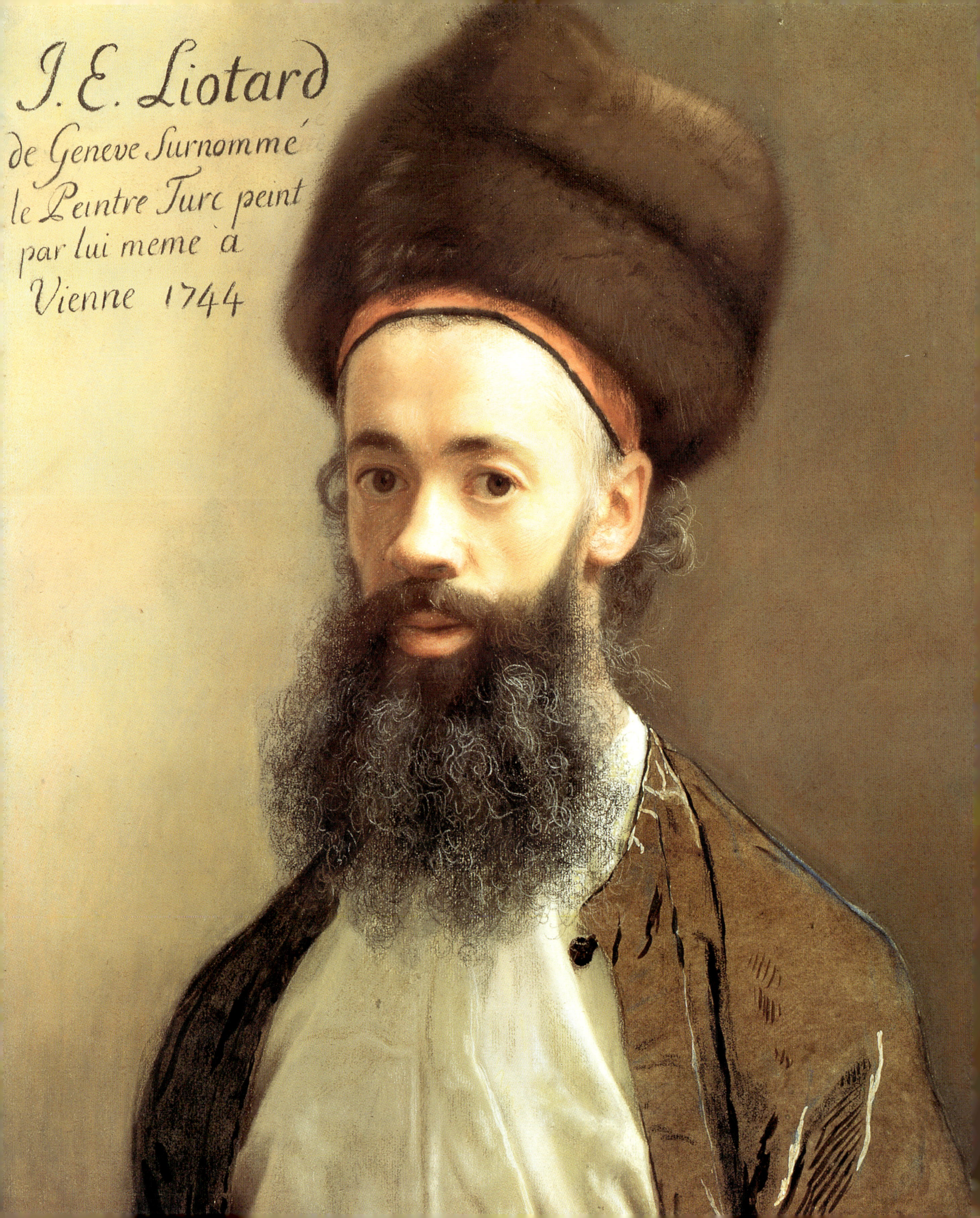
I. E. Liotard
de Geneve Surnommé
le Peintre Turc peint
par lui meme à
Vienne 1744

wearing in a jacket with broad fur lapels. He himself indulged his taste for exotic dress: when he was presented to the Empress Maria-Teresa in Vienna he was dressed as a Turk and sported a long ringletted beard. His several self-portraits show him with an immense beard, his hair worn in the Oriental style, his smile subtly ironic.

Upon his return to Europe, Liotard continued to paint pictures inspired by the Orient and these include his most successful works, notably the *Young Woman in Oriental Costume, Reading*, which was begun in 1738 and of which he made three versions between 1743 and 1753. It has been suggested that they feature Madame Chénier, the mother of the poet André Chénier, or even Madame Marie-Adélaïde de France. During the same period he also completed *Girl in Turkish Costume with Tambourine*, a work that gives the young musician a dignity that transcends her peasant features and physique. Here he again produced three versions that differ only slightly. But gradually the opportunities to use Oriental themes became increasingly rare as an interest in the East was starting to wane, but he used them when he could. In 1750, when he was living in Paris, he painted the portrait of the Countess of Coventry, who was reputed to be one of the most seductive women of her time. She is seated on a low divan, her chin resting on her hand. As usual, he used very few accessories and the wall behind her is completely bare. This was to be his last work in this intimate genre. He was now forced to devote himself to portraits that are much more formal and, with very few exceptions, have much less charm and vitality.

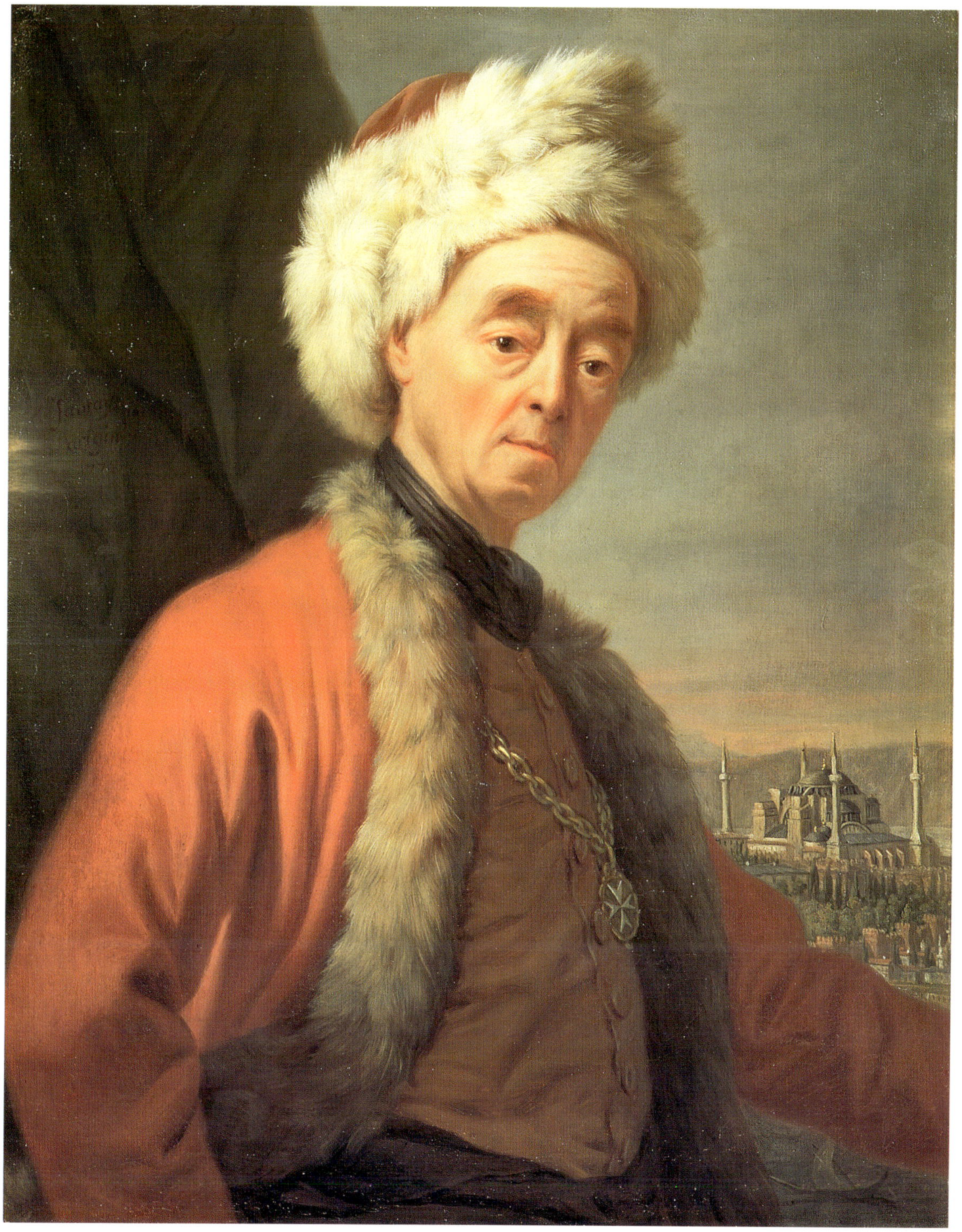

Self-portrait, Antoine de Favray, 1778
Oil on canvas, 79 x 63 cm
(Uffizzi Gallery, Florence).

Opposite
Self-portrait, Jean-Étienne Liotard, 1744
Pastel on card, 61 x 49 cm
(Uffizzi Gallery, Florence).

A Knight of Malta at the Court of the Caliph

The career of Antoine de Favray resulted, as was frequently the case in the 18th century, from a singular set of circumstances. When in 1728 De Troy was appointed head of the Académie de France in Rome, replacing Natoire, he asked Favray to accompany him; and it was in Rome that Favray made the acquaintance of the Knights of Malta, who suggested that he should return with them to Malta. In Valletta he received a number of Church commissions, including a series on the history of the Order and a portrait of Grand Master Pinto, who in 1751 made him a "knight servant at arms." Favray was particularly fond of depicting both the landscape and also the costumes of the attractive Maltese women. But an odd and unexpected turn of events caused him to leave Malta. In October 1760, an Ottoman galley put into the port of Valletta: the Christian rowers who manned the ship had mutinied and seized the vessel. This created a serious diplomatic

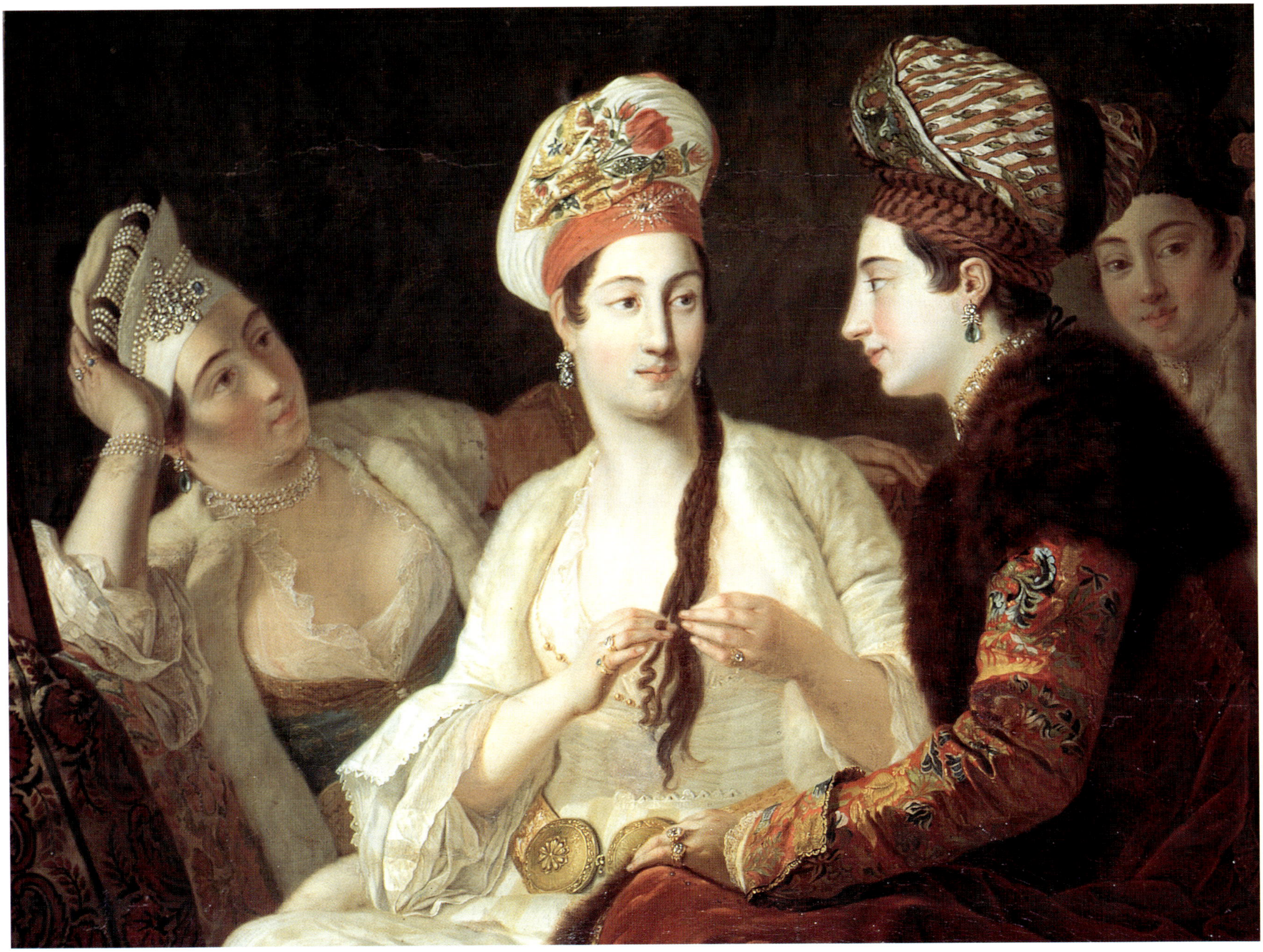

Turkish Women, Antoine de Favray, c. 1754
Oil on canvas, 93 x 124 cm
(Musée des Augustins, Toulouse).

Opposite
Maltese Women,
Antoine de Favray, undated.
Oil on canvas, 93 x 124 cm
(Musée des Augustins, Toulouse).

problem, and finally the King of France bought the ship in order to give it back to the Grand Turk. So on 19 January 1762 the French frigate *Oiseau* accompanied the galley into the port of Constantinople. Favray, who was on board the frigate, was overwhelmed by the view of the Bosporus gradually unfolding before his eyes. The French ambassador, Monsieur de Vergennes, who wanted to do everything he could to prolong Favray's stay in Constantinople, took him into his service. It did not take him long to become acquainted with the cultivated French community in the capital, thanks largely to remarkable personalities like Madame Chenier and Monsieur Guys, a merchant and man of letters. The view from the French embassy was superb, but Favray preferred the view from the Russian embassy, where he could also work undisturbed. After eight years in the Turkish capital he completed his major work, his *View of the Bosporus and the Golden Horn*. He painted this view several times, determined to capture it as truthfully as possible. One of these versions, painted in 1762, was purchased by Monsieur Guys, another by the French embassy. Favray also presented a version to one of his patrons, Chevalier Turgot, in gratitude for his support. In 1774, in a long letter to Turgot from Malta, Favray describes the picture in detail. "On the left of the picture as you look at it is the beginning of the city of Constantinople, separated from Galata and Pera (from which this view is seen) by the port. The great mosque with six minarets is

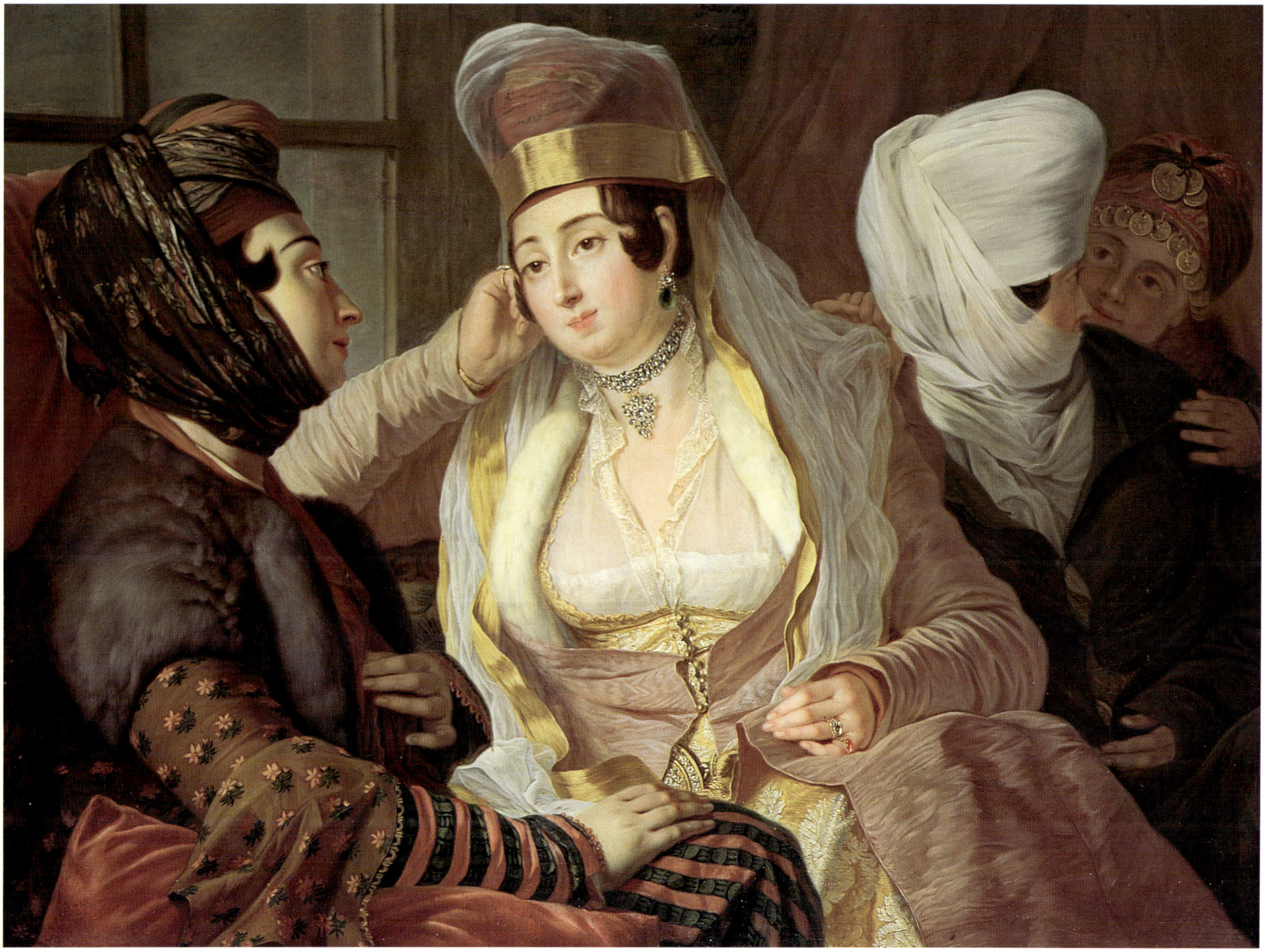

the mosque of Sultan Ahmed I, built on the site of the former Hippodrome. The small, lead-roofed dome at the foot of the mosque is the sultan's tomb. Beyond is a glimpse of Hagia Sofia with its four tall minarets, separated from the walls of the Seraglio by no more than the width of the street, which widens at that point. Beyond Hagia Sofia, the area full of trees is the Seraglio or Seray, where Sultan Mahmud built the little apartments you can see. The kiosk, the green-painted pavilion, which comes right at the tip, is the kiosk of Amurat; it was from there that he embarked on the Babylonian expedition [...] In the middle of the Seraglio there is a steeple like those on our village churches; below it is the Hall of the Divan, where ambassadors dine with the Grand Vizier on the same day that they have their audience with the Great Sultan. The building near Hagia Sofia, the one with the little dome like a copper, was formerly the church of St. John Chrysostom and is now an armory where the magnificent weapons of the Greek emperors are kept. Next to this building is the entrance to the first court of the Seraglio. The Harem, or women's quarters, has its windows on the White Sea side, so that no-one can see them." Favray expressed his love for these hallowed places by painting views such as *Shores of the Sweet Waters*, *Castles of Europe and Asia*, and *The Golden Horn*, places that are depicted in their full splendor.

Favray was also a fine portraitist, as indeed his remarkable portrait of Monsieur de Vergennes reveals. The French ambassador is shown wearing Turkish costume, with a red mantle edged with white fur, a yellow robe, and yellow slippers; he holds a chaplet of cornelians in one hand and a Turkish pipe in the other, and there is a dagger in his belt. His ironic expression, however, belies his Oriental guise. When he painted de Vergennes' wife, in a less typical Oriental costume, ornamented with bracelets and a pearl diadem, Favray gave her a curiously theatrical expression. As his *Portrait of Catherine Raulin, Wife of the Embassy Secretary at Constantinople* and his *Portrait of a Greek Woman* show, he knew how to give his sitters gravity and depth, capturing their personality not only through facial expression but also through pose and costume. His most beautiful works of this type are portraits of elegant women, for example *Levantine Women in Indoor Head-dress*, *Levantine Women in Outdoor Head-dress* (1754), *Turkish Women* (c. 1754), *Greek Women in a Garden*, and *Greek Women in the Bazaar*. In such works he provides a sensitive, even intimate view of his subjects. To Western eyes, such women, resplendent in their elaborate costumes, must have seemed strange indeed, though they were hardly more exotic than the extravagantly disguised Venetians during Carnival.

The diplomatic activity that accompanied the war between the Ottoman Empire and Russia gave Favray the opportunity to paint *Audience Granted Monsieur de Saint-Priest by the Sultan*, which was exhibited at the Salon in 1771, and *Audience Granted Monsieur de Saint-Priest by the Grand Vizier in the Camp of Daoud Pasha, 1769*. In time the tense and bellicose atmosphere in Constantinople, and the problems it caused for foreigners, finally induced him to leave. He set sail for Marseilles and from there made his way to Malta, where he received a warm welcome.

In Paris, however, Favray's talents were not appreciated. His *Audience Granted Monsieur Saint-Priest by the Sultan* was criticized by Denis Diderot, who reproached him for "poor composition," though in 1763 Diderot had praised Favray's *Maltese Women Receiving a Visit*. Favray's *Street of the Hippodrome in Constantinople*, exhibited in the Salon of 1779, was also poorly received.

Constantinople through the eyes of Jean-Baptiste Hilair

Almost nothing is known of Jean-Baptiste Hilair's training. He was probably influenced by his mentor, Le Prince, who traveled in Russia and throughout Asia Minor. Hilair's destiny was also closely linked to that of the Count of Choiseul-Gouffier, whom he accompanied on his travels when the count was preparing to publish his *Voyage littéraire de la Grèce* (Literary travels in Greece), the first volume of which appeared in 1782. The work was very successful, with its author being voted a member of the Académie Française and appointed ambassador to the Sublime Porte. A number of

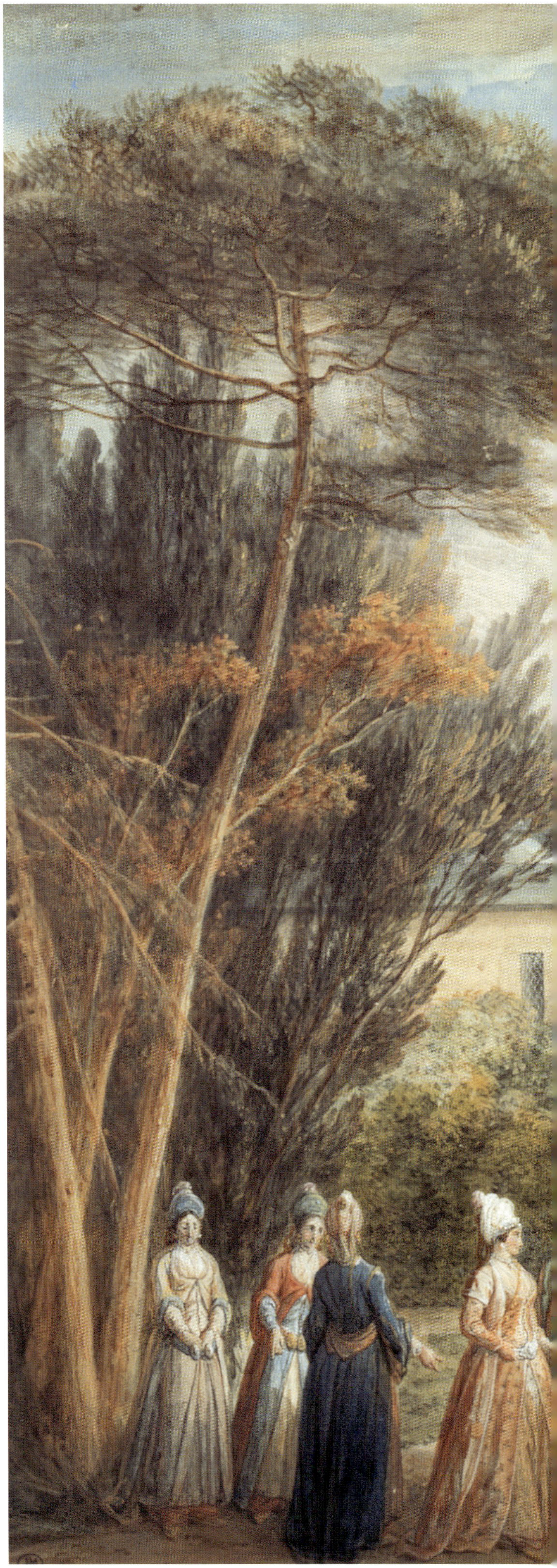

Promenade,
Jean-Baptiste Hilair, 1797
Ink and watercolor, 35 x 46 cm
(Musée du Louvre, Départment des Arts Graphiques, Paris).

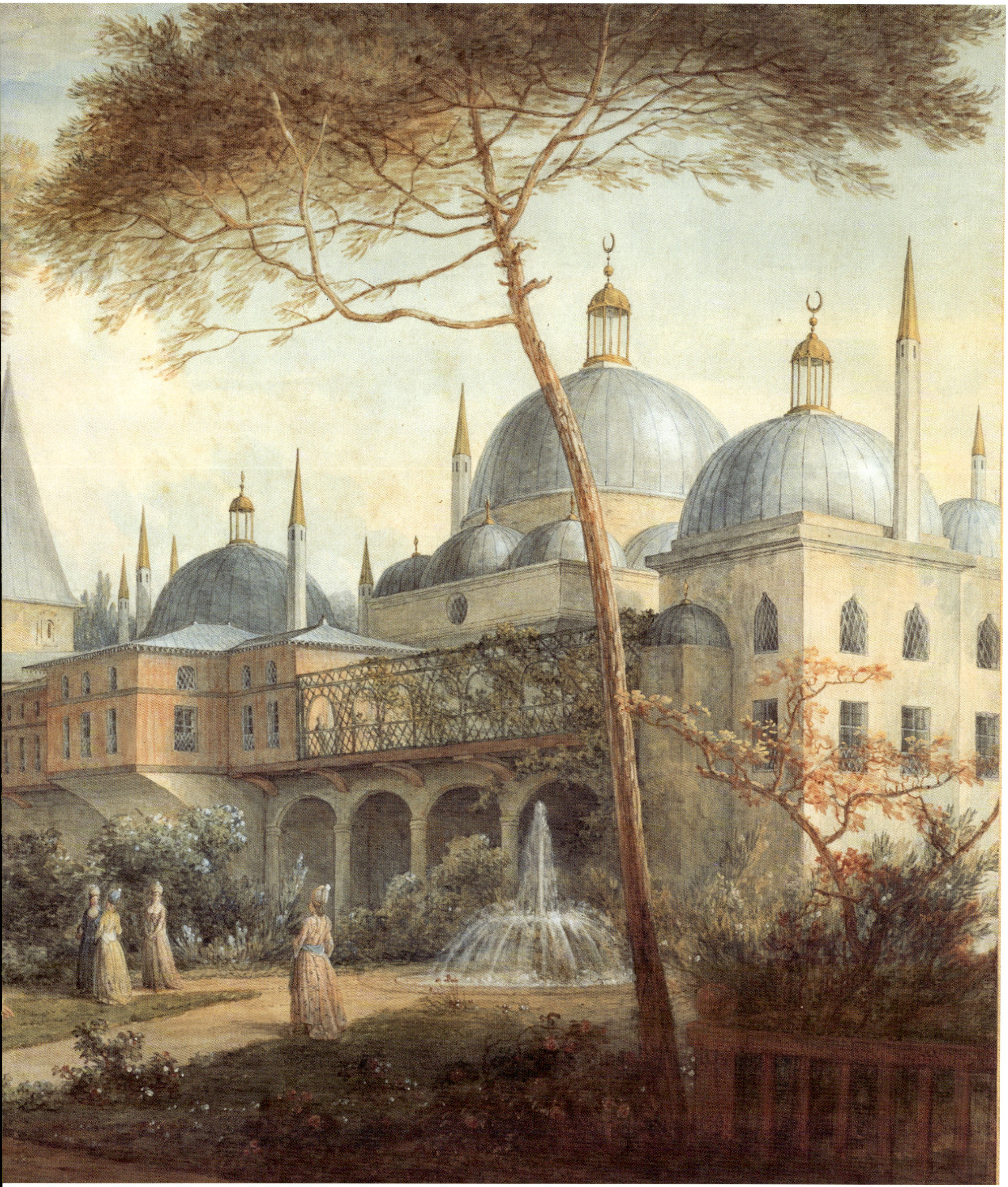

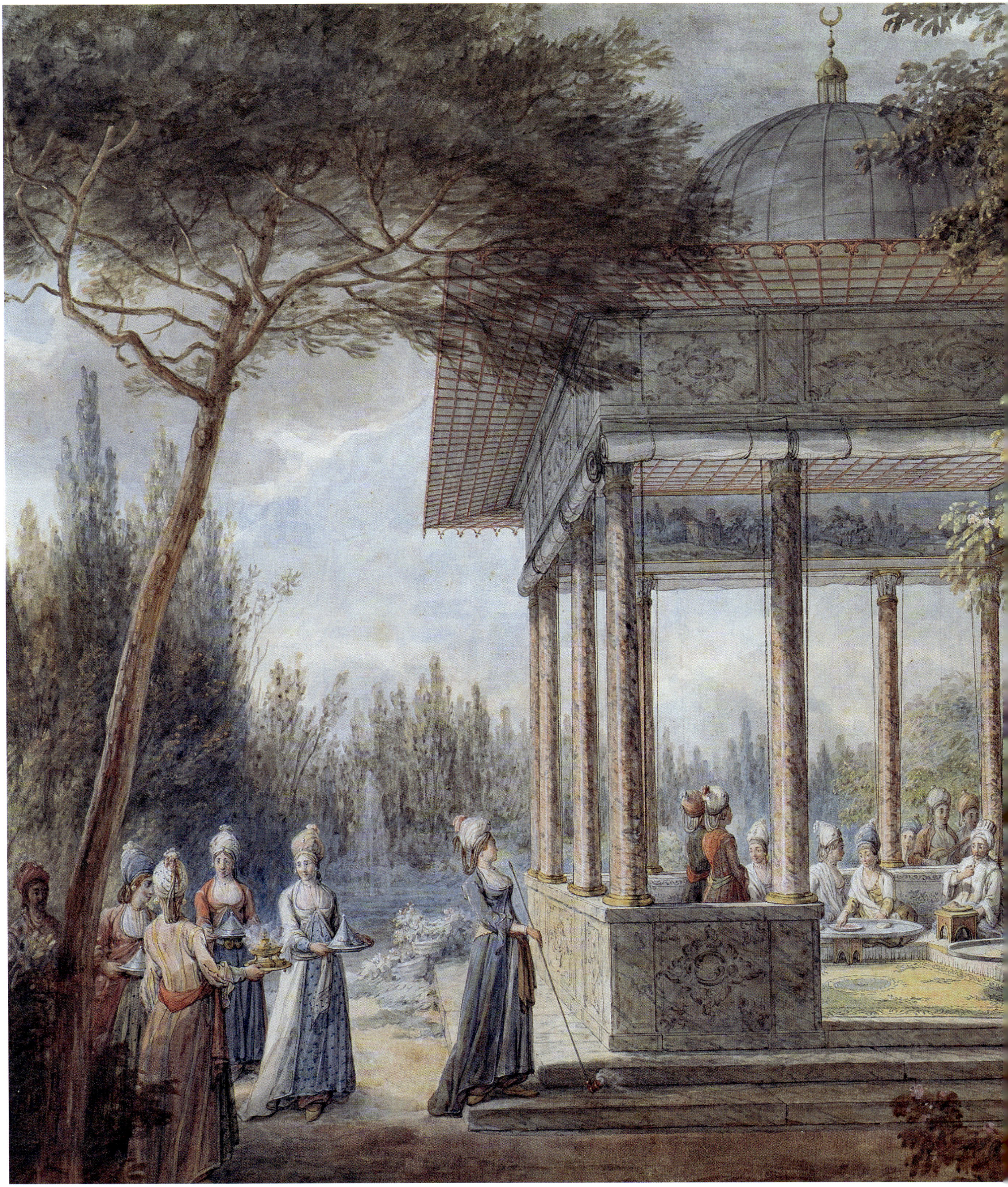

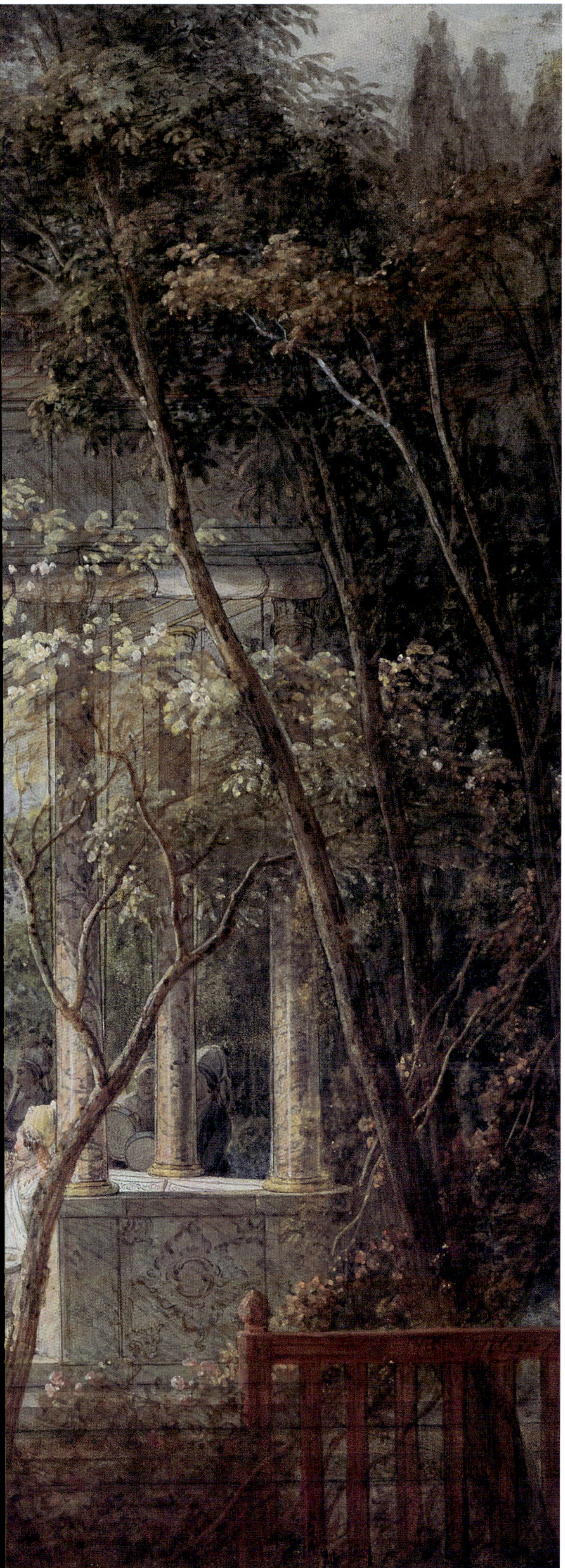

Harem Scene,
Jean-Baptiste Hilair, undated.
Ink and gouache,
33 x 44 cm (Musée du Louvre,
Graphic arts section, Paris).

Following double page.
View of Sultan Ahmet's mosque
(or *The blue mosque*), Louis-François
Cassas, between 1787 and 1791
Pen and ink and watercolor on white
laid paper, 59 x 100 cm
(Musée des Beaux-Arts, Tours).

artists were involved in the production of this book, including Tillard, Choffard, Lemire, and Aliamet, though Hilair produced most of the illustrations. The count liked to show the illustrations to his friends, and in the evenings, as Lady Craven wrote on 25 April 1786, when the day's work was over, they often gathered around the great portfolios to examine the drawings at their leisure. By then the young artist had already completed a number of impressive paintings and drawings. He produced many landscapes, a good example being *View of Seraglio Point from Galata*, a watercolor depicting Constantinople from the European shore. It features small rowing boats and sailing craft, and a great sailing ship bearing aloft huge oriflammes and a large flag. Another fine landscape is his *View of Constantinople*, an oil painting that shows the Topkapi Palace. He also painted the pleasure gardens, as in *The Sweet Waters of Europe*, where we see a terrace on the shores of the Bosporus, and *The Sweet Waters of Asia*, which shows three men in front of a log cabin in an idyllic natural scene. He particularly excelled in scenes from life in the imperial palace, examples being *Harem Scene*, a pen and watercolor drawing of the women of the court and their servants in a kiosk in a park that also features a small lake and fountain; and *Promenade*, in which a group of women stroll peacefully in a closed garden while a man converses with a group of young beauties. He painted touching interiors – such as *Christian Women*, in which a group of women are shown in their summer apartments – and a number of portraits, notably *Oriental Woman*, a gouache that is said to be of Aimée Dubuc, who was abducted by pirates and sold to Sultan Abdulhamid I, who named her Naksh-I-Jill. Hilair also painted a striking portrait of Abdulhamid I, resplendent in his strange feather-plumed turban. As the sultan refused to sit for his portrait it is not known how Hilair accomplished it. However he managed it, he achieved a striking likeness of the man, who is portrayed in front of buildings with blue-gray cupolas set against a greenish-blue evening sky. Several picturesque scenes, such

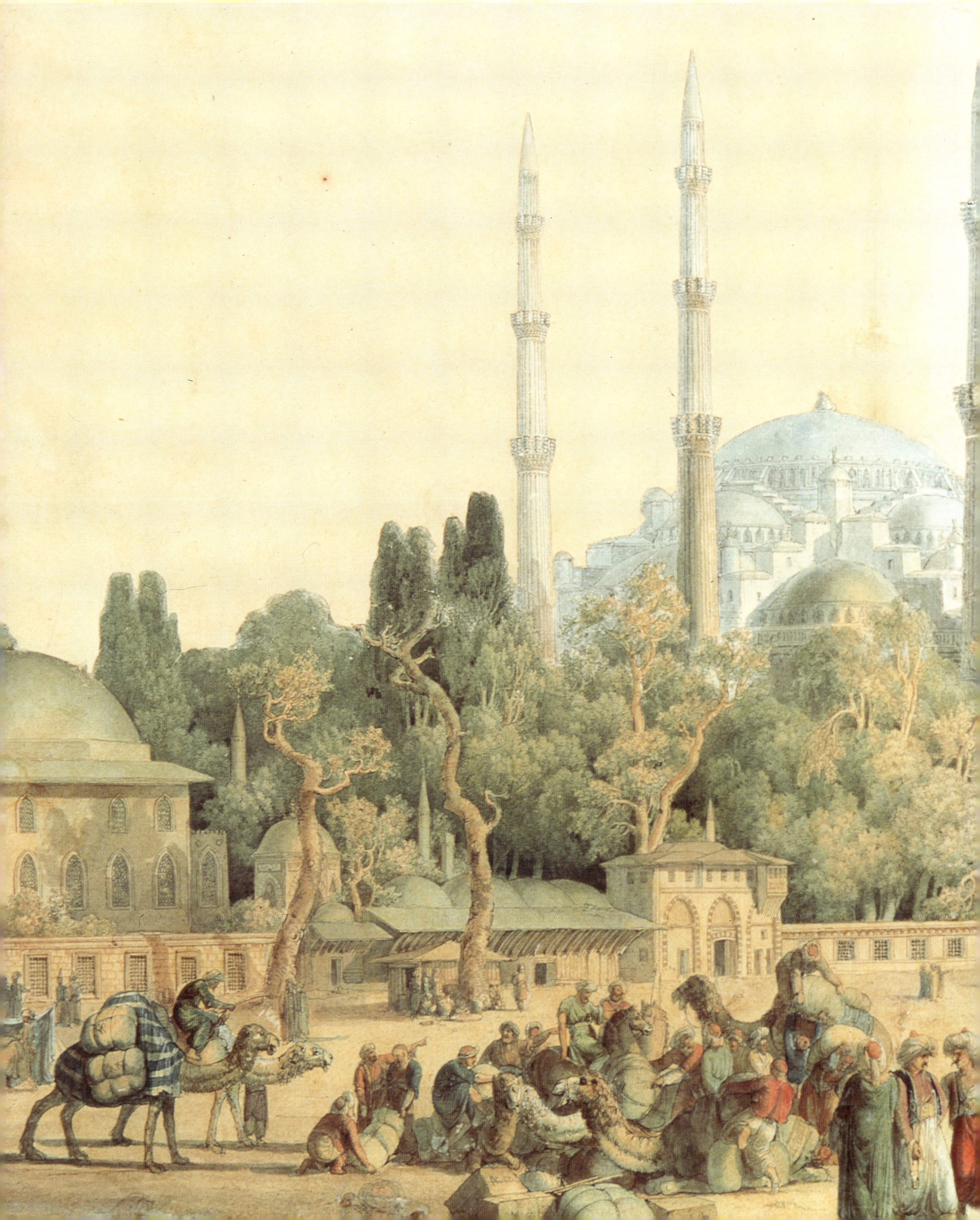

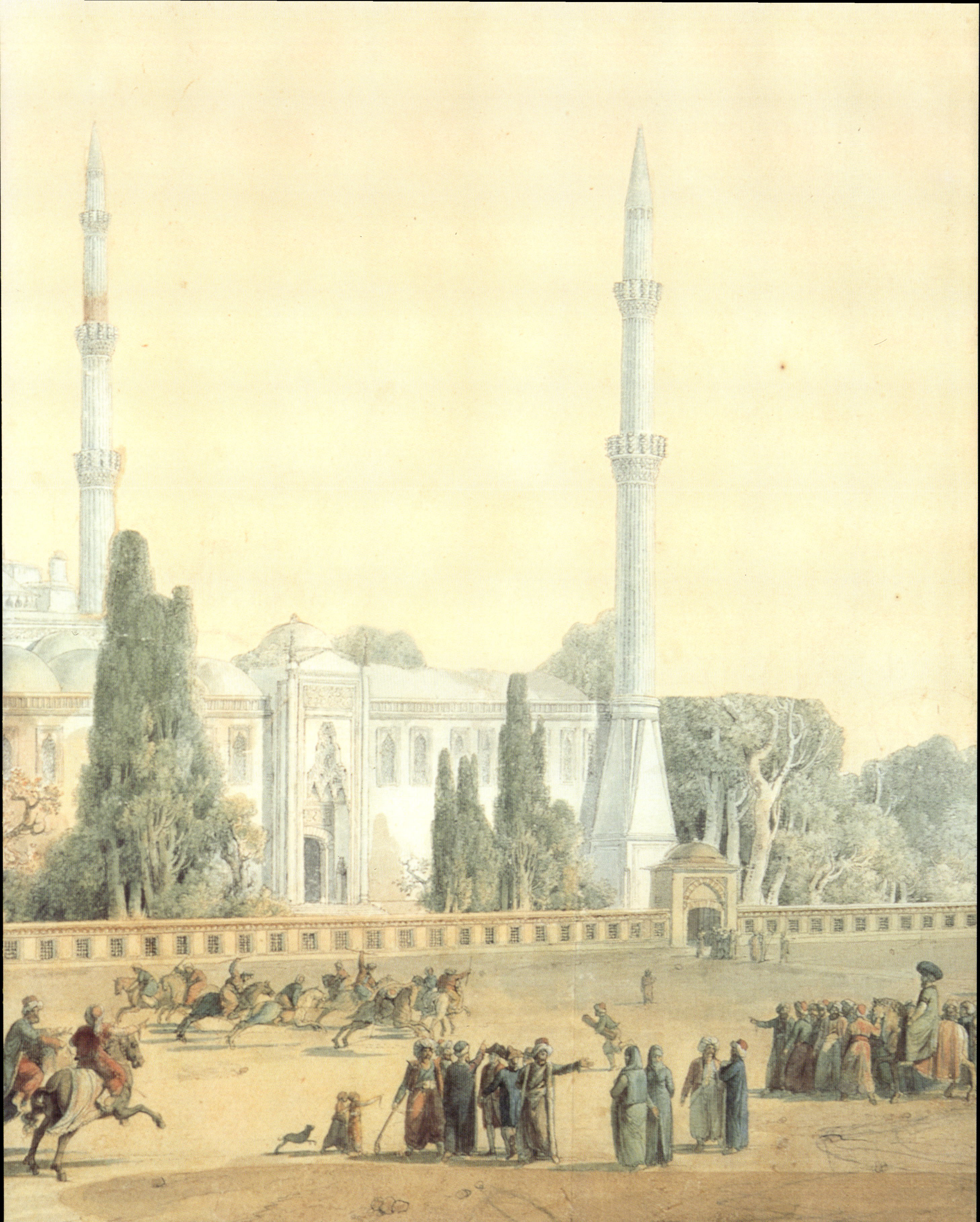

as *Turkish Festival* and *Greek Dance*, feature as engravings in the *Voyage pittoresque en Grèce* (Picturesque journey through Greece). Others, along with detailed descriptions of monuments, appear in the *Tableau général de l'Empire othomane* (General description of the Ottoman Empire), a survey written by the very learned Armenian scholar Mouradgea d'Ohsson; the first volume was printed in Paris in 1788, the last volume not appearing until 1820.

On returning to France Hilair commissioned Langlois and Malbeste to undertake engravings for a collection of prints illustrating Oriental costumes, and he himself painted a series of Oriental landscapes, one of which now hangs in the Louvre.

Cassas and Goethe

For seven years the French artist Louis-France Cassas followed the Duc de Chabot in his travels throughout Italy, Sicily, and Dalmatia. The drawings he produced during these journeys persuaded Count Choiseul-Gouffier to take him into his service. So, on 4 August 1784, Cassas took ship with the count and his retinue of painters and draftsmen, arriving in Constantinople on 23 September. A month later he was aboard the *Poulette*, bound for the Lebanon. He traveled through Syria, Palestine, and Egypt for 14 months, producing around 300 drawings during his journey. He continued to work for Choiseul-Gouffier in Rome, where he was given the job of acquiring works of art, and quickly built up a reputation for his own works, with people flocking to him to admire his drawings, which had "escaped the Arabs." The German poet Goethe was one of his visitors. On 15 September 1787 Goethe wrote in a letter, "Cassas' work is extremely beautiful. It made me think of a lot of things I'd like to tell you." And, two days later, writing in his journal, he describes the drawings he has seen in great detail. "The Seraglio of Constantinople viewed from the sea with part of the city and the Mosque of Hagia Sophia. On the very end of the point, the most delightful in Europe, is the dwelling of the Great Sultan, which is built in as pleasant a manner as may be imagined. High trees are respected, planted one behind the other in great groups that are generally linked together: between them there are no great walls or fences, but small houses, grilles, galleries, kiosks, and carpets, and all with such an intimate feeling, so small-scale and so delightfully pell-mell that it is a pleasure to see. The drawing is colored, which makes for a very attractive effect. A beautiful inlet bathes the coast where these buildings are situated. The opposite shore is Asia, and the eye plunges into the straits which end in the Dardanelles." He also describes the *Turkish Tombs*, noting that the "girls cultivate flowers on the tombs with the greatest care."

On the outbreak of the French Revolution, Count Choiseul-Gouffier left his post. Cassas made his way to Paris and managed to persuade the Committee for Public Safety to publish a selection of the drawings as *Voyage en Syrie* (Syrian journey). However, only 30 copies came out as the count forbade publication since he had paid all the artist's expenses and therefore had a legal right to the drawings. Cassas' drawings are remarkable for their freshness and their lightness of touch; they have the spontaneity of the original sketches.

His paintings are also very distinctive. The gouache *View of Constantinople and Seraglio Point* is enlivened by a nautical festival in the foreground; in another view in pen and watercolor he keeps the idea of the nautical festival, but places a dense wood and a cemetery in the foreground. Cassas could handled the picturesque deftly, as we can see in the different versions of *The Sultan's March on the Day of Bayram* and *View of the Suleymaniye*. His skill lay in his ability to render the architecture and costumes with a meticulous attention to detail that vividly evokes, for Western eyes, the exotic character of the people and events depicted. In *Wrestlers*, he shows the athletes confronting one other in front of the Pasha's tent in a military camp. French officers are present among Oriental figures dressed in the most varied costumes. Occasionally, Cassas comes close to sentimentality, and the gouache *Choosing a Slave* shows that he sometimes gives way to a facile dexterity. On his return to Paris he continued, with a modest success, to produce works with an Oriental character, such as *Walk in the Seraglio Gardens*, a late gouache of 1822.

Melling: artist, and architect to his highness

Antoine-Ignace Melling, an artist from Lorraine in France, arrived in Constantinople in 1785. Frédéric Gisberg van Dedem van Gelder, Dutch envoy for 27 years, recalled: "He was then attached to the Russian embassy; Monsieur de Bulgakov

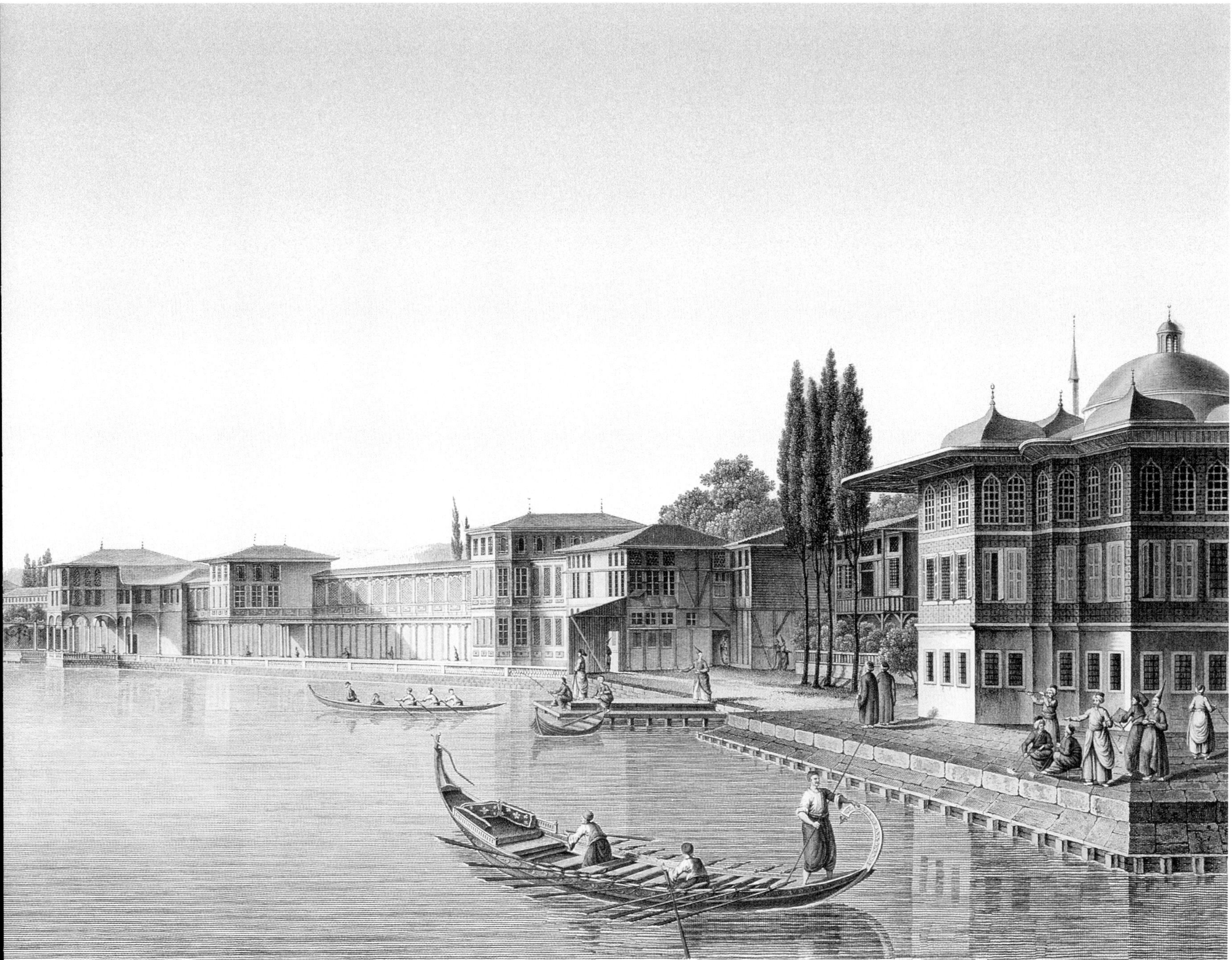

allowed him to give my sister and myself lessons and it was from him that I received the first elements of that art which was to prove so useful when traveling and which was a great help to me in my expeditions in Asia and Egypt."

Melling was then living in the Russian embassy in Pera and at the Bulgakov residence in Büyükdere, a short distance north of Constantinople, and also spent time in a superb residence shared by Baron de Hübsch, Baron of Grossthal, and the Danish consul. He quickly established a high reputation in embassy circles in the Ottoman capital, and even in the court of the new sultan, Selim III, who ascended the throne in 1789 with the firm intention of undertaking major reforms.

It was Kadidja, the sultan's favorite sister, who made Melling a royal favorite. She commissioned him to design a garden as beautiful as the one he had created for the envoy of the King of Denmark at his palace, Nebad Abad, on the point of Defterdar Bümu at Ortakoy. Melling, who then had his private apartments in the palace of the Pasha of Erzerum, designed for the sultana a garden in the form of a labyrinth, using lilac, rose, and acacia. "The winding paths were so designed that nearly all the ways led to the center, and so it was easy to find the way out." After this initial success he was

View of Constantinople (Beçitaç Palace),
Antoine-Ignace Melling, between 1807 and 1816
Etching, 69 x 93 cm (Château de Fontainebleau).

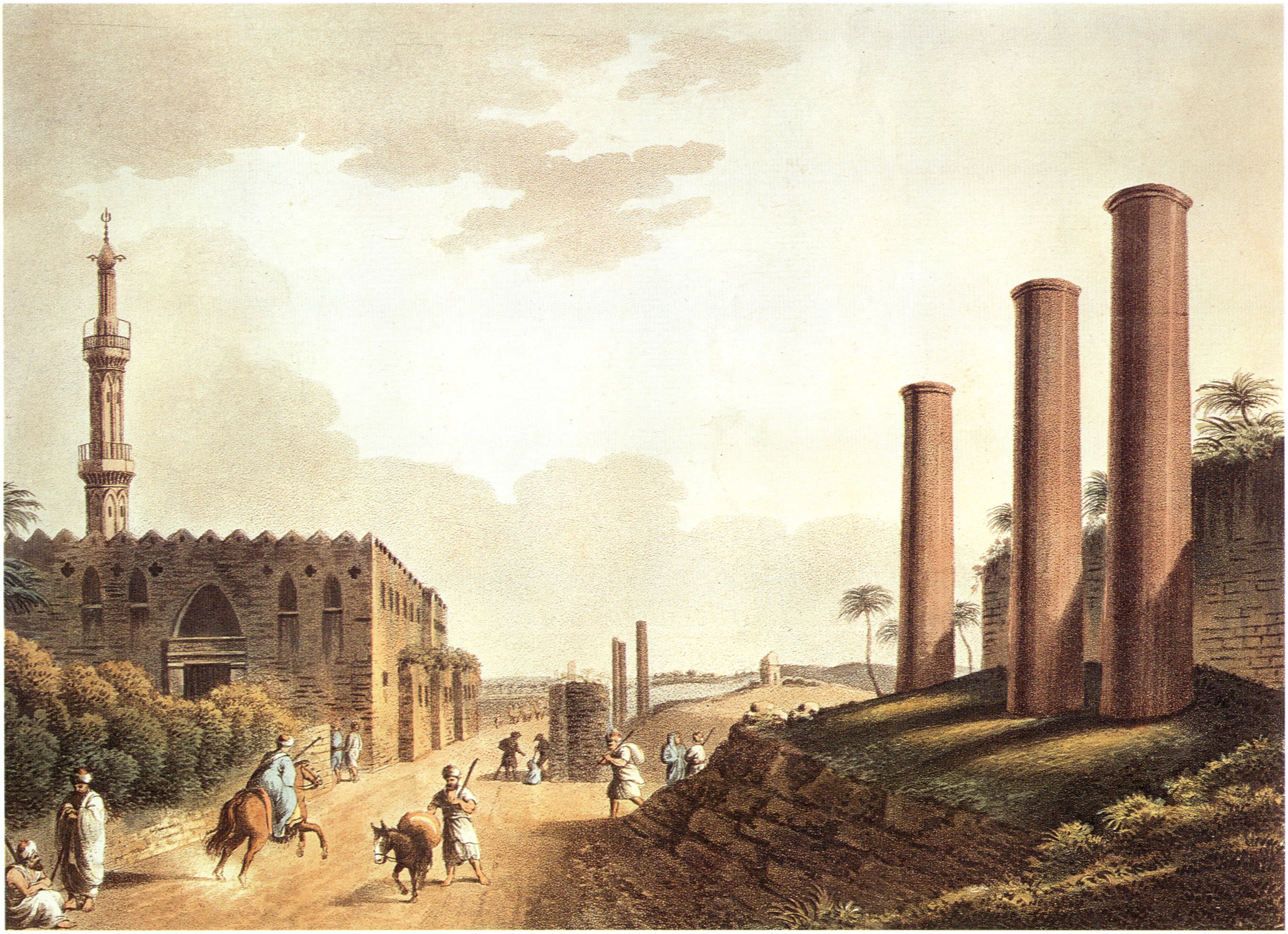

commissioned to build a small mansion that was to form part of the sultan's palace. He designed a one-story building inspired by the principles of the Italian Renaissance architect Vignola and furnished with an undecorated pediment and a Doric colonnade. It was divided into five bays, the three central ones forming a projecting pavilion. On the side where the quay was situated, Melling decided on a balustrade, which was also in the Doric order. He created a second design in which the pavilion was prolonged with a long open gallery on which there was a kiosk where one could, he wrote, "enjoy the pleasures of fishing." For the Sultan's summer palace at Beçitaç, he designed a kiosk resembling a Greek temple, built of wood and featuring eight Ionic columns of white marble and a gallery in the Corinthian order. Selim III, who was wholly delighted, accorded Melling the distinction of a pelisse (a robe of office) and awarded him the title of Architect to His Highness. He next requested him to draw up the plans of a building for Seraglio Point, a project that was later abandoned. But Melling did prepare interior decoration for the sultan's palace, declaring that he wanted to replace "the luxury of gilding and colors that left no rest for the eye" with something far simpler. He was so well respected at court that he had the right to examine everything that was bought for the harem, drawing the robes, belts, and shawls of the favorites, and organizing the décor for the festivities.

These architectural projects did not, however, prevent him from producing drawings, gouaches, and watercolors; quite the contrary. His work for the Great Sultan and his sister gave Melling the greatest possible freedom to travel the country. This allowed him to work on his album *Voyage pittoresque de Constantinople et les rives du Bosphore* (Picturesque journey from Constantinople and the shores of the Bosporus), which he considered his most important project and on which he spent the whole of 1801.

Leaving Turkey in July 1802, he arrived in France in 1803. He exhibited his drawings at the Salons from 1804 to 1810, gaining a gold medal, while preparing 13 volumes of his major work, his album, under the patronage of the statesman Talleyrand. The project was dedicated to Napoleon in 1807, though the first volume did not appear until December 1819. It contained views of the ancient fortresses of the Bosporus, Seraglio Point, a café interior, Tophané Square, and many views of Constantinople from a wide range of locations. Also included were his depictions of traditional costumes and of ceremonies, such as marriages, and the Sultan's march on the day of Bayram.

Minor artists of Pera

The embassies of the great European powers played a major cultural role in Constantinople during this period. Official receptions offered the opportunity to meet wits and scholars, travelers, archaeologists, men of letters, artists, and people of wealth, an elegant and brilliant microcosm of society. In Pera, the European quarter of Constantinople, the French embassy, the Dutch envoy's salon, the British legation, and the Russian embassy were intellectual centers of exceptional brilliance at a time when the Seraglio (the sultan's palace) was undergoing a period of cultural rebirth that made it relatively open to Western ideas.

Many painters spent time in Constantinople, called in by diplomats to take part in missions that meant maintaining the best possible relations with the Great Sultan on the one hand, and, on the other, satisfying Europe's ever-growing curiosity about the civilization that had developed under Turkish rule.

François Favel stood out from his colleagues because he was himself a career diplomat, while also being a painter, engraver, and archaeologist. He made a journey in Egypt in the company of the son of the Dutch ambassador, and then worked with the indefatigable Choiseul-Gouffier, who sent him on a reconnaissance mission in Greece to catalog the ancient monuments. He was also appointed vice-consul in Athens and became an expert on Greek archaeology – Chateaubriand claimed that Favel knew Athens better than anyone else of his day. For half a century he remained the final source of information for connoisseurs of the Orient.

Armand Carafe stayed for some time at the Académie de France in Rome, then made a great journey that allowed him to discover Constantinople, Greece, Egypt, and the islands of the Archipelago.

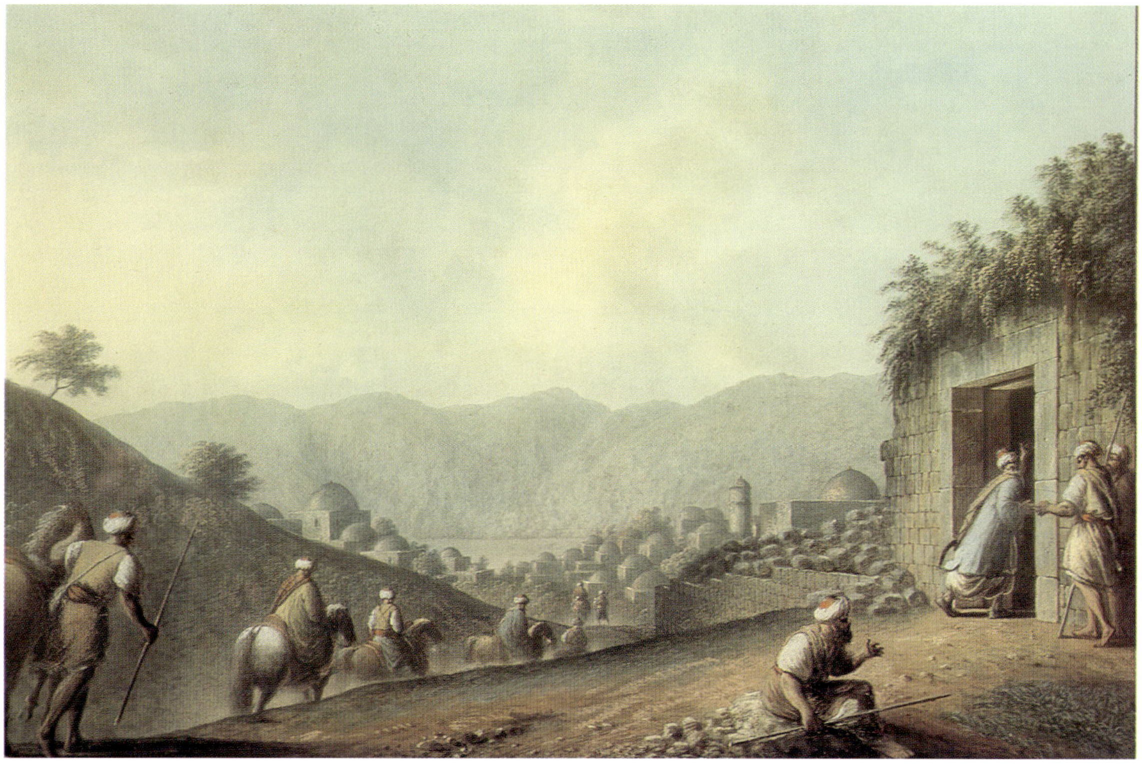

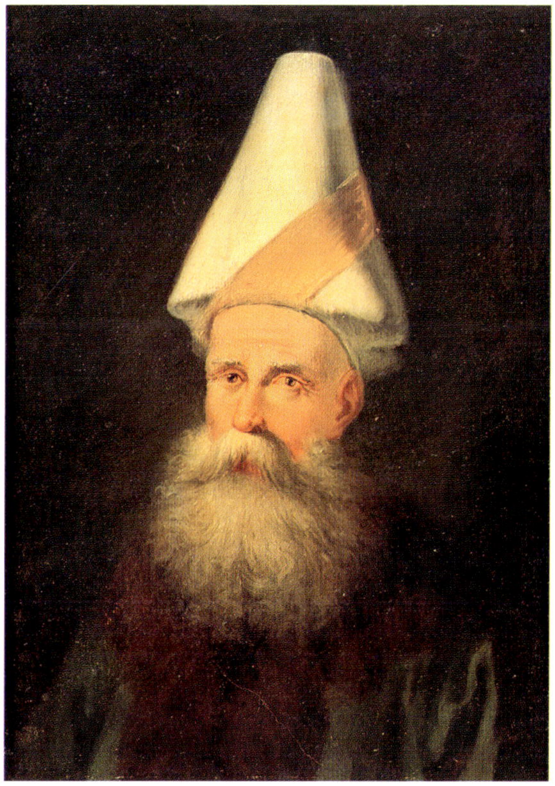

Comidas de Carbognaro, a dragoman to the Legation of the Two Sicilies, worked on a major description of Constantinople for the Count Ludolf, though it turned out to be a rather mediocre work.

Luigi and Chiara Mayer were also employed by the count, their role being to draw the monuments and sites of Turkey. Luigi Mayer produced images of great finesse, selecting original views of the famous sights of the Bosporus and documenting official ceremonies with a very delicate touch. His wife, Chiara, focused her attention on picturesque events, especially dance scenes.

Ferdinando Tonioli worked for de Juliani, the Venetian envoy. He left some very curious portraits, including those of Abdulhamid I and his vizier, Youssouf Pasha. Tonioli paid considerable attention to the two men's astonishing head-dresses, which stand out strikingly against very dark backgrounds.

Above
View of Bethany with the Entrance to the Tomb of Lazarus, Luigi Mayer,
Pastel, (Roy Miles Gallery, London).

Left
Portrait of Youssouf Pacha, Grand Vizier in Constantinople from 1785 to 1789,
Ferdinando Tonioli 1788,
Oil on canvas, 37 x 27 cm
(Musée National du Château de Versailles).

Opposite
Granite Columns of the Canope Portico in Alexandria, Luigi Mayer, 1802
Engraving from *Vues d'Egypte*
(Bibliothèque Nationale de France, Paris).

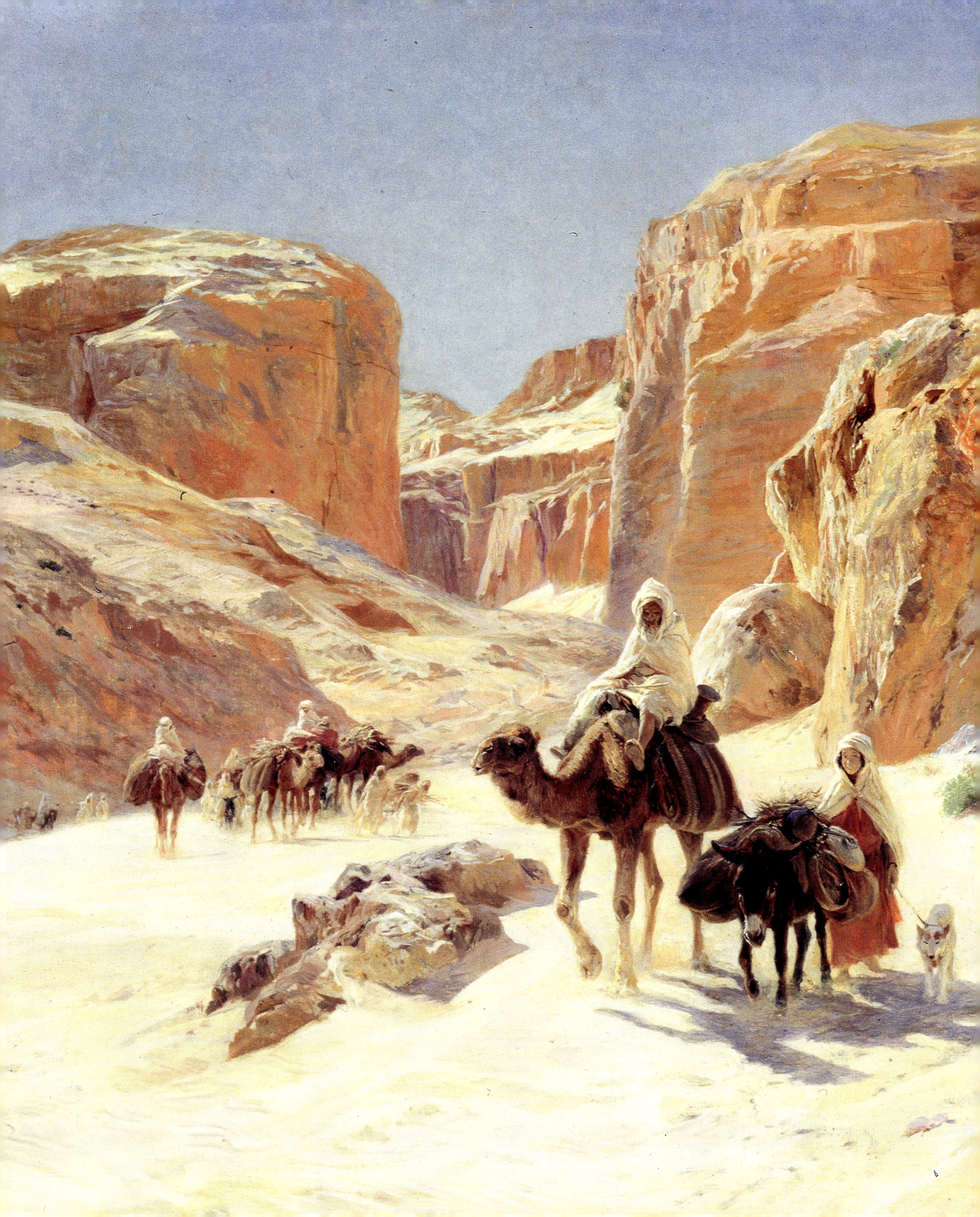

CHAPTER III

Orientalism in the 19th Century

The reasons for the emergence of Orientalism, which was in essence a product of the 19th century, were numerous and complex. Past centuries had slowly paved the way for this fascination until finally the dramatic events of modern history brought it into being. During the 19th century the 'Eastern Question' – Europe's role in the East – had become increasingly significant in European foreign policy and was causing stormy debates. The orientalist adventure began in Egypt in the wake of Napoleon Bonaparte's campaign, a military event that soon turned into a scientific, and indeed a cultural, expedition.
But Egypt had long captivated the European imagination – ever since the time when the esoteric cults of its gods were taken up in ancient Rome, then capital of the Western world.

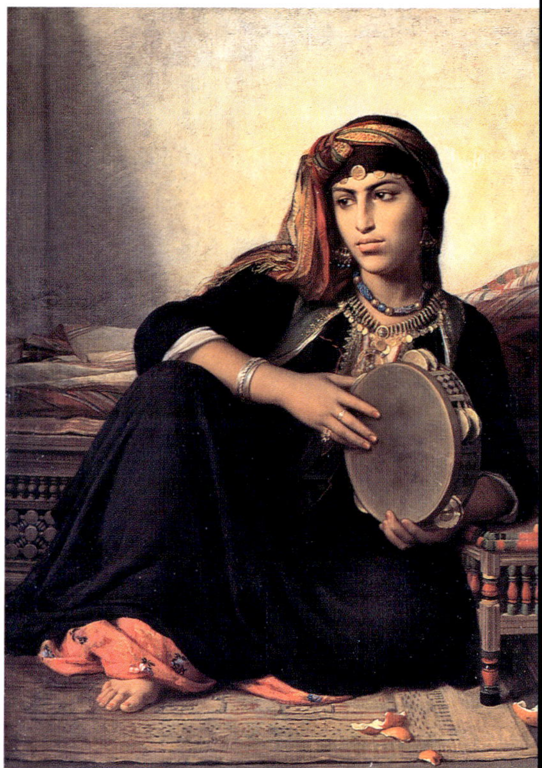

The Conquest of Egypt

Page 86
Caravan in the Dunes at Bou-Saâda,
Eugène Girardet, c.1898
Oil on canvas, 67.7 x 108.7 cm
(Musée des Beaux-Arts, Nantes).

Previous page
The Daughter of Sheik El Bahalede, Playing the Tambourine, Félix-Auguste Clément, between 1862 and 1875
Oil on canvas, 117 x 80 cm
(Musée des Beaux-Arts, Lyon).

Opposite
Al Makhamah (The Cadi Tribunal),
Franck Dillon, 1869
Watercolor and pencil, 29.7 x 52.7 cm
(Victoria and Albert Museum, London).

Egypt's appeal before Bonaparte

A fascination with the ancient and mysterious civilization of Egypt did not begin with Bonaparte's adventure. The two sphinxes found in the church of St. John Lateran in Rome had in all likelihood been placed there as early as 1222–1224. The first recorded archaeological finds in the Eternal City can be traced back to 1460 or thereabouts, when a statue of Antinous was found in the ruins of Hadrian's Villa (Antinous was a young friend of Emperor Hadrian who drowned in the Nile; Hadrian, who encouraged the cult of Isis and had Egyptian elements incorporated into the architecture of his villa at Tivoli, turned Antinous into a god). Shortly afterwards, the artist Pinturicchio used the figure of the Egyptian bull deity Apis when he decorated the Borgia apartments at the Vatican, making it a symbol of Pope Alexander the XI's good fortune. Archaeological finds would henceforward be a constant spur to artists.

In fact Egypt had long been a part of Western culture. Egypt's religious cults were accepted in Rome and in time became integrated into the established religion, especially during the reign of Emperor Caracalla; for the Romans, the mysteries of Isis were a sensation. And in spite of the efforts of the Church Fathers to eradicate any mention of them, the gods of the Egyptian pantheon survived the Middle Ages, as is shown by a curious 12th-century fable that presents Isis as a goddess of ancient gaul. It was also claimed that the pagan Frankish kings had worshipped her. One temple to Isis (it was claimed) had once stood on the site where the church of Saint Germain-des-Prés was built, and Isis herself was closely linked by some (largely through corrupt etymology) to the very foundation of Paris. The 14th-century Italian writer Boccaccio, in his *De genealogiis deorum gentilium* (Genealogies of the pagan gods), rolled into one the Egyptian Isis and the Greek Io, a maid who was changed into a cow by Zeus in order to protect her from the jealousy of his wife, Hera. Poetic fancy would soon have Isis enter the evangelic realm: in the early 15th century the French writer Christine de Pisan used her as an allegory for the Immaculate Conception; Isis had become a mysterious messenger from far distant, pre-Christian times.

The growing interest of Renaissance scholars in the remains of ancient times was not confined to the Greek and Roman civilizations, as is shown by the presence of several figures based on the Antinous statue in Raphael's fresco *Fire in the Borgo* in the Vatican (c. 1514). In France, the Pavillon des Armes in the palace at Fontainebleau, the decoration of which was completed by Rosso Fiorentino in 1530, shows that he too was inspired by the same statue of Hadrian's friend. Five years later, sphinxes adorned a fine French residence known as the *Batie d'Urfé*, built by the diplomat Claude d'Urfé; and five years after that, Giulio Romano and his pupils used hieroglyphs to decorate the ceiling of the Muses' Loggia in the Palazzo del Tè in Mantua. The discovery in 1559 of the Bembine Table – a 1st-century A.D. bronze table-top decorated with hieroglyphics – spurred imaginations with the wealth of its designs. And in 1589, an obelisk found in the Circus Maximus in Rome was erected in the Eternal City, in the Piazza del Popolo.

A remarkable and unique book, Francesco Colonna's *Hypnerotomachia Polifili* (1499), became the obligatory reference for all things to do with ancient Egypt. The missal of Cardinal Pompeo Colonna bears this out in its frontispiece, which is decorated with Egypt-inspired vignettes. At the end of the 16th century, the Italian humanist and scholar Pierio Valeriano wrote a treatise entitled *Hieroglifica sive de Sacris Aegyptiorum Literis Comentarii*, a bizarre attempt at deciphering hieroglyphs. His example was followed by Athanasius Kircher, a German priest who between 1636 and 1678 wrote no less than ten treatises on obelisks and hieroglyphics, among them *Œdipus Aegyptiacus* (1652).

By the 17th century there was a marked taste for things Egyptian. In France, Louis XIV's court raved about shows and ballets that included characters from Pharaonic cosmology. Lully and Quinault's opera *Isis*,

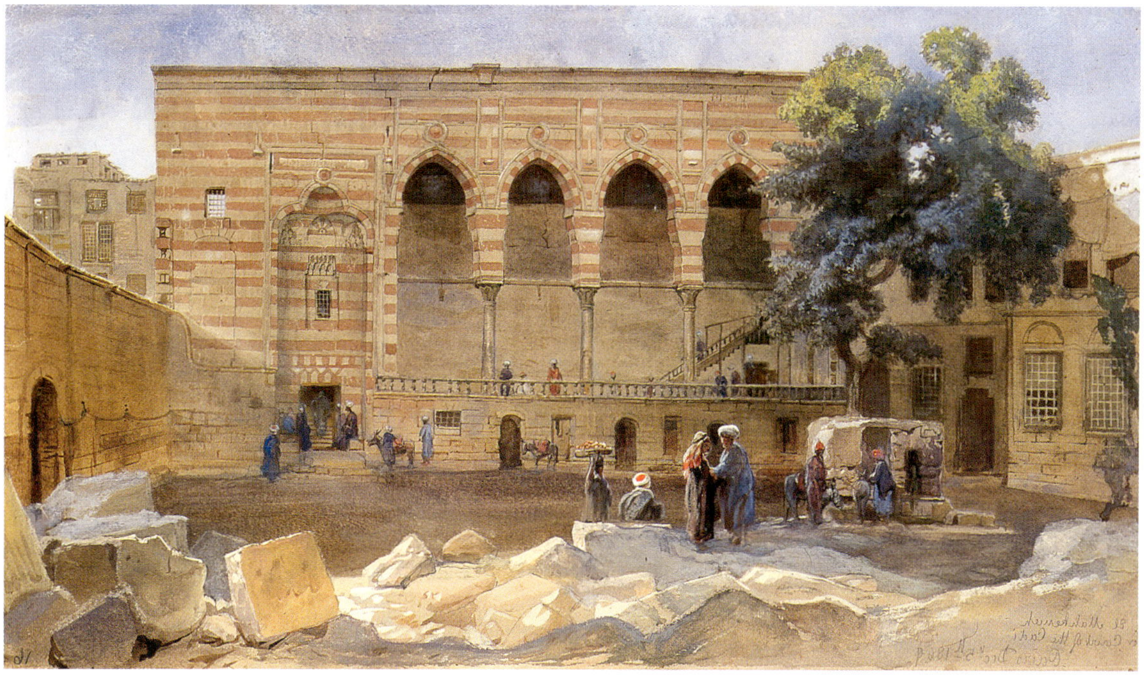

first performed in 1671, is an interesting testimony to this trend. Such was the craze that in 1666 a Father Menestrier spoke out against these Egyptian tales, which he dismissed as pernicious nonsense. In Rome, the sculptor Bernini, almost literally taking a leaf from Francesco Colonna's book, designed for the Piazza Santa Maria sopra Minerva a marble statue of an elephant that bears the obelisk that had been found in the excavation of the Isis Temple on the Campo Marzio (the work being realized by Bernini's pupil, Ercole Ferrata). The French sculptor Lespagnandel created a female sphinx for the gardens at Fontainebleau in 1664; a much-imitated sphinx ridden by a cupid, sculpted by Louis Lerambert, was placed on the terrace of the Orangerie at Versailles in 1665; and about 1680 female-busted sphinxes were set at the entrance to the Hôtel Fieubert on the Quai des Celestin in Paris. The use of Egyptian elements in architecture was gradually spreading.

The following century would show an avid interest in all things exotic, with Egypt occupying a place somewhere between *chinoiseries* and *turqueries*. Pyramids, obelisks, and sphinxes were now standard elements in architecture and garden design. Starting in the 1730s, the vogue of Anglo-Chinese gardens started to spread; this often included structures in the Egyptian style set amid buildings inspired by Japanese art, Gothic ruins, and of course, Chinese architecture. Pyramids were being built all over Europe: Charles Bridgemen erected one at Stow in England in 1739; Charles Cameron insisted on one in the gardens of Tsarskoye-Selo near St. Petersburg in Russia (1770–1780) and on another in the Alley of Tombs in Wilhelmshöle near Cassel in Germany (1775); and Louis Carrogis (Carmentelle) enhanced the Duc de Chartres' property at Monceau in France with one in 1779, and rounded it off with an obelisk. Moreover, François de Monville and François Barbier design the icehouse in the Désert de Retz in the shape of a pyramid (1774–1784). A project by Jean-Baptiste Kléber (the Revolutionary general who would be on Bonaparte's staff in Egypt) dated 1787, for the Parc d'Étupes on the Princes of Montbéliard's estate, comprised a small Egyptian temple with typical grooved cornices, a winged sun-disk, and invented hieroglyphics. Shortly after that, Dubois the Elder designed an Egyptian temple for Monsieur Davelouis' park at Soisy-sous-Étiolles in France, and in England Charles Tatham drew up plans for a winter garden in the shape of an Egyptian temple.

The large collections that this passion for Egypt encouraged now made it possible to get to know Egyptian artefacts at first hand. The Antinous statue, discovered in 1460, was added to the Greek Room in the Vatican in 1780. Two years later, a room in the Villa Borghese in Rome was opened and the first pieces brought from Egypt were presented to the public in a pseudo-Egyptian setting – the German Neo-classical artist Anton Raphael Mengs pioneered this genre of décor, decorating the Papyrus Room in the Vatican between 1772 and 1776 with sphinxes, lions, and mummy cases inscribed with hieroglyphics. After 1775, the French architect Charles-Nicolas Ledoux submitted designs for factories and workshops that came straight from Egypt. Even Egypt's funereal architecture could not fail to strike the imagination of the Enlightenment's architects and builders. Thus Michel-Ange Slodtz built a memorial to Bishop Armand de Montmorin in the choir of the Saint-Maurice Church in Vienna in the purest Baroque style, a pyramid-shaped obelisk that would be a source of inspiration for other memorials. Louis-Jean Desprez, on the occasion of his trip to Italy (1779–1784), drew imaginary tombs that owe everything to Egyptian funereal art as it was then understood. The mausoleum for the Earl and Countess of Buckinghamshire submitted by Joseph Bonomi in 1794 was a pyramid with entrances in the classical style. Étienne Louis Boullée endeavored to create a cenotaph in the "Égitien" (sic) style that is in effect a stepped pyramid; his sarcophagus-shaped "cenotaph for a warrior" is trimmed with an Antinous frieze. Finally, when a ceremony was organized in commemoration of those who had died on the 10 August 1792 (when an insurrection in Paris led to the fall of Louis XVI), a pyramid was erected in the Jardins des Tuileries to glorify the heroic victims of the day that sealed the fate of the French monarchy.

The knowledge of Egyptian remains was now no longer restricted to the few artifacts unearthed in the great excavations undertaken in Italy. Artifacts had already been brought in from Egypt when trading centers were established at the end of the Renaissance, in particular after the voyages of Pietro della Valle and Paul Lacas. John Greeve, an English astronomer, visited Egypt in 1738–1739 and conducted one of the earliest studies of the pyramids. The Frenchman Claude Sicard, who set off for Egypt in 1721, identified the site of Thebes, the City of a Hundred Gates described by Homer. Frederik Ludwig Norden traveled the Nile Valley in 1737 and recounted his progress in his *Journey to Egypt and Nubia* of 1741, which contains numerous drawings. Richard Pococke published his important *Description of the East* between 1743 and 1746, in which monuments are discussed in detail, particularly the zodiac discovered in the temple at Denderah. Art history also played a part: in 1764 the German art historian Johann Winckelmann, the pioneer of Neoclassicism, completed his seminal *Geschichte der Kunst des Altertums* (History of ancient art); and in France in 1785, Quatremère de Quincy received a prize from the Académie des Inscriptions et Belles-lettres for his essay "The state of architecture in Egypt, and what appears to have been borrowed by Greece." In 1782 Constantin François Chassebœuf Volney published *Voyage en Égypte et en Syrie* (Journey to Egypt and Syria), essentially a geographic and political treatise. Claude Étienne Savary, a distinguished translator of the Koran, described his visit to Egypt in 1776 in his *Lettres sur l'Égypte* (Letters on Egypt), in which he describes both the Egyptian landscape and the Arab lifestyle; it was published to great acclaim between 1785 and 1786. The first reconstructions of ancient monuments appeared in 1799 in a chapter of Count de Choiseul-Gouffier's *Voyage pittoresque de la Syrie* (A picturesque journey to Syria). It was he who started the fashion for "picturesque" travel, even though his book is largely historical in content. Published from 1782, still incomplete 1804, it appeared with 180 illustrations by Jean-Baptiste Hilair.

The arts followed where the scientists led. The playwright Mattheson created his *Cleopatra* in 1704. In 1731, Abbé Terrasson published his long novel *Séthos*, which eight years on would become a tragedy in verse under the pen of Alexandre Tannevot. In 1737, Handel composed his oratorio *Israel in Egypt*, and in 1751 the French composer Jean-Philippe Rameau created the ballet *La naissance d'Osiris* (The birth of Osiris) using a treatment by the choreographer Cahusac; Rameau had already created a ballet on Eastern themes, *Les Fêtes de l'Hymen et de l'Amour, ou les Dieux d'Égypte* (The festivals of Hymen and Love, or the Gods of Egypt), which was performed at Versailles in 1747. And in 1791, the year the Italian composer Sebastiano Nasolini created his opera *La morte di Cleopatra* (The death of Cleopatra), Mozart's opera *Die Zauberflöte* (The magic flute) was performed in Vienna – a work that was the culmination of this fascination with the esoteric cults of ancient Egypt, here with Masonic rites thrown in for good measure. The stage sets by Gayl and Nessthaler, low-key though they were, featured an Egyptian pyramid in the second act of the opera.

In art and design, the French sculptor Clodion produced several terracottas of Egyptian figures in varied poses between 1775 and 1780. The interiors of the aristocracy were taken over by Egyptified artifacts and furniture. Queen Marie-Antoinette's apartments epitomize the new cult, with sphinxes appearing in her bedchamber at Versailles and her boudoir at Fontainebleau; Jean-Baptiste Séné crafted sphinx-busted furniture for her private drawing room in the palace at Saint-Cloud. Others also subscribed to this desire to use these inscrutable and melancholy figures unearthed from desert sands. In 1786 Charles III of Spain ordered an Egyptian room for the Escorial near Madrid from Jean-Démosthène Dugourc, and in Britain Josiah Wedgwood created a range of ceramic designs to satisfy the Egyptian vogue.

The great forerunner in Egyptian-inspired design was undoubtedly the Italian graphic artist Gianbattista Piranesi, whose *Diverse manieri d'adornare i camini*, a collection of prints illustrating interior design, was printed in Rome in 1769. For a Europe eager for the exotic, this became the essential catalog of the Egyptian style. The engravings show religious scenes, hieroglyphic friezes, mythological characters, deified animals, including the crocodile and the falcon, canopic jars, scarabs, and, naturally, sphinxes. Nine years earlier, he had been able to employ this Egyptian aesthetic in his designs for the décor of the Caffè degli Inglesi, which opened on Piazza di Spagna in Rome. Looking on the painted walls, visitor were able to immerse themselves in the open prospects of Egypt's varied landscapes, which were depicted complete with pyramids, obelisks, tombs, and colossal ruins. Contemporaries commented on the rather gloomy character of the place!

By the end of the 18th century, Egyptomania was well established. Its presence in painting, though discreet, was symptomatic. Until the 17th century, representations of Cleopatra's suicide – an artistic alternative to countless bosom-stabbing Lucretias – formed history painting's single link with Egypt (a link that in fact came through Roman history). Only gradually did artists begin to feel the need to establish more direct and specific references to Egyptian antiquity. The French artist Nicolas Poussin dutifully places a very peculiar sphinx in *The Finding of Moses* to make it more authentic. The English painter William Hogarth, also treating the same subject of Moses rescued from the Nile, goes one better by including a mummified crocodile, a pyramid, a sphinx,

The Mosque of Kaid Bey (Cairo),
Louis-Claude Mouchot, undated,
Oil on canvas, 130 x 91 cm
(Diplomatic Club, Cairo).

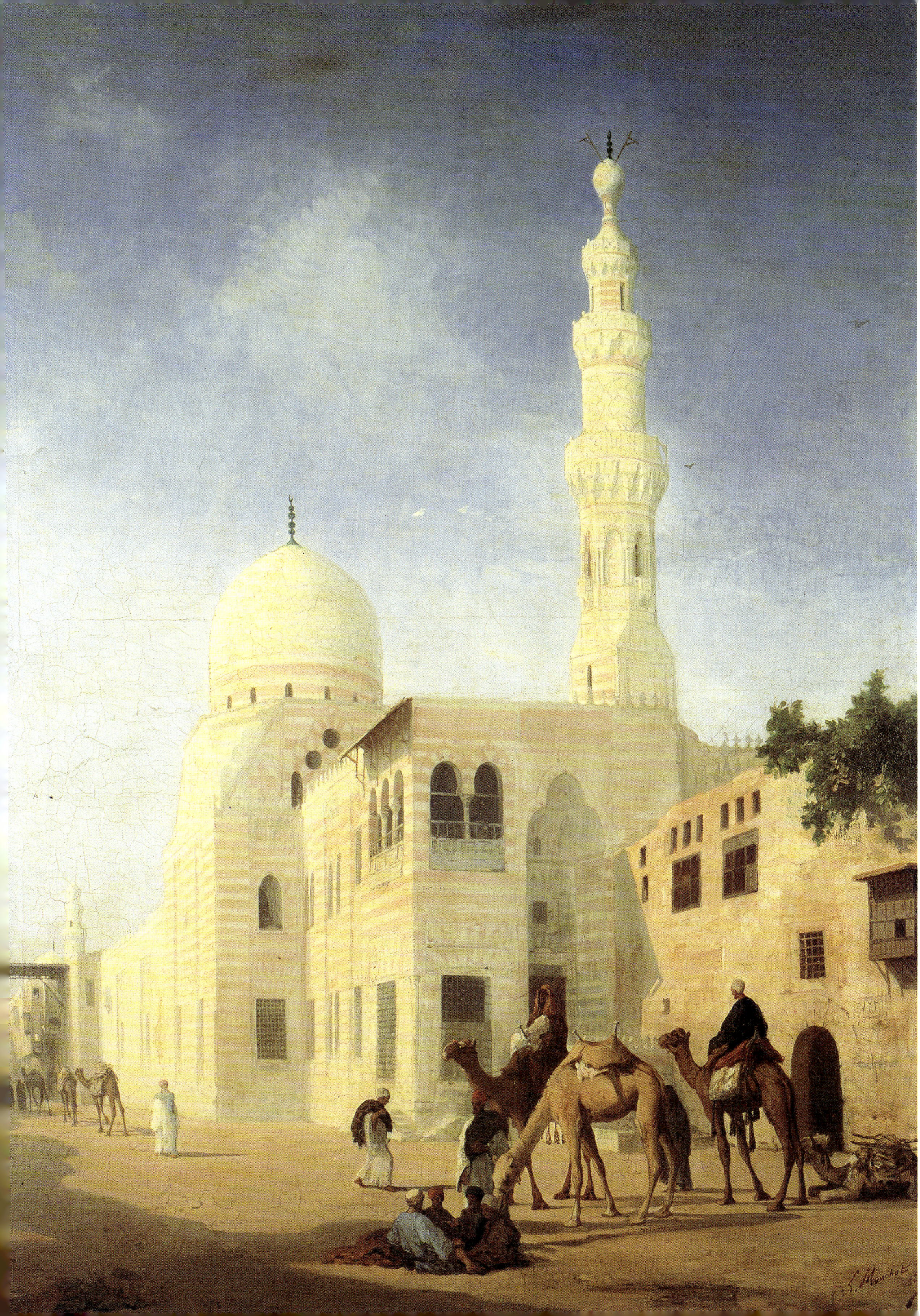

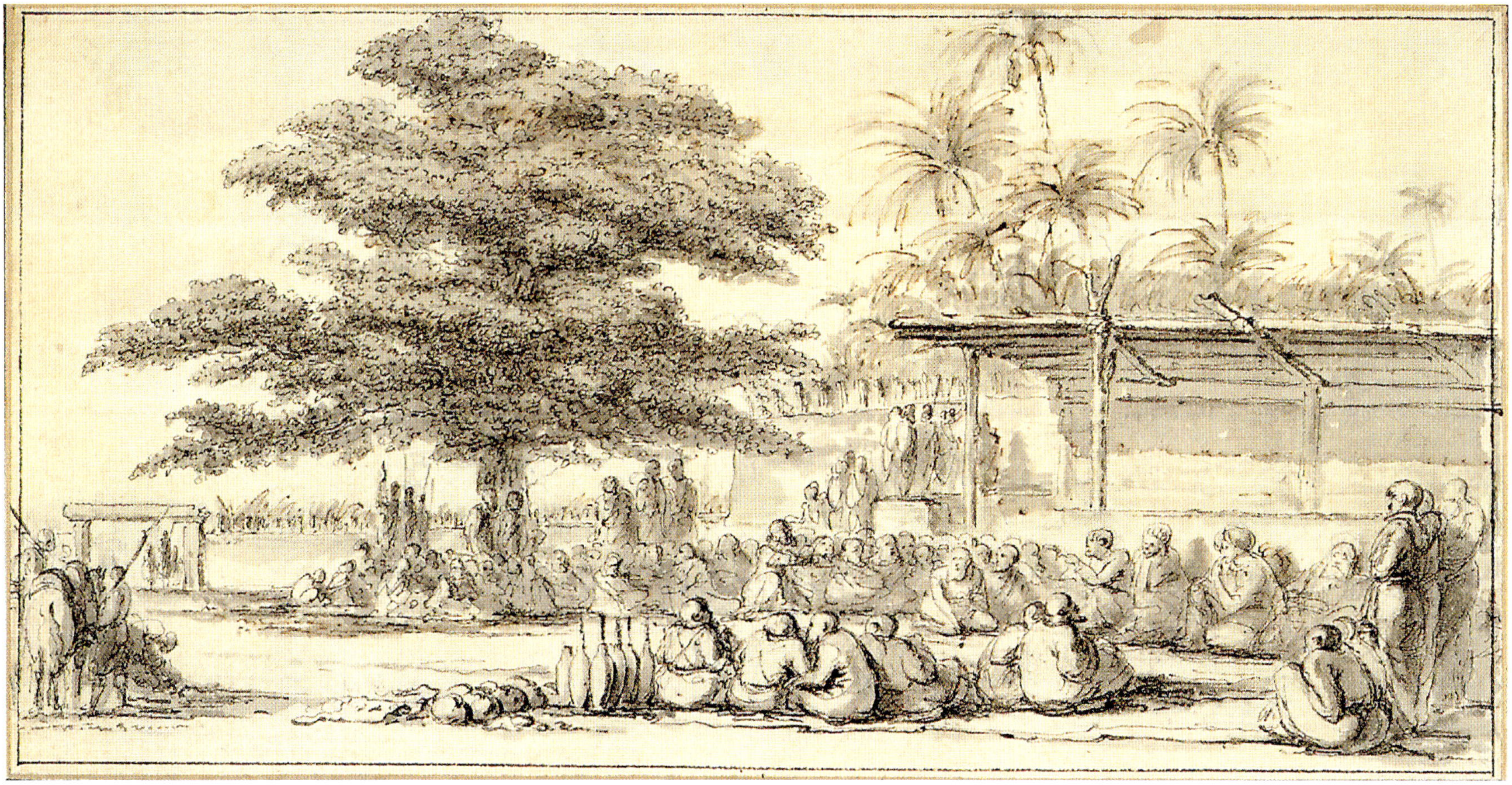

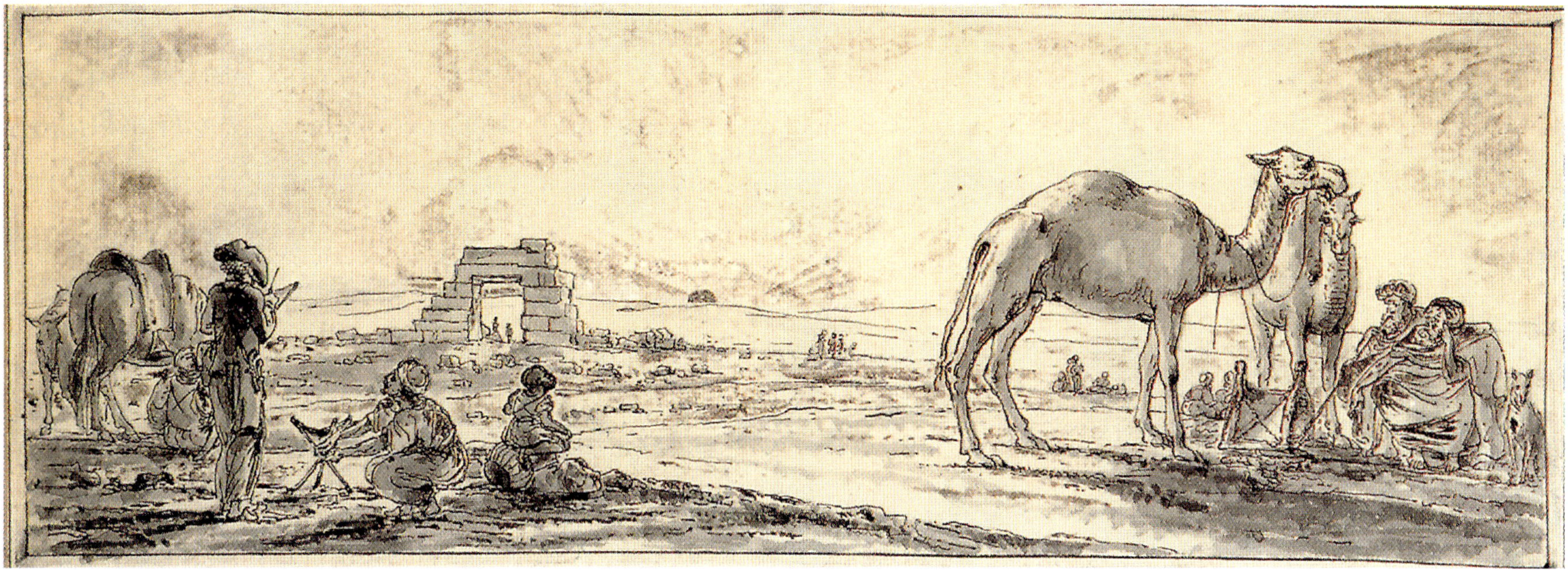

Top
Arab Council, Dominique Vivant Denon, 1802
Brown pen and ink drawing with gray wash, 14 x 28.2 cm
(British Museum, London).

Opposite
Dominique Vivant Denon in Egypt, Armand-Philippe-Joseph Béra, 1804
Oil on canvas, 41 x 32.7 cm
(private collection).

Above
Denon Drawing the Ruins at Hierakonpolis, Dominique Vivant Denon, 1802
Black pen and ink drawing with gray and brown wash, 11.4 x 32.7 cm
(British Museum, London).

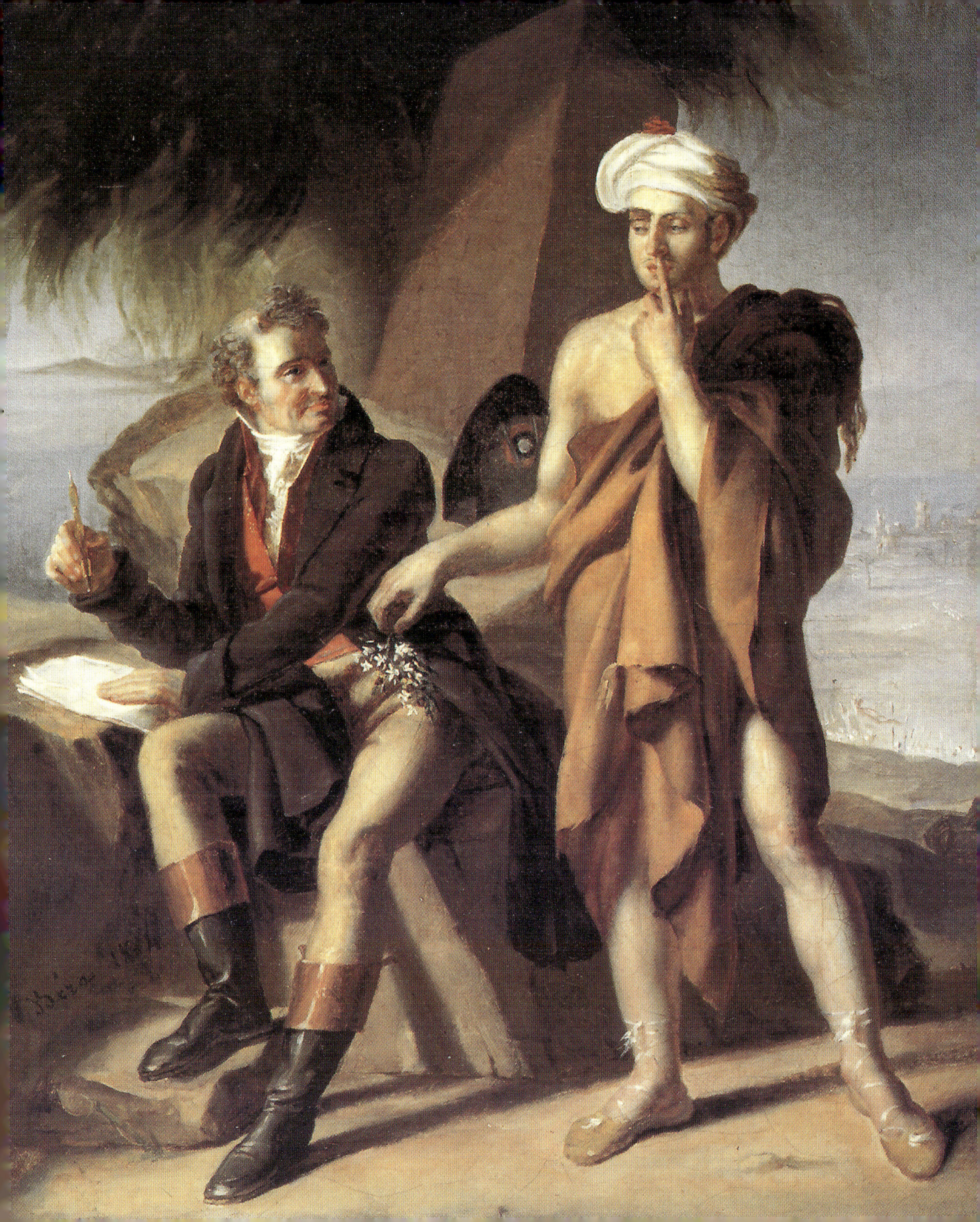

BONAPARTE'S EGYPT

"Napoleon would soon outdo Bonaparte. He was about to receive on ancient wisdom's sacred land, the mysterious sanction of forty centuries of majesty, and return to a rapturous France with the authority of a conqueror and the prestige of a magus."

Théophile Gautier

and made-up hieroglyphics. For the most part, however, the allusions are fleeting, as in Joseph Vernet's *Port with Pyramid* (1751) and Nicolas de Larguillère's *Portrait of Madame Berton with her Son, Balthazar-Bruno*. Egyptian elements are as a rule introduced in the spirit of what might be called archaeological nostalgia, a melancholy musing on ancient ruins. Examples include Hubert Robert's *The Fountain* (c. 1765), which features an Egyptian woman, a lion, and an obelisk covered in hieroglyphics; and his *Classical Ruins* (1798), in which there is a broken obelisk, pyramids, and a sphinx. The oddest of his paintings is undoubtedly *Peasants by a Fountain in an Italian Landscape* (c. 1770), in which he introduces the cordonata lion into a remote Italian countryside by turning it into a carved fountain.

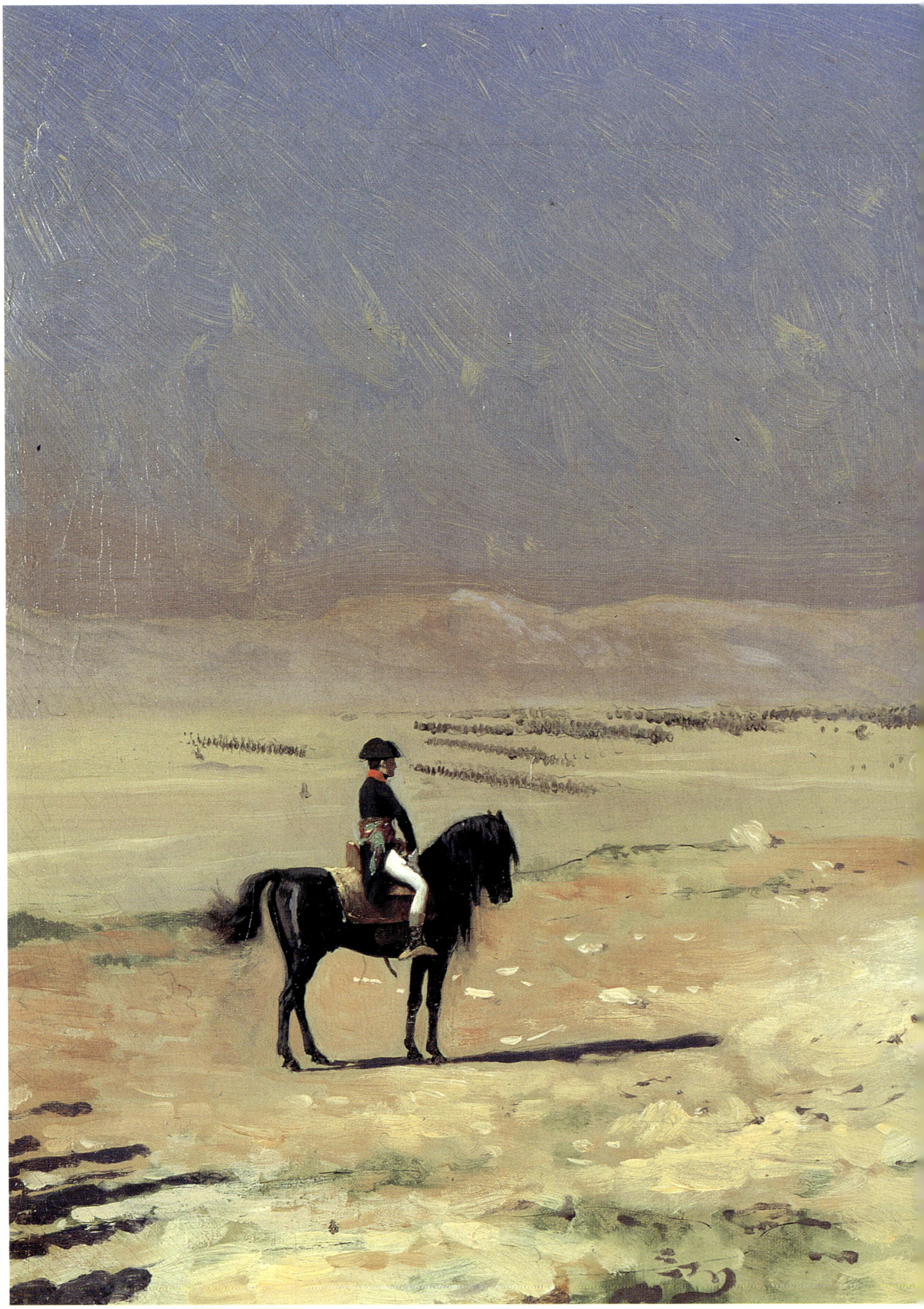

On 16 August 1797 General Bonaparte sent to the Directoire a letter claiming that the seizure of Egypt would be a highly effective means of reducing British influence in the Mediterranean. This scheme had already been considered by Choiseul under Louis XV, and the acquisition of Corsica in 1768 had been undertaken with this in mind. Bonaparte put together a 38,000 strong army in utmost secrecy. But it was not to be solely a military campaign: he believed that such an expedition had also to have civilizing and scientific aims. On 26 Ventose, year VI of the Revolutionary calendar (16 March 1798), he created the Commission des Sciences et des Arts de l'Armée d'Orient (Sciences and arts commission of the army of the east). He put General Cafarelli du Falga in charge, together with Gaspard Monge, founder of the École Polytechnique and author of *De l'Art de fabriquer des canons* (The art of canon building; 1794), and the chemist Claude Louis Bertholet as the academic linchpins of the operation. They were able to bring in their distinguished colleagues from such institutions as the École Polytechnique, the Muséum, the Observatoire de Paris, the Ponts-et-Chaussées, and the Langues Orientales. Among many others, they invited to the commission the writers Antoine-Vincent Arnault and François Auguste Parceval; the musicians Henri-Jean Pugel and Guillaume-André Villoteau; the illustrators Jean-Gabriel Caquet and André Dutertre; the painters Joly and Michel Pugo, and the sculptor Jean-Jacques Castex. France's most distinguished artist, Jacques-Louis David, declined to join the venture, no doubt still smarting from the consequences of his involvement with the

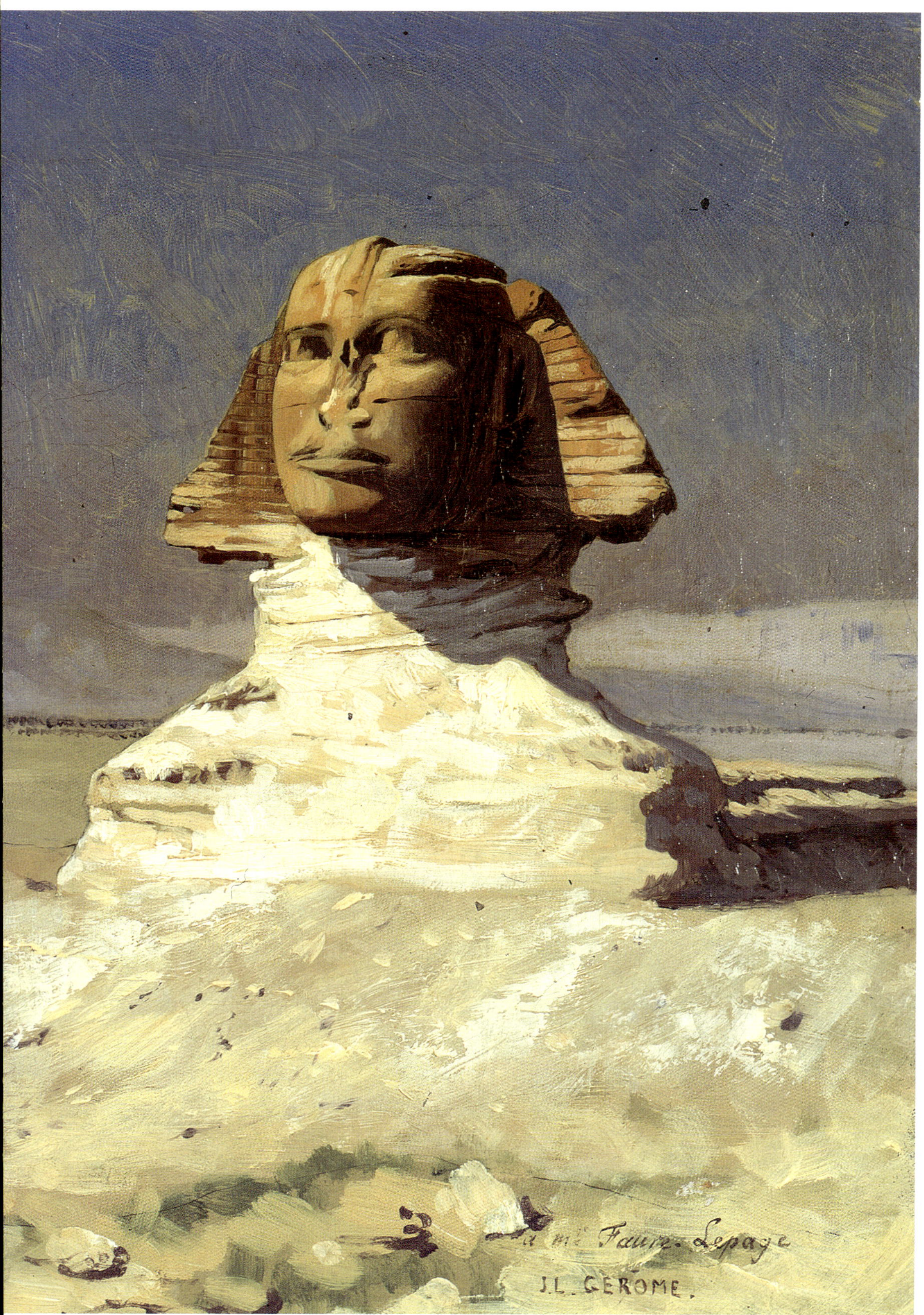

Œdipe (Oedipus, or General Bonaparte in Egypt), Jean-Léon Gérôme, 1867–1868
Oil on canvas, 30.2 x 45.6 cm
(Diplomatic Club, Cairo).

Jacobins, whilst Gros bemoaned being overlooked: "I would have painted Oriental costumes, Mamelukes, arab and turkish horses," he lamented. By contrast, Dominique Vivant Denon's bid for an archaeological survey, something Bonaparte had not considered, was successful and he too was taken on. All together, the Commission was 167 members strong. They set sail on 30 Floreal, year VI (19 May 1798) from Toulon, the most distinguished members sailing on the *Orient*. Among the personnel assembled – the balloonists, astronomers, engineers, physicians, surgeons, pharmacists, naturalists, carpenters, mechanics, and students at the École Polytechnique – some were old hands who had been with Bonaparte on his Italian campaign.

On 2 June they witnessed the fall of Malta, an island they could then admire at their leisure. On 25 June they docked at Alexandria, where the doctors and apothecaries immediately set up a hospital. On 2 July, Bonaparte had his *Proclamation aux Égyptiens* (Proclamation to the Egyptian people) printed as he marched on Cairo. On 7 July, scientists were dispatched to Rosetta. On 10 July, Egyptian forces were defeated at the Battle of Shubrakhit and again on the 21 July at the decisive Battle of the Pyramids; the gates of Cairo were now open to Bonaparte, who entered the city as a conquering hero three days later. But on 13 August he suffered a naval disaster at the hands of the British at Aboukir, a defeat that deprived him of his fleet and cut him off from reinforcements and supplies. For good measure, Sultan Selim III now saw an opportunity to take advantage of Bonaparte's apparent weakness and so declared war on the French, enlisting the support of the Russian navy. At the end of August, Desaix started on his long chase after the Egyptian leader Murad Bey, who had withdrawn to Upper Egypt.

Over the worst, Bonaparte turned his attention to the government of an Egypt now free of the Mamelukes, the powerful warrior caste. Abd Allah Cherkaoui was elected president. On 21 October, however, Cairo rose up in revolt, though the rebels were swiftly suppressed. Three days later, several Ottoman and Russian ships attacked Alexandria and tried to seize Fort Aboukir.

Despite the constant military operations, Bonaparte found time to create the Institut pour les Arts et les Sciences d'Égypte (Egyptian institute for Arts and Sciences) on 21 August. In September the scientists finally settled down in a fine house in Nashried, a suburb of Cairo. A museum was planned (which would in due course house the Rosetta Stone), and learned discussions were arranged; at one of these, Gaspard Monge presented a paper on "the phenomenon of mirages." On 19 September, Bonaparte visited the pyramid in the company of scholars. Soon geographers and surveyors were ordered to draw maps of Cairo and to survey the entire region.

All these scholars, technicians, and artists were faced with a wide range of tasks, including the planning of celebrations for the first day of the Republican year, 1 Vendémiaire, year VII (22 September 1798); the launching of balloons; and even military parades. Nicolas Jacques Conté was active on all fronts. He built a furnace to make canon balls; devised a technique to stop guns and canons from rusting; built flourmills; set up fire hydrants and water tanks; and had scientific instruments made to replace those that had been destroyed during the insurrection in Cairo. Manufacturing works were brought into being. The printing press from the Congregation of the Inquisition in Rome, commandeered by Bonaparte during his campaign in Italy, began printing a newspaper, the *Courrier de l'Égypte*, from 29 August and also a review, the *Décade Égyptienne*. Another paper was even printed in Arabic: *El Tambyeh* (the warning). And as Desaix continued to sail up the Nile in pursuit of an elusive enemy who attacked swiftly only to vanish again, civil engineers busied themselves with the reconstruction of the Nile Delta's canals.

Vivant Denon followed the 21 Brigade for six months, ceaselessly drawing and making notes. He had had a varied career. Once Madame de Pompadour's engraver, a diplomat at the Bourbon court, a provider of works of art to the royal collections during his tenure in Italy, and a member of the Académie de Peinture (painters' academy), he was rescued from the Terror's avenging arm by J.-L. David; the Directoire even put him in charge of all French museums.

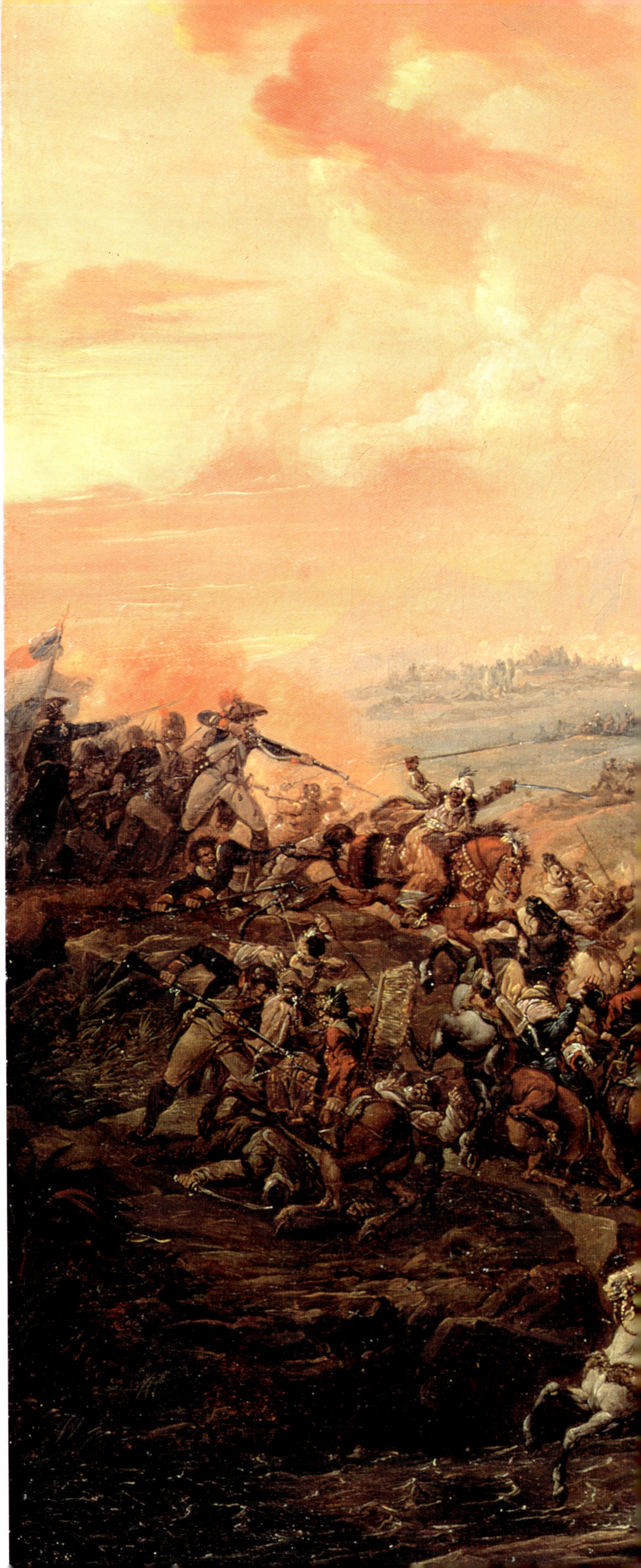

Battle of the Pyramids, 21 July 1798,
François Louis Joseph Watteau, 1798–1799
Oil on canvas, 92 x 120 cm
(Musée des Beaux-Arts, Valenciennes).

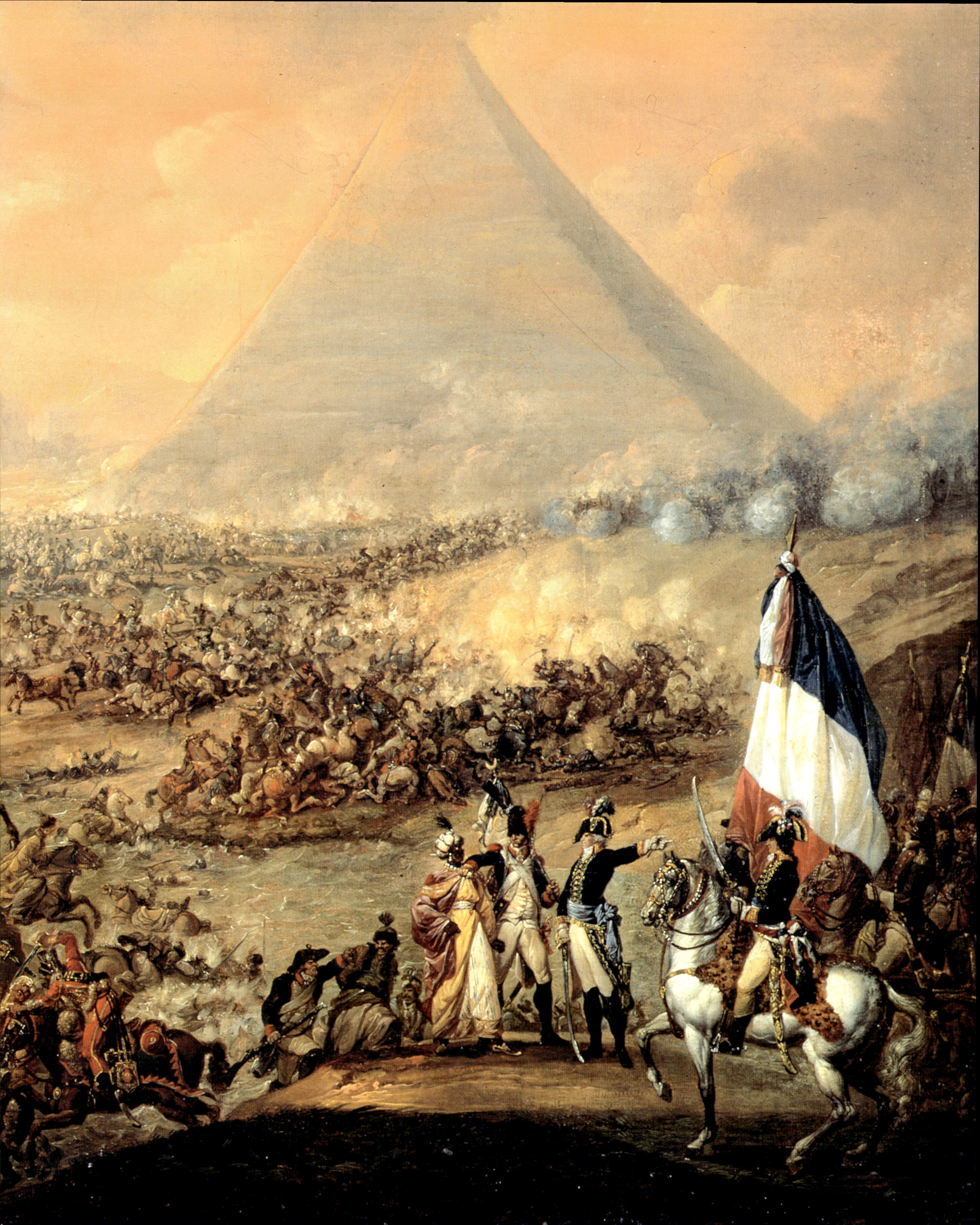

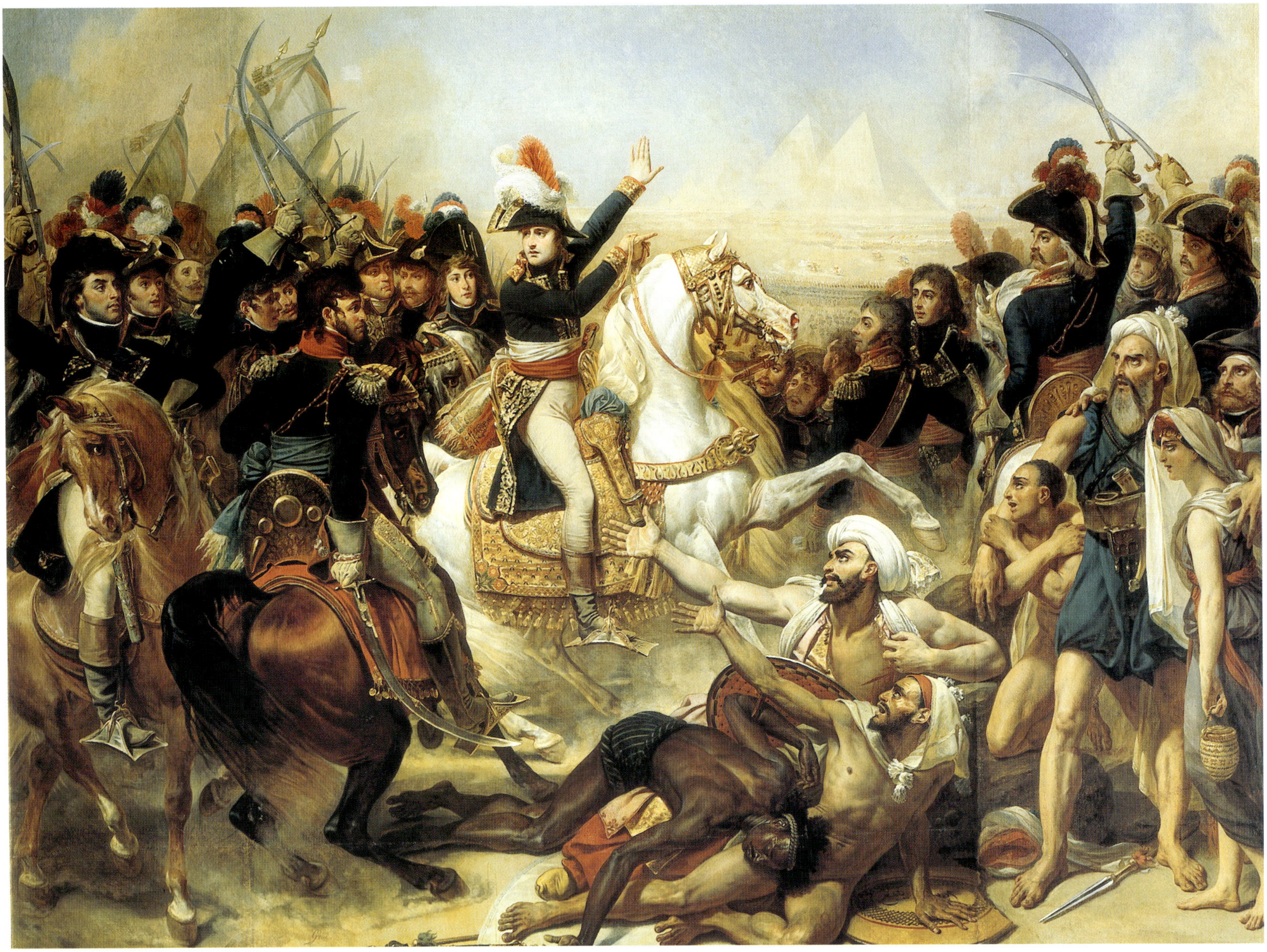

In Egypt he witnessed skirmishes and, when his military duties allowed, visited undiscovered sites, drew maps and plans, and set up archaeological digs. He didn't always do as he pleased, of course, and in his *Voyage dans la basse et haute Égypte* (A journey in lower and upper Egypt), published 1802, he described vividly the ups and downs of an expedition that was more military than archaeological: "That evening we went to bed at Melaui, half an hour away from Achmounin. Even as I write, I hear the reader say to me: 'Am I to understand that having bored me with lengthy descriptions of buildings, you are now to leave Hermopolis in haste – just as I'm about to become interested? What's the hurry? Aren't you an art-loving officer? Have you not got three hundred men at your disposal?' All this is true, but circumstances beyond this traveler's control are at work: the general was well disposed but his curiosity soon satisfied, and he informed the artist: these three hundred men have been on horseback for ten hours, and I must find them food and shelter before nightfall." These endless set backs notwithstanding, Denon brought back enough information to provide a new insight into both ancient and modern Egypt.

Other members of the commission worked wonders in archaeology. The architect Charles-Louis Balzac studied Alexandria's ancient monuments from Philae to Karnak; Geoffroy Saint-Hilaire researched the subject of embalmed animals; André Dutertre conducted a range of topographical surveys; Jean-Baptiste-Prosper Jollois, a *polytechnicien* who with his colleague Edouard de Villiers du Terrage worked at Thebes and Denderah, undertook digs and made important drawings.

At the end of December, with Suez taken, Bonaparte started an offensive against Syria. By March 1799, he had already taken Al Arich, Gaza, and Jaffa, where he visited the victims of the plague (a scene famously depicted by Gros). He laid siege to Saint Jean d'Acre, but was not successful and in May decided to withdraw. Meanwhile, on 25 May, the Ottoman forces were defeated at Aboukir. But the situation in Europe had worsened, and Bonaparte decided to return to France; when he departed, on 23 August, he left General Jean-Baptiste Kléber in command. But Kléber, an excellent administrator and an

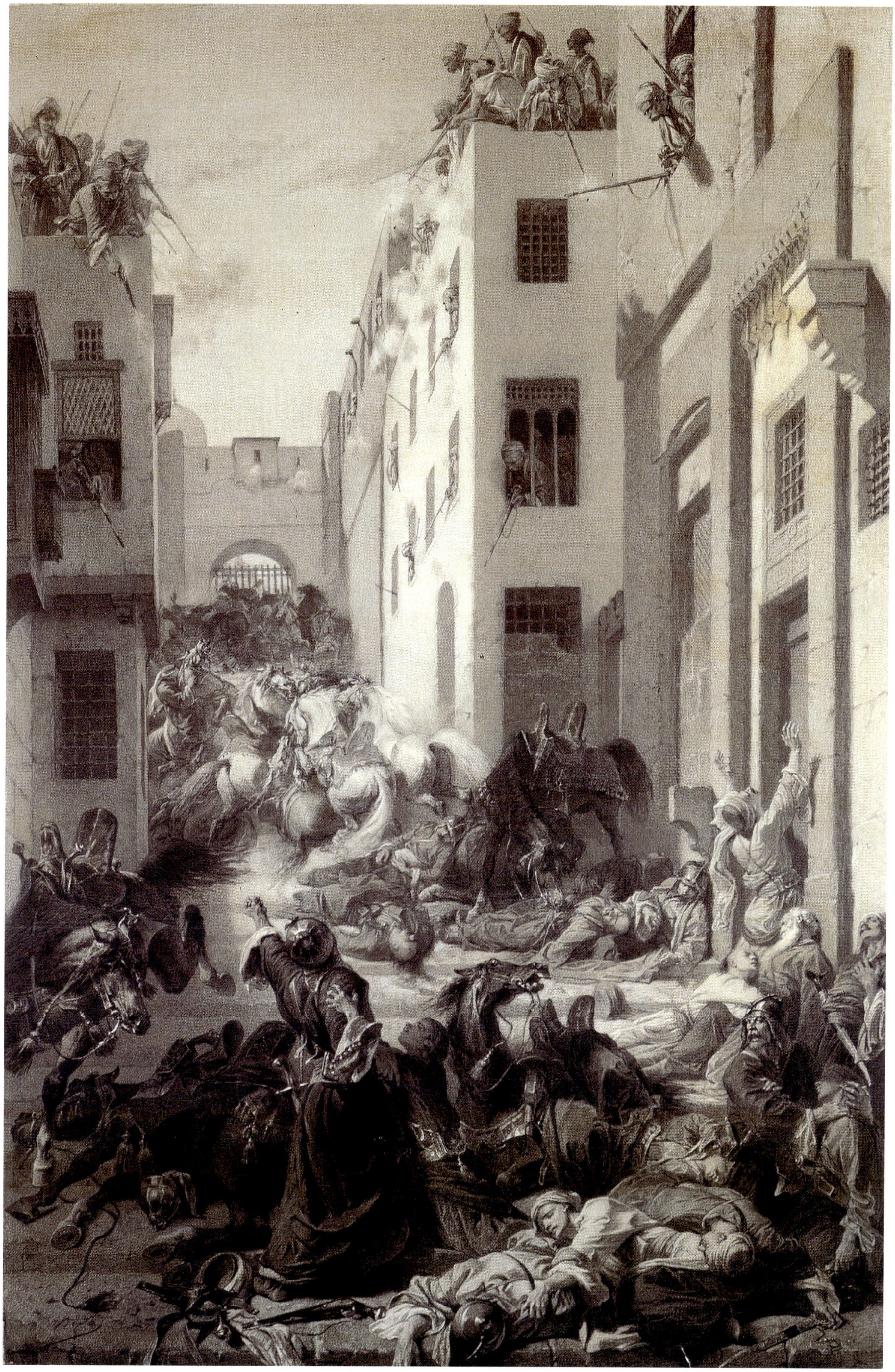

Opposite
Battle of the Pyramids (Bonaparte Encouraging his Army at the Battle of the Pyramids, 21 July 1798), Baron Antoine-Jean Gros, 1810
Oil on canvas, 389 x 311 cm (Musée National du Château, Versailles).

Massacre of the Mameluks, Alexandre Bida, 1861
Black pencil, graphite, and scraping on paper, 92 x 69 cm (Musée du Louvre, Département des Arts Graphiques, Paris).
This scene depicts a tragic event that took place in 1811 in the citadel of Cairo during the reign of Mehemed Ali. It was a widely used artistic theme in the 19th century: Horace Vernet produced a large painting of it, which was exhibited in the Salon from 1819 onwards; Alexandre Bida presented his version to the Salon in 1861; Willem de Famars Testas made it the subject of a watercolor in 1869.

Following double pages
The Battle of Aboukir (Cavalry Charge Led by General Murat at the Battle of Aboukir, 23 July 1799), Baron Antoine-Jean Gros, 1806
Oil on canvas, 578 x 968 cm (Musée National du Château, Versailles).

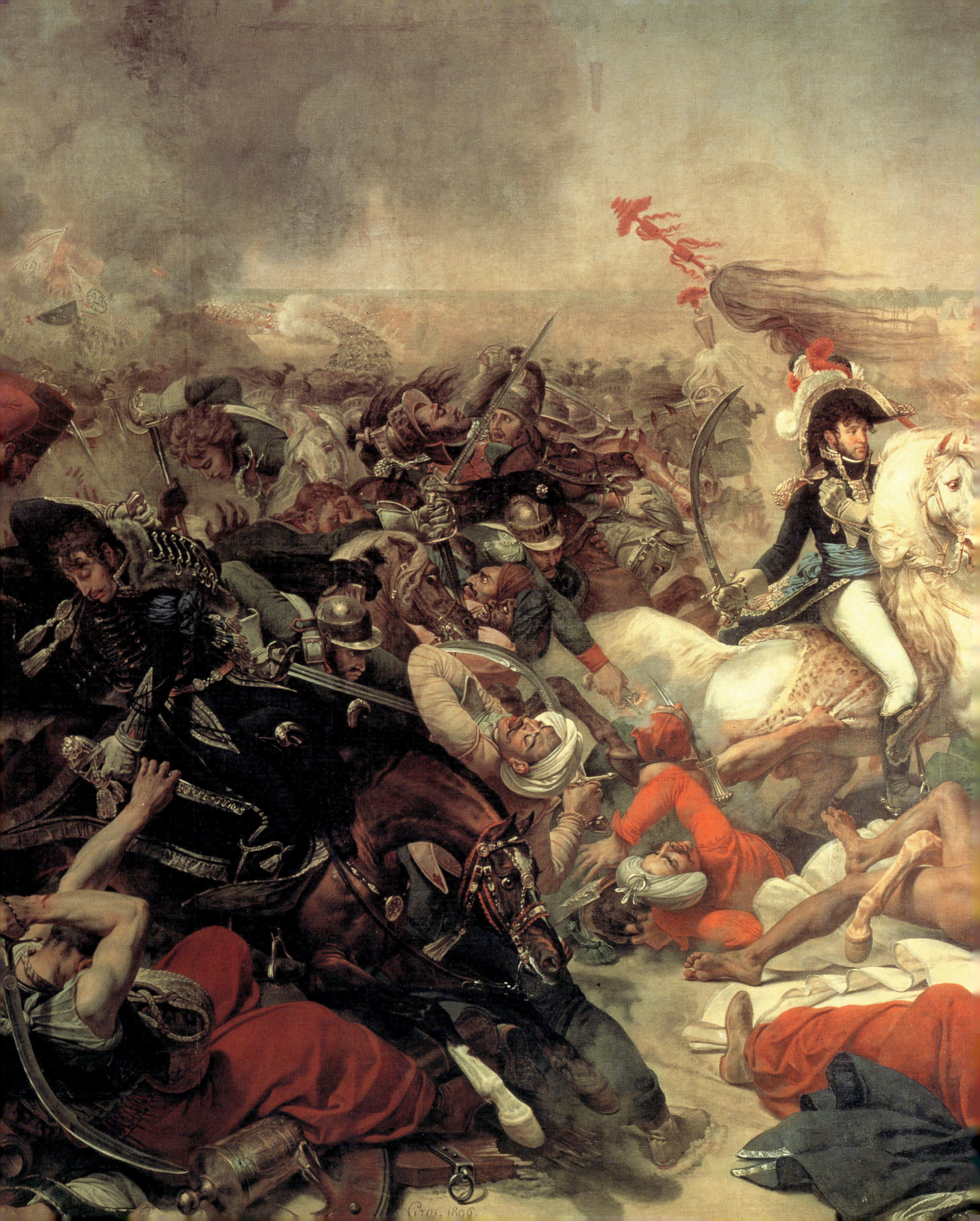
Gros. 1806.

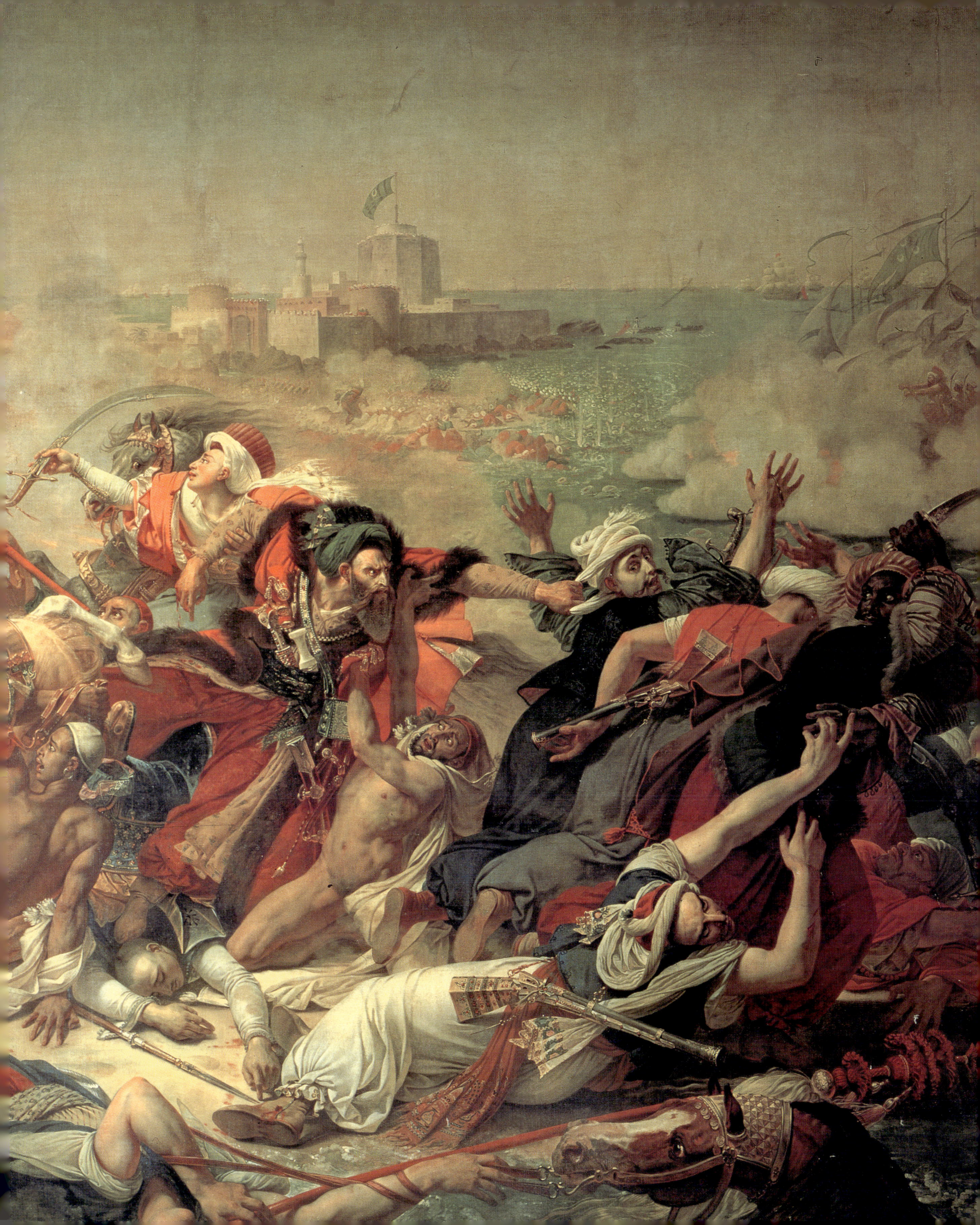

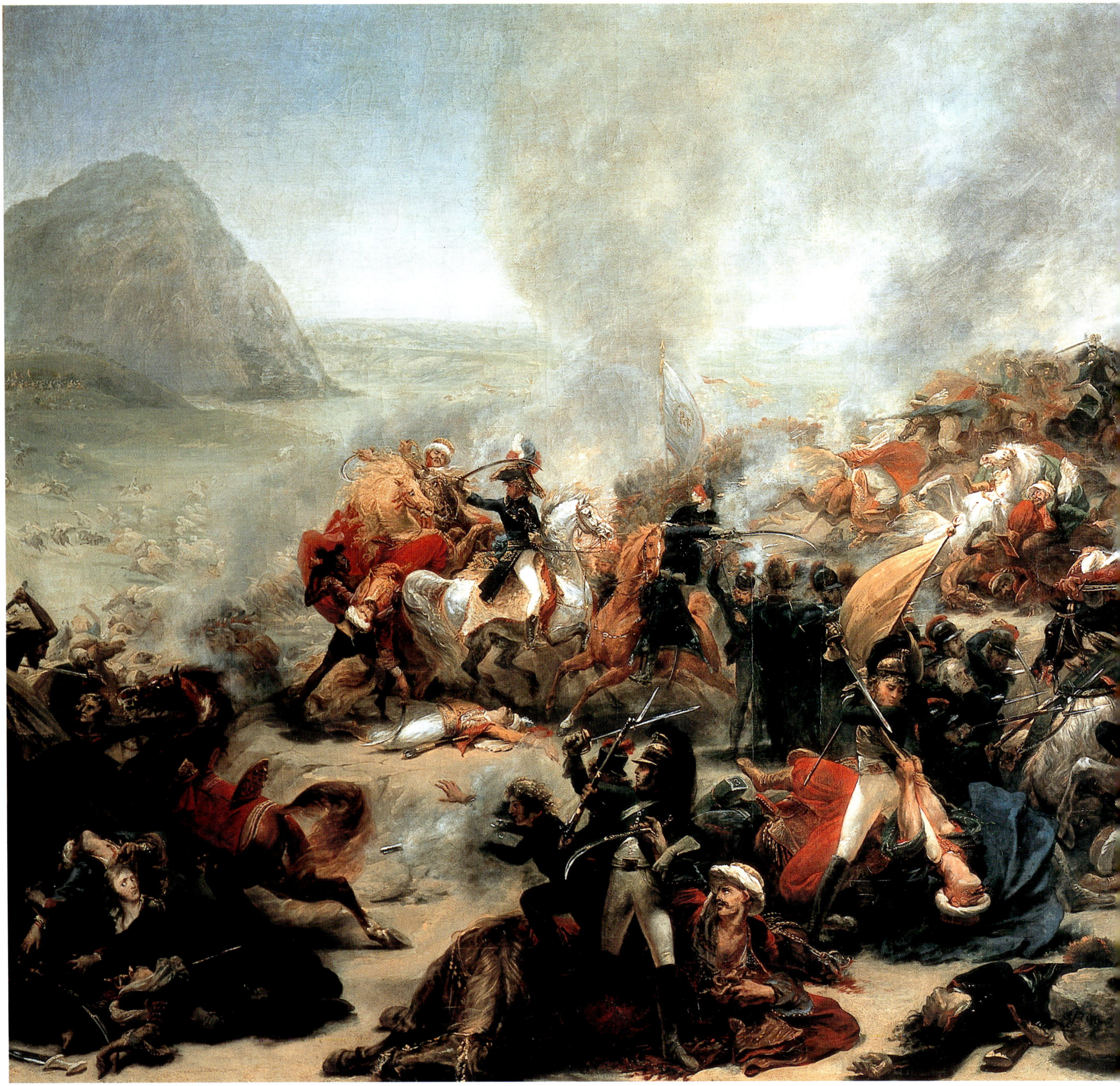

Battle of Nazareth, 8 April 1799,
Baron Antoine-Jean Gros, 1801,
Oil on canvas, 135 x 195 cm
(Musée des Beaux-Arts, Nantes).

outstanding tactician, was murdered on 14 June; his replacement, Jacques Menou, did not have the military skills required and was dealt defeat after defeat until finally he capitulated to the British on 2 September 1802. The French were left to sail back to France, leaving behind them the best part of the archeological finds, which included the famous Rosetta Stone, gathered together in the new museum. Bonaparte's grand scheme, that of retracing the steps of Alexander the Great, had failed. Egypt was once again under the Ottomans, who were now closely watched by Perfidious Albion.

The Egyptian campaign ended in an inglorious but more or less dignified departure. One

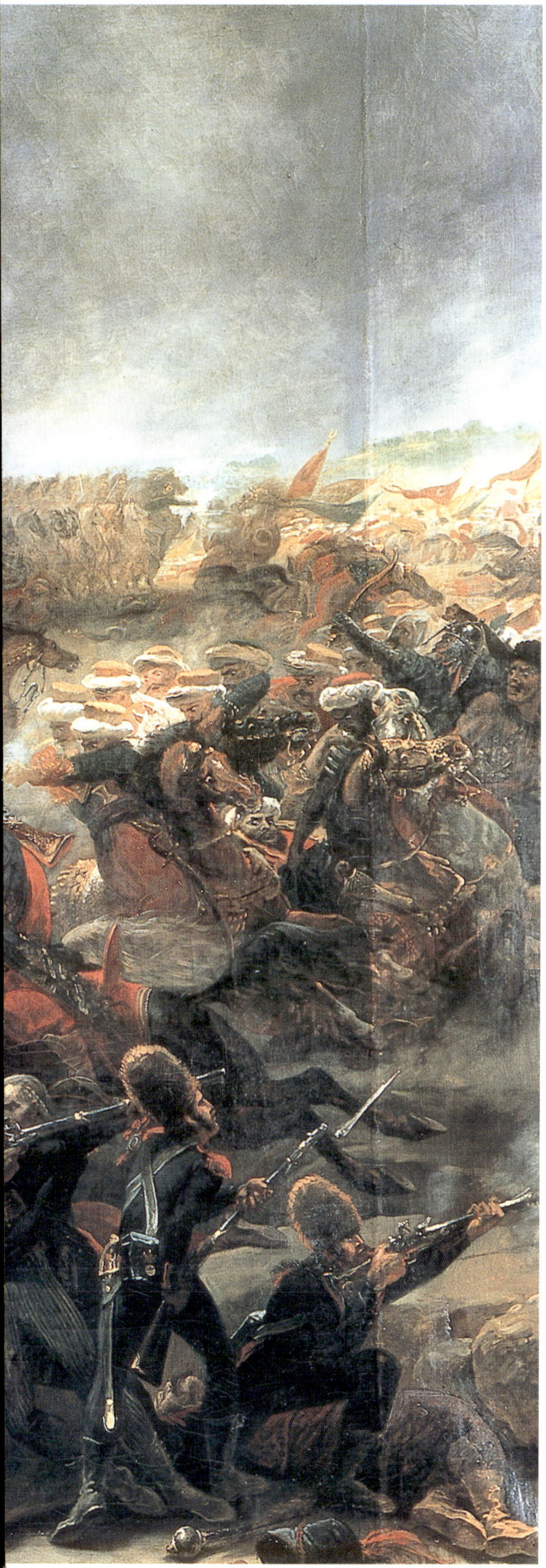

Plague House at Jaffa (Bonaparte Visiting those Stricken by the Plague in Jaffa, 11 March 1799), Baron Antoine-Jean Gros, 1804
Oil on canvas, 523 x 715 cm
(Musée du Louvre, Paris).

Below
The Cairo Insurgents (21 October 1798), Anne-Louis Girodet-Trioson, 1810
Oil on canvas, 365 x 500 cm
(Musée National du Château, Versailles).

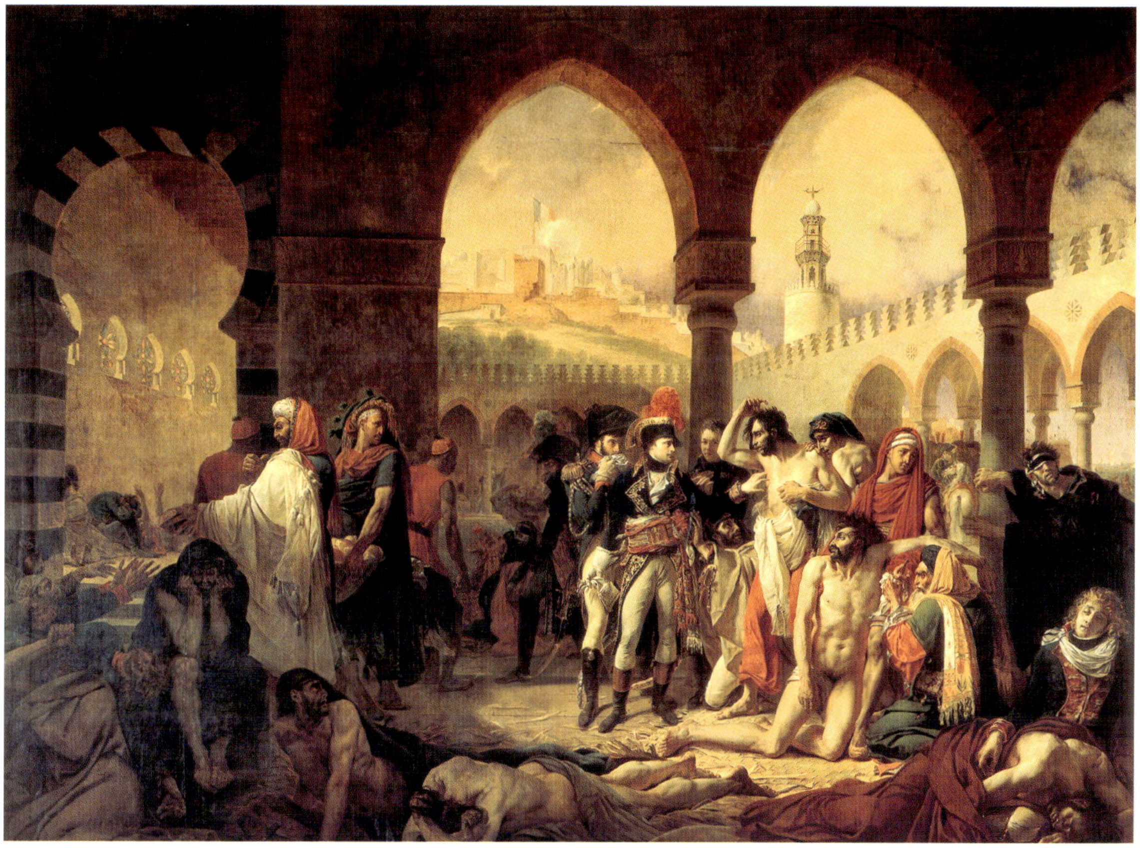

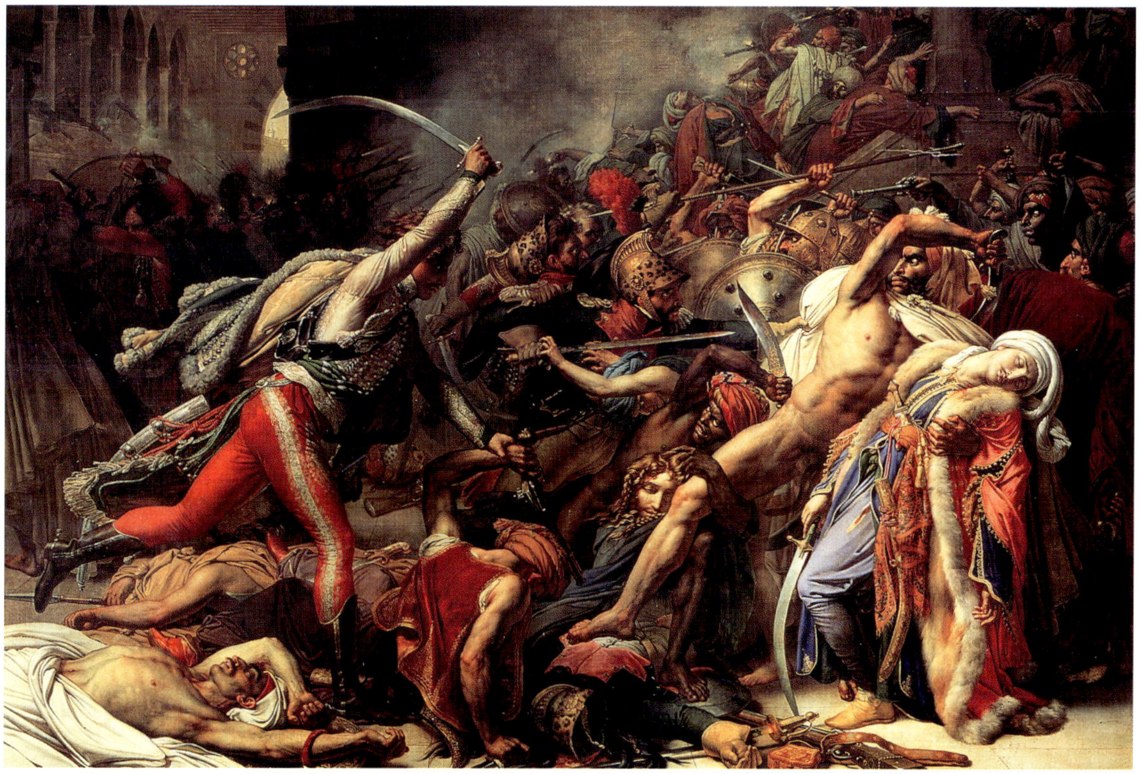

consequence of the withdrawal was the Treaty of Amiens, signed in 1802, which provisionally ended the conflict between France and Britain. For a France emerging from the Revolution, this adventure in the Orient had become a triumph for the arts and sciences.

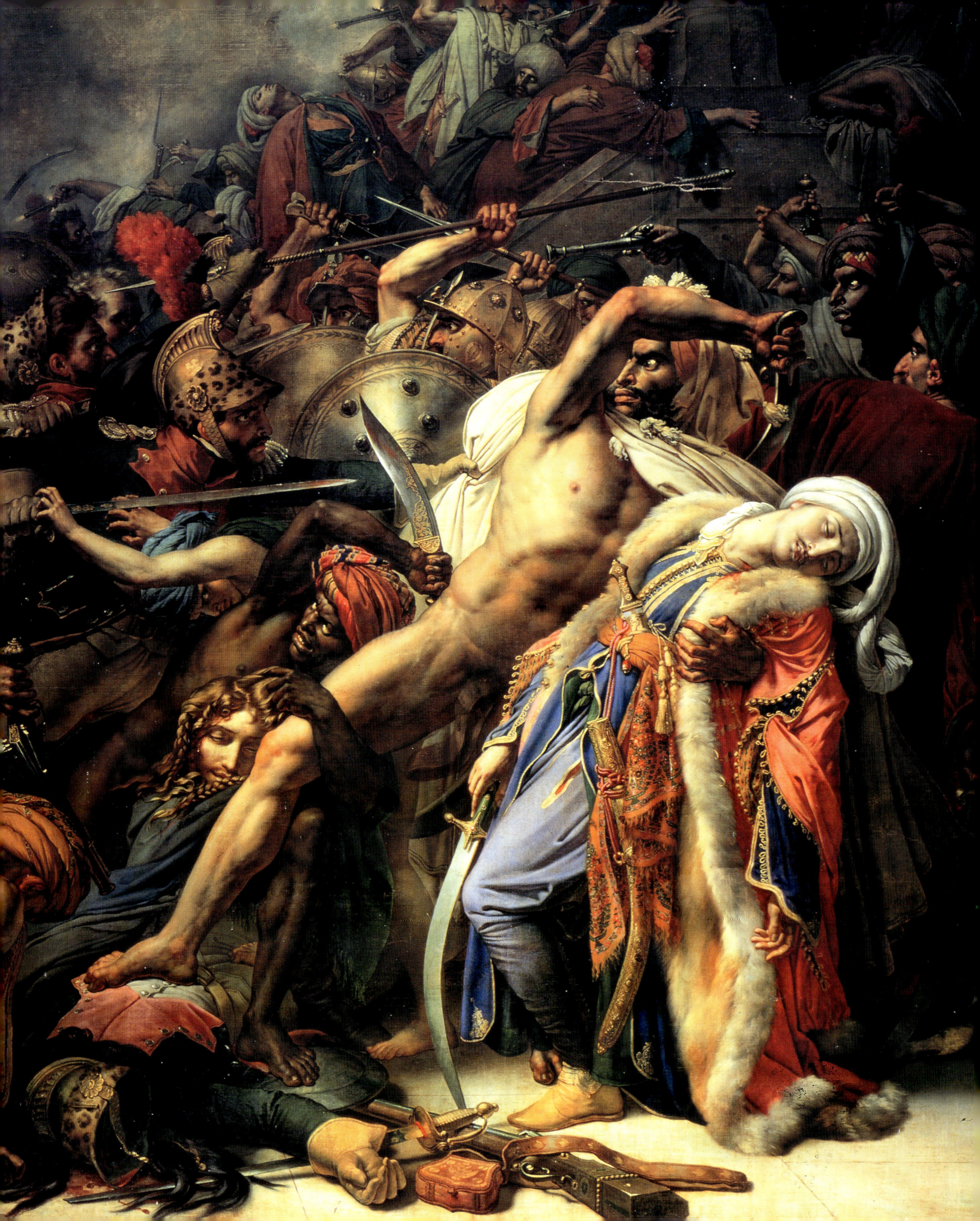

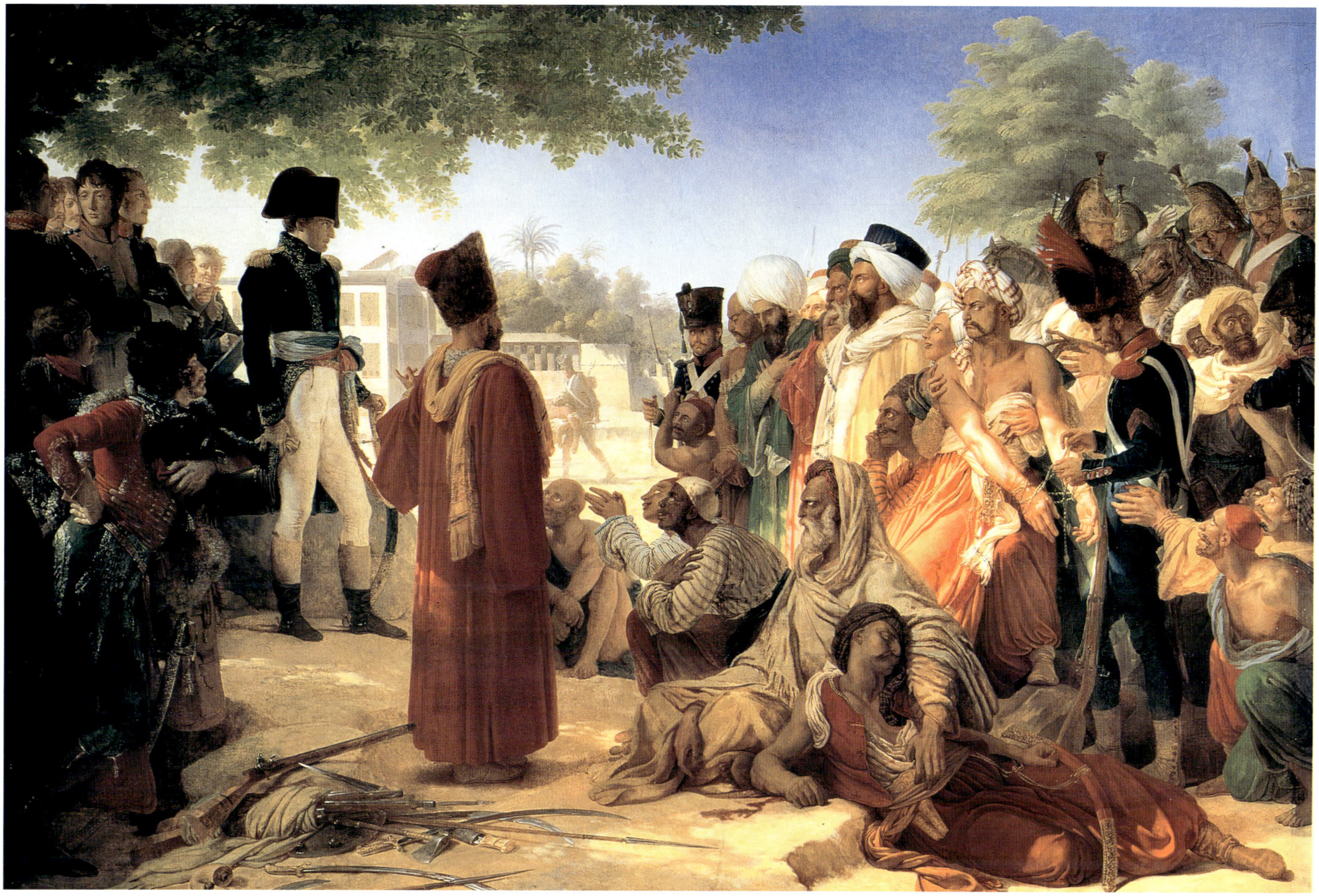

GLORIFYING BONAPARTE'S CAMPAIGN

"Great names are made in the East."
Napoleon Bonaparte

The military feats of the campaign were carefully recorded by the artists accompanying Bonaparte; Vivant Denon, for example, painted *The Battle of the Pyramids*, and also created an imposing portrait gallery of those illustrious colleagues who had shared the venture. He became the obligatory adviser to artists asked to paint one or another episode of this eventful campaign. An example is provided by the competition organized to commemorate the Battle of Nazareth. The competition was won by Gros, who set to work immediately; but Denon soon advised him, discreetly, to set aside the painting as it drew too much attention to the heroism of the battle's victor, Junot. He suggested that Gros should turn to another theme, one that would flatter the young, all-conquering Consul: Bonaparte showing mercy to Cairo's insurgents. Denon also asked Gros to start work on *The Battle of Aboukir*, having already furnished him with ample documentation for his *Plague House at Jaffa* (1804). Gros wrote to Denon: "I have the greatest need to have in my studio the Eastern cloths, covers, and weapons you so obligingly offered to lend me [...] An artist benefits immensely from painting as close as possible to life [...] May I remind you to send that blue-tinged damask sword, which in a well-practiced hand would whisk enemy heads off like as much stubble."

Throughout this time, the Salon in the Louvre became little more than a showcase exalting the glory of the Grande Armée and its generals, above all Bonaparte. In 1801, Louis François Lejeune exhibited his painting *Battle of Mount Tabor, 16 April 1799*; in

Bonaparte Pardoning the Insurgents in Cairo (23 October 1798),
Pierre Narcisse Guérin, 1808
Oil on canvas, 365 x 500 cm
(Musée National du Château, Versailles).

The Cairo Insurgents (*21 October 1798*),
Anne-Louis Girodet-Trioson, 1810 (detail)
Oil on canvas, 365 x 500 cm
(Musée National du Château, Versailles).

Following double page
The French Army Halts at Aswan in Upper Egypt (2 February 1799),
Jean Charles Tardieu, 1812
Oil on canvas, 112 x 164 cm
(Musée National du Château, Versailles).

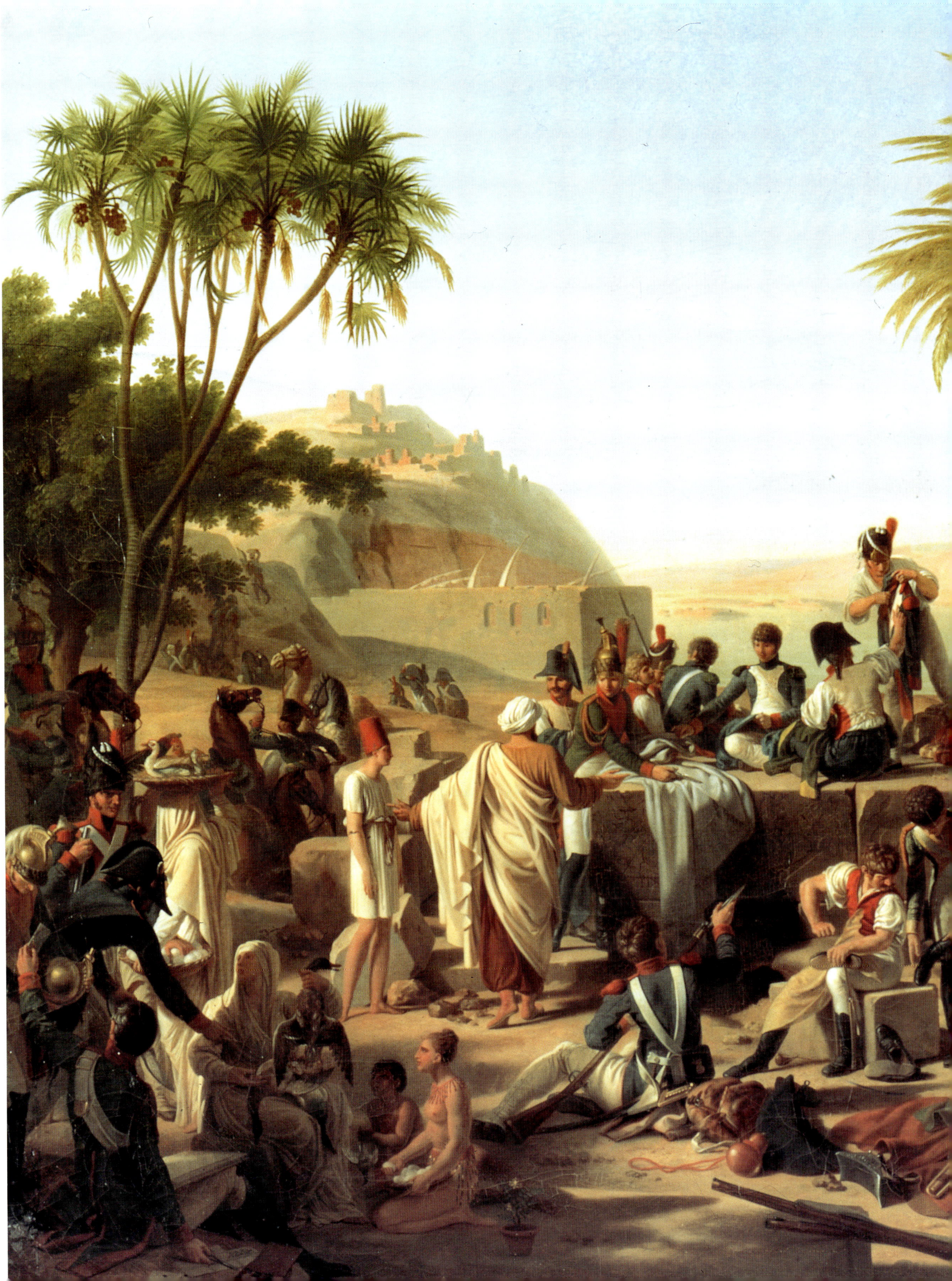

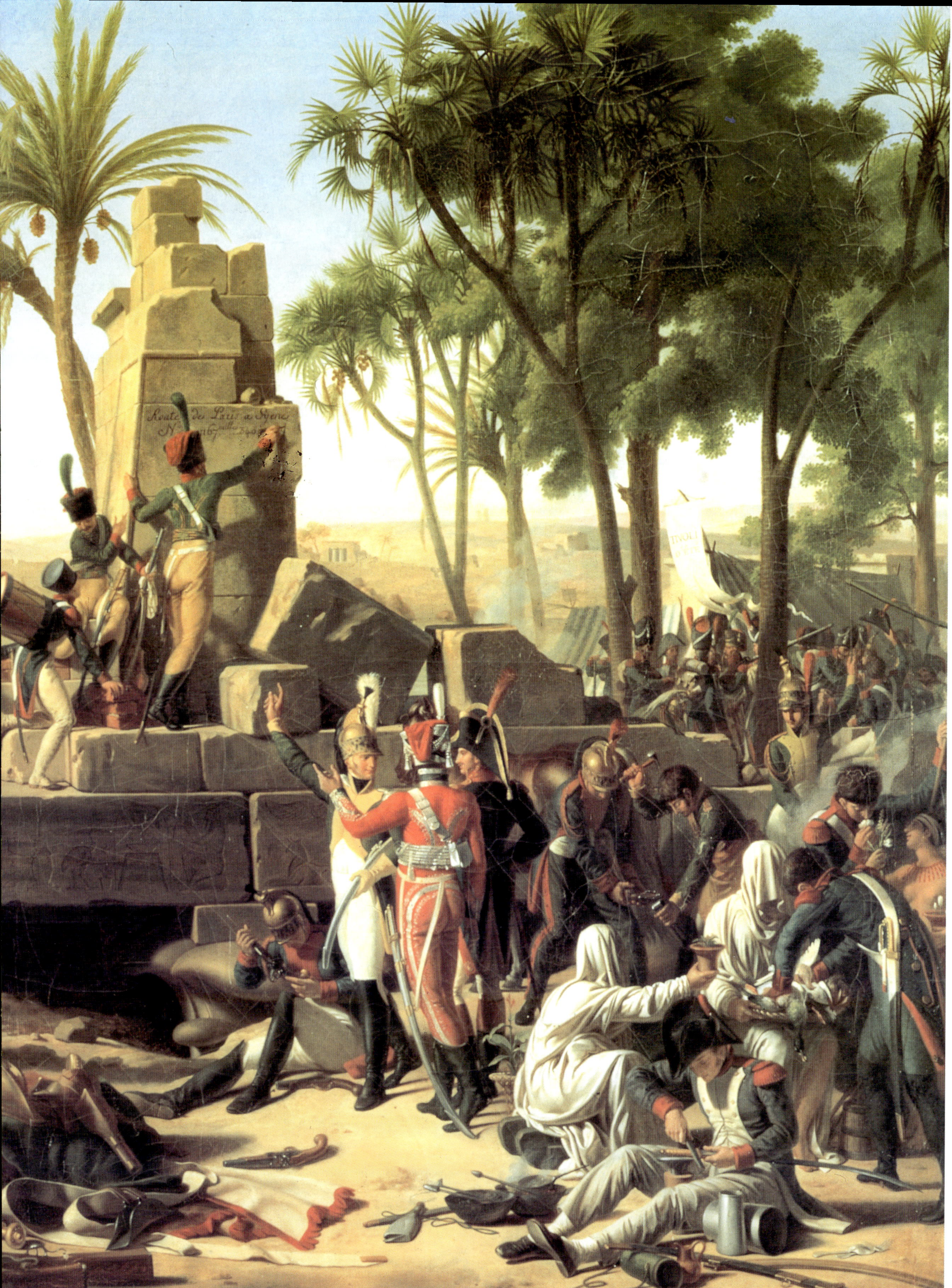

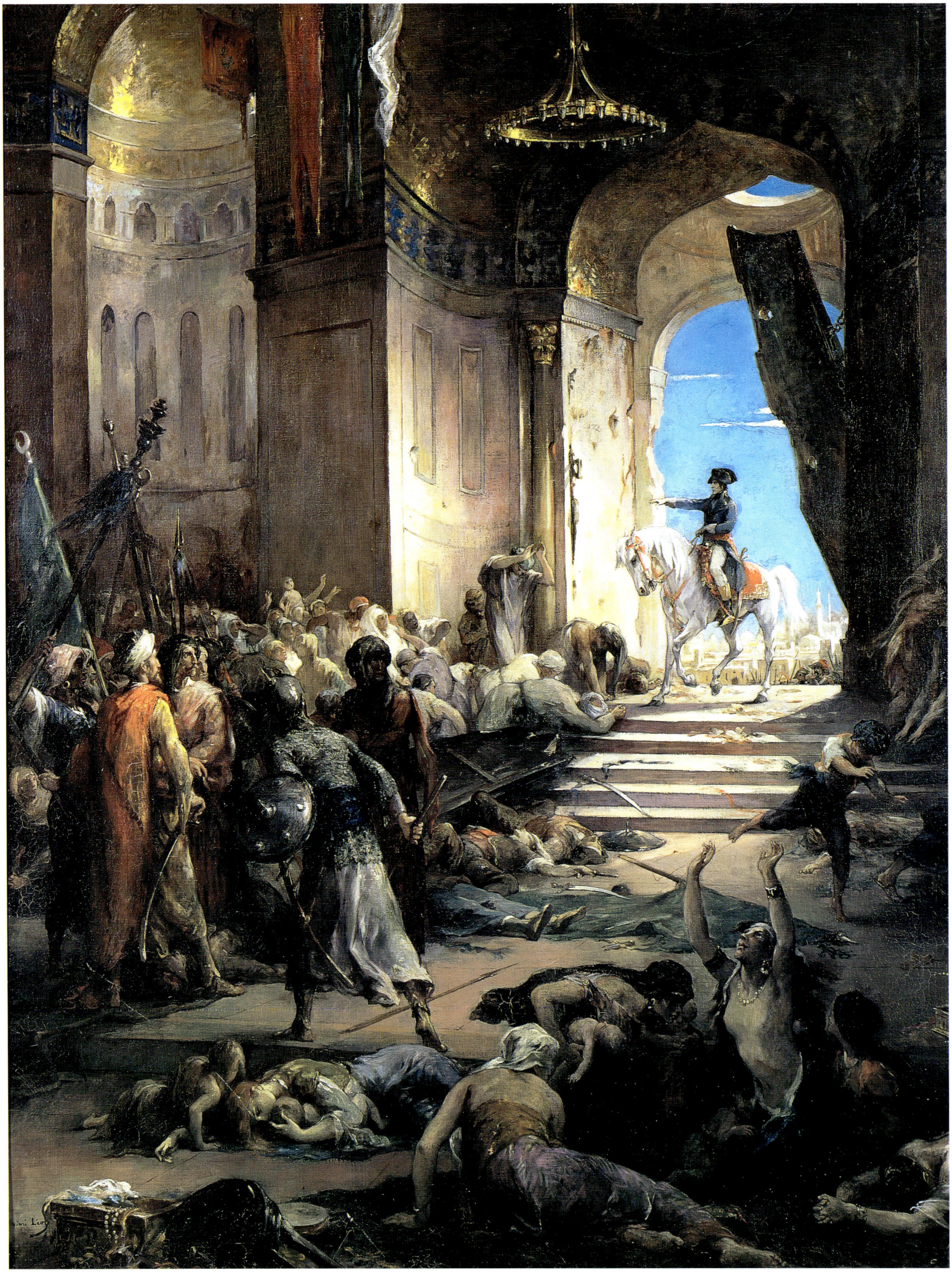

1804 he exhibited his *Battle of Aboukir*, which appeared along with Gros' powerful evocation of the plague hospital in Jaffa being visited by Bonaparte. The following year Gros hung his version of the Battle of Aboukir in the Salon Carré in the Louvre. In 1810 Anne-Louis Girodet-Trioson created a stir with the work *The Cairo Insurgents*, which Stendhal described in the following terms: "Imagine a viper's nest discovered as an old vase is moved: it is almost impossible to follow the same body, and if you look for a long time, your eyes waver."

Between 1800 and 1812, no less than 70 paintings dealing with the Egyptian campaign were produced under the leadership of Vivant Denon, including *Bonaparte Suppressing Sedition in Cairo* (1806) by Pierre Narcisse Guérin, and *The French Army Halts at Aswan, Upper Egypt, 2 February 1799* by Jean Charles Tardieu, shown at the 1812 Salon.

Even after Bonaparte had fallen from power, the subject continued to attract artists like Vernet, who in 1819 painted *Massacre of the Mamelukes*, which was exhibited in the 1821 Salon. Other artists who continued to be drawn to the subject include Bonnat, Gérôme (*Œdipe*, featuring Bonaparte at Giza), Decamps, and Henri-Léopold Lévy. All of them used Denon's *Voyage* as a source. Léon Cognet, who painted a fine portrait of Champollion, was entrusted with an important project for the Salle des Papyrus in the Louvre that took him seven years to complete, from 1828 to 1835. His general theme: *The Egypt expedition under Bonaparte's command; surrounded by scientists and artists, He directs both their work and the military operations that protect Them.* In order to make his depiction more authentic, Cognet directed his attention not only to the travel writings and journals the Egypt campaign had pro-

Bonaparte at the Great Mosque in Cairo, Henri Lévy, undated.
Oil on canvas, 150 x 116 cm
(Musée des Beaux-Arts, Mulhouse).

The Egypt Expedition under Bonaparte's Command, Léon Cogniet, 1832
Painting on the ceiling of the Salle Campans (Musée du Louvre, Paris).

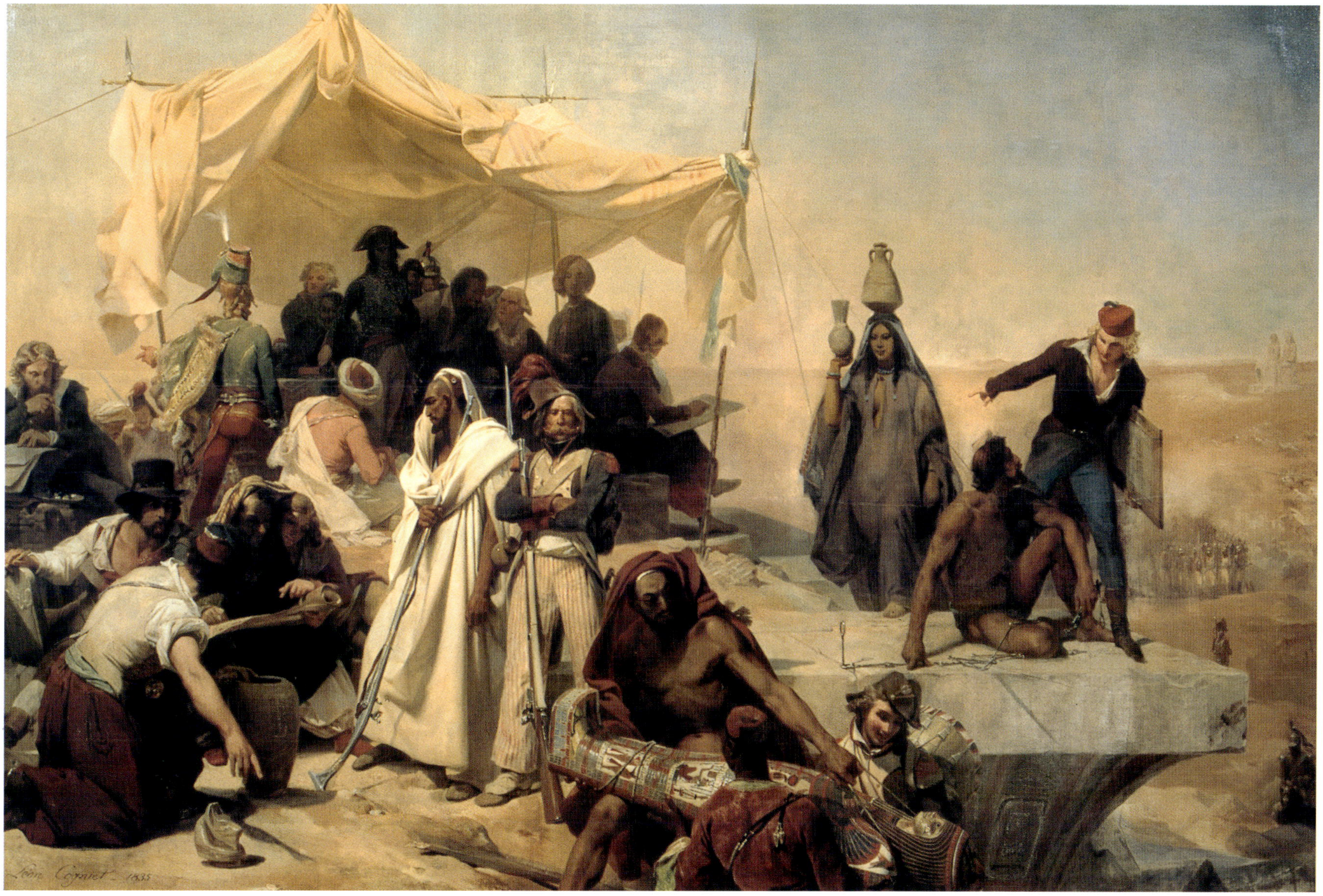

duced, but also to the Louvre's own greatly enhanced collection of Egyptian artifacts.

Egypt and the Arts

Anxious to put his inglorious exit from Egypt behind him, in March 1802 Bonaparte ordered work to start on the monumental *Description de l'Égypte* (Description of Egypt). The realization of this project, with the first volume appearing in January 1803, continued until 1826, when the last engraving was presented to King Charles X. In all it comprises 23 volumes, 13 of which are illustrated with more than 900 engravings and some 4,000 drawings, and covers three main topics: Ancient Egypt, contemporary Egypt, and the natural sciences. Five volumes are dedicated to archaeology and include reconstructions of ancient monuments. It would remain the standard work on Egyptology until the end of the 19th century.

After the Revolution, the love for all things Egyptian grew even greater than under the *ancien régime*. Paradoxically, the craftsmen Percier and Fontaine, who had fought long and hard against the trend, created the first Egyptian-style piece of furniture: a bureau bookcase with two seated Egyptian women in bronze wearing the plume head-dress of the goddess Maat, a grooved cornice, and a winged sun-disk, together with hieroglyphs, sphinxes, and various Egyptian gods. Yet again it was left to Vivant Denon to set the tone by his decision to have his own apartments decorated in this imposing style. This featured a commanding medal cabinet in the shape of a monolith, crafted by M.G. Biennais after Denon's own drawings, and a magnificent bookcase, ordered from Charles Morel, to hold the 23 volumes of the *Description de l'Égypte*.

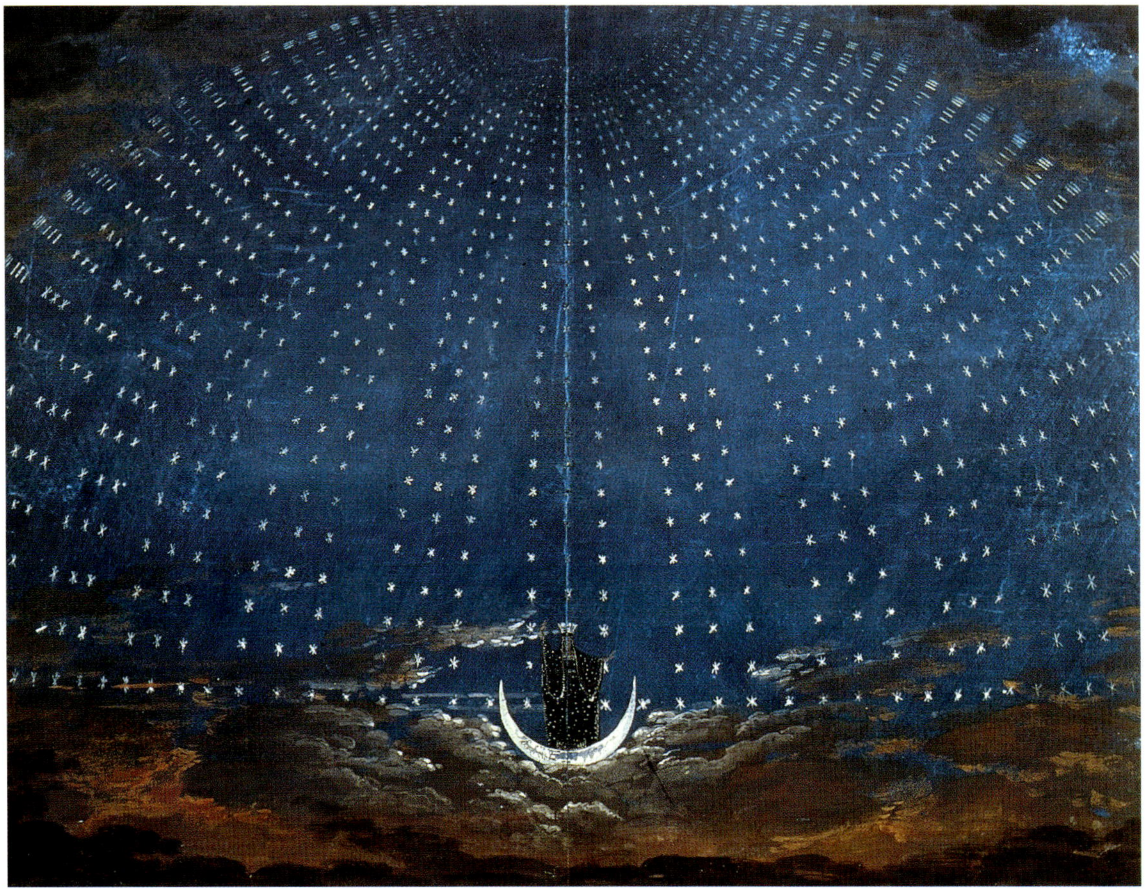

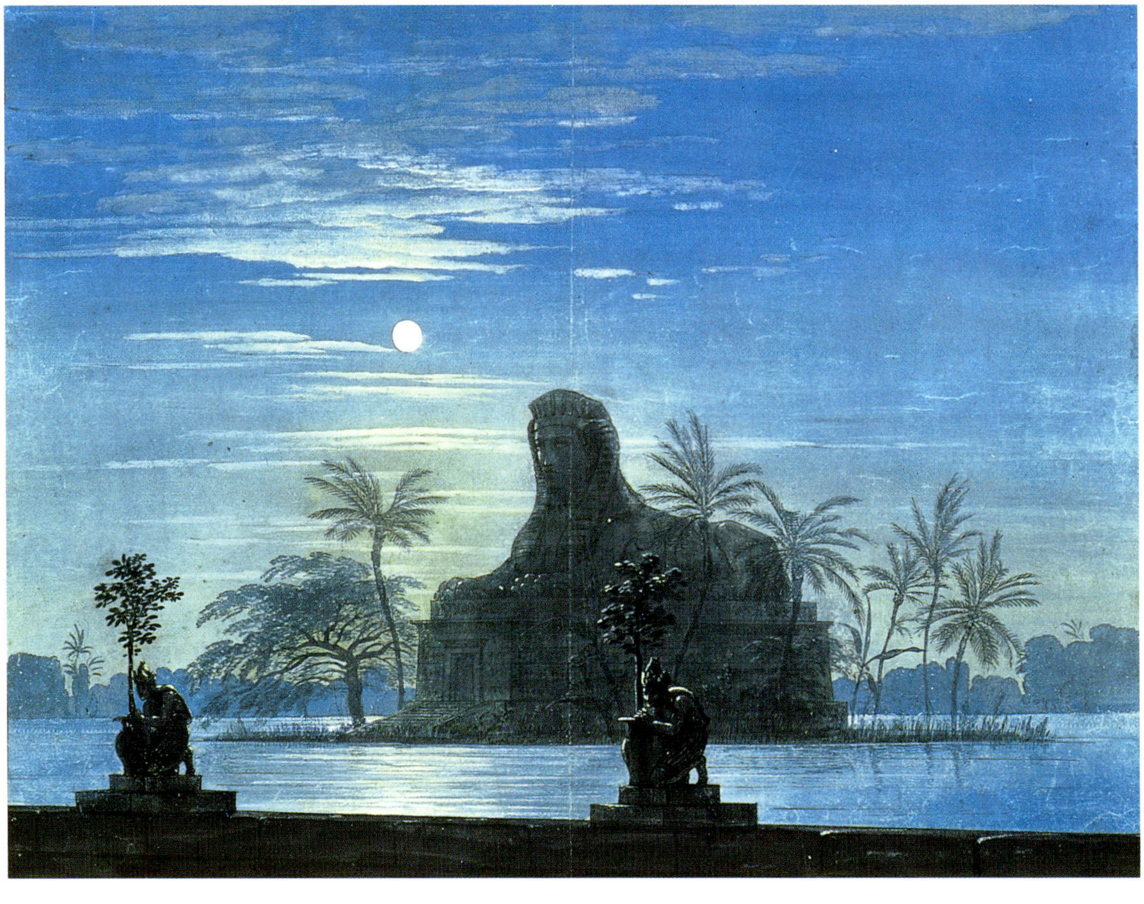

It is not by chance that the Empire style was first known as the *style retour d'Égypte* (return from Egypt style). Egyptomania could be seen everywhere. Important decorative projects were carried out in the Egyptian style, notably the emperor's rest room at the palace of Saint-Cloud; the portico of the Hôtel de Beauharnais in Paris (c. 1807) by Nicolas Bataille; and the many fountains built in the capital city, including the Fontaine du Fellah (1806–1809), the monumental fountain on the Place Dauphine (1799), and, on the Place du Châtelet, the fountain of the Apport-Paris (1806). At the Sèvres factory, a magnificent table set was created – it included dessert, tea, and coffee sets, and an amazing seven-meter-long white biscuit centerpiece – that in 1805 Napoleon gave to Tsar Alexander I. This was followed by the celebrated "Coffee Service" of 1810, and the "Egyptian Service" of 1811.

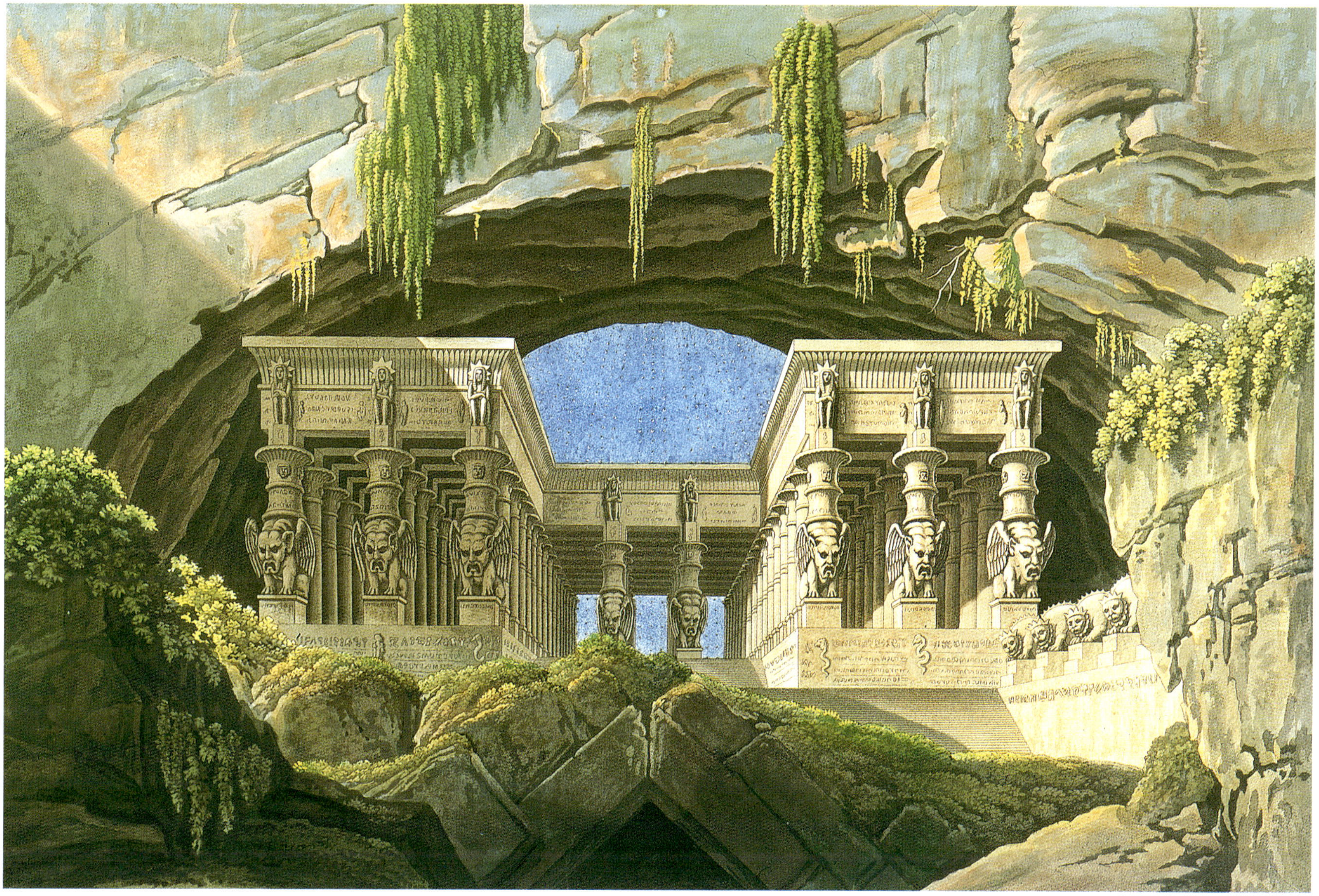

This Egypt-led fashion was not confined to France; England also adopted it with a passion. It finds its finest expression in the Egyptian Room in Thomas Hope's house in London (1799–1804), James Randall's Egyptian Mansion (1806), the famous Egyptian Hall (1812) in London conceived by Peter Frederick Robinson, and Thomas Hope's Egyptian furniture (1819). Likewise, the Italian architect and designer Antonio Basoli had a taste for sets with Egyptian or Persian character, a taste he indulged in his designs for (among other things) a production of Meyerbeer's opera *Semiramide riconosciuta* (Semiramide rewarded), first performed in Turin in 1819. Basoli, the last representative of the great Bibiena family of designers, drew upon an extensive range of sources – including Denon's *Voyage* and Lebrun's *Voyage en Perse* (Travels in Persia) – to produce a monumental work on theater design, the first four volumes of which came out in 1811: *Cose egizie. Studio sopra li monumenti antichi del Egitto. Altri initiati da moderni autori*. This is an encyclopaedia for scene designers that exceeded its original objectives by achieving a comprehensive synthesis of architectural and design knowledge in this field. In 1829, Basoli published 24 lithographs representing 24 capital letters in shapes fashioned from the architectural forms of Persia, India, China, Cambodia, Greece, and of course Egypt: his *Raccolta de pensieri pittorici composti di ogetti comincianti della singole lettere afabetiche*. This compendium of ornamental letters was the first use of eastern architectural forms in typography.

Musicians and choreographers were not exempt from the trend. A version of Mozart's opera *Die Zauberflöte* (The magic flute) was performed in Paris in 1801 under the name *Les Mystères d'Isis* (The mysteries of

Above
The Portico of the Queen of the Night's Palace, décor for Mozart's opera *Die Zauberflöte* (The magic flute) (act I, scene I)
Karl Friedrich Schinkel, 1815
Sepia aquatint, 28 x 40 cm
(Deutsches Theatermuseum, Munich).

Opposite
In the Palace of the Queen of the Night, décor for Mozart's opera *Die Zauberflöte* (The magic flute) (act I, scene VI),
Karl Friedrich Schinkel, 1815
Aquatint in gray and blue, 28.5 x 40 cm
(Deutsches Theatermuseum, Munich).

The Garden of Sarastro by Moonlight, with Sphinx, décor for Mozart's opera *Die Zauberflöte* (The magic flute) (act II, scene VII), Karl Friedrich Schinkel, 1815
Aquatint in gray and blue, 28.4 x 40 cm
(Deutsches Theatermuseum, Munich).

Isis); Jean Aumer created a ballet entitled *Les amours d'Antoine et Cléopâtre* (Anthony and Cleopatra in love; Paris, 1812); and Pierre Gardel, using a score by the composer Henri-Montan Berton, staged the ballet *L'Enfant Prodigue* (The prodigal son), with lavish sets painted by Jean-Baptiste Isabey, who drew on the familiar Egyptian repertoire, temples, obelisks, columns with Hathoric capitals, and sphinxes. But the most accomplished work in this field was undoubtedly Schinkel's enchanting set for the Berlin Opera's 1815 production of Mozart's *Die Zauberflöte*.

In literature, Goethe was one of the first on the trail. During his trip to Italy in 1797 he was fascinated by Egyptian remains and took home casts of hieroglyphics. In the following year he wrote *Der Zauberflöte, zweiter Teil* (The magic flute, part two); that same year, the German writer Novalis began his novel *Die Lehrlinge zu Sais* (The disciples of Sais), and Schiller wrote a poem on Sais. In France, Chateaubriand completed in 1804 what is in effect a Christian epic, *Les Martyrs* (The martyrs). Retracing the steps of early Christians, the narrator, Eudore, travels up the Nile Valley, where he discovers Memphis, the "funereal gates of Egypt": "Close by, and as if in the shadow of these dwellings of the void, stands Memphis surrounded by graves and steeped in the waters of the Acheron, across which Charon ferries the dead. On the edge of the Plain of Tombs, it seemed poised to begin the journey that will take it down to join its generation in Hades." Two years earlier, Chateaubriand had been able to fulfill his dream of a pilgrimage around the Mediterranean, a journey he wanted to make in order to find the authentic images he needed for *Les Martyrs*. The result, his *Itinéraire de Paris à Jérusalem et de Jérusalem à Paris* (Journey from Paris to Jerusalem and from Jerusalem to Paris), was the model for a new literary genre: travel writing. Though not of course the first of its kind, this book, completed in 1810, launched a new literary ambition: writers now took upon themselves the task of describing the world, and more specifically the Middle East, to their fellow countrymen. His journey, which took him from Greece to Tunisia, gave rise to a chapter on Egypt. His account of the Land of the Pharaohs, however, is brief and in the end much less effective than the one he would invent using classical texts, for the Nile was in flood and he suffered an ill-timed bout of illness when sailing around Rosetta Island. But he did write a poem, indeed a hymn: "Ancient mother of divine arts and fables, / Whose glory seated in the midst of ruins / arrests even brilliance and confounds our pride, / Venerable Egypt where, from the depth of a tomb, / Your colossal grandeur defies our dreams..." The French writer Prosper Mérimée exploited this new vein with *L'Amour africain* (African love; 1825) and *La Guzla* (1827), which purports to be a collection of Illyrian folk songs. And in 1829 Victor Hugo, who never set foot on African soil, nor even visited the Mediterranean, published a collection of poems called *Les Orientales* (The Orientals). Such works mark the point at which non-European themes began to play an important role in French literature.

Egyptology, in its infancy just after Bonaparte's campaign, was at first little more that a huge treasure hunt led by colorful, larger-than-life figures. There was, for example, Bernardino Drovetti, who was French consul to Egypt from 1810 to 1814. From 1821 to 1829 he was in charge of the dig in Thebes; he also put together the core of the Turin Museum collection, built up the collection in the Louvre, and initiated the one in Berlin. Henry Dalt, who wrote an account of a journey through Abyssinia, and who was British consul between 1816 and 1827, procured remarkable antiques for the British Museum and also sold pieces to the Musée Charles X in Paris. Jean-Jacques Riffaud, a sculptor from Marseilles, lived for 40 years in Egypt and became an authority on the country and its people. A Swiss, Jean-Louis Burckhardt, discovered the temple at Abou Simbel in 1813 and in 1819 published an account of his travels in Nubia. Giovanni Battista Belzoni, hired by the viceroy Mehmed Ali, was the first person to enter the temple at Abu Simbel, and it was he who discovered tombs in the Valley of the Kings. In 1817, he organized a very important exhibition of drawings and casts in the Egyptian Hall in London.

Apart from these archeology-prospectors, for whom science and business were often one and the same thing, science was progressing rapidly, especially under the direction of the celebrated French scholar Jean-François Champollion. It was he who in 1822 succeeded in deciphering hieroglyphs, publishing *Précis du système hieroglyphique des anciens Égyptiens* (A precis on ancient Egypt's

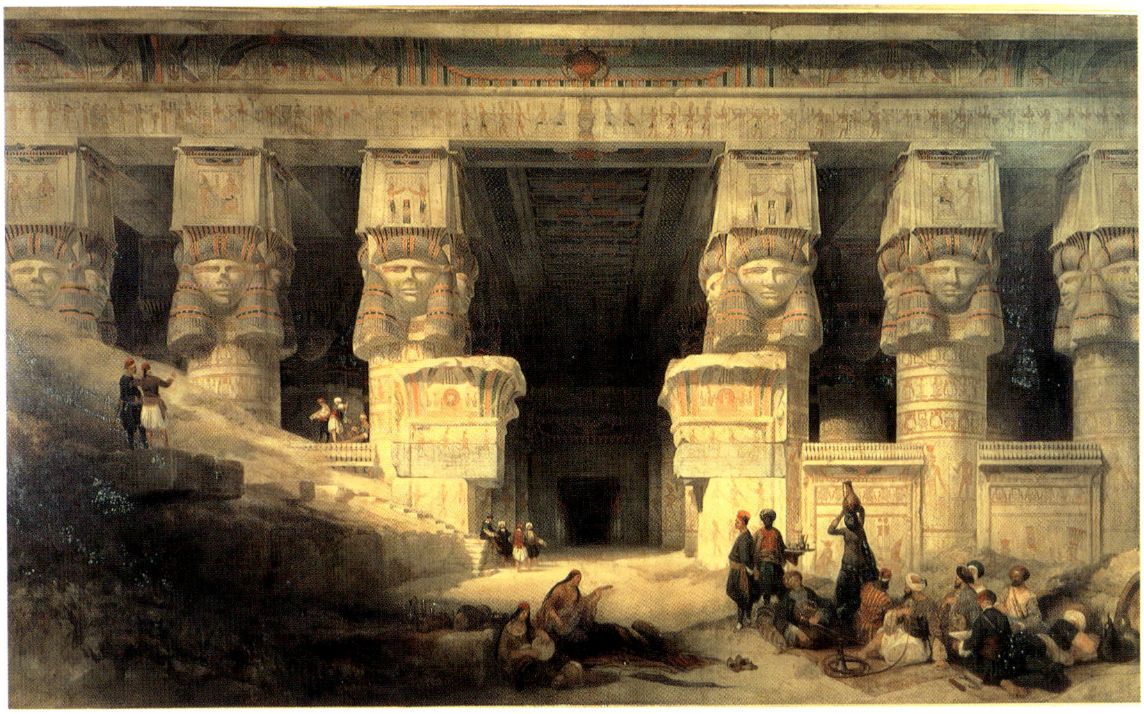

system of hieroglyphs) in 1824. Sizeable expeditions were mounted. The first, from Prussia, began operations in 1820 under the management of Baron Heinrich Carl von Minutoli, who explored Upper Egypt as far as the oasis at Siwa. Painters and draftsmen were on hand, among them Louis Faure, who painted on his return *Henrich Carl von Minutoli Resting at Siwa Oasis, 1823*. The Franco-Tuscan archaeological mission of 1828 comprised Egyptologists like Champollion, but also painters like Nestor L'Hôte, who would subsequently be attached to the viceroy's court; and Giuseppe Angelelli, who around 1836 painted *The Franco-Tuscan Expedition in the Midst of the Ruins at Thebes*, where Champollion is pictured dressed as a pasha wearing a saber. In 1842, the king of Prussia backed another expedition, this one conducted by Karl Richard Lepsius, founder of the Egyptian museum in Berlin; this led to the publication of the 12-volume *Denkmäler aus Ægypten und Æthiopien* (Egyptian and Ethiopian monuments), which became an invaluable source for scholars and archaeologists. Here again several artists were taken along, including Jacob Frey, who commemorated the event with the startling, almost laughable *Installation of the Prussian Flag on the Pyramid at Cheops under the Command of Professor Lespius, 15 October 1842*. Meanwhile in France, the publication in 1819 of the Comte de Forbin's *Voyage dans le Levant en 1817 et 1818* (Journey to the Levant, 1817 to 1818), which was illustrated with numerous colored lithographs, and the publication between 1825 and 1827 of the works of the artist Louis Dupré, once a pupil of J.-L. David, greatly improved Europe's understand of these far-off lands.

The most famous and undoubtedly the most talented of the painters who went to Egypt to bring home detailed descriptions of antique monuments was the Scotsman David Roberts. Self-taught and highly gifted, he first came into contact with the Middle East in an unusual way – through his sets for a production of *Aladin* at the Theatre Royal in London, where he worked for 14 years. On the advice of the artist Joseph Mallord William Turner, he decided to travel

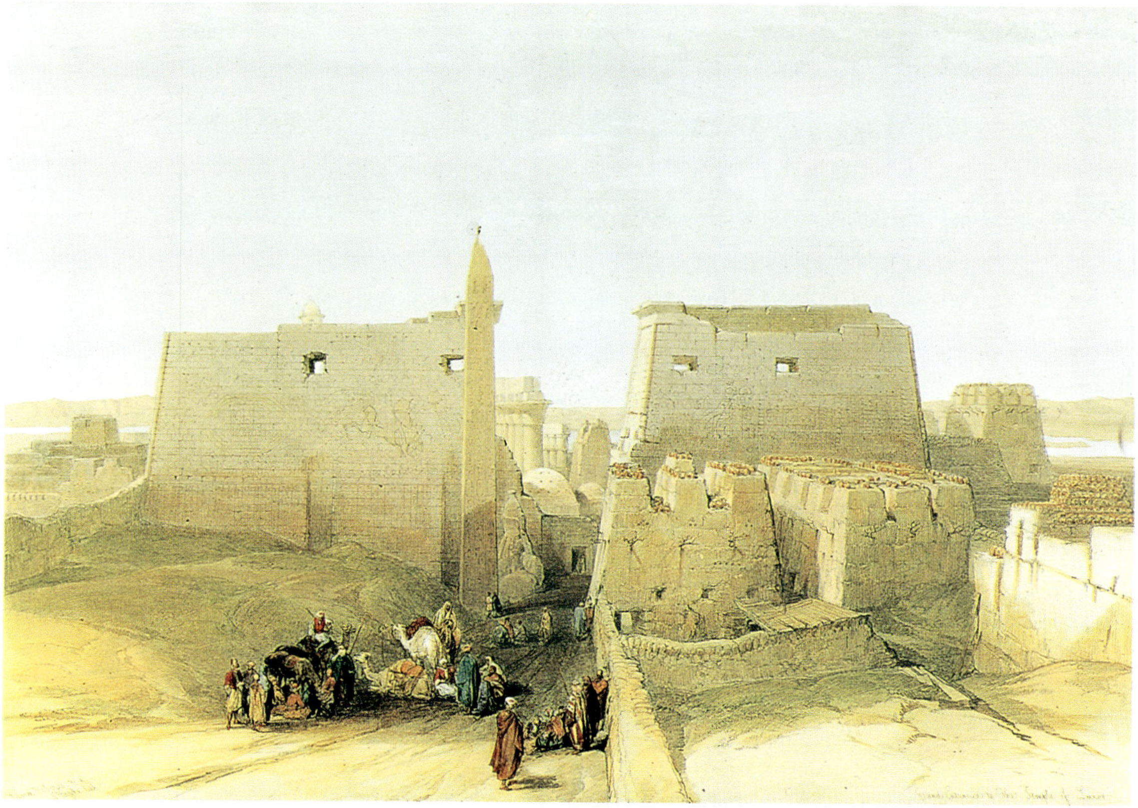

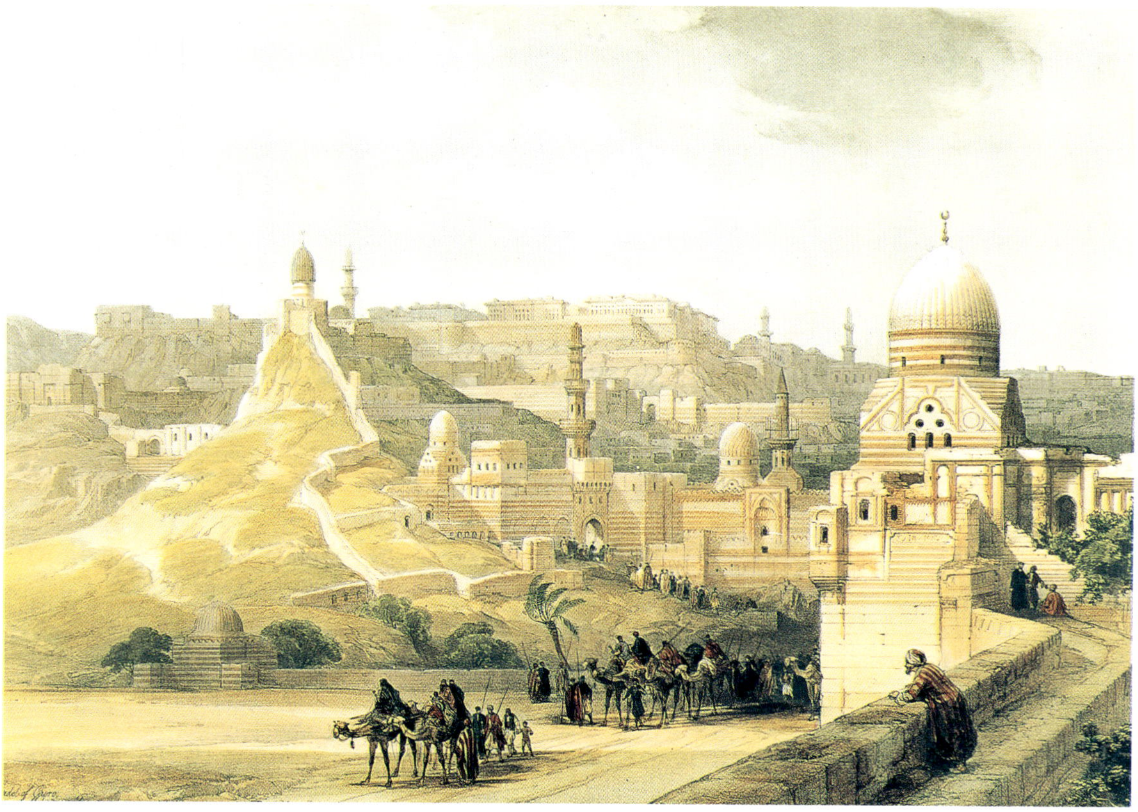

Opposite
The Temple at Dendera,
David Roberts, 1841
Oil on canvas, 119 x 212 cm
(City Museum and Art Gallery, Bristol).

Top
Main Entrance to the Temple at Luxor,
lithograph 1846–1850 by Louis Haghe based on a watercolor by David Roberts, 1838–1839
Plate taken from *Views in the Holy Land, Syria, Idumea, Arabia, Egypt and Nubia* 1846–1850 (Victoria and Albert Museum, London).

Below
The Citadel of Cairo, lithograph by Louis Haghe based on a watercolor by David Roberts, 1838–1839
Plate taken from *Views in the Holy Land, Syria, Idumea, Arabia, Egypt and Nubia* 1846–1850 (Victoria and Albert Museum, London).

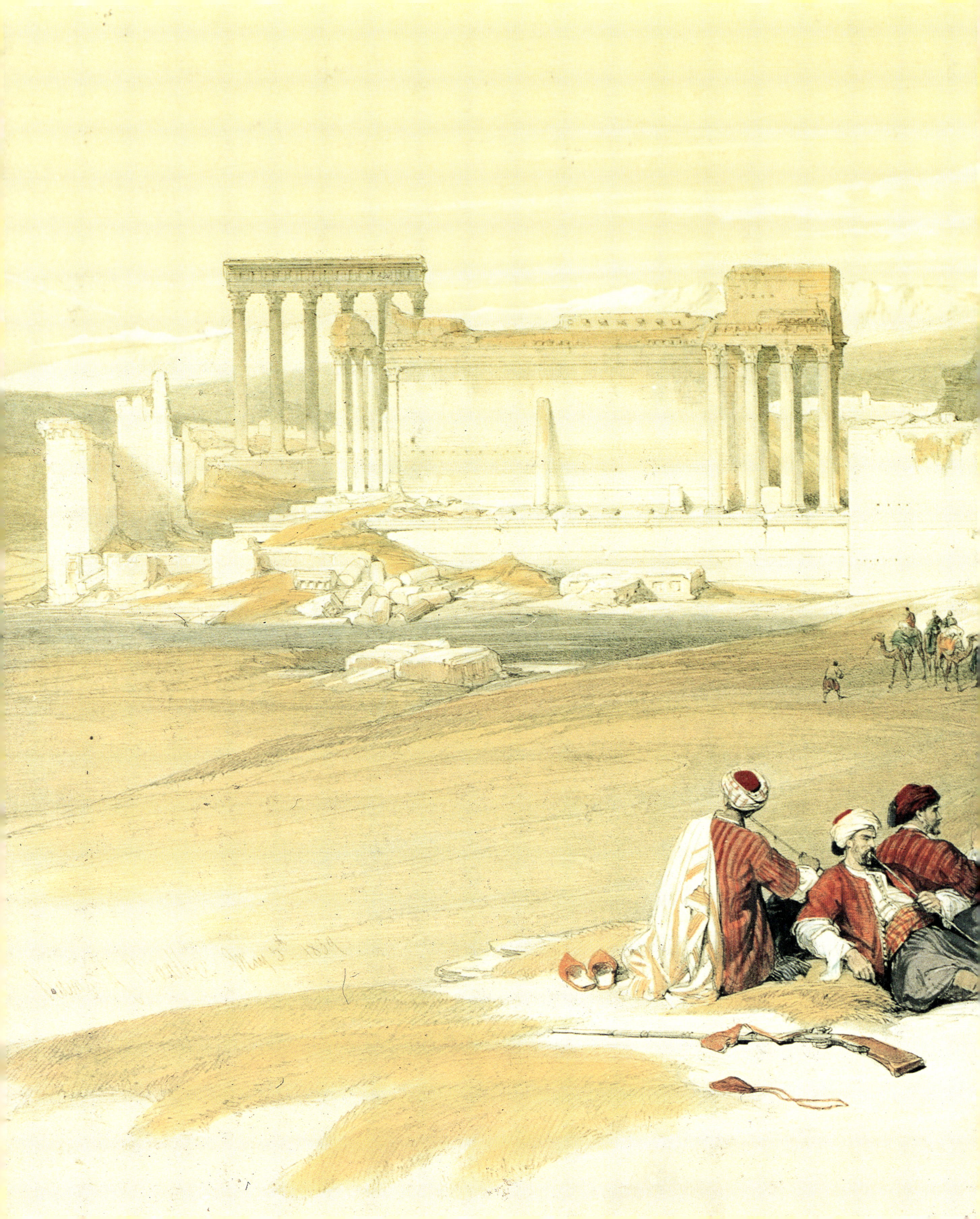

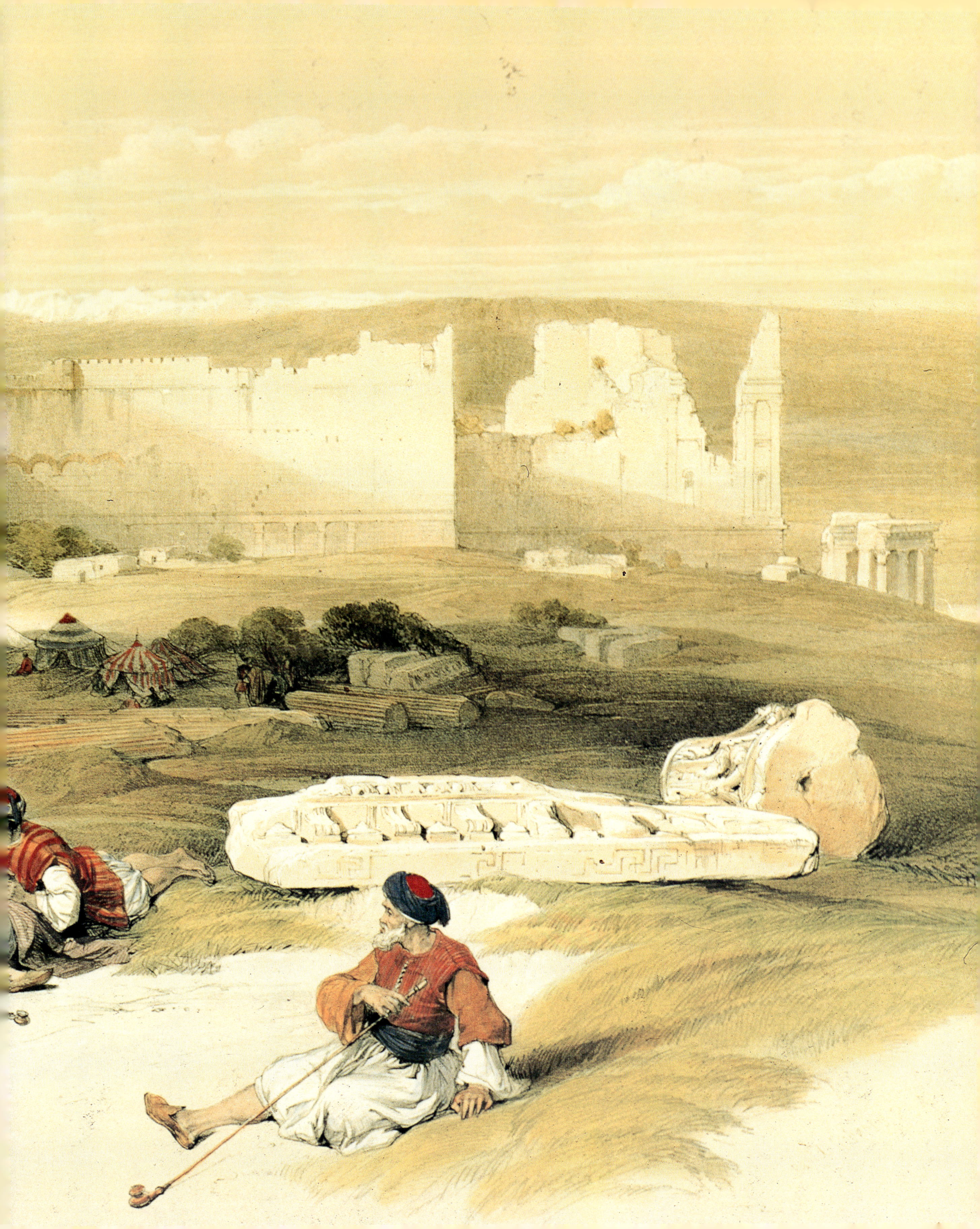

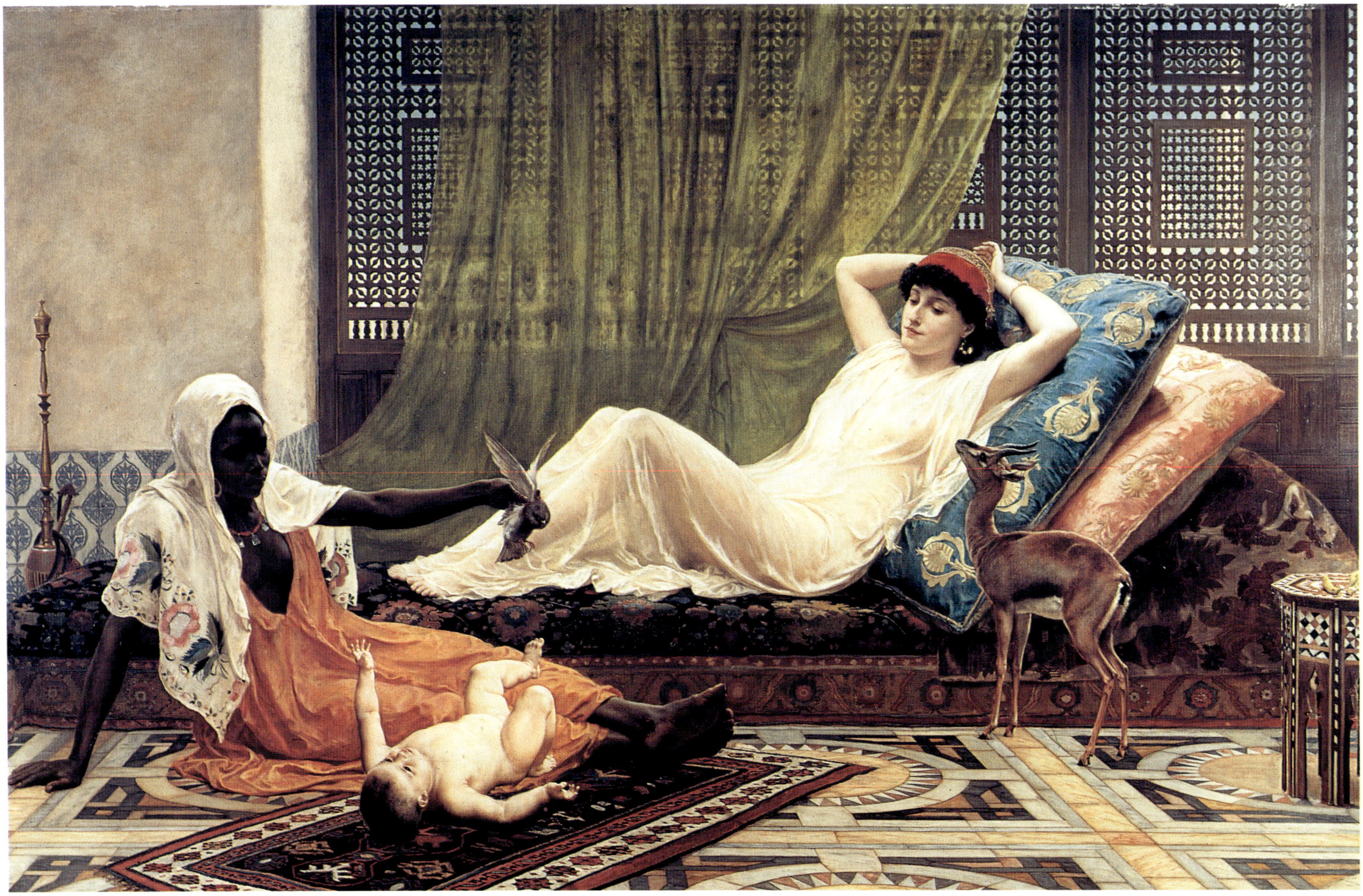

abroad. In 1832 he discovered Morocco, where he was completely captivated by Islamic art. When he sailed up the Nile he was, as he noted in his journal, completely won over by the majestic beauty of the temples, in particular those at Luxor and Karnak, which seemed beyond compare. During the seven months of his trip he drew all of 272 sketches, and on his return to London entrusted Louis Haghe with the task of preparing lithographs from his watercolors. Out of this enormous undertaking came the six volumes of *Views in the Holy Land, Syria, Idumea, Arabia, Egypt and Nubia*, which has 247 plates. Their powers of evocation rest both on the angle with which he viewed the architectural remains, which emphasizes their grandeur, and on his ability to suggest the vast scale of the buildings by dotting about them groups of Arabs, a device that also introduces a contemporary dimension to his pictures. In other words

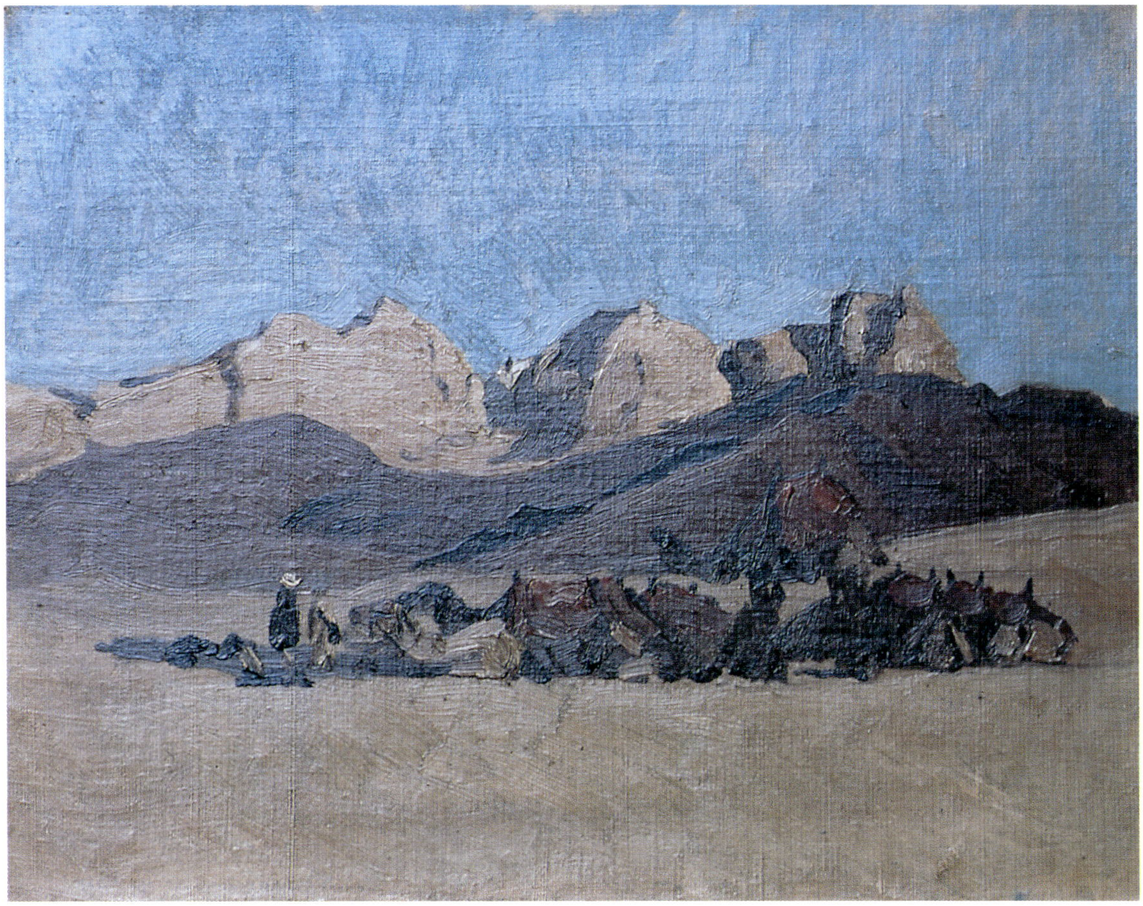

they provided viewers with both archaeological authenticity and local color. Moreover, his finished prints remained as fresh and vibrant as his first sketches. Roberts' achievement was to create an approach to Egypt that brought together the present and the past, the poetic and the documentary.

The works of the Italian artist Ippolito Caffi marked a turning point in Western art's attitude to the Middle East. This talented painter from Veneto first visited Malta, Greece, and Constantinople. He was then able to travel to Egypt, where he managed to join a caravan traveling from Suez to Alexandria; having reached Cairo, he followed the Nile into Nubia. He drew many sketches, and from these he derived the 23 paintings he exhibited on his return to Italy.

Though strongly influenced by the works of Roberts, Caffi placed a greater emphasis on the presence of the contemporary Arab world, for which he had a deep respect. As a result, he often places ancient monuments and desert dwellers in dynamic juxtaposition. We can see this in *A Caravan at Rest* (1844), where the great pyramid forming the background of the colorful contemporary scene appears to dissolve into the whitish light of an already high sun. He let his imagination give a dramatic tone to his paintings in such works as *Simoon in the Desert* (1844), in which camel-riding travelers in front of the pyramid of Cheops (Khufu) gaze intently at the setting sun; the brooding sphinx is shown in profile. He also left works noted for their poetic mood, including *Cairo*, *Island on the Nile*, *Karnak*, and *Caravan in the Desert*, all from 1843. Caffi's works signal two of the trends that will characterize Orientalist art: the dramatic and the poetic.

Egypt, from which such a fascinating and mysterious past was being exhumed, was soon trawled by an increasing number of artists from all over Europe, keen to pay homage to a civilization that never failed to impress. The British artist Frederick Goodall, already a well-established and highly esteemed artist, traveled through Egypt in 1858–1859. What he found enchanted him, inspiring several strange compositions, such as *Mystery of the Past*, in which the Giza Sphinx, surrounded by a dark and stormy sky, is aglow with an intense red light. In fact he was often keen to give a dramatic or symbolic interpretation to the archaeological remains he depicted, as in *Memphis* (1882), in which a thoughtful man leaning on a stick is shown contemplating the old temple whilst his cattle drink at a pool surrounded by ibis. Even when he came closer to his own times and depicted the people he met, he was inclined to give a free rein to his imagination and transport his subject to earlier times, as in *Desert's Gate*, which shows a young woman with the demeanor of a princess holding out a cup to a proud and handsome man, the very image of a classic hero atop his camel.

Of the many artists of all nationalities who developed the approach established by David Roberts, the following should be mentioned: James Müller, who in 1843 accompanied the archaeologist Charles Fellows to Anatolia before visiting the Nile valley (*The Ramseseum in Thebes*; *Sunset*, 1840; *Pyramids*, 1843); André Schranz (*Seti I's Temple at Gourna*; *Thebes*, 1843); Jacob Jacobs

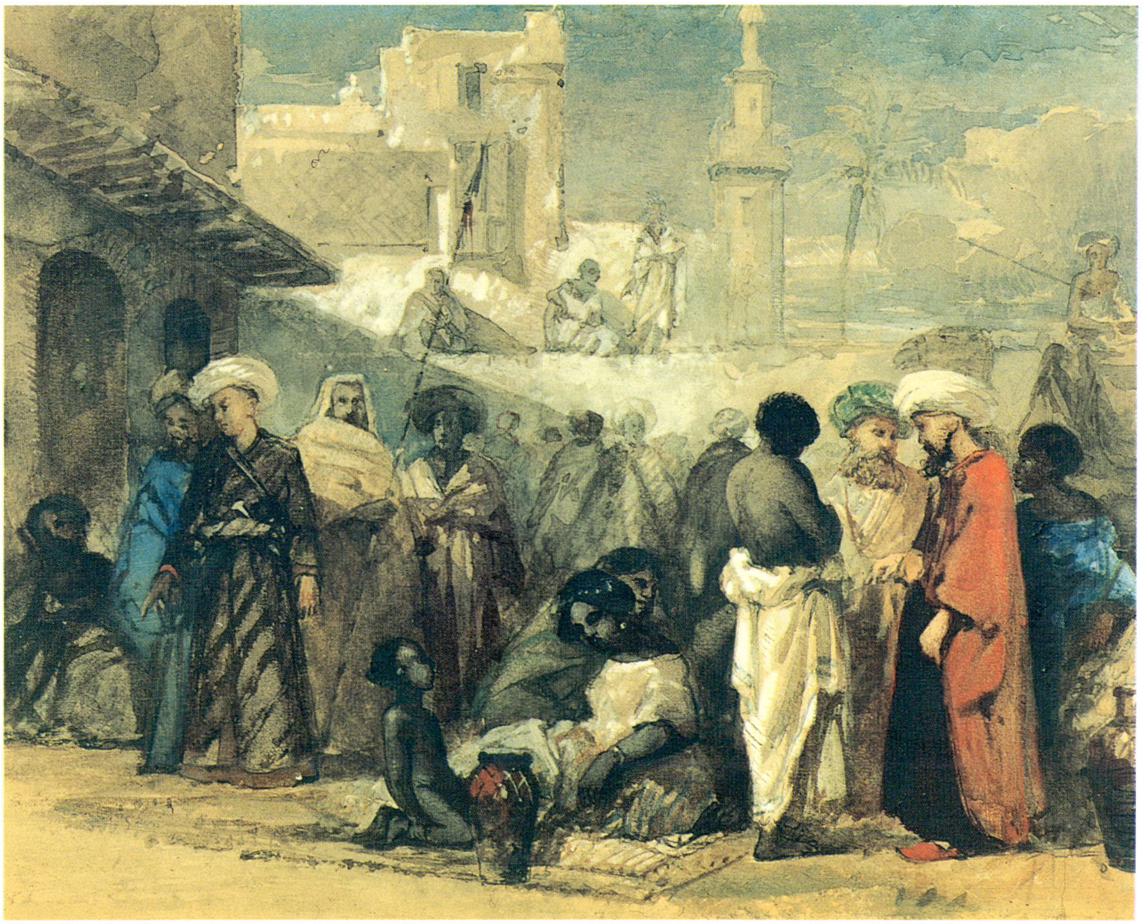

Previous double page
Ruins at Baalbek, lithograph by Louis Haghe based on a watercolor by David Roberts, 1838–1839
Plate taken from *Views in the Holy Land, Syria, Idumea, Arabia, Egypt and Nubia* (Victoria and Albert Museum, London).

Opposite, top
A New Attraction in the Harem, Frederick Goodall
Oil on canvas, 122 x 213.5 cm
(Sudley Art Gallery, Liverpool).

Opposite, below
Simoon in the Desert, Ippolito Caffi, c. 1844
Oil on canvas, 45 x 63 cm
(Ca' Pesaro, Galleria d'Arte Moderna, Venice).

The Cairo Slave Market, William James Müller, 1838–1839
Pencil and watercolor, 25.5 x 33 cm
(The Whitworth Art Gallery, Manchester).

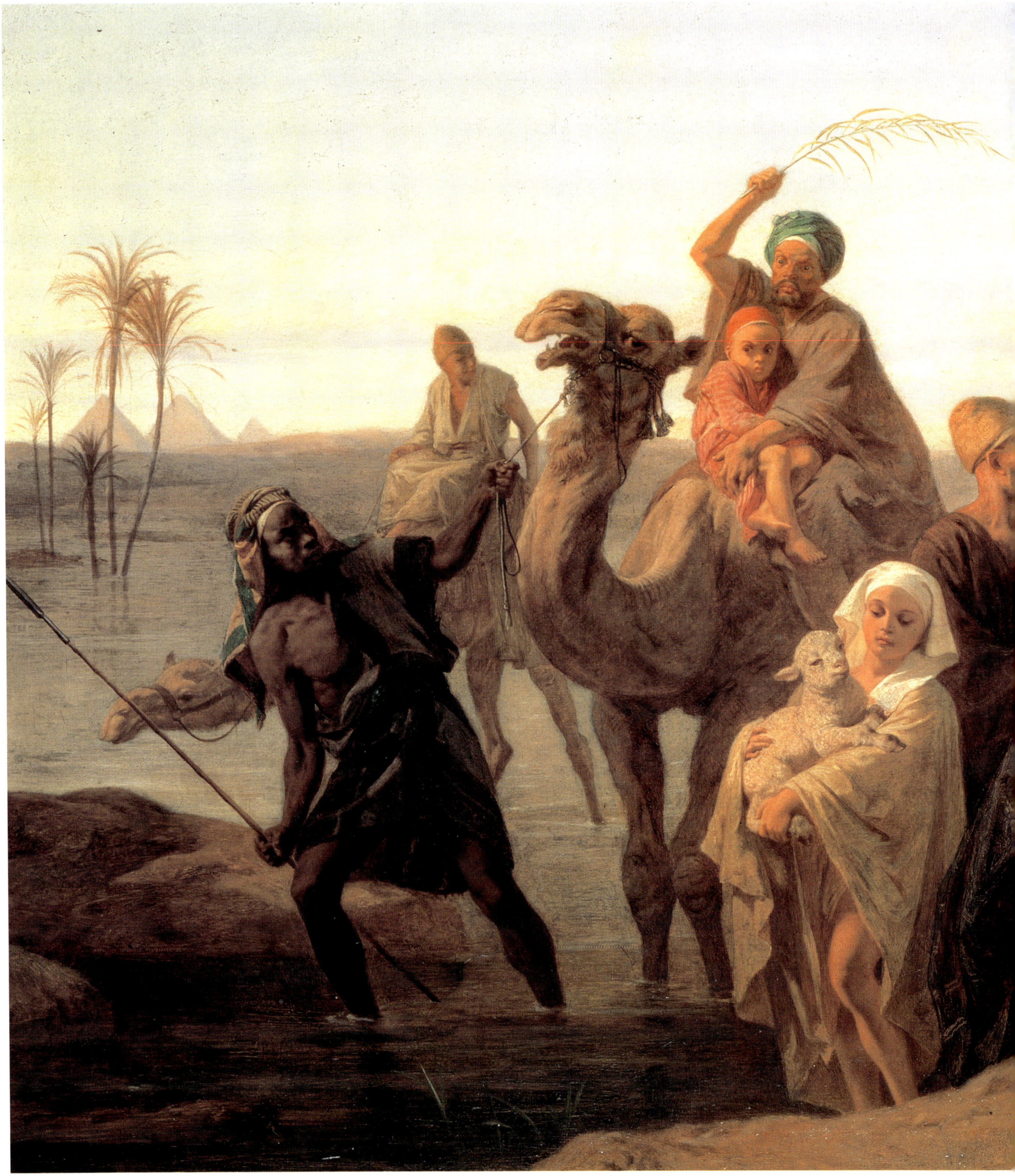

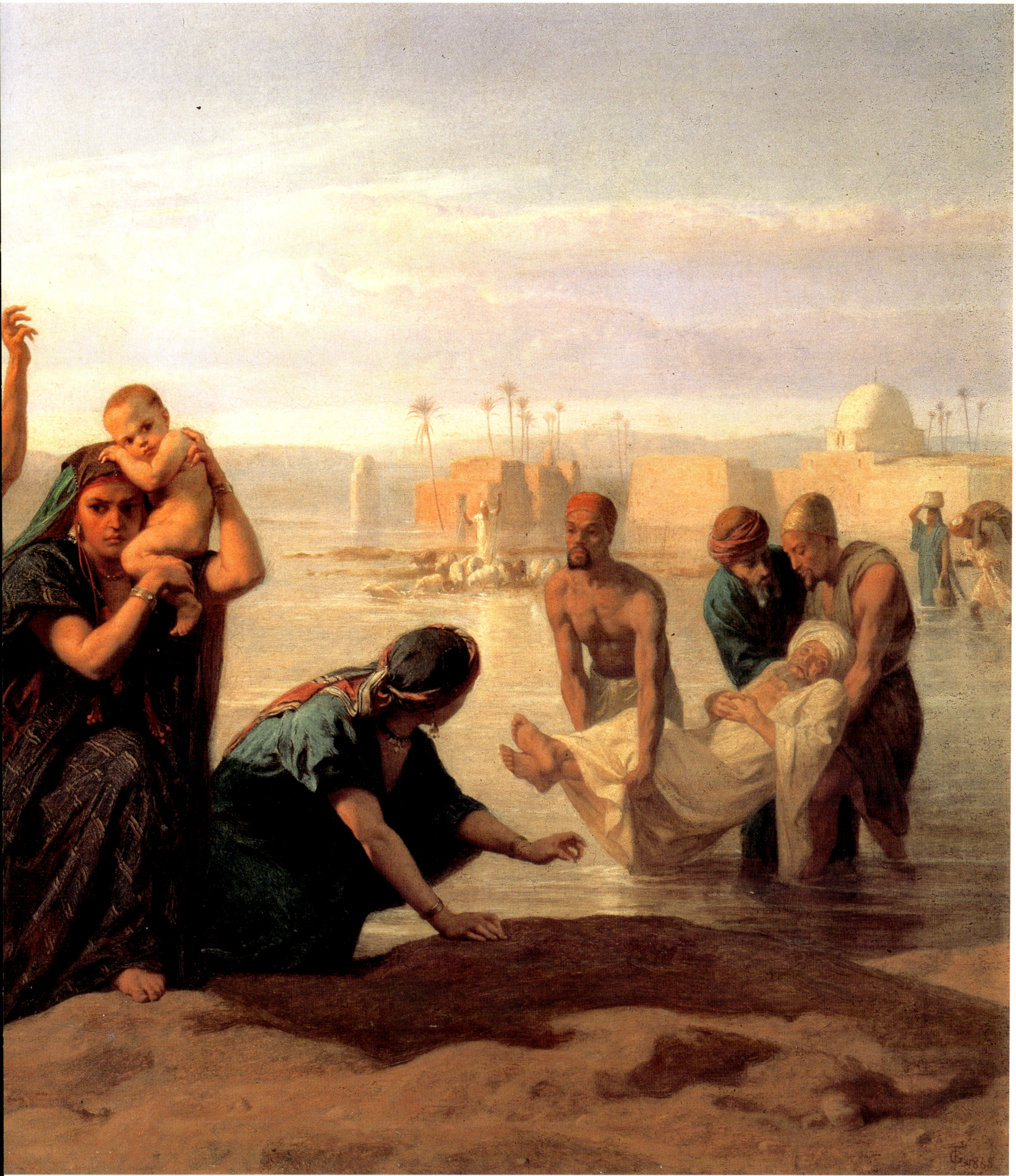

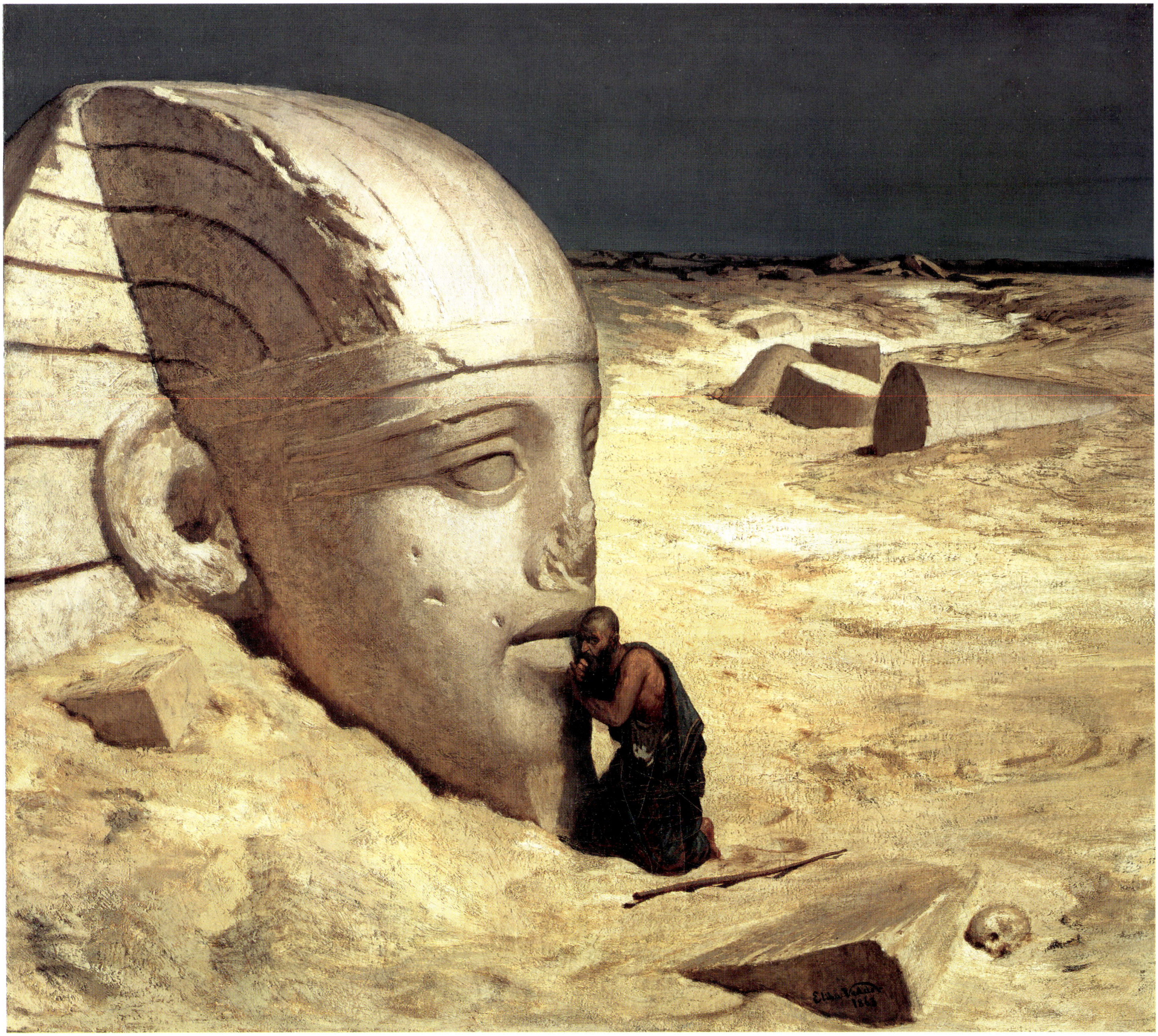

Previous double page
The Flood Waters of the Nile,
Frederick Goodall, 1865
Oil on canvas, private collecton (City Museum and Art Gallery, Bristol).

The Questioner of the Sphinx, Elihu Vedder, 1863
Oil on canvas, 91.5 x 106 cm
(Museum of Fine Arts, Boston).

(*Visit of the Ruins of the Temple at Karnak*, 1847; *The Ruins of the Temple at Karnak*, 1856); François Barry (*Sunset on the Pyramids*, 1873); Karl Paul von Eckenbrecker (*Sunset*, 1883); C.F.H. Werner (*Temple of the Goddess Mut, Karnak*, 1867; *The Portal between Courtyard of Isis and the Small Temple called the Pharaohs' Bed, Philae*, 1873); and Walter Prell (*The Kings' Temple*).

On occasions, one of these meticulous landscapists would seize the opportunity to transform what he saw into an arcane allegory. A striking example is *The Questioner of the Sphinx* (1863) by the American artist Elihu Vedder: a man on his knees turns an ear to the Giza Sphinx's stone mouth as he awaits an answer to his questions about the eternal mysteries of life. Like many others at this time, Vedder no longer regarded these monuments merely as mute witnesses of illustrious, far-distant historical dynasties, but as symbols of mysteries still very much alive in the Western imagination.

THE NEW GRAND TOUR

"Then I saw Cairo beneath me; to my right the desert with camels gliding along escorted by their shadows; ahead of me, beyond the floodplain and the Nile, the Pyramids."

Gustave Flaubert, *Voyage en Égypte*

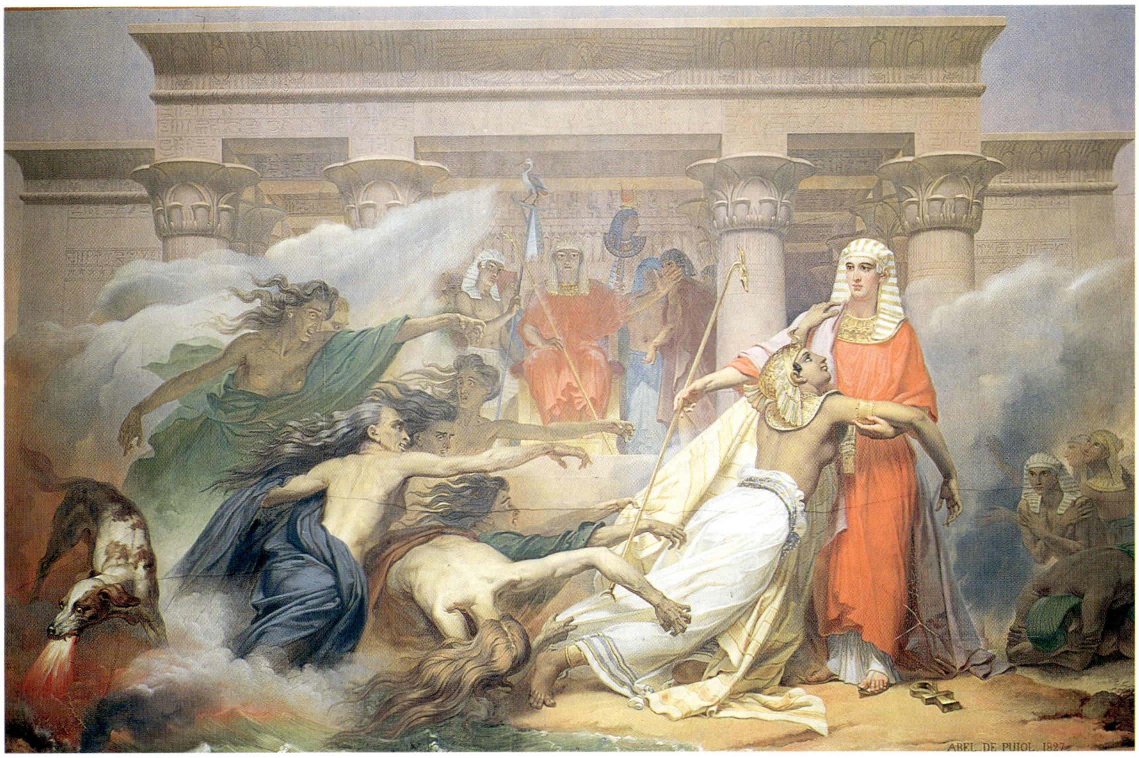

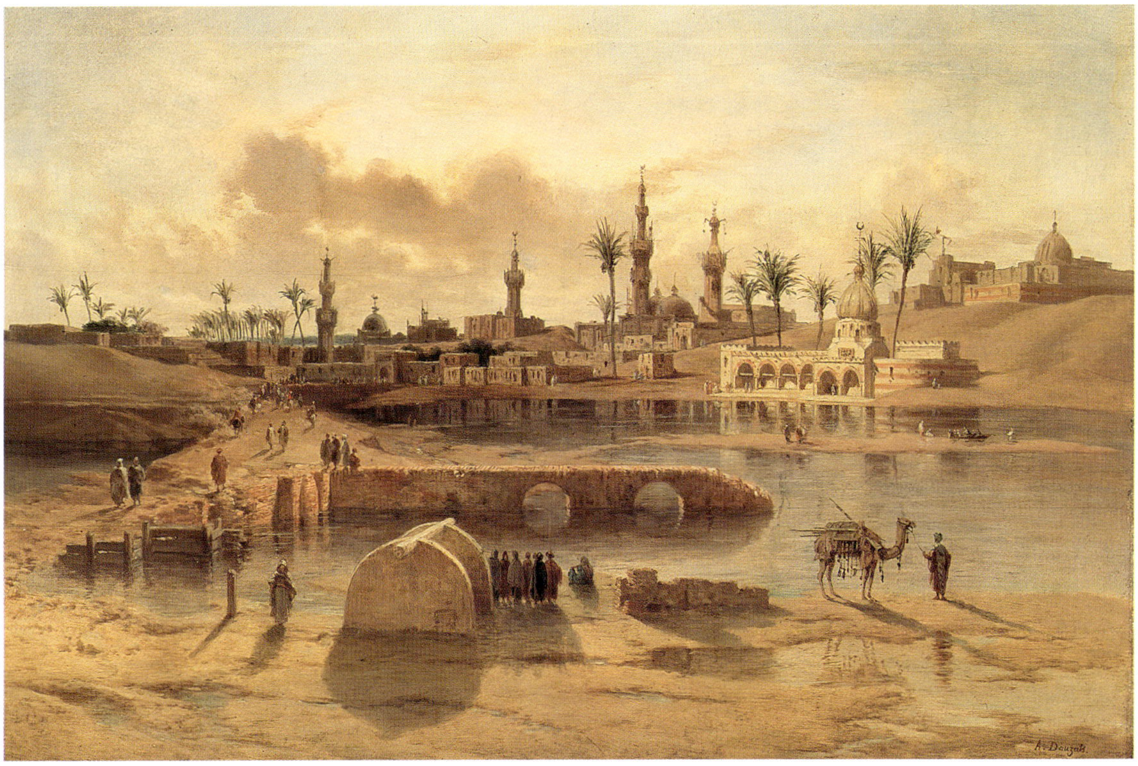

If Orientalism in French art can be given a formal date of inauguration, it was the year 1827: the official opening of the rooms dedicated to Egyptian artifacts in the Musée Charles X in Paris. The first room boasted a ceiling painted by François-Édouard Picot (*Learning and Genius Revealing Antic Egypt to Athens*), the second room a ceiling by Abel Pujol: *Egypt Saved by Joseph*. Despite this official sanction, however, it was the more popular Salon of that year that won over the Parisian public, with watercolors by Calande de Champmartin, who went to Cyprus, Jerusalem, and Constantinople and returned with a violent *Janissaries' Massacre* (1826), a brilliant pendant to the *Mamelukes' Massacre* exhibited by Horace Vernet at the 1821 Salon. Also on display was Champmartin's more pacific scene depicting a group of Turkish smokers, *Smokers in an Alleyway in Constantinople*, along with small canvases by Decamps that also depicted everyday urban scenes.

At this time, just as their predecessors had undertaken a Grand Tour of Italy on the advice of Goethe and Wincklemann, artists now began to travel to the Middle East, only rarely passing Egypt by as that was the land that had acquired a deeply mysterious and mythical nature. Between 1815 and 1817, Jules-Robert Auguste, a sculptor who had once been awarded the Prix de Rome, traveled all the way around the Mediterranean and returned both with some interesting pastels and an immoderate passion for all things Middle Eastern. In the early 1820s he brought together in his studio in Paris a range of fellow enthusiasts, among them Prosper Mérimée, author of *L'Amour africain* (1825) and *La Guzla* (1827); the artist Delacroix, whose *Turk Sitting on a Couch and Smoking* was completed around 1826; and the English painter Richard Parkes Bonington, who was just then starting on works inspired by the Middle East, such as the two charming watercolors *Turk Resting* and *Médora*. Bonington, though he never traveled beyond Italy, was helpful when Delacroix needed documentation to complete his *Massacres on Chios* (1824), lending him Eastern artifacts. The publication of Victor Hugo's poetry collection *Orientales* in 1829 gave artists one more reason to make exotic subjects an essential part of their work. Some would take their text directly from the poet's verses, notably Alexandre Colin with *Sara Bathing* (1838)

Egypt Saved by Joseph, Alexandre-Denis Abel de Pujol, 1827–1833
Painting on the ceiling of Room C of Egyptian Antiquities (Musée du Louvre, Paris).

View of Damanhur during the Flooding of the Nile, Adrien Dauzats, undated
Oil on canvas, 40 x 60 cm
(Guezireh Museum, Cairo).

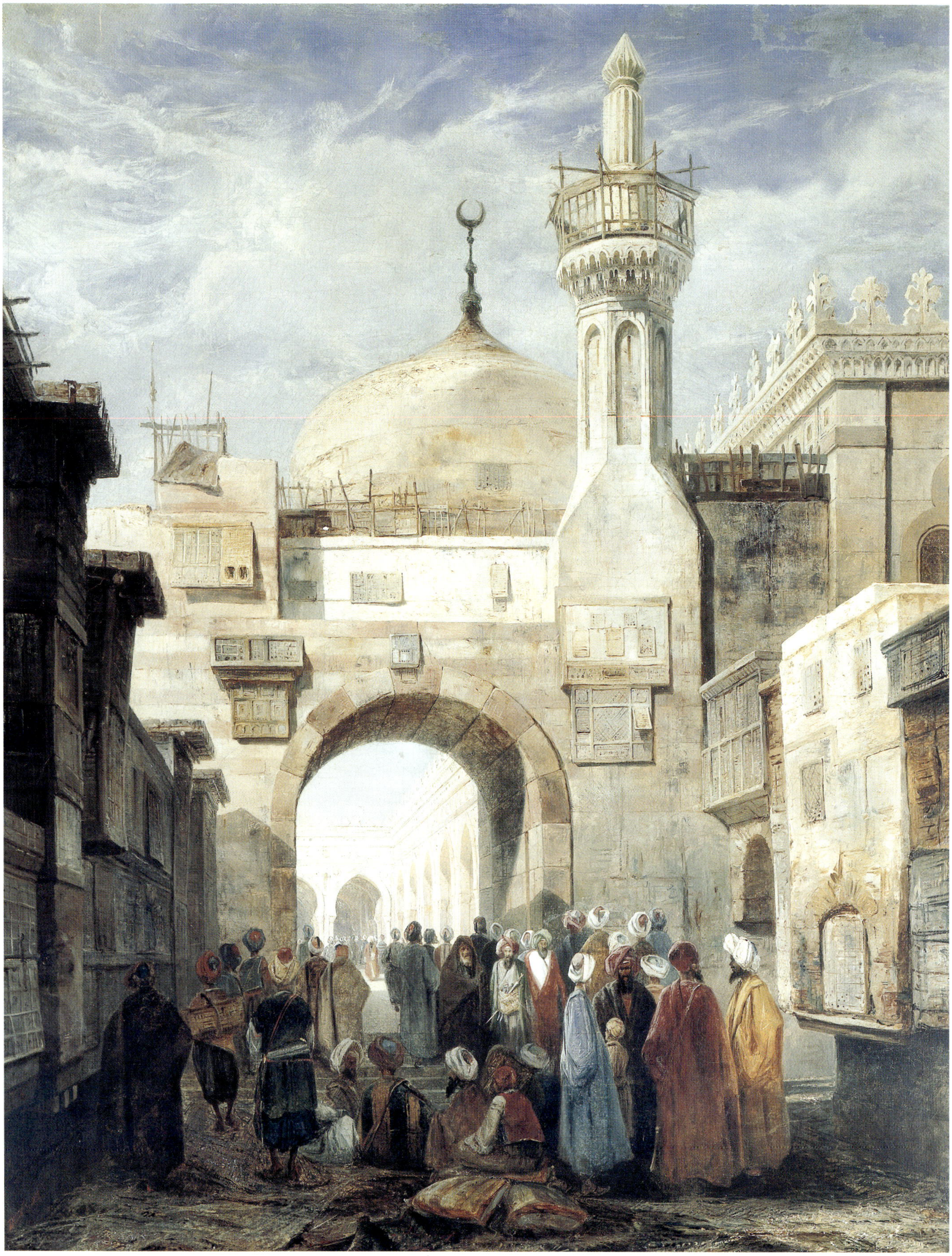

Mosque of Al Azhar in Cairo,
Adrien Dauzats, 1831
Oil on canvas, 100 x 80 cm
(Assemblée Nationale, Paris).

The Convent of St. Catherine at Mount Sinai,
Adrien Dauzats, c. 1845
Oil on canvas, 130 x 104 cm
(Musée du Louvre, Paris).

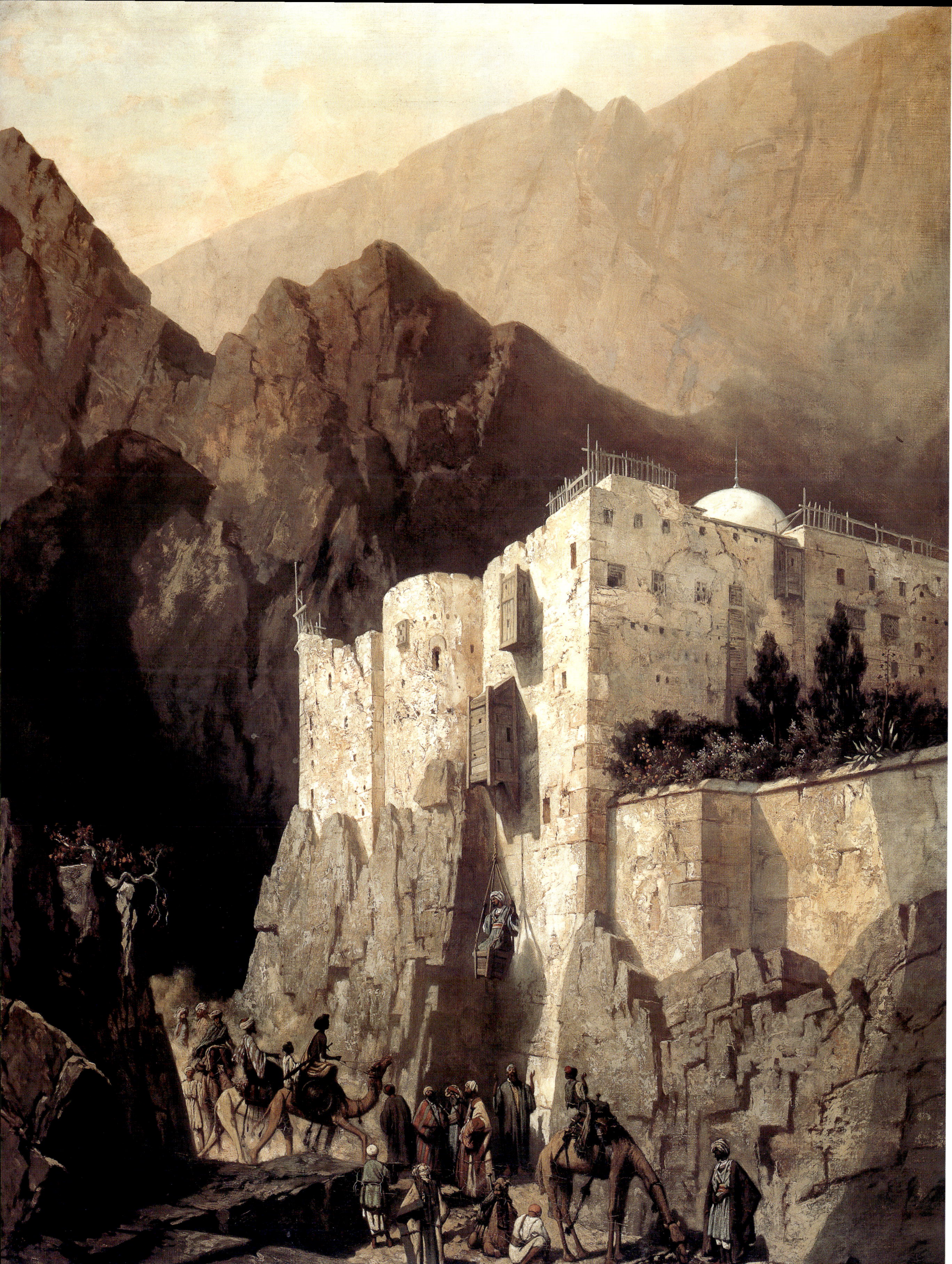

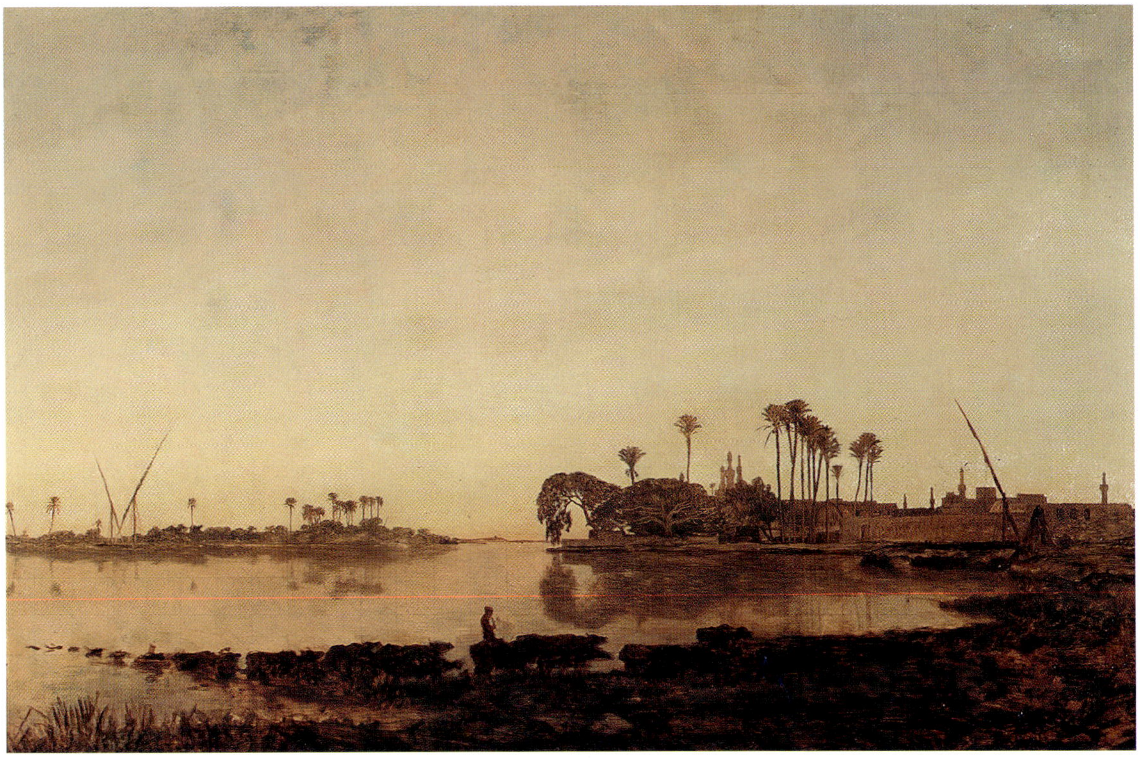

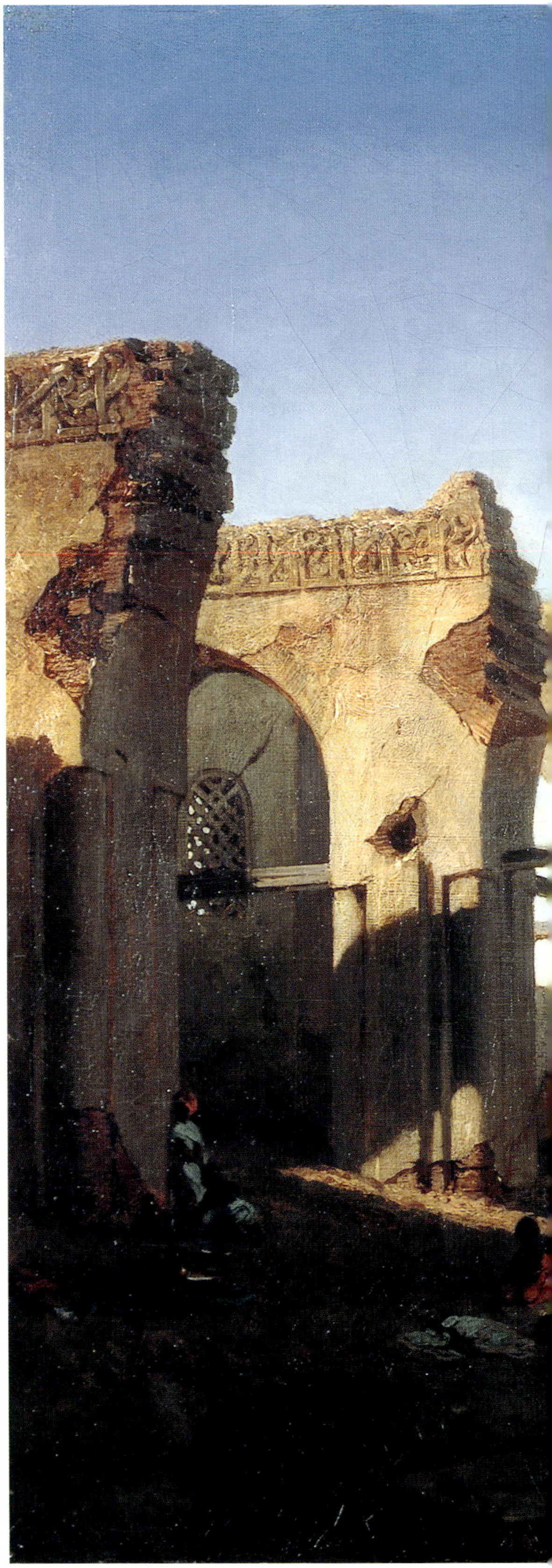

The Banks of the Nile at Damanhur,
Prosper Marilhat, c.1843–1844
Oil on wood, 31 x 45 cm
(Diplomatic Club, Cairo).

The Ruins of the El Hakim Mosque in Cairo,
Prosper Marilhat, 1840
Oil on canvas, 84.5 x 130.7 cm
(Musée du Louvre, Paris).

Previous double page
Syrian Arabs on a Journey,
Prosper Marilhat, 1844
Oil on wood, 28 x 50 cm
(Musée Condé, Chantilly).

and in due course Louis Boulanger, who painted *Fire from the Sky*.

While most painters were happy to create a Middle East they imagined from the comfort of their studios, assiduously collecting authentic artefacts, prints, and first-hand accounts of foreign travel, some did not shrink from setting sail from Marseilles on an adventure in search of new subjects and new experiences.

Adrien Dauzats from Bordeaux was without doubt a pathfinder for this kind of expedition, which was far from trouble- or danger-free. In 1830 he had the opportunity to go to Egypt for six months with Baron Taylor, who was both soldier and archaeologist. Dauzats had already worked with him, providing the illustrations for Taylor's attractive *Voyages pittoresques et romantiques dans l'ancienne France* (Picturesque and romantic travels in the France of old). Taylor was in Egypt to negotiate with Mehmed Ali the transportation to France of the Luxor Obelisk. Dauzats and Taylor visited the Nile valley and stayed in Sinai, where Dauzats fell under the spell of Saint Catherine's Convent, which he painted several times between 1845 and 1850. Keen to portray contemporary Arab life, he went out of his way to depict Muslim monuments, as in *Sultan Kalaoun's Grave in Moristan, Cairo*, and *Fountain by Sultan Hanan's Mosque*, which appeared in the Salon of 1836.

The French artist Prosper Marhilat left for the Levant in April 1831, accompanying Baron von Hügel, a wealthy military man who had switched his interests from war to politics and amateur botany. The two men first visited Greece and then Egypt, taking the opportunity to pass through Syria, the

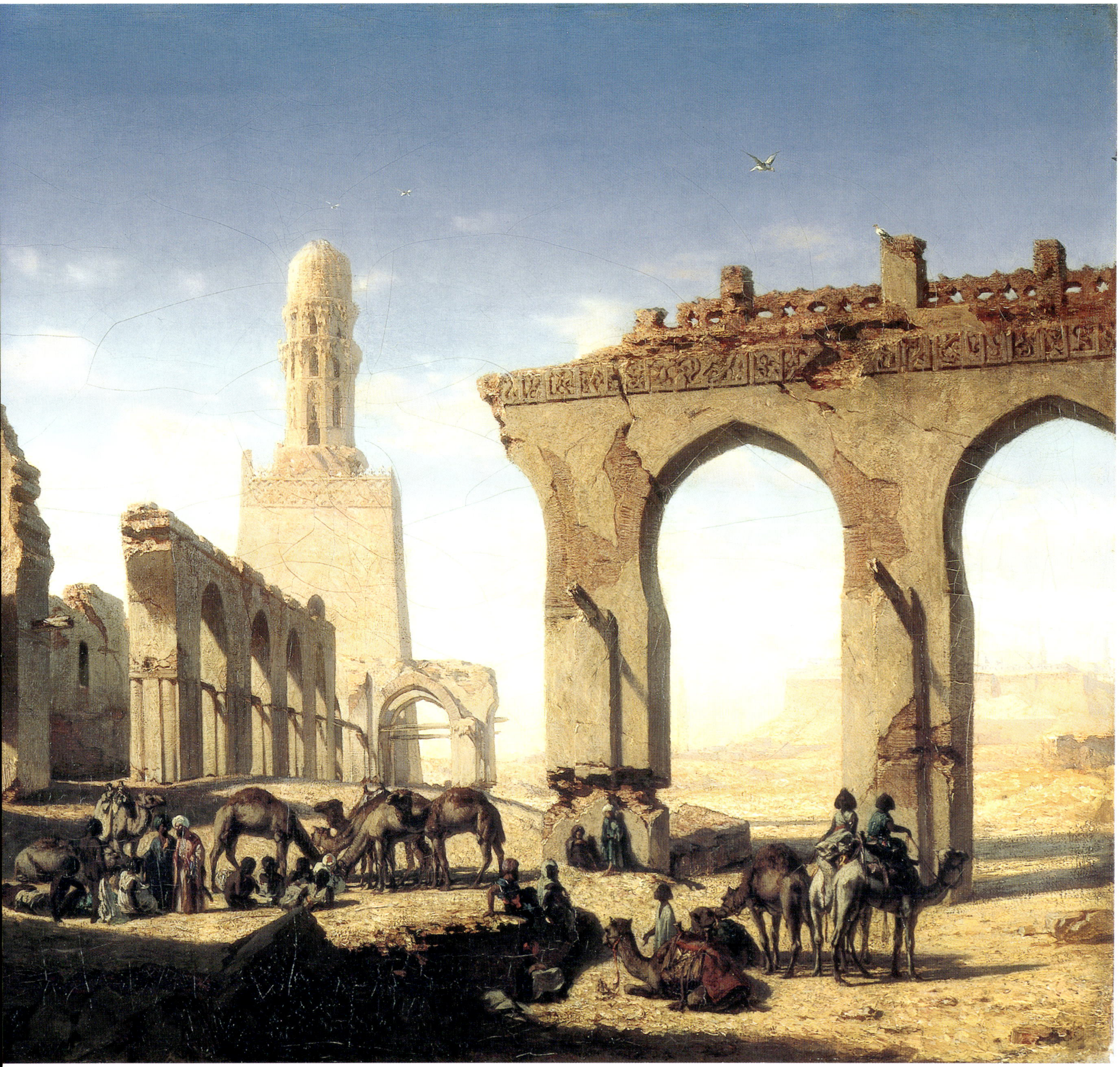

Lebanon, and Palestine. Marhilat was fascinated by Egypt, to which he returned at the end of 1832, living in Alexandria and just about making a living from a few commissions. He painted the portrait of Sultan Mehmed Ali, patron of the arts, and of the great Egyptologist Prisse d'Avennes. He was also asked to design sets for the city theater, but at this point began his travels in the Nile Delta. The result was that when he returned to France in May 1833 on board the *Sphinx*, the ship transporting the Luxor Obelisk, Marilhat, who had been drawn to Egypt by "the stark figures of its ancient hieroglyphs" and "their grotesque granite faces," returned with a completely different view, purged of the dusty weight of archaeology. His submissions to the 1834 Salon were accepted and warmly received. Théophile Gautier was enthralled by one of his paintings, *Esbekieh Square*, and wrote that this evocation of the Coptic quarter caused him "to pine for a Middle East, where I have never set foot. I felt I had just recognized my true homeland, so that when I took my eyes off the enchanted painting I felt an exile." He would mention it again in the long

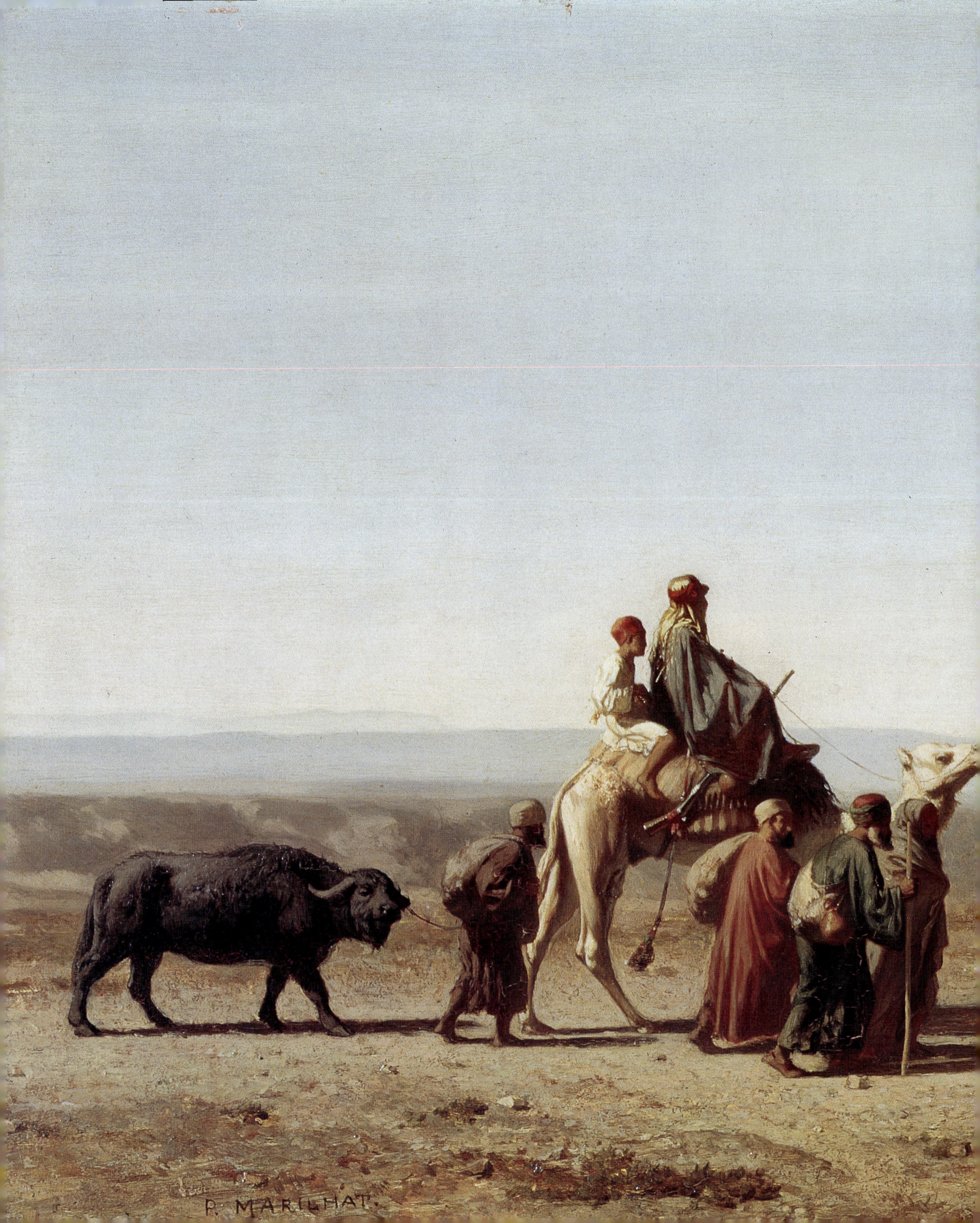
P. MARILHAT.

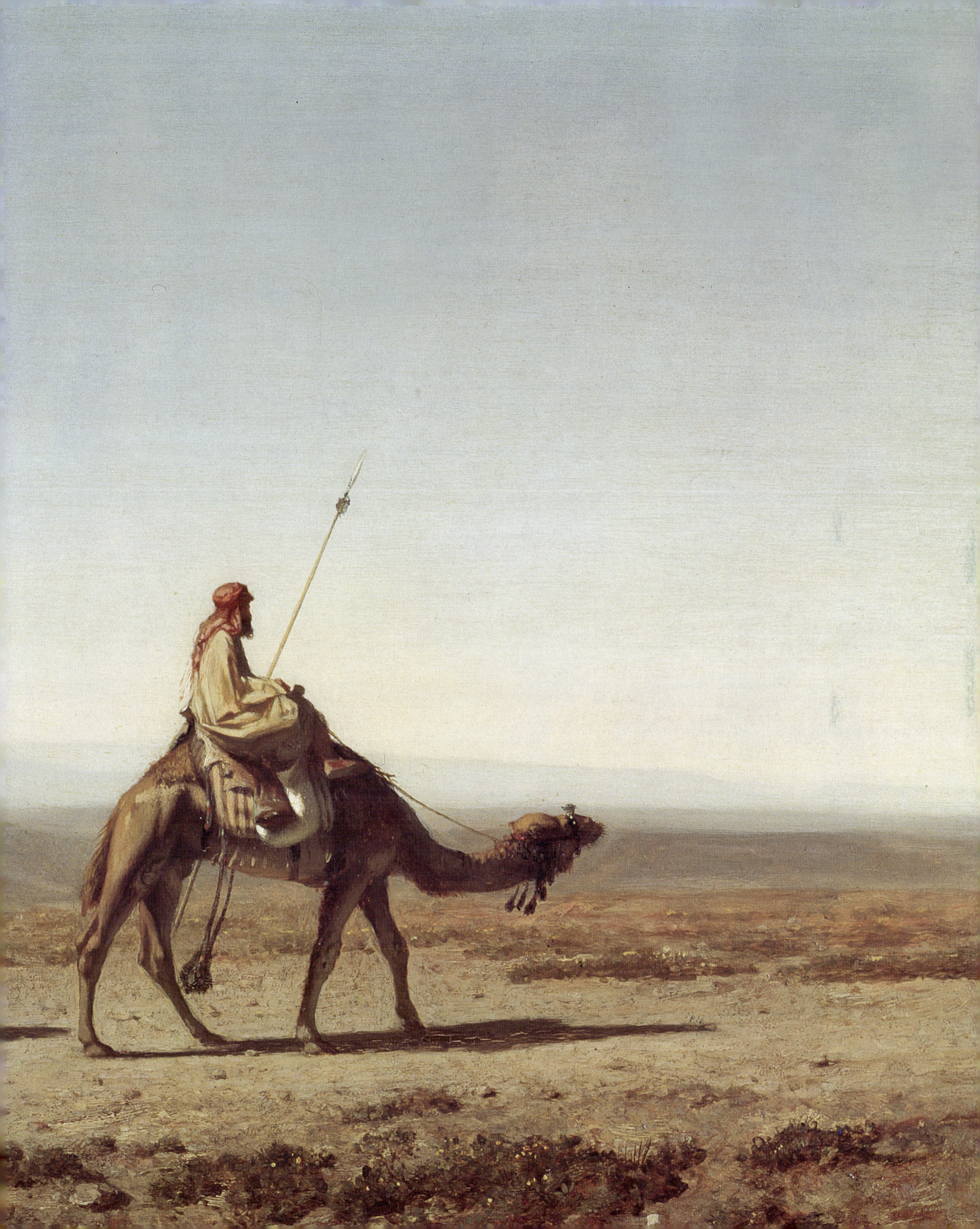

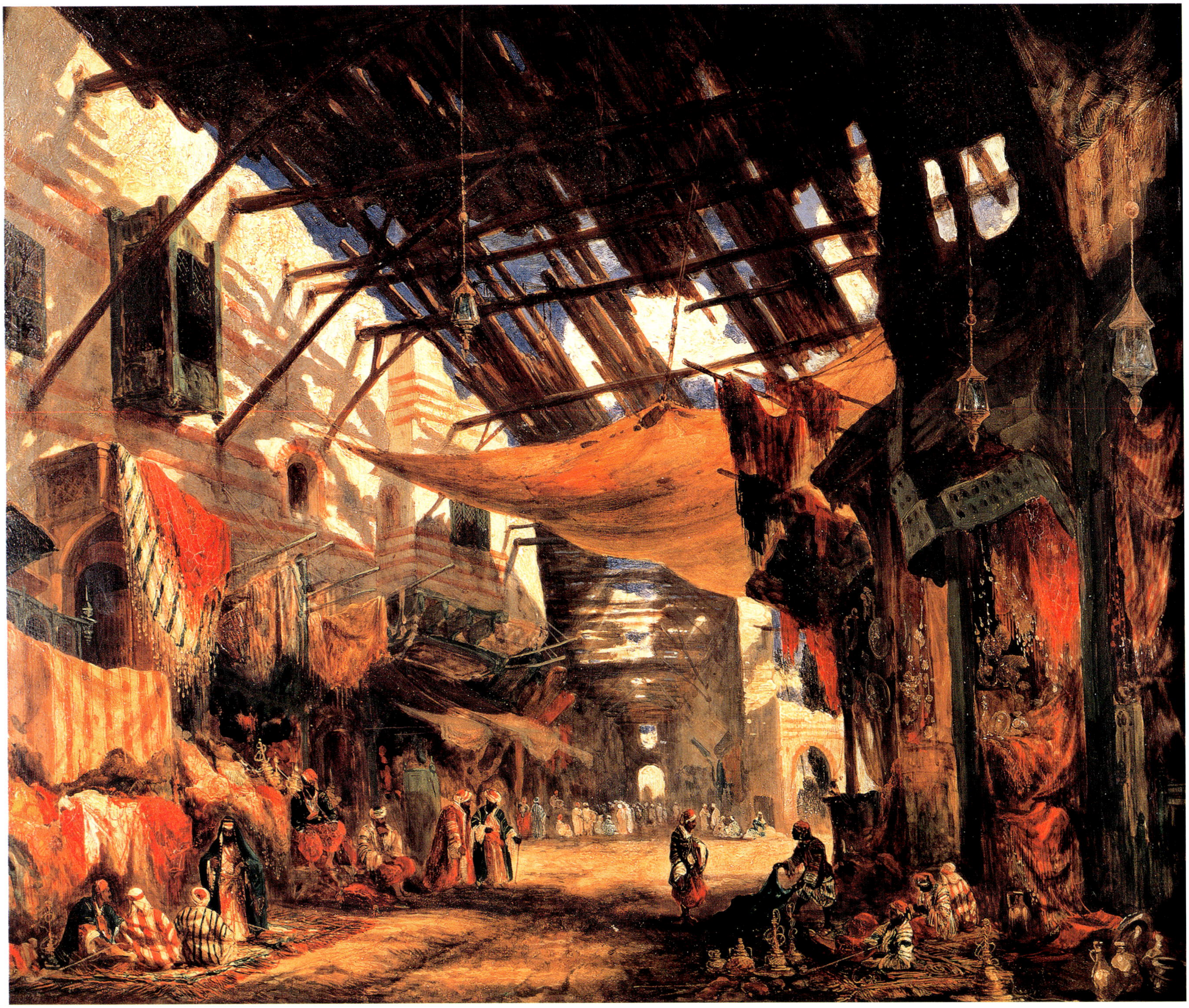

article he dedicated to the artist, who died prematurely in 1847, in the journal *Revue des Deux-Mondes*. In this moving homage, an obituary brimming with warm friendship and light on solemnity, Gautier quoted several of the painter's letters, which told of his many very real difficulties, but also of his enchantment with the sights set before him: "Try to imagine in the midst of this desolation three or four thousands camels, white, red, black, eating the dried grass and scattered over the plain like as many dots; a Bedouin camp made up of twenty or thirty black tents, uniformly black, made of camel hair, thrown together in no particular order..." His letters give a good impression of his paintings. In 1840, Marilhat painted *The Ruins of the El Hakem Mosque in Cairo*, in which he shows himself wonderfully adept at capturing the play of light. He was a great success at the 1844 Salon with his *Souvenir of the Banks of the Nile, Village near Rosetta, Egyptian Town at Nightfall, Café on a Syrian Road*, and *View from Tripoli*. He toyed with the idea of returning to Egypt but the mental illness that beset him suddenly took a turn for the worst and he died in Paris quite insane.

The Swiss painter Marc-Gabriel-Charles Gleyre, who spent a year in Upper Egypt from 1835 to 1836, was amazed at the number of artists who, like him, had rushed to the country in search of new themes: "I don't know where to go," he wrote in his diary, "to avoid the society of fellow painters. I find here at least a dozen of them all brimming with talent, if they are to be believed. They have ruined Cairo for me." He traveled along the banks of the Nile as far as Nubia. At Abydos, he sketched *Lost Illusions*. At Aswan, he wrote: "Must remember the little girl on the Nile at Philae..." Upon reaching Abu Simbel he exclaimed: "what peace, what silence; the broad river flows majestically; the palm trees swing their disheveled heads gracefully. The softened forms of the temple mountain assumes this night a more imposing air..."

Gleyre was not exaggerating: painters were flocking in droves to this part of the world. Théodore Frère, who already knew Algeria well, discovered Egypt in 1851 after a journey to Constantinople and Syria. He returned in 1869 with Empress Eugénie's retinue and completed a series of 13 watercolors. Among the Orientalist paintings he exhibited at the Salon are *Philae* (1869), *Charity in a Cairo Street* (c. 1855), *A Market near Cairo*, and *At Cairo's Gates*. The British artist William James Müller spent several years in Cairo, painting popular subjects like *The Carpet Bazaar in Cairo* (1843) and *The Market at Cairo's Gates*. Stefano Ussi, a hero of the Risorgimento, the movement to unify Italy, left Italy when he found his political ideals betrayed. A disappointed man, he lived as an exile in Egypt, changed his style and worked mainly on small oil paintings. When he eventually returned to Italy, he continued to paint orientalist compositions. Meanwhile, the British artist Henry Wallis pored over the Arab world through the fastidious magnifying glass of the Pre-Raphaelite Brotherhood.

The British were indeed the most numerous visitors to this artistic new world. British governments had long been aware of Egypt's commercial and strategic importance, and British artists were keen to explore the many cultures that had mingled there. Edward Lear gave Orientalism a new impetus by bringing to it a very personal touch. This outstanding figure, famous for his nonsense limericks and his ornithological expertise, had begun his career by painting exotic birds for the London Zoological Society and private patrons before

The Carpet Bazaar in Cairo,
William James Müller, 1843
Oil on wood, 62.2 x 74.9 cm
(City Museum and Art Gallery, Bristol).

Dancing Fakir, Stefano Ussi, undated
Oil on wood, 23 x 35 cm (Palazzo Pitti, Galleria d'Arte Moderna, Florence).

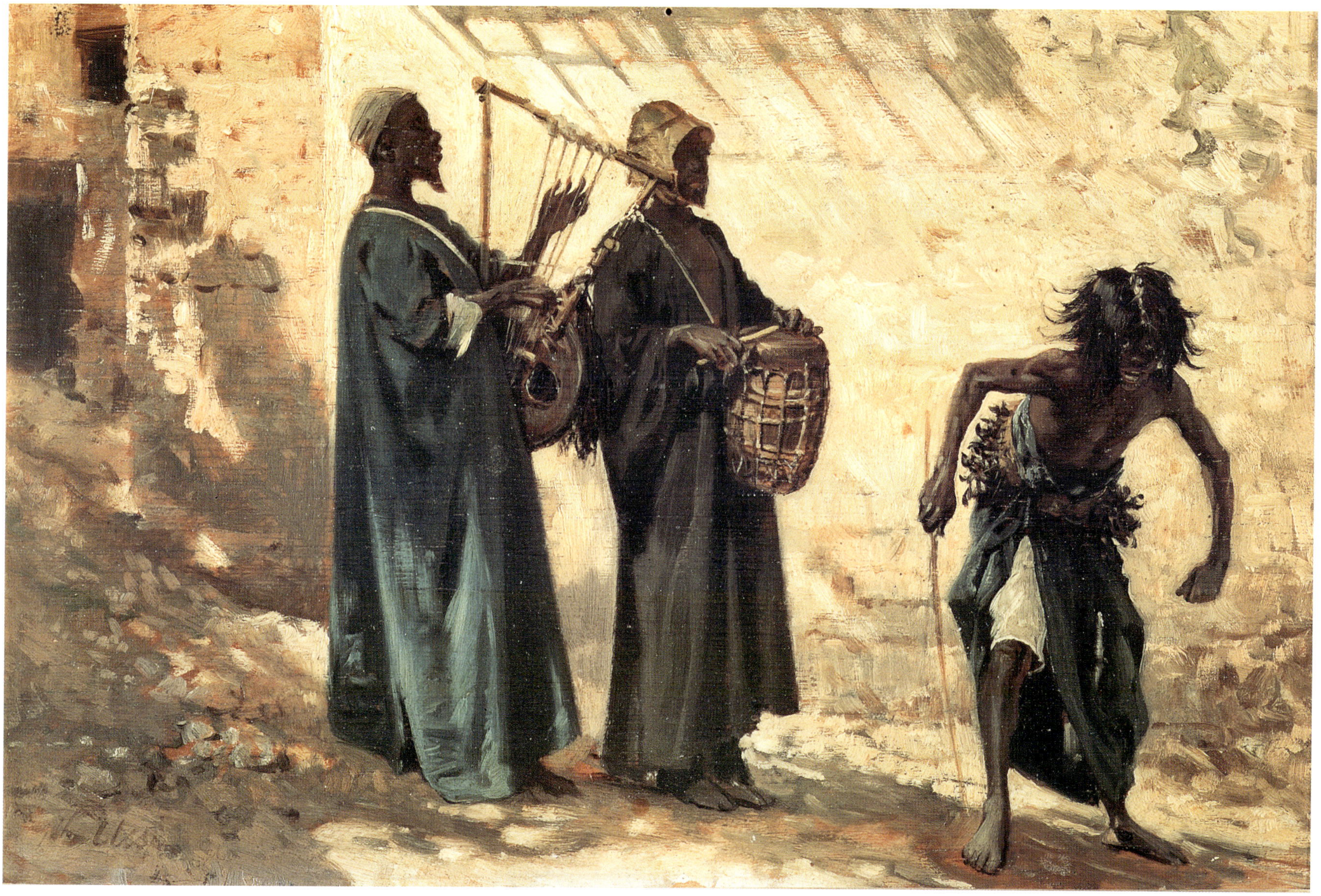

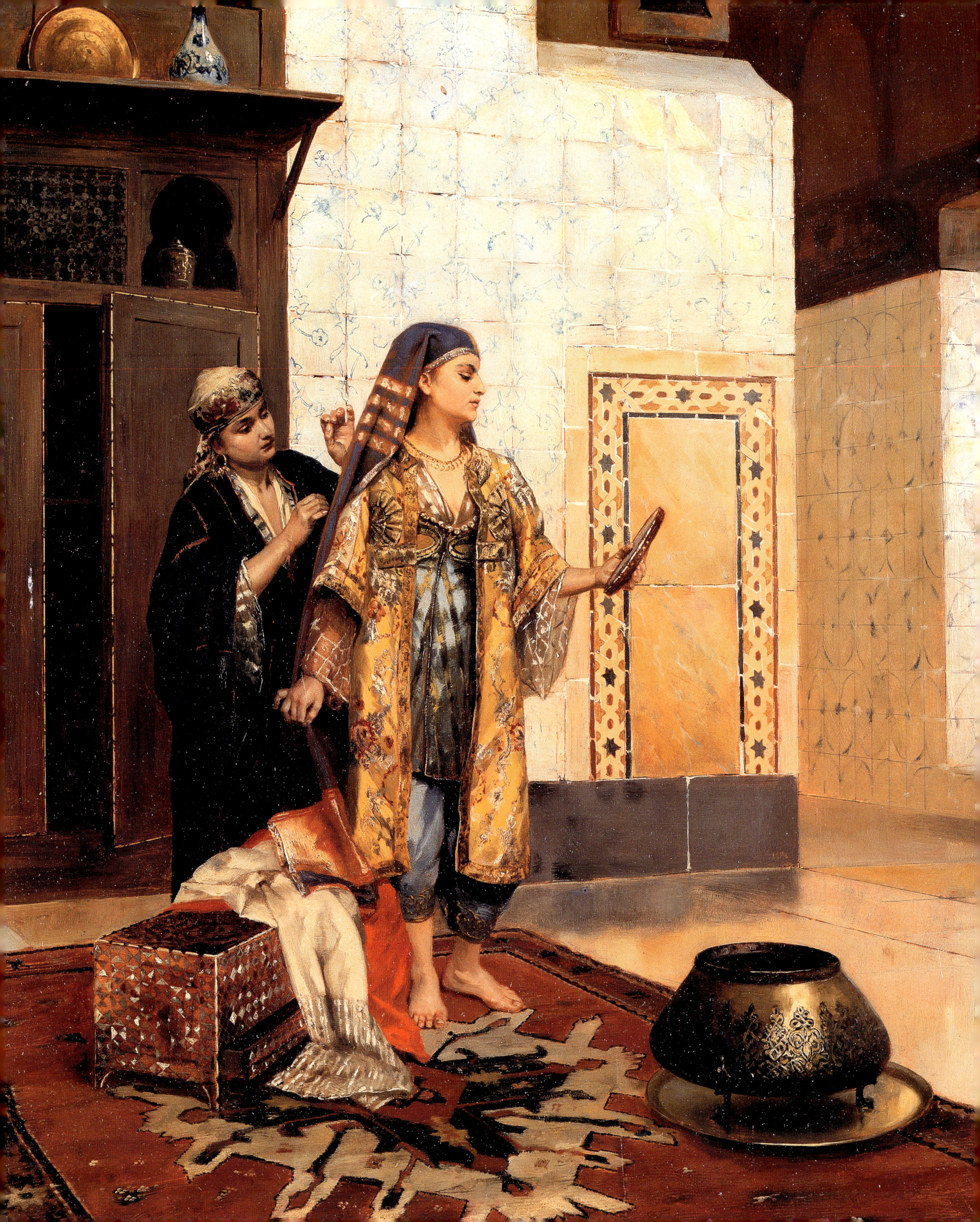

After the Bath, Rudolf Ernst, 1889
Oil on paneling, 61 x 48.2 cm
(private collection).

Inside Sheik Sadat's Harem (Cairo),
Franck Dillon,
Watercolor, 75 x 57 cm (Victoria and
Albert Museum, London).

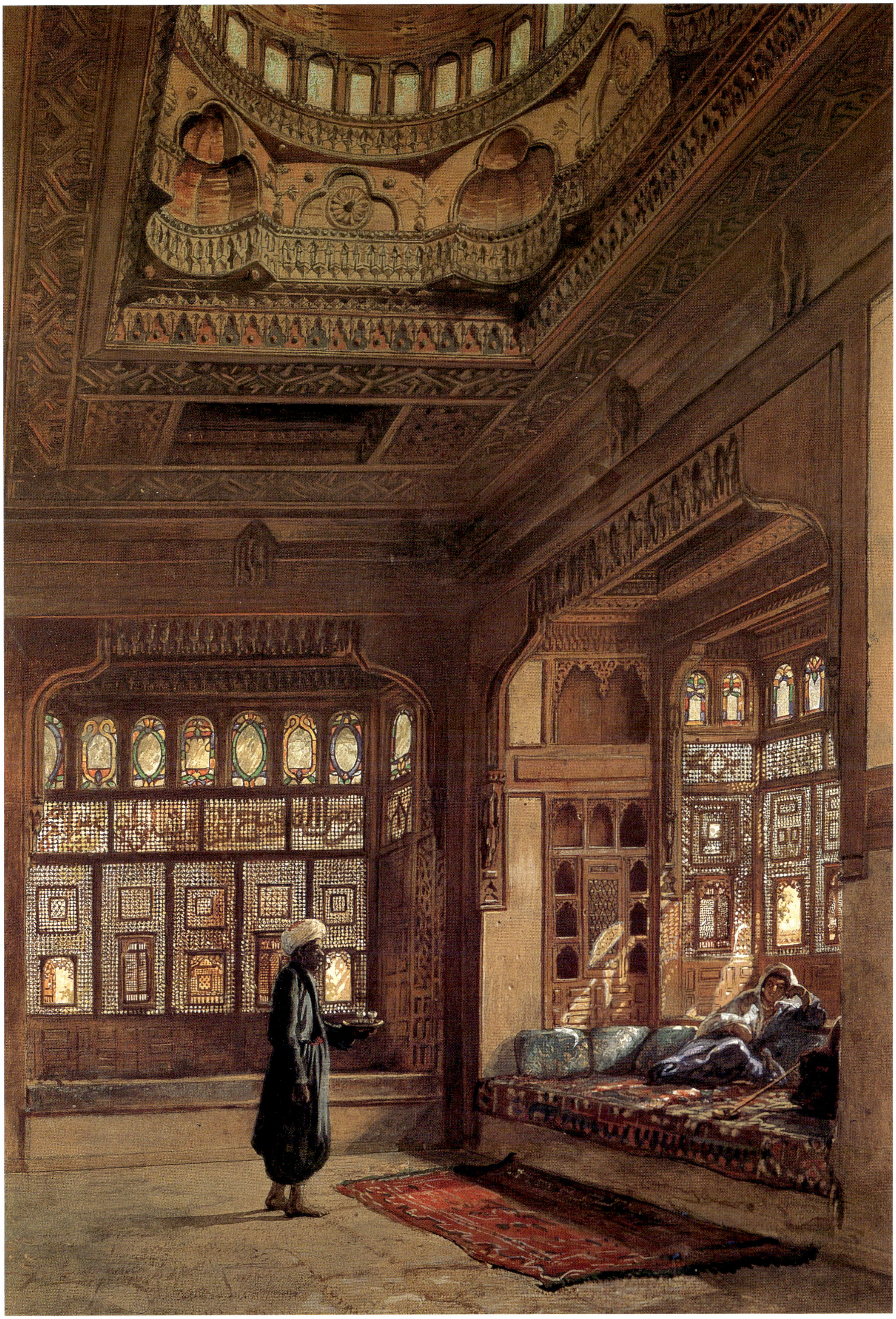

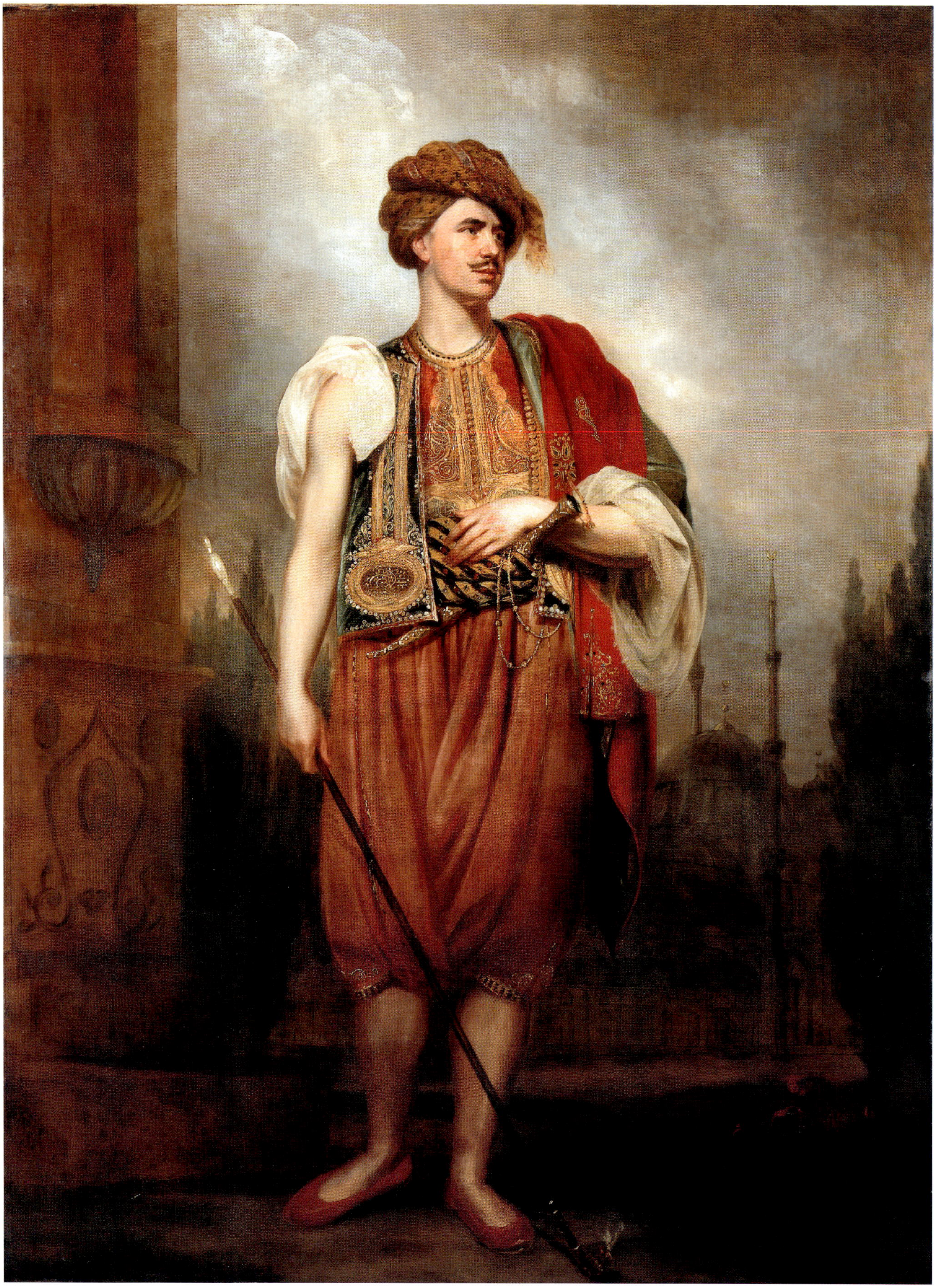

The Hookah Smoker, Rudolf Ernst,
Oil on paneling, 46 x 37 cm
(private collection).

The Brass Workers, Rudolf Ernst, c. 1888
Oil on wood, 61.6 x 48.9 cm
(Dahesh Museum, New York).

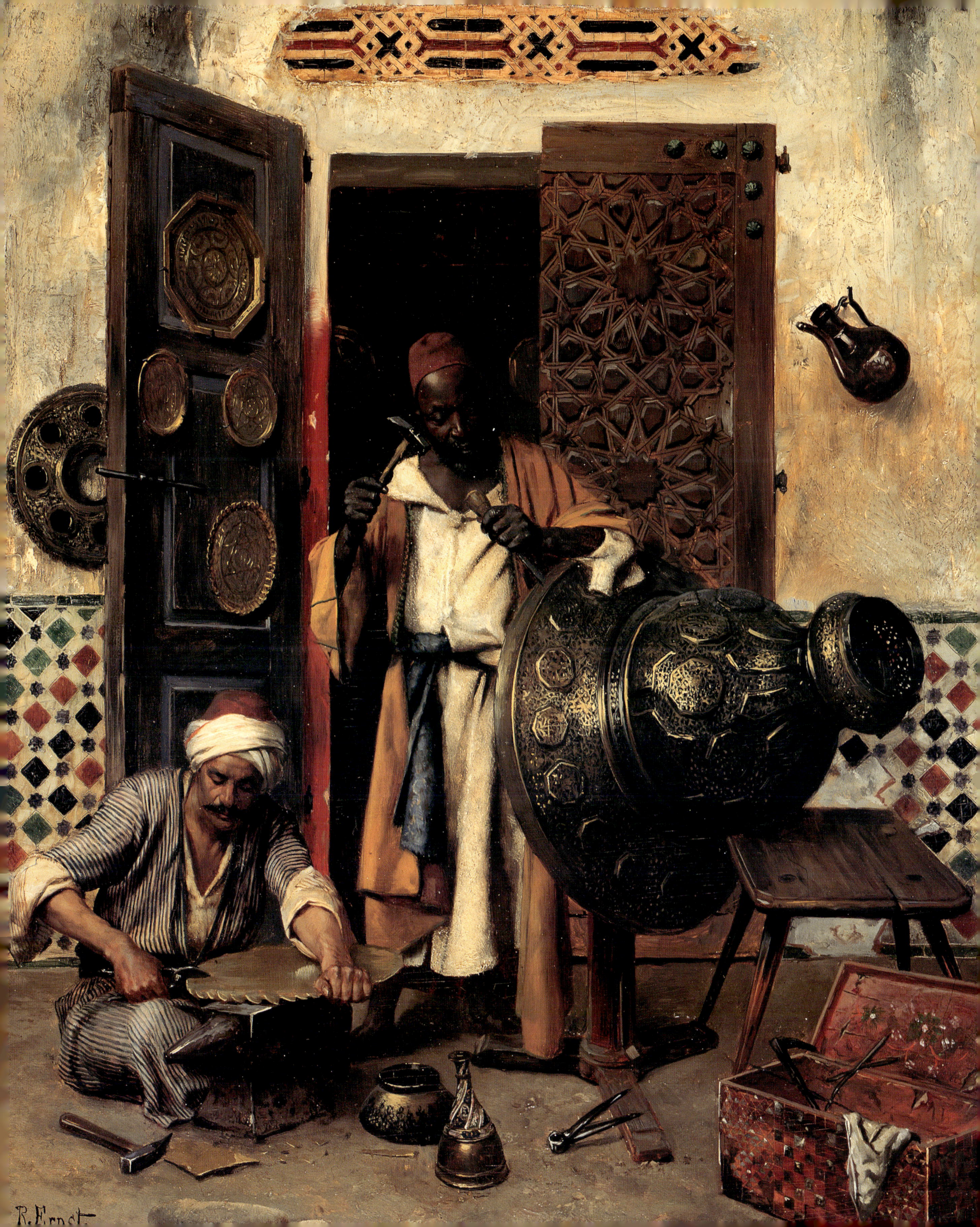
R. Ernst.

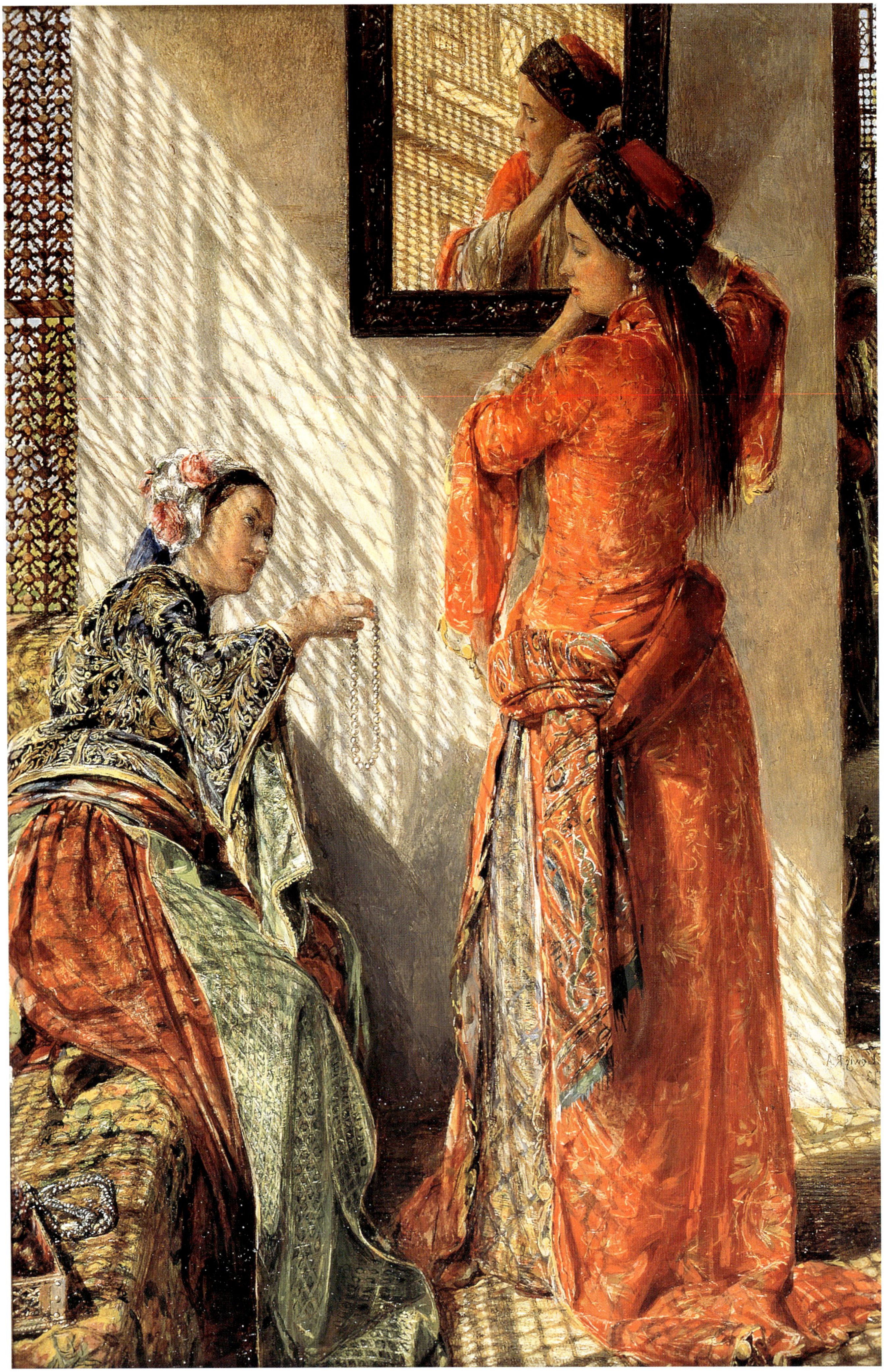

Private Conversation,
John Frederick Lewis, 1873
Oil on wood, 30.5 x 20.5 cm
(The Whitworth Art Gallery, Manchester).

Imaginary Egyptian Harem,
Richard Dadd, 1865
Watercolor on colored paper with white highlights, 27.5 x 17.9 cm
(Ashmolean Museum, Oxford).

turning to landscape. As his health was poor, he had to seek warmer climates, and so traveled widely, his first voyages talking him to southern Europe, the islands of the Mediterranean, Turkey, and the east coast of Africa. In 1851, he published his *Illustrated Journals of a Landscape Painter in Albania and Illyria*. He then traveled to Constantinople and finally embarked for Egypt; he would sail up the Nile on several occasions. He loved the island of Philae and produced several watercolors of it, one of the best known being *Philae seen from the Opposite bank of the Nile*. He was always on the lookout for an unexpected view of a subject, which he would sometimes find after hours spent walking, or scanning the landscape with field glasses. He would then rapidly draw numerous sketches. The resulting paintings, fresh as the original sketches, stand out for their unparalleled individuality of vision. A fine example is his sensational *The Pyramids Road, Gizah* (1873), in which the road to Cairo, shown sheltered by overarching trees, is teeming with merchants and travelers.

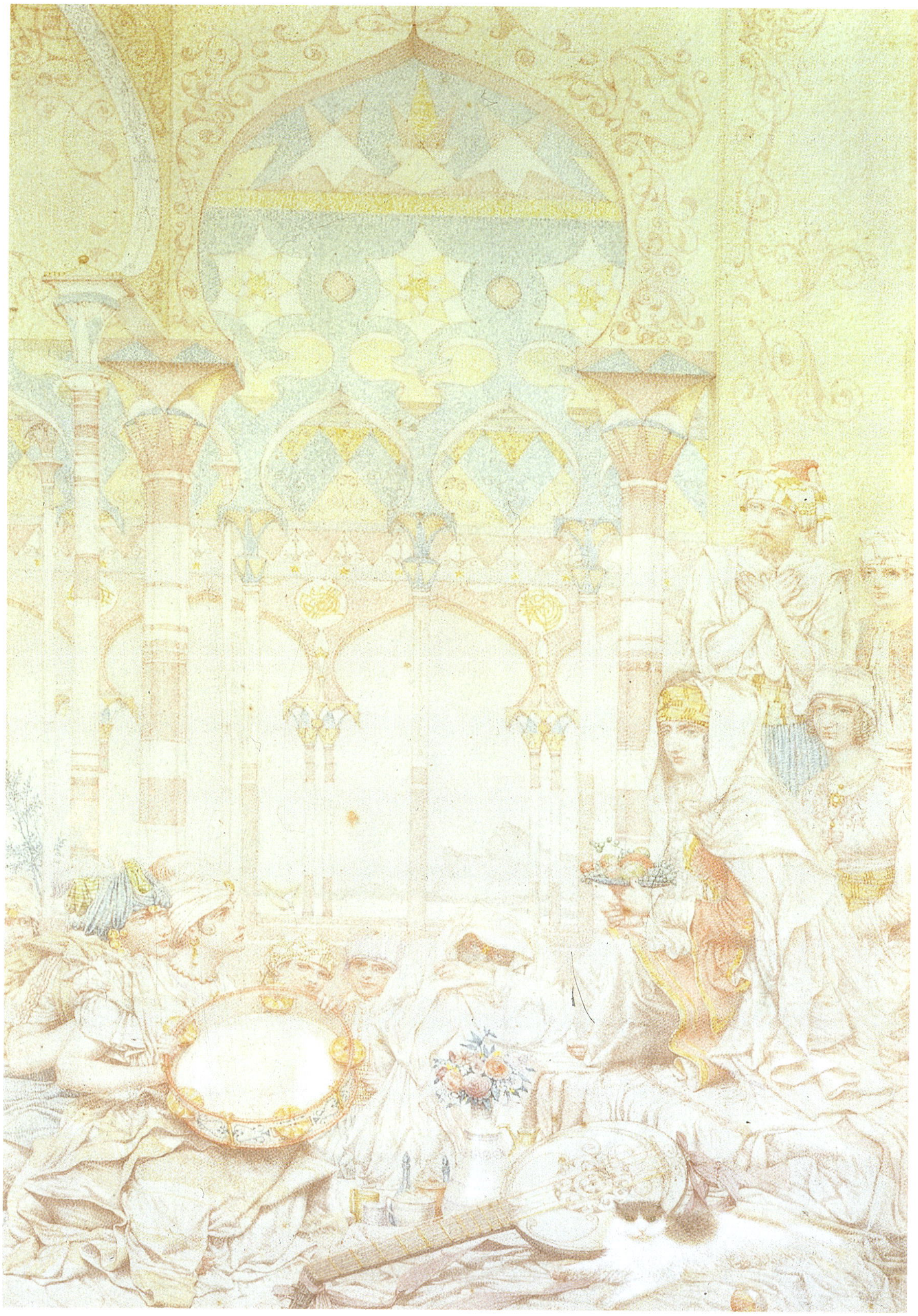

John Frederick Lewis, son of an engraver whose passion for animals he shared, had soon made his mark as an artist, exhibiting at the Royal Academy in London when only 21. After this first success he turned his attention to watercolor. He toured Spain in 1823, bringing back a project for two volumes of lithographs. In 1837 he set off to visit Paris and then Italy, where for two years he lived in Rome. He then traveled through Albania and Greece to Constantinople, which so fascinated him that he stayed for nearly a year. Finally, he embarked for Egypt, where he was to stay ten years, an unusual length of time for a Western artist of that period. Living in a fine house in the Esbekieh suburb, not far from Sultan Hassan's mosque, he played host to his many friends, among them the novelist William Thackeray, who in *A Journey from Cornhill to Grand Cairo* describes him as a "Lotus-eater," dressed in a "long yellow gown, with a long beard, somewhat tinged with grey, with his head shaved, and wearing on it first a white wadded cotton night-cap, second, a red tarboosh..." A man who wholeheartedly adopted an Eastern lifestyle, and loved the desert above all else, Lewis devoted himself completely to depicting the extraordinary beauty and splendor of life in Egypt. This artist's works include *An Intercepted Correspondence, Cairo* (1869), *And Faith will Save the Sick* (1872), *The Hósh (Courtyard) of the House of the Coptic Patriarch* (1864), and *The Midday Meal, Cairo* (1875). He endowed such intimate scenes of public and family life with an unparalleled splendor, stressing the opulence of architectural and the decorative arts, the magnificence of the costumes, and the majesty of the people, whether they were dignitaries, mere passers-by, or even beggars, as in *The Carpet Seller* (1860) and *View of the Street of Al-Ghouri Mosque* (1876). In *Harem* (1858) and *Life in the Harem* (1858) he created works that are at once sensual and realistic. Lewis devoted his artistic life to sharing his deep love for a country he knew

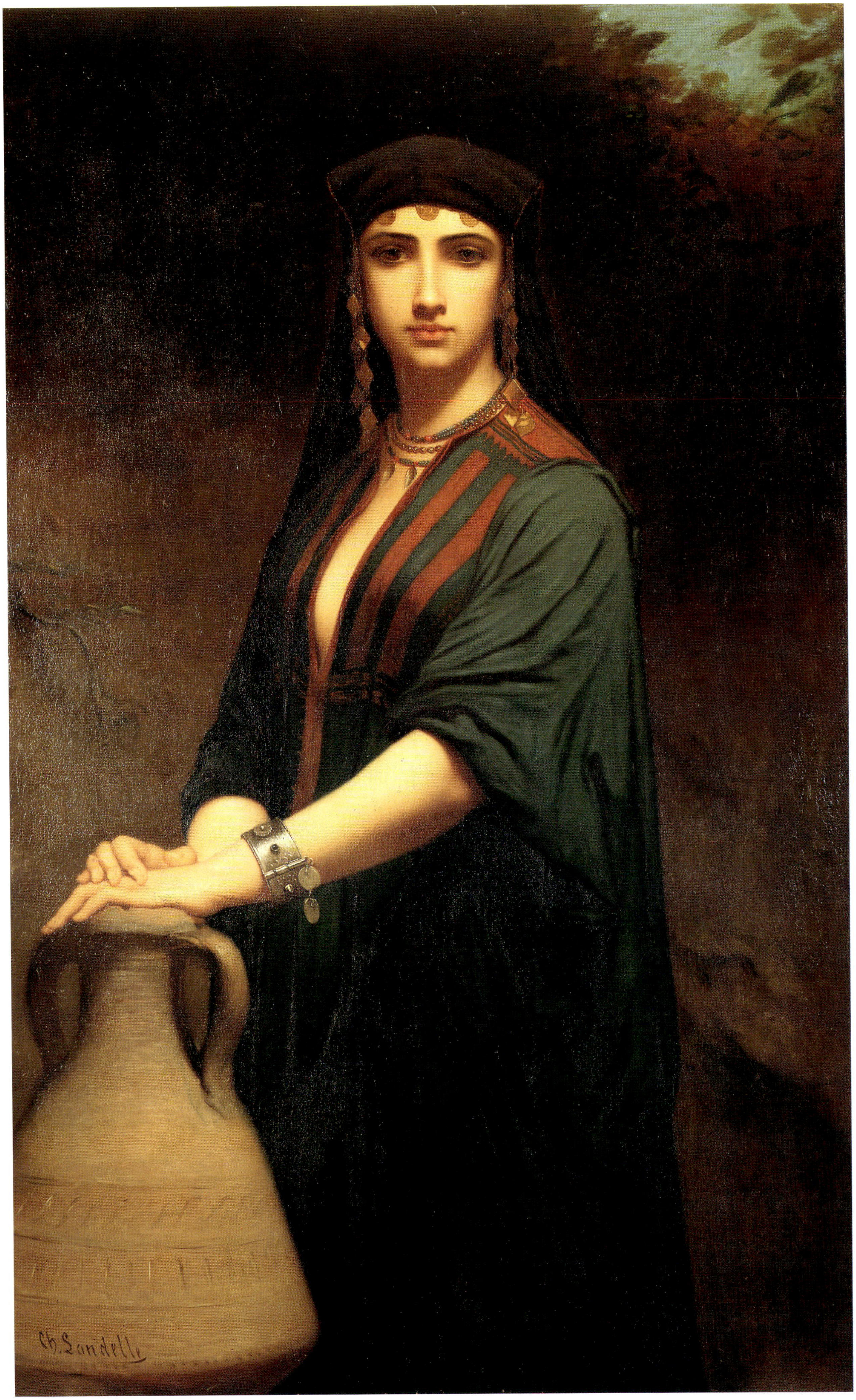

Peasant Woman, Charles Landelle, 1866
Oil on canvas, 131.5 x 84 cm
(Musée du Vieux-Château, Laval).

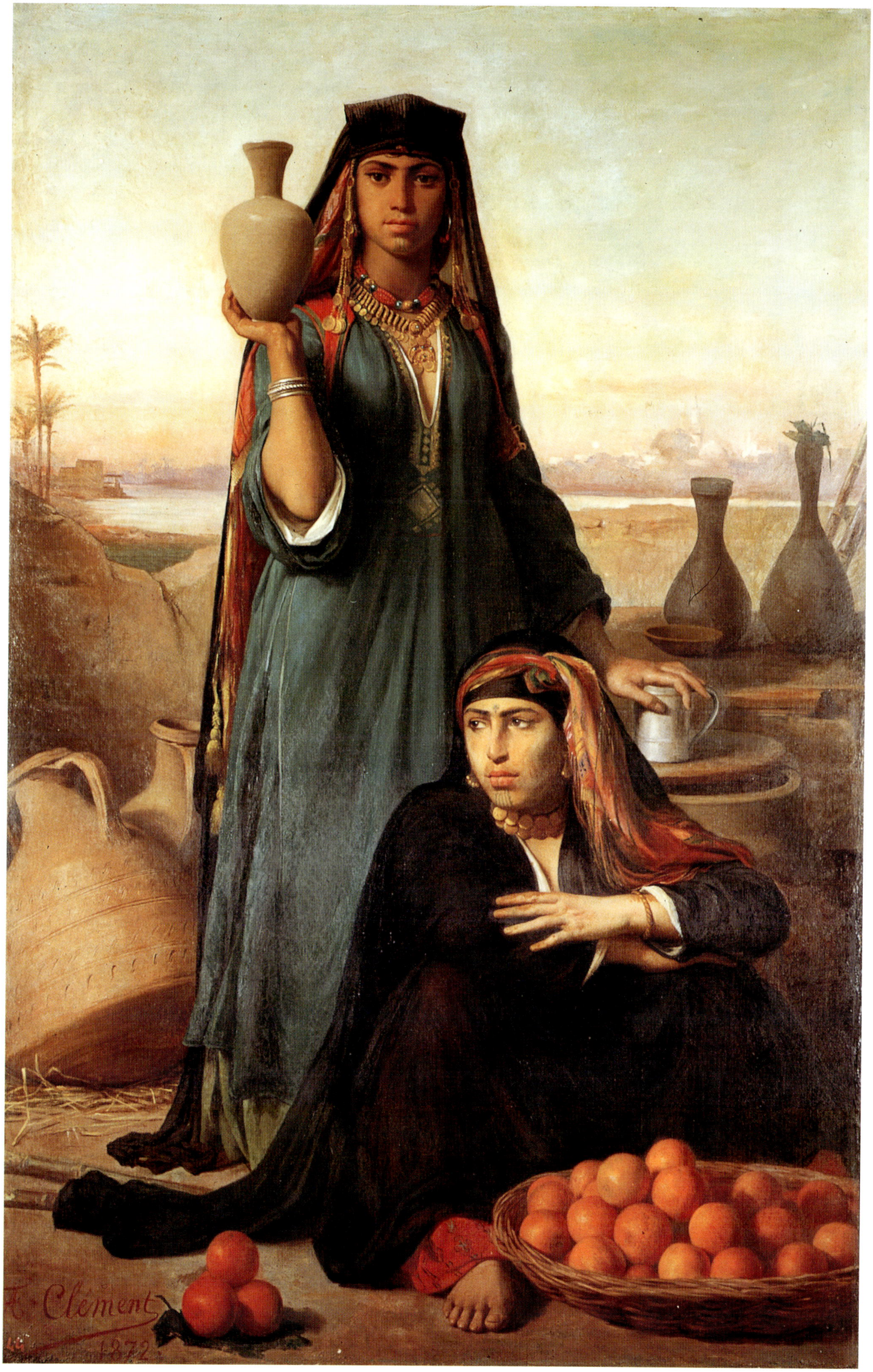

Women Selling Water and Oranges on the Road to Heliopolis, Near Cairo,
Félix-Auguste Clément, 1872
Oil on canvas, 185 x 122 cm
(Musée des Beaux-Arts, Nice).

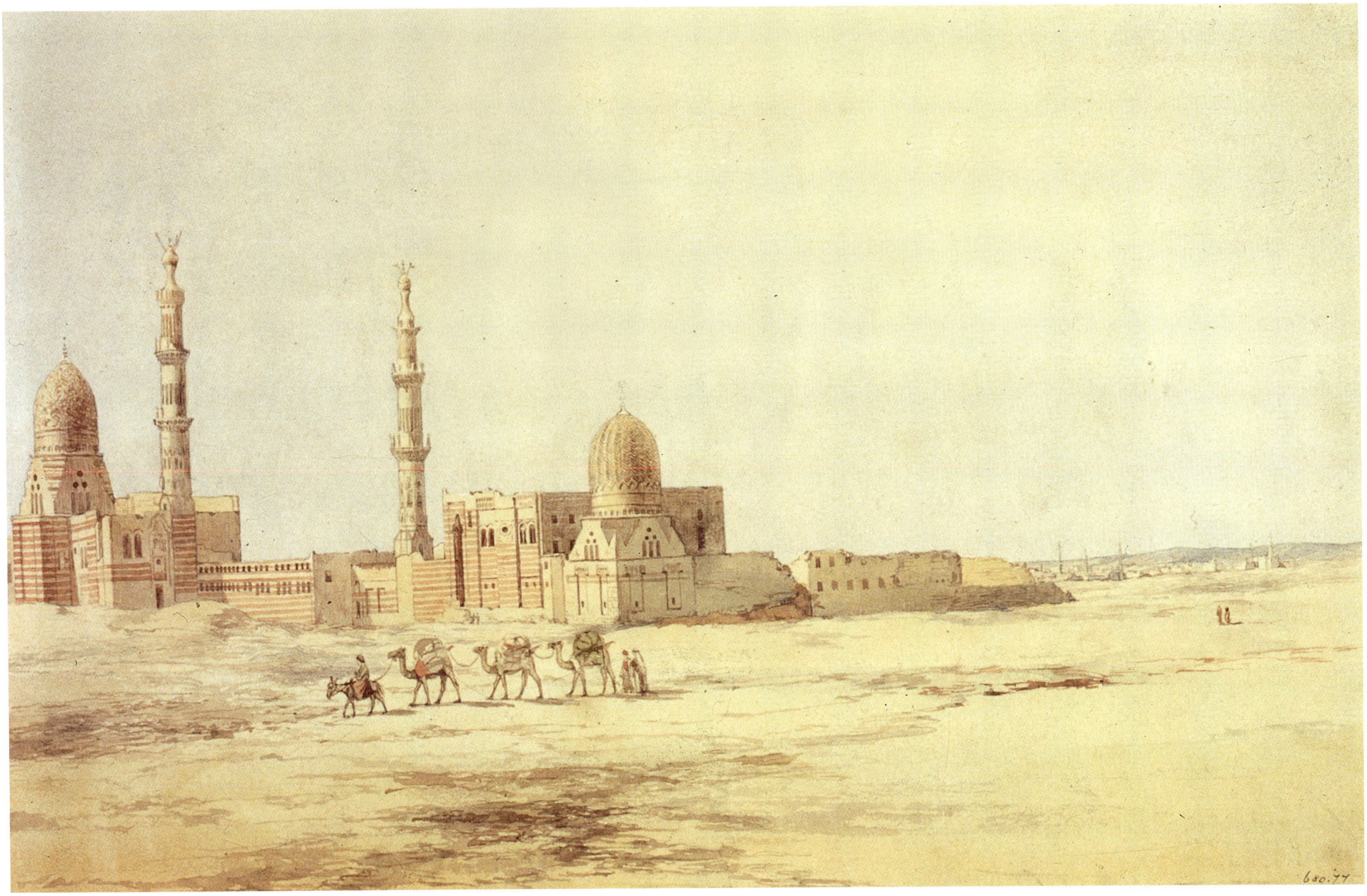

The Tombs of the Caliphs, Richard Dadd, 1843
Watercolor, 24.2 x 36.8 cm
(Victoria and Albert Museum, London).

Old Damascus: The Jewish Quarter, Lord Frederick Leighton, 1873–1874
Oil on canvas, 129.5 x 104.1 cm
(private collection).

intimately, and whose greatness and culture he wanted to depict as honestly as possible.

Like Marilhat, the English artist Richard Dadd suffered from severe mental illness. In 1842, he had the chance to undertake a long trip that took him from Germany to Italy and then from Greece to Anatolia. He subsequently visited Syria and Palestine and finally arrived at Cairo, where he was delighted to meet up with his fellow countryman, Lewis. Excited by his discovery of the Middle East, he created fine canvases, notably *Caravan Halt by the Sea* (1843). But his mental health deteriorated as his excitement grew. Back in England, though staggering from one emotional crises to another, he nonetheless continued to paint very moving and subtle recollections of his travels, including *The Tombs of the Caliphs* (1843), but also improbable inventions such as *Imaginary Egyptian Harem* (1865), a watercolor of unique design and rare sensitivity. Having killed his father in a fit of madness, he spent many years in an asylum, where he continued to paint.

In 1855 Joseph Farquharson decided to emulate his contemporaries and travel through Egypt. From his trip he evolved a characteristic style for picturesque scenes in which the most humble aspects of Arab life are depicted in highly structured compositions full of evocative details, as in *The Orange Seller*, and the evocative *Guerizah Island Ferry on the Nile* (1878). He had a marked preference for market scenes (*A Market in Egypt*) and for prayer time in the mosques (*Inside Sultan Hassan's Mosque*).

In the case of the celebrated English artist Lord Frederick Leighton, Orientalism became a part of his life rather than an aspect of his art. One of the leading exponents of academic painting, he imbued his works with a melancholy pining for classical antiquity; his universe has a tragic and deathly character, as though his works are

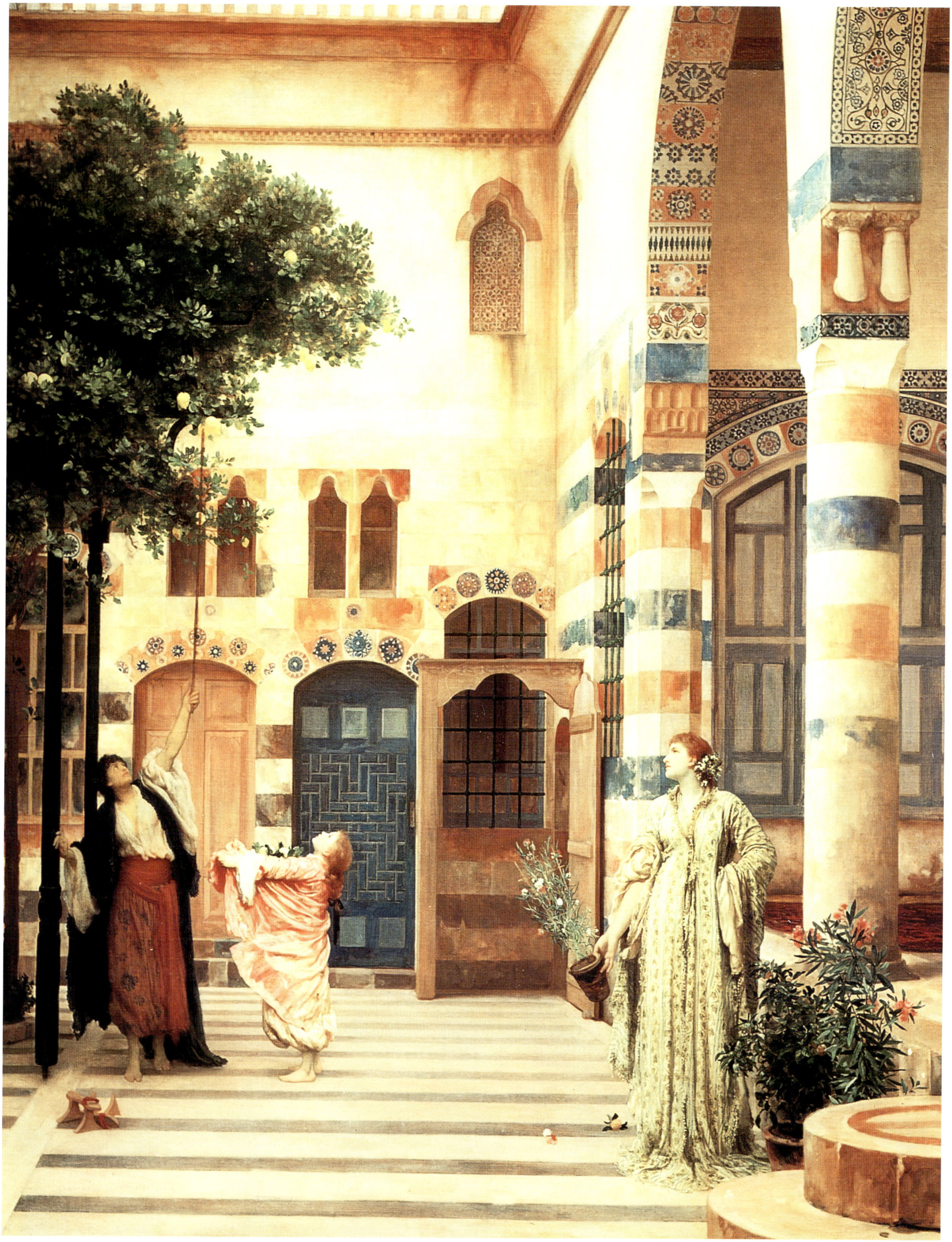

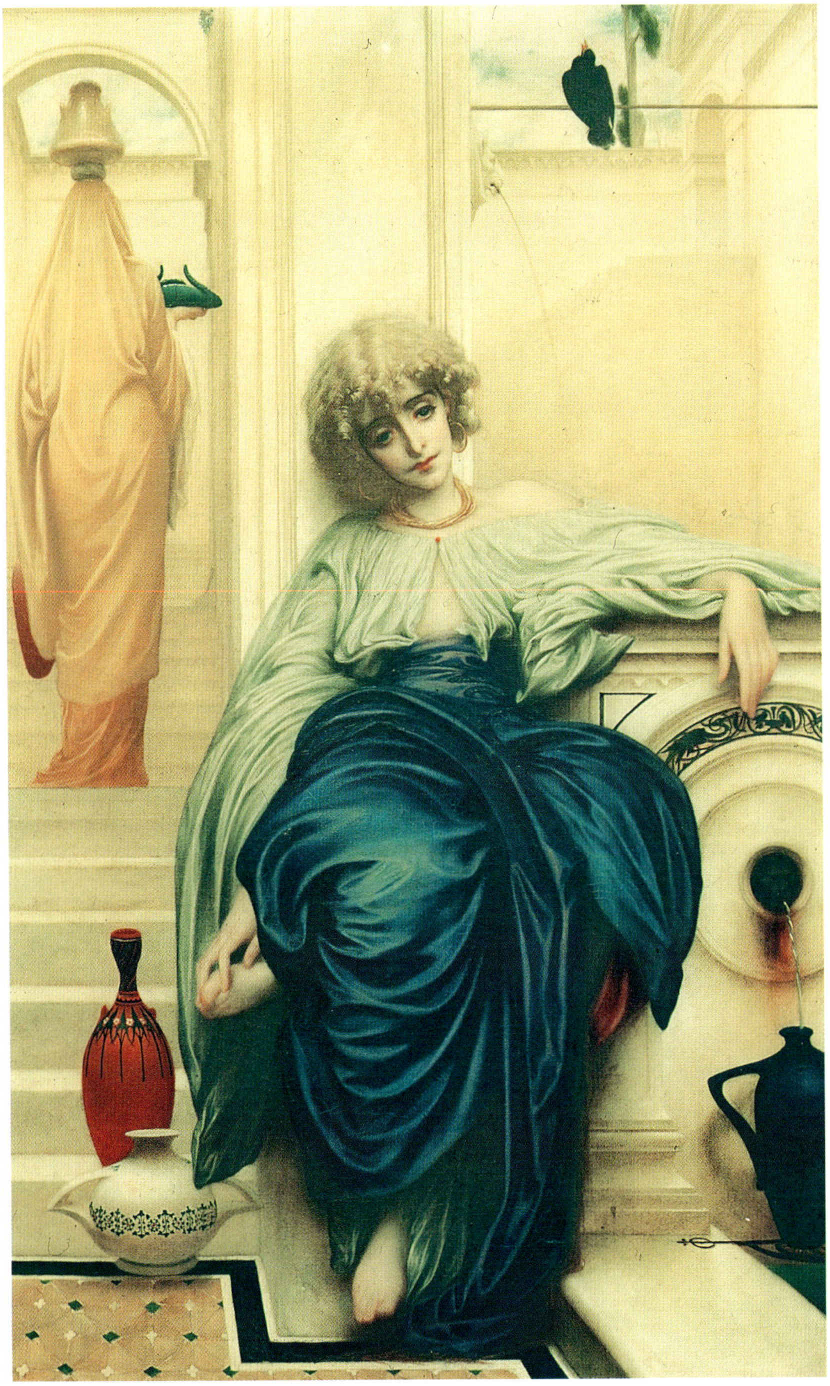

From left to right
Songs Without Words,
Lord Frederick Leighton,
1860–1861
Oil on canvas
101.7 x 63 cm
(Tate Gallery, London).

Egyptian Widow,
Sir Lawrence Alma-Tadema,
1872
Oil on wood,
73.9 x 98.1 cm
(Rijksmuseum, Amsterdam).

Egyptian Juggler,
Sir Lawrence Alma-Tadema,
1870
Oil on canvas mounted on
wood, 78.7 x 49.5 cm
(private collection).

portents of the approaching demise of academic art itself. His genuine love for the Middle East rarely found an expression in his paintings. After a long stay in Florence, he continued to study in Germany and then in Rome. Established in London after a three-year spell in Paris, at the end of the 1850s he was taken with the desire to travel farther, and so embarked on a tour that took him from Italy to Algeria, Constantinople, and Egypt. He sailed the Nile in 1868 but was both disappointed by what he termed "an unchanging antiquity" and also transported by the splendor of the sunsets over the sacred river, as he recorded in his diary: "Another wonderful sunset tonight. Like yesterday the east bank was low, brown, green; and, as yesterday, it came alive with bird song. On the Eastern side, the long rock face which seems to close off the whole Nile Valley became liquid or almost liquid at the water's edge: what intense glory it reflected!" Yet despite such reactions he returned from his many trips with only a few beautiful watercolors, such as *The City of Tombs* and *An Empty Street Corner* (1865).

In his splendid London home, however, he created what he called his Arab Room, an authentic reconstruction by the architect Aitchison, who had made detailed drawings of Moorish architecture in Spain. It was lined with period tiles from the 13th to 17th century, and a verse from the Koran was placed above its entrance. The fountain in its center was carved out of black marble. A wealth of ornamentation was added: *Moucharabieh*, a frieze of Persian designed by the illustrator Walter Crane, a copper crown created by Aitchison, marble columns sculpted by Edgar Boehm, and a ceiling whose windows incorporate Damascus stained glass. Reality and fiction merged in this room, where the artist long dreamt of an Orient that was the very antithesis of the West.

Recreating Ancient Egypt

Ancient Isis bequeathed her veils
To the Nile's modern daughters;
And under the headband, stars
Shine with a pure and subtle fire.

Théophile Gautier, *Émaux et Camée*

Théophile Gautier's novel *Roman de la momie* (The story of the mummy) was serialized from 11 March to 6 May 1857. Its publication was a momentous event for it was the first historical novel – worthy of the name – to deal with Ancient Egypt. The writer had embellished his fiction with a wealth of archaeological details, and it was not by chance that he dedicated his work to Egyptologist Ernest Feydeau, who a year earlier had published in the journal *Le Moniteur* a major work on the history of ancient peoples' funereal rites and burial chambers. Feydeau had provided Gautier with the wealth of factual information he needed in order to tell a believable story. Gautier, who had been able to go to Greece and Constantinople in 1852 (a stay from which he drew a thick tome of recollections), dreamt above all of Egypt. He had in fact written novels with an Egyptian theme before – *Une nuit de Cléopâtre* (Cleopatra's night; 1838) and *Le Pied de la Momie* (The mummy's foot; 1840) – but he did not get an opportunity to visit the country until 1869, when, in his capacity as special correspondent of the *Journal Officiel*, he was able to witness the opening of the Suez Canal. Unfortunately his stay was brought to an abrupt end by a bad fall and he was able to

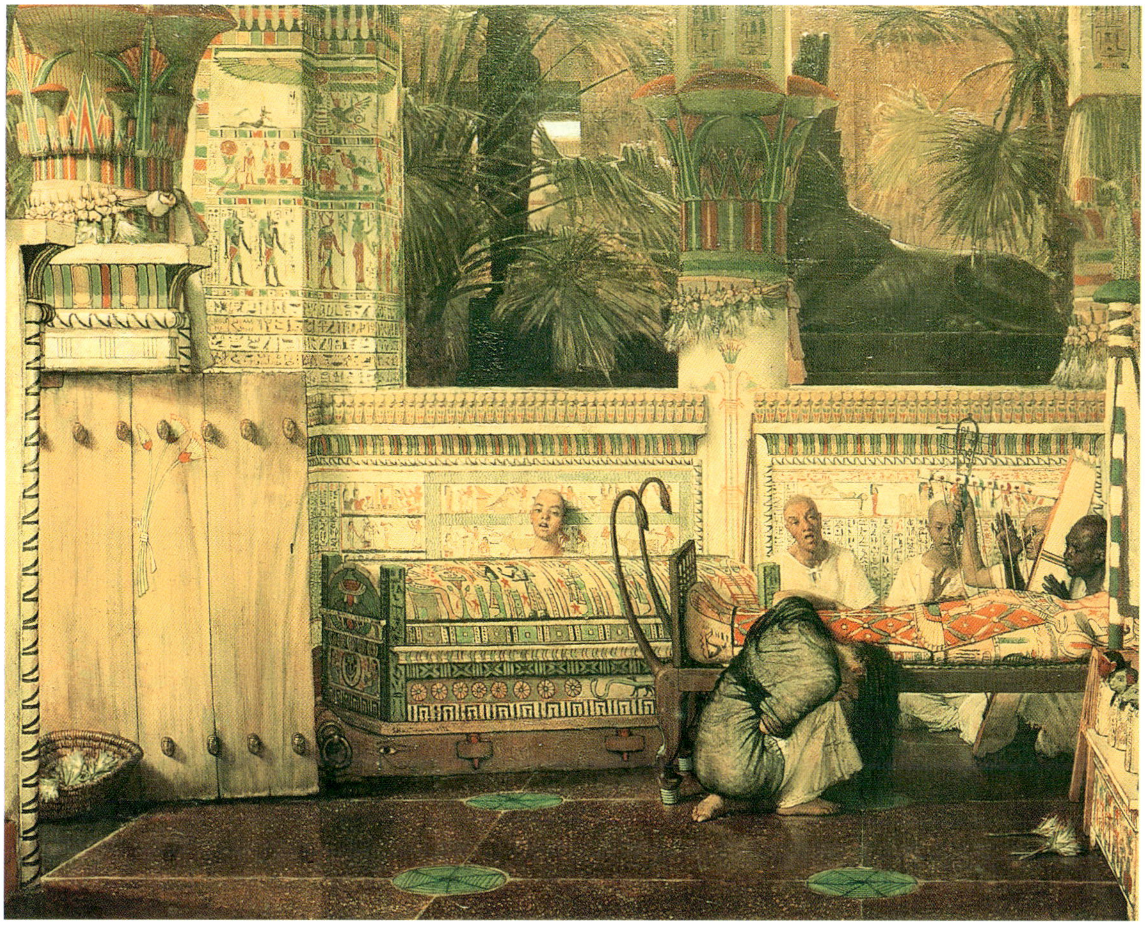

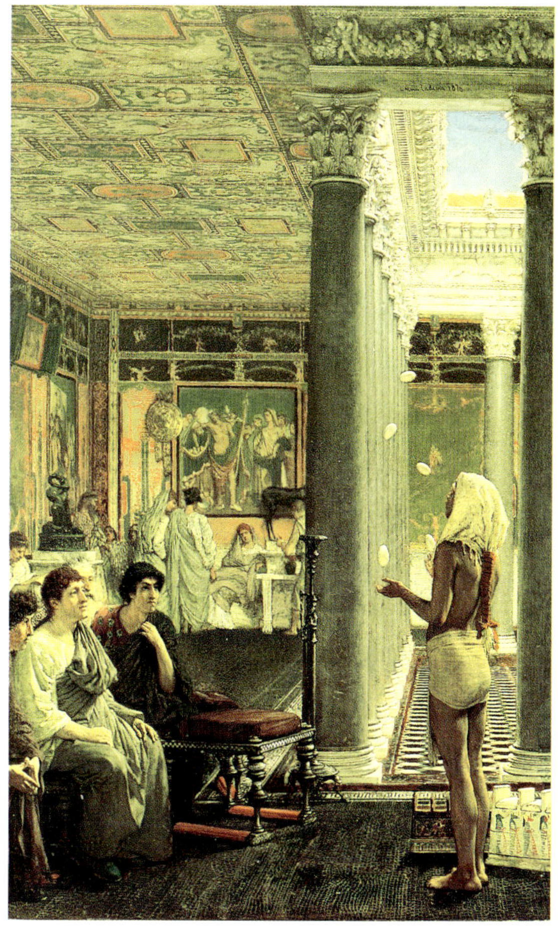

file only six reports. He was not now able to sail down the Nile, the mere thought of which had inspired many pages of richly evocative prose from his pen.

Though a pure fiction, *Le Roman de la Momie* passed as a scholarly reconstruction of the life of the Egyptians of old. It inspired the French artist Jules Lecomte du Noüy, who from 1885 to 1886 created an absorbing triptych entitled *Ramses in His Harem*. The panel on the left represents music, that on the right, dance. From that same novel the artist drew other compositions, notably the celebrated *Bearers of Bad News*, which he exhibited at the 1876 Salon, and *Pharaoh's Sorrow*.

The English artist Benjamin Haydon, who did not travel to the Middle East, was one of the first painters systematically to apply the knowledge recently unearthed by Egyptology to the visual arts. He produced five paintings on biblical themes in Egyptian settings, and for these he studied both Vivant Denon's drawings and the volumes of *Description de l'Égypte*; talked to the Italian adventurer Giovanni Battista Belzoni; and examined anything Egyptian he could find in British collections.

A similar approach was taken by Sir Lawrence Alma-Tadema in 1863 for his *Entertainment in Ancient Egypt*, which reveals a scrupulous attention to historic authenticity – it features harpists from the tomb of Ramses III, furniture on show at the British Museum, and information gleaned in diverse written works, including those of Prisse d'Avennes. Though he preferred to concentrate on scenes from Imperial Rome – to much acclaim – he did not neglect Egypt, explaining when asked the reason for this attachment: "Where else should I have commenced when I first began to make myself familiar with the life of the ancients? The first thing the child learns of ancient times leads him into the courts of the Pharaohs, to Goshen in Egypt, and when we go back to the source of the art and science of the other nations of antiquity how often we reach your Egypt!" His striking *Egyptian Widow* (1872) is an attempt to grasp the meaning of death in Ancient Egypt. Similarly, in works like *Egyptian Game* and *Egyptian in Front of his House* his main aim is to provide as vivid a depiction as possible of what life might actually have been like in Ancient Egypt.

Another renowned English artist, Sir Edward J. Poynter, also a fervent admirer of Ancient Rome, imitated Alma-Tadema, but largely in terms of his own interest, which was military history; a celebrated example is *A Faction in Pharaoh's Times*. But he also had a keen interest in the esoteric rites of Egypt's polytheist religion, as we can see in his *Adoration of the God Ra* (1867), *An Offering to Isis*, and *Young Girl Feeding the Sacred Ibises in the Hypostyle Room at Karnak*. The English artist Edward Long also ventured into the sacred, his very vivid imagination producing *The Gods and Their Makers* (1878) and *Alethe Walking the Sacred Ibises to the Temple of Isis in Memphis* (1888). His *Crown of Justification*, a theme taken from the Ancient Greek historian Diodorus Siculus, is an attempt at creating an image of the ultimate tribunal: the deceased is received in the Kingdom of the Dead, anointed with sacred oils, and crowned with white lotus flowers before being set on a barge to be taken to his new dwelling place.

In France, Georges Rochegrosse specialized in the Egyptian genre. Two of his most notable works are *After the Bath, Ancient Egypt*, an image of bathing women; and the striking

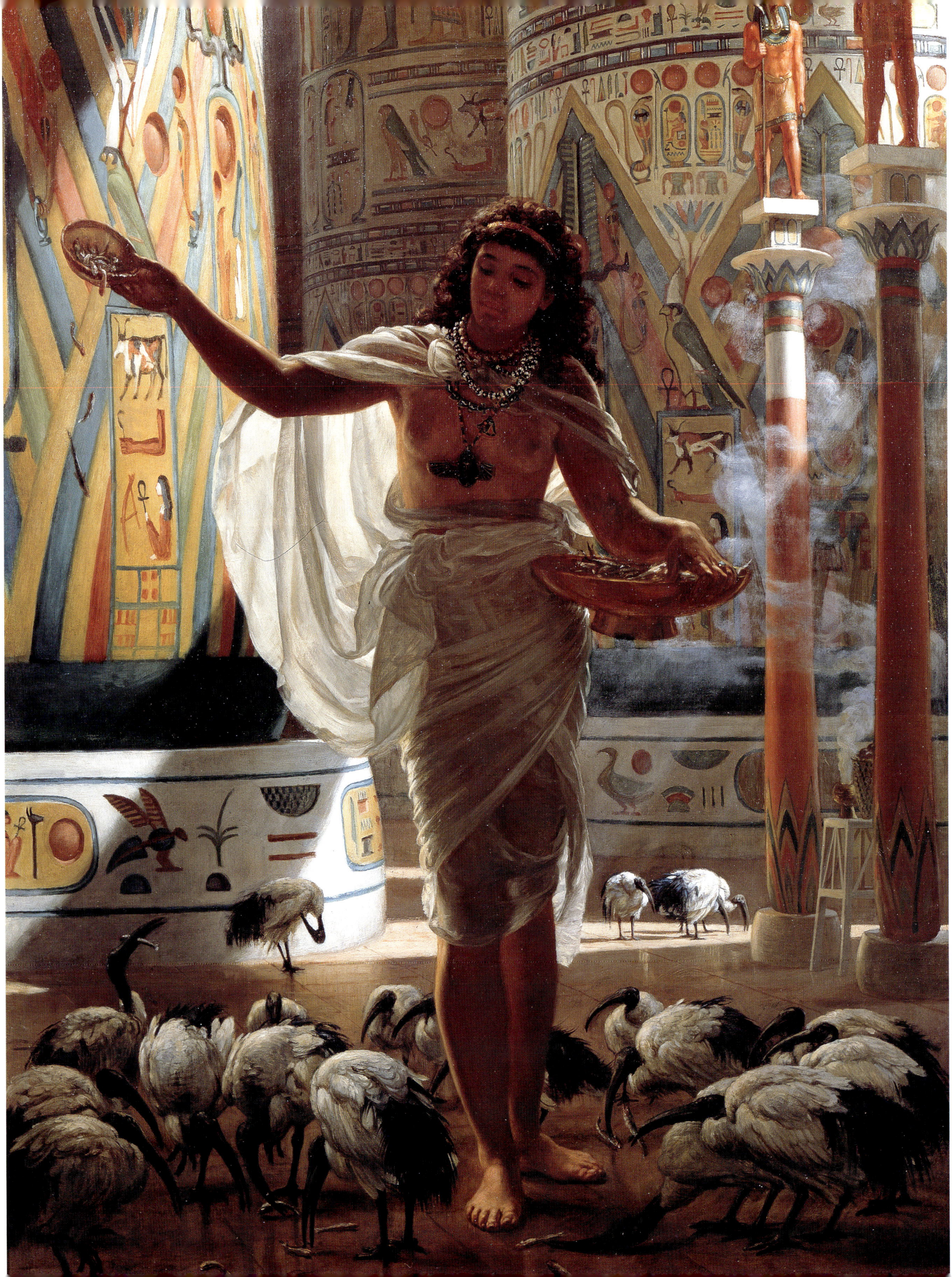

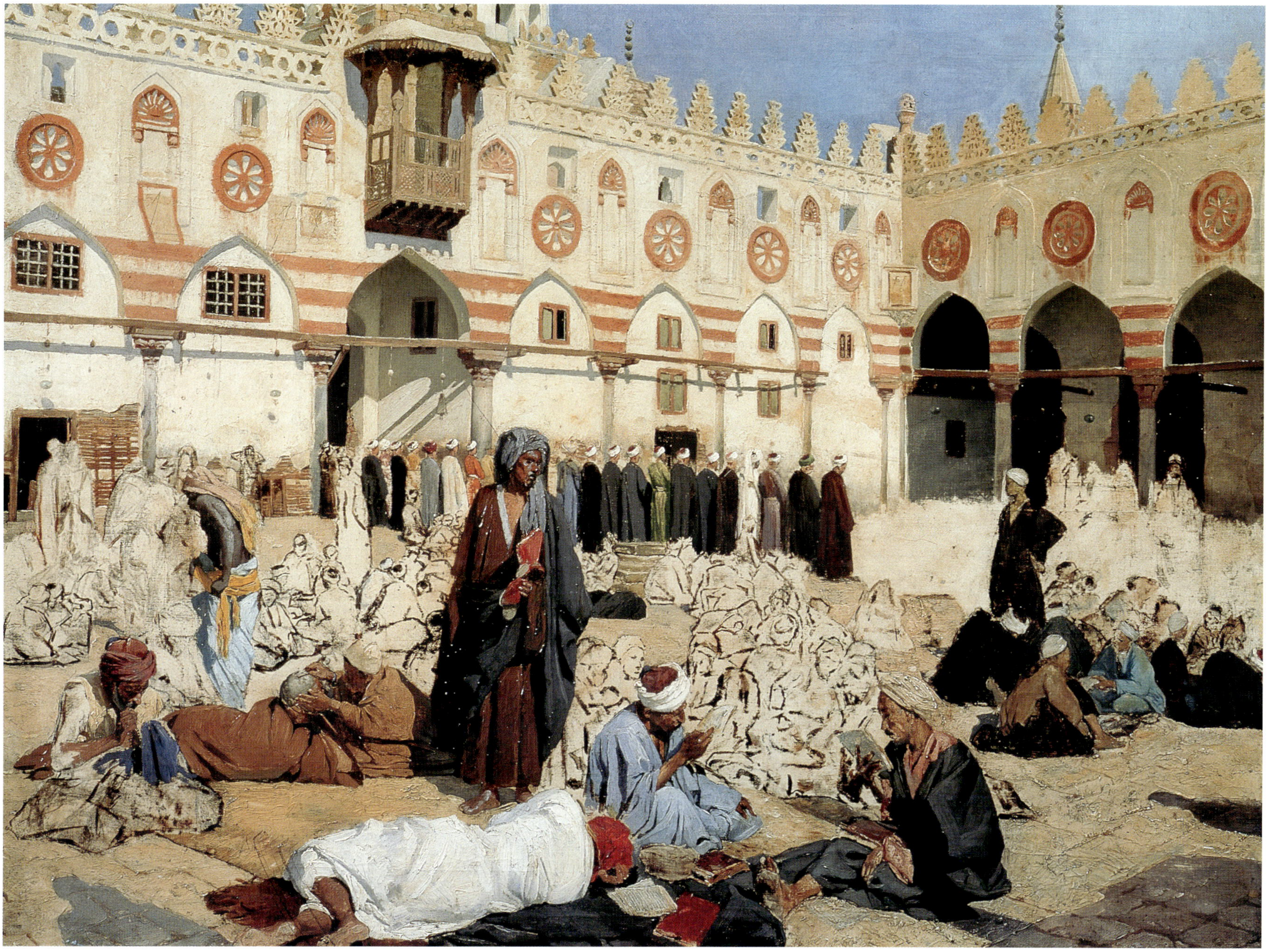

In Pharaoh's Day (1887), in which a young man pays court to a girl who is stroking the cat on her lap. Another French artist, P. de Neuville, painted *Female Musician*, whilst the German painter Ludwig Deutsch produced *In the Temple* (1892).

Among the many Egyptian subjects that had attracted both artists and public one was of particular significance: the life and tragic death of Cleopatra. The queen of Egypt exercised an irresistible fascination over 19th-century artists. She was the only Egyptian theme to belong to Western art by virtue of her place in Roman history. Her story was seized upon by many painters, including Gustave Lasalle Bordes (*The Death of Cleopatra*); Alexandre Cabanel, (*Cleopatra testing poisons on condemned prisoners*, 1887); Reginald Arthur (*Cleopatra's Suicide*, 1892), and many others. Perhaps only T. Buchanan demonstrated any real originality in the treatment of this theme, with his *Cleopatra Embarking*. The Austrian artist Hans Makart, who arrived in Egypt with a quasi-princely retinue took home an opulent and sensual *Cleopatra* (1875) that was perhaps the last word on this theme.

El Azhar Arab University of Cairo,
Ludwig Deutsch, 1890
Oil on canvas, 73.5 x 99.5 cm
(private collection).

Opposite
Young Girl Feeding the Sacred Ibises in the Hypostyle Room at Karnak,
Sir Edward John Poynter, 1871
Oil on canvas, 92.6 x 69.2 cm
(The Bridgeman Art Library, London).

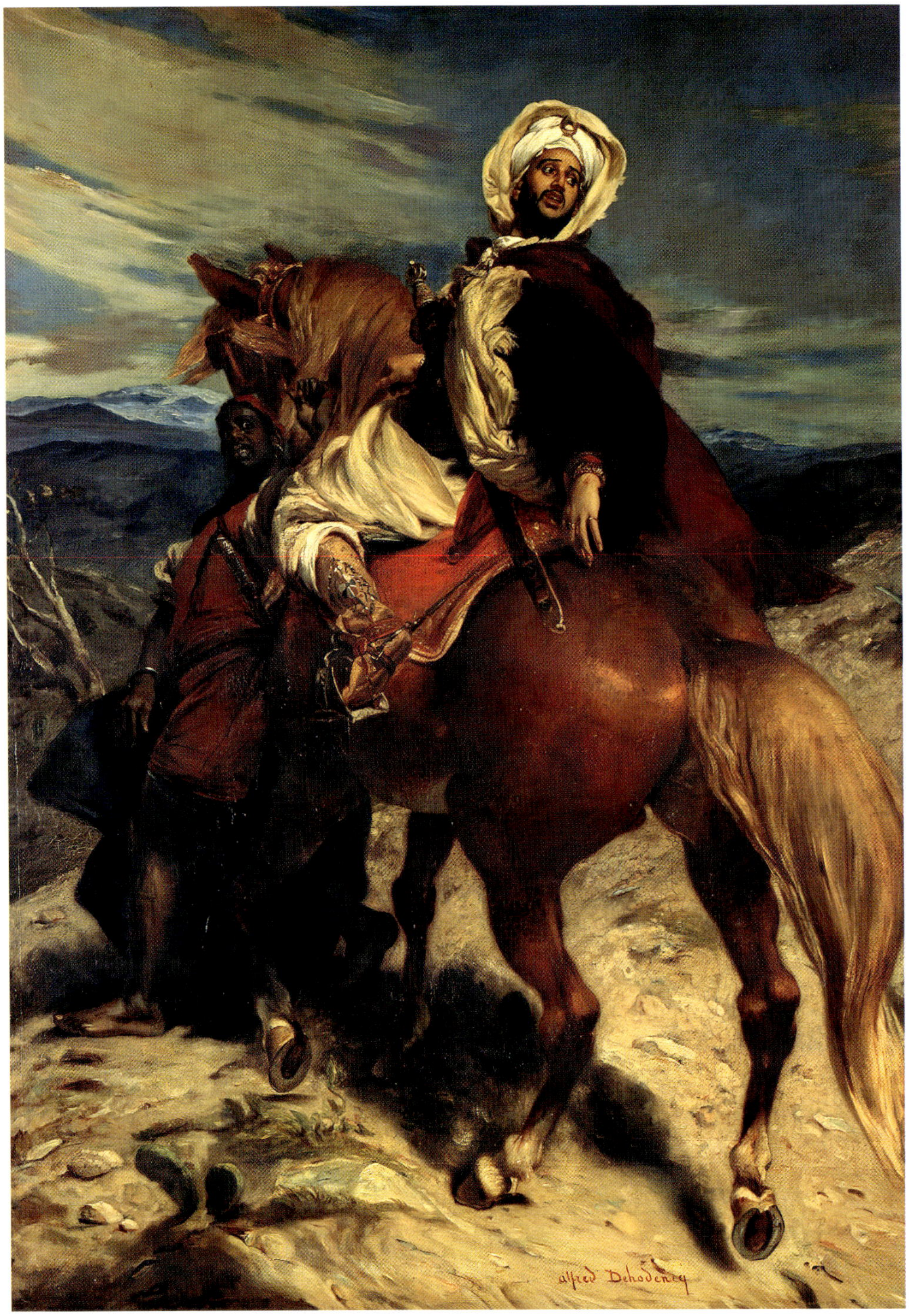

Boabdil's Farewell,
Alfred Dehodencq, 1869
Oil on canvas, 377 x 275 cm
(Musée d'Orsay, Paris).

Spain, Gateway to the East

In terms of overseas cultural adventures, the discovery of the Middle East was the main preoccupation of the West during the 19th century, though this sometimes took unexpected courses. Strange as it may seem at first, Spain came to be considered an important introduction to the Orient; Victor Hugo claimed that "Spain is half African." An Iberian tour, though still a difficult and at times risky expedition during the romantic era, offered the possibility of poring over the Moorish civilization's astonishing legacy. Lord Byron visited Spain and had both Childe Harold and Don Juan sojourn there. Chateaubriand stayed there in 1807 and 20 years later set his *Aventures du dernier Abencérage* (The Adventures of the last Abencerage) there. The German poet Heinrich Heine found there the theme for his fierce attack on the Inquisition, "Almanzor." And Théophile Gautier traveled the length and breadth of the country in 1840, the result being his *Tra los montes*, a colorful tale that served as a vibrant tract in favor of Spain.

Following the writers, several painters soon crossed the Pyrenees. In 1825, David Wilkie set out on his Continental tour, which took him from Rome to Madrid, where he studied the paintings of Velazquez and Murillo; he exhibited his "Spanish" works at the Royal Academy in 1828 to great acclaim. The Frenchman Baron Taylor was hot on his tracks with a view to finding canvases for the Louvre collections; he returned with a precious sketchbook of his own drawings. Giroult de Pongrey spent many months in the production of an essential guidebook, *Les Monuments arabes et mauresques de Cordoue, Séville et Grenade* (Arab and Moorish buildings in Cordoba, Seville, and Granada). In 1832 it was David Roberts' turn to be enthralled by what he found; Spain, in his eyes, was Europe's artistic hunting ground, "wild and unspoilt." He set about making many drawings, among them studies of the Alhambra, and compiled a volume of "picturesque sketches" from Spain, published in 1835. Thereafter he crossed to Gibraltar to make his first real contact with the East, an experience that would be the defining moment in his career. John Frederick Lewis was also in Spain at the time. He stayed a while at the house of a friend, the writer Richard Ford, in Seville, and it was Ford who asked the British ambassador in Madrid to facilitate a "sightseeing tour" to enable Lewis to prepare illustrations for an edition of Byron. In Madrid, Lewis worked intensively, making 60 copies of Spanish masterpieces in the Prado; then, like Roberts, Lewis visited Morocco, though taking good care not to meet Roberts! On his return to England, Lewis immediately busied himself with the preparation of two volumes of lithographs, one of which was entirely dedicated to the Alhambra. His works were so well received that he became known as "Lewis the Spaniard," and he continued to exhibit Spanish works long after leaving Spain.

Lewis was soon imitated by others, notably the French artist Alfred Dehodencq. Dehodencq, having suffered severe trauma during the 1848 revolution, went to convalesce in the Pyrenees. While there he seized the opportunity to go on to Madrid, where he fell under the spell of Velazquez and above all Goya. His canvases depict Spanish life in a dashing, heroic style, his favorite subjects being bull races and the colorful Andalusian gypsies. In 1869 he exhibited *Boabdil's Farewell* at the Salon in Paris, a painting awash with the heroic Romanticism of Victor Hugo.

On arriving in Rome after winning a scholarship, Mariano Fortuny y Marsal, a Catalan, was soon sent by the City of Barcelona to join the North African expedition of General Prim y Pratas, which acquired Tangiers and the Tetuán region for Spain in 1859. It was Fortuny who attracted both Henri Regnault and Georges Clairin to Spain. Regnault was entirely captivated by the Alhambra: "My divine mistress, the Alhambra, beckons; she has sent forth one of her lovers, the Sun, to tell me that all is ready to receive me." Chateaubriand, whose lyricism was less febrile, declared that the Alhambra "seemed to me worthy of close attention, even after Greece's temples," and that there was something "voluptuous, religious and warlike appearing to breathe in this splendid building; this cloister of love, this mysterious retreat where the Moorish kings tasted all pleasures, forgot all life's calls."

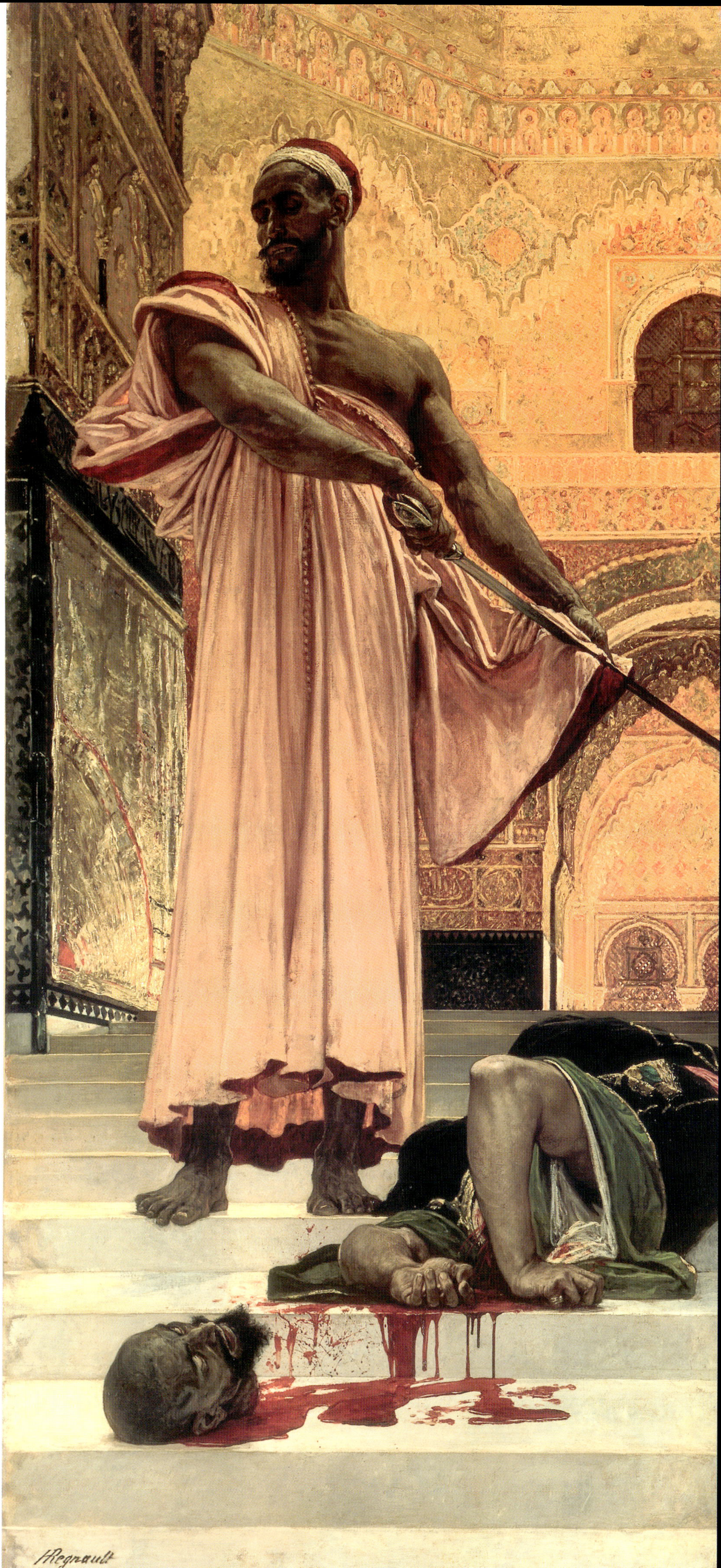

Execution Without Trial,
Henri Regnault, 1870
Oil on canvas, 302 x 146 cm
(Musée d'Orsay, Paris).

Art and the Eastern Question

The Massacres on Chios,
Eugène Delacroix, 1824
Oil on canvas, 419 x 354 cm
(Musée du Louvre, Paris).

The Greek war of independence

The Rediscovery of Greece

Two factors brought modern Greece to Europe's attention. First, from the end of the 18th century the Greek islands were seen as having strategic significance, particularly by the British, the French, and Ottoman Turks. Second, a European-wide philhellenism continued to grow in importance, inspired by an admiration both for the culture of Ancient Greece and the plight of the modern Greeks. Finally, in 1812, after several thwarted attempts, there was an armed uprising against Turkish rule in Greece. The Greek patriot Alexandros Ypsilantis, who had served as an officer in the Russian Imperial Guard, founded the Sacred Battalion and had the first revolutionary declarations printed. Soon the first foreign volunteers started arriving. The following year at Epidaurus, the Greek insurgents declared independence and drafted a constitution. Fierce fighting continued and not long after the declaration the Ottoman Turks carried out a notorious massacre on the island of Chios. In 1823 a new Greek government was installed at Nauplia and in the same year Lord Byron arrived in Greece to support the fight for independence; he died a year later at Missolonghi. Two civil wars took place in 1824, and the landing in the Peloponnese of forces from Turkey and Egypt seriously threatened the bid for freedom; at the end of August Athens was besieged. However, the defeat of the Ottoman fleet at Navarino by a joint British, French and Russian naval force, together with General Fabvier's successful campaign on Chios, speeded up peace negotiations and at the Poros Conference the borders of a new Greek state were mapped out. In 1832 there was a vote on a royal constitution and Otto of Bavaria became king of Greece. Nationalist unrest started afresh, however, in 1836; the "Greek problem," closely linked to the complex and intractable problems in the Balkans, was to last until the Great War.

The fight for Greek liberation, a sorry succession of battles, revolts, massacres, naval engagements, fratricidal clashes, betrayals and reversals stirred a deep sympathy in Europe. In part this can be ascribed to the archaeological passion that gripped the educated middle-classes and in which a concept of the glory of Ancient Greece played a central role. But also significant was the Romantic concept of the autonomous nation-state, which in the wake of Napoleon's meteoric career had made a deep impact on the Western psyche.

Greece was "rediscovered" during the Enlightenment, largely as a result of the digs conducted in Italy, which unearthed Greek statues, and its culture became the object of eager attention. In 1754, Julien David Le Roy published *Ruines des plus beaux monuments de la Grèce* (Ruins of the finest monuments in Greece) and in 1788 Abbé Barthélemy's *Voyage du jeune Anacharsis en Grèce* (The journey of young Anacharsis to Greece) appeared. Other publications that made readers graphically familiar with both ancient and modern Greece were books of prints; they included – to give just French examples – those illustrated by Jean-Baptiste Van Mour, *Receuil de cent estampes représentant différentes nations du Levant* (Collection of one hundred engravings depicting the different nations of the Levant); by François Boucher, *Recueil de diverses figures étrangères* (A collection of various foreign figures; 1740); and by Nicolas Lancret *La Belle Grecque* (The handsome Greek). Books such as *Voyage littéraire de la Grèce* (A literary voyage through Greece) by Pierre Augustin Guys (1776), and *Voyage pittoresque* (Picturesque journey) by Comte de Choiseul-Gouffier (1782–1822), with plates by Augustin de Saint-Aubin, Moreau le Jeune, Jean-Baptiste Hilair and others, rounded off a library that would prove invaluable when political interest in Greece grew under the Consulate. The journey to Greece soon became an integral part of the Middle Eastern tour. Chateaubriand, Alphonse de Lamartine, and Théophile Gautier undertook this voyage in the footsteps of Antoine Laurent Castellan, author of *Lettres sur la Morée* (Letters on Morea; 1808) and *Lettres sur la Grèce...* (Letters on Greece...; 1811).

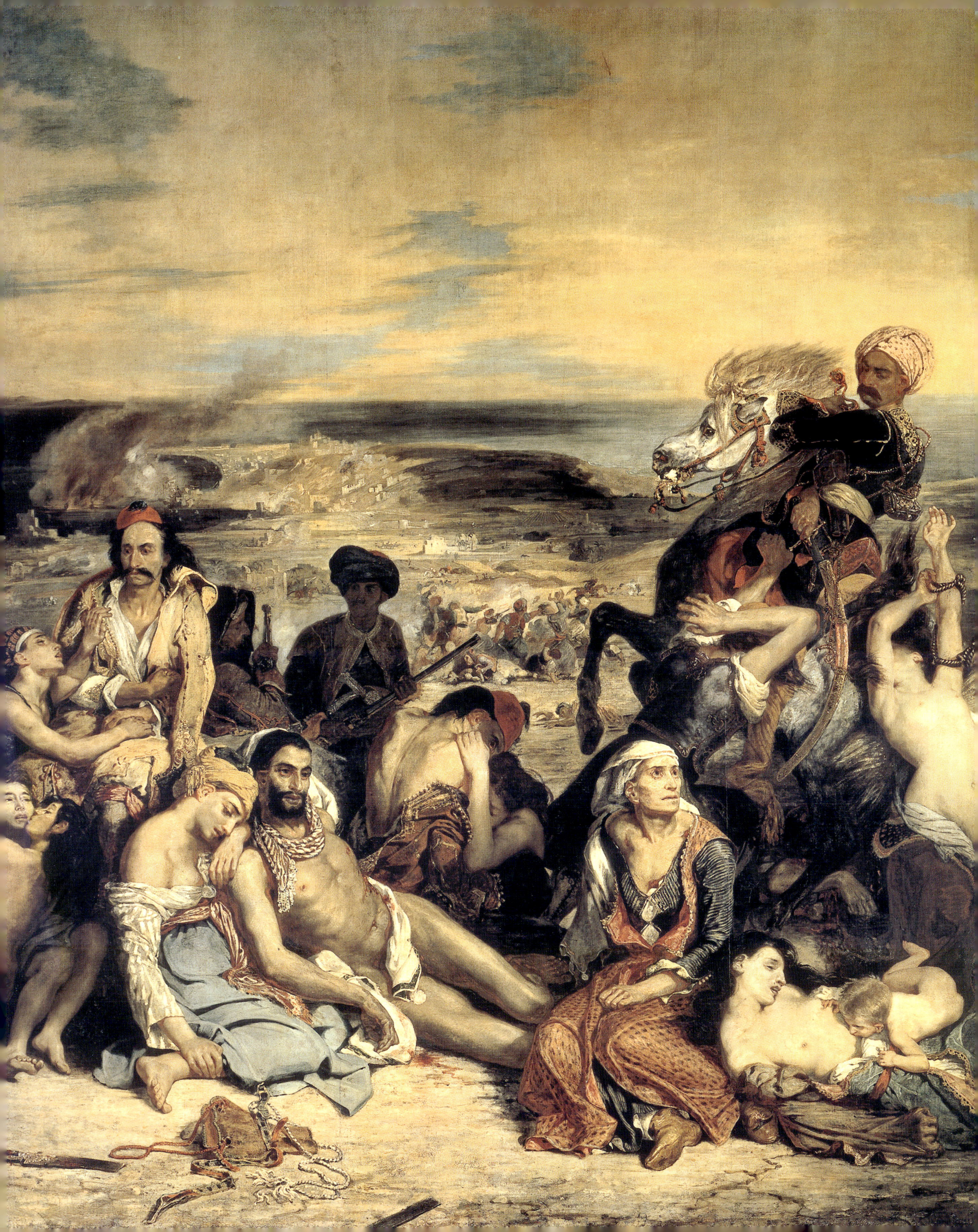

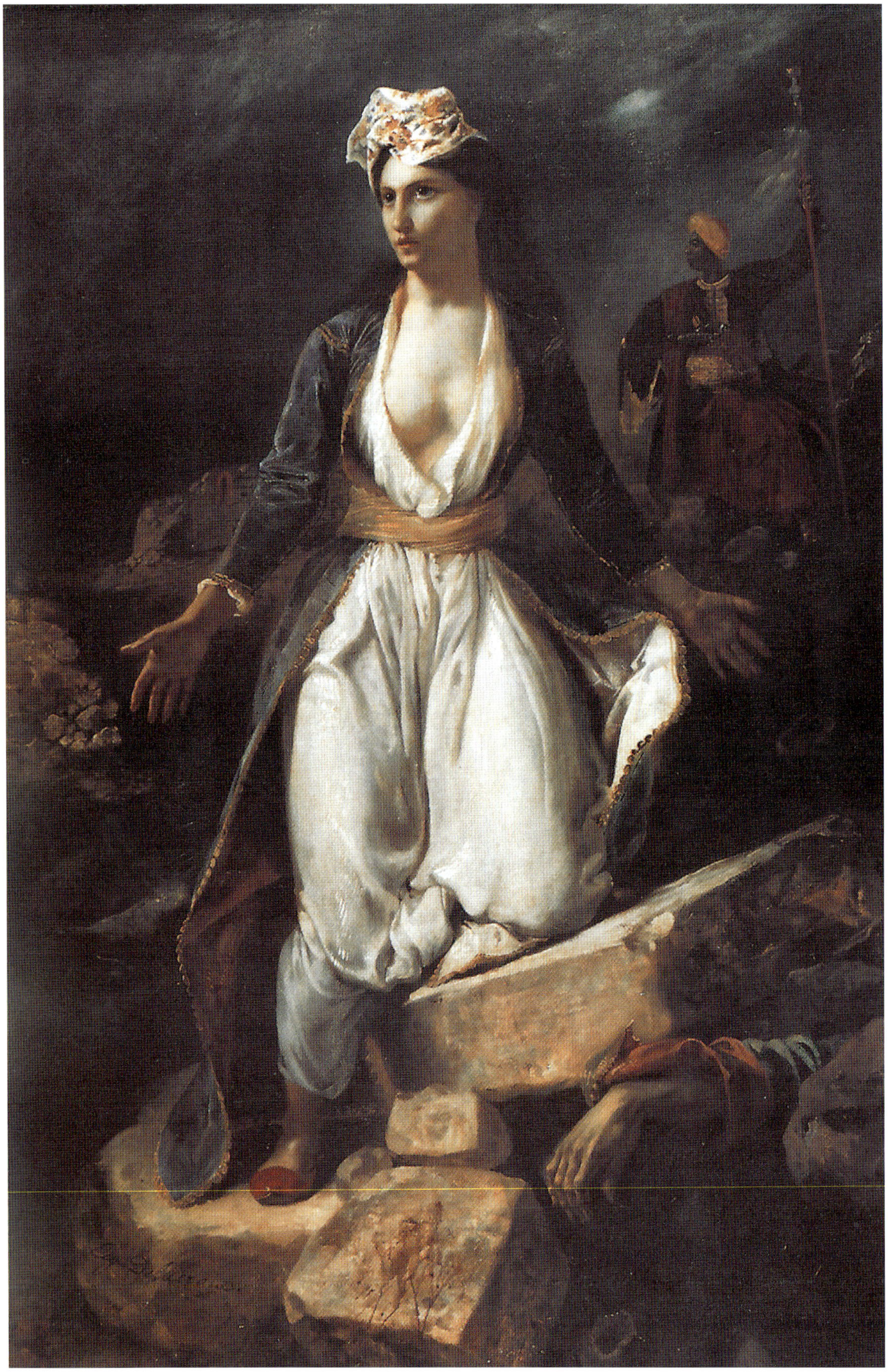

Greece on the Ruins of Missolonghi,
Eugène Delacroix, 1826
Oil on canvas, 209 x 147 cm
(Musée des Beaux-Arts, Bordeaux).

Artists and Political Commitment

Lord Byron's poetic works, in which a rebellious and martyred Greece was evoked (for example his "Siege of Corinth," which refers to a war in 1715), together with his personal action in support of the Greek insurgents, were typical of a trend developing across Europe in support of a proud people determined to free themselves from the Ottoman yoke. Artists began to visit this inhospitable, often dangerous country, among them Sir Charles Eastlake. Having made a great deal of money out of his portraits of Napoleon, Eastlake set off to Rome, where he became friendly with the Nazarenes (the German counterparts of the British Pre-Raphaelites) and where he also became fascinated by classical antiquity. In 1818, he visited Corfu and then Athens, producing etchings such as *The Temple of Erechteion* (1821). He underwent a complete change of attitude after the insurrection and his characters began to express his dislike of the Turks. His watercolors, livelier than his Neo-classical oil paintings, provided a wide-ranging record of Greek life and customs.

In France, public opinion was deeply moved by the fate of the Greeks. A young artist born in the Low Countries, Constantin Guys, joined forces with Byron in Greece when he was only twenty. First a horseman in a dragoons regiment, then a private tutor, Guys became a correspondent for the *Illustrated London News*, which gave him leave to roam the world from 1848 to 1860. This artist of fashionable life in Paris, who delighted in the company of girls he never tired of sketching when he saw them in the streets, theaters, cafés, or brothels of the capital, brought back from the Levant drawings of outstanding vitality. He depicted war with the expert knowledge of a military man, his images having a frankness and realism ahead of their time; he was skilled in showing life raw. The French poet Charles Baudelaire, who wrote a celebrated study of him, and who was able to see his sketchbook, was deeply impressed by the sense of reality that characterizes Guys' depictions of battlefields, hospitals, and cavalrymen during the Crimean War. He admired the depth of his insight into foreign lands: "Here we are at Schumla, at the house of Omar-Pasha: Turkish hospitality, pipes, and coffee; all the visitors, lined up on couches, take to their lips pipes which are as long as blowpipes and whose bowls stand on the ground at their feet."

In response to the war in Greece, the Société de la Morale Chrétienne (Society for Christian Morals) and the Société Française Philanthropique en Faveur des Grecs (French Philanthropic Society in Defense of the Greek People) set up committees (in 1823 and 1825 respectively) where people from all walks of life came together to offer help, among them Alphonse de Chateaubriand, the Duc de Choiseul, and Ambroise Firmin-Didot. The second of these organizations also arranged auctions and, more significantly, spectacular art exhibitions, one of which took place from 17 May to 3 July 1826 at the Galerie Lebrun in Paris, and again from 16 July to 14 October. These would become known as the "Greeks' Salon," for there was no official salon that year. Close on 30,000 people paid to see works by Géricault, Guérin, Granet, Horace Vernet, Prud'hon, David, Lejeune, Cogniet, Delacroix and others. In 1827 another exhibition presented paintings that had not been accepted by the official Salon, but this exhibition met with much less success. Among the general public at least, the enormous emotion stirred by the Greek revolt was already beginning to wane.

The main attraction at the Galerie Lebrun exhibition was without doubt *Greece on the Ruins of Missolonghi* by Delacroix. Two years earlier, the young Delacroix had shown the remarkable *The Massacre on Chios, with Greek Families Awaiting Death and Slavery*; in a terse program note, he was content to state as an explanation of his work: "See various accounts and the newspapers of that period." Delacroix aimed to stress the burning relevance of the event (the French government was trying to remain neutral) and to translate into graphic terms the feelings the tragedy inspired. His composition is noticeable for the multiplicity of scenes it includes, each of which tells its own terrible story. It is a composition that was carefully calculated to drive the message home: the Turkish horseman who drags away a bare breasted girl manages to cut a dramatic and violently heroic figure, but behind him opens a vista that reveals the vast scale of the devastation wrought by the Turkish forces. With *The Massacre on Chios*, Delacroix sought to alert his contemporaries to the human tragedy of the conflict, and to do so created vivid images of fear and horror. In *Greece on the Ruins of Missolonghi*, by contrast, he turned to allegory. A homage to Byron, who died at Missolonghi, this work is an evocation of the year-long siege that ended in April 1826 when the Greek survivors committed mass suicide. In an early and intensely emotional study, Delacroix depicted Greece as a martyr in the midst of children's corpses. But when he came to the painting itself, he depicted a young woman who is half kneeling on a collapsed building; she is dressed in blue and white, the colors both of Greece and the Virgin Mary. Only some scattered evidence of the tragedy remains, the flotsam and jetsam of a people stricken by history's violence. A similar allegorical approach is to be found in an earlier lithograph of 1822 by Ravault, and in an engraving by Achille Devéria for Casimir Dealvigne's *The Women of Messenia*. Delacroix gave this figure of a young Greek woman a new dimension by alluding to the tragic event through the ruins of the city and the haughty but distant figure of a Turkish soldier. Delacroix would return to this theme in 1856 with a canvas entitled *An Episode in the Greek War*.

The Salon of 1827 was remarkable for the number of paintings depicting the Greek conflict. Ary Scheffer was the most vehement in his expression of support for the Greek cause. At the exhibition at the Galerie Lebrun, he exhibited *The Remnant of the Missolonghi Garrison at the Moment of Setting Fire to the Mine that will Destroy Them*. The previous year, he had already painted *A Young Greek Defending his Father* and *Greek Exiles on a Rock*, in which Greek refugees in Corfu gaze darkly at the sea, thinking of their violated homeland. In 1827 he would earn renown with *The Heroines of Souli*, which depicts the sacrifice of the women of Souli, who at the end of 1803 threw themselves off a cliff in order to avoid being taken prisoner by Turkish soldiers. Here he dropped the Neo-classical style, the hallmark of his style to date, for a freer manner, taken from Géricault, that intensified the dramatic tension of the scene. Narcisse Diaz de la Peña treated the same subject in *The Women of Souli*, whilst Jean-Baptiste Vinchon painted *A Modern Greek Subject after the Samothrace Massacre*, showing an old man who, sitting by a dead woman, holds her child on his knee. Finally, Apollodore Callet, taking his text from Baron d'Ordre's poem *Les Exilés de Parga* (The Parga exiles), created *The People of Parga Embarking*, a theme that also attracted Théodore Géricault. A lover of justice, passionately inspired by the Declaration of Human Rights, Callet could not have remained indifferent to the tragedy besetting the Greek people. Between 1822 and 1823 he painted *Scene of the Greek War of Independence*, often taken to be a plague scene, where the sick and the dying are seen lying amid deep shadows. The painter's own feelings towards these historical events is revealed by the picture's taut composition. Around 1822, he painted *Greek on a Rock*, which is not a depiction of a specific incident, but rather an allegory (in the best classical tradition) of melancholia, in this instance the pining for a lost country. Around the same time, he painted *Oriental on a Rock*, which employs an identical iconography but without any specifically Greek connotations.

The philhellenic vein seemed inexhaustible. Louis Dupré, who would publish a remarkable book of colored plates in 1828, exhibited *A Greek* at the 1824 Salon. In 1825 Henry Serrur painted an episode during the capture of Tripolis, then capital of the Peloponnese: *Injured Greek Soldier*. Vincent Raverat submitted *Young Messenian Deacon Dying* at the Galerie Lebrun in 1826, the year when Louis Devousges signed yet

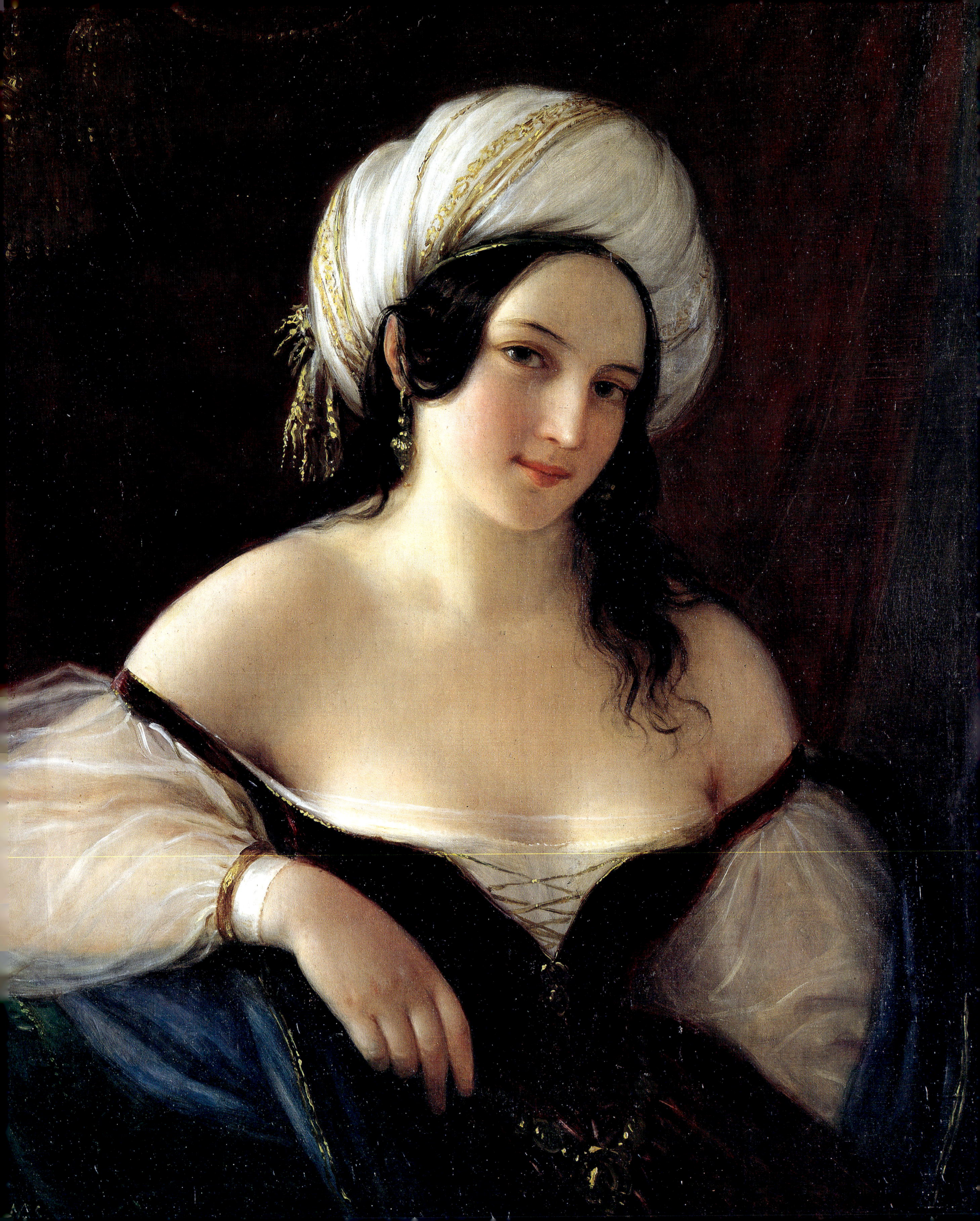

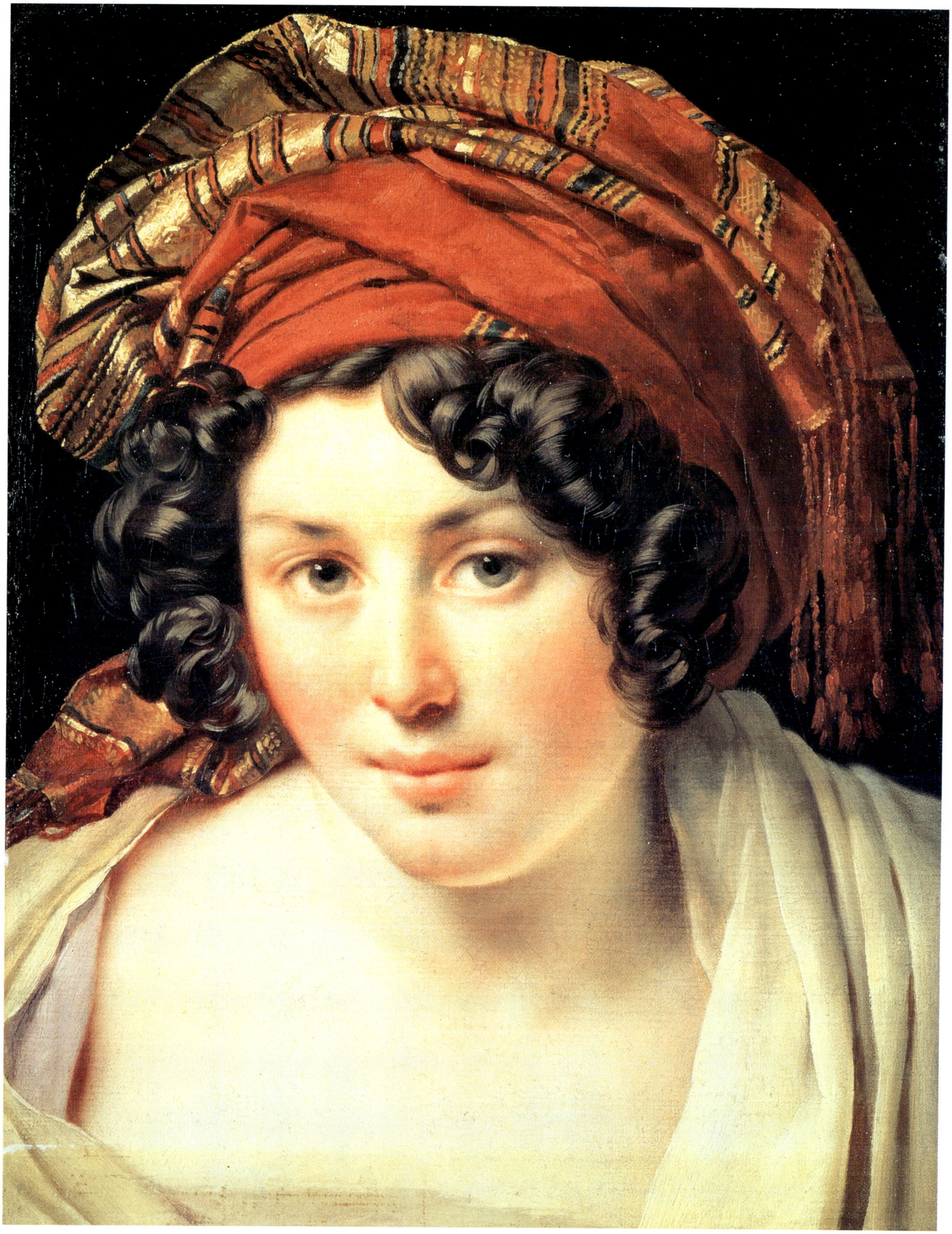

Opposite
Odalisque, Natale Schiavoni, c.1840
Oil on canvas, 81.5 x 66 cm
(Civico Museo Revoltella, Trieste).

Above
Head of Young Woman Wearing a Turban,
Anne-Louis Girodet de Roussy-Trioson,
Oil on canvas, 41 x 33.5 cm
(The Hermitage Museum, St Petersburg).

Passing Through the Iron Gates, Adrien Dauzats, 1853
Oil on canvas, 146 x 105 cm
(Musée des Beaux-Arts, Orléans)

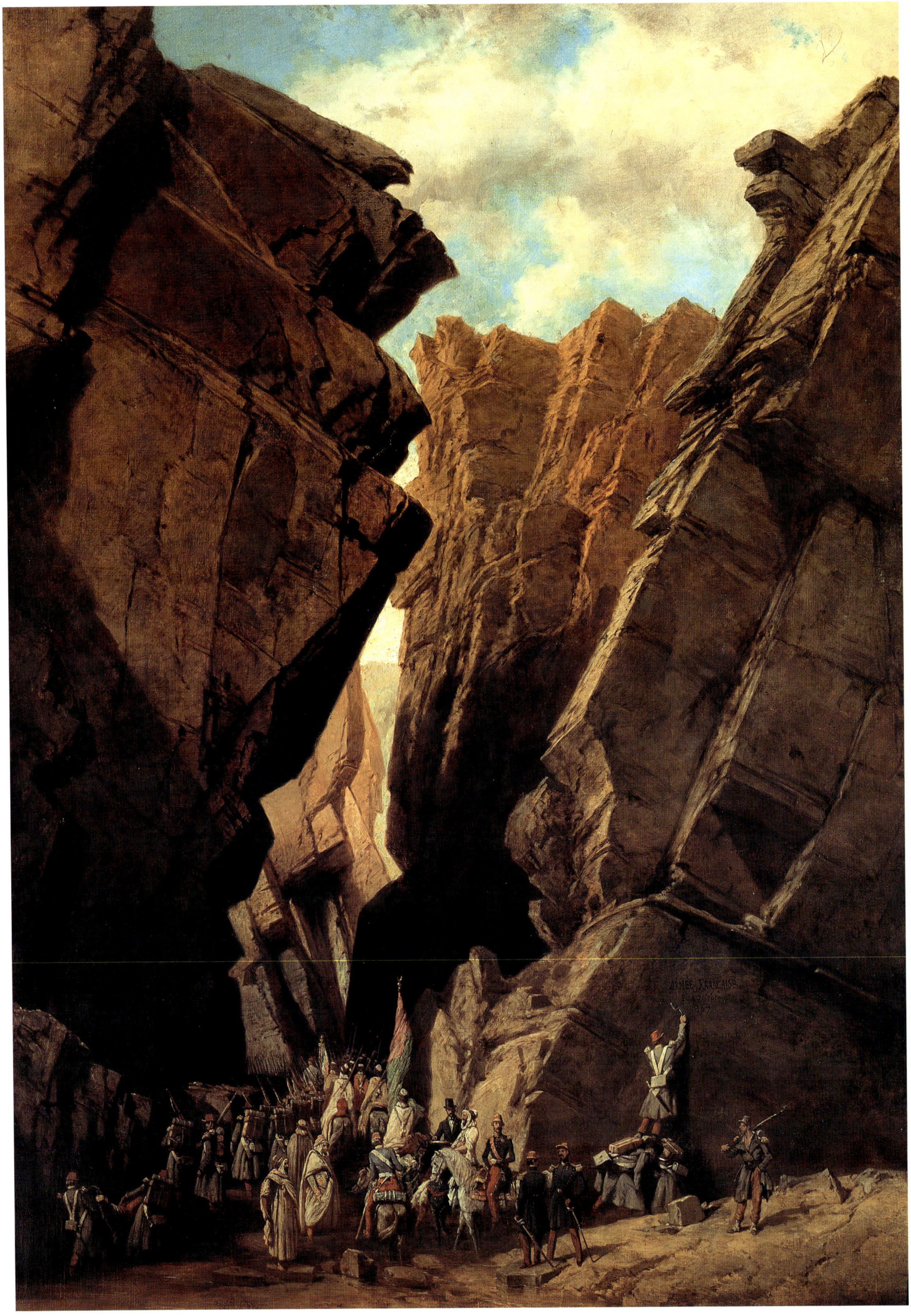

another *Missolonghi*. In 1827, Horace Vernet completed *The Defeat*, and François-Émile de Lansac *Incident During the Missolonghi Exodus*, in which a woman kills herself after killing her own child.

The 1830 Revolution in France largely put paid to French compassion for the insurgents' fate. German painters took over when in 1832 Otto, Prince of the Royal House of Bavaria, was called to the throne of the nascent Greek nation, which he would rule as king until 1862. He invited to Greece competent artists like Peter von Hess, who painted *Pillikares of Athens* during his nine-months stay in 1829, and also *The Entrance of King Otto to Nauplia*. On his return to Munich, Hess decorated the Hofgarten Gallery with scenes illustrating the Greek War of Independence. In 1835, Karl Willhelm von Heideck painted *The Philhellen's Camp During the War of Insurrection*, which shows Bavarian troops in Greece during the fight for independence; and Karl Kraizeisen, an officer during the war against the Ottomans, painted a series of watercolors. Karl Rottman, called to King Otto's court in 1834, specialized in landscapes and groups in traditional Greek costumes. Adolf Teick created *Greek Prisoners Under Mameluke Guard* in 1836. Italian painters came, too: Raffaello Ceccoli held a chair at Athens' School of Fine Arts from 1843 to 1852, and Vincenzo Lanza made his name treating Orientalist subjects. The best Greek painters were sent to Munich to study, some of them – Nicolas Ghyzis and Theodore Ralli, for example – meeting with considerable success.

Once independence had been won, artists soon lost interest in Greece. Prosper Marilhat, who visited it twice, in 1831 and 1833, was not particularly impressed by the country, even though he conceded that the landscapes had "grandeur, and superlative beauty." However, writers like Lamartine, Gautier, and Flaubert, to quote a few of the better-known names, were still curious. For them, the image of an independent Greece still had a wild, dangerous quality; this was fully exploited in Edmond About's *Le Roi des Montagnes* (The king of the mountains), which was illustrated by Gustave Doré. The painter Camille Corot must have been one of the very few artists left to dream of this world between East and West; his *Haïdée* (1872), a delightful canvas which exudes a dreamy nostalgia, was inspired by Lord Byron's poem *The Corsair* (1814). The poem tells of a Greek pirate called Conrad, who leaves his fiancée Medora to launch a desperate attack on the Ottomans; he is taken prisoner but escapes, only to find that Medora, thinking he was dead, has committed suicide.

French colonization of the Maghreb

Algeria

During the 19th century, European powers were increasingly brought into conflict with the Ottoman Turks over control of the Mediterranean. The decline of the once-powerful Osmanli dynasty was now plain to see and Western powers were quick to take advantage of the weaknesses of the Ottoman Empire. King Charles X of France saw an opportunity to make advances in Maghreb, and Algiers, the capital of Algeria, fell to French forces on 5 July 1830. Emir Abd al-Quadir's stubborn resistance, however, did not end until 1847, when he finally surrendered. Whatever the real facts of France's occupation of Algeria, the military feats of the French expeditionary force were given an epic character; even Victor Hugo played with the idea of a collection of poems named after the country, *Les Algériennes*. Painters were invited to accompany the French army, among them Crépin, Baron Gudin, and Isabey, who took home with him several canvases, including *Minaret of the Mosque in Bab Azoun Street* (1835), *Commandant Théodore*

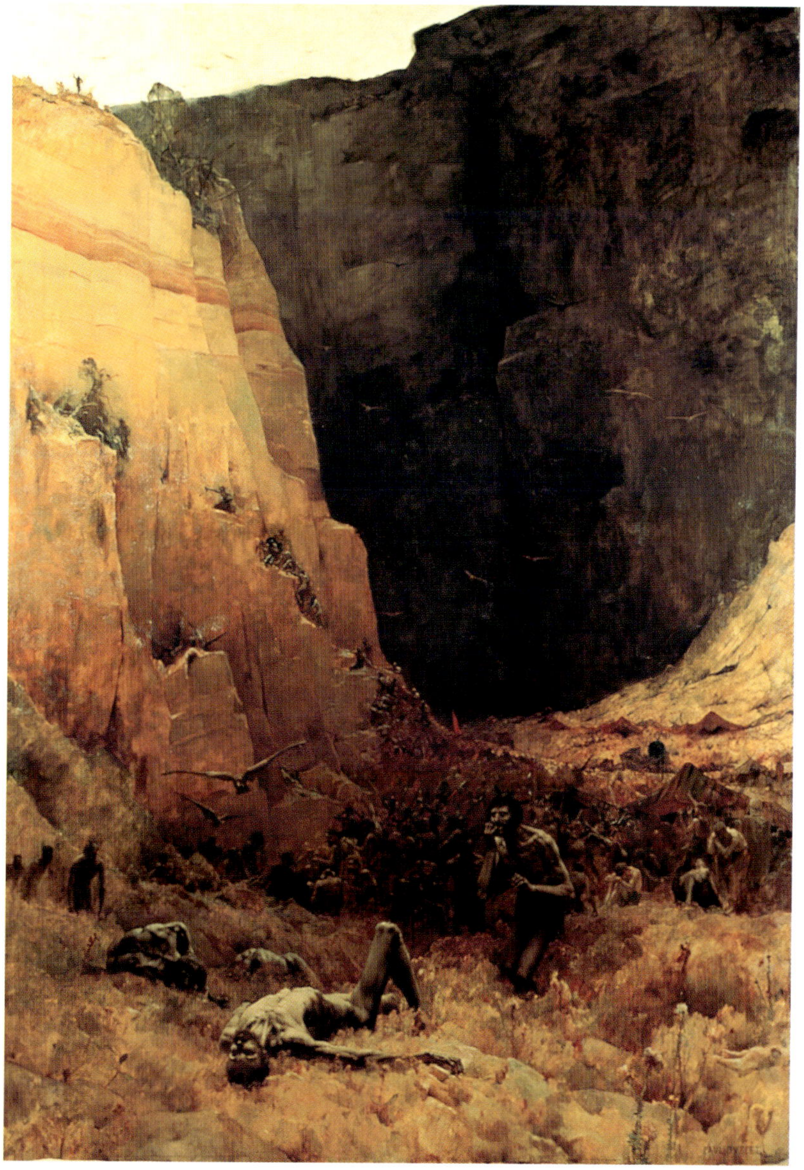

The Narrow Pass at La Hache, Paul Buffet, 1894
Oil on canvas, 400 x 284 cm
(Musée des Beaux-Arts, Nantes).

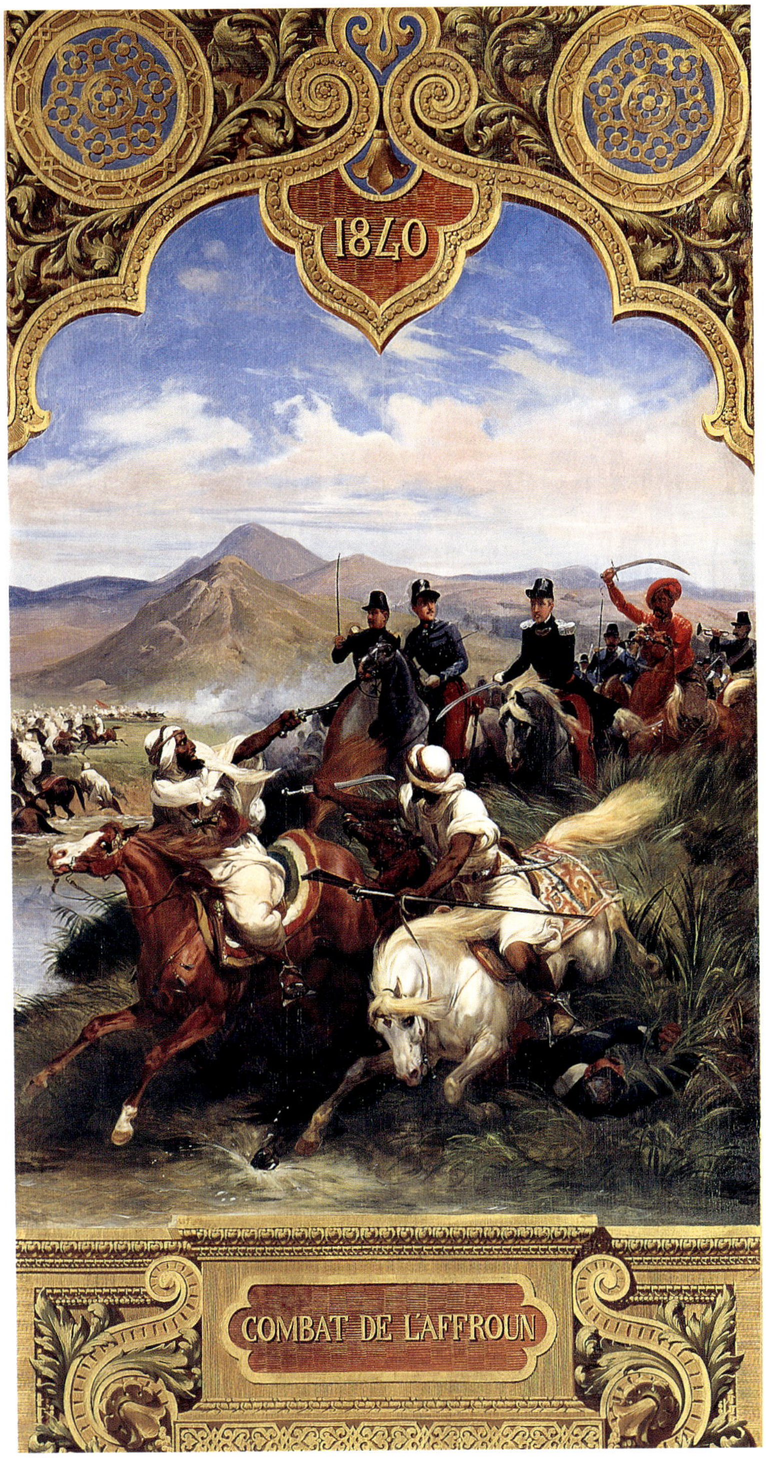

The Battle Below the Hills of Affroun (The Duke d'Aumal's Victory Over the Cavalry of the Caliphate of Millianah, 27 April 1840)
Horace Vernet, c. 1845
Oil on canvas, 288 x 153 cm,
Above the door in the Salle Constantine
(Musée National du Château, Versailles).

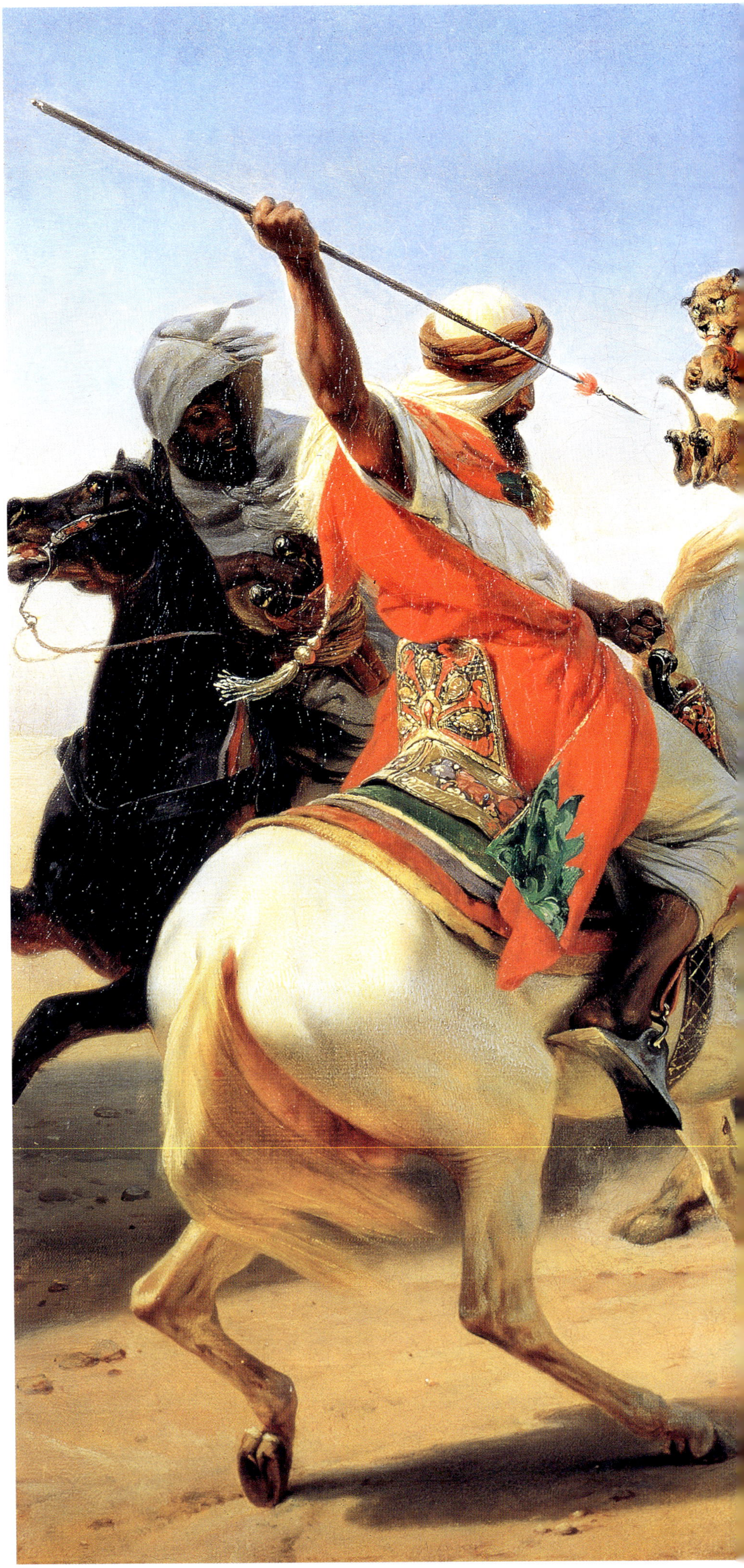

Lion Hunt, Horace Vernet, 1836
Oil on canvas, 57.1 x 81.7 cm
(Wallace Collection, London).

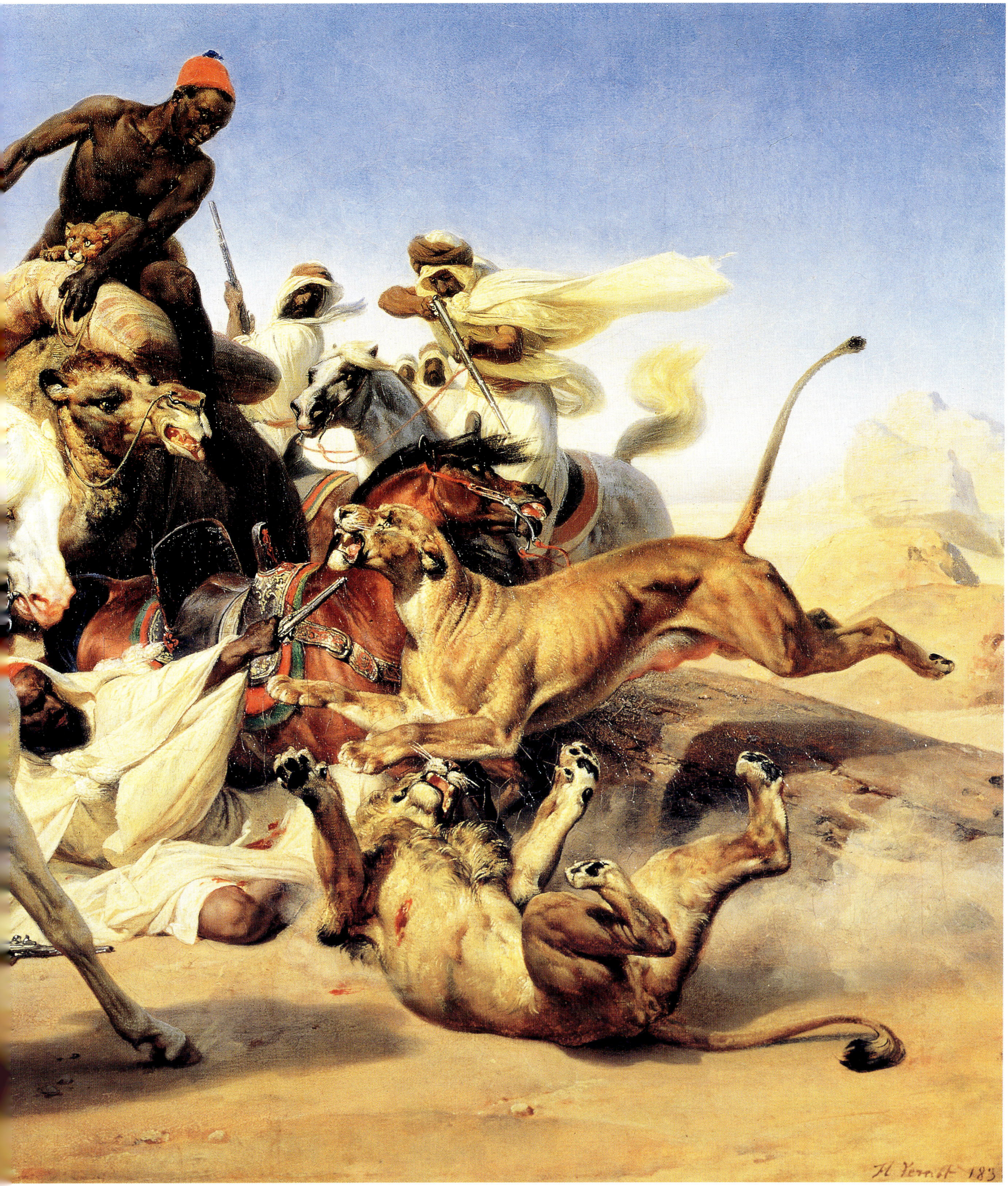

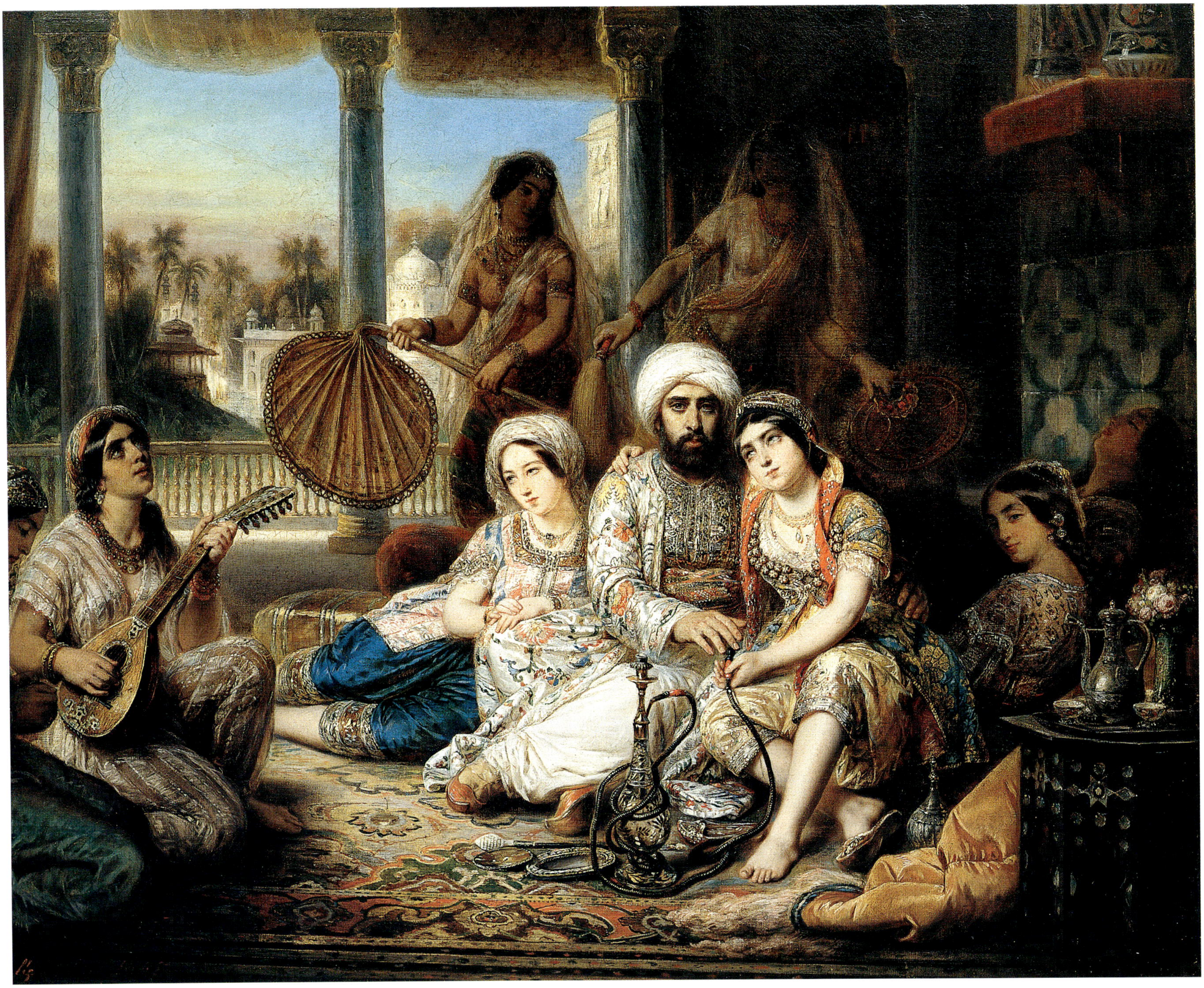

The Pasha and his Harem,
François-Gabriel Lépaulle, undated
Oil on canvas, 92 x 73 cm
(private collection).

Algerian Woman and Her Slave,
Ange Tissier, 1860
Oil on canvas, 130 x 97 cm
(Musée des Arts d'Afrique et d'Océanie, Paris).

Leblanc, Killed at the Battle of Constantine (1837), and *Dyeing Workshop in the Rue du Divan* (1937). When resistance to the French was at its height, Adrien Dauzats traveled with the Duc d'Orleans' army, along with Charles Nodier, the writer who in 1844 published *Journal de l'expedition des portes de fer* (Journal of the Expedition to the Iron Gates), illustrated by Dauzats. Dauzats returned to France with several impressive landscapes, including *Passing Through the Iron Gates* and *The Bibans Pass*; some still show his predilection for Roman remains, for example *The Arc de Triomphe, Djemilah* (c. 1854). Five of his watercolors were shown at the 1841 Salon.

Horace Vernet left behind the running of the Villa Medici in Rome to take part in the Algerian adventure. He took a close interest in military operations, as is shown by *The Attack on Constantine, October 1837* (1839), and the vast canvas, 21 meters (69 feet) long, *The Capture of Abd al-Qadir's Retinue* (c. 1843–1844). Though criticized because of its historical inaccuracy, this work has some fine passages, notably the depiction of the women of the Arab court. He had previously commemorated *The Fall of Bône*, exhibited at the 1835 Salon, *The Fall of Bougie*, and *The Battle of Isly*. His eulogizing of the campaign earned him the contemptuous

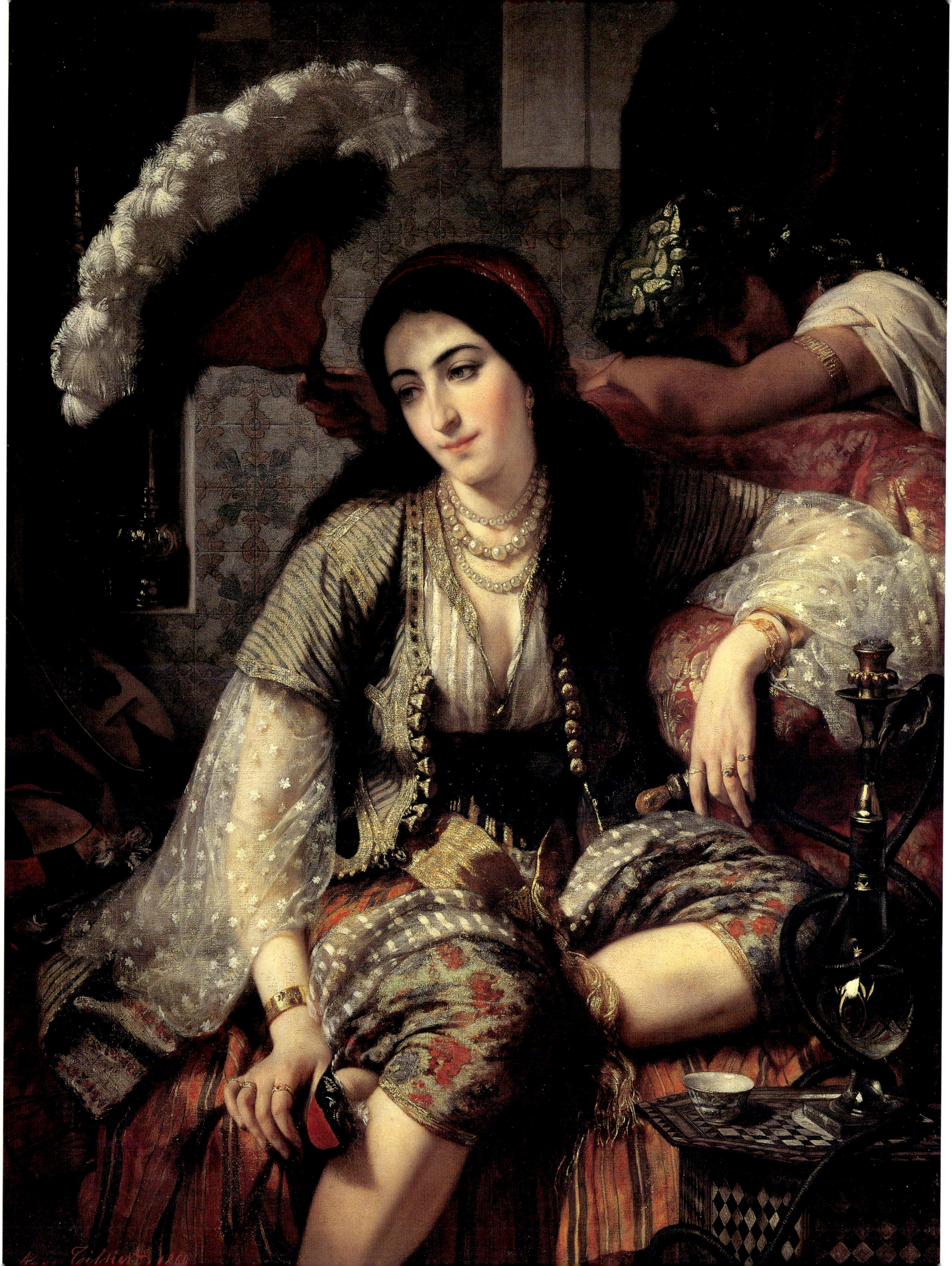

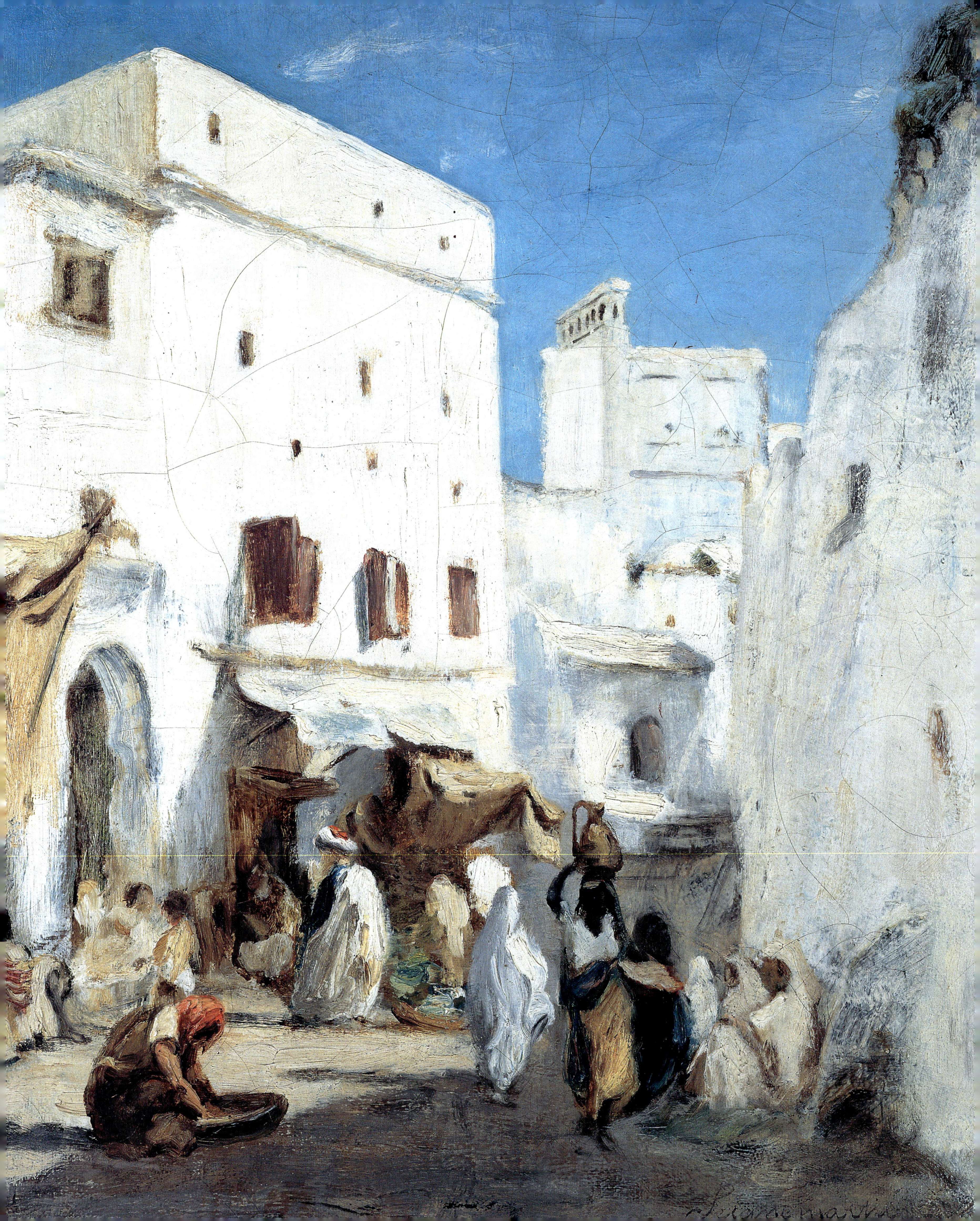

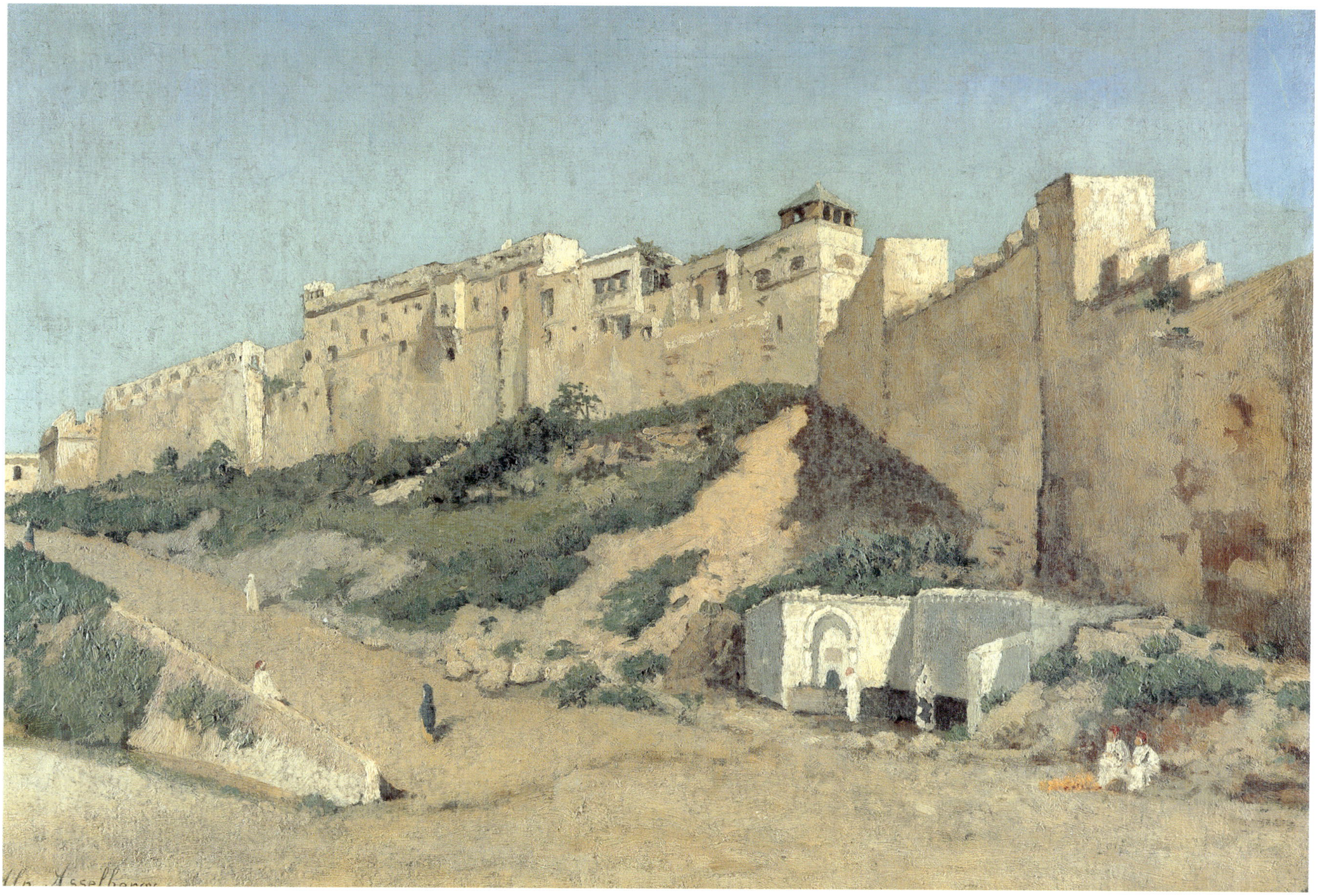

nickname "the Raphael of the canteens," and also Baudelaire's barb that he was essentially a "soldier dabbling in painting." He would continue to travel until 1853, seeking not only to immortalize the colonial army's valor and chivalry – as in *Adopted Child* (1848), a propaganda work in which a Zouave gives a mother something to drink whilst her child is being nursed at a ewe's udder – but also to capture the customs of the Algerian people, as in his *Arabs Listening to a Story Inside their Encampment*, a canvas exhibited at the 1834 Salon. His *Mass in Kabylia* (1852) illustrates his astute grasp of the political, and also his unerring flair for finding the symbolic value of an incident. Though he was often criticized for the detachment in his style, Vernet was emulated by Eugène Ginon and Capitaine Leblanc; Raffet, too, would imitate him, producing lithographs glorifying the colonial army.

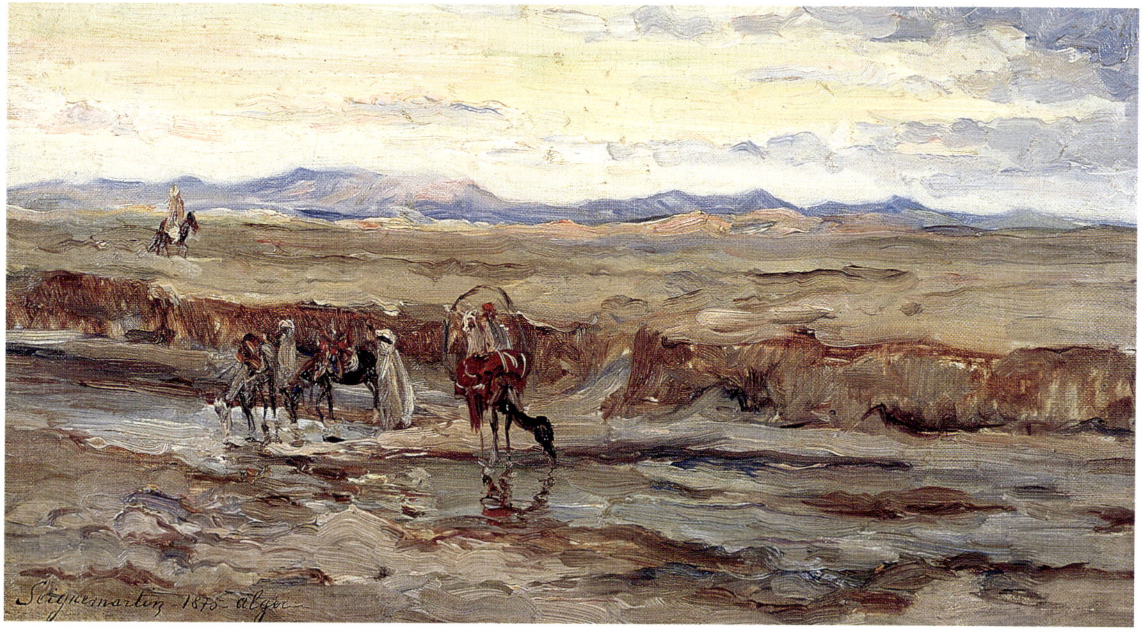

Opposite
A Street in Algiers,
Jean Seignemartin, 1875
Oil on canvas, 46 x 38 cm
(Musée des Beaux-Arts, Lyons).

Top
The Casbah of Algiers, Alphonse Asselbergs, c. 1873–1874
Oil on canvas, 47 x 65 cm
(Musée d'Orsay, Paris).

Above
Winter Landscape, Southern Algeria,
Jean Seignemartin, 1875
Oil on wood, 22 x 39 cm
(Musée d'Art Moderne, Saint-Étienne).

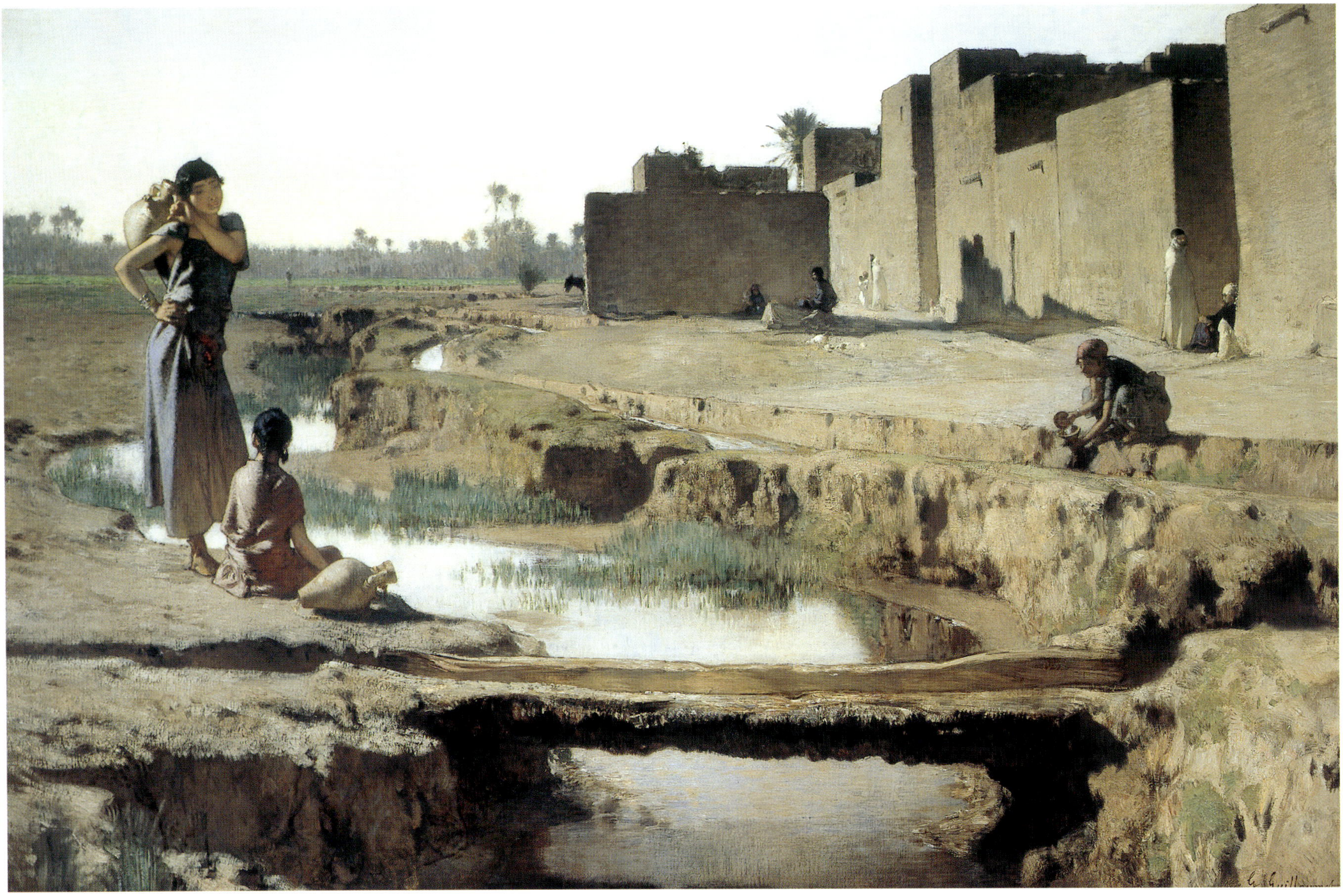

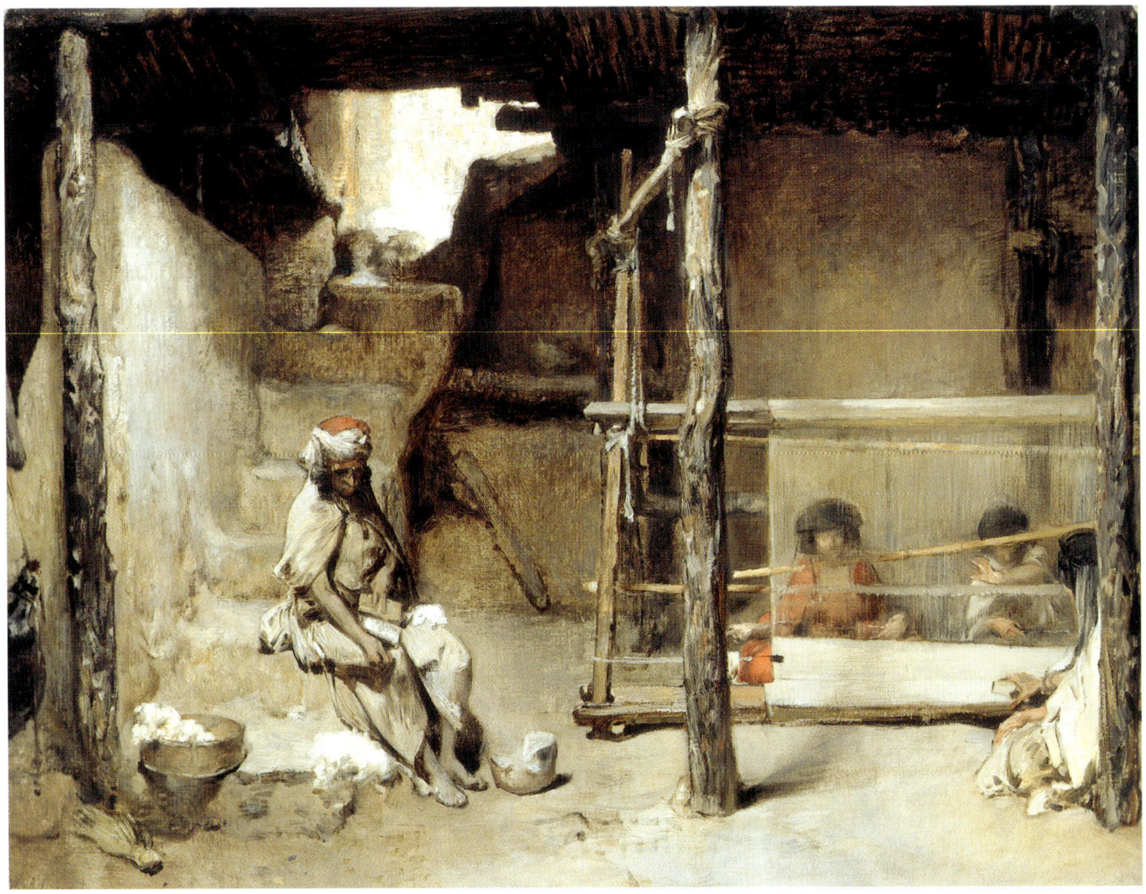

Above
La Seguia, Near Biskra, Gustave Guillaumet, 1885
Oil on canvas, 100 x 155 cm (Musée d'Orsay, Paris).

Right
Weavers at Bou-Saâda (formerly *Spinners at Bou-Saâda*),
Gustave Guillaumet, undated
Oil on canvas, 95 x 112 cm (Musée d'Orsay, Paris).

Opposite, top
Evening Prayer in the Sahara, Gustave Guillaumet, 1863
Oil on canvas, 135 x 182 cm (Musée d'Orsay, Paris).

Opposite, bottom
Laghouat, Algerian Sahara, Gustave Guillaumet, 1879
Oil on canvas, 122 x 181 cm (Musée d'Orsay, Paris).

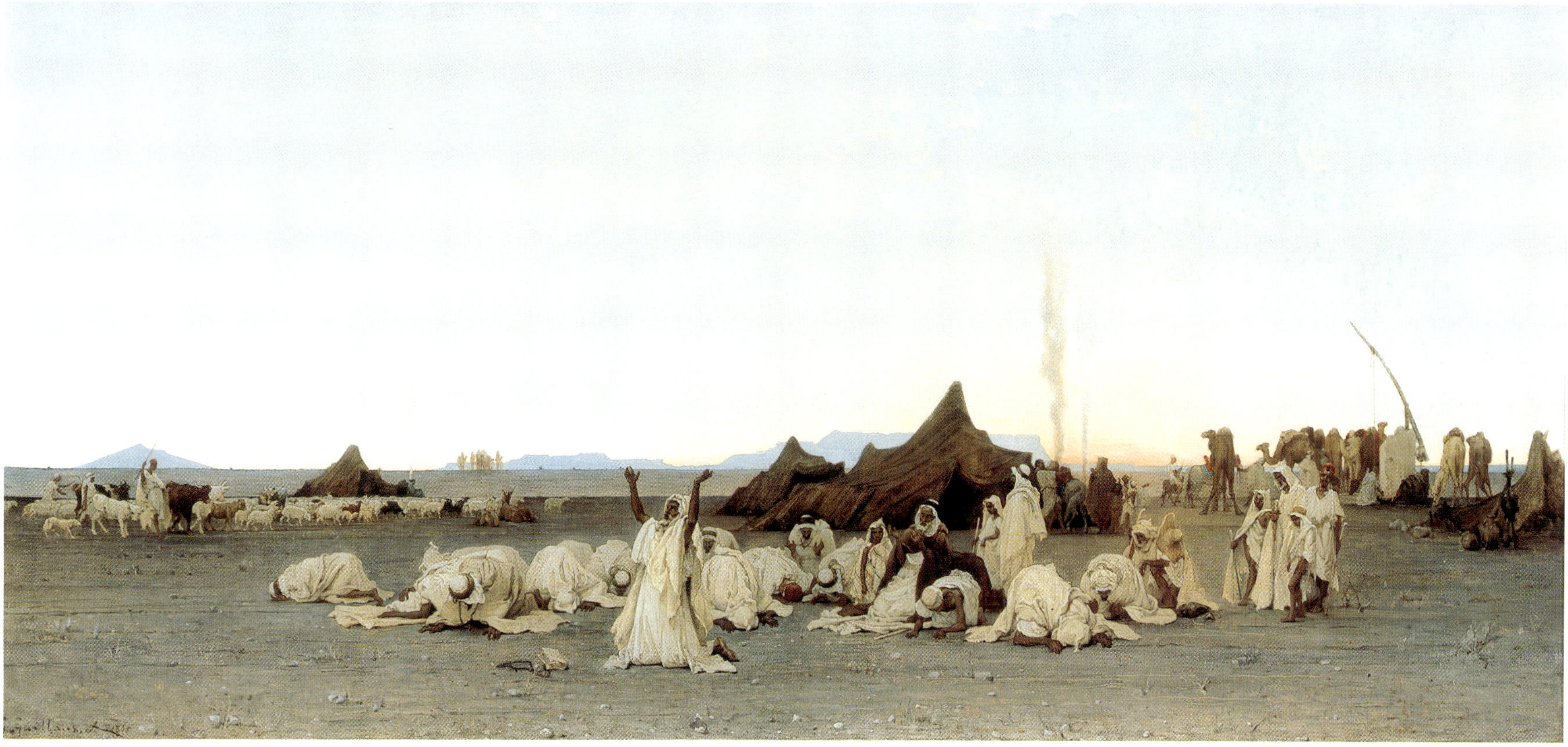

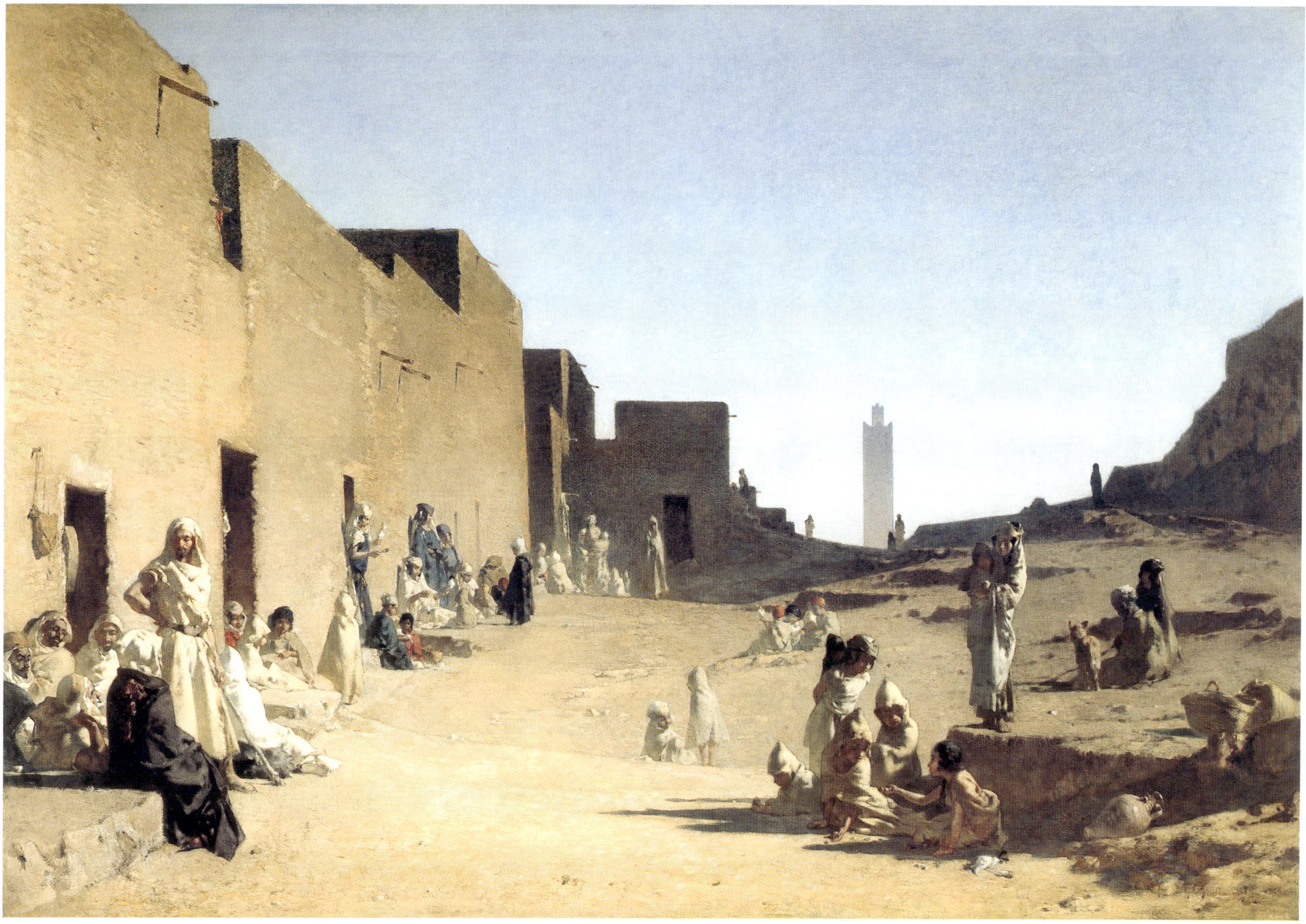

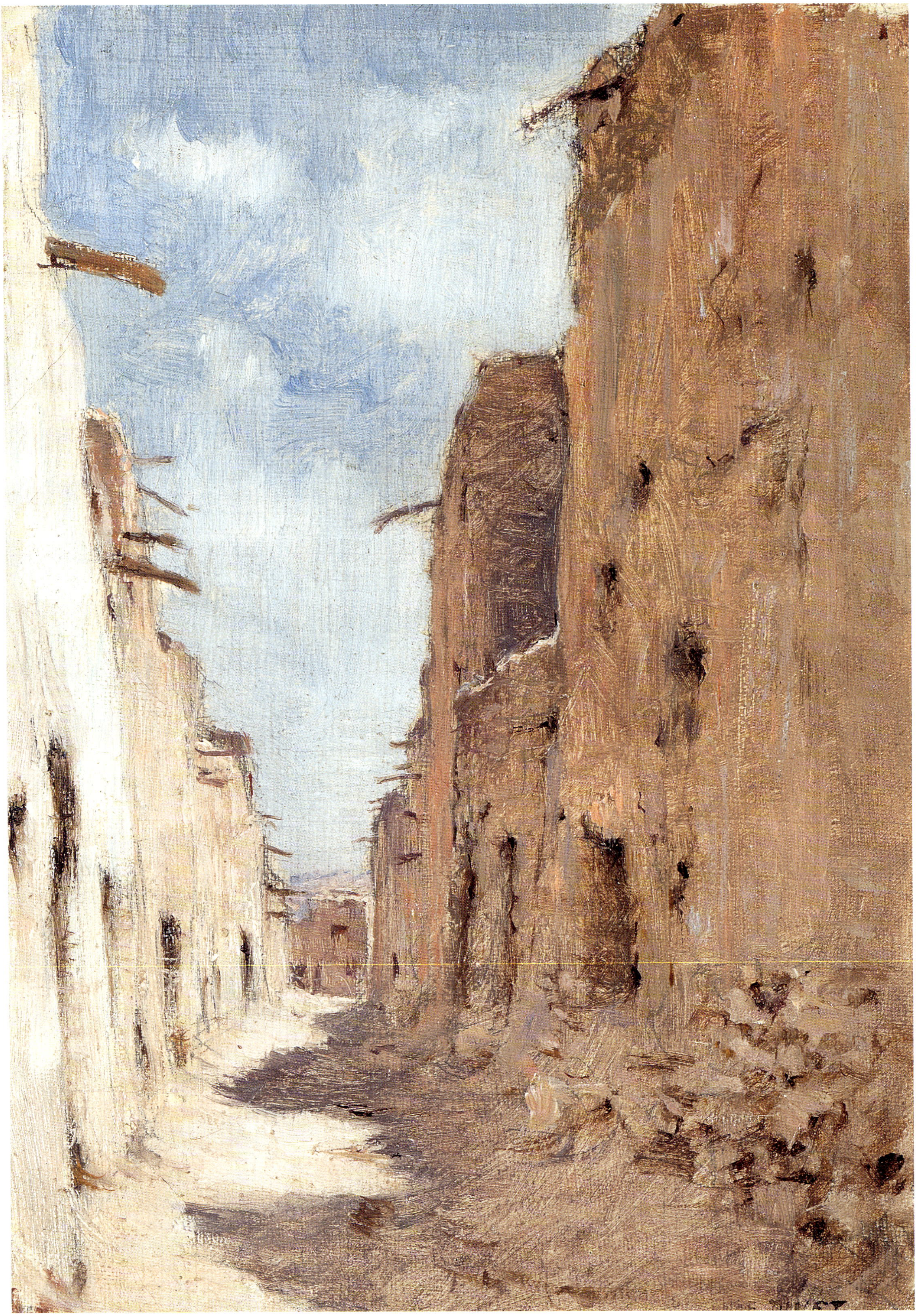

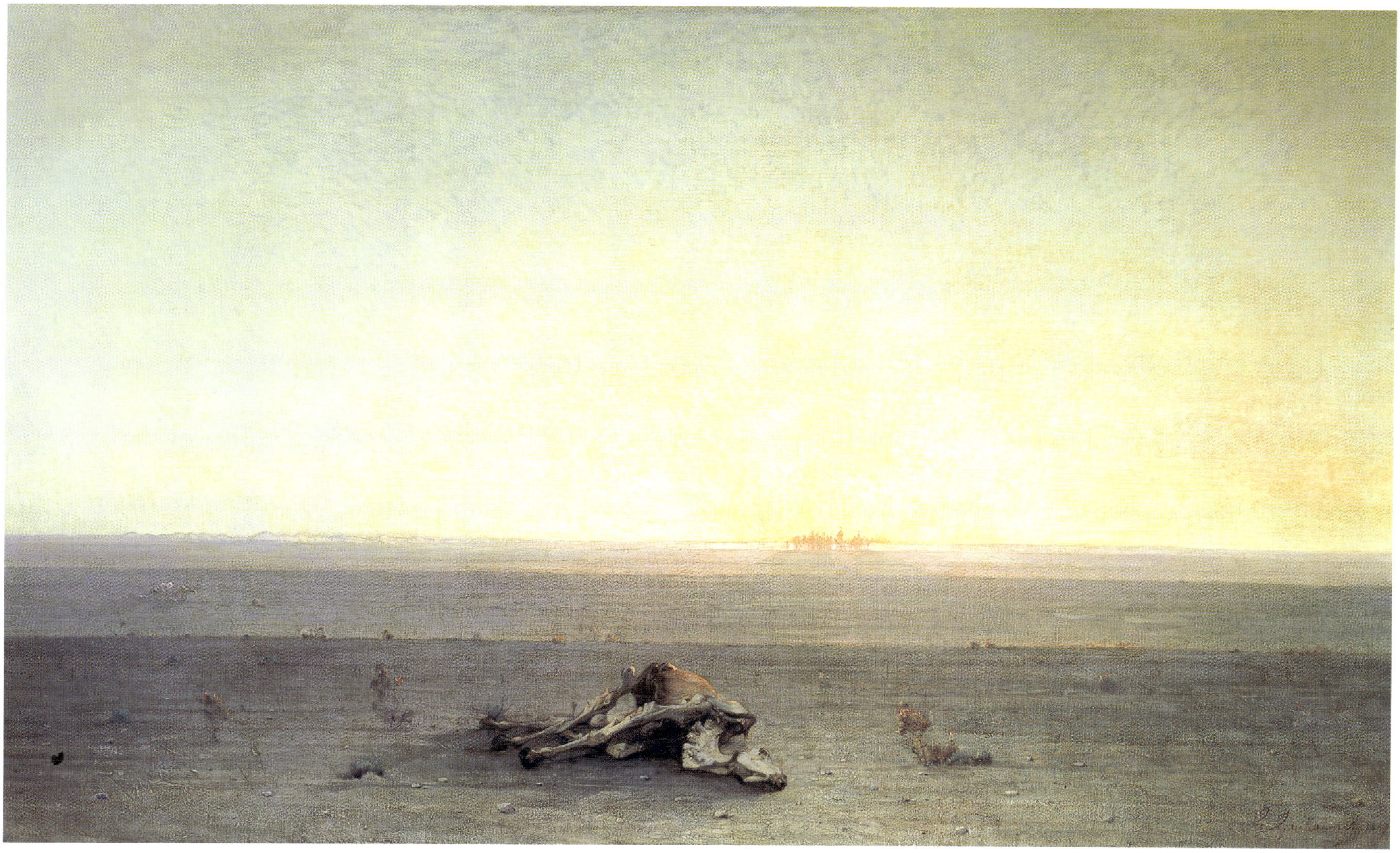

Desert heroics and appalling sieges, however, left others indifferent, among them William Wyld. Wyld was hailed by Gautier as a pioneer of Orientalism: "He was among the first to push his way to the Moorish banks, complete with palette, when Algiers still shone in all her barbarian glory and the whole city had a uniquely Moorish quality now to be found only on the Heights of Sidi Mohamed Sherriff." Wyld's work in, say, *Algerian Shops*, a gouache from 1833, clearly expresses his preoccupation with authenticity, his determination to get to the essence of his subject. In 1835 he and his friend Lessore published their fascinating *Voyage dans la Régence d'Alger* (Journey around the Algerian Protectorate). Théodore Frère first visited Algeria in 1835, taking home the conviction that this world must be painted with a cold, neutral precision; having returned three years later, he sent to the Salon a number of canvases, one of the finest being *On Algiers Heights*.

With the main exception of Eugène Fromentin, artists were far less interested in Algeria during the second half of the 19th century. Another exception was Gustave Auguste Guillaumet, who, visiting it for the first time in 1862, described it with respect and humility. He made laudable efforts to come to grips with the Muslim world and also, traveling far into the south, attempted to gain a deep knowledge of Algeria. His particular technique, using small separate dabs of paint, sets his works apart from that of his contemporaries. With *An Arab Market in Algeria* he put behind him the earlier, rather mawkish canvases he had exhibited in the Salon during the 1860s. And there were a few other artists. Albert Girard overdid everyday life in Algeria and Kabylia, if *A Sacrifice of Chickens at Babel Oued* (1875) and *Algerian Festival* are anything to go by. Georges Rochegrosse ended his life in Algiers, in his luxuriously decorated villa of El-Biar, with its garish pottery, pools, and marble fountains. In his old age he painted Algerian scenes whose bold colors are striking even today. Étienne Dinet, who visited Algeria first in 1882, finally settled there for good.

Above
The Sahara (The Desert),
Gustave Guillaumet, 1867
Oil on canvas, 110 x 200 cm
(Musée d'Orsay, Paris).

Opposite
A Street in Laghouat, Algeria,
Étienne Dinet, 1887
Oil on wood, 30 x 22 cm
(Musée d'Orsay, Paris).

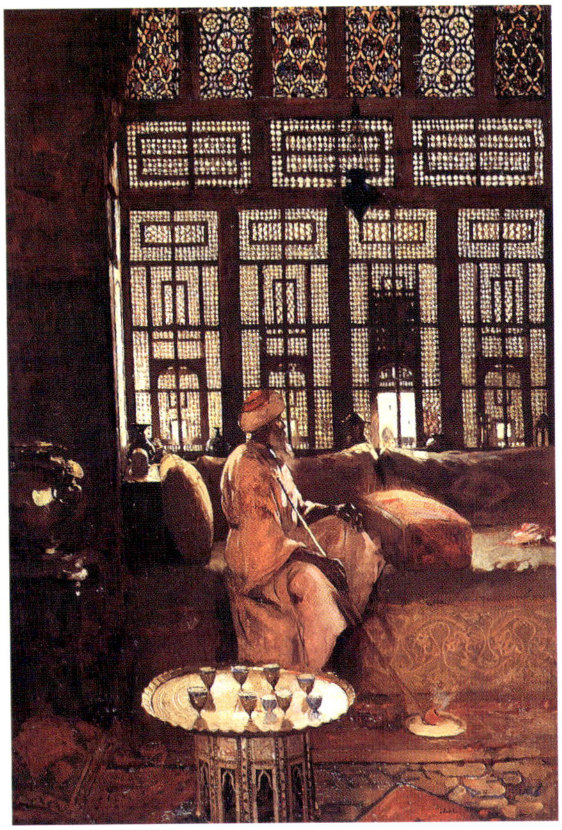

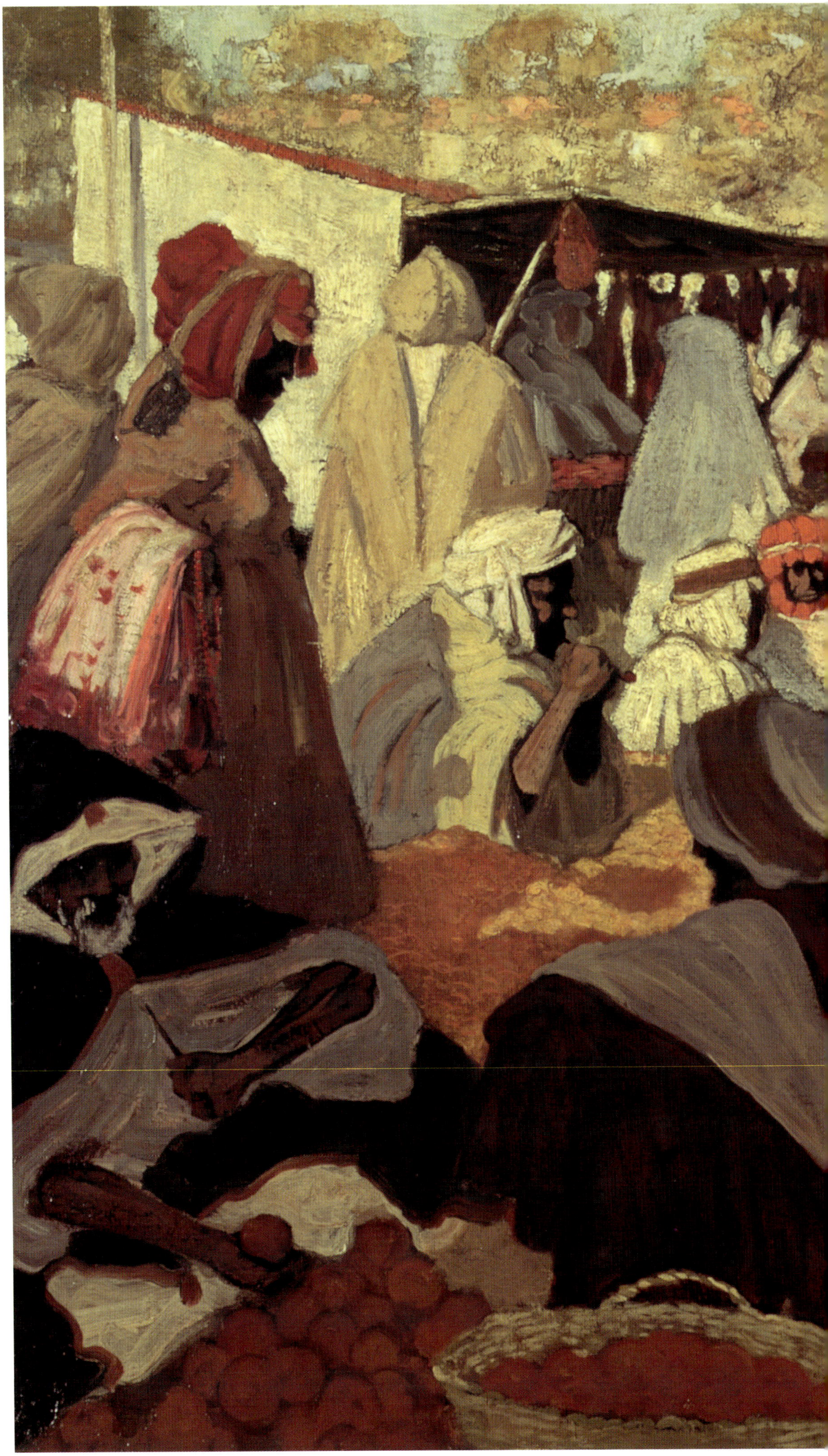

Above
Arab Interior, Arthur Melville, 1881
Oil on canvas, 94 x 71 cm
(National Gallery of Scotland, Edinburgh).

Right
Orange Market in Blidah,
Henri Evenepoel, 1898
Oil on canvas, 81 x 125 cm
(Musées Royaux des Beaux-Arts de Belgique, Brussels).

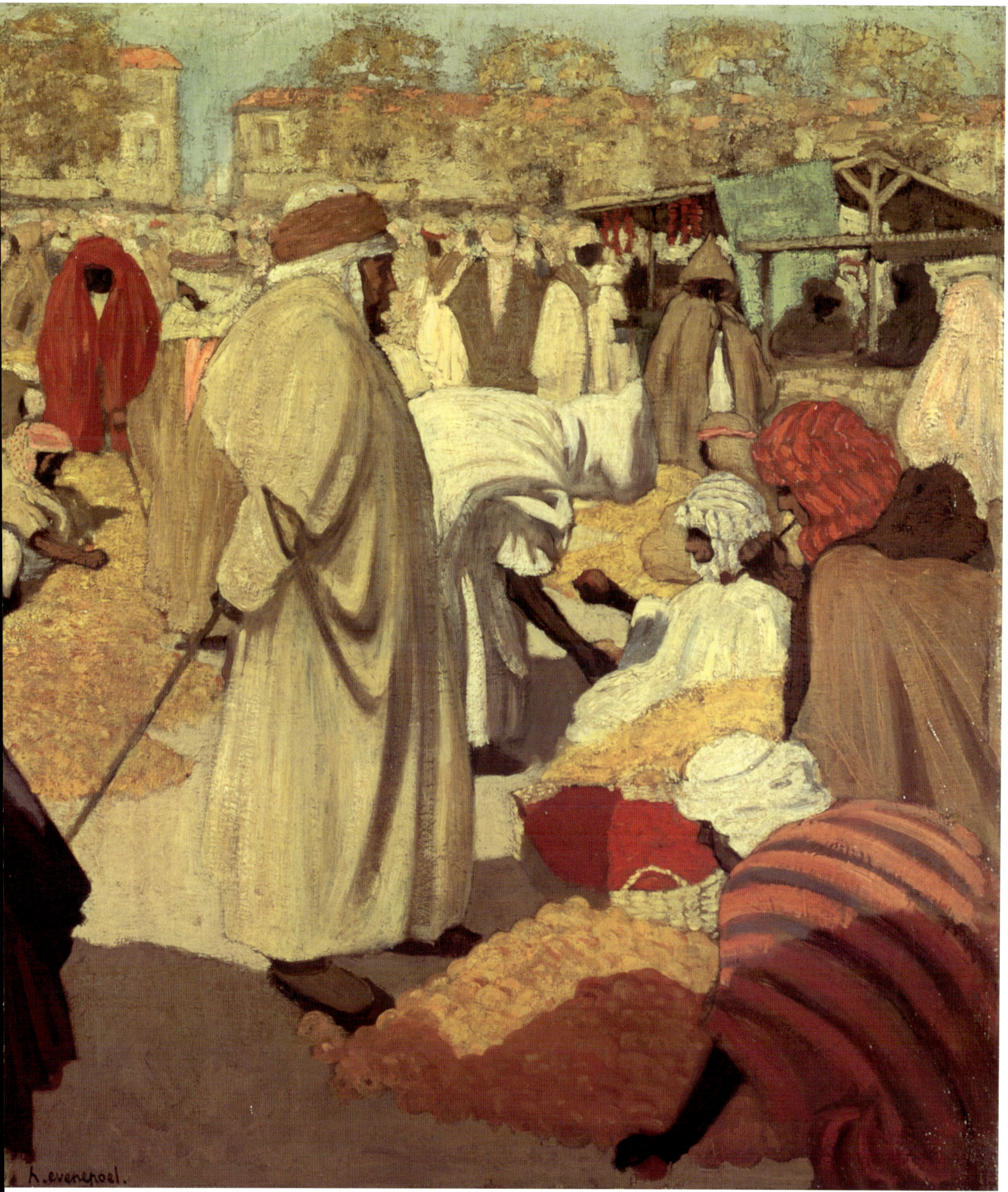
h.evenepoel.

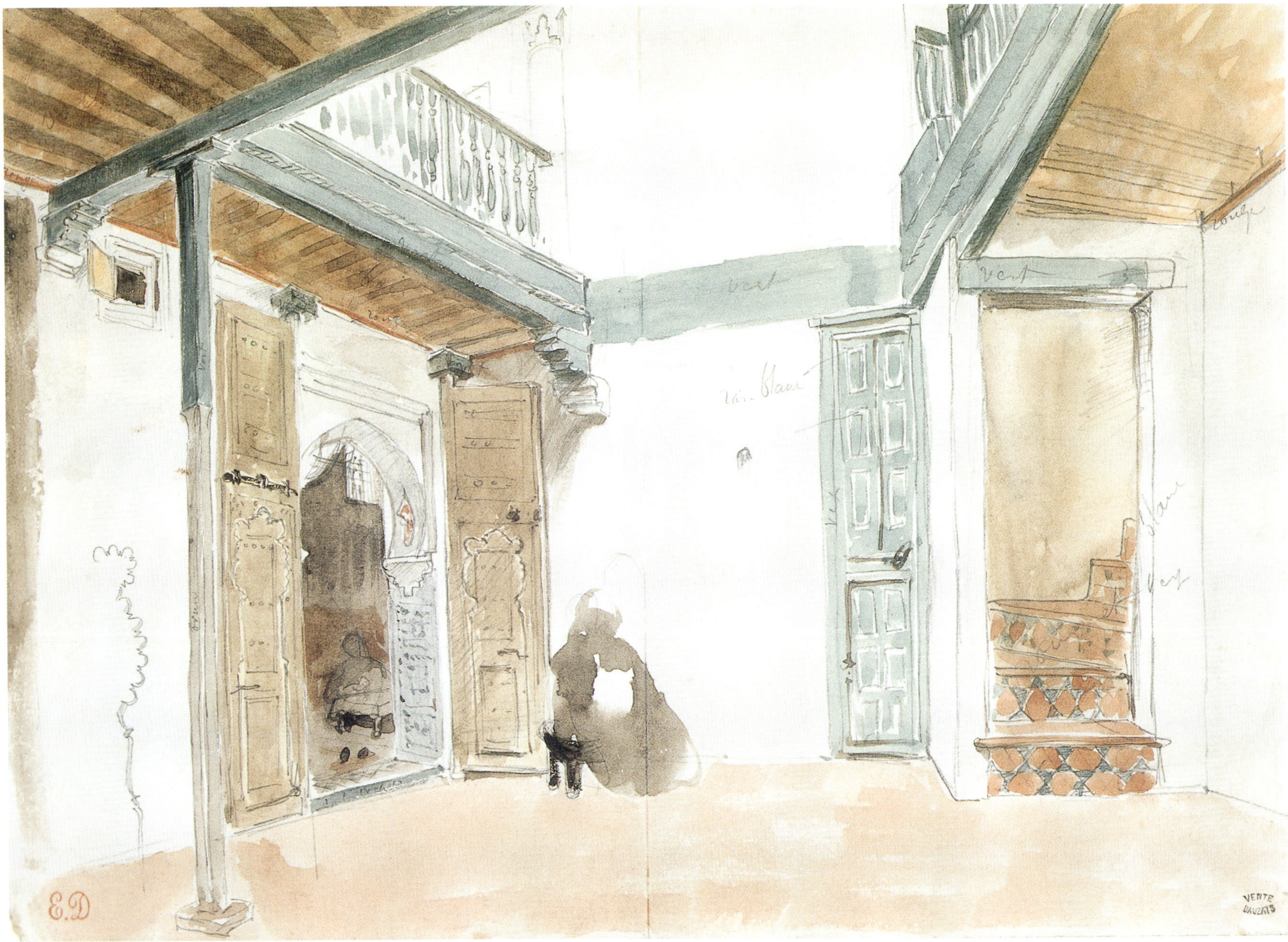

A Courtyard in Tangiers,
Eugène Delacroix, 1832
Watercolor over graphite drawing,
20.7 x 29.4 cm
(Musée du Louvre, Paris).

He converted to Islam, and, having performed the obligatory pilgrimage to Mecca, adopted the name of Hadji Nasr Ed Dine Dini. This self-proclaimed champion of the beauties of the Muslim world ended up producing color prints whose eroticism is highly questionable.

On the whole, however, the best accounts of Algeria were to be provided by French writers, notably Théophile Gautier, Guy de Maupassant, and Jean Lorrain.

Morocco

In the 19th century Morocco had little in common with Algeria. The country had never fallen under Turkish domination and had maintained the same dynasty on its throne without interruption. Horace Vernet, a great lover of the bleak Algerian countryside, warmed even more to what he could see of the accessible regions of the Shariffian kingdom. The French public made its first acquaintance with the country through Pierre Blanchard's painting *Funeral in Tangiers*, which was exhibited at the 1841 salon. It was left to Eugène Delacroix to make Morocco sublime in the eyes of generations to come. Henri Regnault went to Tangiers, one of the rare cities open to foreigners, and painted, among other works, *Halt in the Desert* (1869) and the *Execution Without Trial*, which strongly influenced Benjamin-Constant, who visited Morocco in 1872.

Alfred Dehodencq, who lived in southern Spain, went for long visits to Tangiers and Tetuán from 1853 onwards, and was able to visit Rabat, Mogador, and Salé. He was gripped by Morocco's potent assault on the senses: "I can still hear the snake charmer's

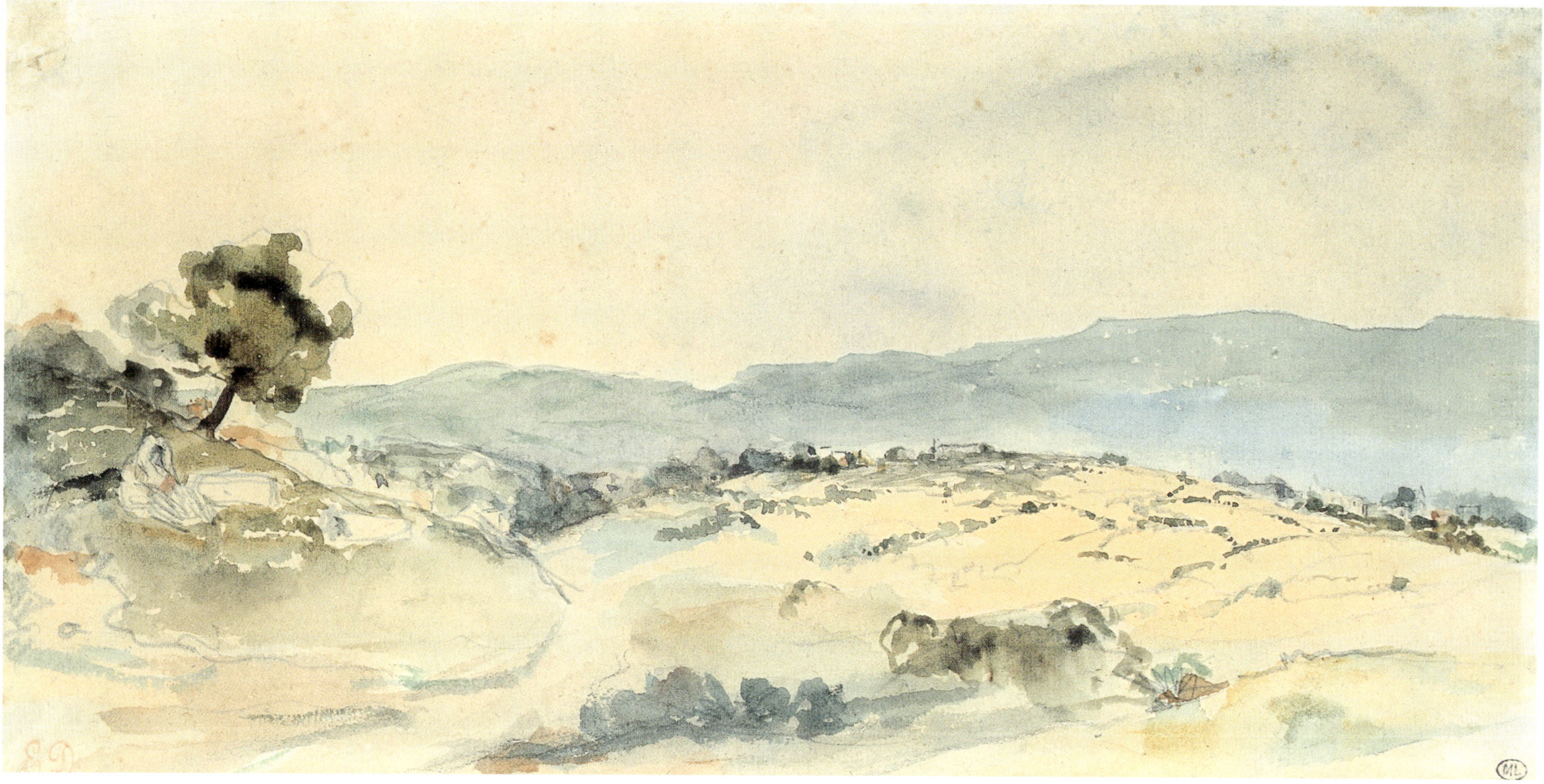

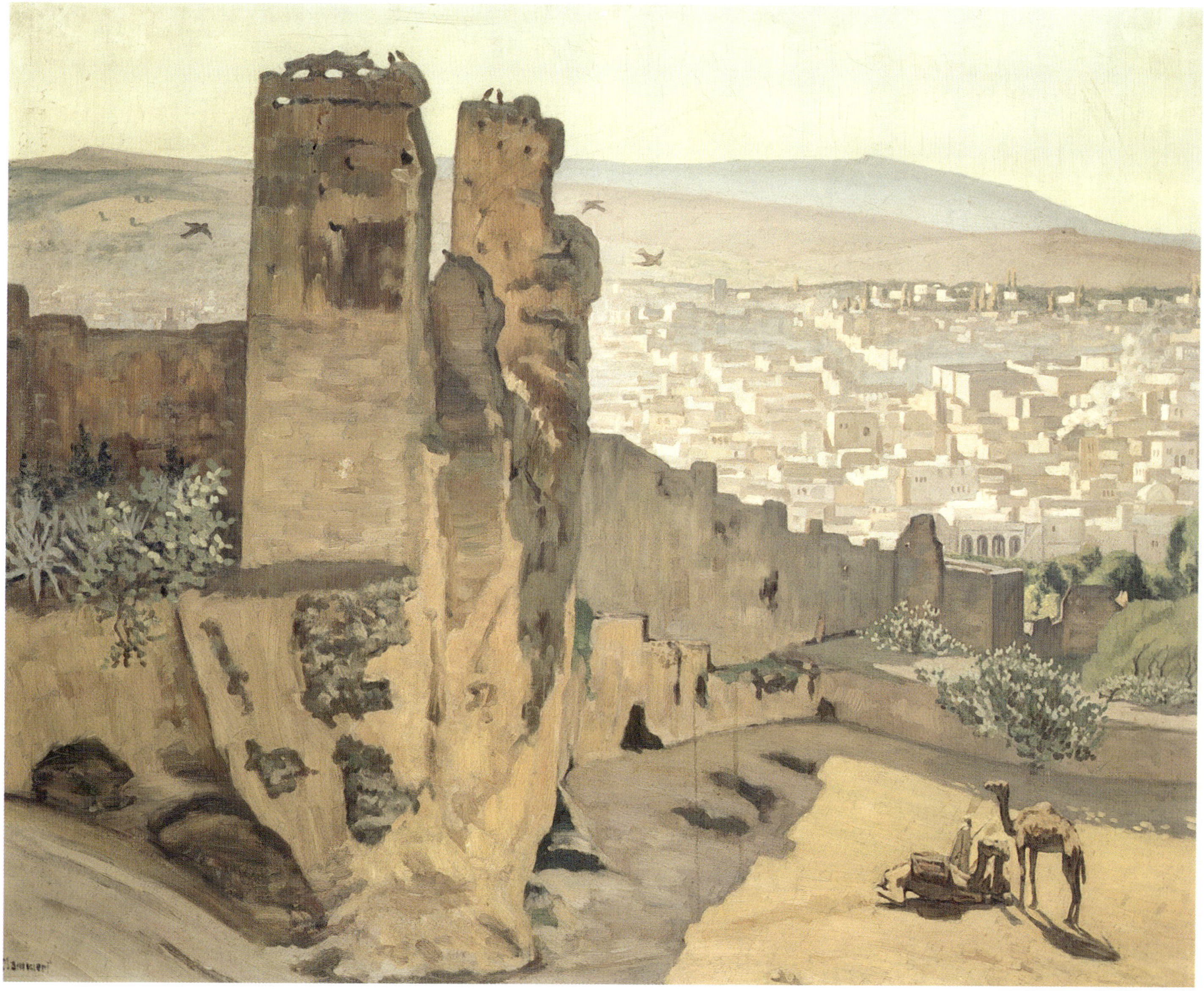

Moroccan Landscape near Tangiers,
Eugène Delacroix, 1832
Watercolor with gouache highlights over graphite drawing, 13.9 x 28.8 cm (Musée du Louvre, Département des Arts Graphiques, Paris).

View of Fez, Azouaou Mammeri, undated
Oil on canvas, 70 x 90.2 cm (Musée d'Orsay, Paris).

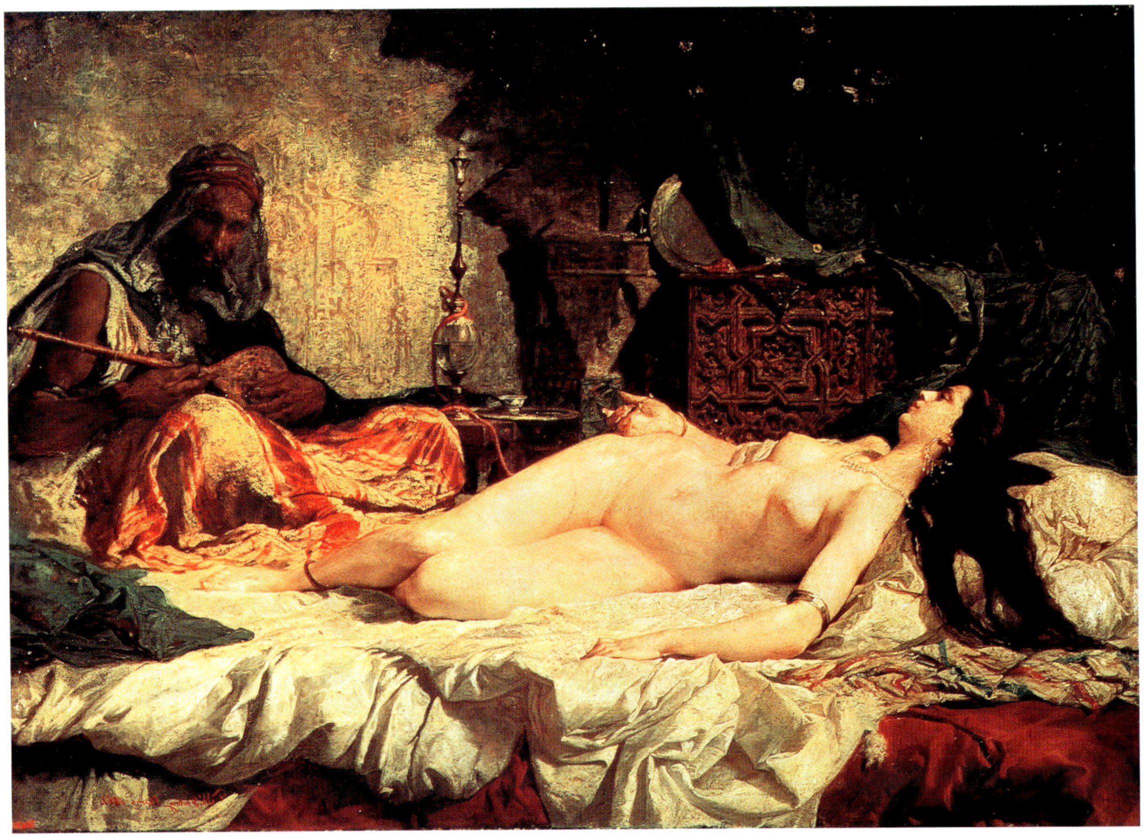

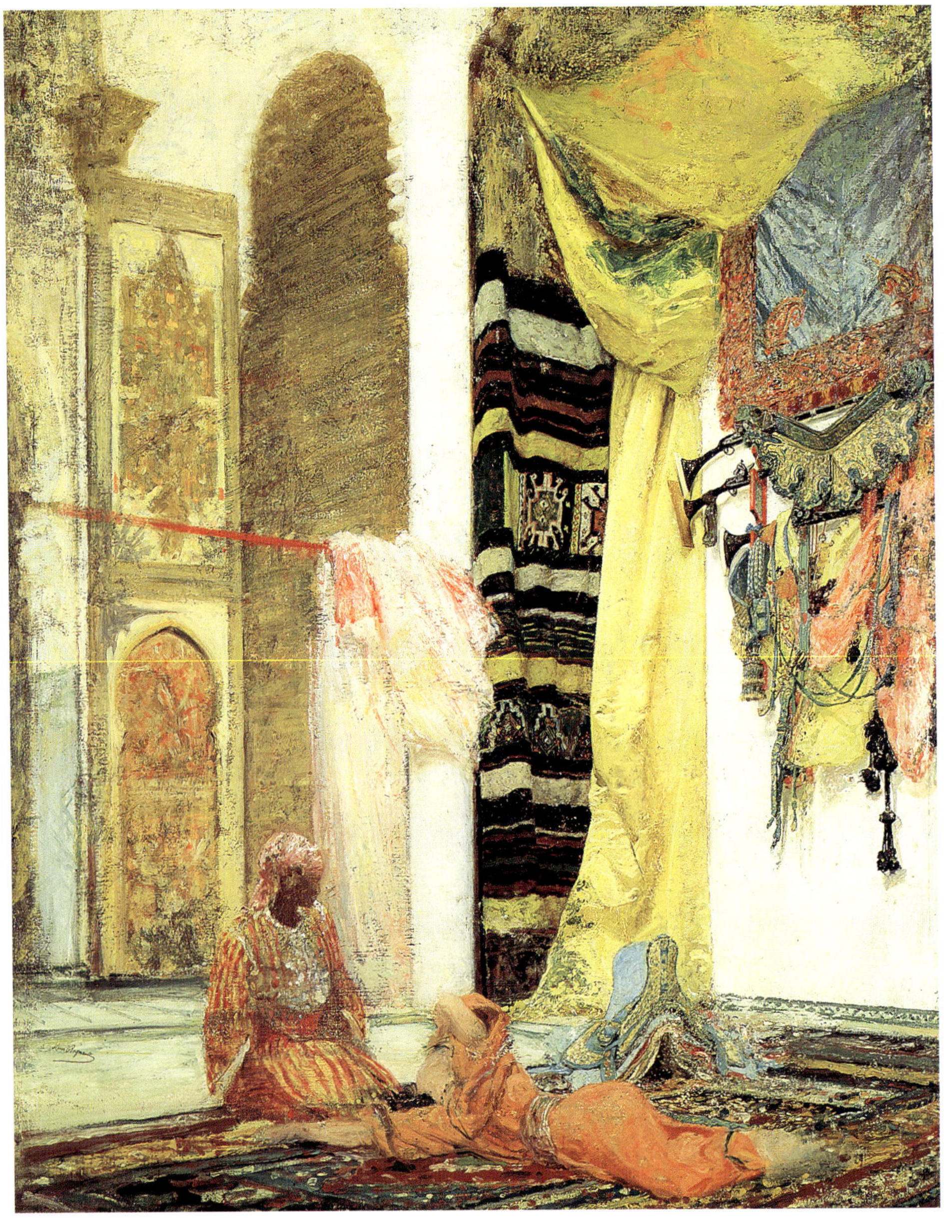

pipe and the oboe. Dreaming, nostrils wide open, I breathe in this smell of old hay, of butter and dust, which is heaven to me, a smell which grabs hold of you at the first step you take on Moroccan soil." He took enormous personal risks and was almost stoned to death when drawing sketches for his *A Jewish Girl's Execution*, a sordid incident in which a poor girl who pretended she had converted to Islam was put to death. He was not averse to exaggeration in aid of 'local color,' however, as we can see in such works as *The Pasha's Justice*, *Robbers Punished*, *A Jew Arrested in Tangiers*, *A Beating in the Casbah*, and *The Pasha on an Outing*. He focused his attention in particular on the Jewish community, which furnished him with his main models; examples include *Jewish Concert*, *Jewish Wedding*, and *Jewish Feast in Tangiers*. His *Black Women Dancing*, however, was not well received at the 1879 Salon, and on his return to France, where he continued to paint Moroccan scenes, his style, characterized by bold strokes and splashes of color, failed to please.

The Catalan painter Mariano Fortuny y Marsal had an unqualified success with his Oriental paintings at his first exhibition in Paris in 1870. Sent to Morocco by the City of Barcelona to commemorate the Spanish victory of Tetuán – a painting he would never complete – he was won over by the intense colors of North Africa. His brisk, lively style was well suited to the exuberance he sought to capture in works like *Arab Fantasy* of 1867. He returned to Tangiers and Tetuán in 1871 in the company of Georges Clairin, whose enthusiasm for the vitality and passion of the land and the people

Odalisque, Mariano Fortuny y Marsal, 1861
Oil on card, 56.9 x 81 cm
(Museo de Arte Moderno, Barcelona).

Patio in Tangiers, Henri Regnault, 1869–1870
Oil on canvas, 117.5 x 95 cm
(Guezireh Museum, Cairo).

Opposite
Jewish Girl in Tangiers, Charles Landelle, undated.
Oil on canvas, 61.4 x 50.5 cm
(Musée des Beaux-Arts, Reims).

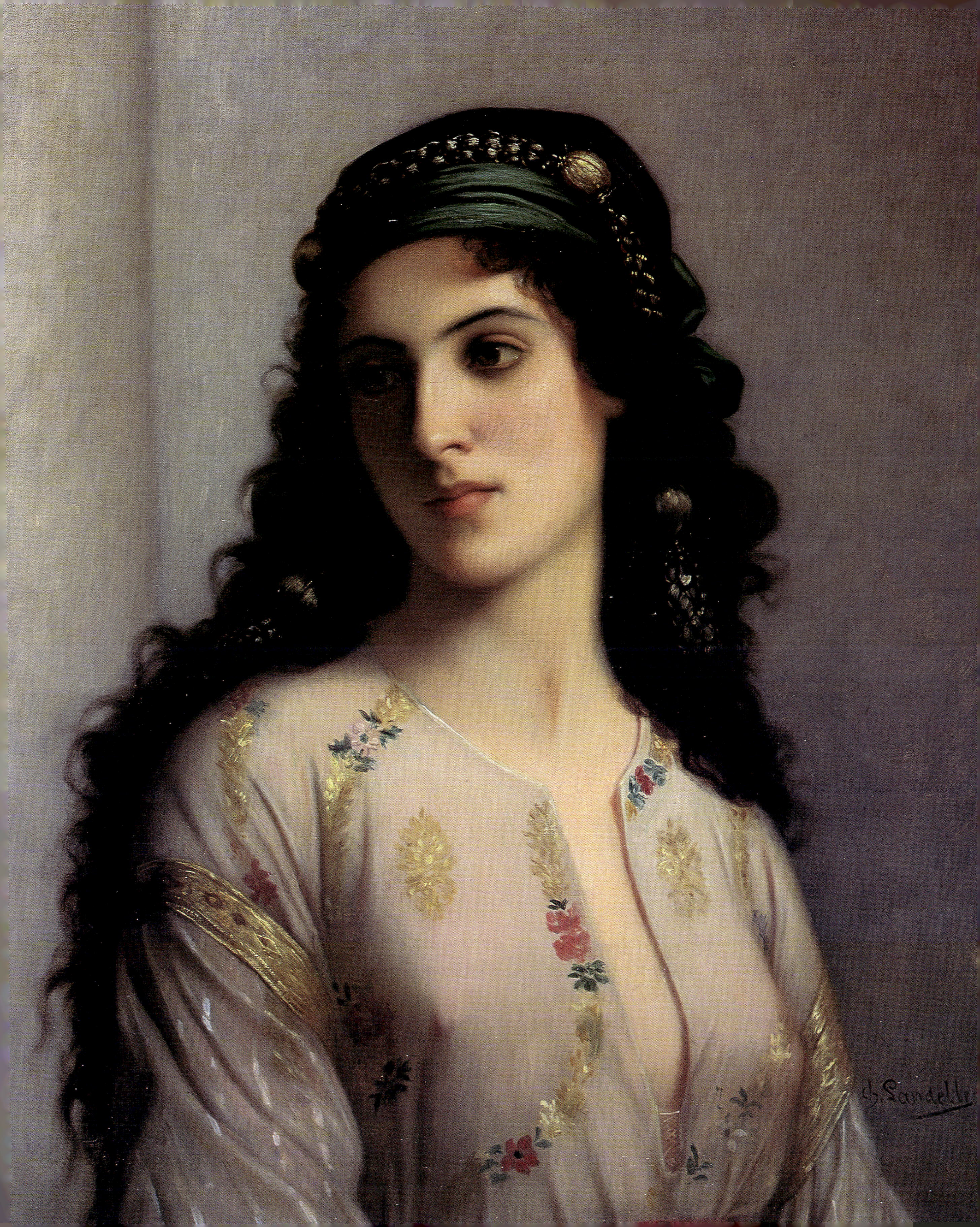
Ch. Landelle

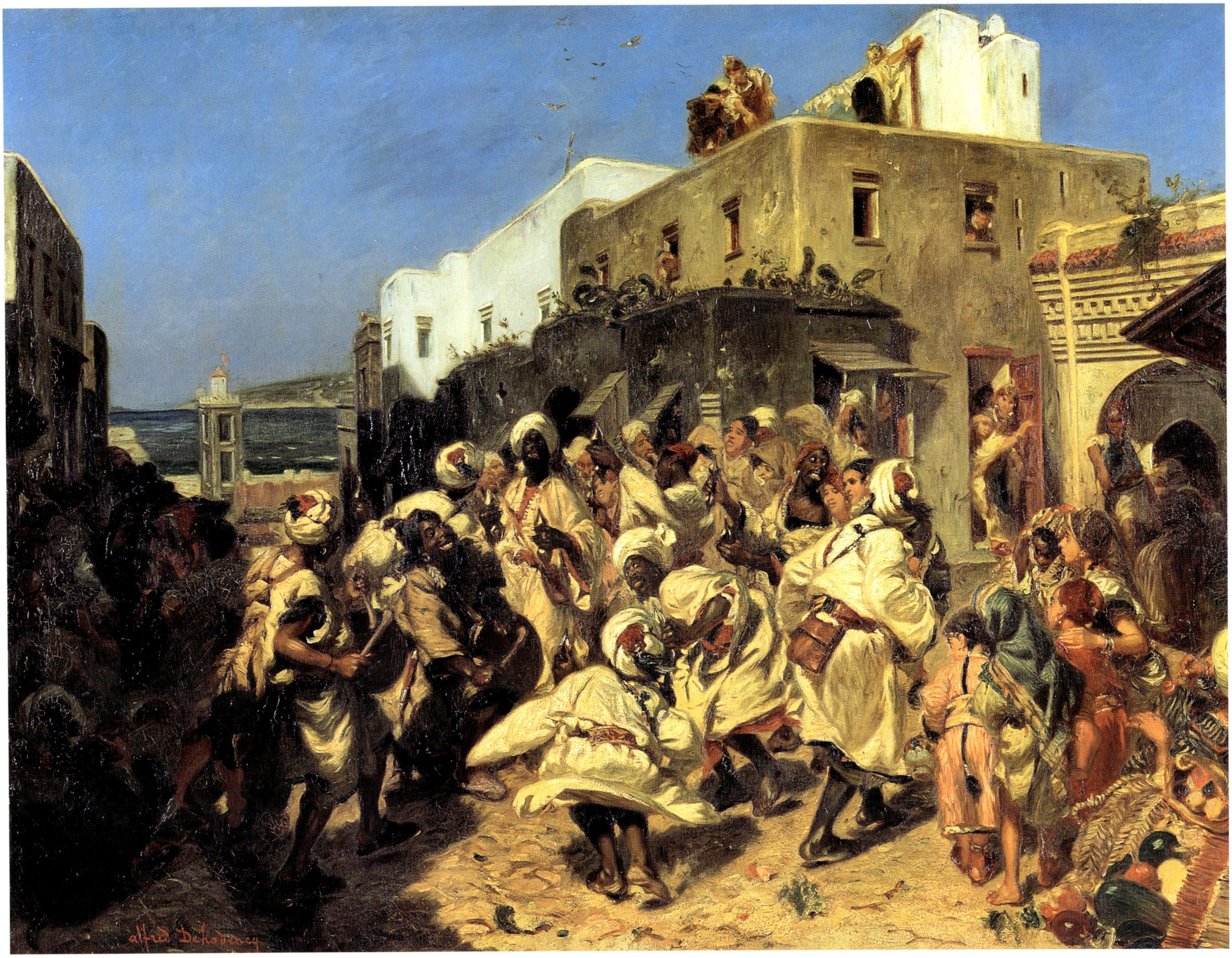

Black Women Dancing,
Alfred Dehodencq, c. 1874
Oil on canvas, 152 x 202 cm
(Musée d'Orsay, Paris).

The Pasha's Justice,
Alfred Dehodencq, 1866
Oil on canvas, 162 x 132 cm
(Musée Salies, Bagnères de Bigorre).

Pages 172-173
Rest in Egypt,
Luc Olivier Merson, 1880
Oil in Canvas, 77 x 133 cm
(Musée des Beaux-Arts, Nice).

prompted him to say: "The color of the East, the smell of the East, its remoteness, its mystery, its glory. Another life, another dream of a life!" He would return to Morocco after the Franco-Prussian war, this time staying for a year and a half, during which he was able to visit the holy city of Fez. His oil paintings may look a little overworked, but his watercolors are a delightful and faithful account of Moroccan life in the last third of the 19th century.

Benjamin-Constant, who lived in Morocco for two years, is among the last Orientalists of any worth to follow in the footsteps of Henri Regnault and Clairin. His first Moroccan canvas, *Women of the Rif*, was exhibited at the 1873 Salon. Thereafter, he would insist on introducing a profusion of original details that generally make his canvases overblown. His *Arabs at Home*, *Moroccan Harem*, *Evenings on the Terraces*, *Women in the Harem*, and in particular *Tamed Leopard*, are all paintings whose evocative powers are based on a lavish use of decorative effects.

Italian painters also went to Morocco, among them two Middle East veterans: Cesare Biseo and Stefano Ussi, who both accompanied the first Italian ambassador on his official visit of 1875, along with the writer Edmondo de Amicis, whose account they illustrated on their return. Ussi, an old Egypt hand like Biseo, was asked to paint *The Reception of the Italian Embassy in Morocco*, for which he chose a horizontal format pro-

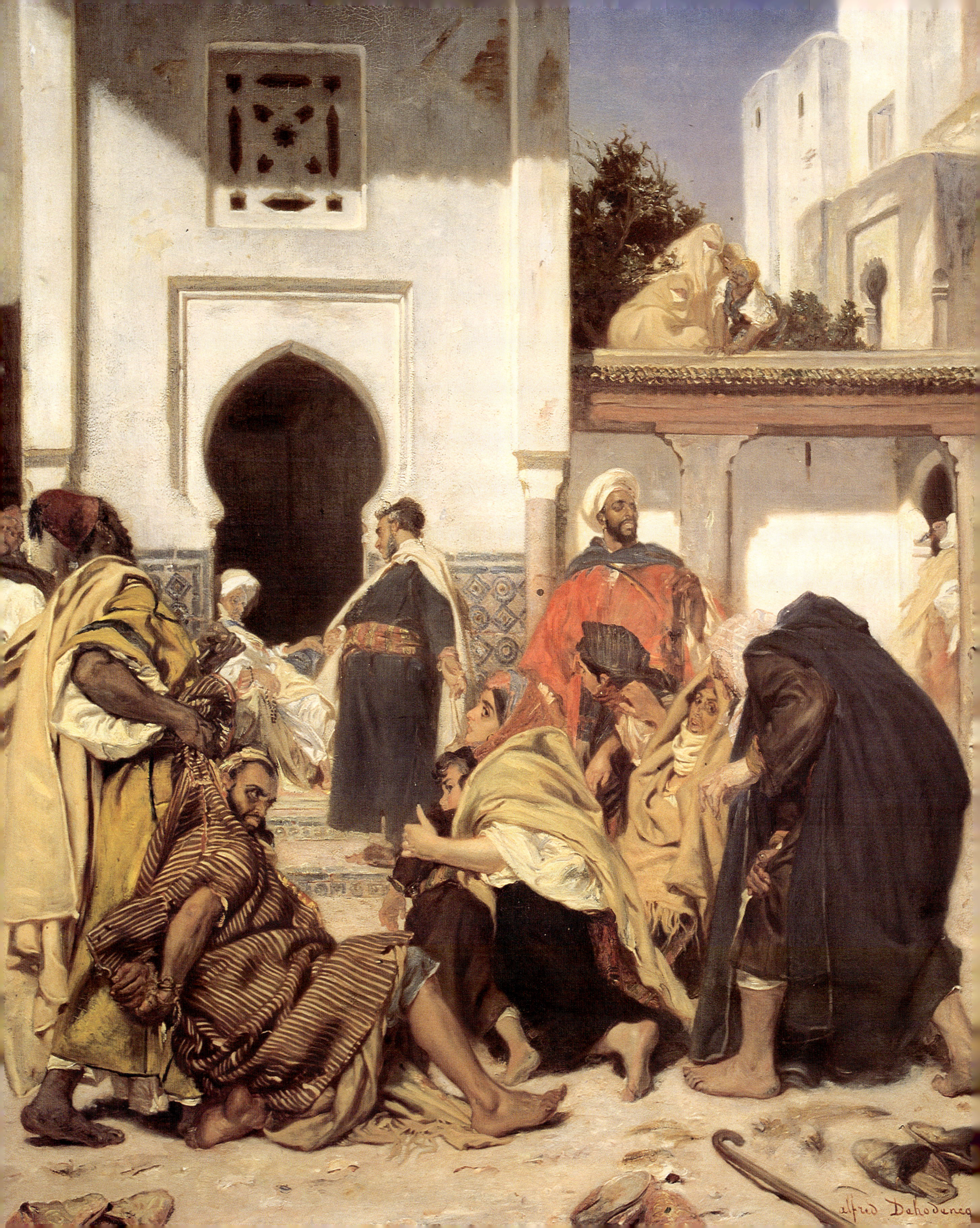
alfred Dehodencq

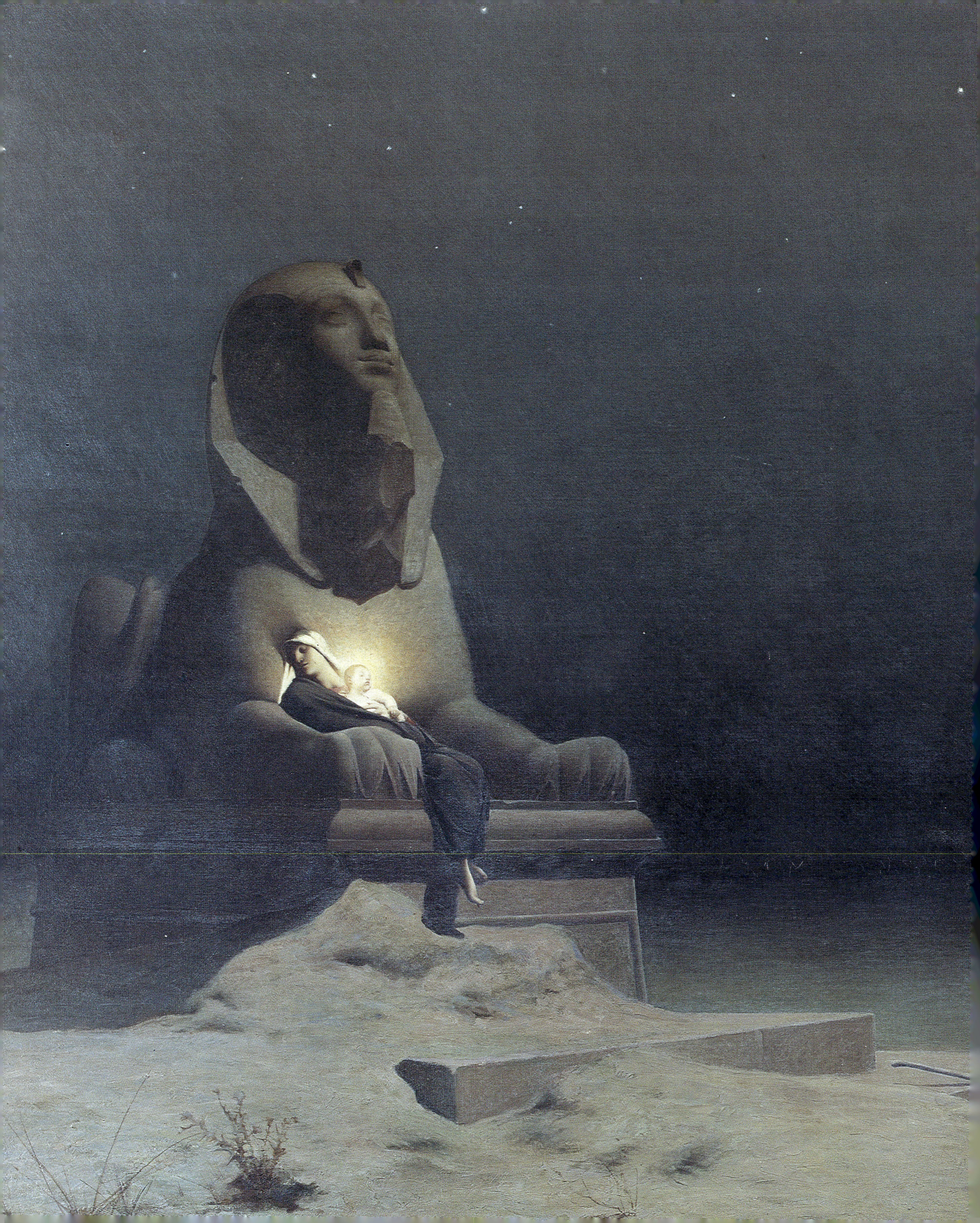

LVC OLIVIER-MERSON

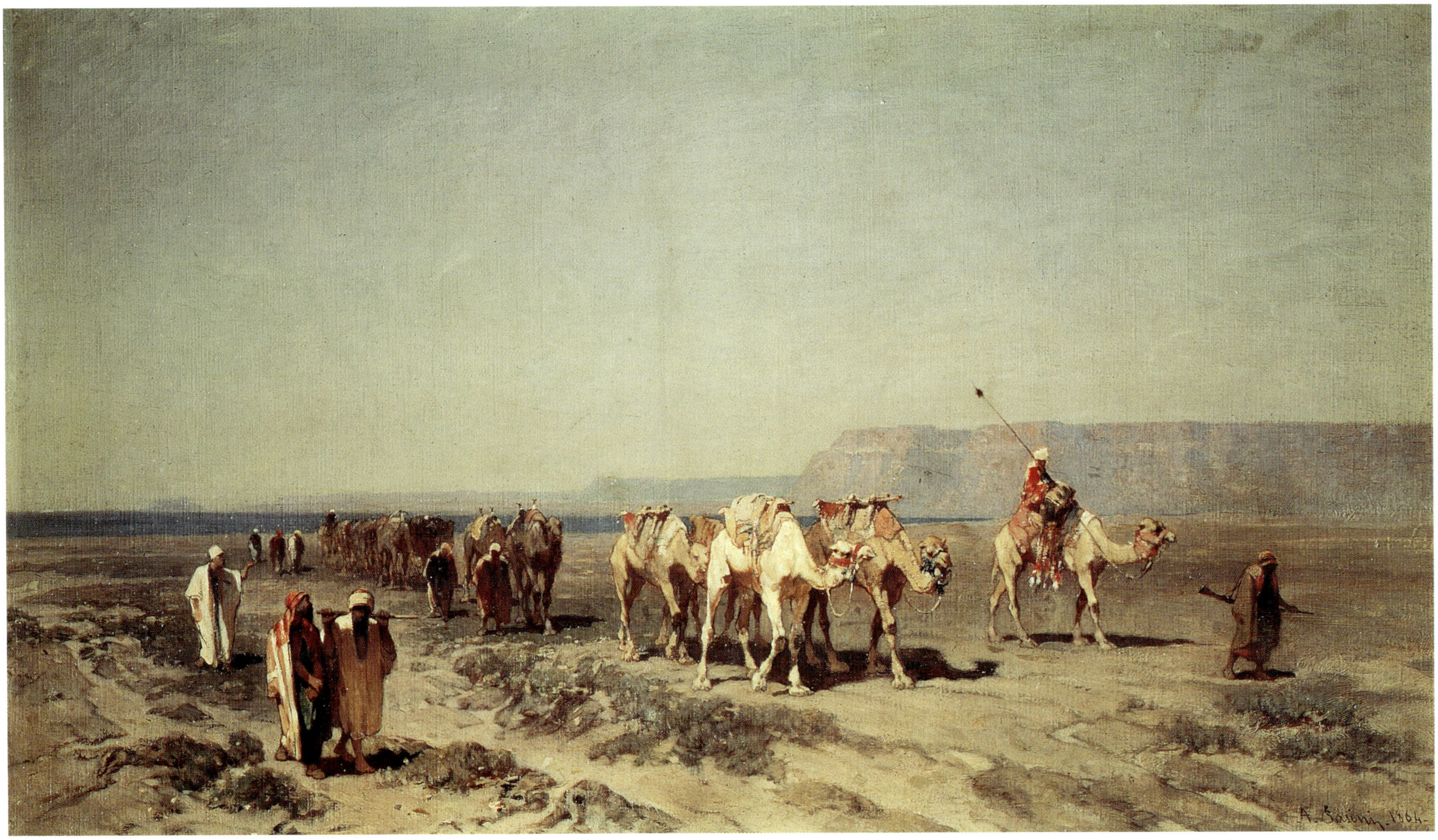

viding a panoramic view. He would also paint *Governor Ben Ouda and his Son Escorting the Italian Embassy in Morocco*, *The Feast of Muhamad in Tangiers*, and *Moroccan Man* (1877).

But on the whole, painters gradually lost interest in Morocco, though there were a few individualists who continued to find inspiration there. One was the American Louis Comfort Tiffany, who left a stunning *Snake Charmer in Tangiers*, dating from 1875. Then there was the outlandish figure of Hercules-Brabazon Brabazon. This great art collector, wealthy and urbane, lived in Tangiers from 1868 to 1884, painting thousands of watercolors good enough to impress John Singer Sargent, who organized a posthumous exhibition of Brabazon's work in 1896. The style of the French artist Levy-Dhumer flourished in Morocco, as is shown by the fine *Mosque at Rabat* (c. 1920), a composition that is a symphony of mauves and pinks.

Pilgrimage to the Holy Land

The Challenge of Palestine

In his *Itinéraire de Paris à Jérusalem et de Jérusalem à Paris* (Journey from Paris to Jerusalem and from Jerusalem to Paris), Chateaubriand observes that "Judea is the only country in the world to present the traveler with memories of both human travails and heavenly matters, a combination that moves the soul to feelings and thoughts that no other place can inspire." He exults: "The burning sun, the untamed earth, the barren fig-tree, all the poetry, all the imagery of the Scriptures is here."

From the beginning of the 19th century the rapid development of archaeology greatly enhance direct knowledge of the Holy Land. However, many were to be disappointed by their actual experience of a land so weighed down with history and religious significance, not least Chateaubriand himself. A few years later, Gustave Flaubert was appalled, and the English poet and painter Edward Lear expresses his disappointment in the Holy City with characteristic wit: "Oh my nose! Oh my eyes! Oh my feet! How you suffered in this vile city. Let me tell you, physically Jerusalem is the foulest and odiousest place on earth. A bitter doleful soul-ague comes over you in its streets. And your memories of its interior are but horrid dreams of squalor and filth, clamour and uneasiness, hatred and malice and all uncharitableness."

It is not surprising, therefore, that translations of Holy Scripture into images were frequently based on the inspiring discoveries of Pharaonic Egypt rather than on the accounts of travelers to the Holy Land, even well written ones like those of David Roberts. The traveler-painters who drew inspiration from Palestine can be counted on the fingers of one hand, and they were usually British. Richard Dadd painted a few fine watercolors of the Holy Land on his return to England, where he spent many years in an asylum. David Wilkie, who had done many promising sketches, fell ill and died in Malta before he could fully develop his Holy Land themes. All told, only Edward Lear and Thomas Seddon returned with paintings that

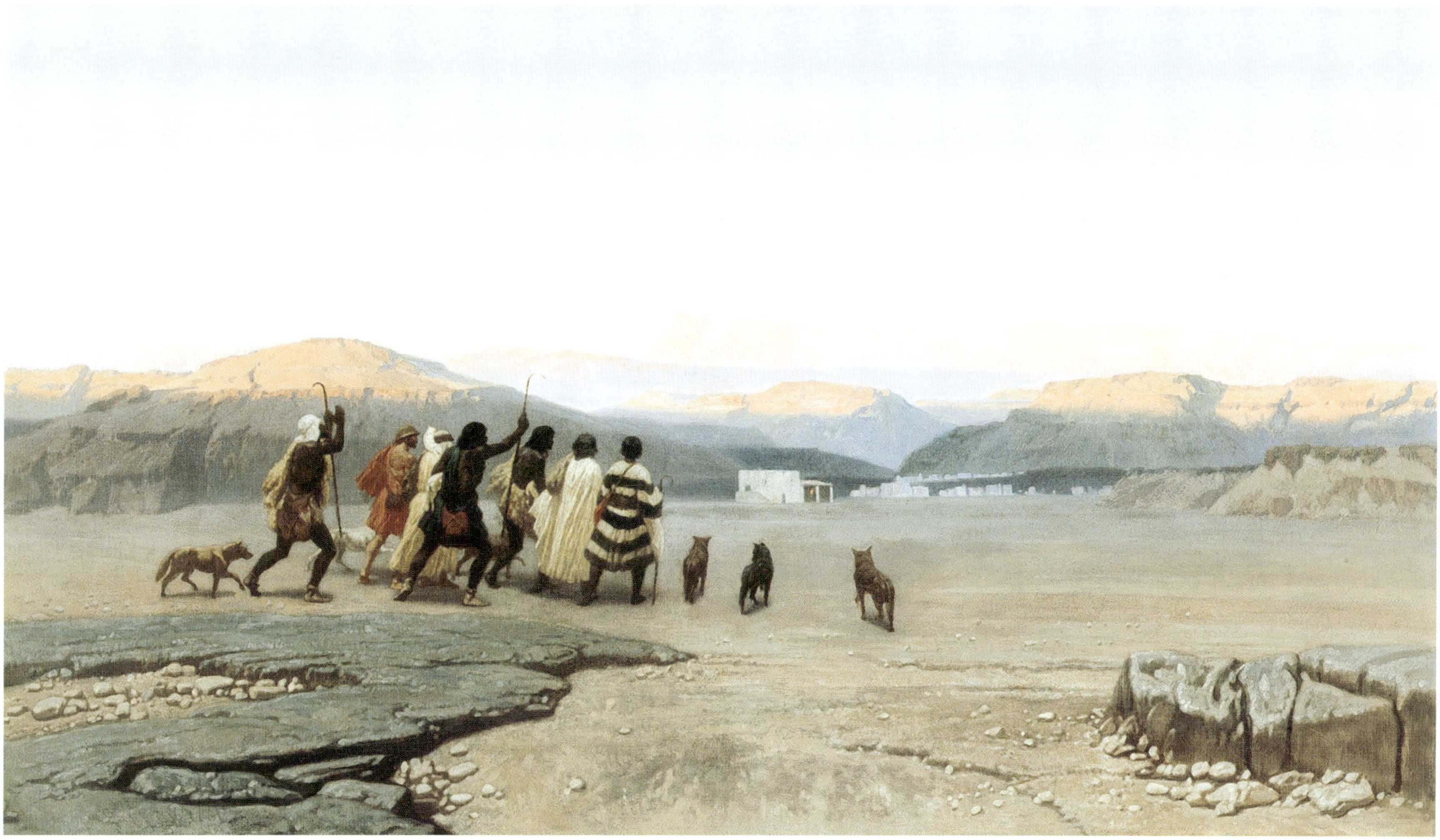

show genuine sensitivity and ability. Seddon was to meet William Holman Hunt on Hunt's perilous travels in the Middle East.

In his visionary compositions, the English painter John Martin, the matchless illustrator of John Milton's *Paradise Lost*, used genuine architectural details taken from Egypt or Sumer and Babylon, but constructed from them vast fantastical palaces shown in dizzying perspective; examples include *The Seventh Plague of Egypt* (1824) and *The Death of the First Born*. Martin was not interested in the illusion of reality; quite the reverse. He always chose to set his scenes in huge brooding and dramatic settings that have an apocalyptic power that puts them firmly in the realm of fantasy. He was, therefore, an exception; most Orientalists were concerned with evoking a sense of place.

As a rule, 19th-century religious art showed a marked preference for Old Testament episodes set in Egypt. This is clearly demonstrated by the treatment of the story of Joseph. It was depicted by numerous

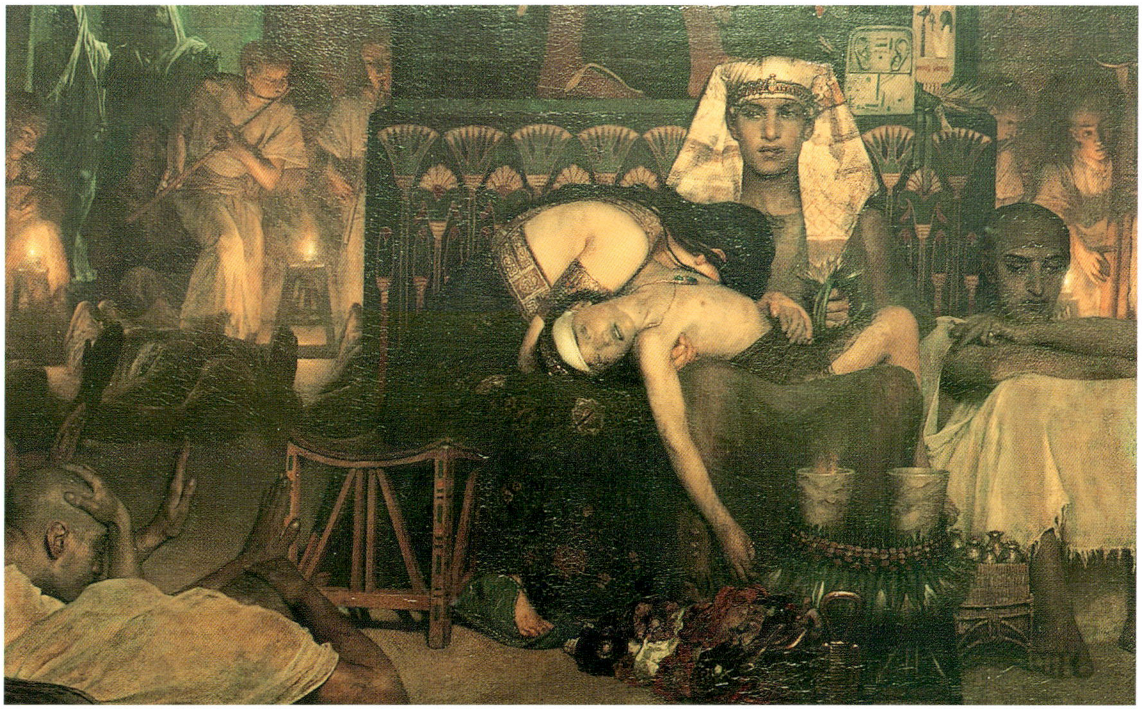

Above
The Shepherds, Guided by the Star, Come to Bethlehem, Octave Penguilly-L'Haridon, 1863
Oil on canvas, 70 x 120 cm
(Musée d'Orsay, Paris).

Left
The Death of the First Born, Sir Lawrence Alma-Tadema, 1872
Oil on canvas, 79.9 x 124.5 cm
(Rijksmuseum, Amsterdam).

Opposite
Caravan on the shores of the Red sea, Alberto Pasimi, 1864
Oil on canvas, 37 x 64 cm
(Galleria d'Arte Moderna, Florence).

Pages 176–177
The Finding of Moses, Sir Lawrence Alma-Tadema, 1904
Oil on canvas, 137.5 x 213.4 cm
(private collection).

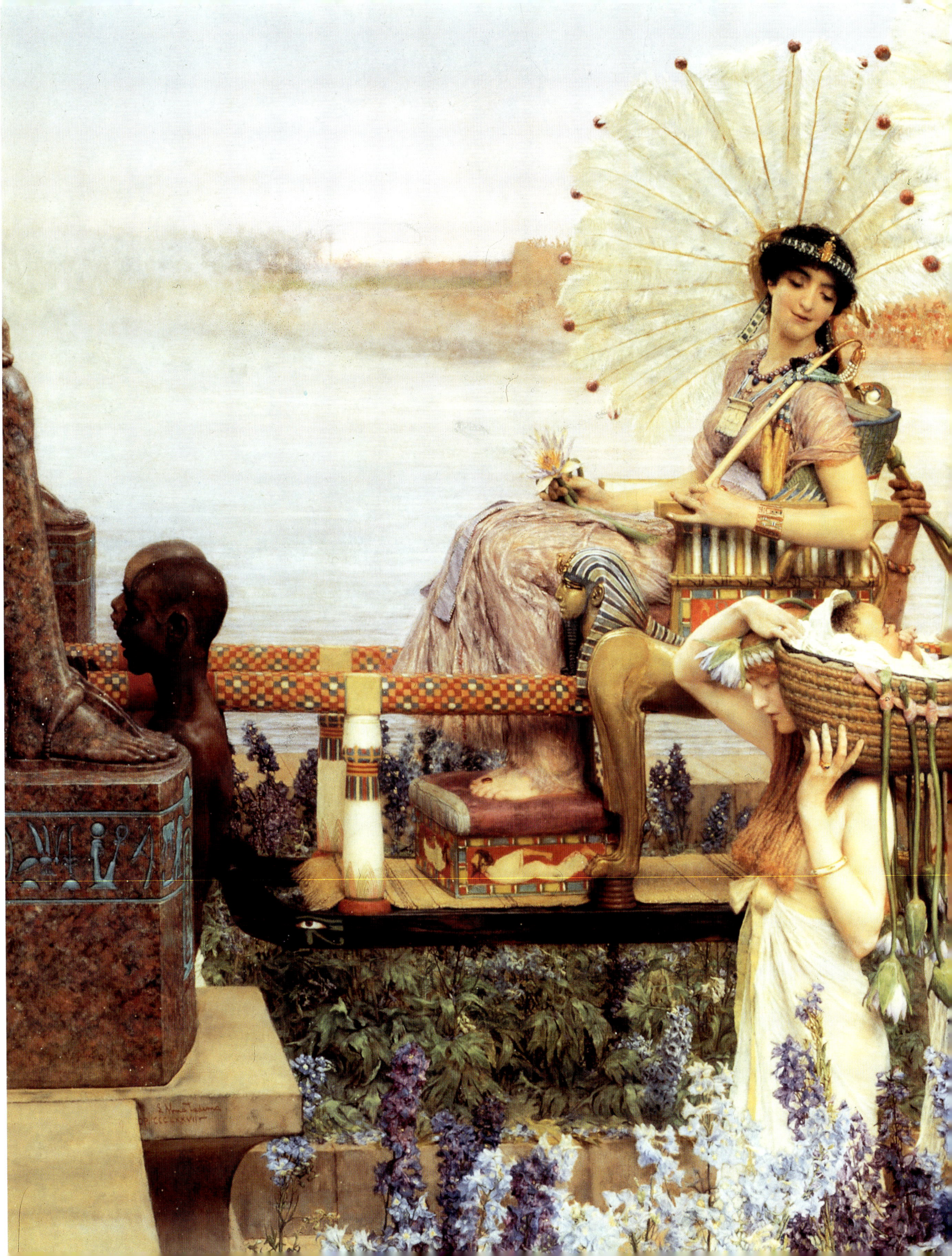

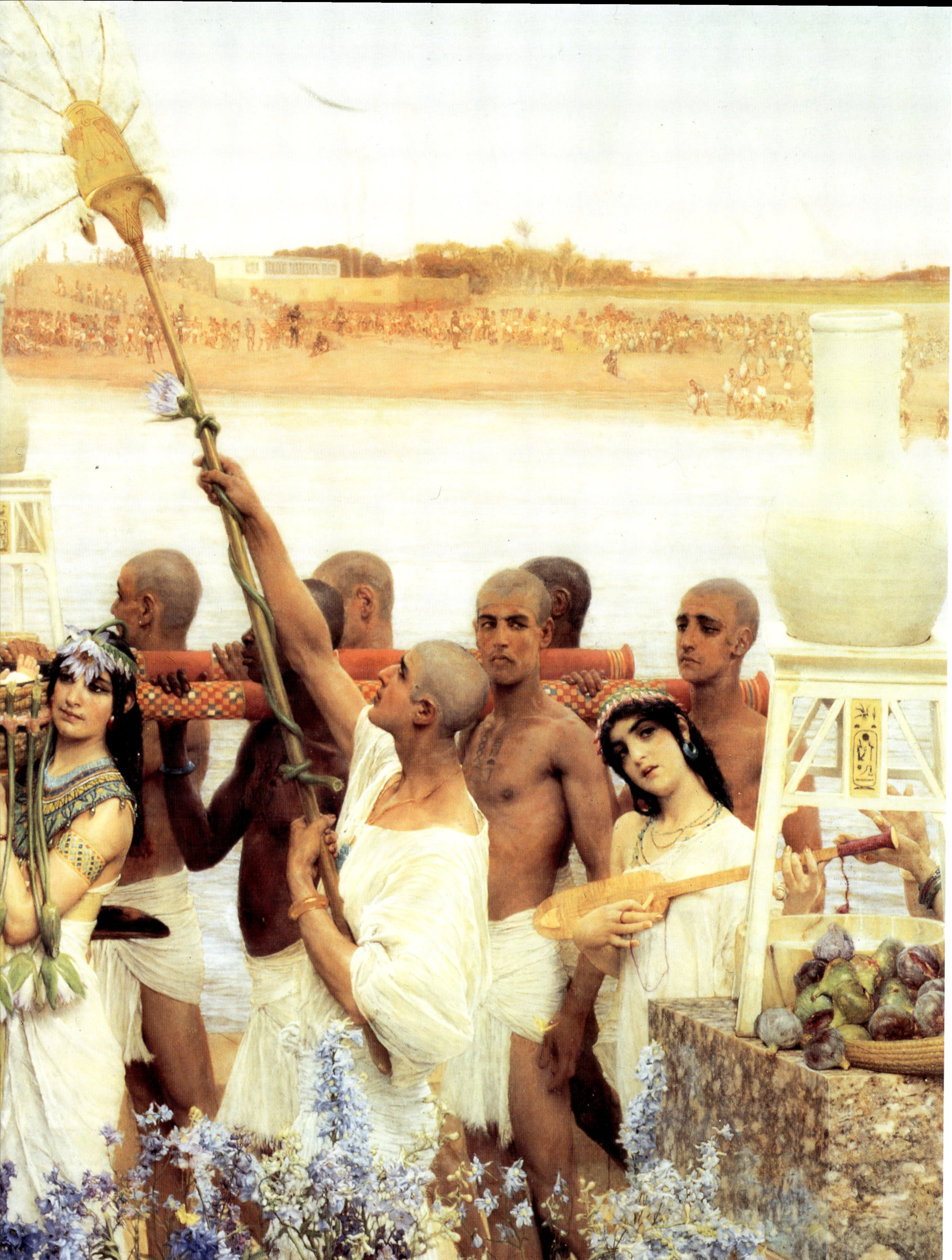

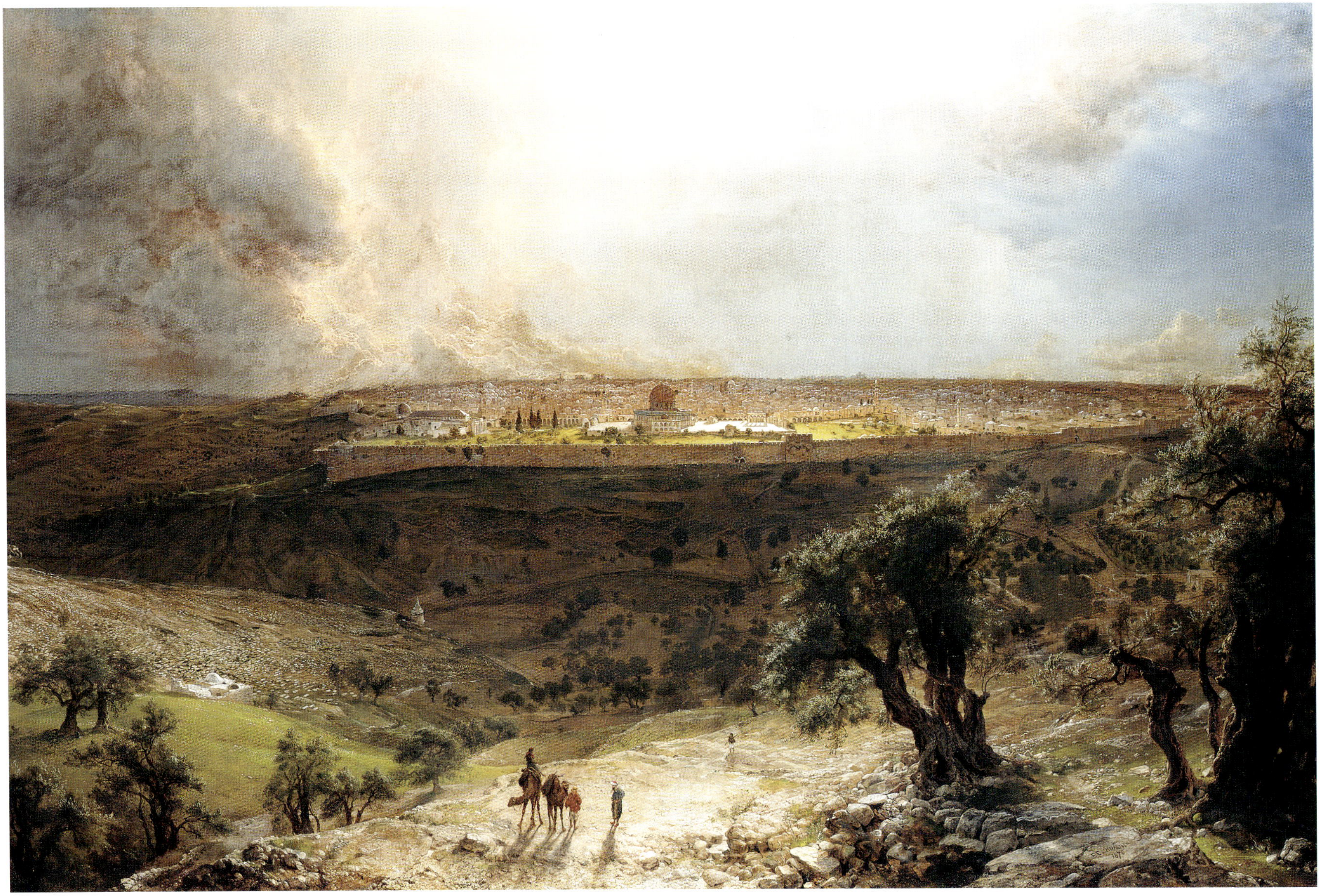

Above
Jerusalem Seen from Mount Olive,
Frederic Edwin Church, 1870
Oil on canvas, 137.2 x 213.4 cm
(Nelson-Atkins Museum of Art, Kansas City, Missouri).

Opposite
The Lost Sheep,
William J. Webb, 1864
Oil on wood, 33.1 x 25.1 cm
(City Art Galleries, Manchester).

artists, starting with Abel de Pujol and his Louvre ceiling: *Egypt Saved by Joseph* (1827). David Roberts painted his *Israelites Leaving* before his trip to Egypt. Adrien Guignet took on the theme in *Joseph Explaining Pharaoh's Dreams*, a painting he created for the 1845 Salon; his research included checking his facts with Prisse d'Avennes and drawing direct inspiration from the zodiac recently found in the temple at Denderah in Egypt. In a like manner, the English artists Edward Poynter (*Israel in Egypt*, 1867) and Sir Lawrence Alma-Tadema (*Joseph Watching Over Pharaoh's Granaries*, 1874) also depicted scenes from the Scriptures in the light of modern archaeological discoveries.

Also popular among Old Testament subjects were the life of Moses and the liberation of the Jewish people from the tyranny of Ramses II. Of the many artists who attempted these themes we can cite John Martin; Christopher Wilhelm Eckersbery, *The Crossing of the Red Sea* (1813); Sir Lawrence Alma-Tadema, *The Finding of Moses* (1904) and *The Death of Pharaoh's Eldest Son*; Frederick Goodall, *Moses Amid the Bulrushes* (1885); Dominique Papety, *Moses Amid the Bulrushes*; Edwin Long, *The Finding of Moses* (1904), and so on. Although examples are few and far between, the New Testament also gave rise to compositions inspired by Ancient Egypt, such as Adrien Guignet's *Flight into Egypt* (1849); Edwin Long's canvases from 1883; and, undoubtedly the most unusual of them all, Luc Olivier Merson's *Rest in Egypt* (1880), in which the Blessed Virgin Mary is seen sleeping against the vast paw of the Sphinx at Giza.

Illustrations of the Bible by major artists like John Martin, Gustave Doré, and Edward J. Poynter also bear witness to the tendency to place Christian subjects in an Egyptian

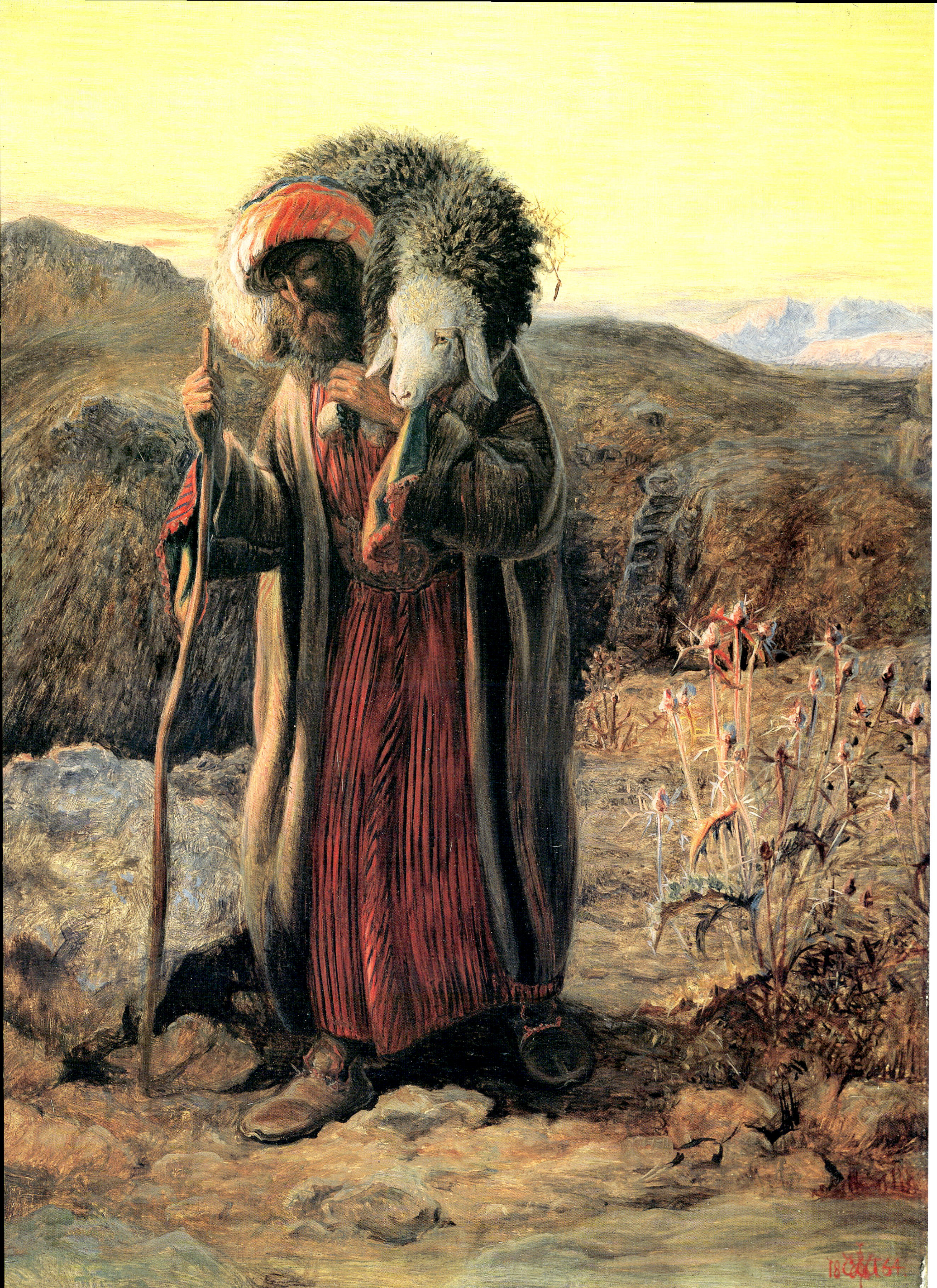

setting. Traditional Christian art, however, was barely affected by this development, the clergy remaining faithful to artistic clichés. It is hardly surprising that Ernest Renan's iconoclastic *Vie de Jésus* (Life of Jesus), written after a stay in Palestine alongside an archaeological mission, caused a scandal. Even painters as adventurous as Chassériau and Delacroix become rather tame when treating a religious subject (though this would not apply to Delacroix's work in the Chapelle des Saints Anges in the church of Saint-Sulpice in Paris). But there are two rare exceptions who deserve a mention. David Wilkie, who arrived in Jerusalem in 1840, created several works that reflect his direct study of the Holy Land, notably *Christ Before Pilate*, *Nativity*, and *Supper at Emmaus*, in which, for example, his characters wear Turkish dress while Jesus is dressed in Palestinian clothes. Similarly, the Russian artist Alexander Ivanov visited the Holy Land in order to give his religious works, and in particular his celebrated *Christ Appearing to the People* (c.1840), greater authenticity.

Another interesting example of the use of Palestine in religious art is provided by the painter Horace Vernet. Generally seen as a conformist bereft of imagination and of limited ability, Vernet asked what Nicolas Poussin would have done if, "like us, he had lived in the midst of Abrahams and Jacobs?" Behind this rhetorical question was Vernet's close relationship with the Islamic world. In 1848, his address to the Académie des Beaux-Arts on "the links between ancient Israelites' dress and that of modern Arabs," subsequently published in the *Illustration* of 12 February, caused a sensation. He advocated abandoning the pseudo classic style inherited from the Renaissance and widely used during the Baroque, arguing that contemporary Arab dress would be very like that worn by the Jews of biblical times. As early as the 1830s he had decided to adopt Arab dress styles for his religious subjects, as is shown by *Rebecca at the Fountain* (exhibited at the 1835 Salon). He would act on the same principle in some ten biblical scenes he created (nearly all of which, interestingly, revolve around the theme of seduction). In *Hagar Dismissed by Abraham* (1835), he used a dramatic composition that was actually revealed to him when in Algeria. He had been reading in his tent the Old Testament passage where Rebecca, a pitcher on her shoulder, offers a drink to Eliezer; at that very moment Vernet saw "a young woman giving a drink to a soldier and reenacting the scene I was trying to visualize." Among Vernet's works that stand out for their dual allegiance to a Classical style and to Orientalist authenticity are: *Judah and Tamar* (1840), in which Tamar is seen disguised as a prostitute and seducing her father-in-law in order to continue her family line; *Joseph Betrayed by his Brothers* (1853); and *Joseph's Coat* (1853). Reactions were on the whole hostile; Gautier objected violently to Vernet's rejection of "biblical severity," and Fromentin asserted harshly that "dressing up the Bible is tantamount to destroying it."

The works of the Venetian artist Francesco Hayez marked a new departure in Orientalism. Once a pupil of the celebrated Neo-classical sculptor Canova, he sought throughout his career a balance between his Neo-classical training and his highly romantic nature. With religious subjects he took a bold line, his aim being to present biblical figures in authentic settings. His Rebecca wears clothes that are no longer the conventional garb of Western religious art, and the landscape is clearly that of the real Middle East. This desire to create a Holy Land free of the overblown imagery of Baroque art can be seen in works such as *Bathsheba Bathing* (1834), the superb *Esau Meeting Jacob* (1844), and the very sensual *Tamar*. Though he never in fact visited the Middle East, he felt the need to bring into his art believable images of the people and places of the Bible. He entitled his last painting, intended as an artistic testament, *The Destruction of the Temple of Jerusalem* (1867), a work that was meant to give full dramatic significance and historical veracity to the Diaspora.

Though he never left his hometown of Naples, the Italian painter Domenico

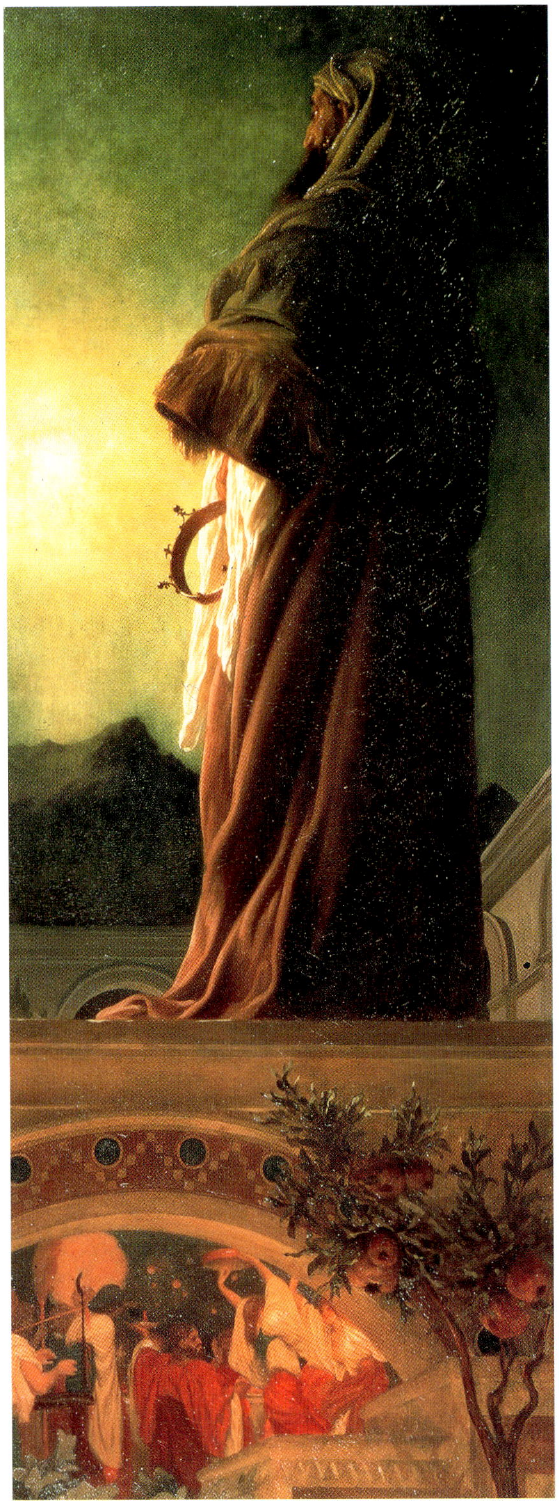

The Star of Bethlehem,
Lord Frederick Leighton, 1862
Oil on canvas, 152.4 x 59.7 cm
(Eagle Art Partners).

Opposite
Judah and Tamar, Horace Vernet, 1840
Oil on canvas, 129 x 97.5 cm
(Wallace Collection, London).

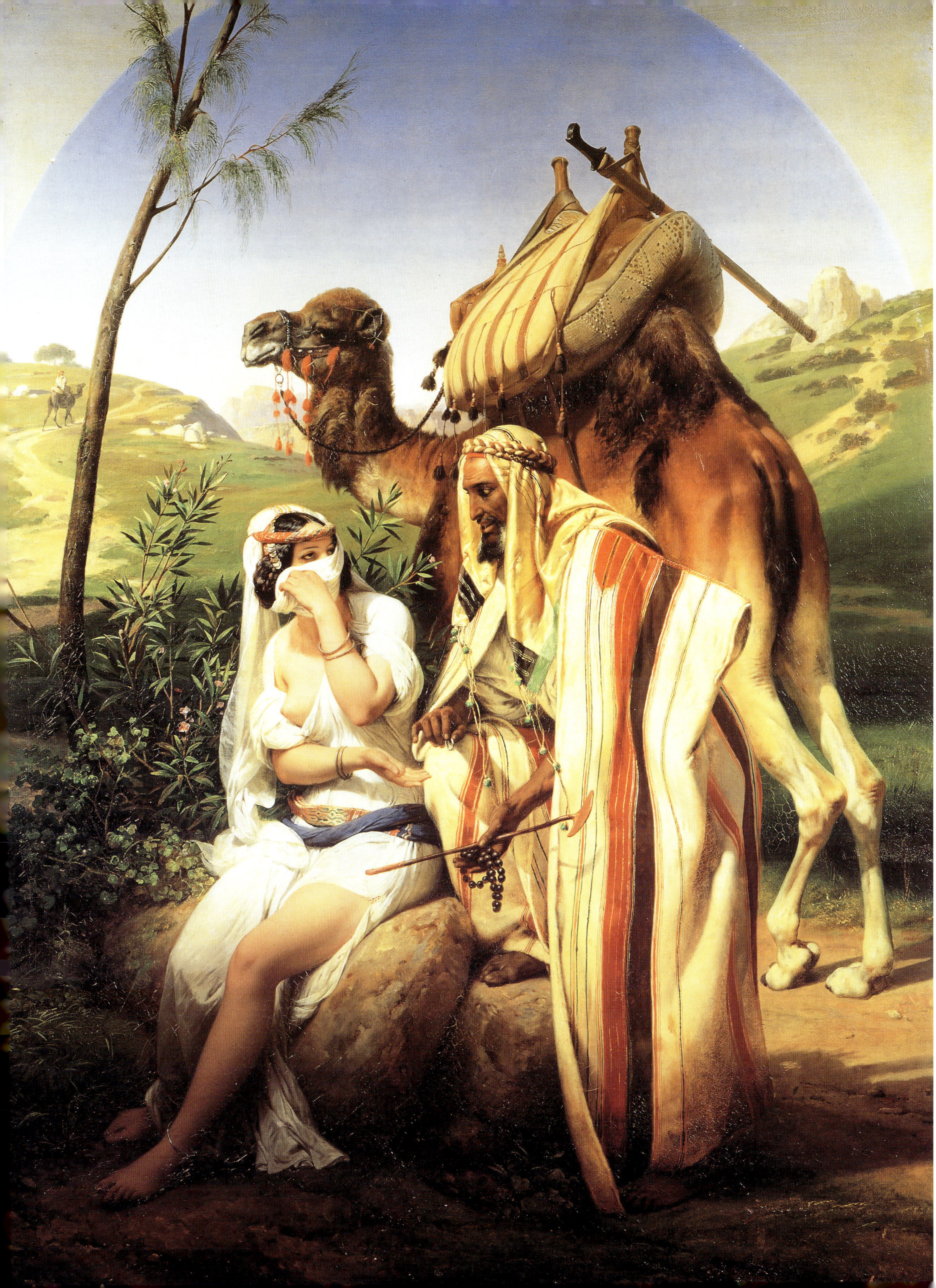

Morelli established a high reputation as an Orientalist. His typical handling of biblical scenes, in which he takes the utmost care over the authenticity of his settings, can be seen in *Potiphar's Wife*, where a very credible Egyptian fresco serves as a backdrop and all the furniture is true to period. Relying on a wealth of documents, he placed his characters in credible settings, as in *Mary Magdalene*, *Christ in the Desert*, and *The Temptation of St. Anthony*. Unconventional, and immensely well read, Morelli was among the very few Western artists to have taken a keen interest in the Koran; this found expression in four paintings of Muhammad, including *Muhammad with His Soldiers*.

The French artist James Tissot, painter par excellence of Paris high society, became deeply religious after the tragic death of his mistress. He left for Egypt and Palestine on 15 October 1885, his 50th birthday, with the intention of completing a series of watercolors and gouaches for a lavishly illustrated edition of the New Testament. He also seized this opportunity to complete a few canvases, including *Sojurn in Egypt* (1894) and *The Marriage Feast at Cana* (1895). For Tissot, there was a tragic urgency in his trip, for, as he wrote, "what facts still exist ... will disappear ... in this era of railway and engineers, irresistibly pushed out by all-invading modernity." He visited the major historical sites of the Bible and returned with a huge and scholarly body of drawing and notes. On his return to Paris he created 365 illustrations for the New Testament, which came out in two volumes in 1896 and 1897 under the title *La Vie de Notre Seigneur* (The Life of Our Lord). He made two other visits to Palestine, the last in 1896, this time to prepare illustrations for

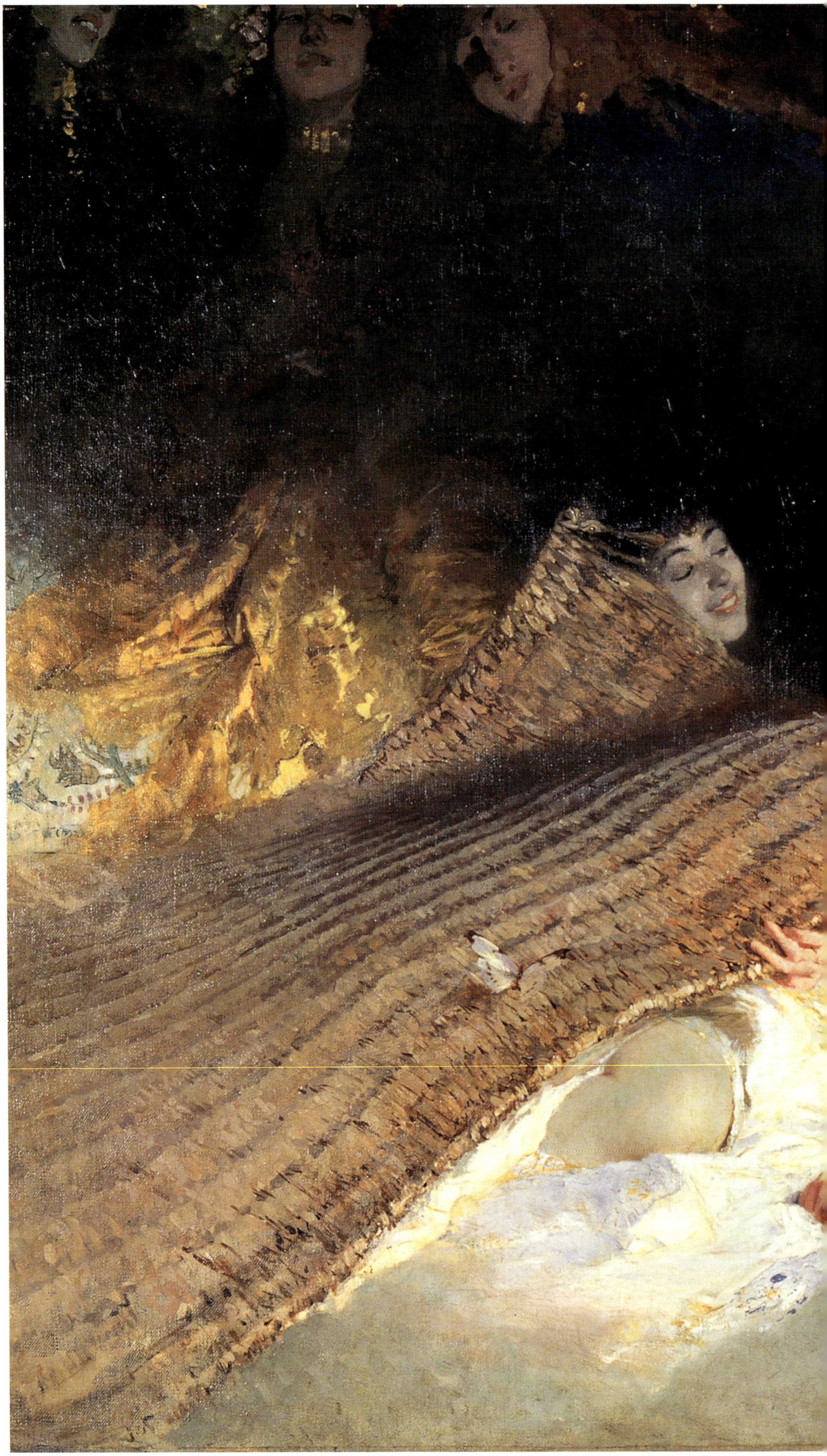

The Temptation of St. Anthony,
Domenico Morelli, c. 1878
Oil on canvas, 137 x 225 cm (Galleria Nazionale d'Arte Moderna, Rome).

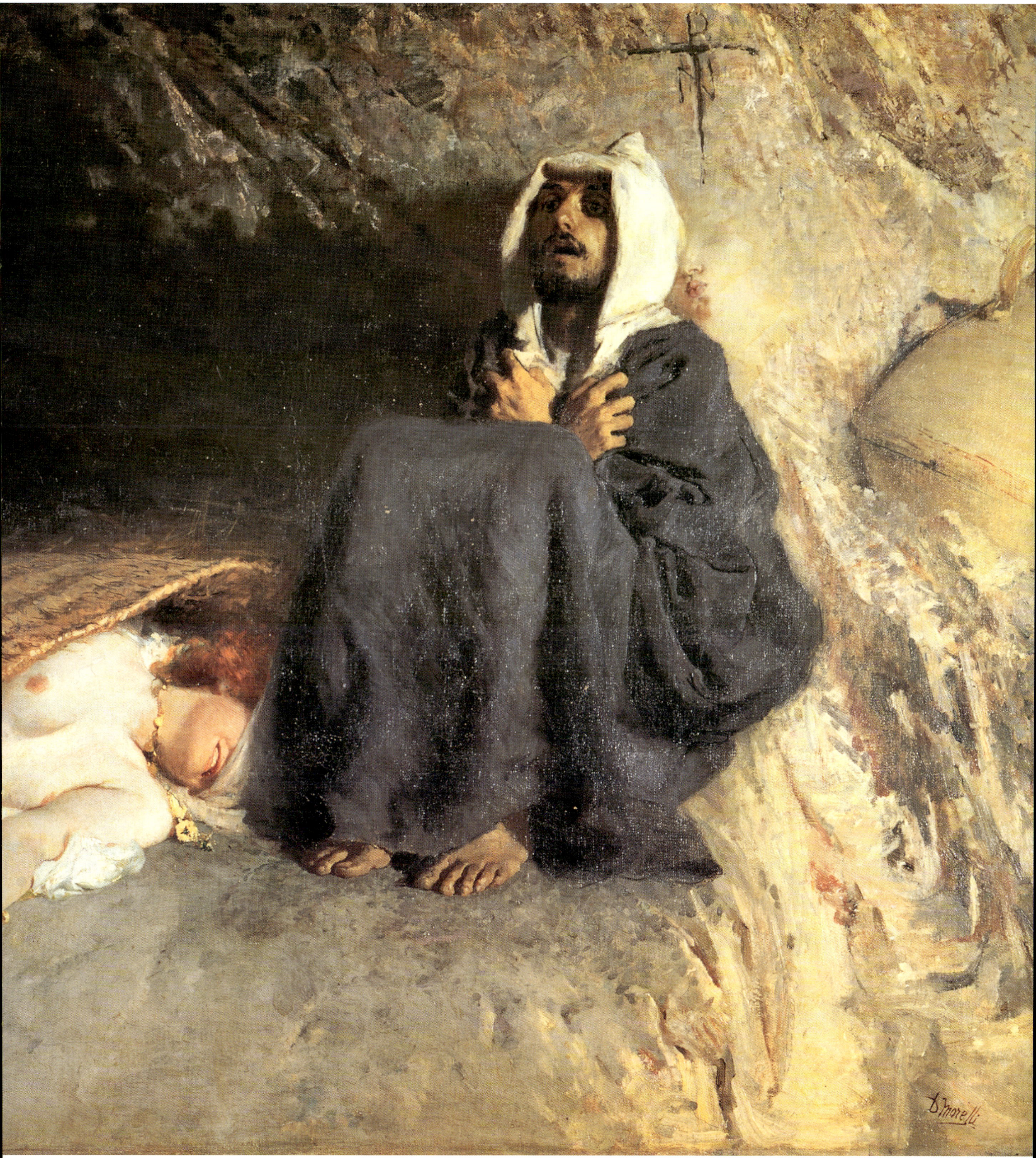
D Morelli

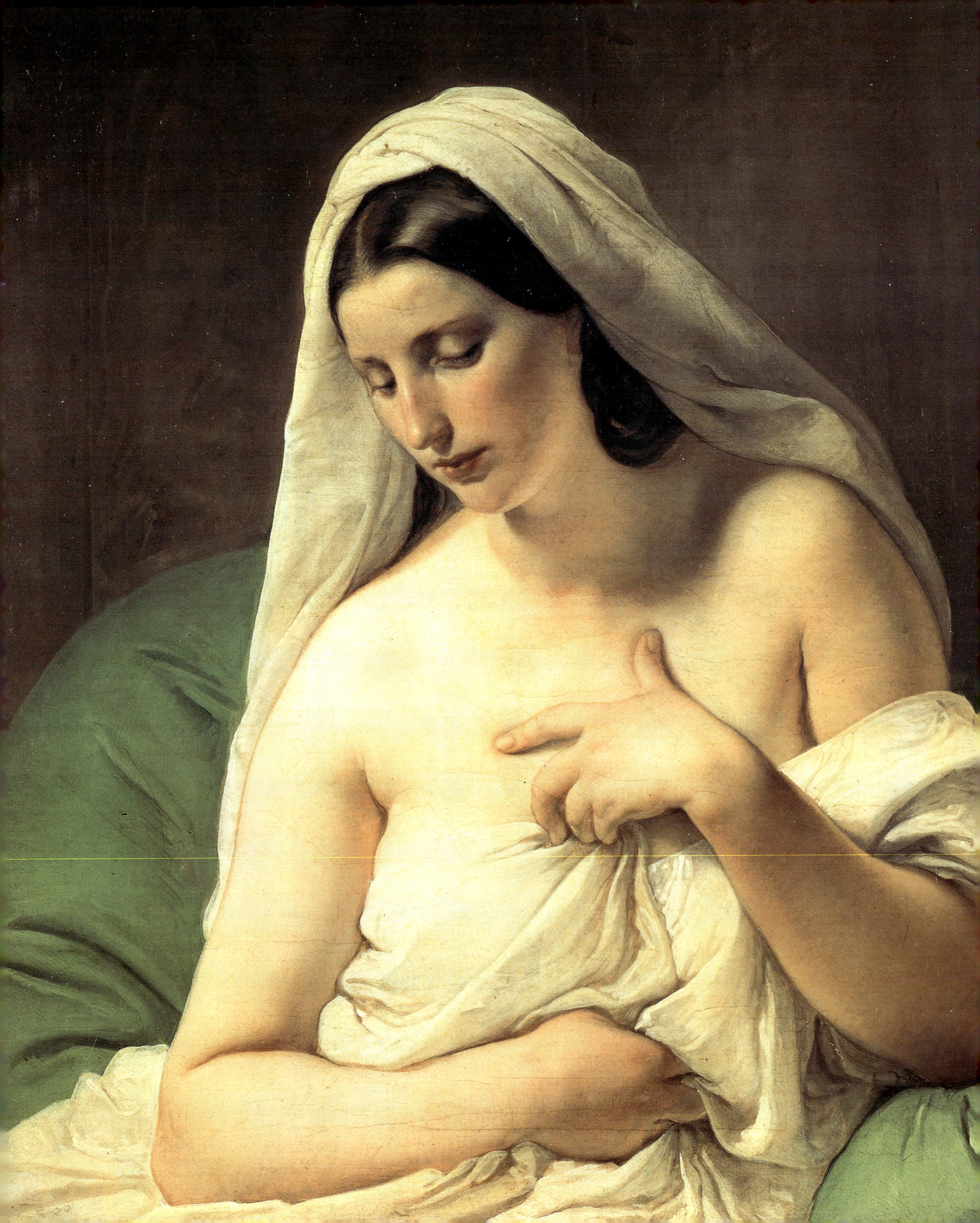

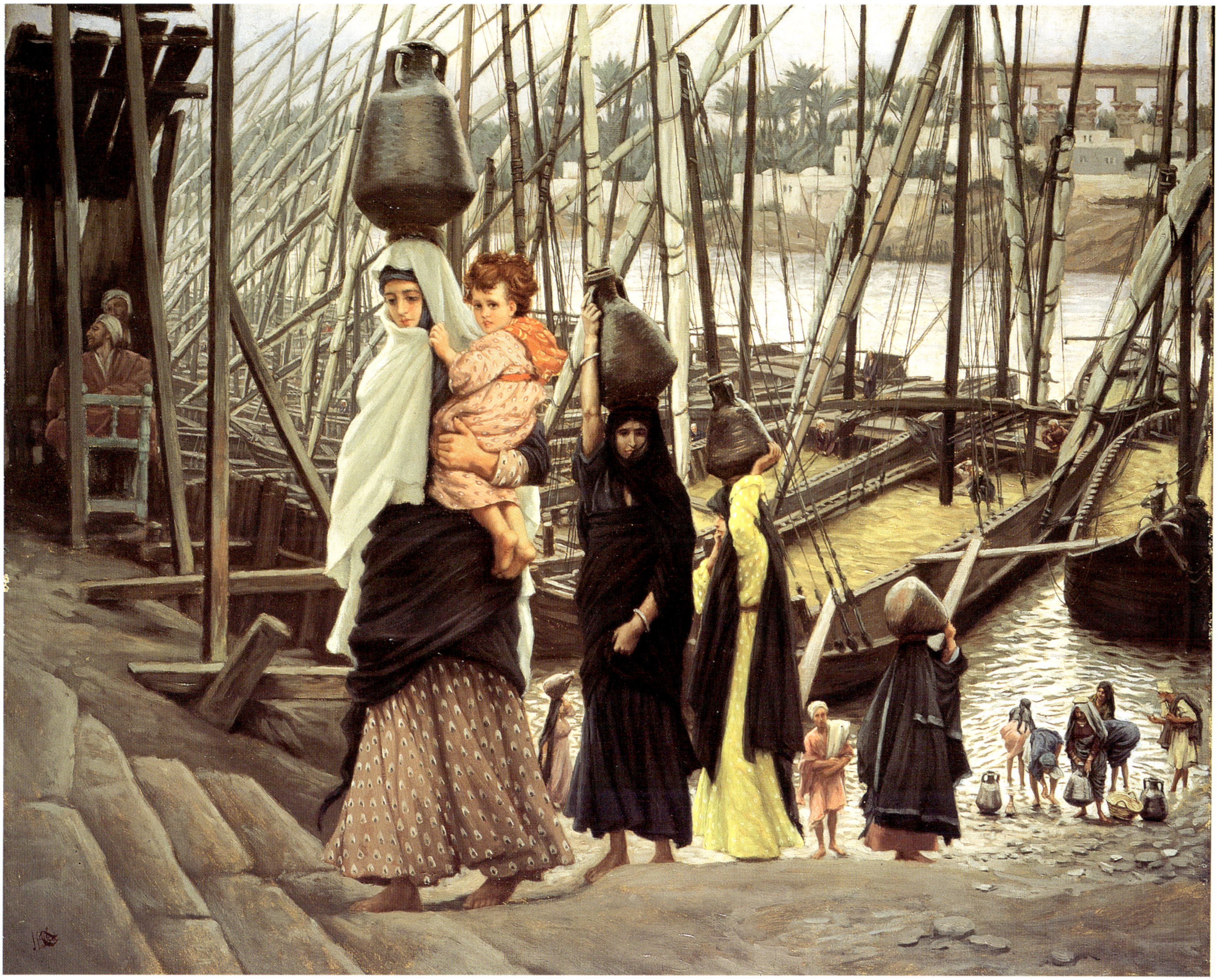

an edition of the Old Testament. He died in 1902, but not before creating half of the 400 intended drawings.

William Holman Hunt

A promising student of the Royal Academy in London, but exasperated by the conventional teaching delivered there, William Holman Hunt was, in 1848, one of the founding fathers of the Pre-Raphaelite brotherhood. All his life he would remain faithful to the Pre-Raphaelite aesthetic, as well as to the moral ideals the young artists of the group had set themselves. However, instead of turning to the Middle Ages or the Renaissance for inspiration, as many of the Pre-Raphaelites did, he stuck to an uncompromising quest for "truth to nature." This took the form of a frank, painstaking, and to his mind strictly Anglican exploration of religious themes, as we can see in such works as *A Converted British Family Sheltering a Christian Missionary from the Persecution of the Druids* and his celebrated *Light of the World* (1853). It was on completing this canvas that he set off for the Middle East.

Standing on Egyptian soil he experienced a revelation: "At one fell swoop, I hit upon the means of escaping the artificiality of civilization. Nature was there in all its simple raw grace, and life seemed to resume the appearance of its beginnings." In con-

Above
Sojourn in Egypt, James Tissot, between 1886 and 1894.
Oil on canvas, 69.2 x 85.4 cm
(The National Gallery of Ireland, Dublin).

Opposite
Odalisque, Francesco Hayez, 1839
Oil on canvas, 80 x 64 cm
(Pinacoteca de Brera, Milan).

trast to the artists that came before him, he dreamt of immersing himself in ancient history. However, this did not prevent him from depicting an amusing scene witnessed in a Cairo street, *A Street Scene in Cairo; the Lantern-maker's Courtship* (1854), a painting which breaks with the best Orientalist traditions by concentrating on a light-hearted scene in which, moreover, we catch an ironic glimpse of a Westerner in a top hat. He also

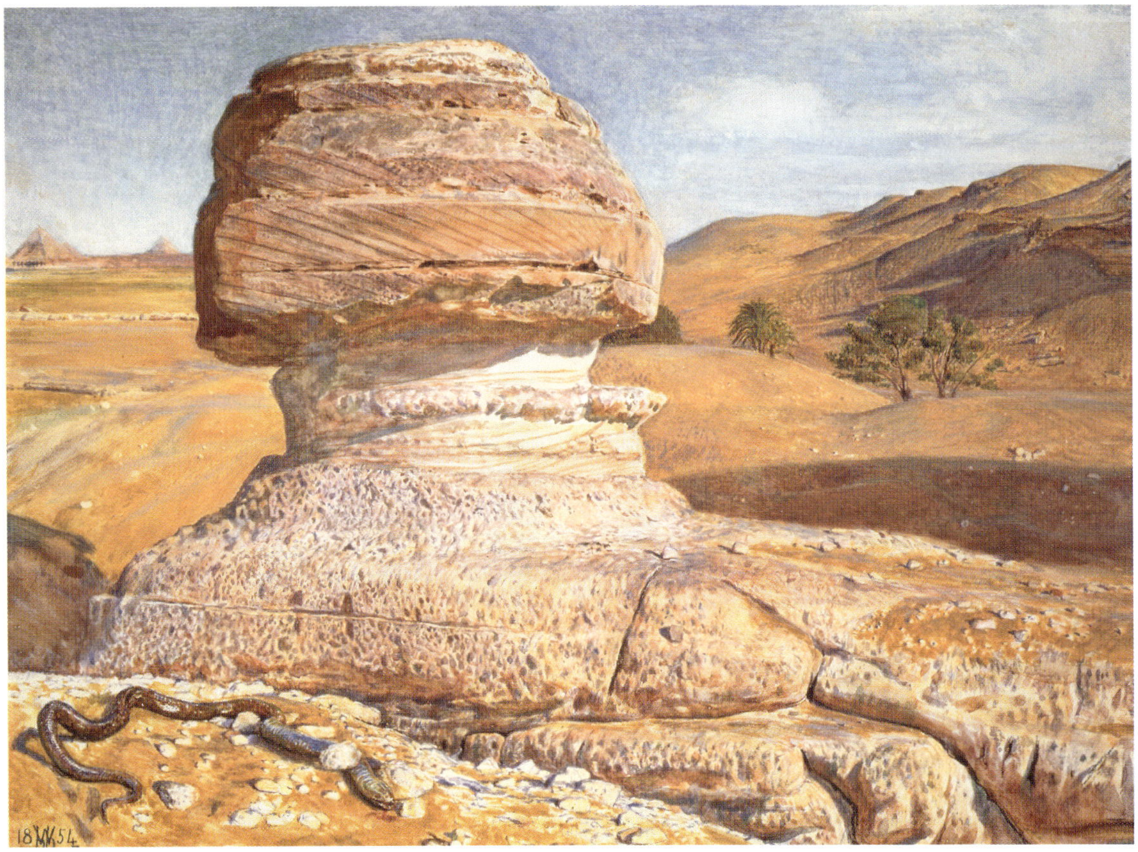

The Sphinx, William Holman Hunt, 1854
Watercolor, 25.4 x 35.5 cm (Harris Museum and Art Gallery, Preston).

painted *The Afterglow in Egypt*, a strange allegory in which we see a young woman holding a sheaf of corn on her head and a green vase in her hand, surrounded by birds of many different kinds.

Before continuing on to Jerusalem, Hunt stayed at the home in Giza of his friend Thomas Seddon, who had adopted an Arab lifestyle. Hunt's striking canvas *The Finding of the Saviour in the Temple* (1860), for which he sought out Jewish models, is a remarkable evocation of ancient Jerusalem. In the face of rabbinical hostility, however, Hunt temporarily abandoned work on this canvas and turned to his famous *The Scapegoat*. To create this brilliant and bizarre work he traveled to the banks of the Dead Sea, taking with him a white goat.

Hunt described in his diaries the eventful incidents that punctuated his lengthy preparations. There he sat, by the Dead Sea, on whose shore he tethered the poor animal, with a brush in one hand and a gun in the other for fear of attack from Arab marauders (as indeed happened). In a note written for the critic John Ruskin, he related the circumstance of this long and perilous enterprise: "while Crimean heights were white under the tents of war and the cruel passions of Europe's nations flared high and deadly over countless corpses, a peaceful English tent was pitched hard by an empty sea and an English heart's passion was spent painting a hapless goat dying a slow death on a salt beach. The surrounding countryside was stagnant and pestilential, poisoned by the rotten plants the River Jordan churns in its current. The bones of beasts who died on the bank lay like wrecks picked dry by the vultures and whitened by the salted silt."

The result of these endless sessions, during which the countryside turned into a landscape that the light of the setting sun turned into an intense, surreal vision, prompted Ruskin to say that this work had become a de-composition, ultimately the opposite of what the artist had sought. Hunt continues: "Every minute the mountains became more gorgeous and solemn – the whole scene more unlike anything ever portayed before . . . I had planned all my work so carefully the previous evening – marking in the shadows and noting the tints – that, although the effect was, till past the middle of the day, quite different, I was able – counting with certainty upon a cloudless sunset to correct all – to lay in my day's work boldly."

The goat died of exhaustion and thirst after 12 days, and Hunt had to spend three dispiriting months searching for an immaculately white he-goat as a replacement. When he finally left the Edom mountains, he had still not completed the picture, and so took with him crates of bones, sand, salt, and rocks. When the painting was finally exhibited, reviewers were outraged by this stark allegory of Christ's sacrifice in the shape of

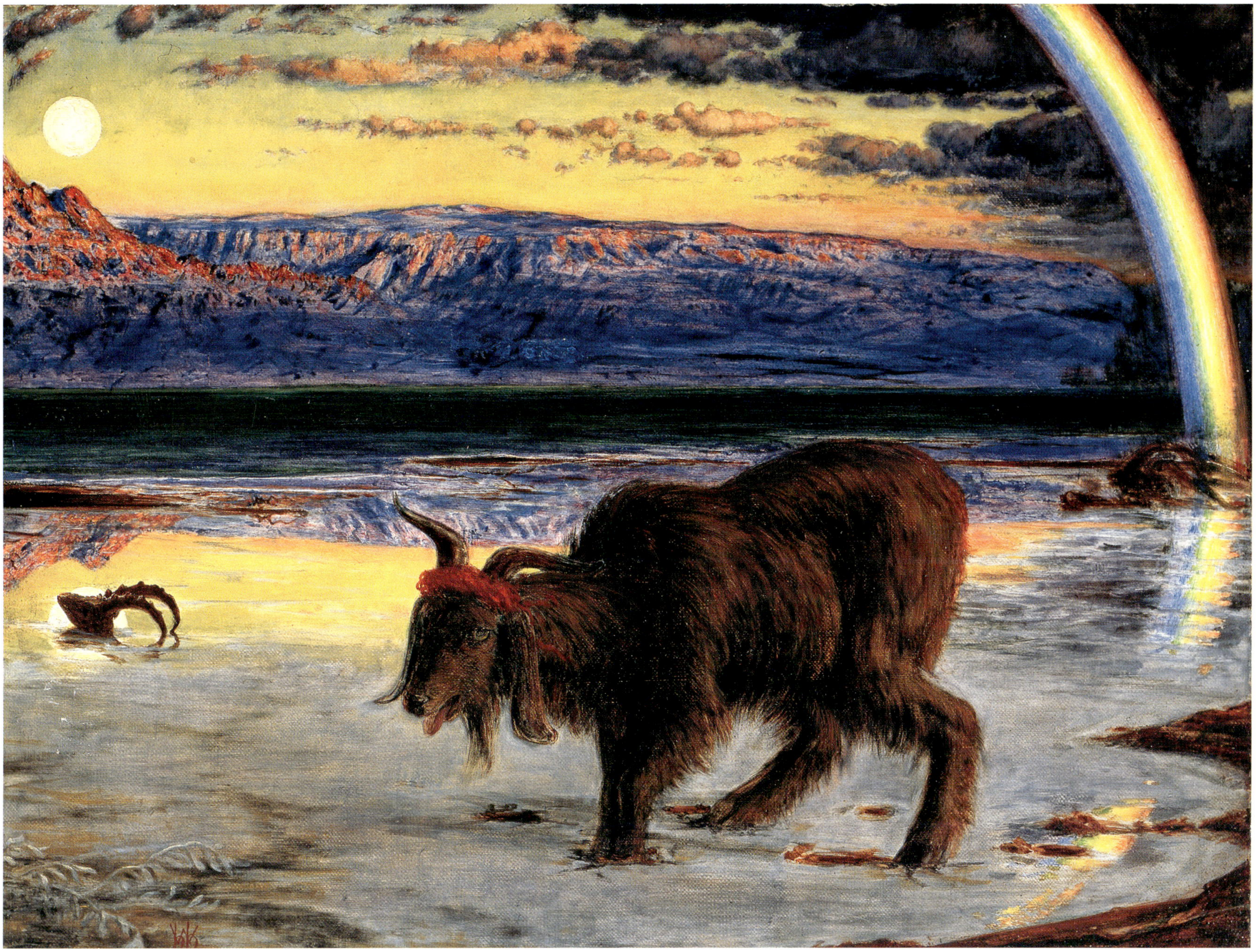

a helpless, bleating goat dying in a dead and dying desert landscape.

Before returning to England, Hunt pushed on into Syria, finally succeeding in visiting Baalbek, which delighted him. From his eventful journey, Hunt brought back ideas and sketches for several works, including *The Plain of Rephaim from Zion*; a watercolor, *The Golden Age of Haroun Al-Rachid*, an illustration for a poem on the Arabian Nights by Alfred Lord Tennyson; and some marvelous watercolors of desert landscapes. He then started on what for him was a major work, his *Triumph of the Innocents*, showing the Holy Family on their flight into Egypt surrounded by the souls of the new-born massacred by Herod, shown here as putti. It would take him ten years to complete this strangely intense work. He undertook a last trip to Palestine during the years 1869 to 1872, and soon after started a new work whose uninhibited mysticism makes it quite remarkable: *The Miracle of the Holy Fire*. Among the many artists who visited the Middle East, Hunt, fired by his desire to combine realism with an intense and sincere religious vision, stands out for the originality and richness of the imaginary world he conjured from the Holy Land.

The Scapegoat, William Holman Hunt, 1854–1858
Oil on canvas, 33.7 x 45.9 cm
(City Art Galleries, Manchester).

Constantinople

Recollection of Asia Minor,
Charles de Tournemine, c. 1865
Oil on canvas, 43 x 64 cm
(Musée des Augustins, Toulouse).

Turkish Women Out Walking – Sunset,
Charles de Tournemine, 1863
Oil on canvas, 68 x 125 cm
(Musée Fabre, Montpellier).

From the beginning of the 19th century, Ottoman Turkey and its capital Istanbul (which in the West was still widely known as Constantinople) were a compulsory part of the journey to the East. In the early decades of the century, however, when the Ottomans were seen as the cruel oppressors of a Greece struggling heroically for its independence, visitors did not stay long in the capital of the Ottoman Empire; Chateaubriand hated what he saw as a sprawling metropolis. But the French poet Lamartine, visiting in 1832, was entranced by Byzantine remains, the evocative remnant of the "Roman Empire in the East," and tried to share with his countrymen his fascination with the pomp and magnificence of the Sultan's court. With the end of the Greek conflict, the Ottoman Turks ceased to be the enemy and Lamartine, who was a member of the French Chamber of Deputies, promoted an alliance with Turkey (a policy adopted during the Crimean War).

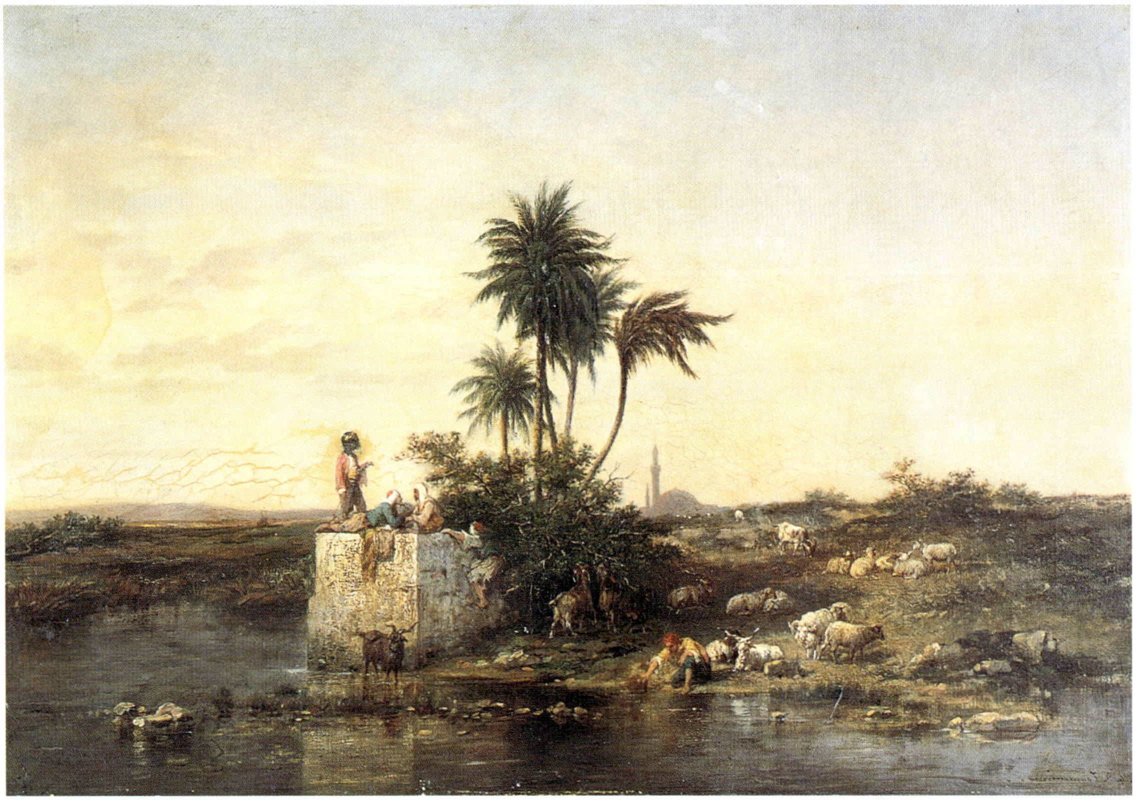

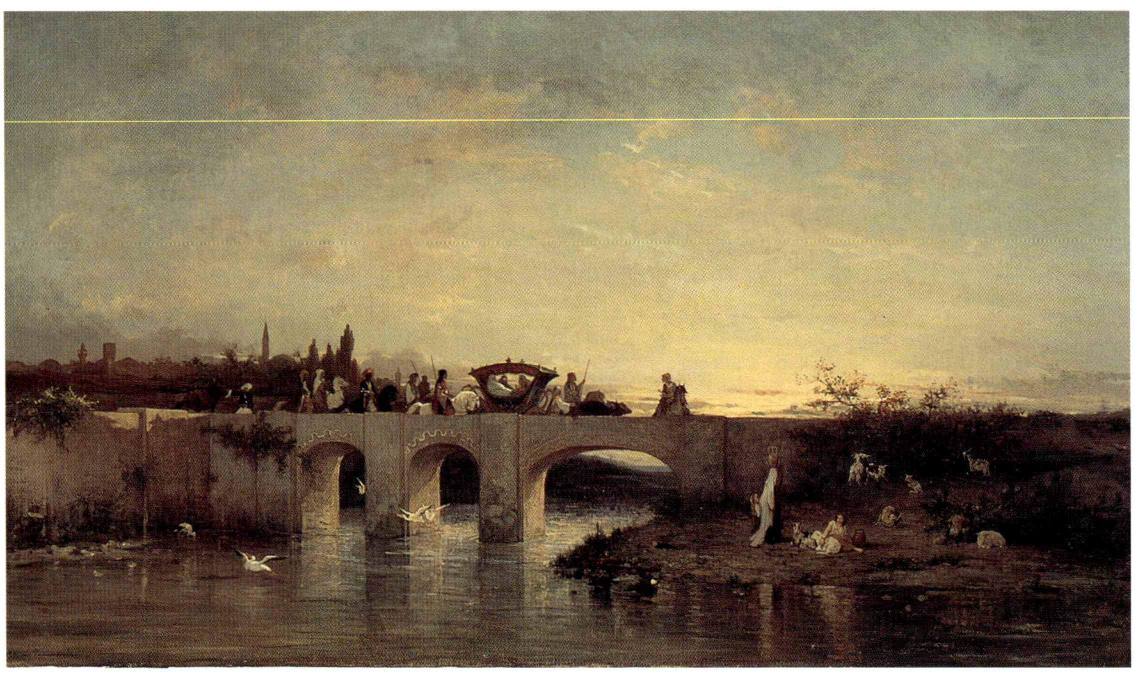

So in time Constantinople and Turkey again became legitimate objects of curiosity, one result being the setting up of a number of important archaeological digs in Anatolia. Charles Fellows scoured south-west Anatolia during the 1840s, exploring particularly Lycia and having the Nereid monument at Xanthus moved to the British Museum. Another English scholar, Layard, was for his part conducting the digs at Nimrud, Niniveh, and also at Assur in 1847. The Halicarnassus frieze found at Bodrum was in turn moved to London. Travelers were increasingly numerous and in 1854 the essential *Murray's Guide to Turkey* came out. There were also expensive albums of illustrations devoted to Constantinople's splendors. One of the finest was by the Italian architect Caspare Fossati, published in 1852, which features 25 prints of Hagia Sophia, which had been restored between 1847 and 1849.

Great writers made Turkey the highlight of their Eastern tour. Gérard de Nerval in 1843, Gustave Flaubert and Maxime Ducamp in 1851, Théophile Gautier in 1852, Edmondo De Amicis in 1877, Edmond About in 1884, and finally Pierre Loti and Claude Farrère at the turn of the century, helped to create a new myth of the country. It was a myth that largely ignored the crisis of power at the heart of this huge empire, and that was in part a fantasy world conjured up by an increasingly industrialized Europe.

The first painters to stay in Constantinople were usually lesser artists, though their works often had charm. There was, for example, the Frenchman François Dubois, who painted public occasions well, and also the polish artist Sandor Alexander Swoboda,

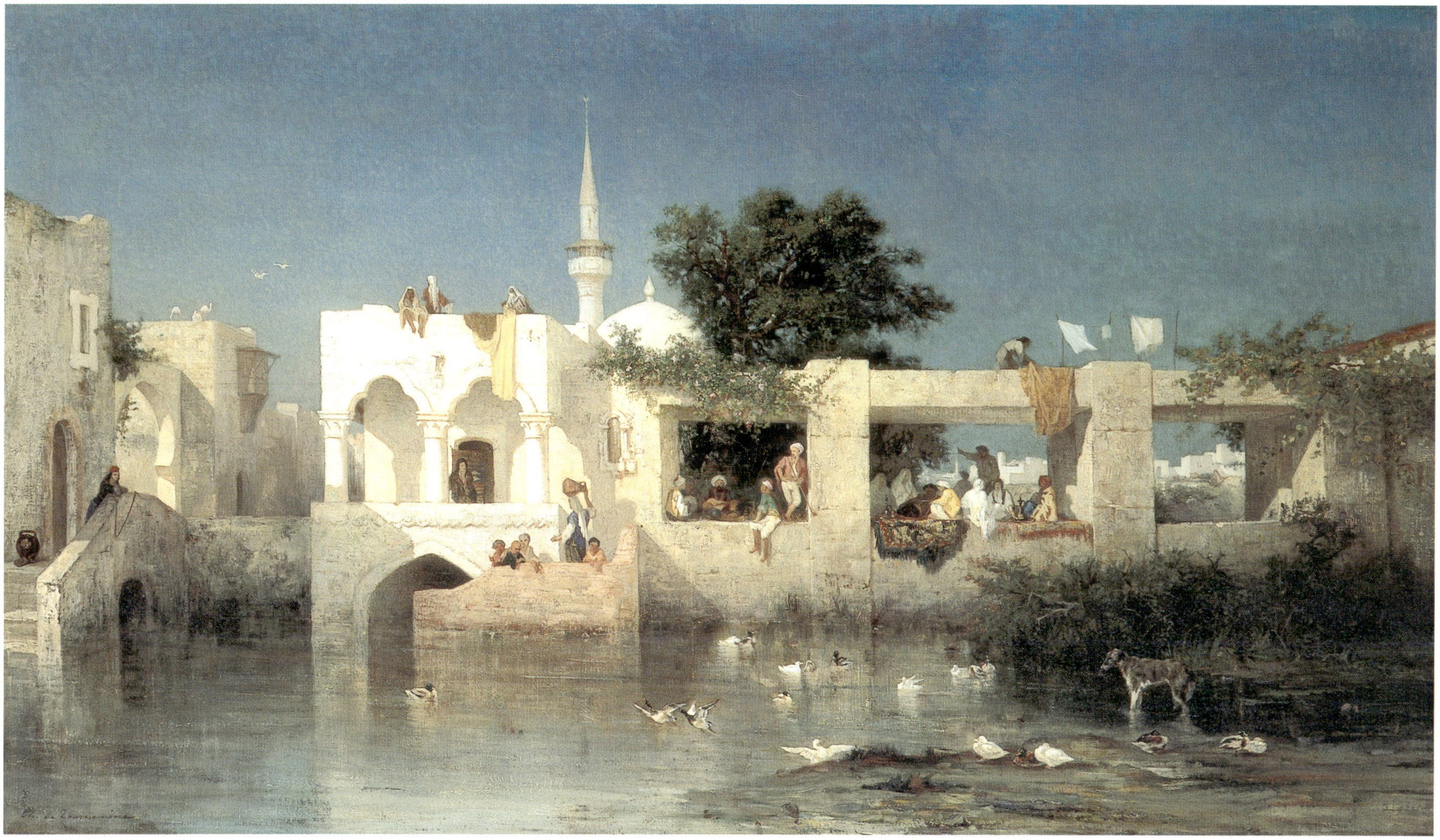

Above
Café in Adalia, Asian Turkey (formerly *Turkish Houses near Adalia*),
Charles de Tournemine, c. 1856
Oil on canvas, 69 x 124 cm
(Musée d'Orsay, Paris).

Right
A Break in the Journey, Near Constantinople,
Karl Pavlovitch Briullov, c. 1835
(National Museum of Russia, St Petersburg).

Following double page
The Slave Market, Sir William Allan, 1838
Oil on wood, 129 x 198 cm
(National Gallery of Scotland, Edinburgh).

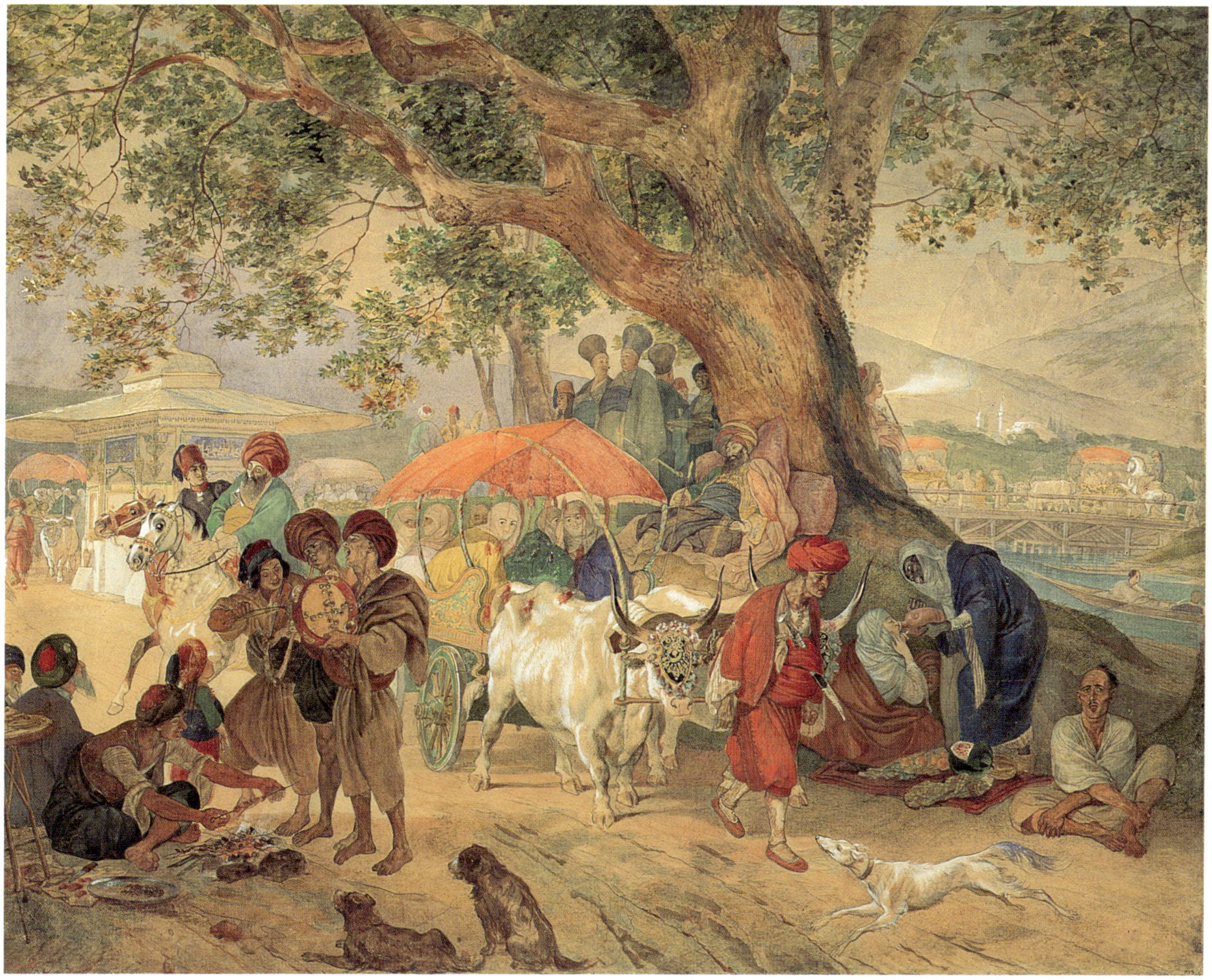

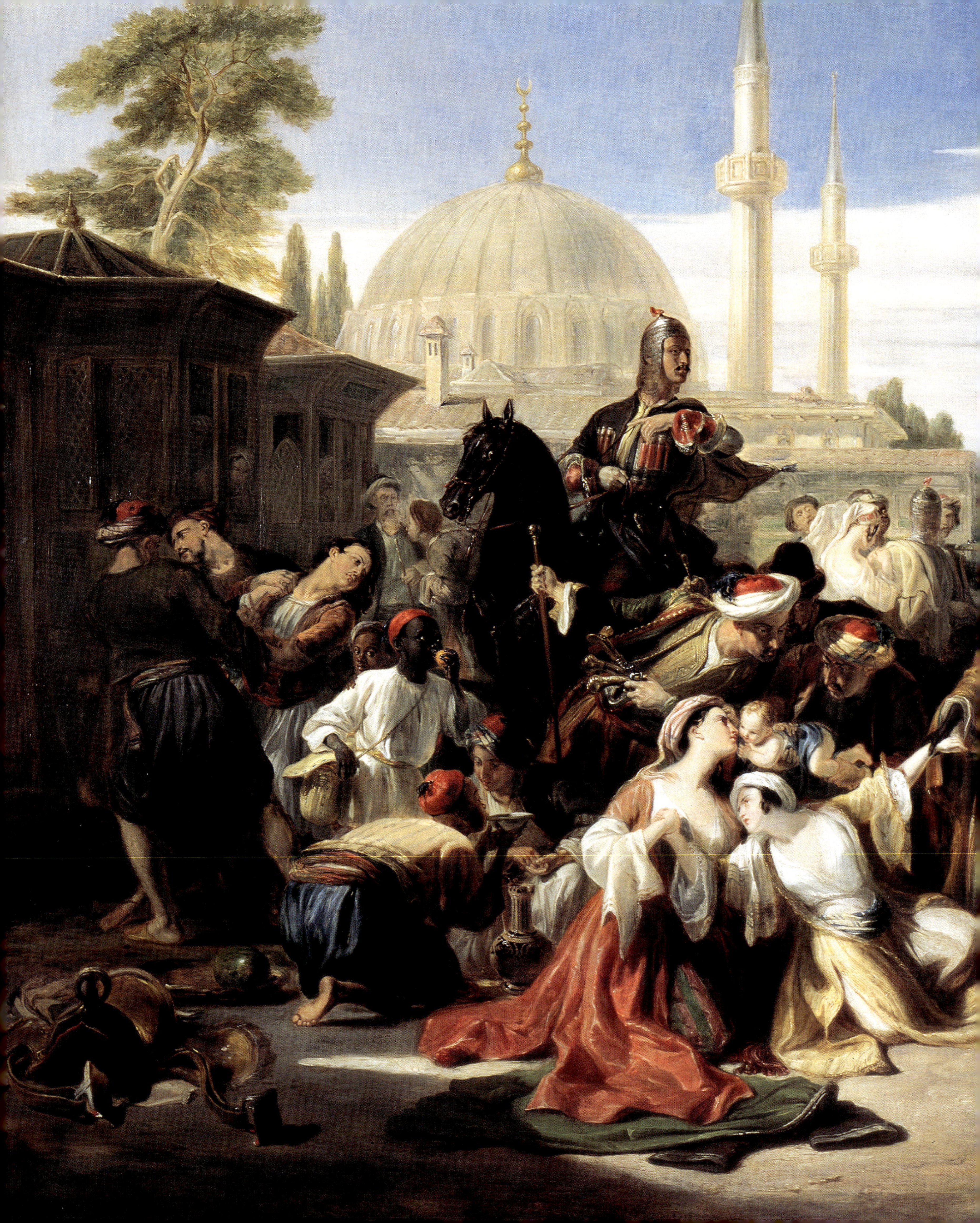

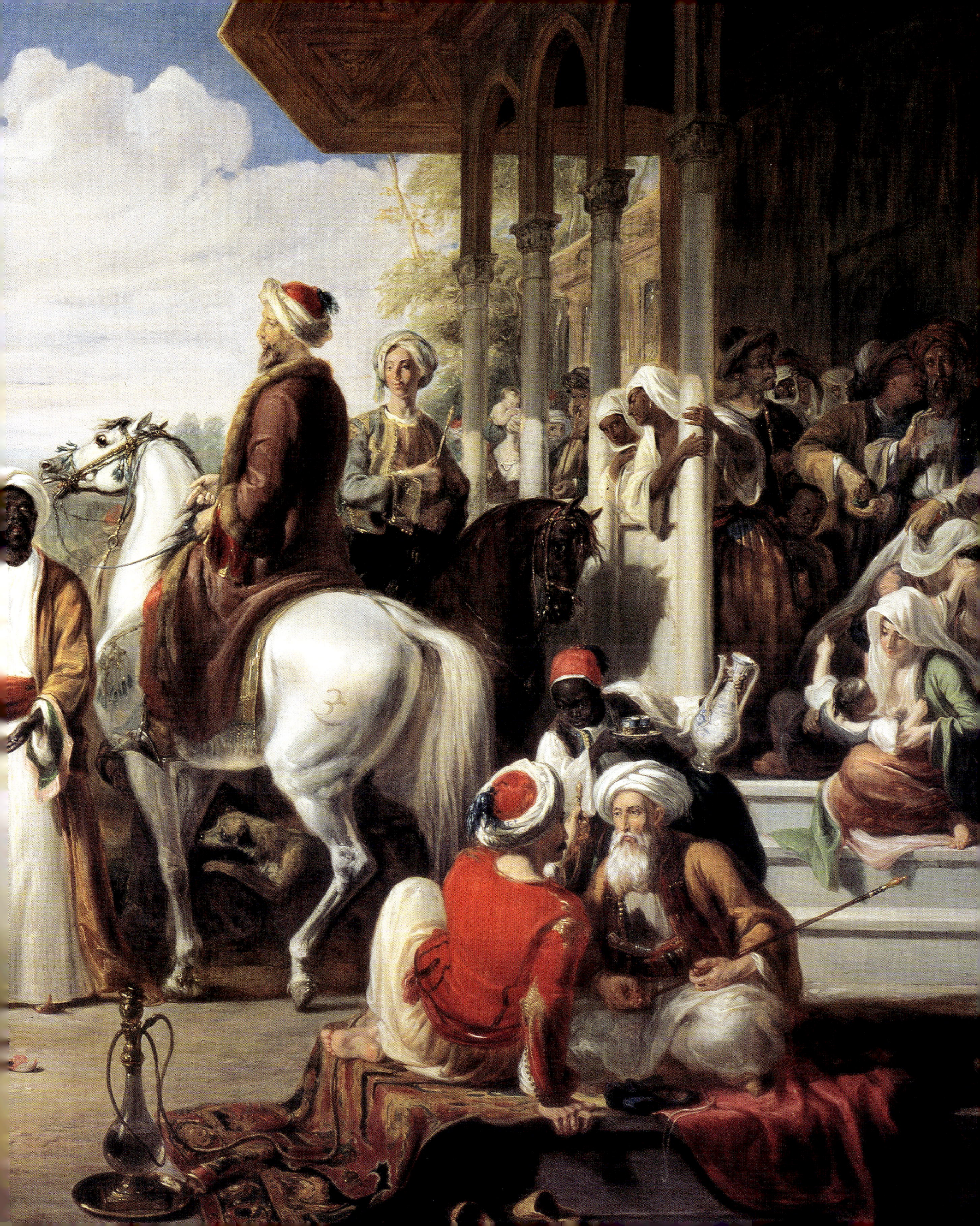

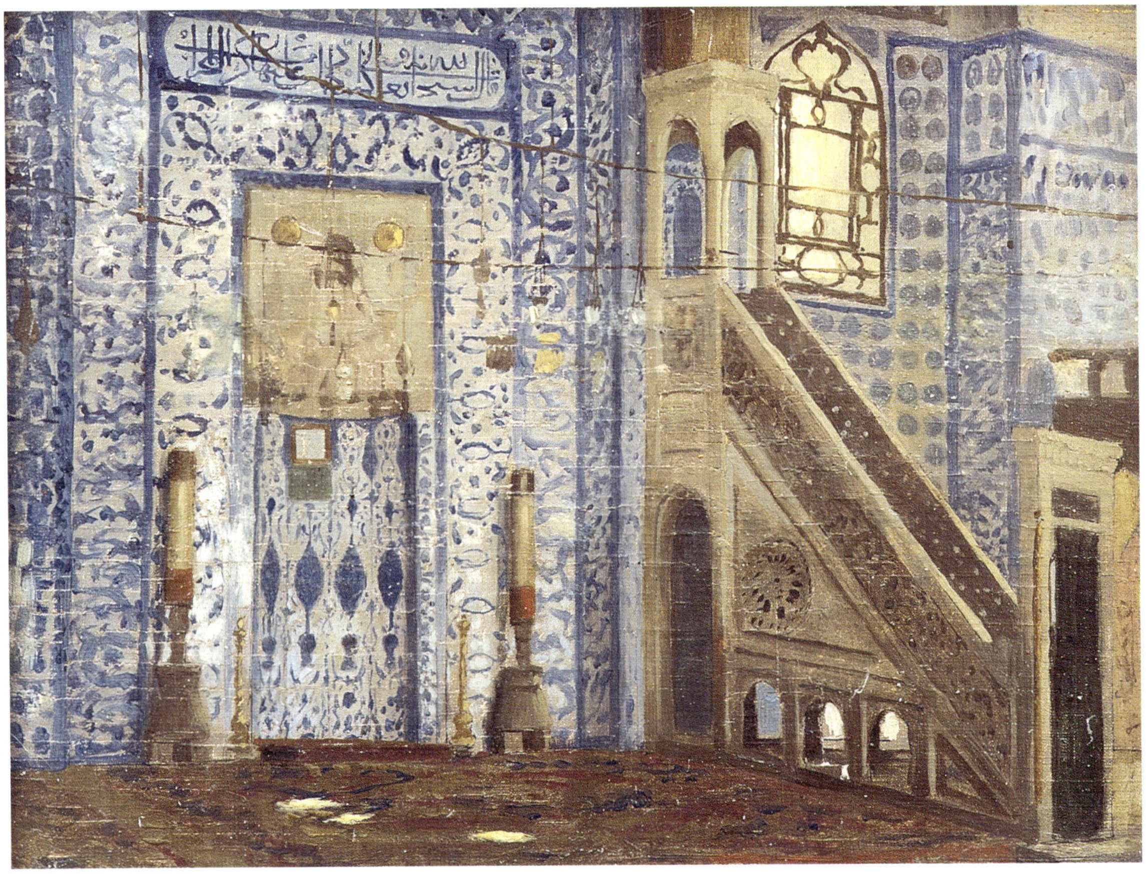

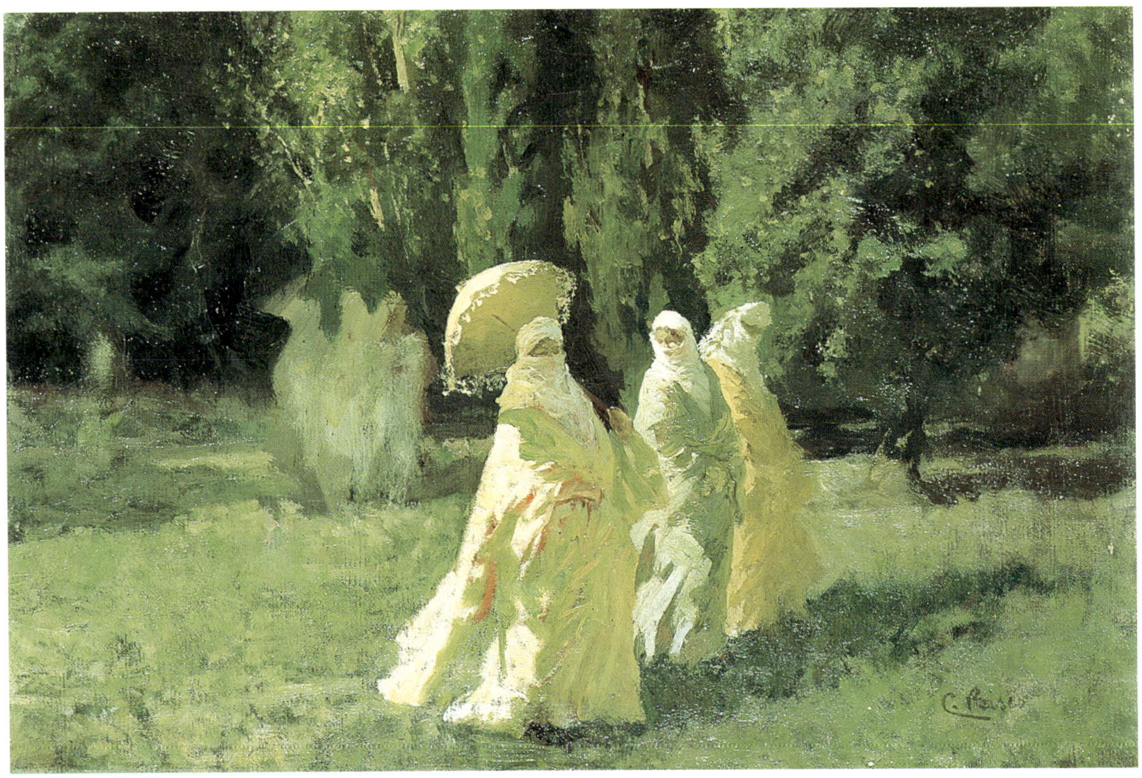

Interior of a Mosque, Jean-Léon Gérôme, undated
Oil on canvas, 22 x 31 cm
(Musée Georges Garret, Vesoul).

The Favorites from the Harem in the Park,
Cesare Biseo, c. 1880
Oil on canvas, 41 x 62 cm
(Galleria d'Arte Moderna Ricci Oddi, Piacenza).

whose harem women are painted with undeniable delicacy and artlessness.

It fell to the Scotsman David Wilkie to introduce modern Constantinople to the West. Having traveled widely in Europe, visiting Italy, Spain, and France, where he visited and was very impressed by Delacroix, he was appointed "painter-in-ordinary to the king" (George IV) on his return to Britain in 1828. In 1840 he set off for the Middle East, intending to visit the Holy Land. But he reached Constantinople just as war with Egypt broke out, the forces of Muhammad Ali of Egypt having invaded Syria. As Wilkie was not allowed to move about the country, he spent several months painting portraits of ordinary people of the city and sketching genre scenes, gradually acquiring a deep respect for a culture of which he had known nothing on his arrival. He wrote: "It is by comparison with the customs and friendships of our native land that we estimate, perhaps unfairly, those of the less advanced race that surround us here, forgetting that the Eastern people were earlier in the advance of civilisation than we, and though now far behind, supplied much of that from which our civilisation has sprung." In 1840 he painted the portrait of the young Sultan Abdulmecid, and the following year *Mr Coloquhan's dragoman Satori* and *Portrait of Master James William Whithall Holding a Gun*, for which he asked the child sitter to don Turkish costume. He also painted on wood the *Turkish Letter Writer*; remembering the scene that inspired him, he wrote: "Saw at the outer court of a mosque a scribe of most venerable appearance. He was reading a letter or paper he had been writing for two Turkish young women—one very handsome: the way they were placed made an excellent composition for a picture." Finally he was able to continue his journey, and reached Palestine, which for him was the highpoint of his travels. Sadly, he died on the return journey to Britain, before being able to use his impressions of the Holy Land; no less a figure than Turner paid homage to Wilkie by painting *Burial at Sea*.

In France, Ottoman lifestyles would be popularized by the artist Alexandre-Gabriel Decamps. He arrived in Turkey in 1828 and settled provisionally in Smyrna, where he managed to fix up a studio of sorts. Back in France in 1829, he completed seven paintings from the watercolor or pencil sketches he had made in Turkey; these were exhibited at the 1831 Salon to great acclaim. He was particularly fond of representing the simple life of soldiers, butchers, the boys at the local school, and small shopkeepers. Throughout his career, he continued to portray characters of very modest background, as in *Turkish Child at the Fountain* (1846). He sometimes also tackled more ambitious compositions, like *The Torture of the Hooks* (1837). But no court commissions were forthcoming and he left the country a disappointed man, destroying his travel diaries and most of his Turkish sketches. He would, however, return to his favorite themes in a number of canvases and remained one of the leading French Orientalists until his death.

Amadeo Preziosi of Malta arrived in Constantinople at the end of 1842, endlessly walking the streets of the old district in order to capture picturesque scenes at the bazaar, craftsmen at work, family occasions, idyllic landscapes... a colorful world in which different ethnic groups lived and worked side by side, Jews, Armenians, Bulgars, Greeks, Turks, and many others. He published several albums of lithographs, including *Stamboul, souvenir de l'Orient* (Istanbul, memories of the Orient) in 1861. He exhibited his paintings in Paris in 1858 and 1867, in London in 1863, and finally at the Istanbul Club in 1880 and 1881. In recognition of his achievement, he was made official painter at the court of Abdulhamid II.

During his long Eastern journey with Sir Thomas Philip, the English artist Richard Dadd arrived in Constantinople at the end of 1842. He had crossed Italy, where he had been enthralled by the paintings of Tintoretto and Veronese in Venice, traveled all over Greece (Corfu, Patras, the Peloponnese, Athens, Thebes, and finally Delphi), and had finally reached Anatolia, where he visited Smyrna. He never set off without his sketchbook, which was assiduously kept up to date as he moved from one place to the next. In Constantinople he did pencil drawings and completed a painting of Sir Thomas in Oriental dress. These two indefatigable travelers would return on horseback, having visited Bodrum (ancient Halicarnassus) on their way to Lycia.

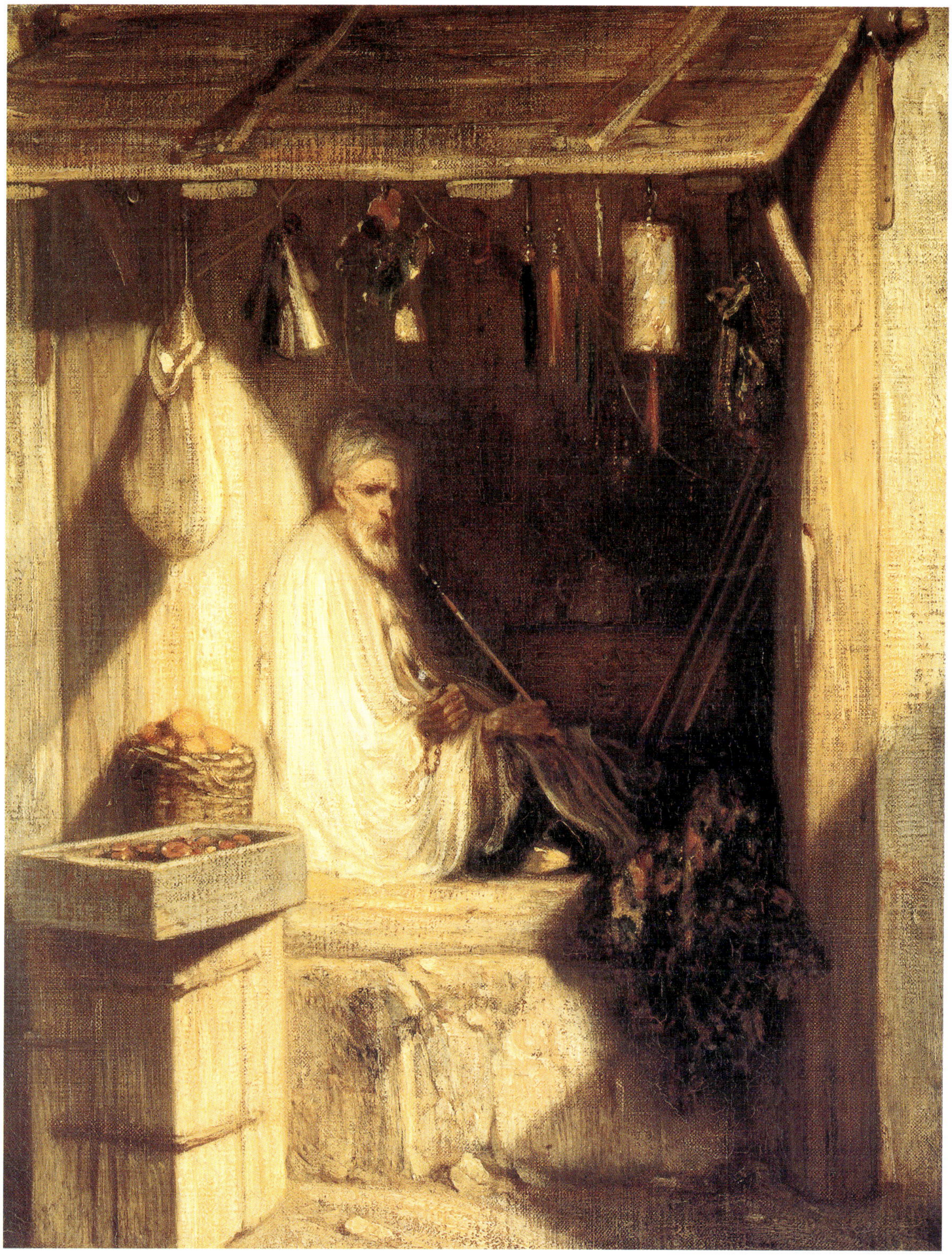

Turkish Merchant Smoking in his Shop,
Alexandre-Gabriel Decamps, 1844
Oil on canvas, 36 x 28 cm
(Musée d'Orsay, Paris).

The Russian painter Ivan Constantinovich Aivazosky was fortunate enough to sail with Grand Duke Constantine along the Anatolian coast in 1845, and to spend some time in Constantinople. He returned twice under Abdulmecid's reign, and painted the portrait of his successor Abdulaziz in 1874. His landscapes, though in the Neo-classical style, are imbued with deep poetry; examples include *Eyüp in the Moonlight* (1874) and *Sarayburnu* (1874).

Among the many artists who arrived with the first influx in the middle of the century was Germain-Fabius Brest. He stayed on for four years, developing a sure hand in depicting both the busy streets of the city and the surrounding countryside. Characteristically subtle works include *Uskudar, in Front of the Mosque, The Turkish Coffee House, The Banks of the Bosporus,* and *A View of the Bosporus.* Jean Brindesi had two remarkable albums published by the French publisher Lemercier in 1856, both containing 24 lithographs; the first depicted costumes, the second scenes in Constantinople. His works show a scrupulous realism combined with great intensity.

In 1856 Félix Ziem, a tireless traveler, undertook his grand tour of Eastern Mediterranean, and was as taken with Constantinople as with Cairo or Venice. On his return he painted a great many views in which the Bosporus and the Golden Horn are seen under vast skies and awash with a scintillating light that gives the scenes an almost unreal quality. As time went by, Ziem's imagination never ceased to work on the memories of that trip, moving from a considered realism to whimsical visions of glowing twilights and enchanting dawns.

As Sultan Abdulaziz wished to develop and modernize the visual arts in his country, he encouraged Western artists to live and work in the capital. To this end he gave permission for the opening of Pierre Désiré Guillemet's Académie de Peinture et de Dessin (Academy for painting and drawing), which was attended by Turkish artists, some of whom had considerable talent. One was Sarkis Direnyam, who between 1874 and 1875 painted several portraits of the sultan and of the ladies at his court; he also worked on wall painting at the Dolmabace Palace, and took part in official exhibitions in Constantinople between 1873 and 1877, the year of his death.

The French artist Jean-Léon Gérôme arrived in Constantinople in 1875, probably intent on broadening his already considerable knowledge of the Islamic world. Completely captivated by this thriving city of contrasts, he returned four years later. He showed a particular interest in colorful Turkish soldiers and the sultan's guards, and often used photographs to ensure authenticity; for his settings, he frequently used the Topkapi Palace. He also taught many of the Turkish painters who, by the end of the 19th century, had established reputations: Osman Hamdi, Seker Ahmed Pasha, Halil Pasha, Ali Cemal, and Théodore Ralli, who studied in Gérôme's Paris studio – a generation of Turkish artists

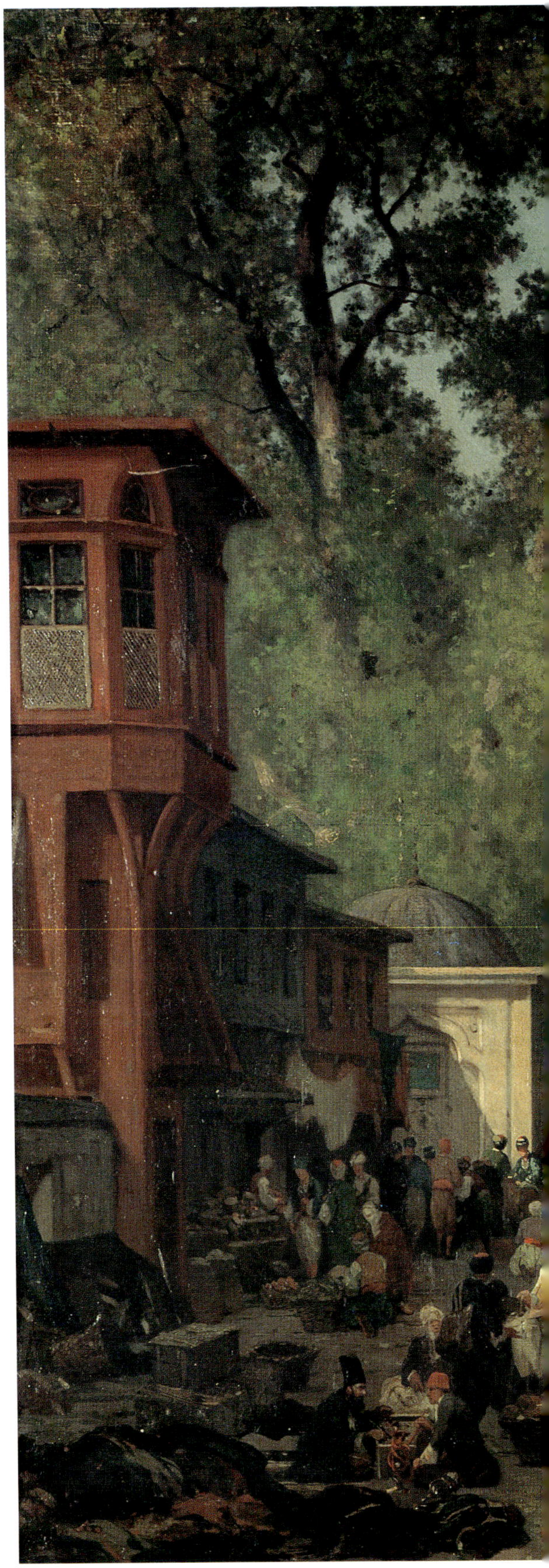

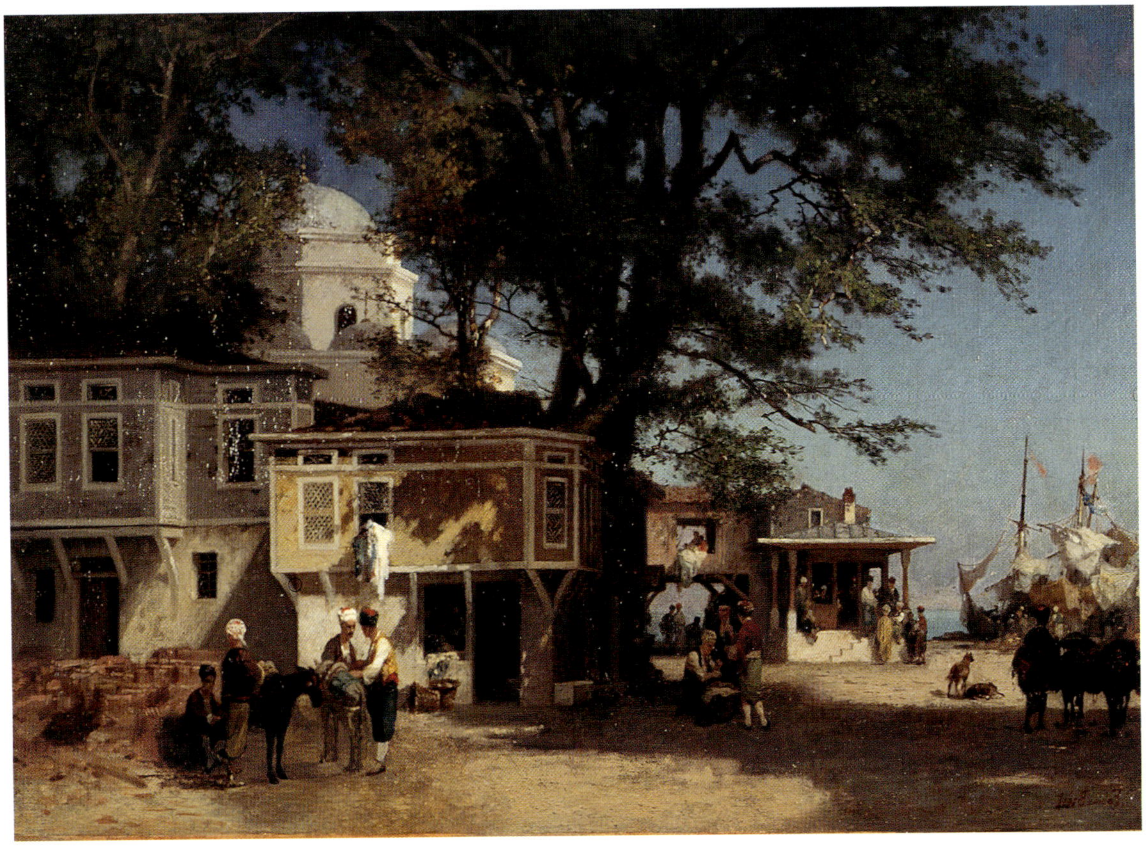

were influenced by his style and approach. When Seker Ahmed Pasha set up the first collection of contemporary Western art for Sultan Abdulaziz, he both sought advice from Gérôme and also gave him pride of place in the exhibition.

Several Italian painters came to Constantinople in search of subjects and inspiration.

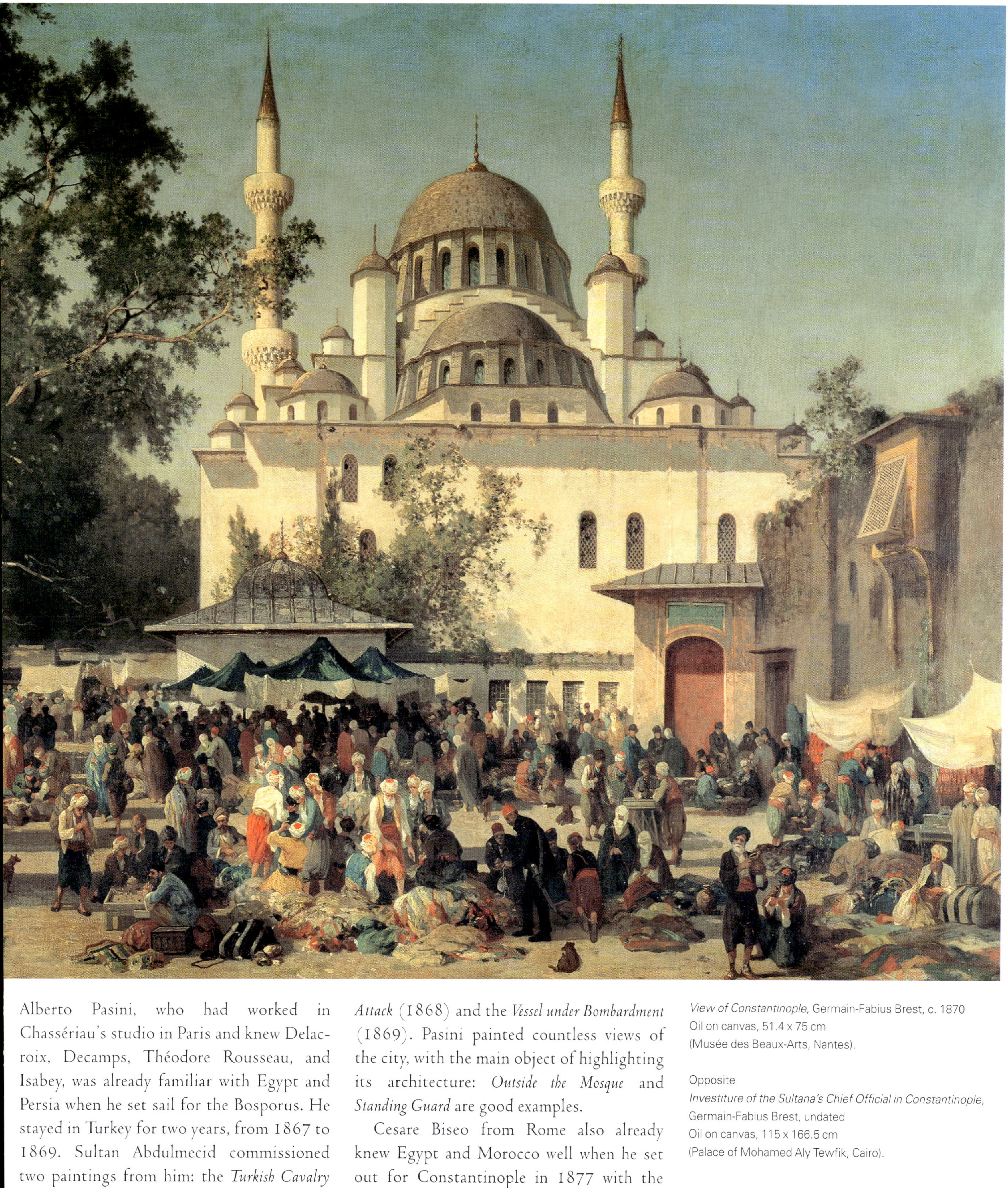

Alberto Pasini, who had worked in Chassériau's studio in Paris and knew Delacroix, Decamps, Théodore Rousseau, and Isabey, was already familiar with Egypt and Persia when he set sail for the Bosporus. He stayed in Turkey for two years, from 1867 to 1869. Sultan Abdulmecid commissioned two paintings from him: the *Turkish Cavalry Attack* (1868) and the *Vessel under Bombardment* (1869). Pasini painted countless views of the city, with the main object of highlighting its architecture: *Outside the Mosque* and *Standing Guard* are good examples.

Cesare Biseo from Rome also already knew Egypt and Morocco well when he set out for Constantinople in 1877 with the

View of Constantinople, Germain-Fabius Brest, c. 1870
Oil on canvas, 51.4 x 75 cm
(Musée des Beaux-Arts, Nantes).

Opposite
Investiture of the Sultana's Chief Official in Constantinople, Germain-Fabius Brest, undated
Oil on canvas, 115 x 166.5 cm
(Palace of Mohamed Aly Tewfik, Cairo).

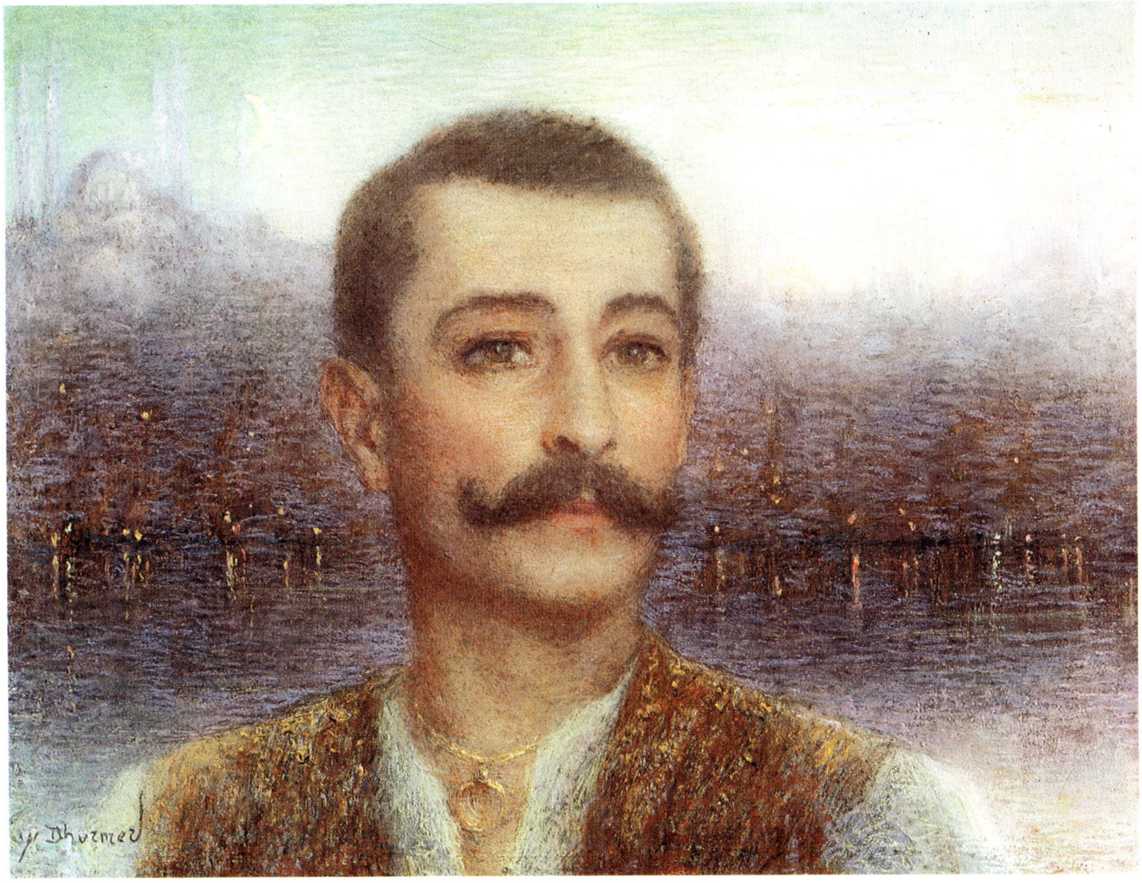

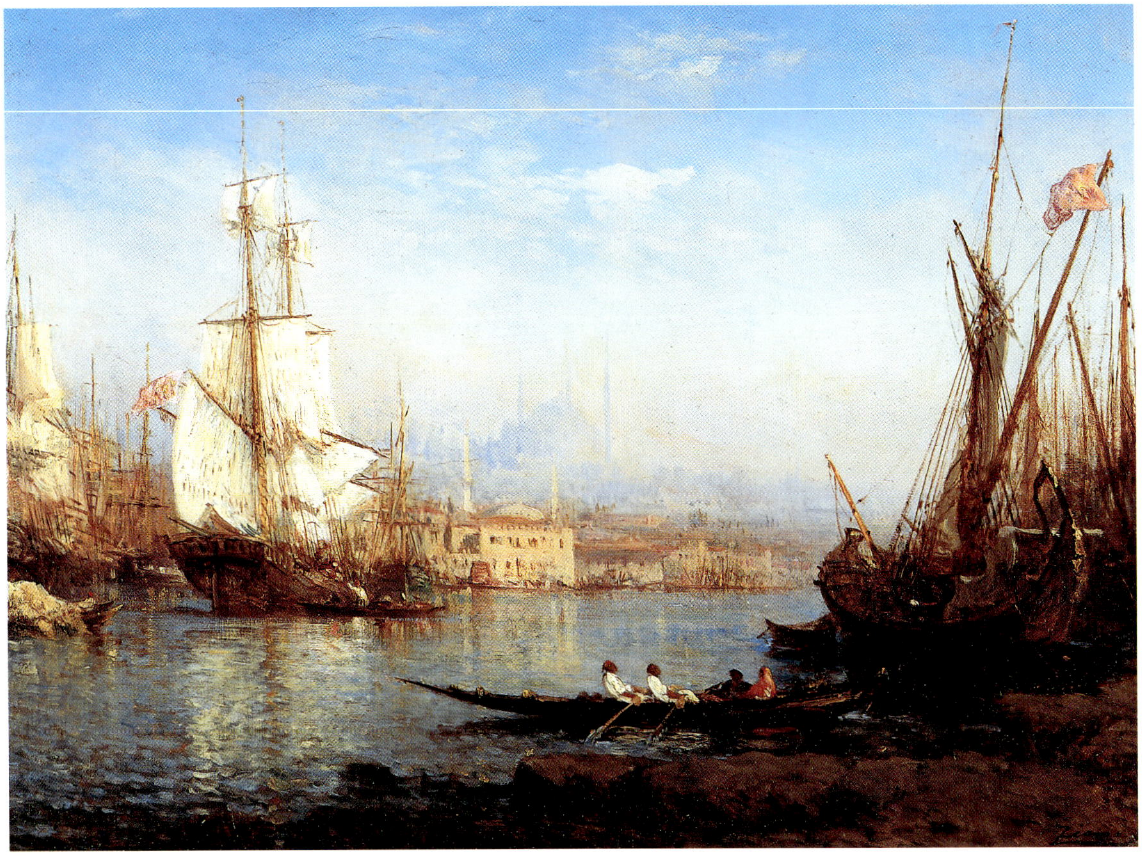

Portrait of Pierre Loti, 'Ghost of the Orient',
Lucien Lévy-Dhurmer, 1896
Pastel, 42 x 56 cm
(Musée Basque, Bayonne).

The Bosporus, Félix Ziem, 1883
Oil on canvas, 53 x 70 cm
(Musée des Beaux-Arts, Reims).

writer Edmondo De Amicis; he was to illustrate the writer's account of the city. His images form an important record of the way the city looked at the time. Salvatore Valeri arrived in the Ottoman capital at the beginning of the 1880s and was given a position in the new arts academy in 1883, a position he held until 1913. He painted highly evocative landscapes (*View of Kagithane*) and was strongly drawn to the life of the ordinary people (*Water Carrier*, *Man playing the Guitar*, *Gypsy*). Leonardo de Mango arrived in the 1880s; he had visited Egypt, Libya, and Syria, where he lived for several years. He painted the various quarters of Constantinople: *Impression of a Street in Eyup*, *Night in Fener*, and *At the Fountain*, and *Friday*. He lived there until his death in 1930, with a break in Libya during the Italian conquest of Libya in 1911. In 1891, the young Paduan painter Fausto Zonaro, just married, decided to settle in Constantinople after a rootless youth. He focused on the depiction of city life, his works often having a certain Venetian quality: *Ladies Getting into a Caique*, *The Fire Brigade*, and *Military Parade Crossing the Bridge of Karakoy* (1896). Appointed painter to the Sultan in 1896, he was granted a studio overlooking the Bosporus. Though he could not visit the women of the harem, he was able to paint them thanks to his wife, who was allowed to photograph them. His dervishes, itinerant scribes, and odalisques conjured up a dual vision of Turkey: on the one hand it reinforced Western preconceptions, and on the other it brought to light unfamiliar aspects of Turkish society.

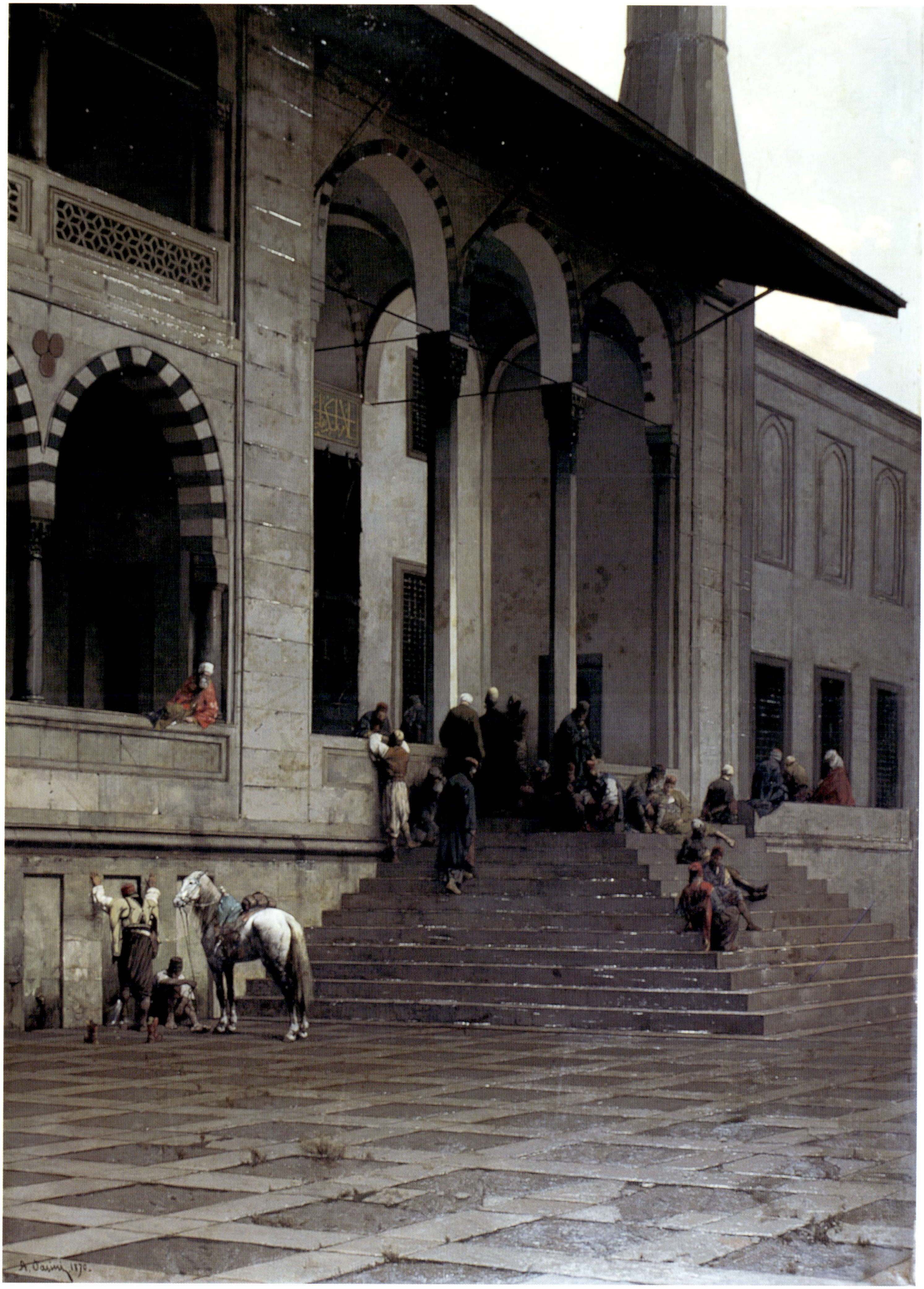

The Door of the Yeni-Djami Mosque in Constantinople, Alberto Pasini, 1870
Oil on canvas,
156.8 x 115.5 cm
(Musée des Beaux-Arts, Nantes).

Jean Auguste Dominique Ingres

For Baudelaire, Ingres' great distinction was "his love of women." He went on to say that Ingres' "libertinism is intentional… if the Isle of Cythera had passed its command to Monsieur Ingres, you may rest assured that it would not appear light-hearted and blissful, as in Watteau's painting, but sturdy, sustaining like ancient love." According to the Vicomte Delaborde, Ingres was thinking of his *Turkish Bath* – one of his major works and certainly one of the finest products of Orientalism – as early as 1819. There is nothing to confirm this claim, but it can not be denied that from 1807 onwards, when he painted *Half-Length Bather*, he had embarked on an extraordinary artistic adventure that was to occupy him throughout his career. Here, the bather wears a kind of turban not unlike the one worn by Raphael's *La Fornarina*, a portrait of Raphael's model and lover. This head-dress forms a common element in Ingres' nude paintings right up to the masterpieces of old age; it appears, for example, in the so-called *Valpinçon Bather*. As for the six separate versions of the *Nude Woman Asleep*, they are, by contrast, bereft of all adornment. None of the restraint of the previous paintings remains and they radiate an unbridled, deeply pagan sensuality that finds its full expression in his *Golden Age*, a hymn of praise to paganism.

In his *Grande Odalisque* of 1814 (of which he painted several versions), Ingres moved a little closer to the Orient by including a number of Eastern accessories – a fly-swatter, Turkish pipe, a stool, and the famous turban. In 1822, however, he worked on a copy of

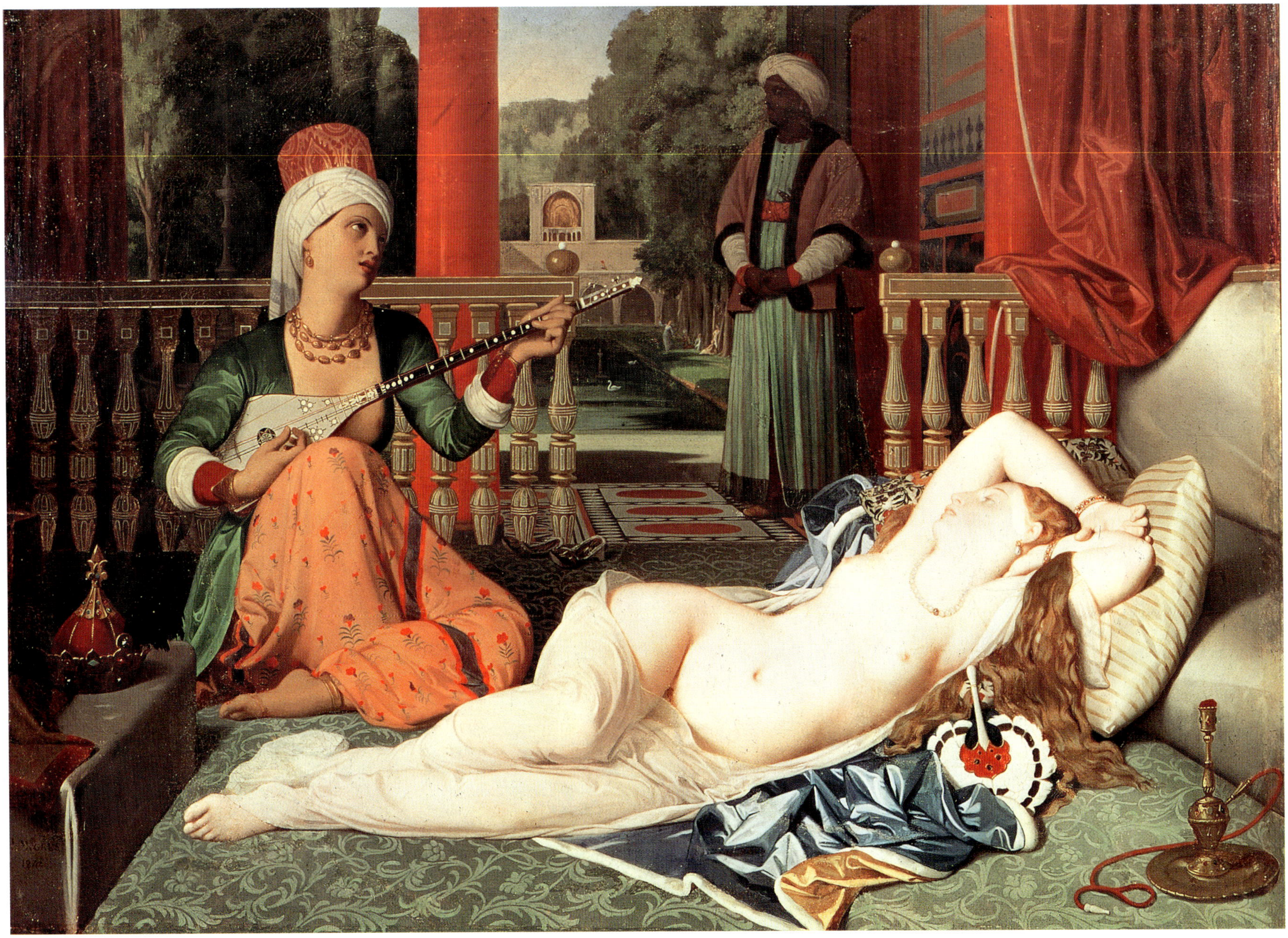

Odalisque with a Slave,
Jean Auguste Dominique Ingres,
1842
75 x 105.4 cm
(Walters Art Gallery, Baltimore).

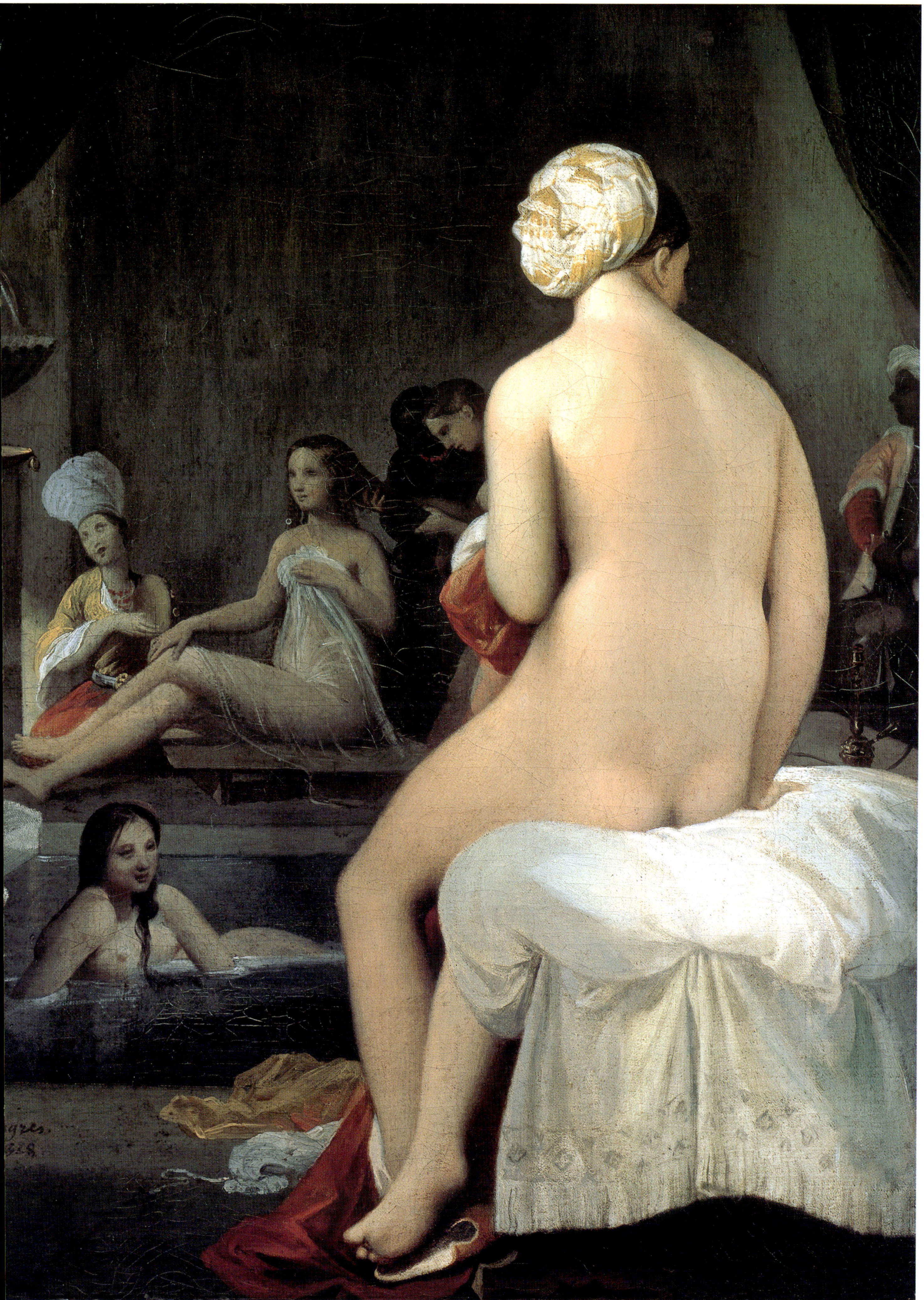

Little Bather, or Inside a Harem,
Jean Auguste Dominique Ingres, 1828
Oil on canvas, 35 x 27 cm
(Musée du Louvre, Paris).

Following pages
Grande Odalisque,
Jean Auguste Dominique Ingres, 1814
Oil on canvas,
91 x 162 cm
(Musée du Louvre, Paris).

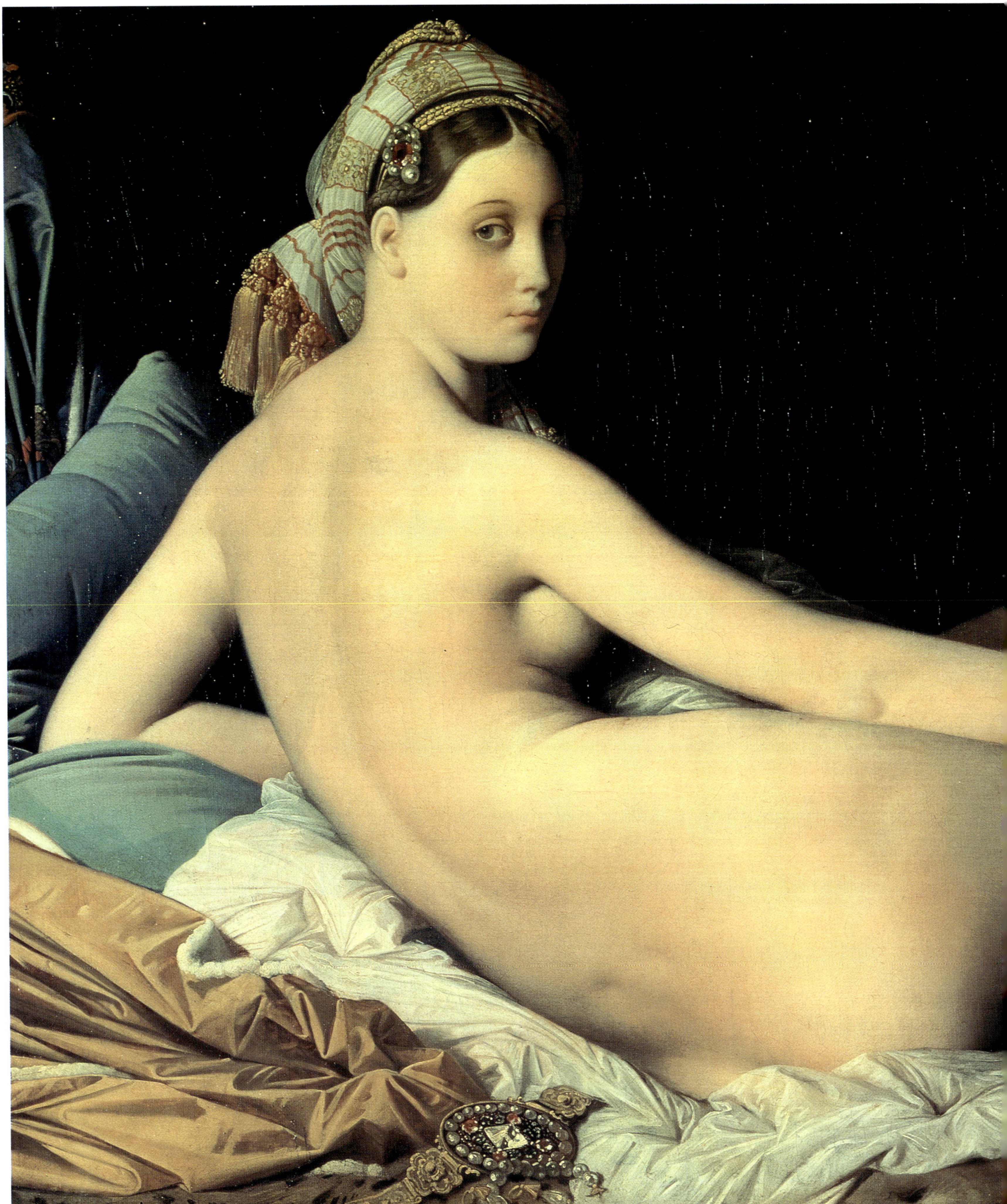

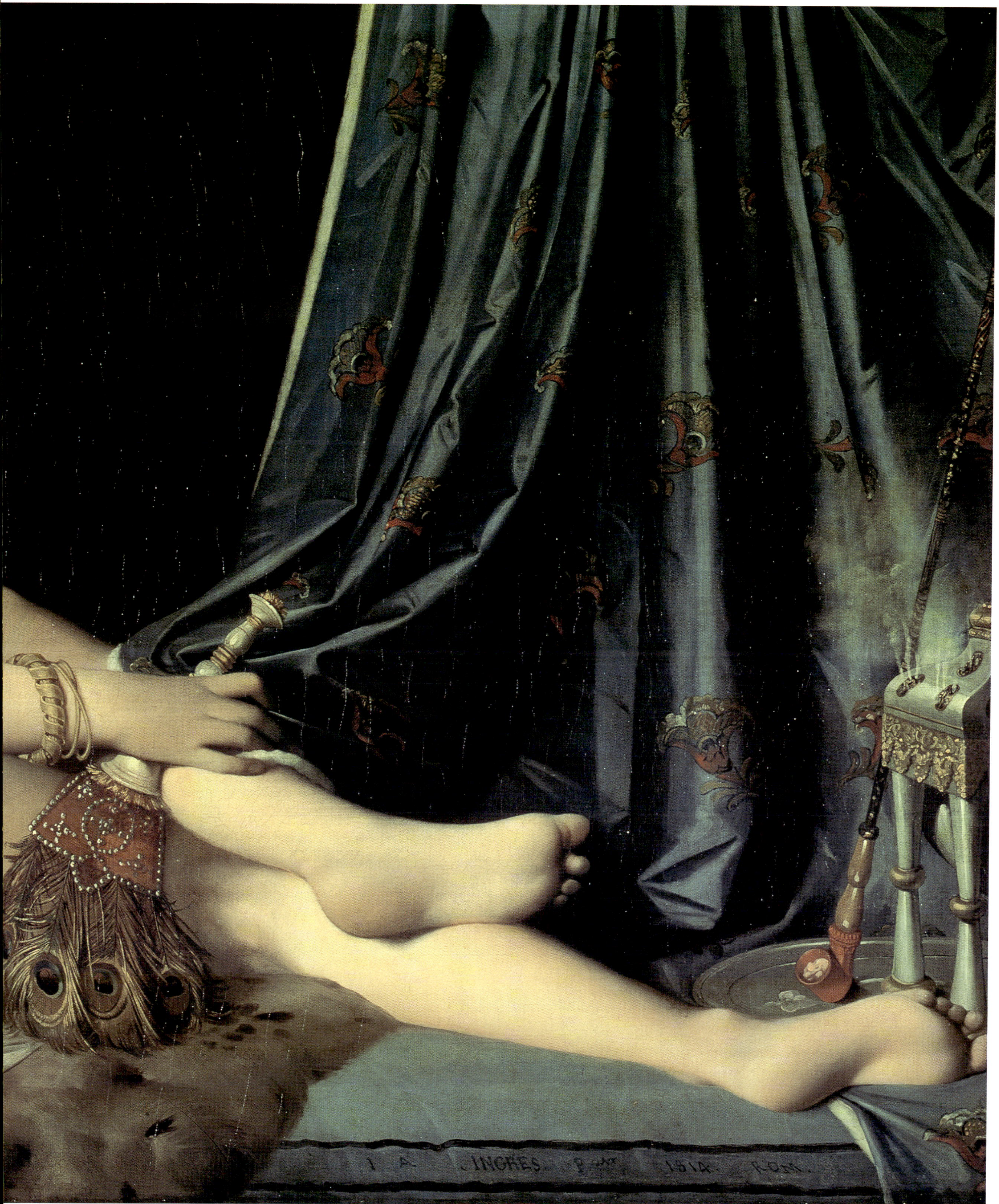
INGRES
1814.

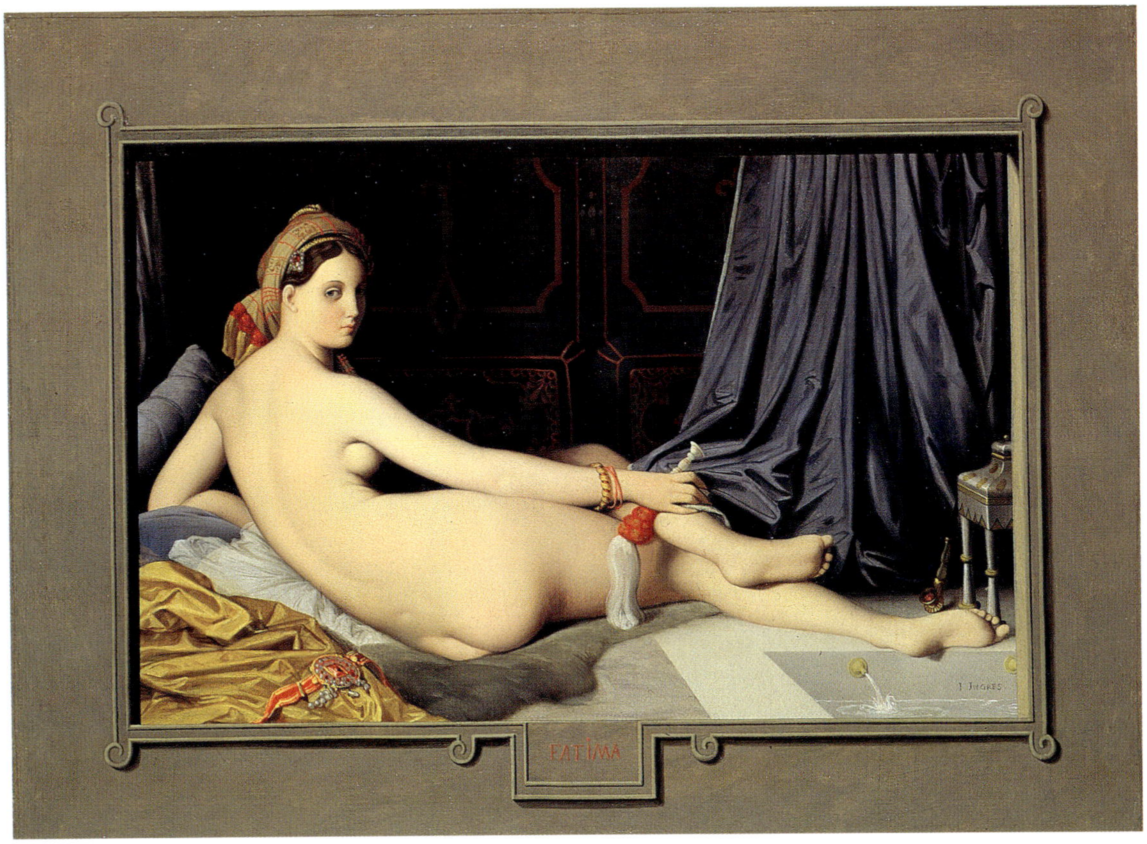

Titian's *Venus of Urbino*, as though he felt the need to return to his roots in Western art before pursuing his strange imaginary exploration of the Orient. In 1828 he completed his *Little Bather, or Inside a Harem*. Here the central figure can be seen as a reincarnation of the *Valpinçon Bather*; that of a young girl combing her hair which is taken from an engraving by Haussard from his album *Cent estampes qui représentent differentes nations du Levant* (One hundred prints representing different peoples of the Levant; Paris 1714-1715). In fact, as Ingres never traveled beyond Italy, the theme of the harem was drawn wholly from his reading, notably from the letters of Lady Mary Wortley Montagu, written on her stay in Constantinople, during the early years of the 18th century. On 1 April 1717 she enlightens one of her friends with a very precise description of the Baths at Andrinople, an account that Ingres copied into his notebooks. The passage which drew his attention contains the following lines: "There were many amongst them as exactly proportioned as ever any goddess was drawn by the pencil of Guido or Titian, and most of their skins shiningly white, only adorned by their beautiful hair divided into many tresses hanging on their shoulders, braided either with pearl or riband, perfectly representing the figures of the Graces." He went on to create other versions of this theme, but rather than continuing his exploration of the Turkish baths, he returned to the subject of the seraglio and in 1830 painted *Odalisque with a Slave*. The young woman lying with arms stretched backward looks very like his earlier *Nude Woman Asleep*. A slave kneeling beside her plays some oriental version of a mandolin, while a eunuch behind a balustrade keeps a discreet and respectful distance. As always, Ingres has used a number of sources; he took the décor from Persian miniatures, and he reproduced the Turkish objects in his own highly individual style, without stressing their Eastern origin. In this first version, the woman is within an enclosed space; in the second version, painted in 1842, she has a garden for background.

In 1848, he finally put the last touches to his *Venus Anadyomène*, first sketched 40 years earlier; and in 1851 he completed *Jupiter and Antiope*, in which the young woman adopts the same position as that seen in *Odalisque with a Slave*. He painted *La Source* in 1856, yet another painting started in his youth and of which he produced two versions. His *Golden Age*, on which he worked from 1842 to 1849, was an important stage on his path to *Turkish Bath*; it offers a vision of humanity before the Fall, with bodies intertwined in an innocent sensuality and voluptuousness.

It would still be another four years before Ingres could feel satisfied with his *Turkish Bath*. The round format, unique in Ingres' output, resulted from the client's shocked reaction, as Jacques-Émile Blanche tells us: "The *Turkish Bath*, an order from Prince Napoleon, went from being a square to a circle: apparently because of the indecent posture of the Almeh to the right, who in a sketch of which I have a photograph, leans back in such a suggestive pose that the artist had eventually to do away with the lower part of her body..." In this canvas, the *Valpinçon Bather* can be identified in the musician shown from behind, and also in the half-length bather; the odalisque from *Odalisque with a Slave* can be recognized in the next figure, still seen from behind; and the figure in *Nude Woman Asleep* is the girl lying down. All told, Ingres has summed up in this canvas the essential features of his ideal female, an ideal closely bound to his artistic ideal. J.E. Blanche (who has not been the only one to see something odd in the picture) observed that "it is a strange painting, apparently cold and yet more heady than the smoke from harem's oil burners, more oriental than a Russian ballet or a Persian miniature." The artistic testament of the aged Ingres in 1863 – the year Manet exhibited his *Olympia*, a nude that scandalized critics and public alike – is an erotic testament. It is more than likely that he opted for Orientalism early in his career in order to provide a counter aesthetic to that of his pupil, Chassériau, to the Romantic movement generally, and especially to his arch-rival, Delacroix. Now, at the age of 80, he had nothing to prove or to defend. Ingres had interiorized the Orientalism that pervaded his era because it allowed him to translate into images an intensity of desire that could declare itself only through the very remoteness of the subject. The *Turkish Bath* is Orientalism pushed to its limit by an artist who rejected all its premises; for Ingres, Orientalism was a means of exploring the limits of an aesthetic of eroticism.

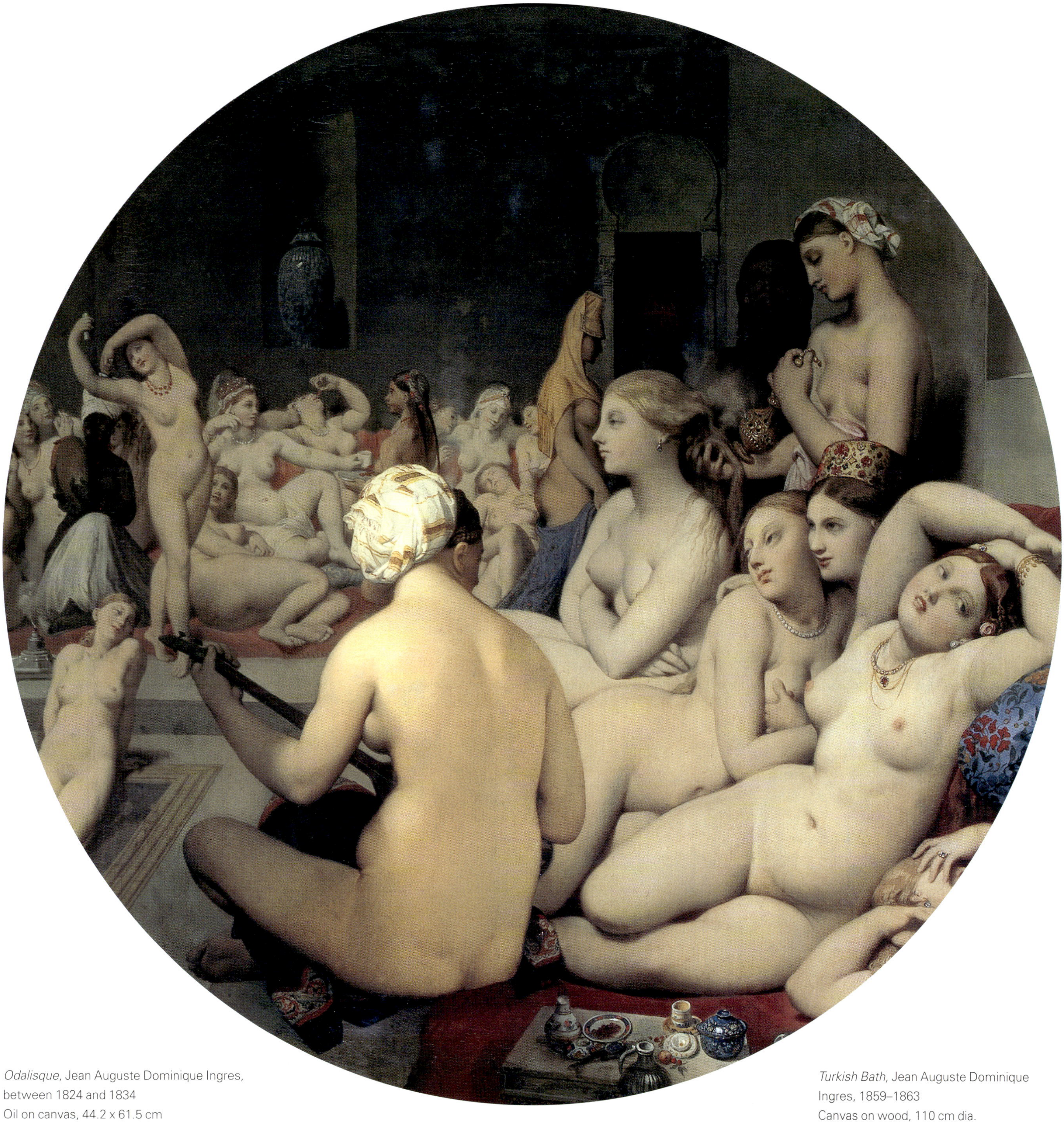

Odalisque, Jean Auguste Dominique Ingres,
between 1824 and 1834
Oil on canvas, 44.2 x 61.5 cm
(Mahmud Khalil Museum, Cairo).

Turkish Bath, Jean Auguste Dominique
Ingres, 1859–1863
Canvas on wood, 110 cm dia.
(Musée du Louvre, Paris).

Eugène Delacroix

"Morocco belongs to Delacroix, who discovered and mastered it: for him it was a pasha's domain."

Théophile Gautier

Right
The Death of Sardanapalus, Eugène Delacroix, 1827
Oil on canvas, 392 x 496 cm
(Musée du Louvre, Paris).

Below
Fight Between the Giaour and the Pasha, Eugène Delacroix, 1827
Black lithograph on ivory paper,
35.8 x 26 cm (private collection).

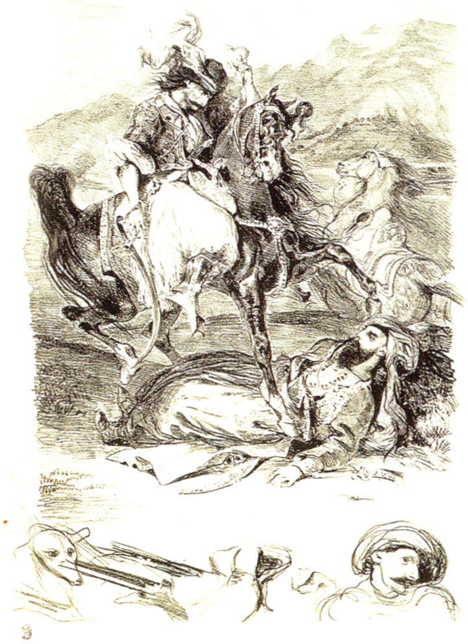

Eugène Delacroix had a close and intense relationship with the Orient long before he set off for Morocco. As we have seen, it went back to the Greek war of independence, which provided him with the perfect opportunity to set out his philosophy of painting. His Greece-inspired works are among his best: *The Massacre on Chios* (1824), *Greece on the Ruins of Missolonghi* (1826), and *Scene in the War Between the Greeks and the Turks* (1827), which he would treat again 30 years later in *An Episode in the Greek War*. His Orientalism was further developed in *The Death of Sardanapalus*, an enormous canvas he prepared for the Salon of 1827. It follows in the tradition of the great tragic works that includes Girodet's *Revolt in Cairo*, Géricault's *Raft of the Medusa*, and Pierre-Narcisse Guerin's *The Burning of Troy*, described by Charles Baudelaire as an "intoxicating universal atrocity." Delacroix's painting depicts a cruel and exceptionally brutal episode of ancient history recently retold by Lord Byron: the story of Sardanapalus, an Oriental ruler who, knowing that his forces were defeated, had all the women in his harem put to death along with his "favorite horses and dogs." Significantly, Delacroix avoided any clear reference to Byron's Sardanapalus, who is an ambiguous figure, essentially liberal and committed to his people's happiness; Delacroix's Oriental ruler is an example of tyrannical cruelty. Delacroix often drew inspiration from great writers, notably Dante, Shakespeare, Tasso, and Walter Scott, though it was undoubtedly Lord Byron who drew his attention to the Orient. By 1825 he had painted two little canvases that echo one other, the *Seated Turk Smoking* and *Odalisque Lying on a Couch*, an erotic vision of a fabulous Orient. By that time, he has read Byron's *The Giaour* in translation and been completely enthralled by it. He wrote in his journal on 11 May 1824:

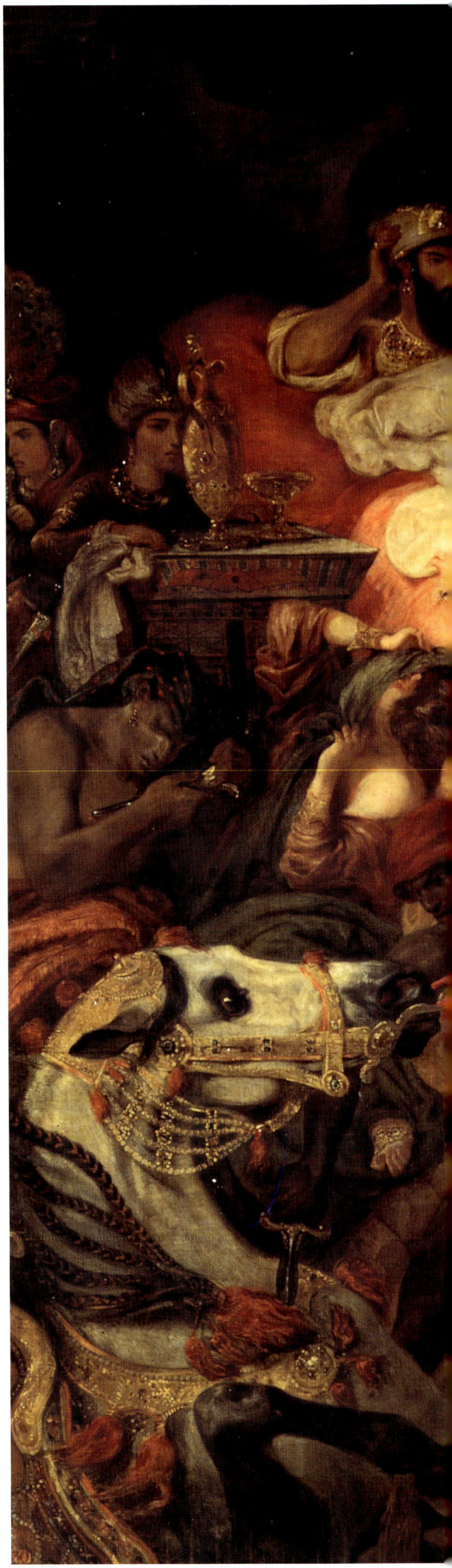

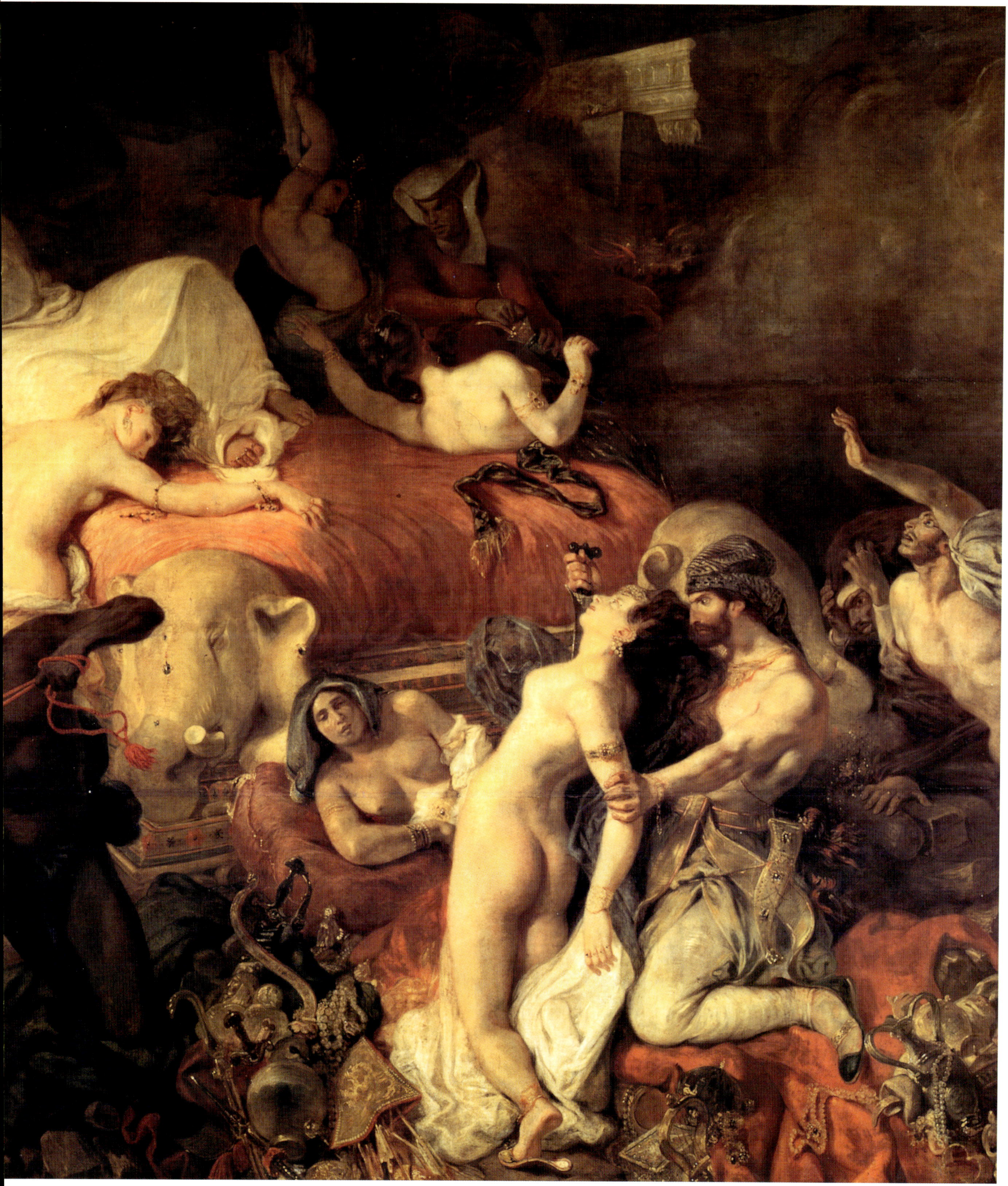

Right top
Men and Women in an Interior (the Bouzaglos' Home),
Eugène Delacroix, 1832
Graphite and watercolor,
23.5 x 36.8 cm
(Musée du Louvre, Paris).

Right bottom
Young Arab in His Room
(or *Moroccan Dressed in White, Young Moroccan Chief*),
Eugène Delacroix, 1832
Watercolor over graphite drawing, 19 x 29.8 cm
(Musée du Louvre, Paris).

Opposite, top
The Coast of Africa Seen from the Strait of Gibraltar,
Eugène Delacroix, 1832
Watercolor, with gouache highlights over a graphite drawing, 16.3 x 23.7 cm
(Musée du Louvre, Paris).

Opposite, bottom
Encampment in Morocco, Between Tangiers and Meknes, Eugène Delacroix, March 1832
Watercolor, graphite and gouache highlights over graphite drawing,
9.5 x 16 cm
(Musée du Louvre, Paris).

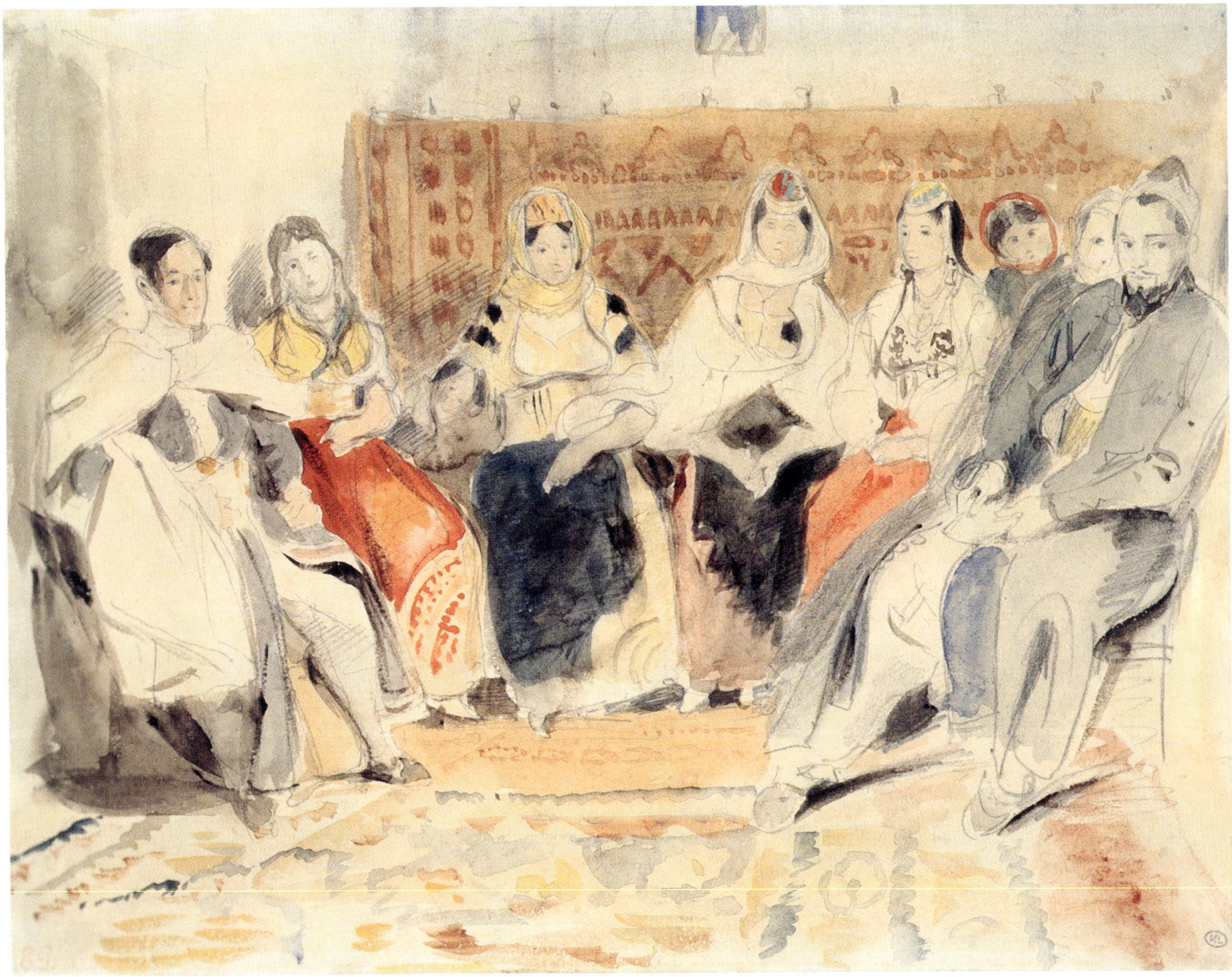

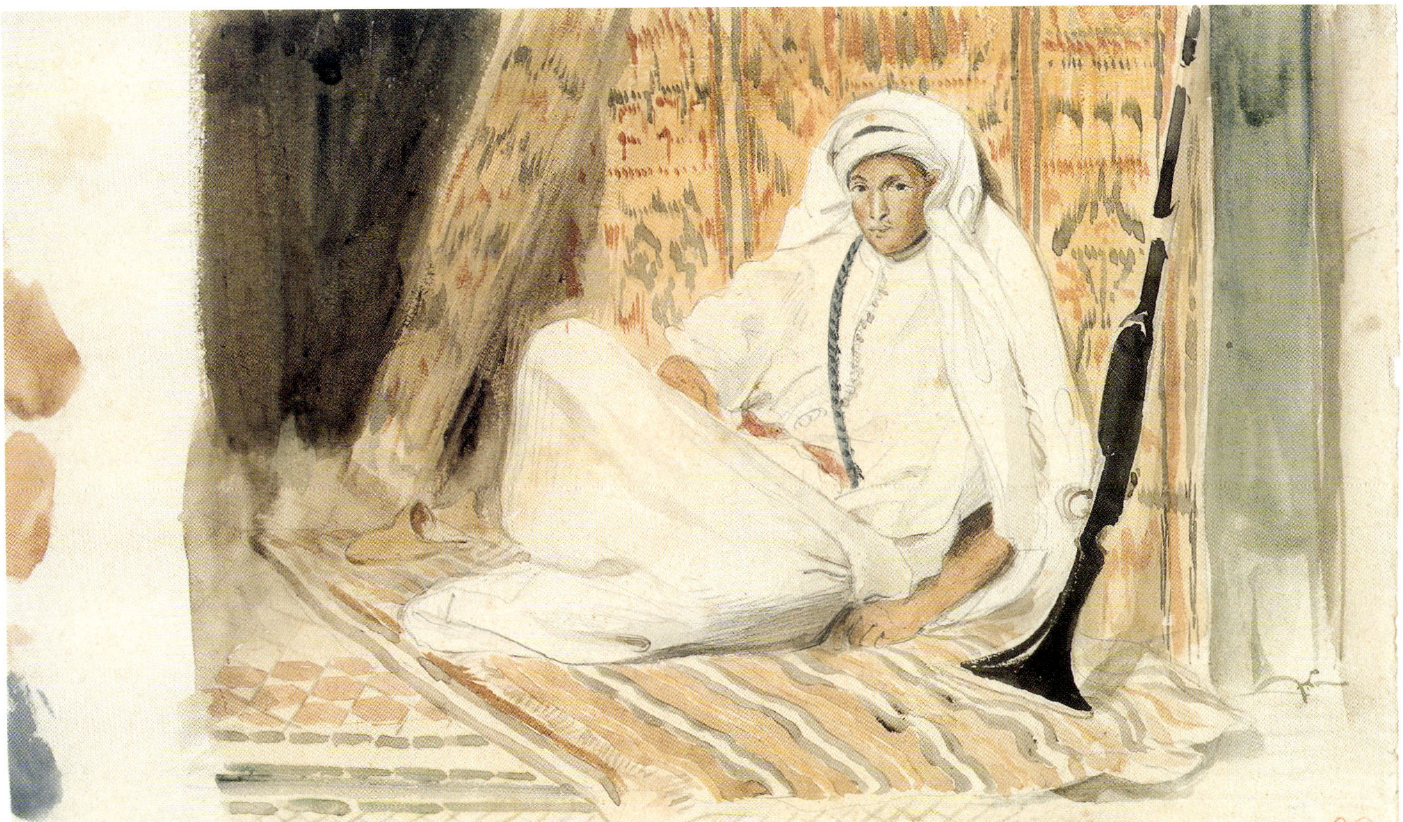

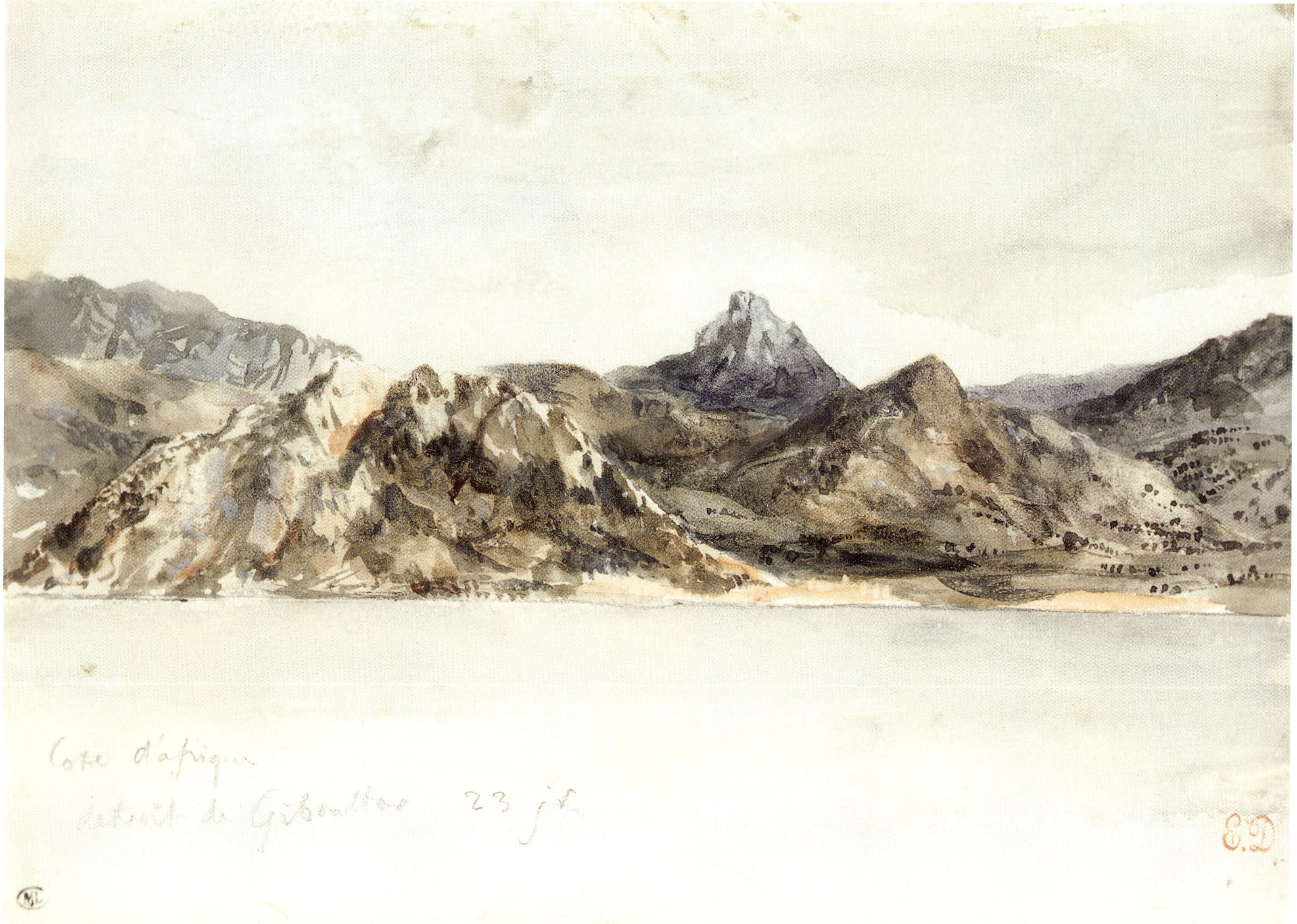
E.D

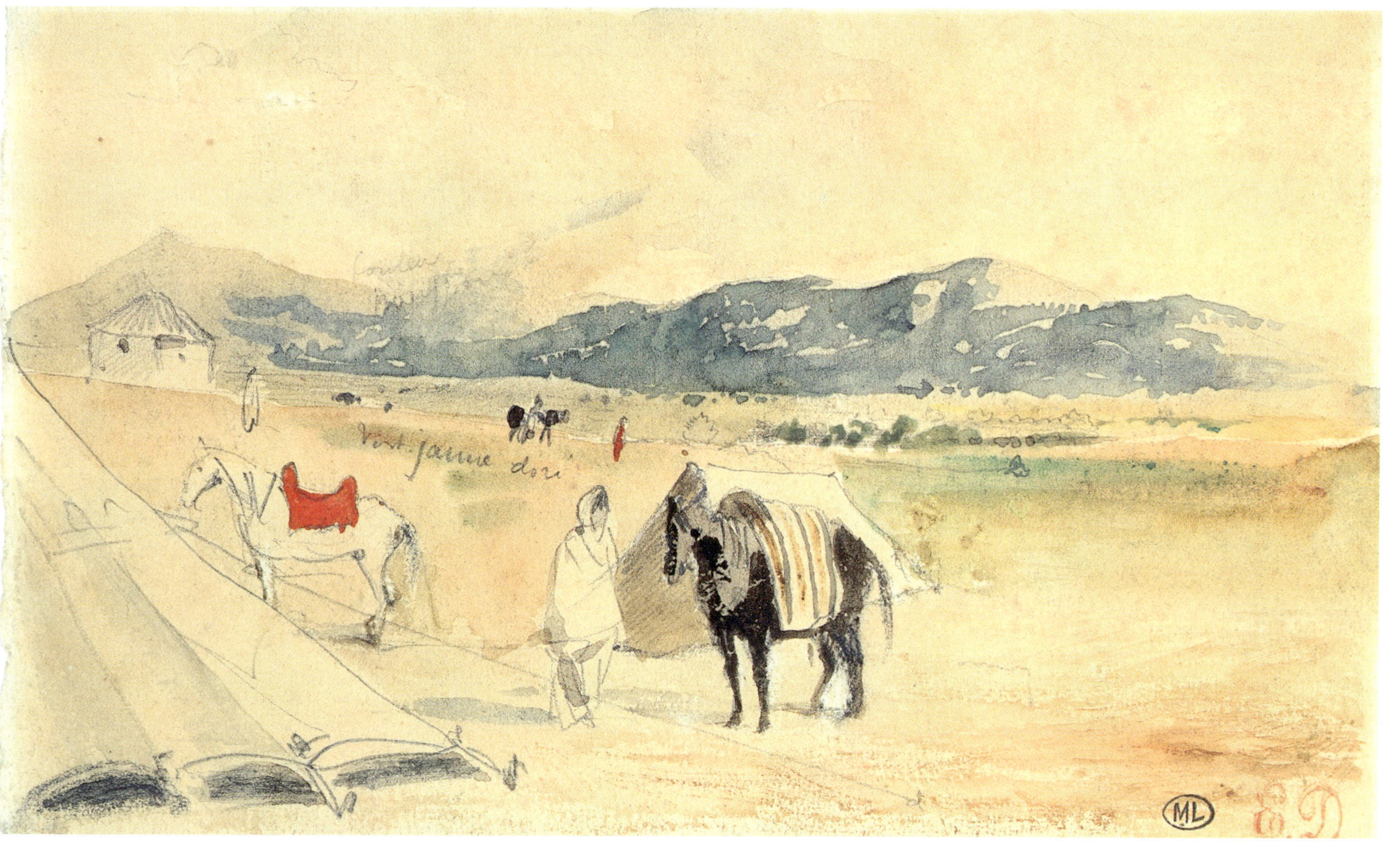
E.D

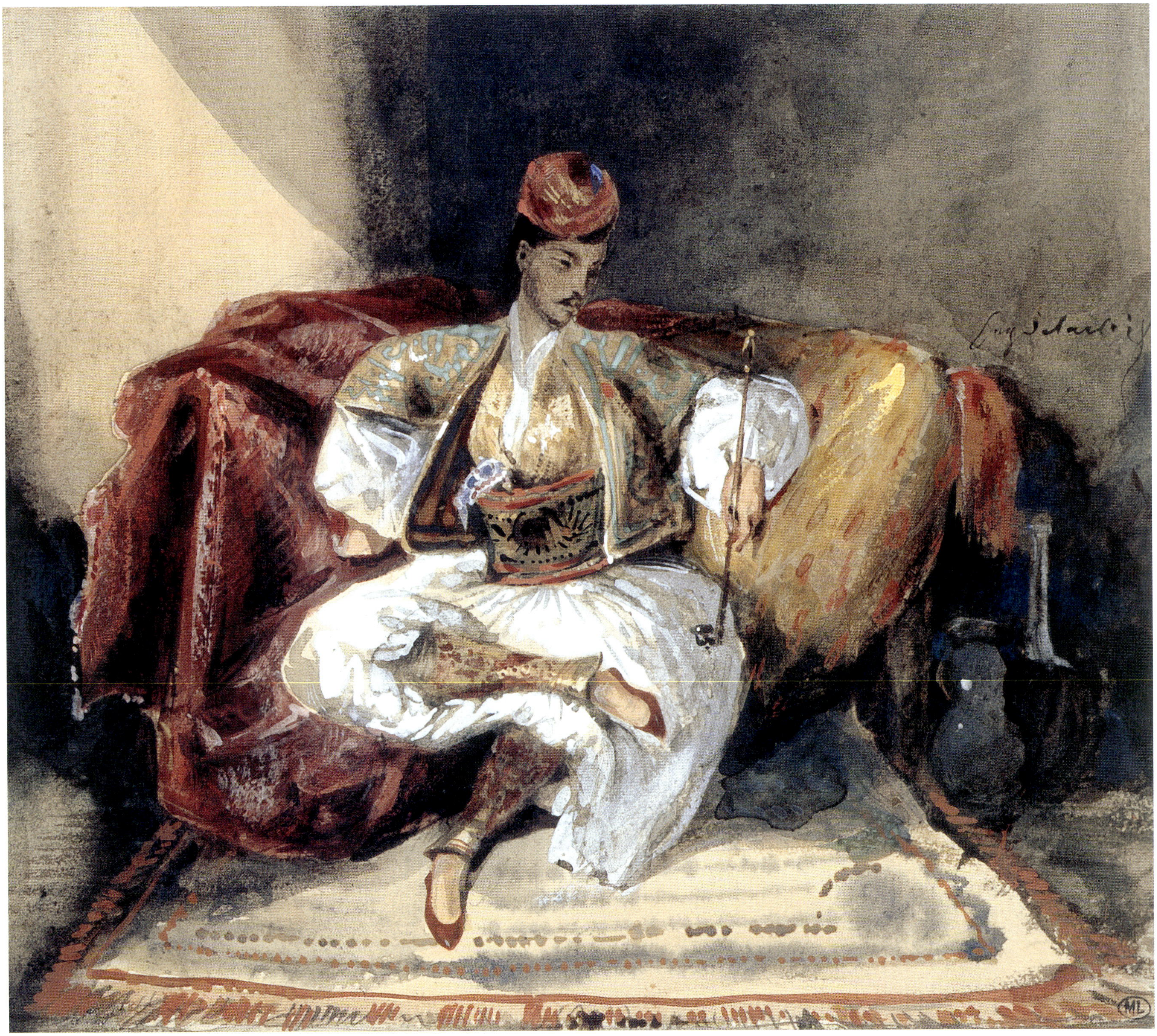

"Poetry is full of riches; always remember certain passages from Byron, they are an unfailing spur to the imagination, they are right for you. The ending of the *Bride of Abydos*; *The Death of Selim*, his body tossed about by the wave and that hand – especially that hand – held up by the waves as they break and die upon the shore. This is sublime, and it is his alone. I feel these things as they can be rendered in painting." *The Giaour* was a particular source of inspiration: he derived his first painting from it in 1826, a work which he exhibited at the Gallerie Lebrun in the exhibition held in support of the Greek cause. The tragic love of the Giaour for Leyla the slave-girl, who is tied up in a sack and thrown out to sea on the orders of her powerful master, Hassan, haunted Delacroix for years. In 1835 he painted *Fight Between the Giaour and the Pasha*, the following year *Giaour and Hassan*, and in 1856 *The Giaour and the Pasha*. As Delacroix observed in his journal, Byron was a constant spur to his imagination. Another Byron poem that appealed to him was the beautiful, violent love story of the *Bride of Abydos* (1813), which ends in bloodshed and despair; he would also return to this story several times. It tells of the beautiful and unfortunate Zuleika; promised to a man she does not love, she tries to run away with Selim, a cousin she thinks is her brother, who is killed as they try to elope; in the last scene she dies of a broken heart.

On 20 April 1824, Delacroix, writing in his journal, ironically dismisses the general

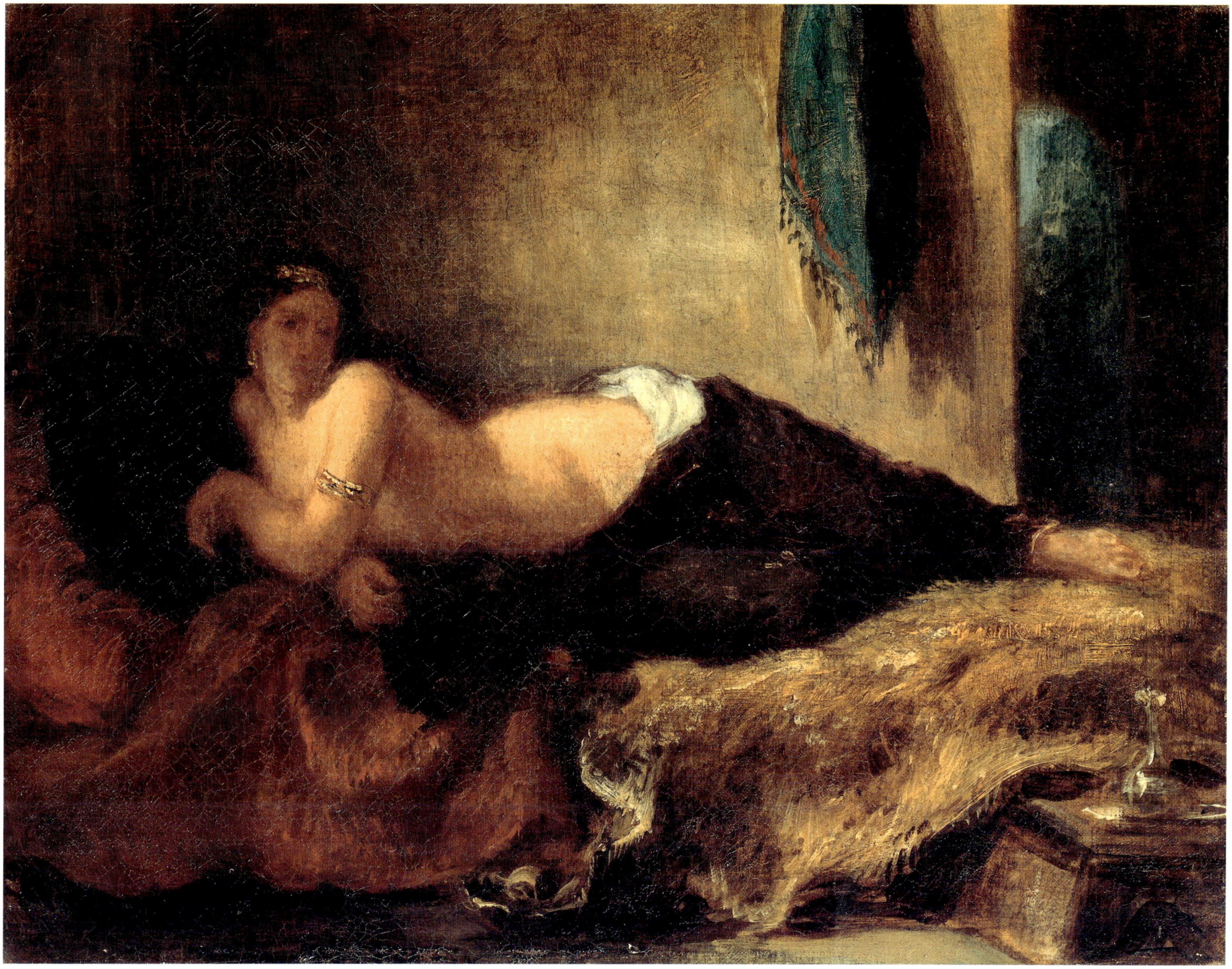

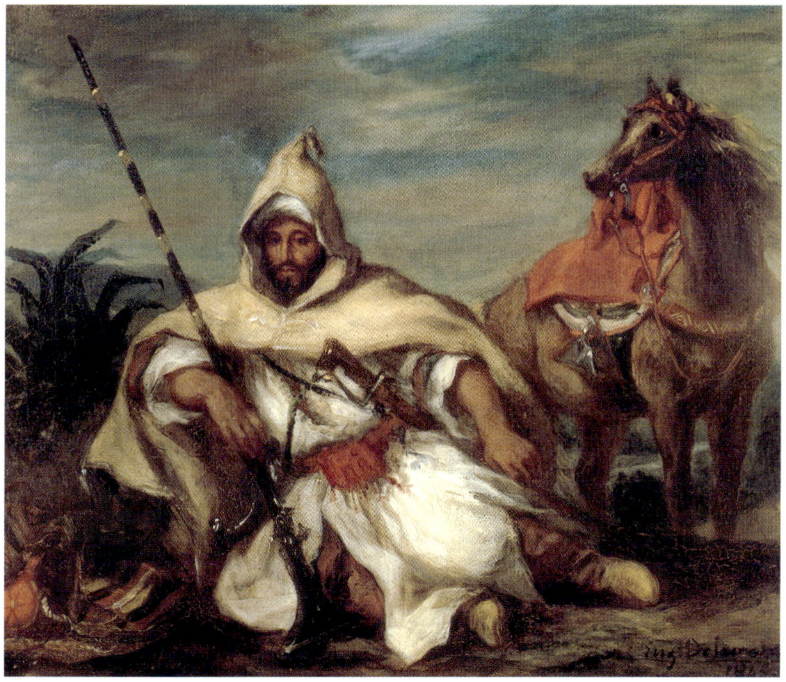

Above
Odalisque Lying on a Couch,
Eugène Delacroix, 1846
Oil on canvas, 24 x 32.5 cm
(Musée du Louvre, Paris).

Left
A Moroccan from the Sultan's Guard,
Eugène Delacroix, 1845
Oil on canvas, 32 x 41 cm
(Musée des Beaux-Arts, Bordeaux).

Opposite
Seated Turk Smoking,
Eugène Delacroix, c. 1824–1825
Watercolor with gouache, 17.2 x 20.1 cm
(Musée du Louvre, Paris).

They have, [...] and this is their chief attraction, small naked white feet, barely covered by pointed slippers; these, which are open at the back, reveal their delightful pink heels. When they are at home, they abandon these little shoes and those charming feet tread freely on carpets or matting. The lower part of their legs is adorned by very broad silver anklets which embellish this bare flesh and draw attention to it in a most graceful manner.

Eugène Delacroix,
Souvenirs d'un voyage dans le Maroc (Recollections of a Moroccan journey), 1832

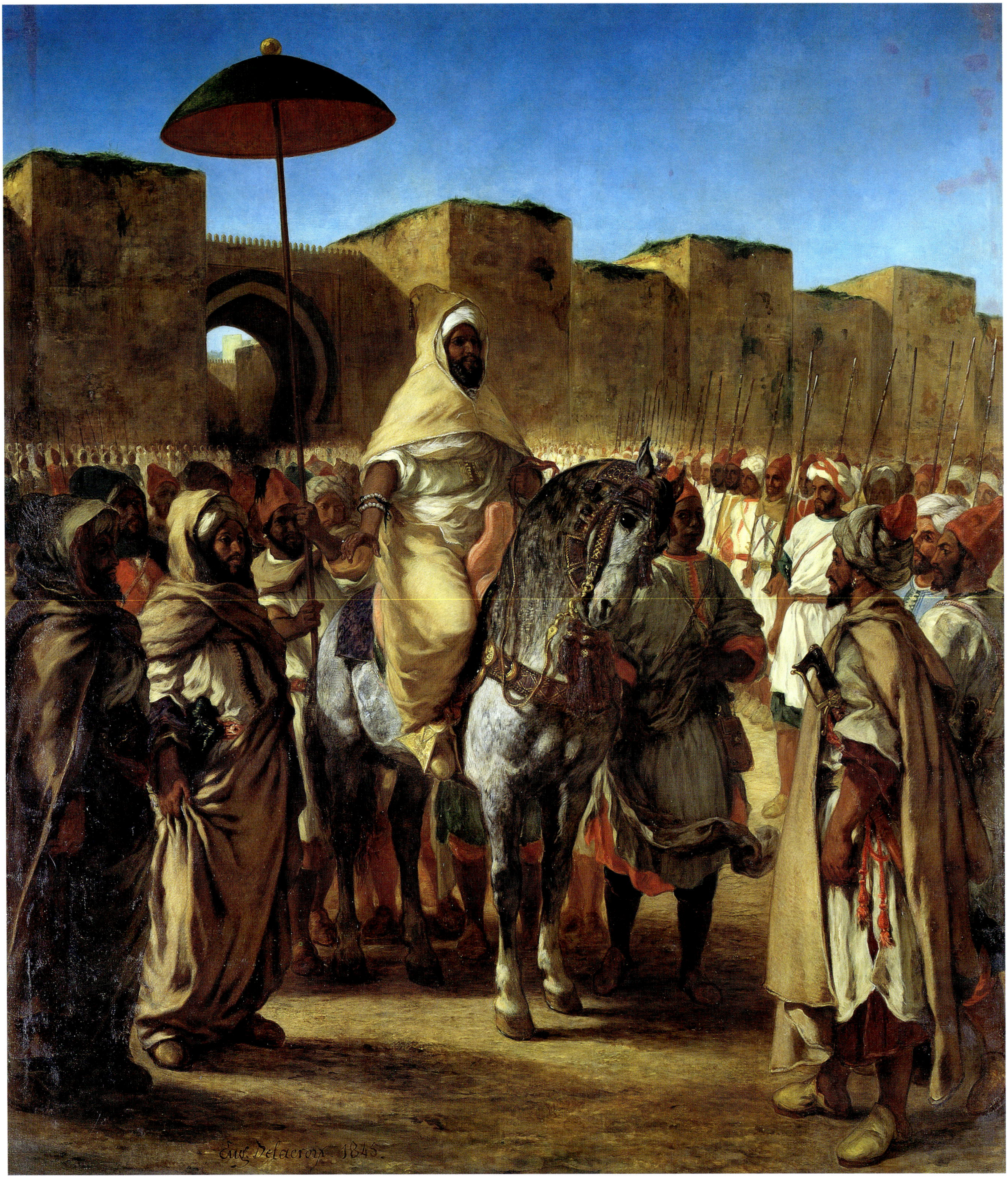
Eug. Delacroix. 1845.

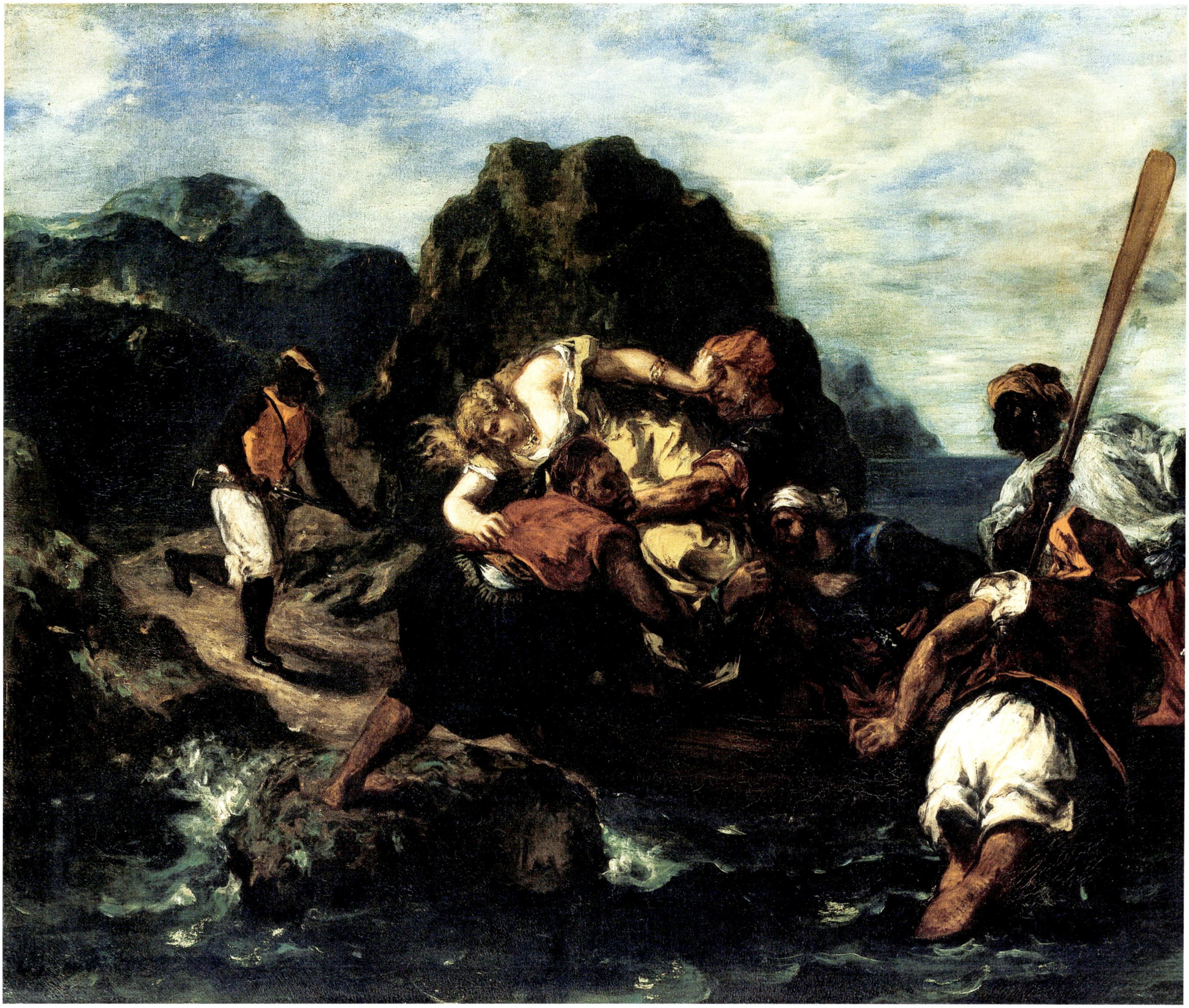

fad for long Eastern tours: "What can Egypt be like? Everyone is mad about it. And if it only costs as much as visiting London?" Morocco, however, was to be a different matter. In the face of insurgency in the Oran region, the French king, Louis-Philippe, decided to send a delegation to Abd al-Rahman, Sultan of Morocco, with a view to resolving matters. The artist Eugène Isabey was called upon to accompany the diplomat Charles Edgar de Mornay on his mission, but he declined. Delacroix was then asked. On 10 January 1832 the French delegation embarked on the corvette *La Perle*, arriving in Tangiers on the 25 January. From the beginning, Morocco fascinated, surprised, and delighted Delacroix. His desire for new experiences was never exhausted in Tangiers; it was for him "a place conceived for painters… there is real beauty here, not the beauty vaunted in fashionable works." He wanted it to be known in Paris that "at every step, you find readymade paintings that would ensure wealth and glory for twenty generations of painters," adding that "the sublime is here in abundance." During the six months spent in North Africa, he filled seven large sketch-books and created an album of 18 water-

Above
African Pirates Abducting a Young Woman,
Eugène Delacroix, 1853
Oil on canvas, 65 x 81 cm
(Musée du Louvre, Paris).

Opposite
Mulay Abd al-Rahman, Sultan of Morocco, Leaving his Palace in Meknes, Surrounded by his Guard and his Chief Officers,
Eugène Delacroix, 1845
Oil on canvas, 377 x 340 cm
(Musée des Augustins, Toulouse).

colors that he presents to the Comte de Mornay at the end of the trip. Sometime later he confided in Théodore Silvestre that things were not always easy for him: "I had to sketch quickly, and with great difficulty, because of the Muslim prejudices against images." Whatever the hardships he had to endure, he found a great deal worth painting.

On 21 February, when in Tangiers, he had the opportunity to attend a Jewish wedding, which he drew in one of his sketchbooks, complete with a wealth of detailed notes. Nine years later he painted *Jewish Wedding in Morocco*, which was accepted by the Salon. In the April issue of the *Journal des Débats*, the critic Delécluze complained that "when you look closely at the canvas, everything becomes muddled and vague"; that the eye "is unpleasantly distracted" by brush strokes in pink, yellow, and blue, which seem to him to go in every direction. As it happens, this negative review was a very perceptive description of the artist's intentions, for he was trying to introduce into art a new relation between the painting and its subject, a relationship that his passionate response to Morocco had encouraged. The subject and its treatment are as it were harmonized: the spectator is transported to this celebration, a festival of light translated into a blaze of colors. In his sketchbooks Delacroix had already recorded the place in which to set his characters, a courtyard in Tangiers that he scarcely altered for his composition, with the exception of the white walls, which are replaced with a play on light and shade.

On 5 March Delacroix left for Meknès, where the Sultan was finally to meet the French delegation. Over the ten days of their

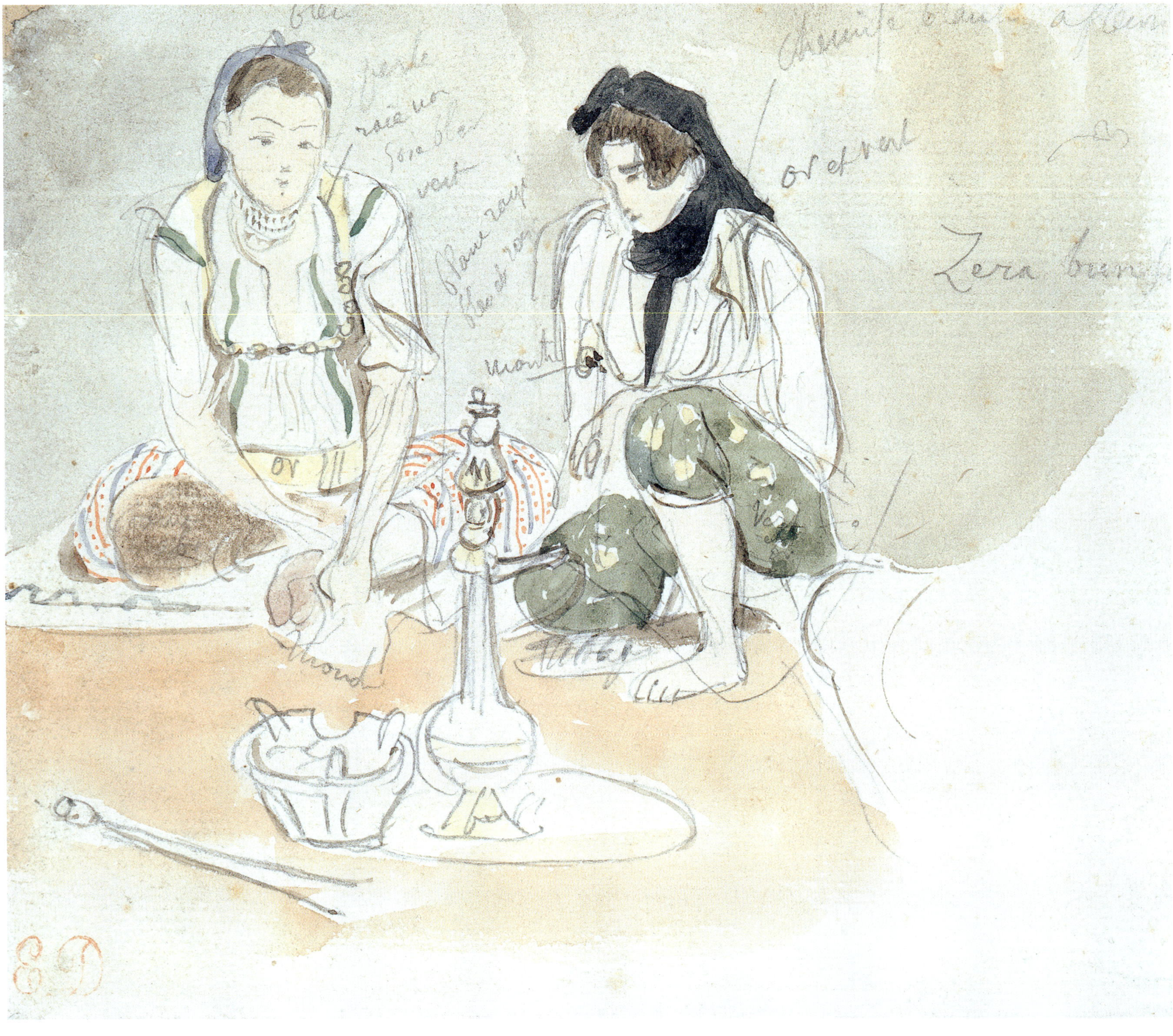

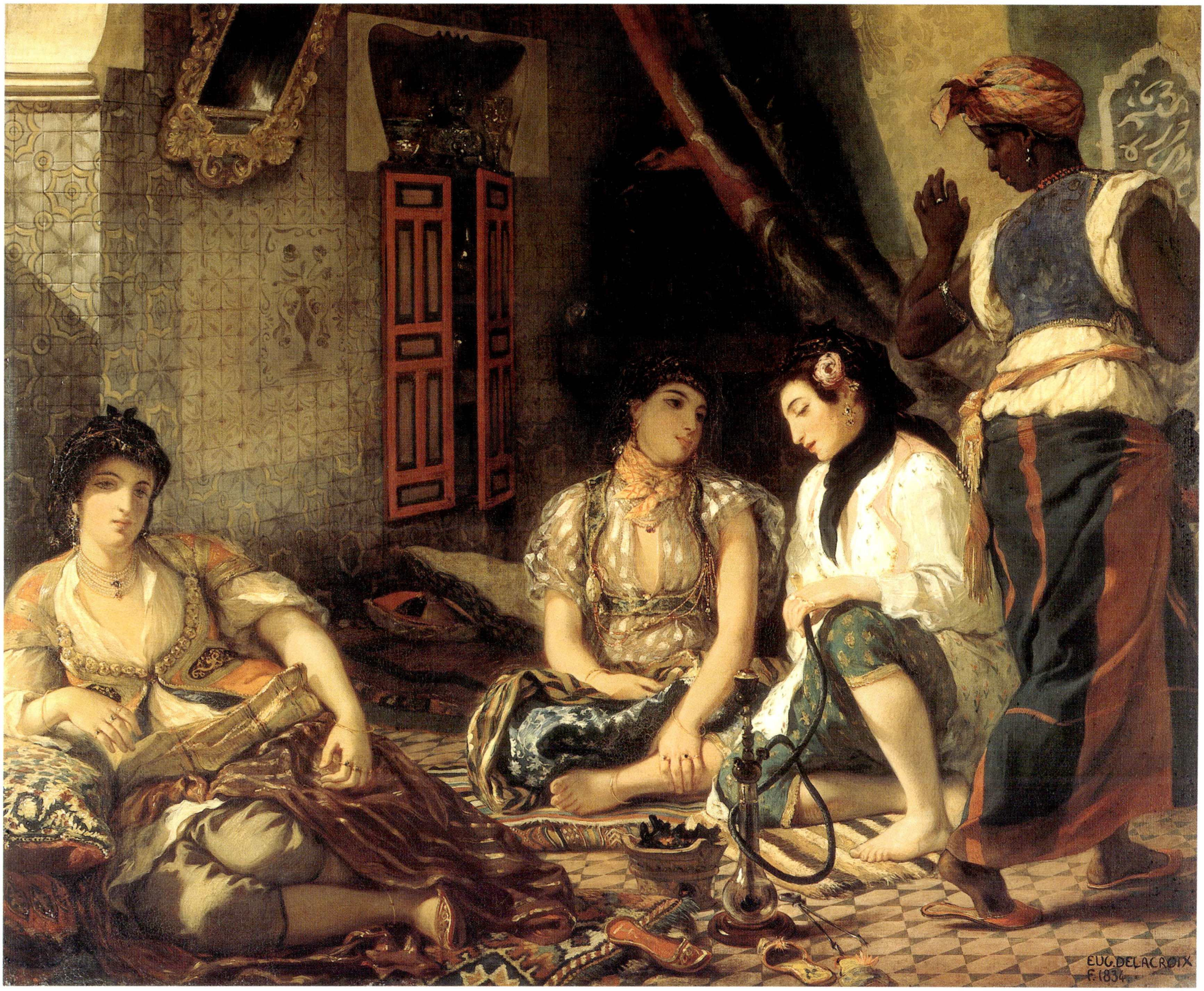

journey, Delacroix was able to explore many aspects of the country and its people; he had ample opportunity to store up a great many subjects he would exploit in the fullness of time. For instance, on 12 March they camped on the banks of the river Sebou, in a stark landscape he would recall for a painting of 1858, though in recreating it he gave it a softer, an almost European character that makes it almost idyllic. On 22 March, the French ambassador was received in the holy city by the Sultan of Morocco, and Delacroix made an imposing portrait of the sultan and his favorite, Muchtar, surrounded by the king's guards. When it was exhibited at the 1845 Salon, the program notes stated that the artist had recorded "exactly" an "audience at which the author was present." Well, perhaps not "exactly": he changed the scene a good deal, emphasizing in particular the crowds at the city gate. Here history was imaginatively re-invented; not through a desire to falsify, but through a need to create a commemoration that would have an artistic rather than simply factual integrity. He would produce two smaller versions of this official portrait in 1856 and 1862.

On his way back to France in June, Delacroix stopped over in Algiers for three days. Is that where he conceived the canvas

Above
Algerian Women in Their Apartments,
Eugène Delacroix, 1834
Oil on canvas, 180 x 229 cm
(Musée du Louvre, Paris).

Opposite
Two Arab Women Seated (study for *Algerian Women in Their Apartments*),
Eugène Delacroix, c. 1832
Watercolor over graphite drawing,
10.7 x 13.8 cm (Musée du Louvre, Paris).

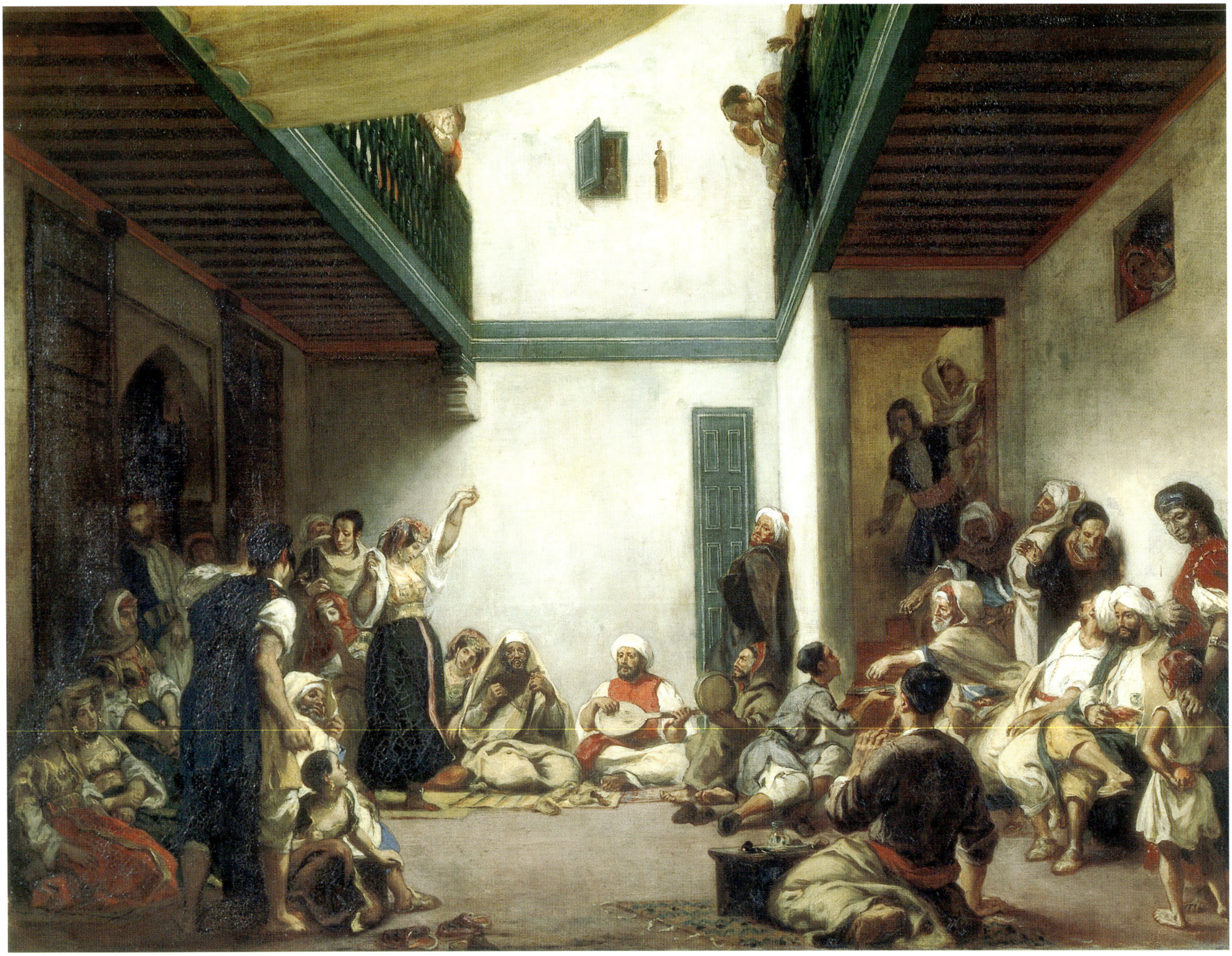

Jewish Wedding in Morocco,
Eugène Delacroix, 1837–1841
Oil on canvas, 105 x 140.5 cm
(Musée du Louvre, Paris).

Opposite
Jewish Musicians of Mogador,
Eugène Delacroix, 1847
Oil on canvas, 46 x 55.5 cm
(Musée du Louvre, Paris).

entitled *Algerian Women in Their Apartments* (1834), a work widely considered one of his masterpieces? There is no solid evidence to that effect, even though Charles Cornault claims that the Reis (unlike most Arabs) would have allowed him to see his wives. His watercolor sketches do indeed show women (*Moûni Bensoltane, Moûni and Zorha Bensoltane*…) and in poses similar to those adopted by the handsome Oriental women in his final painting. The details of their clothing are carefully noted: "pearl blue – black chalk – blue silk (or white?) – green and white striped – blue and pink (red?) – watch." Back in Paris he started on several preparatory studies, among them the superb pastel *Algerian Woman Seated*. Delacroix constructed his *Algerian Women in Their Apartments* around a dynamic balance between a "classical" composition, probably inspired by the Venetian masters he so much admired, and a dramatic use of vibrant colors that creates a sensual and highly charged atmosphere. If the Romantic excesses of this work had an unsettling effect on purists like Delécluze, they were even more astonished by the second version, submitted to the 1849 Salon, in which most of the furnishings have begun to dissolve into a blaze of reds and yellows.

It is clear from his sketchbooks and from his correspondence that Delacroix's visit to Morocco helped him to develop a new approach to his art. In a letter from Tangiers, he exclaims: "It's so beautiful, it's like the days of Homer!" And: "Rome is no longer in Rome." He explains to another correspondent: "Romans and Greeks are here, outside my door; I couldn't help laughing at the Greeks of David's compositions... I have met them." He sees everywhere "Catos and Brutuses... just as pleased with themselves as Cicero might have been on his magistrate's seat... all this in white, like Roman senators, like the Athenian panathenaea." Thus he arrived at an unforeseen definition of Classicism – for him a Classicism that actually existed in his own time, but under other climes. For Delacroix the Orient was in effect the purest manifestation of a modern Classicism. This concept soon had a following, and many orientalists – even those who did not did not in fact adopt his style – took it to heart.

After his visit to Morocco, the Orient as a subject became second nature to Delacroix. He would create no less than 80 Orientalist paintings, of which 15 depict imaginary hunting scenes. These bear out in particular his passion for horses; he claimed that cavalcades "cause me utmost pleasure." Among his many Orientalist works are: *Young Turk Stroking his Horse* (1827); *Turk Saddling his Horse* (1828); *Turkish Officer on Horseback* (1830); *Moroccan Fantasy* (1832); *In Front of the Meknés Gate*; *Arab Horsemen's Assault* (1844); *Moroccan Soldier Sat by His Horse* (1845); *Moroccan Military Exercise* (1847); *Horse-riding Lesson* (1855); *Arab Saddling His Horse* (1855); *Arab About to Saddle His Horse* (1857); and *Arab Horseman Giving a Signal* (1857).

He also loved scenes of festivals, theater, and music: *Jewish Musicians of Mogador*, and *Arab Clowns and Jesters* (1848) are proof of his

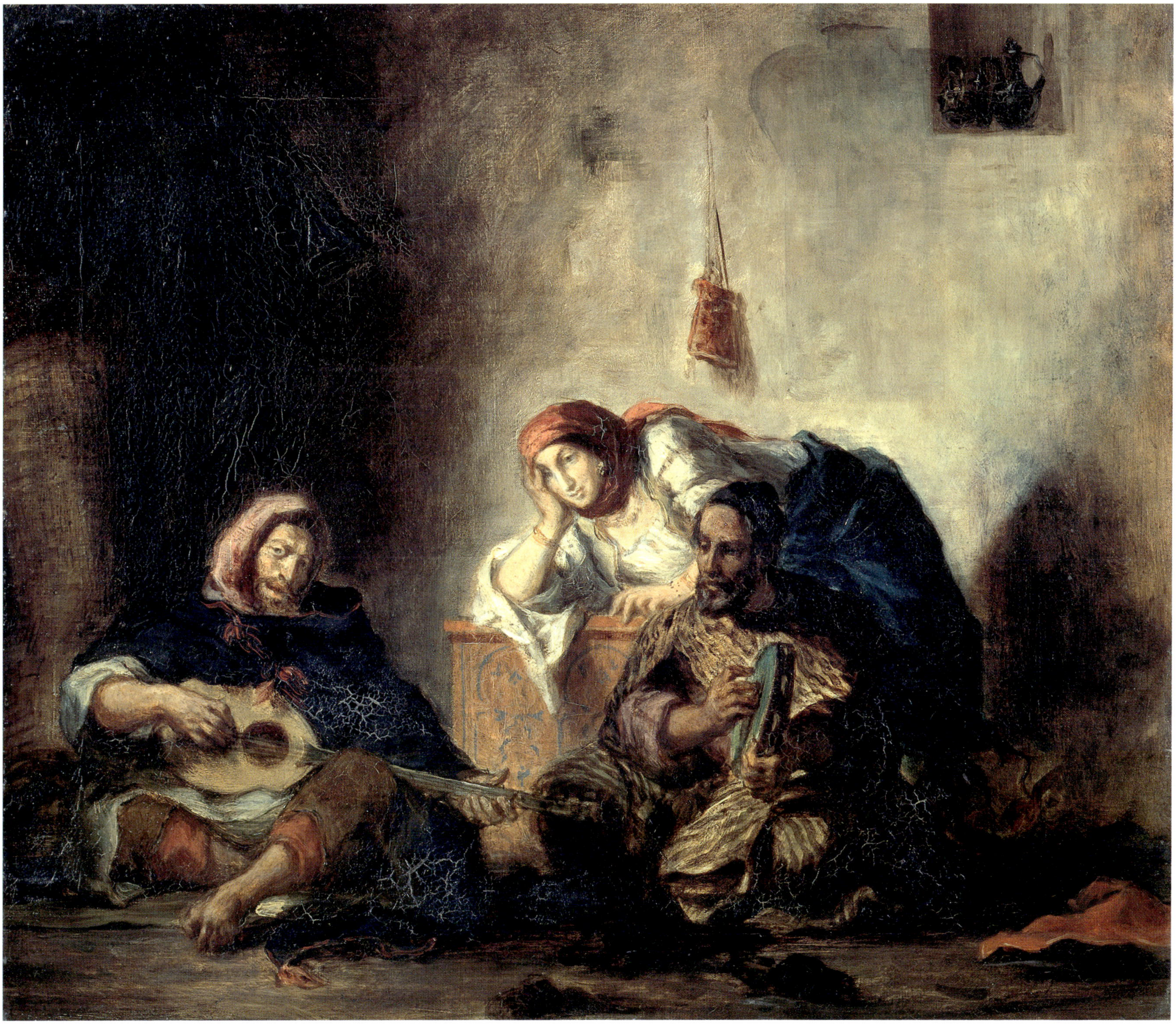

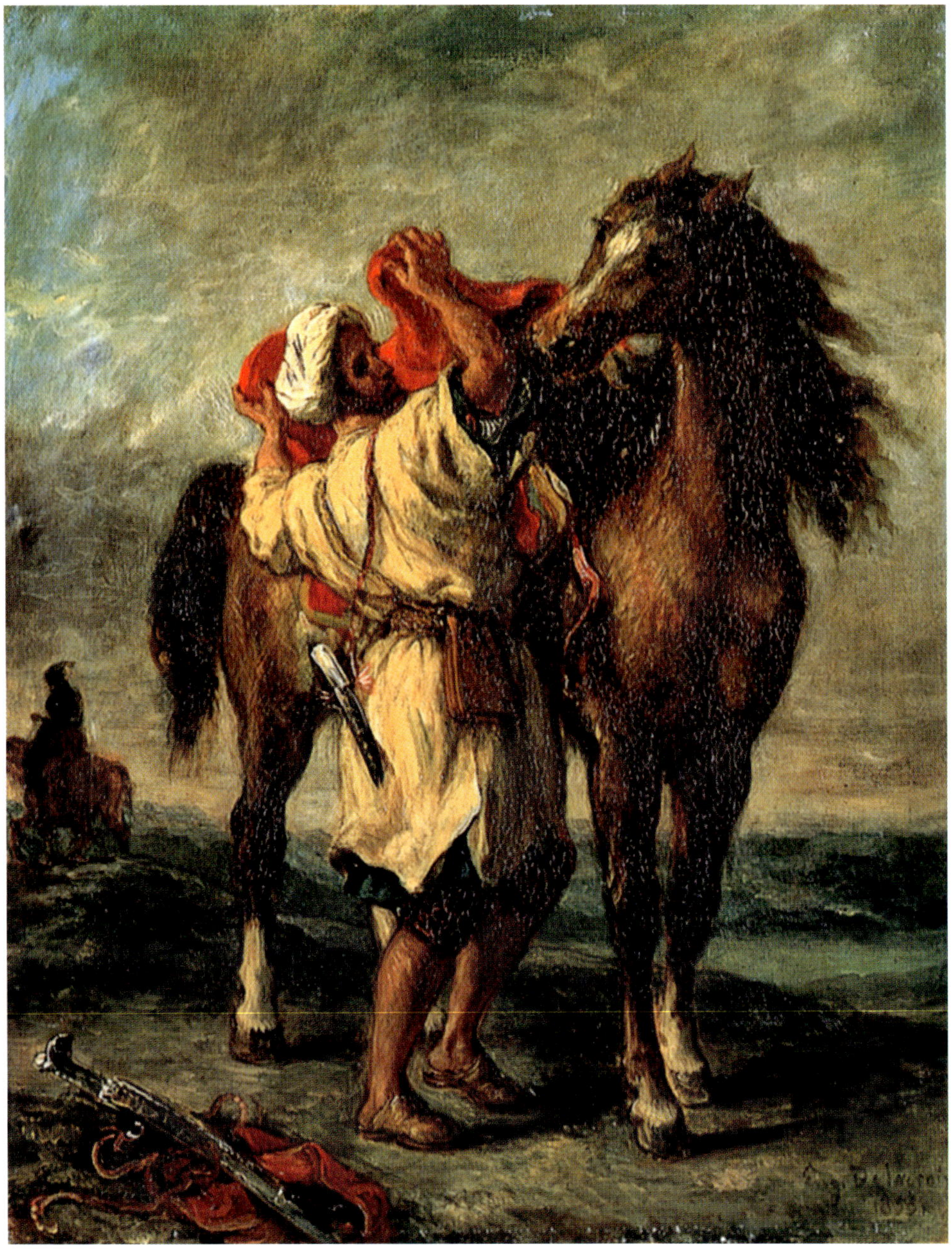

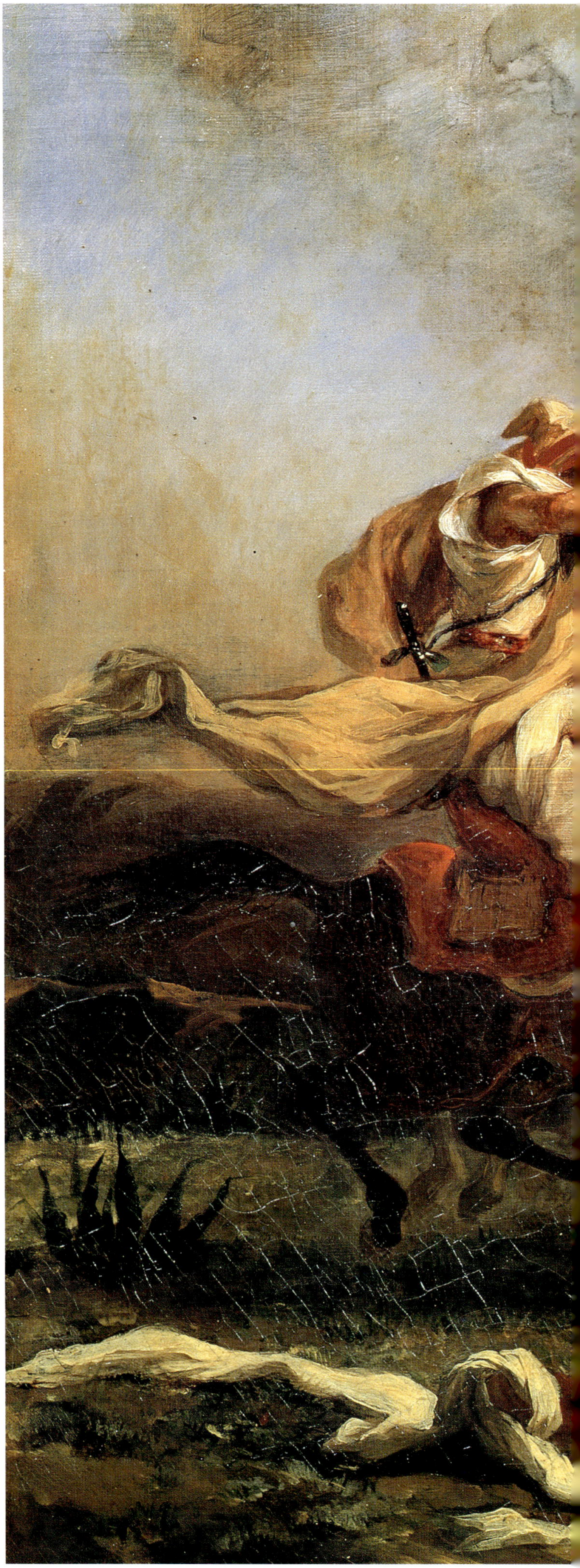

Arab Saddling His Horse,
Eugène Delacroix, 1855
Oil on canvas, 56 x 47 cm
(The Hermitage Museum, St Petersburg).

The Collection of Arab Taxes
(or *Clash of Arab Horsemen*),
Eugène Delacroix, 1863
Oil on canvas, 81 x 99 cm
(The Walters Art Gallery, Baltimore).

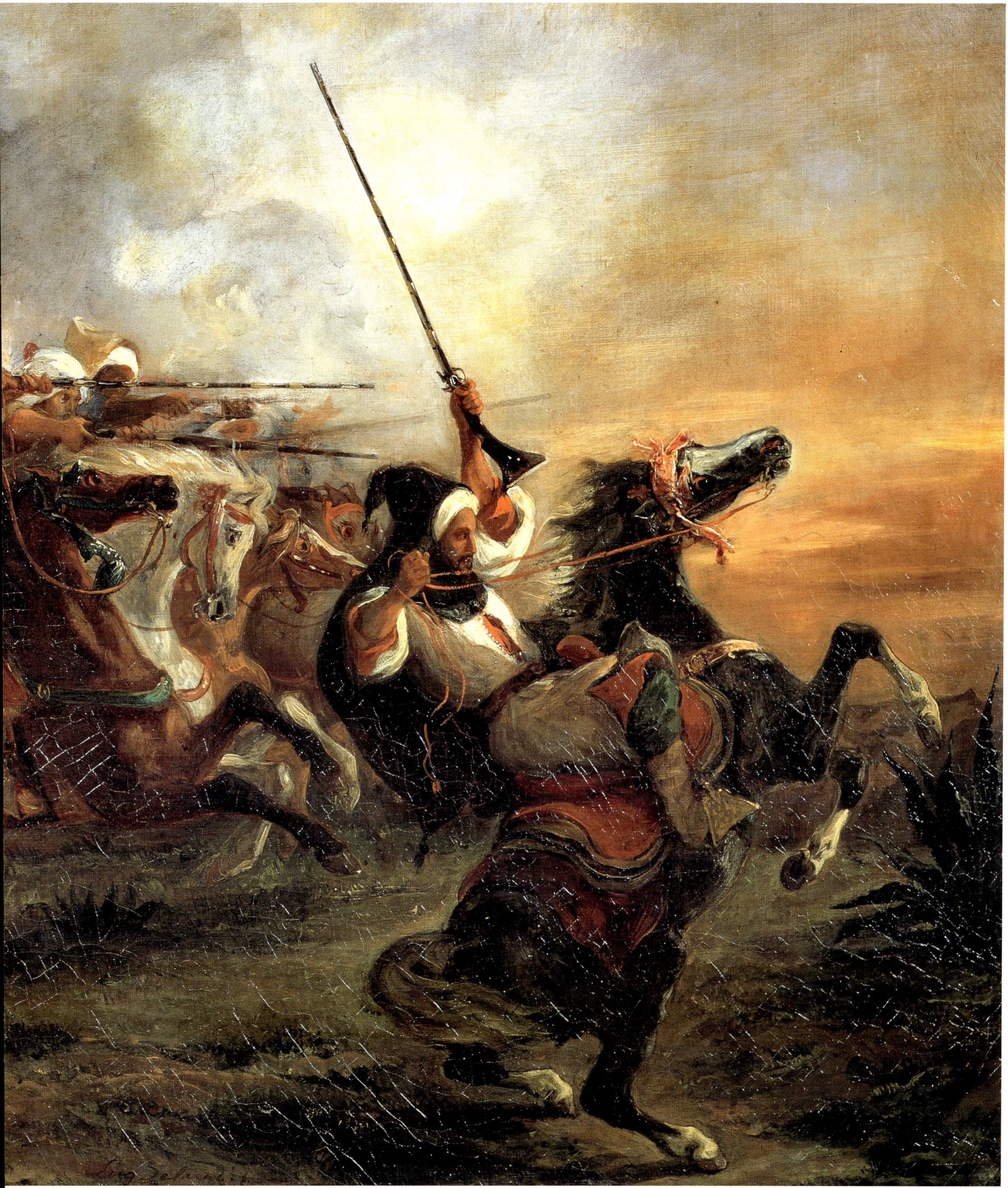

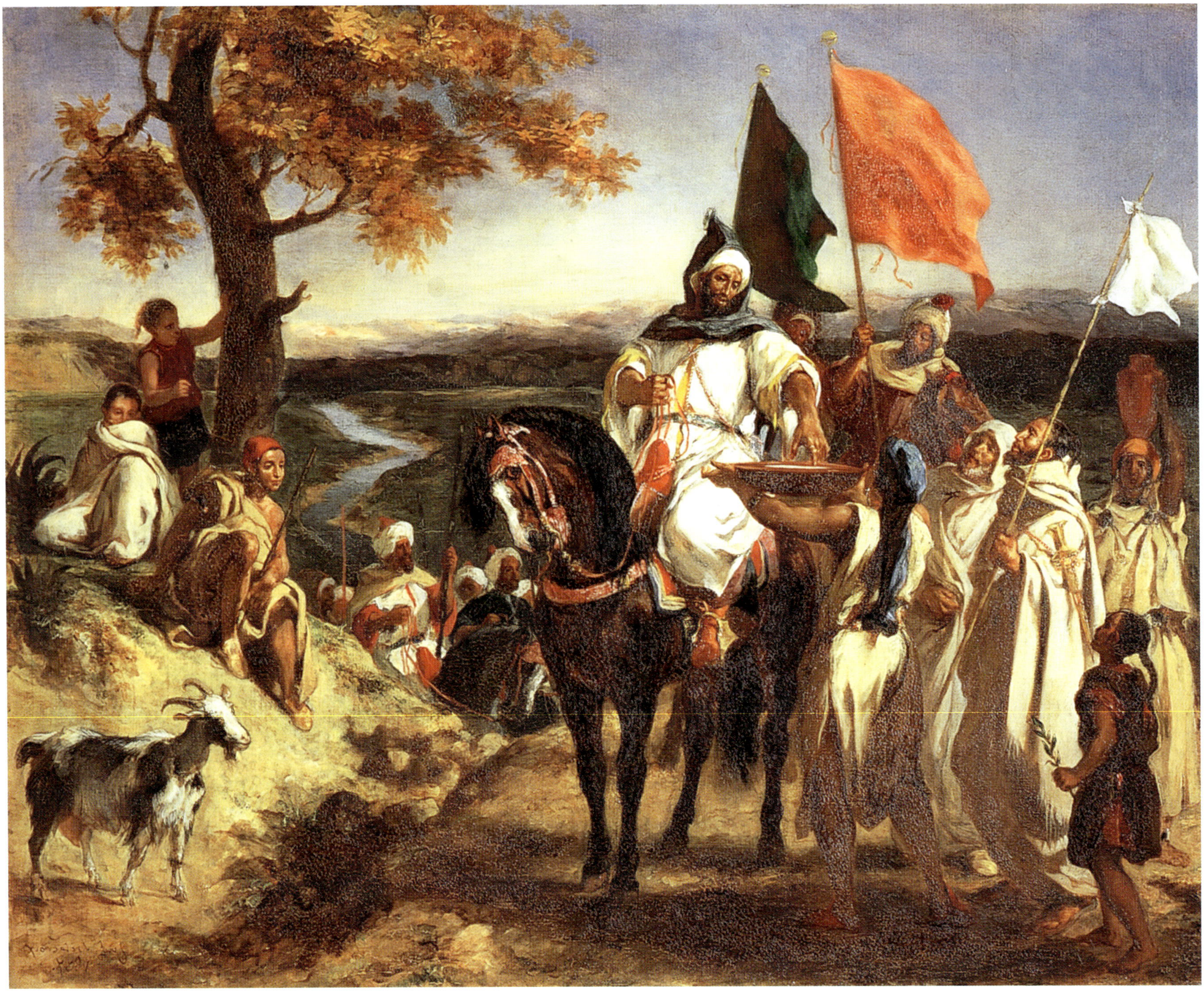

Moroccan Chieftain Receiving Tribute,
Eugène Delacroix, 1837
Oil on canvas, 98 x 126 cm
(Musée des Beaux-Arts, Nantes).

Moroccan Military Exercises,
Eugène Delacroix, 1847
Oil on canvas, 66 x 82 cm
(Sammlung Oskar Reinhart, Winterthur).

warm feelings for showmen and entertainers, here given an Oriental setting. The fact is, nothing in Algiers seems to have left Delacroix indifferent; anything could set off extraordinary pictorial digressions – the Dionysiac *Aïssaouas* (1834), the awesome *Ecstatics of Tangiers* (1857), the intriguing *View of Tangiers* (1858), or even *Arabs Playing Chess* (1848), in which he invests this simple street scene with a rare, indeed a classical, dignity. He never tired of the subjects he took back from the Maghreb; just a few months before his death, he painted *The Collection of Arab Taxes*.

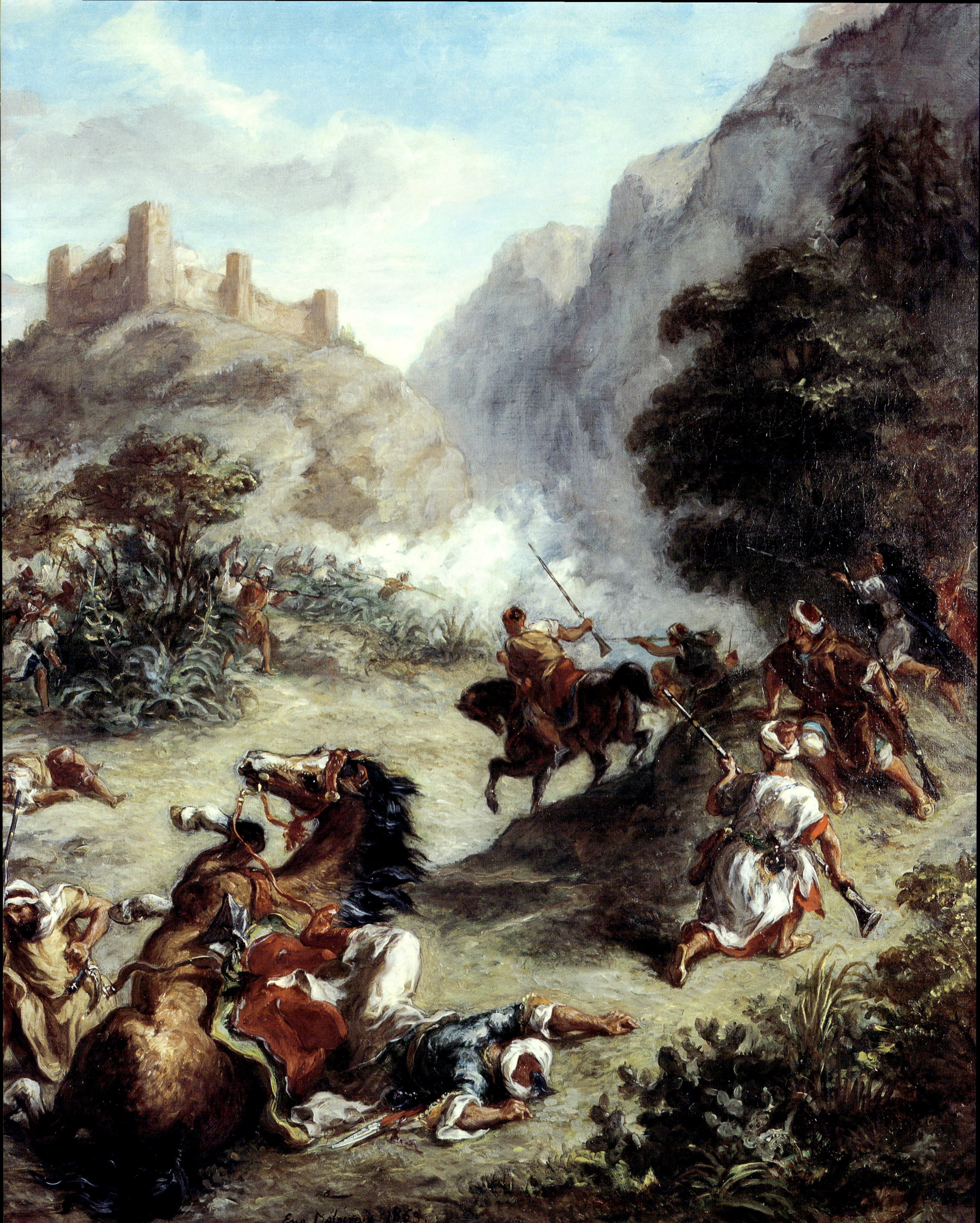

A Painter's Paradise

Turkish Bodyguards on the Road from Magnesia to Meander, Alexandre Gabriel Decamps, 1833
Oil on canvas, 91 x 155 cm
(Musée Condé, Chantilly).

Opposite
Turkish Children Playing with a Tortoise, Alexandre Gabriel Decamps, 1836
Oil on canvas, 72 x 91 cm
(Musée Condé, Chantilly).

If the Eastern tour did not quite replace the artist's traditional pilgrimage to Italy, it was still the ambition of many artists who believed that by reaching the shores of Africa or the Middle East they would be able to fire their imaginations with new experiences and new themes. Orientalism as a genre was felt as an irresistible call, though of course, for some, the Orient itself was not always within reach.

The French artist Narcisse Diaz de la Peña liked to attend the Romantic circle that gathered in the Rue du Doyenné, the preserve of Gerard de Nerval and Théophile Gautier that Prosper Marilhat and Alexandre Dumas père often visited. He found there an aesthetic based on both Germanic legends and Oriental tales; the group once organized a great feast for which Camille Roger painted on wood several "Oriental and Hoffmanesque fantasies."

Diaz de la Peña was fully in tune with the inspirations of this community of aesthetes. Having lost a leg to in an accident, however, he was unwilling to go beyond the woods around Paris; he particularly enjoyed his painting trips to Barbizon and to the Gorge d'Apremont. His friend Félix Ziem, who would sometimes accompany him on these outings, confirmed the young artist's will to join "in spirit" his friends fortunate enough to travel to mysterious places: "I saw Diaz painting in the forest the magic touches of the Orient, unexpected mirages, real, sunny. A trunk, some greenery were enough for a poem heightened by truly enchanted rays."

In his *Fountain in Constantinople* (c. 1845), Diaz represented a group of Turkish men at leisure; they are sitting in the shade of a mighty tree in front of a carved fountain; in the background rises a tall mosque, the minaret of which stands out against the sky. By contrast, in the *Oriental Woman and Her Daughter* (1865), his characters are set amid dense greenery that blocks the view; a very young woman, her head turned away, a hand resting on her hip, holds her little girl close to her. Here Diaz plays on the contrast between the familiarity conjured up by a traditional natural setting and the distance suggested by the exotic costumes.

Adolphe Monticelli, a friend of Diaz and Ziem, was also an Orientalist at second hand; he never traveled farther than Marseilles. That did not, however, stop him from creating in his imagination many images of the secret world of the harem, or of fearless Arab horsemen. In both *Oriental Scene* and *Algerian Scene* (1880) he pictured a crowd of turbaned men gathering at the door of a mosque.

For most contemporary artists, however, when they had enough money or were appointed to a scientific or military mission, they wasted no time in packing up and boarding ship. The Orient seemed to offer a painter's paradise.

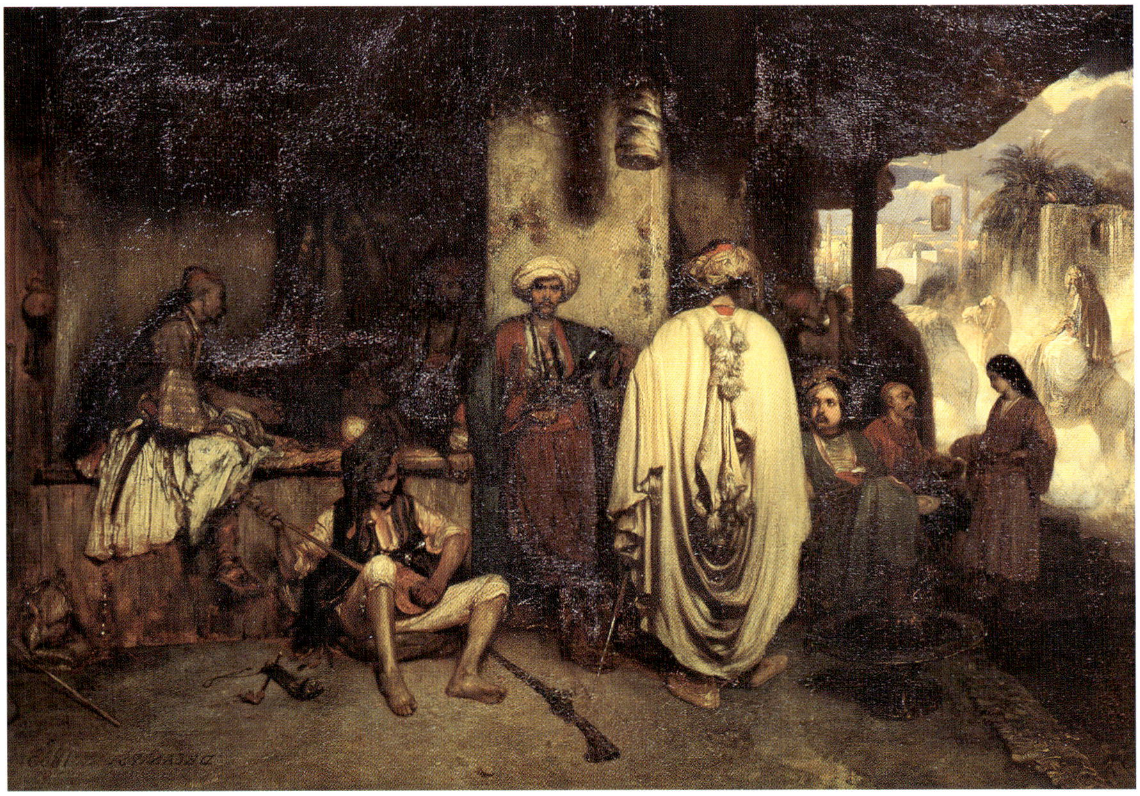

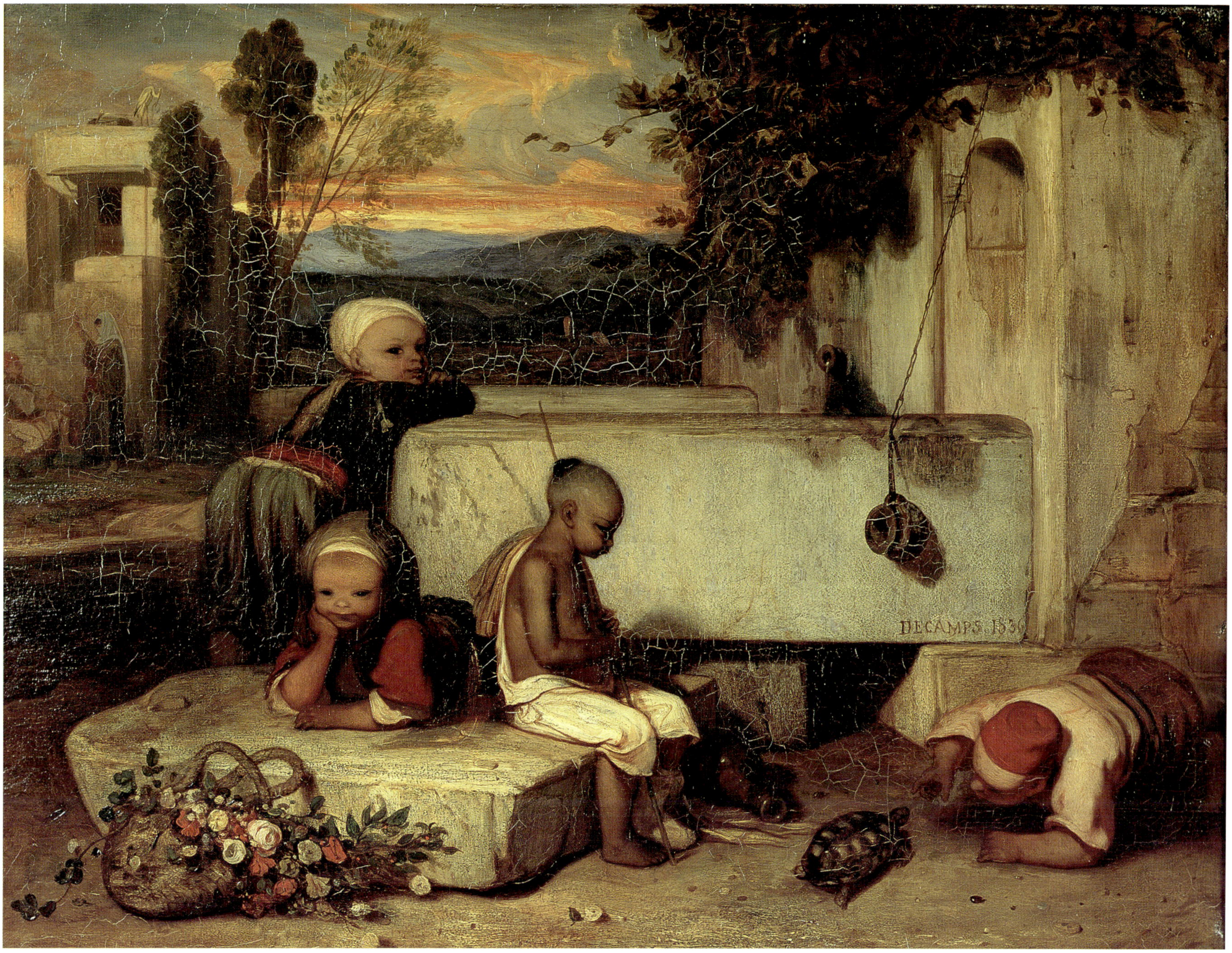

Alexandre Gabriel Decamps

Having spent a part of his childhood in Picardy, young Alexandre Gabriel Decamps became a pupil in the studio of an artist called Bauchot, a friend of his father's, and then in that of Abel de Pujol. As soon as Decamps could sell small paintings, he left Pujol and busied himself painting the daily lives of the craftsmen and merchants of the Paris suburbs. A great admirer of Ingres, he also loved Murillo and Rembrandt, whose works were on view at the Louvre. Between 1822 and 1823, he contributed to the periodical *L'Album*, producing lithographs such as *Poor Negro!* and *The Massacre on Chios*. Unsympathetic to Restoration politics, he drew many political caricatures, such as *King Charles X Hunts in His Apartment Suite*.

When he finally had the opportunity to travel, he set off on his Grand Tour, traveling to Italy via Switzerland. Then a commission sent him on his travels again, this time to Greece: he was to work with Ambroise Louis Garneray on a large commemorative painting of the Battle of Navarino, at which, in October 1827, English, French, and Russian ships had defeated the Egyptian and Ottoman navy. He was not particularly keen on the project, and in any case did not get along well with Garneray. Disappointed, he then set off alone through Anatolia and discovered Constantinople. Dazzled at the busy life of Anatolian cities, he set up a studio as best he could in Smyrna in February 1828. Previously, his love of the Orient, probably inspired by Abel de Pujol, had led him to create the usual fanciful scenes full of fictitious architecture; an example is his *Soldier in the Vizier's Guard*, which Decamps exhibited at the Salon. But now he was armed with first-hand knowledge of Ottoman civilization, and as soon as he returned to France in 1829, he published a book of lithographs depicting everyday life in Turkey, including such scenes as *The Old Shopkeeper*, *A School in Turkey*, and *Turkish School Children*. Two years later, he exhibited his *Night Watch* and *Turkish House* at the Salon, which earned him instant fame.

His characteristic technique (in which paint is applied thickly and in which there

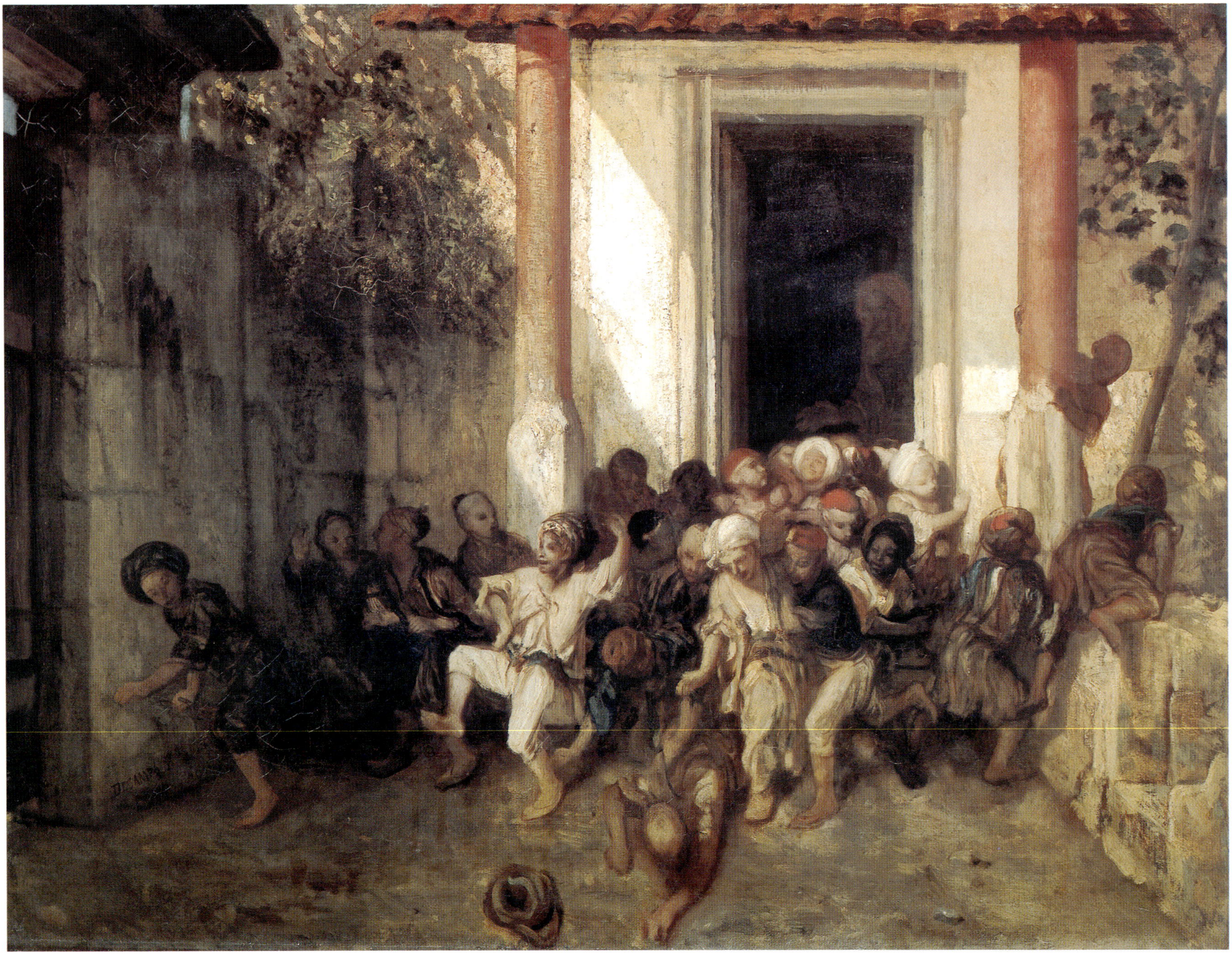

are sharp contrasts of light and dark), his realism, and his simple taste for everyday scenes created an attractive and accessible image of the Middle East. In 1834, he exhibited the *The Defeat of the Cimbri* and *Guardroom*, which confirmed his popularity with both the public and critics. He was to produce a wide range of works: *The End of a Turkish School Day*, *A Street in Smyrna*, *Turkish Child by a Fountain*, and many others, all of which were the result of his single journey to the East. In 1855 he was asked for 50 canvases to show at the World Exposition in Paris; among the works he presented was *Turkish Butcher*.

In addition to his paintings showing the ordinary city people of the modern Ottoman Empire, Decamps painted scenes inspired by the Old and New Testaments, for instance *Samson*, *Joshua*, *Lot*, and *The Miraculous Draught of Fishes*. He even began working on a *St. Jerome in the Desert*, but could not recapture the insight and evocative power of his Oriental works. He was still very popular when he died in 1860, after a hunting accident.

Above
The End of a Turkish School Day,
Alexandre Gabriel Decamps, 1836
Oil on canvas, 66 x 89 cm
(Musée du Louvre, Paris).

Opposite, left
The Caliph of Constantine, Ali-Hamed, Chief of the Harakta, Followed by his Escort,
Théodore Chassériau, 1845
Oil on canvas, 260 x 325 cm
(Musée National du Château, Versailles).

Opposite, right
Jewesses at the Balcony,
Théodore Chassériau, 1849
Oil on wood, 35 x 25 cm
(Musée du Louvre, Paris).

Théodore Chassériau

An 18-year-old from Santa Domingo was the sensation of the 1836 Salon: it was Théodore Chassériau, who won plaudits for two religious paintings, *The Return of the Prodigal Son* and *The Curse of Cain*. A pupil of Ingres, Chassériau was to learn fast. His *Venus Anadyomène* and his *Suzanna Bathing*, both shown at the 1839 Salon, were still in the Neo-classical style, but now Delacroix's influence could be discerned. Commissions to decorate several Paris churches (for example Saint-Merri in 1843) and his *Descent from the Cross* (1842) confirmed his talent but not his daring. His *Andromeda* of 1842, however, and his *Esther Preparing to Appear before Ahasuerus*, which though accepted for the Salon of 1842 went largely unnoticed, showed that he had changed sides – that he had gone over to the Romantic camp. When he created the three female figures for his *Esther*, he introduced a distinctly Oriental tone that had only been hinted at in his earlier biblical works. In 1857, Théophile Gautier commented on the insistent melancholy that pervades the work, and also on its strong leaning towards the exotic: "It feels as though we have already seen them [the three female figures] in a dream or in a far-off land in times when we did not exist, in the middle of strange towns, in forests of unknown foliages. They could have been barbarian captives brought into our civilization draped in their garish clothes, bedecked in tribal jewelry and huddling together with the fearful grace of trapped gazelles." Still in thrall to the East, in 1844 Chassériau painted *The Death of Cleopatra*, but destroyed it because it was rejected by the jury for the following year's Salon; only an etching of it remains.

In 1845, Ali-Hamed, the Caliph of Constantine in Algeria, asked to be painted on

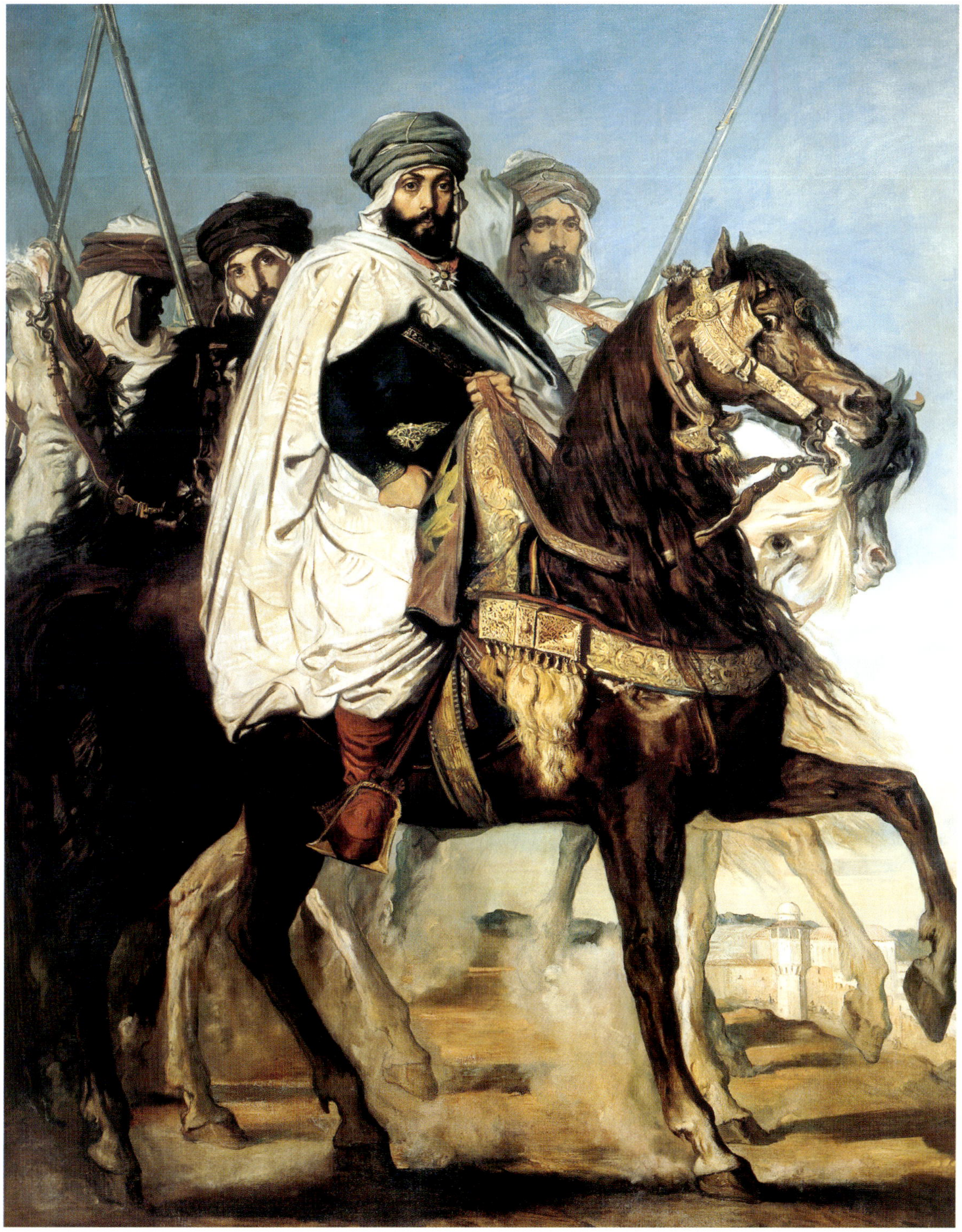

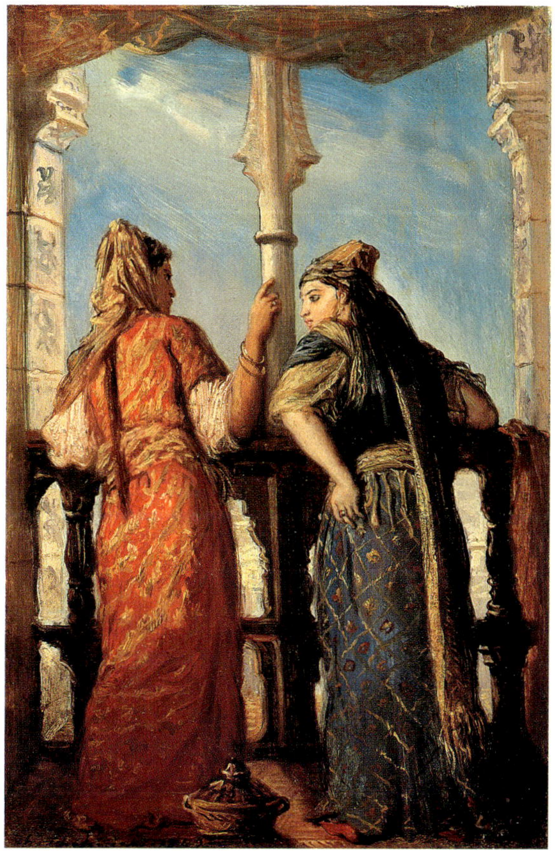

horseback. Chassériau treated his subject and his retinue in a highly original manner (it was at this time that Delacroix exhibited his *Portrait of Abd al-Rahman*). In his *Curiosités esthétiques* (Aesthetic curiosities), Charles Baudelaire noted that Chassériau's "long line of horses and tall horsemen has some of the tranquil daring of the Great Masters." The Arab potentate was equally impressed and invited the young artist to join him in Constantine. Dazzled by Algeria, Chassériau noted in the margin of a sketchbook: "The country is very beautiful, very new. I am in the *Arabian Nights*. I am going to be able to

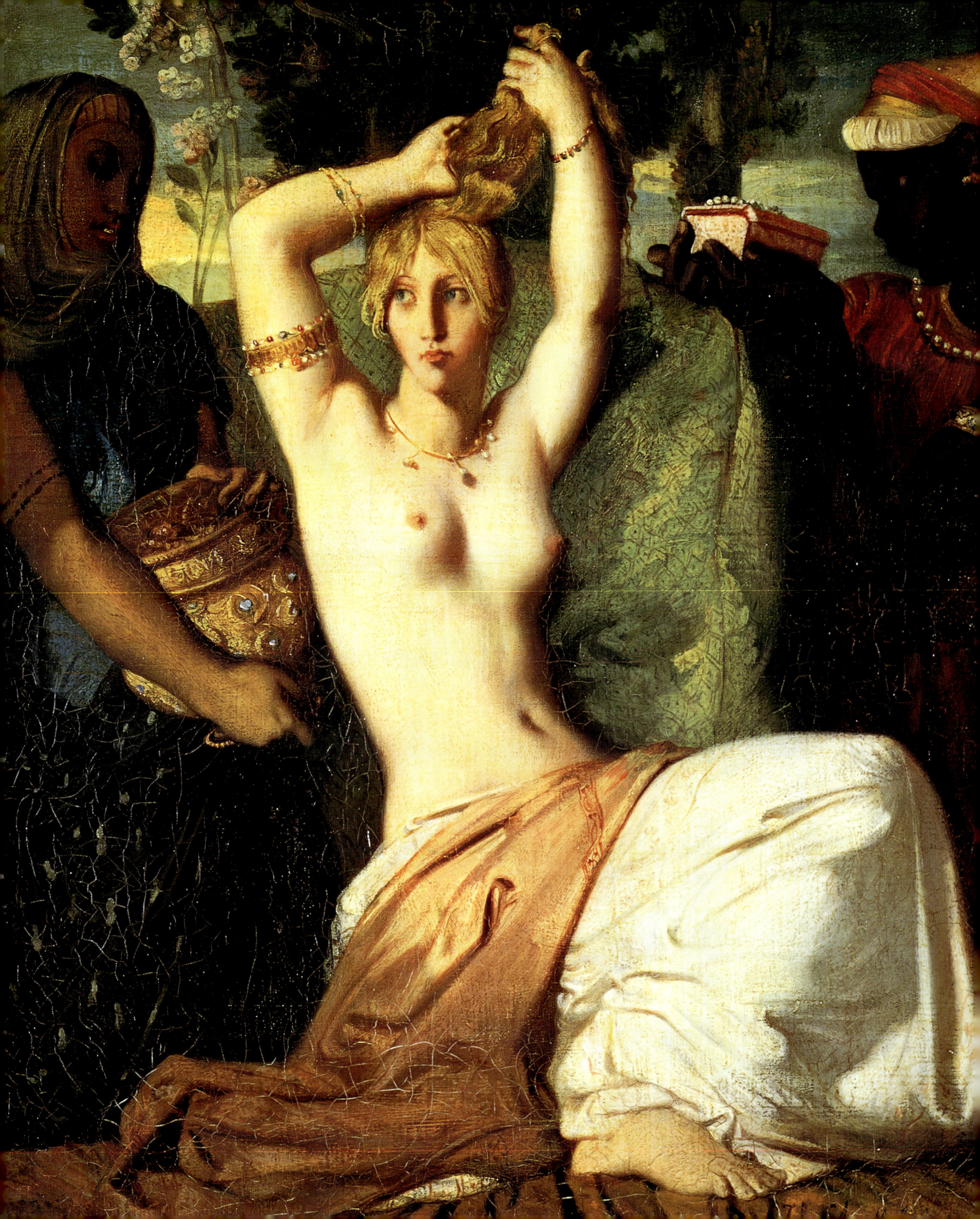

make the best of this. I work and I watch." He committed to paper all that was worth remembering. He was entranced by the landscapes: "The exquisite blue of the sky, the mountains, ordinarily lapis lazuli blue during the day, the gold-dusted air which gives off a wonderful vapor; the thicket intensely blue and luminous close to emerald-green water, here and there, holes exploding with sunlight." He was equally fascinated by the resplendent costumes: "Green velvets, yellow materials, headdresses in all colors, bright blue, red, mauve, often black; they are very beautiful, these powerful, vivid figures against these white backgrounds, the brilliant colors of the East." It was not unusual for him to anticipate the effects he would be able to achieve in his studio: "In order to offset large, drab areas of gray wall, all I need is a simple dash of gold in the odd place." He does his utmost to keep his experiences fresh: "Never forget that the blazing towns of the South have satin tones in the shadows and radiant lights; the sky a searing blue, green, then red tones, reddish, then gray tones." And when he commits a few lines to paper about Algiers, the composition of a potential painting come through: "Algiers, the blue sea, the city like white stucco or marble; the pink, bluish horizon; above the sea, the light, luminous blue sky, opalescent. Old men with their singular, Oriental faces starkly set against the white walls; the pure beauty of the children with that pale pink hue to their complexion; the white houses, often with subdued silvery or gold undertone."

On his return to France, Chassériau gave his Paris studio an entirely Eastern character. In 1857, shortly after Chassériau's death, Gautier visited his studio and described it admiringly: "On the little settee, where he sometimes rested, *yataghans*, *khandjars*, Persian daggers, Circassian pistols, Arab rifles, old damask blades, nielloed with Koranic verses, riffles encrusted with silver and coral… this charming, barbarous clutter, beloved of the painter, arranged like trophies along the walls; hanging loosely, *gandouras*, *haiks*, burnooses, caftans, silver and gold embroi-

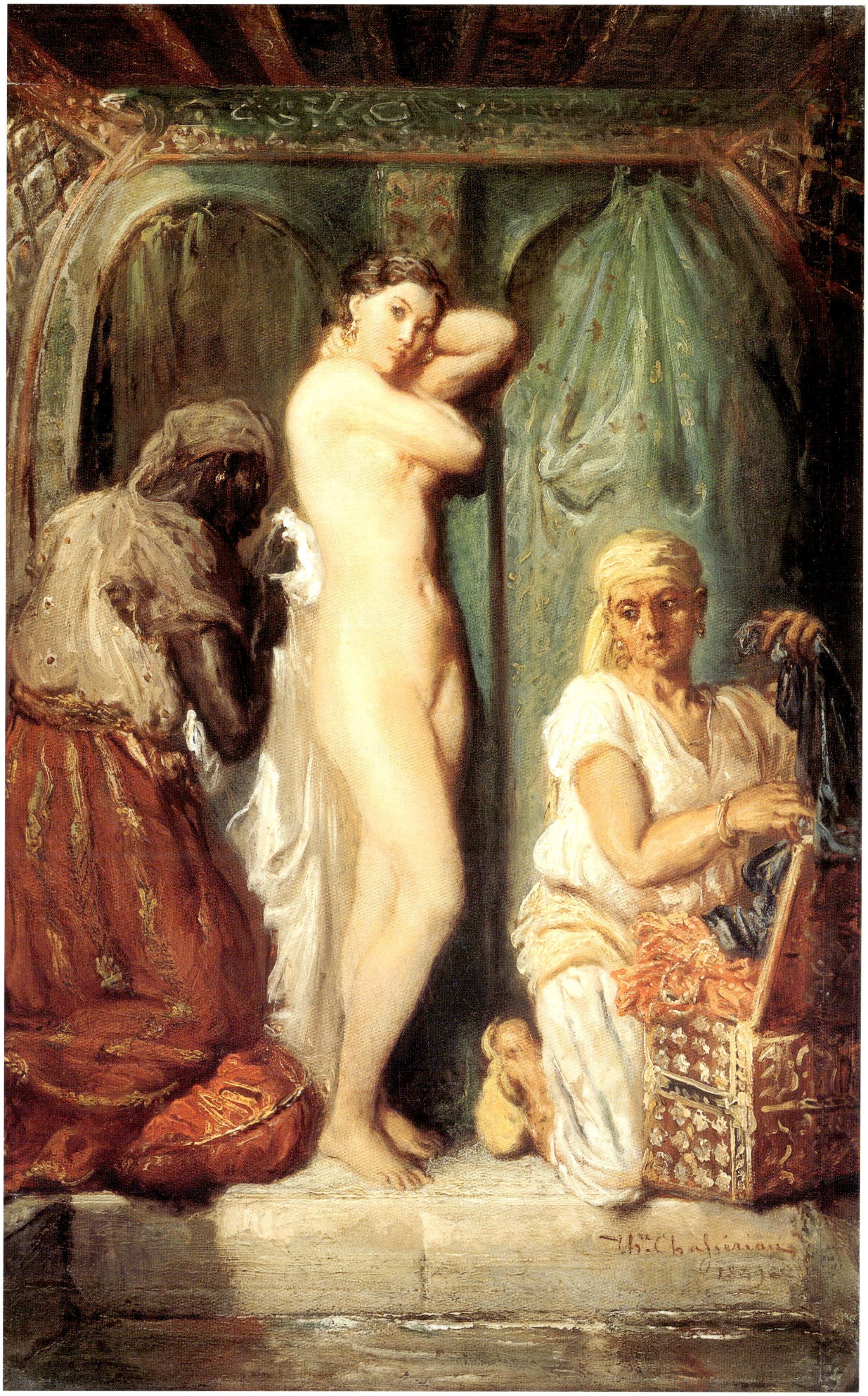

Esther Preparing to Appear before Ahasuerus,
Théodore Chassériau, 1841
Oil on canvas, 45.5 x 35.5 cm
(Musée du Louvre, Paris).

Young Woman Coming out of the Bath,
Théodore Chassériau, 1849
Oil on wood, 50 x 32 cm
(Musée du Louvre, Paris).

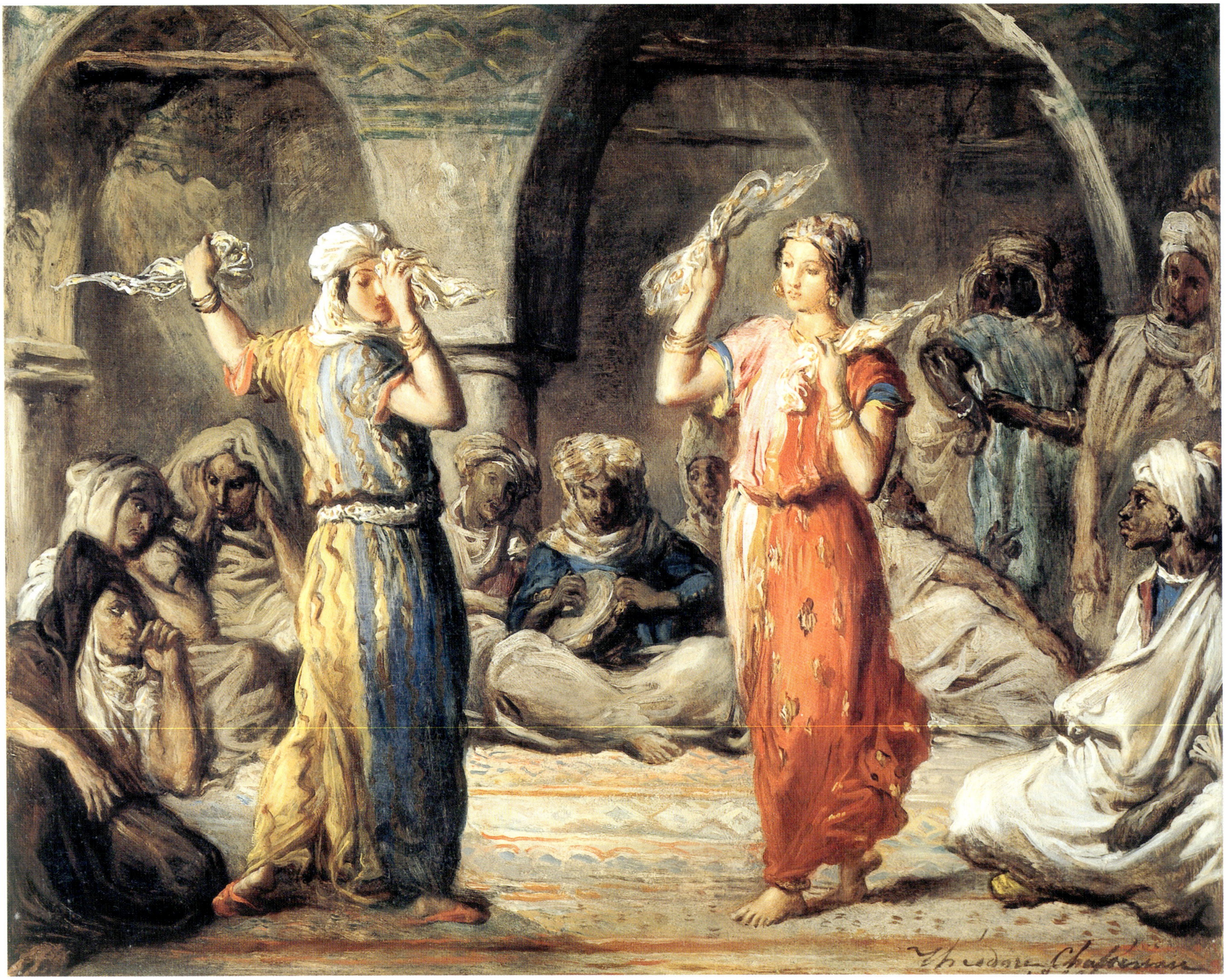

dered jackets delighted the eye with colors fit to help an artist forget the dull shades of our cheerless attire and seemed to hold in their creased and sheeny pleats the rays of the African sun." After 1848, Chassériau would never tire of returning to Algerian subjects. He created countless sketches and 50 paintings of war scenes and episodes in the lives of Moorish or Jewish women, among the finest being *The Sabbath in Constantine's Jewish Quarter*, *Jewesses at the Balcony*, and the astonishing *Dance of the Kerchiefs*. A little later he painted *Moorish Woman Nursing her Infant* (1850). This very young woman with her child in her lap and an older woman, probably her own mother leaning gravely over the child, is treated with such candor and simplicity that the painting seems an expression of personal longing. In the same year he painted a Moorish woman and girl playing with a gazelle and also *Constantine Jewesses Soothing a Child to Sleep*, a strange composition in which two Jewish women are seen almost in full face on either side of a cradle suspended by four ropes from a beam in a narrow, stone-tiled room. Chassériau submitted eight works for the Salon of 1850, among them *Arab Horsemen Carrying Away Their Dead After an Encounter With the Spahis*. Gautier praised this composition in honor of the defeated: "*Arab Horsemen* constitutes one of the finest themes he has brought back from Africa, spurred on by the sight of these patriarchal and alien lifestyles. There is Homeric grandeur in the proud simplicity of these groups so nobly turned out. The Greeks and the Trojans couldn't have been very different (...) What heroi cally delicate faces on these young warriors shrouded in their veils, like women's with their great somber eyes, their languid mouths, and their exhausted appearance." In 1851, Chassériau opted for a return to Romantic Greece with his *Mola Fisherman's Wife Kissing a Child*. Two years later he completed one of his masterpieces, *Tepidarium*, in which he combined his taste both from classical culture and Oriental

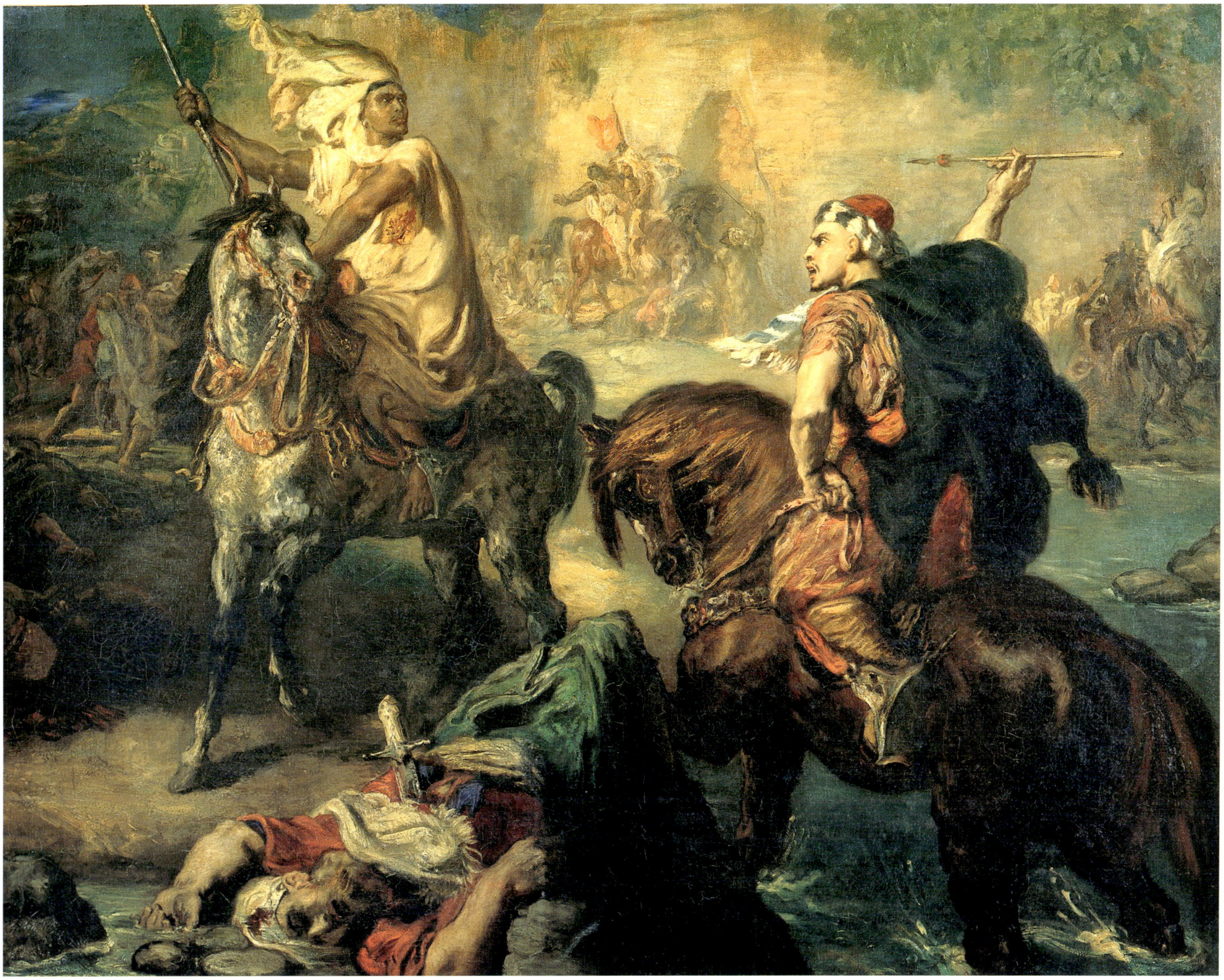

sensuality, a combination also seen in *Young Woman Coming out of the Bath*, *Odalisque Lying Down*, and *Oriental Toilette*. In 1852, he presented at the Salon a painting to parallel the *Arab Horsemen*, the *Arab Chiefs Challenging Each Other to Single Combat*. Both these works appeared at the 1855 World Exposition. One of the last canvases he painted before his untimely death was *Interior of the Harem*, which he left unfinished. It shows "two women sitting against cushions, their head thrown back. Though it is little more than an outline, it remains a delightful painting. Two women in dazzling costumes lean back against the cushions of a couch in tired, languid poses, their listless gestures those prompted by the enclosed harem and the presence of the black eunuch..." This harem, his artistic legacy, is not an erotic fantasy but a meditation on women, a meditation that had its origins in Algeria, when he noted: "Moorish women's interior – one lying down, naked under gold spangled russet gauze. In her face, capture the pale-skinned type with fine black eyes..."

Arab Chiefs Challenging Each Other to Single Combat, Théodore Chassériau, 1852
Oil on canvas, 91 x 118 cm
(Musée d'Orsay, Paris).

Opposite
Dance of the Kerchiefs,
Théodore Chassériau, 1849
Oil on wood, 32 x 40 cm
(Musée du Louvre, Paris).

Arab Falconer,
Eugène Fromentin, 1863
Oil on canvas, 108 x 73 cm
(Chrysler Museum of Art,
Norfolk, Virginia).

Opposite, top
The Tribal Tents,
Eugène Fromentin, 1850
Oil on canvas, 44.3 x 85.2 cm
(Musée Fabre, Montpellier).

Opposite, bottom
Moroccan Burial,
Eugène Fromentin, 1853
Oil on canvas, 32.5 x 56 cm
(Musée du Louvre, Paris).

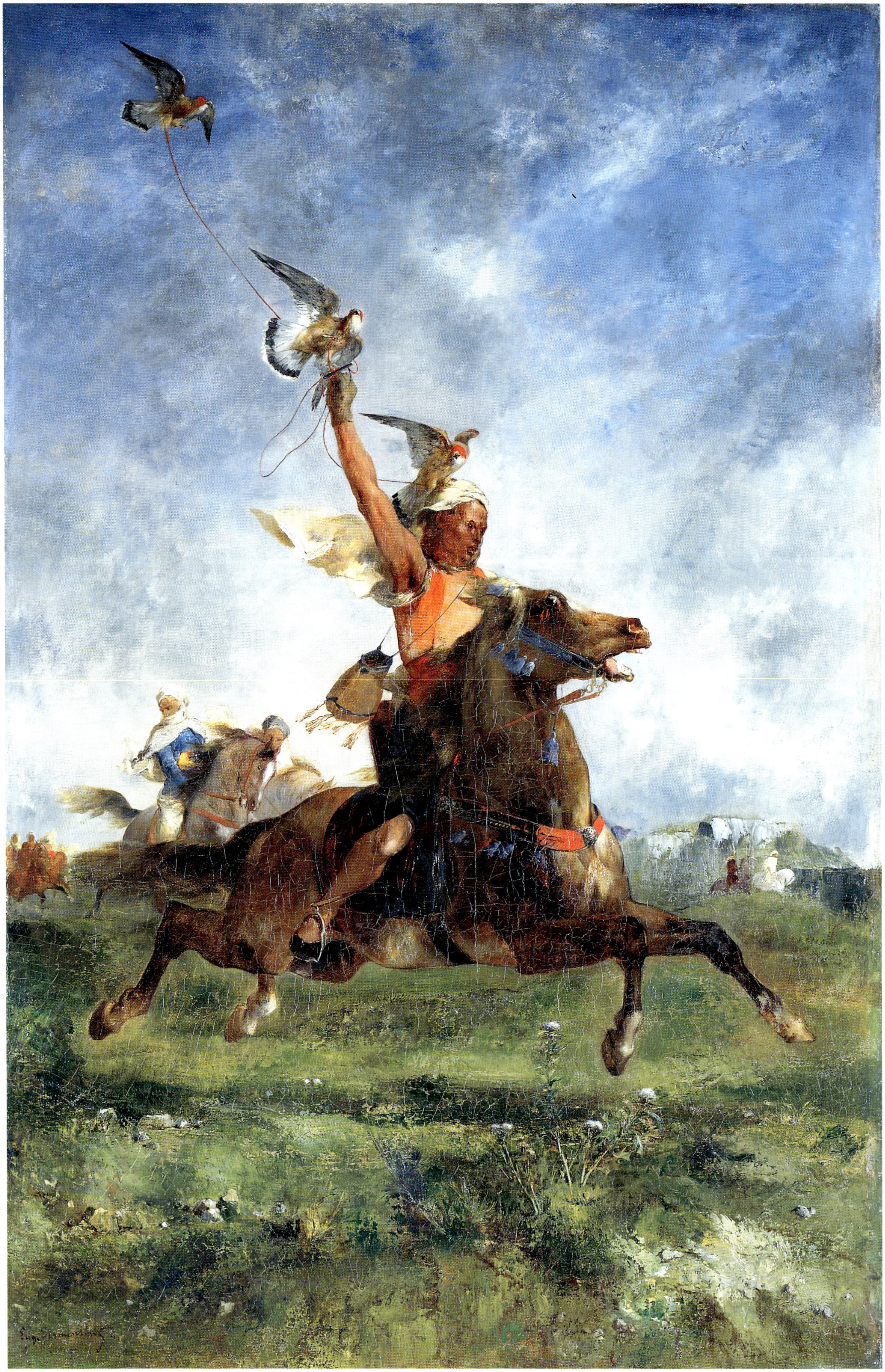

Eugène Fromentin

Though the son of a doctor who in his youth had himself been drawn to painting, Eugène Fromentin did not meet with much sympathy when he tried to persuade his father that his heart was not in law but in art. He was taught by Louis Cabat between 1844 and 1845 and soon began to write reports on the paintings at the Salon for a journal. Nothing predisposed him to the Orient. In the spring of 1847, however, he visited Algeria to attend a friend's wedding and though he stayed a mere five weeks he was completely captivated; the trip was to have a deep and lasting effect on him. The following year, he exhibited two canvases expressing his new fascination: *The Chiffa Gorge* and *A Mosque Near Algiers*. In 1847, he wrote to his father: "I have now the right to paint in the Oriental style. I don't feel that, hitherto, anybody has truly understood that country. I cried at the sorrow of having to abandon so many treasures I had only just discovered. Another might go in my place who will discover new ones. But no two men will see things in the same way… I may be mistaken, but this trip, the new possibilities it has opened my mind to, the excellent lesson I have learned in that country about light, color, bold shapes, all that has given me a new impetus, has stimulated me, strengthened me." On 24 September 1847 he set off again with two friends and this time stayed in Algeria until May 1848. He dearly loved the city of Algiers, of which he would later write: "You always go upwards, always climb, criss-cross. The rooftops almost meet, narrowing the sky to an azure ribbon. Doors, green or

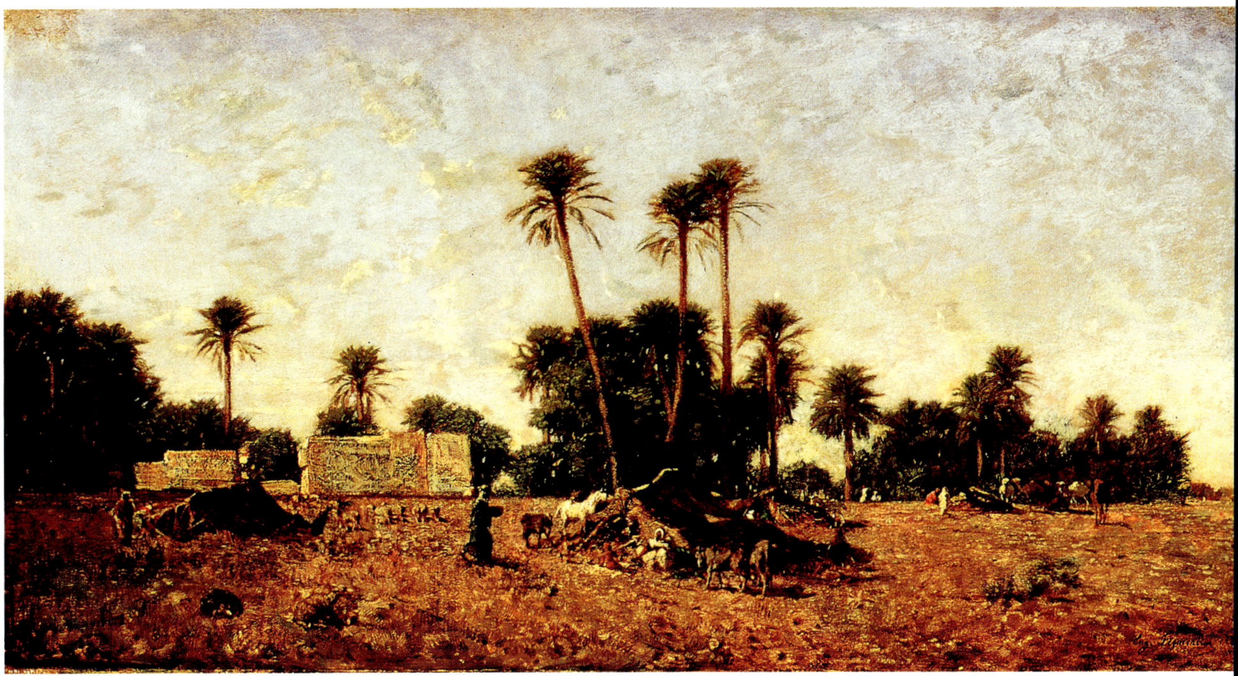

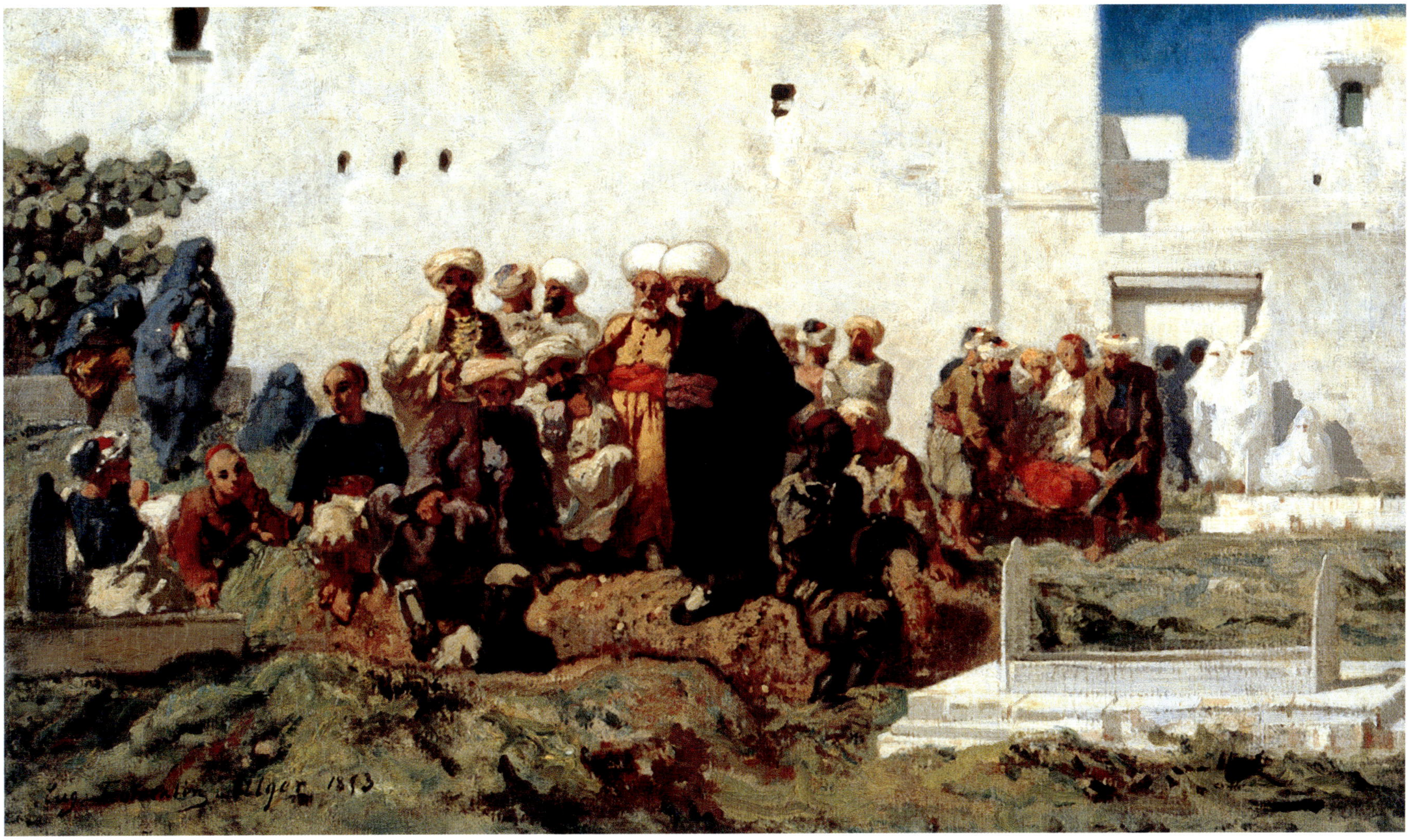

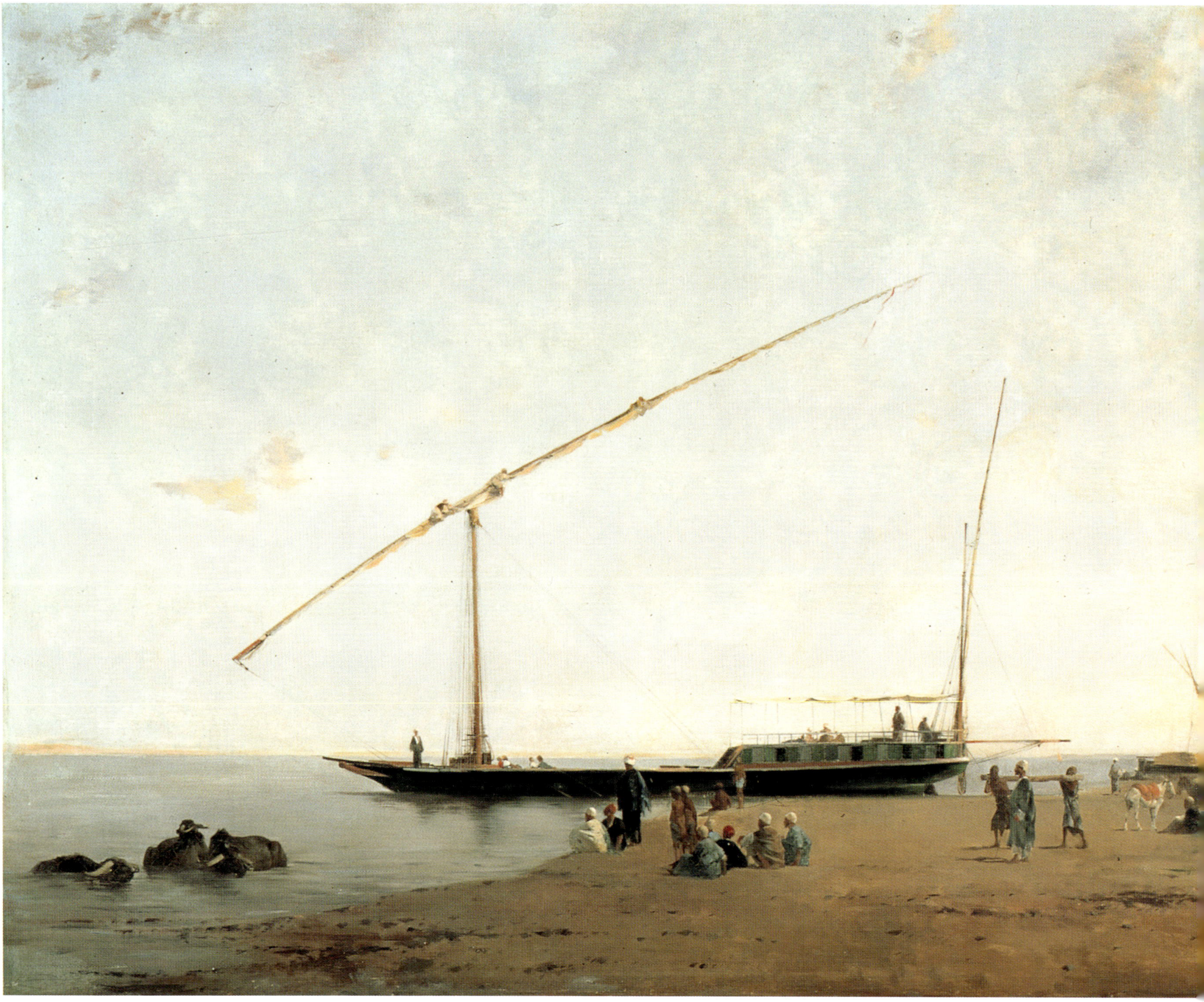

black, are closed, a red hand marked on them like a drop of blood… you feel life seep from behind these walls, these narrow grills. Rumors come through: forlorn women's songs, quarrels. And still you climb… A few women in white walk down; they look you over, a brazen laughing irony in their eye. Some Arab scratches at a little door, gives a mysterious password, bends under the door and pushes the bolts shut behind him." He visited the city of Constantine and also, more importantly, Tolga, in the south. Back in his studio, he painted passionately and was in a position to send five canvases on Algerian subjects to the Salon of 1849. The following year he had 11 paintings ready, also accepted by the Salon, including *Moroccan Burial*, *Merchants Resting at El-Aghouat*, *Desert Encampment*, and *Arabs Under Attack in a Mountain Gorge*. He had only just got married when he decided to make a third – and last – journey to Algeria, between 5 November 1852 and 5 October 1853, a trip which took him to Laghouat and Aïn-Madhy. On his return he immediately started writing his first book, *Un été dans le Sahara* (A summer in the Sahara), which was published in instalments from June 1854 in the *Revue de Paris*. It is a book passionate in its evocation of the desert and in its praise for those who dwell in it: "Don't you see that what moves the soul of these people, inspires them and delights their spirit, is the vision of another age? Yes, these people – and these people alone – have true greatness because they alone in the midst of civilization, they have remained simple in their life, in their practices, in their traveling. It is beautiful above all because not being naked, it shows total plainness in its garment (…) It alone, by some wonderful privilege, has preserved something of a biblical inheritance, like a fragrance of olden days."

Left
On the Nile, Near Philae,
Eugène Fromentin, 1871
Oil on canvas, 63.8 x 110.6 cm
(The Art Institute, Nickerson Collection, Chicago).

Below
View of the Nile, Eugène Fromentin, c. 1870
Oil on wood, 32.5 x 41 cm
(Musée d'Orsay, Paris).

Bottom
The Nile (Upper Egypt),
Eugène Fromentin, 1876
Oil on canvas, 102 x 143 cm
(Mahmoud Khalil Museum, Cairo).

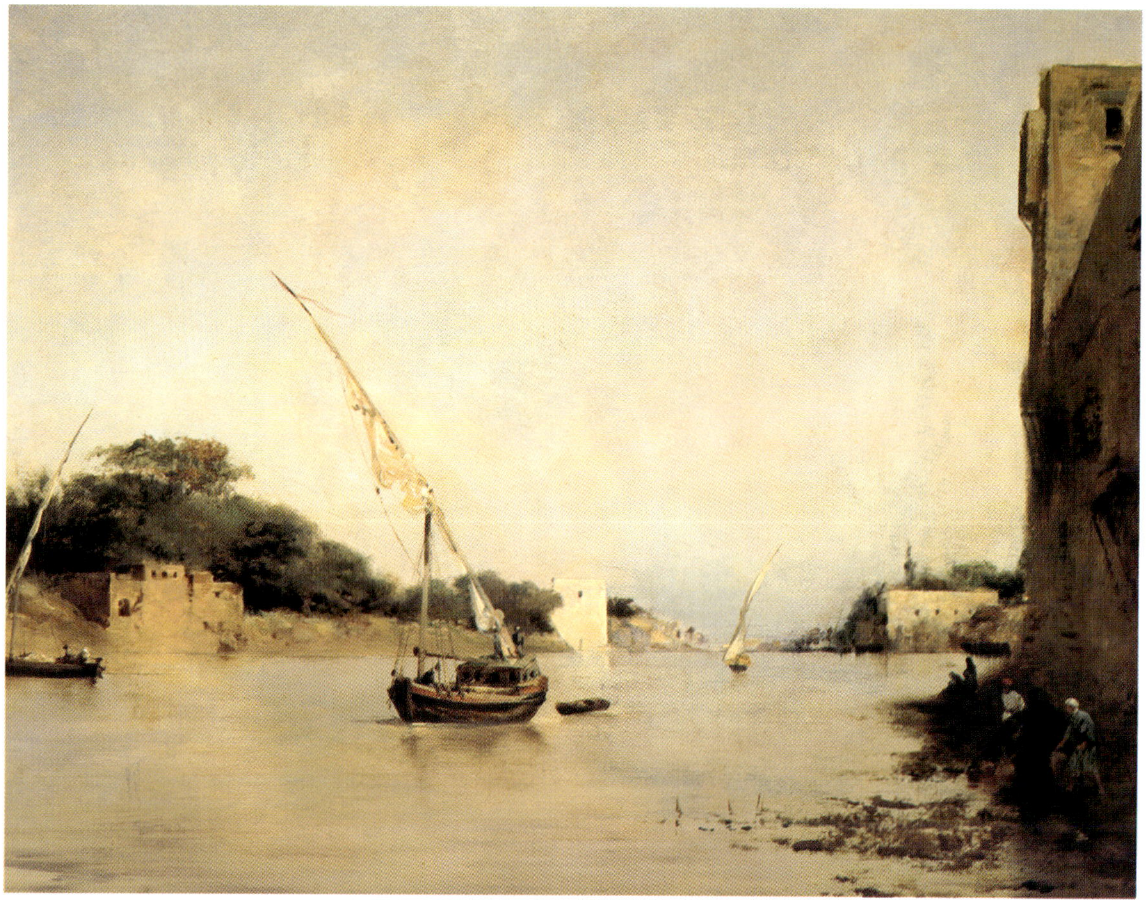

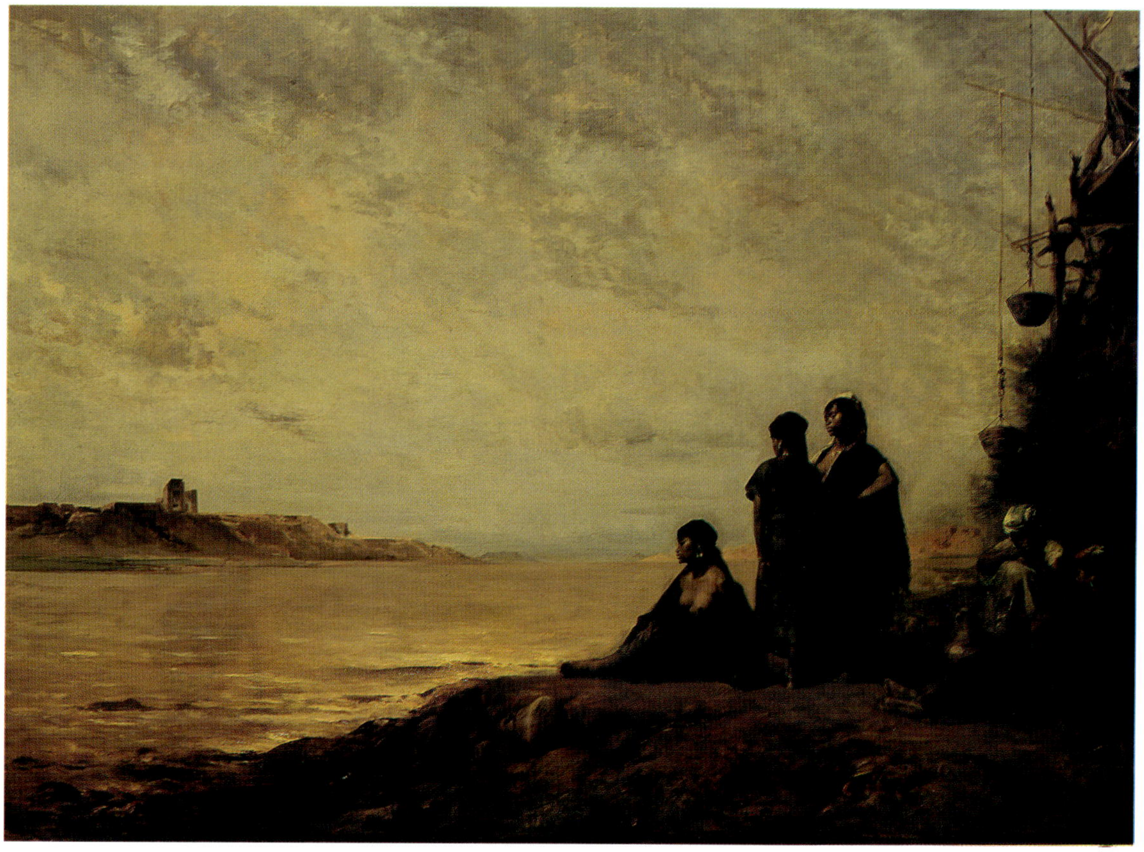

From then on he would divide his time between painting and writing; whilst sending three canvases for the 1857 Salon, he had the first edition of *Une année dans le Sahel* (A year in the Sahel) published; it appeared in the journal *Revue des Deux-Mondes* at the end of 1858. Five of his paintings shown in the 1859 Salon were praised by Théophile Gautier and earn him the Légion d'honneur. He continued to exhibit regularly, always choosing to evoke with passion, but also with a fitting reticence, the people and landscapes of Algeria. After 1861, he started to use gray tones, probably taking a leaf from Camille Corot's work; this enabled

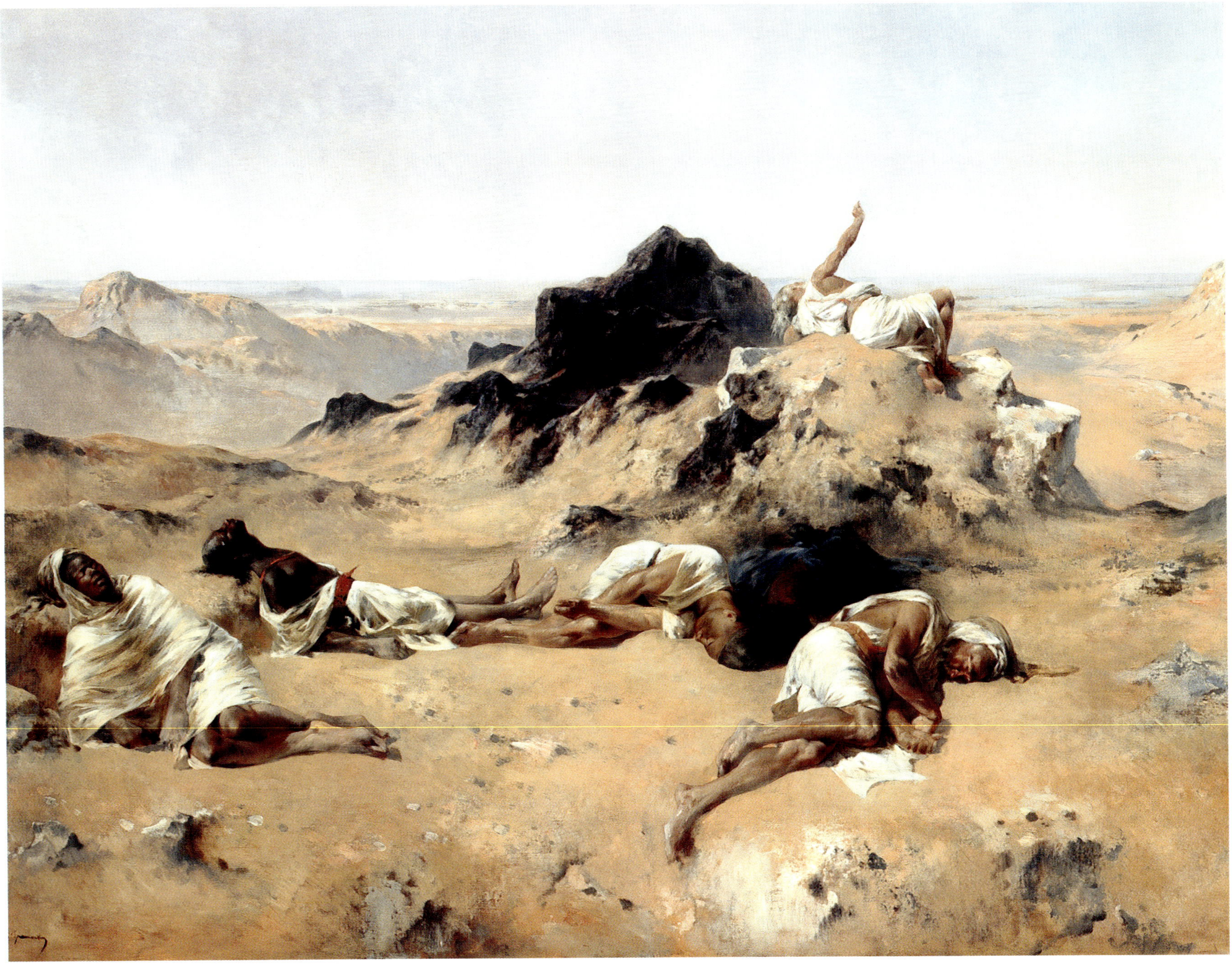

The Land of Thirst, Eugène Fromentin, 1869
Oil on canvas, 103 x 143.2 cm
(Musée d'Orsay, Paris).

Right
Algerian Town, Eugène Fromentin, 1853
Oil on canvas, transferred to board,
17.8 x 26 cm
(Musée des Beaux-Arts, La Rochelle).

Opposite
A Street in El-Aghouat,
Eugène Fromentin, c. 1859
Oil on canvas, 142 x 103 cm
(Musée de la Chartreuse, Douai).

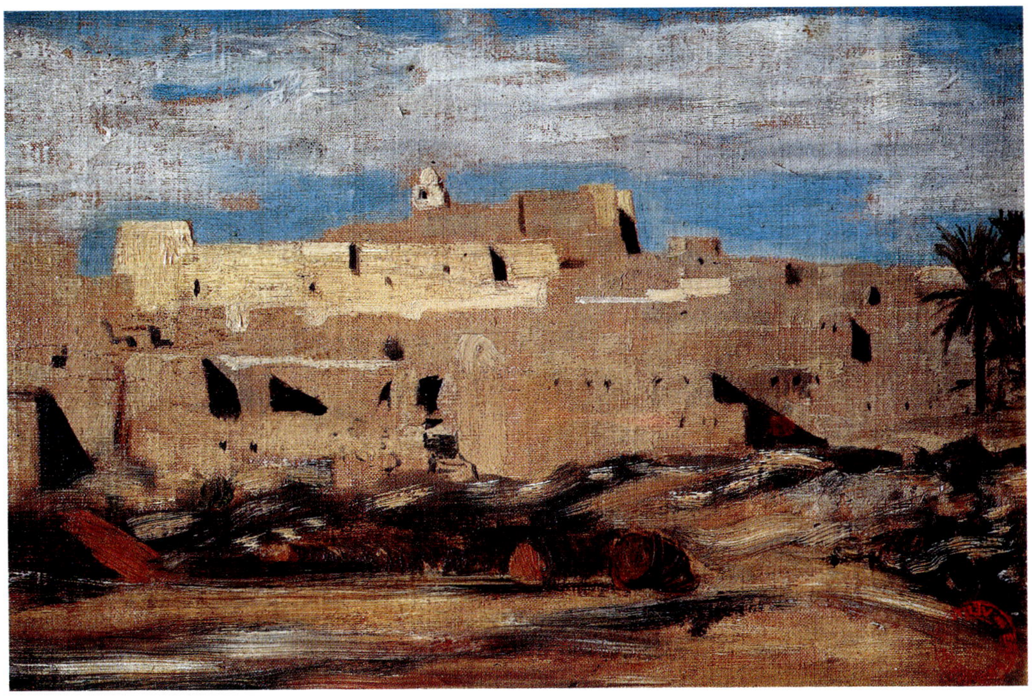

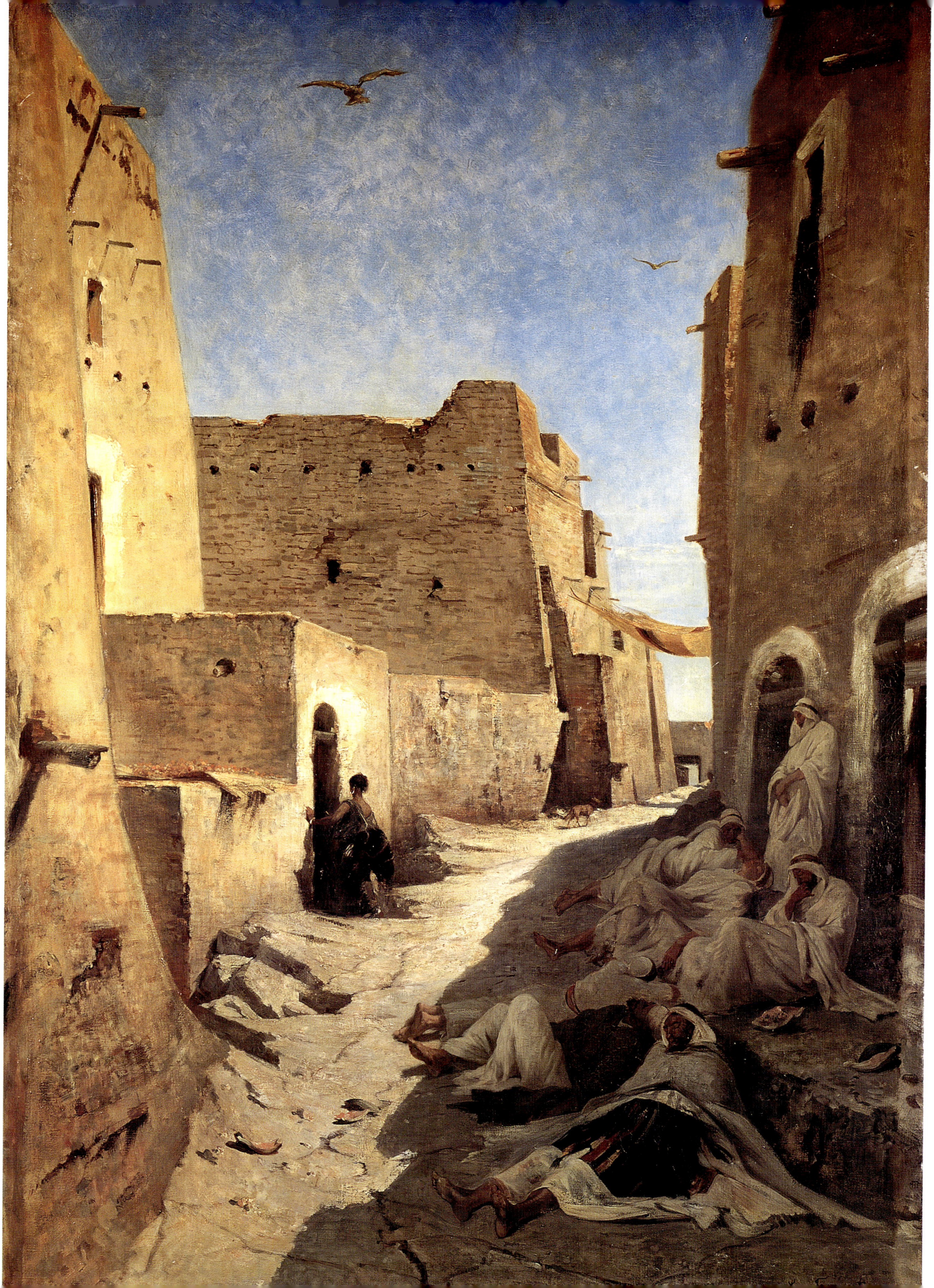

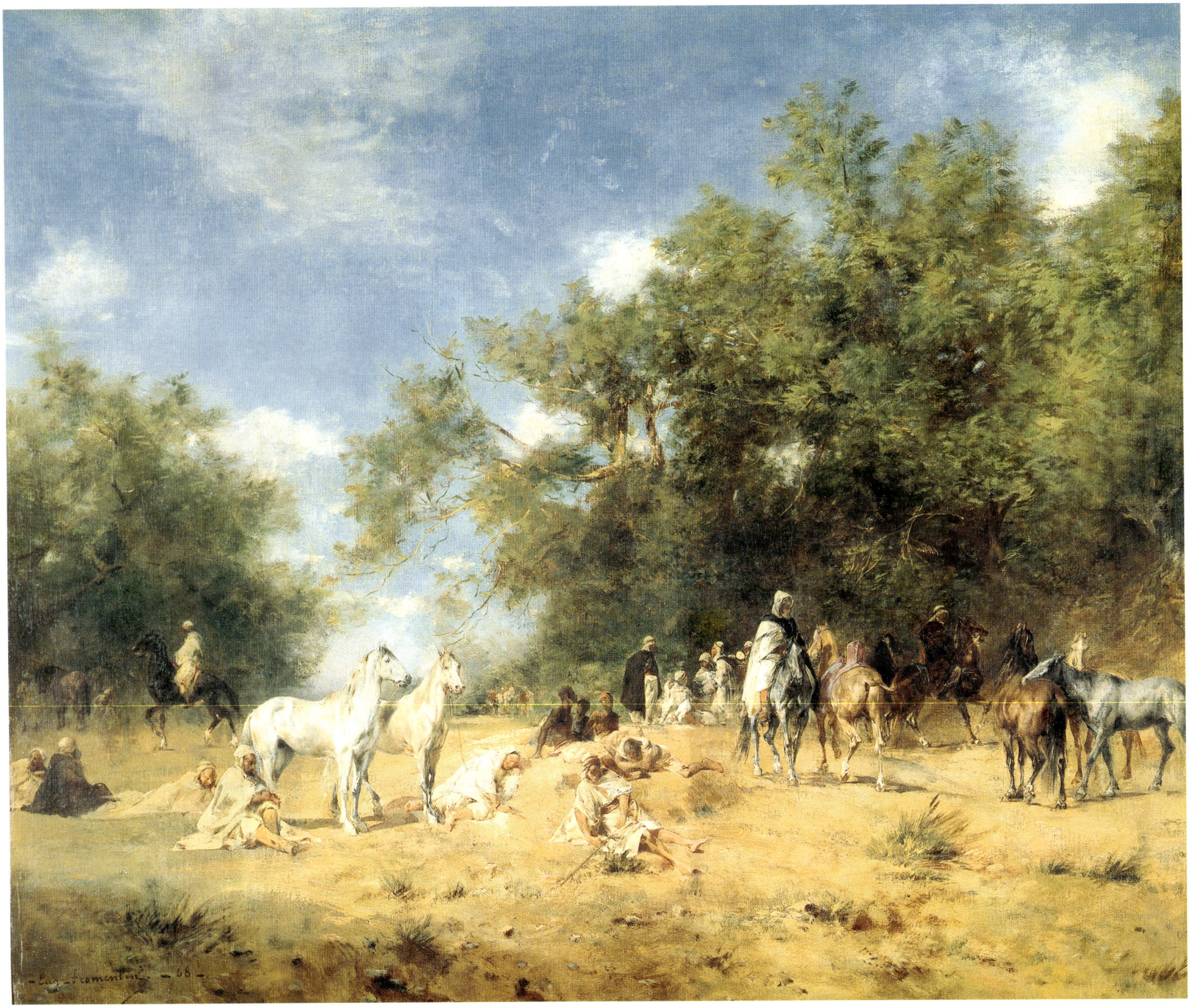

him to achieve a greater subtlety of tones and color. Becoming well established did not deter him from seeking new adventures and experiences. He chose a mythological subject for the 1868 Salon, though he soon realized that he had made a bad mistake. The following year, he wisely returned to safer ground with *Algerian Fantasy* and the *Muleteers' Rest*.

In 1869 Fromentin traveled to the Middle East for the opening of the Suez Canal. He made notes and drew a number of sketches. When he wrote to Edmond de Goncourt, he was clearly under the sway of contradictory impressions: "Egypt, Egypt, it distresses me to write a few pages on this country... Imagine... a sludgey land, something ... like rubber... A pale sky... All you have known is a clear, crystalline Orient... here on every plane, barely visible veils of vapor which become more intense as they move away... Here black and blue figures, it is rare to spot a dash of red... I can see all these small figures with a flash of light on the forehead and at the collarbone... I just have not found the painting mode which would account for all this..." He found Cairo both squalid and too "civilized," though that did not prevent him from deriving two of his finest compositions from it. Influenced in turn by Marilhat, Decamps, and Delacroix, Fromentin sought to show North Africa as truly noble, without emphasizing its "local color" or falsifying its beauty. His *Arabs Hawking* (1865), *Heron Hunting*, and *Hawking* (1873) all express an underlying Classicism that still allows him to show intense feeling. Reserve and control are part of his way of remaining faithful to his vision of the landscape, the people, and culture of North Africa.

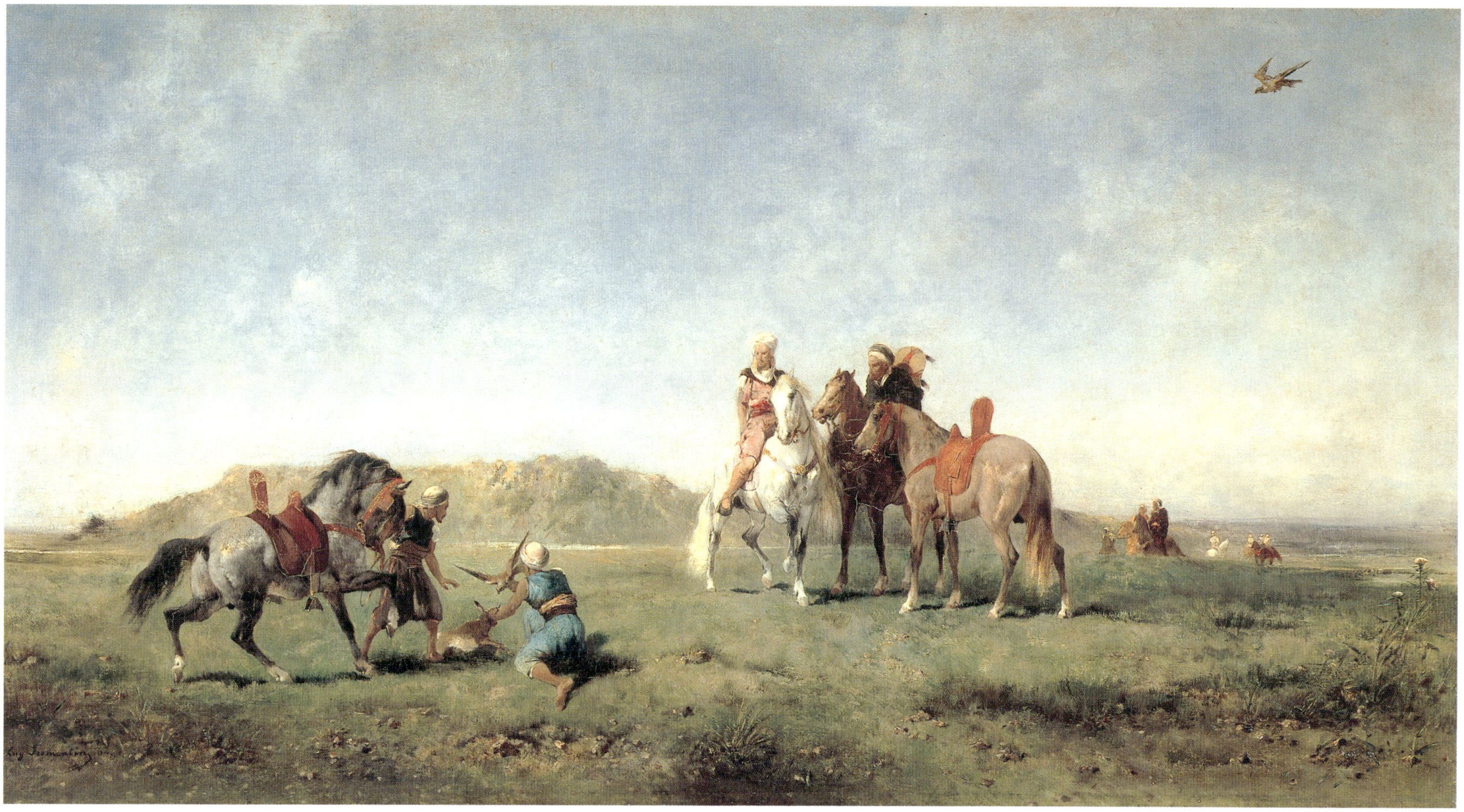

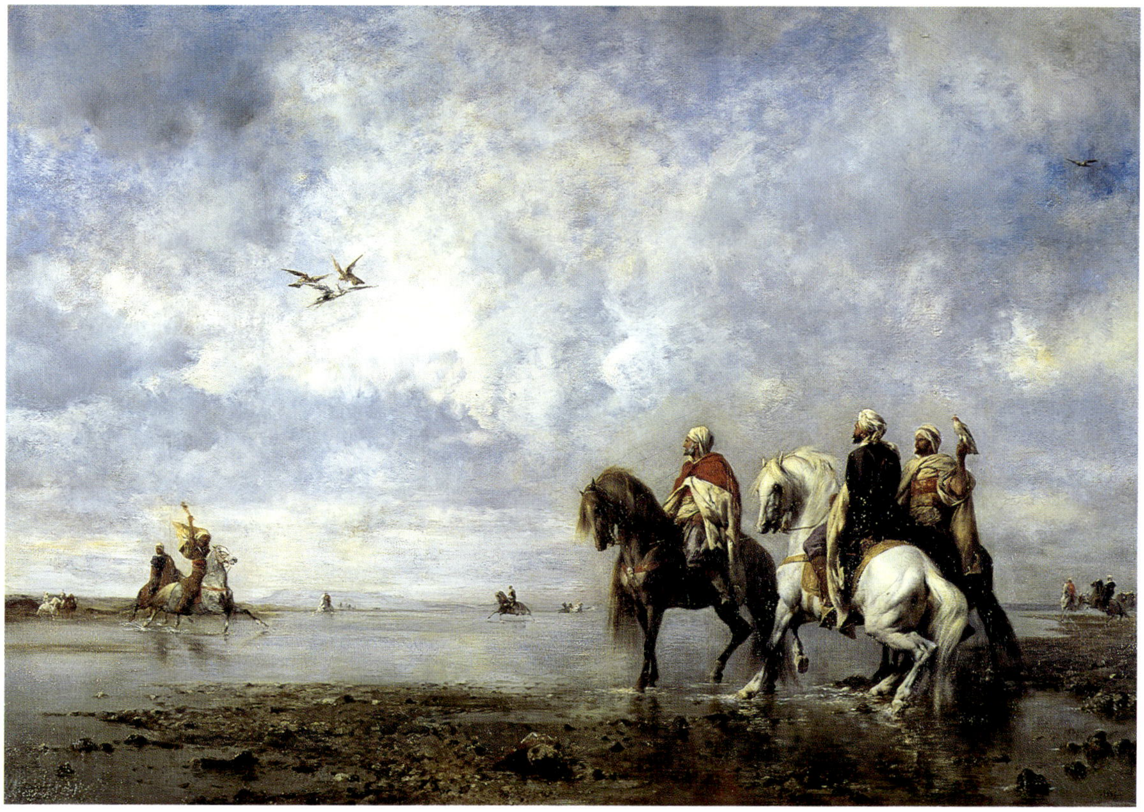

Above
Hawking in Algeria,
Eugène Fromentin, 1863
Oil on canvas, 162.5 x 117.8 cm
(Musée d'Orsay, Paris).

Left
Heron Hunting,
Eugène Fromentin, 1865
Oil on canvas, 99 x 142 cm
(Musée Condé, Chantilly).

Opposite
Arab Horsemen Resting,
Eugène Fromentin, 1868
Oil on canvas, 54.5 x 64.5 cm
(Musée d'Orsay, Paris).

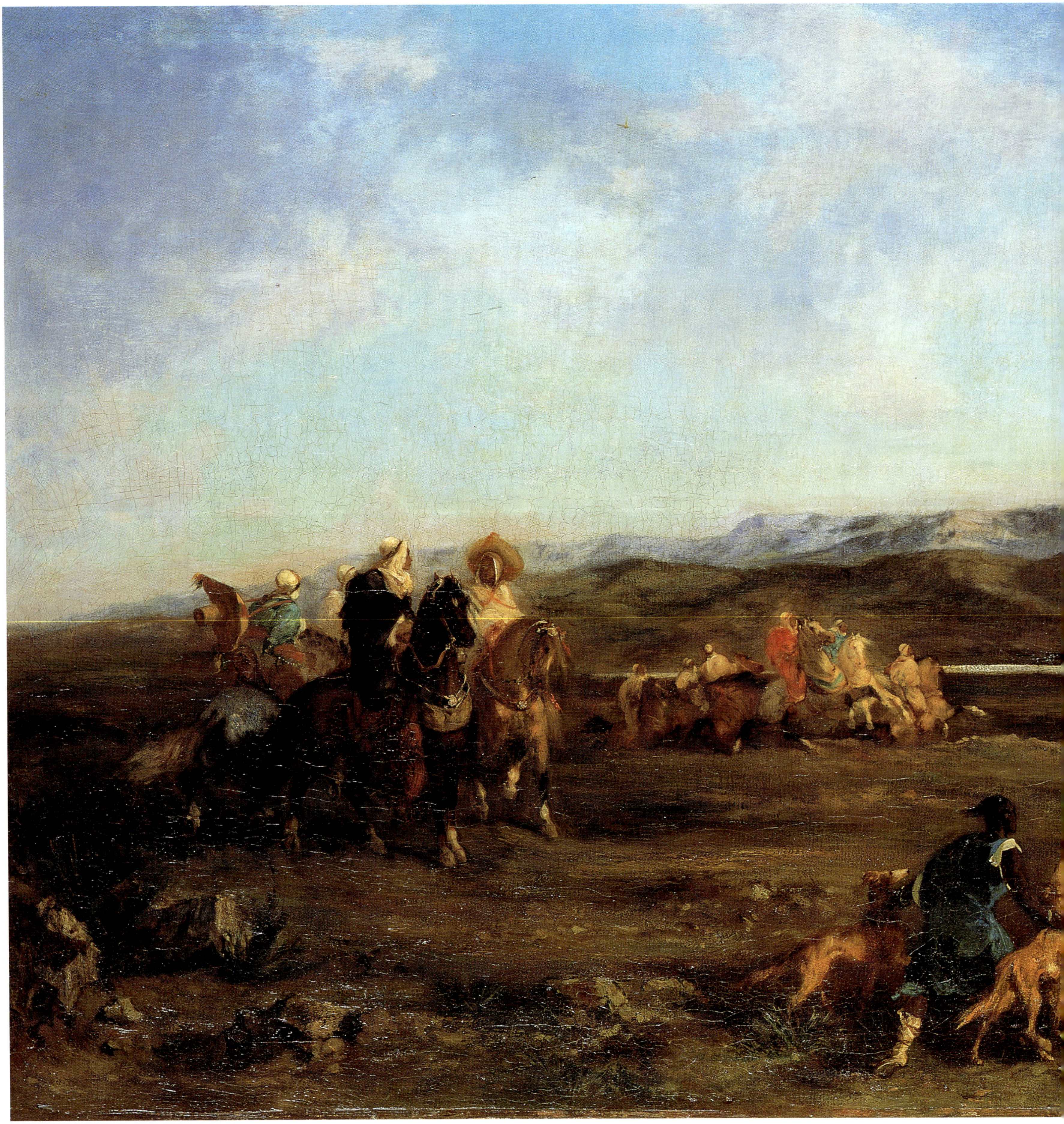

Gazelle Hunting in Hodna,
Eugène Fromentin, 1856
Oil on canvas, 98 x 195 cm
(Musée des Beaux-Arts, Nantes).

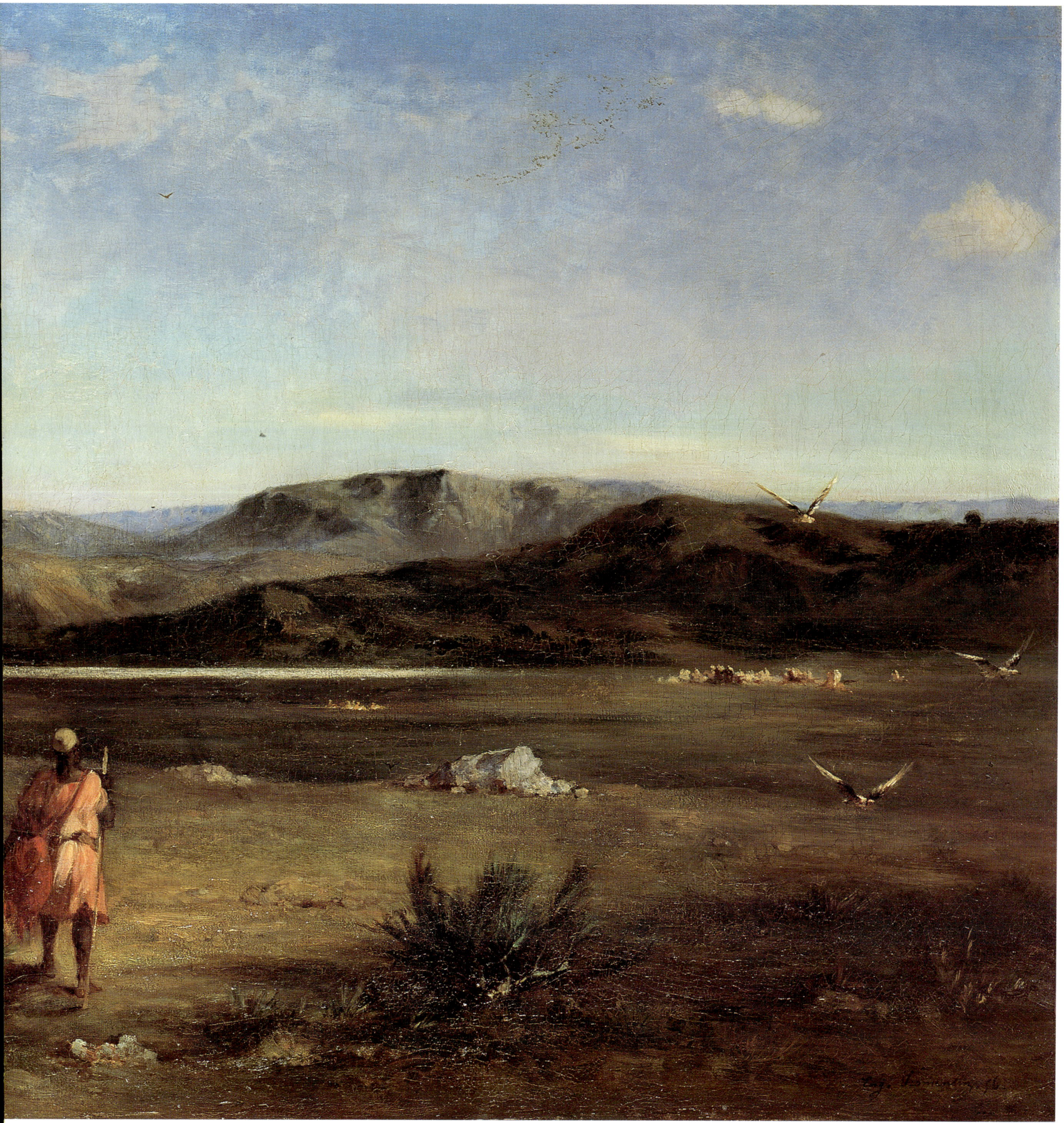

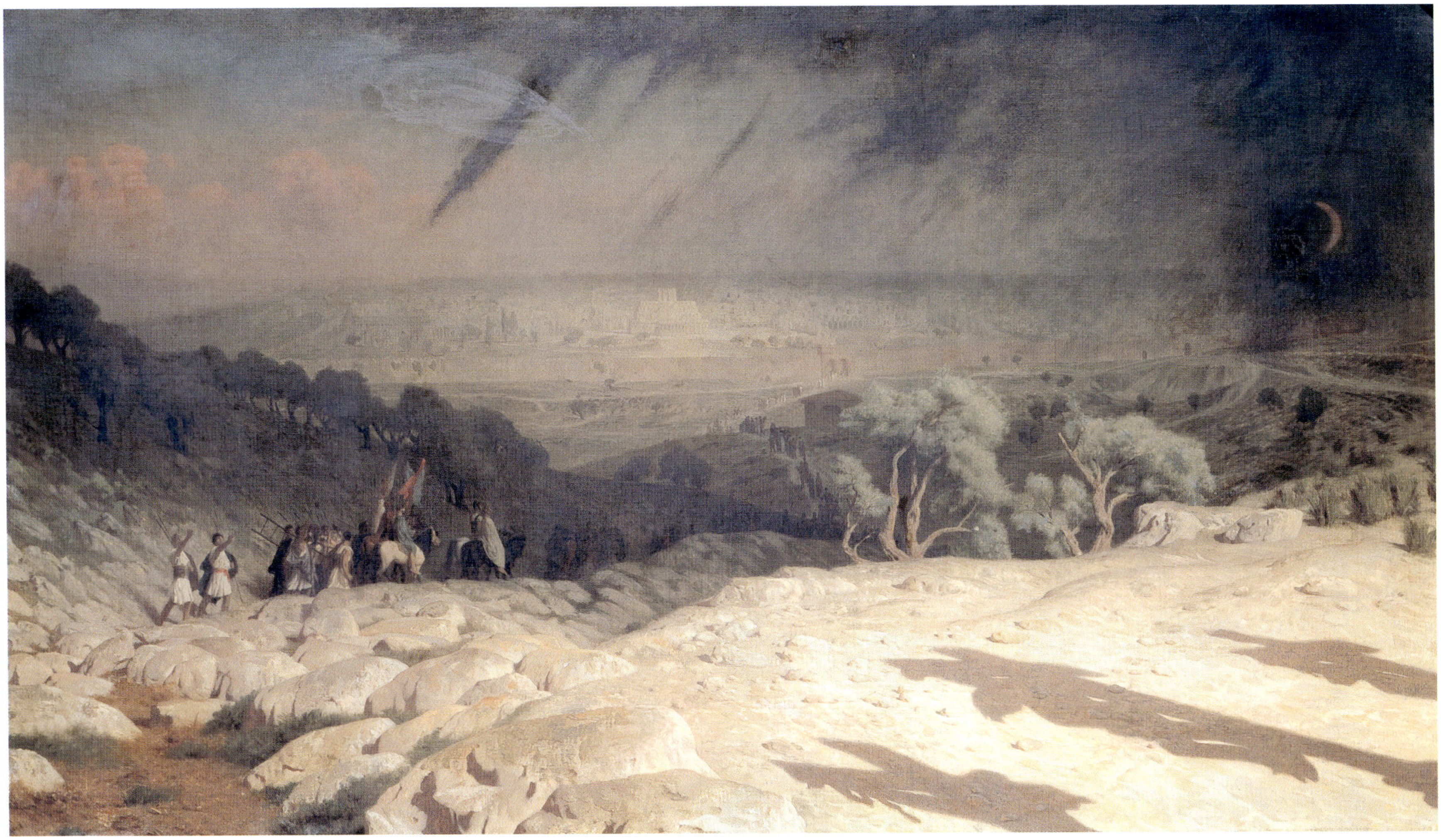

JEAN LÉON GÉRÔME

Taught by Paul Delaroche, Jean Léon Gérôme was a born leader and formed with studio friends a small group that met at the Café Procope. He joined Charles Gleyre's studio in 1844 and spearheaded the Neo-Greek movement. His hour of glory came at the Salon of 1847 with his *Cockfight*, which set out his notion of Classicism. In 1852, he set off for Russia, but as war was threatening he traveled down the Danube to the Black Sea and set sail for Constantinople. It was his first contact with the Middle East. He became infected with the urge to travel and announced: "I have always had a wandering soul." The following year he was off again, traveling through Germany and Hungary, and stopping at Galatz, where he painted the Russian soldiers' camp, the *Camp Recreations, Souvenir from Moldavia*, which was exhibited at the 1854 Salon. He then decided to go to Egypt with the playwright Léon Augier, the sculptor Auguste Bartholdi, and several painter friends. For Gérôme the trip was immensely enjoyable for he was able to soak up the atmosphere of a country that inspired him greatly. He noted in his diary: "We hired a boat and spent four months on the Nile, hunting and painting, from Damietta to Philae. Back in Cairo, we spent another four months in one of Soliman Pasha's houses, which he rented to us." This tour produced many paintings in a new vein, showing a broadening of his artistic approach; this can be seen in *Arnauts Playing Chess* (1859) and *Arnauts' Guardroom in Cairo* (1861). When Gérôme returned to his studio on the Rue Notre-Dame-des-Champs in Paris, Théophile Gautier visited him and was very taken with what he found: "Gérôme was kind enough to allow us to leaf through his rich portfolio and to study one by one the sketches he had taken down as quickly as his pencil would go, quick notations, snatched from reality, without fuss, with no construction, no system, just a sincere effortlessness and charming informality. The least of Gérôme's drawings shows such a firm, pure, precise stroke in its casualness, that you are left wondering what could be achieved by a more protracted effort. The traveler-artist has drawn in lead pencil several likenesses of local types: *fellaheen*, Copts, Arabs, mixed-blood Negroes, men so finely observed that they would be quite appropriate in an anthropological paper."

Gérôme presented one of his first Egypt-inspired paintings at the 1859 Salon; from 1862, when he returned to Egypt, he would concentrate almost entirely on his Orientalist work. He also discovered Syria and Jerusalem, thus broadening his stock of places and human types. On his return to Paris in 1863, Gérôme married Marie Goupil, the daughter of a rich and influential art dealer, and in that same year showed *The Prisoner* and *Turkish Butcher* at the Salon. In 1864, by then a teacher at the École des Beaux-Arts, he chose a more daring subject, *Almeh*, which shows a dancer in a state of undress displaying her abundant charms. Even-handedly, he submitted the *Prayer* for the 1865 Salon. In 1868, he started on an extended tour that took him to Egypt and Asia Minor in the company of Edmond About, the writer, who as a result of the trip was to publish a novella

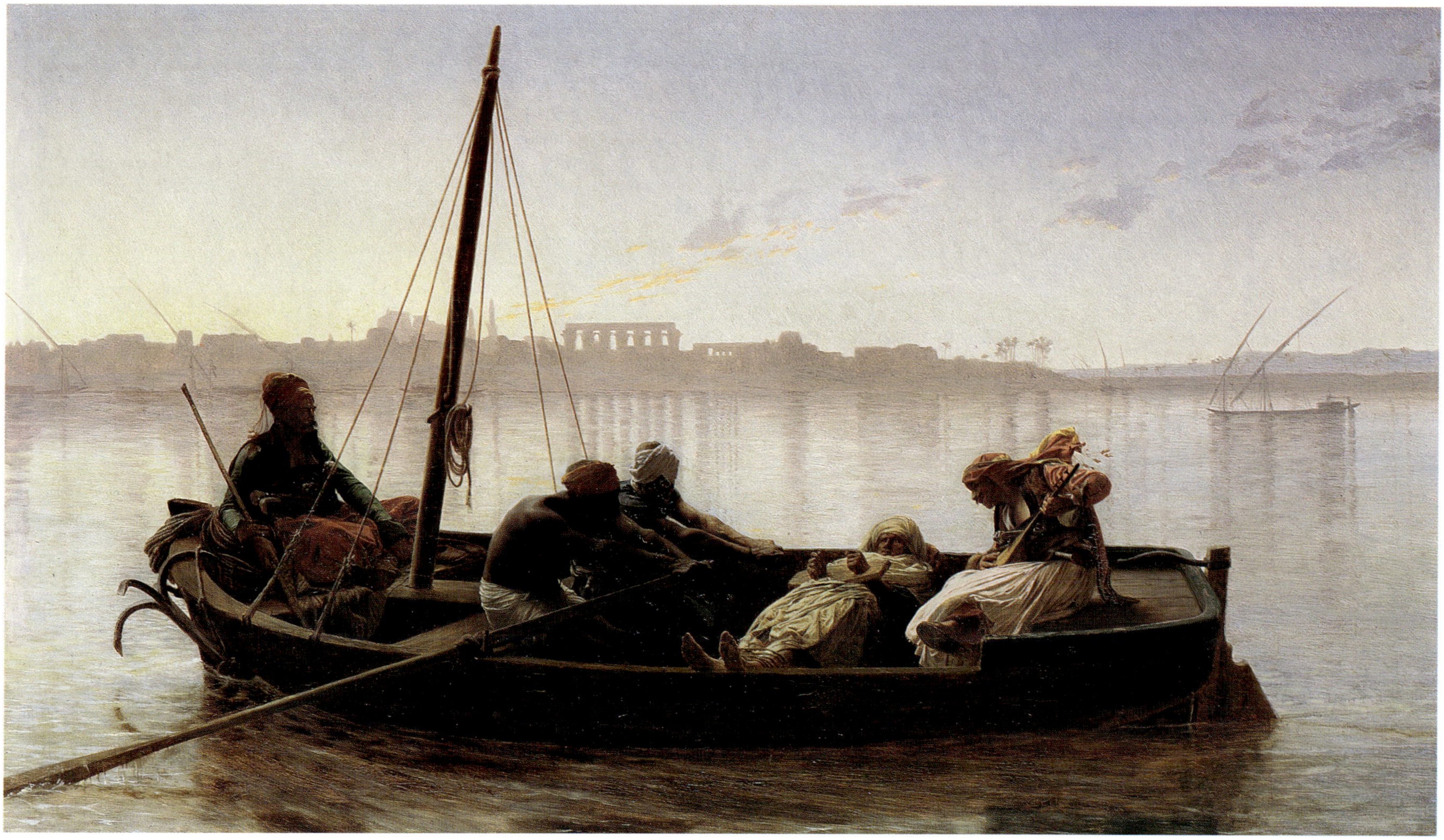

called *Le Fellah* in 1870. They traveled around the Red Sea, visited the Monastery of Saint Catherine on Sinai, were attacked by bandits at Petra, and ended their long journey with a stay in Jerusalem, where Gérôme painted *Golgotha* (exhibited at the 1868 Salon).

Gérôme was soon back in Egypt, where he witnessed the opening of the Suez Canal. He then went on to visit Alexandria, Cairo, and Ismailia before returning to Upper Egypt. After several months in London he visited Turkey in 1871, Spain and Algeria in 1873,

Above
The Prisoner, Jean Léon Gérôme, 1861
Oil on wood, 45 x 78 cm
(Musée des Beaux-arts, Nantes).

Left
The Red Sea, Jean Léon Gérôme, c. 1869
Oil on canvas, 22 x 31 cm
(Musée Georges Garret, Vesoul).

Opposite
Jerusalem, Jean Léon Gérôme, 1867
Oil on canvas, 81 x 146 cm
(Musée d'Orsay, Paris).

Following double page
Harem Outing, Jean Léon Gérôme, c. 1869
Oil on canvas, 120 x 178 cm
(Chrysler Museum of Art, Norfolk, Virginia).

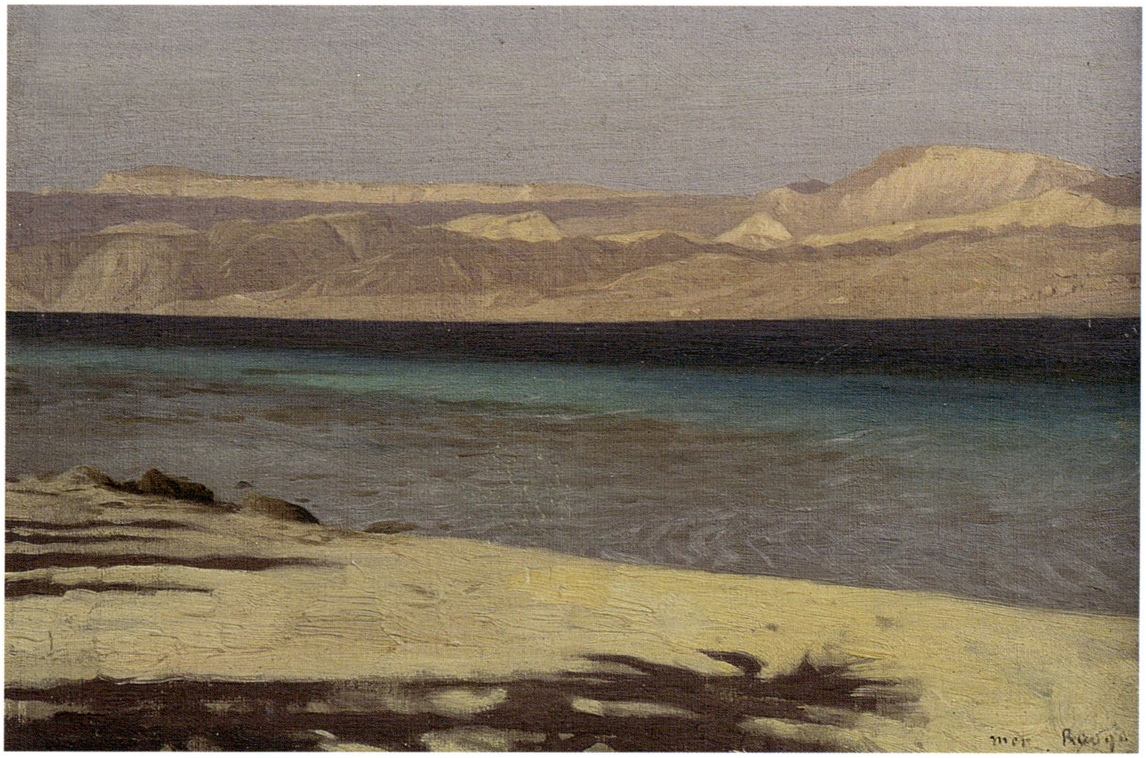

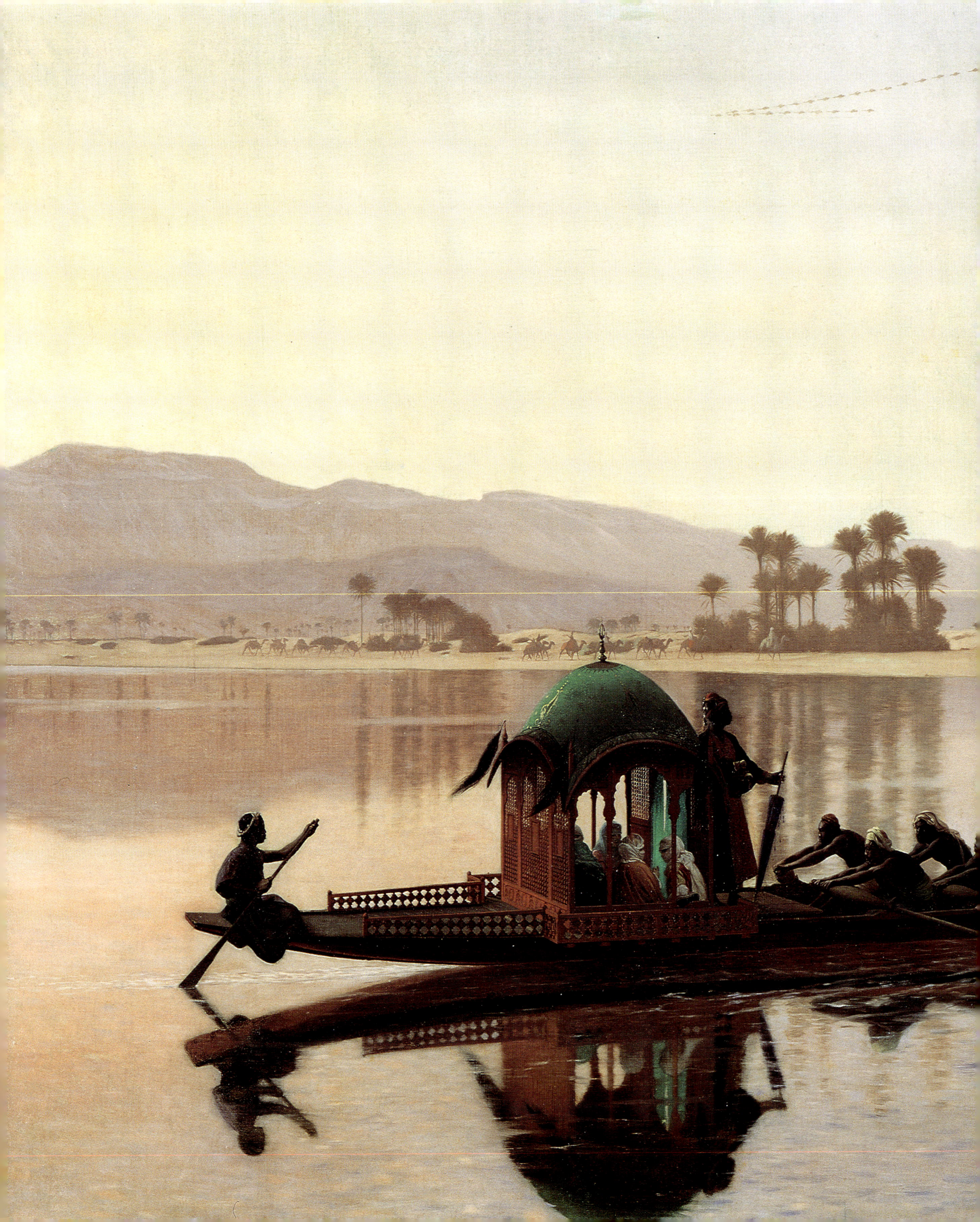

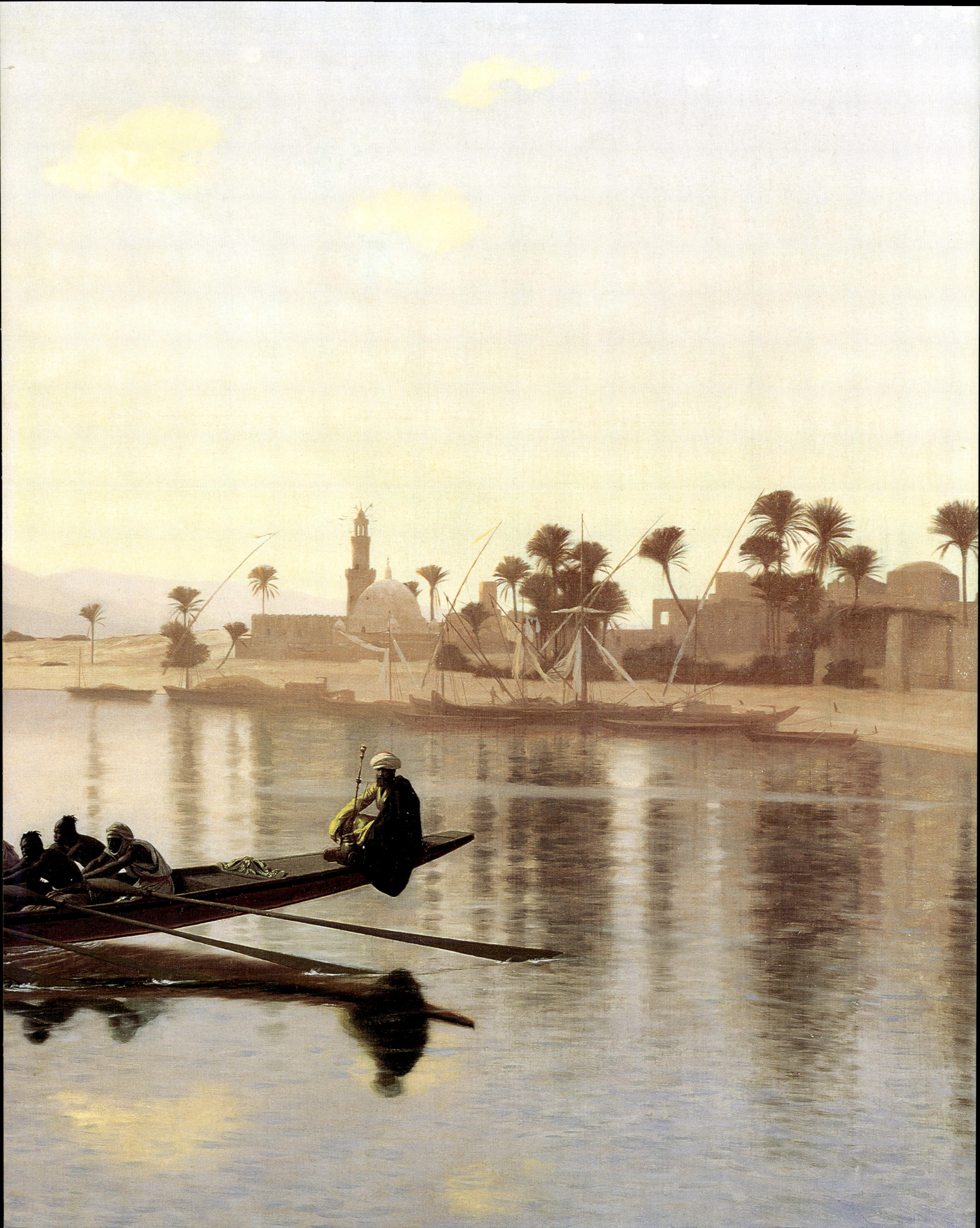

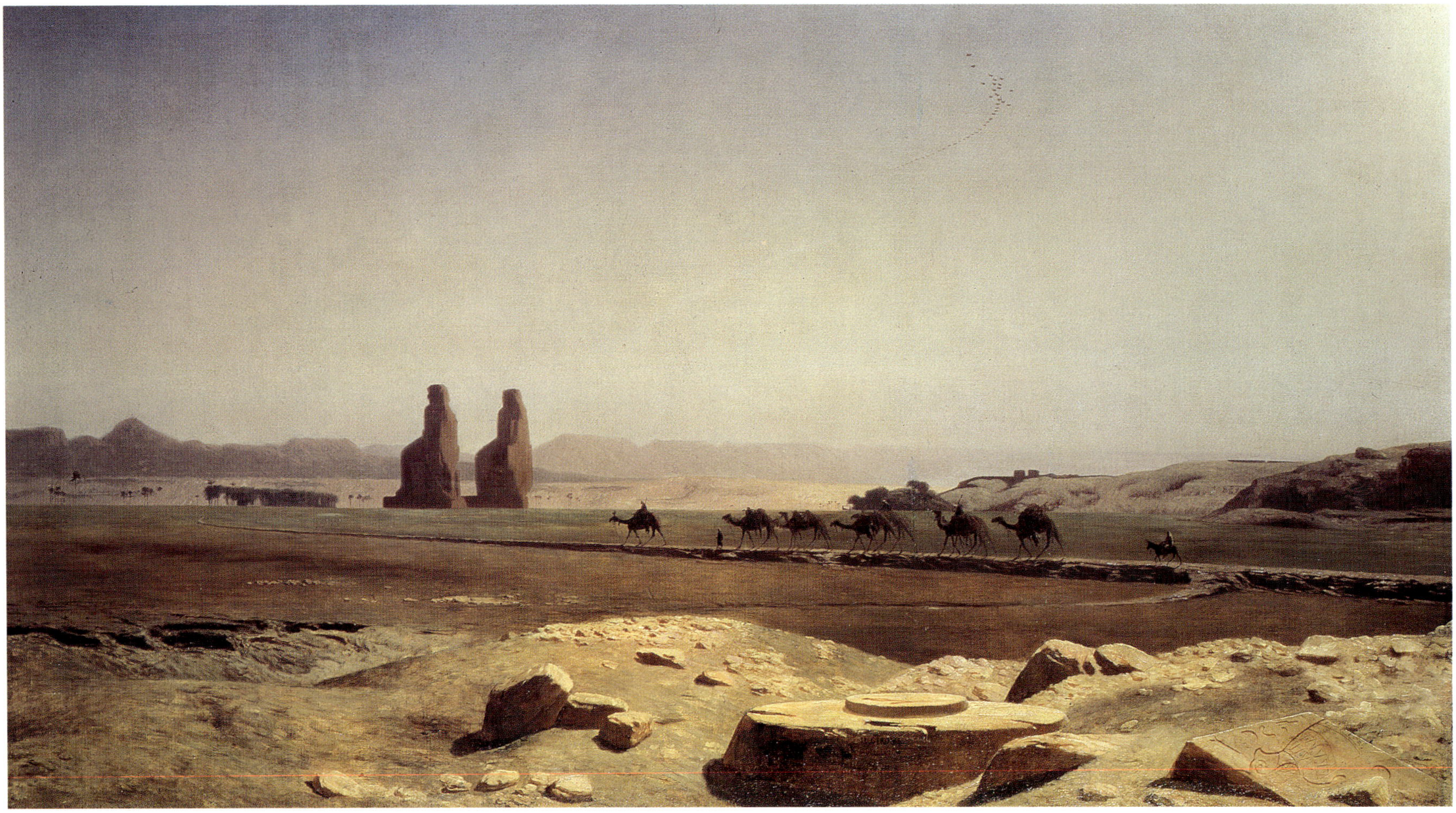

and Egypt again in 1874. After that, he renewed his acquaintance with the Ottoman world, Greece, and Egypt from 1879 to 1880. His growing interest in Ottoman Turkey can be seen in *The Great Bathhouse at Brousse*, *Saber Dance in a Coffee House* (1875), and a view of Constantinople. Narrowly Neo-classical and the sworn enemy of change (he loathed Manet and the Impressionists), bereft of originality, Gérôme nevertheless showed exceptional dexterity, faultless technique, and peerless visual precision. Though his compositions are cold, stilted, and devoid of genuine feeling or emotion, he had some uniquely successful moments, a good example being his small portrait *An Egyptian Girl*. His scrupulous technique and powers of observation can be seen in *Public Prayer in a Mosque* (1870) and *Arab with His Dog* (1877). He was not averse to taking his text from literary work, for example his *Pasha's Sorrow*, which is derived from Victor Hugo's poetry collection *Orientales*. In later years Gérôme occasionally painted works that combine an academic style with erotic subjects, the best-known being *The Slave Market* (1866). He also showed a fascination with public baths: *Steam*, *Harem Bathers* (1889), *The Great Bathhouse at Brousse* (1885), *Female Nude* (1889), and others. Famous throughout his career (he died in 1904), and wielding considerable influence over his many pupils, he was the archetypal academic painter, an artist whose Orientalism was a display of technical facility rather than the expression of an engaged imagination.

Above
A View of the Plain of Thebes in Upper Egypt,
Jean Léon Gérôme, 1857
Oil on canvas, 76 x 131 cm
(Musée des Beaux-Arts, Nantes).

Right
The Colossi of Thebes: Memnon and Sesostris,
Jean Léon Gérôme, 1857
Oil on canvas, 22 x 31 cm
(Musée Georges Garret, Vesoul).

Opposite
Moorish Bath, Jean Léon Gérôme, 1870
Oil on canvas, 51 x 41 cm
(Museum of Fine Arts, Boston).

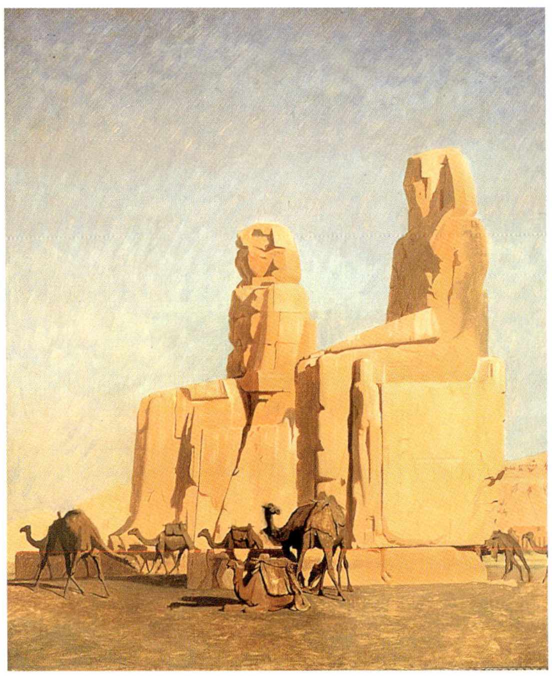

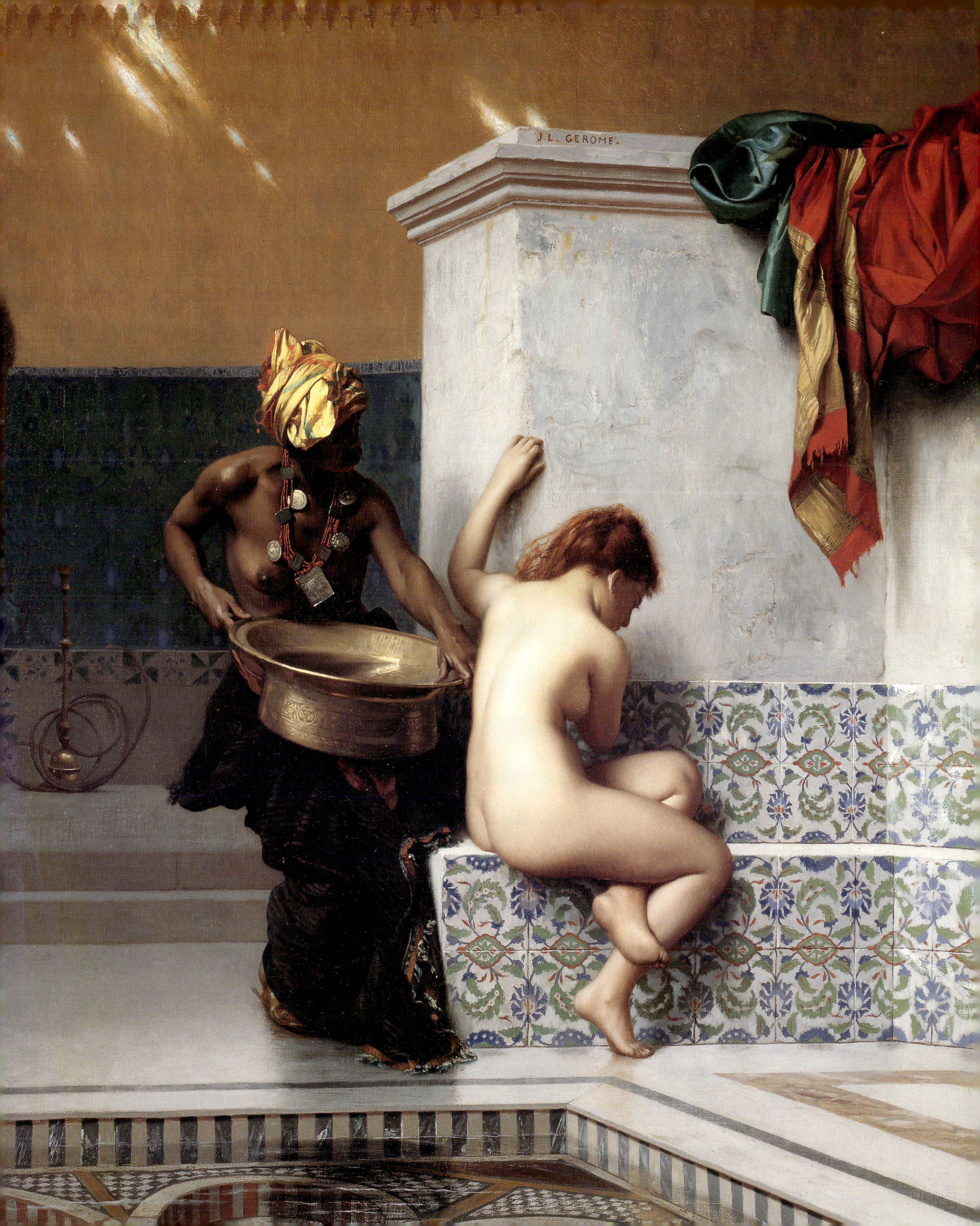
J.L. GEROME.

The Road to Isfahan

While the Mediterranean Middle East had throughout the 19th century been widely explored, written about, and painted, Persia remained remote and unvisited; artists rarely risked the long journey there. It was only by chance that the young French painter Jules Laurens found himself in this ancient world, which was almost closed to Western visitors. A student of Paul Delaroche, Laurens was unsuccessful when he entered for the Prix de Rome, but he was fortunate enough to make the acquaintance of the geographer Xavier Hommaire de Hell; after an improbable interview, the latter appointed him to join his expedition to Persia. So, in 1846, he set off on the long and arduous journey that took him right across Europe and Turkey, to Persia. He stayed until 1849, when Hommaire de Hell was struck by cholera. The years spent in this kingdom of a bygone age were very productive: he made a phenomenal number of drawings, 300 of which are now kept at the École des Beaux-Arts, in Paris. He lived for a long time in Semnan, in the desert region of Khorasan, and was particularly fascinated by the Fet Ali Shah mosque, a Quajar building that has turrets in colored bricks, and is decorated with enameled terracotta. So strong were the impressions that remained with him after his odyssey in *terra incognita* that, once back in Paris, he would constantly return to his drawings as an inspiration for paintings.

In 1863 he showed a canvas inspired by the fortified village of Laguir. Upon discovering the village he had written to his brother, Bonaventure: "Imagine an adobe construction the form and shape of the Nîmes Arena or thereabouts and covered with two external stories; and, inside, terraces of houses. Today, time has given these Babel-sized masses all the traits of the wildest of rocks (...) what it encloses by ways of rubble, garbage, tatters, and cries could be described only by the pen that wrote the wondrous chapter on the *cour des miracles* [a passage in Victor Hugo's novel *Notre Dame de Paris*]."

He was a contributor to the album *Voyage en Turquie et en Perse, 1854–1860* (A journey to Turkey and Persia, 1854–1860) and regularly exhibited at the Paris Salon; his *Roman Road in Bithynia* was accepted in 1864. He was deeply affected by a fire he witnessed when he first arrived in Kashan, and was obsessed with the idea of painting his *Sodom Ablaze*. Teheran's ancient brick quarries and all his archaeological memories combined to provide a striking backdrop to this biblical drama, which can unquestionably be seen to be his most intriguing work.

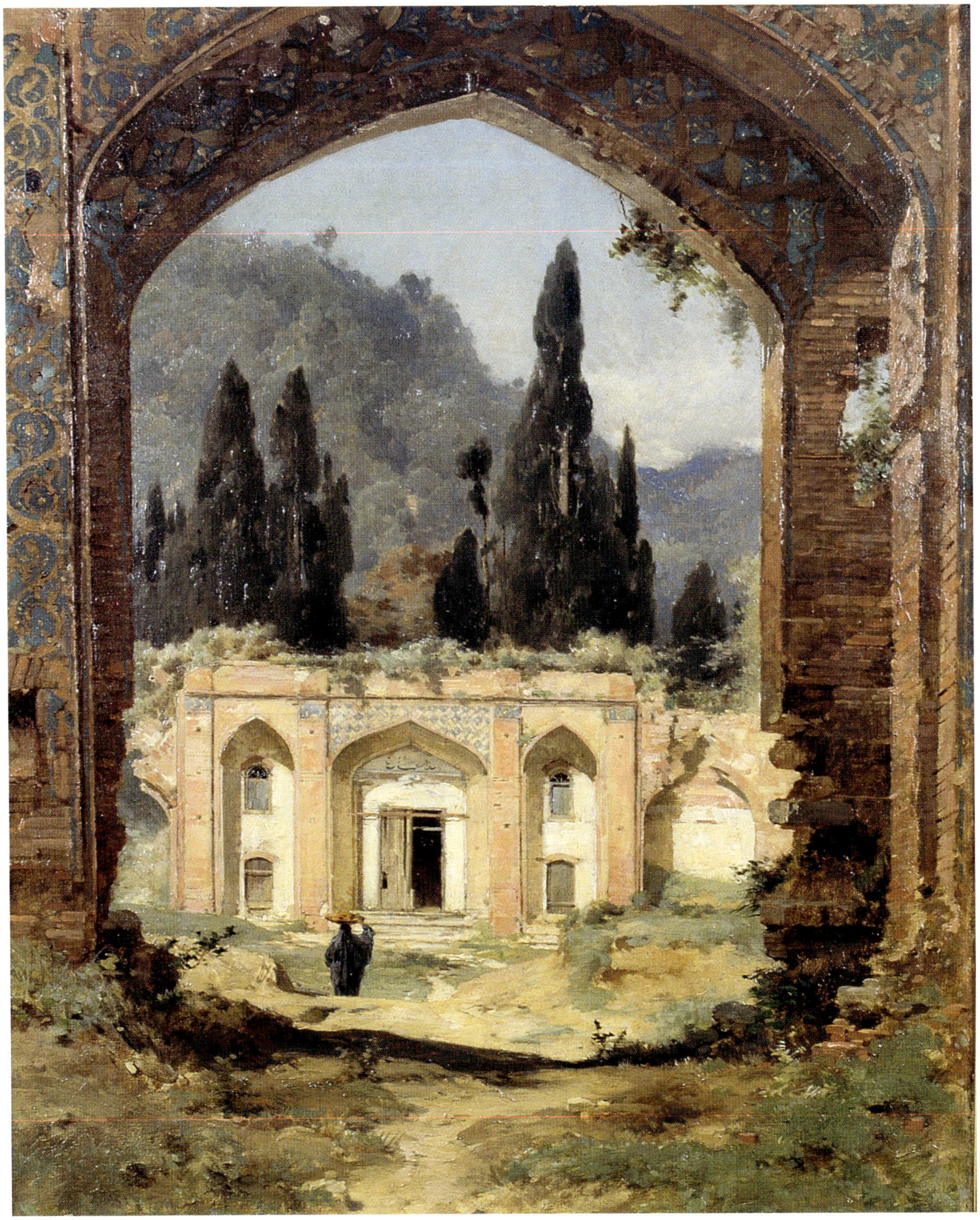

Left
Ruins of the Palace of Asraf,
Jules Laurens, undated.
Oil on canvas, 65 x 55 cm
(Bibliothèque Inguimbertine, Carpentras).

Vann's Rock (Kurdistan),
Jules Laurens, 1880
Oil on canvas, 134 x 88 cm
(Musée d'Orsay, Paris).

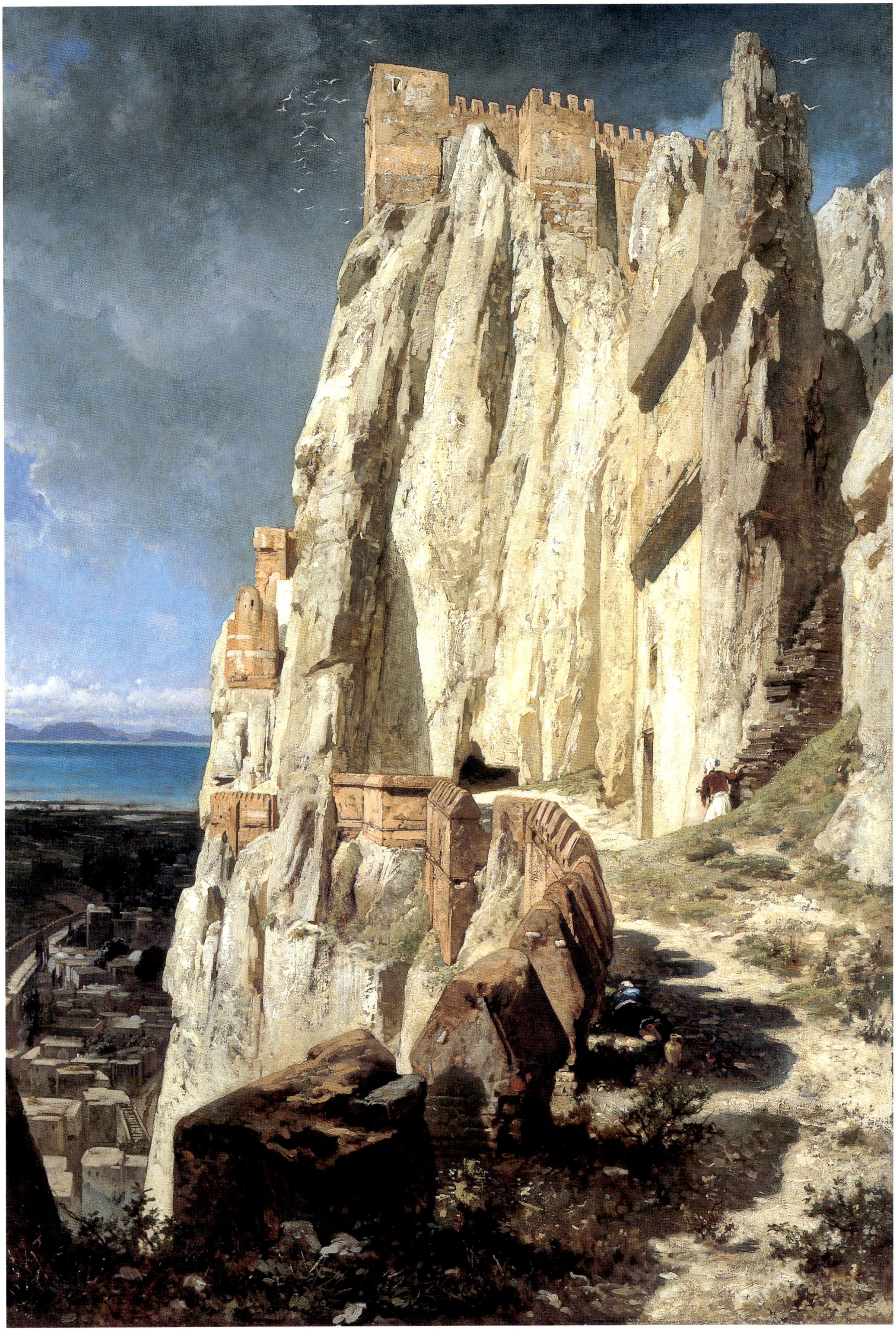

Palace of the French Mission in Teheran (Persia), Jules Laurens, between 1846 and 1849
Drawing and watercolor, 50 x 32 cm
(A. Gharagozlou Collection).

Harem Interior in Teheran (Persia), Jules Laurens, 1848
Drawing and watercolor, 44 x 34 cm
(A. Gharagozlou Collection).

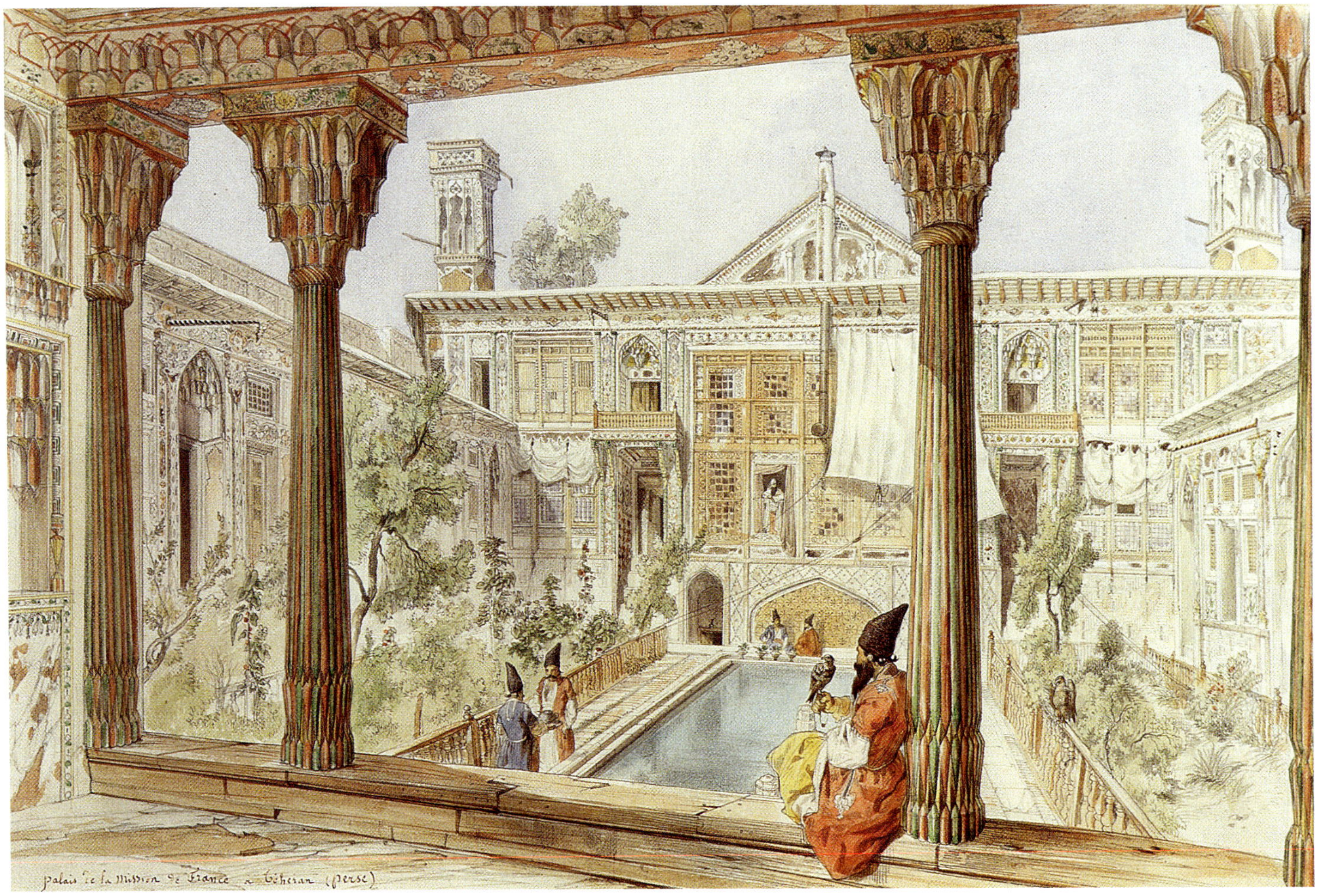

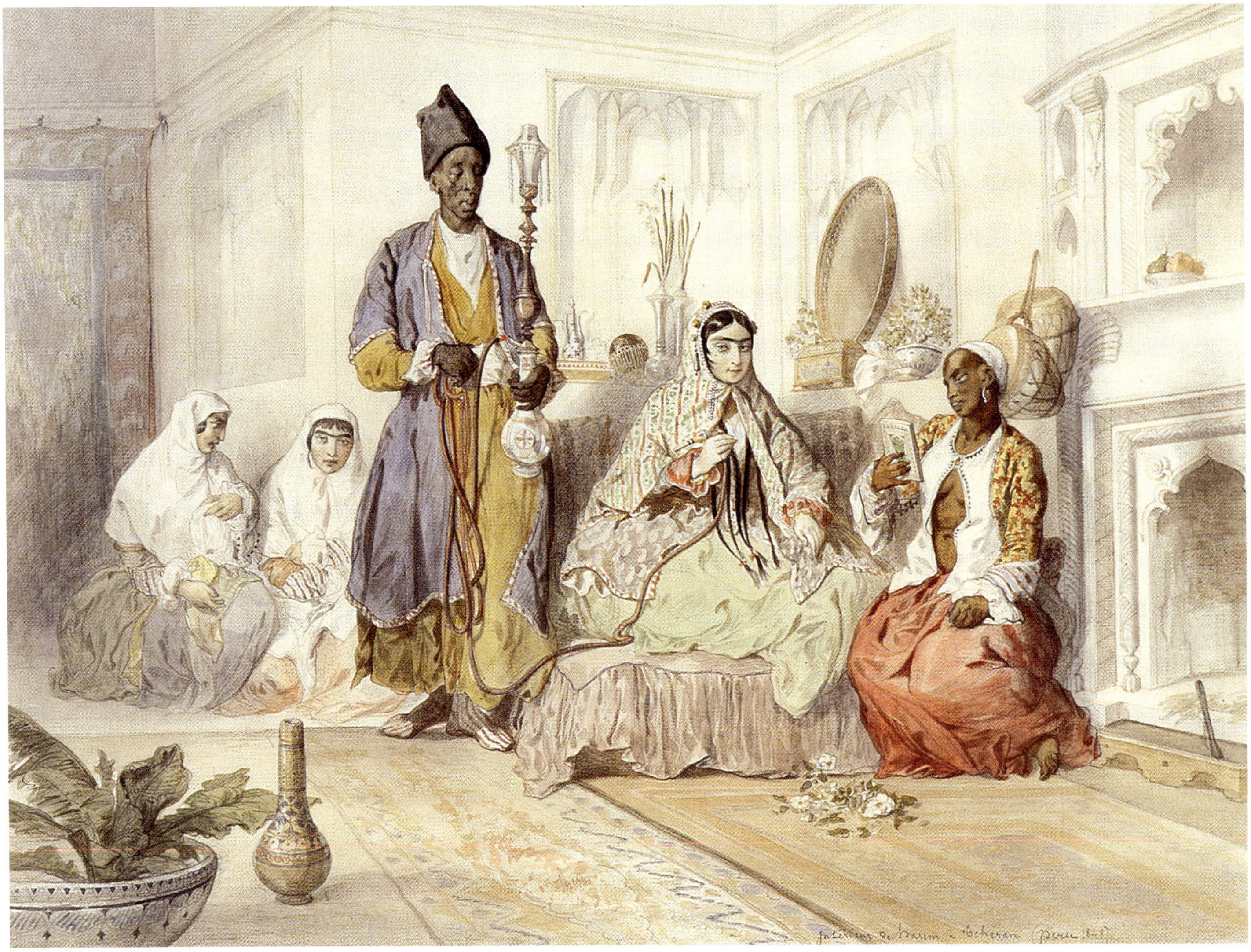

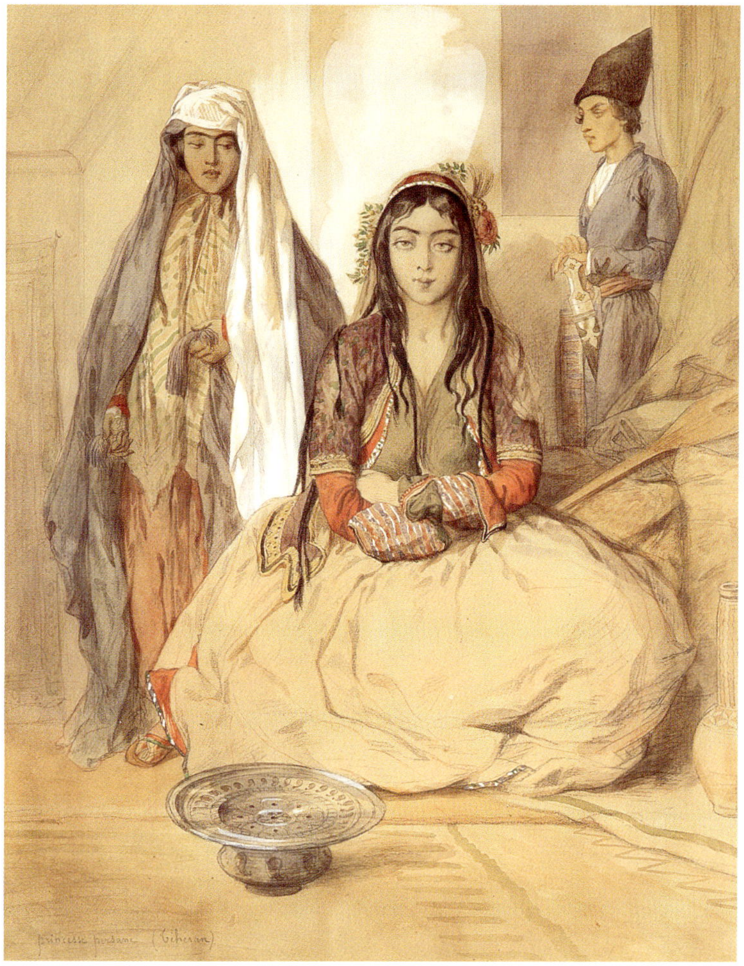

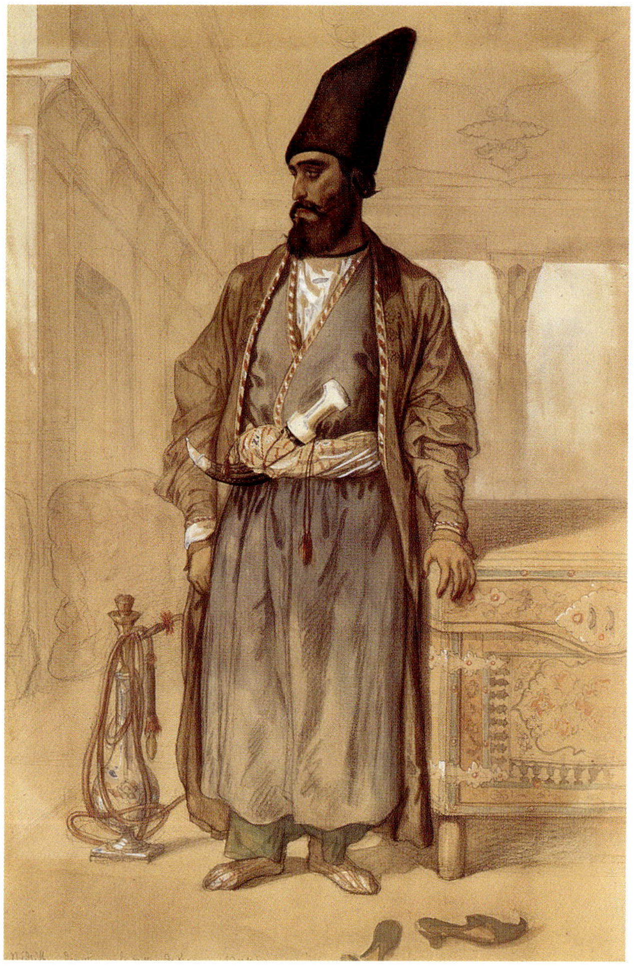

Far left
Persian Princess (Teheran),
Jules Laurens, between 1846 and 1849
Drawing and watercolor,
37 x 30 cm
(A. Gharagozlou Collection).

Left
Nedjeff, Manservant at the French Mission,
Jules Laurens, between 1846 and 1849
Drawing and watercolor,
30 x 42 cm
(A. Gharagozlou Collection).

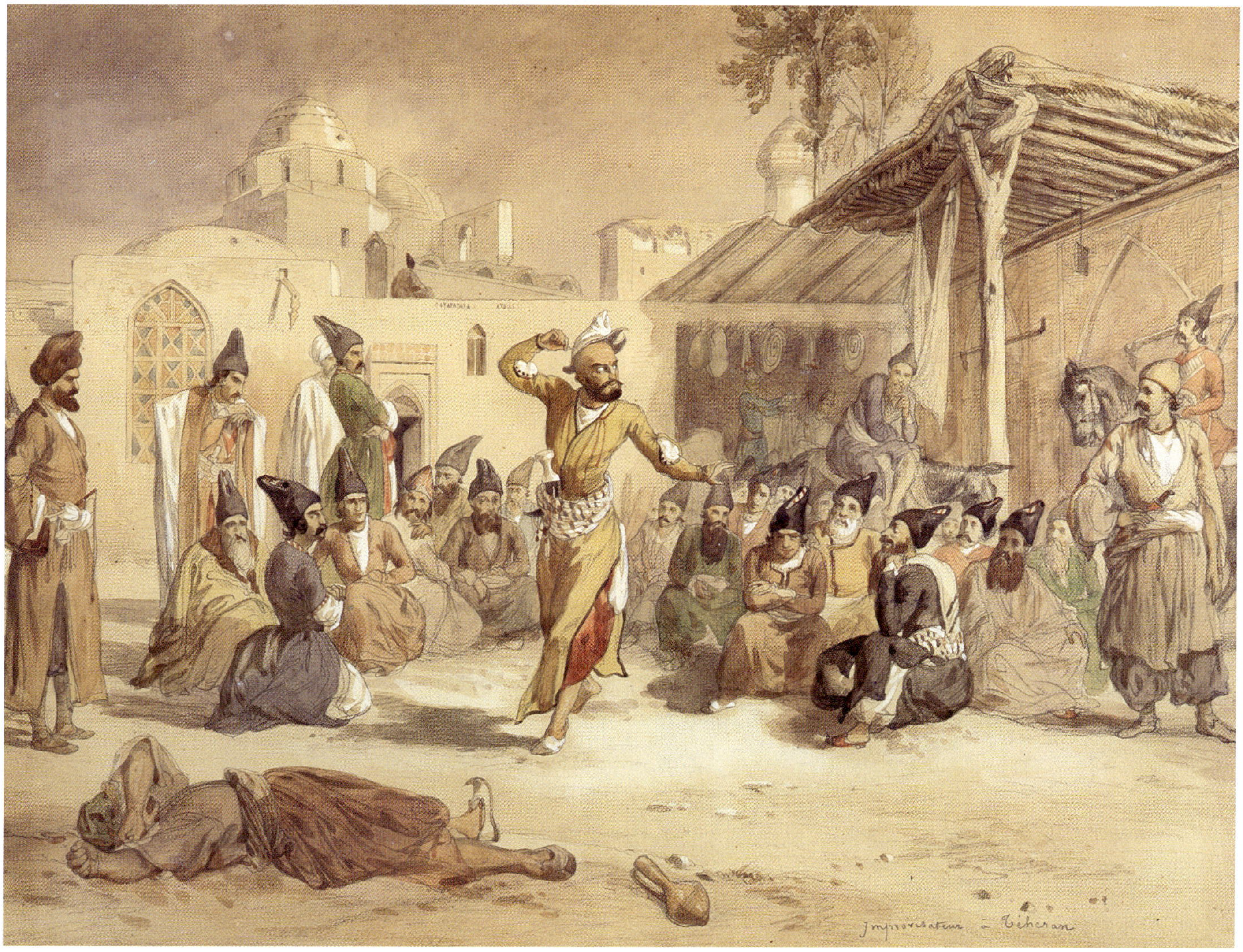

Bottom
Dragoman in Teheran, Jules Laurens, between 1846 and 1849
Drawing and watercolor,
35 x 28 cm
(A. Gharagozlou Collection).

Félix Ziem

Félix Ziem, the son of a Polish immigrant, worked first as a clerk of the works in Marseilles. Finding that he could sell his drawings successfully, he opened an art school and later settled in Nice. He went on his first journey in 1843, accepting an invitation from Prince Gagarin to join him in his Novaseliza Palace in Russia. Ziem spent nine months in St. Petersburg in 1844 and did several paintings of Russian landscapes in 1846. After the death of his mistress, that same year, he settled in Florence; from there he went to Venice, which made a profound impression on him. Over the years, he painted a large number of works in which he sought, like Turner, to capture the mists and the enchanting light of the City on the Lagoon. For Ziem, Venice was the gateway to the exotic: "The Orient is Venice."

In 1847, still traveling, he stayed in Naples, taking in Herculanum and Pompeii before visiting Sicily and Rome. He stayed in Paris for several months and then set off for Holland, but he was still drawn to Venice and returned there for the month of October. After visiting London and Edinburgh, he returned to Holland (1853). In 1854 he embarked for Egypt and discovered Tunisia in 1855.

The desire to travel never left him. In his diary on 25 January 1855 he wrote: "I am increasingly thinking of traveling again, to refresh what I know by new studies taken from life, but to where?" A few months later, on 7 May, he noted: "I have in mind a trip to Constantinople. Why? I know that talent can grow and be developed without resorting to this inspirational frenzy that traveling produces at every turn. But an irresistible force always urges me on, in the belief that new horizons will provide more quickly and more clearly the key to the mystery I crave to solve."

On 10 July 1856, he set sail down the Danube bound for Constantinople; he stayed there for six weeks then moved on to Egypt via Smyrna, Alexandretta, and Rhodes. From 8 October to 20 November 1856 he traveled around Egypt, which

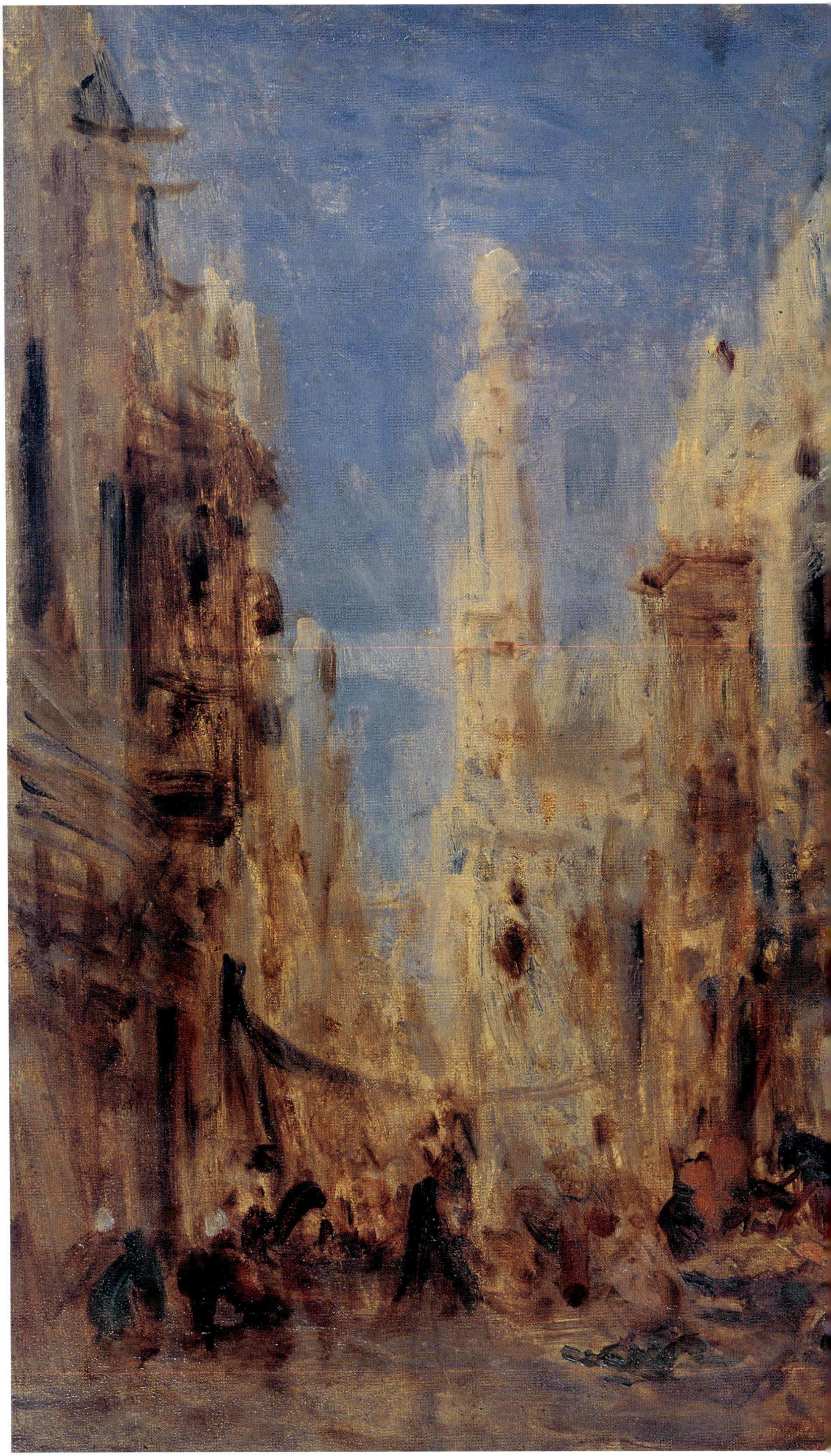

inspired fiery, almost unreal visions of twilight. At the 1857 Salon, he took the opportunity to show such paintings as *Venice Under Water* and *Constantinople: The Golden Horn*, which were praised by Gautier: "Monsieur Ziem painted the Golden Horn, an unrivaled sight, the most beautiful in the world… Shapes are of secondary importance to the luminous flaring of colors, the exuberant play of the brush." Gautier identified the essence of the painter's originality: a vaporous mist charged with gold or diaphanous colors, and a spirited, light-hearted, quirky treatment that produced vivacious compositions.

From then on, Ziem concentrated on two broad subjects: Venice, of which he never tired and which he painted in a range of styles; and the Middle East. He particularly loved Cairo, which he often sketched, but also other Egyptian cities, for example Damanhour: *Damanhour, Sunset* was shown at the 1859 Salon. Gautier said that it was "an inferno, that canvas. It glows, it blazes, it dazzles and almost forces you to avert your eyes." Ziem also found time for the capital city of the Ottoman Empire, painting a great many views of the Bosporus and the Golden Horn. He would combine seascapes with great ships at anchor, caiques, wharves, harbors, bridges, the region's famous landmarks, and views of the city. *Constantinople, Entrance of the Sweet Waters of Europe* was shown at the 1859 Salon; he also painted *The Mosque at Scurati* and genre scenes, such as *Oriental Dancer*.

Ziem visited Algeria in 1858 and produced several paintings showing, indeed glorifying, the city of Algiers: *Algiers* (1858); Old Street, Algiers (1870); *Market, Algiers* (1858). He would say of one of them: "The whole of Algiers is there, its temperament, its very nature. But this charm, this *je ne sais quoi* of which you dream, does not exist…" As a rule Ziem endeavored to recreate as accurately as possible the rich and varied spectacles he was fortunate enough to witness on his constant travels. It is the light, its gleam, its fast and ever-changing touch, which spurred him on to create, though his

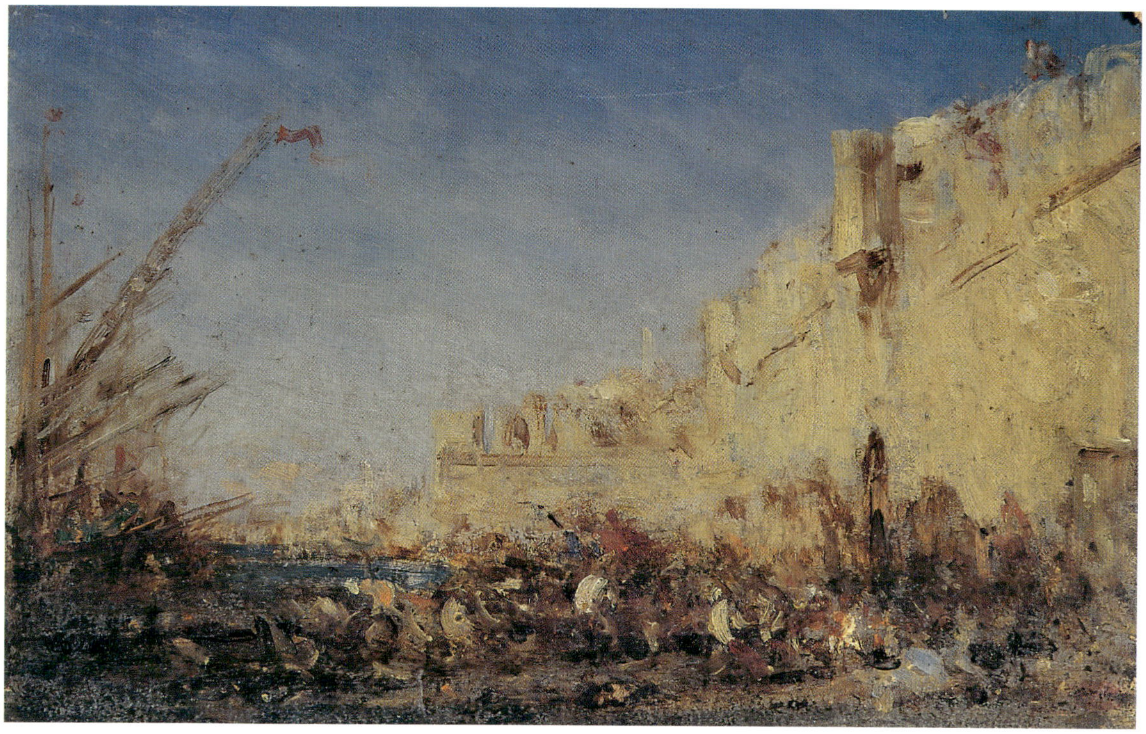

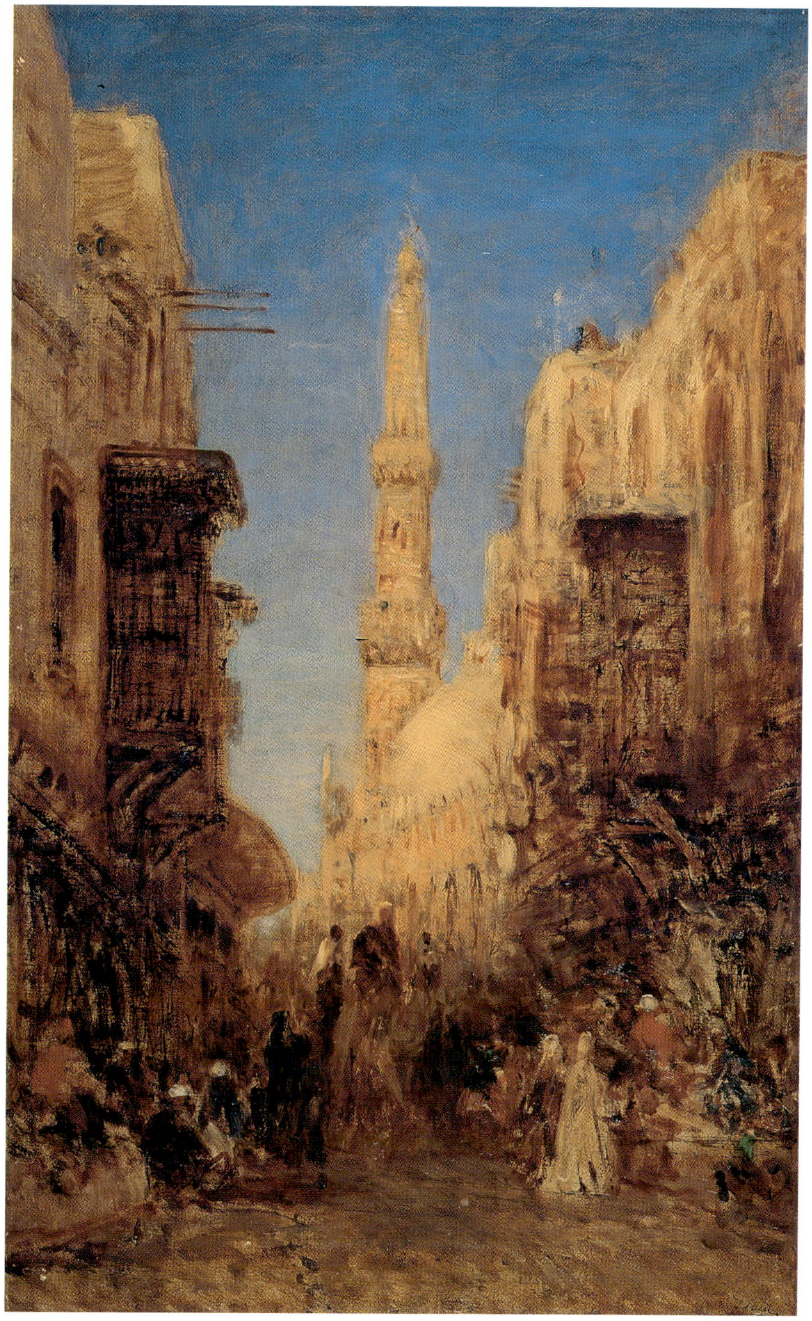

Above
The Ramparts, Algiers,
Félix Ziem, between 1860 and 1870
Oil on card, 28 x 44 cm
(Musée Ziem, Martigues).

Right
Street in Old Cairo, Félix Ziem, undated.
Oil on canvas, 112 x 68.5 cm
(Musée du Petit Palais, Paris).

Opposite
Cairo Street, Félix Ziem, 1856–1860
Oil on card, 62 x 36 cm
(Musée Ziem, Martigues).

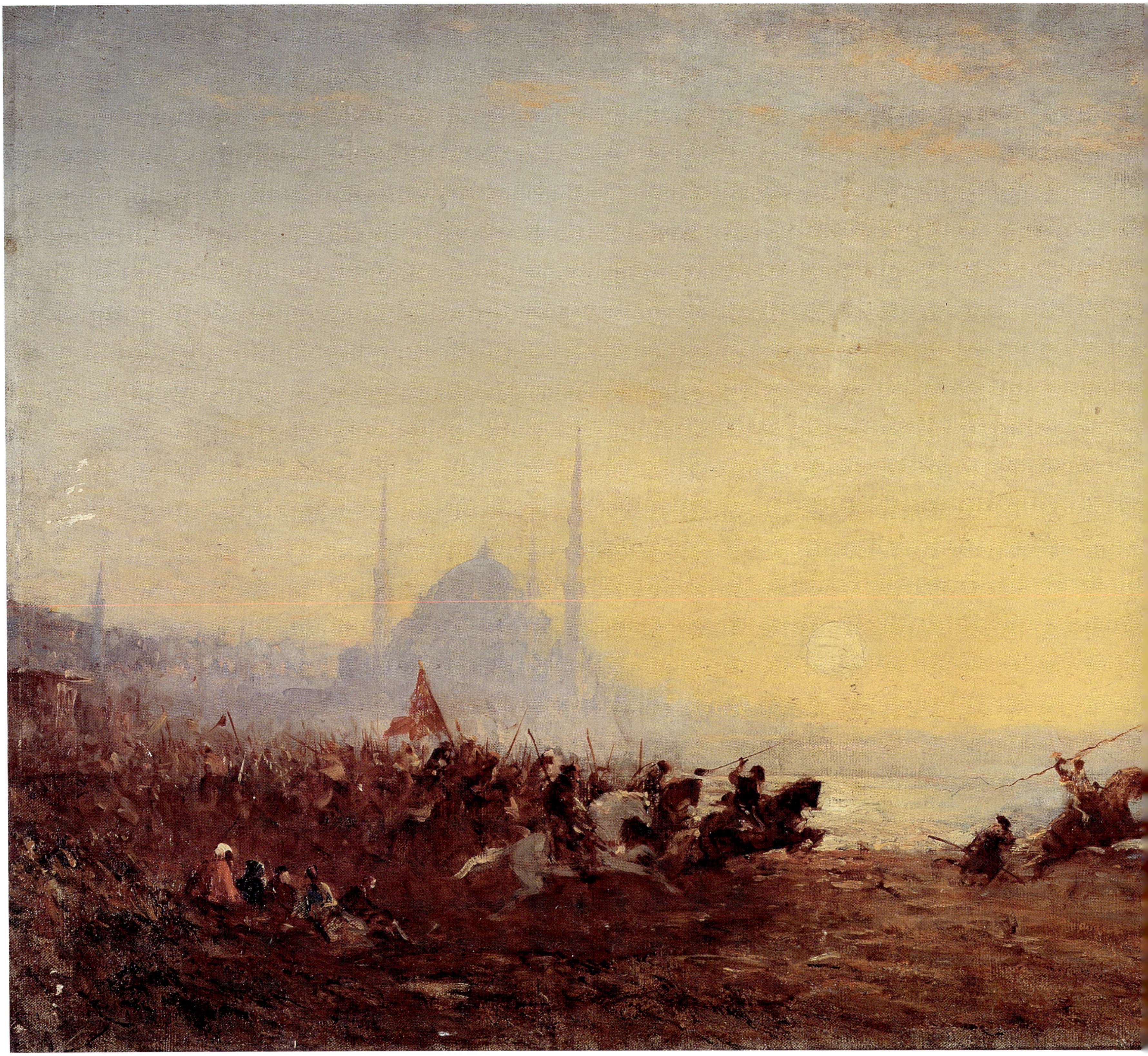

Constantinople, Fantasy, Félix Ziem, undated.
Oil on canvas, 68 x 117.5 cm
(Musée du Petit Palais, Paris).

concern was essentially with form rather than appearance. He occasionally gave free rein to his imagination, as can be seen in the remarkable *Fantasy on the Banks of the Bosporus* (1874) and *Constantinople, Fantasy* (1890, 1900). Anxious never to work to a formula, Ziem showed throughout his career an astonishing ability to question both his technique and his style, so that he often depicted the same scene in two very different ways. He kept abreast of the revolution that rocked the French artistic world in the second half of the 19th century, not championing its cause but not rejecting its premises either.

The Ramparts, Algiers, Félix Ziem, 1858
Oil on wood, 11 x 15 cm
(Musée Ziem, Martigues).

Oriental Dancer, Félix Ziem,
between 1880 and 1890
Oil on wood, 54 x 80 cm
(Musée Ziem, Martigues).

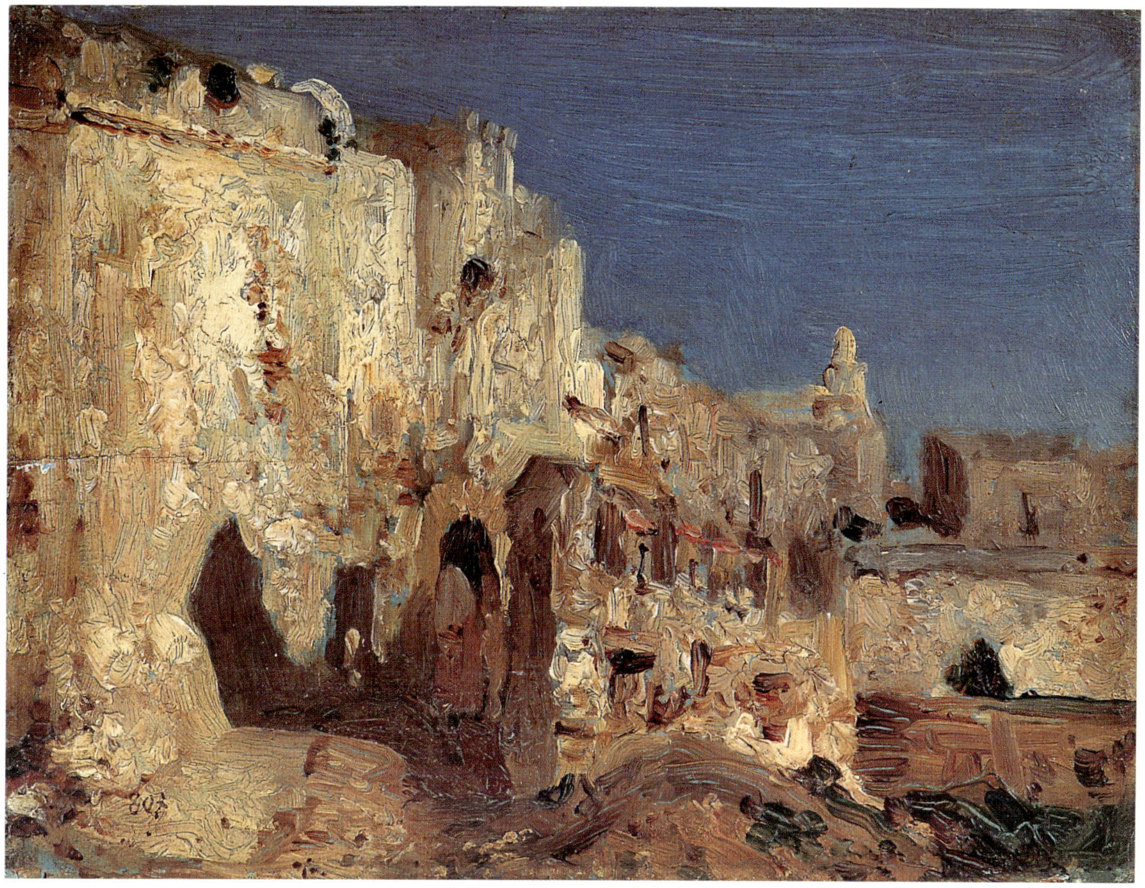

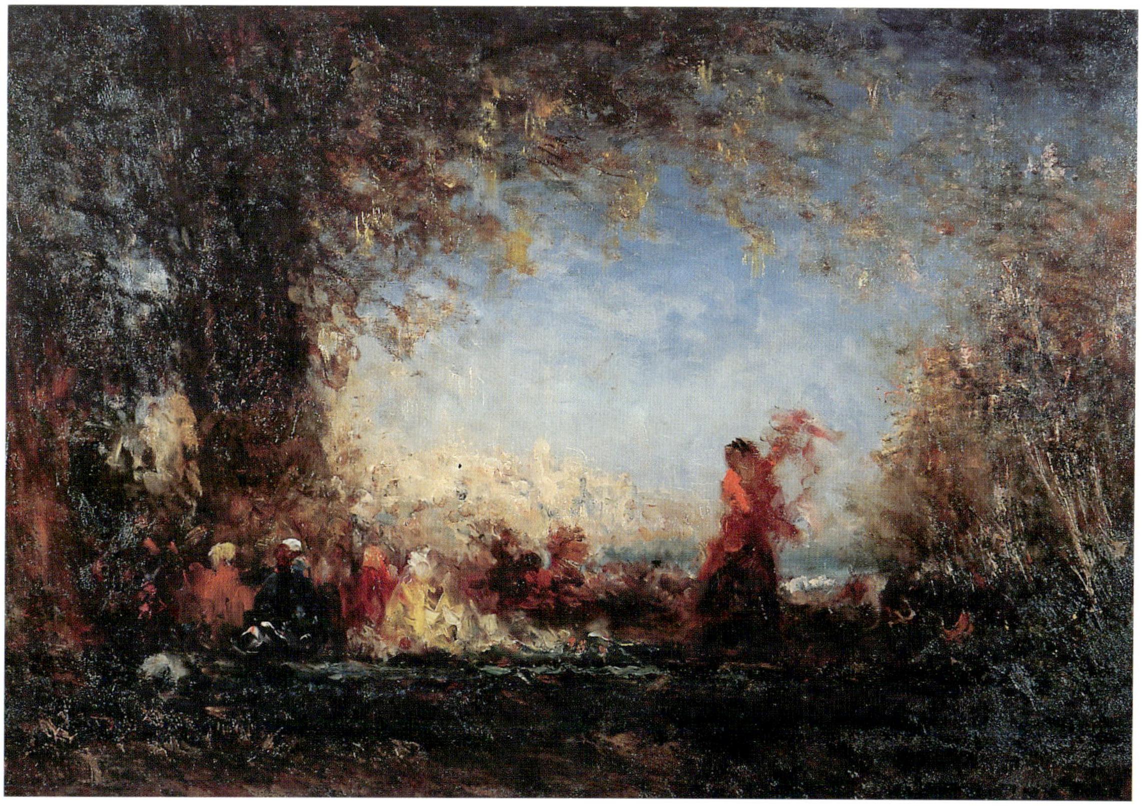

Gustave Moreau

The French artist Gustave Moreau brought a new and highly personal dimension to Orientalism. Having started his career with a thorough review – and reinvention – of classical mythology, crowding his paintings with chimeras and muses, he came to the Orient through his fascination with Salome. Seductive and dangerous, Salome, who had danced before Herod in order to obtain the head of John the Baptist, fully occupied Moreau from 1875 to 1876. He began a remarkable cycle of works with *Salome in Prison*, in which the youthful beauty leans pensively against an enormous column in the darkness of a lugubrious chamber. He painted three versions of *The Apparition*, the watercolor version being shown at the 1876 Salon. He gave these three images of the *femme fatale* an entirely personal sense of the Orient by depicting Salome tattooed, and by adding fantastical architectural details and a huge throne. The naked young woman in the king's enchanted palace, a palace that at times appears to be a temple, has stopped dancing, her arm now raised in the direction of the martyr's head shown floating at the center of the composition in a gleaming circle of light; she seems to be gazing intently into the Baptist's eyes. There are no witnesses to this vision apart from the executioner, who stands motionless and spectral near the throne.

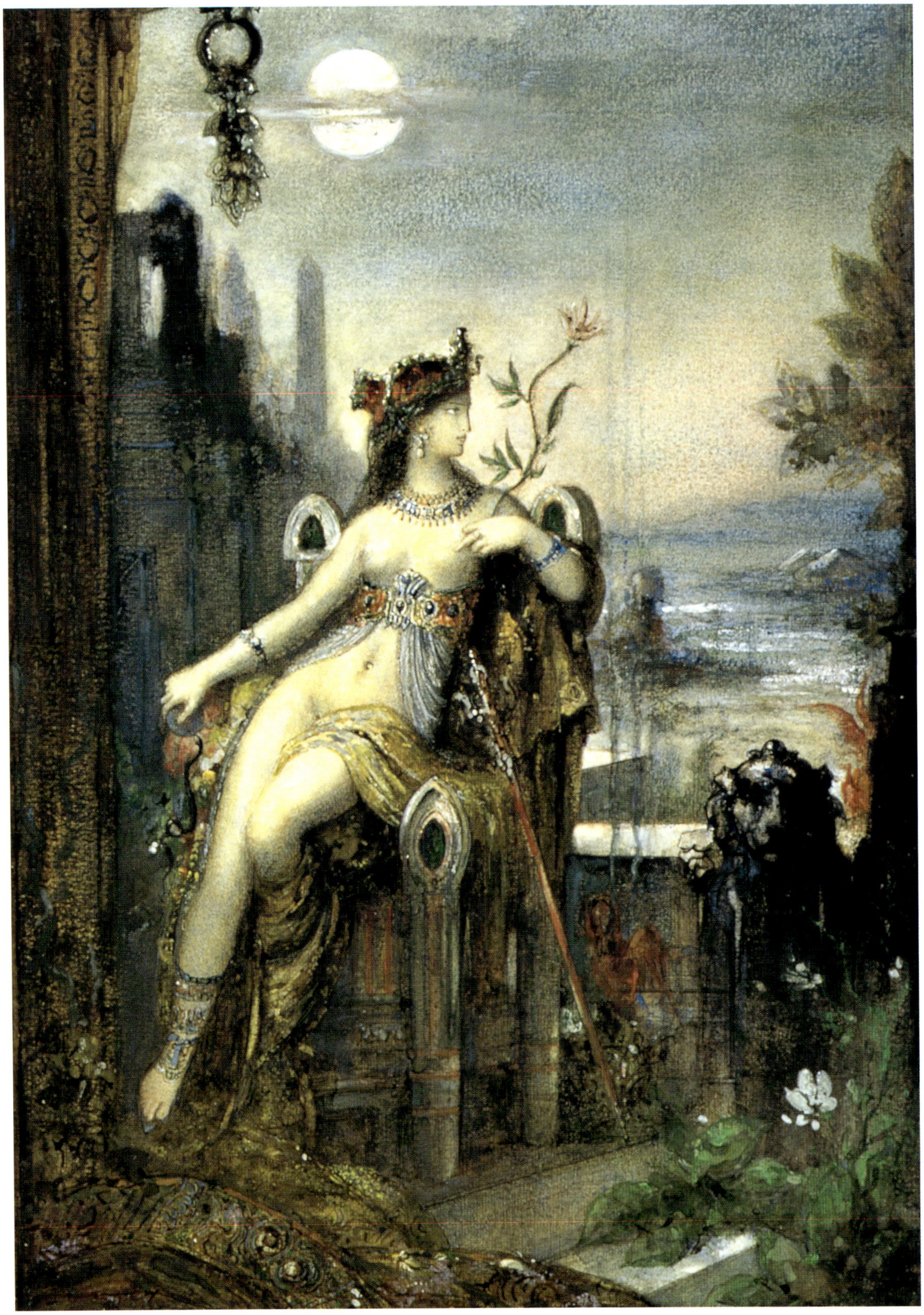

In 1878 Moreau painted a last watercolor and gouache of his beguiling heroine: *Salome in the Garden*. Here, she walks absentmindedly in front of an area of foliage, carrying the Baptist's severed head on a platter. She is walking as in a trance, her eyes almost closed. Moreau spelt out how he envisaged this tragic moment: "This woman represents the eternal feminine, a delicate bird, often deadly, who walks through life with a flower in her hand in search of some vague, often dreadful ideal; walking, always, and trampling underfoot even geniuses and saints. Her dance is performed, her mysterious dance conducted in the face of Death, who watches her incessantly, yawning and intent, and before the executioner of the striking sword. She is the emblem of the awesome future reserved for the seekers of nameless ideals, of sensuality, of lasciviousness. A saint and a severed head are at the end of a road strewn with flowers. It all takes place in a mysterious sanctuary conducive to gravity and the contemplation of higher things." In these works the New Testament is forgotten in favor of a personal vision of the prophet's execution, a dark vision that sees life as a clash of wills and ideals, as a conflict in which protagonists are

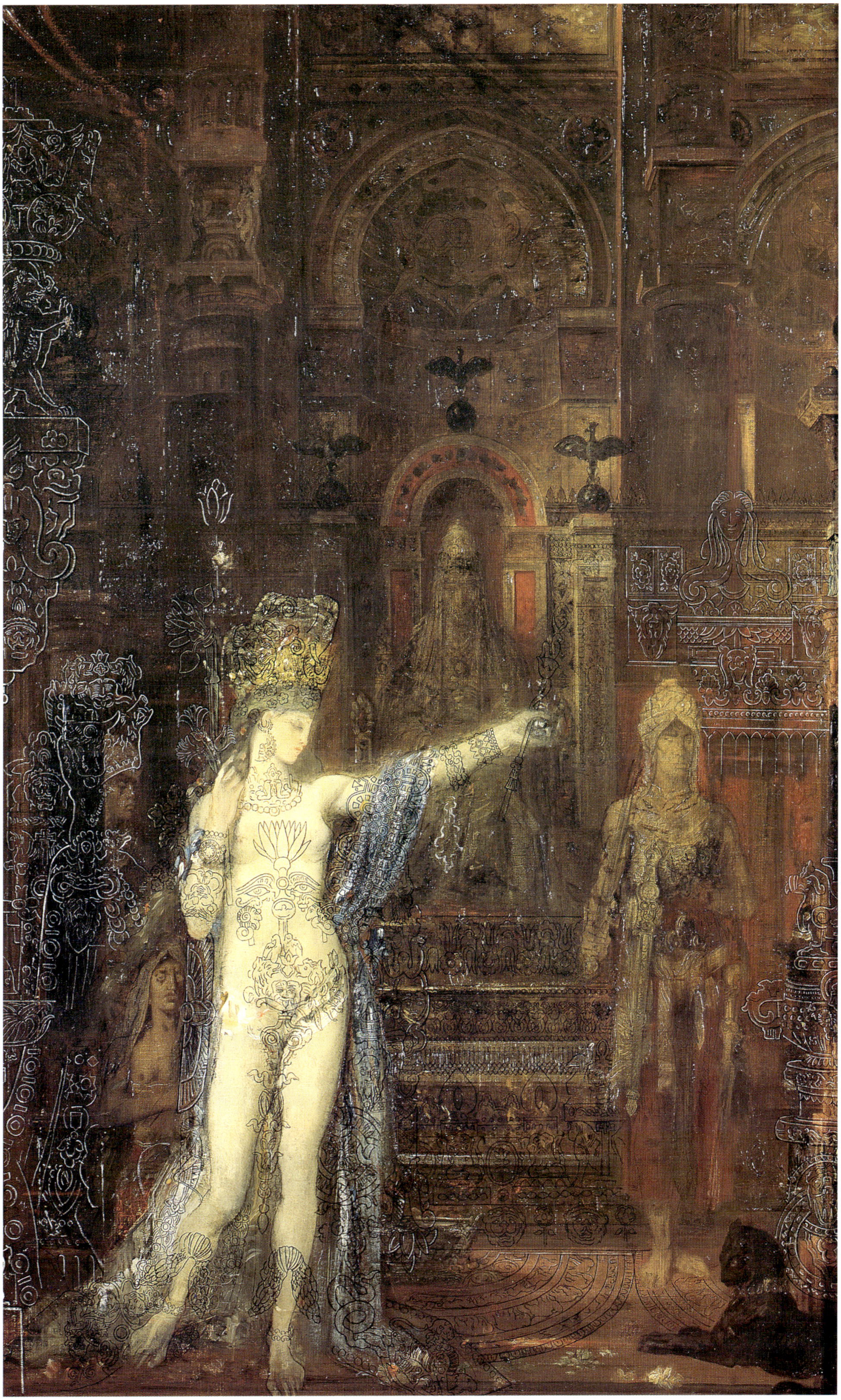

Opposite
Cleopatra, Gustave Moreau, c. 1887
Watercolor with gouache highlights,
40 x 25 cm (Musée du Louvre,
Département des Arts Graphiques,
Paris).

Salome Dancing (or *Tattooed Salome*),
Gustave Moreau, c. 1876
Oil on canvas, 90 x 60 cm
(Musée Gustave Moreau, Paris).

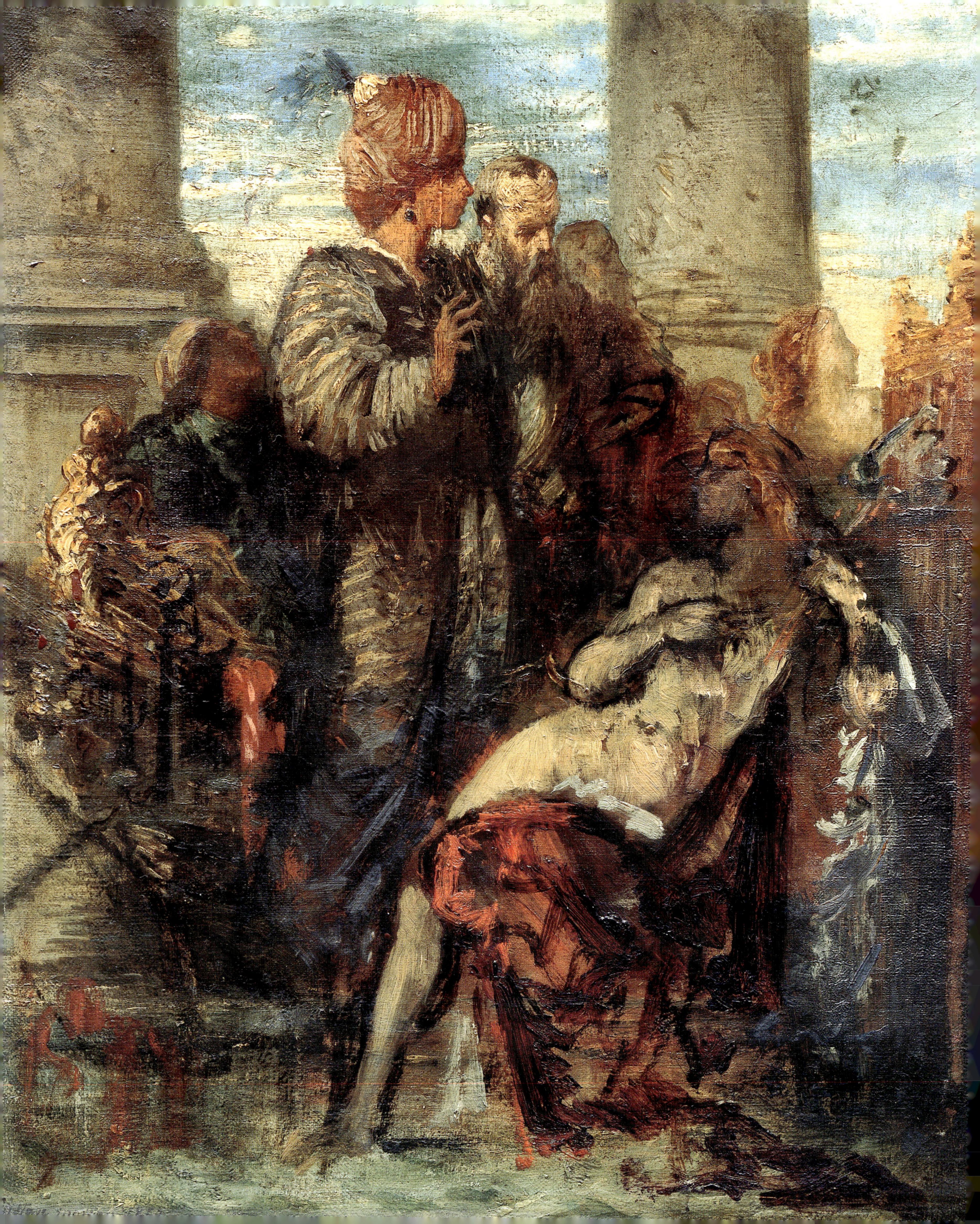

inextricably locked in a dance of death. His superb and evil Salome, amoral yet proud in her unrepentant vice, is another in the long line of mythical women created to satisfy male fantasies: Galatea, Helen, Semele, Andromeda, Leda, Aphrodite, Sappho, Deianeira, Messalina... The same type is behind Moreau's *Bethsheba* (c. 1886), and also his interest in Delilah, who obsessed him from 1882 to 1885, Salome's double – her irresistible beauty will cause the downfall of the man who trusts her.

In his evocation of Cleopatra, Moreau eschewed all visible signs of Ptolemaic Egypt, choosing to set her in a totally unreal world. Similarly, the figure of Suzanna in *Suzanna and the Elders* (1897) is alone in a palace that is a temple, almost naked (like all his heroines), and sublimely beautiful. All she wears is a tiara – as do Cleopatra, Salome, and the other women who haunt Moreau's imagination.

Moreau's only painting with an Oriental setting that at least draws on some traditional elements is *The Finding of Moses* (1878). Here he has set Egyptian ruins on both sides of the Nile – though they have little to do with archaeological reality – and put a sphinx on top of an imagined building. Though its poetic impact cannot be denied, his Egypt is a fantasy. For Moreau: "This civilization, with its mummies, sphinxes, fixed looks, and still eyes" is the very opposite of that represented by the Child Moses, "this fine human fruit brimming with life."

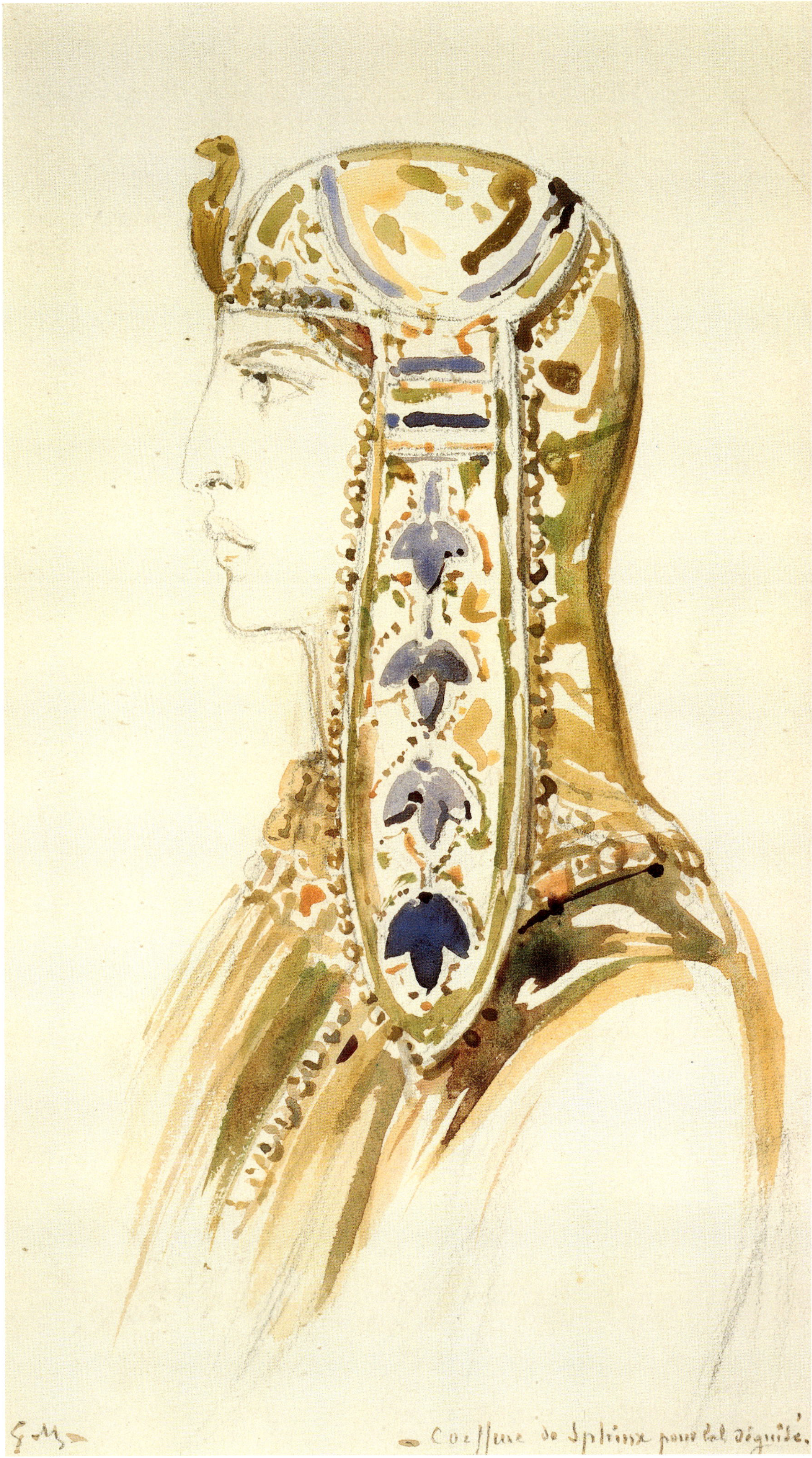

Opposite
Sultana, Gustave Moreau, c. 1850
Oil on canvas, 40.5 x 32 cm
(Musée Gustave Moreau, Paris).

Sphinx Headdress for a Masked Ball,
Gustave Moreau, 1879
Watercolor, 26 x 15 cm
(Musée Gustave Moreau, Paris).

Orientalism and the Impressionists

The Batignolles school, later better known as the Impressionists because of a jibe at Monet's *Impression, Sunrise*, had its beginnings in the quiet Café Guerbois in Paris. There Édouard Manet, Claude Monet, Auguste Renoir, Camille Pissaro, Alfred Sisley, sometimes Paul Cézanne, Émile Zola, and Théodore Duret, would meet to talk about art and life. It was even possible to find in their ranks a minor Orientalist painter, Tobar. But there was little talk of setting sail for far-flung lands. At the Salon, Manet's sworn enemy was Gérôme, the most famous Orientalist of the day. No, these young artists had two concerns: with modern urban life, and with nature shown at its simplest and most enticing. The advent of a new aesthetic concept, *japonisme*; a determination to reject a grim and narrowly defined realism; and a new focus on the city and contemporary life – all these ambitions drove these young artists away from Orientalism.

Édouard Manet, who was a dedicated admirer of Delacroix – among his early works is a copy of Delacroix's *The Barque of Dante* – did not travel to Morocco after him. He chose Spain, which he visited once in 1865, and where he took a special interest in dance and the bullfight. His sole concession to the mystique of the Orient, at a time when France

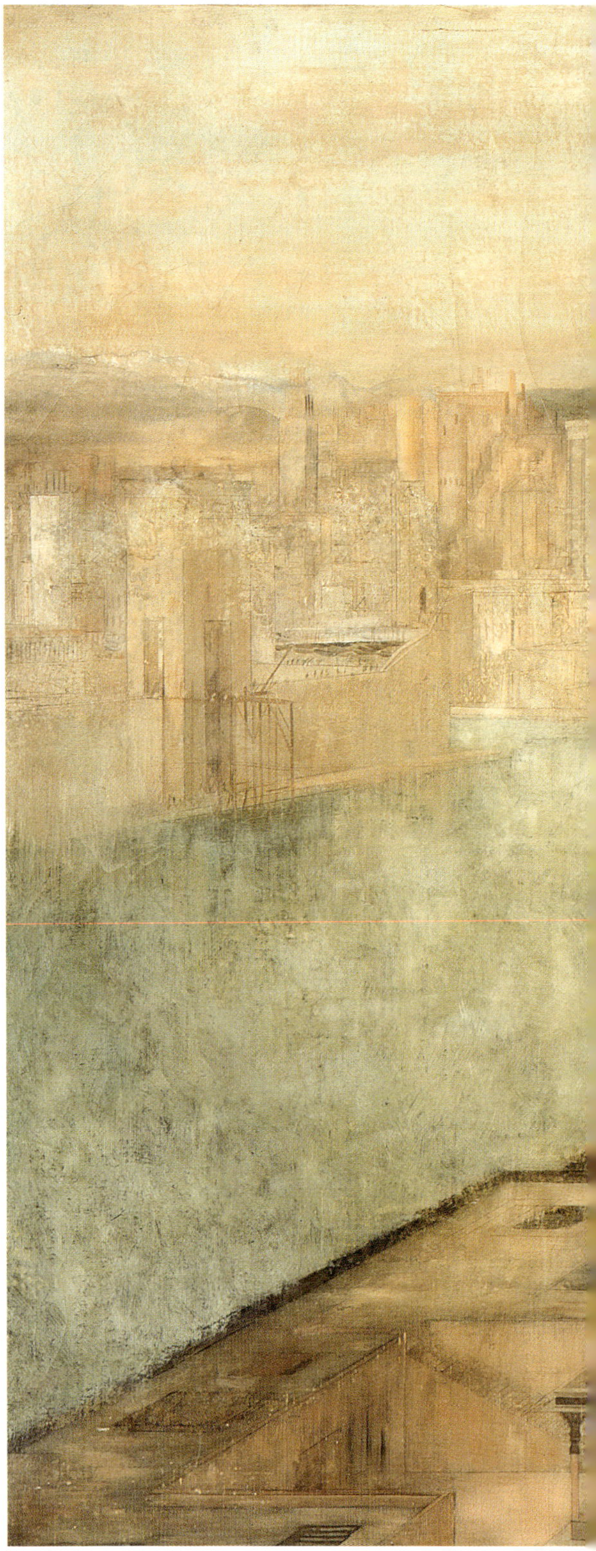

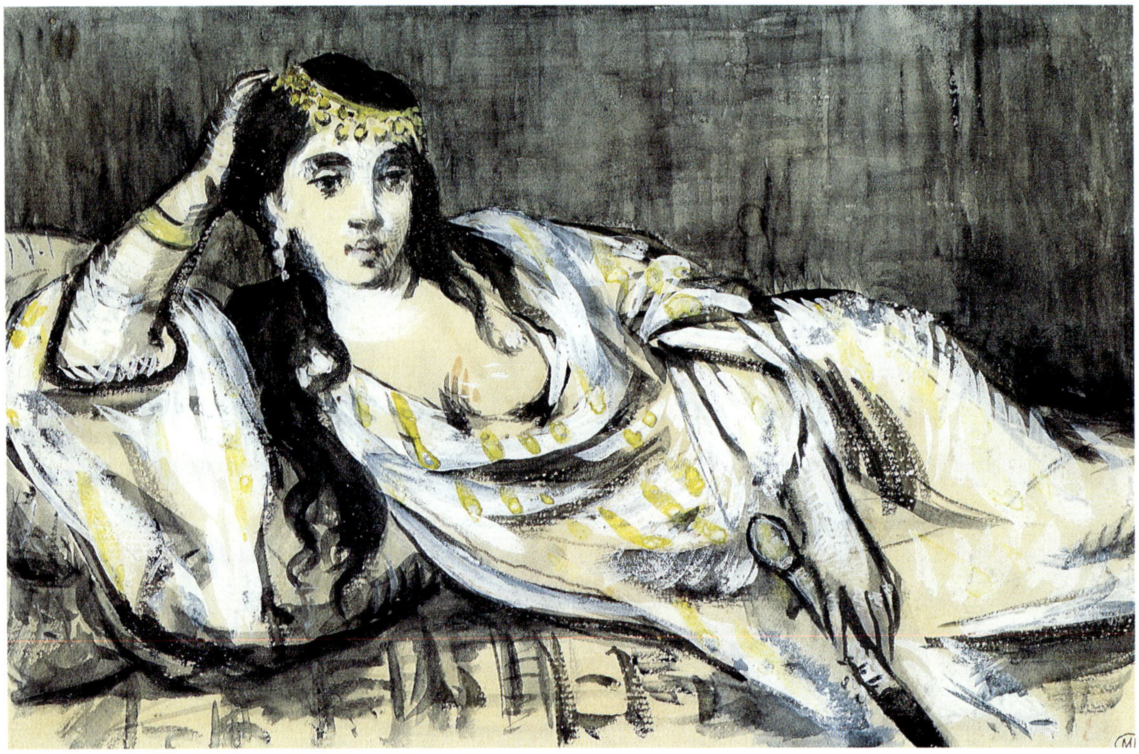

Odalisque, Édouard Manet, between 1862 and 1866
Watercolor, Indian ink, gouache highlights, 13 x 20 cm
(Musée du Louvre, Orsay Collection, Paris).

Above
Semiramis Building Babylon, Edgar Degas, c. 1861
Oil on canvas, 151 x 258 cm
(Musée d'Orsay, Paris).

Following pages
Odalisque (or Algerian Woman), Auguste Renoir, 1870
Oil on canvas, 69.2 x 122.6 cm
(National Gallery of Art, Chester Dale Collection, Washington).

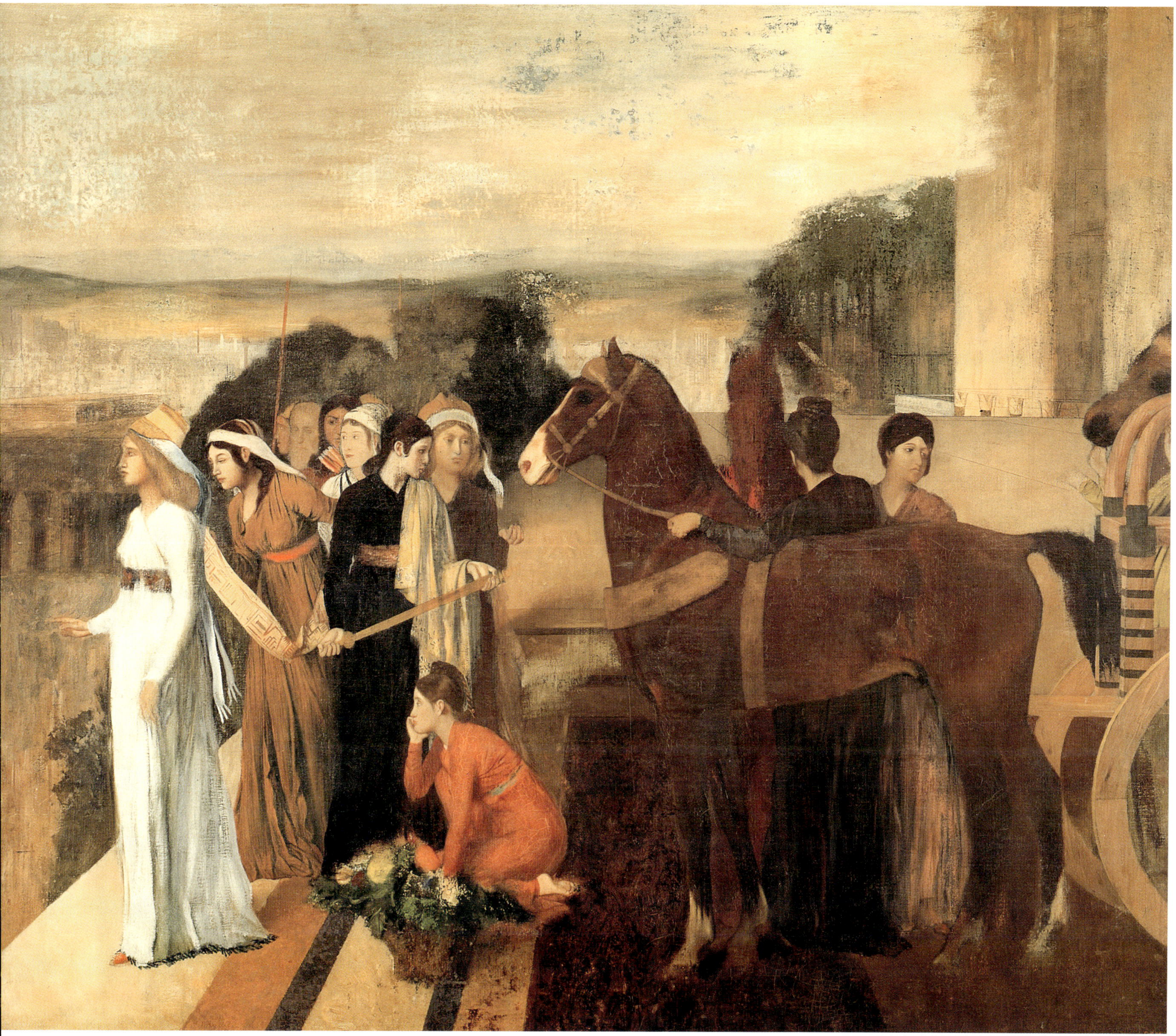

was busy colonizing North Africa and had interests in Egypt, was a charming odalisque, a small drawing in watercolor and ink (c. 1862) of which an engraving was made. Manet's exoticism was largely restricted to the young black servant girl in his celebrated *Olympia*, the painting that caused a furore at the 1863 Salon des Refusés.

These young painters were not interested in the Oriental fascination of their elders. Not Edgar Degas, whose only allusion to the East was *Semiramis Building Babylon*, a late and very untypical work done in homage to Delacroix. Not Claude Monet, who was entirely given over to the new fad for things Japanese – as we can see in his painting *Japonerie* (1876) – and to Venice. Not Sisley, nor Pissaro, and certainly not Cézanne, who was completely absorbed in his protracted study of Mont Sainte-Victoire in his native Aix-en-Provence. But there were two exceptions: Frédéric Bazille and Auguste Renoir.

Though he was a southerner, Bazille made contact with the Orient only in 1869, when he painted a fine *Female Moor*; standing against a pinky-gray wall where a sheathed blade and black-and-white striped burnous are hanging, she idly plays with her belt. The following year he painted *Toilette*, inspired by Veronese's *Mystical Marriage of St. Catherine*. The young woman, sitting on a fur-covered couch, has placed her hand on the shoulder of her black servant who, kneeling before her wrapped from the waist in a multicolored cloth, is drying her mistress. On the other side a woman is shown standing, holding up

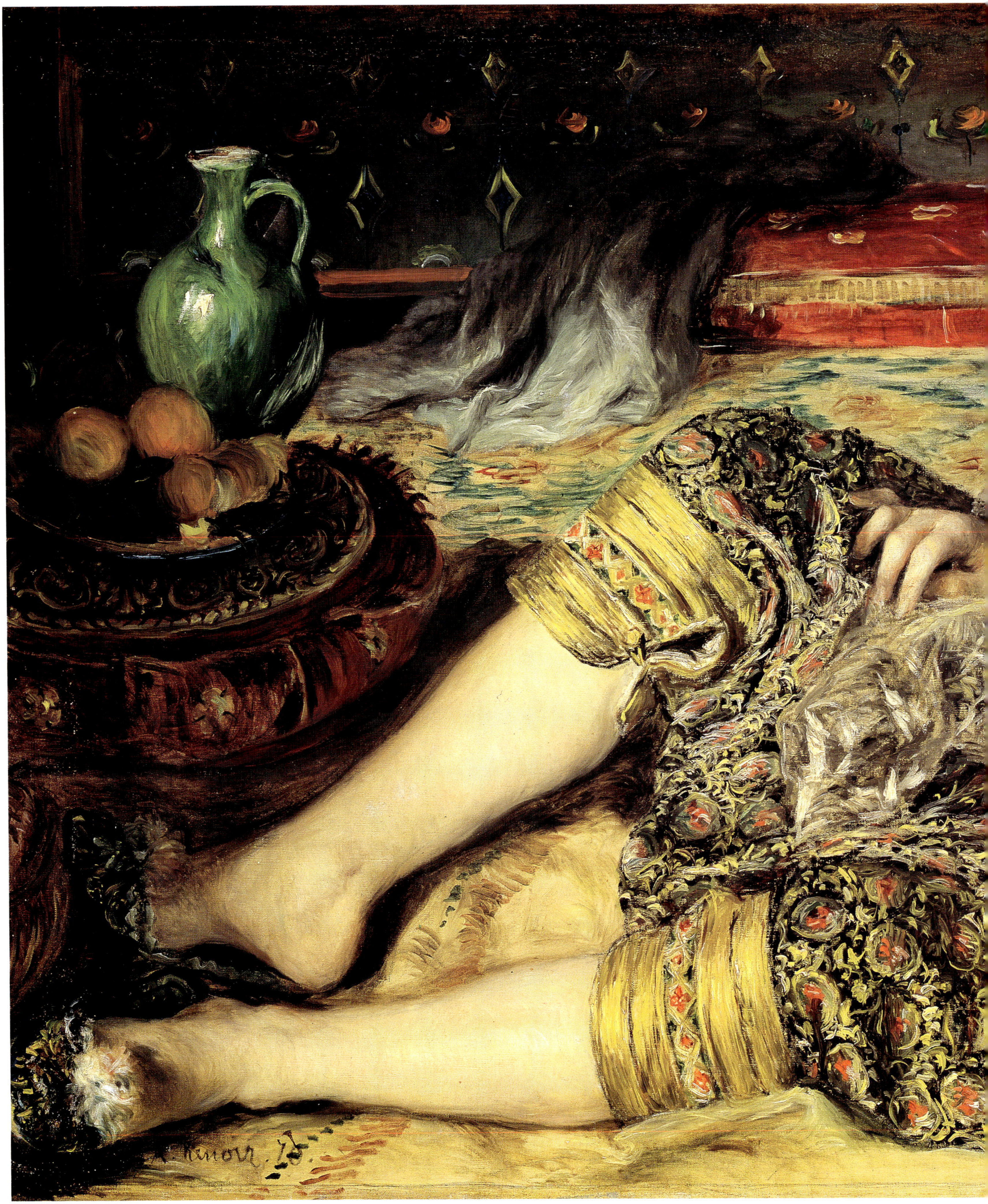

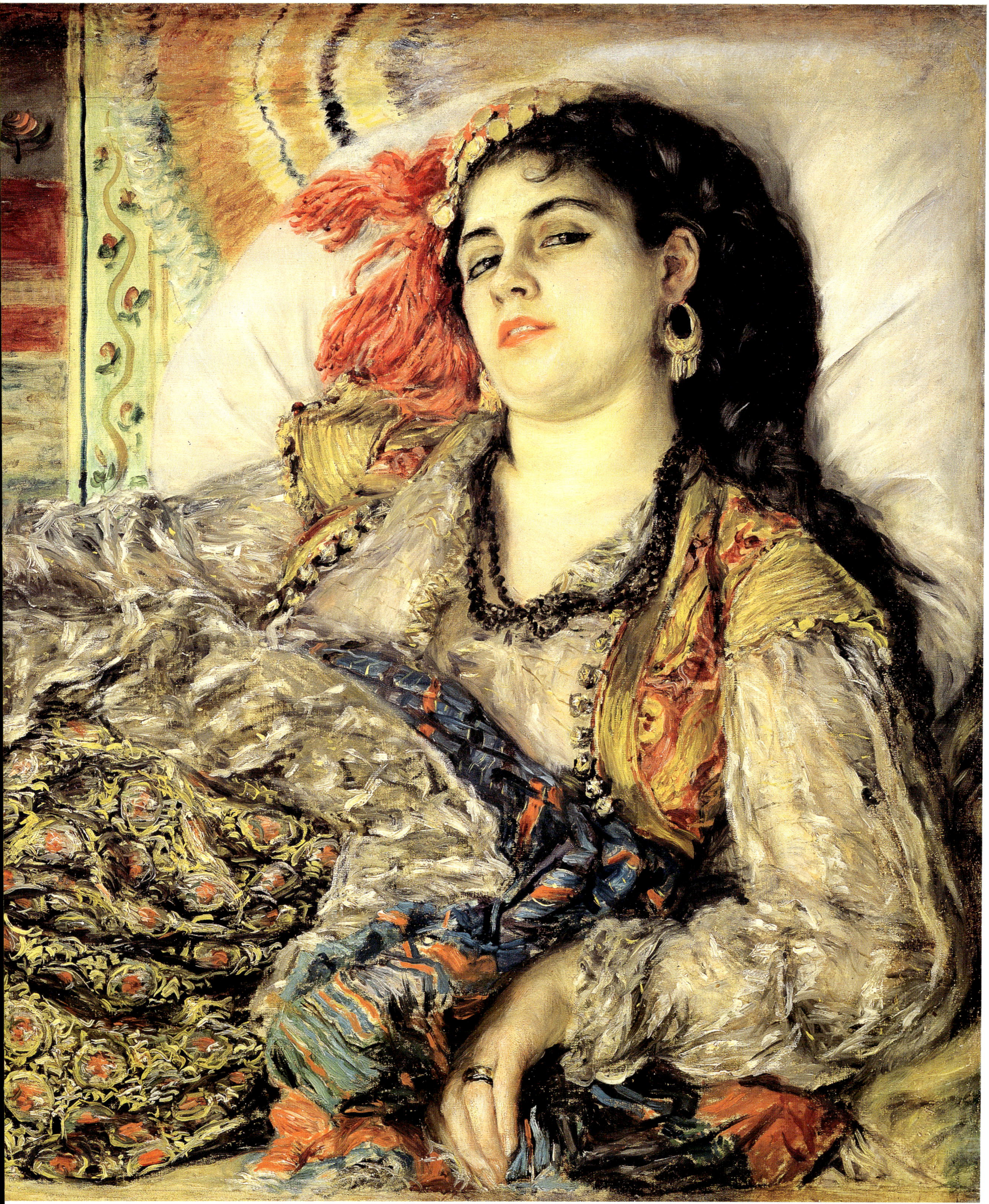

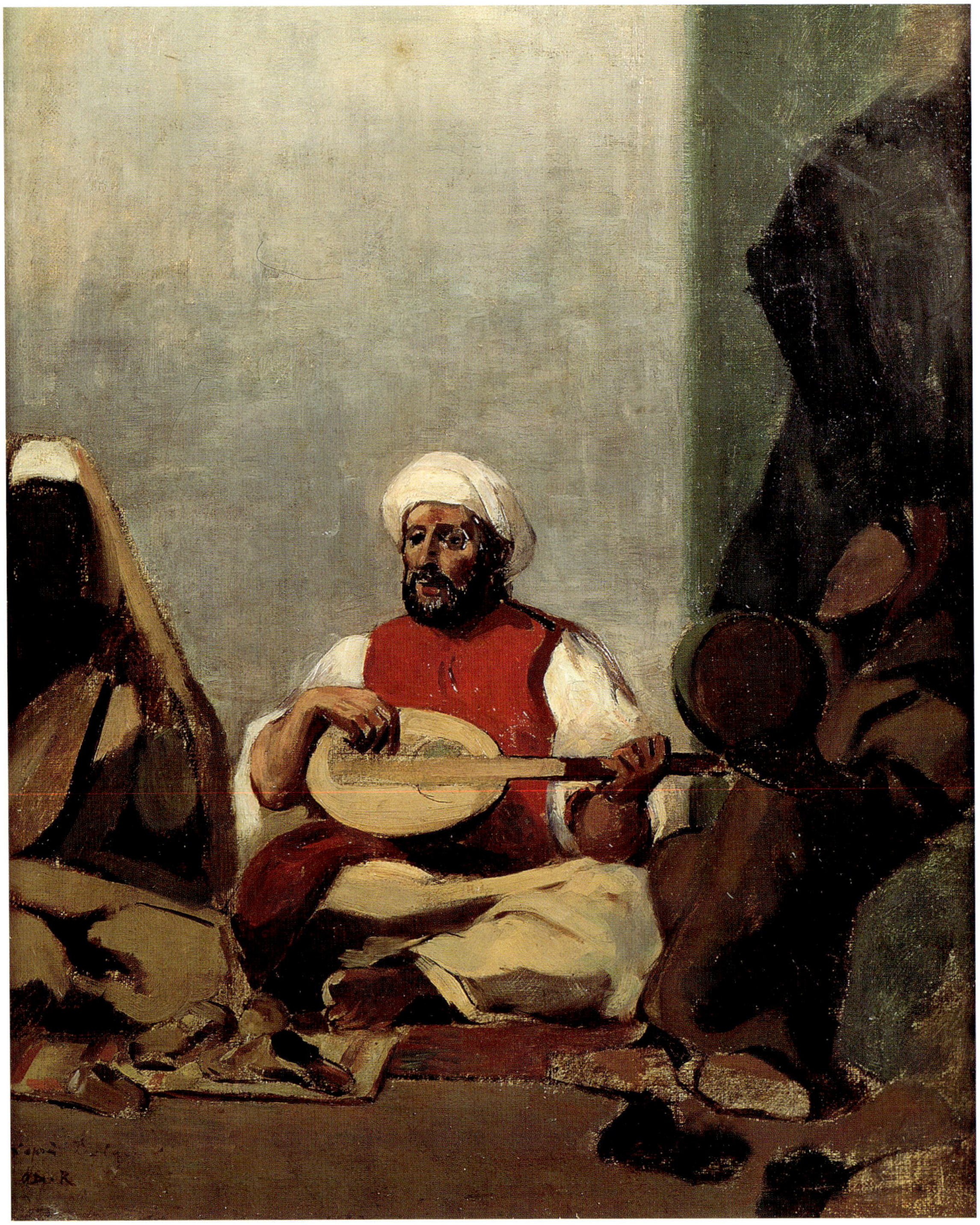

Jewish Wedding (copy of a detail of a painting by Delacroix),
Odilon Redon, undated.
Oil on canvas, 40 x 32.2 cm
(Musée d'Orsay, Paris).

Opposite
Toilette, Frédéric Bazille, 1869–1870
Oil on canvas, 132 x 127 cm
(Musée Fabre, Montpellier).

a red dress trimmed with bright flowers; she herself wears a black-and-white striped dress. Curiously, Bazille painted this at the same time as he painted another toilette scene, *Coming out of the Bath*, which adheres firmly to Western traditions. It was as though the two images were meant to form a diptych on the theme. The black woman present in the first of these two canvases appears in two other works dating from the same year: the *Black Woman with Peonies* and *Second Black Woman with Peonies*; soberly exotic, they hint at an interest in lands far south of Bazille's native Languedoc. This interest would lead to the creation of one of his finest canvases: *Ruth and Boaz*, in which the young Ruth, lying down, her head on one hand, gazes at the crescent moon while aged Boaz, dressed all in white, sleeps peacefully; they are set in a barren landscape interspersed with oddly shaped hillocks. This austere composition indeed, continues the Renaissance perception of the East. With the Franco-Prussian war going badly for France, Bazille joined the Zouaves and set off for Algeria; billeted in Philippeville, he was, however, deeply disappointed, for "this country has no African traits." Before returning to the war in France, he was given leave to visit Constantine, but died before he was able to make the journey.

The Orient that first appeared to Auguste Renoir was the Orient of the bazaar: he was asked by a dealer in carpets and North African goods, Nathan Stora, to paint a portrait of his wife. This portrait, *Madame Clémentine Stora in Algerian Costume*, was clearly an homage to Delacroix, even though references to North Africa remain discreet. In the same year, Renoir sent *Algerian Woman* to the Salon, a work that took its inspiration directly from Delacroix; it was well received by the Salon. He remarked to a friend, Julie Manet: "After completing this, I can sleep at ease." The indolent woman, who looks seductively at the spectator through half-shut eyes, and who is resplendent in her vibrant finery, is a reworking of Delacroix's unforgettable *Algerian Women in Their Apartments*. Two years later, Renoir produced another fantasy drawn from Delacroix, *Parisian Women in Algerian Dress*, also known as *Inside a Montmartre Harem*. The artist Paul Signac noted that the latter was more like "a scene in a brothel than in a harem," something that had not escaped the jury of the Salon, which this time rejected his picture. It is in fact a free reworking of Delacroix's painting, the Oriental element being restricted to the embroidered muslins the women are wearing and a garish carpet. In fact, Renoir's intentions are partly ironic, his homage to Delacroix being balanced by a parody of the Orientalist fashion. These paintings are in effect a magnificent demon-

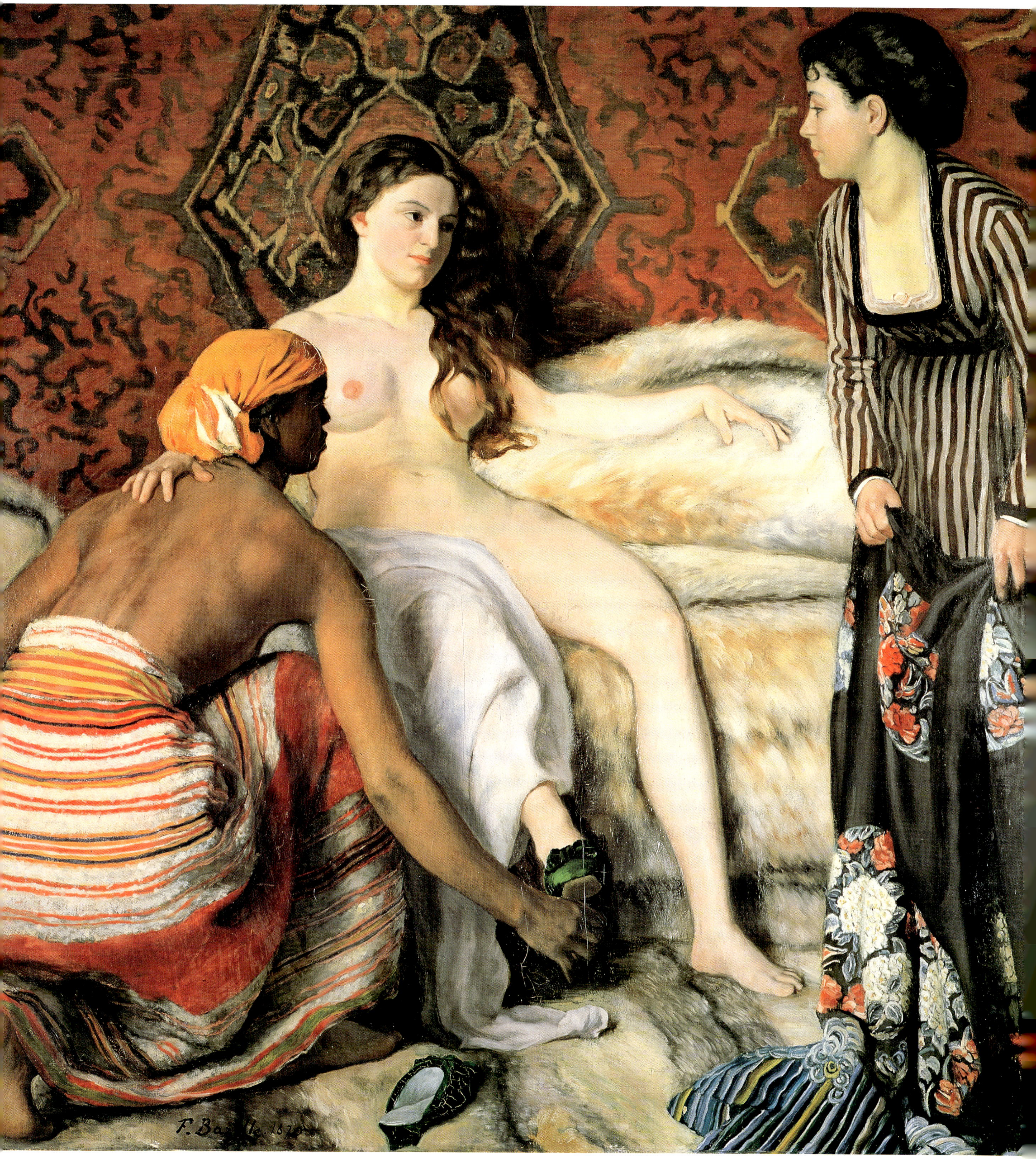

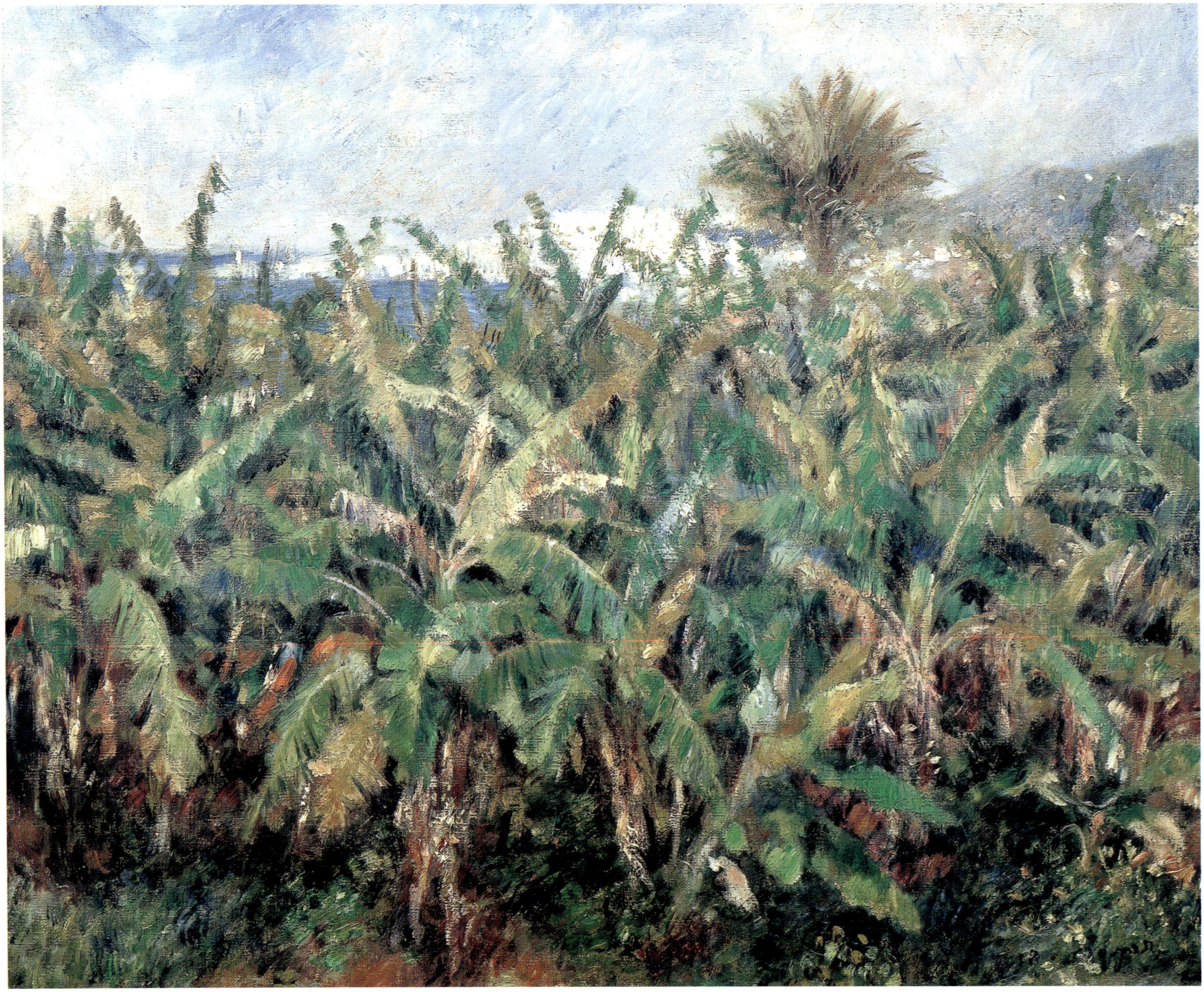

stration of Renoir's aesthetic program, which was to use the Oriental fantasy as a means of creating works in which the expression of sensuality would no longer be a forbidden dream but an honest reality.

Renoir finally arrived in Algeria early in 1881, and was delighted by the climate and the lush vegetation. He soon painted *Algerian Landscape*, in which he used a deep tonality for the shadows, particularly when depicting the Barbary fig trees and the aloes of the Birmandrais Valley. He then began work on *Mosque* (sometimes referred to as the *Arab Fête*), in which he depicts a large village square where a crowd forms a circle around clowns and musicians. The white buildings on the square, set under an intensely blue sky, echo the white burnouses of the audience. "In Algeria," he stated, "I discovered white. Everything is white, burnouses, walls, minarets, the road." He returned to Algeria a second time after a long visit to Italy, and stayed six weeks. On this trip he painted more canvases, mostly of people – *Algerian Woman and Her Child*, *Seated Algerian*, *Old Arab Woman* (two versions), *Algerian Child* – and made a number of drawings. He also painted city views and landscapes, for example *The Steps of the Mosque* and above all the superb *Garden*. After this intense preoccupation with Algeria, with its people and places, its intense colors and light, Renoir lost all interest in Orientalist inspiration. It had, perhaps, served its purpose.

The American painter John Singer Sargent was born in Florence and brought up in Italy, where he also studied; he settled in Paris in 1874 where he studied for the next two years with the fashionable society portraitist Carolus-Duran. He started on his first tour of North Africa in 1880, visiting Tunis and Tangiers before renting a small Moorish house in Tetuán. In a letter he described it as being flooded with light and as having typical Arabic features, namely horseshoe arches,

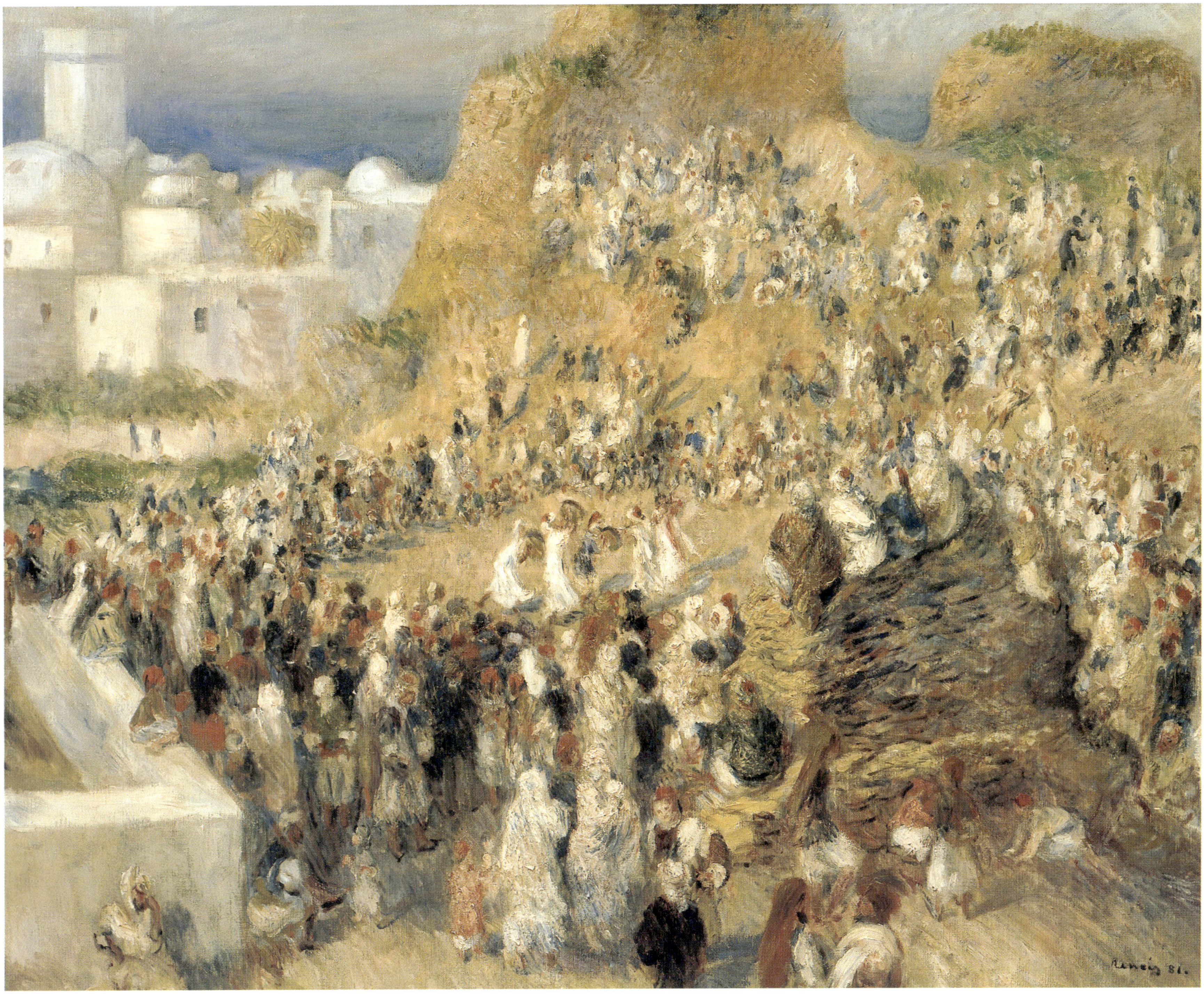

tiles, and Moorish ornaments. He drew many sketches of the area surrounding the town, focusing in particular on the light-soaked architecture. Meanwhile, inside his house, he started on one of the most outstanding early works. It shows a young woman, standing, who is pulling her long white dress over her head in order to smell the aroma rising from an oil burner set at her feet; it is ambergris, reputed to have aphrodisiac powers. She is standing in front of a wall recess decorated with a rounded pilaster. Apart from the carpet and the magnificent floor tiles, Sargent has composed a symphony in white. He cannot have been too happy with his effort, for his friends noticed his dissatisfaction. He continued working on it back in France. His sister Emily wrote to her friend Vernon Lee: "John returned to Paris about a month ago, leaving Tangier in haste as the rain had begun, & he could not continue his picture of an Arab woman which he was painting in the Patio of the little house his friend & he hired for a studio. He had sent us a little water-colour sketch to give us an idea of the picture. It is a figure all draped in white." It was completed just in time to be shown at the 1880 Salon. Paul Mantz referred to it in the journal *Le Temps* as a "melodic fantasy"; others referred to its "refined voluptuousness." It fell to

Mosque (or *Arab Fête*), Auguste Renoir, 1881
Oil on canvas, 73 x 92 cm
(Musée d'Orsay, Paris).

Banana Plantation, Auguste Renoir, 1881
Oil on canvas, 51 x 63 cm
(Musée d'Orsay, Paris).

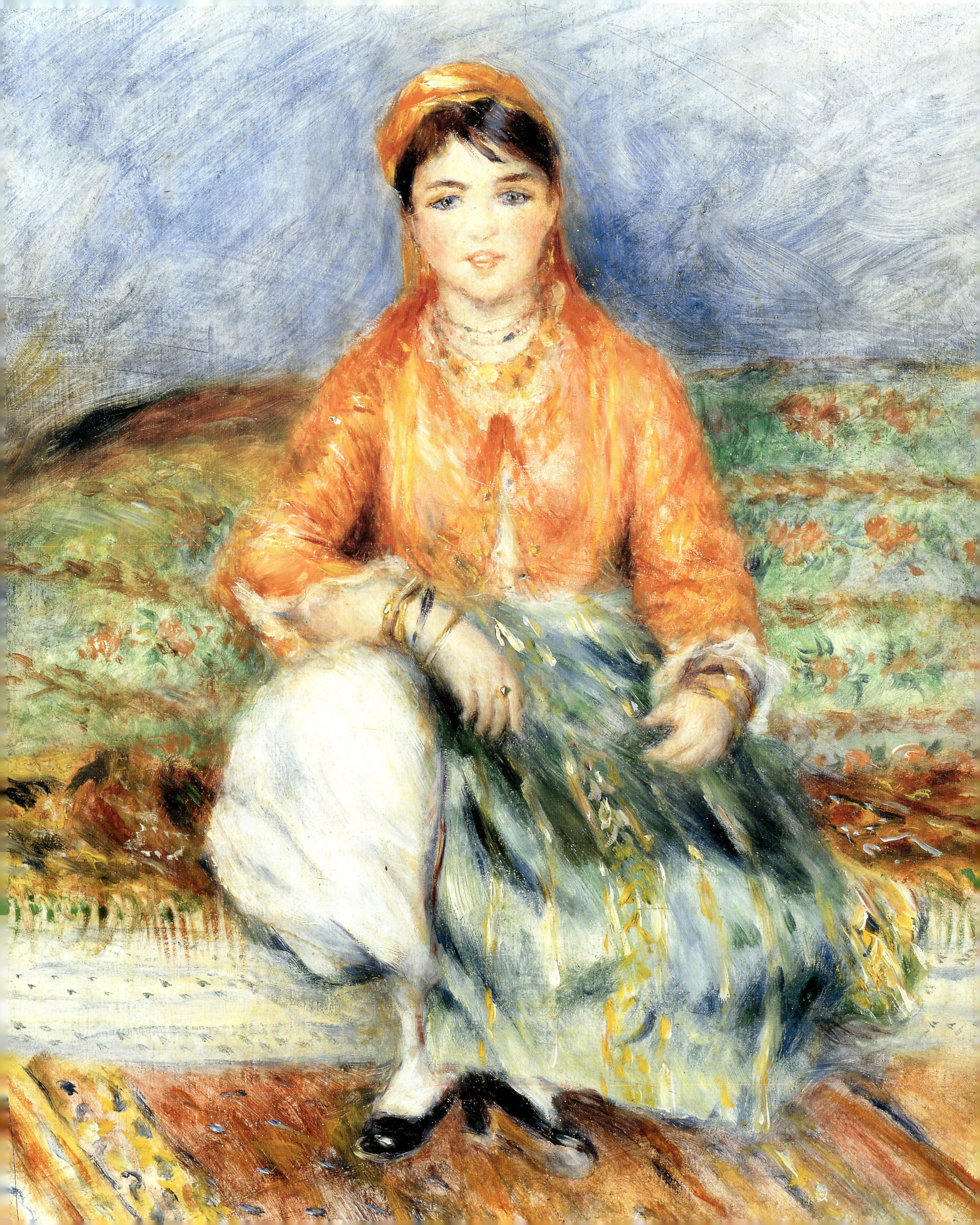

Henry James to give this canvas, named in French *Fumée d'ambre grise* (Ambergris fumes), the praise it deserves in his column in *Harper's Bazaar* in 1887. "I know not who this stately Mohammedan may be, nor in what mysterious domestic or religious rite she may be engaged; but in her muffled contemplation and her pearl-coloured robes, under her plastered arcade, which shines in the Eastern light, she is beautiful and memorable. The picture is exquisite, a radiant effect of white upon white, of similar but discriminated tones."

Sargent made two further visits to the Middle East. The first took place in 1891, when he spent the month of January in a rented studio in Cairo. He sailed the Nile to Luxor and then, in April, visited Constantinople and Anatolia. He once again embarked on an Oriental subject when commissioned to decorate the Boston Public Library; he was asked to create a series of murals on the theme "The Triumph of Religion." Sargent's second visit to the Orient was in November 1905, when he visited Syria and Palestine with his manservant and the painter Alberto Falchetti. On this trip he visited Baalbek, the Sea of Galilee, the Jordan Valley, Nazareth, and Jaffa. The death of his mother in 1906, however, cut short his trip, on which he had wanted to "restock for his decorative work." Despite this curtailment, he was able to paint a dozen canvases and forty watercolors. *Bedouins*, did indeed find its way into one of the Boston paintings. The East continued to appear in his work, sometimes in a roundabout way, as in *Almina, Daughter of Asher Wertheimer* (1908), in which a young woman is dressed in an ivory-white Persian costume, topped with a green-patterned white jacket, and holds in her hand an Indian musical instrument. In 1907, while on holiday in the Italian Alps, Sargent had some relatives sit for him: the result was *The Game of Chess*, which shows a young man and woman in Turkish clothing playing chess in a sun-splashed meadow. Here Sargent created a loosely Impressionist interpretation of the Oriental reverie in terms of his own distinctive artistic sensitivity.

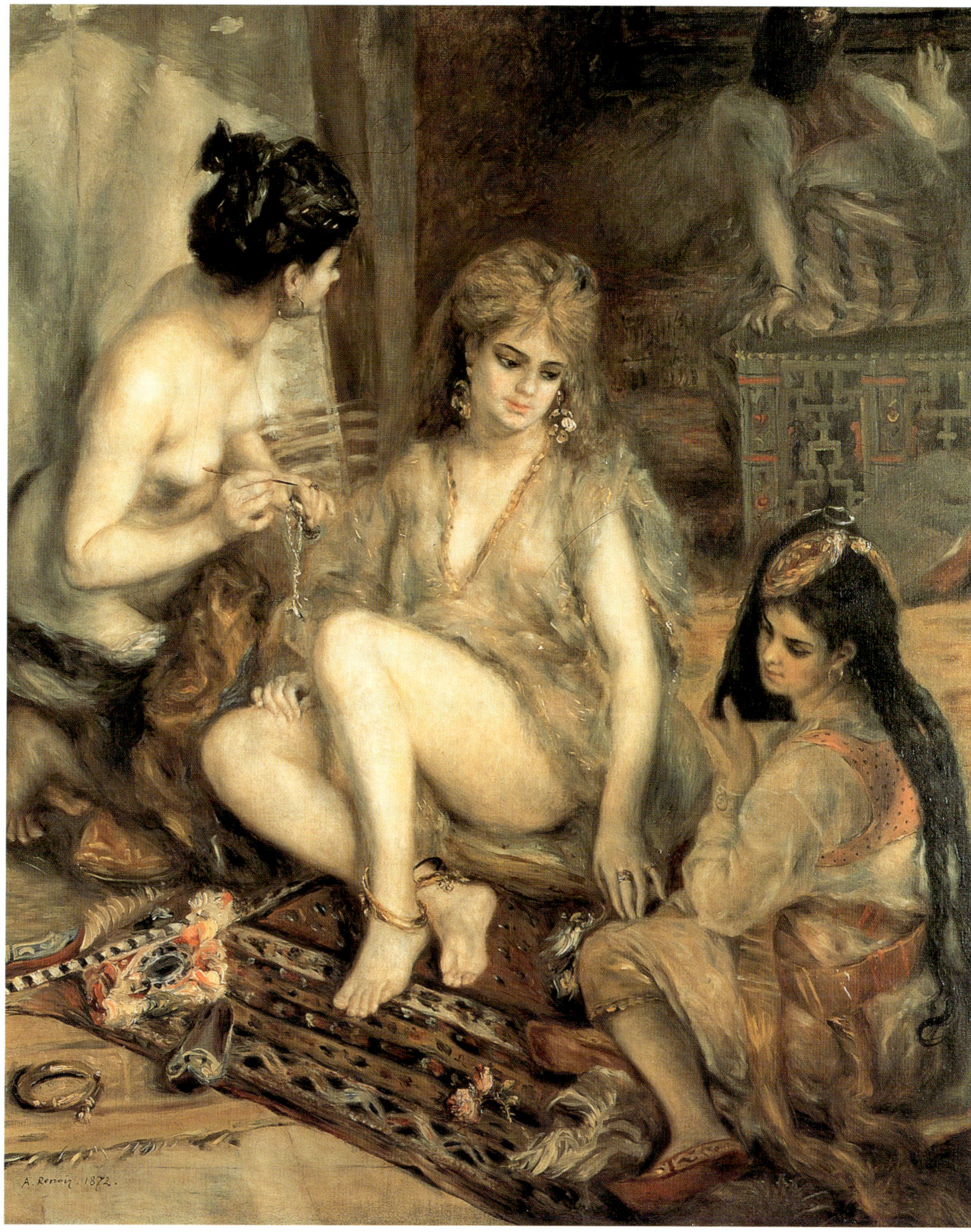

Opposite
Seated Algerian, Auguste Renoir, 1881
Oil on canvas, 51 x 41 cm
(Museum of Fine Arts, Boston).

Parisian Women in Algerian Dress (or *Harem scene in Montmartre*),
Auguste Renoir, 1872
Oil on canvas, 156 x 129 cm
(The National Museum of Western Art, Matsukata Collection, Tokyo).

Orientalists from the Orient

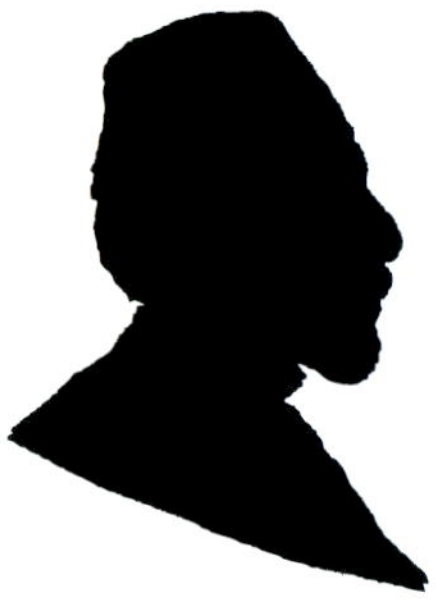

Self-portrait silhouette of Osman Hamdi Bey.

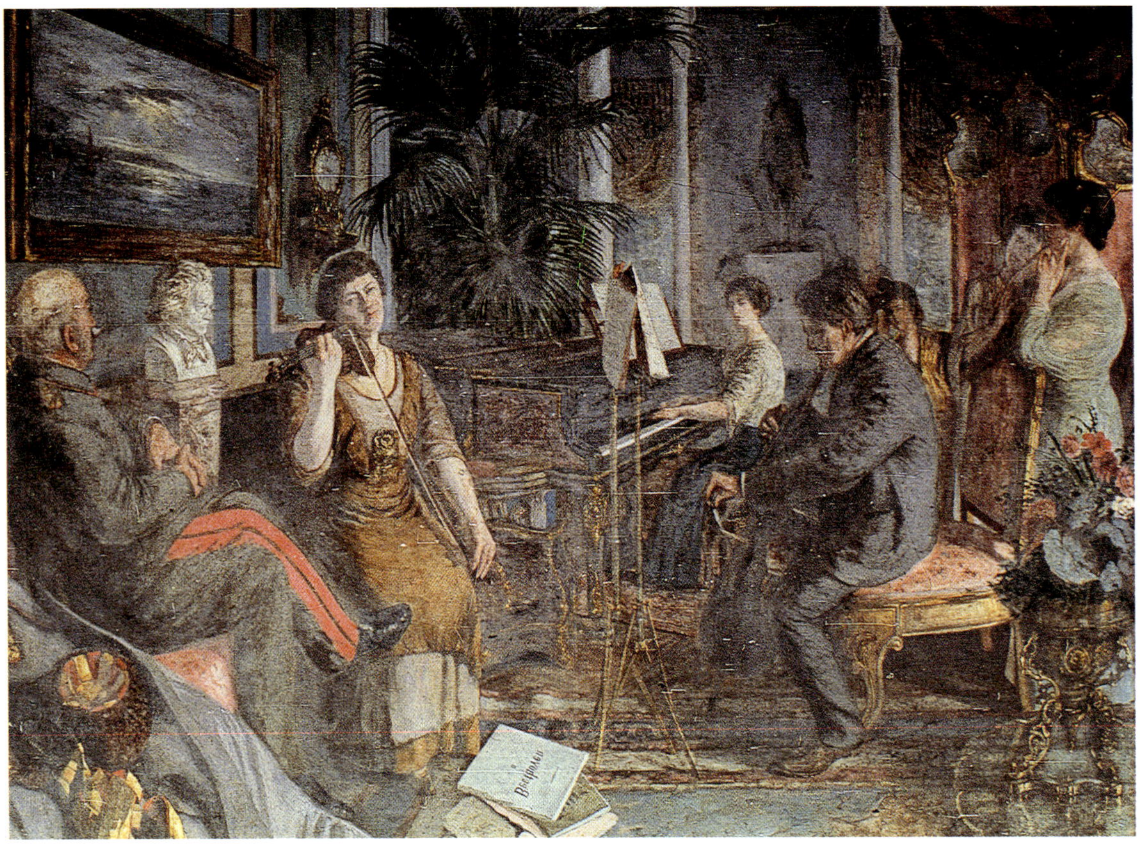

Beethoven at the Palace, Prince Abdulmecid, 1900
Oil on canvas, 154 x 221 cm
(Museum of Painting and Sculpture, Istanbul).

In Turkey during the 19th century, and especially during the Reforms Era, the traditional *nakka* or court painters gradually disappeared and the art of the miniature fell into disuse. Ottoman sultans now wanted to develop links with European powers and adopt Western lifestyles. The arts follow suit. Many foreign artists were invited to work at the court in Istanbul: Fausto Zonaro, from Padua, was appointed Abdulhamid's official painter; Salvator Valeri from Rome taught for 25 years at the School of Fine Arts in Constantinople; and Joseph Warnia-Zarzecki, who had studied in Warsaw and then Munich, and had worked in Bavaria for ten years, arrived in Turkey in 1874. There were also Russian artists in the Ottoman capital.

The emergence of a specifically Turkish school of painting came about in rather curious circumstances. When Sultan Selim III created the Imperial School of Military Engineers, modern teaching subjects and methods were introduced, including geometry and along with it perspective. From 1832 lessons in drawing and painting were taught in order to introduce young officers to linear perspective, a notion foreign to their culture. In 1847, a Spanish artist named Chirans was put in charge of training teachers and pupils. From 1851, this form of teaching was used in all the schools of the Empire. By then, the most promising students over the last decade or so had been sent to Europe to study in the studios of well-established artists. From this unique experience a school of landscape painting arose that was the preserve of military painters. General Ibrahim Pasha (1815–1889) and General Tevfick Pasha (1819–1866), along with Commandant Husnu Yusuf (1817–1861), were the main figures in the development of art training in Turkish schools.

In his travel book *De Pontoise à Stamboul* (From Pontoise to Istanbul), the French writer Edmond About tells of an unexpected encounter: "Our guide was a member of the Sultan's military staff, Ahmed, who had completed his studies in Paris, not as one would expect at the École d'État-Major – but in Gérôme's studio. As a painter he was good enough for Courbet to ask him for one of his landscapes, and to be granted an award from the Salon jury."

Army officers also established a secondary school for children from deprived backgrounds, the Darussafaka School, which opened in 1873. Pupils were introduced to graphic arts and then, if they showed promise, to painting in oils and in watercolor. At the same time, they were taught plane geometry, perspective, shading, decorative painting, and technical drawing. The best would be sent to the École des Beaux-Arts in Paris after a stay in the École Ottomane, which was open between 1860 and 1874.

The artists produced by this army-inspired education understandably show a commonality of style and subjects. As the works are often anonymous, it is now difficult to trace the development of the school as a whole, and as Islam prohibits the representation of the human figure, the artists had to confine themselves to landscapes. For his part, the

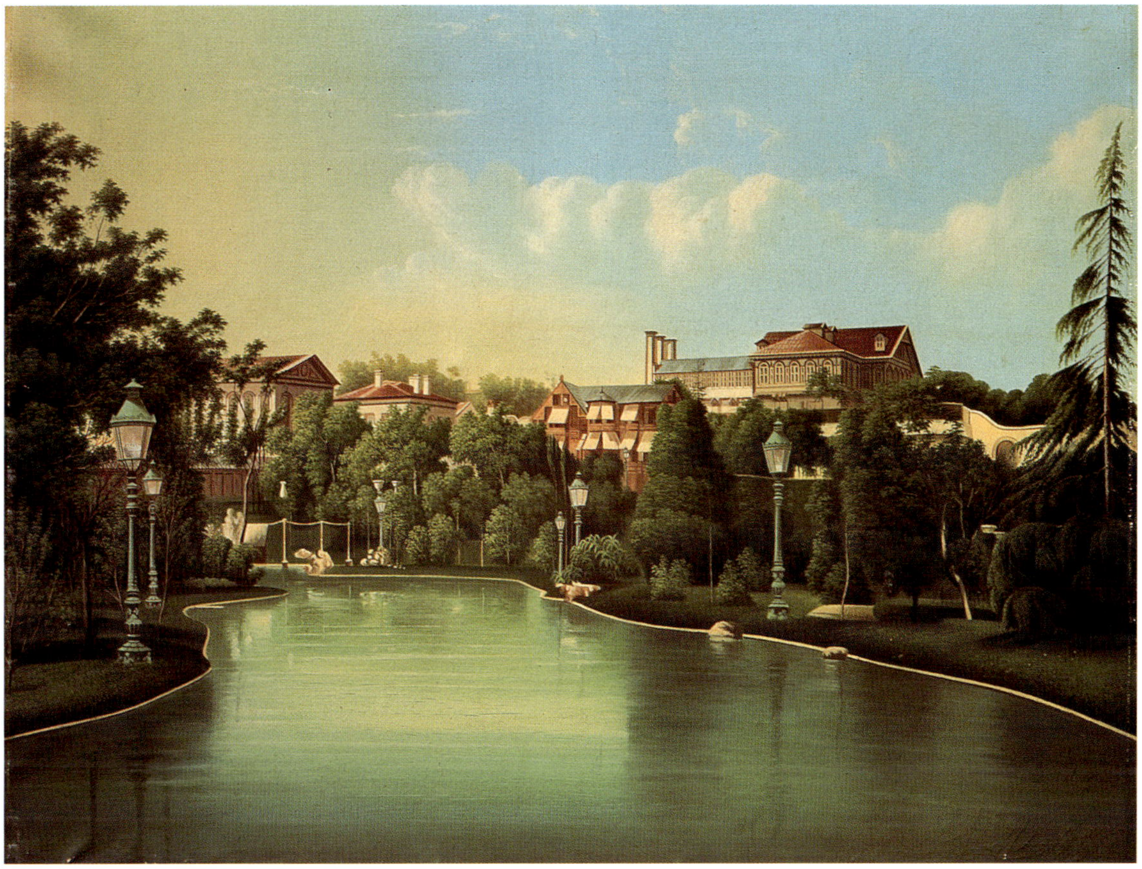

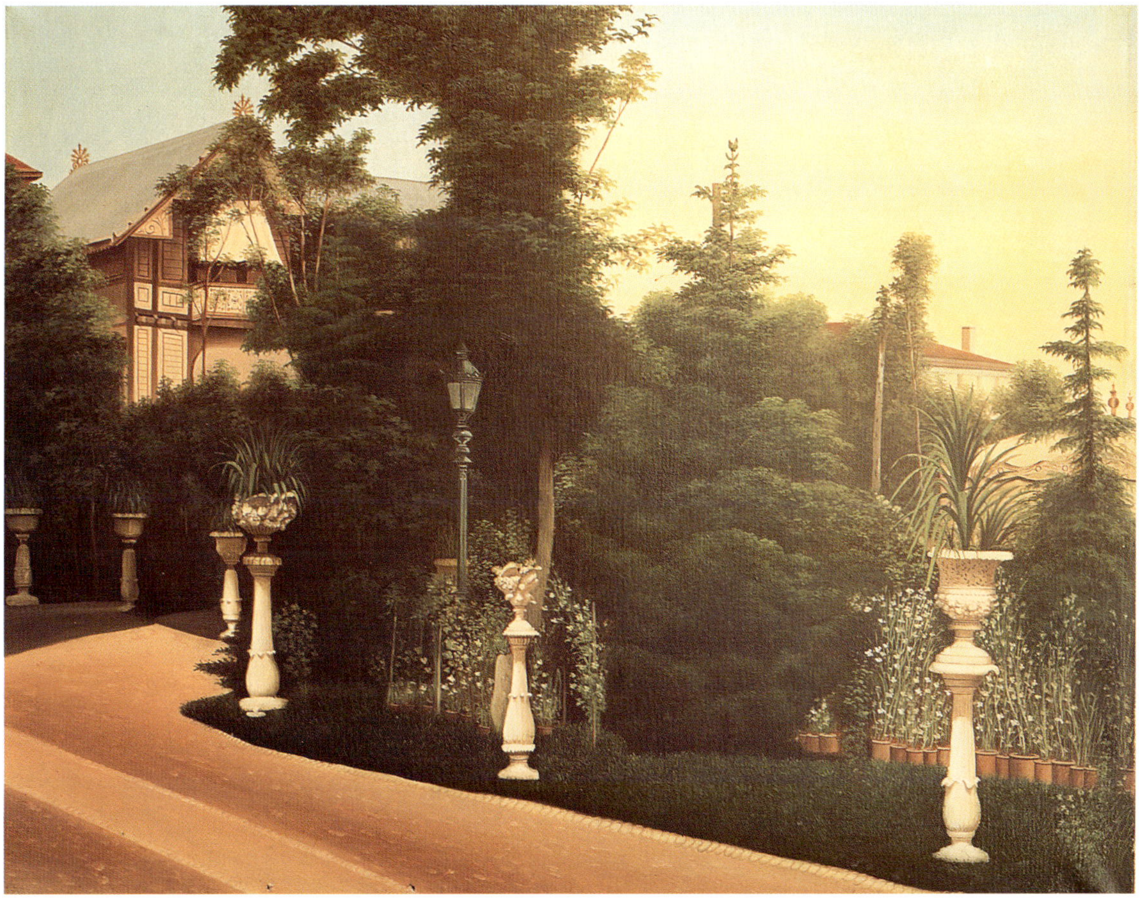

Page 267
Views of Yildiz Park, artist unknown, mid 19th century
(Museum of Painting and Scultpure, Istanbul)

sultan offered students an album of photographs of the imperial palaces, Dolmabace and the enchanting park of Yildiz. Their task was to paint these same views from life. The results are often a little awkward, stilted, or contrived, the colors a little shrill; yet these compositions have unmatched poetry and charm, making up in appeal what they lack in technical virtuosity. All these views, besides providing an extraordinary document on the splendor of the imperial palaces and gardens, reveal an art form that instinctively found a balance between the Eastern tradition of the miniature and the new style brought in from the West.

Three 19th-century Turkish artists stand out in particular. One of them, Ahmet Ali, who was active during the first third of the century, painted delicate landscapes of the Istanbul countryside and also elegant still-lifes. Huseyin Zekai Pasha produced a great many works, among them *The Ablutions Fountain at Hagia Sophia* (1904) and *The Sultan's Bench at Hagia Sophia* (1905). He was probably the first Ottoman painter to introduce human figures into his paintings. Last comes Seker Ahmed Pasha, who, specializing in still-lifes, displayed a dazzling stylistic freedom.

The first painting academy to appear in Constantinople was created by Guillemet, a French painter attached to the court of Sultan Abdulaziz. But it is a Turkish artist, Osman Hamdi Bey (1842–1910), who takes the credit for establishing the Imperial School of Fine-Arts in Constantinople in 1883. This extraordinary figure, who ran the Ottoman Imperial Museum and played a central role in archaeological work in his country, was also a very fine portraitist – though because of the ban on depictions of the human form his contemporaries would often hide their portraits, especially those of women. A mere glance at *The Lady of the Mimosa* (1906) or *Young Woman in Profile* shows that he had broken free of academic art and was sensitive to the most innovative trends in European art. Other fine examples of his work include *Mirah* (1901), which shows a young girl in traditional costume seated in the midst of books scattered on the ground; and his delightful *Reader*,

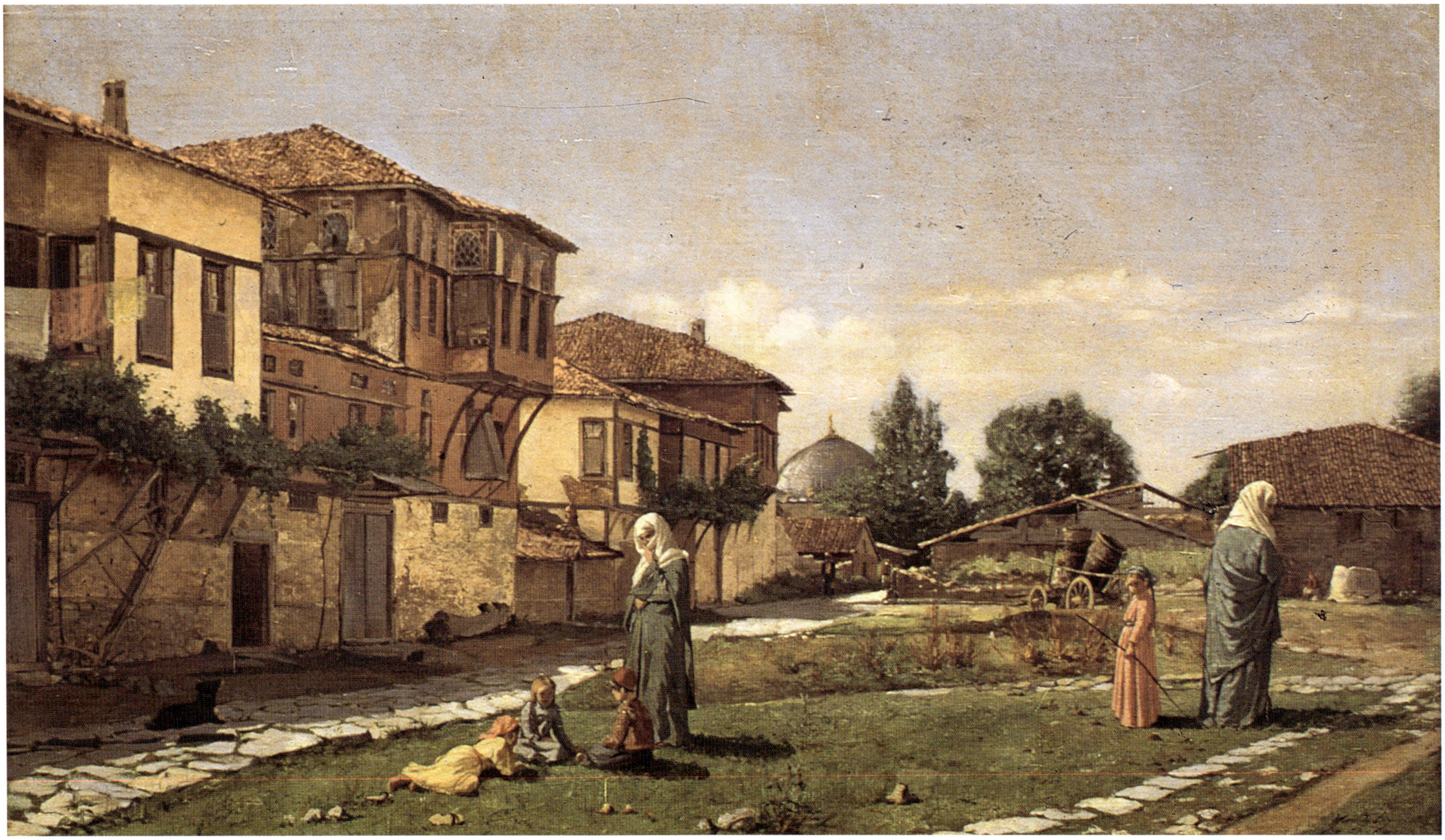

which also shows a young woman reading; this time it is a huge tome, and she is stretched out on a low couch. By comparison, his formal works are far more traditional and austere, even stuffy: *Hodja in a Yellow Caftan* (1905), *The Miraculous Fountain* (1904), *The Mosque Door*, and the celebrated *Man with Tortoises* (1906), which introduces a note of humor. There are two versions of this painting, as there are of many of his works, for he was in the habit of making a copy of most of his paintings to send to the exhibitions in Paris. He showed much vivacity and gaiety when treating scenes of city life, such as the very enticing *Turkish Women on a Walk at the At-Meidan* and the attractive *Turkish Women at the Entrance of a Mosque*. With Osman Hamdi Bey the East effectively appropriated the Orientalist genre at the very moment when the world on which it was based was about to disappear.

Others would walk in his footsteps, notably Ahmet Ziya Akbulutu, Hoca Ali Riza, who so loved the idyllic scenery of the Bosporus; and Halil Pasha, whose suggestive and nonchalant *Woman Lying on a Couch* was painted in 1917. Halil Pasha painted mainly in the open air, depicting the fine suburb mosques and the old streets of the capital, his subjects dressed in clothes soon to be replaced by Western dress.

Even Prince Abdulmecid, last of the caliphs, who should have acceded to the Ottoman throne under the name of Murat

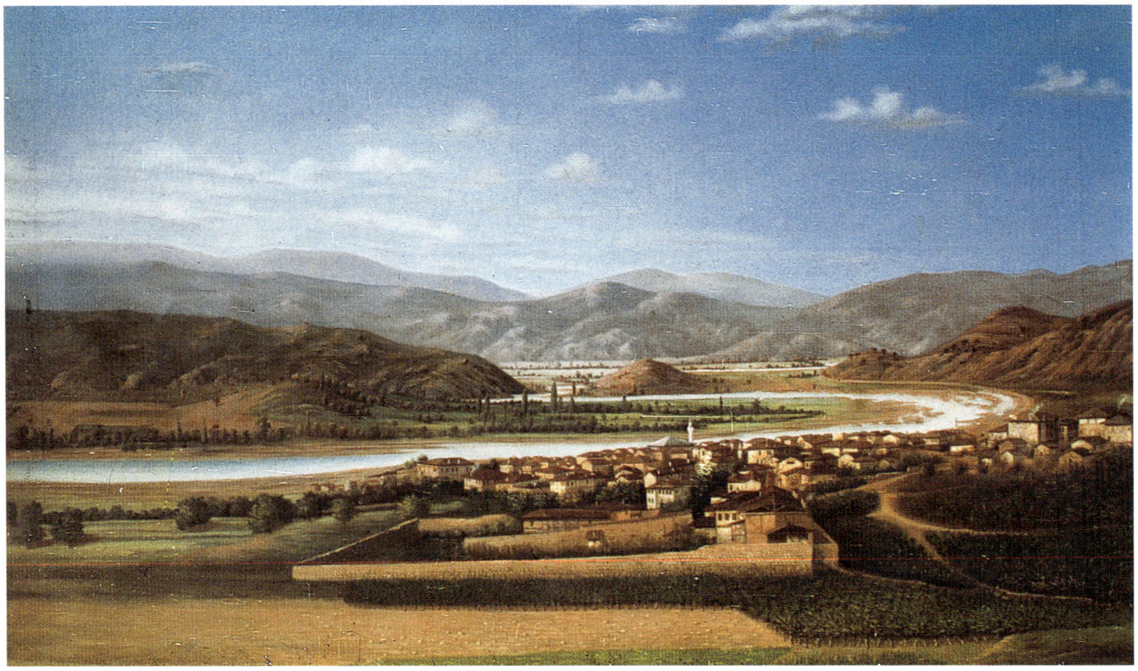

Unknown artist, mid 19th century,
Oil on canvas
(Museum of Painting and Sculpture, Istanbul).

IV, was a talented painter. He spent much of his life in exile, summoning up the court's splendors, now lost for ever. Examples include *Ottoman Princesses Embarking on an Outing on the Bosporus* (c. 1924) and *A Reading of Goethe in the Seraglio* (1920), a strange and melancholy echo of an earlier painting in which he depicted himself in uniform attending a concert at court, *Beethoven at the Palace* (1900).

Prince Abdulmecid took with him into exile a certain conception of figurative arts in Turkey. With the birth of the Turkish Republic in 1923, Turkish art was to undergo a transformation.

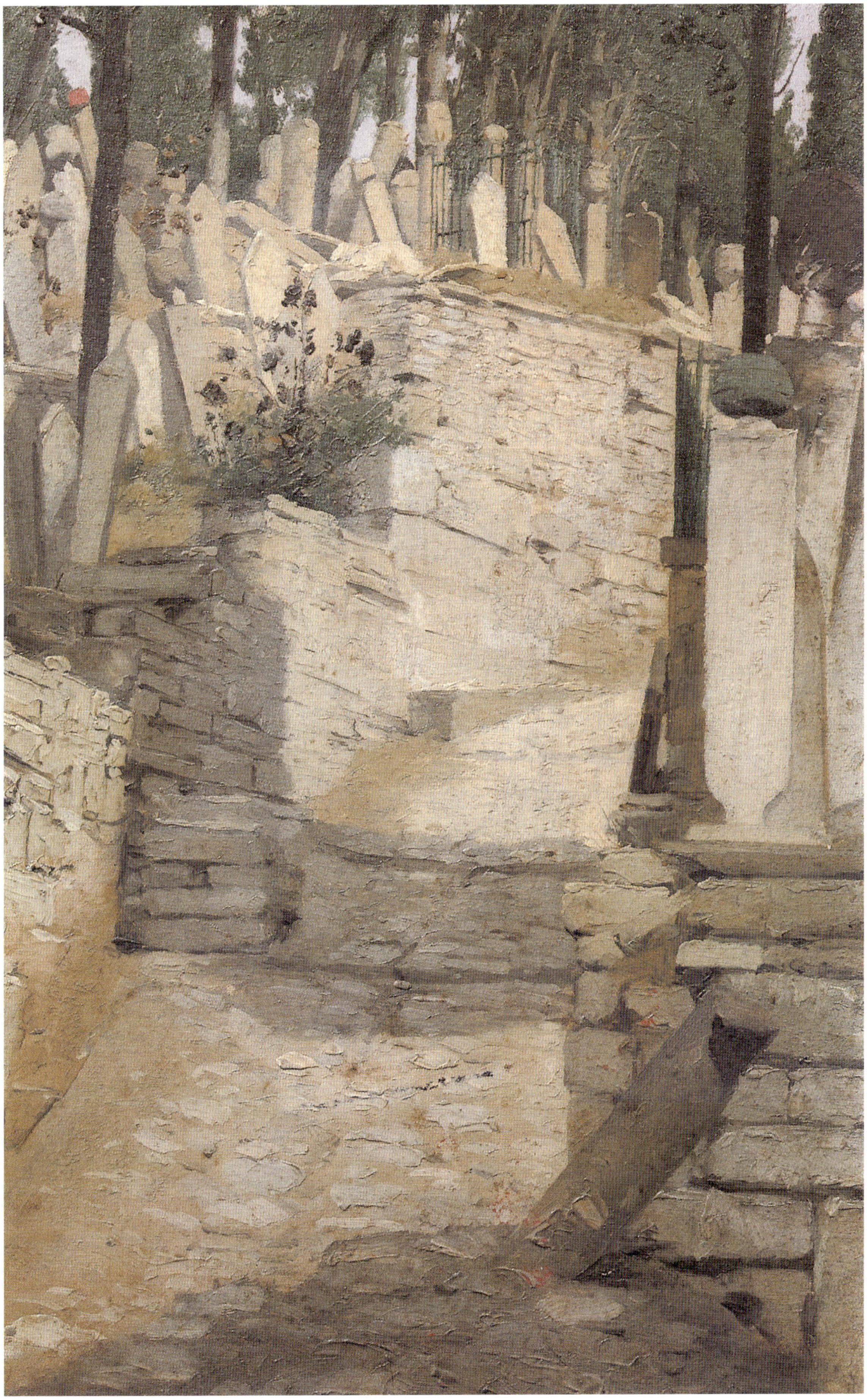

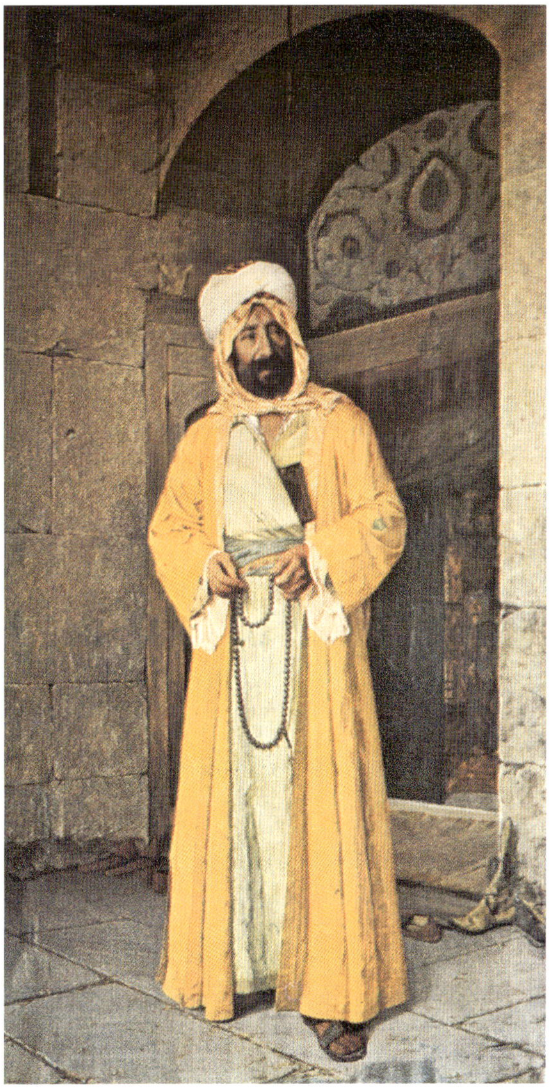

Hodja in a Yellow Caftan, Osman Hamdi Bey, 1905
Oil on canvas, 220 x 120 cm (Museum of Painting and Sculpture, Istanbul).

Cemetery, Osman Hamdi Bey, 1880
Oil on card, 20.7 x 31.6 cm
Museum of Painting and Sculpture, Istanbul.

The Last Orientalists

By the end of the 19th century, Orientalism was often closely linked with eroticism. Admittedly, the great exponents of the form – Chassériau, Delacroix, and Ingres, with his astonishing *Turkish Bath* – had already set the tone. But with the triumph of academic painting, this eroticism acquired a more dubious character. The austere Gérôme did not tire of his bath scenes – such as *Steam, Female Nude, Women's Bath*, all completed in 1889 – which are little more than an exercise in prurience. Artists quickly turned the Turkish bath and, of course, the harem into erotic clichés. Eugène Giraud, Paul-Louis Bouchard, Frederick Arthur Bridgeman, Francesco Ballesio, Attilio Simonetti, Giuseppe Aurelli, Jean-Baptiste Huysmans, Gustavo Simoni and many more described in minute and titillating details women's realms to which they had no access. All told, the only artists reaching beyond the art establishment's well rehearsed formulae were Paul-Désiré Trouillebet, with such works as *Servant of the Harem* (1847), and Jean-Jules Antoine Lecomte du Nouÿ, with his *White Slave*, exhibited at the 1888 Salon. His "white slave," who exudes a strong and sensual aura, is a buxom young woman shown smoking.

In 1893, 14 artists established the Société des Peintres Orientalistes Français (Society of French Orientalist Painters); Léonce Bénédicte, director of the Musée du Luxembourg was its president. It is clear from their inaugural statement that they in effect supported France's colonial objectives in North Africa and in the Middle East, but

The Fortuneteller,
Jean-Baptiste Huysmans, 1875
Oil on canvas, 50 x 73.5 cm
(private collection).

The Egyptian Dancing Girls,
Paul-Louis Bouchard, 1893.
Oil on canvas, 160 x 133 cm
(Musée d'Orsay, Paris).

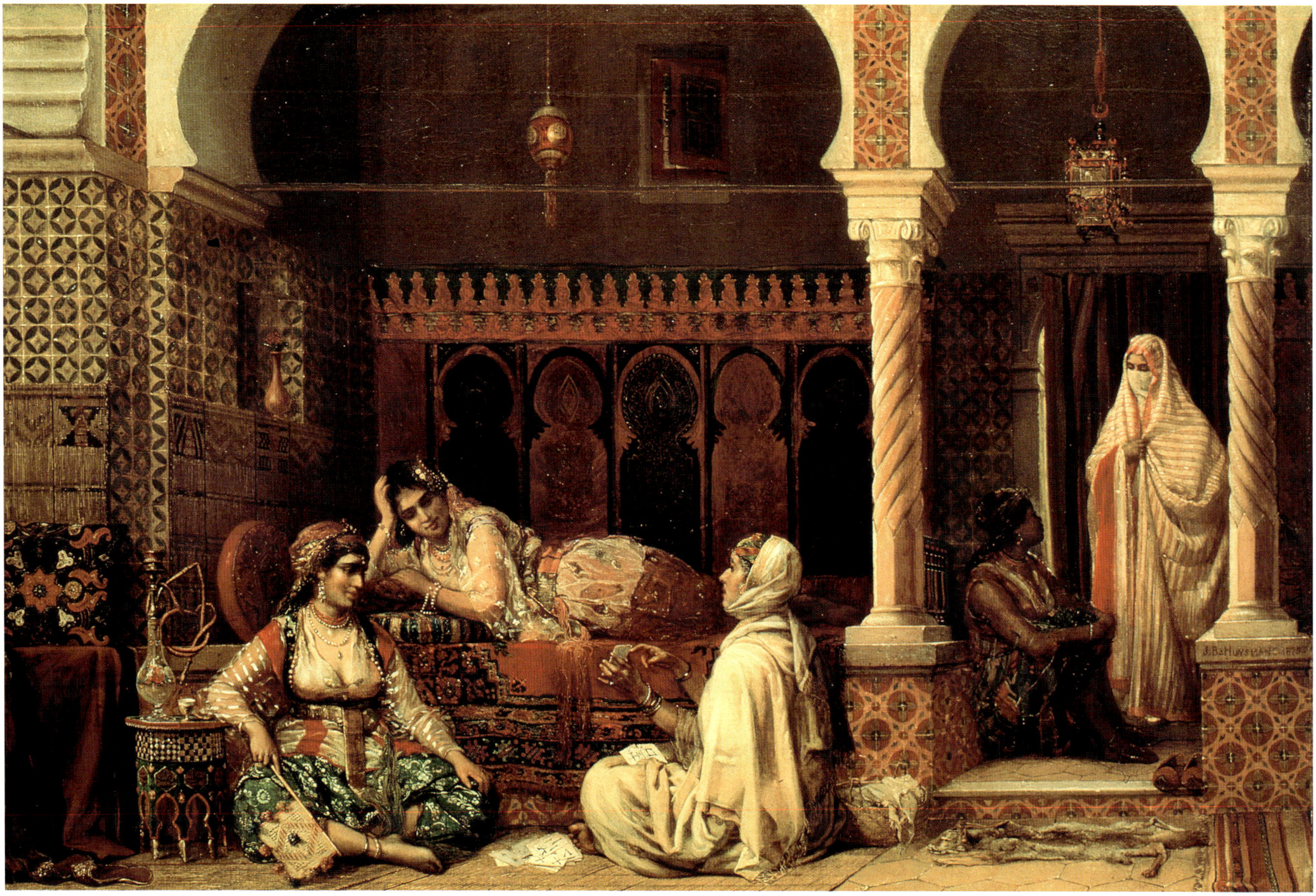

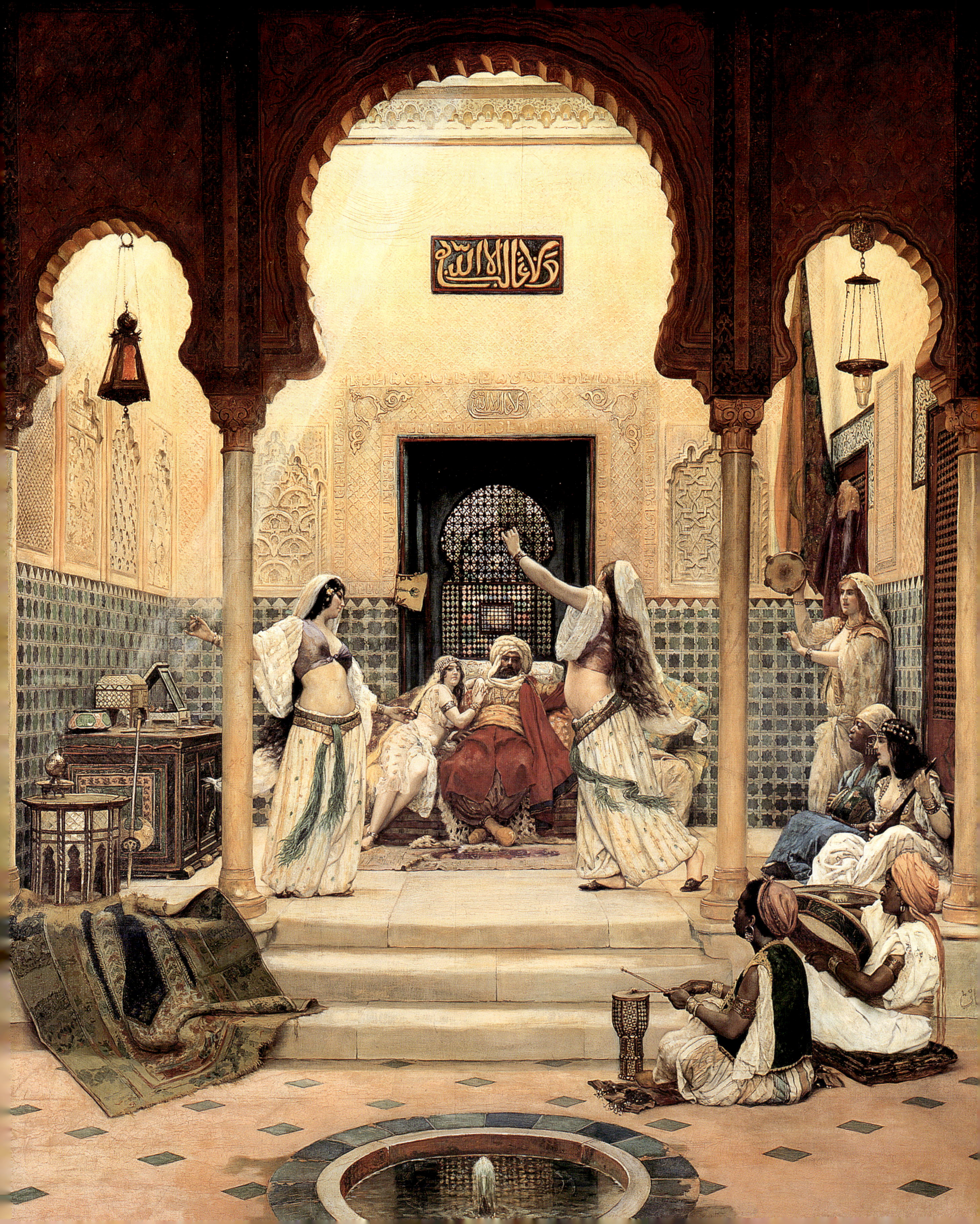

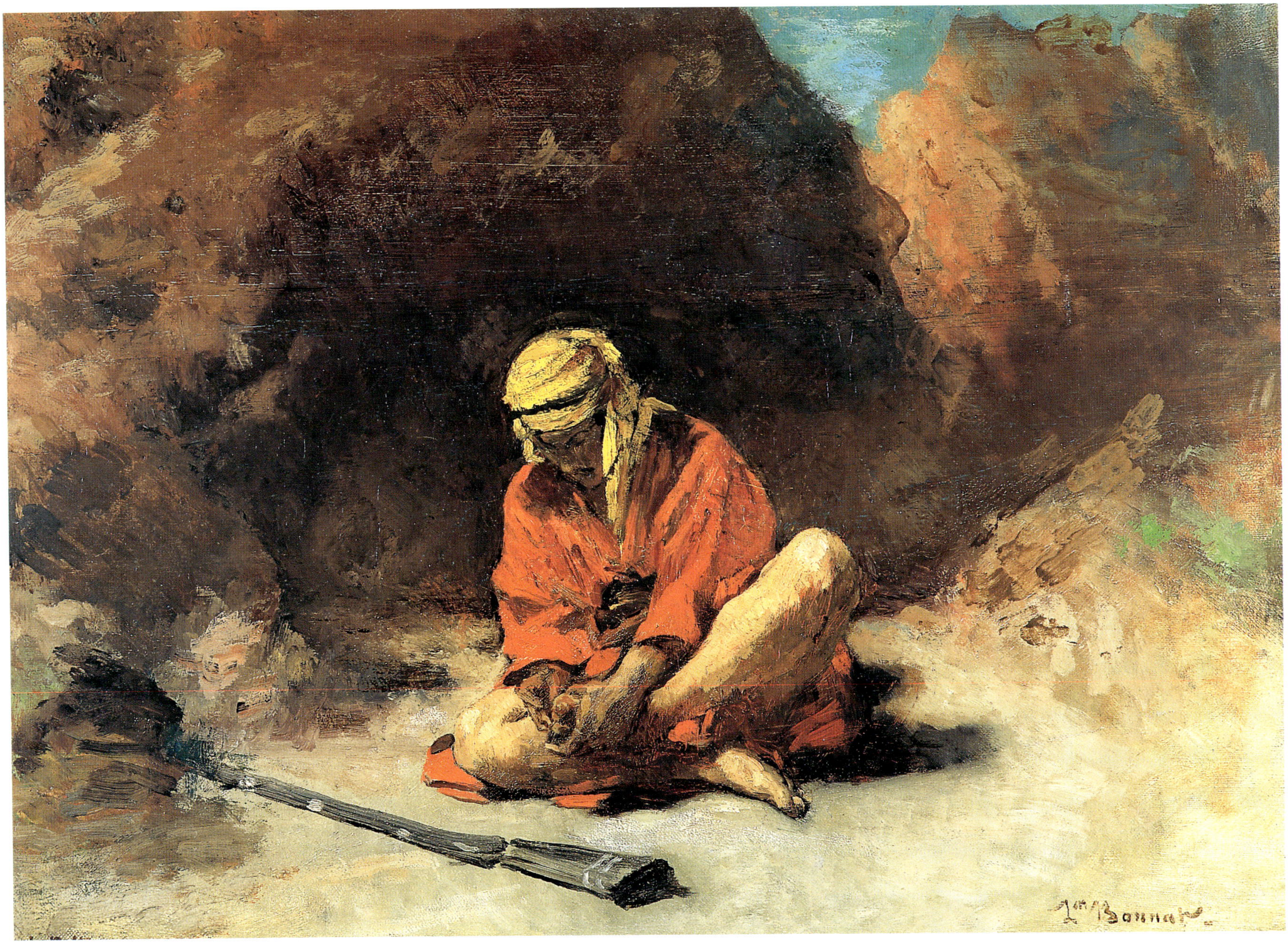

Arab Removing a Thorn from his Foot,
Léon Bonnat, 1870
Oil on canvas, 43 x 60 cm
(Musée des Beaux-Arts, Dijon).

Right
The Cairo Street in the 1889 World Exhibition, C. Bussilliet, 1889
Oil on card, 37 x 27 cm
(Musée Carnavalet, Paris).

Opposite
The Harem Servant,
Paul-Désiré Trouillebert, 1874
Oil on canvas, 130 x 97 cm
(Musée des Beaux-Arts, Nice).

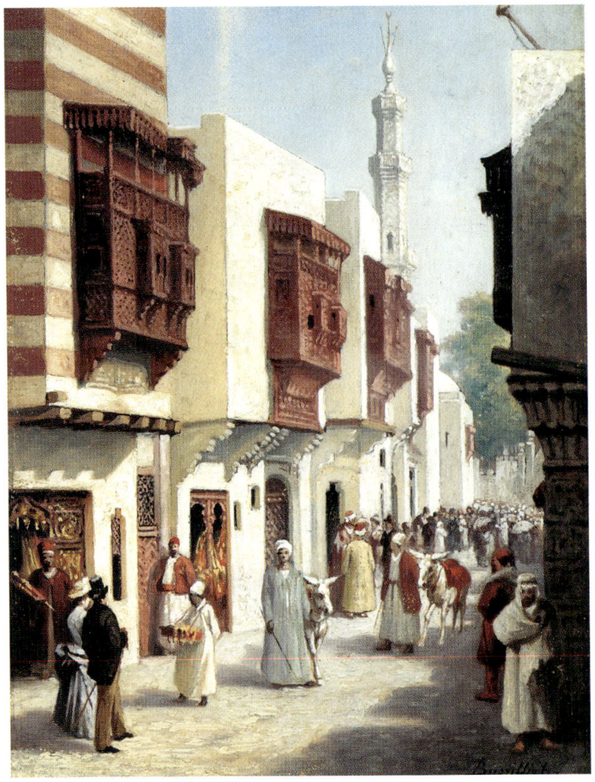

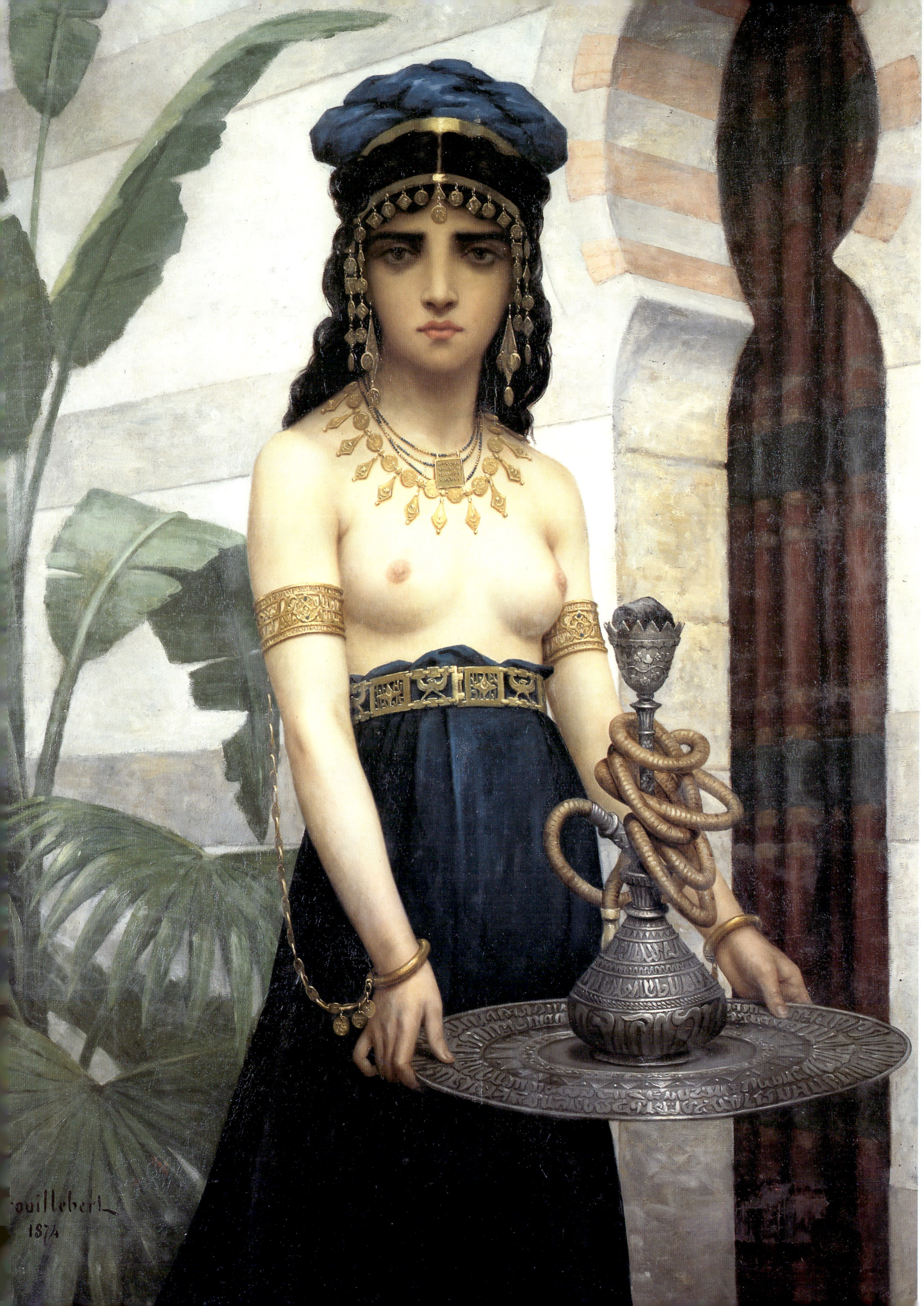
ouillebert
1874

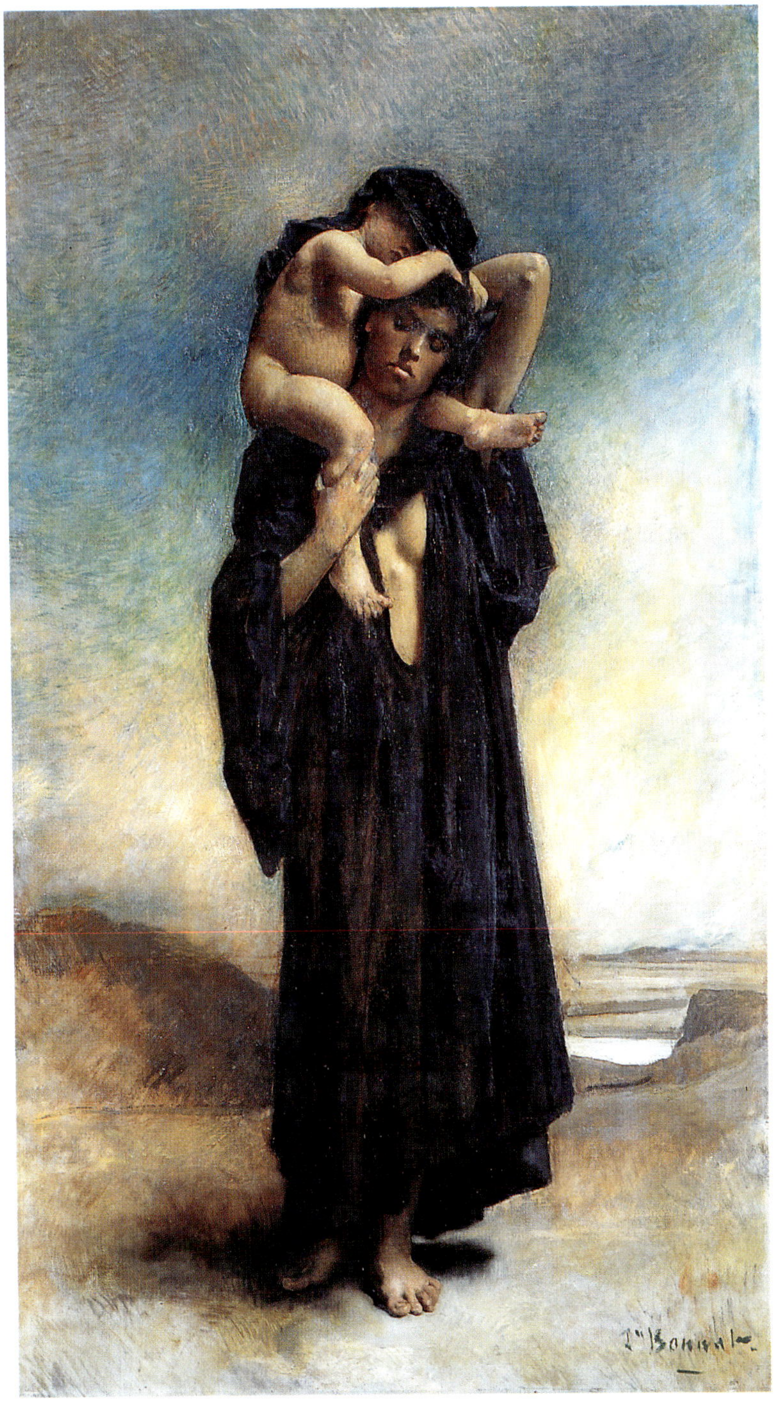

Peasant Woman and her Child,
Léon Bonnat, 1870
Oil on canvas, 258 x 138 cm
(Musée Bonnat, Bayonne).

Twilight in Marrakesh,
Lucien Lévy-Dhurmer, 1932
Oil on canvas, 93.5 x 125.3 cm
(Musée des Beaux-Arts, Brest).

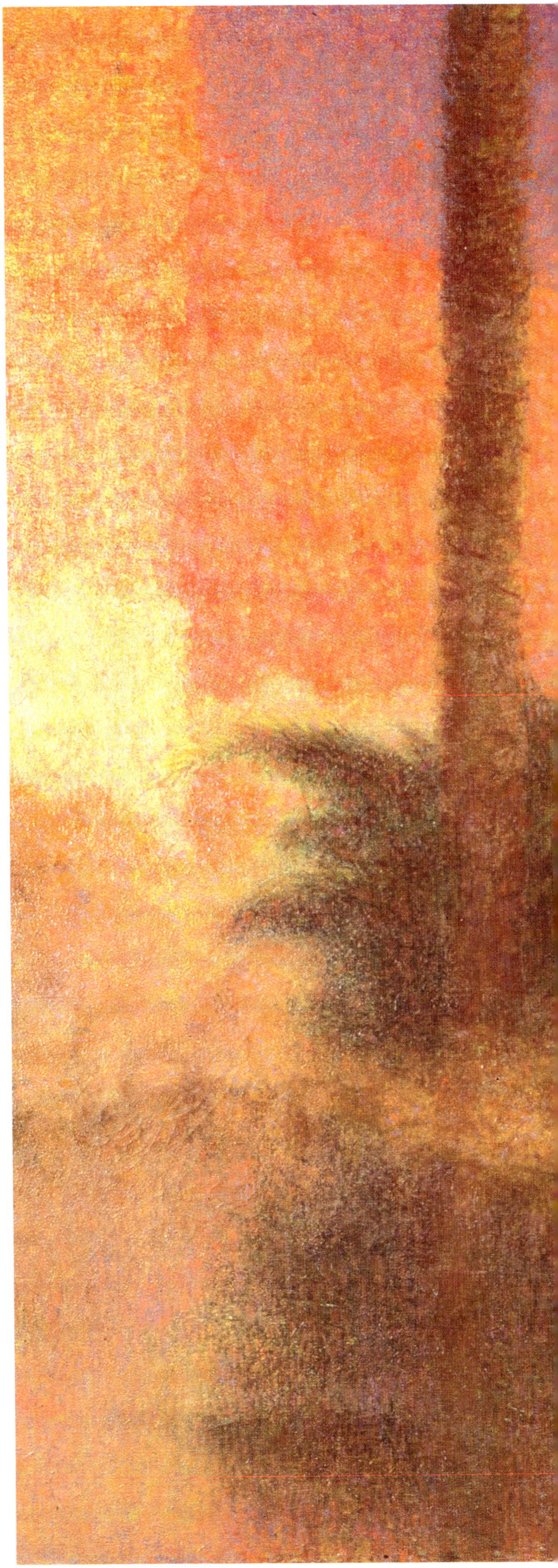

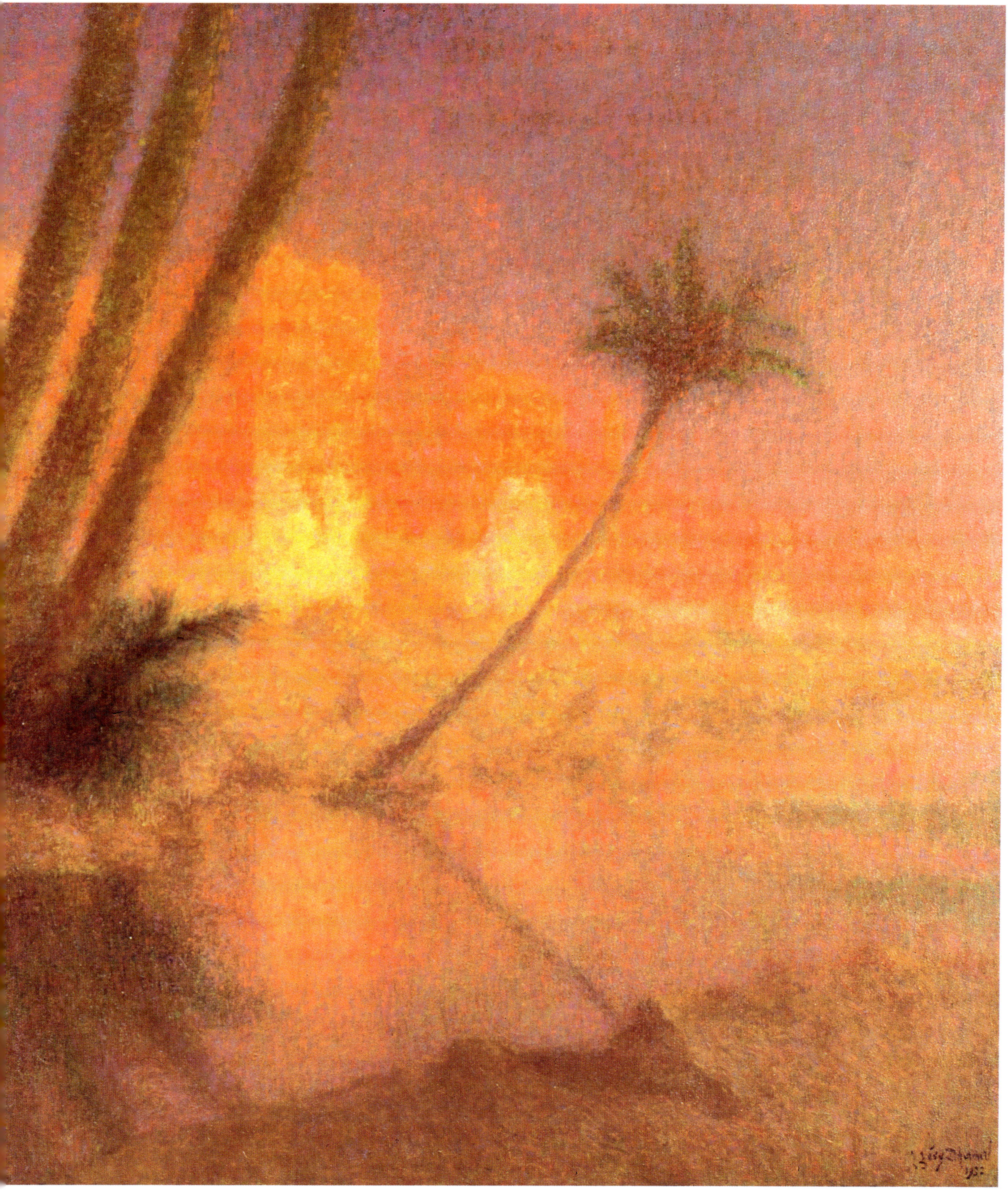

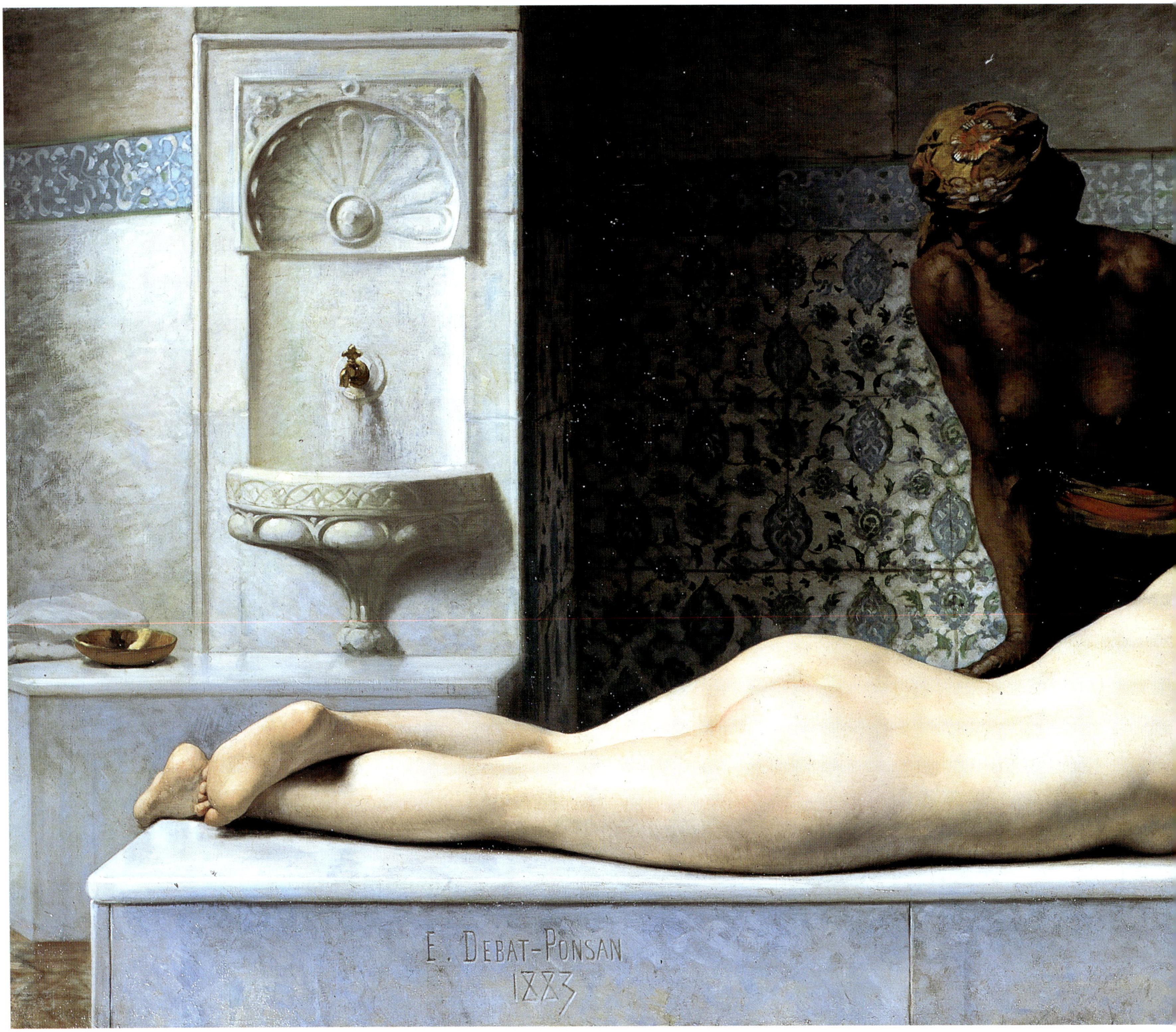

The Massage: Scene from the Turkish Baths, Edouard Debat-Ponsan, 1883
Oil on canvas, 127 x 210 cm
(Musée des Augustins, Toulouse).

it is also clear that they had a genuine interest in preserving the authentic cultures of the Orient. In their first year they organized an exhibition in which Muslim art took its place alongside the works of Delacroix, Chassériau, and Camille Roger, illustrator of Théophile Gautier's *Turquie*. Several years later the society set up an exhibition of Moslem arts at the Paris Musée des Arts Décoratifs (museum of decorative arts), under the curatorship of Gaston Migeon, who had written extensively on Muslim art. At the same time they opened an artist's residence in Algiers, in the fine Abd el-Tif Villa. One year later, the Musée Municipal d'Alger (which in 1930 became the Musée National) was opened. Salons were organized in Algiers and also in Tunis, their aim being to promote both Arabic and French art.

The painters gathered in the Société des Peintres Orientalistes had a sincere love for the Orient, but they in fact sustained a concept of Orientalism that reflected out-

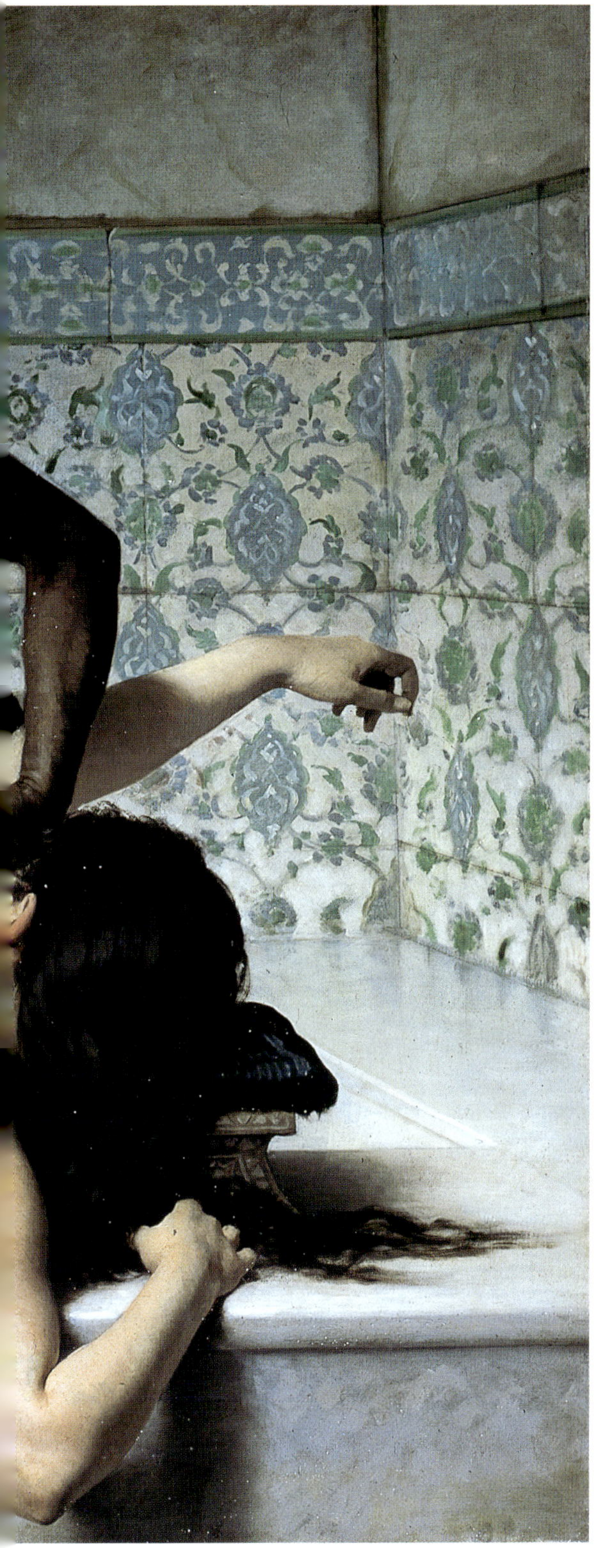

White Slave, Jean-Jules Antoine Lecomte du Noüy, 1888
Oil on canvas, 149.5 x 183 cm
(Musée des Beaux-Arts, Nantes).

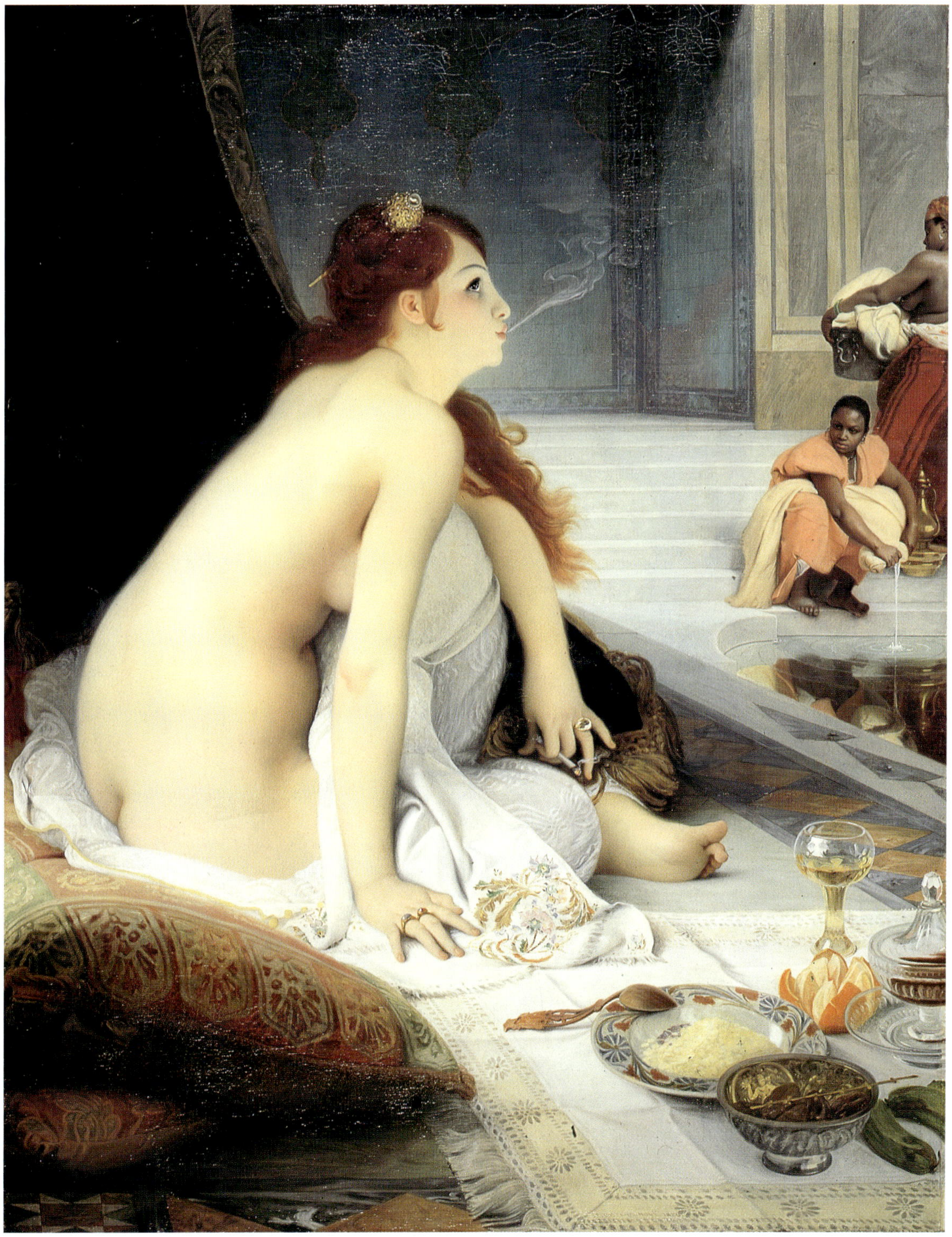

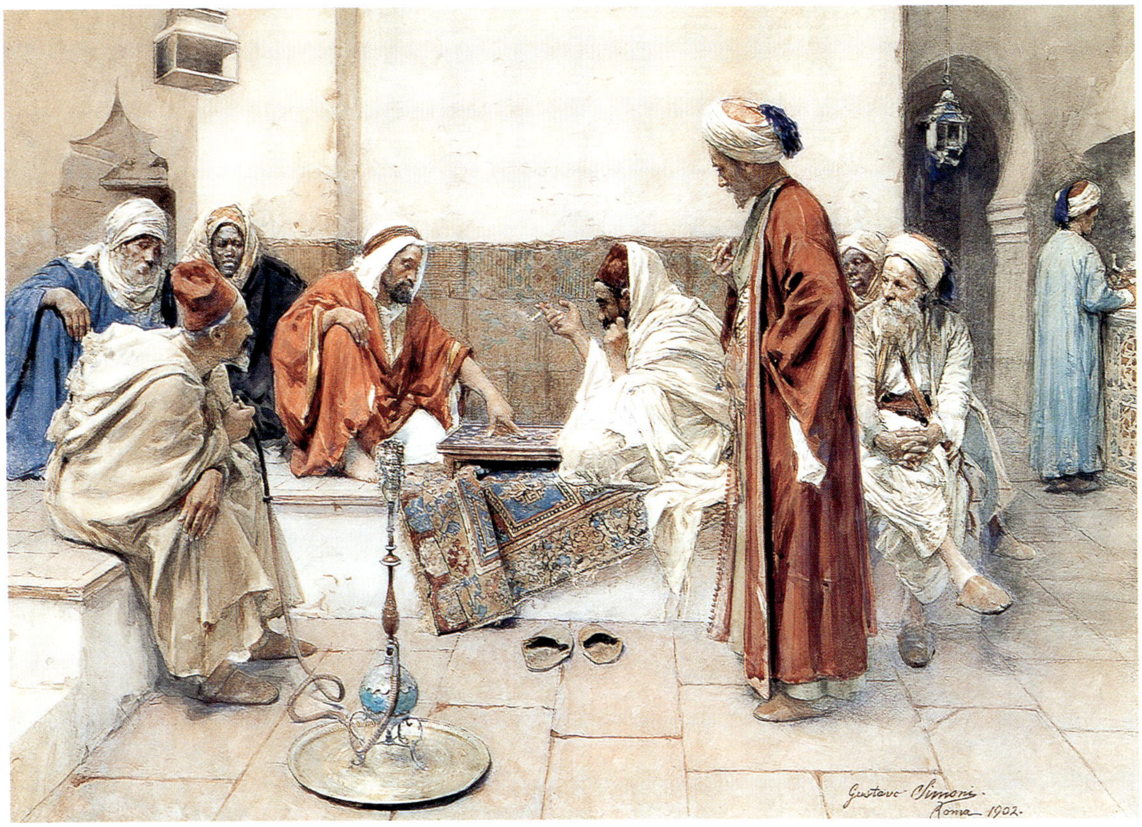

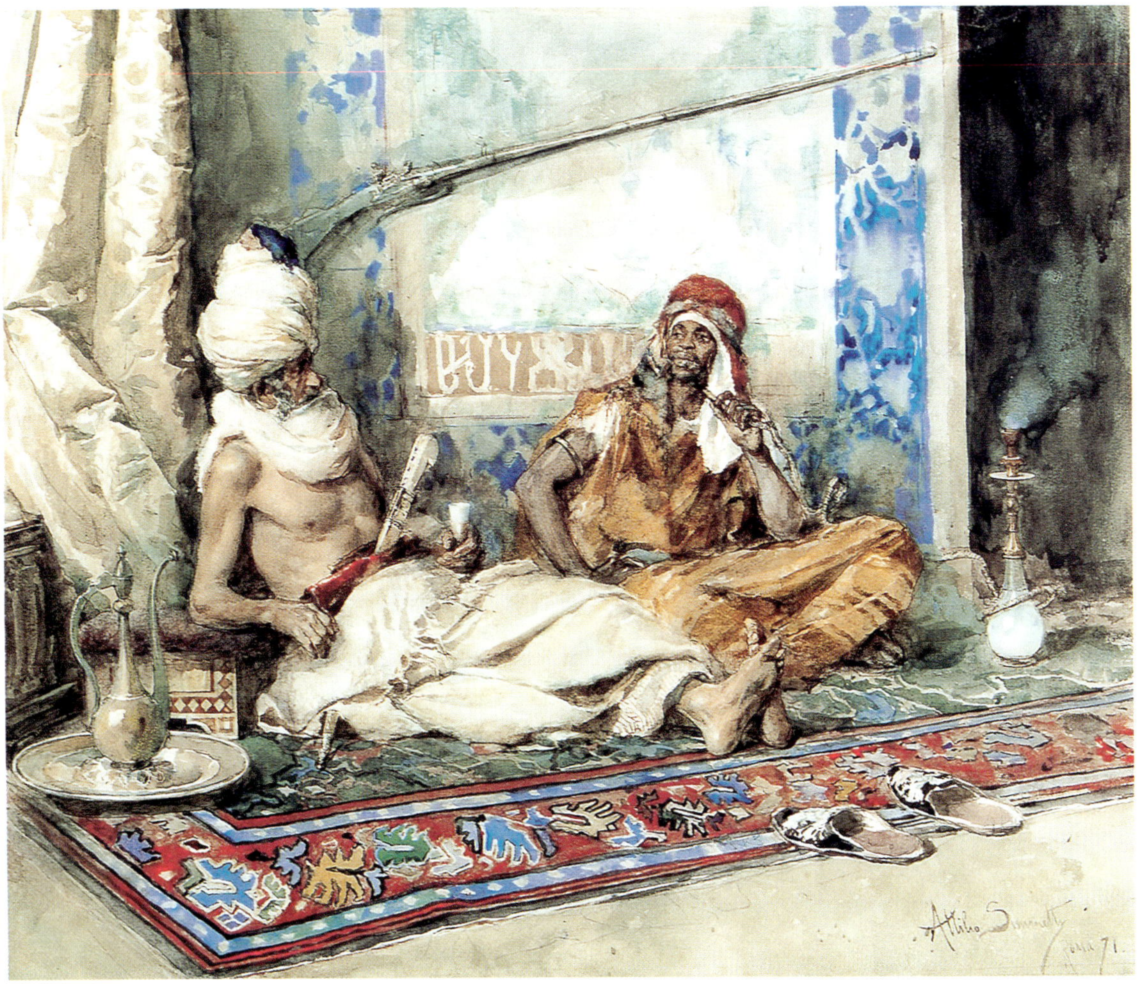

Top
Checkers Players,
Gustavo Simoni, 1902
Watercolor on paper, 53.7 x 76.2 cm
(private collection).

Above
Arabs in an Interior,
Attilio Simonetti, 1871
Pencil and watercolor on paper,
35.5 x 43.8 cm (private collection).

Opposite
Cairo Citadel, Seen from Iman Chafi,
Paul Leroy, c. 1884
Oil on canvas, 30 x 22.6 cm
(Musée des Beaux-Arts, Nantes).

dated and self-serving attitudes, political as well as cultural. Étienne Dinet, for example, a pupil of Bouguereau, may have challenged his master's teaching, but he had neither the capacity nor the desire to go beyond anecdotal painting. He worked in Algeria from 1884 to 1929, and took a genuine interest in local traditions and lifestyles; indeed, in 1912 he converted to Islam. Such canvases as *Springtime of the Hearts* (1904), which took its theme from a book by Soliman Ben Ibrahim that Dinet had illustrated in 1902, and *Mirages* (1906), well-meaning but unambitious works, were well received in France.

Paul Alexandre Leroy was also well versed in Islam and in his style was influenced by Persian miniatures; Arabic speaking, he lived for many years in Biskra in Algeria. As late as 1941 he painted *Interior of a Mosque in Constantinople*, a work that harked back to a bygone era. Painters taking part in local exhibitions showed little appetite for a fight against the genre's traditions. Exceptions were few and included Russian-born Alexander Roubtzoff, a student of the St. Petersburg Academy, lived in Tunis from 1915, painting unusually sensitive landscapes, and portraits of considerable insight.

All in all, the Société des Peintres Orientalistes opened the last chapter in the annals of a genre that no longer reflected either the realities of history, nor the demands of art.

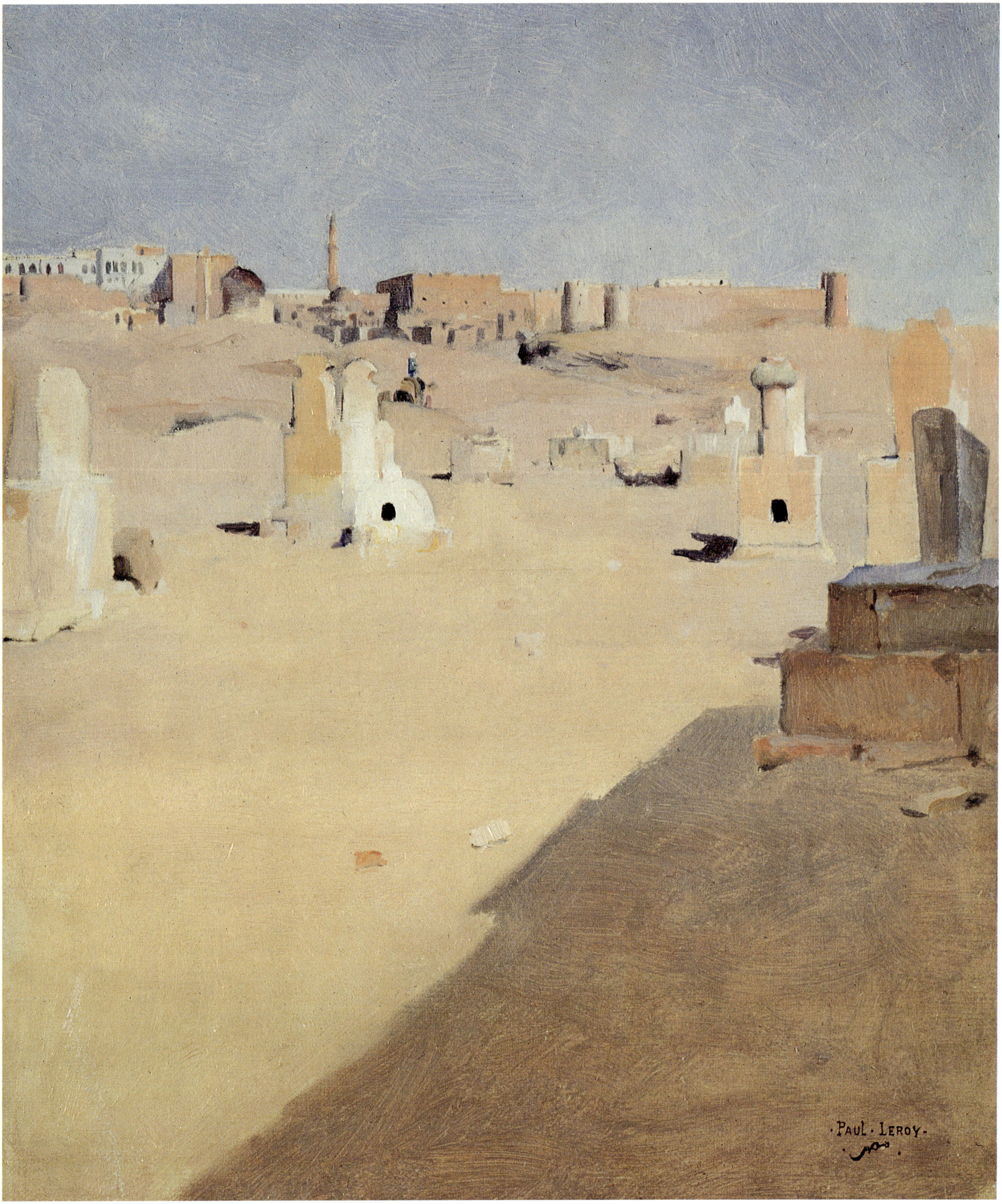
·PAUL·LEROY·

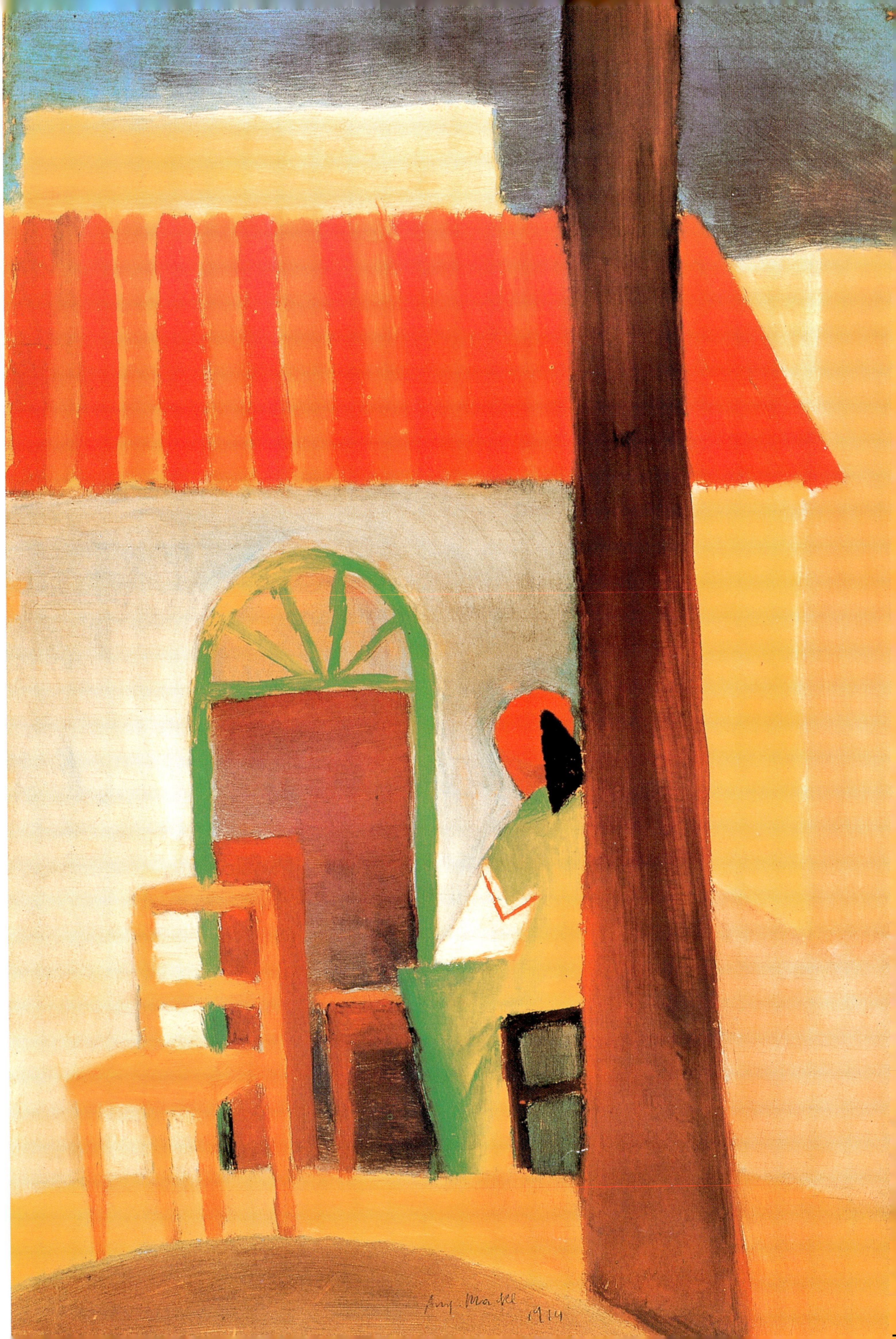
Aug Macke 1914

CHAPTER IV

Orientalism Today

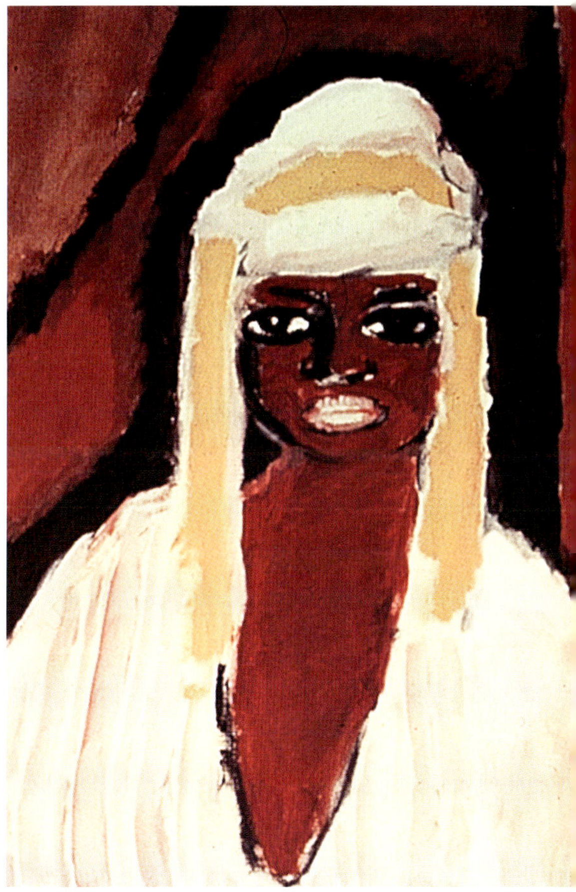

I got up while it was still dark and climbed to the bridge from where I saw the day slowly dawning. [...] Beyond the mist, as if through a screen, indistinct shadows became visible; there seemed to be a tangible presence behind the veil. Suddenly, in a bright chink in this airy tissue, there appeared the sharp point of a minaret and the dome of a mosque. The air began to turn slightly pink. [...] All of a sudden, just above the water, the narrow column of a cypress shot into view, as if its sharp spurt had broken a spell. Was that the enchanter's palace, those massive white towers that now came into view?

Escales en Méditerranée
(Ports of call on the Mediterranean),
Henri de Regnier, 1931

A Shift in the Center of Gravity

Turkish Café I, August Macke, 1914
Oil on chipboard, 35.5 x 25 cm
(Städtisches Kunstmuseum, Bonn).

The Young Arab, Kees Van Dongen, 1910 (detail)
Oil on canvas, 131 x 82 cm
(private collection).

With the development of modern art, the Orientalist genre started to lose both its prestige and its raison d'être. During the second half of the 19th century there was a profound change in the focus of aesthetic interest, with a taste for things Japanese dominating from the 1860s onwards. The opening of Japan to the Western world after Commodore Perry's show of force in 1853 revealed a great civilization that had up until then been virtually impenetrable. Europeans marveled at the delicacy and sumptuousness of Japanese crafts and visual arts, and in particular Japanese prints. The growing craze for Japan was encouraged by a number of factors. In 1867 Japan began to take part in the World Expositions, travelers, now becoming real connoisseurs of the Eastern arts, brought back treasures, and the first specialist publications appeared. It would, however, have been merely another passing fashion, like the 18th-century crazes for things Chinese and Turkish, if artists had not been so deeply influenced by it. The innocent *japonaiseries* were transcended by an artistic movement that took shape under the name of *japonisme*. The boldest artists of the late 19th century, such as Manet, Moreau, Monet, Van Gogh, Rodin, Whistler, Vuillard and Vallotton, started to collect woodblock prints from the Edo period. It was not a question of sacrificing themselves on the altar of a far-flung exoticism. They discerned something revealing in this art, an art that was both popular and highly sophisticated. Through their study of Japanese art, they were able to question the fundamental rules governing the formal structure of Western painting and sculpture. This Far Eastern art provided them with an example of a more flexible form of representation in which perspective was shown symbolically and sometimes simply abolished. The French writer Edmond de Goncourt, an experienced collector and the author of works on Utamaro and Hokusai, stated in 1884 that Japan had "revolutionized Europe's perspective."

Whistler and Manet were among the first important artists to reflect Japanese influence, though they had several precursors. Whistler was inspired by the work of Hiroshige when he produced *The Golden Screen* in 1864, whilst Manet's *Portrait de Zacharie Astruc* of 1866 made a telling allusion to Japan by placing a small, brown book near the sitter, a book of Japanese prints. There was nothing superficial in such allusions. Whistler's entire works are impregnated with this Japanese atmosphere and his sublime *Peacock Room*, begun in 1876, for F.R. Leyland's apartment in London, is a supreme expression of this aesthetic. Manet gave prominence to a print by Kuniaki II on the wall that serves as the background in his *Portrait of Zola* (c. 1868). Many other works owe much to Japanese art: Fantin-Latour's extraordinary *Rhododendron* (1874), the works of Puvis de Chavannes and Toulouse Lautrec, and Monet's *Japonerie* (1876). Japanese art allowed such artists to accomplish the most sacrilegious acts by demonstrating that great (Japanese) artists had long preceded them on this road. In Van Gogh's portrait *Père Tanguy* (1887), the background is again a wall on which there are Japanese prints. The French artist Maurice Denis (who amused himself by painting fans between 1891 and 1895, as Dégas had done before him), not to mention Gustave Moreau, Pierre Bonnard and Félix Vallotton, also owed much to Japanese influence. The enormous success of Puccini's opera *Madame Butterfly* (1904) was a clear sign of a groundswell that was overturning the most firmly established canons of art.

Another area of exotic interest emerged as well; an enthusiasm for Pacific cultures. Paul Gauguin, who fled Europe and its over-sophisticated culture to take refuge on the island of Tahiti, was the first fully to exploit this region in aesthetic terms and consequently the first to give it status in Western art. This increasing recognition of Pacific art went hand in hand with the ever more marked desire to "return to roots," to a more natural way of life, a feeling which had affected the entire 19th century. It was expressed by the Barbus, the young emulators of the French Neo-classicist Jacques-Louis David; by the German Nazarenes; by

Ingres; by the English Pre-Raphaelites; and by various artists and writers' groups who harked back to the Middle Ages, from Pugin and William Morris in England to Viollet-le-Duc and Sérusier in France. However, it was the 'discovery' of African art – known, with contempt for some and familiarity for others, as 'negro art' – which caused the major impact. The first collections, some of which were lovingly put together by artists, served as influences rather than as the direct inspiration of the German Expressionsts, the Fauves, and the Cubists. In time, however, it was the impact of masks and statues from black Africa, combined with several other exotic influences, that underlay the advances made by artists determined to change the course of Western art.

Ancient Egyptian sculptures and bas-reliefs also had a role to play in the story of modern art. In 1909 the German art historian Wilhelm Worringer used Egyptian art to support his twin concepts of "empathy and abstraction"; and before him, Paul Gauguin had drawn direct inspiration from Egyptian painting, recalling a painting from a Theban tomb, of which he had a reproduction, for the figures in *Te Matete* (The Market), which he painted in 1892. The Italian artist Amedeo Modigliani was also profoundly affected by these sources, as can be seen in his characteristic portraits of long-necked women. The French naïve painter Henri Rousseau is credited with a revealing observation: he told Picasso that he [Rousseau] was "the best at the Egyptian style."

In this context, Rousseau's *The Dream*, the last picture he exhibited at the Salon des Indépendants in Paris before his death, is a very personal tribute to the Orientalists and perhaps, more specifically, to Gérôme, the art teacher who advised him to retain his naïve style. From 1891 onwards he painted his wholly unreal jungles, such as *Surprised* or, in 1904, the *Fight Between Tiger and Buffalo*, in which beasts that look as though they had come from a circus poster live amid luxuriant, disproportionate, dreamlike vegetation. In 1907 he painted *The Snake-Charmer*, in which a girl who is blacker than coal plays a flute by

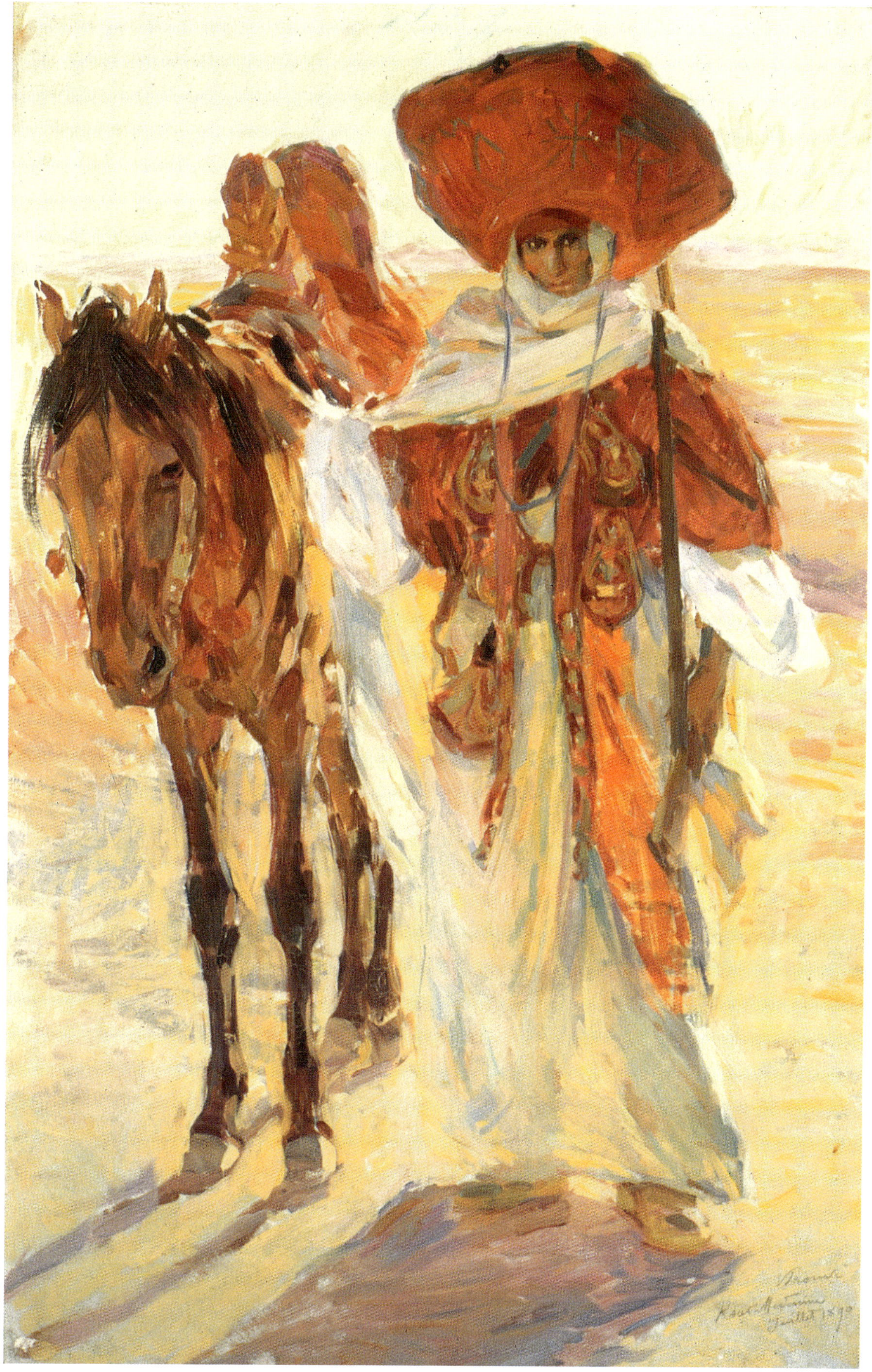

Arab Horseman, Victor Prouvé, 1890
Oil on canvas,
(Musée de l'École de Nancy)..

Victor Prouvé, one of the leaders of the Art Nouveau movement, did not lapse into its common fault of idealism: he portrays the Orient in its most carnal and hedonistic colors.

moonlight on the edge of a river bordered with impenetrable forest. She seems to be accompanied by an exotic pink and gray bird, which appears not far from the snake that has risen in response to her music. She echoes the *Sleeping Gypsy* of 1897, one of his best known canvases, in which a lion stands over a figure sleeping peacefully on the ground.

From this time onwards, the basis of Orientalism changed and it developed in ways that had little to do with Orientalism of previous centuries. Despite the mistrust of some sections of the avant-garde, Orientalism was to enjoy a final, magnificent flowering.

Victor Prouvé, the Precursor

In 1889 The French artist Victor Prouvé traveled to Tunisia in the company of his friend Émile Friant. Prouvé was overwhelmed by the capital city: "Tunis the white! And what a white! White, but such a beautiful white: pure, colored, flavored, vibrant, enveloping and rather disconcerting when one looks at the palette." He made over a thousand drawings while he was there, drawings that were a storehouse of inestimable value throughout his career. On his return to Nancy in France, he immediately got down to painting a large number of imagined scenes. But his own decisive influence was not so much on painting as on the applied arts. He employed Islamic themes in the Art Nouveau décor of the École de Nancy, and he was certainly the inspiration behind the Moorish glassware of the celebrated glassmaker Émile Gallé and the Arabic-style enamels of Camille Martin. Thanks to Prouvé the radical revolution accomplished by architects, decorators, craftsmen and painters was enriched with decorative elements which, once transformed, integrated marvelously in a multifaceted style that was continuously being renewed. His contribution to design is as important as that of the architect Antonio Gaudí in Barcelona, and the designers Carlo Bugatti in Turin and Ernesto Basile in Palermo, all of whom employed elements of the Egyptian or Moorish styles.

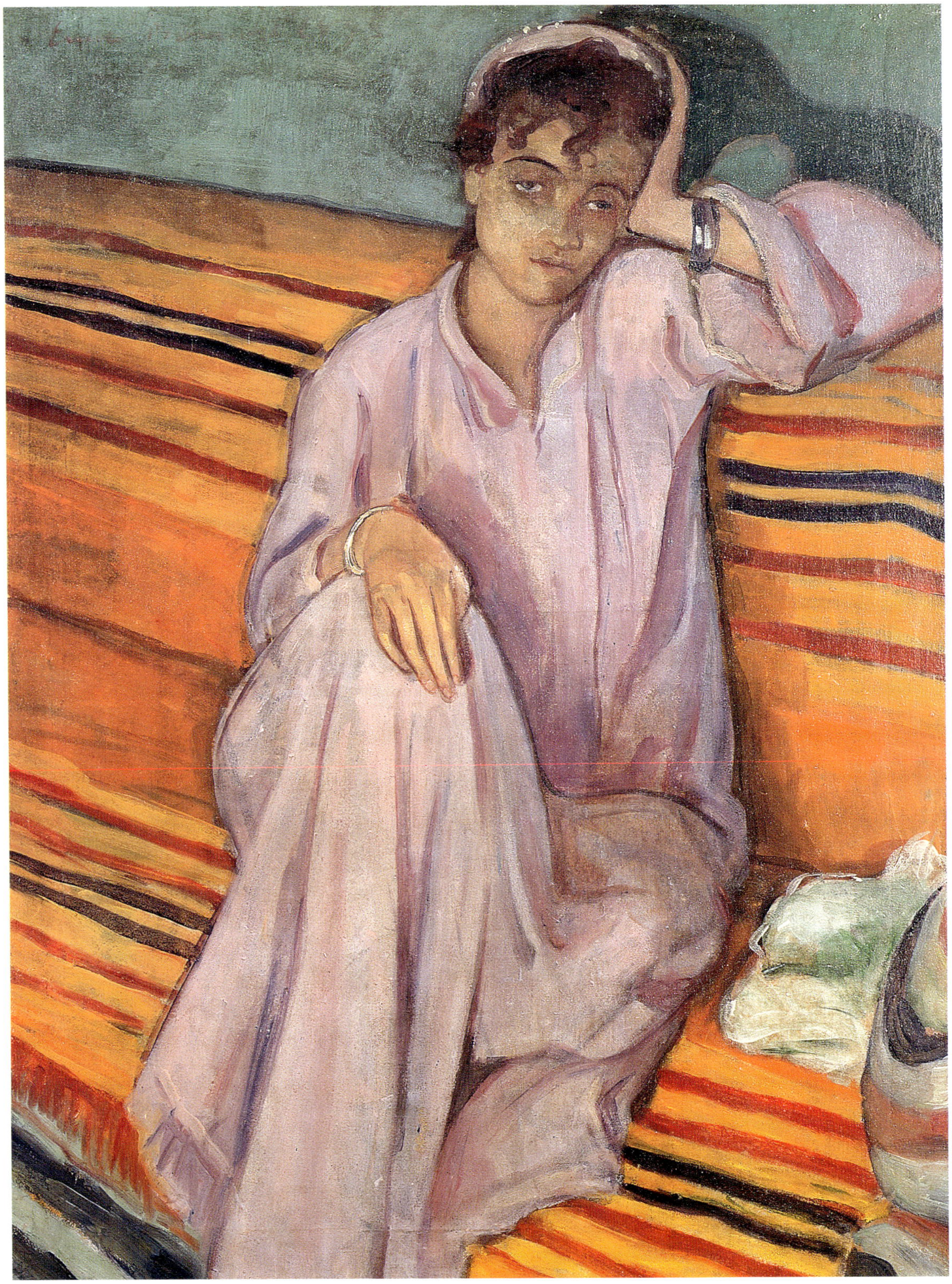

Émile Bernard, the first modern Orientalist

Of all those who took part in the artistic adventure in Brittany with Paul Gauguin, the French artist Émile Bernard remained the most deeply marked by his stay in Pont-Aven and Poldu in 1888. Unable to deal with life in Paris, and then having finally fallen out with Gauguin, he eventually decided to leave Pont-Aven. In 1893 he reached Italy; he visited Florence, then Rome, Pisa, and Genova, embarking there for Constantinople, where he painted views of the port and a beautiful panorama showing a park on a hill with a wooden bridge crossing a lake. He then went on to the island of Sámos, Jerusalem, and Jaffa before arriving in Egypt, where he landed at Port Said. He spent several months in Cairo and Alexandria, capturing many scenes from daily life: *Cloth Merchant* (1893), *A Street in Cairo* (1894), and *Women in the Market*, together with numerous still-lifes and women's portraits. He was fascinated in particular by

Arab café society, as can clearly be seen in his drawing *Café-concert* of 1900. However, his major work from this period is undoubtedly *Harem* (1894), in which he attempted to break with the West's clichéd view of Eastern women. His sitters are clothed in long, dark costumes. There is nothing languorous about them and, with the exception of one musician playing the cymbals, his recluses exude an air of impressive austerity.

In a letter to his mother he attempted to describe the transcendent value of life on the other side of the Mediterranean: "You cannot imagine what great visions I have had from the sight of the *fellaheen*. Almost naked, powerfully muscular, burnt by the sun and dressed in sober fabrics with majestic folds, for me they were a revelation of life at its simplest and most noble. In them I found the freedom of man and woman far from that of our misshapen civilization. Their life is truly biblical and divine, for there is nothing more supernatural for us nowadays than the purely natural. When I speak of the sacredness of Art, I mean the beauty which emanates from the simple, basic life of the desert and the fields, the beauty of men and women naked under the sun."

Émile Bernard immersed himself in the Egyptian way of life, and married a Syrian woman, Sett Hannah Saati. He never tired of

Opposite
African Woman (My Wife on a Sofa), Émile Bernard, 1895
Oil on canvas, 111.5 x 86 cm
(Folkwang Museum, Essen).

Below
Woman Smoking Hashish (or *Woman Smoking a Tombac*), Émile Bernard, 1900
Oil on canvas, 86 x 113 cm
(Musée d'Orsay, Paris).

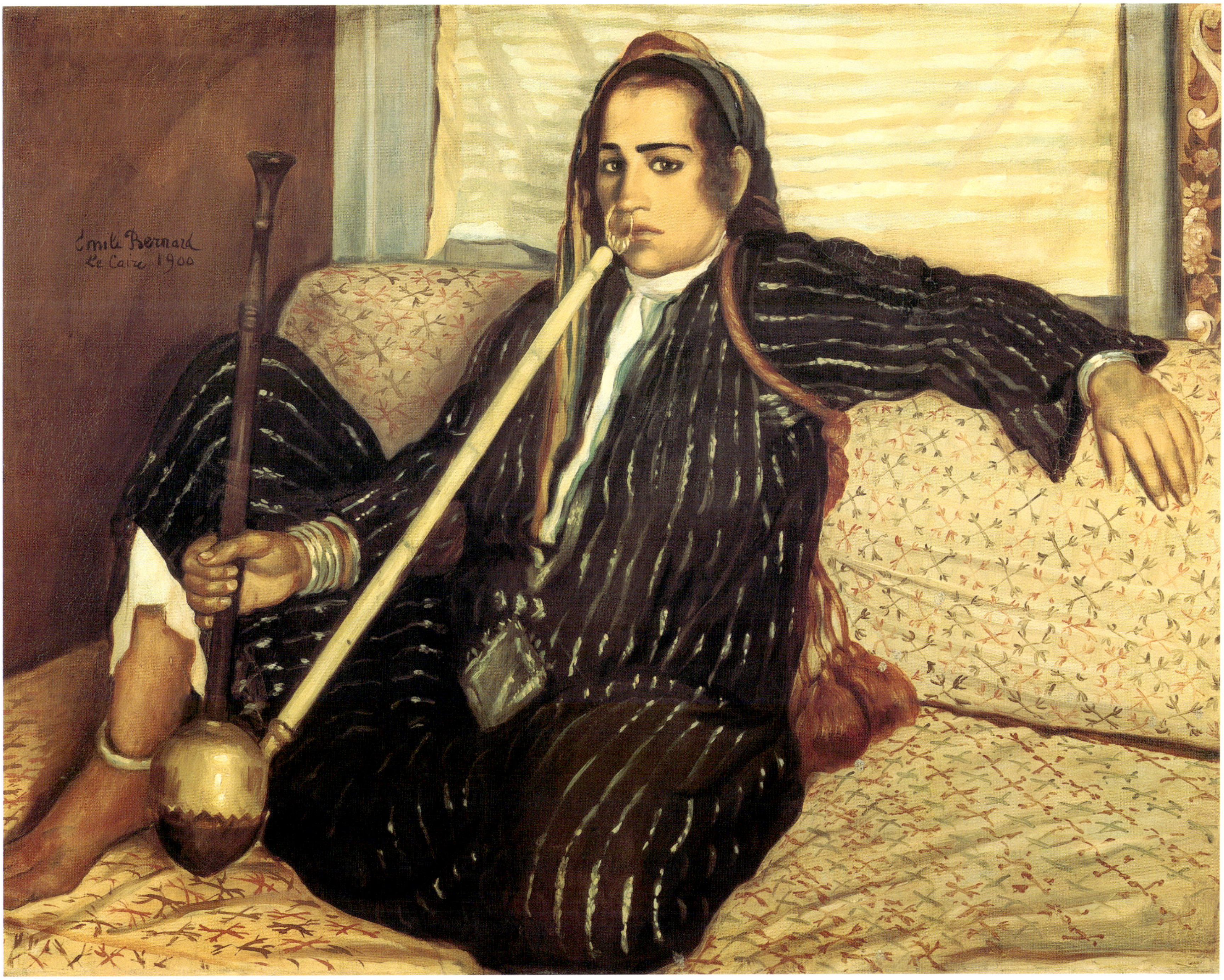

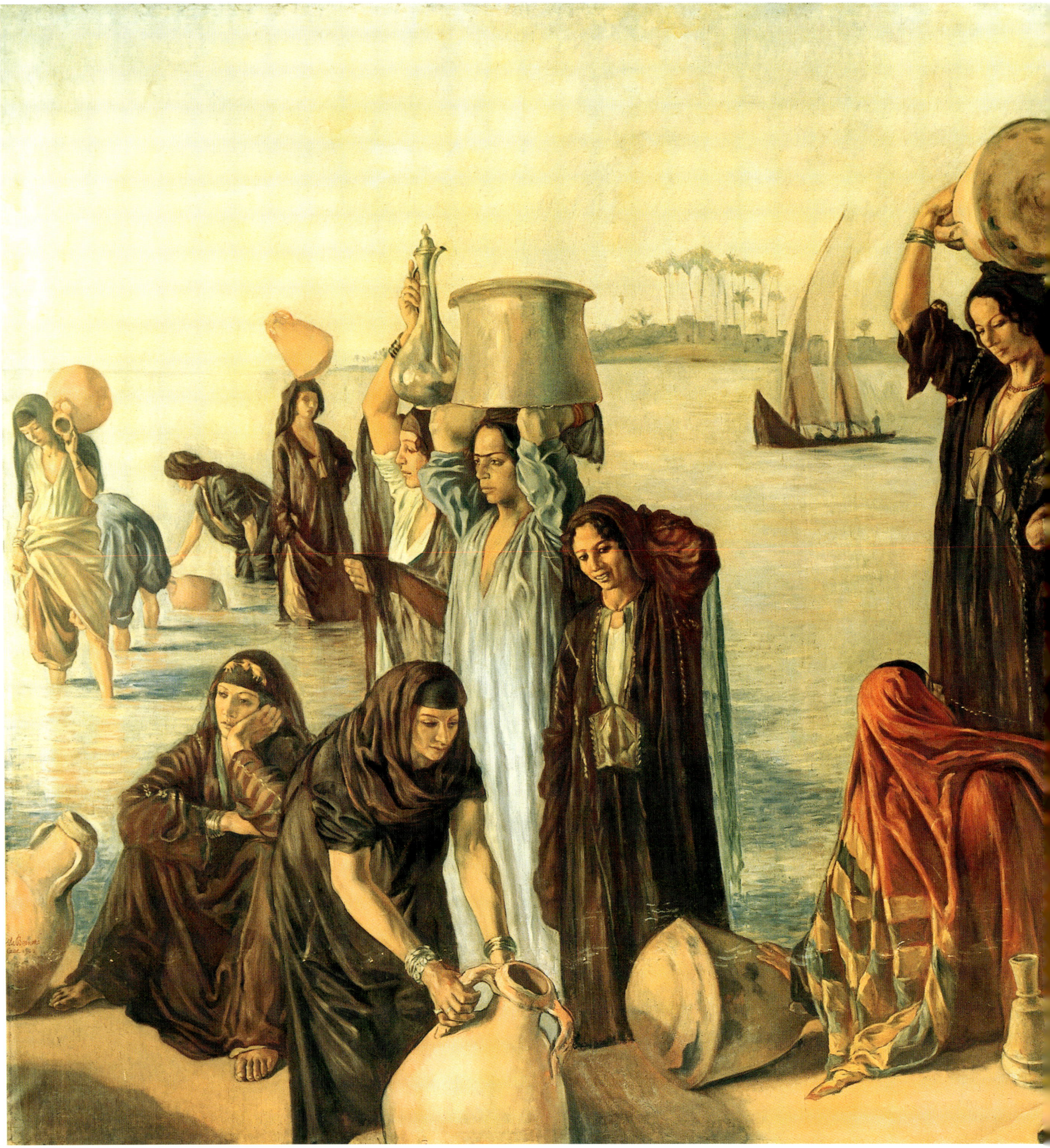

Vision of Egypt (or *Women on the Banks of the Nile*),
Émile Bernard, 1898–1900
Oil on canvas, 200 x 300 cm
(Musée des Beaux-Arts, Lille).

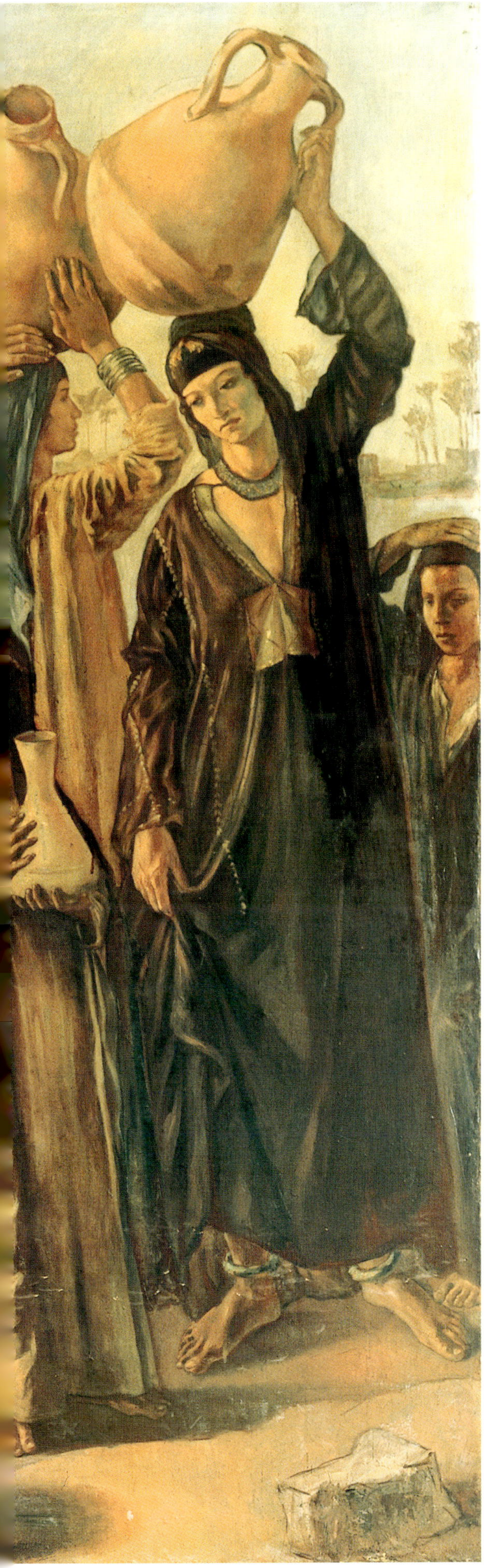

lamenting the twilight of the authentic world he was trying to recapture, a world that was the exact opposite of the modern (Western) world. He was exasperated by the Egyptian élite, who as far as he was concerned had betrayed the values of their country: "The Egyptians, civilized though they believe themselves to be since they abandoned the robes of their fathers for the European suit, are nothing less than people on the border between a state of things which is on the way out and a new state of things which is coming in. They belong neither to yesterday nor to tomorrow, offering only the deplorable spectacle of uncertain men who will leave no lasting work." He also railed violently against the destruction of old Cairo, opposed to the fact that, "ancient buildings are abandoned or sold off cheap to Syrians, Greeks and Armenians who have destroyed the gardens round these palaces and filled them with haphazard buildings which they rent any way they can!"

You cannot imagine what great visions I have had from the sight of the fellaheen. Almost naked, powerfully muscular, burnt by the sun and dressed in sober fabrics with majestic folds, for me they were a revelation of life at its simplest and most noble. In them I found the freedom of man and woman far from that of our misshapen civilization. Their life is truly biblical and divine, for there is nothing more supernatural for us nowadays than the purely natural. When I speak of the sacredness of Art, I mean the beauty which emanates from the simple, basic life of the desert and the fields, the beauty of men and women naked under the sun.

Lettre à sa mère (Letter to his mother),
Émile Bernard, *undated.*

On his return to Paris in 1901 he exhibited at Ambrose Vollard's gallery in Paris, showing a number of the works that had been done in Egypt, notably *Vision of Egypt*, a large canvas showing a group of women on the banks of the Nile bearing water-jars; for Bernard they were a symbol of the Orient of our dreams. His works were the visual expression of the last refuge of the imaginary. "I love the East," he wrote, "as much as one can love it while wishing for it to retain its own character. I want the East to remain the land of the sun, a great garden, the last glimmer of Eden. I want the East to be the place where beauty matches desire and enjoys civil rights under the pure blue sky." His watercolors are full of mauve, red, green, and yellow, with clear almost transparent harmonies, accentuated with white and the use of black outlines. From 1894 onwards his works became less diaphanous and the tones became warmer. In their extreme simplicity and sobriety, his paintings, reduced to the basics of the art of painting, are attempts to create visions of a bygone world.

After his exhibition in Paris he returned to Cairo accompanied by the sister of the poet Paul Fort, in order to remain there permanently. Living in the East he realized both his pictorial and his philosophical ideal. He fulfilled the dream that had sprung to life on the wild coast of Brittany.

Kandinsky in Tunisia

From 1904 onwards, after problems with the Phalanx, an experimental art school he had founded in Munich, the Russian artist Wassily Kandinsky began to travel more frequently. Trained as an ethnologist, the young artist wanted to broaden his knowledge of the world and of the varied artistic expressions and customs of the societies he encountered. He spent several days in Venice, made a second visit to the Low Countries, and traveled to Odessa and Moscow. He was greatly influenced by the exhibition of Islamic art that he had seen in Munich in 1903 and wished to discover this artistic aesthetic world for himself, one founded on theoretical bases quite opposite to those of Western art. Late in September, or more probably December, he arrived in Tunis. On his French naturalization papers he noted: "1904, a trip to Tunisia, strong impression of surroundings, fantastic [...] lots of studies, drawings, 'sheep festival'..." He produced a large number of views of the city of Tunis in oil on card, more sketches than finished works, and *Arab Town* in tempera on card in a larger format, which he submitted to the Paris Salon d'Automne of 1905. Even though it is almost impossible to know exactly how many months he spent in North Africa, the profound effect it had on him may be seen in the works executed five years later, when he founded an avant-garde art group, the Neue Künstlervereinigung (new artistic association) in Munich.

The first work, *Arab Cemetery*, shows that he had assimilated the various methods with which he had previously experimented; above all, he had started to see the theories of abstraction formulated by the German art historian Wilhelm Worringer embodied in his art; Worringer, whom he had recently met, strongly influenced the direction of Kandinsky's work. The lively, luminous colors in this painting, which still respects the main figurative conventions, accompany a deliberate lack of definition about the faceless figures. The second painting is the most accomplished of all: *Oriental*, a horizontal composition that brings together many divergent influences. Here the vibrancy of pure color (close to that attempted by the Fauvists) and the very spirit of nascent Expressionism mix and sometimes harmonize, sometimes clash. Kandinsky was here

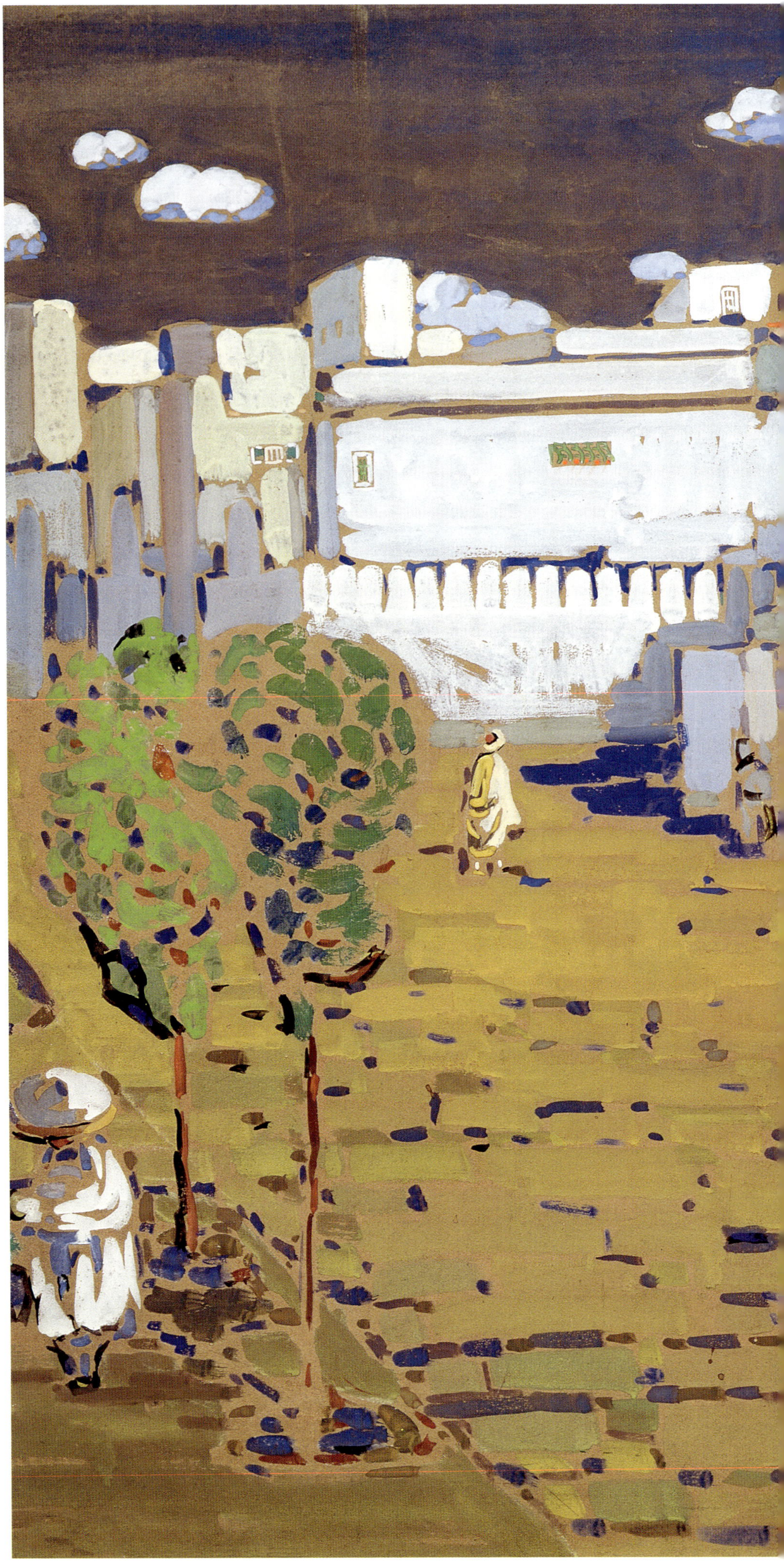

Arab Town, Wassily Kandinsky, 1905
Tempera on card, 67.3 x 99.5 cm
(Musée National d'Art Moderne,
Centre Georges Pompidou, Paris).

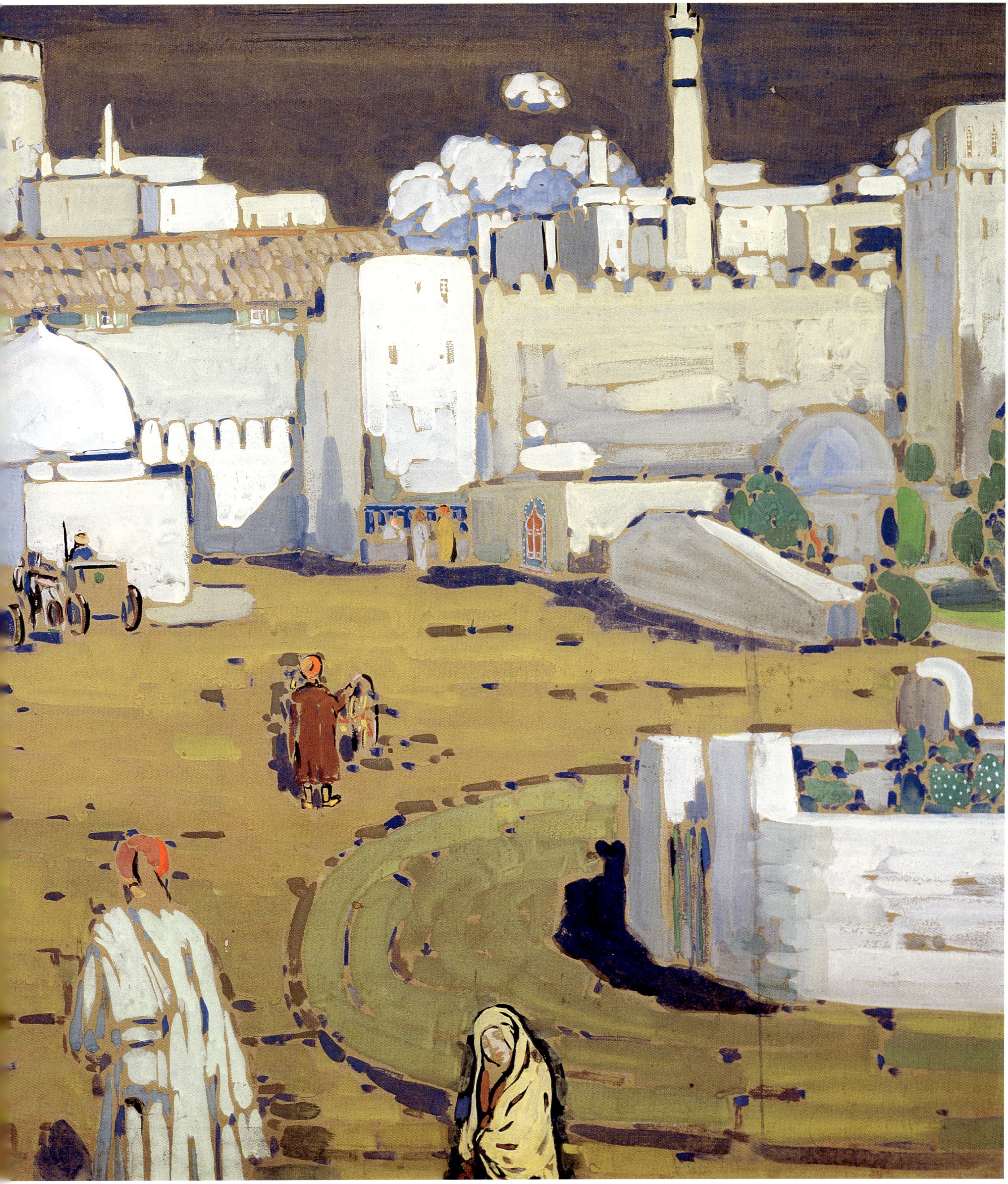

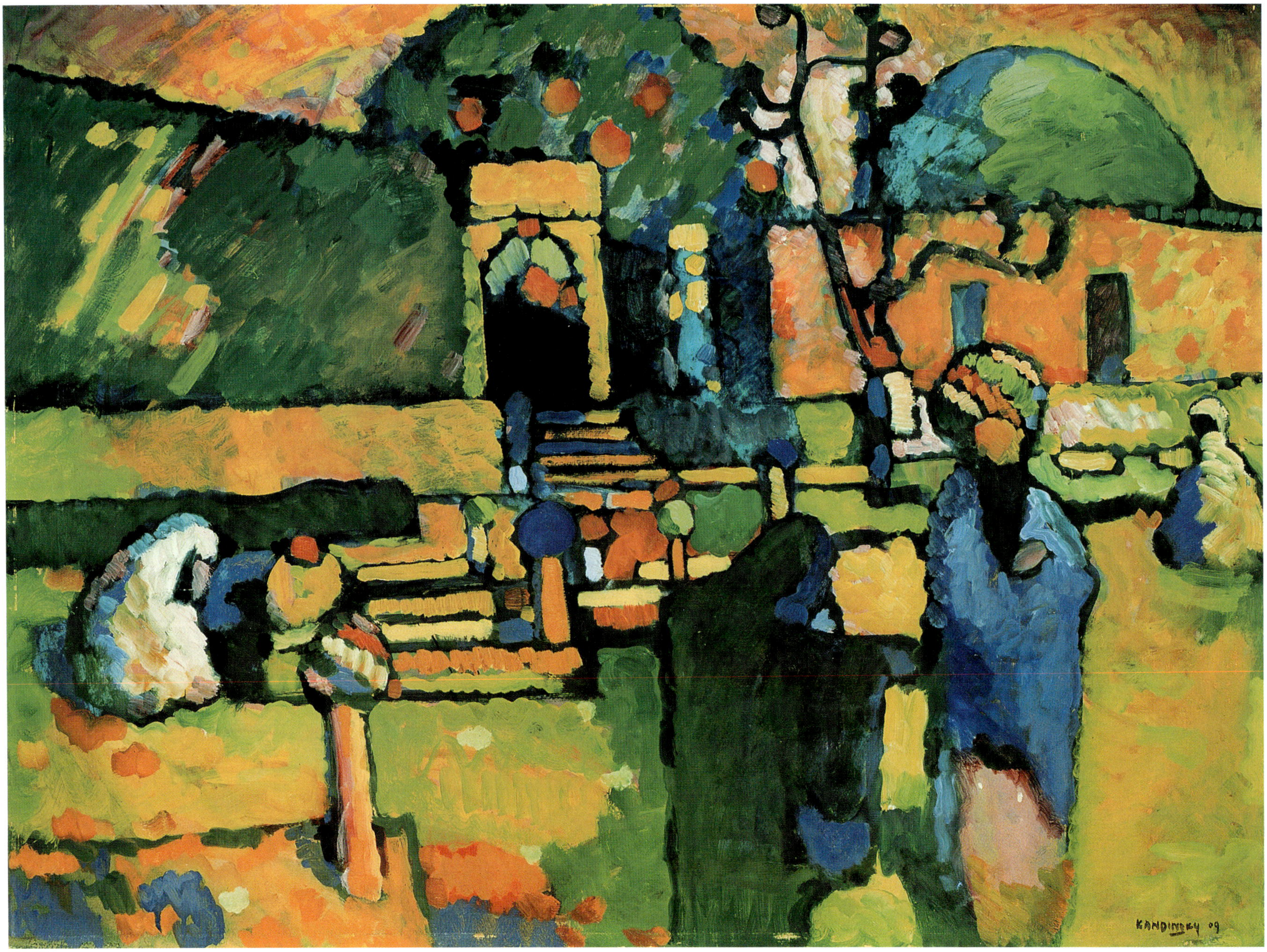

Arab Cemetery, Wassily Kandinsky, 1909
Oil on card, 71.5 x 98 cm
(Kunsthalle, Hamburg).

Opposite
Improvisation VI (or *The African*),
Wassily Kandinsky, 1909–1910
Oil and gouache on canvas,
107.5 x 96 cm (Städtische Galerie,
Lenbachhaus, Munich).

trying to use color to reach beyond mere depiction. Though the picture is perfectly readable, with the figures seated in the foreground, the buildings in the background belong to an imaginary domain. Where the sky is concerned, it is a purely abstract arrangement of colors. This fantasy seems to be the summation of the reflections he tried to define the same year in his celebrated book *Über das Geistige in der Kunst* (On the spiritual element in art). The third picture, *Improvisation VI (The African)*, was conceived in a novel fashion; here color and form take equal roles in defining the figurative system, with a very clear range of strong colors working in relation to the stark white of the beaches. The two people in the foreground are Arabs, but recognizable only from very general features. This painting is part of the series of 35 improvisations that mark the passage to pure painting, that is, to abstraction. Oriental elements are visible in a number of his *Improvisations*, which are a synthesis of the painter's experiences, but also go far beyond them. Between 1909 and 1911, Kandinsky painted three pictures with the same title: *Arabs*. The first work in this trilogy was exhibited in Salon 2 of the World Exposition at Odessa, which opened on 6 February 1911. The last of these canvases is one of the works that are halfway between the figurative and the abstract. In the foreground is the figure of a veiled woman lying down near a vase. Behind her the shape of a white horse is visible on the right and on the other side is a man in a turban dancing in

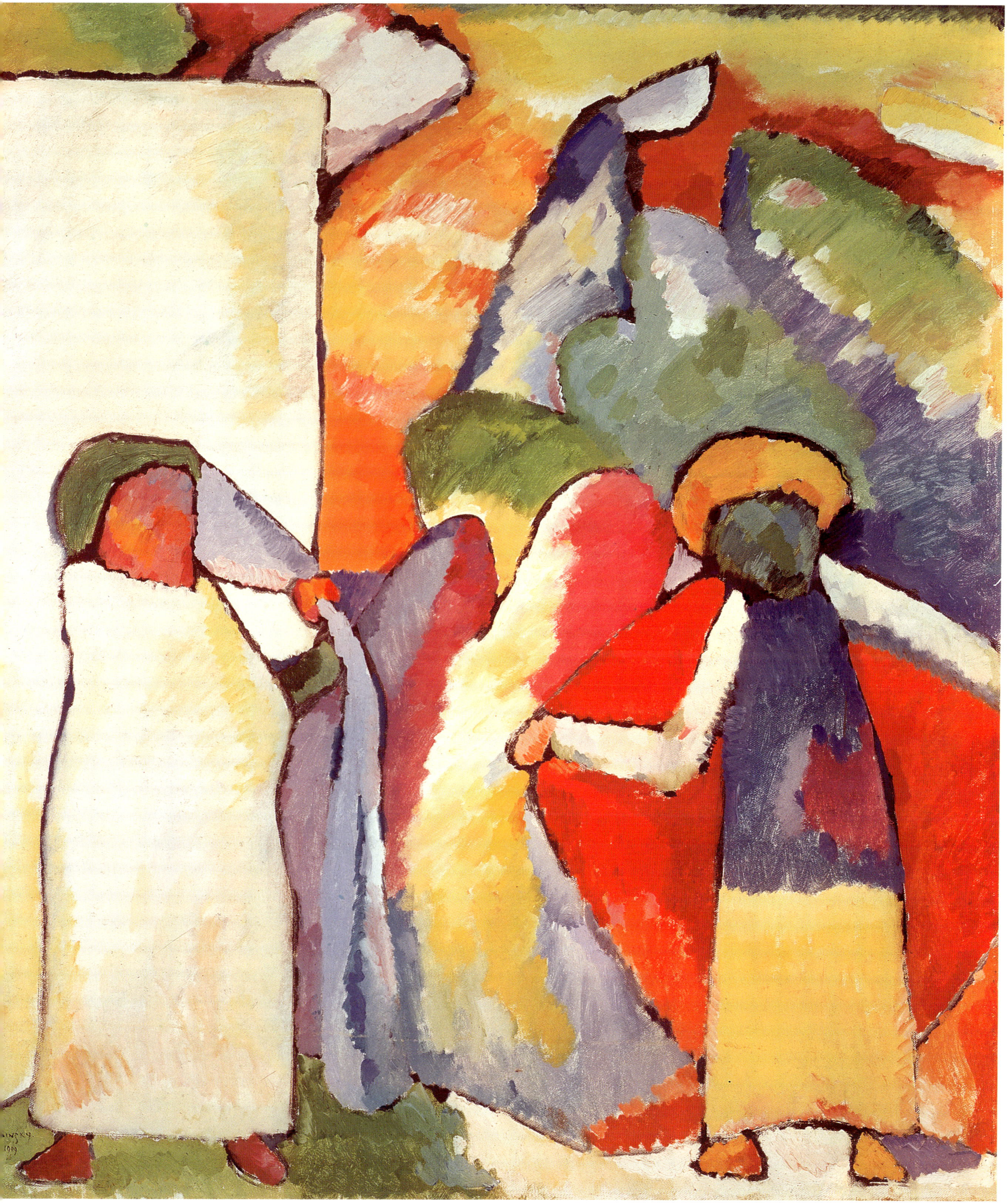

front of another white-clad figure, who is hard to make out. The rest of the surface is an 'abstract' arrangement of colored areas.

During this very long stay in Tunisia, Kandinsky's Russian background also came into play; in effect, Russia became a parallel Orient, encouraging him to look searchingly at the Western tradition. For Kandinsky, his love of the streets of Moscow and Russian culture in general were crucial to his development; the profound impact made on him by the distant provinces are revealed in *Looking Back* (1913). He insisted that the houses of the little villages he went through taught him "to move around in the picture, to live in its bosom." This feeling must have deepened in North Africa.

During this prolific period he wrote articles for the review *Apollon* in which, in December 1910, he enthusiastically recalled an exhibition of Islamic art in Munich that "passed all expectations." He was also excited by the Persian miniatures he discovered in the Kaiser Friedrich Museum in Berlin. "I had the impression that I was standing in front of something which arose all on its own, a gift from Heaven, like a revelation." He explains what attracted him to this form of expression: "It is of an almost barbaric simplicity. An almost vertiginous complexity. The exquisite side of a more refined people, more consciously perfect. The seriousness, the rigor, sometimes the severity of the drawing, as in old icons. It is a beauty of lines that are gentle, flexible, sometimes even malicious. The primitivism of the color tones like a dye. And it is so conceptually sensitive and sensory in terms of its simple tones, so spare in its combination and arrangement, that this primitive coloring is unexpectedly elevated to the very heights of painting. An infinite depth, an expressive depth to which everything else is subordinated, to which immeasurable beauty itself is subordinated and the exterior aspect itself." In short, Kandinsky's great theoretical maelstrom was fed by his sense of the Orient; it strengthened his will to adhere to the culture of "eternal Russia" and to draw this culture into the mainstream of avant-garde Western culture.

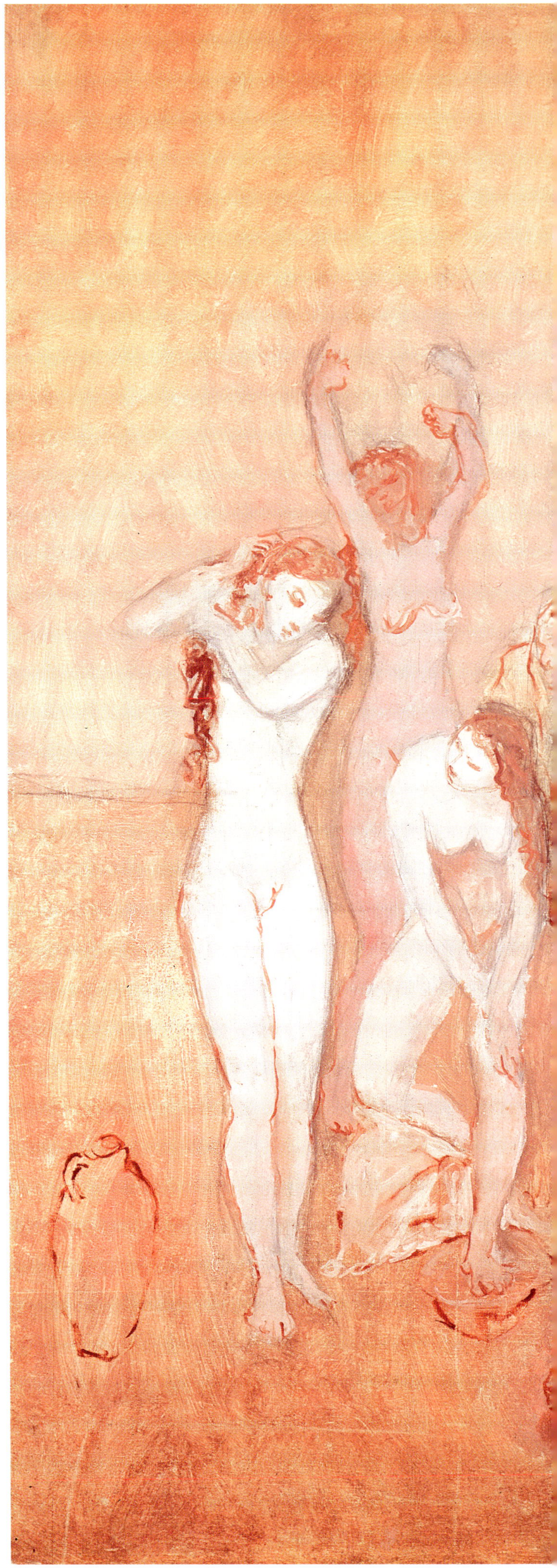

The Harem, Pablo Picasso, 1906
Oil on canvas, 154.3 x 109.5 cm
(The Cleveland Museum of Art, Cleveland).

By combining the profound influence that Ingres had on him with the warm ochers of Iberian art, Picasso was paving the way with his *Harem* for the violent scene of his celebrated *Les Demoiselles d'Avignon* 1907.

Opposite
Women of Algeria, after Delacroix, Pablo Picasso, 1955
Oil on canvas, 114 x 146 cm
(Ganz Collection, New York).

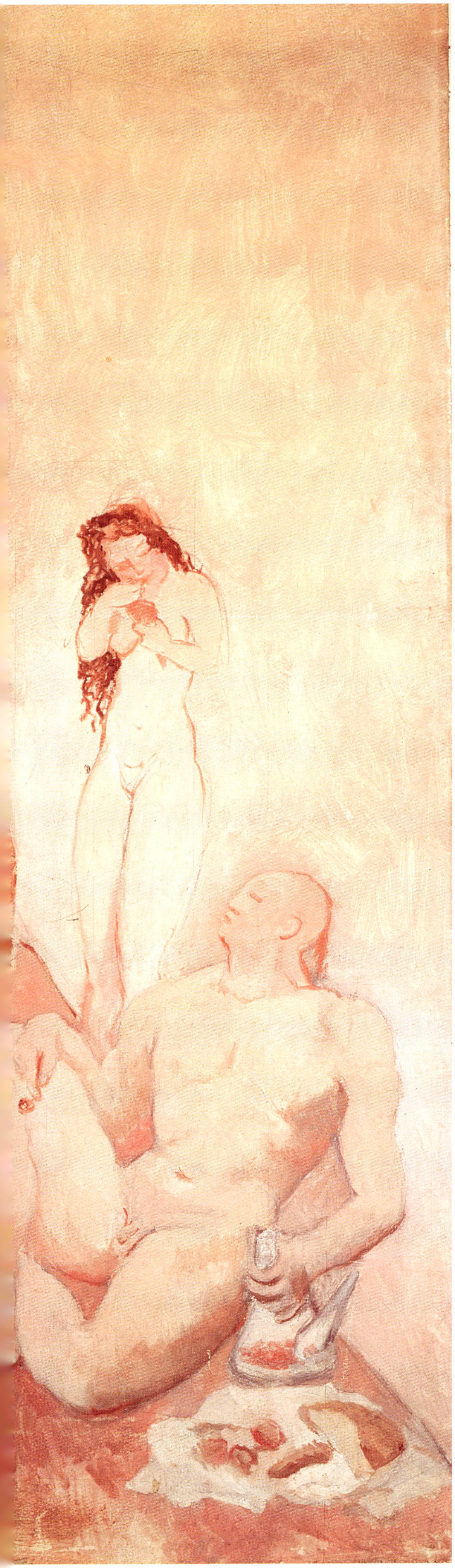

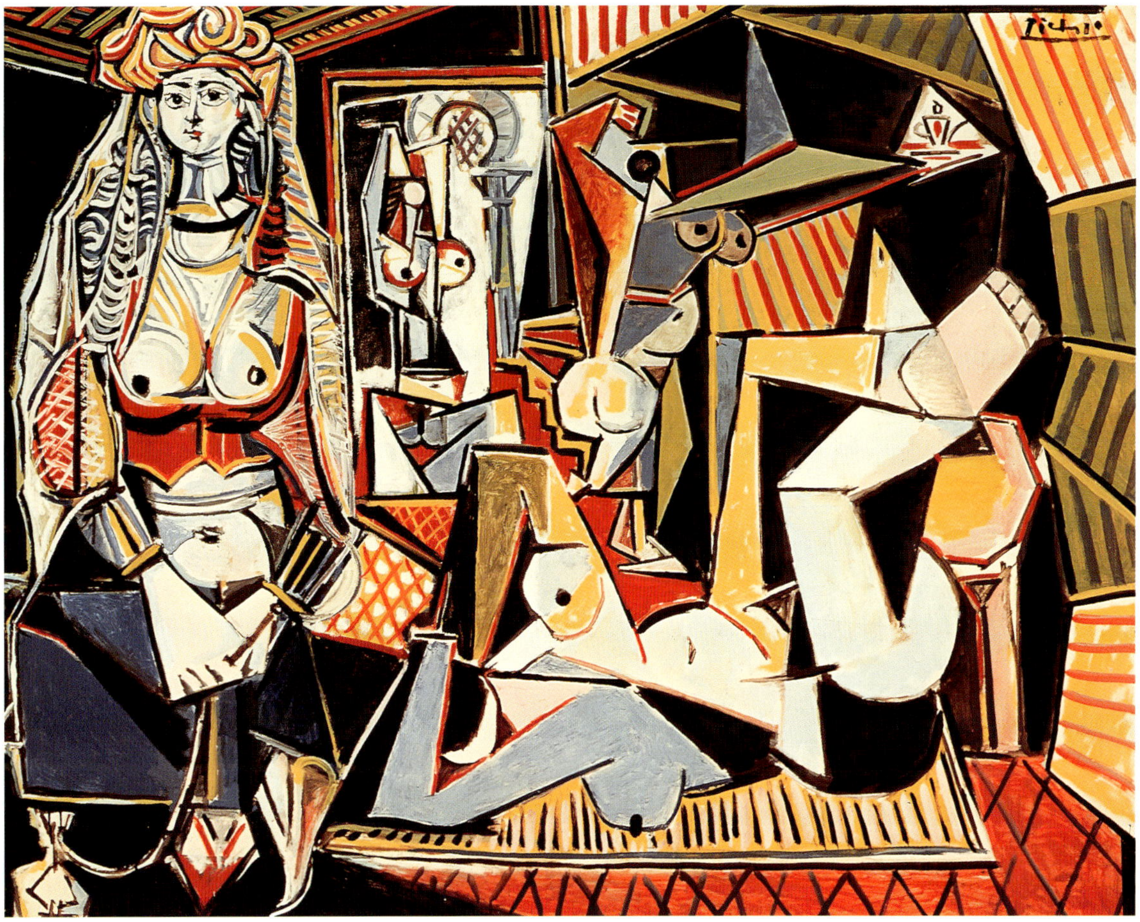

Pablo Picasso and *Les Demoiselles d'Avignon*

The Spanish artist Pablo Picasso, who was hardly at all interested in the art of black Africa at the dawn of the Cubist period, felt no particular attraction for Oriental art either. Even so, the Orient plays a far from negligible role in the thinking that led to the creation of his seminal work *Les Demoiselles d'Avignon* (1907). Picasso drew his inspiration from the work of Ingres, whom he greatly admired, and especially from his last work, the *Turkish Bath*, one of the key works of Western Orientalism. Ingres' languid, voluptuous female bathers and the more virile bathers by Paul Cézanne were to mingle in Picasso's mind, resulting in the left-hand side of the famous picture, which has been called "Cubism's manifesto." A large painting entitled the *Harem* further illuminates this close but iconoclastic relationship with Ingres. Beautiful young women are bathing in the presence of a seated male figure (very likely a eunuch) in a pale red-ocher setting. But the dreamlike, almost phantasmagoric quality of this work, which was created at Gósol during the summer of 1906, was not to reappear in Picasso's brutal *Les Demoiselles d'Avignon*, a work which, formerly known as *Le Bordel philosophique* (The Philosophical Whorehouse), was his tribute to the inhabitants of a brothel in "Avignon street" in Barcelona.

With the exception of odalisques, who form an archetypal theme in Western painting, Picasso made no direct move towards the Orient. He once declared, however: "Matisse is dead; he left me his odalisque." But it was in fact Eugène Delacroix who brought him closer to North Africa when Picasso revisited Delacroix' *Women of Algiers* in a series of 15 variations on this theme between December 1954 and February 1955. This tribute, translated into a monstrous, sublime pastiche, is an Orientalizing fantasy that allowed Picasso to make his own journey to the East by proxy.

Landscape Viewed from a Window, (or *Window in Tangiers*),
Henri Matisse, 1912
Oil on canvas, 115 x 80 cm
(Pushkin Museum of Fine Art, Moscow).

Small Mulatto Woman,
Henri Matisse, 1912
Oil on canvas, 36 x 28 cm
(Musée des Beaux-Arts, Grenoble).

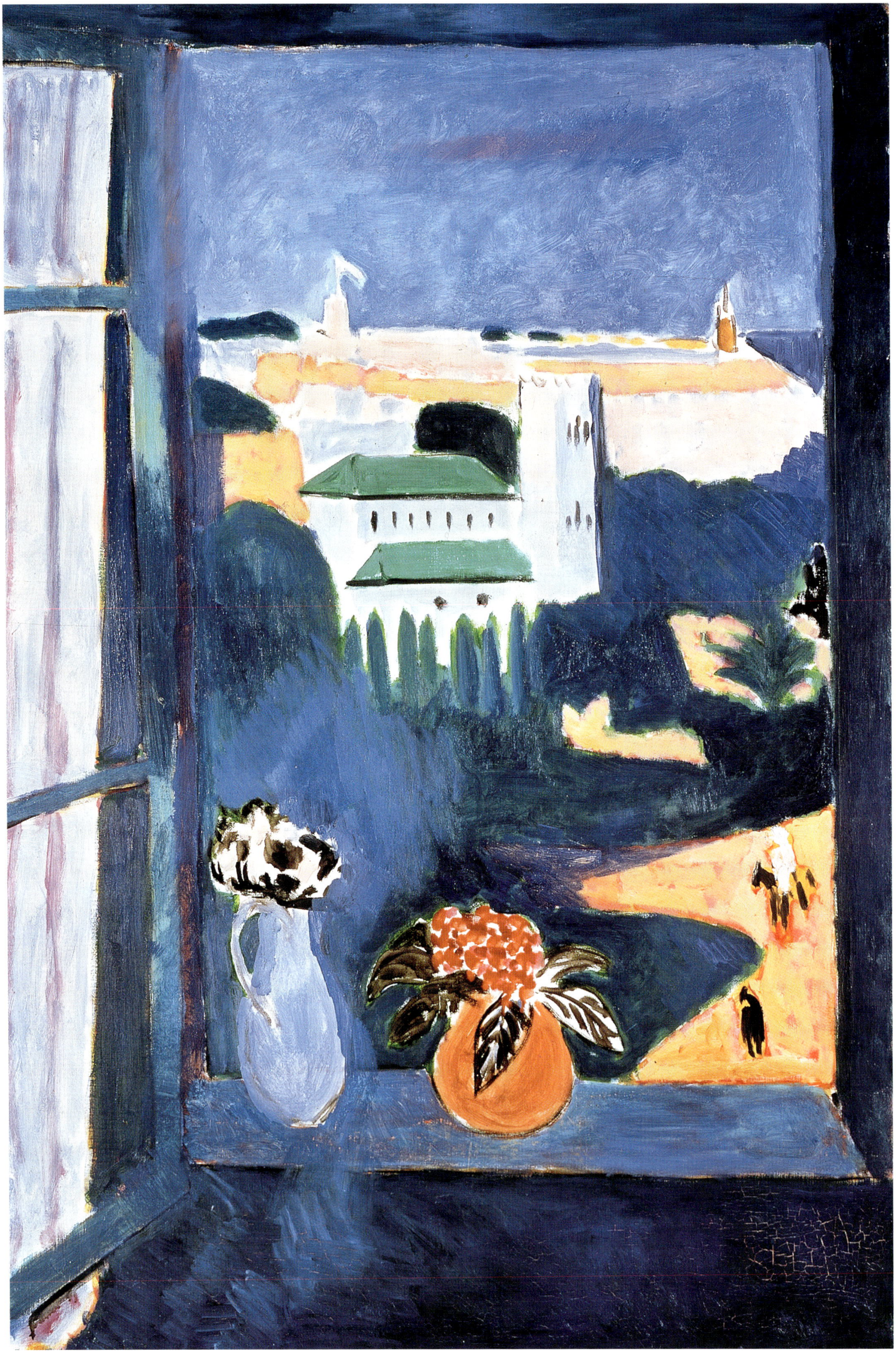

Henri Matisse and the image in the carpet

The first trip Matisse took to North Africa was fairly disastrous. He embarked at Perpignan and sailed for the coast of Algeria on 10 May 1906. Unfortunately, he didn't really like the country where he had been hoping to rediscover what he had caught glimpses of in Islamic art. He declared that Algiers was like Paris but "even more repellent," and Constantine struck him as an "appalling" place. The desert was no better: "Imagine an enormous sand and pebble beach (at low tide)," he wrote to his friend, the painter Henri Manguin: "I kept looking for the sea on the horizon. In the sun, and that's how it almost invariably is, the light is totally blinding." Nor did he find any of the enticing local color he had been expecting: "As for the belly-dancing side of things, I haven't even tried to find it in Algiers, and it was only quite by chance that I saw a quarter of an hour of it in Biskra. And as for the famous Ouled Naïl, who are they kidding? It was ten times better at the Exhibition." It was only from the Biskra oasis that he managed to derive any aesthetic pleasure, but he could not find anything that really engaged his attention as a painter: "It is quite obvious that you would have to spend several years in this country to get anything new out of it, and that you can't just pick up your palette and try to apply your usual methods." All that this unfortunate trip produced was the *Blue Nude*, subtitled *Souvenir of Biskra*, which he worked on a year later in France. In fact it was not until 1909 that he thought again about his days in North Africa, when he was busy on *The Algerian Girl*, the portrait of a curvaceous young woman who, though carelessly reclining on a cushion, gives a paradoxical impression of intense energy, in part because her pastel-colored dress contrasts effectively with the bright reds of the furnishings. This painting belongs in fact to a series of exotic figures Matisse painted, including *The Spanish Girl* and *The Gipsy Girl*.

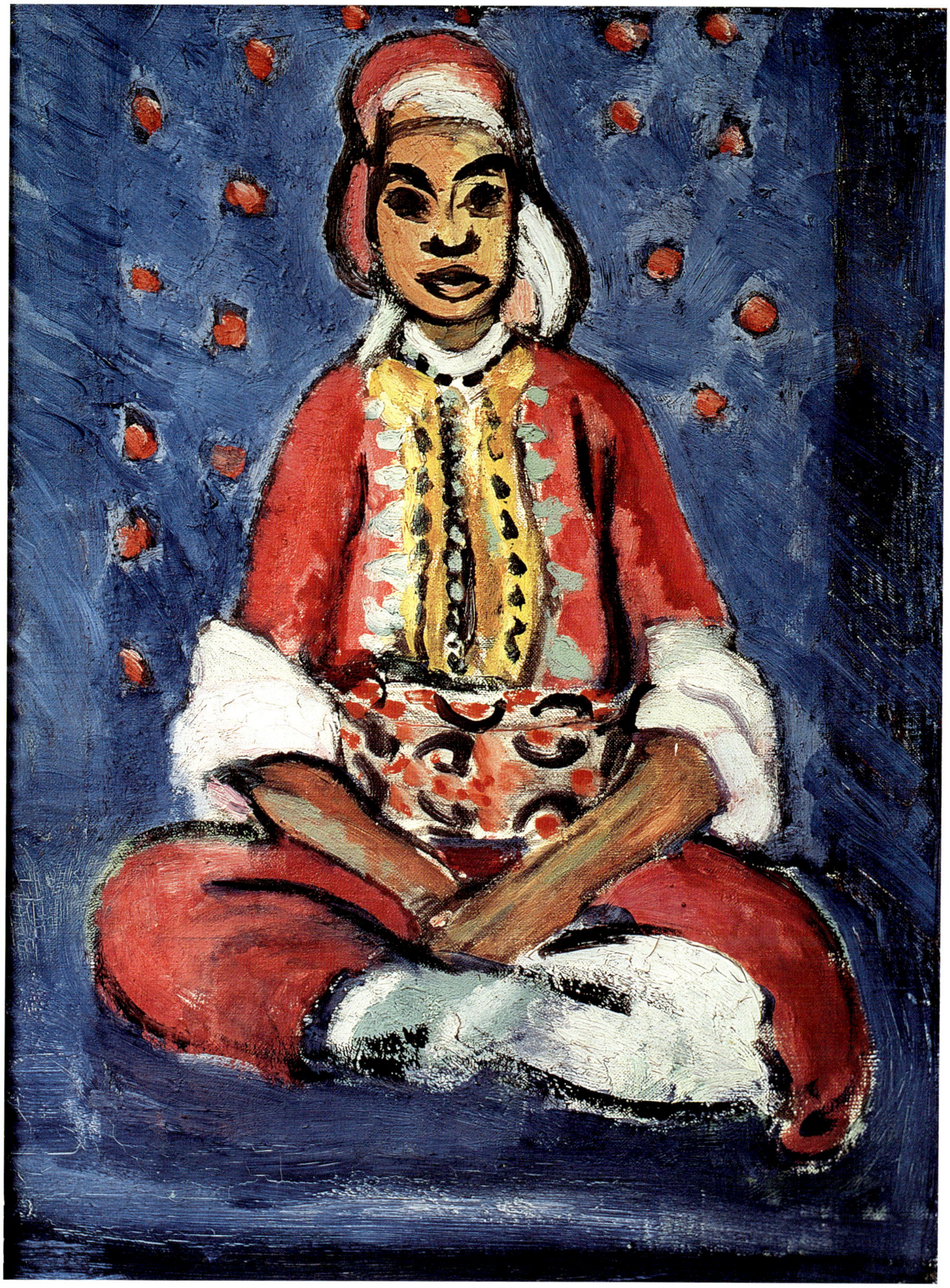

Matisse had long been an admirer of Islamic art, probably from as early as 1900. He loved the exhibition of Islamic art at the Marsan Pavilion, which was on show in Paris in 1903. In 1910 he visited the exhibition of ancient Islamic art in Munich, accompanied by Marquet and at the invitation of Hugo Van Tsudi, the gallery's director and a great admirer of Islamic art. Matisse told Gaston Diehl: "The Orient has always been a revelation to me. In Munich I have found further confirmation of all that I have been looking for. In the Persian miniatures, for example, I discovered a new depth of sensation. The visual props in this form of art give a feeling of greater space, a really tangible space. This has helped me to get away from overly 'intimate' paintings." His experience of Islamic art was in fact one of the most important factors in his meditations on the nature of painting. At the end of his life, he recalled the (apparently) contradictory nature of his development: "The influence of the Impressionists, of the Neo-Impressionists, of Cézanne, and of the Orientals." The "Orientals" was an influence he always cited.

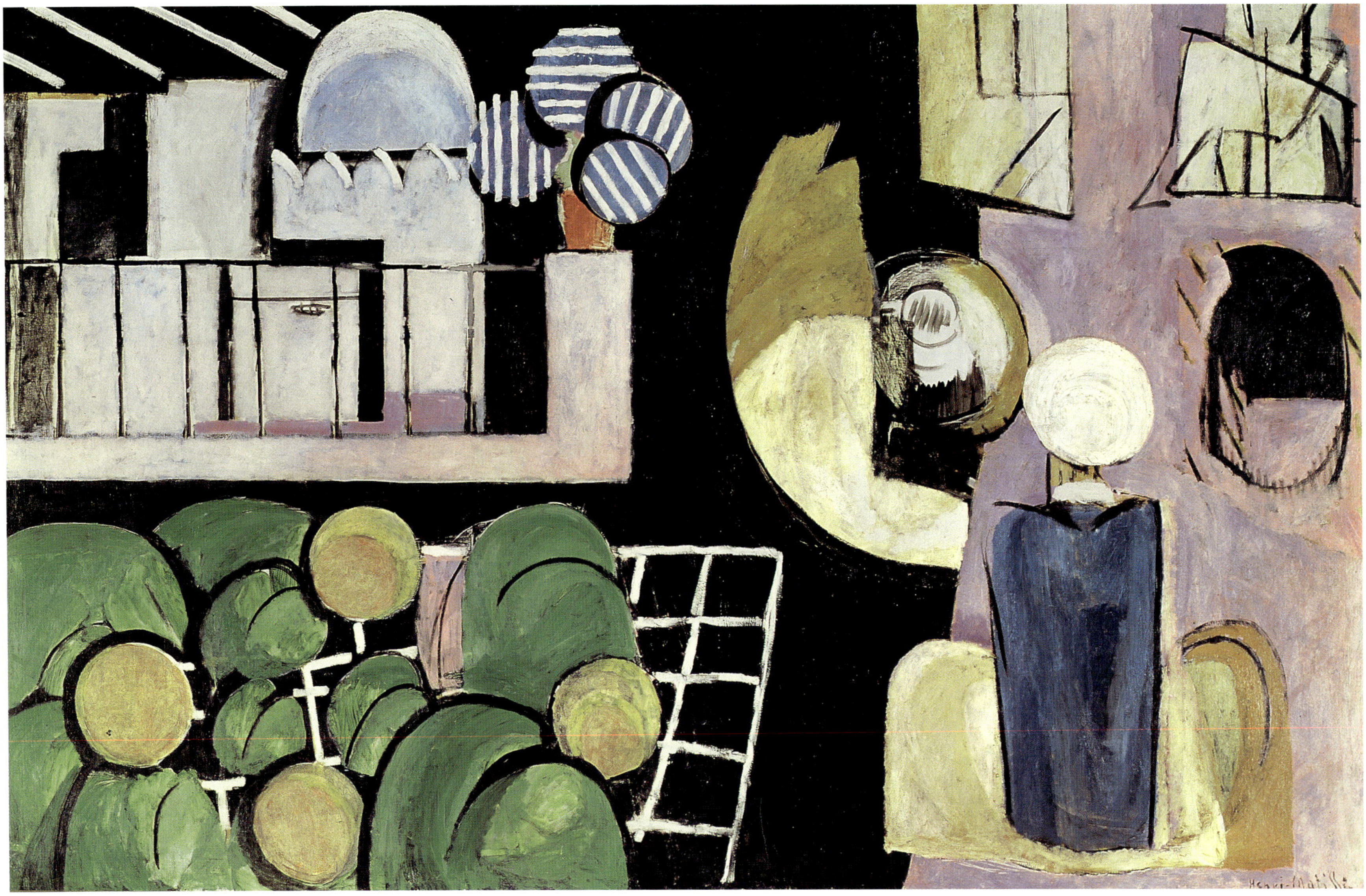

The Moroccans, Henri Matisse, 1915–1916
Oil on canvas, 181.3 x 279.4 cm
(The Museum of Modern Art, New York).

On the Terrace, Henri Matisse, 1912–1913
Oil on canvas, 116 x 80 cm
(Pushkin Museum of Fine Art, Moscow).

He was also captivated by the vogue for all things Japanese, which was all the rage among the Parisian intelligentsia; it had won over artistic circles all over the world, and contributed to the shift in the concept of perspective that brought about a total change in Western painting. But he was not ultimately satisfied with the partial abolition of classical perspective that emerged as a result. Islamic art, by contrast, opened up new horizons. And his interest went beyond Persian miniatures; he was also fascinated by Islamic applied arts, ceramics, fabrics, and most of all by rugs. He was in effect following the advice of Paul Gauguin, who wrote: "You painters who are looking for a way of using color, study the rugs, you will find all the skill there can possibly be, but, who knows, the book may be in a hidden code, you may not be able to read it. [...] Color that is determined by its own peculiar charm, not through a portrayal of objects as seen in the real world." Matisse took this advice literally and used it to transform his paintings into surfaces meaningful in themselves, patterned surfaces that are an essential part of the painting's message. Proof of this can be found in *Interior with Eggplants* (1911), in which a five-leaf motif and garlands of vegetables fill the entire surface of the painting. Stylization, repetition, the complete saturation of the surface, geometric patterns formed by abstract or figurative motifs, an arrangement of lines that continue the elements of the motif, the abolition of barriers between different genres, between high art and applied arts – all this contributed to the subtle revolution that Matisse undertook on the fringes of Fauvism, a movement which, though vital to his development, left him ultimately unsatisfied. But his enthusiastic response to Oriental art needs to be understood correctly: for Matisse it was a matter of Westernizing the ideas he borrowed from Oriental art, not of Orientalizing

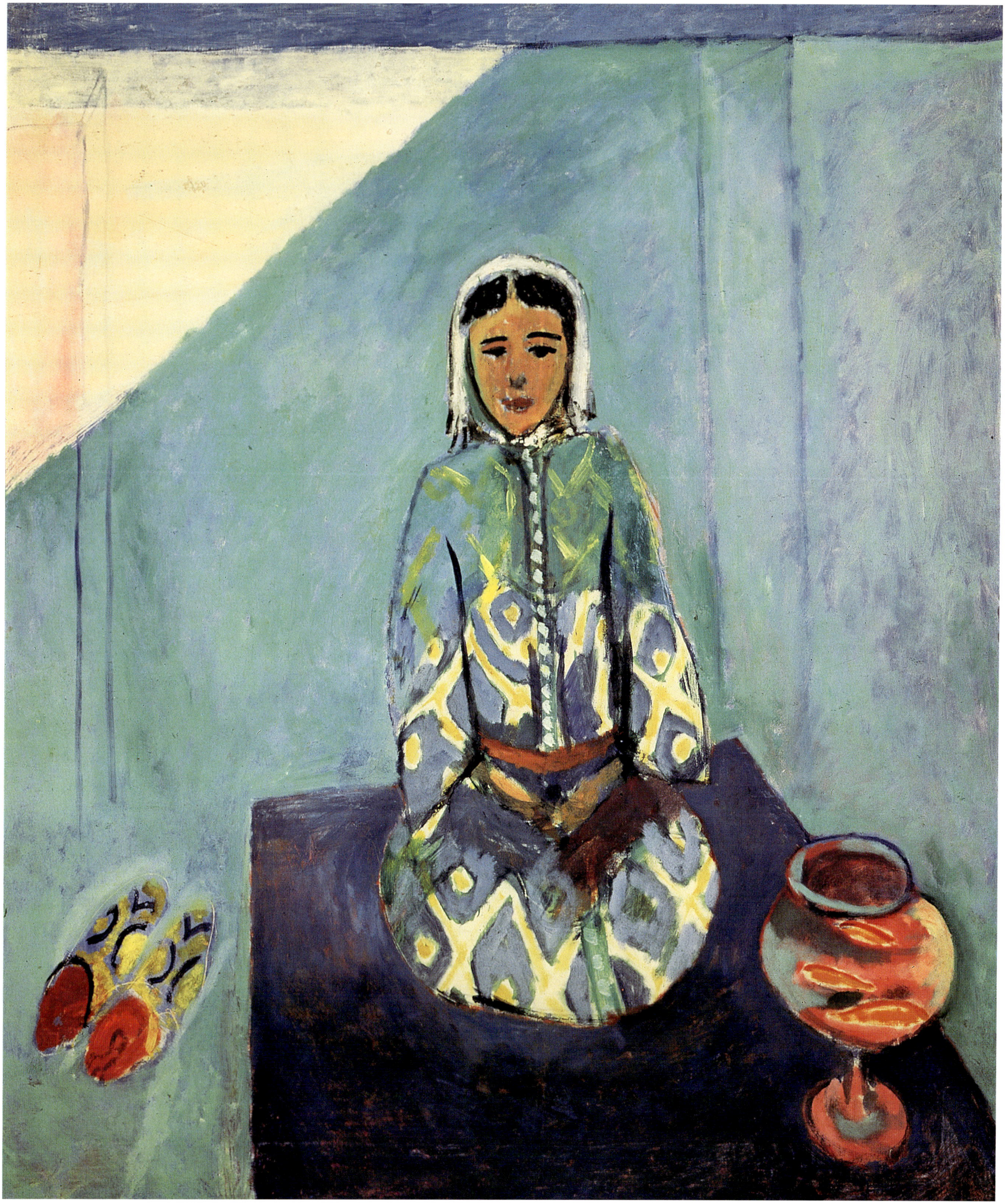

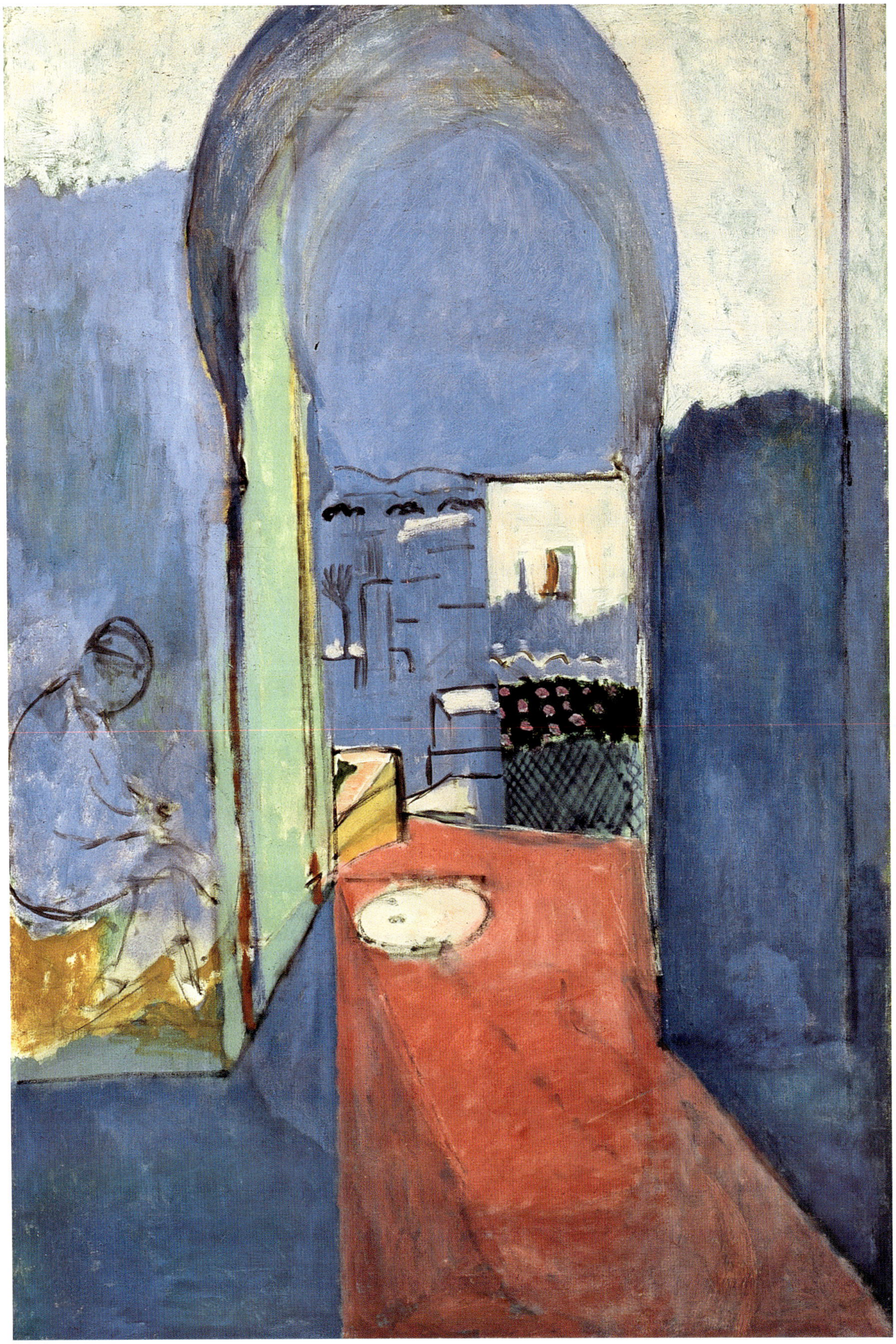

Western art; he was not attempting to create an image of the "mythical Orient."

Matisse decided to make a second trip to North Africa, this time to Morocco. He sailed from Marseilles on 29 January 1912, with the intention of spending the whole winter in Morocco. His friend Albert Marquet had suggested this idea to him, and Matisse had allowed himself to be convinced despite the poor impression the trip to Algeria had made on him. Shortly after his arrival, he sent a postcard to his daughter from the Villa de France, where he was staying, telling her, "I have started on a bunch of blue irises"; and the *Vase of Irises* is in fact the very first of his Moroccan paintings. Doubtless he chose this rather mundane subject because of the incessant rain that prevented him from going out. He also painted *Still-life with Oranges*, another composition probably chosen because of the rain. As soon as he was able, he did some sketches for *Landscape Viewed from a Window*, a painting that he hoped to send to the Russian collector Ivan Morozov, but which he did not manage to complete in Tangiers.

It was the garden that really fascinated him, and as a result he started on a major painting to which he gave the title *Periwinkles* (also called *Moroccan Garden*). The sky is pink and the tree trunk is reddish brown; there are shades of mauve and ocher, a bit of yellow, and above all lots of pale green. The flowers themselves appear in the foreground and seem to be insignificant in the midst of this triumph of nature, which has been translated into the abstract language of colors and forms. He never tired of these enchanted gardens, which he often compared to the Garden of Eden.

The rain lasted more than a month and seriously hindered his work, but he also noted that dull gray weather would clear all of a sudden, offering "green to the onlooker, like an almond glistening when the shell is cracked open." Green was Matisse's great discovery in Morocco. He used it so much that he radically changed his palette, with all the other colors being determined by its presence. The artistic intuition seen in *Periwinkles* is repeated in *The Palm*, a painting in which he displays an approach that is almost disconcertingly radical. In this canvas he tried to go beyond simple plant forms, so that they become scarcely more than abstract symbols. It is only the vibrancy of the colors, the balance and the sudden transitions between foreground and background, and the dizzy verticality of the space, crossed by the slanting tree trunks, that give the work a perceptible and intelligible structure. *Acanthus (Moroccan Landscape)* takes its title from a border of leaves in the foreground, while the trees and tufts of greenery stand out against the intense mauve of the sky and the periwinkle blue seen in the background.

Matisse next decided to paint the portrait of the young boy who worked at the hotel. His name was Amido, and he posed in traditional dress, with a pale green waistcoat over a white shirt, violet trousers, a bright orange scarf, and a bag with a gilt strap. Matisse painted him rather in the manner of a Russian icon (he had recently been on a trip to Moscow and had seen some wonderful examples), or of a Persian miniature. The room that forms the background is depicted as simply as possible, with flat stretches of light ocher for the walls and of pink for the floor, and curtains of a plain white.

Having returned to France in mid-April, Matisse went back to Tangiers on 8 October. At the end of November, his wife, Amélie, joined him, accompanied by the painter Charles Camoin. This time, Matisse allowed himself to be completely seduced by the country. He now found "the Moroccan landscape to be exactly as portrayed in the paintings of Delacroix," and saw Morocco as a magical and wonderfully evocative world. He decided to paint several portraits of a young woman, and in October 1912 wrote: "I have started to do a Moorish girl on the terrace, to form a pair with the little Moroccan boy I did last year." The model was a beauty by the name of Zorah, and the canvas Matisse painted was finally called *Fatma, the Mulatto Girl*. Dressed in a turban and a long bright green dress, the girl stands out against a dark green background. The portrayal of her facial features is limited to a few simple strokes. There is nothing formal about her pose; her right hand rests on a piece of furniture, her left is tucked inside her white belt, and she is gazing into the distance. Here Matisse has done away with details, and any indication of place or time. He had already use this young woman as a model the previous winter; it was she who had posed for *The Yellow Dress*, and for studies of heads. He subsequently had some problems with the young woman's brother, who ended up objecting to the sittings. Matisse was astonished to discover that she was a prostitute, though this in fact made it easier to continue working with her: from that point on, Matisse and Camoin would go to the brothel from time to time to paint the girls there. Camoin observed that "in Tangiers, I worked together with him on some prostitutes in their own setting. Matisse used to say to me: 'Watch out, you know that we're like doctors when we're in there.'" Matisse started on a portrait of Zorah on the terrace at the end of 1912, or at the very beginning of 1913. He had now moved on a stage in the development of his art. Wearing a blue, cream, and green dress, her hair covered by a white veil, she is shown kneeling on a blue-purple carpet; her Turkish slippers, set to one side, emphasize the vertical lines of the canvas. A single strong diagonal in the top left of the painting, which forms the boundary between the bluish-green of the scene from a small triangular area of white, helps to counteract the impression of what at first seems a somewhat arbitrary composition.

A similar rather hieratic air emanates from *The Standing Riffain*, also called *Moroccan Youth Standing, Dressed in Green*, a painting he described to his family on 21 November

Opposite
The Casbah Gate, Henri Matisse, 1912–1913
Oil on canvas, 116 x 80 cm (Pushkin Museum of Fine Art, Moscow).

Moroccan Café, Henri Matisse, 1912–1913
Tempera on canvas, 176 x 210 cm (The Hermitage Museum, Saint Petersburg).

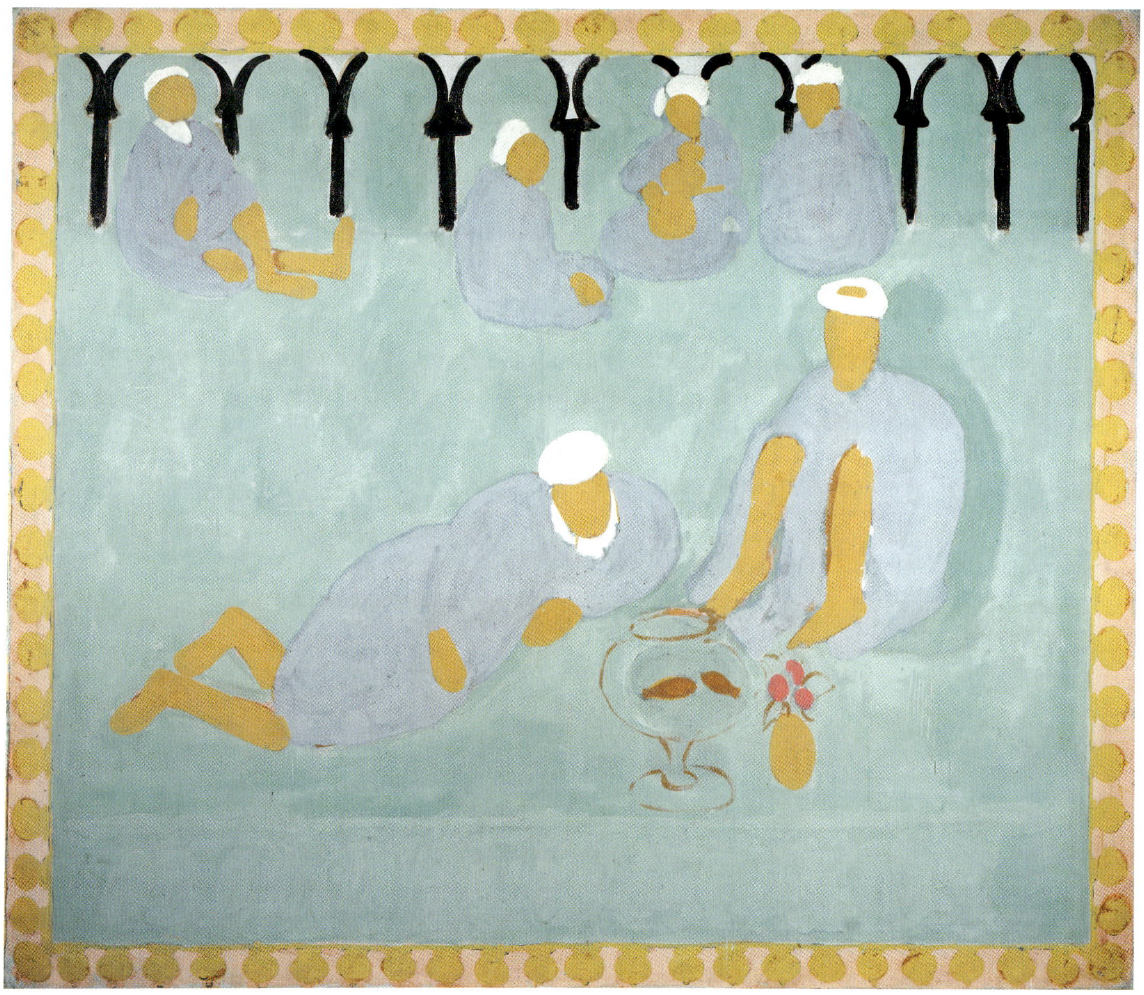

1912. He announced that he had chosen "a canvas the size of Choukine's Red Fish [sic]. It's the portrait of a certain Riffain, a magnificent man from the mountains, as wild as a jackal." In fact he did another painting of the same subject, *The Seated Riffain*. The figure's expression is haughty and distant, but his wild nature is played down by the gentle tones of the background. Only the intense green of his clothes and his unflinching gaze give a hint of solemnity and toughness, allowing us to guess at a warrior's indomitable soul.

But there was another project that was close to Matisse's heart, *The Casbah Gate*. Here yet again he employs the technique of a foreground frame revealing a landscape, which in this case is the distant view of some vegetation and a little of the town. He got rid of the figure that was originally standing in front of the tall gateway and replaced it with one that dissolves into the blue of the left-hand wall; his use of blocks of strong color is so unreal that this little section of street has lost all direct relation with reality.

He had already completed *Zorah Seated* and now started work on *Zorah Standing*, in which she appears in a long turquoise dress with a black and white geometric pattern, her figure standing out against a red background. In this painting Matisse emphasized the fundamental elements first found in *Amidon, the Moroccan Boy*. In the Zorah picture, the arbitrary manner of depicting reality is further accentuated, and the figure is clearly portrayed in an iconic manner. At the end of his stay, he completed *Arum Lilies on the Veranda* and *Arums, Iris, and Mimosa*. The first of these is composed in a color scheme of yellows and pale violet, while the second employs a harmonious combination of greens, blues, and yellows. Before he left, Matisse had begun to erase all allusions to the Orient, or at least all explicit references, pouring all his Oriental experiences into a subject that avoids any direct link with the time he spent in Tangiers.

However that may be, among his baggage on his return was a masterpiece, *Moroccan Café*. This large tempera painting had been preceded by two preparatory sketches, *Café I* and *Café II*. The composition is very simple: two men in pale gray *gondourahs* in the center, one seated, the other lying down, are contemplating a bowl in which two goldfish are swimming, and a flesh-colored vase containing a few pale-red flowers. In the background, in front of a long arcade of slender black arches, four men can be seen seated, one of them playing a musical instrument. The space is a uniform area of very pale bluish green, and Matisse has even painted the picture frame to further underline the decorative nature of the picture. He described it with enthusiasm, aware that he had accomplished an extraordinarily good piece of work: "I have my fish bowl and my pink flower. That's what really struck me! These great big fellows who can sit for hours looking at a flower and some goldfish! Now, if I make them the reddish-gold color they should be, the vermilion will make my flower look pale purple! And so? I want my flower to be pink! Otherwise, it's no longer right! While my fish could be yellow, it really doesn't matter, they'll be yellow!" In this painting Matisse captured the essence of café life; it is the epitome of a hedonistic philosophy of life that appeared in earlier manifesto works like *La Joie de Vivre*, *The Dance*, and *Music*.

Though Matisse was never to return to North Africa, the Orient never ceased to haunt him. In particular, he could not shake off the theme of Oriental women, as can be seen from *Two Odalisques – The Terrace* (1921); *Odalisque in Red Trousers* (1922), in which the young woman, seen from an oblique perspective, is lying on an ottoman with her arms stretched languorously behind her head; and *Odalisque in an Armchair* (1928). *The Moorish Screen* (1922) shows two contemporary women dressed in white set against Arabic-style décor, with shimmering rugs, golden wall decorations, and a large screen with a violet pattern on a white background. *The Red Jacket*, painted in 1917, is reminiscent of *The Standing Riffain* and the various *Zorah* pictures. Moreover, he never abandoned the Oriental rug as a paradigm for his system of painting. Matisse lived his dream of the

Odalisque with Red Trousers, Henri Matisse, 1922
Oil on canvas 65 x 90 cm (Musée National d'Art Moderne, Centre Georges Pompidou, Paris).

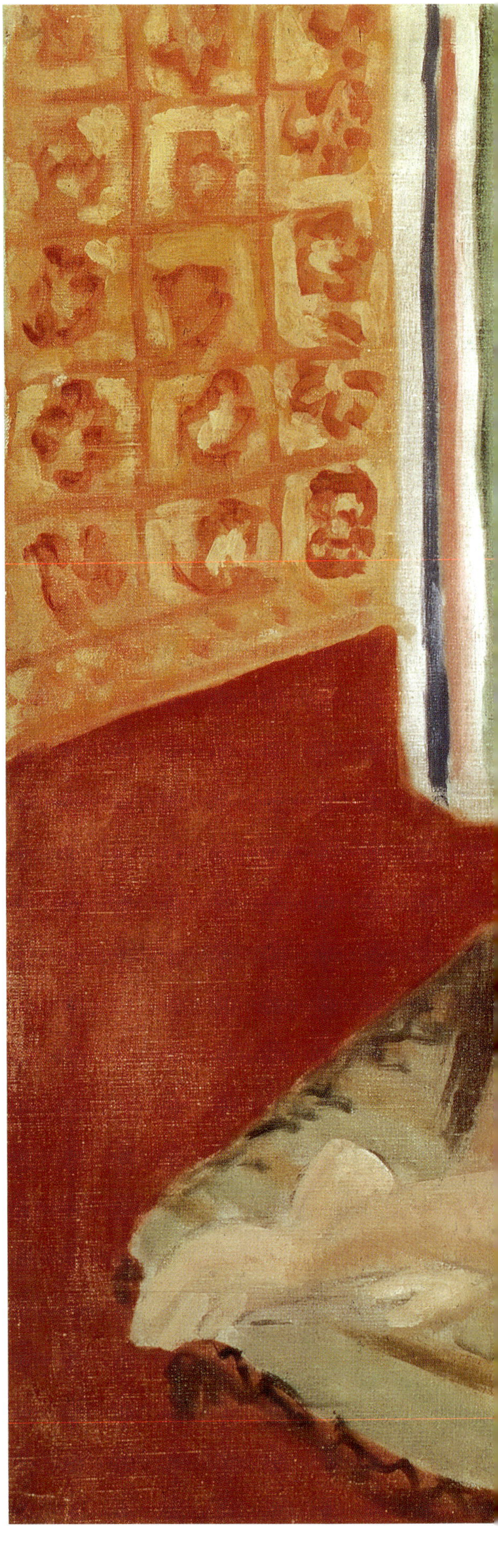

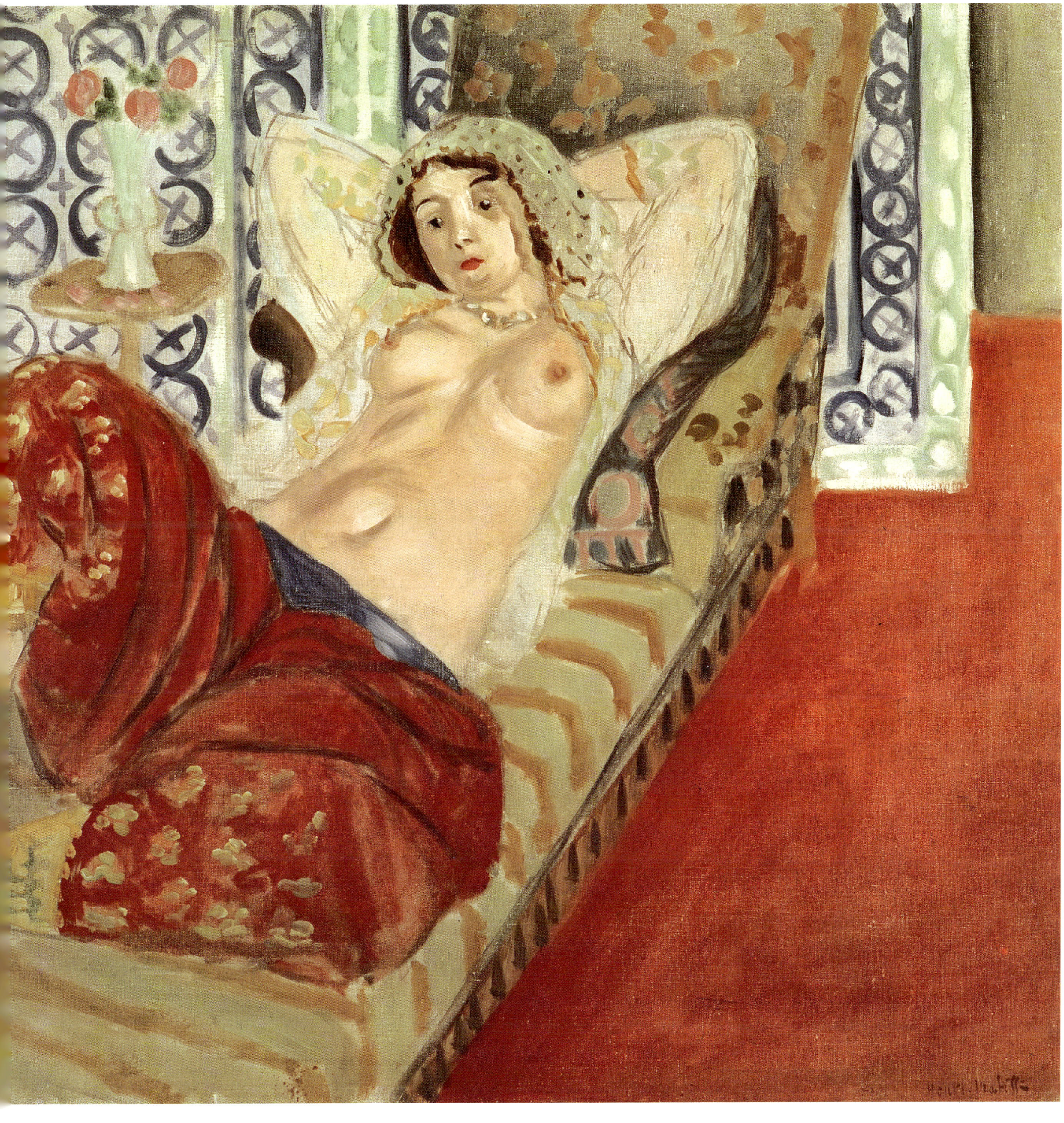

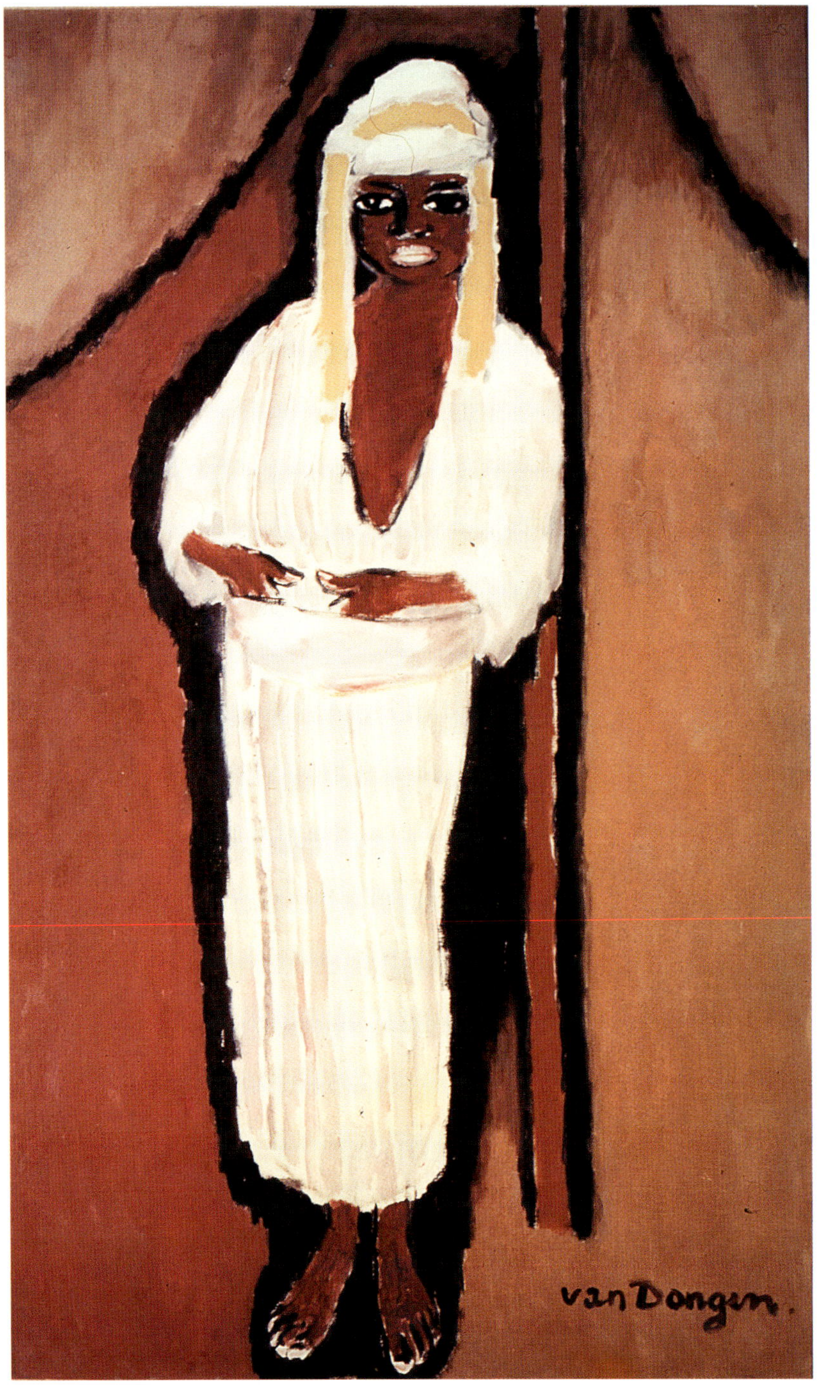

The Young Arab,
Kees Van Dongen, 1910
Oil on canvas, 131 x 82 cm
(private collection).

Moorish Dancing Girl,
Kees Van Dongen, 1910
Oil on canvas, 131 x 82 cm
(private collection).

Orient through his painting, in a relentless search for a lost paradise that he never ceased trying to recreate.

Matisse's last voyage was to Tahiti, a destination that had already seen its share of artists. He set off without any materials, and found there "the continuous surprises of travel." He hoped to benefit from this in time, and his thoughts turned again to the author of *Noah Noah*, Gauguin, who had advised artists to take inspiration from Oriental carpets. He wrote: "I am convinced that exactly the same happened to Delacroix with his journey to Morocco. It was ten years later that the colors started to emerge in his paintings."

Kees Van Dongen, Charles Camoin, and Albert Marquet in the Maghreb

Towards the end of 1910, the Dutch artist Kees Van Dongen traveled through Spain to winter in Morocco. He had already been interested in the East since 1906, the year of the "wild beasts' cage" (a description of a celebrated Fauvist exhibition), when he painted *Fatima and Her Troupe*. This exotic dancer performed in public, accompanied by an orchestra composed entirely of women. He painted several versions of "the celebrated Fatima," fascinated by this colorful and controversial figure who enthralled Paris with her lascivious dancing. Out of this early fascination with the Orient came a wonderful painting, *The Young Arab* (1910), which is of an unusual simplicity, with the body of the young man standing out against a plain, pale background, his "Fauvist" red skin contrasting with his white clothes. During his time in Africa, however, he did not always work with bright, luminous colors; some of his work is very somber in tone, for example *Djilali* (1911). Here the face of the wild Moroccan is of an intense brown, emphasized by his black beard. The dark blue background, which is only slightly relieved by a dazzling green and by the grayish white of his burnous, gives the whole painting an atmosphere that is both unreal and slightly menacing. In 1913 he painted *The Egyptian Girl*, a colorful study in which his palette ranges from bright orange to purple. The young woman's face and arms combine shades of green and white that give her a melancholy expression, in complete contrast to the gay and shimmering colors of her clothes and the background. This painting dates from the time he spent in Egypt. He also took from Egypt the idea for a painting that is strikingly different from everything that he had previously composed, *Peasants Beside the Nile*, which is treated like a black and white drawing. This "pseudo sketch," showing two women walking away from the water's edge with large jars on their heads, gives a hint of a new direction in his approach to painting, though in fact it was not one he chose to pursue. In 1918, he completed the illustrations for the book *Hassan-Badreddine-Bassaraoui, conte des 1001 Nuits* (Hassan-Badreddine-Bassaraoui, a story from the 1001 Nights), which was published by Éditions de la Sirène. For this book, Van Dongen chose a linear and humorous treatment of his subject.

For many years the Oriental influence on his style was barely discernible, but in 1946 he produced a strange and intriguing still-life that hints at his former fascination. On a table, next to a bunch of red and white peonies, he has arranged a pile of books. Placed conspicuously on top of novels by

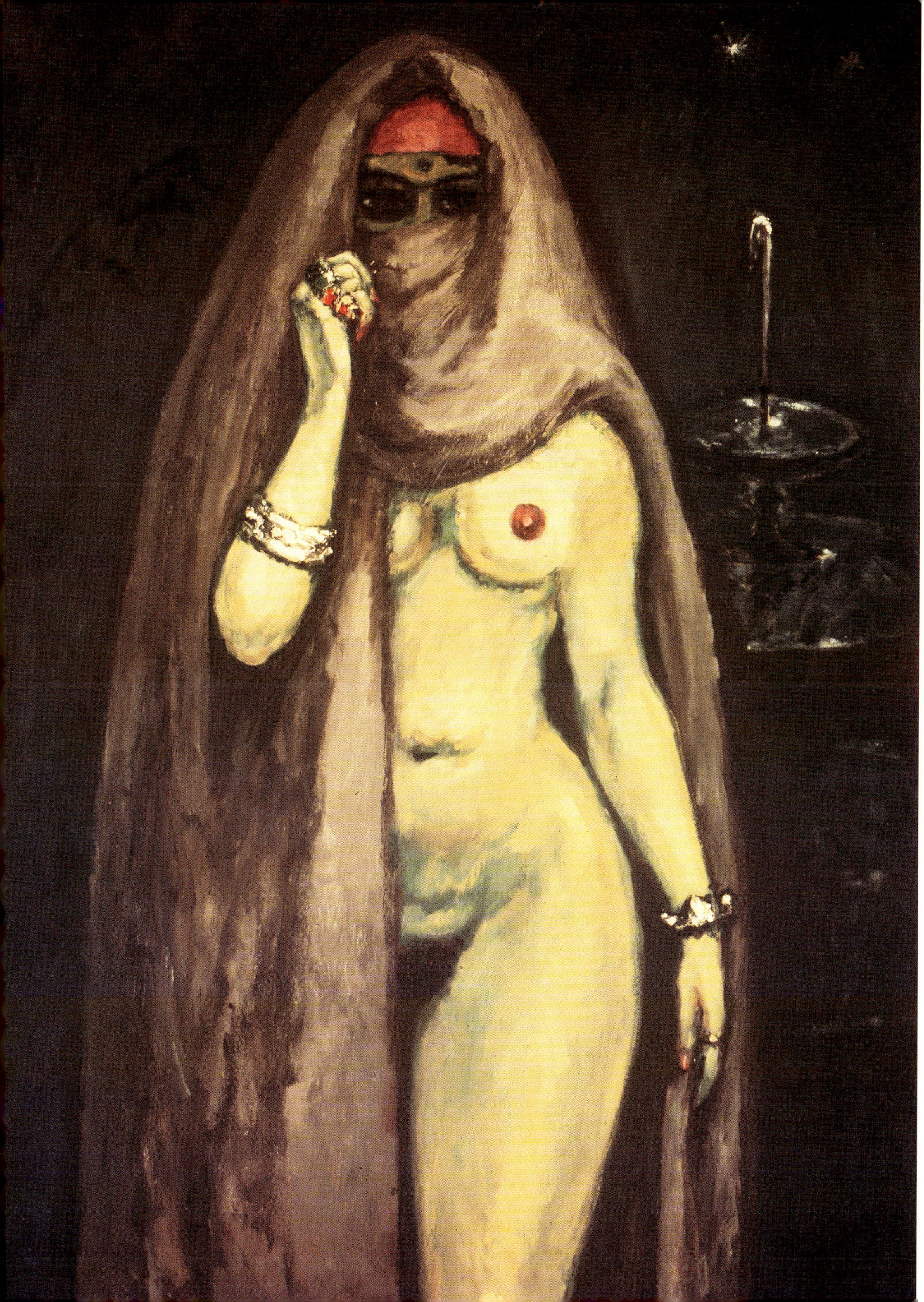

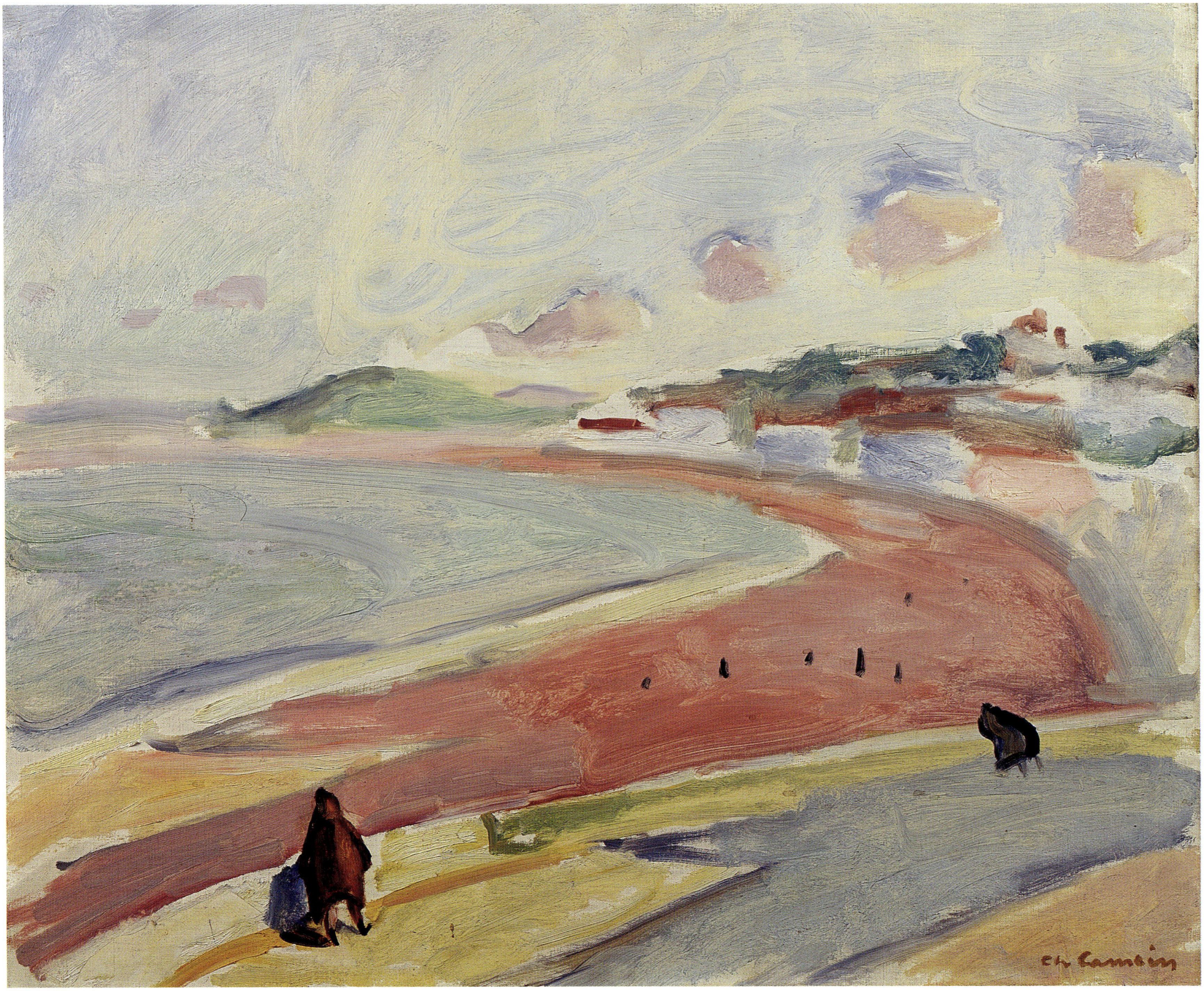

Beach at Tangiers,
Charles Camoin, 1913
Oil on canvas, 60 x 73 cm
(Musée des arts d'Afrique et d'Océanie, Paris).

Minaret in Tangiers,
Charles Camoin, 1913
Oil on canvas, 65 x 81 cm
(Musée des Beaux-Arts, Grenoble).

Stendhal and Balzac, surely not by chance, is a book by the French novelist and traveler Pierre Loti, a reminder of his time on the other side of the Mediterranean.

As was mentioned above, Charles Camoin, a friend of Amélie Matisse from the time when they both used to visit Gustave Moreau's studio, accompanied her in mid-November 1912 when she went to join her husband, who had settled in Tangiers for the second time. A companion from Matisse's Fauvist phase, Camoin had distanced himself from Matisse because of Matisse's "excessive theorizing," though he was still on excellent terms with his old friend. However, there is no denying that he strongly resisted Matisse's systematic approach, and the way his friend always wanted to argue about the aims and methods of painting. In retrospect, he described Matisse as a man who was "very argumentative and always wanted to prove everything by mathematical equations." Nevertheless, in time he allowed himself to be won over by Matisse's arguments, and by the method of painting that was the logical outcome. He learned how to detach himself more and more from the subject – from its specific reality – and concentrate on the painting as a painting, as an artifice with its own logic. On 25 February he wrote to Matisse (who had now returned to France) to

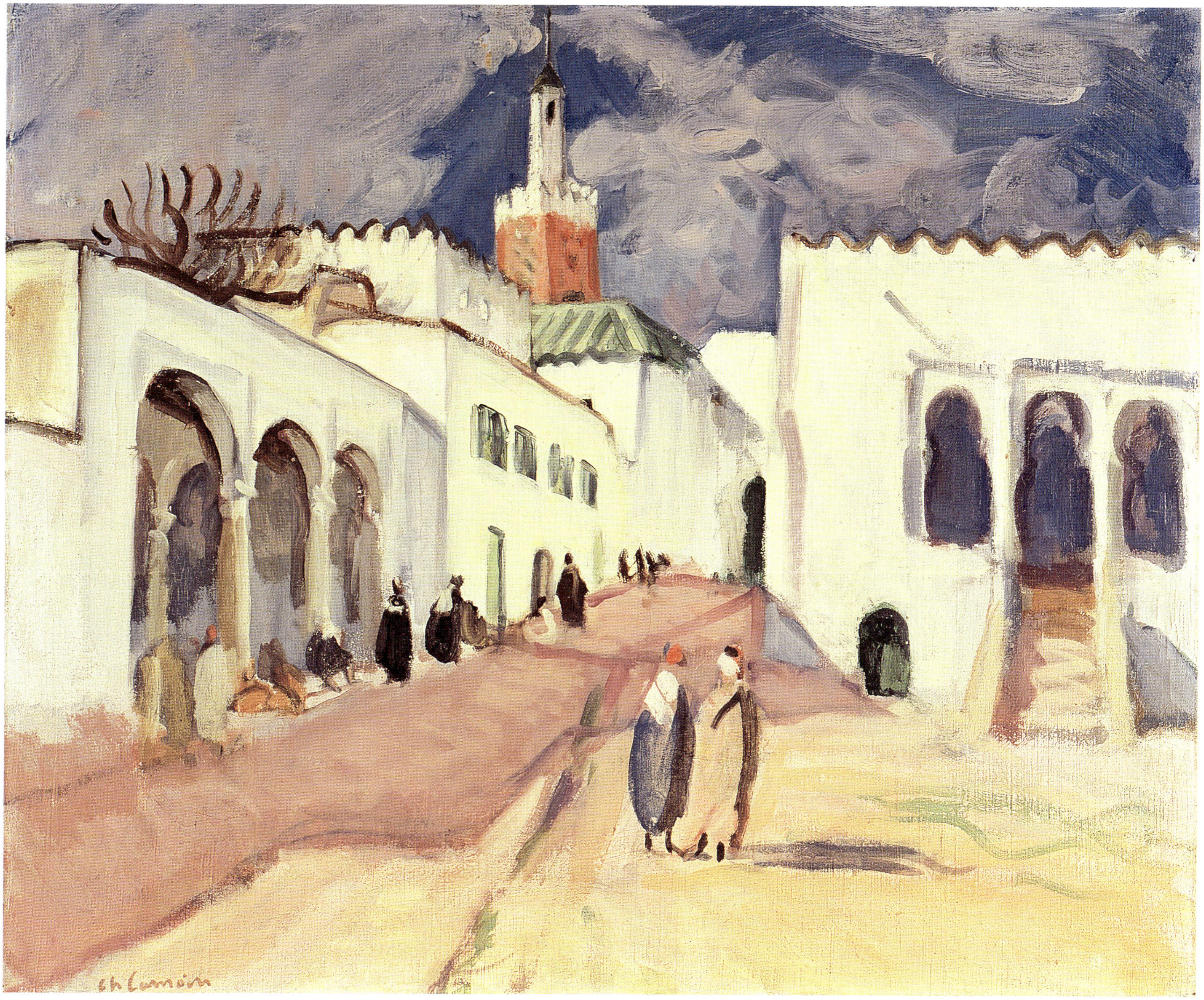

impress on him that he (Camoin) had in fact changed his style of painting, and that he had made this change "in order to get away from this habit of instantaneous impressions of nature." He felt a strong personal bond with Matisse, and 40 years later he recalled how "at that time Matisse was a very close friend [...] He was an excellent rider and introduced me to this noble sport, to which his wife always rather objected. We had a very happy time together in those days." Matisse also recalled "those wonderful times in Morocco." When he left again in February, Camoin hastened to write to him from Morocco: "I so enjoyed the winter that I spent here with you, in one of the most beautiful countries that I have ever seen, not to mention the wonderful desire to work that I could not help but feel in your company." The two artists often used the same subjects, just as Monet and Renoir had at Grenouillère near Paris in the early days of Impressionism. But despite his gradual acceptance of Matisse's approach, in time their standpoints diverged more and more. While Matisse accomplished a "Copernican revolution" in his approach to painting, Camoin developed in a direction that distanced him more and more not only from his earlier Fauvism style, but also from Matisse's ceaseless searching and experimentation.

When it came to doing drawings and sketches based on a particular subject, however, Matisse and Camoin were remarkably similar. This can be seen, for example, in the way they both treated a house with trellises, which had captured both their imaginations. But the manner in which they *painted* this subject was radically different. *The Moorish Café* by Camoin is the opposite of the version by Matisse. Camoin was primarily concerned with respecting the actual appearance of the place and would seek to emphasize its specific character, with the foreground remaining in the shade while the room at the back is depicted by lighter

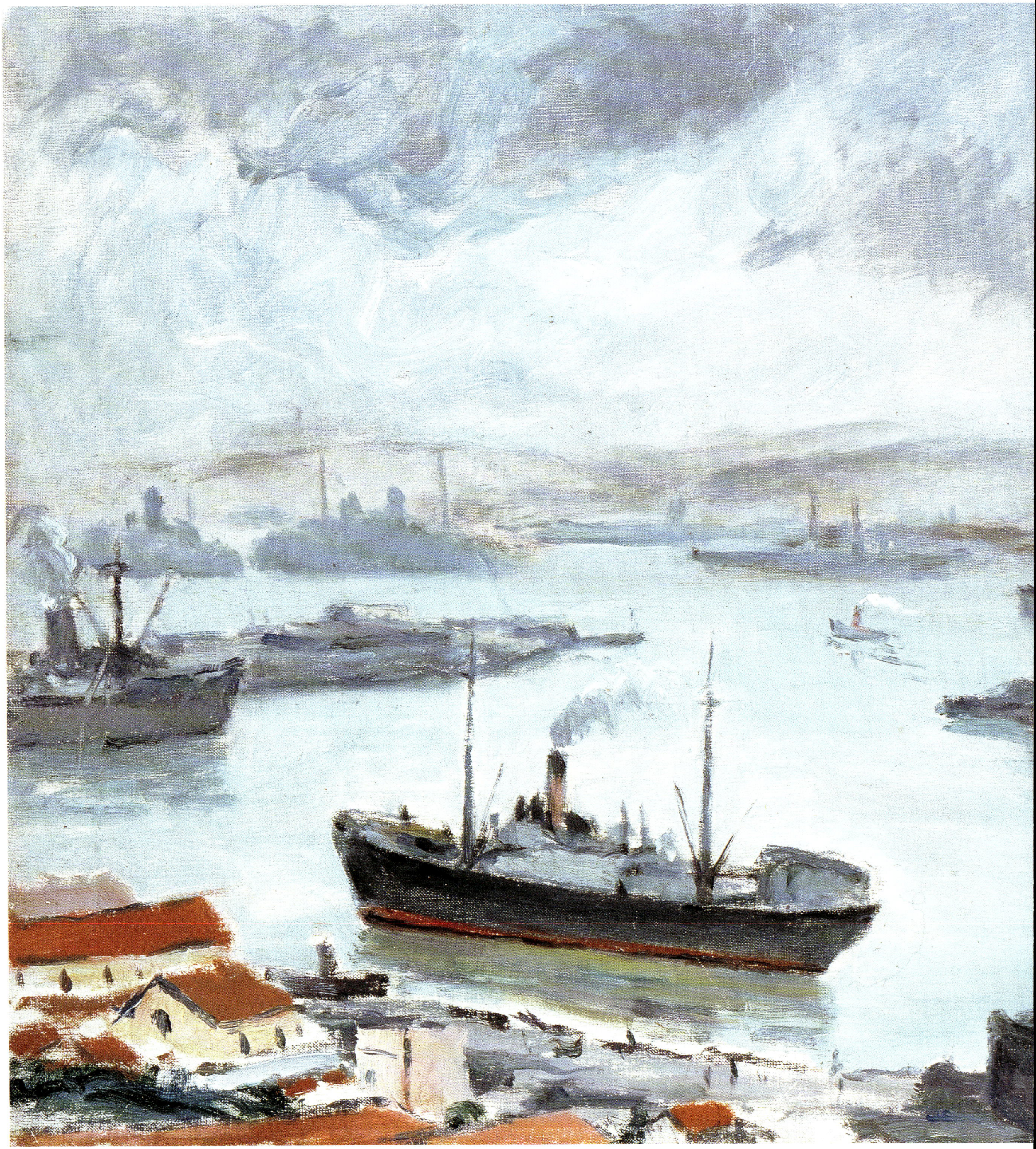

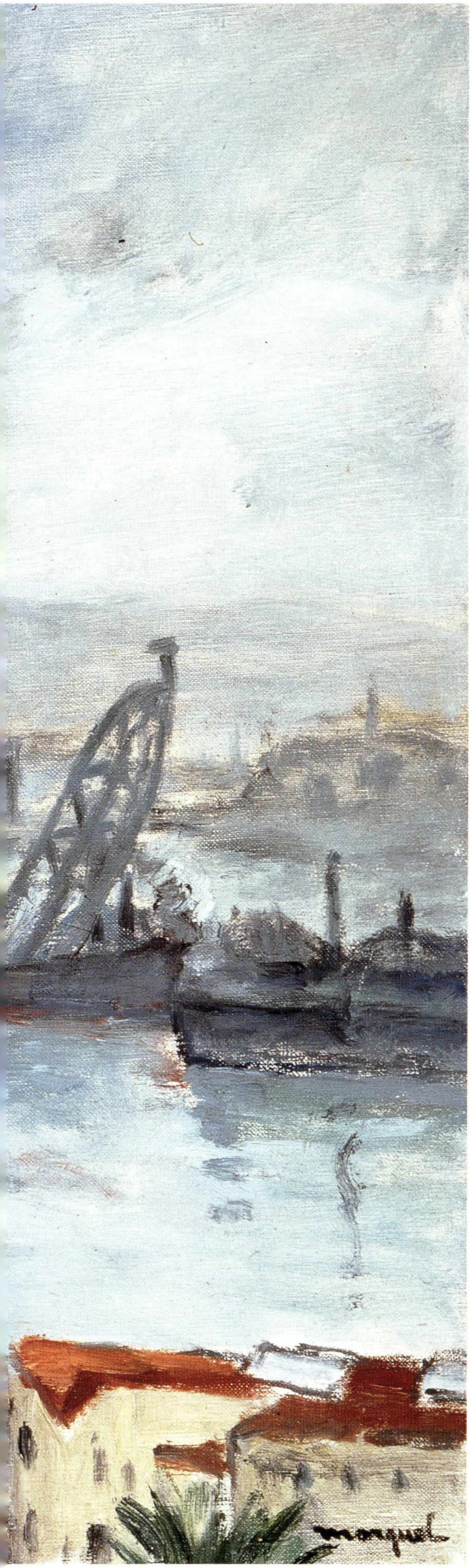

colors – a harmony of browns and blues with figures dressed in white. Composition and a sense of space are created largely by means of color and bold outlines. For his part, Matisse was searching for the quintessence of cafés in general and not the features that characterized one particular café. Similarly, when Camoin painted his *Young Moroccan Boy* and *Young Moroccan Girl Serving Tea*, he tried to express the truth of what he saw before him, though at the same time exaggerating their features and producing an arrangement of colors that were quite independent of the scene itself. For Camoin, the beach at Tangiers, which was an inexhaustible source of luxuriant color (he produced four paintings on this theme), the city's streets and inhabitants (he was very keen on the mosque's minaret, the medina, and so on) allowed him to use harmoniously linked blocks of color, the keynote of the canvas being brightness and translucence, with white playing an essential role. Quite obviously Camoin had reached a very important stage in his development. But he used the Orient essentially to cure himself of the speculative methods of his Fauvist phase; on his return to France he destroyed about 80 canvases from his earlier period. The exhibition he mounted in February–March 1911 at the Druet Gallery in Paris gave him the opportunity to show eleven of his Moroccan paintings, out of a total of 60 paintings he exhibited.

The Bay of Algiers, Albert Marquet, 1924
Oil on canvas, 65 x 81 cm
(private collection).

The French artist Albert Marquet traveled to Morocco in August of 1911 accompanied by his friend Eugène Monfort. They visited Tangiers, Rabat, Fez, Tetuán, and Casablanca. Marquet's African trip was a holiday, which he enjoyed to the full, and so he did not produce any paintings. He confided this to Henri Matisse in a letter sent on 31 August: "At the moment I am in Tétouan, which we have reached after twelve hours on horseback [...] Not done any painting yet." He extended his stay, dazzled by this country, but did not feel the need to recall his impressions on paper.

At the end of January 1912, Matisse wrote to Marquet asking him to come to Tangiers. During his second stay in North Africa, Matisse renewed his efforts, enticing him with pleasures of life in Tangiers: "We live it up every day. Camoin and I can hardly stand up any more. [...] When are you arriving?" Marquet did not even reply. He turned down a great meeting of artists, out of carelessness, perhaps no longer feeling the need to share his artistic ideas with his old friends.

It was only in 1920 that he returned to North Africa, on the advice of the French art historian Élie Faure, who advised him to travel to a sunny climate to avoid the recurring bouts of influenza, from which he suffered so much during the winters in Paris. He embarked at Marseilles during January. On 26 January he sent a postcard to Faure announcing that "the weather is beautiful here in Algiers," adding that he was "thinking of working here." It was at this time that he made the acquaintance of Marcelle Martinet, a young French woman born in Algeria, who took him with her along "the little paths" that she loved, "which, crossing through gullies and orchards, twisted and turned in the hills above Algiers." At the beginning of spring, he crossed the Sahara with Jean Launois. From this time onwards, he returned to Algiers every year when the winter became a threat to his health. He now began, with passionate enthusiasm, to paint North African landscapes. He also painted several scenes of harbor life, including *View from the Pier* and *The Port of Algiers*, which he

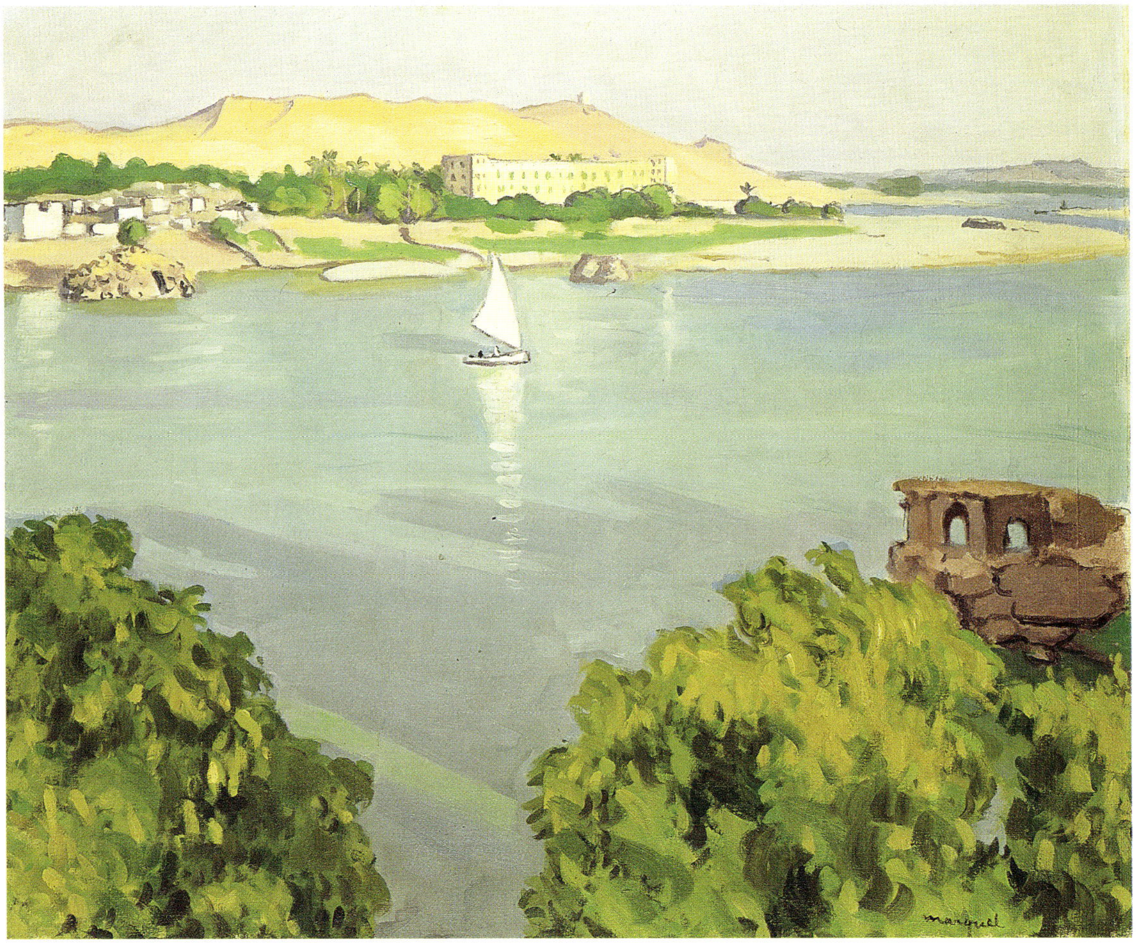

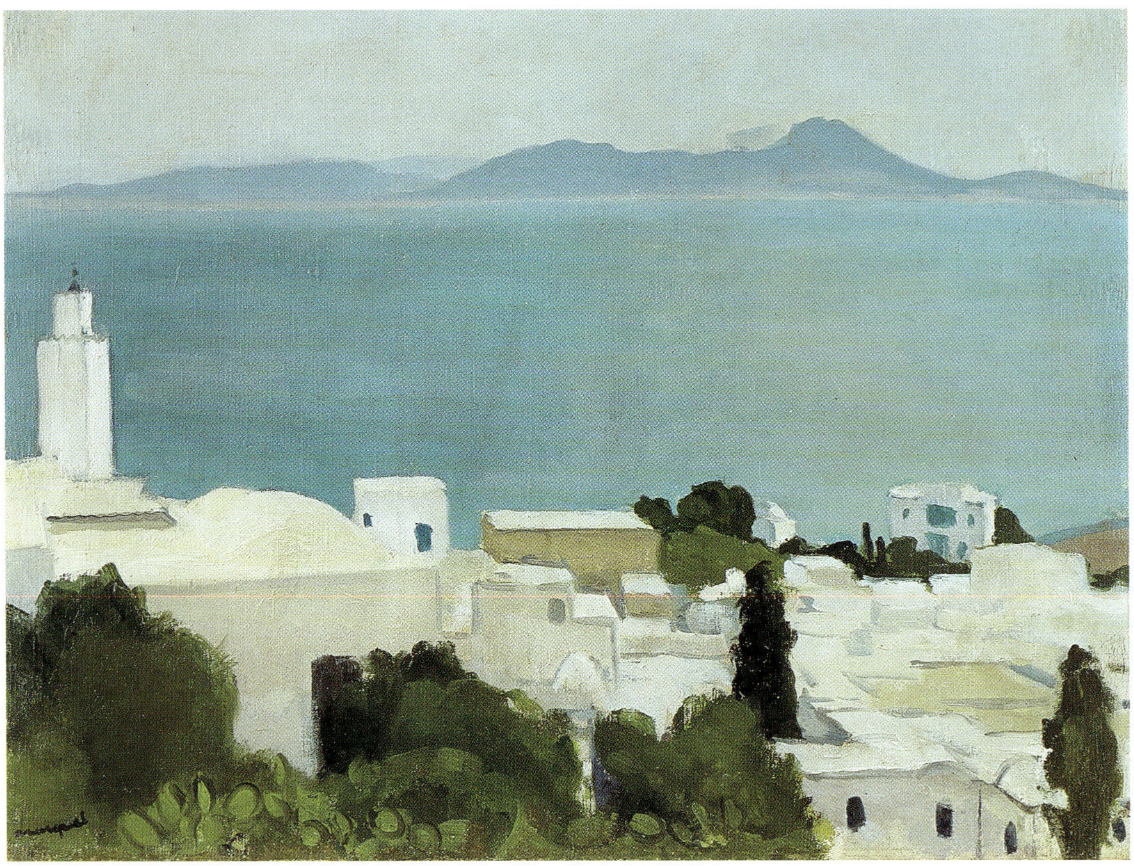

Assouan, Morning, Albert Marquet,
Oil on canvas, 64.8 x 80.5 cm
(Guezireh Museum, Cairo).

The Minaret at Sidi Bou Saïd, Albert Marquet, 1923
Oil on panel, 22 x 27 cm
(private collection).

exhibited at the Salon d'Automne in Paris in 1921. That year he spent several weeks in Laghouat, which he liked a great deal and which inspired several of his paintings, including the *Women of Laghouat*. He also traveled in southern Algeria and completed a beautiful painting called *View of the Casbah*. In 1921 he headed south once more, traveling from Touggourt to Nefta. He continued to paint the port, producing among other paintings *The North Jetty at Algiers*, *Algiers*, and *Seaside Health*.

The following year he married Marcelle Martinet, and they traveled to Tunisia, visiting Tunis and then ancient Carthage. Entranced by what he saw, but also a little disappointed by what the remains of the distant past suggested to him, he saw "ruins in a noble landscape but the sea a bit too far off, the hotel isolated, no foreground, barely enough material for three or four paintings." Later they went to Sidi Bou Saïd and discovered with delight, in the words of Marcelle, "white houses, blue woodwork, cacti, agave, fields covered in flowers [...] looking out over a vibrant sea." They settled there for six months, and Marquet painted *The Farm at Sidi Bou Saïd*, *Woman in the Street at Sidi Bou Saïd*, and *The Minaret at Sidi Bou Saïd*. From one year to the next he continued his patient exploration of the "white town." "Every winter," recalled Marcelle, "we used to return to Algiers, to a different hotel or house. Marquet knew that I was very attached to my country and that he would never be short of subjects to paint." In 1924 he painted *The Bay of Algiers*, and in 1927 he did several views of the Place du Gouvernement (he could see the whole of the square from the window of the Hôtel de la Régence, where he was staying). A whole stream of other paintings followed, including: *The Pine Tree at Algiers* and *The Bay of Algiers* in 1932; *The Port at Algiers in Calm Weather* in 1933; *View of Algiers* in 1939; *The Port at Algiers* in 1941; *The Allied Squadron at Algiers* in 1942; *The Garden at Algiers* in 1943; and *The Port of Algiers in Fog* in 1944.

The two months he spent with his wife in Bougie during 1925 were a rich source of marvels. In her memoirs, Marcelle recalls the

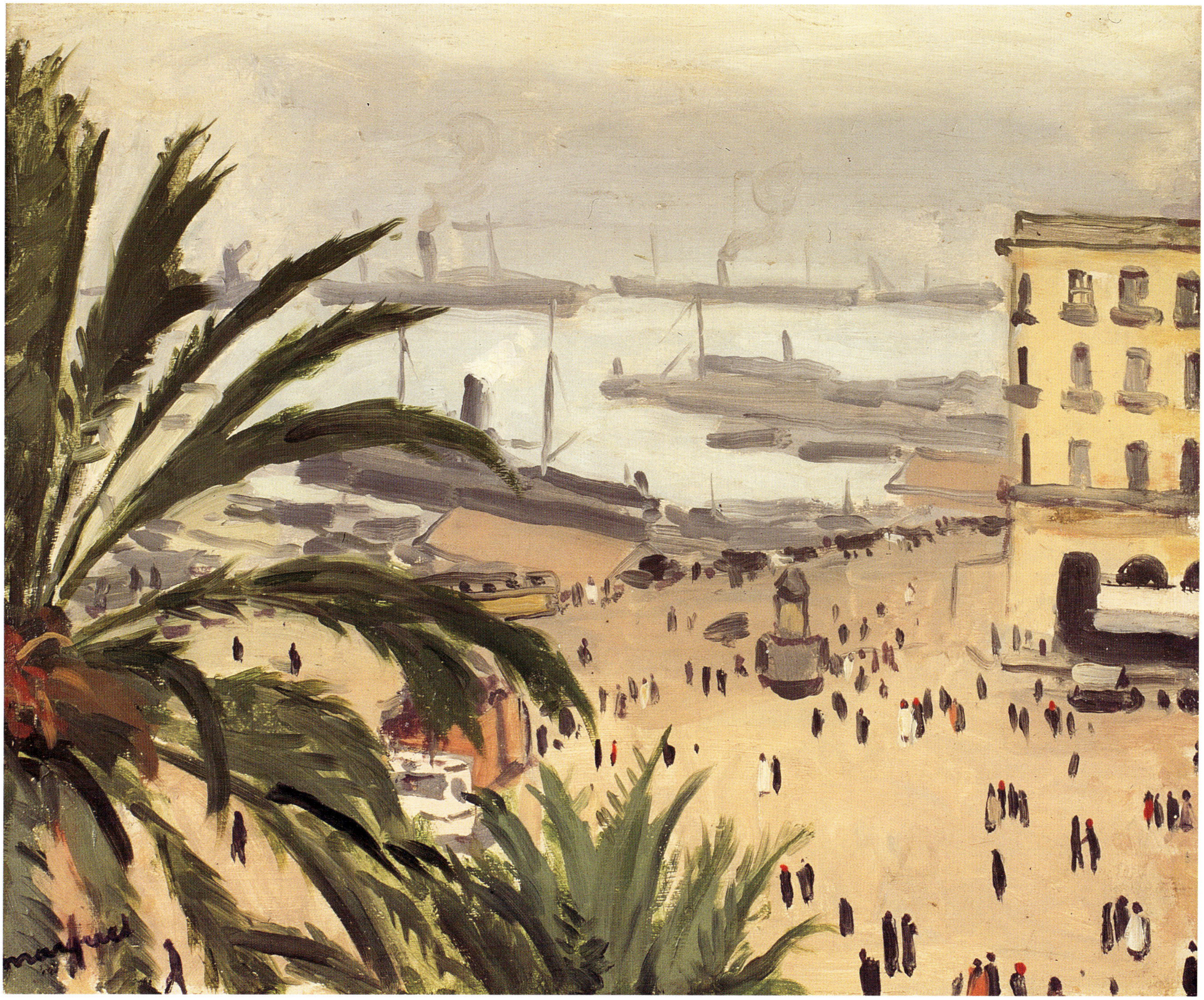

character of this beautiful city on the coast of the Mediterranean: "A forgotten harbor, often empty but in such a beautiful setting. Marquet used to say, 'a landscape made for Poussin,' trees hundreds of years old, enormous carob trees [...] fruit trees [...] Violent storms and calm weather followed one another in quick succession." Marquet's output was huge; he left nothing unpainted: the port installations, the gulf, the trees in flower, and the streets, in works such as *In the Port of Bougie*, and *The Road to Bougie*. The Marquets stayed for a time at the entrance to Tunis harbor, which proved to be a prime source of inspiration, as can be seen from *La Goulette*, *Window at La Goulette*, and *Storm at La Goulette*. In 1927 he went to Istanbul, where he painted the Bosporus with great intensity, before sailing for Palestine in order to visit Jerusalem. A year later, at the end of January, the Marquets were in Cairo for an exhibition of French art. They visited the capital and also Aswan, and Marquet started several paintings on the banks of the Nile. Another journey through the Sahara brought them once again to Laghouat, where Marquet was inspired to work with great fervor, producing several paintings, numerous watercolors, and a large series of drawings. 1930 saw them traveling in Spain, between Barcelona and

Place du Gouvernement, Algiers,
Albert Marquet, 1927
Oil on wood, 35 x 44 cm
(Musées de la Cour d'Or, Metz).

Cadiz; they crossed the straits of Gibraltar and stopped in Tetuán for a while. From here he wrote to Camoin, telling him: "Tetuán is wonderful; after lunch we're leaving for Tangiers." They returned to Algeria by way of Fez, Tlemcen, and Oran. A period spent in Rabat was equally inspirational, as can be seen from *Rabat, Seen from Les Oudaïas*. Marcelle recalls with delight the luxurious house that they were offered the use of: "Its terrace opened straight out on to the river and looked down on to a blue and white Moorish café, which was frequented at certain hours of the day by customers of a nonchalant attitude, who provided Marquet with models, without his even having to wish that they would slow down."

From 1941 to 1945, they lived in Algiers. He worked without pause and exhibited often. It was there that he produced one of the most curious works of his late career, *Window at Djenan Sidi Saïd*. In this painting a window is shown wide open but with its shutters half closed; in the shadows a climbing plant is blossoming. It is the antithesis of what he had been striving for since his youth; previously in his works a window had, as it were, been the aperture of a *camera obscura*, a privileged and secure observation point from which he could view the world beyond. Barely a year later he painted *Window in Algiers*, which no longer reveals a wide landscape, but the building opposite, as if his field of vision was being reduced.

Louis Moilliet, Paul Klee, and August Macke in Tunis

Though the German artist August Macke painted Oriental subjects in watercolors before 1910, it was his visit to the great exhibition Masterpieces of Islamic Art, in Munich, that really awakened his interest. When Paul Klee finally persuaded his childhood friend, Louis Moilliet, to come with him to North Africa to test out the theories about light and color propounded by the French artist Robert Delaunay, Macke met these two young men, who finally persuaded him to join them. Klee wanted nothing more from this trip than a rigorous and exacting period of study, and the opportunity to work together, with each of them supposedly "stimulating the others to work." The three artists finalized their travel plans at Christmas in 1913. August Macke set off first, at the beginning of April 1914, and awaited his traveling companions in Marseilles. He went to see a bullfight, which made a strong impression on him, and he did a drawing of it. The three artists finally sailed on the *Carthage*; on arrival in Tunis, Klee and his friend settled at the house of Doctor Jaeggi, an old acquaintance of Moilliet, while Macke stayed in a room at the Grand Hôtel de France.

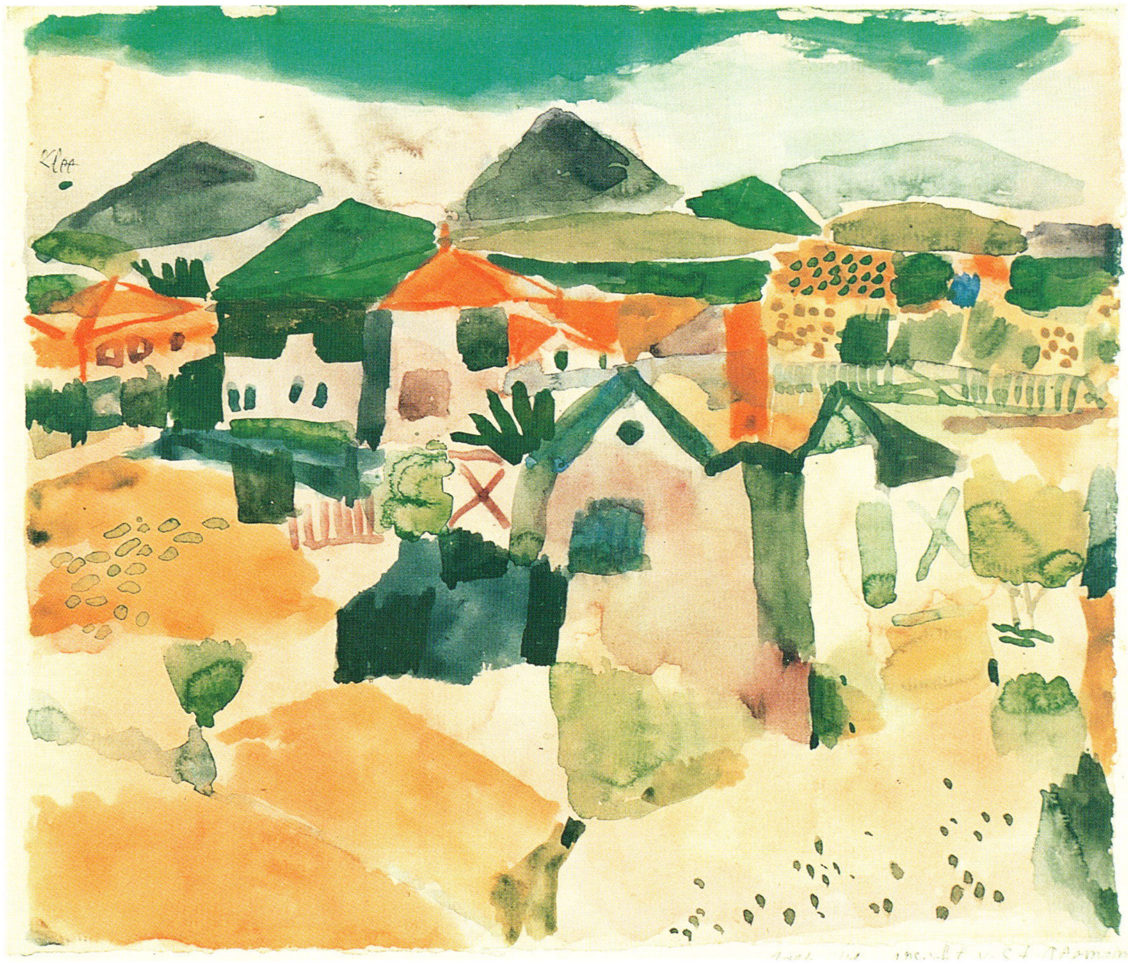

The diary kept by Paul Klee makes it possible to follow exactly what these three men got up to in their brief stay. On Wednesday 8 April they visited the Arab quarter together, taking with them their painting materials to do a watercolor. The following day they headed for the port of Tunis, where Macke painted his first watercolors of the trip. On the Friday they were invited to spend a few days at Doctor Jaeggi's country house in St. Germain. The friends saw this as an opportunity to get down to work. Klee wrote: "Some watercolors on the beach and looking down from the balcony. The watercolor of the beach is still too European in method [...] In the watercolor from the balcony I managed to depict Africa for the first time." Macke was totally enraptured, and, like Klee, began to feel the charm of this Africa, whose hidden power affected him more and more: "Right in the middle of the African landscape, we draw and we write; Klee does watercolors. This morning I went for a walk in the town and did some work. [...] You only have to turn your head to find thousands of subjects to paint, and today I have already done 50 sketches. Yesterday it was 25. I am in the grip of a creative frenzy such as I have never experienced before now. The African landscape is even more beautiful than that of Provence. I could never have imagined it. Two hundred yards away there is a Bedouin encampment, with black tents, herds of donkeys, and camels, etc., which wander about freely among us..." During these work sessions, Macke and Klee began to influence each other directly. Klee increasingly began to question the meaning of his own work. In his notebook he wrote on 13 April: "Spent the morning painting and swimming. An enormous great scarab beetle has been working away in front of me. I shall also work like that; continually testing whether it rolls, unloading, measuring. One day it will work. As for action, I too am walking backwards with my little load, to reach my goal." In the evening Klee returned to Tunis, and was overcome by a feeling of pure ecstasy: "The city stretches out so majestically up there, and looks far, far out over the sea, which, in one great breath, rises up on the horizon as we climb higher. Stop at a garden gate where I do a quick watercolor. Thalassa! Next went back to the small town where Jaeggi was having coffee in front of a large mosque." The next day they went for a drive with the doctor, who took them to see Sidi Bou Saïd. Macke produced several very successful watercolors there, including *Gorge* and *Rocky Landscape*.

Next they went on to Hammamet, where Klee painted *Landscape Near Hammamet*. He summed up the day in these words: "Painted a lot, strolled around a lot. Evening spent at the café, with the blind bard accompanied by a young boy beating a drum, a rhythm never to be forgotten!" And he added: "On the small terrace at the entrance to the hotel, I intend to do a watercolor, in which I shall totally transpose everything, whilst still remaining completely faithful to nature." They reached Kairouan on 15 April. Yet more delight. Yet more watercolors. Macke did three different versions of *Kairouan*. In Tunis, between 17 and 22 April, Moilliet noted that there were "artistic fantasies" to be done there. Klee recalled that his friend kept insisting on the "feasts of color." He did not waste the opportunity. He was aware that a complete transformation was taking place inside him. "Color possesses me," he wrote. "No need to try to seize it. It possesses me; I feel it. This is what is meant by a happy moment: color and I have become one. I am a painter." This was the revelation of the methods that he would follow for all the years to come. On 19 April he had to abandon this aesthetic euphoria and return to Switzerland. Macke and Moilliet made the return journey in a more leisurely manner, stopping in Palermo and Rome, where they stayed until the end of April.

From this very short but highly productive trip, these three artists drew very different conclusions. Paul Klee viewed his stay there as a revelation about the nature of art. He had been able to verify Robert Delaunay's ideas on color; he had translated some passages of Delaunay's *Essai sur la lumière* (Essay on light) and subsequently had them published in the

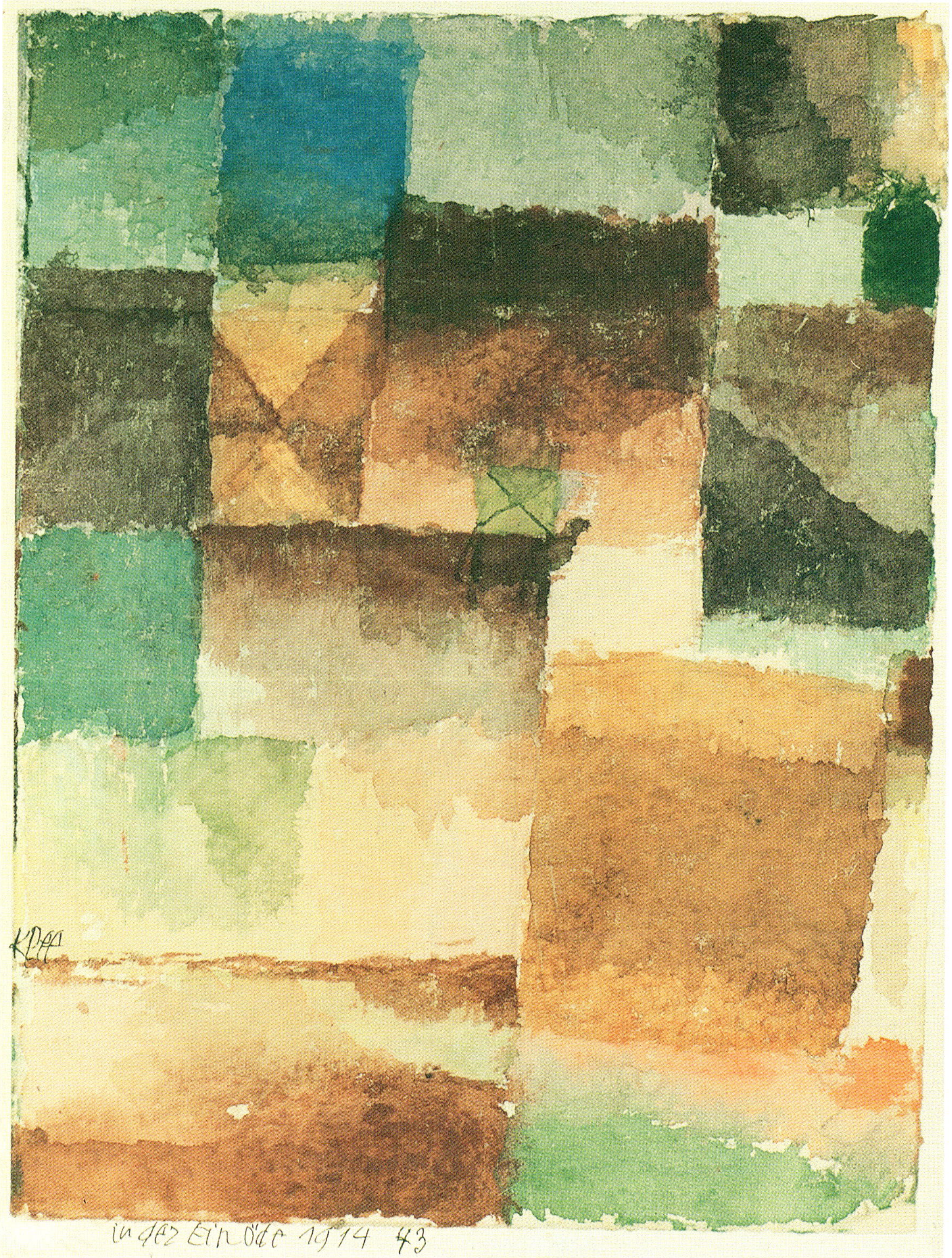

Camel in the Desert, Paul Klee, 1914
Watercolor on Japan paper, 27.6 x 23.7 cm
(Collection Franz Mayer, Zurich).

View of Saint-Germain, Paul Klee, 1914
Watercolor, 23 x 28 cm
(Museum of Arts, Columbus, Ohio).

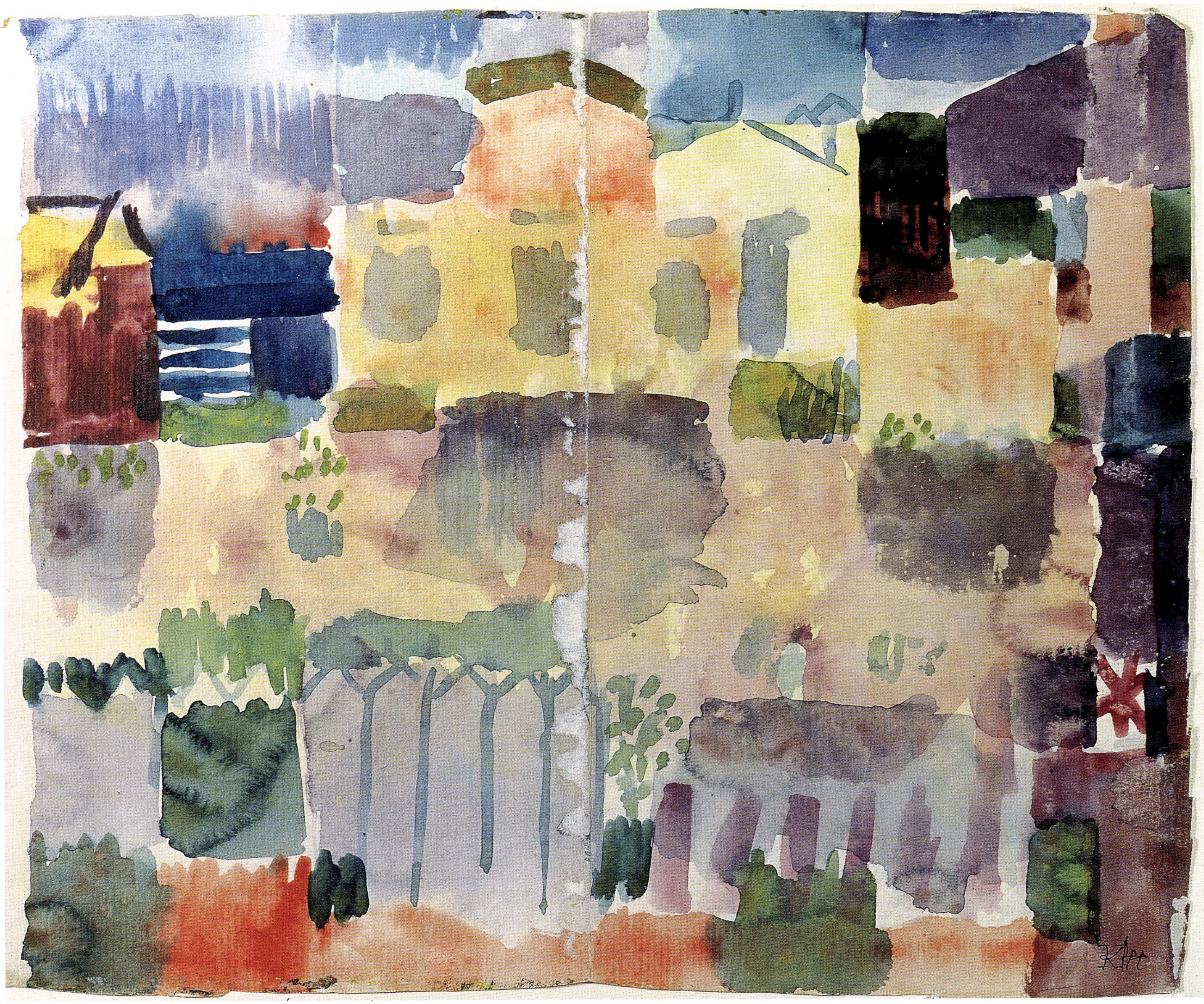

Garden of the European Colony of Saint-Germain in Tunis, Paul Klee, 1914
Watercolor, 20 x 27 cm
(private collection, Paris).

El Halfaouine Square in Tunis,
Paul Klee, 1914
Watercolor, 24.5 x 18 cm
(private collection, Berne).

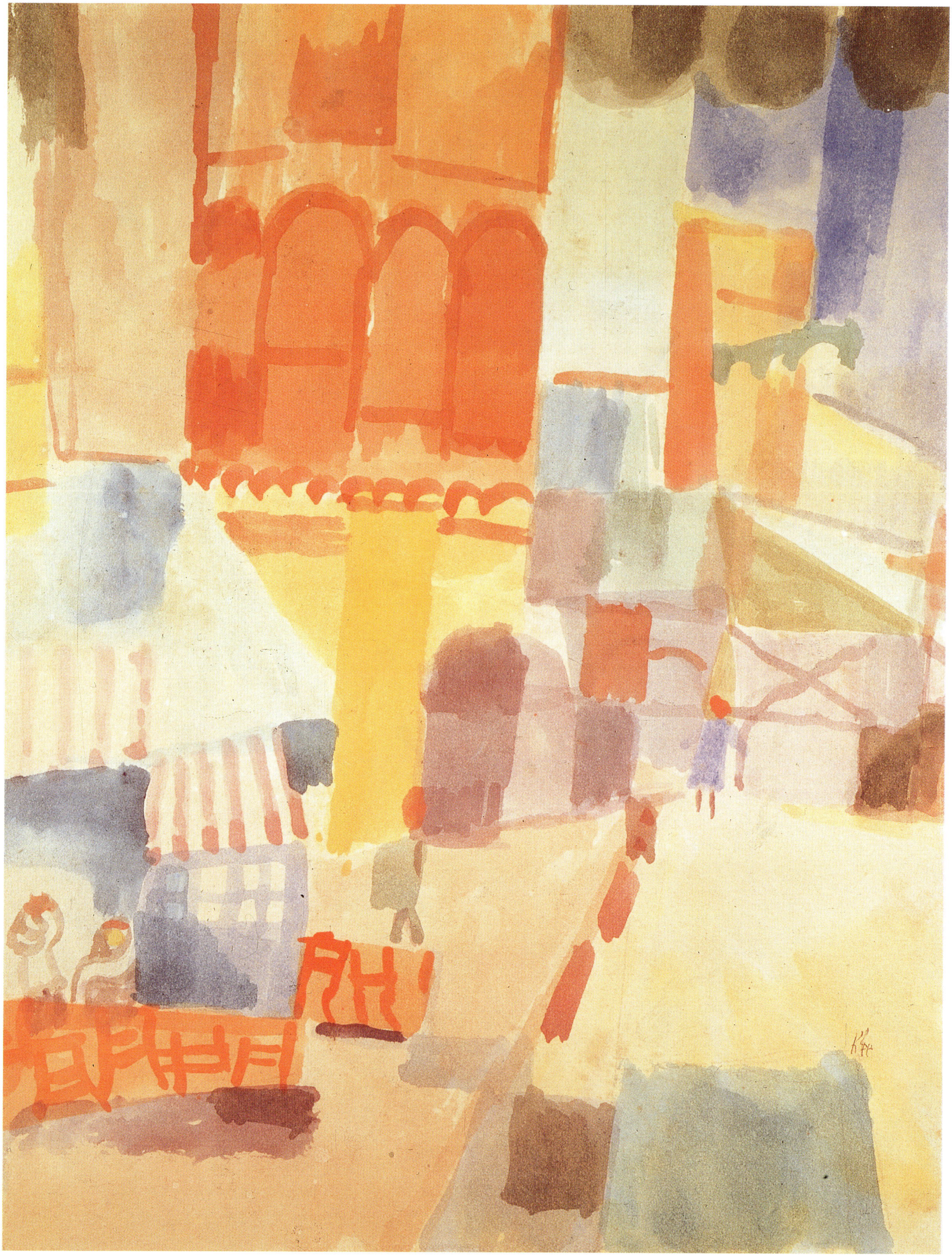

avant-garde German review, *Der Sturm*. But Klee had now been able to go beyond the experiments Delaunay had set up in his studio, shutting the blinds and making a hole to allow a ray of light to pass through, the result being paintings composed according to a "cubist" grid, abstract, and iridescent with the colors of the prism: *Fenêtres simultanées* (Simultaneous windows). Klee's *Homage to Picasso*, in 1914, was a result of this burst of enthusiasm on the other side of the Mediterranean. On his return, he painted several watercolors from memory, including *Hammamet and its Mosque*, which was a pure exercise in color, based on subtle modulations, ranging from green to red, by way of yellow and pink. He has included some reference points (rows of dots, crosses, lines, and so on), with the minarets of the mosque sharply outlined against a dull blue sky.

Apart from this decisive influence of Oriental art on Klee's very approach to art, Oriental themes also recur in his work. *Carpet of Memory*, painted in 1914, makes use

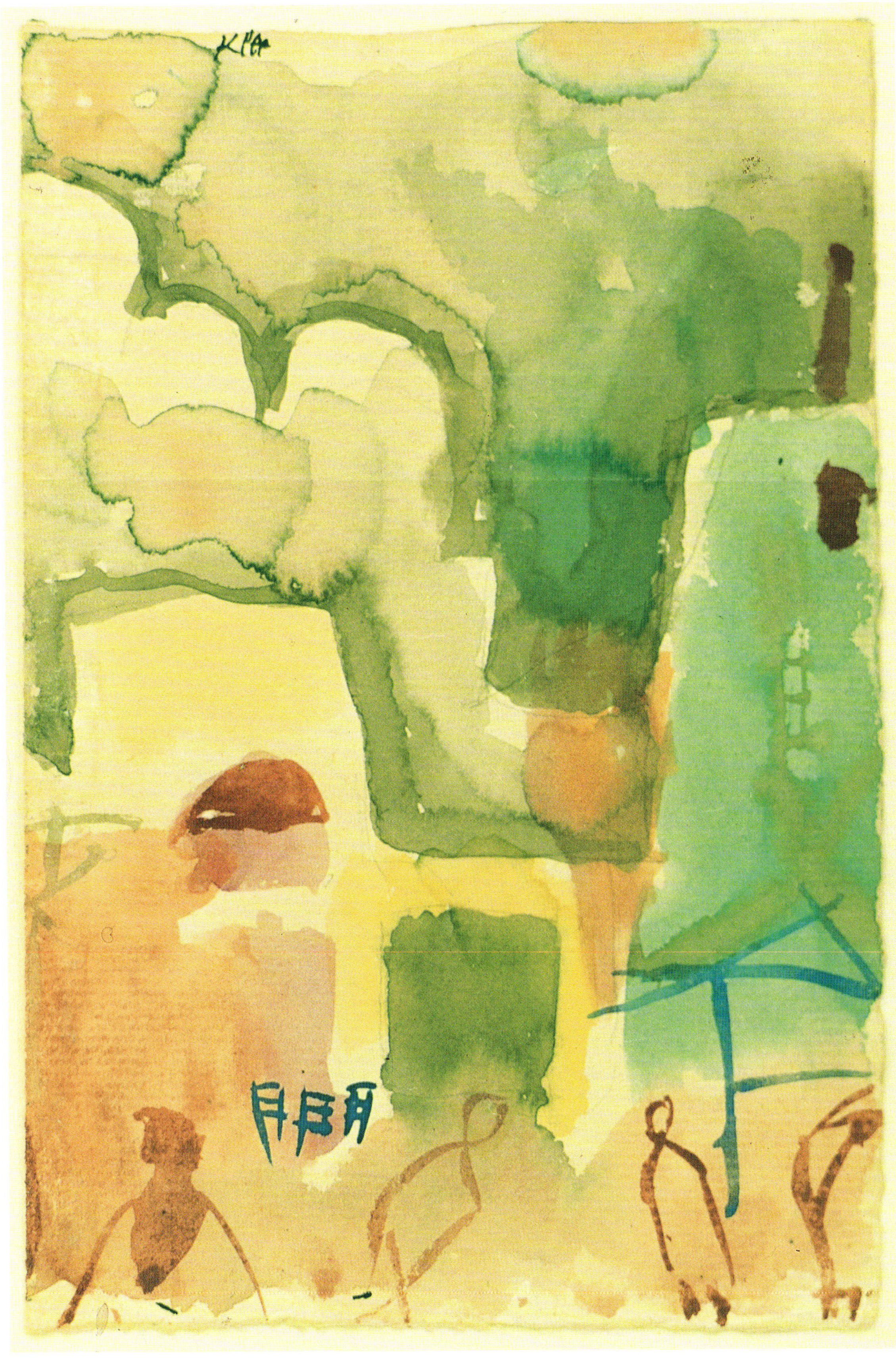

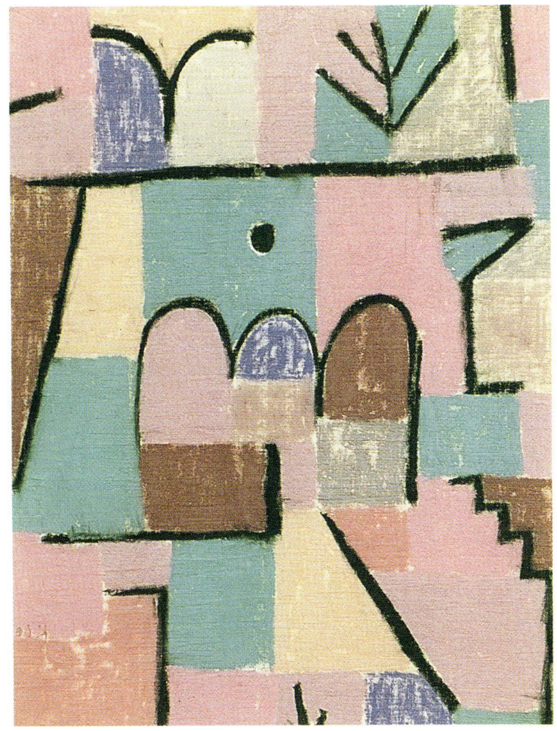

Above
Oriental Garden, Paul Klee, 1937
Pastel, 36.1 x 28.2 cm
(Alsdorf Collection, Chicago).

Left
Tunisian Sketch, Paul Klee, 1914
Watercolor, 17.9 x 12.2 cm
(private collection, Switzerland).

Opposite
Oriental Architecture, Paul Klee, 1929
Watercolor on Canson paper,
24.5 x 31.5 cm (private collection).

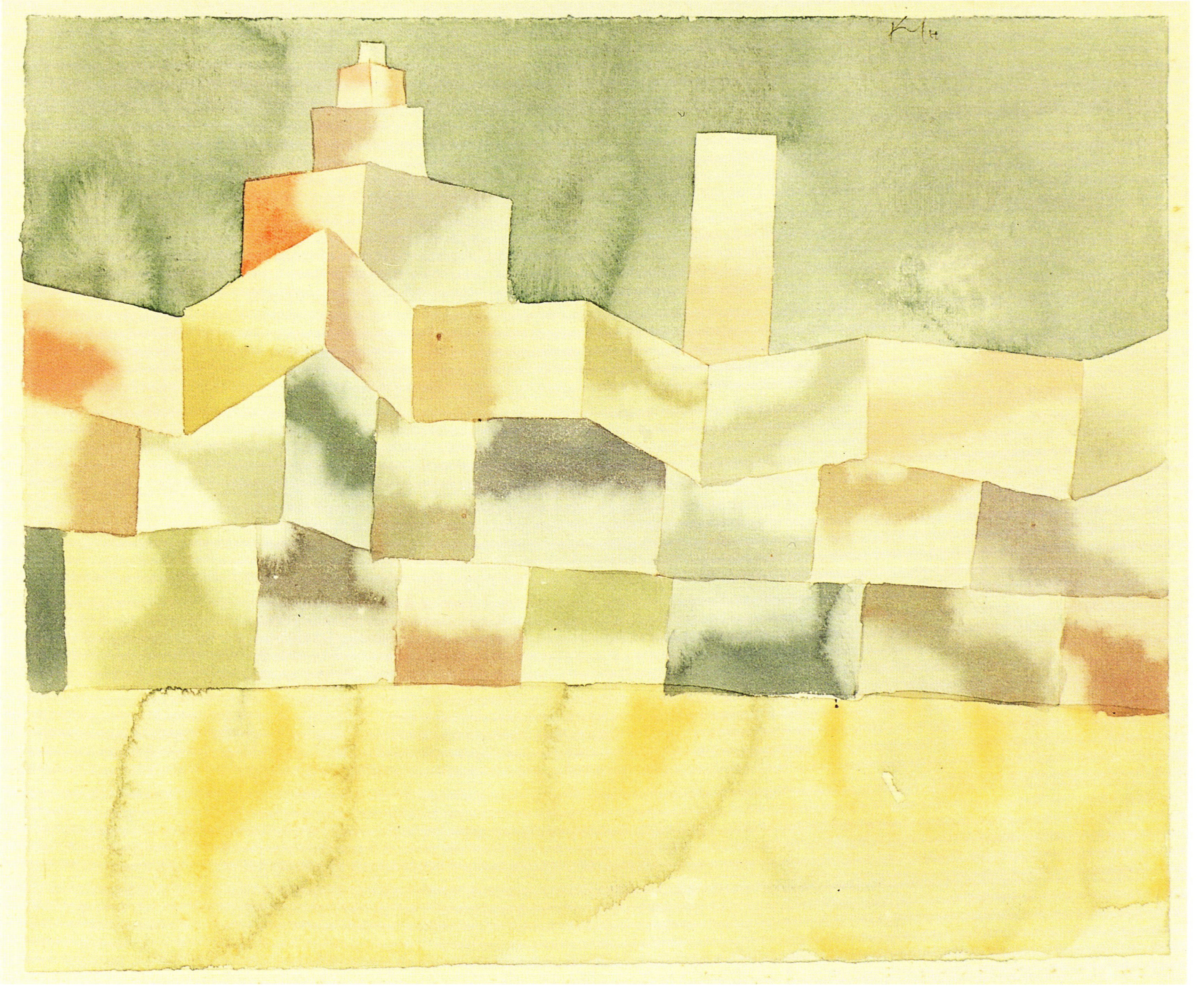

of the geometric style of decoration, applied in a very particular way to lend structure to the surface of the painting. *Small Sketch for Egypt*, a small watercolor of 1918, is developed in the manner of a dream, while *Entrance to the Seraglio*, a pen and ink drawing of 1926, is a work in which the Orient is the realm of pure fantasy. The artist's son, Felix Klee, rightly observed: "My father was always extremely sensitive to the call of the South." A good example is his *Battle Scene for a Comic Opera: The Sailor* of 1923, a watercolor inspired by the voyages of Sindbad in the famous chapter of *A Thousand and One Nights*. In it the sailor can be seen battling with gigantic fish in the middle of a sea composed of a tight grid pattern overrun by gradations of color that go from black to white, passing through purple, blue, and green. And in his *Journal*, Klee remarked on the subject of the southern moon: "She will be my fiancée. My other self. An invitation to find myself. Because that is me, the southern moon, at the moment when she is rising." It is therefore not at all surprising that so many crescent moons rise above his imaginary landscapes, figurative or otherwise.

The attraction of the African continent remained very strong for Klee. He had the opportunity to visit Egypt in 1928, after spending some time in Sicily. He stayed a whole month in Egypt, but it was not as picturesque as he was expecting; it fell far short of what he had imagined it to be. Despite this, he found something that stirred him in the linear outlines of the monuments, in the infinite space of the sandy desert, in the long stretches of water, and in the pale light of a sky that was overrun by colors. In a letter addressed to his wife, Lily, he declared: "I am painting a landscape, *Monument in a Fertile Land*, which is a bit like the view that one has from the top of the Vallée des Rois, over a land covered in fruit trees." This painting, totally abstract in conception, plays on

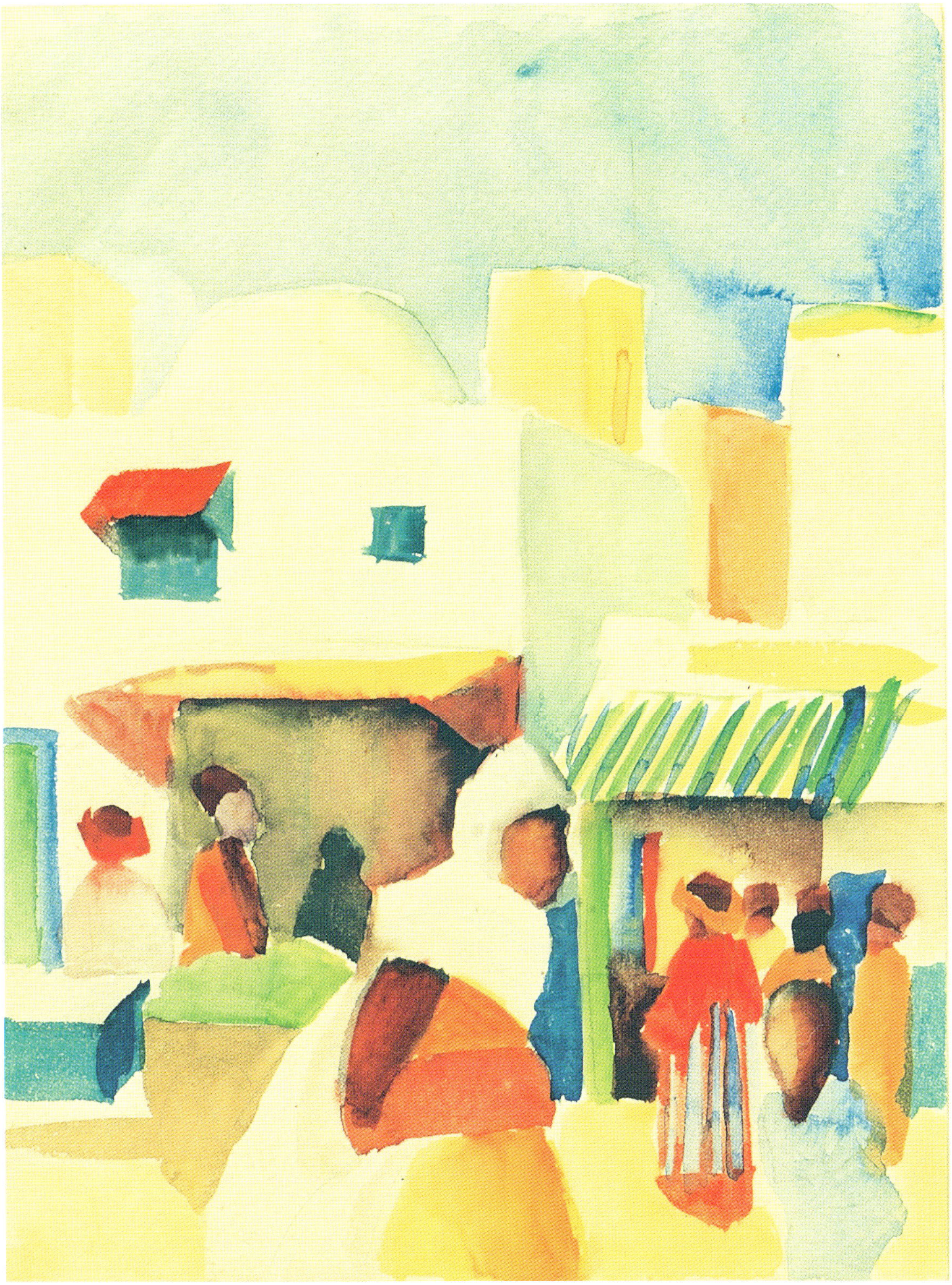

The Market in Tunis, August Macke, 1914
Pencil and watercolor on card, 29 x 22.5 cm
(private collection).

Woman on a Sofa, August Macke, 1914
Watercolor, 27 x 20 cm
(Thyssen-Bornemisza Foundation, Madrid).

the verticality of the painted surface, and so is reminiscent of the multicolored grid patterns formed by cultivated fields when seen from the air. He repeated this type of composition the following year with *Main Road and Side Streets*; also in 1929, he drew *Mountains in the Desert*. Later, he occasionally returned to a subject that evoked ancient Egypt, as in *A Sphinx at Rest* of 1932, which is a parody of one of the sets designed by the German artist and architect Karl Friedrich Schinkel for a production of Mozart's opera *Die Zauberflöte* (The magic flute). He also used the architecture of a traditional Arab town, with its terraced roofs and close-knit interlocking buildings, which seem the center of a labyrinth, in compositions such as *Arab Song* and *Town with Red Dome*, where he has emphasized the arid reality of the landscape by using a rough jute canvas. At the end of his life he took pleasure in pencil drawings, such as *And One More Camel*, and in a watercolor silhouette of an oriental woman dubbed the *Egyptian Girl*.

For Macke the situation was very different. He learned several lessons from this African adventure. Like Klee, he wanted to create works solely by organizing arbitrary blocks of color in terms of an order determined in and for the design itself. But the Orient haunted his imagination, too. When he got back to his studio in Bonn, he hastened to translate all that he had experienced during these enchanted weeks of work into the specific language of paint. Of the 38 watercolors and a hundred or so drawings (some of them done from memory), not to mention the 52 photographs that he brought back from Tunisia, there emerged nine exceptional paintings. Some of these watercolors are perfectly finished pieces of work in themselves, such as *Interior Courtyard of the House at Saint-Germain*, *The Market in Tunis*, and *View of a Narrow Street*. These are in the same vein as the paintings done in Bonn during the spring and summer of 1940. Confirmation of this may be found in *Tunisian Landscape*, in which the geometric outline of the space in the foreground is accentuated by white buildings and, in the background, by the shape of

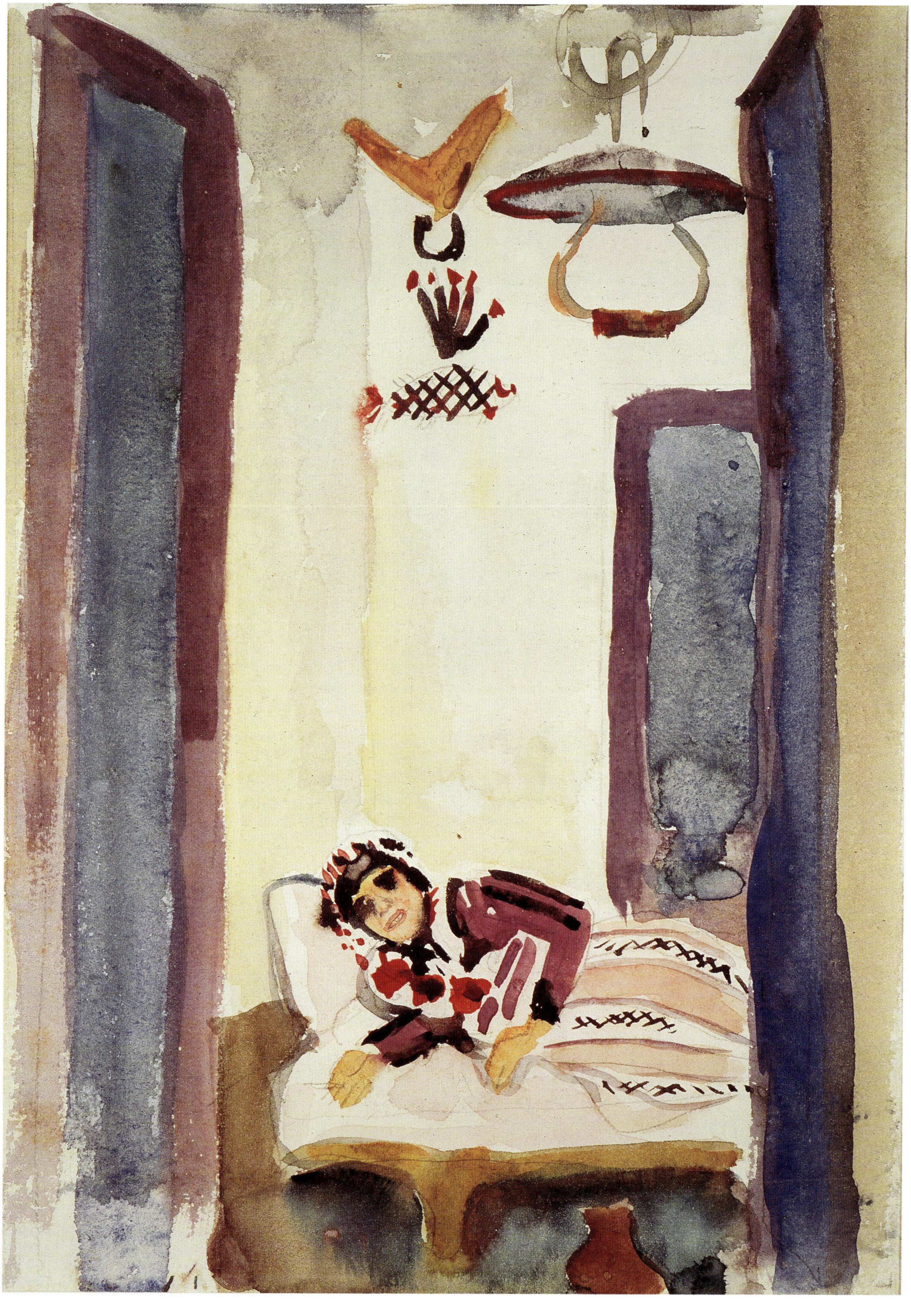

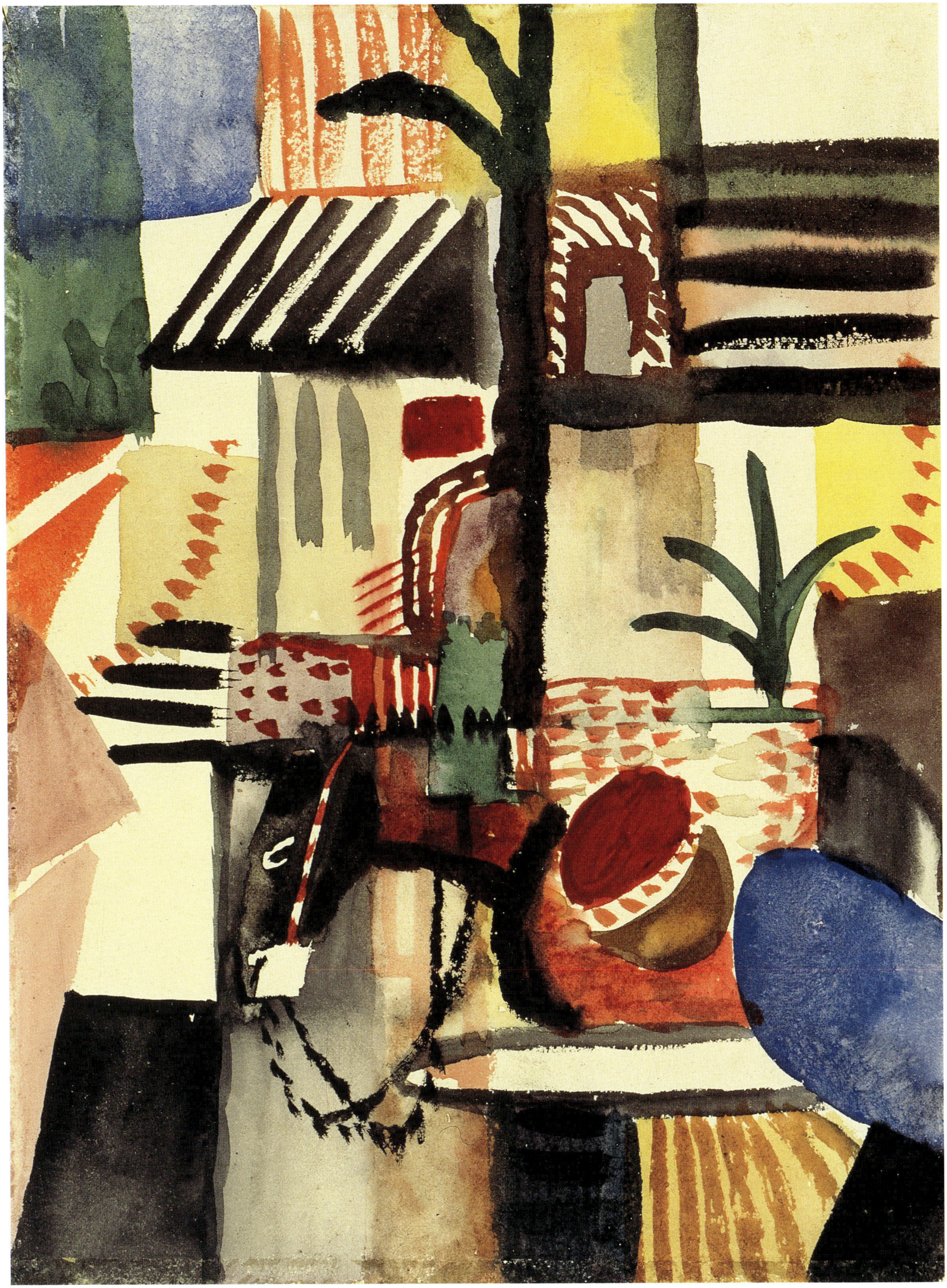

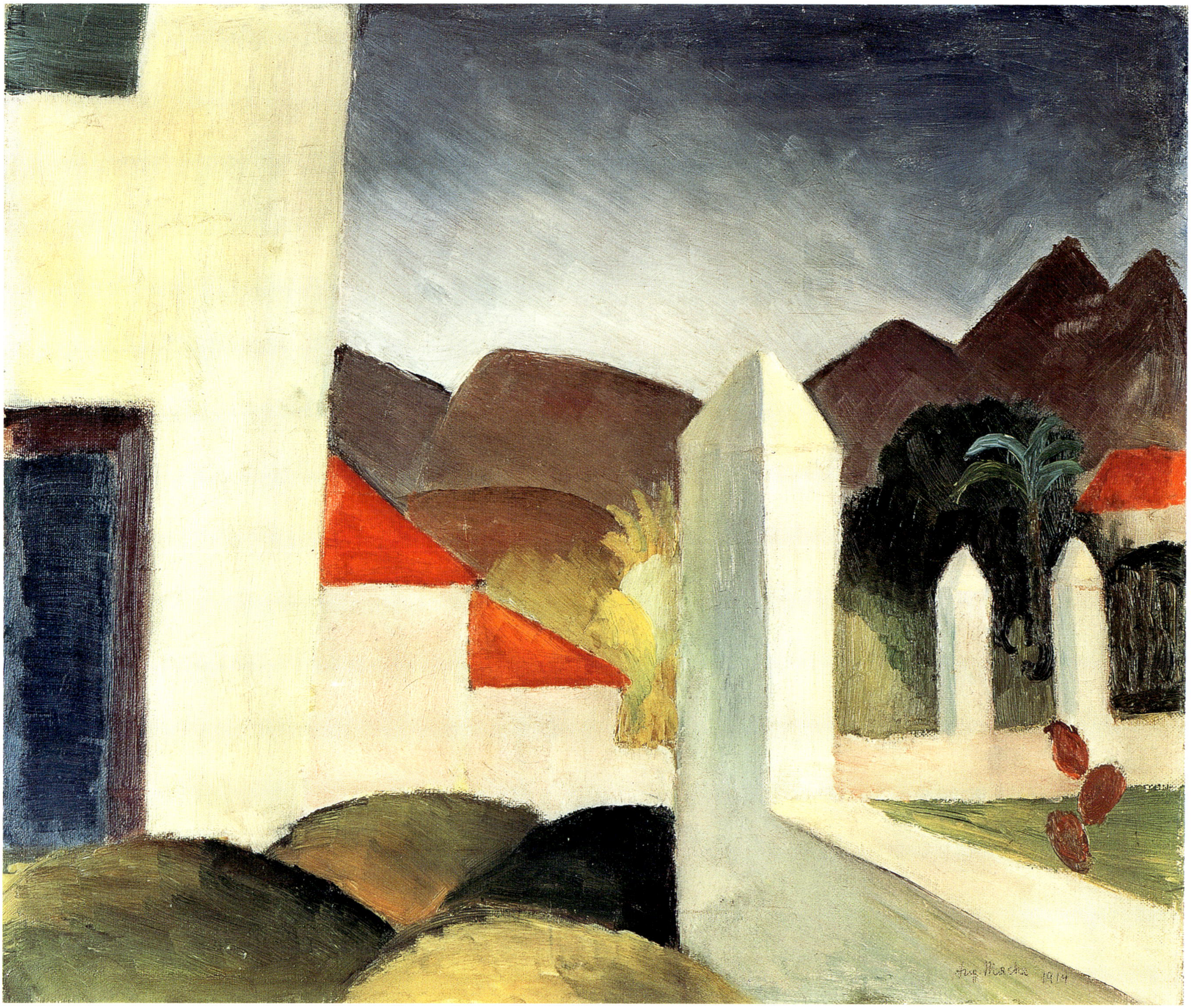

mountains. *The Market in Tunis*, on the other hand, is intended as a synthesis of various scenes and impressions, with figures, objects, architectural elements, and fragments of landscape distributed on different planes. Of the café scenes that he so loved, Macke has left us three paintings, one of them a small composition, *Arab Café – Small Turkish Boy*, which emphasizes details of the café's decoration. Of the other two, known as *Turkish Café I* and *Turkish Café II*, the former concentrates far more on a man sitting almost with his back to us, wearing a fez. *The Donkey in the Palm Grove* is seen from a similar viewpoint, since the landscape seems almost real while the donkey is a transformed, unreal image of this animal, a donkey from the realms of fantasy. But the strangest and most captivating painting is without any doubt *Landscape with Cow and Camel*, since in it two opposing universes are brought face to face: the German countryside and the arid regions of North Africa.

Macke was called up on 8 August 1914. We will ever know how he might have pursued his Oriental dream, for he was killed a few weeks later, on 26 September, one of the early casualties of the Great War.

Tunisian Landscape, August Macke, 1914
Oil on canvas, 45 x 55 cm
(Städtische Kunsthalle, Mannheim).

Man with Donkey, August Macke, 1914
Watercolor, 26.6 x 20.8 cm
(Kunstmuseum, Berne).

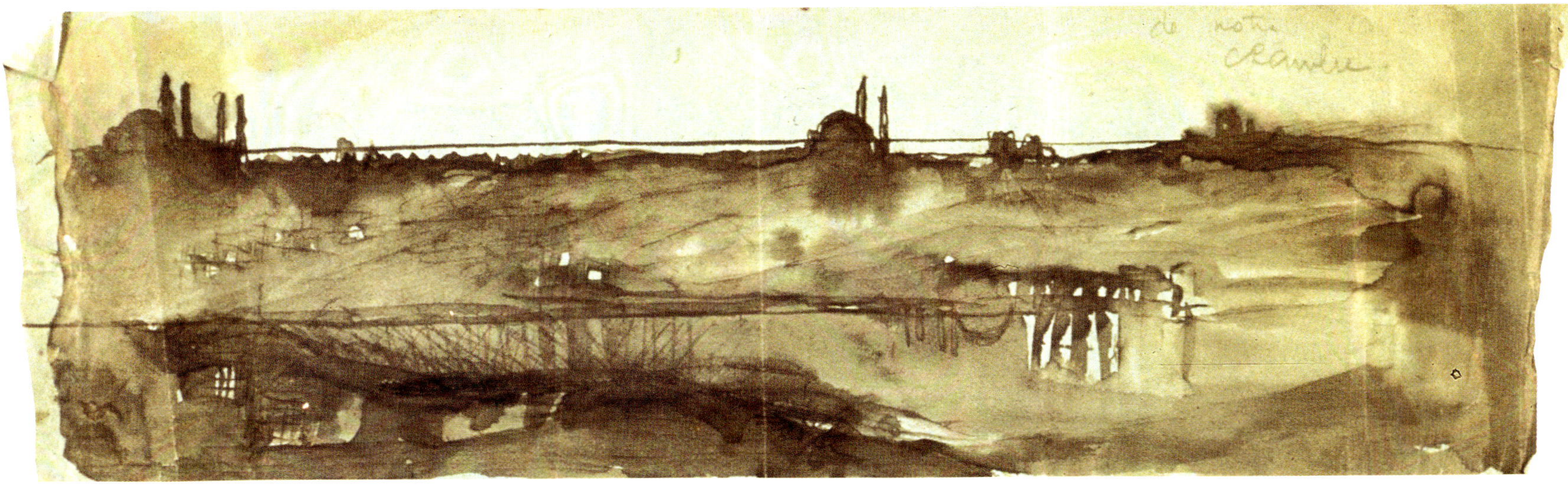

Le Corbusier and the Light of the Orient

Charles Édouard Jeanneret – better known as Le Corbusier – was 20 years old when, on the advice of L'Eplattenier, one of his teachers at the Ateliers d'Art in La Chaux-de-Fonds in Switzerland, he went to Italy to study Florentine Gothic and the Italian Primitives. He traveled throughout Tuscany, stayed one month in Florence, visited Ravenna, and ended his tour in Venice. Five years later he went on a second tour, from autumn until spring, this time in Germany. In May 1911, he went abroad again for six months, visiting Berlin first of all, then crossing Hungary, Romania, and Bulgaria, finally reaching Constantinople, and going as far as Bursa. He returned via Greece and Italy.

From this long tour of Eastern Europe, Ottoman Turkey, and Greece, Le Corbusier came back with an account that he was to publish at the end of his life, in 1965; he published his notes, however, in the journal *Feuille d'Avis* in La Chaux-de-Fonds as soon as he returned. The account he published in the 1960s is a work of undeniable literary merit, proving that Le Corbusier had not only great sensitivity but also the ability to record the impressions of his travels in a style that is subtle and vivid. He also had the discerning eye of a painter (he was in fact a painter of considerable ability), as he demonstrated in the chapter on a small café in Istanbul, and in the impression of this same town that he recorded in *Deux féeries, une réalité* (Two visions of enchantment, one reality).

Le Corbusier brought back with him a large number of watercolors and 300 drawings, which he described as "rough sketches," and at least 200 photographs. His two ambitions were revealed by these two complementary activities: on the one hand, painting, on the other, architecture. There is no doubt that the Orient had a profound influence on his architecture, where light plays a central role.

Raoul Dufy in the Garden of the Pasha

It was fairly late in life that the French artist Raoul Dufy discovered North Africa: in 1926, when he went on a journey to Morocco with his friend Paul Poiret. Poiret had already gone there first in 1919, and during the early 1920s had produced paintings inspired in particular by Arab clothes, the *jellabas*, burnouses, and *gandouras*. Together the two artists visited Fez, Casablanca, Marrakesh, Demaat, Meknes, and lastly Tangiers, before traveling through the south of Spain. In the

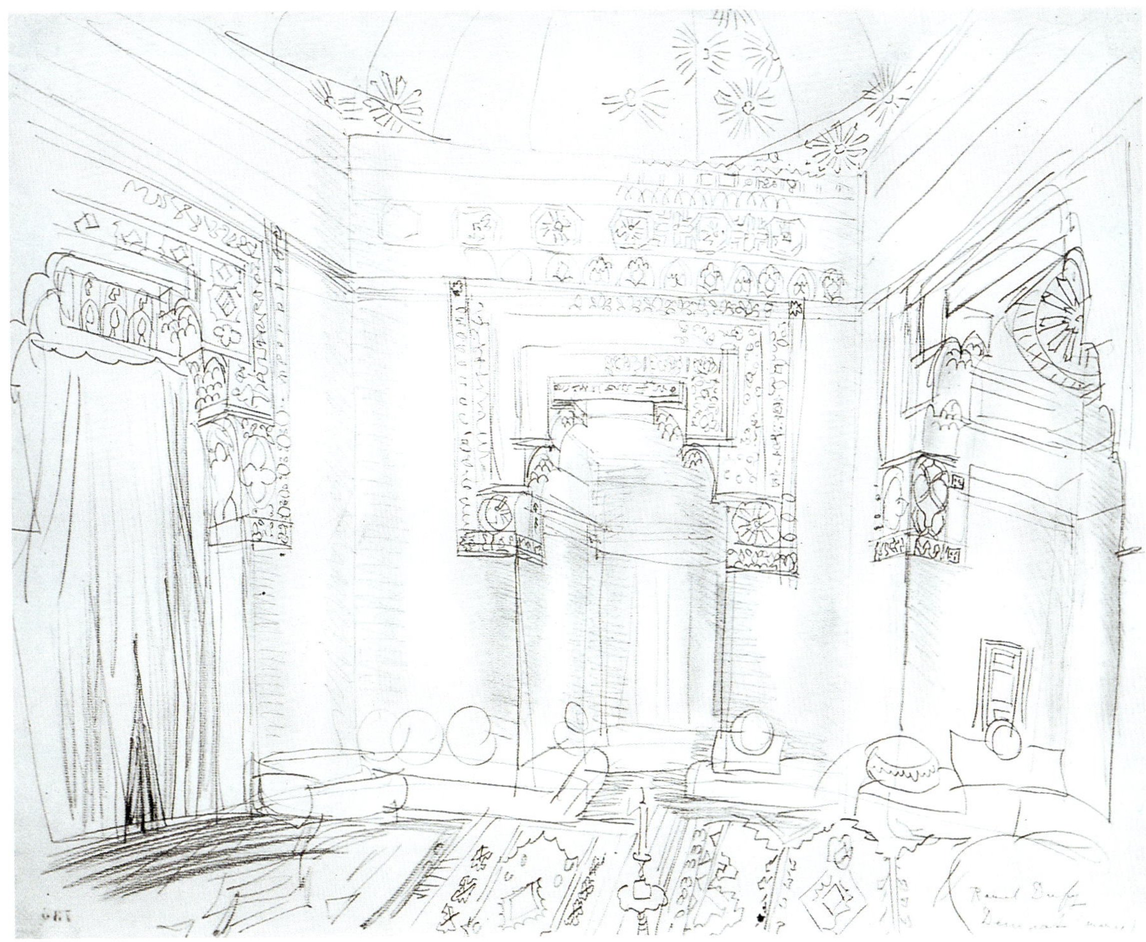

course of his "enchanted travels," Dufy produced a large number of drawings and watercolors. He was full of enthusiasm, finding there the inspiration that had been found by earlier artists, notably Eugène Delacroix, Eugène Fromentin, and Émile Bernard: "Imagine all the biblical characters [...]," he wrote; "we are rubbing shoulders with the descendants of the tribes of the Old Testament." He returned to France with some very beautiful watercolors, notably *The Pasha's Garden* and *Café in Morocco*. He was so delighted with this trip, and with the artistic inspiration it provided, that he wrote to a friend: "How can I describe to you this fantastic experience of art at work [...] I am bringing back about forty watercolors and about twenty drawings [...]. I shall exhibit them at Berheim." This exhibition of 40 watercolors did indeed take place, from 17 to 28 May of the same year.

In 1934, he had a second opportunity to visit North Africa, this time visiting Algeria. A Doctor Roudinesco, who represented a group of book lovers and art enthusiasts, had commissioned him three years earlier to produce lithographs to illustrate a reprint of the novel *Tartarin de Tarascon* by Alphonse Daudet. Dufy had little liking for Daudet, but he took the work very seriously, visiting first Tarascon in southern France and then, in 1934, Algiers and Constantine. Dufy returned to Marrakesh for the last time in 1946 and found it as charming as ever. "I shall take back travelers' notes and landscapes, for the rest of it is beyond the reach of painting," he wrote to his friends. Sadly, and despite his initial enthusiasm, he subsequently ceased to find in the Orient a fertile source of inspiration.

Wyndham Lewis, a filibuster in Barbary

The Englishman Wyndham Lewis was both a painter and a man of letters. He founded the London Vorticist group and in 1914 he started the avant-garde magazine *Blast*. In 1919, after war service as a gunner on the Western Front in France, he took up another fight, for art and literature, publishing a small volume entitled *The Caliph's Design*, which was mainly addressed to architects, but also to artists. The book opens with a tale in which the Caliph of Baghdad, seated on his golden bed, takes up his turquoise quill to express his disgust for his city and to draw design for a new one. The potentate wants to redefine town planning by putting it on a modern footing, a Vorticist one, which is to say one according to the Futurist principles that Lewis had set out in his writings and works of art shortly before the Great War broke out. From the Orient Lewis took the idea of the absolute ruler, an enlightened despot, who would have the power to make the plans for a completely new city and impose them without any discussion. In 1927 he translated his thoughts into pictorial terms in a picture entitled *Baghdad*. The vision he offers us is a totemic one: a long, narrow spiral staircase leading to the top of a minaret contrasts with the somber colors of the architectural elements and an enigmatic sculpture. The upper part of this ideal city is the outline of a magical garden.

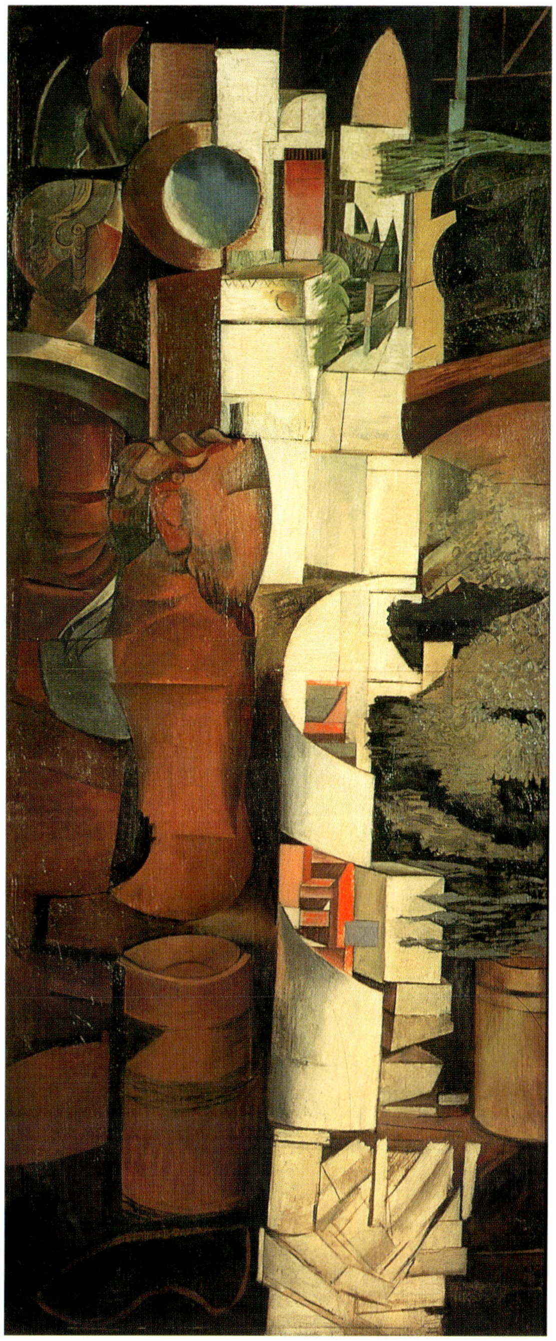

Opposite top
A View of the Hill of Istanbul,
Le Corbusier, 1911

Opposite bottom
Moroccan Interior, Raoul Dufy, 1926
Graphite, 47.5 x 61.3 cm
(Musée National d'Art Moderne, Paris).

Baghdad, Wyndham Lewis, 1927
Oil on plywood, 183 x 79 cm
(Tate Gallery, London).

Lewis's own meeting with the Orient came several years later, during the summer of 1931, when he visited North Africa. While there he wrote several articles that he sent to English newspapers; they deal with subjects as varied as farm workers, the town of Casablanca, and the *Café-chantant*. In 1932 he brought these together in a volume he entitled *Filibusters in Barbary*. He came back from his journey with a number of drawings, many depicting Berber culture and landscapes of the High Atlas. He selected a number of these for a collection, *Islamic Sensations*, dedicated to "tous les aimables visiteurs qui viennent si nombreux chercher ici du ciel blue, de l'air pur et embaumé . . . ainsi que des sensations d'Islam!." Although careful to respect his subjects, he nonetheless depicted them in the angular style derived from the geometrical construction of his Vorticist period during 1912–1915.

New Visions of the Orient

While Europe was being devastated by World War II, a new artistic order was being created by a generation of young American artists. Deeply influenced by Picasso, Masson, Miró and the Surrealists in general, many of whom had followed André Breton and exiled themselves to New York, they constructed the basis of what was to be known, particularly in France, as "lyrical abstraction" – abstract art that favored spontaneous, gestural forms rather than simple geometrical ones; the best-known example was Action Painting. Some were to look beyond Europe (French art in particular had dominated the pre-War years) to the Far East for a model of a new aesthetic that went beyond the figurative. A West Coast artist, Mark Tobey, for example, attempted to adapt the key principles of Zen painting to a modern pictorial language. The same was happening in France: from Henri Michaux to Jean Degottex, the references used were always linked to the ancient arts of China or Japan. Degottex even broadened the field of his concerts to include the cuneiform writing of Mesopotamia. Typical of his approach is *Métasignes*.

Brion Gysin, who lived in Tangiers during the 1950s, was almost the only Western artist to use Arabic calligraphy as a resource for the painting of signs. He started by depicting desert landscapes, enigmatic, but always changing, vibrant and unreal. Then he used only invented pictograms, derived from Japanese ideograms and from the Arabic alphabet, forming them into sequences or constructing grids (since Japanese calligraphy is written vertically and Arabic horizontally) that effectively form a magic square. Gysin's works are not mimetic, but metaphorical; his signs are inventions that obey only their own internal rules, infinite echoes of an imaginary writing.

In 1947 the French artist Jean Dubuffet, who had recently spent time in Switzerland studying what he called Art Brut (the art of children and the insane) and who had just exhibited for the first time, in Pierre Matisse's gallery in New York, decided to make a trip to North Africa. There he discovered El Goléa and became passionate

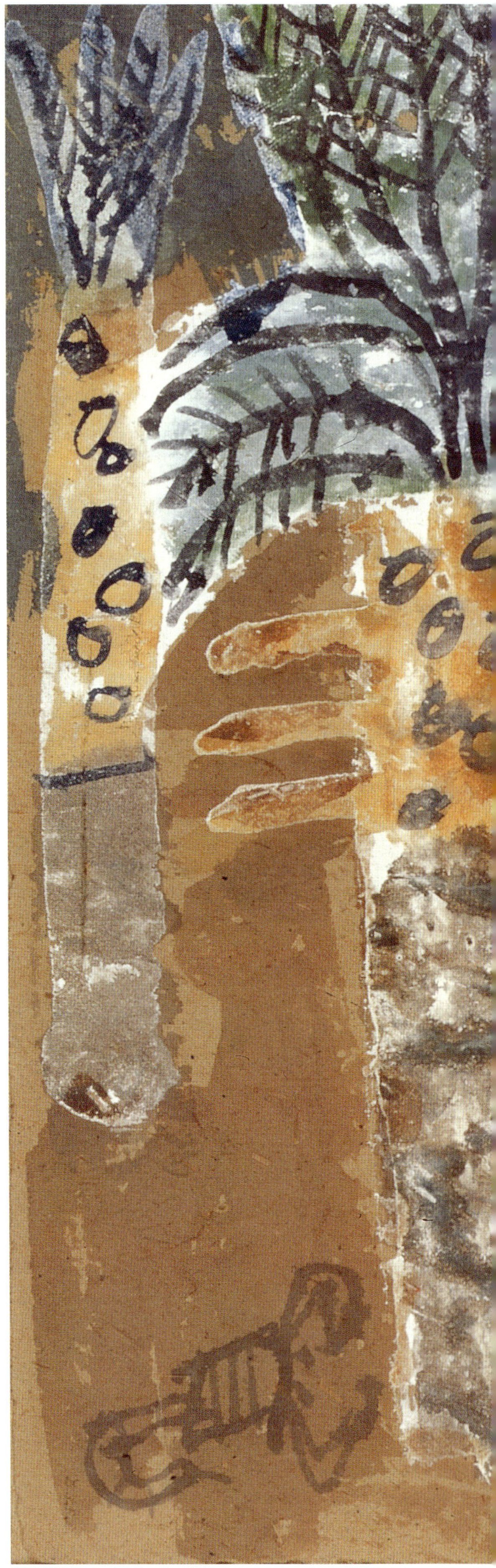

Palm Grove with Scorpions, Jean Dubuffet, 1948
Gouache on paper, 24 x 33 cm
(Union Centrale des Arts Décoratifs, Paris).

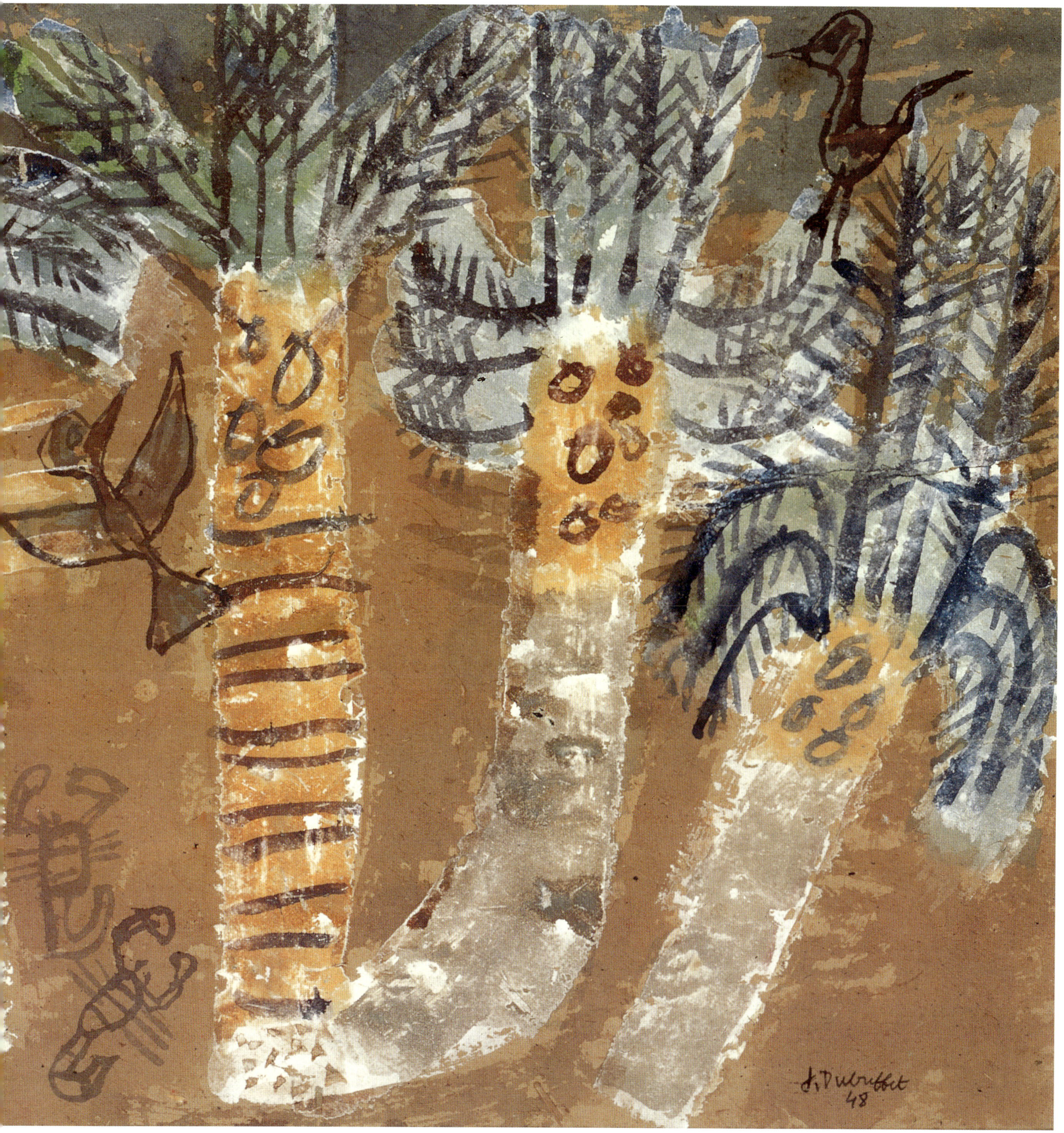
J. Dubuffet
48

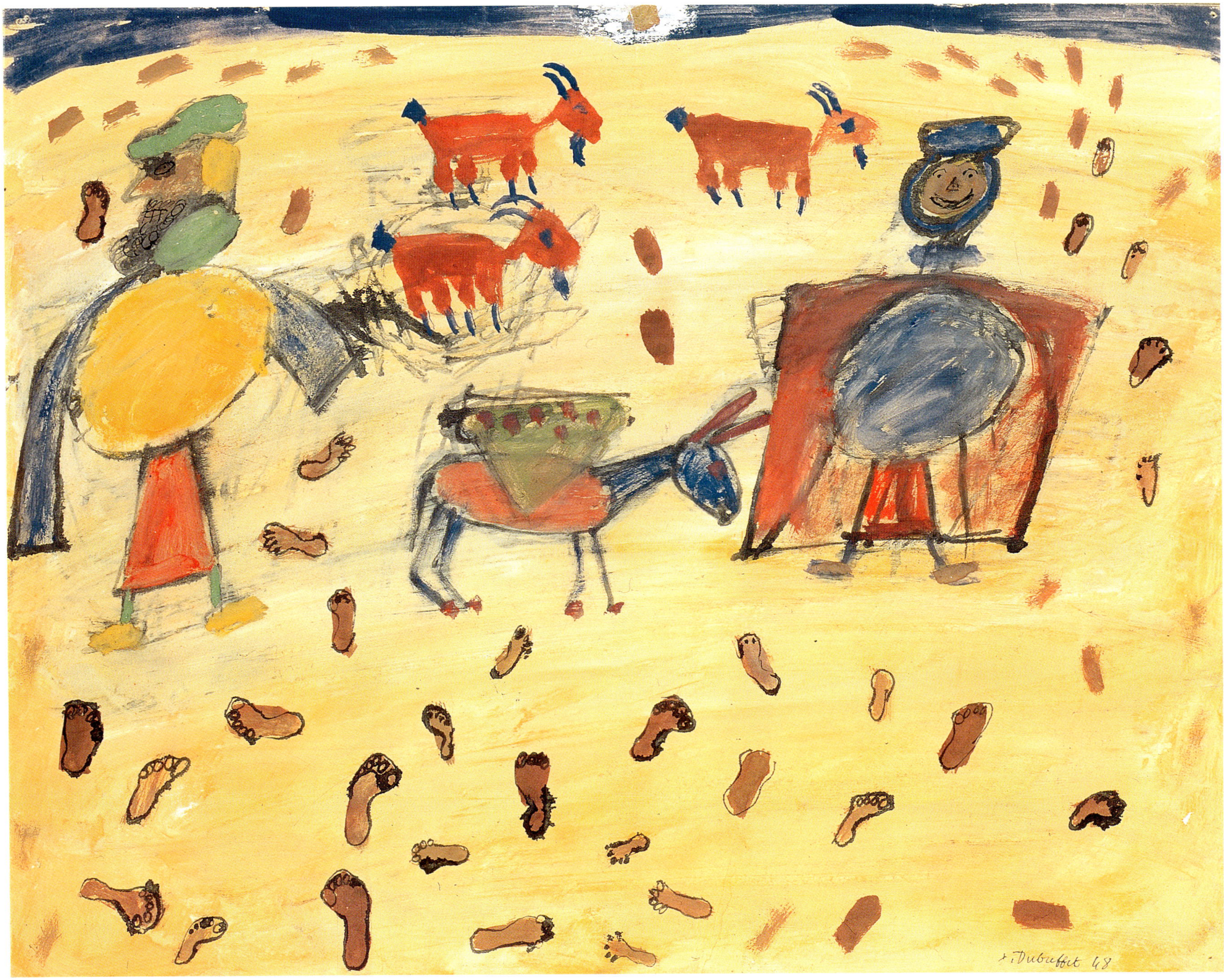

about this area of the Sahara, returning there twice, in 1948 and 1949. From these trips he brought back numerous works on paper; landscapes or Oriental scenes in gouache, ink, gum arabic, or colored pencils. He expressed himself with surprising variety and energy, accentuating the grotesque character that he had already begun with his series of writers' portraits. He created a very individual vision of the desert, which he saw as the last wilderness. In stressing this trait, and in denaturing the forms, which are at times exaggeratedly infantile and ostensibly derived from images produced by the insane, he in fact achieves, paradoxically, drawings of unequalled freshness and humor. This unique phase of his career was fundamental because it was for him the moment when his art freed itself, his imagination flowing with uninhibited spontaneity.

Eastern artists themselves have long explored the intrinsic value of written characters, calligraphy being the highest art form both in the Islamic world, where it is the sacred art par excellence, and also in the Far East. The contemporary Iraqi artist Shakir Hassan Al-Saïd introduces fragments of writing on to a broken surface that brings to mind a wall eroded by time, weather, and chance. The Algerian Ben Bella saturates his works with graphic signs; they swarm and run together, in all the colors of the spectrum, producing a semantic mass that is almost organic in nature. In Turkey during the 1980s, the writer and artist Ferit Edgu created a visual world embodying a creative tension between two poles, the first Eastern and the second Western and modern. Contrary tensions, attractions and reciprocal repulsion, contrasting aspirations: the result of this confrontation is the appearance of a scriptural constellation whose elements make the space where they are deployed vibrate. The characters deform themselves, retract, dilate, broadening out, dividing, stretching themselves and forming spheres or spirals. The work concerns the ceaseless play of thought, applied as a deregulation of codes which, within the abstract volume the canvas suggests, resonate like so many notes assembled for an improvised fugue.

Such modern Orientalists explore the relationship between calligraphy and the experimental art developing in the West. By contrast, one artist has renewed a figurative approach that was believed to have disappeared for ever. Having been one of the main figures in the Parisian avant-garde in the 1960s and 1970s, Aldo Mondino later started work on a project with a decidedly Orientalist theme. From his journeys to the Near East he brought back drawings and pictures that related to the traditions and ceremonies of these regions. His work brings together two attitudes, one Eastern, the other Western. In *Hanging Carpets* (1985) he creates a feeling of accumulation by cutting out the contour of the works typical of the Islamic decorative arts and then superimposing them, playing on their infinite variations of color and line. He comes close to ironic caricature with his *Card Players*, in which he humorously illustrates different aspects of daily life in Egypt and North Africa. Mondino is not content merely to plagiarize stereotypes of Western Orientalism, as in *General Bonaparte* (1986), in which he created a ferocious pastiche of the clichés of Western historical painting. In 1985 he produced *Harvest at Prayer*, a sort of large Islamic prayer mat whose geometrical patterns were made from corn, white haricot beans, peas, green and red lentils, sunflower seeds, and so on. Shortly afterwards he went to Israel and brought back whirlwind visions of the dances and the most unusual aspects of Jewish ritual. Similarly, in Turkey he was fascinated by the ceremonies of the Whirling

Opposite
The Desert Theater, Jean Dubuffet, 1948
Gouache on paper, 31 x 40.5 cm
(Union Centrale des Arts Décoratifs, Paris).

Below
Untitled, Brion Gysin, 1960
(Archives Galeries de France, Paris).

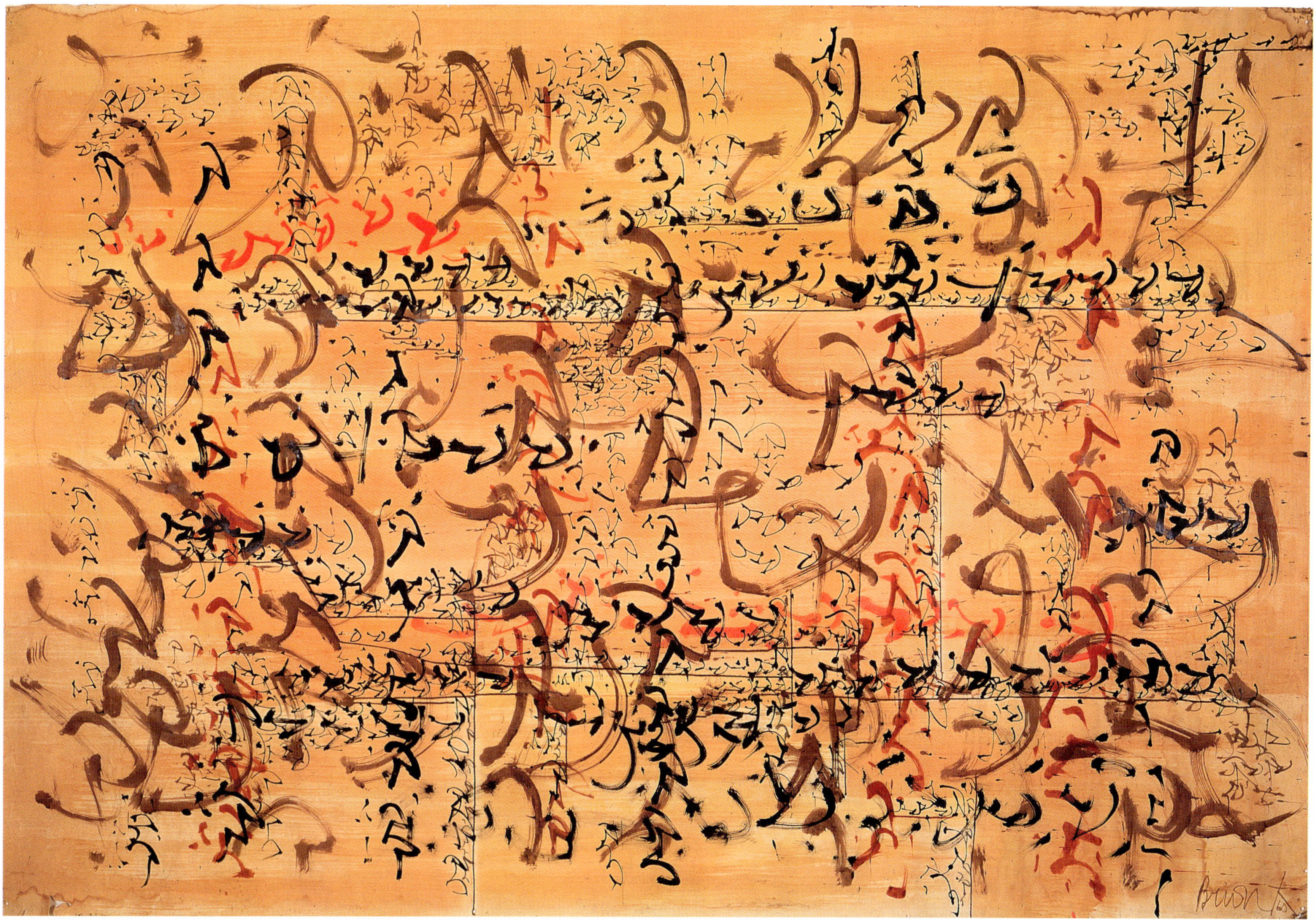

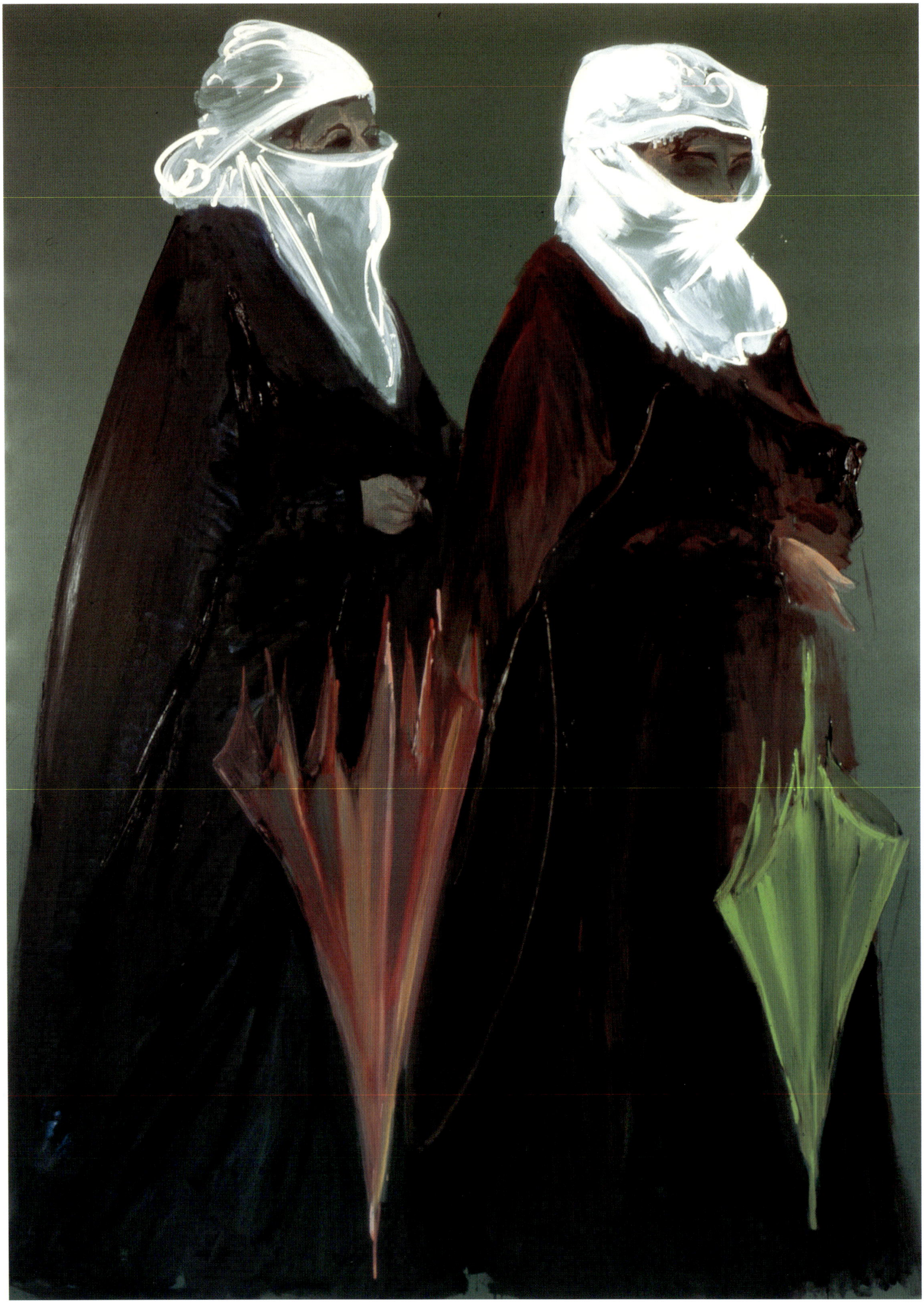

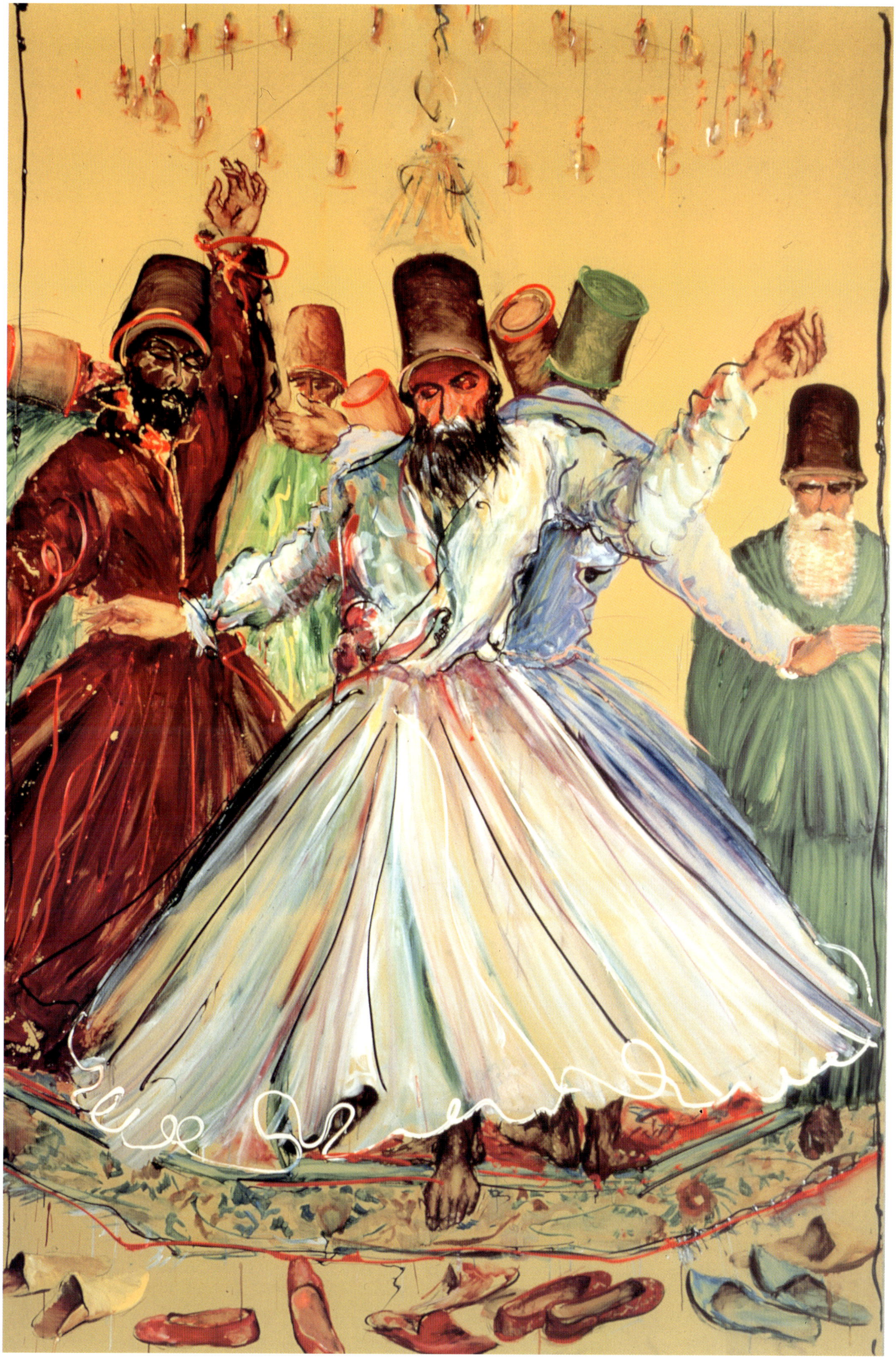

The Walk,
Aldo Mondino, 1989
Oil on linoleum,
200 x 140 cm
(Cremniter Laffanour
Collection, Paris).

Dervishes,
Aldo Mondino, 1989
Oil on linoleum,
240 x 190 cm
(Cremniter Laffanour
Collection, Paris).

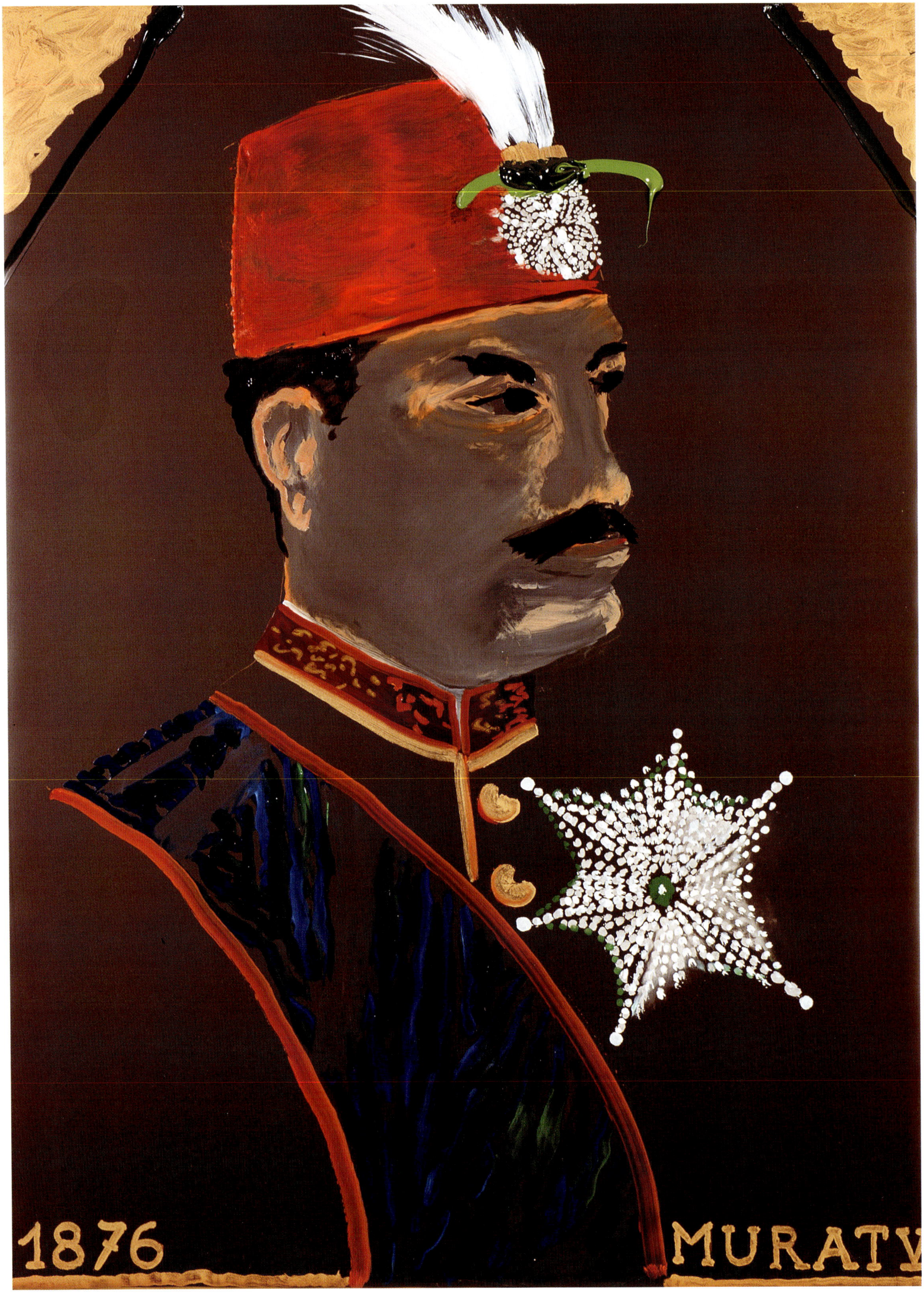

Murat V,
Aldo Mondino,
1989-1990
Oil on linoleum
80 x 60 cm
(private collection).

Dervishes and translated their unsettling beauty onto canvas. Between 1989 and 1990 he decided to bring together a complete gallery of the sultans of the Osmanli dynasty, who reigned over the Ottoman Empire from the 13th century to the start of the 20th century. This *Sultans* cycle, although drawing upon originals, is not without irony. The elements he used – such as the two copper plates glued above the head of Abdulhamid I; the mosaic impression given by the pointillist touches on the portrait of the ferocious Murat IV; the words "San Remo" written in red on the picture of the unfortunate Murat V, who was deposed by Kemal Ataturk, a derisive symbol of his exile during which he devoted himself to painting – all bear ample witness to his irony. In 1997 he created a large sculpture entitled *Dinojarres*, made of slender jars that are inserted one into the other to form a long snake of terracotta and metal which undulates in space. Mondino endowed Orientalism with a new meaning, full of paradoxes, using surviving examples of ancient beauty while introducing a certain humor and a critical distance, though it is not a distance that implies indifference.

The Orient reappears in a disturbing manner in the work of several contemporary Western painters. The Spanish artist Victor Mira, for example, inspired by the monastery of Montserrat, a center of the mysticism that occupies such an important place in the religious life of Spain, made the connection between the Desert Fathers and this place loved by the celebrated Spanish architect Antoni Gaudí. Mira paints pictures that show austere and ludicrous anchorites perched on pillars and melting like candles or drying out like overripe fruit under an implacable sun. They are undergoing their exacting spiritual trials in a desert of intense blues and disturbing black where, here and there, we may distinguish no more than the skull of an animal which has died of thirst.

Similarly, though from a quite different perspective, the Italian artist Marco Del Re shows great expanses of ocher deserts, often enveloped in whitish mists where long trains

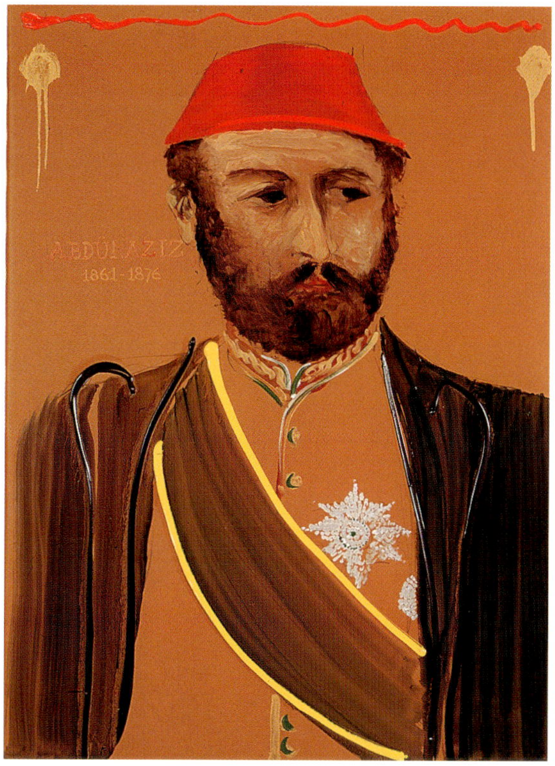

Abdulaziz, Aldo Mondino, 1989–1990
Oil on linoleum, 80 x 60 cm
(private collection).

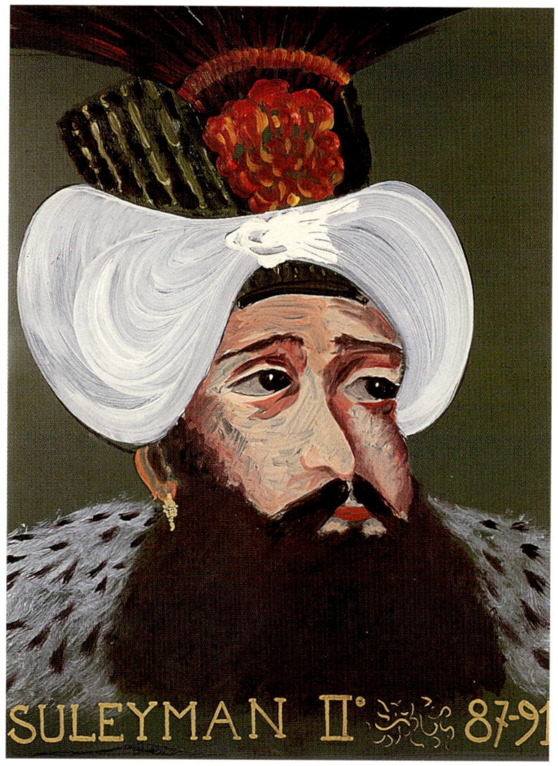

Suleyman II, Aldo Mondino, 1989–1990
Oil on linoleum, 80 x 60 cm
(private collection).

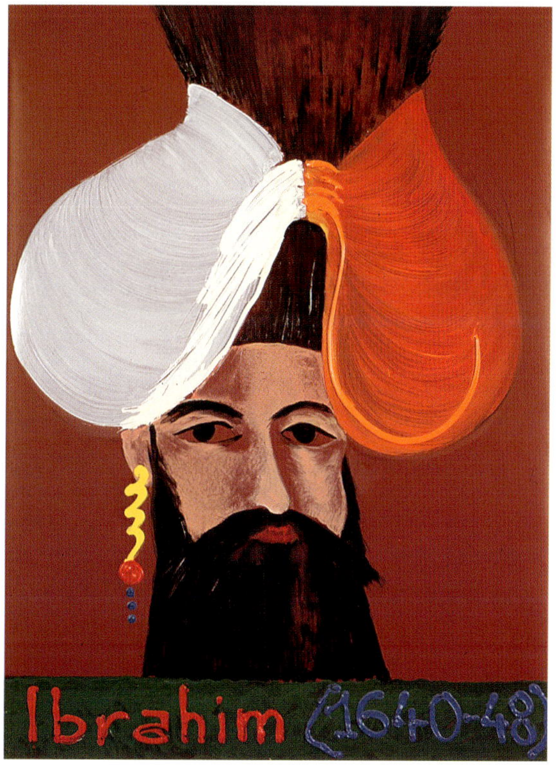

Ibrahim, Aldo Mondino, 1989–1990
Oil on linoleum, 80 x 60 cm
(private collection).

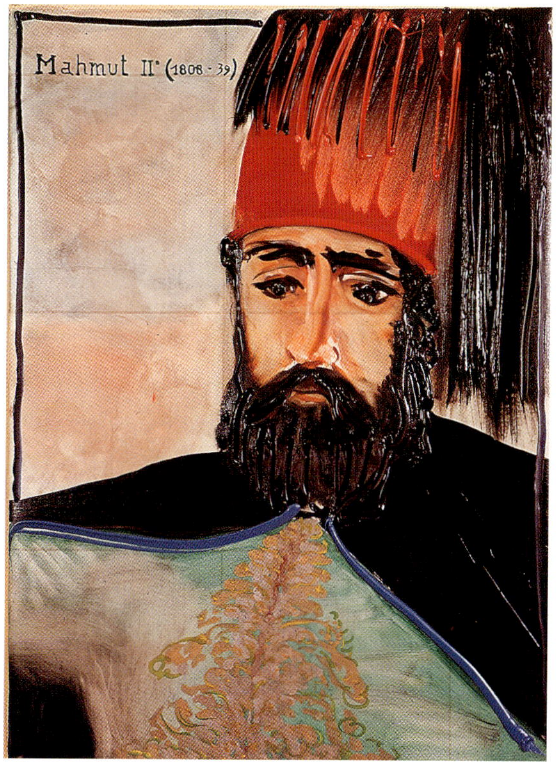

Mahmut II, Aldo Mondino, 1989–1990
Oil on linoleum, 80 x 60 cm
(private collection).

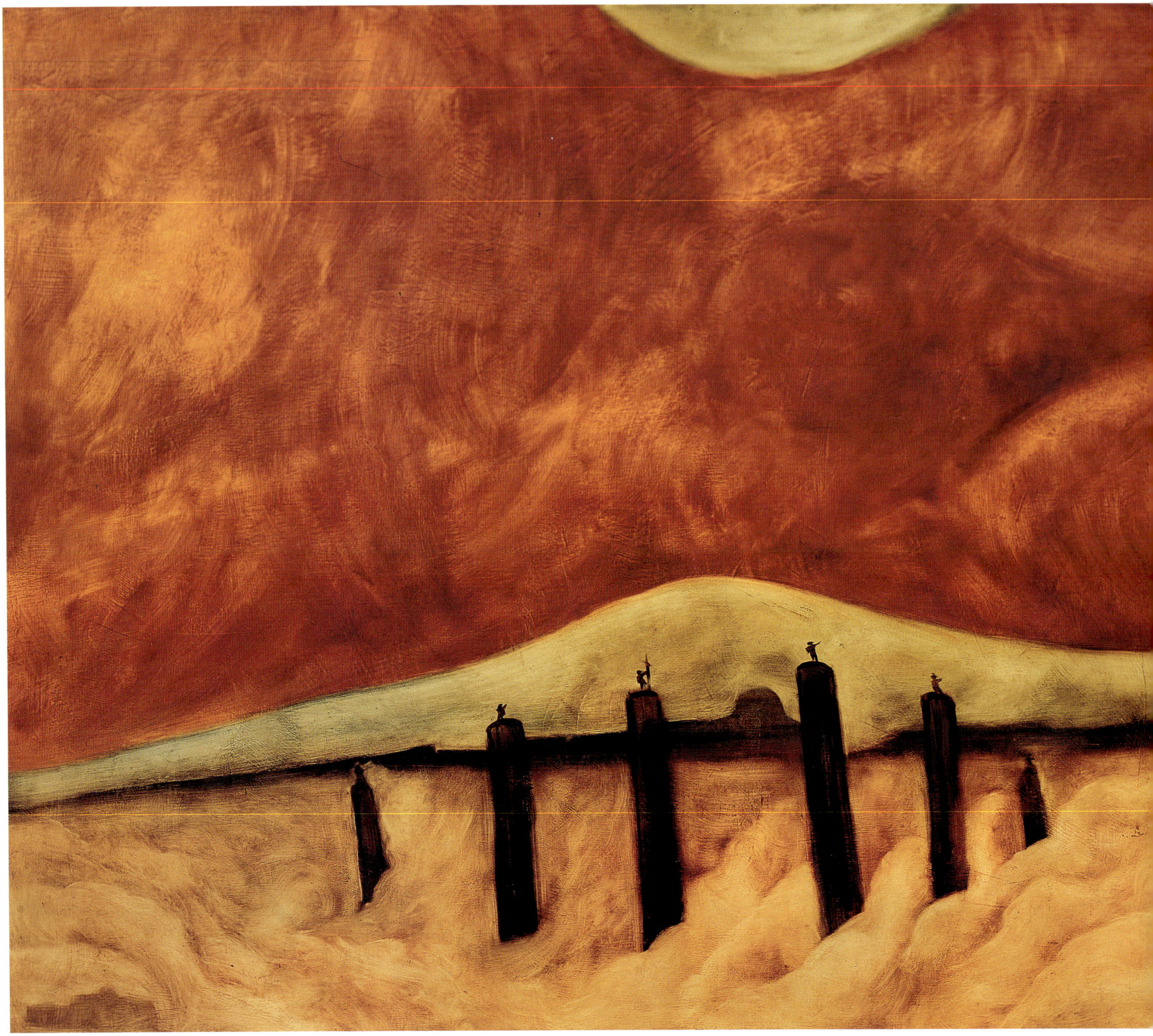

One pillar short of Wisdom
Marco Del Re, 1988,
Oil on wood, 150 x 250 cm.

Opposite
Dinojarres
Aldo Mondino, 1197
Terracotta and iron, 300 x 700 cm
(Galeria Astuni, Fano).

of poets wander after being expelled from the city; or where high columns stand out against an opaque sky. On top of these columns stylites pray and gesticulate, reduced to faintly ridiculous signs. Sometimes there is nothing to be seen but the tops of columns hidden by an impenetrable mist and the anthracite black silhouettes of the saintly men immersed in vehement prayer or malediction. These somber lands, skies which resemble earth, the cities which have been torched and burn on the horizon, the exiles fleeing after being condemned to death, all evoke the troubled times of the great wave of mysticism that broke over Sinai in the early centuries of the Christian era.

These two artists – a Spaniard and an Italian – refer to the Orient of early Christianity, a subject which has been little dealt with up to now and which, in their imagination, takes on an intense and tragic value. In the East, a number of artists have

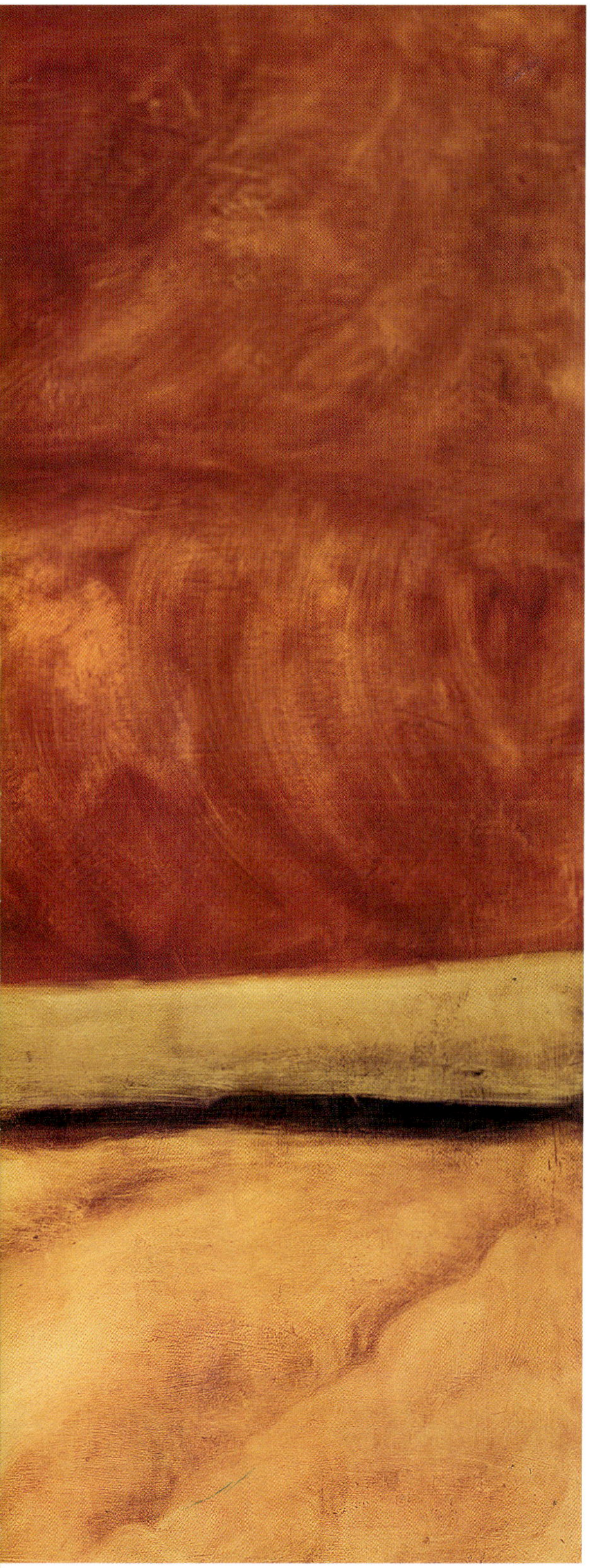

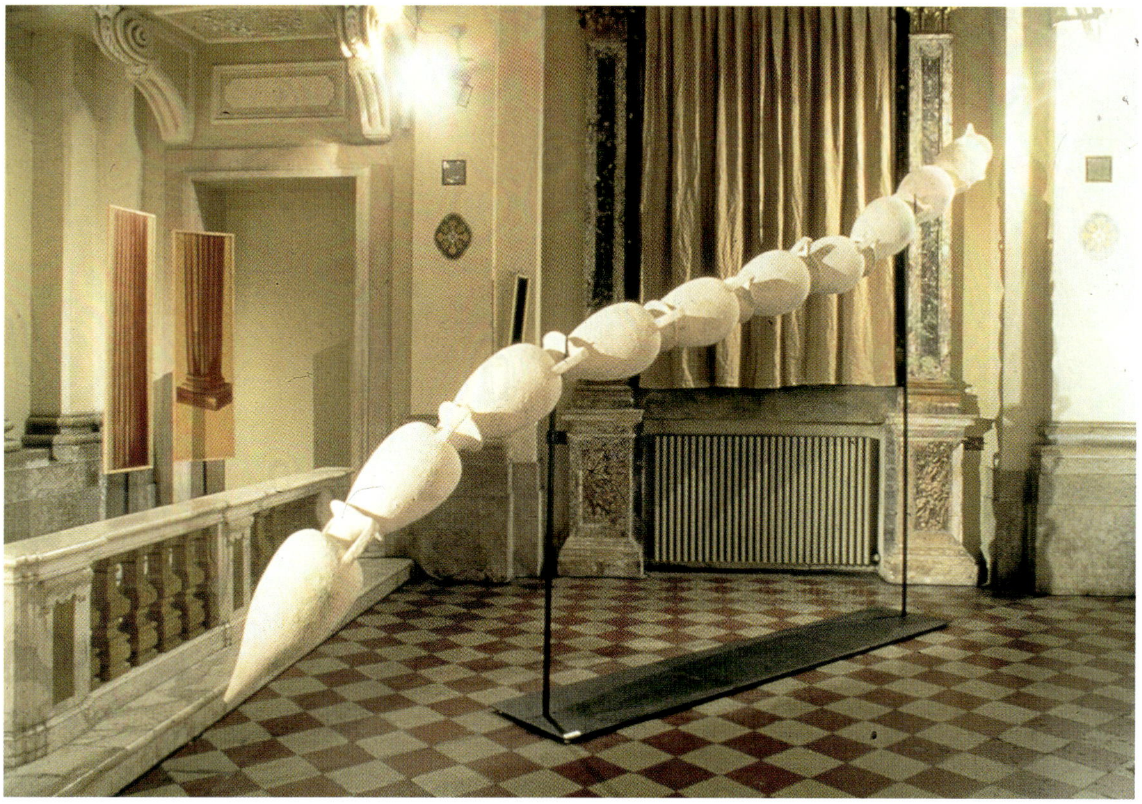

attempted to ally a traditional artistic language with a modern one. This has been the case for Turkish painter and sculptor Selma Gürbüz. Throughout the 1990s Gürbüz created an imaginary world based on the magic of *A Thousand and One Nights*. It is a source she completely reinvented, peopling it with improbable beings and phantasmagoric scenes, which exist only in strange and uneasy visual combinations, transforming her pictures into bewitching dream-like sequences. But her art does this on the condition of taking her creations for what they really are – namely dreams that occur and have meaning only in and through the laws of art. The forms she models and remodels in constructing the fictional characters are derived from Oriental painting, especially from Persian and Arab miniatures and Turkish painting of the 17th century, but also from medieval illuminated manuscripts such as those of Catalunya in Spain. This incessant moving from one world to the other in her painting always concludes with Oriental culture predominating, even if the pictorial principles she employs are, for the most part, of a Western character.

Selma Gürbüz

When in 1990 she took on the task of evoking the cafés of Constantinople in the days of Murat IV, when the sultan persecuted these little oases of tranquillity with their innocent pleasures, she chose to show the different types of people found in them – *narghile*-smokers, people in conversation, dancers, storytellers, and audiences on the evenings of Ramadan – as though they were figures in scenes from the Karagöz shadow theater. She comments on the figures on paper as follows, "I have received an inheritance of innumerable images. It is these images, or rather the memory of them, their instantaneous reminiscences, which inspired me to create these visions of Constantinople café society in the Ottoman period. For me, they remain the cafés of literary and aesthetic pleasure. I have chosen to show this kaleidoscopic spectacle of bygone days by depicting them on a flat surface; a shadow theater of people and objects simplified in the most absolute way."

During 1991, in the cycle of paintings and drawings brought together under the title *Hand Games*, she was essentially describing erotic games, couples entwined or embracing, women kneeling, naked women waiting. Although the style was unambiguously linked to the history of Western art, she brought to it a visual dimension that was undeniably linked to the East. But this East has no clear, unambiguous references, except perhaps for the head of one of the young lovers, which has the form of an Egyptian goddess' head-dress.

Her artistic intuition also leads her to create a universe of fables that mingles European medieval and Renaissance mythology and cosmology with imagery from calligraphy or Turkish miniatures. The pictures in her *Zodiac* series (1998) are brilliant exam-

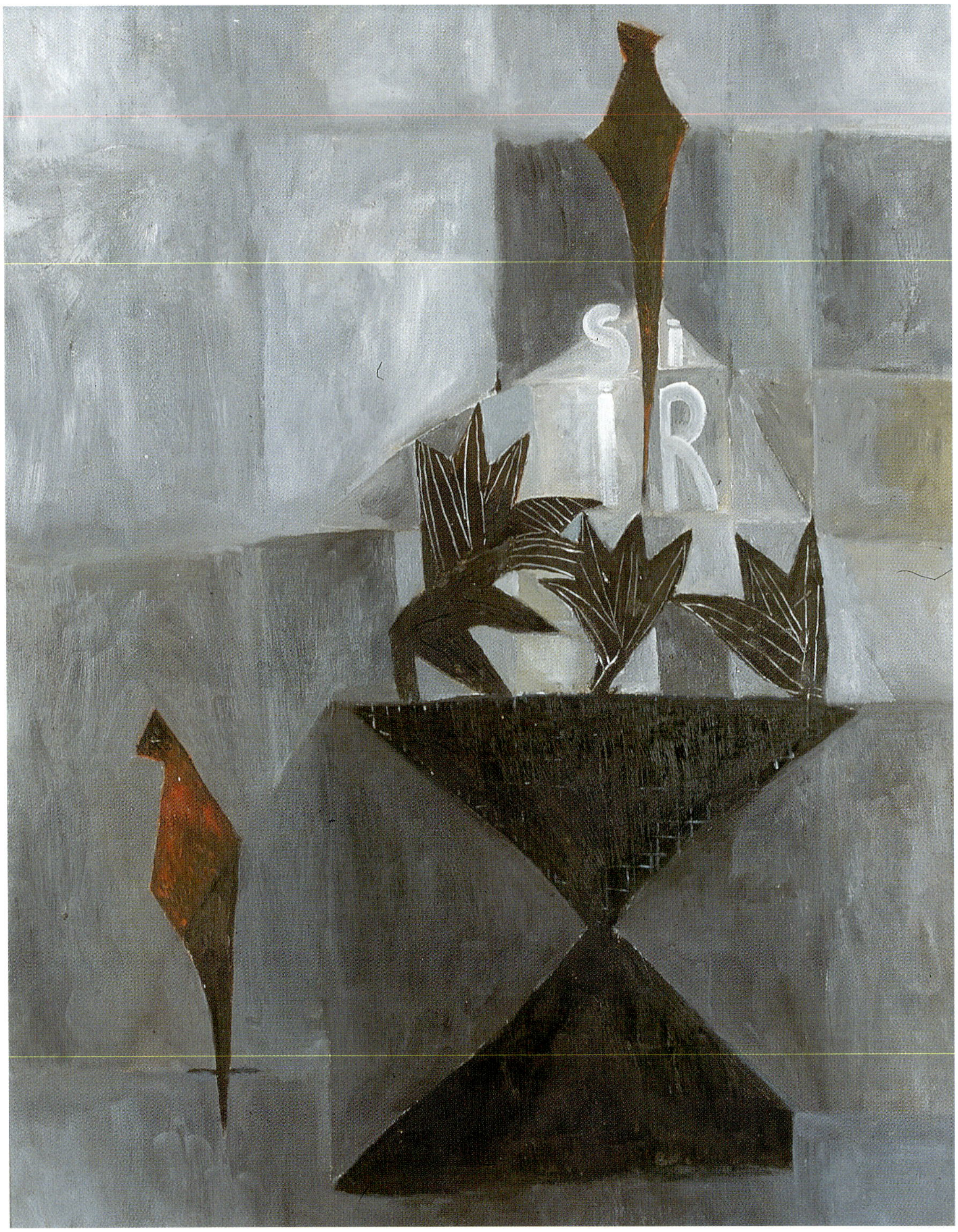

Opposite
Women in the Turkish Bath,
Selma Gürbüz, 1993
Oil on canvas, 130 x 112 cm
(Collection of Mr and Mrs Gügüs).

Oriental Still Life,
Selma Gürbüz, 1993
Oil on canvas, 130 x 112 cm
(Collection of Mr and Mrs Gügüs).

ples of this tendency, as are the works of two years before in which she used black inks to create facetious graphic fantasies afterwards called *Gray Magic*, and the oil paintings in her *Mundus elementaris* period (1997).

The great, thick, woollen carpets in the Anatolian tradition that Gürbüz wove in 1998 and 1999 make use of ancient Islamic decorative style, but she lends them a certain ambivalence; they belong to a composite culture, as did the art of the late Ottoman empire. While the majority of Oriental artists attempt to imitate the most radical creations of contemporary art of East or West, Selma Gürbüz wants to explore the ambiguity of that meeting; she wants to push the conflict-ridden conjunction of these two ways of understanding the world to the very limit, using nostalgia and modernity as the twin poles of her meditations.

As the works of these contemporary artists demonstrate only too clearly, though Orientalism may appear to be over and done with, certainly in the West, it would be unwise to make any facile assumptions about its lack of a future.

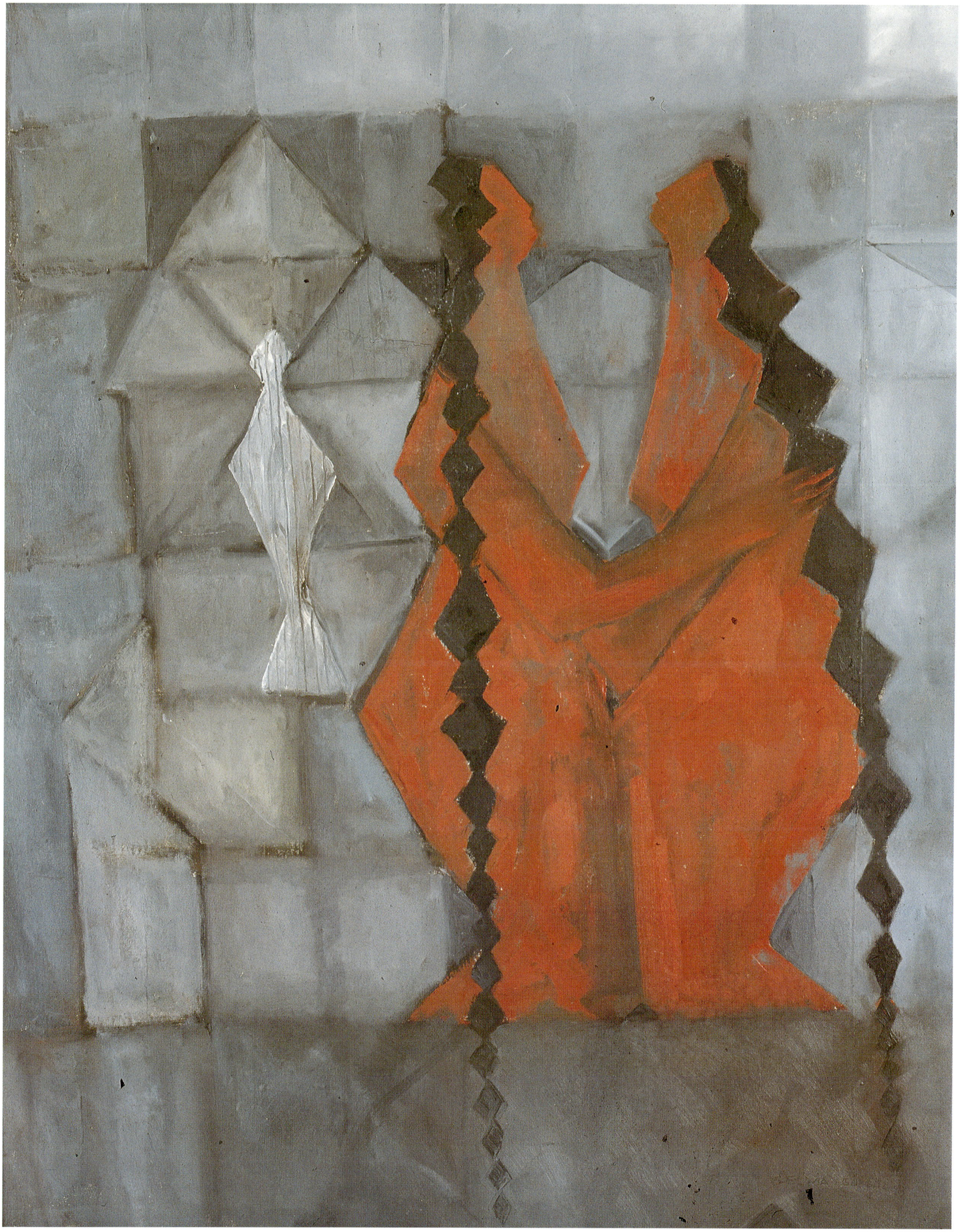

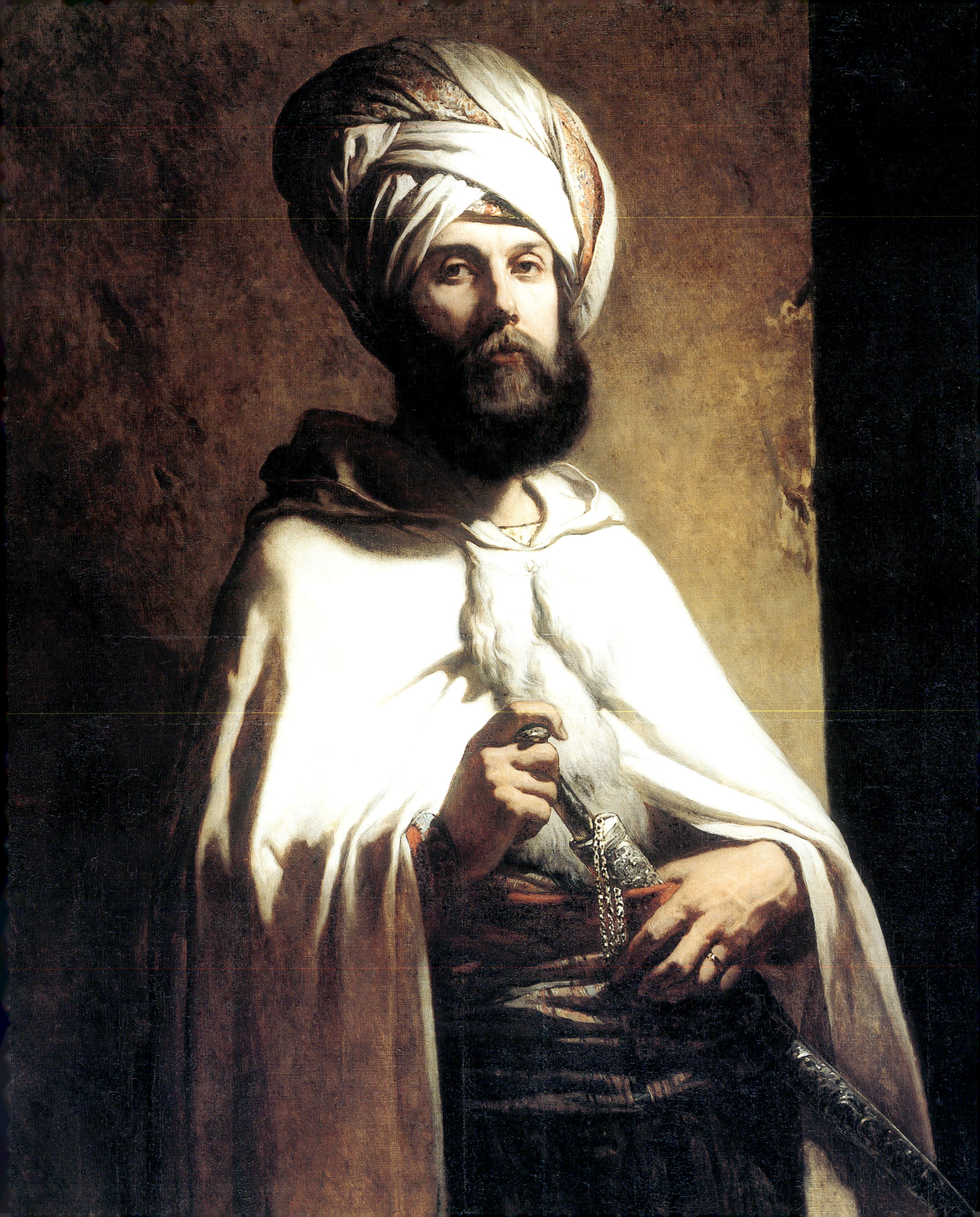

Appendix

Portrait of the Belgian Painter and Engraver, Charles Cousin, in Algerian Costume,
Louis Gallait, 1838
Oil on canvas, 140 x 97 cm
(Musée des Beaux-Arts, Lille).

ABEL DE PUJOL, Alexandre Denis (Valenciennes 1787–Paris 1861) French painter. A pupil of J.-L. David, he was awarded a medal at the Salon of 1806. In 1810 a gold medal and the Prix de Rome brought him wide recognition. He was responsible for the decoration of one of the Egyptian rooms in the Musée du Louvre in 1827. In the reign of Louis Philippe he received several commissions for pictures for the historical museum at Versailles. He also painted murals for the Paris stock exchange and the church of Saint-Sulpice in Paris.

AHMED PASHA, Seker (Turkey 1841– 1907) Turkish painter who pioneered oil painting in Turkey. In 1862, he studied under Boulanger and Gérôme, though Western ideas did not cause him to lose his affinity with the East.

AIVAZOVSKI, Ivan Konstantinovich (Theodosia 1817–1900) Russian painter. He studied at the Academy of Saint-Petersburg and in 1840 went on a journey round Europe (Italy, Holland, Spain, England). Back in Russia, he was appointed painter-in-chief to the Russian Imperial Navy. He painted above all landscapes and seascapes, which he exhibited in European art centers and in particular in Paris in 1843.

ALMA-TADEMA, Sir Lawrence (Dronrijp 1836–Wiesbaden 1912) Dutch-born British painter. He was admitted to the arts academy in 1852. After winning a gold medal, he settled in Brussels in 1864. He moved to London in 1870 and became a British subject in 1873. He exhibited at the Royal Academy, where he had great success. He discovered Egyptian art at the British Museum, but it was only in 1902 that he went to Egypt.

ANGELELLI, Giuseppe (Coimbra 1803–1846) A Portuguese painter who studied at the Academy in Florence. He accompanied the archaeologists Rossellini and Champollion on their expedition to Egypt in 1827. Rossellini's *Monuments d'Egypte et de Nubie* (Monuments of Egypt and Nubia) is illustrated with almost 400 drawings by Angelelli. He also painted some landscapes and portraits.

ARTHUR, Reginald (19th century) English painter. From 1881 to 1896 he exhibited in London, at the Royal Academy and in Suffolk Street as well as at the autumn exhibitions in Liverpool. Until 1895, he often painted ancient historical subjects. The Egyptian subjects were inspired by visits to the British Museum.

AUGUSTE, Jules Robert (Paris 1789–1850) French painter and sculptor. He entered the École des Beaux-Arts in Paris in 1806, in Cartelier's studio. In 1810, he won the Grand Prix de Rome with his work *The Last of the Spartans*. The East had a fascination for him that he transmitted to Delacroix. A fine example of his Orientalism is *Odalisques*.

AURELI, Giuseppe (Rome 1858–Anzio 1929) An Italian painter who studied at the Academy in San Luca, and exhibited in Rome, Turin, and Bologna between 1883 and 1907, in Munich between 1880 and 1900, and at the World Exhibition in Paris in 1889. He was a history painter and a portraitist for the Italian royal family. Though he never went to the Near East, he painted scenes of harems and Arab bazaars, adorning his canvases with exotic musical instruments, Moorish objects, and scenes taken from photographs.

BALLESIO, Francesco (Turin 1860–Tivoli 1923) Italian painter. Having studied in Turin, he settled in Rome. He painted Islamic scenes taken from photographs, since he never went either to North Africa or the Near East. He strove in particular to portray with great precision the various shimmering materials and details of Islamic architecture.

BARBAULT, Jean (Viarmes 1718–Rome 1762) A French painter who studied under Jean Restou. He settled in Rome in about 1747, where he was resident at the Académie de France from 1749. He participated in the memorable Turkish Masquerade in Rome in 1748. He was expelled in 1753 after copying a work by Raphael for the principal of the academy. He attracted attention because of his wit, his frivolity, and the freedom of style, as can be seen in *The Four Corners of the World*.

BARRY, François Pierre Bernard (Marseilles 1813–Saint-Laurent-du Var 1905) French painter. He first studied painting in Marseilles, going to Paris in 1840, where he worked in Gudin's studio. The same year he won a medal for two seascapes exhibited at the Salon; almost all of his seascapes draw their inspiration from the harbor in Marseilles. Barry went to Egypt with Napoleon and brought back several pictures depicting Egyptian themes, for example: *The Ruins of Carnak*, *Valley of the Tombs of the Caliphs*, and *View from the First Cataract*.

BAZILLE, Frédéric (Montpellier 1841–Beaune-la-Rolande 1870) French painter. An important figure among the early Impressionists, he met Cézanne in Paris, and also established links with Manet, Monet, Sisley, and Renoir. He gave up the study of medicine to work in Gleyre's studio. He painted with Monet in the forest of Fontainebleau and in Honfleur. His works include: *Girl Washing* and *View of a Village*, both exhibited at the World Exhibition of 1900.

BELLY, Léon-Adolphe (Saint-Omer 1827–Paris 1877) French painter who studied to enter the École Polytechnique in Paris but then decided to devote himself to painting, studying under under Picot and the landscape artist Troyon. He went to the East for the first time in 1850 as artist for the scholar L.F. Caignart de Saulcy, traveling through the Lebanon, Egypt and Palestine in order to study the historical geography of the region. He went to the East again in October 1855, this time to Egypt. He crossed the Sinai with Narcisse Berchère, and sailed down the Nile with Gérôme and the sculptor Bartholdi. He went back again in 1857. He presented works inspired by his trips at the Paris Salons of 1856, 1857, and 1859.

BENJAMIN-CONSTANT (François Jean-Baptiste Constant) (Paris 1845–1902) French artist. A descendant of the writer Benjamin Constant, he studied at the École des Beaux-Arts in Toulouse then at the École des Beaux-Arts in Paris, in Alexandre Cabanel's studio. He exhibited at the Salon for the first time in 1869. He took part in the Franco-Prussian war of 1870, then visited Spain, where he was captivated by Moorish influenced Spanish architecture. He traveled to Morocco with Charles Tissot, where he stayed for nearly two years. He replaced Cabanel at the École des Beaux-Arts in 1883, then in 1888 he replaced Boulanger at the Académie Julian. He went to New York in 1887, where he acquired a reputation as a portrait painter. Appointed a member of the Institut in 1893, he was responsible for the large-scale decoration work at the Sorbonne and the Opéra-Comique in Paris.

BERCHERE, Narcisse (Étampes 1819–Asnières 1891) French painter. He studied at the École des Beaux-Arts in Paris. He failed to win the Prix de Rome, and so went to Provence and then traveled in the Balearic Islands and in Spain. He went to Egypt, Asia Minor, and Greece between 1849 and 1850. He took part in the World Exhibition in Paris in 1855, where he was awarded a medal. He went to Egypt and the Sinai with Léon Belly in April–May 1856, then traveled in Upper Egypt with Gérôme and Bartholdi. In 1860, Ferdinand de Lesseps persuaded him to do some drawings of the excavation of the Suez Canal. In 1863, he published a series of letters to the French artist Eugène Fromentin. In 1869, he was able to return to Egypt for the opening of the Suez Canal. He was one of the founders of a private museum in Étampes.

BERNARD, Émile (Lille 1868–Paris 1941) French painter who studied in Cormon's studio, where he met Toulouse-Lautrec, Van Gogh, Cézanne, and Odilon Redon, and in 1886 worked in Pont-Aven in Brittany, where he met Gauguin. From 1893 to 1904, he traveled in Italy, the Near East and in Egypt, where he lived for six years.

BISEO, Cesare (Rome 1843–1909) Italian painter. He gained attention thanks to a frieze he produced for the Caffè degli Convertiti in Rome. He was sent to Egypt in 1868 during work on the Suez Canal, and stayed for two years. He did decoration work on public buildings, in particular on the Cairo Opera House, which was inaugurated in 1869. In 1875 he set off again, this time for Morocco with the writer Edmondo De Amicis, on the occasion of the first Italian diplomatic mission. In 1884, he was given the responsibility of portraying the meeting that took place at the Quirinal between the king and the emissaries of the Negus of Ethiopia. Three years later he completed a picture commemorating the battle of Dogali in Eastern Africa, at which 600 Italian soldiers were massacred.

BLANCHARD, Henri Pierre Léon Pharamond (Lyon 1805–Paris 1873) French painter. He entered the École des Beaux-Arts in 1819, in Gros' studio, and exhibited regularly at the Paris Salon from 1834. In 1833, he traveled in Spain, North Africa, Mexico, and Russia and brought back numerous sketches. Among his works are: *Bull Race in a Small Spanish Town, José-Maria, a Spanish brigand, A Delegation of Russian Officers Talking to a Persian Diplomat.*

BONNAT, Léon Joseph Florentin (Bayonne 1834–Monchy-Saint-Éloi 1922) French painter. He studied first of all in Spain, then in Paris in Léon Cogniet's studio. He made his début at the Salon of 1857, then he set off for Italy, where he stayed for several years studying the masterpieces of classical art. From Rome, he sent *The Good Samaritan* to the Salon. In 1861, he painted *Adam and Eve Discovering the Body of Abel*, which won him an official award. In 1870, he traveled in the East but this venture into Orientalism did not last long. He afterwards devoted himself to portrait painting.

BONINGTON, Richard Parkes (Arnold, near Nottingham 1801–London 1828) English painter. Working largely in France, he soon got to know Delacroix and in 1819 entered the École des Beaux-Arts, where he was admitted to Gros' studio. He proved to have a gift for landscapes and watercolor seascapes. He traveled first of all in Normandy and the north of France, then in 1825 he went with Delacroix to England, where he saw Turner's paintings. In the spring of 1826 he went to Italy, visiting Naples, Florence, Milan, Bologna, and Venice. This stay enabled him to produce several works of art, including: *View of the Grand Canal*, and *The Ducal Palace in Venice*.

BOUCHARD, Paul Louis (Paris 1853–1937) French painter. A pupil of Boulanger and Lefebvre, he exhibited regularly at the Paris Salon between 1880 and 1930, and in particular at the Salon des Artistes Français. He made his début with historical compositions inspired by medieval history, then extended his horizons to the East and Russia. Examples of his work include: *Soliman II and Roxelane*; *The Moskava River*, and *Winter in Moscow*.

BOUCHER, François (Paris 1703–1770) French artist. The son of a dealer in engravings, in 1720 Boucher entered the studio of Lemoyne, then he was admitted to that of J.F. Cars. He went to Rome in 1727 and stayed there for nearly four years. He returned to Paris and in 1733 was married. He illustrated several publications: (Molière, 1734– 1736; *Les Cris de Paris* (The cries of Paris) 1735; *Les Livres des Fontaines* (The books of fountains), 1736; *Le Livre de Vases* (The book of vases); and *Le Bréviaire de Paris* (The Paris breviary), from 1736. He was admitted to the Académie in Paris in 1734 along with Renaud and Armide. He produced décor for the opera and drew designs for the royal factories, receiving commissions from both the king and Madame de Pompadour. He worked on the ceiling of the Queen's bedroom at Versailles from 1735 and painted two pictures for the gallery of the Petits Appartements at Versailles. Between 1742 and 1748, he took the responsibility for the Opéra from Servandoni. In 1755 he was appointed Chief Inspector of the Gobelins factory. He specialized in mythology, sentimental allegory, and exotic scenes. These brought him a success that lasted till the death of Madame de Pompadour.

BOULANGER, Louis (Vercelli 1806–Dijon 1867) French painter. He was admitted to the École des Beaux-Arts in 1821 and exhibited at the Salons of 1831 to 1864. Louis Boulanger played an active role in the Romantic movement and was an intimate friend of Victor Hugo. He painted among other works: *The Sabbath Dance* 1828, *Petrarch's Triumph* in 1836, *Virgil's Georgics* in 1864.

BREST, Fabius (Marseilles 1823–1900) French artist. A pupil of Émile Loubon, he went to Asia Minor and lived there between 1855 and 1859; he felt a particular attraction for Turkey and stayed there for four years. The first pictures he showed at the Paris Salon represented Constantinople, the Bosporus, and various regions of the East. He continued to paint canvases depicting the East until 1875, but from 1860 preferred views of Venice and the south of France.

BRIDGEMAN, Frederick Arthur (Tuskgegee 1847–Rouen 1928) American painter. He studied at the National Academy of Design in New York. He was able to go to France in 1866 thanks to a scholarship and studied at the École des Beaux-Arts in Paris, in Gérôme's studio. He made several journeys to Egypt and Algeria between 1870 and 1880. He was happy to work from photographs and depicted ancient Egypt and Assyria as well as modern scenes. In 1890 he published *Winters in Algiers*. He was invited to the World Exhibitions of 1878, 1889, and 1900 and each time he was awarded a silver medal.

CABANEL, Léon (Montpellier 1823–Paris 1889) French painter admitted to the École des Beaux-Arts in 1840. He studied in Picot's studio. He won the Prix de Rome in 1845. He became a teacher at the École des Beaux-Arts in 1863, the year he exhibited his celebrated *Birth of Venus* at the Paris Salon.

CAFFI, Ippolito (Bellun, 1809–Lissa 1866) Italian painter. He studied at the school of fine arts in Venice 1827–1831. He settled in Rome in 1832, where he worked as a scene painter. He went on a long journey to the East in 1843 (Malta, Greece, Constantinople, the Near East, Egypt, Nubia) and on the return journey the following year traveled through Palestine and Asia Minor. On his return, he exhibited 23 pictures inspired by Egypt and Nubia. He was in Paris in 1845, the year he decided to join the Civil Guard to fight for the independence of Italy. In 1865, he designed a temple in the Moorish style in the park of the villa Marini Missana at Carpenedo. When hostilities resumed with Austria in 1866, he set sail on the warship *Re d'Italia*. He drowned during a naval battle at Lissa.

CALLANDE DE CHAMP-MARTIN, Charles Émile (Bourges 1797–La Neuville-en-Hez 1883) French painter. He was admitted to the École des Beaux-Arts in 1815, where he worked under Guérin. He exhibited in the Salons from 1819 to 1848. Examples include: *The Flight into Egypt*; *St John the Baptist*, and *St Stephen*.

CALLET, Alphonse Appollodore (Paris 1799–1831) French painter. He was admitted to the École des Beaux-Arts in 1816, where he became the pupil of J.-L. David and Regnault. He obtained a medal in 1827. His works include *The Condemnation of Sejanus* and in Rouen *The Embarkation of the Pargiotes*.

CAMOIN, Charles (Marseilles 1879–Paris 1965) French artist. The son of a painter, he settled in Paris in 1885 and studied at the Lycée Montaigne. He attended classes in drawing at the École des Beaux-Arts in Marseilles, where he obtained the first prize for figure drawing. He was admitted to the École des Beaux-Arts in Paris in 1898 and left to go to the Académie Camillo. He exhibited at the Salon des Indépendants in 1904 and at the Berthe Weill gallery (with Manguin, Marquet, Matisse, and others). In 1905, he again took part in the Salon des Indépendants and exhibited in the famous room VII at the Salon d'Automne. He traveled in Spain (Madrid, Seville, Grenada, Barcelona). In December 1912, he set off for Tangiers to join Matisse. He returned to Paris in March 1913 and exhibited pictures that he had painted in Tangiers at the Druot Gallery and took part in the Post-Impressionist exhibition in London in October. He worked in the manner of Cézanne from 1920.

CARAFFE, Armand Charles (Paris 1762–1822) French painter. Resident at the Académie de France in Rome in 1788, he then traveled in Egypt, in the Ottoman Empire, and in Russia until 1789. He exhibited his Orientalist drawings in several Salons (1796, 1799, 1800). He was one of the artists who illustrated Brugnière and Olivier's *Atlas pour servir au Voyage dans l'Empire ottoman* (Atlas for traveling in the Ottoman Empire).

CASANOVA, Francesco Giuseppe (London 1727–Bruhl 1802) Italian artist. Brother of the writer and adventurer Giacomo Casanova, he followed his parents to Venice where his gift for drawing became obvious. He worked there under Francesco Guardi, then he entered the studio of Francesco Simonini, where he produced above all battle scenes. He went to Paris in 1751 where worked in Charles Parroncel's studio. He included Turks in the military scenes and carved out for himself a reputation for being a connoisseur of the East without ever having been there. He refused his brother's help to join the Académie Royale. Then he settled in Dresden, where he copied pictures in the Elector's collection. In 1761, he obtained a great success with a battle scene exhibited at the Palais du Luxembourg. Two years later, he was admitted to the Académie and his talents recognized at the Salons of 1765 and 1767. He lived in Austria from 1787. He painted large-scale scenes commemorating the victory over the Turks for the Empress of Russia. In 1795 he worked for Prince Esterhazy. During the Consulate, a tapestry manufacturer in Beauvais produced as tapestries his *Military Convoys* and *Fêtes Champêtres*.

CASSAS, Louis-François (Azay-le Ferron 1756–Versailles 1827) French painter. Studied under Vien, Lagrénée the Younger, and De Leprince. He went to Constantinople in 1784 with the Count of Choiseul-Gouffier, the new French ambassador at the Sublime Porte. Cassas carried out dangerous missions in various regions of the Ottoman Empire and returned to Constantinople in 1786. He then lived in Italy and France, where he worked on the illustrations for *Voyage Pittoresque de la Syrie, de la Phénicie, de la Palestine et de la Basse Egypte* (A picturesque journey through Syria, Phoenicia, Palestine, and Lower Egypt) of which the first volume appeared in 1799, and which remained unfinished. He collected many pictures, watercolors, and drawings depicting Turkish society.

CHASSERIAU, Théodore (El Limón, Santo Domingo 1819–Paris 1856) French artist born at Santo Domingo, but was taken to Paris in 1822, where he was brought up by his elder brother. He soon became one of Ingres' pupils; Ingres even asked him to follow him to Rome when he was appointed director of the Villa Médicis, but Chassériau refused. He began to exhibit at the Salon of 1839 with *Susanna Bathing*. He was close to Doyenné's circle, where he mixed with Prosper Marrilhat, Théophile Gautier, and Gérard de Nerval. Despite his Neo-classical training, he was an admirer of Delacroix, and was attracted by the East. Having produced a portrait of the Caliph of Constantine, which was presented at the Salon of 1845, he was invited by the caliph to visit Algeria the following year. There he made many studies of horses and was fascinated by the lives of the Arabs and the Jews. He died at the early age of 37.

CLAIRIN, Georges (Paris 1843 – Belle-Ile-en-Mer 1919) French painter. Attracted to distant lands, he went to Spain with his friend Henri Regnault to support the Republicans. He then went to Madrid, Barcelona, and Granada, where he was fascinated by the Alhambra. He joined Regnault in Tangiers in 1870. He returned to Morocco after the Paris Commune and stayed there a year and a half, becoming friendly with the artist Mariano Fortuny. He later accompanied the French plenipotentiary to Fez, on his return worked with Charles Garnier on the decoration of the Paris Opéra; he created decorative scenes for a number of big houses, casinos, thermal baths, and castles. He traveled to Italy, Spain, Algeria, and Egypt in 1895, where he traveled with the archaeologist Morgan and went up the Nile with the composer Camille Saint-Saëns. He depicted Orientalist themes throughout his career.

COGNIET, Léon (Paris 1794–1880) Studied at the École des Beaux-Arts in Paris, he won the Prix de Rome in 1817. A teacher at the École Polytechnique and at the École des Beaux-Arts, he influenced many pupils, some of whom became leading Orientalists.

COLIN, Alexandre-Marie (Paris 1798–1873) French painter. A friend of Delacroix and Bonington, he exhibited at the Paris Salons from 1819. He was appointed teacher of drawing at the École des Beaux-Arts in Nîmes. A fine portrait painter, he also produced paintings with romantic themes, views of Italy, and scenes from the Greek war of independence inspired by the works of Lord Byron.

COROT, Jean Baptiste Camille (Paris 1796–Ville d'Avray 1875) French painter. Corot traveled a great deal, making three trips to Italy and visiting many parts of France. There is a dreamlike feel to his landscapes and even more to the women he painted, whom he dressed as gypsies or as Italian, Greek, and Oriental women. Corot's work is much more complex than it appears at first sight; he has been described as a "modernist in spite of himself," for although he remained attached to the classicism in which he had been trained, he also went along the road that led to Impressionism, though without ever becoming an Impressionist.

COYPEL, Antoine (Paris 1661–1722) French painter. The son of Noël Coypel, he studied under his father and accompanied him to Rome when he became head of the Académie de France there (1673–1675). He took studied the masters of the Renaissance and early Mannerism. In 1681 he was admitted to the Paris Académie with *Allegory of Victories*. He received many commissions from the French king and from the Dukes of Orleans. Among his religious scenes are: *Esther and Ahasuerus*; *Athaliah Chased from the Temple*; *The Sacrifice of Jephthah*; and *Susanna Vindicated*. He participated in major decorating tasks, for example the Aeneas Gallery at the Palais-Royal (from 1703), and the ceiling of the chapel of the Château of Versailles (1709). He was appointed chief painter to the King and director of the Académie des Beaux-Arts in 1721.

DADD, Richard (Chatham 1817–Berkshire 1886) English painter. He entered the Royal Academy Schools in 1837 and exhibited the next year at the Society of British Artists; he later became a member of the Painters' Etching Society. Highly gifted, he won awards and exhibited in different institutions in 1839 and 1840. He set off with Sir Thomas Phillips for a journey that took him to Switzerland, Italy, Greece, Turkey, Syria, Palestine, and Egypt. He was one of the most original of the Orientalists, his gift for observation combining with a strangely intense imagination. He suffered fits of madness, and after killing his father, spent many years in an asylum. His works include *The Flight into Egypt* in 1849, and *Puck, Titania Asleep*, and *Oberon and Titania*. In 1853 he began to illustrate the Passion. In 1864 he was moved to Broadmoor Hospital in Berkshire, where he produced wall paintings and stage sets between 1873 and 1874. He painted his last work, *Tlos in Lycia* in 1883 and died on 8 January 1886.

DAUZATS, Adrien (Bordeaux 1804–Paris 1868) French painter. He studied stage design in Bordeaux at his father's instigation. From 1827 he worked with Baron Taylor on his *Voyages pittoresques et romantique dans l'ancienne France* (Picturesque and romantic journeys through old France). He went to Egypt with him in 1830 when the obelisk of Luxor was presented to France. He crossed the Sinai desert and stayed for a few days in St. Catherine's monastery, painting a memorable picture of it. Then he went to Palestine and Syria. He wrote an account of his journey with Alexandre Dumas, *Quinze jours au Sinaï* (A fortnight in Sinai), which appeared in 1839. He presented his first Orientalist work to the Salon in 1831. He went to Spain in 1837 with Baron Taylor, spending much of his time in Andalusia. In 1839, he went to Algeria with the writer Charles Nodier to follow the military expedition placed under the orders of the Duke of Orleans. He illustrated Nodier's *Journal de l'Expédition des Portes de Fer* (Journal of the expedition to the Gates of Iron), published in 1844. He took charge of the Association des Artistes created by Baron Taylor in 1840.

DECAMPS, Alexandre Gabriel (Paris 1803–Fontainebleau 1860) French artist. He entered the studio of Bouchot, a painter of historical subjects, when he was young, then joined the studio of Abel de Pujol. In 1828, he went to Greece to paint a commemorative picture of the naval battle of Navarin. Losing interest in this project, he went to Turkey and set up a studio in Smyrna in 1829. Then he traveled to Switzerland, Italy, Greece, Egypt, and Turkey. He exhibited at the Salon of 1831, mainly scenes of daily life in Turkey. He persisted with this genre, which was very popular. In spite of his success, however, he did not obtain any important commissions. He withdrew to the country and destroyed his travel notes, his studies, and his sketches. He took part in the World Exhibition in Paris in 1855. This marked both his recognition and his decline. A good many of his paintings were destroyed during the Paris Commune (1871).

DEHODENCQ, Alfred (Paris 1822–1882) French painter. He studied in Léon Cogniet's studio at the Paris École des Beaux-Arts and began his career by painting religious canvases. He went on a journey to Spain in 1850 and was strongly influenced by Velazques and Goya. He married there and settled in Andalusia. He went to Morocco for the first time in 1853 and was overwhelmed. Between 1854 and 1863, he went back several times to this country, staying mainly in Tangiers, which became the inspiration for many of his compositions. He did not return to France till 1863 but regularly sent pictures to the Salon during his long absence. On his return to France he had great difficulty re-establishing himself, and had to devote himself to genre scenes, mainly sentimental. His lack of success finally drove him to suicide.

DELACROIX, Ferdinand Victor Eugène (Charenton-St-Maurice 1798–Paris 1863) French painter. Delacroix studied under Pierre-Narcisse Guérin at the École des Beaux-Arts in Paris; he also studied the Old Masters in the Louvre and was strongly influenced by the slightly older Théodore

Géricault. He débuted at the Salon with *The Barque of Dante* (1822). At first his Orientalism was expressed through his interest Lord Byron' poetry (*The Giaour and the Pasha*, 1856) and his passionate commitment to the Greeks in their struggle for independence from the Ottoman Turks (*The Massacre on Chios*, 1824). He first experienced the East came when he accompanied a French diplomatic mission to Morocco in 1832. The impact of North Africa was profound and he continued to work on themes inspired by his trip for the rest of his career. His works include *Algerian Women in Their Apartments* (1834) and *Jewish Wedding in Morocco* (1837).

DEL RE, Marco (Rome 1950–) Italian artist who spent his childhood in Brussels. Having studied architecture in Rome, he later devoted himself to the avant-garde theater and turned towards painting at the beginning of the 1970s. He entered the Schwartz Gallery in Milan in 1976. He exhibited in Italy and in other European countries, taking part in major international events such as the Venice Bienniale (1982), the Rome Quadrennial (1982, 1998), the Milan Triennial (1986, 1992), the Istanbul Biennial (1989). He also exhibited in major traveling exhibitions, notably *Les Cafés littéraires* (Literary cafés) from 1989, *Le Cirque* (The circus) from 1996, and *L'Univers n'existe que pour un livre* (The universe only exists in a book) from 1998. He has exhibited regularly at the Maeght Gallery in Paris and in Barcelona since 1988.

DEUTSCH, Ludwig (Vienna 1855–1935) Austrian-born French painter. He studied at the art academy in Vienna and began to exhibit at the Paris Salon of 1879. He went several times to Egypt between 1880 and 1890, and exhibited works inspired by Egypt from 1883. He adopted a style of an Impressionist nature towards 1909 and abandoned it a few years later.

DEVERIA, Achille (Paris 1800–Pau 1857) French artist. A pupil of Laffitte and Girodet, in 1848 he was appointed assistant curator of the print collection at the Louvre, and in April 1857 became its curator. His drawings are not very important; the best are the cartoons for the stained-glass windows that can be seen at the museum at Versailles. He was above all a talented lithographer: he produced 450 portraits that constitute the most valuable collection of portraits of Romantic society. Among them are images of Victor Hugo, Marie Dorval, Lamartine, Vigny, and Liszt.

DEVERIA, Eugène (1805–1865) French painter. A major figure in the Romantic movement, he showed *The Birth of Henri IV* at the Salon of 1827, a work that established his reputation. The decoration of the cathedral in Avignon was entrusted to him. Ill from 1841 onwards, and retired to Pau. Eastern themes are a secondary but significant part of his work.

DEVOUGES, Louis (Paris 1770–1842) French painter. A pupil of Regnault, J.-L. David, and De Marne, he exhibited at the Paris Salon from 1793 to 1839, where he showed pictures with pastoral themes. He also produced several portraits and during a stay in Russia painted a large number of pictures for the gallery of Prince Narishkin.

DILLON, Frank (London 1823–1909) English painter. The son of a silk merchant, he studied painting under James Holland, a traveling painter who specialized in views of Venice. He made many journeys to Norway, Spain, Egypt, and Japan. He went to Egypt for the first time in 1854–1855 and returned there in 1861–1862, in 1869–1870, and finally in 1873–1874. He produced many watercolors of Islamic monuments and fought vigorously to prevent their destruction. He led the struggle to save the island of Philae, which was threatened by the first dam in Aswan. He exhibited regularly at the Royal Academy in London and took part in the World Exhibitions of 1862 and 1868.

DINET, Etienne (Paris 1861–1929) French painter. He studied art at the Académie Julian, in the studios of Bourgereau and Robert-Fleury. He exhibited for the first time at the Salon in 1882, presenting religious scenes and portraits. Two years later he traveled in the Algerian desert. He developed a passionate interest in this country and decided to paint different aspects of its social and private life, trying to reveal its culture and the spirit of its religion. He went to Egypt with his friend Leroy, also a painter, in 1889. In 1904, he settled in Bou-Saâda, and retired to a villa in Algiers in 1924. He regularly took part in the Salon of the Société des Peintres Orientalistes Français (society of French Orientalist painters), in the colonial exhibitions of 1906 and 1922, and in the Salon in Algiers. He wrote several books: *Antar* (1898); *Le Printemps des Coeurs* (Spring in your hearts) (1902); *Mirages* (1906); and *Le Désert* (The desert) (1911); *Khadra* (1926), and a biography of Muhammad (1918). He converted to Islam in 1913 and went on a pilgrimage to Mecca in 1929.

DUBOIS, François (Paris 1790–1871) French painter. He was a pupil of Regnaut at the École des Beaux-Arts in Paris, which he entered in 1813. He won the second Prix de Rome in 1817 and the first prize in 1819. He exhibited at the Paris Salon from 1814 to 1861. His portraits include: *François I, Emperor of Austria*; his religious subjects: *St. Leu Freeing the Prisoners*; and his mythological subjects: *Daphnis and Chloe*.

DUBUFFET, Jean (Le Havre 1901–Paris 1985) French painter. He devoted himself to painting in 1942, increasingly influenced by the art of children and the insane, his works often crudely naïve and heavily worked. In terms of Orientalism, he was particularly drawn to the Sahara. He produced a large number of works organized into series: *Marionettes of Town and Country* (1943); *Mirobulus, Macadam & Co.* (1945); *Notes for the Very Well Read* (1946); *Anti-cultural Positions* (1951); *Women's Bodies* 1951; *Paris Circus* 1962; *Earth and Ground* (1952). He painted *Castilian Landscapes* in 1974.

DUFY, Raoul (Le Havre 1877–Forcalquier 1953) French painter. He entered the Paris École des Beaux-Arts, studying in Bonnat's studio and making his début at the Salon of 1901. He exhibited with the Indépendents from 1903, and was fascinated by Matisse's *Luxe, Calme et Volupté* at the Salon d'Automne 1905. His style is noted for its bright colors and free forms. With Friesz in Munich, Marquet at Sainte-Adresse, Braque at l'Éstaque and La Ciotat he gave expression to his taste for beaches. He traveled in the United States in 1937, to Venice in 1938 and again in 1952, when he obtained the 1st prize at the Biennial in Venice.

DUPRÉ, Louis (Versailles 1789–Paris 1837) French painter. One of J.-L. David's many pupils, he was appointed court painter by the King of Westphalia. He sent to the Salon paintings, drawings, and watercolors from 1817–1837. From a journey from Athens to Constantinople he brought back a large number of scenes painted from nature.

DUTERTRE, André (1753–Paris in 1842) French painter and engraver. A pupil of Vien and Collet; in 1796 he sent to the Salon several drawings based on the frescos of Raphael in the Vatican. He appeared at the Salon in 1804 and 1812 with portraits, in particular one of General Kléber, and with pictures representing Muslim figures and Egyptian scenes.

EASTLAKE, Charles Lock (Plymouth 1793–Pisa 1865) English painter. In 1814 he visited Paris, after studying in London with Haydon. In 1815, when Napoleon arrived in Plymouth, Eastlake took the opportunity of painting a celebrated portrait of the emperor, standing on the ship's deck, surrounded by his officers. Then he visited Italy in 1817 and Greece in 1819. He stayed in Italy for 14 years. He was elected to the Royal Academy in London in 1830. Several of his works represent the costumes, customs, and habits of Greece and Italy.

ECKENBRECHER, Karl Paul von (Athens 1842–Berlin 1921) German painter. A pupil of Achenbach in Dusseldorf, he made his début in Berlin in 1866; he painted a large number of landscapes during his travels throughout the whole of Europe.

FARQUHARSON, Joseph (Edinburgh 1846–Finzean 1935) Scottish painter. He was elected a member of the Royal Academy in London in 1900. In 1877, he had a notable success with *The Joyless Winter Day* and was considered primarily a painter of the snow and sheep. Then left for the continent and during the winter of 1885–1886 made a journey to Egypt, where he painted scenes of daily life in Cairo.

FAUVEL, Louis-François (Clermont-en-Beauvais 1753–Izmir 1838) French painter. He accompanied the Count of Choiseul-Gouffier to Constantinople when he became French ambassador to the Sublime Porte. Fauvel was later appointed vice-consul in Athens. Several of his drawings are engraved in the album *Voyage pittoresque de la Grèce* (Picturesque journey in Greece) (3 volumes).

FAVRAY, Antoine de (Bagnolet 1706–Malta 1798) French painter. Becoming friendly with the Knights of Malta during his stay in Rome, he went to Malta in 1744, where he painted pictures of churches, portraits of the Grand Master, and episodes in the history of the Order. He set off for Constantinople in 1762 and worked for the French ambassador, the Comte de Vergennes. He drew panoramas of the town, depicted audiences in the palace of the Grand Sultan and the Grand Vizier, and also portraits of upper-class ladies. His drawings in red and black chalk constitute an invaluable source of information on the customs of the Levant.

FLANDRIN, Eugène (Naples 1803–Paris 1876) French painter. He exhibited for the first time at the Salon in 1836, with views of Venice. He accompanied the French expeditionary corps to Algeria the following year. He took part in the Salon of 1839 with his first Orientalist pictures. In 1840, he went to Persia with the architect Pascal Coste, the two men making an exhaustive inventory of the monuments both ancient and modern. They traveled through the regions of the northwest without a map and discovered Isfahan, Shiraz, and Persepolis. He returned to France two and a half years later, traveling via Mosul, Aleppo, and Constantinople. They published the sketchbook of their journey in six volumes in 1851; Flandrin also wrote a personal account of his journey. He exhibited pictures of Persia at the Salon in 1853. While continuing to exhibit regularly at the Salon, he published an album (1856) that consisted of four volumes and numerous articles.

FORTUNY Y MARSAL, Mariano (Reus 1838–Rome 1874) Spanish painter. Left an orphan very young, he nevertheless managed to get into the academy of fine art in Barcelona. Sent to Rome on a bursary in 1860, he was suddenly sent to Morocco by the city of Barcelona in order to accompany the military expedition of General Prim y Pratas. He returned in 1862, this time to make a large picture commemorating the victory of the Spanish at Tetuán. He stayed in Paris in 1866, where he became friendly with, among others, Gérôme and Meissonnier. The art dealer, Goupil, offered him a contract for the exclusive rights to his works. He exhibited his work in 1870 with notable success. A great collector, he had in his studio an impressive number of Arab objets d'art. He died, very young, of a fever.

FRAGONARD, Jean Honoré (Grasse 1732–Paris 1806) French artist. He studied in Paris, destined to become a notary's clerk, but chose to be a painter and trained under Boucher and Chardin. He won the Prix de Rome in 1752 and spent three years in Italy from 1756. He made friends with Hubert Robert, who took him to Tivoli and Naples. Back in Paris in 1761, he presented his entrance piece to the Académie and was given a studio in the Louvre, but did not produce his final reception piece for the Académie, preferring to paint light, pleasant subjects. In 1769, he painted a portrait of Diderot, who had admired his work at the Salon of 1765. One of the great Rococo artists he enjoyed great success, but was criticized by the supporters of Neo-classicism for the frivolity of his style and subjects. He traveled in Italy and Austria in 1773 and 1774. After his return, his star faded and he was nearly ruined by the Revolution, but J.-L. David, who had been his pupil, got him appointed curator of the future Louvre Museum. This prolific painter, sometimes frivolous, sometimes serious (when he took his inspiration from the Northern masters), also had a taste for *chinoiserie* and things Turkish.

FRANCKEN II THE YOUNGER, Frans (Antwerp 1581–1642) Flemish Painter, a pupil of his father Frans Francken I, Frans Francken II excelled in all genres from mythology to biblical scenes. He soon developed a style very different from his father's and outclassed him. He painted The *Allegory of Fortune*, *The Witches' Sabbath*, and *King Midas's Meal*, and a magnificent series of 12 paintings inspired by the Old Testament.

FRERE, Charles-Théodore (Paris 1814–1888) French painter. Although his father wanted to steer him towards a musical career, he studied with Jules Cogniet and Camille Roqueplan. He traveled throughout France and exhibited at the Salon for the first time in 1834. He went to Algeria in 1837 and was deeply impressed, presenting his first Orientalist works at the Salon two years later. He visited Constantine shortly after its capture by the French army, and in 1851 embarked on a long journey that took him from Malta to Greece, and from Syria to Egypt, traveling as far as Nubia. He returned to Egypt several times and the Egyptian government gave him a studio in Cairo where he was known as Frère Bey. He worked for the Empress Eugénie at the opening of the Suez Canal in 1869. He exhibited regularly at the Salon until 1887.

FREY, Johann Jakob (Basle 1813–Frascati 1865) Swiss painter. He studied first in Basle, then in Munich, Rome, and Naples. After visiting Sicily and Spain, he joined the Egyptian archaeological expedition under the German archaeologist Karl Richard Lepsius, then he settled in Rome.

FROMENTIN, Eugène (La Rochelle 1820–Saint Maurice 1876) French painter and writer. He studied law in Paris from 1839 to satisfy the demands of his father, a doctor in La Rochelle, then decided to devote himself to painting. He attended the classes of Rémond and the landscape artist, Cabat. In 1844, he discovered Orientalist art through the canvases of Prosper Marilhat and Decamps. He went on his first journey to Algeria in 1846 and went from Algiers to Blidah. He stayed there on two other occasions between 1847 and 1848 (when he stayed eight months, going to Biskra and the edges of the Sahara) and between 1852 and 1853 when he stayed nearly a whole year at Mustapha and Blidah with his young wife. He presented his first Algerian pictures at the Salon of 1847. He published in 1856 *Un Été dans le Sahara* (A summer in the Sahara) and two years later *Une Année dans le Sahel* (A summer in the Sahel). In 1863, he published a novel, *Dominique*. His literary work builds up his reputation more than his painting. He discovered Egypt in 1869, on the occasion of the opening of the Suez Canal.

GEROME, Jean- Léon (Vesoul 1824–Paris 1904) French painter. The son of a goldsmith, he went to school in Vesoul and entered Paul Delaroche's studio at the École des Beaux-Arts in Paris in 1842. When the studio was closed, he went to Italy where he stayed a year. He then studied under Charles Gleyre but only stayed three months. A fervent Neo-classicist, he became the leader of a group of young artists – known as the neo-Greeks or Pompeiists – among whom were Hamon, Boulanger, Picou, and Aubert. He was awarded a medal for *The Cock Fight*, which he presented at the Salon of 1847. The World Exhibition of 1855 enabled him to establish himself as leader of the French Orientalists. He went to Egypt in 1856 and sailed for four months along the Nile, and then stayed for another four months in Cairo. He traveled frequently, visiting Italy, Turkey, Greece, Palestine, and North Africa. He became a teacher at the École des Beaux-Arts in 1864. He married Marie Goupil, the daughter of the major art dealer.

GIRARD, Paul Albert (Paris 1839–1920) French painter. He entered the École des Beaux-Arts in Paris in 1857, was awarded the Prix de Rome in 1861, and exhibited in the Paris Salon from 1859 to 1880. He produced large Orientalist panels and pictures that illustrate daily life in Kabylia and Algiers, such as *Sacrifice of Chickens at Bab-el Oued* and *Arab Huntsmen in the Mountains of Blidah*.

GIRAUD, Eugène (Paris 1806–1881) French painter. He entered the École des Beaux-Arts in 1821, obtained the Prix de Rome for engraving in 1826, and appeared at the Salon from 1831 to 1866 with portraits and historical pictures.

GIRODET DE ROUCY TRIOSON, Anne-Louis (Montargis 1767–Paris 1824) French painter. One of David's pupils, he obtained the Prix de Rome in 1789. In Italy he painted *Endymion's Dream*, which was exhibited at the Salon of 1793. His *Deluge* created a sensation at the Salon of 1806. He took his inspiration from Chateaubriand to paint *Atala's Funeral*, which was presented at the Salon of 1808. He also illustrated the work of Racine.

GOODALL, Frederick (London 1822–1904) English painter. He left school to learn the job of an engraver alongside his father, who also taught him anatomy and animal painting. In 1836 he received a prize from the Society of Arts for an architectural drawing. Four years later, he won a medal at the exhibition of the Society of Arts. He traveled in Ireland and Wales, then went to France. He stayed in Egypt in 1858; when he returned, his canvases were well received. He went to Egypt again in 1870 and traveled through the desert. He became a member of the Royal Academy in London in 1863, and took part in the World Exhibition of 1867 in Paris.

GLEYRE, Charles (Chevilly 1818–Paris 1874) French painter. In 1834, he had the opportunity of accompanying an American, John Lowell, on a journey to Greece, Turkey, and Egypt. Lowell then went on to India, while Gleyre stayed on in the Near East until 1838. When he returned to Paris, he was almost blind. He exhibited his Orientalist works at the Salon of 1843.

GRANET, François Marius (Aix-en-Provence 1775–1849) French painter. He was with Bonapart at the siege of Toulon. In Paris, he entered David's studio and set off for Rome in 1802, staying there until 1819. In 1824, he was appointed assistant curator in charge of the royal museums, and later Louis-Philippe appointed him director of the historic galleries of Versailles; he was made an officer of the Légion d'honneur in 1837. One of his most famous works is *Stella Passing through an Image of the Virgin Mary on the Walls of her Prison*.

GROS, Antoine Jean, Baron (Paris 1771–Meudon 1835) French painter. In 1786 he entered the studio of J.-L. David, whom he admired unreservedly. Suspected of loyalties to the *ancien régime*, he went to Genoa where Madame Bonapart took him into her service; he accompanied her to Milan. In Genoa, he studied the work of Rubens, which added a more emotional note to his paintings. Bonapart gave him the responsibility of selecting the works of art taken as war tribute. He exhibited for the first time at the Salon of 1798 with a portrait of General Berthier, and became best known for depictions of Bonapart. He created the pictures on the dome of the Panthéon. He committed suicide on 26 June 1835.

GUÉRIN, Pierre Narcisse, Baron (Paris 1774–Rome 1833) French painter. He worked with Regnault and obtained the Prix de Rome with *The Death of Cato of Utica*. At the same time he painted *The Return of Marcus Sextus*. His canvases had outstanding success, particularly *Phaedra Accusing Hippolytus in Front of Theseus* 1802; *Andromache* 1810; *Dido*; and *Clytemnestra*, 1817. As a teacher he started Delacroix, Géricault, and Cogniet on their art studies. In 1829, Charles X made him a baron.

GUIGNET, Jean-Adrien (Annecy 1816–Paris 1854) French painter. He entered the École des Beaux-Arts in Paris in 1836 and appeared at the Salon from 1840 to 1848. He painted: *The Defeat of Attila*, *Belshazzar's Feast*, and *The Gardens of Armida*.

GUILLAUMET, Gustave (Paris 1840–1887) French painter. After studying at Académie des Beaux-Arts in Paris, he won the second Prix de Rome. He went to Algeria in 1862 and contracted malaria. He returned to Algeria nine times, sending to the Salon canvases evoking life in North Africa. He collected the articles he had published in *La Nouvelle Revue* into a work entitled *Tableaux Algériens* (Algerian pictures) in 1888.

GÜRBÜZ, Selma (Istanbul 1961–)Turkish artist. Born in Istanbul, she has divided her time between Turkey and France. A painter and sculptor, she has exhibited regularly in Paris and Istanbul. In addition, she has shown her work at the Mira Phalaina complex in Montreuil, at the Institut Français in London, and at the Alliance Française in Buenos Aires. She has taken part in many group exhibitions, for example *Mediteranea* (Bari); the *Second Biennial* (Istanbul); *Parigi* (EUR, Rome); the *Cafés Littéraires* (Literary cafés) (Graz, Istanbul, Prague, Bratislava, Caen, Buenos-Aires, Montevideo, Santiago, etc.); *L'Ennemi* (The enemy) (Georges Pompidou Center in Paris); *Les Femmes artistes dans la République* (Women artists in the republic) (Archaeological Museum, Istanbul); *Paris Cosmopolite* (Cosmopolitan Paris) (Prague); *Double Jeu* (Double game) (Barcelona); *Ex-Libris* (Paris, Barcelona, Saragossa, Buenos-Aires); *Tapis Volants* (Flying carpets) (Paris, Cairo, Istanbul, etc.); *Le Cirque* (The circus) (Paris, Montreuil); *The First Biennial* (Kwanju, Korea). She was responsible for the cover of the magazine *L'Ennemi (Londres Revisité)* (The enemy, London revisited), Christian Bourgeois Éditeur, 1995.

GUYS, Constantin (Flessingue 1802–Paris 1892) French artist. The son of a chief administrator in the Navy, in 1822 he set off to fight alongside the Greek rebels. Then he joined a dragoon regiment but left it towards 1830. From 1842 to 1848, he was tutor to the grandchildren of the English painter of watercolors, Girtin, and then a correspondent to the *Illustated London News* until 1860. He did drawings of the Revolution of 1848 and of his travels in Germany, round the Mediterranean, and in particular to the East. He followed the military operation in the Crimea in 1855. He excelled in scenes of Parisian life and these won him the esteem of Gautier and of Baudelaire, who devoted an important essay to him, *Le Peintre de la Vie Moderne* (The painter of modern life) 1863.

GYSIN, Brion (Great Britain 1916–Paris 1986) British-born painter. Spent his childhood in Canada, and in 1934 arrived in Paris and got in touch with the Surrealist group. In 1939, he had his first private exhibition at the Les Quatre Chemins gallery. In 1940, he went to the United States, where he worked on Broadway. He then became Japanese translator for the American and Canadian armies. After the war he went to France, and later settled in Tangiers, where he opened the restaurant Les Mille et une Nuits (The thousand and one nights). He went several times to the Sahara where he painted many watercolors. Between 1958 and 1964, in Paris, he met the American novelist William S. Burroughs, with whom he worked. He invented the literary techniques of fold-in and permutations. He exhibited in New York, Rome, and Naples, and took part in several group exhibitions in Paris. In 1964, he went to New York where he worked with Burroughs on *The Third Mind*. He returned to Tangiers to write his novel *The Process*. In 1973 he settled in Paris, and exhibited in Paris, London, and Brussels.

HALIL PASHA (Constantinople 1859–1939) Turkish portrait painter. A pupil of Gérôme and Courtois, he won a bronze medal at the 1889 World Exhibition. He also exhibited in 1900.

HAMDI BEY, Osman (Constantinople 1842–1910) Turkish painter. From 1857–1869 he studied in Paris under Boulanger and Gérôme. He acquired a considerable reputation particularly as an archaeologist and art collector, and founded the Museum of Constantinople. He was also responsible for major excavations in Asia Minor and Syria.

HAYDON, Benjamin (Plymouth 1786–London 1846) English painter. He studied at the Royal Academy, the first picture he sent to the Exhibition being *The Holy Family Resting* 1807. Though he never traveled to the East, he attempted to incorporate Egyptian discoveries into several of his canvases. In spite of some success, he experienced all of the difficulties associated with the life of an artist, and committed suicide in 1846.

HAYEZ, Francesco (Venice 1791–Milan 1881) Italian painter. The best-known representative of the Italian academic school, he painted various mythological and literary pictures, such as *Rinaldo and Armida* and *Aristides*, then appeared as a history painter, as in *The Sicilian Vespers* and *The Refugees from Parga*. Frescos by him can be seen in the Vatican. In the choice of his themes, he moved towards Romanticism.

HEIDECK, Karl Wilhelm von (Saaralben 1788–Munich 1861) German painter. He studied in Zurich and took part in the Spanish war against Napoleon and in the Greek war of independence in 1826. His first exhibition was in Munich in 1823. He produced frescoes, lithographs, and etchings.

HESS, Peter von (Düsseldorf 1792–Munich 1871) German painter. He devoted himself almost exclusively to history painting, and so accompanied the Prince of Wrede during the campaign of 1813 to 1815, visited Switzerland and Italy, and accompanied Prince Otto to Greece. He painted the major battles of 1812 for the Emperor of Russia.

HILAIR, Jean-Baptiste (Audun-le-Tiche 1753–Paris 1822) French painter. He collaborated closely with the Count of Choiseul-Gouffier and was the principal illustrator of the count's *Voyage Pittoresque de la Grèce* (Picturesque journey through Greece). He was also the illustrator of the *Tableau de l'Empire ottoman* (Picture of the Ottoman Empire) by M. d'Hosson.

HUNT, William Holman (London 1827–1910) English painter. A student at the School of the Royal Academy in London, where he exhibited in 1845, he was drawn to the Flemish Primitives after a trip to France and Belgium in 1849. He also visited Egypt and Palestine in 1854 and 1892 and these visits gave him the inspiration for works such as *The Finding of the Saviour in the Temple* (1860), and the celebrated *The Scapegoat*. Among his late religious paintings was *Triumph of the Innocents* (1885).

HUYSMANS, Jean Baptiste (Antwerp 1826–Hove 1906) Belgian painter. From 1856 he traveled in Greece, Turkey, Syria, Palestine, Egypt, and Algeria. He spent several years in Paris and then returned to Antwerp. He composed vast religious compositions for churches in Jerusalem. He published his memoirs in *Voyage en Italie et en Orient* (Journey to Italy and the East) in 1856–1857, and *Voyage en Espagne et en Algérie* (Journey to Spain and Algeria) in 1862.

INGRES, Jean Auguste Dominique (Montauban 1780–Paris 1867) French painter. Son of a minor artist and decorator, Ingres learned the rudiments of his trade from his father. He was admitted to David's studio and won the Prix de Rome in 1801. It was only in 1806 that he went to Italy, after painting two portraits of Bonapart, and returned to Paris in 1826. He was appointed director of the Académie de France in Rome in 1835, staying there until 1841. He completed one of the major work of Orientalism, *Turkish Bath*, in 1863. He never went to the East, his vision being created by literature. Other works include *Harem*.

ISABEY, Jean Baptiste (Nancy 1767–Paris 1855) French painter. He went to Paris in 1786 and worked in particular with J.-L. David. A close friend of Bonapart and Josephine, he knew how to flatter princes and so was also painter to Louis XVIII and Charles X, and was just as fortunate under Louis-Philippe, becoming known as the "painter of kings." At the Salon of 1793, he made his début with several miniatures and in 1805, he was appointed chief painter to the Empress. Isabey was the most brilliant miniaturist of his time and was one of the first painters to do lithographs.

IVANOV, Alexander Andreyevitch (St. Petersburg 1806–1858) Russian painter. A student at the Academy of St. Petersburg, he went to work in Italy, and painted scenes from Russian history and biblical subjects. Among his works are *Jesus appearing to Mary Madelene*, *Ecco Homo*, and *Christ Appearing to the People* (c. 1840), on which he worked for 22 years. He spent a large part of his life in Rome.

JACOBS, Jakob (Antwerp 1812–1879) Belgian painter. A student at the art academy in Antwerp, he later studied in Italy and Greece and visited Russia, Scandinavia, and France. In 1847, he visited Germany with Wappers, and was later appointed Landscape Professor at the Academy of Antwerp. He is best known for his seascapes. He was awarded a medal at the 1836, 1842, and 1845 Salons.

KANDINSKY, Wassily (Moscow 1866–Neuilly-sur-Seine 1944) Russian painter. In Munich, where he founded the school called the Phalanx, he met Paul Klee. In 1906, he stayed in Paris where he painted *Landscapes in the Tower* in 1908. He painted *First Abstract Watercolor* in 1910 and the same year he wrote his book *Über das Geistige in der Kunst* (On the spiritual element in art). Returning to Russia in 1914, he founded the Museum of Pictorial Culture in 1919, and the Academy of Artistic Sciences in 1921. He then set off again for Germany and taught at the Bauhaus from 1922 to 1933, later settling in Neuilly-sur-Seine in France. Kandinsky was one of the first abstract artists.

KLEE, Paul (Münchenbuchsee, near Berne 1879–Lugano 1940) Swiss artist. He entered the academy of art in Munich in 1898. In 1902 he traveled in Italy and became interested in Byzantine art. He then produced series of etchings *The Virgin in the Tree* 1903, and *The Senile Phoenix* 1905. He met Kandinsky, Macke, and Robert Delauney. In 1914, a journey to Tunisia with Macke and Moilliet had a deep effect on him. He worked from the notes he took on his journey and painted in the same year *On a Hammamet Motif, Kairwan*. He exhibited at the Der Sturm Gallery in Berlin from 1917 and settled in Munich in 1919. In October, he joined the Weimar Bauhaus, where he taught from 1921. His first exhibition in New York was in 1924, and he held an exhibition at the Vavin-Raspail Gallery in Paris. He returned to Berne when the Nazis came to power in 1933. In 1940, he painted his most dramatic works: *The Timpanist*, *Death and Fire*, and *Rowing Desperately*.

LA HYRE, Laurent (Paris 1606–1656) French painter. He studied under his father, Étienne de la Hyre, and then in Georges Lallemand's studio. A music lover, he was also a mathematician and had a passion for archaeology. He received his first commission in 1630. He was particularly fond of representing life in Paris, and also painted religious works in a Baroque style. He decorated several townhouses and from 1640 produced cartoons for tapestry. He was also interested in landscapes, at which he excelled, and showed a care for historical truth in his ancient, mythological, and biblical compositions. He was one of the founders of the Paris Académie des Beaux-Arts in 1648.

LANCRET, Nicolas (Paris 1690–1743) French painter. He studied under Dulin, then Gillot, and was admitted to the Académie des Beaux-Arts in 1719. An admirer of Watteau, he specialized in pictures of fêtes galantes (outdoor festivities) and this brought him many commissions; he found a particularly good patron in Frederick II of Prussia. He painted *Tiger Hunt* for the series of nine *Exotic Hunting Scenes* (1736). He worked at the château of Fontainebleau in 1737 and at Versailles in 1738, with his *Seasons*. He preferred genre scenes and cultivated a taste for fables under the influence of the writer Jean de la Fontaine.

LANSAC, François Émile, Count of (Tulle 1803–Paris 1890) French painter. A pupil of Scheffer and Langlois, he appeared at the Salons from 1827 to 1878 and won medals in 1836 and 1838.

LAURENS, Jules (Carpentras 1825–Saint-Didier 1901) French painter. At first he was the pupil of his brother, Bonaventure, before entering the École des Beaux-Arts in Montpellier in 1837. He went to Paris in 1842, being admitted to the studio of Paul Delaroche. He exhibited at the Salon of 1845 but failed to obtain the Prix de Rome. The geographer, Xavier Hommaire de Hell, engaged him for one of his scientific missions to Turkey and Persia.

LEAR, Edward (Holloway 1812–San Remo 1888) English artist. The twentieth child of a stockbroker who suffered a severe reversal of fortune, Lear began his career in London with illustrations and drawings, specializing in pictures of exotic birds and later landscapes. In 1837 he set off for Rome where he stayed several years. He regularly exhibited at the Royal Academy and gave drawing lessons to Queen Victoria and the Prince of Wales. In 1846, he went to Malta, Sicily, Greece, Turkey, Palestine, Syria, and Egypt, where he sailed up the Nile several times. Most of his life was spent traveling. In 1860, he settled in San Remo, though he lived in India and Ceylon for three years (1872–1874). He became famous as a writer of books for children and for his nonsense limericks. He began to produce sketch-books of his travels from 1851.

LECOMTE DU NOÜY, Jean Jules Antoine (Paris 1842–1923) French painter. In 1861, he entered Gleyre's studio and a little later frequented the studios of Émile Signol and of Gérôme. It was the latter who urged him to go to the East in 1865, and he visited Greece, Turkey, Asia Minor, and Egypt. He exhibited for the first time at the Salon of 1863 and won several medals between 1868 and 1889. He was influenced by Théophile Gautier and composed a series of pictures inspired by Gautier's novel *Roman de la momie* (The story of the mummy). He worked on the decoration of the Église de la Trinité in Paris. He then obtained the second Prix de Rome and went to Venice with the painter Charles Toché. In 1876, he was awarded the Légion d'honneur and went to Morocco, where he discovered Tangiers and Tetuan. In 1895, he went to Constantinople, passing through Bucharest, and then returned to Egypt and Algeria.

LE CORBUSIER (Charles-Édouard Jeanneret) (La Chaux-de-Fonds 1887–Roquebrune-Cap Martin 1965) Swiss architect. A dominant architectural figure of the first half of the century, he was also a fine painter. He traveled in North Africa from 1907 to 1911. He exhibited his first canvases in 1917 and signed the Purist Manifesto. He also published *Après le Cubisme* (After Cubism). He met Léger at the beginning of the 1920s. He painted *Still-life with a White Jug on a Blue Background* in 1919; he introduced the human form into his work from 1930 with *Dangerous Harmony*.

LEIGHTON, Lord Frederick (Scarborough 1830–London 1896) English painter. The son of a doctor, he took art courses in Florence, Rome, and Frankfurt. He painted his first canvas in Brussels in 1850. He stayed in Paris and then returned to England, where Queen Victoria bought his *Cimabue* in 1855. He exhibited at the Royal Academy from 1855–1896, excelling in scenes of classical mythology. He settled permanently in London in 1860, and six years later traveled to Spain and Egypt. He was president of the Royal Academy.

LEJEUNE, Louis-François, Baron and General (Strasbourg 1775–Toulouse 1848) French painter. An officer in Bonapart's expeditionary corps in Egypt, he specialized in battle scenes. He became curator of fine arts and director of the museum of Toulouse.

LE PRINCE, Jean-Baptiste (Metz 1734–Saint-Denis-du-Port 1781) French painter. From a family of sculptors, he studied with Boucher and Vien. He went to Italy in 1754, then traveled in northern Europe before going to Russia, traveling as far as Siberia. He worked on decorations for the Winter Palace of St. Petersburg between 1758 and 1763. He was admitted to the Académie des Beaux-Arts in Paris in 1765 with a subject inspired by his long stay, *The Russian Christening*. He published engravings of life in Russia, and produced tapestry cartoons on the same theme for the royal factory in Beauvais 1767–1770.

LE ROY, Paul Alexandre (Paris 1860–1942) French painter. He began his studies at Odessa, then he was Cabanel's pupil in Paris. From 1885 to 1887 he was in Egypt and then visited Algeria every year, going sometimes as far as Constantinople or Persia. In 1899, he founded the Society of Orientalists. His love of the East prompted him to paint religious and moral subjects, such as *Blind Men in Jericho*.

LEVY, Henri Léopold (Nancy 1840–Paris 1904) French painter. He was a student under Picot, Fromentin, and Cabanel at the École des Beaux-Arts in Paris, to which he was admitted in 1856. He took part in the Paris Salon from 1865, won a first class medal at the World Exhibition of 1878, and received the Légion d'honneur in 1872.

LEVY-DHURMER, Lucien (Algiers 1865–1953) French painter. He made a journey to Italy in 1895. From 1882, he showed paintings at the Salon des Artistes Français, where he won many awards.

LEWIS, John Frederick (London 1805–Walton-on-Thames 1876) English painter. He studied art under his father, who was a distinguished engraver, but soon started to study animal painting under the direction of Edwin Lanseer. He exhibited in 1820 at the British Institution and the following year at the British Academy. From 1825, he devoted himself exclusively to watercolors. In 1824, he set off for Switzerland and Italy, and lived in Spain and Morocco 1832–1834. Because of his Spanish works he was nicknamed Lewis the Spaniard. In 1837 he traveled to Paris and visited Rome between 1838 and 1840. In 1840, he made an extensive journey to the East, visiting Greece, Turkey, and the Middle East, then in 1841 went to Egypt; he lived for ten years in Cairo and adopted an Egyptian way of life. He produced many portraits and strove to portray as authentically as possible the life of the people of Cairo. When he returned to England, he became president of the Old Watercolor Society, a position he held until 1858, and exhibited regularly at the Royal Academy.

LEWIS, Percy Wyndham (off Amherst, Nova-Scotia 1882–London 1957) British artist. He studied art at the Slade School in London from 1898 to 1901. He traveled in Europe from 1902 to 1908. He was back in London in 1909 but often went to Paris. He published his first short stories in the *English Review*. In 1909 he met the American poet Ezra Pound, and was one of the founders of the Camden Town Group, whose first exhibition took place in 1911. In 1912, he took part in the exhibition of the Allied Artists' Association andin Roger Fry's Post-Impressionist exhibition. He also worked for the Omega Workshops and took part in the second Post-Impressionist exhibition of the Camden Town Group. He broke with Fry and the Bloomsbury group to create the Vorticist movement, and launched the review *Blast*, which had only two editions between 1914 and 1915. In 1916, he enlisted in the army and fought in France as a gunner. In 1918, he published his first novel *Tarr*. In 1930, he traveled to Morocco, published several articles in England and a book *Filibusters in Barbary* in 1931. He wrote many works of fiction, essays, poetry, and drama while continuing to paint.

LIOTARD, Jean-Étienne (Geneva 1702–1789) Swiss artist. A merchant's son, he started painting early. In 1723, he went to Paris to study engraving and the painting of miniatures. He entered the service of the Marquis of Puysieux, French ambassador to the Kingdom of the Two Sicilies in 1735. He went several times to Rome, then to Florence in 1737. There he met Lord Ponsonby, with whom he set off for the Levant, visiting Malta and the Ionian Islands. In August 1738, he arrived in Constantinople and stayed there till September 1742. He produced many portraits of Europeans in Oriental costumes and of Turkish people. In 1742 he was invited to Moldavia and stayed ten months. From 1743 to 1745 he stayed in Vienna, where he worked for the Empress, Marie Theresa. In 1745, he set off for Venice and returned to Paris the following year where he stayed for eight years. From 1751, he exhibited at the Académie de Saint Luc. In 1765, he became a friend of the writer Jean-Jacques Rousseau, whose portrait he painted five years later. In 1772, he returned to Paris to paint Marie-Antoinette's portrait, then returned to Holland. Between 1773 and 1775, he was in London again, where he exhibited at the Royal Academy. In 1777 and 1778, he was in Vienna. In 1781, he published *Le Traité* (The treaty).

MACKE, August (Meschede 1887–Perthes-les-Hurlus 1914) German painter. He studied art in Düsseldorf. In 1905, he went to Italy for the first time and the following year he traveled in Holland, Belgium, and England; in 1907 he went to Paris. Between 1907 and 1908 he studied with Louis Corinth in Berlin. He returned to France and Italy in 1908. In 1910 he met Franz Marc. He visited the Matisse exhibition and saw major works of Islamic art in Munich. In 1911, he visited Switzerland, where he met Paul Klee. He took part in the first Blaue Reiter exhibition (1911) and in the second (1912). In 1912, he went to Paris with Marc and there they met Delaunay; later Delaunay and the French poet Guillaume Apollinaire visited him in Bonn. He took part in several group exhibitions in Bonn and Berlin. In 1914, he went to Tunisia with Louis Moilliet and Klee. He returned to Germany at the end of April. Mobilized in 1914, he was killed in France.

MAKART, Hans (Salzburg 1840–Vienna 1884) Austrian painter. A history painter, he studied briefly in Vienna and then in Munich under Piloty. He began to exhibit in 1861 and was invited to the World Exhibition in Paris in 1867. It was three pictures he produced in 1868 that brought him to public notice: *Modern Love*, *Children Sprawling on Heaps of Gold*, and *The Plague in Florence*. He made several journeys to Egypt in 1875–1876 and to Belgium and Spain in 1877. When he returned to Austria, a special class of historical painting was created for him at the academy in Vienna.

MANET, Édouard (Paris 1832–1883) French painter. Though from a middle-class background, when he was very young he became a cabin boy aboard a ship, *Le Guadeloupe*, which took him to Rio de Janeiro. At 18 he joined Thomas Couture's studio later traveling in Holland, Germany, and Italy. He was very influenced by Spanish and Japanese art. At first he was reviled by critics, though his *The Guitar Player* in 1861 won an award. He was a friend of the poet Mallarmé, and was strongly supported by the writer Émile Zola. His portrayal of nude figures in *Déjeuner sur l'Herbe* caused a scandal in 1863, but *Le Bon bock* was admired and accepted at the Salon of 1873. His enemies were disarmed by *Jeanne* in 1882. Though stricken by serious illness, he still produced *Monsieur Perthuiset*, and worked with pastels, which were less tiring than brushes.

MARILHAT, Prosper (Vertaison 1811–Paris 1843) French painter. He spent his childhood at the Château de Sauvagnat in the Auvergne. At 18, he tried to launch himself in the cutlery trade in Thiers. After his business failure, he went to Paris to study painting in Camille Roqueplan's studio. In 1831, he exhibited at the salon for the first time. He was employed by the German politician and botanist, Baron von Hügel: from 1831–1833, he traveled with him in Greece, Egypt, Palestine, and Syria. In Egypt, he painted many portraits and did decorations for several buildings in Cairo, among them a new theater. He sailed along the Nile. He came back to France with ten big sketchbooks of drawings, sailing on the *Sphinx*, which brought back the Obelisk of Luxor. The canvases he exhibited at the Salon of 1834 were a revelation to his contemporaries, and Théophile Gautier sang his praises. The following year, he won a medal. The Salon of 1844 was also a triumph for him. He sank gradually into madness, however, and died prematurely.

MARQUET, Albert (Bordeaux 1875–Paris 1945) French painter. He entered the École Nationale des Arts Décoratifs (national school of decorative arts) in 1902. There he met Matisse and was able to join the studio of Gustave Moreau, later meeting

Manguin and Camoin. He exhibited for the first time (along with Matisse) at Berthe Weill's gallery in 1902. In 1904, he illustrated Charles-Louis Philippe's *Bubu de Montparnasse* (Bubu from Montparnasse). In 1905 he took part in the Salon d'Automne, well known because of the scandal of the Fauves. Between August and October 1911 he was in Morocco, accompanied by Eugène Montfort. Declared unfit for service in 1914, he settled in Marseilles and only returned sporadically to Paris. As he was often ill in the winter, he went to Algeria in 1920. He went there regularly and painted many views of the capital. In 1923, he married Marcelle Martinet in Algiers. He made many journeys to France, to Egypt (1928), to Romania (1933), to the U.S.S.R. (1934), to Morocco (1935), to Italy and Switzerland (1936), to Holland and Sweden (1938). He spent the war period in Algiers, dying of cancer in June 1947.

MARTIN, John (East Land Ends 1789–Douglas, Isle of Man, 1854) English painter. He settled in London in 1806 and began to exhibit at the Royal Academy from 1811. He is best known for his grand, apocalyptic subjects, usually taken from the Bible.

MATISSE, Henri (Le Cateau 1869–Nice 1954) French artist. In 1893 he entered the École des Beaux-Arts in Paris in the studio of Gustave Moreau, who interested him in Muslim art. He was drawn to Gauguin, Cézanne, and Lautrec. From 1896 onwards he traveled often (Collioure 1904, Algeria 1906, Italy 1907, Morocco 1911 and 1913, Russia, Spain, England). After his travels he painted the "Moroccan triptych," the centerpiece being *Interior with Eggplants*. His travels in Morocco and his visits to the exhibitions of oriental art in Munich in 1910 and in Paris in 1912 provided the inspiration for *Moroccan Café*. Next he settled in Nice, where he treated the theme of the *Odalisques* with its overloaded Oriental décor. He painted *The Egyptian Curtain* in 1948. Among his Orientalist works are *Periwinkles* (also called *Moroccan Garden*) and *The Standing Riffain*.

MAYER, Luigi (Rome c. 1755–London 1803) Italian painter. Between 1776 and 1793 he worked in Constantinople for the English ambassador, Sir Robert Ainslie. He produced many drawings representing Constantinople but also painted in Palestine, Syria, and Egypt.

MELLING, Antoine Ignace (Karlsruhe 1763–Paris 1831) German painter. He studied under his father, Joseph Melling, a pupil of Carle Van Loo. Antoine traveled in Italy, Egypt, and Anatolia. He settled in Constantinople, where he became the official designer and architect to the Sultana, Hadidge. There he worked on his album *Voyage pittoresque de Constantinople et des rives du Bosphore* (Picturesque journey in Constantinople and the banks of the Bosporus), published in 1819 with 48 engraved plates. After 18 years on the banks of the Bosporus, he acquired a great reputation, taking advantage of the fashion for things Turkish. He became the official painter of Louis XVIII.

MERSON, Luc Olivier (Paris 1846–1920) French painter. He débuted at the Paris Salon in 1867 with a history painting *Leucothea and Anaxandra*. Another typical example of his work is *St. Michael* (1875). He treated allegorical subjects and also illustrated the works of Victor Hugo, Musset, and Mérimée.

MIRA, Victor (Saragossa 1949–) Spanish artist. Since his first two personal exhibitions in Madrid and Munich in 1979, he has exhibited regularly in these two countries and also in the United States, Mexico, Austria, and Holland. He has taken part also in large traveling exhibitions, such as *Cafés littéraires* (Literary cafés) (from 1989 to 1998) and *L'Univers n'existe que dans un livre* (The universe only exists in a book) (from 1998).

MOILLIET, Louis (Berne 1880–La Tour de Peiltz 1962) Swiss painter. As an adolescent he met Paul Klee, and later trained in Germany and in the art colony at Worpswede on the North Sea from 1901 to 1903, then at the art academy in Stuttgart in 1904. In 1907–1908, he visited Rome, Provence, Sicily, and Tunisia. He took part in the first autumn Salon in Berlin in 1913 and exhibited with the Blaue Reiter group in Germany. He returned to Tunisia in 1914, with Klee and Macke, and there worked exclusively in watercolors. From 1913 to 1939, he stayed frequently in southern countries, traveling in North Africa, Spain, and the south of France.

MONDINO, Aldo (Turin 1938–) Italian artist. He settled in Paris at the end of the 1950s. In 1960, he had his first private exhibition at the Bellechasse Gallery. From then on, he exhibited in France, Italy, and many European countries, in the United States and Japan. He took part in international exhibitions such as the Venice Biennial (1976; 1993), the Rome Quadrennial (1993; 1999). He settled in Milan at the beginning of the 1980s. From 1986 he began to draw his inspiration from the East with the series *Hanging Carpets* in 1986 and 1990 which is exhibited in the Sperone Westwater Gallery in New York. He continued experimenting as his travels took him to North Africa, Israel, and Turkey.

MONTICELLI, Adolphe (Marseilles 1824–1886) French painter. His artistic education was based on frequent visits to the Louvre, and he met Delacroix. Living in Marseilles until 1863, he then stayed in Paris until the siege of 1870. In spite of his success in Paris, where his painting pleased and sold well, it was in Marseilles that he felt at home, fascinated by the nearness of the East, by gypsy music, and by the light and the smells of the Mediterranean.

MOREAU, Gustave (Paris 1826–1898) French painter. He entered the École des Beaux-Arts in 1846, studying in Picot's studio. He chose Chassériau as his master and painted in his memory *The Young Man and Death* (1865). He visited Italy in 1857 to 1859 and admired Michelangelo and Carpaccio. Moreau was often awarded medals at the World Exhibition. Among his best known works are: *The Song of Songs* (1853), *Oedipus and the Sphinx* (1864), and *Jacob and the Angel* (1878). Moreau, who never went to the East, drew the highly personal exoticism of his canvases largely from Delacroix. The teacher of many pupils, including Matisse, Georges Rouault, Marque and others, he had a considerable influence on modern painting.

MOREAU, Jean-Michel, (Paris 1741–1814) French artist. He studied engraving in Lebas' studio, producing excellent works of everyday life. It was only in 1759 that he established himself in watercolors, an example being *Louis XIV Reviewing the Regiments of the French Guards* and *The Swiss on the Sablon Plain*. His works, engraved by Lebas, won him the appointment as artist to the king. From 1781 to 1810, Moreau exhibited a large number of drawings in the Salon and won several prizes. In 1785, he traveled to Italy. Moreau illustrated the main classical authors, in particular Ovid, Molière, La Fontaine, Rousseau. He was also royal artist to Louis XVIII.

MORELLI, Domenico (Naples 1823 or 1826–1901) Italian painter. He studied in Naples followed by a period in Rome. In 1900 he was awarded a gold medal at the World Exhibition in Paris. He was best known as a history painter.

MÜLLER, Léopold Carl (Dresden 1834–Weidlingen 1892) German painter. He studied under his father, who was a lithographer, then followed the classes of Karl von Blaas and Christian Ruben in Vienna. He traveled in the Balkans and in Turkey, and visited Egypt during the winter of 1873–1874, returning nine times in 12 years. Back in Vienna in 1874, he presented his first canvas inspired by Egypt at the Künstlerhaus. In 1875, he invited Hans Makart to join him in Cairo. He became director of the arts academy in Vienna in 1877. In 1877–1878 he worked for the German Egyptologist and novelist Georg Ebers. In 1881, he went to Upper Egypt and stayed two months in Aswan. He regularly exhibited his work in London.

MÜLLER, William James (Bristol 1812–1845) English painter. In 1827, he entered the Bristol Institution and attended the classes of the landscape artist James Baker Pyne. He exhibited for the first time at the Bristol Institution in 1829 and the following year he received an invitation from the British Society of Artists. He exhibited at the Royal Academy from 1833. The following year he set off for seven months to visit Belgium, Germany, Switzerland, and Italy, returning via France. In 1838, he went to Greece and Egypt. He settled in Cairo and visited Thebes in 1839. He continued to travel in Greece, Turkey, France, and Malta. In 1845, he returned to Bristol very ill and died there a few months later.

NATOIRE, Charles-Joseph (Nîmes 1700–Castel Gandolfo 1777) French painter. A pupil of Lemoyne and Galoche, he won the Prix de Rome in 1721 and visited Italy again between 1724 and 1727. Back in Paris, he was accepted at the Académie in 1734. He executed extensive decorative schemes in churches; worked at Versailles and also for private patrons; and produced many cartoons for the Gobelin works, notably *The Story of Don Quixote*. He was particularly fond of historical and mythological subjects. In 1751, he was appointed director of the Académie de France in Rome, where he devoted himself to teaching. He worked for Saint-Louis-des-Français and produced many views of Rome and the countryside around it. He retired to Castel Gandolfo in 1775.

NATTIER, Jean-Marc (Paris 1865–1766) French artist. He was the son of a member of the Académie, Marc Nattier, and younger brother of Jean-Baptiste, the history painter. He engraved *The Story of Marie de Medici* between 1700 and 1710, then worked for Pierre le Grand in Holland and in Paris in 1717. He was admitted to the Académie in 1718. He collaborated with Watteau on the pictures of the King meant for Crozat in 1721, and with J.B. Massé to decorate the Main Gallery at Versailles (1723–53). He became painter to the House of Orléans. He decorated the Temple from 1734 to 1748, and was appointed painter to the royal family.

PAPETY, Dominique Louis (Marseilles–1815–1849) French painter. One of Cogniet's pupils, he won the Grand Prix de Rome in 1836. He visited Greece, Syria, and Palestine. Ingres, who thought highly of his talent, influenced him greatly.

PARROCEL, Charles (Paris 1688–1752) French painter. He studied in La Fosse's studio. Enlisting in the cavalry in 1705, he produced war pictures. From 1712 to 1721, he was resident at the École de France in Rome. On his return to Paris he was accepted at the Académie des Beaux-Arts. He painted *The Entrance* and *The Departure of the Turkish Ambassador* in 1721, and between 1736 and 1738 painted hunting scenes for Versailles. He accompanied several campaigns of the royal army and painted the Battle of Fontenoy. He produced ten cartoons of the war in Flanders for the Gobelin works.

PASINI, Alberto (Busetto 1826–Cavoretto 1899) French artist. Left an orphan at an early age, he studied lithography at the arts academy in Parma, and later published a sketchbook of the history and the architecture of the region. In 1851, he went to Paris to work for a publisher, and there studied under Eugène Ciceri. He met the diplomat, Prosper Bourée, who asked him to accompany him on a mission to Persia, along with Arthur de Gobineau. Pasini left in 1855 and crossed through Egypt, Arabia, the Yemen, and the Persian Gulf. He spent a year and a half in Teheran. In 1856, he returned to France, this time going via the Black Sea and Constantinople. He exhibited his canvases inspired by Persia at the Salon. In 1868–1869 he returned to Constantinople, and then to Asia Minor, Syria, and the Lebanon in 1873. He also went to Venice and Spain with Gérôme. In 1880 and again in 1898, he exhibited at the National Exhibition in Turin, where a room was reserved for him to present 300 sketches.

PICASSO, Pablo (Malaga 1881–Mougins 1973) Spanish artist. One of the major artists of the 20th century, Picasso explored a wide range of styles, passing through his so-called Blue Period and Pink Period to his development of Cubism, inspired in part by Iberian and African culture. Among his many friends were Matisse, Braque, Rousseau, and Apollinaire. His notorious *Les Demoiselles d'Avignon* appeared in 1907. In 1917, he discovered post-war Italy and moved towards a painting of traditional inspiration, often copying the classics. After the Spanish Civil War, which moved him deeply, he lived in the south of France. He often studied the great works of the past, as for example in the series *Women of Algiers* (1954–1955) after Delacroix, and the series *Maids of Honor* (1957) after Velazquez.

PICOT, François Édouard (Paris 1786–1868) French painter. A pupil of Vincent and J.-L. David, he exhibited at the Salon from 1819 to 1839. He collaborated with Hippolyte Flandrin on the monumental paintings of the frieze of the sanctuary of Saint-Vincent de Paul.

POYNTER, Sir Edward John (Paris 1836–London 1919) English artist. Having studied in London he traveled in Italy in 1853 and in 1856 attended Gleyre's classes in Paris. In 1860 he returned to London, where he began to exhibit at the Royal Academy, producing drawings, illustrations, miniatures. He was appointed president of the Royal Academy in London.

PREZIOSI, Amadeo (La Valletta 1816– Constantinople 1882) Italian painter. Having studied in Paris, in 1842 he settled in Constantinople, where he opened a studio, his works an attempt to represent the daily life of the capital. Lemercier published his lithographs between 1858 and 1861.

PRINCEP, Valentine (Calcutta 1836–London 1904) British painter. She studied at the Royal Academy, then in 1859 went to Paris to study under Gleyre. In 1862, she exhibited for the first time at the Royal Academy, and was awarded a bronze medal at the World Exhibition in Paris in 1889.

PROUVE, Victor (Nancy 1856–Sétif 1943) French painter. His first decorative composition was already colored by the East: *Sardanapolus*. In 1888, he stayed for six months in Tunisia and the following year went on a second journey. He brought back more than a thousand drawings.

RAFFET, Auguste (Paris 1804–Genoa 1860) French painter. He was inspired by the wars in Algeria and the campaigns in the Empire, although he did not follow them personally. In 1857, he went to Hungary, Moldavia, the Crimea, Smyrna, and Constantinople. On his return to Paris, he published the plates of his *Voyage en Crimée* (Journey to the Crimea). Continual journeys filled the rest of his life: Spain, London, Holland, Scotland, Austria, and San Donato during the Italian War.

RALLI, Théodore (Constantinople 1852–Lausanne 1909) Greek painter. A pupil of Gérôme and of the École des Beaux-Arts in Paris, he appeared at the Salon from 1875, then at the Salon des Artistes Français, and later exhibited at the Royal Academy in London. Ralli traveled in North Africa and the Middle East, bringing back drawings and sketches.

RAVAULT, Ange René (Montargis 1766–1845) French painter. He was a student at the École des Beaux-Arts from 1793. He painted *Adoration of the Angels* for the church of Montargis and at the Salon of 1795 exhibited *Battle in Which Armida and her Family are Defeated* and *Bonapart Invoking Fortune*.

RAVERAT, Vincent (Moutier-Saint Jean 1801–Paris 1865) French painter. A pupil of Abel de Pujol, from 1831 he exhibited historical subjects at the Paris Salon, including *The Martyrdom of St. Andoche* and *The Dying Christ* (for the church of Saulieu).

REGNAULT, Paul (Paris 1843–Buzenval 1871) French artist. After failing twice, he finally obtained the Prix de Rome in 1866. During his stay in Rome, he discovered the work of Mariano Fortuny y Marsal. He went to Spain in 1869 and returned to Rome with a number of Orientalist works, among them *Judith and Holofernes*. He returned to Spain with his friend, the painter Clairin, and was captivated by the Alhambra in Granada. He later went to Morocco, settling in Tangiers in a house he decorated with oriental motifs. He sent a *Salome* to the Salon of 1870. He returned to France to take part in the defence of Paris and was killed in battle at Buzenval.

RENOIR, Auguste (Limoges 1841–Cagnes 1919) French painter, one of the leading Impressionists. He went to evening classes in drawing and in 1862 was admitted to the École Supérieure des Beaux-Arts in Paris. He met Bazille, Monet, Cézanne, and Pissarro. He was admitted to the salons of 1864 and 1865. He showed *Odalisque* ("an Algerian woman which Delacroix could have signed") in 1870. On the occasion of the first Impressionist exhibition in 1874, he showed *The Dancer*, *The Theater Box*, and *A Parisian Woman*. His first exhibition was held at the Gallerie de la Vie Moderne in 1879. He traveled in Italy in 1881, where he particularly admired the works of Raphael. Stricken with illness, he spent the winter in the south of France, finally settling at Cagnes in 1903. He painted mythological scenes (*The Judgement of Paris*); odalisques; portraits, such as *Gabrielle with a Rose* (1911), and *Gabrielle with Jewels*; and bathing scenes, *Women Bathing* (1918).

RIXENS, Jean André (Saint Gaudens 1846–Paris 1924) French painter. A pupil of Gérôme at the École des Beaux-Arts in Paris, he made his début at the salon of 1868, where he obtained many prizes, likewise at the World Exhibition. His favorite themes were scenes from history and mythology, as well as portraits of well-known people.

ROBERTS, David (Stockbridge 1796–London 1864) Scottish painter. He served his apprenticeship with a house painter in Edinburgh for seven years. Then he worked as a scene painter for the

Royal Theatre in Edinburgh from 1822, then for Drury Lane and Covent Garden in London. He made several sets for Charles Dickens and became a friend. His first exhibition took place in 1824 at the Society of British Artists. Also in 1824 he visited Europe, and in particular Normandy. He went to Spain and Morocco in 1832. He went to Egypt in 1838 and traveled in Upper Egypt and Nubia for several months. The following year, he went to Sinai, to Syria, Palestine, and the Lebanon. A plague epidemic cut short his journey. Back in London, he was elected corresponding member of the Royal Academy in 1839 and became a member two years later. Between 1842 and 1849 he published the six volumes of lithographs of his *Views of the Holy Land, Syria, Idumea, Arabia, Egypt and Nubia*, which had a considerable success.

ROTTMANN, Karl (Handschuhsheim 1798–Munich 1850) German painter. Working in Munich from 1822, he traveled in Italy, then went on a long trip to Greece, from where he brought back many canvases. He was commissioned by Louis I to paint 23 Greek landscapes; he also painted frescos of Italian landscapes.

ROUBTZOFF, Alexander (St. Petersburg 1884–Tunis 1949) Russian painter who obtained French nationality in 1924. He was a student at the Imperial Academy of Fine Arts of St. Petersburg. He traveled in the Crimea, Poland, France, Spain , Italy, Estonia, and Finland. Towards the end of his life he settled in Tunis, becoming particularly interested in Islamic and Bedouin art. He exhibited at the Société des Peintres Orientalistes and the Salon Artistique de l'Afrique Française, at the Tunisian Salon, from 1920. He painted many Europeans living in Tunis, the Tunisian landscape, and architecture. He was deeply saddened by the modernization of Tunis.

ROUSSEAU, Henri (known as Le Douanier Rousseau) (Laval 1844–Paris 1910) French painter. Self-taught, he painted in a naïve-seeming style. He was noticed by the French writer Alfred Jarry, who gave him the nickname of Le Douanier (the customs officer). Apollinaire, Delaunay, and Picasso were his closest friends. In his most famous canvases, he gave free rein to his imagination in exotic landscapes shown with little or no traditional perspective. He painted: *Sleeping Gypsy* (1897); and a series of jungle paintings, such as *The Hungry Lion* (1905), *The Snake-Charmer* (1907), and *The Dream* (1910).

SAINT-AUBIN, Augustin de (Paris 1736–1807) French artist. He was accepted at the Académie Royale in Paris in 1771, the year he exhibited drawn portraits and engraved portraits; in 1773 he exhibited more portraits and the drawings *The Concert* and *The Evening Ball*. In 1776, he was appointed engraver to the King's library. Examples include the portraits engraved after Cochin: *Madame de Pompadour*, and *Moreau the Younger*, among others.

SARGENT, John Singer (Florence 1856–London 1925) American painter. Born in Italy of American parents, he spent his childhood traveling in Europe. In 1874, he was in Paris where he met Carolus-Duran, under whom he studied painting. In 1876, he met Monet and the following year he was admitted to the École des Beaux-Arts. In 1878 he exhibited at the first exhibition of the Society of American Artists. In 1879 he exhibited at the Salon in Paris and obtained an honorable mention. He traveled to Spain at the end of the summer and copied canvases by Velazquez at the Prado. He exhibited a *View of Venice* at the Salon of 1881 and two Venetian interiors at the Grosvenor Gallery in London. He visited Monet at Giverny in 1885 and painted *Monet Painting on the Edge of a Wood*. He settled in London in 1886. In 1889, he took part in the campaign to get the French State to acquire *Olympia* by Manet. In 1890, he began to work on the wall decorations for the public library in Boston, and at the end of the year went to Egypt, visited Alexandria, and rented a studio in Cairo. In April 1891, he went to Greece and Turkey, to Sicily in 1897, and to Switzerland and Italy during the autumn of 1900. In 1903 he traveled in Spain and Portugal. In 1905 he exhibited at the Royal Academy in London, and the Museum of Fine Art in Boston acquired his *Artist in his Studio*. He went to Syria and Palestine during the winter, and in 1907 traveled to Venice and Central Italy.

SCHEFFER, Ary (Dordrecht 1795–Argenteuil 1858) French painter. He exhibited for the first time in 1805 and in 1810 sent a portrait to the exhibition in Amsterdam. In 1811 he worked in Guérin's studio. He obtained a prize in Antwerp with his picture *Abraham and the Three Angels* and became appreciated by the middle class public for pictures painted in the 'romance' genre. From 1812, he exhibited at the Salon and continued till 1855. Art teacher to the children of the Duc d'Orléans, he did a large part of the work on the historical frescos commissioned for the museum in Versailles.

SCHINKEL, Karl Friedrich (Neuruppin 1781–Vienna 1841) German artist and architect. In 1803 he brought back from Italy drawings of landscapes, costumes, and monuments; examples include *View of the Flowering of Greece*, *The Six Hours of Day*. Then, back in Germany, he became known as a painter and architect. Friedrich obtained for him the job of set designer for the theater in Königsberg. Between 1816 and 1824, he built many Neo-classical monuments in Berlin.

SEDDON, Thomas (London 1821–Cairo 1856) English painter. The son of a distinguished cabinet maker, he went to France, living in Paris, Barbizon, and Dinan. In 1852, he exhibited for the first time at the Royal Academy in London. He went to Egypt the following year and met the English scholar Richard Burton; his celebrated portrait of Burton shows him in Arab costume. This lithographed portrait illustrates the account that Burton wrote of his journey to Mecca, published in 1855, *Personal Narrative of a Pilgrim to Al Mahdinah & Meccah*. In 1854, he went to Palestine with William Holman Hunt, returning to Dinan in November. The following year, a personal exhibition was organized for him. He returned to Cairo and died there of rheumatic fever. John Ruskin then launched a national subscription to acquire one of his major works, *Jerusalem and the Valley of Jehoshaphat, Seen from the Mount of Temptation*.

SERRUR, Henry (Lambersart 1794–Paris 1865) French painter. One of Regnault's pupils and a student at the Académie des Beaux-Arts in Paris, which he entered in 1837. He exhibited at the Salon from 1819 to 1850.

SIMONETTI, Attilio (Rome 1846–1926) Italian painter. A student at the Academy of Fine Art in Rome and member of the group *The Twenty-Five of the Roman Countryside*, he specialized in landscapes and seascapes. Among his Orientalist works are *The Sultan's Favorite* and *The Scribe*.

SIMONI, Gustavo (Rome 1846–1926) Italian painter. A student at the Academy San Luca in Rome, he worked in Paris, Spain, and Africa, painting lively scenes of Oriental life.

SISLEY, Alfred (Paris 1839–Moret-sur-Loing 1899) English painter, a noted Impressionist. He often visited Gleyre's studio in Paris and in 1862 became friends with Monet, Renoir, and Bazille. Freeing himself from the academicism of Gleyre, Sisley embarked on a great artistic adventure. In 1874, he organized an exhibition which caused a scandal and which earned its main exhibitors the nickname 'Impressionists.' The following years were very eventful as these artists exasperated the public and Sisley's canvases sold at very low prices and only to close friends; he died in poverty. It was only in the late 1890s that his work was better received and began to command high prices.

TIFFANY, Louis Comfort (New York 1848–1933) American painter. He was a member of the National Academy of America, of the National Society of Fine Art in Paris, and of the Imperial Society of Fine Art in Tokyo. During his stay in Paris, his canvases were influenced by the art of the Far East, especially Japanese decorative art. He was the founder of a factory of blown glass art, and decorated public and religious buildings (the mosaics in the cathedral of St. John the Divine in New York City, for example). His paintings date from before 1900. Among his Orientalist subjects are: *The Mosque of Mohammed Ali*, *Tombs of the Mamelukes in Cairo*, and *The Last Rays of Sunlight on the Mosque in Aswan*.

TINTORETTO (Jacopo Robusti) (Venice 1518–1594) Italian painter. The son of a silk dyer, he served a brief apprenticeship with Titian (broken by their rivalry). He was attracted by the Mannerist style that had come from Tuscany and Rome, and was greatly influenced by Michelangelo (he may have visited Rome in 1547). He painted *The Last Supper* in 1547, and the cycle of St. Mark in 1548 for the Scuola Grande di San Marco in Venice. Towards 1550, his feeling for the landscape become more noticeable, as in *Episodes in the Old Testament* in the

Scuola della Trinità. He worked again at the Scuola San Marco from 1562. For the Scuola di San Rocco in 1564 he painted such works as *The Discovery of the Body of St. Mark* and *The Removal of the Body of St. Mark*. He then began the second cycle of San Rocco in 1576 and finished it in 1588. He also produced many portraits.

TISSOT, James (Nantes 1836–Buillon 1902) French artist. In 1856 he entered the École des Beaux-Arts in Paris, where he met Whistler and Degas. He collected Japanese works of art. He exhibited for the first time in 1858. He went to London in 1869 and produced his first illustrations for *Vanity Fair*. He took part in the defense of Paris in 1870, making many drawings during the siege. Having settled in London in 1871, he visited Venice with Manet in 1874. He published his first etchings in 1876. In 1855, he had a vision at the church of Saint-Sulpice, which he portrayed in *Inner Voices*. In 1886, he set off for the Near East to work on the illustrations of the life of Our Lord. He exhibited the 270 drawings of this work at the Salon at the Champ de Mars. He later traveled in Palestine to work on the illustrations for the Old Testament, first exhibiting his first Old Testament drawings in 1901.

TROUILLEBERT, Paul Désiré (Paris 1829–1900) French painter. He made his début at the Salon of 1865 and one of his 'bathers' attracted a great deal of attention at the Salon of 1882. All his works reveal Corot's influence. He produced pleasant paintings, particularly landscapes and portraits.

TROY, Jean de (Toulouse 1638–Montpellier 1691) French painter. He was the son of Antoine de Troy, and became his pupil. In 1680, he founded an academy in Toulouse and was its director till 1688. He painted many portraits and history paintings. His religious paintings include *Mary Magdalene in the Desert* and *St. Joseph's Dream*.

TROY, Jean François de (Paris 1679–Rome 1752) French painter. He studied under his father, Jean de Troy, and was admitted to the Académie des Beaux-Arts in Paris in 1708. He lived in Italy from 1699–1706. At first, he devoted himself to biblical themes at which he excelled, such as *Susanna and the Elders* (1721), *Bathsheba Bathing* and *Lot and His Daughters*. Next he tried mythological pictures. He was appointed a teacher at the Académie in 1716, he worked for the Palace of Versailles and painted one of the nine *Exotic Hunting Scenes, Lion Hunt* (1736). He produced eight tapestry cartoons for *The Story of Esther* for the Gobelin factory (1736–1740). He was appointed director of the Académie de France in Rome in 1738. He was made a member of the Académie de Saint-Luc in 1744. He fell out of favor in 1751 and had to give up his position to Natoire.

USSU, Stefano (Florence 1822 or 1832–1901) Italian painter. He studied at the Academy of Fine Art in Florence and Rome, and later settled in Egypt. For the Khedive of Egypt he painted *The Carpet Festival* and *The Pilgrimage to Mecca*.

VALERI, Sylvestro (Rome 1814–1902) Italian painter. He débuted in Rome. He was a teacher at the Academy of Saint Luke and an honorary member of the Institute of Fine Art in Urbino.

VAN DONGEN, Kees (Delfshaven 1877–Monte-Carlo 1968) Dutch painter. In 1897 he moved to Paris, settling in Montmartre. He was involved in Fauvism and exhibited at the Salon d'Automne of 1905. He was invited to Dresden, to the exhibition of the German Expressionist group Die Brücke in 1908. In 1911 he traveled in Spain and Morocco.

VAN LOO de PRUSSE, Charles Amédée Philippe (Rivoli 1719–Paris 1795) French painter. A pupil of his father, he became a member of the Paris Académie in 1747. He was appointed one year later to the court of Frederick II of Prussia. He returned to France in 1758 and visited Prussia again in 1763 and 1769. He produced large historical and mythological pictures but he was not averse to more intimate scenes. He produced many cartoons for the Gobelin factory between 1773 and 1775, notably the tapestries of the *Hanging of Turkish Costume*, which included *The Sultana and Odalisques* and *A Sultana Dressing* (1774).

VAN MOUR, Jean-Baptiste (Valenciennes 1671–Constantinople 1737) French painter. He worked for the Dutch ambassador in Constantinople, Cornelis Calkoen, whose portrait he painted, as well as those of the Grand Sultan Ahmed III and various Ottoman notables. He painted many ceremonies and the social life of the town. He then worked for the French ambassador, the Marquis de Bonnac. He also painted a celebrated portrait of Lady Montagu Wortley.

VEDDER, Elihu (New York 1836–Rome 1923) American painter. He studied at the Academy of Sherburne and then went to Paris to enter Picot's studio, later continuing his studies in Italy. In 1865, he became a member of the National Academy of New York. He settled in Rome in 1867.

VERNET, Claude Joseph (Avignon 1714–Paris 1789) French painter. After studying in Aix-en-Provence, he set off for Italy where he was the pupil of both Pannini and Locatelli, painting Italian landscapes. He was admired at the Salon of 1750 and admitted to the Académie des Beaux-Arts three years later. He produced the series of the ports of France for the château of Marigny (1754–1765).

VERNET, Horace (Paris 1789–1863) French painter. The descendant of a celebrated family of painters, and the son of Joseph Vernet, a famous painter of seascapes, he obtained a first class medal in 1811. He was made a chevalier of the Légion d'honneur three years later. He was appointed director of the Villa Médici in 1828. In 1833, he went to the East for the first time. Very early he took his inspiration from the Romantic works of Victor Hugo and of Lord Byron, as in *Le Giaour* 1827. In 1833, he went on his first journey to Algeria with the English painter, William Wylde. He went back there several times and became the official recorder of the conquest of Algeria. His nephew, Frédéric Goupil-Fresquet, who traveled with him from Greece to Egypt and Morocco, wrote an account of their journey in *Le Voyage en Orient avec Horace Vernet en 1839 et 1840* (Journey to the East with Horace Vernet in 1839 and 1840). He produced more than 500 pictures and lithographs.

VERONESE (Paolo Caliari) (Verona 1528–Venice 1588) Italian painter. He studied with Badile and Caroto, and absorbed the lessons of Parmesan, Guilo Romano, and Titian. From 1548, he demonstrated his talent with *The Virgin and Child with Saints and Donors*. In 1553, he was summoned to Venice where he decorated the ceiling of the Council of Ten in the Doges' Palace. He produced several paintings for the Doges' palace, then began the major decoration of the sacristy and altarpiece of the church of San Sebastiano in 1555. He almost certainly visited Rome at that time and studied Michelangelo's frescos. He also produced a series of decorations for the Villa Barbaro (Maser) in 1562, then his most famous works, such as *The Wedding at Cana*, *Darius's Family before Alexander*, and *The Last Supper* (1573).

VIEN, Joseph-Marie (Montpellier 1716–Paris 1809) French painter. One of Natoire's pupils, he won the Grand Prix de Rome and in 1744 went to Italy, where he stayed six years. There he was influenced by Le Guerchin and the Bolognese painters. He devoted himself to painting large Biblical scenes such. He took an active part in the Turkish Masquerade of 1748, organized by the students of the Académie de France in Rome. After visiting the excavations of Herculanum in 1760, he became one of the supporters of Neo-classicism. He was appointed teacher in 1759, then, from 1775 to 1781, was director of the Académie in Rome. He was admitted to the Académie de Saint-Luc in 1776. He devoted himself to large mythological compositions or subjects drawn from ancient history.

VIGÉE-LEBRUN, Élisabeth (Paris 1755–1842) French painter. She was a pupil of her father, Louis Vigée, then of Vernet and Greuze. In 1776 she married the art dealer, J.B. Lebrun. In 1779, she became the official painter of Marie-Antoinette and painted some 30 portraits of her. She was admitted to the Académie in Paris in 1783. Many of her works were portraits of artists and self-portraits. During the Revolution, she left for Italy, where she lived from 1789 to 1793, then Vienna from 1793 to 1794, and finally to St. Petersburg between 1795 and 1802. She was admitted to the Académie de Saint-Luc in Rome and the Academy of St. Petersburg. In 1802, she was in France but she continued to travel in Europe. She lived in England until 1805, and in Switzerland between 1808 and 1809. She published her *Souvenirs* (Memoires) between 1835 and 1837.

VINCHON, Jean-Baptiste (Paris 1789–Bains d'Ems 1855) French painter. He obtained the Prix de Rome in 1814 and on his return from Italy worked particularly on frescos and at the church of Saint-Sulpice in Paris. One of his best-known projects is the series *Scenes from the Life of St. Maurice*. Other examples of his work include *The Dead Christ* in the church of Saint-Paul.

WALLIS, Henry (London 1830–Croydon 1916) English painter. Studying first at the Royal Academy in London, he then went to the École des Beaux-Arts in Paris to study in Gleyre's studio. He went to Italy, Egypt, and Turkey, and exhibited in London from 1854 to 1893, particularly at the Royal Academy. Two representative examples of his Pre-Raphaelite style are *The Death of Chatterton* and *The Stone Breaker*.

WATTEAU, Jean Antoine (Valenciennes 1684–Nogent-sur-Marne 1721) Flemish-born French painter. He studied in J.A. Gérin's studio in Valenciennes, then in Paris where he copied Flemish pictures. From 1703, he created paintings on subjects of Italian comedy, and in 1708 worked on the decoration of the Château de la Muette, where he expressed a sure taste for exoticism. His discovery of Rubens' Medici cycle completely transformed his style. He was still passionately interested in the theater and was particularly fond of masquerades. He was engaged by the Royal Treasurer, Crozat, towards 1712 and was able to get to know the collection at the Château of Chantilly. In 1717, he showed *L'Embarquement pour Cythère* (Setting sail for Cythera) which was his reception piece at the Académie. In 1719, he went to London where he received some commissions. On his return, he produced *L'Enseigne de Gersaint* (Gersaint's shopsign).

WERNER, Karl Friedrich (Weimar 1808–Leipzig 1894) German painter. He was a student at the art academy in Leipzig, then in Munich (1829). In 1833, he went to Italy where he stayed for nearly 20 years. He visited Spain in 1857, Palestine in 1862 and 1864, Greece in 1875, Sicily 1877–1878, and Rome 1891. He often exhibited in London.

WILKIE, David (Cults 1785–near Malta in 1841) Scottish painter. He entered the Royal Academy in London as a student in 1805. Rapidly becoming successful, he traveled a widely and was particularly influenced by the Spanish masters. In Constantinople, he painted portraits of the Sultan. He also visited Smyrna, Rhodes, Beirut, Jerusalem, and Alexandria. He died on the way to Gibraltar. His album *Sir David Wilkie's Sketches in Syria and Egypt in 1840 and 1841* was published in 1843.

WYLDE, William (London 1806–Paris 1889) English artist. A merchant's son, he entered a diplomatic career and spent four years in Calais as secretary to the English consul. Abandoning that career, he became a champagne merchant in Épernay. He then spent six years studying the technique of oil painting, and in 1833 set off for Algeria with Horace Vernet, later traveling in Spain and Italy. He began to sell his pictures in Rome. In 1835 he published a sketchbook of lithographs, *Le Voyage Pittoresque dans la Régence d'Alger exécuté en 1833* (Picturesque journey through the protectorate of Algiers in 1833). From 1839 he exhibited at the Salon du Louvre and from 1848 began to exhibit at the Royal Academy and the British Institution. In 1855, he exhibited at the World Exhibition in Paris in the French section and received the Légion d'honneur. He was elected to the Royal Institute of Painters in Watercolour in 1879.

ZIEM, Félix (Beaune 1821–Paris 1911) French painter. From 1834 he studied under the architect Lemaire. He enrolled at the École des Beaux-Arts in Dijon in 1837, but was expelled the following year. In 1839, he went to live with his brother in Marseilles and in 1840 opened his own studio. In 1842, he made a journey to Italy (Genoa, Florence, Venice) and then discovered Germany. In 1843 he was invited to Russia by Prince Gagarin, and he stayed several months in St. Petersburg. In 1845 he settled in Nice but he left the following year after the death of his mistress. After a brief stay in Florence in 1847 he went to Constantinople. After several months in Rome, in 1848 he settled in Paris where he opened a studio. He exhibited for the first time at the Salon of 1849. During the early 1850s he visited Flanders, Holland, Italy, England, and Scotland. He set off for Egypt in 1854 and to Tunisia the following year. In 1856, he again went to Constantinople and continued his travels in Egypt and Syria. He was in Algeria in 1857. In 1859 he went to Genoa, to the Balearic Islands and Tunisia, then to Venice, to which he returned many times. In 1870, he took part in the defense of Paris and was wounded. When he was not traveling, he divided his time between Paris, Barbizon, Martigues, Nice, and Marseilles. In 1897, Camille Mauclair published *L'Art de M. Félix Ziem* (The art of Mr Felix Ziem).

ZONARO, Fausto (Masi 1854–San-Remo 1929) Italian painter. Having settled in Constantinople, he became painter to the Sultan. He exhibited mostly in Italy.

Bibliography

(I) General works

ABOUT, Edmond, *De Pontoise à Stamboul*, Paris, 1884.
ACKERMAN, Gerald, *American Orientalists*, Paris, 1994.
ACKERMAN, Gerald, *Les Orientalistes de l'école britannique*, Paris, 1991.
AGERON, Charles-Robert, *Histoire de l'Algérie contemporaine. De l'insurrection de 1871 au déclenchement de la guerre de libération (1954)*, Paris, 1979.
ALAZARD, Jean. *L'Orient et la peinture française au XIXe siècle, d'Eugène Delacroix à Auguste Renoir*, Paris, 1930.
ARAMA, Maurice, *Itinéraires marocains*, Paris, 1991.
BALTRUSAITIS, Jurgis, *La Quête d'Isis, essai sur la légende d'un mythe*, Paris, 1985.
BENDINER, Kenneth Paul, *The Portrayal of the Middle East in British Painting, 1835–1860*, Ph.D. Thesis, Columbia University, New York, 1979.
BÉRAUD, Edmond, *Souvenirs du baron Gudin, peintre de la marine (1820–1970)*, Paris, 1921.
BERCHET, Jean-Claude, *Le Voyage en Orient.Anthologie des voyageurs français dans le Levant au XIXe siècle*, Paris, 1985.
BEZOMBES, Roger, *L'Exotisme dans l'art et la pensée*, Paris, 1953.
BOPPE, Auguste, *Les Peintres du Bosphore au XVIIIe siècle*, Paris, 1911.
BOUDJEDRA, Rachid, *Peintre de l'Orient*, Cadeilhan, 1996.
BUISINE, Alain, *L'Orient voilé*, Cadeilhan, 1993.
CARRÉ, Jean-Marie, *Voyageurs et écrivains français en Égypte*, Cairo, 1932.
CLAYTON, Peter, *The Rediscovery of Egypt: Artists and Travellers in the 19th Century*, London, 1982.
DAVIDSON, Angus, *Edward Lear: Landscape Painter and Nonsense Post* (1812–1888).
DE AMICIS, Edmondo, *Contantinople*, Paris, 1883.
DENON, Dominique-Vivant, *Voyage dans la Basse et la Haute Égypte*, introduction by Jean-Claude Vatin, Le Caire, 1989.
DU CAMP, Maxime, *Souvenirs littéraires*, volume 1, 1822–1850, volume 2, 1850–1880, Paris, 1906.
ESQUER, Gabriel, *Iconographie historique de l'Algérie depuis le XVIe siècle, jusqu'à 1871*, Paris, 1929.
ÉTIENNE, Roland et Françoise, *La Grèce antique, archéologie d'une découverte*, Paris, 1990.
L'Exotisme, cahiers CRLH-CIRAOL, no. 5, textes réunis by Alain Buisine and Norbert Dodille, Paris 1988.
FARRÈRE, Claude, *Mes voyages, tome 2: En Méditerranée*, Paris, 1926.
FLAUBERT, Gustave, *Voyage en Égypte*, with an introduction by Pierre-Marc de Biasi.
FOUCART, Bruno, *Le Renouvau de la peinture religieuse en France (1800–1860)*, Paris, 1987.
FOX, Wyndham Lewis, *Journeys into Barbary*, (1983).
GAUTIER, Théophile, *L'Art modern*, Paris, 1854.
GAUTIER, Théophile, *Portraits contemporains*, Paris, 1874.
GAUTIER, Théophile, *L'Orient*, Paris, 1877.
GAUTIER, Théophile, *Voyage en Égypte*, with an introducton by Paolo Tortonese, Paris, 1991.
GAUTIER, Théophile, *Constantinople*, with an introduction by Gérard-Georges Lemaire, Paris, 1991.
GONCOURT, Edmond and Jules de, *Manette Salomon*, Paris, 1993.
GOURNAY, Jean-François, *L'Appel du Proche-Orient. Richard Francis Burton et son temps, 1821–1890*, Paris, 1983.
HARAMBOURG, Lydia, *Dictionnaire des peintres paysagistes français au XIXe siècle*, Neuchâtel, 1985.
HENTSCH, Thierry, *L'Orient imaginaire. La vision politique occidentale de l'Est méditerranéen*, Paris, 1988.
Histoire de la peinture turque, collected work, Geneva, 1988.
HONOUR, Hugh, *The Image of the Black in Western Art*, Paris, 1989.
HUMBERT, Jean-Marcel, *L'Égyptomanie dans l'art occidental*, Paris, 1989.
HUNT, William Holman, *"Painting 'The Scapegoat'*, The contemporary Review 52 (1887).
JOURDA, Pierre, *L'Exotisme dans la littérature française depuis Chateaubriand*, tome 1, *Le Romantisme*, Paris, 1938; tome 2, *Du romantisme à 1939*, Paris, 1956.
JULER, Caroline, *Les Orientalistes de l'école italienne*, Paris, 1994.
JULLIAN, Philippe, *Les Orientalistes: la vision de l'Orient par les peintres européens du XIXe siècle*, Fribourg, 1977.
LAMARTINE, Alphonse de, *Voyage en Orient*, Paris, 1914.
LAMARTINE, Alphonse de, *Nouveau voyage en Orient*, Paris 1877.
Le CORBUSIER, *Le Voyage d'Orient*, Marseilles, 1977.
LELIÈVRE, Pierre, *Vivant Denon, hommes des lumières, "Ministre des arts" de Napoléon*, Paris, 1993.
LEMAIRE, Gérard-Georges, *Les Préraphaélites*, Paris, 1989.
LEMAIRE, Gérard-Georges, *Constantinople, L'Ennemi*, Paris, 1991.
LEMAIRE, Gérard-Georges, *Istanbul*, Geneva, 1997.
LOTI, Pierre, *Voyages (1872–1913)*, Paris, 1991.
MACKENZIE, John M., *Orientalism. History, Theory and the Arts*, Manchester and New York, 1995.
MAUPASSANT, Guy de, *Lettres d'Afrique*, présenté par Michèle Salinas, Paris, 1997.
MONNERET, Sophie, *L'Orient des peintres*, Paris, 1989.
MONTAGU, Lady Mary, *Embassy to Constantinople: The Travels of Lady Mary Montagu*, ed. Christopher Pick, London, 1988.
MOURA, Jean-Marc, *Lire l'exotisme*, Paris, 1992.
MOUREAU, François (ed.), *L'Œil aux aguets ou l'artiste en voyage*, Paris, 1995.
NERVAL, Gérard de, *Voyage en Orient, in Œuvres II*, intro. by Albert Béguin, Jean Richer, Paris, 1962.
NODIER, Charles, *Journal de l'Expédition des Portes de Fer*, Paris, 1844.
L'Orient de Théophile Gautier, Bulletin of the Société Théophile Gautier, no. 12, Montpellier, 1990.
L'Orient des Provençaux, texts by André Miquel, Jean-Claude Garcin, Robert Mantran, Camille Aboussouan, and Jacques Thullier, Marseilles, 1982.
PELTRE, Christine, *L'Atelier du voyage. Les peintres en Orient au XIXe siècle*, Paris, 1995.
PELTRE, Christine, *Retour en Archadie. Le voyages des artistes français en Grèce au XIXe siècle*, Paris, 1997.
PELTRE, Christine, *Les Orientalistes*, Paris, 1997.
PLAZAOLA, Jean, *Le Baron Taylor. Portrait d'un homme d'avenir*, Paris, 1989.
POTOCKI, Jan, *Voyage en Turquie et en Égypte, en Hollande et au Maroc*, with an introducton by Daniel Beauvoir, Paris, 1980.
PRADIER, Jean, *Notes artistiques sur Alger*, Tours, 1875.
RODINSON, Maxime, *La Fascination de l'Islam*, Paris, 1980.
SAID, Edward W., *Orientalism*, New York, 1978.
SOUBIRAN, Jean-Roger, *Le Paysage provençal et l'école de Marseille avant l'impressionisme, 1845–1875*, Paris and Toulon, 1992.
THALASSO, Adolphe, *L'Art ottoman, les peintres de Turquie*, Paris and Istanbul, 1988.
THÉVOZ, Michel, *L'Académisme et ses fantasmes. Le réalisme imaginaire de Charles Gleyre*, Paris, 1980.
THORNTON, Lynne, *The Orientalists: Painters and Travellers*, Paris, 1983.
THORNTON, Lynne, *La Femme dans la peinture orientaliste*, Paris, 1983.
THORNTON, Lynne, *Du Maroc aux Indes, voyages en Orient*, Paris, 1998.
TZIGAKOU, Fanny-Maria, *La Grèce retrouvée. Artistes et voyageurs des années romantiques*, Paris, 1984.
VATIN, Jean-Claude (ed.), *D'un Orient à l'autre. Les Métamorphoses successives des perceptions et connaissances*, Paris, 1991.
VERTOUTTER, Jean, *À la recherche de l'Égypte oubliée*, Paris, 1986.

(II) Exhibitions (in order of date)

Exposition du centenaire de la conquête de l'Algérie, 1830–1930, Palace of Fine Art, Paris, May–June 1930.
Bonaparte en Égypte, Paris, Musée de l'Orangerie, 1938.
Orient–Occident. Rencontres et influences durant 50 siècles d'art, Paris, Cernuschi Museum, 1958–1959.
Occident–Orient. L'art moderne et l'art islamique, Strasbourg, Ancienne Douane, 1972.
Équivoques, Peintures françaises du XIXe siècle, Paris, Musée des Arts Decoratifs, 1973.
Le Musée du Luxembourg en 1874. Peintures, Paris, Grand Palais, 1974.
De David à Delacroix. Le peinture française de 1774 à 1830, Paris, Grand Palais, 1974–1975.
L'Orient en question. De Missolonghi à Suez, ou l'orientalisme de Delacroix à Flaubert, Marseilles, Cantini Museum, 1975.
Une autre XIXe siècle. Peintures et sculptures de la collection Tanenbaum, Ottowa, 1978.
L'Orientalisme dans les collection du Musée de Tours, Tours,

Museum of Fine Art, 1980.
Orientalism: The Near East in French Painting, 1800–1880, Rochester, Memorial Art Gallery of the University of Rochester, 1982.
Orients. Collection du XIXe siècle. Nantes, Museum of Fine Art, 1982.
The Islamic Perspective: An Aspect of British Architecture and Design in the Nineteenth Century, London, Leighton House, 1983.
The Inspiration of Egypt: Its Influence on British Artists, Travellers, and Designers 1700–1900, Royal Pavilion, Brighton, 1983.
Les Orientalistes provençaux. Orient réel et mythique, Marseilles, Borély Museum, 1982–1983.
L'Aquarelle en France au XIXe siècle, Paris, Musée du Louvre, 1983.
Les Peintres orientalistes, 1850–1914, Pau, Museum of Fine Art; Dunkirk, Museum of Fine Art; Douai, Musée de la Chartreuse, 1983.
The Orientalists: Delacroix to Matisse, London, Royal Academy of Art, 1984.
Peintres dans la lumière de la Méditerranée, Jerusalem and Marseilles, 1987.
Lord Byron. Une vie romantique, Paris, Maison Renan-Scheffer, Museum of Romantic Life, 1988.
The East: Imagined, Experienced, Remembered. Orientalist Nineteenth Century Painting, Dublin, The National Gallery of Ireland, 1988.
Pintura orientalista española (1830–1930), Madrid, Fundación Banco Exterior, 1988.
Europa und der Orient (1800–1900), Berlin, Martin-Gropius-Bau, 1989.
La Peinture française du XIXe siècle. Collection Chester Beatty de la Galerie nationale d'Irlande, Calais, Quimper and Poitiers, 1989.
La Tradition et l'innovation dans l'art français par les peintres des Salon, Fukuoka (Japan), Municipal Museum, 1989.
Voyage en musique. Cent ans d'exotisme, Boulogne-Billancourt, Cultural Center, 1990.
Delacroix au Maroc. L'orientalisme au Musée Condé, Chantilly, Condé Museum, 1992.
Souvenirs de voyages. Autographes et dessins français du XIXe siècle, Paris, Musée du Louvre Department of Graphic Art, 1992.
Album de voyage. Des artistes en expédition au pays du Levant, Tel-Aviv, Museum of Art; Bayonne, Léon-Bonnat Museum; Paris, Hébert Museum, 1993.
Voyages d'opéra, Paris, Museum Library of the Paris Opera, 1993–1994.
Egyptomania. L'Égypte dans l'art occidental, 1730–1930, Paris, Musée du Louvre, 1994.
Les Oubliés du Caire. Chefs-d'œuvre des Musées du Caire, Paris, Musée d'Orsay, 1994–1995.
Le Baron Taylor, l'association des artistes et l'exposition du Bazar Bonne-Nouvelle en 1846, Paris, Taylor Foundation, 1995.
Peintres de la couleur en Provence, 1875–1920, Marseilles, Provence-Alpes Hotel, Côte d'Azur; Paris, Musée Luxemburg, 1995.
Les Années romantiques. La peinture française de 1815 à 1850, Nantes, Musée des Beaux-Arts; Paris, Grand Palais; Plaisance, Palazzo Gottico, 1996.
La Grèce en révolte. Delacroix et les peintres français, 1815–1848, Bordeaux, Museum of Fine Art, 1996; Paris, Eugène-Delacroix National Museum, 1996; Athens, Pinacothèque nationale, 1997.
Le Roman de la momie: les amours d'une princesse égyptienne, Saint-Gérard-de-Brogne (Belgique), 1997.
Gli orientalisti italiani, cento anni di esotismo, 1830–1940, Turin, Palazzo di Caccia di Stupinigi; Marsilio, Venise, 1998–1999.

(III) Individual artists

BELLY, Léon
Léon Bely, exhibition catalog, Saint-Omer, Musée de l'hôtel Sandelin, 1977.
BERNARD, Émile
Aquarelles orientales d'Émilie Bernard, 1893–1904, exhibition catalog, Saint-Germain-en-Laye, Musée du Prieuré, 1983–1984.
CAFFI, Ippolito
Ippolito Caffi, viaggio in Oriente, 1843–1844, exhibition catalog, Venice, Galleria d'arte Modern, Cà Pesaro, 1988.
CAMOIN, Charles
Charles Camoin, Rétrospective 1879–1965, exhibition catalog, Lausanne, Fondation de l'Hermitage; Musée de Marseille, 1997–1998.
Correspondance Charles Camoin–Henri Matisse, with an introduction by Claudine Grammont, Paris, 1997.
CHASSÉRIAU, Théodore
Prat, Louis-Antoine, *Musée du Louvre. Cabinet des dessins. Inventaire général des dessins. École française. Dessins de Théodore Chassériau (1819–1856)*, Paris, 1988.
Sandoz, Marc, *Théodore Chassériau. Catalog raisonné des peintures et estampes*, Paris, 1974.
COGNIET, Léon
Léon Cogniet, 1794–1880, exhibition catalogue, Orléans, Museum of Fine Art, 1990.
DADD, Richard
Allderidge, Patricia, *The Late Richard Dadd*, exhibition catalog, The Tate Gallery, London, 1974.
DAUZATS, Adrien
Adrien Dauzats ou la tentation de l'Orient, exhibition catalogue, Bordeaux, Museum of Fine Art, 1990.
Plazaola, Juan, *Le Baron Taylor. Portrait d'un homme d'avenir*, Paris, 1989.
DECAMPS, Alexandre-Gabriel
Alexandre-Gabriel Decamps, 1803–1960, exhibition catalog, Williamstown (Massachusetts), Sterline and Francine Clark Art Institute, 1984.
Mosby, Dewey, *Alexandre-Gabriel Decamps*, New York, 1977.
DEHODENCQ, Alfred
Séailles, Gabriel, *Alfred Dehodencq: histoire d'un coloriste*, Paris, 1885.
DELACROIX, Eugène
Delacroix, Eugène, *Selected Letters, 1813–1863*, edited and translated by Jean Stewart, London, 1971.
Delacroix, Eugène. *Journal*, translated by Lucy Norton, London, 1951.
Delacroix in Morocco, exhibition catalog, Paris, Institut du Monde Arabe, 1994–1995.
Delacroix, Eugène, *Souvenirs d'un voyage dans le Maroc*, edition of Laure Beaumont-Maillet, Barthélémy Jobert and Sophie Join-Lambert, Paris, 1999.
Daguerre de Hureaux et Guégan, Stéphane, *ABCédaire de Delacroix et l'Orient*, Paris, 1994.
Dumur, Guy, *Delacroix et la Maroc*, Paris, 1988.
Guégan, Stéphane, *Delacroix et les Orientales*, Paris, 1994
Johnson, Lee, *The Paintings of Eugène Delacroix. A Critical Catalog*, Oxford, 1981–1989.
Sérullaz, Maurice, *Inventaire général des dessins. École française. Dessins d'Eugène Delacroix (1798–1863)*, Paris, 1984.
DEL RE, Marco
Lemaire, Gérard-Georges, *Del Re, La Ville d'or*, exhibition catalog, Tarascon, Château du roi René; Saragossa, Pablo Gargallo Museum, 1989.
DINET, Étienne
Brahimi, Denise and Benchikou, Koudir, *La Vie et l'œuvre d'Étienne Dinet*, Paris, 1984.
DUBUFFET, Jean
I Dubuffet di Dubuffet, exhibition catalog, Milan, Spazio Oberdan, 2000.
DUFY, Raoul
Cogniat, Raymond, *Raoul Dufy*, Paris, 1962.
Pérez-Tibi, Dora and Forneris, Jean, *L'ABCédaire de Dufy*, Paris, 1997.
DUPRÉ, Louis
Dupré, Louis, *Voyage à Athènes et à Constantinople*, Paris, 1825.
FORTUNY, Mariano
Davillier, Baron C., *Fortuny, sa vie, son œuvre, sa correspondance*, Paris, 1875.
Fortuny (1838–1874), exhibition catalog, Barcelona, Cultural Centre of the Caixa de Pensions Foundation, 1989.
FROMENTIN, Eugène
Beaume, Georges, *Fromentin*, Paris, *Colloque Eugene Fromentin*, Lille, 1979.
Eugène Fromentin au Musée des Beaux-Arts de La Rochelle, catalog, La Rochelle, Museum of Fine Art, 1988.
Fromentin, Eugène, *Correspondance*, colleced texts categorized and annotated by Barbara Wright, Paris, 1995.
Fromentin, Eugène, *Œuvres complètes*, established texts, introduced and annotated by Guy Sagnes, Paris, 1984.
Wright, Barbara, *Eugène Fromentin: A Biography*, London, 1973.
GÉRÔME, Jean-Léon
Ackerman, Gerald, "Gérôme's Oriental Paintings and the Western Genre Tradition," *Arts Magazine*, March 1986, pp. 75–80.
Ackerman, Gerald, *Jean-Léon Gérôme: His Life, His Work*, Paris, 1987.
Jean-Léon Gérôme (1824–1904), catalog, Dayton, The Dayton Art Institute, 1972; Minneapolis, The Minneapolis Institute of Arts, 1973.
Leonoir, Paul-Marie, *Le Fayoum, le Sinaï et Petra. Expédition dans la Moyenne Égypte et l'Arabie Pétrée sous la direction de J. L. Gérôme*, Paris, 1872.
GIRODET DE ROUCY-TRIOSON, Anne-Louise (Girodet-Trioson)
Coupin, P. A., *Œuvres posthumes de Girodet-Trioson, peintre d'histoire, suivies de sa correspondance, précédée d'une notice historique*, Paris, 1829.
Girodet, 1767–1824, exhibition catalog, Montagris, Girodet Museum, 1967.
GROS, Antoine-Jean
Gros, ses amis, ses élèves, exhibition catalog, Paris, Petit Palais, 1936.

Lemonnier, Henri, *Gros*, Paris, 1907.
Tripier Le Franc, J., *Histoire de la vie et de la mort du Baron Gros*, Paris, 1880.
GUIGNET, Adrien
Adrien Guignet (1816–1854), exhibition catalog, Autun, Rolin Museum; Annecy Château Museum, 1978.
GUILLAUMET, Gustave
Guillaumet, Gustave, *Tableaux algériens*, Paris, 1888.
GÜRBÜZ, Selma
Lemaire, Gérard-Georges, *Selma Gürbüz, Jeux de mains*, exhibition catalog, Paris, Thorigny Gallery, 1992.
Lemaire, Gérard-Georges, *Selma Gürbüz, La Mille et troisième nuit*, preface by Jean-François Bory and Bernard Comment, exhibition catalog, Paris, Thorigny Gallery, 1994.
Lemaire, Gérard-Georges, *Selma Gürbüz, Magie grise*, exhibition catalog, Prague, French Institute, 1996.
HAMDI, Osman
Cezar, Mustafa and Edgü, Ferit, *Osman Hamdi, Bilinmeyen resimleri*, Istanbul, 1986.
Osman Hamdi ve sanayi-I nefise mektebi, "Toplu Sergiler" 8, Istanbul, 1983.
HUNT, William Holman
Amor, Ann Clark, *William Holman Hunt, The True Pre-Raphaelite*, introduction by Diana Holman-Hunt, London, 1989.
Hunt, William Holman, *Pre-Raphaelitism and the Pre-Raphaelite Brotherhood*, London, 1905.
The Orientalists: Delacrox to Matisse, exhibition catalog, London, Royal Academy of Art, 1984.
The Pre-Raphaelites, exhibition catalogue, London, The Tate Gallery, 1984.
William Holman Hunt, exhibition catalogue, Liverpool, Walker Art Gallery; London, Victoria and Albert Museum, 1969.
INGRES, Jean Auguste Dominique
Bajou, Valérie, *Monsieur Ingres*, Paris.
Ingres, catalog, Paris, Petit Palais, 1967–68.
Le Bain turc d'Ingres, Les Dossier du département des peintures, no. 1, exhibition catalog, Paris, Louvre Museum, 1971.
Rosenblum, Robert, *Ingres*, New York, 1967.
Schlenoff, Norman, *Ingres, ses sources littéraires*, Paris, 1956.
Vigne, Georges, *Ingres*, Paris, 1995.
Wildenstein, Georges, *Ingres*, London, 1954.
ISABEY, Eugène
Miquel, Pierre, *Eugène Isabey, La marine au XIXe siècle*, Maurs-la-Jolie, 1980.
KANDINSKY, Wassily
Kandinsky: collections du Centre Georges Pompidou, Musée national d'Art moderne, exhibition catalog, Nantes, Museum of Fine Art, 1998.
Kandinsky et la Russie, exhibition catalog, Martigny, Pierre Gianadda Foundation
KLEE, Paul
Klee, Paul, *Journal*, Paris, 1959.
Grohmann, Will, *Paul Klee*, Cologne, 1951.
Ferrier, Jean-Louis, *Paul Klee*, Paris, 1998.
LAURENS, Jules
Labande, L. H., *Jules Laurens*, Paris, 1910.
Laurens, Jules, *La Légende des ateliers. Fragments et notes d'un artiste peintre de 1842 à 1900*, Carpentras, 1901.
LEAR, Edward
Hofer, Philip, *Edward Lear as a Landscape Draughtsman*, Cambridge (Mass.), 1968
Hyman, Susan, *Edward Lear in the Levant: Travels in Albania, Greece and Turkey, 1848–1849*, London, 1988.
Lehmann, J., *Lear and His World*, London, 1977.
Travellers, Beyond the Grand Tour, The Fine Art Society, 1980.
LECOMTE DU NOÜY, Jean-Jules Antoine
Montgailhard, G. de, *Lecomte du Noüy*, Paris, 1906.
Souvenirs de voyages, exhibition catalog, Paris, Hahn Gallery, 1995.
LÉVY, Henri-Léopold
Henri Lévy et la tentation symboliste. Peintures, dessins, exhibition catalog, Nancy, Musée des Beaux-Arts, 1996.
LEWIS, John Frederick
John Frederick Lewis, R.A. (1805–1876), Orientalist and Animal Lover, exhibition catalog, London, The Tate Gallery, 1985.
Lewis, Michael, *John Frederick Lewis R.A.*, Leigh on Sea, 1978.
LEWIS, Percy Wyndham
Lemaire, Gérard-Georges, *Wyndham Lewis et le vorticisme*, Paris and Aix-en-Provence, 1982.
Michel, Walter, *Wyndham Lewis, Paintings and Drawings*, introduction by Hugh Kenner, London, 1971.
Tomlin, E. W. F., *Wyndham Lewis, an Anthology of his Prose*, London, 1969.
MACKE, August
Mœller, Magdalena, M., *August Macke, le Voyage en Tunisie*, Paris, 1991
MARILHAT, Prosper
Menu, Danièle, "L'Orient de Prosper Marilhat d'après quelques inédits," *L'Information d'histoire de l'art*, 1973,
pp. 62–69.
Prosper Marilhat, exhibition catalog, Clermont-Ferrand, Bargoin Museum, 1973.
MARQUET, Albert
Marquet, exhibition catalog, Bordeaux, Gallery of Fine Art, 1975–1976.
Marquet, exhibition catalog, Milan, Lodève Museum, 1998.
MATISSE, Henri
Flam, Jack D., "Matisse in Morocco," *Connoisseur*, vol. CCXI, 1982, pp. 65–71.
Le Maroc de Matisse, exhibition catalog, Paris, Institute of the Arab World, 1999–2000.
Matisse au Maroc, peintures et dessins, 1912–1913, Paris, 1999.
Matisse in Morocco: The Paintings and Drawings, 1912–1913, exhibition catalog, Washington, National Gallery of Art, 1990.
Schneider, Pierre, *Matisse*, Paris, 1984.
MIRA, Victor
Lemaire, Gérard-Georges, *Victor Mira*, exhibition catalog, Barcelona, Carlos Taché Gallery, 1989.
MONDINO, Aldo
Lemaire, Gérard-Georges, *Mondino, The Sultans*, New York, Sperone Westwater Gallery, 1990.
Mondino, The Sultans, historical notes by Paolo Maltese, exhibition catalog, New York, Sperone Westwater Gallery, 1990.
MOREAU, Gustave
Lacambre, Geneviève, *Gustave Moreau, 1826–1898*, exhibition catalog, Paris, Grand Palais, 1998.
Mathieu, Pierre-Louis, *Gustave Moreau*, Oxford, 1977.
PASINI, Alberto
Botteri Cardoso, Vittoria, *Pasini*, Genoa, 1991.
PRECIOZI, comte Amedeo
The People & Places of Constantinople, Watercolors by Amedeo Count Preciozi, exhibition catalog, London, Victoria and Albert Museum, 1985.
REGNAULT, Henri
Duparc, Arthur, *Correspondance de Henri Regnault*, Paris, 1872.
Henri Regnault (1843–1871), exhibition catalog, Saint-Cloud, Municipal Museum, 1991.
RENOIR, Auguste
Renoir, exhibition catalog, London, Hayward Gallery; Paris, Grand Palais; Boston, Museum of Fine Arts, 1985–1986.
Renoir en Italie et en Algérie, preface by Albert André, introduction by Georges Besson, Paris, 1955.
ROBERTS, David
David Roberts, Artist Adventurer, 1796–1864, exhibition catalog, Scottish Arts Council, 1980–81.
David Roberts, exhibition catalog, London, Barbican Art Gallery, 1986.
Guiterman, Helen, *The Life of David Roberts, R.A., 1796–1864*, London, 1978.
Rachet, Guy and Simoën, Jean-Claude, *David Roberts. Voyage en Égypte*, Paris, 1992.
SARGENT, John Singer
Elaine Kilmurray and Richard Ormond, *Sargent*, exhibition catalog, London, The Tate Gallery, 1998–1999.
Ormond, R., *John Singer Sargent*, London and New York, 1970.
VAN DONGEN, Kees
Chaumeil, Louis, *Van Dongen, l'homme et l'artiste, la vie et l'œuvre*, Geneva, 1967.
Diehl, Gaston, *Van Dongen*, Paris, 1976.
VERNET, Horace
Blanc, Charles, *Une famille d'artistes. Les trois Vernet, Joseph, Carle, Horace*, Paris, [1898].
Durande, Amédée, *Joseph, Carle et Horace Vernet*, Paris, 1863.
Goupil-Fesquet, Frédéric, *Voyage d'Horace Vernet en Orient*, Paris, 1843.
Horace Vernet, 1789–1863, exhibition catalog, Rome, Academy of France; Paris, National School of Fine Art, 1980.
WILKIE, David
Cunningham, Alan, *The Life of Sir David Wilkie*, London, 1843.
Sir David Wilkie of Scotland (1785–1841), exhibition catalog, Raleigh, North Carolina Museum of Art, 1987.
ZIEM, Félix
Félix Ziem, peintre voyageur, 1821–1911. Peintures, exhibition catalog, Martigues, Ziem Museum, 1994.
Miquel, Pierre, *Félix Ziem, 1821–1911*, Maurs-la-Jolie, 1978.
Ziem, Félix, *Journal, 1854–1898*, texts compiled by S. Biass-Fabiani and G. Fabre, Arles, 1994.

Glossary

ACADEMY (Latin academia, Greek akademia), body, institution or society for the promotion of artistic or academic study and education. The term "academy" is believed to refer to a garden near Athens which was dedicated to the Attic hero Academus and contained facilities for gymnastic training. A favorite spot of Plato, he named the school of philosophy which he established in 387 B.C. after it. The idea of the academy spread throughout Europe during the period of absolutism. The main models for the establishment of academies are the Académie Française, founded in 1635, and the Académie Royale de Peinture et de Sculpture, 1648. The term "academic" style is frequently used in comparison to the innovative movements of Impressionism, Expressionism, and the Secession and refers to a more conservative, static form of painting according to tradition.

ANCIEN RÉGIME (French "old regime"), refers particularly to the absolutist form of government in the 17th and 18th centuries, against which the French Revolution of 1789 rebelled.

BERBER A collective term for the different ethnic groups of North Africa, most likely of European-Mediterranean descent, who speak Berber dialects. With the Arabic invasion in the 8th century, the Berbers converted to Islam.

CALIPH/CALIPHATE (Arabic, "successor, representative") An Islamic title for a ruler. According to the dominant Sunni point of view, the caliph was a successor to the prophet Muhammad. However, Umayyad and subsequent caliphs were regarded as God's representatives or God's shadows on earth. Their claim to an all-encompassing religious authority could not be enforced in practice. The dispute over the successor of the prophet, who had not established any prescriptions for this before he died, was the cause for the greatest schism in Islam – mainly between the two most prominent strands of Muslim faith, the Sunnis and the Shiites.

CASBAH (Arabic: Qasaba,) A castle or fortress (citadel) in the cities of the North Africa.

CLASSICAL Relating to the culture of ancient Greece and Rome (classical antiquity). The classical world played a profoundly important role in the Renaissance, with Italian scholars, writers, and artists seeing their own period as the rebirth (the "renaissance") of classical values after the Middle Ages. The classical world was considered the golden age for the arts, literature, philosophy, and politics. Concepts of the classical, however, changed greatly from one period to the next. Roman literature provided the starting point in the 14th century, scholars patiently finding, editing and translating a wide range of texts. In the 15th century Greek literature, philosophy and art – together with the close study of the remains of Roman buildings and sculptures – expanded the concept of the classical and ensured it remained a vital source of ideas and inspiration.

COPPERPLATE ENGRAVING A method of printing using a copper plate into which a design has been cut by a sharp instrument such as a burin; an engraving produced in this way.

COPTIC CHRISTIANS The Coptic Church is the national church of Egypt. It rejected the resolutions laid down by the Council of Chalcedon (451), according to which Christ was declared a single person with two natures, one divine and one human. The Coptic Christians continued to practice monophysitism, i.e. the view that Christ is not only one person, but also only had one nature. Following the Arabic conquest of Egypt in 640, the Copts were extensively arabized, but have still been able to retain their characteristic individuality to the present day.

CUBISM (Latin: cubus, "cube") Stylistic direction after 1907, in which the natural forms are reduced to their basic cubic structure. Picasso, Braque and Delaunay are the main proponents.

DER BLAUE REITER The title of an 1910 almanac with art historical texts edited by Wassily Kandinsky and Franz Marc. The name later became synonymous with an artistic movement, which under the influence of Cubism turned against the academic painting styles and Impressionism. The movement was concerned with the search for an abstract visual vocabulary and the expression of the "spiritual essence" of art.

DERVISH (Persian, "poor") The members of an Islamic order who live according to the vows of poverty. Through religious training they endeavor to reduce their bodily functions in order to free the soul from all physical compulsions. This includes 40 days of intense meditation with fasting and little sleep. In some orders listening to music and the dhikr, a combination of prayer and invocations of God with physical movement, are also practiced.

ENGRAVING A print made from a metal plate that has had a design cut into it with a sharp point. Ink is smeared over the plate and then wiped off, the ink remaining in the etched lines is transferred when the plate is pressed very firmly onto a sheet of paper.

FAUVISM (French: les Fauves, "the wild ones") In the first decade of the 20th century, Henri Matisse and a group of Post-Impressionists initiated the movement in French painting which rejected the representation of dimensionality and spatiality in favor of pure color.

FUTURISM A modern art movement in Italy prior to World War I focused on the celebration of machines and the future.

GENRE PAINTING The depiction of scenes from everyday life, appropriate to a particular time and place. Most commonly associated with depictions of domestic interiors.

GOUACHE Opaque watercolor. The paint differs from transparent watercolor in that the pigments are bound with glue and the ligh ter tones are obtained by mixing white pigment.

GRAND TOUR An expression from the 18th century used to denote a trip by educated art-lovers to Italy. In the 19th century, the term was used to denote any journeys serving to promote artistic refinement or education in general. Destinations were expanded to include oriental countries and Egypt, as well as Spain and Greece.

GRISAILLE (French: gris, "gray") Painting in gray monochrome; a type of painting that deliberately omitted colors and only used stone colors, shades of brown or gray. It was often used in paintings to imitate stone sculptures.

HAMMAM (Arabic, "to warm") A structural design for a bath house dating back to antiquity. The bath house could be erected as an independent structure or as part of a palace complex. The main rooms are the frigidarium (cold bath), the caldarium (warm bath), and the harara (sweating room). In the middle of the building is a large central domed room surrounded by smaller domed rooms. In the Islamic world the bath house is still a part of daily life.

HISTORY PAINTING Genre of painting concerned with the representation of scenes from the Bible, history (usually classical history), and classical literature. From the Renaissance to the 19th century it was considered the highest form of painting, its subjects considered morally elevating. It was typical of the "academic style."

LEVANT (Latin, Italian: from levarsi, "to stand up, rise [sun]") Designation for the countries in the eastern part of the Mediterranean (Turkey, Syria, Lebanon, Israel, Egypt, Cyprus). As a passageway for the main trading routes, the Levant was a fiercely contested area. During the Crusades, Crusader nation states were established in parts of the territory, which were only able to withstand the superior strength of the Muslims for a few years. The last areas of occupation were Antioch, which survived until 1268, Tarabulus (Lebanon) until 1289, and Acre, which fell in 1291.

MANNERISM A movement in Italian art from about 1520 to 1600. Developing out of the Renaissance, Mannerism rejected Renaissance balance and harmony in favor of emotional intensity and ambiguity. The term has been extended to cover any form of art where the subject is expressed mainly through severe distortions of perspective and scale; complex and crowded compositions; strong, sometimes harsh or discordant colors; and elongated figures in exaggerated poses.

MEDINA (Arabic, "town") The word medina designates whole towns or parts of towns.

MINARET (Arabic: manara, "place where fire or light is") A tower-shaped building either erected on its own or as a component of the Friday mosque, from which the daily calls to prayer are made.

MOORS (Spanish: moriscos) The Muslims in Spain forcibly converted to Christianity after 1492 who, although baptized as Christians, still observed their Muslim beliefs in secret. At the start of the 17th century they were finally expelled from Spain – mostly to North Africa, but also to the Ottoman empire and France.

MOSQUE (Arabic: masjid, Turkish: cami, "place of prostration") The general term masjid refers to mosques that could be used every day. The communal Friday worship is held in the particularly important Friday (or congregational) mosques. The meaning of the word as a place where one prostrates oneself in prayer leaves worshippers free to choose where they pray and is not linked to any particular building; even the Koran leaves no instructions on any given form of place for praying. Muhammad's house in Medina became the starting point for the development of the Arab courtyard mosque. This house resembled those from the Arab Peninsula, with an open rectangular, walled courtyard within a square ground plan. The courtyard mosque included some elements of the original house type: in front of the qibla wall, indicating the direction of prayer, a prayer hall was built with many pillars and aisles, and in front of this was an open area. Each mosque was also supplemented by one or several minarets.

MUSLIM (Arabic, "devotion to God") The one who practices the devotion to God is a Muslim. The acceptance of Islam is fulfilled with the profession of the faith (shahada). The shahada is the first of the five pillars of Islam – followed by worship (salat), giving alms (zakat), fasting (saum) and the pilgrimage to Mecca (hajj).

NEO-CLASSICISM The dominant movement in European art and architecture in the late 18th and early 19th centuries, characterized by the desire to recreate the spirit of classical Greece and Rome. The interest in classical art was revived by the discoveries at Pompeii and Herculaneum. The order, clarity, and reason of Greek and Roman art reflected the convictions of the Enlightenment and was associated with a change of social outlook and a desire to restore the strong classical values to everyday life. The painting of Jacques Louis David is exemplary for the period style.

ODALISQUE (Turkish-French, "for the private chamber intended") An odalisque was a white, Turkish lady of the harem. The figure became a popular motif in painting when Ingres presented her in his painting *Grande Odalisque* in 1814. The work was the result of his search for a new possibility of depicting a beautiful nude woman without having to integrate her into a historical narrative. Even into the 20th century, many painters – such as Picasso, Matisse, Courbet and Manet – took this as an example. Particularly in the face of prudish bourgeois such Oriental subjects enabled artists to present sensuality and eroticism to a larger public.

ORIENTALISM A special form of a general exotic trend in European art in the 18th and 19th centuries. Oriental influences were introduced to European art and culture through travel descriptions and the opening of the Near East and Egypt for scientific and archeological purposes. The fascination for all things oriental culminated in the 19th century in French painting. The thematic spectrum reached from realistic genre paintings of everyday life and interior scenes to imaginary landscapes and Biblical representations.

PASHA (Persian: from padishah, "great ruler") A title for high-ranking Ottoman dignitaries. In the Turkish Republic, the title was replaced by the position of general.

PRE-RAPHAELITES English artistic circle in the mid-19th century. William Morris and John Ruskin were the most significant proponents of the group. They rejected the academic painting of their time and adopted the Italian Renaissance painting from the time prior to Raphael as their role model.

ROMANTICISM Artistic movement in the late 18th and early 19th centuries. The movement had various manifestations, but the main emphasis was on individual experience. It formed a reaction to the rationalism of Neo-classicism. Both the Romantic and the Classical artist focus on ideals, but whereas the classical artist concentrates on real possibilities for improving society, the Romantic envisages the unattainable, beyond the limits of society and human adaptability. Romanticism is an attitude rather than a set of stylistic traits and is the outgrowth of an expression that tends to be more narrative than visual. Hence, a ruined temple is more significant in the eyes of the Romantic than a new one because it is more suggestive of the passage of time and human frailty. Romantic art reflects the infinite and the transcendental, forces exceeding the boundaries of reason, and essences that are ambiguous rather than concrete.

SHARIF (Arabic, "noble, sublime") In pre-Islamic times, a term used to denote those of noble descent and distinguished character. In Islam, sharif became an honorary title for a man who could trace his genealogy back to Muhammad and his family.

SOUK (Arabic) A market or bazaar in the older part of the city. Usually characterized by narrow winding streets.

SULTAN (Arabic, "authority and rule") Islamic title of authority, which was already applied in the 10th century to independent rulers, who did not come under the control of the central power of the caliph. The title was not officially recognized until the 11th century, when it was adopted by the Turkish dynasty of the Seljuks, in order to emphasize their claim to universal dominion. All the Ottoman rulers were also called Sultans.

VEDUTA (Italian, "view") A primarily topographical representation of a town or landscape that is depicted in such a life-like manner that the location can be identified.

Index

Picture Credits

p. 6 : National Portrait Gallery, Smithsonian Institution (Washington)
p. 9 : Musée des Beaux-Arts, La Chaux-de-Fonds
p. 10 : RMN – R.G. Ojeda, Paris
p. 11 : Marseille, Musée des Beaux-Arts / Giraudon
p. 12-13 :, RMN – R.G. Ojeda, Paris
p. 14-15 : Marseille, Musée des Beaux-Arts / Giraudon
p. 16-17 : Lauros-Giraudon / ADAGP
p. 18 : RMN – G. Blot
p. 19 : AKG Paris
p. 21 : AKG Paris
p. 22-23 : Scala, Florence
p. 24-25 : AKG Paris
p. 26 : RMN – G. Blot, Paris
p. 27 b. : AKG Paris
p. 28 : AKG Paris
p. 29 : Scala, Florence
p. 30 : AKG Paris / Cameraphoto
p. 31 : Alinari – Giraudon
p. 33 : Quimper, Musée des Beaux-Arts / Giraudon
p. 34-35 : Musée des Beaux-Arts de Rennes / Giraudon
p. 36 : © Yves Delfour/musée de Périgueux
p. 37 : Scala, Florence
p. 38-39 : AKG Paris
p. 40 : RMN – C. Jean, Paris
p. 41 : Studio Image'in, Montluçon
p. 42 : AKG Paris
p. 43 : AKG Paris
p. 44 : Bridgeman-Giraudon, Paris
p. 45 : Petit Palais, Musée des Beaux-Arts de la Ville de Paris / Giraudon
p. 46 : Giraudon, Paris
p. 47 : RMN – Arnaudet ; Schormans, Paris, Paris
p. 49 : Musée du Petit-Palais / Giraudon, Paris
p. 50-51 : Photo Scala, Florence
p. 52 : Musée des Beaux-Arts, Nice – © M. de Lorenzo
p. 53 : Rouen, musée des Beaux-Arts / Lauros-Giraudon
p. 54 : RMN – G. Blot, Paris
p. 55 : RMN – G. Blot, Paris
p. 56 : RMN – Berizzi, Paris
p. 58 t. l. : Musée des Beaux-Arts, Nice – © M. de Lorenzo
p. 58-59 : RMN – Arnaudet ; Schormans, Paris
p. 60 : Bridgeman-Giraudon, Paris
p. 61 : RMN, Paris
p. 62 : RMN – Hervé Lewandowski, Paris
p. 63 : RMN – Hervé Lewandowski, Paris
p. 64-65 : RMN – Arnaudet, Paris
p. 65 t. r. : AKG Paris
p. 65 b. r. : AKG Paris
p. 66 : By Courtesy of the National Portrait Gallery, London
p. 67 : RMN – R.G. Ojeda, Paris
p. 69 : Petit Palais, Musée des Beaux-Arts de la Ville de Paris / Giraudon
p. 70 : Giraudon, Paris
p. 71 : Giraudon, Paris
p. 72 : Scala, Florence
p. 73 : Scala, Florence
p. 74 : Giraudon, Paris
p. 75 : Giraudon, Paris
p. 76-77 : RMN – Michèle Bellot, Paris
p. 78-79 : RMN – Michèle Bellot, Paris
p. 80-81 : Musée des Beaux-Arts de Tours – Photo Boyer
p. 82-83 : RMN – Lagiewski, Paris
p. 84 : Jacqueline Hiegel – Giraudon, Paris
p. 85 t. : Bridgeman-Giraudon, Paris
p. 85 b. : RMN – Arnaudet, Paris
p. 86 : A. Guillard – Ville de Nantes – Musée des Beaux-Arts
p. 87 : Studio Basset, Lyon
p. 89 : Courtesy of the Trustees of the V&A, London
p. 91 : J. Hyde
p. 92 t. : The British Museum, London
p. 92 b. : The British Museum, London
p. 93 : RMN – M. Bellot, Paris
p. 94-95 : J. Hyde
p. 96-97 : RMN – R.G. Ojeda, Paris
p. 98 : RMN – Arnaudet ; J. Schormans, Paris
p. 99 : RMN – Michèle Bellot, Paris
p. 100-101 : RMN – Peter Willi, Paris
p. 102-103 : RMN – Musée de Nantes
p. 103 t. : RMN, Paris
p. 103 b. : RMN – Arnaudet / J. Schormans, Paris
p. 104 : RMN – Arnaudet / J. Schormans, Paris
p. 105 : RMN – Arnaudet / J. Schormans, Paris
p. 106-107 : RMN – Gérard Blot, Paris
p. 108 : Mulhouse, Musée des Beaux-Arts / Giraudon
p. 109 : RMN – C. Jean, Paris
p. 110 t. : Bridgeman-Giraudon, Paris
p. 110 b. : Bridgeman-Giraudon, Paris
p. 111 : AKG Paris
p. 112 : City of Bristol Museum and Art Gallery / Bridgeman-Giraudon
p. 113 t. : AKG Paris
p. 113 b. : AKG Paris
p. 114-115 : AKG Paris
p. 116 t. : Board of Trustees of the National Museums and Galleries (Walker Art Gallery, Liverpool)
p. 116 b. : Osvaldo Böhm, Venice
p. 117 : AKG Paris
p. 118-119 : City of Bristol Museum and Art Gallery / Bridgeman-Giraudon, Paris
p. 120 : Bequest of Mrs. Martin Brimmer / Courtesy, Museum of Fine Arts, Boston
p. 121 t. : RMN, Paris
p. 121 b. : J. Hyde
p. 122 : RMN – P. Bernard, Paris
p. 123 : RMN – C. Jean, Paris
p. 124 : J. Hyde
p. 124-125 : RMN – C. Jean, Paris
p. 126-127 : Lauros-Giraudon
p. 128 : City of Bristol Museum and Art Gallery / Bridgeman-Giraudon
p. 129 : Scala, Florence
p. 130 : Private Collection, London
p. 131 : London, Victoria and Albert Museum / Bridgeman-Giraudon
p. 132 : with permission of Mr. Gros and Delettrez, Paris – ArtGo (Marc Guermeur)
p. 133 : Dahesh Museum, New York
p. 134 : The Withworth Art Gallery, The University of Manchester
p. 135 : Artephot/Bridgeman
p. 136 : Musée du Vieux-Château, Laval, Leportier, Laval
p. 137 : Musée des Beaux-Arts, Nice – © M. de Lorenzo
p. 138 : Artephot-Bridgeman
p. 139 : AKG Paris
p. 140 : AKG Paris
p. 141 l. : AKG Paris
p. 141 r. : AKG Paris
p. 142 : Artephot-Bridgeman
p. 143 : with the permission of Mr. Gros and Delettrez, Paris – Ph. Sebert
p. 144 : RMN – Gérard Blot, Paris
p. 145 : RMN – Jean Schormans, Paris
p. 147 : RMN – Hervé Lewandowski, Paris
p. 148 : Musée des Beaux-Arts, Bordeaux
p. 150 : Alinari-Giraudon, Paris
p. 151 : Scala, Florence
p. 152 : Bulloz, Paris
p. 153 : Musée des Beaux-Arts – Ville de Nantes – P. Jean
p. 154 : RMN – Gérard Blot, Paris
p. 154-155 : Bridgeman-Giraudon, Paris
p. 156 : Private collection, London
p. 157 : RMN – Arnaudet, Paris
p. 158 : Studio Basset, Lyon
p. 159 t. : RMN – Lagiewski, Paris
p. 159 b. : Saint-Étienne, Musée d'Art Moderne – Photo Yves Bresson
p. 160 t. : RMN – Jean Schormans, Paris
p. 160 b. : RMN – Hervé Lewandowski, Paris
p. 161 t. : RMN – Hervé Lewandowski, Paris
p. 161 b. : RMN – Hervé Lewandowski, Paris
p. 162 : RMN – Hervé Lewandowski, Paris
p. 163 : RMN – Gérard Blot / Jean Schormans, Paris
p. 164 : National Gallery of Scotland
p. 164-165 : Musées royaux des Beaux-Arts de Belgique, Bruxelles – Photo Speltdoorn
p. 166 : RMN – Bellot, Paris
p. 167 t. : RMN – Bellot, Paris
p. 167 b. : RMN – Hervé Lewandowski, Paris
p. 168 t. : Scala, Florence
p. 168 b. : J. Hyde
p. 169 : Musée des Beaux-Arts de la Ville de Reims – Photo Devleeschauwer
p. 170 : RMN – Gérard Blot, Paris
p. 171 : Musée Salies, Bagnères de Bigorre
p. 172-173 : Musée des Beaux-Arts, Nice – © M. de Lorenzo
p. 174 : Scala, Florence
p. 175 t. : RMN – Hervé Lewandowski
p. 175 b. : AKG Paris
p. 176-177 : Bridgeman-Giraudon, Paris
p. 178 : The Nelson-Atkins Museum of Art, Kansas City, Missouri (Gift of the Enid and Crosby Kemper Foundation)
p. 179 : Manchester City Art Gallerie
p. 180 : AKG Paris
p. 181 : Bridgeman-Giraudon
p. 182-183 : Scala, Florence
p. 184 : Scala, Florence
p. 185 : Reproduction of *The Rest in Egypt* by courtesy of the National Gallery of Ireland
p. 186 : Preston, Harris Museum and Art Gallery
p. 187 : Manchester city Art Galleries
p. 188 t. : Musée des Augustins © B. Delorme
p. 188 b. : Musée Fabre, Montpellier – Frédéric Jaulmes
p. 189 t. : RMN – Jean Schormans, Paris
p. 189 b. : Scala, Florence
p. 190-191 : National Gallery of Scotland
p. 192 t. : Musée Georges Garret, Vesoul

© Studio Fotografico Elli Manzotti
p. 193 : RMN – Hervé Lewandowski, Paris
p. 194 l. : Musée des Beaux-Arts – A. Guillard – Ville de Nantes
p. 194-195 : J. Hyde
p. 196 t. : Lauros-Giraudon / All rights reserved
p. 196 b. : © Musée des Beaux-Arts de la Ville de Reims – Devleeschauwer
p. 197 : P. Jean – Ville de Nantes – Musée des Beaux-Arts
p. 198 : Scala, Florence
p. 199 : RMN – Arnaudet – Schormans, Paris
p. 200-201 : RMN – Hervé Lewandowski, Paris
p. 202 : J. Hyde
p. 203 : RMN – Gérard Blot, Paris
p. 204 l. : Photograph courtesy of the Art Institute of Chicago
p. 204-205 : RMN – Hervé Lewandowski, Paris
p. 206 t. : RMN – J. G. Berizzi, Paris
p. 206 b. : RMN – Michèle Bellot, Paris
p. 207 t. : RMN – R. G. Ojeda, Paris
p. 207 b. : RMN – Jean Schormans, Paris
p. 208 : RMN – J. G. Berizzi, Paris
p. 209 t. : RMN – C. Jean, Paris
p. 209 b. : RMN – A. Danvers, Paris
p. 210 : Giraudon, Paris
p. 211 : RMN – C. Jean, Paris
p. 212 : RMN – Gérard Blot, Paris
p. 213 : RMN, Paris
p. 214 : RMN – Jean Schormans, Paris
p. 215 : RMN – Jean Schormans, Paris
p. 216 l. : Scala, Florence
p. 216-217 : Giraudon, Paris
p. 218 l. : Musée des Beaux-Arts – Ville de Nantes – H. Maertzns
p. 219 : Bulloz, Paris
p. 220 : Giraudon, Paris
p. 221 : Giraudon, Paris
p. 222 : RMN – Jean, Paris
p. 223 l. : RMN – D. Arnaudet / G. Blot, Paris
p. 223 r. : RMN – D. Arnaudet, Paris
p. 224 : RMN – R. G. Ojeda, Paris
p. 225 : RMN – D. Arnaudet, Paris
p. 226 : RMN – D. Arnaudet, Paris
p. 227 : RMN – Jean Schormans, Paris
p. 228 : Chrysler Museum of Art, Norfolk, VA. Gift of Walter P. Chrysler, Jr.71. 643
p. 229 t. : Musée Fabre, Montpellier – Frédéric Jaulmes
p. 229 b. : RMN – Jean SchormansParis
p. 230-231 : Photograph courtesy of the Art Institute of Chicago
p. 231 t. r. : RMN – Gérard Blot, Paris
p. 231 b. r. : Private Collection
p. 232 t. : RMN – Hervé Lewandowski, Paris
p. 232 b. : La Rochelle, Musée des Beaux-Arts
p. 233 : RMN, Paris
p. 234 : RMN – Gérard Blot, paris
p. 235 t. : RMN – Jean, Paris
p. 235 b. : Giraudon, Paris
p. 236-237 : Giraudon, Paris
p. 238 : Giraudon, Paris
p. 239 t. : Giraudon, Paris
p. 239 b. : Musée Georges Garret, Vesoul
p. 240-241 : © Chrysler Museum of Art, Norfolk, VA
p. 242 t. : Giraudon, Paris
p. 242 b. : Musée Georges Garret, Vesoul
p. 243 : Gift of Robert Jordan from the Collection of Eben D. Jordan / Courtesy, Museum of Fine Arts, Boston
p. 244 : Bibliothèque Inguimbertine, Carpentras
p. 245 : RMN – Jean Schormans, paris
p. 246 t. : Private Collection, Ziai – Gharagozlou
p. 246 b. : Private Collection, Ziai – Gharagozlou
p. 247 t. l. : Private Collection, Ziai – Gharagozlou
p. 247 t. r. : Private Collection, Ziai – Gharagozlou
p. 247 b. : Private Collection, Ziai – Gharagozlou
p. 248 : Martigues, Musée Ziem / Frédéric Aubert
p. 249 t. : Martigues, Musée Ziem / Frédéric Aubert
p. 249 b. : Bulloz, Paris
p. 250-251 : Bulloz, Paris
p. 251 t. : Martigues, musée Ziem / Frédéric Aubert
p. 251 b. : Martigues, musée Ziem / Frédéric Aubert
p. 252 : RMN – J. G. Berizzi, Paris
p. 253 : RMN – R.G. Ojeda, Paris
p. 254 : RMN – R.G. Ojeda, Paris
p. 255 : RMN – R.G. Ojeda, Paris
p. 256 : RMN – C. Jean, Paris
p. 256-257 : RMN – Hervé Lewandowski, Paris
p. 258-259 : © Bob Grove, Board of Trustees, National Gallery of Art, Washington
p. 260 : RMN – C. Jean, Paris
p. 261 : Musée Fabre, Montpellier – Frédéric Jaulmes
p. 262 : RMN – Gérard Blot, Paris
p. 263 : RMN – C. Jean, paris
p. 264 : Juliana Cheney Edwards Collection / Courtesy, museum of Fine Arts, Boston
p. 265 : Matsuka Collection. The National Museum of Western Art, Tokyo
p. 266 : Museum of Painting and Sculpture, Istanbul
p. 267 t. : Museum of Painting and Sculpture, Istanbul
p. 267 b. : Museum of Painting and Sculpture, Istanbul
p. 268 t. : Museum of Painting and Sculpture, Istanbul
p. 268 b. : Museum of Painting and Sculpture, Istanbul
p. 269 l. : Private Collection, Istanbul
p. 269 r. : Museum of Painting and Sculpture, Istanbul
p. 270 : with permission of Mr. Gros and Delettrez, Paris
p. 271 : RMN – J. G. Berizzi, Paris
p. 272 t. : © Musée des Beaux-Arts, Dijon, donation Granville
p. 272 b. : Photothèque des Musées de la Ville de Paris – cliché Joffre
p. 273 : Musée des Beaux-Arts de Nice
p. 274 : V. Minard, Musée Bonnat, Bayonne
p. 274-275 : J. Bocoyran, Musée Municipal de Brest/ All rights reserved
p. 276-277 : Giraudon, Paris
p. 277 r. : A. Guillard – Ville de Nantes – Musée des Beaux-Arts
p. 278 t. : Private Collection, London
p. 278 b. : Private Collection, London
p. 279 : A. Guillard – Ville de Nantes – Musée des Beaux-Arts
p. 280 : Städtisches Kunstmuseum, Bonn
p. 281 : Artephot / A. Held, Paris
p. 283 : Musée de l'École de Nancy – © Jean-François Brabant-M.E.N
p. 284 : Museum Folkwang, Essen, Germany
p. 285 : RMN – C. Jean, Paris
p. 286-287 : RMN – P. Bernard, Paris
p. 288-289 : Lauros- Giraudon, Paris
p. 290 : Artephot/Artothek, Paris
p. 291 : Artephot/Artothek, Paris
p. 292-293 : Artephot / © Estate Picasso
p. 293 r. : Scala, Florence / © Estate Picasso
p. 294 : Artephot/M. Plassart / © Estate H. Matisse
p. 295 : Scala, Florence / © Estate H. Matisse
p. 296 : Artephot/M. Plassart / © Estate H. Matisse
p. 297 : Scala, Florence / © Estate H. Matisse
p. 298 : Scala, Florence / © Estate H. Matisse
p. 299 : Scala, Florence / © Estate H. Matisse
p. 300-301 : Scala, Florence / © Estate H. Matisse
p. 302 : Artephot/A. Held, Paris
p. 303 : Artephot/A. Held, Paris
p. 304 : RMN – Arnaudet, Paris
p. 305 : Artephot/Artothek, Paris
p. 306-307 : Artephot/Artothek, Paris
p. 308 t. : J. Hyde
p. 308 b. : © Artephot/Artothek, Paris
p. 309 : © Metz, Musées de la Cour d'Or – Jean Munin
p. 310 : AKG Paris
p. 311 : AKG Paris
p. 312 : Lauros-Giraudon, Paris
p. 313 : Lauros-Giraudon, Paris
p. 314 l. : AKG Paris
p. 314 r. : AKG Paris
p. 315 : AKG Paris
p. 316 : AKG Paris
p. 317 : Scala, Florence
p. 318 : Artephot/Artothek, Paris
p. 319 : Artephot/Artothek, Paris
p. 320 t. : © F.L.C./ADAGP, Paris 2000
p. 320 b. : Musée National d'Art moderne, Paris
p. 321 : © Tate, London 2000
p. 322-323 : © Musée des Arts décoratifs, Paris – Laurent-Sully Jaulmes
p. 324 : © Musée des Arts décoratifs, Paris – Laurent-Sully Jaulmes
p. 325 : Archives Galerie de France, Paris
p. 326 : All rights reserved
p. 327 : All rights reserved
p. 328 : All rights reserved
p. 329 top l. : All rights reserved
p. 329 t. r. : All rights reserved
p. 329 b. l. : All rights reserved
p. 329 b. right : All rights reserved
p. 330-331 : © Photo Galerie Maeght
p. 331 right : All rights reserved
p. 332 : Selma Gürbüz, Private Collection
p. 333 : Selma Gürbüz, Private Collection
p. 334 : RMN – Quecq d'Henripret

© Adagp, 2000 : pp. 9, 16-17, 162, 281, 283, 284, 285, 286-287, 288-289, 290, 291, 302, 303, 304, 305, 306-307, 308 top et b., 320 t. et b., 322-323, 324